The Regions of Italy

See the map opposite and on the Inside back cover.

Piazza del Campidoglio, Rome
© Rene Mattes / Mauritius / Photononstop

THEGREENGUIDE
Italy

How to...

Plan Your Trip

Understand Italy

Discover Italy

Green Guides - Discover the Destination

Main sections

PLANNING YOUR TRIP
The blue-tabbed section gives you **ideas for your trip** and **practical information.**

INTRODUCTION
The orange-tabbed section explores **Nature, History, Art and Culture** and the **Country Today.**

DISCOVERING
The green-tabbed section features Principal Sights by region, **Sights, Walking Tours, Excursions,** and **Driving Tours.**

Region intros

At the start of each region in the Discovering section is a brief introduction. Accompanied by the region maps, these provide an overview of the main tourism areas and their background.

Region maps

Star ratings

Michelin has given star ratings for more than 100 years. If you're pressed for time, we recommend you visit the three or two star sights first:

★★★ Highly recommended

★★ Recommended

★ Interesting

Tours

We've selected driving and walking tours that show you the best of each town or region. Step by step directions are accompanied by detailed maps with marked routes. If you are short on time, you can follow the star ratings to decide where to stop. Selected addresses give you options for accommodation and dining en route.

Addresses

We've selected the best hotels, restaurants, caffès, shops, nightlife and entertainment to fit all budgets. See the Legend on the cover flap for an explanation of the price categories. See the back of the guide for an index of where to find hotels and restaurants.

Other reading

- Green Guides to Rome, Venice, Tuscany, or Sicily
- Must Sees to Milan, Venice, Rome, or Italy
- Michelin Local Maps of Italy
- Michelin Regional Maps of Italy
- Michelin Italy Country Map or Road Atlas

Welcome to Italy

For centuries Italy has been one of the world's foremost tourism destinations, attracting visitors for its art, cuisine, wine, design, fashion, and lifestyle. The Italian lifestyle, which prompts the enjoyment of these treasures to the fullest, extends to visitors as well. Culture enthusiasts will find more UNESCO World Heritage sites in Italy than anywhere else in the world, while history buffs have the thrill of seeing mysteries revealed through archaeological excavations. Beauty abounds in nature, too, from the coastline prized by Italians for basking in their seaside vacations, to the craggy mountains in the North for climbing and skiing, voluptuous mountain meadows for picnicking and hiking in Central Italy, hillsides dotted with vineyards, volcanoes to climb or even observe erupting, while other thermal phenomena is transformed into sybaritic baths. Paths followed by religious pilgrims and crusaders offer tranquil retreats for all to enjoy, often leaving glorious tributes of art and architecture. The marvel of Italy being so densely packed with wonders is that one could do all of these in a single day. It's also a reminder that Italy caters to a wide range of ages and interests. Italy's outdoor caffès and cosy wine bars beckon visitors to stop and savour these experiences in their myriad variety.

San Gimignano, Tuscany © Shargaljut / Dreamstime.com

Planning Your Trip

Introducing Italy

Discovering Italy

Abbazia di Montecassino, Lazio
© Raimund Kutterimageb / age fotostock

Regions of Italy

Southern Italy p142

Rome and Lazio (pp146-189)

More than a lifetime is required to explore Rome, the ancient city that serves as the capital of both Italy and the region of Lazio. The Coliseum and Vatican Museums vie for the largest number of visitors, while Rome's many other treasures tend to overshadow Lazio's other highlights, which include UNESCO heritage sites of an emperor and a Renaissance cardinal in Tivoli, medieval tranquillity in Viterbo and Etruscan ruins in Tarquinia. Montecassino houses a massive Benedictine monastery, a scene of conflict during World War II. Volcanic hills, forests, lakes and farmland give way to the coast, where vestiges of ancient Rome are in evidence even while sunbathers relax.

Abruzzo and Molise (pp190-199)

Mountains etched with tracks from ancient cattle-drives and sprawling parklands, like Parco Nazionale d'Abruzzo, define most of Abruzzo and Molise. Dense forests give way to medieval towns. Along the way to monasteries, abbeys, and ancient ruins such as Pietrabbondanza and Saepinium, gourmet meals and superb wines await. The pleasantly rugged coast still preserves some spindly fishing wharves.

Naples and Campania (pp200-255)

Campania epitomises the balmy, Mediterranean ideal. Glamorous seaside getaways on the Amalfi Coast and Isle of Capri have long attracted the elite. The Bay of Naples is a heart-stopping stunner of deep blue waters framed by the volcanic Mount Vesuvius. The volcano destroyed nearby Pompeii, the eerie ruins of which are among Italy's most visited sights. Naples, the capital and cultural heart, is a fast-paced jumble of Baroque art, regal buildings and superb cuisine.

Puglia (pp256-272)

Puglia has quickly become a favourite tourist haunt, which is not surprising. Its long seashore boasts bustling harbours, sandy beaches and dramatic cliffs, which are particularly impressive along the Gargano Promontory, the 'spur' of Italy's boot. Alberobello is sprinkled with 'trulli,' curious dome-shaped homes. Meanwhile, the city of Lecce is famed for its splendid historic centre, a Southern apotheosis of the Baroque. The landscape is dotted with mysterious dolmen and menhirs amidst ancient olive groves. Puglia's 'heel' alternates wild coastline with lovely seaside towns, curving back up toward Calabria in the busy port of Taranto.

Calabria and Basilicata (pp273-280)

Tropea is the jewel of Calabria's long coast, while Greek bronze statues lure visitors to Reggio. Whereas in smaller Basilicata, the rock dwellings of Matera are so evocative of ancient eras they've been used as film sets by Pasolini and Gibson.

Naples and the Mount Vesuvius
J. Fuste Raga/Bridge/Photononstop

Isola dell'Asinara, Sardinia
© Sandro Bedessi/Fototeca ENIT

Sardinia (pp281-294)

Sardinia is the second-largest Mediterranean isle. Its unique island culture includes a pocket of Catalan heritage in and around the city of Alghero. From the altitudes in Barbagia to the dry and craggy landscapes with cork trees bent by the wind, Sardinia seems largely untamed. The prehistoric *nuraghi* structures add mystery. Conversely, the Emerald Coast, Sardinia's key attraction, draws an elite clientele to the area's exclusive resorts. Cagliari, the capital, is a busy port.

Sicily (pp295-337)

The great island of Sicily, the Mediterranean's largest isle, is prized by travellers for its extensive Greek and Roman ruins, which stand majestically at Agrigento, Segesta and Taormina, among others. Modern Sicilian life bustles in Palermo, a capital that reflects millenia of conquests, while to the east Catania is closer to Mount Etna, an active volcano and the island's highest point. Sun-drenched and spoiled for sights, the island melting pot of Sicily produces some of Italy's best cuisine from Norman, Greek, Arab, Spanish, and French influences.

Northern Italy p338

Valle d'Aosta and Piemonte (pp342-366)

The north western regions of Italy contrast the Valle d'Aosta basking in the shadow of Mont Blanc and defined by mountains, with Piemonte in the fertile Po River Plain. The Valle d'Aosta shares many traditions with its French neighbours, as does Turin. Piemonte's capital, Turin transformed dramatically from industrial city to genteel cultural centre, enchanced by the 2006 Olympics.

Liguria (pp367-384)

A sliver of a region, Liguria possesses almost everything to wish for on a trip to Italy, including Alpine vistas, warm Mediterranean breezes and colourful coastal villages of the Cinque Terre that make the heart sing. Liguria's coast curves along the Gulf of Genova, named for the illustrious maritime capital.

Valle d'Aosta
© inevio doz / age fotostock

Lombardy and the Lake Region (pp385-433)

Affluence is evident in Lombardy, from the stunning villages of the region's Lake District (Regione dei Laghi) to Milan, where Italy's chic designers, bright business minds and savvy media players maintain a very visible presence. Though Lombardy is the epitome of modern Italy, it is not without its heritage trail, which marches right through Milan, by way of the Duomo and Leonardo da Vinci's *Last Supper*, to the photogenic and refined.

Veneto and Friuli-Venezia Giulia (pp434-476)

Connected via canals and alluring bridges, Venice, the capital of the Veneto, is instantly recognisable and boasts a unique culture derived from its days as one of the Mediterranean's most prominent seafaring powers. The Veneto and Friuli-Venezia Giulia, a small region that was once a part of Austria's domain, possess cities of quiet charm, such as Verona, Padova, and Trieste, and are known for their superb wines from full-bodied red Amarone to whites like sparkling Prosecco.

Trentino-Alto Adige /Südtirol (pp477-495)

Tucked firmly into the Dolomites, the dual autonomous provinces of Trentino and Alto Adige /Südtirol make up this region. Spectacular mountain passes have made Trentino-Alto Adige a pristine skiers' paradise. However, its relative isolation over the centuries has resulted in a pervasive Germanic culture, whereby most towns have both German and Italian names. The Iceman, in Bolzano's archaeological museum, is a favourite attraction.

Bologna and Emilia Romagna (pp496-527)

Love of food has steered many a tourist to Emilia Romagna, Italy's culinary centre. Indigenous items from the region's pantry include balsamic vinegar from Modena, prosciutto ham and Parmesan cheese from Parma and numerous pasta varieties. Bologna, the regional seat, has a lovely historic centre of medieval towers and Renaissance squares. Ravenna, a former capital of Byzantium, astounds with its trove of ancient mosaics. Ferrara has the Este castle and Palazzo Diamante, known for the quality of its art exhibits.

Vineyards of Chianti, Tuscany
© JR Photography / Fotolia.com

Central Italy p528

Tuscany (pp534-601)

Home to the art centre of Florence, Pisa's famous Leaning Tower and the vineyards of Chianti, Tuscany is the region that is most familiar to travellers. Its dizzying collection of must-see sights goes beyond the well-known diversions to include Renaissance cities such as Arezzo, Lucca and Pienza, medieval enclaves in Siena and San Gimignano, and natural wonders such as the thermal baths in Montecatini Terme. Indeed, all of Tuscany begs to be explored. Coastal areas often have Etruscan archeological sights within easy reach and to the north the marble quarries of Carrara, supplier to Michelangelo among others, remain active.

Urbino, Le Marche
© José Antonio Moreno / age fotostock

Umbria and Le Marche (pp602-635)

Landlocked and green with forests, Umbria is a quiet region of hill towns and undulating landscapes, from which both saints and artists have drawn inspiration. The main attraction is Assisi, the town where the great basilica to St Francis beckons millions of devoted pilgrims each year. Umbria's pleasant capital Perugia, a strategic town since Etruscan times, has an impressive cache of art and artefacts in its museums. Le Marche is known primarily for its hill towns, bordered by the Sibillini Mountains and by the dramatic coastal cliffs of the Conero that frame the Adriatic beaches near the port and capital of Ancona. Nestled in the mountain forests is Urbino, the birthplace of master painter Raphael, and one of the most elegant cities of the Renaissance.

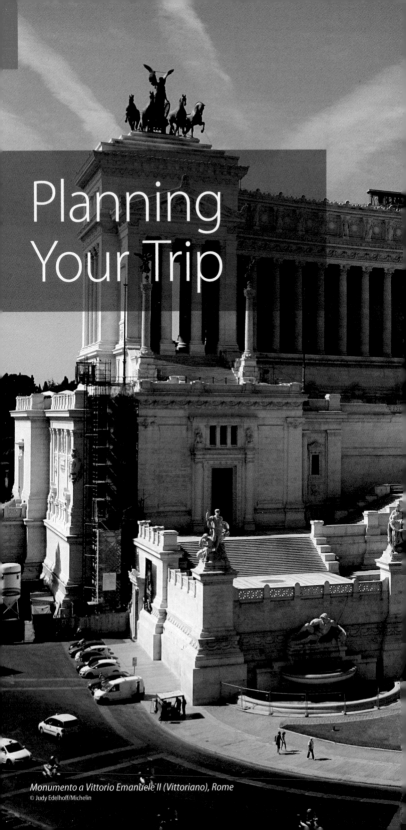

Planning
Your Trip

Monumento a Vittorio Emanuele II (Vittoriano), Rome
© Judy Edelhoff/Michelin

Planning Your Trip

Inspiration

WHAT'S HOT

– **Gastronomy** (see p29, 43, 73) has become a major focus for travellers, from agritourism to cookery classes and regional culinary tours.

– The Salone Internazionale del Mobile, the most important appointment in the global design calendar, is held in **Milan** (see p386) 12–17 Apr 2016

– The Architecture Biennale in **Venice** (see p435) is underway 28 May–27 Nov 2016 with related dance, theatre and film festivals. The Art Biennale returns 2017.

– **Mantua** (see p160) has been chosen as Italian culture capital in 2016.

– The **Vatican** (see p160): Pope Francis has declared an Extraordinary Jubilee Year for the Church. The "Holy Year of Mercy" begins on Dec 8, 2015 (the 50th anniversary of the end of the Second Vatican Council) and concludes on 20 Nov 2016 (the Feast of Christ the King).

Piazza San Pietro, Vatican City © I. Pompe / hemis.fr

Italy's Must See Cities

Will it be the sensuality of Venice, gliding along her canals, or the vibrant energy of Naples? An aperitivo amidst the grandeur of Rome or scoping MIlan's best of design and fashion? Spend a long weekend in each…

BOLOGNA See p497

Prosperous Bologna, known for its rich cuisine, keeps its lively edge with its large university student population, a presence here for over 1,000 years. Not to be missed is San Petronio Basilica.

FLORENCE See p535

Nowhere does Renaissance splendour shine so bright and so concentrated as in Florence, a jewel box of treasures that testifies to the genius of the artists themselves, as well as their patrons. No wonder it was here that Stendhal experienced the syndrome later named for him. The David statue and the Uffizi are musts, but so is a pause for good Tuscan fare and glass of Chianti or Brunello, or for a drink in a grand piazza to recover from so much beauty.

GENOA See p368

The great maritime port city of Genoa, home of Christopher Columbus, has the feel of the Riviera with an intriguing hillside rabbit warren of streets lined with fine palaces and art.

MILAN See p386

Italy's financial and fashion capital pulses with commerce and innovation. Spot new design trends enroute to see the Last Supper and the Duomo.

NAPLES See p201

The "it" place for the Grand Tour travellers, energy abounds in Naples, from the frantic streets to the looming volcano Vesuvius, lit by the sparkling light from the bay. The elegance of the grand palaces shares space with its ancient past, beautifully so at the Archaeological Museum and Capodimonte. Capri and Ischia beckon for an island interlude.

PERUGIA See p603

Umbria's capital and university town, Perugia shows its Etruscan and medieval heritage. Paintings by Pinturicchio and Perugino are inspired by nearby landscapes. The hilltop town of Assisi offers sublime tranquillity and masterpieces by Giotto and other great artists who adorned the cathedral.

Basilica di San Pietro, Rome

ROME 👤See p149

Epicentre of the Roman Empire, Rome is still a compelling draw. A walk between the ancient architectural wonders of the Colosseum and the Pantheon offers astonishing contrasts, with Baroque piazzas and fountains, in turn perfect settings for a drink and glimpse to see what remains of the *Dolce Vita*. Across the Tiber, where perfectly groomed Romans whiz across bridges on motorbikes and in cars, the Vatican Museums lure visitors in for a seemingly endless collection of artistic treasures, not the least of which is the Sistine Chapel.

TURIN 👤See p343

Turin, master of reinvention, has kept its literary trade and transformed into a genteel city of technology and culture. It guards the famous Shroud and is home to arguably the best Egyptian museum outside Cairo, as well as excellent chocolate. A mummy, a book and hot chocolate, perhaps?

VENICE 👤See p435

La Serenissima, Her Most Serene, could be none other than Venice.

TOURIST OFFICES

www.italia.it/en
Italian State Tourist Office – ENIT (Ente Nazionale Italiano per il Turismo). For information, brochures, maps and assistance in planning a trip to Italy, apply to the ENIT in your country or consult the ENIT website, www.enit.it. The main tourist offices in Italy are given at the beginning of each chapter in the Discovering Italy section, preceded by the symbol 🛈.

UK 1 Princes Street, London W1B 2AY, 📞(020) 7408 1254, italy@italiantouristboard.co.uk, www.enit.it/it.

USA 686 Park Avenue, New York, NY 10111 📞(212) 245 5618. 10850 Wilshire Boulevard, Suite 575, Los Angeles, CA 900254, 📞(310) 820 1898. 500 North Michigan Avenue, Suite 506, Chicago, IL 60611, 📞(312) 644 0996.

Canada 110 Yonge Street, Suite 503, Toronto M5C 1T4, 📞(416) 925 4882.

Once a major sea power embracing the intrigues of exotic traders and doges, seductive in her silver light, Venice still offers canals and narrow streets to navigate, the Doges Palace and St. Marks to explore, and a water transport system where each stop has at its own treasure trove. The Islands of Murano, Burano, and the Lido delight with their own shapes and colours.

VERONA 👤See p467

The ancient Roman Arena, an evocative spot to see a performance, stands near Verona streets that lead to the house of Juliet. Castelvecchio has a lovely art collection and its ramparts offer a fine view of the river and city. A glass of Amarone wine and a hearty meal complete the day.

Historic Italy

A wander through Roman villas in Pompeii or on the Palatine in Rome opens a colourful world of frescoes, which take on divine mystery in the great cathedrals that for centuries served as both spiritual and social centres. Castles and stately villas were grand residences but also important economic forces with trade in agriculture and other commerce; some remain so today as wineries or luxury resorts. Small towns and villages offer their own treasures and at a tranquil pace.

ROMANS

From feats of engineering and architecture to urban planning, aqueducts, and road systems, Ancient Rome is in grand evidence throughout Italy. Glimpses of life are found in the frescoes lingering on villa walls and the mosaics and artefacts found amid the grandeur.

1. Colosseum – p155. Entertainment arena and door of victory (or death) for gladiators, this engineering feat built under the Flavian emperors remains a marvel today.
2. Pompeii – p231. The daily life of a Roman port city had its intimate moments frozen in time and then preserved after the eruption of Vesuvius. Centuries later its glory, daily routine, and secrets were revealed.
3. Pantheon – p164. If Italy has one unmissable sight, it is the Pantheon. This temple dedicated to all the gods looms in harmonious perfection, its interior pierced by a shaft of light.
4. Theatres and Amphitheatres – p329, 467, 254, 173, 614. Even at a fraction of their original splendour, Roman theatres are a grand venue for select performances today from **Taormina** to **Verona**, **Capua**, **Ostia**, and **Spoleto**.
5. Roads – p379, 573, 633, 185. Roads are in part what made the Empire possible. The **Appian Way** is the most evocative, but a visitor can explore almost the entire 'boot' on what once were Roman roads, like the **Aurelia** and **Salaria**.

FRESCOES

Fresco ('fresh'), generally refers to the technique of painting with pigment and water on wet plaster or lime. The painting must be completed quickly – within a day or less – before the plaster dries. The colours sink in and once dried, are set, in many cases remaining vivid over 2,000 years later. The technique was used by Romans and Etruscans and on through later times. Italy has some of the world's most stunning frescoes and arguably the highest concentration of them.

1. Sistine Chapel – p163. Michelangelo painted in the Sistine Chapel twice in the 16C, first the ceiling and 20 years later, the Last Judgement.
2. Villa dei Misteri – p236. Painted in a residence in Pompeii, a young woman is prepared for an initiation rite (perhaps Dionysian); mysterious, momentous, and very Pompeian red.
3. The Last Supper – p400. The compelling drama of the Last Supper painted in Milan by Leonardo Da Vinci remains the benchmark for the theme.
4. Basilica of St. Francis – p609. In the Middle Ages, Giotto ushered in a "brave new style," as found in this basilica in Assisi, where nature and spirituality tell a compelling story.
5. Legend of the True Cross – p596. The tale of an 4C woman who departs Italy to search for the True Cross in Jerusalem, brought to life in Arezzo in the 15C by Piero della Francesca.

CATHEDRALS

Most major cities in Italy have a cathedral worth seeing, as do many small towns: many also contain important historic treasures, themselves imposing structures. All offer an insight into the religious and social life of the community.

1. St. Peter's Basilica – p160. Vatican headquarters and top pilgrimage site for the Catholic church, its monumentality and treasures are unsurpassed.

2. Santa Maria del Fiore – p541. Crowned by Brunelleschi's famous dome, Florence's Duomo along with its baptistry and bell tower, forms a spectacular square.

3. Monreale – p307. Sicily's famous cathedral outside of Palermo is renowned for its mosaics, many of which are golden, and fine architecture with its Moorish and Norman influences.

4. St. Mark's – p438. Next to the Doges Palace the onion domes and splendid balconies of this basilica face Venice's main square.

5. Romanesque cathedrals of Puglia – p258, 270. Evidence of the building boom during the Crusades, cathedrals in Puglia made of luminous local stone set at the edge of the sea – like in **Trani**, or above it like **Otranto** – are memorable under Puglia's particular ivory light.

CASTLES

Italian castles range from fortresses to simple feudal villages or elegant palaces, all of which may be found in every region of Italy.

1. Castel del Monte – p259. Italy has several 13C Frederick II castles to explore, but none more enigmatic than this octagonal structure in Puglia, invested with the symbolism of the number '8' and its astronomical precision.

2. Reggia di Caserta – p253. Built outside of Naples in the late-18C to rival Versailles, its castle, gardens, and sophisticated court life were the epitome of culture and elegance for Grand Tour travellers.

3. Castel Sant'Angelo – p163. Originally Hadrian's mausoleum, this round castle in Rome has served as papal residence with a passageway to the Pope's Vatican apartments, as a fort, a prison, and now a museum.

4. Palazzi Normanni – p299, 212, 260. **Palermo**, Sicily is home to a Norman palace, developed on the site of a previous Arab fortress. The Normans built castles in Italy from the 11C–late-13C: Molise has **Venosa** and **Melfi**; Naples has **Castel dell'Ovo**; and the **Gargano** in Puglia has a castle.

5. Castles of Chianti – p553. The Tuscan countryside around Florence and Siena is dotted with castles on hillsides.

San Gimignano, Tuscany © bluejayphoto / iStockphoto.com

TOWNS

Towns offer an opportunity to slow down the pace a bit and to savour details. Being Italy, each has its masterpiece or two to admire.

1. Taormina – p329. An Ancient Greek theatre overlooks the volcano Etna and the sea offering summer performances and a film festival. This chic town boasts excellent Sicilian cuisine and lovely hotels.

2. Ravello – p246. A sophisticated artsy crowd alights in this perch, lured as much by the famous summer music festival as well as by its commanding views of the sea. Set higher up and further inland than other towns along the Amalfi Coast, this romantic nest has superb hotels and dining.

3. Capri – p240. Hedonistic pleasure was a theme for Emperor Tiberius 2,000 years ago and the 21C island town doesn't disappoint. Jetsetters know that they are an attraction and do their best not to cross paths with daytrippers soaking up the beauty.

4. Tropea – p276. Calabria's glam summer spot on the cliff above the sea can also serve as entry point to one of Italy's least explored regions.

5. Ascoli Piceno – p633. If Le Marche were as 'in' as Tuscany, the crowds that visit San Gimignano would pile into this lovely, more luminous medieval tower town near the Adriatic.

6. San Gimignano – p591. The 14 medieval towers rise up from the Val d'Elsa like skyscrapers. Walk the delightful Tuscany town, then explore the wines producers beyond, from tangy white Vernaccia to the reds of the province from Chianti to Brunello.

7. Suvereto and Bibbona – p573. Superb dining in Suvereto and enchanting shops in Bibbona, make these little Maremma towns in Tuscany worth a stop. Suvereto wineries like friendly Bulichella produce delicious white Vermentino and reds, as well as Tua Rita with its prestigious reds. The Etruscan Coast wine road leads to **Bolgheri**, which boasts Sassicaia and Ornellaia, prized by wine collectors.

8. Assisi – p609. The stunning cathedral with its Giotto frescoes, Roman ruins, and sublime tranquillity make an ideal atmosphere to relax. Savour a languid lunch with Umbrian cuisine and hefty red Sagrantino wine from Montefalco.

9. Ravenna – p511. Full immersion into the Byzantine world includes its marvellous mosaics. The port makes a good spot for lunch near the sea.

10. Sulmona – p194. Set in an Abruzzo valley below an ancient Hercules sanctuary, this airy and flat town makes for a lovely walk. The main market square is bordered by a medieval aqueduct. Nearby vineyards produce good Montepulciano.

VILLAGES

The old section of a town or even neighbourhoods of great cities often seem like villages. Each of these has its own distinctive characteristics.

1. Matera – p280. Once called "Italy's gash of shame" for its poverty, its 'sassi' rock dwellings suggestive of another millennia and place have brought new life to Basilicata as a film set for Biblical epics or evocative refuge for visitors.

2. Alberobello – p265. Constructed initially to avoid taxes, Puglia's cone-roofed dwellings create a fairy-tale effect clustered together. The *cantina sociale* (community winery) in **Locorotondo** produces a wide variety of good wines at very reasonable prices.

3. Erice – p311. Phoenician and Greek in origin, the Norman castle still stands. Foggy and atmospheric in winter, bright Sicily sea view in summer. Nero d'Avola red wine is produced locally.

4. Bellagio and Tramezzo – p426. Situated on Lake Como in Lombardia, these lake villages are filled with flowers, have scenic ports and mountain views.

5. Portofino – p377. Experience the Italian Riviera as haven both to the jet set and fishing ports. Hike the regional park trails or scuba dive.

STATELY HOMES

Stately homes in Italy might be a grand villa or palace. Often they served not only as dwellings, but as major points of commerce, for agricultural products in the country or trade in the city.

1. Villa Rotonda (Valmarana) – p465. The harmony of the sphere and cube, like that of the Pantheon, makes this the most famous of the villas designed by Andrea Palladio. Veneto villas grace the countryside especially near Vicenza, Verona, and the Brenta Canal.

2. Medici villas – p553, 167. The countryside around Florence is dotted with Medici villas, while in Rome, **Villa Medici** hosts the French Academy and lively programs.

3. Villa Rufolo – p247. Perched high in Ravello, this 13C villa shows Moorish and Gothic influences. The garden hosts concerts with the cliffs and sea as backdrop.

4. Villa d'Este – p181. Tivoli in the Castelli Romani hills outside Rome hosts this splendid, frescoed villa. Gardens have rows of fountains and a water clock. Nearby is Hadrian's Villa.

5. Palaces of Strada Nuovo – p371. Genoa's street lined with luxury palaces, some of which host important art museums.

Portofino, Liguria © Dan Breckwoldt/iStockphoto.com

Gourmet Italy

F ood has always been one of Italy's key attractions and no more so than today, when Michelin-starred restaurants make destinations of some especially small villages and towns. These culinary beacons dot a landscape where regional producers and products enjoy wide international fame. Yet beyond the headline items lies an even more varied cuisine and network of producers than that which first made Italian food famous.

WINE REGIONS

Wine is one of Italy's greatest lures and with some 3,000 indigenous varieties of grapes, there are endless wines to taste. Below is a sampling of Italy's best from north to south. Each region has wine routes to explore, defining the countrysides.

1. Barolo – p73, 348, 358. King of the Piemonte wines, other good local red wines to seek out include Barbaresco and Barbera. Piemonte also produces some of Italy's best cheeses.
2. Brunello – p74, 593. Tuscany's bold red is produced in Montalcino. Other important reds include Chianti, Nobile di Montepulciano, and Morellino di Scansano.
3. Franciacorta – p409. This zone of bubbles in Lombardy is Italy's response to Champagne, wine produced using the 'classical method.' Various versions, including a rosé.
4. Two Veneto Wines: Amarone and Prosecco (p73, 471, 449, 473) – Amarone is a deep ruby color and dense, made from grapes that have been left to dry slightly before being pressed. Prosecco, the bubbly white wine, was created in the 19C using a quicker fermentation process, thus is less complex and less costly.
5. Sagrantino – p612. Umbria's full-bodied red wine, produced in the Montefalco area, is ideal for meats like wild boar, sausage, or goose, as well as dishes made with wild mushrooms or truffles. Its *passito* (semi-sweet) version is worth trying, too.

GOURMET DESTINATIONS

Look for establishments that cook and serve artisanal and fresh products, with respect for tradition and some creative flair. Non-wine drinkers can seek out craft beers, grappa, and mineral waters.

1. Sicily – p295. A crossroads of culture and conquests results, Sicily has some of Italy's best and most varied cuisine, from simple to complex. Delicious local products include tuna, pachino cherry tomatoes, blood oranges, and wines from around Etna and across the island, such as Nero d'Avola.
2. Naples – p201. Earthy to refined, Naples has it all, including influences from the French royal court. Pasta, pizza, street food, seafood, mozzarella, and even some of Italy's best chocolates are here. Excellent produce from volcanic soil. Taurasi and Aglianico red wines.
3. Puglia – p256. Excellent seafood at prices that are still reasonable, plus superb local breads and pastas, as well as Primitivo di Manduria red wine.
4. Le Marche – p625. Even *vincis grassi*, the local lasagna, is a bit more complex and flavourful. Emphasis on local produce, from mountain forests to seafood. Unique wine varieties rom white Verdicchio to floral reds.
5. Venice – p435. Ancient trade with the East has left a few exotic spice touches, plus superb fish and waterfowl from the Lagoon. Wide variety of wines from the Veneto and Friuli.

Natural Italy

taly has incredible natural variety, from alpine to coastline – its forests, parks, gardens and islands offer much to explore and admire.

ISLANDS

Sicily and Sardinia are the largest and most important of Mediterranean islands, though our selection includes some smaller highlights. Don't overlook interior islands such as the Lake District islands in Lombardy or Lake Trasimeno in Umbria, each with its own unique habitats, architecture, and features. The ultimate island city is Venice, set on a series of islands.

1. Isole Eolie – p332. Each of these islands off the coast of Sicily has a distinct personality. **Stromboli**'s black sand washes down from its volcano with its ongoing eruptions visible in the evening. **Vulcano** offers thermal mud springs that gurgle and bubble for a soothing soak. **Lipari**, the largest, is a good point for booking boat trips.

2. Capri – p240. Most glamorous of Italy's islands, the elite from Emperor Tiberius to the jet set have called this jewel box home– or at least a favourite port and watering hole.

3. Ischia – p238. Like Capri, near Naples, but larger and lower key, with thermal waters for soaking. Daily life seems a bit more real, with repair shops and vineyards in evidence.

4. Tremiti – p262. Puglia's islands are mostly park, surrounded by bright, clear sea. Ports in Puglia, Molise, and Abruzzo serve the Tremiti Islands. Perfect for a picnic, hike, and swim.

5. Mozia – p312. Less known of Italy's islands, Mozia once was inhabited by Phoenicians. A small boat departs from near the salt flats and windmill (tours available) north of Marsala. The scrubby Sicily island has a small museum, an ongoing archaeological dig, and a project to cultivate ancient grapes for wine.

COASTLINES

Italy's myriad promontories, cliffs, and sandy beaches enshroud a landscape of glittering resorts from the Riviera in the northwest to Venice's Lido in the northeast.

1. Amalfi and Sorrentine Coast – p244, 227. Farmers vie with the forces of gravity to harvest lemons and olives, while travellers enjoy the cliff side view of the coast. Small beaches or rocky platforms are reached by steps, elevators, or boat.

2. Puglia – p256. Rocky and sandy areas alternate along the coast, with lovely ports and inlets along the mythic seacoast of Magna Grecia. The Gargano Promontory juts out to form Italy's spur, with high cliffs and strips of sandy beach. South at the 'heel' in Leuca is the more active sea, which rounds the heel to Gallipoli.

3. Tuscany – p573. Chic Forte dei Marmi is neighbors with the busy marble port of Carrara. The Maremma offers wild vegetation, pine forests, sandy strips, Etruscan tombs, metal and mineral mines, vineyards, Italy's cowboys, and port cities. Departure points to Elba, Giglio and Corsica.

4. Basilicata, Molise, and Abruzzo – p273, 199, 191. These regions have small strips of coast, some quite rugged and unspoiled. The former has a small coastline on both seas, while the other two have ancient spindly fishing piers.

5. Calabria – p274. One of Italy's longest coastlines, Calabria has been very erratically developed, either with beauty or blight. Tropea is its most successful incarnation.

NATIONAL PARKS

National parks provide nature lovers a wide variety of geographic terrain to explore and many activities. Park rangers are wonderful sources of information and often give tours, which might be possible in English with sufficient advance booking.

1. Abruzzo – p191. About one-third of Abruzzo is national park, including Italy's oldest park, Parco Nazionale d'Abruzzo (1934), which is now partly in Molise. Two others are Gran Sasso and Maiella. Hiking, wolf studies, bear spotting, bird watching, and transhumance (cattle drive) trails. Some areas offer winter skiing. The cable car near Camarda goes to the Campo Imperatore, with vast meadows for kids to run, craggy peaks for climbers, food, and lodging.
2. Parco Nazionale delle Dolomiti Bellunesi – p487. Three Dolomite ranges between Belluno and Feltre offer trails, including World War I themes (100th anniversary 2014).
3. Parco Nazionale del Cilento e Diano – p250. A good trip to combine with a visit to Paestum or Salerno.
4. Etna and Vesuvius – p326, 223. These two volcanoes have flora, fauna, lava fields, and volcanic activity.
5. Aspromonte and Pollino – p275, 273. Spectacular Calabria mountain vistas, some with two seas. Even in summer, very few visit Aspromonte.

PARKS AND GARDENS

Gardens in Italy tend to emphasize the forms of trees, shrubs, and plants. When flowers appear, often they are accents rather than the main feature. Fountains are often lavish. Some museums and historic sites have splendid gardens, while some cities and universities have botanical gardens.

1. Palazzo Doria Pamphilj, Rome – p164. Up on the Janicululm Hill, majestic umbrella pines form tall graceful lines on well-kept grounds. Ponds are skated by ducks and swans.
2. Villa Borghese, Rome – p168. Bike rentals, a park train, a zoo, a zoo museum, two cinemas, ponds, fountains, and first-rate art in Galleria Borghese add up to a full offering and refuge from Rome's city noise.
3. Boboli Gardens, Palazzo Pitti and Villa Bardini, Florence – p545. The back gate at Boboli, if open, leads directly to Villa Bardini with its magnificent vista of Florence.
4. Reggia di Caserta – p253. Within the palace's extensive park are fountains with nymphs and goddesses, a waterfall fed by an aqueduct designed by Vanvitelli, and an English-style garden.
5. Villa d'Este, Tivoli – p181. Famed for its variety and number of fountains and water clock, with a small terrace to sit and enjoy the environment.

Mount Amiata region, Tuscany © G. Bere/De Agostini Editore/age fotostock

The Great Outdoors

I taly's varied landscape has something for everyone. The Alps provide footpaths and mountains suitable for all levels of athletic expertise.

The lake district, the mountain streams and rivers are ideal for fishing. Trentino-
Alto Adige /Südtirol, the Riviera del Brenta, Tuscany and Umbria are among the
more suitable regions for cycling. The Maremma offers a perfect landscape for
horse riding. The entire coast of Italy is an Eden for those who enjoy swimming,
wind-surfing and the beach: the Adriatic coast with its shallow waters and long
beaches is ideal for families with children, while the waters of the Gargano, the
Gulf of Policastro, Sicily and Sardinia are renowned for their crystalline purity and
splendid colours, notably the emerald greens of the Costa Smeralda. The Amalfi
coast and the Faraglioni of Capri are perhaps the best-known Italian coastlines;
Versilia, with the Apuan Alps as a backdrop, is an essential venue for habitués of
the beach, and the Ligurian Riviera offers striking views and beaches that nestle
between the hills that lead down to the sea. For information on sporting and
leisure activities see the addresses of information offices for each region or
sight in the introduction to each chapter in the guide.

🏃 HIKING

Club Alpino Italiano (CAI; Via Petrella 19,
20124 Milano 📞02 20 57 231; www.cai.it).

FOOTPATHS

Many people overlook Italy's walks
when they visit but between the
stunning coastlines, rugged mountain
terrain and wild national parks there
are a number of walking and hiking
options – regardless of the traveller's
athleticism and stamina.
Some of the most travelled paths are
the five lands of the **Cinque Terre**.
Capri and neighbouring Anacapri are

© ATL Cuneo / Fototeca ENIT

a hiker's dream with trails that offer
views of Saracen forts, natural grottoes
and the stunning Bay of Naples. The
Pollino Mountains (📞0973 66 93 11,
www.parcopollino.gov.it) between
Calabria and Basilicata offer stunning
walks, with trails through waterfalls
and caves (for guided tours contact
ormenelparco.com), while the **Parco
Nazionale d'Abruzzo, Lazio e Molise**
(📞0863 91 131, www.parcoabruzzo.it) is
one of the most rugged national parks
in the country.
No hiker's trip to Italy would be
complete without a summit to
one of Italy's famous volcanoes.
Both **Mount Etna** (www.funiviaetna.
com) and **Mount Vesuvius** (www.
parconazionaledelvesuvio.it) offer
superb hiking and views.

HUNTING

Federazione Italiana della Caccia
(Via Salaria 298a, 00199 Rome; 📞06 84
40 941; www.federcaccia.org).

CANOEING

Federazione Italiana Canottaggio
(Viale Tiziano 74, 00196 Roma; 📞06 87
97 48 01; www.canottaggio.org)
Federazione Italiana Canoa e Kayak,
(Viale Tiziano 70, 00196 Roma; 📞06 36
85 84 18; www.federcanoa.it).

CYCLING

Federazione Ciclistica Italiana
(Stadio Olimpico, Curva Nord, Via dei
Gladiatori, 00194 Foro Italico, Roma;
✆06 36 85 78 13; www.federciclismo.it).

RIDING AND
PONY TREKKING

**Federazione Italiana di Turismo
Equestre e Trec** (Largo Lauro De Bosis
15, 00135 Roma, ✆06 32 65 02 31,
www.fitetrec-ante.itt).

GOLF

Federazione Italiana Golf
(Viale Tiziano 74, 00196 Roma,
✆06 32 31 825, www.federgolf.it).

SAILING AND WINDSURFING

Federazione Italiana Vela
(Corte Lambruschini, Piazza Borgo
Pila 40, Torre A, 16129 Genova; ✆010 54
45 41; www.federvela.it).

FISHING AND SCUBA

**Federazione Italiana Pesca Sportiva
e Attività Subacquee** (Viale Tiziano 70,
00196 Roma; ✆06 87 98 00 86;
www.fipsas.it).

WATERSKIING

Federazione Italiana Sci Nautico,
(Via Piranesi 44b, 20137 Milano;
✆02 75 29 181; www.scinautico.com).

SPELEOLOGY

Società Speleologica Italiana
(Via Zamboni 67, 40127 Bologna,
✆051 53 46 57; www.ssi.speleo.it).

SKIING

Federazione Italiana Sport Invernali
(Via Piranesi 44b, 20137 Milano;
✆02 75 731; www.fisi.org).

RESORTS

Italy has some of the most enticing
ski resorts in the world with slopes for
beginners, intermediates and experts.
The Dolomites – 🄳 Ufficio Informazioni
Turistiche Dolomiti, Corso Italia 81, 32043
Cortina d'Ampezzo, ✆0436 86 90 86.

USEFUL WEBSITES

www.italiantouristboard.co.uk
www.italiantourism.com
Italian Tourist Board - main
websites for the UK and USA.
www.beniculturali.it
Website of the Ministry of Culture
(in Italian only). Museum details,
cultural event programmes, news
on restorations and publications.
www.060608.it
Official city website; RomaPass
for discounts, hotels, as well for
museums, archaeological sites,
churches, events, transportation,
and the Vatican Museums.
www.firenzeturismo.it
Tourism board website, includes
info on the city, plus towns and
countryside in the province;
hotels, transport, activities for
families and disabled travellers,
sustainable tourism, museums
and events.
http://en.turismovenezia.it
Tourism board website, includes
museums, Chorus churches,
hotels, transportation, updates
on acqua alta (high tide), lagoon,
beaches, as well as activities for
family and disabled travellers.

www.cortina.dolomiti.org. *Skiers flock to*
1200km/746mi of slopes for near year-
round winter fun. Cortina is one of the
top resorts in Europe.
Piemonte – 🄳 Piazza Risorgimento 1,
12037, Saluzzo, ✆0175 46 710. www.
saluzzoturistica.it. *Some of the slopes*
hosted the 2006 Winter Olympics. The
Val di Susa has a particularly beautiful
natural landscape and Limone is one of
the oldest alpine villages in the country.
Courmayeur – 🄳 Piazzale Monte Bianco
3, 11013 Courmayeur Aosta, ✆0165 84
16 12, www.courmayeur.it. With peaks
reaching more than 4 000m / 13 100ft,
Courmayeur is just opposite France's
Mont Blanc and is a great place to
experience alpine Italy.

Michelin Driving Tours

The **Driving Tours** map (💿 *see the following pages*) shows recommended itineraries. The Green Guides to Rome, Tuscany and Venice provide even more detail on these destinations.

1 THE GULF OF GENOVA AND THE ITALIAN RIVIERA

This itinerary follows the Ligurian Coast. Stop and stroll the seaside paths between the Cinque Terre, five coastal villages. Then survey the French-infused chic of the Côte d'Azur before moving inland, passing through the Colle di Tenda *(not recommended for those prone to travel sickness)*.

2 VALLE D'AOSTA TO THE WINE-GROWING MONFERRATO AREA

A route for mountain lovers, this loop reaches the French Alps and includes a cultural stop in Turin, with its splendid museums and Baroque architecture, the nearby Sacra di San Michele, the Olympic Val di Susa and a stop in the wine-growing Monferrato region.

3 FROM THE GREAT LAKES OF LOMBARDY TO THE PO VALLEY

This tour begins in the heart of Lombardy, the frenetic city of Milan. Look past the glamorous shops to discover an equally rich cultural heritage. The route continues to the Bassa Padana, a land of mist and fog with a melancholy charm, poetically described in the stories of Giovannino Guareschi. Finally, Verona is an ideal starting point for the lake district.

4 FROM THE DOLOMITES TO VENICE AND TRIESTE

Start in Venice (💿 *see THE GREEN GUIDE VENICE*) before exploring this area's blend of Italian and central European culture. In Trieste savour the literary atmosphere in the Caffè San Marco. The route continues through the harsh and atmospheric Dolomites between Cortina and Bolzano, with the sounds of the German- and Latin-accented local dialect, before descending to Trento, dominated by the Buonconsiglio Castle with its ancient fresco, "Cycle of the Months". The itinerary concludes in the Palladian town of Vicenza.

5 THE PLAINS' RICH CITIES TO THE ADRIATIC LAGOONS

This itinerary straddles the Veneto, Lombardy and Romagna. This area embraces the Po Delta, Bologna, the mosaics of Ravenna (infused with a Byzantine atmosphere), the noble city of Ferrara, the Palladian villas of the Brenta and the Venetian Lagoon.

6 ART, NATURE AND SPIRITUALITY IN TUSCANY AND UMBRIA

This programme takes in the art cities of Tuscany (💿 *see THE GREEN GUIDE TUSCANY for more detailed information*), starting from Florence and progressing through the area around Lucca with its fine villas, Pisa, the Balze of Volterra and San Gimignano. The heart of Tuscany is embodied by Siena, a city at once gentle and aggressive (home of the *palio* horse race). Here the route explores some of the region's saints: St Bernardino with his sermons that shook the walls, St Catherine and, in Umbria, Sts Francis and Clare.

7 UMBRIA TO THE ADRIATIC

A journey of contrasting landscapes, from gentle Umbrian countryside

Todi, Umbria

and its treasures of art and spirituality (Gubbio, Perugia, Assisi and Spoleto), to the Abruzzi Mountains, the last refuge of bears, wolves and other indigenous wildlife. The route continues to the Adriatic Sea, with a stopover in the piazza of Ascoli Piceno. From Rimini move inland to San Marino and the palace of the Duke of Montefeltro in Urbino.

8 FROM ROME TO THE ABRUZZI

Italy's capital requires several days even for an introduction (♿consult *THE GREEN GUIDE ROME*). Once dubbed the *caput mundi*, head of the world, the Eternal City is rich in history and passion. Explore on foot and by public transport – traffic is intense. Afterwards, explore the region's lakes, castles, gardens and the Etruscan remains of Tarquinia. Finally, proceed to the Parco Nazionale d'Abruzzo and the abbeys of Casamari, Montecassino and San Clemente a Casauria. Nearby, the beach town of Sperlonga, reminiscent of a Greek white-washed village, sits above the Villa of Tiberius.

9 THE TREASURES OF THE NEAPOLITAN COAST

This colourful itinerary combines the intense blue of the sea, magenta bougainvillea and pastel houses overlooking the winding Amalfi Coast (its splendid views are a frequent backdrop for thrillers such as the James Bond film *For Your Eyes Only*). Visit Naples and the surrounding bay, Capri, Mount Vesuvius and its illustrious victims Herculaneum and Pompeii, and then on to Paestum before reaching Calabria and the Gulf of Policastro. The island of Ischia is a restful detour; Capri's cheaper neighbour contains ancient ruins and volcanic hot springs.

10 PUGLIA

This route combines the sea with unusual architecture. Gargano – the "chicken spur" of Italy's boot – is a favourite holiday spot for natives, thanks to the sparkling Adriatic. Pilgrims flock to San Giovanni Rotondo to see the Padre Pio shrine. Drive south to the Terra dei Trulli, with its cone-topped stone huts, then explore the Baroque town of Lecce and down to the Ionian Sea and the Sassi di Matera.

11 SICILY AND CALABRIA

Retrace some of Odysseus' epic journey. At the Strait of Messina, gaze out at the Sirens' rocks, Scylla (a tentacled mythological monster) and Charybdis (a whirlpool). Inland lies Mount Aspromonte, with its vast mountain ranges and sea vistas. Greek ruins line the Ionian shore, but the colonists' descendants still dwell in the Graecanico, mountain villages that were Greek-speaking. Ancient monasteries line the road down to Sicily.

12 SARDINIA

In the north, trace the Emerald Coast, where pink bluffs contrast with the green sea. Mysterious stone structures dot the west coast; Nuraghe Su Naraxi is the most famous. Museums in Sassari and Cagliari, the island's main town to the south, explore this ancient culture.

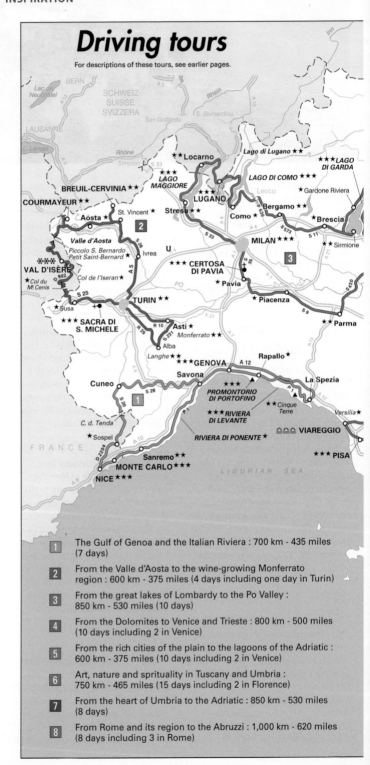

Driving tours

For descriptions of these tours, see earlier pages.

1 The Gulf of Genoa and the Italian Riviera : 700 km - 435 miles (7 days)

2 From the Valle d'Aosta to the wine-growing Monferrato region : 600 km - 375 miles (4 days including one day in Turin)

3 From the great lakes of Lombardy to the Po Valley : 850 km - 530 miles (10 days)

4 From the Dolomites to Venice and Trieste : 800 km - 500 miles (10 days including 2 in Venice)

5 From the rich cities of the plain to the lagoons of the Adriatic : 600 km - 375 miles (10 days including 2 in Venice)

6 Art, nature and sprituality in Tuscany and Umbria : 750 km - 465 miles (15 days including 2 in Florence)

7 From the heart of Umbria to the Adriatic : 850 km - 530 miles (8 days)

8 From Rome and its region to the Abruzzi : 1,000 km - 620 miles (8 days including 3 in Rome)

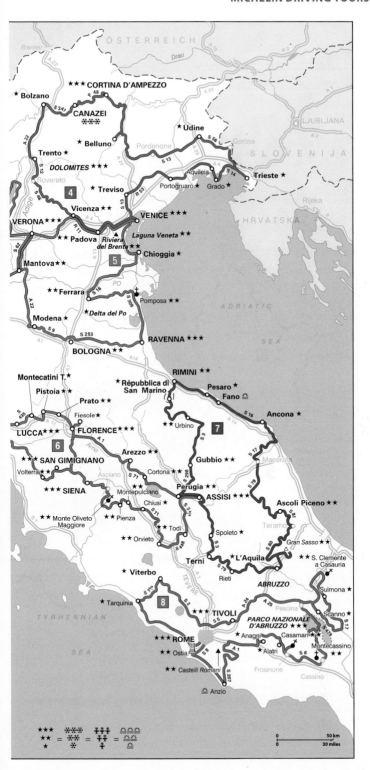

ÖSTERREICH

Brenner
Drau

★ **Bolzano**
★★★ **CORTINA D'AMPEZZO**
CANAZEI
★★★
★ **Belluno**
★ **Udine**
Pordenone
★ **Trento**
DOLOMITES ★★★
Rovereto
★ **Treviso**
Aquileia
Portogruaro ★ Grado ★
★★ **Trieste**
SLOVENIJA
LJUBLJANA

4
★★ **Vicenza**
VENICE ★★★
HRVATSKA
VERONA ★★★
★★ **Padova**
Riviera del Brenta ★★
Laguna Veneta ★★

5
★ **Chioggia**
Mantova ★★
PO
★★ **Ferrara**
Pomposa ★★
ADRIATIC
Delta del Po
Modena ★
RAVENNA ★★★
SEA
BOLOGNA ★★

Montecatini T. ★
RIMINI ★★
Pistoia ★★
★ **Répubblica di San Marino**
Pesaro ★
Fano
★ **Prato** ★★
Fiesole ★
7
Ancona ★
LUCCA ★★★ **FLORENCE** ★★★
★★ **Urbino**

6
Arezzo ★★
Macerata
★★★ **SAN GIMIGNANO**
Volterra ★
Cortona ★★
Gubbio ★★
★★ **Montepulciano**
Perugia ★★
ASSISI ★★★
Ascoli Piceno ★★
★★★ **SIENA**
Chiusi ★
★★ **Monte Oliveto Maggiore**
★★ **Pienza**
★ **Todi**
Spoleto ★
Teramo
Gran Sasso ★★
★★ **Orvieto**
Terni
★ **L'Aquila**
★★ **S. Clemente a Casauria**
Rieti
ABRUZZO

8
★ **Viterbo**
Sulmona ★
★ **Tarquinia**
TEVERE
Pescina
Scanno ★
TYRRHENIAN
TIVOLI
PARCO NAZIONALE D'ABRUZZO ★★★
SEA
★★★ **ROME**
★ **Anagni**
Casamari ★★
★★ **Ostia**
★ **Alatri**
Montecassino ★★
★★ *Castelli Romani*
Frosinone
Cassino
△ **Anzio**

★★★ ★★ ★

0   50 km
0   30 miles

37

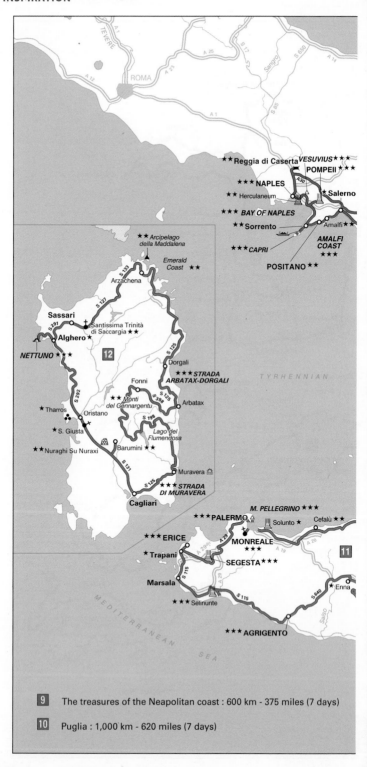

★★ Reggia di Caserta   VESUVIUS ★★★
                        POMPEII ★★★
★★★ NAPLES   Salerno ★
★★ Herculaneum
                        ★★★ BAY OF NAPLES
                        ★★ Sorrento   Amalfi ★★
                                        AMALFI
★★★ CAPRI   COAST
                                        ★★★
POSITANO ★★

★★ Arcipelago
della Maddalena
        Emerald
        Coast ★★
Arzachena
S 133
S 127
Sassari
        Santissima Trinità
        di Saccargia ★★
★ Alghero ★
NETTUNO ★★★
S 291   S 125
                    Dorgali
                                ★★★ STRADA
                                ARBATAX-DORGALI
        Fonni
★★ Monti   S 125
del Gennargentu   Arbatax
S 292
★ Tharros   S 198
        Oristano
                Lago del
★ S. Giusta   Flumendosa
★★ Nuraghi Su Nuraxi
        Barumini ★★
S 131
                Muravera
        S 125   ★★★ STRADA
                DI MURAVERA
Cagliari

TYRHENNIAN

12

11

M. PELLEGRINO ★★★
★★★ PALERMO   Solunto ★   Cefalù ★★
                A 29
★★★ ERICE   MONREALE
★ Trapani   ★★★
                SEGESTA ★★★
Marsala
S 115   A 29   S 640   Enna
                                        Saldo
★★★ Selinunte   S 115

MEDITERRANEAN   ★★★ AGRIGENTO

SEA

9   The treasures of the Neapolitan coast : 600 km - 375 miles (7 days)

10 Puglia : 1,000 km - 620 miles (7 days)

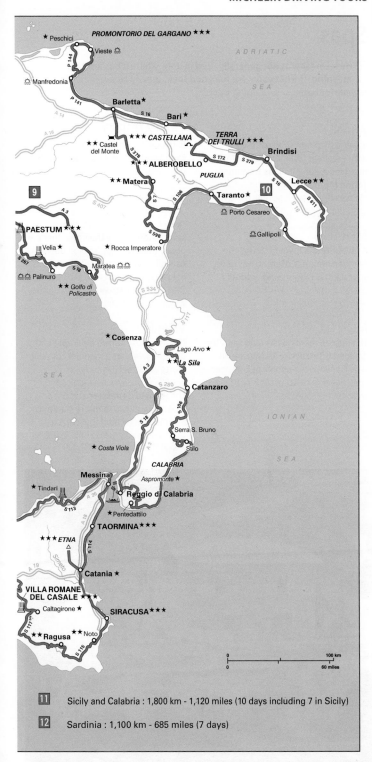

PROMONTORIO DEL GARGANO ★★★

★ Peschici

Vieste ⌂

ADRIATIC

⌂ Manfredonia

SEA

Barletta ★

S 16

Bari ★

★★★ CASTELLANA

★★ Castel
del Monte

**TERRA
DEI TRULLI** ★★★

S 172

S 379

Brindisi

★★ **ALBEROBELLO**

PUGLIA

Lecce ★★

S 16

S 611

★★ **Matera** ○

9

Taranto ★

10

⌂ Porto Cesareo

PAESTUM ★★★

★ Velia

★ Rocca Imperatore

⌂⌂ Gallipoli

Maratea ⌂⌂

⌂⌂ Palinuro

★★ *Golfo di
Policastro*

★ **Cosenza**

Lago Arvo ★

★★ *La Sila*

SEA

Catanzaro

Serra S. Bruno

IONIAN

★ *Costa Viola*

Stilo

CALABRIA

SEA

Messina

★ Tindari

Aspromonte ★

Reggio di Calabria

★ Pentedattilo

TAORMINA ★★★

★★★ *ETNA*
△

Catania ★

**VILLA ROMANE
DEL CASALE** ★★★

Caltagirone ★

SIRACUSA ★★★

Ragusa

★★ *Noto*

0   100 km

0   60 miles

11 Sicily and Calabria : 1,800 km - 1,120 miles (10 days including 7 in Sicily)

12 Sardinia : 1,100 km - 685 miles (7 days)

Spas

The term "spa" is not generally used in Italy, where it has another meaning. If what you want is a good soak, specify *bagni termali* or *piscina termale* for baths or swimming pools.

ABANO
Shaded by pines, this spa town with excellent facilities near Padova numbers among Italians' favourites. **Terme Montegrotto**, (Largo Marconi 8; ☎049 86 66 609; www.abanomontegrotto.it).

MERANO
A favourite spa town of "Sissy", the Austrian empress, **Merano** has good spa facilities indoors and outdoors (Piazza Terme 9, ☎0473 252 000, www.termemerano.it).

MONTECATINI
This Tuscan town boasts nine spas. The grandest is **Tettuccio**, Art Nouveau in style known as the 'temple of European spas' (Viale Verdi 41; ☎0572 77 81, www.termemontecatini.it).

SANT'ANGELO, ISCHIA
Baths cascade down a cliff to the hot sand beach at the **Aphrodite Apollon**, (Via Fondolillo; ☎081 99 92 19, 081 388 308 99, www.terme-ischia.it).

SATURNIA
One of Tuscany's chic spa towns, several hotels have their own thermal pools, while free spirits plop down in natural thermal pools that pop up in fields outside the centre (S.P. Follonata; 58014 Saturnia, ☎0564-600111, www.termedisaturnia.it).

VITERBO
The grandiose **Terme dei Papi** ('baths of the Popes') has a magnificent pool, grotto and hotel (Strada Bagni 12; ☎0761 35 01, www.termedeipapi.it). The **Pianeta Benessere** is more a "beauty farm with a mix of tradition and modern technology" (Strada Tuscanese 26/28; ☎0761 19 70 000; www.hotelsalusterme.it).

Thermal pool in Saturnia, Tuscany

© Fototeca ENIT

Activities for Kids

| n this guide, sights of particular interest to children are indicated with a
KIDS symbol 👥. Some attractions may offer discount fees for children.

THINGS TO DO

In this guide, sights of *particular* interest to children are indicated with a KIDS symbol (👥), though rare these days is the visitor attraction that does not cater in some way for young ones. All attractions offer discount fees for EU children. Inquire about combined passes for families or for extended stays. Here are some of the highlights:

Rome and Lazio
– Colosseum (p155)
– Vatican Museum Mummies (p162)
– Bicycle in Villa Borghese park (p168)
– Tour the catacombs (p172)

Abruzzo and Molise
– Campo Imperatore cable car (p197)
– Bell factory in Agnone (p199)
– Explore Calanchi in Atri (p195)
– Termoli fish market and swim (p199)

Naples and Campania
– Explore Pompeii (p231)
– Hike around Vesuvius (p223)
– Doll hospital in Naples (p201)
– Reggia di Caserta gardens (p253)
– Ferry to Ischia and swim (p238)

Puglia
– Boat ride to Tremiti Islands (p262)
– Castel del Monte (p259)
– Foresta Umbra in Gargano (p262)
– Otranto cathedral mosaics (p270)
– Trulli in Alberobello (p265)

Calabria and Basilicata
– Matera sassi stone dwellings (p280)
– Straight of Messina ships (p276)
– Swim at Tropea (p276)
– Stromboli eruptions (Palmi, p333)
– Pentedattilo ghost town (p277)

Sardinia
– Explore Nuraghi (p292)
– Swim Emerald Coast (p284)
– Li Muri Giant's Tomb (p285)
– Neptune's or Ispinigoli caves (p288)
– Cagliari port and boat ride (p293)

Sicily
– Etna sledding and hiking (p326)
– Salt flats and boat to Mozia (p312)
–Villa Romana del Casale (p317)
– Ferry or boat to Stromboli (p333)

Valle d'Aosta and Piemonte
– Winter Olympics site (p343)
– Egyptian mummies, Torino (p349)
– Po River boat trip (p346)

Liguria
– Train and hike Cinque Terre (p382)
– Genova aquarium (p369)
– Genova port ships (p369)
– Portofino park trails (p377)

Lombardy and the Lakes Region
– Leonardo inventions (p385)
– Climb Duomo in Milan (p388)
– Cremona taste torrone, violins (p417)
– Boat trip Lake District (p422)

Veneto Friuli-Venezia Giulia
– Glass blowing in Murano (p447)
– San Marco or Campanile climb (p438)
– Bike ride and swim Lido (p447)
– Gondola and vaporetto rides (p436)

Trentino-Alto Adige/Südtirol
– Sesto funicular railway (p493)
– Merano thermal pool (p483)
– "Ice Man" in Bolzano (p482)

Bologna and Emilia Romagna
– Bike ride, Castello Estense (p506)
– Po Delta bike ride (p509)
– Rimini beach and swim (514)
– Bike ride in Parma (p521)

Tuscany
– Palazzo Vecchio secret passage (p544)
– Florence museum mummies (p549)
– Siena climb Duomo (p583)
– Florence Boboli gardens (p545)

Umbria and Le Marche
– Cascate delle Marmore (p615)
– Castelluccio plains (p615)
– Grotte di Frasassi (p632)
– Bevagna crafts (p611)

What to Buy & Where to Shop

Italy is rarely a place to find a bargain. But it is still the place to go for quality, good design, expert craftsmanship and fine materials. You can get a good idea for quality objects in museums or in high-end designer shops.

SHOPPING

Italy is noted for its luxe retail goods. Shop for quality leather items in Florence and Padova, for high fashion in Milan (in the so-called Golden Triangle around Via Monte Napoleone), or near Via Condotti in Rome. Naples is famous for its tailors.

Sales are controlled by antiquated government regulations, usually occurring Jan/Feb and July/Aug. For a more personal shopping experience, every region produces beautiful crafts of which it is justly proud.

CRAFTS

Alabaster and stone

Alabaster is mostly crafted in Volterra in Tuscany. Liguria crafts slate objects. Cararra, with some of the world's best stonecutters, sells marble and stone products.

Paper and papier mâché

Fine paper can be found in Fabriano in Le Marche, in Florence, Amalfi, Syracuse in Sicily, Lecce in Puglia, Verona, Venice, and Bassano del Grappa in the Veneto region. Venice and Viareggio have papier mâché masks and figures, which appear in many towns during Carnival time.

Ceramics

Mainly these appear in Romagna (Faenza), Umbria (Deruta, Gubbio, Orvieto, Città di Castello) and Sicily (Caltagirone). Some shops in Orvieto and Tuscany make fine reproductions of Etruscan works. Independent potters are represented throughout Italy by art galleries and specialised shops.

Gold and Coral

Look for fine goldsmiths in major cities like Rome, Venice, and Milan, as well as in gold-trading cities of Arezzo and Vicenza. Coral is popular in Naples, Torre del Greco and Alghero on the island of Sardinia.

Filigree

Liguria (Genova) and Sardinia produce fine metalwork. In Abruzzo (Sulmona, Teramo, Lanciano), *presentosa* filigree pendants are given during proposals.

Shopping in Burano/ © Fototeca ENIT

Wood

Trentino-Alto Adige /Südtirol (particularly in Val Gardena) and Valle d'Aosta are popular for carvings. Look for fine inlaid wood, too.

Textiles, Lace, and Leather

Lovers of lace should head to Burano, the colourful Venetian island. Fine silks are produced near Como and decorator silks near Caserta. Casentino wool for sporty jackets and coats is produced in Tuscany near Poppi, while luxurious cashmere is produced in Umbria, Veneto, and other points. Venice has exquisite silks and velvets. High-tech materials are produced in Prato near Florence and near Mantova. Leather purses and shoes are made near Padova, Le Marche, and Florence, which along with Naples is best for gloves.

Porcelain

Campania, Capodimonte, and Bassano del Grappa in the Veneto produce some porcelain.

Glass

Watch the almost magical creation of glass objects on the island of Murano in the Venetian lagoon, known the world over. Glassblowers also work in Liguria, at Altare, near Savona. Empoli manufactures tableware, including wine glasses. While reading glasses and sun glasses are manufactured in the Veneto and Luxottica (Ray-Ban, Persol) is based in Rovereto.

Gourmet

Food and wine are amongst Italy's most important products. Don't look for these products in supermarkets, instead go to specialised shops and quality markets. This is a country where every town has its own style of bread and rolls.

This is the place to taste it all fresh or aged using various methods and times; hams from Parma and San Daniele, and cheeses like Parmigiano (Parmesan).

Try olive oils, especially from Umbria, Tuscany, Sicily and Puglia to compare styles and olives. Don't buy flavoured oils, which often are substandard oils repackaged. Look for fresh truffles, as most "truffle" oil is synthesised. Mushrooms are delicious fresh, but also dried.

Italy has many famous wines to try, but also has many delicious inexpensive everyday wines. Look for grappa in the Trentino and Veneto. Craft beer is becoming more popular throughout Italy. Mineral drinking waters abound.

Find excellent chocolates in Naples, Tuscany, and Torino.

Festivals & Events

Religious festivals are major events, even in a country that seems to have become more secular. Many Christian festivals were timed to substitute for old pagan rituals, which often marked agricultural or cyclical events.

JANUARY

30–31 JANUARY
Aosta – **St Orso Fair** – Craft fair with sale of articles from the Valle d'Aosta.

FEBRUARY

DATES VARY
Agrigento – Almonds in bloom festival.
Carnivale – Celebrated throughout Italy, most famous is Venice with parties and events in the *calli* and *campi* of Venice.
Ivrea – Folk festival, including the famous battle of the oranges.
Rome – Commedia dell'arte plays in piazzas, horse shows, musicians.
Viareggio – Procession of allegorical floats.
Verona – "Venerdì gnocolar" procession.

MARCH

PENULTIMATE SUNDAY IN MARCH
Rome – **Marathon of Rome** – A racecourse amid Rome's most famous monuments.

FEBRUARY: Carnivale, Venice

FEBRUARY: Ivrea, Battle of the oranges

© AGaeta/istockphoto.com

EASTER DAY (MARCH OR APRIL)
Florence – **Scoppio del Carro** – At noon, in Piazza del Duomo, fireworks display from a decorated float – the fireworks are set off by a dove sliding along a wire from the high altar of the cathedral to the float. Parade in Renaissance costume.

APRIL

1 APRIL
San Marino – Investiture of the regents of the Republic.
Taranto – **Holy Week** (Maundy Thursday and Good Friday).
Holy Week rites – Procession of Our Lady of Sorrows and the Mysteries.

© Olivier Harand/Fotolia.com

MAY

SATURDAY BEFORE THE FIRST SUNDAY OF MAY

Naples – Feast of the Miracle of St Januarius (Gennaro) in the cathedral – this feast day is marked by the "blood miracle" of the city's patron saint. Also in September.

Cagliari – Feast of Sant'Efisio.

Assisi – First Thursday after 1 May **Calendimaggio** – A celebration of the Ides of May rooted in medieval and Renaissance traditions.

FIRST WEEK OF MAY

Bari – Feast of St Nicholas – 7 May: procession in period costume through the city; 8 May: Mass and procession along the shore; the statue is taken out to sea and worshipped.

15 MAY

Gubbio – Ceri ("candle") race – Three teams dressed in medieval garb compete in a dramatic uphill foot race to the Basilica of St Ubaldo.

LAST SUNDAY IN MAY

Sassari – Cavalcata Sarda.

Gubbio – Palio della Balestra in Piazza Grande.

LATE MAY

Venice – Vogalonga – A yearly gathering of rowing enthusiasts from around the world who crowd the city's lagoons with all manner of man-powered boats.

Corsa dei Ceri in Gubbio

Each 15 May in the medieval Umbrian town of Gubbio, the townspeople gather at Piazza Grande, the starting point for a gruelling 4.3km/2.7mi uphill race to the Basilica of St Ubaldo. The race always consists of three ten-member teams who represent the town's three main saints – St Ubaldo, St Giorgio and St Antonio. Each team is required to carry a candle *(cero)*, which stands about 4m/13ft tall and weighs approximately 280kg/616lbs. Locals and tourists line the route to cheer on the *ceraioli* (candle-bearers), even though the winner is predetermined. Following choreography that is centuries old, team St Ubaldo always wins – a tribute to Gubbio's most beloved saint.

LATE MAY–EARLY JUNE

Taormina – Festival of Sicilian costumes and carts.

JUNE

EARLY JUNE

Cavalcata Oswald von Wolkenstein – Tournament and medieval fair inspired by the south Tyrolese poet. Castelrotto, Siusi and Fiè allo Scilia.

JUNE–NOVEMBER, EVEN YEARS

Venice – Biennale art festival.

MAY: Feast of St Nicholas, Bari

© APT Puglia

JUNE: Florence – Calcio Storico Fiorentino, parade in historical costume

16–17 JUNE
Pisa – **Feast of St Ranieri.**

24 JUNE AND TWO OTHER DAYS OF THE MONTH
Florence – **Calcio Storico Fiorentino** – Football game in costume in Piazza S. Croce, accompanied by a procession in 16C costumes.

PENULTIMATE SUNDAY IN JUNE
Arezzo – **Giostra del Saracino** – Saracen's Tournament. Also in September.

LATE JUNE–LATE AUGUST
Verona – Opera season in the Roman amphitheatre.

JULY

Spoleto – **Spoleto Festival** – International theatre, music and dance festival.

Perugia – **Umbria Jazz Festival.**

2 JULY
Siena – **Palio delle Contrade** – Historic horse race. Also in August.

SECOND SATURDAY IN JULY
Ascoli Piceno – **Festa della Quintana** – Procession of representatives of the various districts in 15C costumes; jousting.

Third Saturday in July
Venice – **Feast of the Redeemer** – Fireworks display on Saturday night; religious services and regatta on Sunday.

AUGUST

FIRST SUNDAY IN AUGUST
Ascoli Piceno – **Festa della Quintana** – Jousting.

14 AUGUST
Sassari – **Feast of the candles.**

16 August
Siena – **Palio delle Contrade.**

29 AUGUST AND PREVIOUS SUNDAY
Nuoro – **Feast of the Redeemer.**

LAST WEEK IN AUGUST
Ferrara – **Ferrara Buskers Festival** – Street music festival.

LATE AUGUST–EARLY SEPTEMBER
Venice – International Film Festival at the Lido.

SEPTEMBER

Asti – Festival delle Sagre and "Douja d'or" wine festival.
Lucca – Luminara di S. Croce.

FIRST SUNDAY IN SEPTEMBER
Arezzo – **Giostra del Saracino.**
Venice – **Historical Regatta on the Grand Canal** – Gondoliers in period costume compete in this centuries-old boat race.

7 SEPTEMBER
Florence – **Feast of the Rificolona** (coloured paper lanterns). Musical and folklore events in the various districts.

7–8 SEPTEMBER
Loreto – Feast of the Nativity of the Virgin.

AUGUST: Siena – Palio delle Contrade

SECOND WEEKEND IN SEPTEMBER, IN EVEN YEARS
Marostica – Partita a scacchi – Chess tournament in the piazza with human chess pieces.

SECOND SUNDAY IN SEPTEMBER
Foligno – Giostra della Quintana. Sansepolcro – Palio della Balestra – Crossbow competition in medieval costume.

19 SEPTEMBER
Naples – Feast of the Miracle of St Januarius (Gennaro) in the cathedral.

THIRD SUNDAY IN SEPTEMBER
Asti – Palio di Asti – Historic horse race.

OCTOBER

1 October
San Marino – Investiture of the Republic's regents.

NOVEMBER

MID-NOVEMBER
Asti – Truffle festival and auction.

21 NOVEMBER
Venice – Madonna della Salute Feast.

LATE NOVEMBER–DECEMBER
Bolzano, Bressanone, Merano – Christmas markets.

DECEMBER

8 DECEMBER
Rome – Day of the Immaculate Conception – Statue of Mary in Rome near the Spanish Steps is crowned by firemen.

NIGHT OF 9–10 DECEMBER
Loreto – Feast of the Translation of the Santa Casa.

SEPTEMBER: Venice, Historical Regatta on the Grand Canal

Practical Info

TOP TIPS

Best time to go: Fewer travellers in the major cities Dec–Jan.

Best way around: Walking in historic centres, metro or bus within cities.

Best for sightseeing: Carry as little as possible, take breaks in cafes.

Most authentic accommodation: Agriturismo farm stays, castles, palaces.

Need to know: Many places (shops, museums) still observe an extended lunchtime closing; for 'must-see' sights, morning usually is best.

Need to taste: Wine, olive oil, bread, pasta, pizza, gelato and sorbetto, fresh produce, local meats and cheeses, fish, game, mineral waters.

Before You Go

WHEN TO GO
SEASONS

April, May, September and October are best for city breaks, with cooler temperatures, although not always fewer crowds. However, many Italian cities use the seasons to theatrical advantage and are worth visiting off peak – Venice's winter mists (and floods) lend it an air of mystery, while a crisp winter morning in a deserted Florentine piazza is exceptionally pleasant. June and September are best for beach holidays, providing sultry heat without uncomfortable humidity, high prices and peak crowds. However, in the Alps and Apennines short, cool summers between May and September are optimum times for walking and outdoor activity holidays.
The Italian ski season is typically from December to late March, with year-round skiing on the higher reaches of Mont Blanc.

WHAT TO PACK

Packing light is key in Italy, particularly for travellers using public transportation who don't want to tote overweight luggage onto and off crowded trains and buses. In cool-weather locations, travellers should plan a simple wardrobe and pack a variety of warm hats, scarves and gloves. Warm-weather destinations call for airy shirts, trousers, skirts or dresses. Regardless of the destination or season, a light sweater (to cover bare shoulders) might be necessary for visits to religious buildings. Good, comfortable walking shoes are a must. Many accommodations provide shampoo and soap and travellers can save room in their suitcases by using their hotel's hair

PUBLIC HOLIDAYS	
Jan 1	New Year's Day
Jan 6	Epiphany
Mar/Apr	Easter
Apr 25	Liberation Day
May 1	Labour Day
June 2	Anniversary of the Republic
Aug 15	Assumption of the Virgin
Nov 1	All Saints Day
Dec 8	Day of the Immaculate Conception
Dec 25	Christmas Day
Dec 26	Boxing Day (Santo Stefano)

dryer. A sturdy day bag that zips is nice to have for day trips.

GETTING THERE
BY PLANE

For information on discounts on flights to Italy, see Discounts.
Many international carriers operate services to Rome and the country's major provincial airports (Milan, Turin, Verona, Venice, Genova, Bologna, Florence, Pisa, Naples, Catania and Palermo). Numerous no-frills airlines now offer low-cost flights from many regional airports in the UK, Ireland and other European cities. These usually connect to more remote urban airports or those in regional capitals like Pescara or Verona.
Alitalia (www.alitalia.com)
♦ Heathrow and London City Airports. Customer center, ✆03335 66 55 44 (from UK), ✆89 20 10 (from Italy).
♦ JFK and Newark Airports, ✆1 800 223 5730.
♦ Leonardo da Vinci (Fiumicino) Roma. Customer center, ✆03335 66 55 44 (from UK), ✆89 20 10 (from Italy).
Air Canada (www.aircanada.com)
♦ Flights from Montreal and

Toronto Airports to Rome and other destinations. Customer center, ℘1-888-247-2262 (from Canada), ℘06 835 14 955 (from Italy).

British Airways (www.ba.com)

♦ Waterside, PO Box 365, Harmondsworth, Middlesex UB7 0GB. ℘0344 493 0787.

American Airlines (www.american airlines.it).

♦ Leonardo da Vinci (Fiumicino) Aiport Roma. Customer center, ℘02 3859 1485 (from Italy), 1-800-433-7300 (from U.S. and Canada).

Delta (www.delta.com)

♦ Leonardo da Vinci (Fiumicino) Aiport Roma, http://it.delta.com

Easyjet

♦ Flights from London Stansted and regional airports in the UK; ℘0871 244 2366, www.easyjet.com.

Ryanair

♦ Various destinations; ℘0871 246 0000 (from UK), ℘895 589 5509 (from Italy), www.ryanair.com.

BY SHIP

Details of passenger ferry and car ferry services from the UK and Republic of Ireland to the Channel ports, linking up with the European rail and motorway network can be obtained from travel agents and from the main operators:

P&O Ferries – Dover Ferry Terminal, Travel Centre, Eastern Docks, Dover, CT16 1JA; ℘0800 130 0030, www.poferries.com.

Stena Line – Stena House, Station Approach, Holyhead, Anglesey LL65 1DQ; ℘014 07 60 66 66, www.stenaline.com.

For details of crossing via the **Channel Tunnel** (35-minute high-speed undersea rail link between Folkestone and Calais); ℘084 43 35 35 35 (from UK), ℘0321 00 20 61 (from all other countrie), www.eurotunnel.com.

DFDS Seaways – New Channel Company A/S, Dover Eastern Docks, Dover, CT16 1JA; ℘+45 3342 3010, www.dfdsseaways.com.

BY TRAIN

From London and the Channel ports there are rail services to many Italian towns, including high-speed passenger trains and motorail services. Tourists residing outside Italy can buy rail passes that offer unlimited travel during a specific period. Parties may purchase discounted group tickets on the Italian Railways network.

Italian State Railway ℘89 20 21. www.trenitalia.com.

Rail Europe ℘1 800 622 8600 (from U.S.). www.raileurope.com.

Eurostar ℘03432 186 186 (from UK), ℘+44 1233 617 575 (from all other countries). www.eurostar.com.

Italo ℘06 89371892. www.italotreno.it.

Tickets are also available from the main British and American Rail Travel Centres and travel agencies. Rail is a particularly good way of getting to Milan, Venice and Florence, as the stations are within easy reach of the cities' centres.

BY COACH/BUS

Regular coach services operate from London to Rome and to other large provincial Italian towns and cities. Services from Victoria Coach Station in London to Italy are operated by **Eurolines** ℘08717 818177. www.eurolines.co.uk. Alternatively, contact **National Express** ℘0871 781 8181. www.nationalexpress.com.

BY CAR

⊘*See Documents for details of credential requirements in Italy.* Roads from France into Italy, with the exception of the Menton/Ventimiglia

(Riviera) coast road, are dependent on Alpine passes and tunnels. The main roads go through the Montgenèvre Pass near Briançon, the Fréjus Tunnel and Mont-Cenis Pass near Saint-Jean-de-Maurienne, the Petit-Saint-Bernard Pass near Bourg-Saint-Maurice and the Mont-Blanc Tunnel near Chamonix. Via Switzerland, three main routes are possible – through the tunnel or pass at Grand-Saint-Bernard, through the Simplon Pass, and through the St Gottard Pass, which goes via Ticino and Lugano to the great lakes of Lombardy. Be sure to budget for the Swiss road tax (*vignette*), which is levied on all motor vehicles and trailers with a maximum weight of 3.5 tons, instead of charging tolls on the motorways.

The *vignette* costs 40 Swiss francs and can be bought at border crossings, post offices, petrol stations, garages and cantonal motor registries, or in advance from the Switzerland Travel Centre, 30 Bedford Street, London WC2E 9ED; ℘(020) 0742 04 934; www.stc.co.uk. The Brenner Pass south of Innsbruck greets drivers from Germany and Austria. Remember that most of these tunnels or passes levy tolls (*see By Car in Getting Around, p54*). Use **Michelin maps 719, 721** and **735** or the **Michelin Atlas Europe** to help plan your route.

DOCUMENTS

Passport – Visitors entering Italy must be in possession of a valid national passport. Citizens of European Union countries need only a National Identity Card. Report loss or theft to the embassy or consulate and the local police.

Visa – Entry visas are required by Australian, New Zealand, Canadian and US citizens (if their intended stay exceeds three months). Apply to the Italian Consulate (visa issued same day; delay if submitted by mail). US citizens should obtain the booklet "A Safe Trip Abroad" ($2.75), which provides useful information on visa requirements, customs regulations and medical care for international travellers. Published by the Government Printing Office, it can be ordered by phone (℘(202) 512 0000) or consulted online at http://travel.state.gov.

Driving licence – Nationals of EU countries require a valid national driving licence. Nationals of non-EU countries require an International Driving Permit. This is available in the USA from the American Automobile Association for $15 (an application form can be found at www.aaa.com) and in Canada from the Canadian Automobile Association for $25 (see www.caa.ca for details). If you are bringing your own car into the country, you will need the vehicle registration papers.

Car insurance – If you are bringing your own car to Italy, an International Insurance Certificate (Green Card), although no longer a legal requirement, is the most effective proof of insurance cover and is internationally recognised by the police and other authorities. This is available from your insurer.

DUTY-FREE ALLOWANCES	
Spirits (Whisky, gin, vodka, etc.)	10 litres
Fortified Wines (Vermouth, port, etc.)	20 litres
Wine (not more than 60 sparkling)	90 litres
Beer	110 litres
Cigarettes	3 200
Cigarillos	400
Cigars	200
Smoking tobacco	3kg

Customs Regulations

As of 30 June 1999, those travelling between countries within the European Union can no longer purchase "duty-free" goods. For further information on customs regulations, travellers should contact Her Majesty's Revenue & Customs (HMRC) ☎0845 010 9000; www.hmrc.gov.uk.

The US Customs Service offers a free publication entitled "Know before You Go", which can be downloaded at www.customs.gov.

HEALTH

British citizens should apply to the Department of Health for a European Health Insurance Card (EHIC), which entitles the holder to urgent treatment for accident or unexpected illness in EU countries. It does not provide cover for repatriation in the event of an emergency. The EHIC is free, and can be obtained by calling ☎0800 555 7777 or at **www.dh.gov.uk**. Nationals of non-EU countries should check that their insurance policy covers them specifically for overseas travel, including doctors' visits, medication and hospitalisation in Italy (most take out supplementary insurance). American Express offers its cardholders a service called Global Assist to help in financial, legal, medical or personal emergencies. For further information, consult: www.americanexpress.com. Prescription drugs should always be clearly labelled, and it is also recommended that you carry a prescription copy. Chemists' shops (*farmacia* – green or red cross sign) post a list of colleagues open at night or on Sundays. First aid service (*pronto soccorso*) is at airports, railway stations and hospitals.

♿ACCESSIBILITY

Many of the sights described in this guide are accessible to people with special needs. Sights marked with the symbol ♿ offer full or partial access for wheelchairs. However, it is advisable to check beforehand by telephone.
For further information, contact CO.IN (Consorzio Cooperative Integrate), Via Enrico Giglioli 54/A, 00169 Roma; www.coinsociale.it. The website **www.italiapertutti.it** also provides information on hotels, restaurants, museums and monuments that are accessible to disabled travellers.

DISCOUNTS

Trains

Italy honours the Eurail and InterRail passes (a *supplemento*, an additional fee, may be charged for some services). Ferrovie dello Stato – The train system offers its own discounts, as does a new competitor, Italo.

Airlines

Low budget, no-frills airlines have forced fares down in Europe. Travellers should research the airport's location, transport options and their expense before booking, however. Inquire also about discounts for families, youth, or senior travellers.

On Arrival

GETTING AROUND
BY PLANE

Frequent domestic flights cover the whole country. There are transfer buses to town terminals and railway stations. For further information, contact:

♦ **Airone**: ✆892 444 (+39 091 255 1047 from abroad). www.flyairone.com

♦ **Alitalia**: ✆89 20 10 (✆+39 06 65 649 from abroad). www.alitalia.com.

♦ **Meridiana**: ✆89 29 28 (0871 22 29 319 from UK and 1 718 751 4499 from USA). www.meridiana.it.

BY SHIP

These two islands are linked to the mainland by ferries and hydrofoils, especially popular during the summer months.

Visitors are advised to book early, especially if travelling with a car or if a cabin is required. Deck tickets are available until a few hours before departure at the terminal. Again, it's wise to book ahead, even for less luxurious spots. The main ferry services to Sicily (Catania, Messina, Palermo, Trapani) and Sardegna (Arbatax, Cagliari, Olbia) depart from Genoa, La Spezia, Livorno, Civitavecchia, Fiumicino, Naples, and Salerno Cagliari. Crossings range from about 7–18 hours, depending on departure and arrival ports.

www.aliscafi.it connects Naples to southern ports, including along the Amalfi Coast, Salerno, and the Cilento Coast. From Calabria (Ponte San Giovanni or Reggio) crossings can take 15 to 45 minutes, depending on whether by hydrofoil or car ferry; some are operated by Trenitalia. Some ferries also serve other islands, such as Capri, Ischia, and Malta. The Adriatic Coast has ferry service; most ports serve foreign destinations, but a few ferries serve other Italian Adriatic ports. Check port cities of departure and arrival online under "porto di" and the city name to see additional options, passenger lines, and timetables. For information and reservations, contact:

Caronte&Tourist (Salerno to Sicily)
www.carontetourist.it
Corsica Ferries
www.corsica-ferries.it
Grandi Navi Veloci
www1.gnv.it
Grimaldi Lines
www.grimaldi-lines.com
SNAV
www.snav.it

Palermo port

©Sandro Bedessi/Fototeca ENIT

Tirrenia
www.tirrenia.it
Trenitalia
www.trenitalia.com
UsticaLines
www.usticalines.it

BY TRAIN

The railway network (**www.trenitalia.it**) also enables visitors to travel the length and breadth of Italy. Ticket machines usually have English-language displays and accept credit cards, eliminating long waits and confusing conversations. Whenever possible, reserve a seat or you may wind up huddled in the aisle. Also, be aware that Italy has 10 different services, from the posh Eurostar (ES) to the slow, local Regionale (R).

Mix-ups could result in costly fines and upgrades. Abbreviations indicate a train's type on the display boards and schedules (printed on large yellow and white posters). Special train tickets can be bought once in the country. Super Economy is the least expensive ticket, available for a limited number of seats without refund, change or access to an alternate train. Economy allows for one ticket change prior to departure; no refunds for cancellations or for alternate trains from that booked. The 10 Journey Carnet allows a 20 per cent discount on Frecciarossa and Frecciargento high-speed trains. *Biglietto Base* is the least expensive ticket that allows for a change prior to departure; *Biglietto Flessibile* costs 25 per cent more than Base, but tickets can be changed even after departure time. Groups of 2-5 passengers may also qualify for discounts.

Other special railcards include the *Carta Verde* (for those under 26) and the *Carta d'Argento* (for those over 60), which give 10 and 15 percent discounts on all journeys. Bicycles can be taken on trains (usually all local services) for a supplement.

Italo it's a private rail line was inaugurated. Red high-speed trains connect Milan, Bologna, Florence, Rome, Naples and Venice.

Trenitalia in Italy honours the Eurail and InterRail passes (though a supplemento, an additional fee, may be charged for some services). For additional discounts, including family and group (sometimes a minimum of two) consult the train websites.

For discounts on train fares see Discounts, p52.

BY COACH/BUS

While much of Italy is accessible by train, buses often offer more direct routes and budget fares. There is, however, no national bus company, which can make finding the bus lines between regions difficult. **SITA**, www.sitasudtrasporti.it, has an extensive network, operating in Campania, Puglia and Basilicata. For getting around Toscana, try **BUSITALIA**, www.fsbusitalia.it. For getting around Lazio beyond Rome, try **COTRAL**, ℘800 174 471, www.cotralspa.it.

BY CAR

Italian roads are excellent, and there is a wide network of motorways *(autostrade)* (*see map on p55*). The Italian motorway website can be found at www.autostrade.it.

Highway code

The minimum driving age is 18. Traffic flows on the right. Drivers and front-seat passengers must wear seat belts, also mandatory in the back where they are fitted.

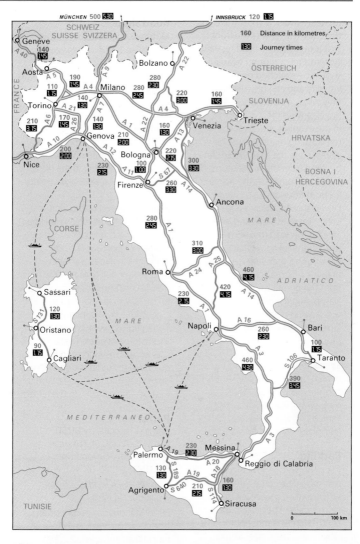

Santa Maria Novella Station, Florence

Y. Kanazawa/MICHELIN

Children under 12 must travel in the back seat, unless the front seat is fitted with a child restraint system. Full or dipped headlights should be switched on in poor visibility and at night; use sidelights only when a stationary vehicle is not clearly visible.

In the event of a breakdown, a red warning triangle must be displayed in the road; these can be hired from the ACI (Automobile Club Italia) offices at the frontier (deposit refunded).

Drivers should watch out for unfamiliar road signs and take great care on the road (there's much truth in the joke that Italian drivers prefer using their horn to their brakes!). At crossroads, cars coming from the right have priority. Flashing lights indicate a driver is not slowing down.

Severe penalties are applicable for drunk-driving offences.

Speed limits

In built-up areas, 50kph/31mph; on country roads, 90kph/55mph; on motorways, 90kph/55mph for vehicles up to 1 000cc and 130kph/80mph for vehicles over 1 100cc.

Parking

Car parks with attendants are common. The crime rate is high, so the extra expense is often worthwhile, especially in the south (Naples is most notorious). Obviously, check rates before parking to avoid unpleasant surprises.

Many large towns limit traffic in their historic town centres (only authorised vehicles may enter), indicated by large rectangular signs saying *Zona a traffico limitato riservata ai veicoli autorizzati.* Parking outside town is advisable anyway, as Italy's old, narrow streets usually have no pavements.

Road signs

Motorways (*autostrade* – subject to tolls) and dual carriageways *(superstrade)* are indicated by green signs; ordinary roads by blue signs; tourist sights by yellow or brown signs.

Road tolls

Tolls are payable on most motorways (www.autostrade.it), calculated according to the distance between the car axles and engine capacity.

At an unmanned booth, press the button for a ticket, which must be presented at the exit.

Motorway fees can be paid in cash (look for lanes with signs representing toll collectors), with the Via Card and by credit card (look for lanes with the Via Card sign and blue stripes on the road surface). The Telepass (www.telepass.it) is a toll pre-pay system that allows cars to pass through road tolls quickly. Unless you have a Telepass don't stray into the signed lane by mistake – it is usually on the far left.

Petrol

Gasolio = diesel.
Super = super leaded (98 octane).
Senza piombo = premium unleaded (95 octane).
Super Plus or Euro Plus = super unleaded (98 octane).

Petrol stations are usually open from 7am to 7pm. Many close at lunchtime (between 12.30pm and 3pm), on Sundays and public holidays, and many refuse payment by credit card.

Attendants do not expect tips and often refuse to issue receipts. Self-service stations have machines that don't give change and have a reputation for malfunctioning. Sometimes a start button or lever activates the flow; however, look around.

Agriturismo in Calabria

Vito Arcomano/Fototeca ENIT

Maps and Plans

Michelin Map 735 at a scale of 1:1 000 000 covers the whole country. At 1:400 000, Michelin Map 561 covers the northwest, 562 the northeast, 563 the centre, 564 the south, 565 Sicily and 566 Sardinia; at 1:200 000, 553 covers Bolzano and Aosta to Milan; at 1:100 000, 115 covers the westernmost stretch of the Italian Riviera. The Michelin Atlas Italy (1:300 000) contains a complete index of towns, 80 plans of the largest cities and covers all of Italy; it is also available in mini format. Folded maps 38 (1:10 000) and 46 (1:15 000) cover Rome and Milano. The Touring Club Italiano (TCI), Corso d'Italia 10, 20139 Milan, ℘02 85 26 800, publishes a regional map series at 1:200 000. www.touringclub.it.
Michelin Travel Publications has created a website to help motorists prepare for their journey. The service enables travellers to select their preferred route (fastest, shortest, etc.) and to calculate distances. Consult www.ViaMichelin.com.

Motoring organisations

Road rescue services – In case of breakdown, contact ACI (Automobile Club Italia), ℘116 (24hrs). This breakdown service (tax levied) is operated by the ACI for foreign motorists. Telephone information in English (and other languages) for road and weather conditions as well as for tourist events: ℘803 116, www.aci.it.

Car rental

There are car rental agencies at airports, railway stations and in all large towns and resorts throughout Italy. The main agencies are Avis, Hertz, Eurodollar, Europcar and Maggiore Budget. Fly-drive schemes or train-and-car packages are available. European cars usually have manual transmissions, but automatic cars are available on request. Many companies won't rent to drivers under-23 International Driving Permit **American Automobile Association** (www.aaa.com) and **Royal Auto Club – RAC** (£8; http://www.rac.co.uk/news-advice) issue these.

PLACES TO STAY AND EAT

BUDGET

The euro has been eroding Italy's reputation for good value. Bills steadily rise and tourists pay the price. However, savvy travellers can still find bargains. Avoid tourist centres and explore off-season. Hotels, in particular, hike up rates in the summer, especially mid-July to the end of August, when Italians go on holiday en masse.

The accommodations and restaurants in the **Address Books** in the guide have been ordered by price categories. Lodgings marked by the symbol ⊖ include campsites, youth hostels and modest but decent hotels and *pensioni* with double rooms for under 70€ (large cities). Restaurants indicated by the symbol ⊖ will charge less than 20€ (large cities) for a three-course meal (excluding drinks) without sacrificing quality: this is Italy, after all, where poor-quality food is scandalous. More charming and comfortable hotels and better-quality restaurants marked by the symbol ⊖⊖. Rooms in this category will cost from 70€ to 100€ for a double (large cities), and expect to pay between 25€ and 35€ for a meal (large cities). For those in search of a truly memorable stay, the category highlighted by the symbol ⊖⊖⊖ includes luxurious hotels, B&Bs and guest farmhouses with great atmosphere, as well as a wide range of facilities. Restaurants in this bracket will satisfy the most demanding tastebuds with prices to match.

Basic meals are cheap and easy to find in Italy: in a pizzeria, expect to pay about 15€ per person, including drinks; a quick snack, especially at lunchtime, will cost around 6€ for a sandwich and 12€ for a simple dish and beverage.

ADDRESSES

⊘ For coin ranges, see the Legend on the cover flap.

Hotel and restaurant listings fall within the descriptions in the Discovering section of this guide. These selections have been chosen for their location, comfort, value and often, their charm. Italian cuisine is as varied as it is exquisite. An array of eateries for their atmosphere, location and/or regional delicacies.

Café in Piazza Navona, Rome

© Jean-Pierre Degas/hemis.fr

STAY
Choosing Where to Stay

Book accommodations well in advance for popular regions and cities, especially from March to October. Typically, prices are lower – and many hotels offer discounts or special weekend deals – from November to March (though not the art cities such as Florence, Venice and Rome). Always check prices before booking, as rates can vary depending on the time of year and availability of rooms.

A law imposes a new hotel tax for the city of Rome.

The fee is intended to financially assist the city's efforts in organising urban services and is aimed at ensuring the standard of the tourists' stay is both highly efficient and of the best quality.

The fee applies to anyone staying in any overnight accommodation inside Rome's boundaries, with the sole exception of hostels, and is paid at the end of each stay. Children under the age of 10 years are exempt from payment. The fee ranges from 1€ to 3€ per person, per night with a maximum of 10 nights (5 nights at campsites).

Hotels And Pensioni

Generally, the word *pensione* describes a small, family-run hotel. Sometimes situated within residential buildings, these offer basic rooms, often with shared bathrooms. A hotel may also be labelled an *albergo* or *locanda*.

Rural Accommodation

Rural guesthouses were originally conceived as an opportunity to combine accommodation and homemade, home-cooked delicacies (among them olive oil, wine, honey, vegetables and meat). Recently some regions have enjoyed an *agriturismo* boom. Some guesthouses are as elegant as the best hotels, with prices to match. Catering could range from a DIY kitchenette to breakfast or a complete menu celebrating the farm's produce. The guesthouses included in the guide usually accept bookings for one night only, but in high season the majority prefer weekly stays or offer half or full board, as well as requiring a minimum stay. Prices for the latter are only given when this formula is compulsory. Many rural guesthouses only have double rooms and prices reflect two people sharing. Solo travellers should ask for, but not expect, a discount. In any case, due to agritourism's ever-increasing popularity, book well in advance. To get an idea of what is on offer, consult www.terranostra.it, www.agriturist.it, www.agriturismo-on-line.com. Information is also available from **Turismo Verde** (Via Mariano Fortuny 20, 00196 Roma; ℘06 32 40 111, www.turismoverde.it).

Bed and Breakfast

Sometimes indistinguishable from a hotel, a B&B may be the hosts' home – an apartment, house or villa with rooms to rent (usually between two and four). Credit cards might not be accepted. Normally, a B&B offers a cosier atmosphere than a hotel.

In Italy the experience is often delightful and reasonably priced. Enquire about curfews before booking, however.

Contact **Bed & Breakfast Italia** (Palazzo Sforza Cesarini, Corso Vittorio Emanuele II 282, 00186 Roma; ℘06 94 80 44 01, www.bbitalia.it). **Also:** www.bedandbreakfast.it; www.primitaly.it/bb/; www.bedebreakfast.it.

Short-Term Rental or Swap

For privacy and authenticity, a short-term rental is ideal. Generally cheaper than hotels, apartments also have basic cooking and facilities. Start your search with companies like **Real Rome** (www.realrome.com), **Life in Italy** (www.lifeinitaly.com/rent) and **ExpatExchange** (www.expat exchange.com). Homeowners can also swap spaces. Find a reputable service, like **Home Exchange** (Post Office Box 787, Hermosa Beach, CA 90254, USA; ℘+1 31 07 98 38 64 (from USA), ℘+44 20 36 08 93 65 (from UK), www.homeexchange.com) or **HomeLink International** (℘422 81 55 75, www.homelink.org). Check references before trading places.

Hostels and Budget Accommodation

Hostel accommodation is only available to members of the **Youth Hostel Association**. Join at any YHA branch for worldwide access. There is no age limit for membership, which must be renewed annually. Apart from official youth hostels there are many establishments, mainly frequented by young people, with dorms, all of which have very reasonable prices.

Visit the websites: www.aighostels.it and www.hostelbookers.com.

For more youth hostelling information, contact www.hiusa.org or www.yha.org.uk.

Italian hostels sometimes inhabit spectacular spaces: villas, fortresses, palaces and old monasteries. Most are run by the **Associazione Italiana Alberghi per la Gioventù** (AIG), situated at Via Nicotera 1 (entrance Via Settembrini 4), 00195 Roma; ℘06 48 71 152, www. ostellionline.org. *Case per ferie* (holiday homes), more common in the big cities, offer decent, cheap accommodations; the only disadvantage being a curfew (typically 10.30pm).

For more information, contact the tourist offices and **CITS, Centro Italiano Turismo Sociale, Associazione dell'ospitalità religiosa**, ℘06 48 73 145, www.citsnet.it.

Campsites

Campsites offer a reasonably priced way of staying close to the city while still enjoying green surroundings. Few wilderness options exist in Italy; the *rifugi* (refuges), some 700 mountain huts, campsites and shelters run by the **Club Alpino Italiano** (℘02 20 57 231; www.cai.it). Expect manicured grounds crowded with tents, caravans (RVs) and bungalows, alongside arcades, shops, discos, pools and restaurants. Happy hordes descend in summertime; reserve in advance. Prices shown are daily rates for two people, one tent and a car. An International Camping Carnet is useful, but not compulsory: **Camping and Caravanning Club**, Greenfields House, Westwood Way, Coventry CV4 8JH, ℘02476 42 20 24, www. campingandcaravanningclub.co.uk. For information contact **Federazione Italiana del Campeggio e del Caravanning**, Via Vittorio Emanuele 11, 50041 Calenzano (FI), ℘055 88 23 91,www.federcampeggio.it.

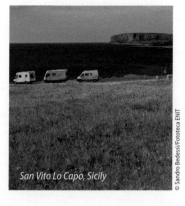

San Vito Lo Capo, Sicily

© Sandro Bedessi/Fototeca ENIT

EAT
Prices and hours

Restaurant opening times vary from region to region (in the centre and south of Italy they tend to open and close later). Generally lunch is from 12.30pm to 2.30pm and dinner from 7.30pm to 11pm. Service is usually included, but tip if you like (a few euros at most, unless the establishment is elite). Restaurants where service is not included are marked; an appropriate percentage for a tip is suggested after the meal's price. By law, the bread and the cover charge should be included, but in some *trattorie* and especially in *pizzerie* they are calculated separately.

♿*For more information on Italian food, see Introduction to Italy.*

Ristorante del Cambio – historic restaurant in Turin
© Giuseppe Bressi/Turismo Torino/Fototeca ENIT

Restaurants, Trattorie And Osterie

The distinction is eroding, but traditionally a *ristorante* offers fine cuisine and service while a **trattoria** or *osteria* is a family-run establishment serving homemade fare in a relaxed setting. In a **trattoria**, the waiter explains the dishes (ask about pricing; seafood, in particular, is sold by weight and expenses mount quickly). Be wary of tourist menus. *Trattorie* used to exclusively serve house wine by the carafe, but now many have wine lists.

Pizzerie

Tasty, quick and affordable, this meal is a staple for tourists and locals alike. We selected exceptional *pizzerie*, but welcome reports of "authentic" establishments from readers.

Wine Bars

Wine bars *(enoteche)* are becoming increasingly popular in Italy. Like *osterie* they often have a kitchen and serve daily specials and light starters, as well as a varied choice of wines served by the glass or bottle. This can be one of the best ways to sample local wines, as well as national or international wines depending on the *enoteca*.

Some coffee bars in major cities have begun to serve a "reinforced" *aperitivo* in the early evenings, more substantial than snacks for an economical light dinner, especially handy for those who have had a large lunch. Likewise a *forno* (bread bakery) might expand its lunch selection to include more than just sandwiches, with a hot dish or two. More effort is being made to accommodate those with dietary needs (vegan, gluten-free, et.c).

Michelin Guide

For a more exhaustive list of restaurants consult the red *Michelin Guide Italia,* which details Italy's hotels and restaurants. Establishments that offer particularly good value are marked with the 😃symbol (good food and service at a reasonable price).

Practical A–Z

ADMISSIONS

Information on admission times and museum- and monument-charges is given in the Sights section of the guide. All are liable to alteration. Due to fluctuations in the cost of living and often in opening times, as well as possible closures for restoration work, the information given here should merely serve as a guideline. Visitors should phone ahead to confirm details.

The admission prices indicated are for single adults benefiting from no special concession. Since 2014 which has ended free entrance to museums for the over-65s, given reductions to under-25s, and free entrance to under-18s and for every first Sunday of the month; parties should be requested on site and be endorsed with proof of ID.

Special conditions often exist for groups, with advance notice. For nationals of European Union member countries, many institutions provide free admission to visitors under 18 and over 65 with proof of identification, and a 50 percent reduction for visitors under 25 years of age. Many museums require visitors to leave bags and backpacks in a luggage deposit area at the museum entrance. Taking photos with a flash is usually forbidden.

During **National Heritage Week** *(Settimana dei Beni Culturali)*, which takes place at a different time each year (usually in the spring), access to a large number of sights is free of charge. A monthly free Sat evening in some state museums is a new service. Contact the tourist offices for details. When visits to museums, churches or other sights are accompanied by a guide, a donation is customary.

BUSINESS HOURS

Most shops in Italy open from 8.30–9am to 12.30–1pm and 3.30–4pm to 7.30–8pm, although in the centre of large towns and cities, shops usually remain open at lunchtime. Credit cards are accepted in most stores, with the exception of small food shops and little markets. In northern Italy,

Santa Croce, Florence

© D. Tondini/hemis.fr

shops often take a shorter midday break and close earlier. Late-night shopping is frequent in seaside resorts. Many tourist resorts have a regular open-air market.

CHURCHES
Churches and chapels are usually closed from noon to 4pm. Notices ask visitors to dress appropriately to a place of worship (no sleeveless and low-cut tops, miniskirts, shorts or bare feet). Tourists should avoid intruding on services.
Try to visit churches early for the best natural light; also some close in the afternoons due to lack of staff. Artworks often have coin-operated lighting.

CONSULATES
♦ **Australia**
Via Antonio Bosio 5, 00161 Roma.
✆06 85 27 21.
www.italy.embassy.gov.au.
♦ **Canada**
Via Zara 30, 00198 Roma.
✆06 85 44 42 911.
www.italy.gc.ca.
♦ **Ireland**
Villa Spada, Via Giacomo Medici 1, 00186 Roma.
✆06 58 52 381.
www.embassyofireland.it.
♦ **UK**
Via XX Settembre 80a, 00187 Roma.
✆06 42 20 00 01.
http://ukinitaly.fco.gov.uk.
♦ **USA**
Via Vittorio Veneto 119a, 00187 Roma.
✆06 46 741.
http://italy.usembassy.gov.

ELECTRICITY
The voltage is 220AC, 50 cycles per second; the sockets are for two-pin plugs. Pack an adaptor to use for hair dryers, shavers, computers, etc.

EMBASSIES
London
14 Three Kings' Yard, W1K 4EH.
✆(020) 7312 2200.
Fax (020) 7312 2230.
ambasciata.londra@esteri.it.
www.amblondra.esteri.it.

Washington, DC
3000 Whitehaven Street NW, 20008-3612
✆(202) 612 4400.
Fax (202) 518 2151.
www.ambwashingtondc.esteri.it.

Ottawa
275 Slater Street, 21st Floor, Ontario K1P 5H9.
✆(613) 232 2401.
Fax (613) 233 1484.
ambasciata.ottawa@esteri.it.
www.ambottawa.esteri.it.

EMERGENCIES
✆113 **General Emergency Services** (soccorso pubblico di emergenza); to be called only in cases of real danger.
✆112 **Police** (carabinieri)
✆115 **Fire Brigade** (vigili del fuoco)
✆118 **Emergency Health Services** (emergenza sanitaria)
✆1515 **Forest Fire Service Environmental Emergencies**
✆803 116 **Automobile Club d'Italia** Emergency Breakdown Service

MEDIA
The main Italian newspapers (available throughout Italy) are *Il Messaggero* and *Il Giorno.* The two national newspapers are *Il Corriere della Sera* and *La Repubblica*. The *Osservatore Romano* is the official newspaper of the Vatican City.

Foreign newspapers are available in the cities and large towns. *Wanted in Rome* magazine keeps expatriates connected in the capital.

MAIL/POST
Opening hours
Post offices are open 8.15am–1.30pm on weekdays, 8.15am–12.30pm on Saturdays. Some branches in city centres and shopping centres are also open on Saturday afternoons. For information, contact ✆800 160 000 or log onto www.poste.it. Stamps are also sold at tobacconists (*tabacchi*) which display a black *valori bollati* sign.

Stamps
Stamps for letters or postcards, up to 20 grams: Zone 1 (Europe inc UK) is 1€; Zone 2 (Americas) is 2.20€. www.poste.it.

MONEY
Currency
The unit of currency is the euro, which is issued in notes (5€, 10€, 20€, 50€, 100€, 200€ and 500€) and in coins (1 cent, 2 cents, 5 cents, 10 cents, 20 cents, 50 cents, 1€ and 2€). Correct change is something of a commodity in Italy. Many bars, for example, are unable to break a 20€ or 50€ note.

Banks
Banks are usually open Mon–Fri 8.30am–1.30pm and 2.30–4pm. Some branches are open in city centres and shopping centres on Saturday mornings; almost all are closed on Sundays and public holidays. Some hotels will change travellers' cheques. Money can be changed in post offices (except travellers' cheques), money-changing bureaux and at railway stations and airports. Commission is always charged.

Credit Cards
Payment by credit card is widespread in shops, hotels and restaurants and also some petrol stations. The *Michelin Guide Italia* and *Michelin Guide Europe* indicate which credit cards are accepted at hotels and restaurants. Money may also be withdrawn from a bank, but may incur interest and charges. Some companies now add a one to three percent conversion fee to credit purchases; avoid using these cards abroad. Finally, inform the company of your itinerary, so a "suspicious activity" block doesn't freeze the account.

PHARMACIES
Crosses (typically in green neon) mark pharmacies (chemists). When closed, each will advertise the name of the duty pharmacy and a list of doctors on call.

PUBLIC HOLIDAYS
Offices and shops are closed in Italy on the following days:

Jan 1	New Year's Day
Jan 6	Epiphany
Mar/Apr	Easter; Mon after Easter
Apr 25	Liberation Day
May 1	Labour Day
June 2	Anniversary of the Republic
Aug 15	Assumption of the Virgin
Nov 1	All Saints Day
Dec 8	Day of the Immaculate Conception
Dec 25	Christmas Day
Dec 26	Boxing Day (Santo Stefano)

Holidays are also observed in cities on local feast days honouring patron saints, including: 25 Apr (St Mark) – Venice, 24 June (St John the Baptist) – Florence, Turin, Genova, 29 June (Sts Peter and Paul) – Rome, 4 Oct (St Petronio) – Bologna and 7 Dec (St Ambrose) – Milan.

TAXES AND TIPPING

Italy adds on a variable tax – averaging 22 percent – to most goods and services. The *Imposta sul Valore Aggiunto* (IVA) mostly lurks unseen, part and parcel of the bill. Visitors from non-EU countries can claim back the IVA on merchandise over 155€. Italians tip about five percent in a pizzeria or humble trattoria, or just round up to the nearest euro.

The rate should rise in more expensive restaurants, but never top 10 percent. 0.50€ tips are appropriate for bar service. Taxi drivers expect around 0.75€, as do cloakroom attendants; porters 0.50€–1€ per bag.

TELEPHONE & INTERNET

The telephone service is organised by TELECOM ITALIA (*www.telecomitalia.it*).

Mobile Phones

Telecom Italia Mobile (TIM) (www.tim.it), Vodafone (www.vodafone.it), Wind (www.wind.it), and 3 (www.tre.it) are the major mobile companies in Italy.

Internet

Many hotels provide a public PC, permit modem hook-ups or have wireless access. Try the following for free access via a laptop: Libero (www.libero.it), Tiscali (www.tiscalinet.it) and Telecom Italia (www.telecomitalia.it). Easy Internet is a reliable connection café; its main outlets are open 24 hours (www.easy.com).

Phonecards

Phonecards (*schede telefoniche*) are sold in denominations of 3€ and 5€ and are supplied by CIT offices and post offices as well as tobacconists (signs bearing a white "T" on a black background). Often,

users must insert a code or tear off a pre-cut corner to activate the card. Also useful for foreigners are New Welcome cards, available in denominations of 5€ and 10€.

Public Phones

Phone boxes (Digito telephone) may be operated by phonecards (sold in post offices and tobacconists) and by phone credit cards. To make a call: lift the receiver, insert payment, await dialling tone, punch in the required number.

Making calls

When making a call within Italy, the area code (eg 06 for Rome, 055 for Florence) is always used, from outside and within the city you are calling.

For international calls dial 00 plus the following country codes:

- 📞 **44** for the UK
- 📞 **61** for Australia
- 📞 **1** for Canada
- 📞 **64** for New Zealand
- 📞 **1** for the USA

If calling from outside the country, the international code for Italy is 39. Dial the full area code, even when making an international call (eg when calling Rome from the UK, dial 00 39 06, followed by the correspondent's number).

Useful Numbers

📞*See also Emergencies, p63.*
The following are subject to a charge:

- 📞 **1254**: Directory Enquiries.
- 📞 **170**: Operator Assisted International Calls.
- 📞 **187**: Telecom Italia's Customer Service.

TIME

Italy lies in the Central European Time Zone and is one hour ahead of Greenwich Mean Time (GMT +1).

Introducing
Italy

Piazzetta San Marco and Palazzo
Ducale from the lagoon, Venice
© Silvio Verrecchia / iStockphoto

Features

Pienza, Val d'Orcia, Tuscany
© Peter Zelei/iStockphoto.com

Italy Today

Italians are masters at knowing how to *arrangiarsi*, which more than making do literally means "to arrange oneself". An art itself done with style, it allows for as much pleasure as possible even in difficult times. No wonder Italy is famous for its way of life, food and wine. For millennia visitors have learned more than a tip or two about the art of living.

A Way of Life

Land of saints, poets, heroes and navigators, Italy's traditions are rooted in an ancient faith. Scars attest to a long struggle for freedom, but the people remain appreciative of life's finer things: art, architecture, cuisine, wine, fashion, design, opera and sultry siestas. Italophile Stendhal noted the Italian predilection for the "art of being happy", something that continues to infuse the modern Italian psyche, despite tumultuous politics and economic uncertainty.

FILM, FASHION AND A FABULOUS LIFE

Italy has long enchanted and inspired the world's imagination. As travel writing's grande dame Jan Morris once observed: "For a thousand years and more, it has been one of the most interesting corners of the earth – not always admirable, but never boring." Indeed, even the peninsula's missteps such as Caligula's cruelties, Christian persecution and the Medici poisonings are the stuff of legend. But Italy is most famous for its sumptuous lifestyle, and rightly so.

One film personifies the country's character: Federico Fellini's *La Dolce Vita*. This 1960 feature captured the glitterati's nightlife in its heyday. As Anita Ekberg frolicked in the Fontana di Trevi, an icon of excess was born. The title – translating as "the sweet life" – passed into everyday English, as did *paparazzo*.

Of course, most Italians do not live silver-screen-style, but most try to infuse a little glamour, a little Good Life, into ordinary existence. Extra virgin olive oil, fresh-baked breads and fine wines are staples. Shoppers select farm-fresh produce among the overflowing stalls in outdoor markets. Pastry shops wrap cakes in lavish paper and ribbons. The sight, the smell, the texture and presentation of food is vital.

The same care translates to fashion. Cashmere, silk, wool and leather hold sway here. Brand names are coveted (and copied frequently by knock-off artists). Through make-up and grooming, the average Italian strives for high style daily. Such *bella figura* – good showing – is only gracious, they believe. Who wants to look at an unkempt person?

People promenade in the evenings, seeing and being seen. Long, languid lunch breaks are common. And the whole country heads to the seashore or mountains for a month each summer. Italians seem to work to live, rather than live to work, yet in recent years Italy has been among the world's top 10 economies.

The formula is not without problems. Passion collides with the Catholic Church's ban on birth control. Governments rise and fall with bewildering regularity. Protests frequently freeze a nation already burdened by Byzantine bureaucracy.

Yet Western civilisation still eagerly takes cues from this small country. Perhaps, as Morris notes, "the world recognises in Italy an essential idea of beauty: beauty of landscape, beauty of learning, beauty of art, beauty of human romance and affectation".

ITALY, THE BEL PAESE

Bel Paese is an affectionate term for Italy, drawn from a book by the Abbot Antonio Stoppani (1824–91) and borrowed by the Galbani dairy in 1906.

Cheese jokes aside, everybody agrees on how beautiful *(bel)* and surprisingly varied the country *(paese)* is. Jutting into the sea, the coastline offers sandy coves and pinewoods, and inlets lapped by emerald water. Inland misty, haunting plains rise to form a wild and rugged terrain where even the snow struggles to settle. Frenetic cities contrast sharply with sleepy hilltop villages, which are still evocative of the Middle Ages. Against this backdrop are mapped the different lives, characters and dialects of this land's inhabitants. For example, Sicilians tease the Milanese about their obsessive punctuality and efficiency. A Neapolitan might marvel over the rhythm, musical tone and humour in the lyrical chatter of the Venetians. And the Romans pity anyone unable to live in the Eternal City, the *caput mundi* – head of the world.

Pizza and Mandolins

Compliments can easily blur into caricatures – and Italy suffers its share of misconceptions. "Pizza, spaghetti and mandolins" is the tourist's knee-jerk perception.

Many Italian traditions – from wheezy accordions to checkered tablecloths and Catholic schoolgirls – are the butt of jokes abroad.

The stereotype was spoofed in *Un Americano a Roma* by **Alberto Sordi** as a xenophile Italian who denounces his origins, but cannot tear himself away from his plate of spaghetti. Yet many long-ridiculed traits have found new vogue: the country's wine, healthy cuisine, the sensual fashion, family values, opportunistic economics and sense of melodrama. Never an easy study, Italy often eludes definition. But that's the charm that leads artists and tourists back to her beauty again and again.

Regions

The 1948 constitution established 20 regions, although it was not enacted until 1970. Five of these (Sicily, Sardinia, Trentino-Alto Adige /Südtirol, Friuli-Venezia Giulia and Valle d'Aosta) have a special statute and enjoy greater administrative autonomy. The regions are subdivided into 95 provinces, which are themselves composed of districts, each headed by a *sindaco* (mayor).

ECONOMY AND GOVERNMENT

Italian politics has long had a reputation for its passionate and precarious nature. In 2006 the centre-left coalition held sway under the leadership of Romano Prodi, former EU Commission president and Italian prime minister in 1998. Prodi's second stint as prime minister lasted less than two years. In 2008 media magnate **Silvio Berlusconi** became Italy's prime minister for a third time. Unable to promise an "Italian Miracle" with regards to the economy, Berlusconi and his conservative coalition was also rocked with scandal. In April 2011 Berlusconi was on trial for a controversy in which he was accused of paying a Moroccan teenage dancer for sex, while charges also continue for his financial misdoings. After Berlusconi resigned in 2011, leaving behind a debt crisis, economist **Mario Monti** led a government of technocrats, remaining until the 2012 budget was passed. In 2013 **Enrico Letta** of the Democratic party was elected leading a coalition government. The next elections are scheduled for 2018, although some predict that general discontent over the economy may force them sooner.

On the international stage, Italy withdrew forces from Iraq in 2006, that same year sending peacekeeping troops to Lebanon. In 2011, Italy participated in the military intervention against Libya. At home, Italy's economy has been facing increasing difficulties, with rising inflation and the impact of fierce international competition on the medium-sized family-owned companies that make up the bulk of its manufacturing industries. In 2008 Italy officially plunged into a recession. The country's public debt, estimated at approximately 126 percent of GDP in 2012, and a fiscal deficit at about 2.9 percent of GDP in 2012, signals a tough economic outlook for the country for at least the next few years. Protests against public spending cuts and pension reforms have been vehement. Meanwhile, Fiat and Alitalia struggle to survive in the increasingly competitive transport market.

Gourmet Italy

L isten to any Italian conversation on the street and chances are it's about food. Italian cooking worldwide is one of the most popular, yet actually is a lavish buffet of regional and provincial cuisines, precisely defined and fiercely defended. The south, especially Sicily and Naples, has among the most sophisticated and varied food, while the north reflects French or hearty Germanic influences. Wine is essential, ranging from wines prized by collectors to marvellous local everyday wines at reasonable prices.

REGIONAL SPECIALITIES: FROM NORTH TO SOUTH

Piemonte

Cooking here is done with butter. A popular dish is **fonduta**, a melted cheese dip of milk, eggs and white truffles *(tartufi bianchi)*. Typical of the region are truffles and *cardi* (cardoons), prepared *alla bagna cauda*, ie with a hot sauce containing oil, anchovies, and garlic. Other dishes include **agnolotti** (a kind of ravioli), braised beef in red Barolo wine, boiled meat, **fritto misto alla Piemontese** and **bonet** dessert (a type of chocolate pudding).

Monferrato and the Langhe hills are also famous for their excellent cheeses, such as **Robiola**, **Castelmagno** and **Bra**, and delicious wines: **Barolo** (one of Italy's great wines), **Barbaresco**, **Barbera**, **Grignolino**, red Freisa wines, white Gavi and dessert wines such as **Asti**, still or sparkling *(spumante)*, and Moscato.

Lombardy

Milan, where cooking is done with butter, gives its name to several dishes: *minestrone alla Milanese*, a soup of green vegetables, rice and bacon; *risotto alla Milanese*, rice cooked with saffron; **costoletta** *alla Milanese*, a fillet of veal fried in egg and breadcrumbs with cheese, and **osso buco**, a knuckle of veal with the marrow-bone. **Polenta**, maize semolina, is a staple food in traditional country cooking.

Also worth trying are the **tortelli di zucca** (pumpkin fritters) from Mantova. The most popular cheeses are the creamy **Gorgonzola**, the hard **Grana** **Padano** and **Taleggio**. **Panettone** is a Christmas bread containing raisins and candied lemon peel and **torrone** (nougat) is a speciality of Cremona. Wines produced include Franciacorta, Italy's sparkling reply to Champagne. Lovely varieties are produced around Garda, and red wines in the Valtellina and Pavia. The Valtellina also makes **pizzoccheri** (a large tagliatelle made from buckwheat) and its **Bitto** cheese.

Veneto

As in the Po Delta, the people of the Veneto eat **polenta**, **bigoli** (a type of spaghetti), **risi e bisi** (rice and peas), **risotto** with fish and **fegato alla Veneziana** (calf's liver fried with onions). The excellent fish dishes include shellfish, eels, dried cod *(baccalà)* and **sardelle in saor** (sardines in brine). Black spaghetti or rice made with cuttlefish ink is a popular Venetian dish.

The most renowned cheese of the region is **Asiago**. **Pandoro**, a star-shaped cake delicately flavoured with orange-flower, is a speciality of Verona. The best red wines come from the district of Verona: **Amarone**, **Valpolicella** and **Bardolino**. Sparkling white **Prosecco** is popular as an *aperitivo*. **Soave** is Verona's white wine.

Trentino-Alto Adige /Südtirol and Friuli-Venezia Giulia

In the Alto Adige, **canederli** (dumplings) made with bread and flour are served with sauce or in a broth. **Gröstl** (potato and meat pie) and smoked pork served with sauerkraut are popular main dishes. Delicious pastries include the **strüdel** fruit tart. Friuli is famous for **cialzons** (a ravioli), **jota** (meat soup), pork-butchers' specialities (ham – **prosciutto di San Daniele**), fish dishes (**scampi**, **grancevole** – spider crabs), **frico** (fried cheese) and montasio cheese. Trentino-Alto Adige / Südtirol is known for its aromatic white wines including Müller-Thurgau, Riesling, Chardonnay, and Pinot Bianco. While reds include Lagrein, Pinot, Cabernet, and Cabernet Franc. Friuli produces white Sauvignon, Pinot and near Udine, Friulano Tocai; red wines are produced, too.

Liguria

Genova's chief speciality is **pesto**, a sauce made with olive oil, basil, pine-kernels, garlic and ewe's cheese. It is served with **trenette** (long, thin noodles) and lasagne (flat pasta leaves). Other dishes include **cima** (stuffed meat parcels) and the excellent **pansotti** (a ravioli) served with a walnut sauce. The delicious seafood includes *buridda* (fish soup), **cappon magro** (fish and vegetable salad) and **zuppa di datteri**, a shellfish soup from **La Spezia**, with which the Ligurians drink white wines Vermentino or Pigato. Sciacchetrà is prized also for a *passito* (sweet) version.

Emilia Romagna

The region has a gastronomic reputation; its pork-butchers' meat is the most famous in Italy: Bologna **salami** and **mortadella**, Modena **zamponi** (pig's trotters), Parma **prosciutto** (ham). *Pasta* is rich and tasty when served *alla Bolognese*, with a meat and tomato sauce. **Parmesan cheese** *(parmigiano)*, hard and pale yellow, is strong yet delicate. Emilia produces **Lambrusco**, a fruity, red, sparkling wine, and white Albana.

Tuscany

Italians claim that the Medici court taught the French how to cook. However, regional fare tends to be hearty and simple. Soup include the famous **ribollita**, pasta the **pappardelle**, a wide noodle. Florence also offers its *alla Fiorentina* specialities: dried cod (**baccalà**) with oil, garlic and pepper; game and meats include **bistecca** – grilled steak fillets with oil, salt and pepper; **fagioli all'uccelletto** or "al fiasco" (white cannellini or borlotti-beans). Livorno produces **triglie** (red mullet) and **cacciucco** (fish soup) and Siena offers **panforte**, a cake containing almonds, honey and candied melon, orange and lemon.

Tuscan cheeses include **pecorino** and **caciotta**. **Chianti** is the most popular red wine, but noteworthy are the **Brunello di Montalcino**, **Nobile di Montepulciano** and reds from the Bolgheri area, while white includes **Vernaccia di San Gimignano** and the sweet **Vin Santo** wines.

Umbria and Le Marche

Like Tuscany, Umbrian cuisine offers bounty from its forests like black truffles (**tartufo nero**), mushrooms, and game. Pork is a speciality, like **porchetta**, a whole suckling pig roasted on the spit. The prized red wine is Sagrantino from Montefalco, while Orvieto produces a vast quantity if not always quality of white wine. Specialities from the Marches include *vincigrassi* (pasta cooked in the oven with a meat and cream sauce), **stringozzi** (a type of hollow spaghetti), stuffed olives, **brodetto** (a fish soup) and **stocco all'anconetana** (dried cod). Le Marche has intriguing wines to try from white Verdicchio) to red Rosso Conero, Rosso Piceno, and Lacrima Moro d'Alba.

Lazio

Rome produces many specialities, most quite simple: **spaghetti** (or other pasta) **all'amatriciana** (tomato with bits of pork cheek) or **alla carbonara** (Parmesan , egg, and bits of pork cheek or bacon), **gnocchi** *alla Romana*, **saltimbocca** (a fillet of veal rolled with ham and a bit of fresh sage and sauteed), and **abbacchio al forno** (roast lamb) or lamb *alla cacciatora* (with white wine or vinegar and herbs).

Roman artichokes are famous, either *carciofi alla Giudia*, fried and crispy, or *alla Romana* boiled with Roman mint then seasoned with garlic and lemon zest. Offal is another speciality.

Pecorino (ewe's milk cheese), **caciotta, ricotta.** Red wines are improving, with Cesanese del Piglio mostly southeast, while other reds are toward Bolsena and Montefiascone. Less distinctive are the white wines of the **Castelli** (Frascati) except for a few good small producers.

Abruzzo and Molise
Among the pasta note **alla chitarra**, which is cut into strings using a guitar-shaped instrument. Lamb and veal are especially good, the coast offers delicious **brodetto** seafood stew. Fresh mountain sheep and even goat cheeses are good, as well as wildflower honey and saffron. **Montepulciano d'Abruzzo** is the famous red wine, while Molise produces litle known but delicous **Tintarella.** For crisp whites try **Passerina** and Pecorino.

Campania
Naples cuisine ranges from sophisticated to earthy. **Spaghetti** is often prepared with shellfish *(alle vongole)*. *Trattorie* and *pizzerie* serve *costata alla pizzaiola*, a fillet steak with tomatoes, garlic and wild marjoram, **mozzarella** in *carrozza* (cheese savoury) and especially **pizza** and **calzone** (a folded pizza), topped with cheese (mozzarella), tomato, anchovy, capers and herbs. The local **mozzarella di bufala** (buffalo mozzarella cheese) is especially delicious. Cakes and pastries often are made with **ricotta** cheese and candied fruit. Wines from volcanic soil have a vivacious, slightly mineral note. For red, don't miss **Taurasi** and **Aglianico.** For white, try Falanghina, Fiano di Avellino, and Greco di Tufo. Even Capri and Ischia produce wines as do the slopes of Vesuvius, red and white **Lacchryma Cristi.**

Puglia, Basilicata and Calabria
Orecchiette con cime di rapa (pasta "ears" with rape), rice with mussels *(cozze)*, stuffed cuttlefish *(seppia)*, the delicious oysters *(ostriche)* of Taranto and **capretto ripieno al forno** (roast kid stuffed with herbs) are some typical Puglia dishes. **Primitivo** is the hefty red from Manduria and Vultura in Basilicata. Other wines are produced, around Locorotondo, San Severo and Castel del Monte. The specialities of Basilicata include **pasta alla potentina** and a range of lamb and mutton dishes, as well as fish, and a good selection of cheeses *(caciocavallo, scamorza* and ricotta). Calabria offers some of Italy's spicier cuisine using **peperoncino** in 'nduja, a spreadable sausage. Cirò is red wine popular near the coastal areas.

Sicily
Some of Italy's most complex and varied cuisine is from Sicily. **Pasta con le sarde** enchances sardines with wild fennel, while **alla Norma** is rich with aubergines, tomatoes and aged ricotta. Coastal seafood dishes and mountain Nebrode pork and game. The Trapani area serves **cuscusu** (couscous), an Arab import, with fish. Rich in fruit (lemons, oranges, mandarins, olives, pistachios, almonds), some is transformed into pastries and ices. **Cassata**, a semi-frozen cream cake, has chocolate and candied fruits, while **cannoli** is filled with ricotta and candied fruit, as well as almond cakes and marzipan. **Nero d'Avola** and **Etna Rosso** are among Sicily's best red wines, while **Cataratto**, **Malvasia** and the white wines of Etna and Lipari are also delicious. **Marsala** produces a strong golden fortified wine.

Sardinia
Sardinia offers **malloreddus** (pasta shells with sausage and tomato), delicious lobster soup and pork cooked on a spit, with **carasau** a paper-thin crunchy bread. Predominant cheeses **fiore** and **pecorino** are made from ewe's milk. **Sebadas** are fried doughnuts drizzled with honey. Local wines include red **Cannonau** and the white **Vermentino.**

Vegetarian Options
Vegetarians *(vegetariani)* and vegan cuisine is popular, but be very clear: *Non mangio la carne* (I don't eat meat). *Antipasti di verdura* (vegetable starters) are delicious, as are many pasta and **risotto** (rice) dishes *con verdura*.

Italian History

Although Italic tribes date to the 10C or 9C BC, "Italia" was used for the first time only in the 1C BC. "Italy" as a unified country, however, did not exist until the latter part of the 19C. For most of its recorded history, this narrow peninsula was a major stage. Phoenicians and Etruscans set up trade, Greeks colonised, emperors ruled most of the known world, later to become the vanquished. Barbarians, Crusaders, Renaissance courts, bankers, guilds, warrior popes, anti-popes, abdicators,slaves, tyrants, saints, sinners, and coalitions – all have left their mark. The country has a rich and tumultuous history, still very much in evidence today.

» Key Events   p77

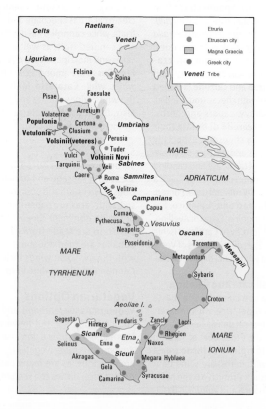

Key Events

Since 2000 BC, Italy has been a crossroads of cultures, the intermingling of Etruscan, Greek and Latin civilisations. The Romans ignited the Italian peninsula, inhabited by Greek colonists, the gentle Etruscans and various Indo-European tribes. They rewrote the rules, from the she-wolf rescuing abandoned babies to Caesar storming across the Rubicon. The Romans spread peace and prosperity from Upper Mesopotamia to the British Isles. Eventually Barbarian invasions and plague weakened the Empire, which split in two and converted to Christianity. Lombards, Franks and Normans ruled the ruins, and later popes and emperors. City-states squabbled through the Dark Ages; then blossomed in the Renaissance. Italians finally cast off foreign rulers – the French and Spanish – under the dashing leadership of Giuseppe Garibaldi in 1871. Following the horrors of Fascism and 1970s political terrorism, Italy stabilised and joined the European Union. The tumultuous journey from "head of the world" to member-state left behind a rich cultural and historical legacy, treasured by travellers.

GREEK COLONISTS (8C–4C BC)

After the **Phoenicians** had settled at Carthage and set up trading posts, the Greeks founded a large number of colonies on the coasts of Sicily and southern Italy (8C BC), known as **Magna Graecia**. It included Ionian, Achaean and Dorian colonies, named after the Greek peoples who had colonised them. The social unit was the "city".

The 6C and 5C BC marked the zenith of Greek civilisation in Italy, corresponding to the period of Pericles in Athens. Greek seaborne trade was so successful that Syracusae soon rivalled Athens. Syracuse and Taranto were the two main centres of this refined civilisation. Philosophers, scientists and writers settled in Sicily. Aeschylus lived at Gela. Theocritus defined the rules of bucolic poetry and Archimedes was murdered by a Roman soldier in Syracusae. But rivalry between these many and varied cities led to warfare, which, with Carthaginian raids, led to decline, culminating in the Roman conquest at the end of the 3C BC.

ETRUSCAN EMPIRE (8C–4C BC)

While the Greeks were disseminating their civilisation throughout the south of the peninsula and Sicily, the Etruscans flourished in central Italy, from the 8C BC onwards. This powerful empire's growth was checked only by that of Rome (3C BC). They are a little-known people whose alphabet, along with certain tombstone inscriptions, has now been partially deciphered. Some authorities think they were natives; others, following the example of Herodotus, insist they came from Lydia in Asia Minor. The Etruscans at first occupied the area between the Arno and the Tiber (*see map, p76*) but later spread into Campania and the Po Plain. They reached their zenith in the 6C BC. Etruria then comprised a federation of 12 city-states known as *lucumonies,* which comprised the cities of Tarquinia, Vulci, Vetulonia, Cerveteri, Arezzo, Chiusi, Roselle, Volterra, Cortona, Perugia, Veii and Volsinii (present-day Bolsena). Grown rich from ironwork, copper and silver mines, and trade in the western Mediterranean, these excellent artisans and technicians enjoyed a highly refined civilisation.

ORIGINS OF THE ROMAN EMPIRE (753–30 BC)

The mythical foundation of Rome by Romulus coincides also with the dates of artefacts excavated on the Palatine Hill, with more recent finds dating as early as the 9C or 10C BC. Latin peoples began moving down from the surrounding hillsides toward the Tiber. The Iron Age settlement huts grew to trading post, town, kingdom, republic, triumvirate, and dictatorship with a powerful and massive military might and system of governors to rule outposts.

BC

753	Foundation of Rome by Romulus, according to legend. (However, archaeologists unearthed Latin and Sabine villages on the Tiber Island and Palatine from the early 8C.)
750	Rape of the Sabine women.
7C–6C	Royal dynasty of the Tarquins, Etruscan rulers. Power is divided between the king, the senate and the people.
509	Tarquins expelled after the rape of Lucretia. Establishment of the Republic: the king's powers are conferred on two consuls.
451–449	The Law of the XII Tables institutes equality between patricians and plebeians.
390	The Gauls sack Rome.
281–272	War against Pyrrhus, King of Epirus; southern part of the peninsula submits to Rome.
264–241	**First Punic War**: Carthage abandons Sicily to the Romans.
218–201	Second Punic War. **Hannibal** crosses the Alps and defeats the Romans at Lake Trasimeno. Hannibal routs the Romans at Cannae and halts at Capua. In 210 **Scipio** carries war into Spain, and in 204 he lands in Africa. Hannibal is recalled to Carthage. Scipio defeats him at Zama in 202.
146	Macedonia and Greece become Roman provinces. Capture of Carthage.
133	Occupation of Spain, end of Mediterranean campaigns.
133–121	Failure of the policy of the Gracchi, who promoted popular agrarian laws.
122	Senate assassinates democratic reformer Gaius Gracchus.
118	The Romans in Gaul.
112–105	War against Jugurtha, King of Numidia (now Algeria).
102–101	Marius, the vanquisher of Jugurtha, stops the invasions of Cimbri and Teutoni.
88–79	Sulla, Marius' rival, triumphs over Mithridates (King of Pontus) and establishes his dictatorship in Rome.
70	**Pompey** and **Crassus** become masters of Rome.
63	Catiline's plot against the Senate exposed by Cicero.

60	The first Triumvirate: Pompey, Crassus, **Julius Caesar**. Rivalry of the three rulers.
59	Julius Caesar as consul.
58–51	The Gallic War (52: Surrender of Vercingetorix at Alesia).
49	Caesar crosses the Rubicon, driving Pompey from Rome.
49–45	Caesar defeats Pompey and his partisans in Spain, Greece and Egypt. He writes his history of the Gallic War and meets Cleopatra.
Early 44	Caesar appointed dictator for life.
15 March 44	Caesar is assassinated by Brutus, his adopted son.
43	The second Triumvirate: **Octavian** (great-nephew and heir of Caesar), **Mark Antony**, Lepidus.
41–30	Struggle between Octavian and Antony. At Actium, lovers Antony and Cleopatra suffer defeat, retreat to Alexandria and suicide.
27	**Octavian** takes the title **"Augustus Caesar"** and plenary powers.

THE EARLY EMPIRE (27 BC–AD 275)

Aware of the perils that being dictator brought Julius Caesar, Augustus carefully avoided using terms like monarchy. But in effect he had the final word, supported by the military, setting up a dynastic succession of emperors. The empire expanded to its largest under Trajan, then was somewhat reduced by Hadrian. Some historians argue that the beginning of the Empire's decline began under Commodus, who succeeded Marcus Aurelius.

AD	
14	Death of Augustus.
14–37	Reign of Tiberius.
41	**Caligula** assassinated.

Pantheon, founded in 27 BC and rebuilt by Hadrian (118–125)

© Sergey Borisov / Fotolia.com

64	**Nero** rules. Rome burns.
67	**Saints Peter** and **Paul** martyred.
68	**Julio-Claudian dynasty** (Augustus, Tiberius, Caligula, Claudius, Nero) ends.
69–96	**Flavian dynasty**: Vespasian, Titus, Domitian.
96–192	Century of the Antonines, marked by the successful reigns of Nerva, Trajan, Hadrian, Antoninus and Marcus Aurelius, who consolidated the Empire.
193–275 **Severus dynasty**	Septimius Severus, Caracalla, Heliogabalus, Alexander Severus, Decius, Valerian, Aurelian.
235–68	Military anarchy; a troubled period. The legions make and break emperors.
270–75	Aurelian re-establishes the unity of the Empire.

THE LATER EMPIRE AND DECLINE (AD 284–476)

The administration of the empire was divided between East and West in a power-sharing scheme intended to institute better controls under Diocletian, who also ruthlessly persecuted Christians. Constantine established religious freedom and instead of Rome created his base in Constantinople. Over-extended, Rome declined as rivalries and invasions weakened the empire.

284–305	Reign of **Diocletian** ("the age of martyrs"). Empire split into East and West.
306–37	Reign of **Constantine**. By the **Edict of Milan** (313), Constantine decrees religious freedom. Constantinople, the eastern capital, thrives. Rome declines.
379–95	Reign of **Theodosius the Great**, the Christian Emperor, who establishes Christianity as the state religion in 382.
	At his death the Empire is divided between his sons, Arcadius (East) and Honorius (West).
5C	The Roman Empire is repeatedly attacked by the Barbarians: in 410, Alaric, King of the **Visigoths**, captures Rome. Capture and sack of Rome in 455 by the **Vandals** under Genseric.
475	Byzantium is the seat of the Empire. Goths rule Rome.
476	Deposition by **Odoacer** of Emperor Romulus Augustus ends the Western Empire.

ROMAN EMPIRE TO HOLY ROMAN EMPIRE

The Goths and Ostrogoths invasion and rule was later replaced by the Lombards. The Papal States were created during this period, while Charlemagne became King of the Lombards and subsequently Holy Roman Emperor. Anarchy followed for a prolonged period. Otto I later became King of the Lombards and then emperor.

493	Odoacer is driven out by the Ostrogoths under Theodoric.

535–53	Reconquest of Italy by the Eastern Roman Emperor **Justinian** (527–65).
568	**Lombards**, a Germanic tribe, invade led by King Alboin.
590–604	Papacy of **Gregory the Great**, who evangelised the Germans and Anglo-Saxons.
752	Threatened by the Lombards, the Pope appeals to **Pepin the Short**, King of the Franks.
756	Donation of Querzy-sur-Oise. Pepin the Short returns the Byzantine territories conquered by the Lombards to Pope Stephen II, leading to the birth of the **Patrimonium Petri** (**Papal States**) and temporal power of the Pope.
774	Pepin's son, **Charlemagne** (Charles the Great), becomes King of the Lombards.
800	Charlemagne is proclaimed Emperor of the **Holy Roman Empire** by Pope Leo III.
9C	The break-up of the Carolingian Empire causes complete anarchy and the formation of many rival states in Italy. This is an unsettled period for the Papacy, which is often weak and dissolute. Widespread corruption among the ecclesiastical hierarchy.
951	Intervention in Italy of **Otto I**, King of Saxony, who becomes King of the Lombards.
962	Otto I, now crowned emperor, founds the Germanic Holy Roman Empire.

THE CHURCH VERSUS THE EMPIRE

On the cusp of the millennia, the Lombards continued their power struggle with the Normans. The delicate balance between Roman Emperor and Pope shifted as they vied for predominance. A pilgrimage to the Holy Land evolved into a military campaign to capture Jerusalem from the Moslems, with the Pope proclaiming that participants would be absolved of their mortal sins,thus securing a chance to enter heaven, and some sizable booty. Emperor Frederick I was succeeded by his son Frederick II, born in Jesi (Le Marche), who left behind revised codes of law and a network of castles.

9C	Establishment of **Normans** in Sicily and the south.
1076	The **Gregorian Reform** of Pope Gregory VII tries to re-establish the Church's influence. Dispute between the Pope and Emperor Henry IV leads to the **Investiture Controversy**.
1077	Humbling of the emperor before the Pope at Canossa.
1097	**First Crusade** begins, 35,000+ crusaders.
1155	**Frederick Barbarossa** crowned emperor.
	The struggle between the Empire and the Papacy resumes, with the **Ghibellines** supporting the emperor and the **Guelphs** supporting the Pope.

1167	Creation of the **Lombard League**, an association of Guelph leaning cities.
1176	Frederick Barbarossa and Pope Alexander III reconcile.
1216	Triumph of the Papacy on the death of Pope Innocent III.
1227–50	A new phase in the struggle for Empire (Frederick II) and the Papacy (Gregory IX).

FRENCH INFLUENCE AND THE DECLINE OF IMPERIAL POWER

The Anjou dynasty was established in Sicily at the end of the 13C and in the 14C chose Naples as its seat. Seven years later the papacy moved to Avignon for most of the 14C. In the 15C, Florence saw the rise of banking and patronage of the arts. Spain's power rose during this period, further extended with the only two Spanish popes in history and economically with Isabella's funding of Columbus.

13C	Peak of economic prosperity of the Communes.
1265	Charles of Anjou, brother of St Louis, crowned King of Sicily.
1282	**Sicilian Vespers**: massacre of French settlers in Sicily.
1300	First Jubilee declared by Pope **Boniface VIII**.
1302	The **Anjou dynasty** establishes itself in Naples.
1303	Attack of Anagni, instigated by King Philip of France, on Pope Boniface VIII (👁 *see ANAGNI).*
1309–77	The popes established at **Avignon**, France. The Avignon popes included Clement V to Gregory XI, who took the Papacy back to Rome at the instigation of St Catherine of Siena. This period is referred to as the **Avignon Captivity.**

Castel Nuovo (or Maschio Angioino) built in 1282 in Naples by Pierre de Chaulnes and Pierre d'Agincourt, architects of Charles I of Anjou

© onfilm/iStockphoto.com

THE "ROMAN QUESTION"

The Papacy became involved in the Risorgimento during the 19C, when it became clear that the Unification of Italy could not take place unless the Pope was willing to relinquish the temporal power that he exercised over part of the country. When the troops of Victor Emmanuel II entered Rome in 1870, Pope Pius IX retired to the Vatican, declaring himself a prisoner of the Italian State. The "Roman Question" was only finally resolved in 1929, under the Papacy of Pius XI, with the **Lateran Treaty** drawn up between the Holy See and the Fascist government of **Benito Mussolini**. These pacts recognised the sovereignty of the Pope within the Vatican City, as well as over certain buildings and organisations in Rome, and granted the Church specific authority regarding education and marriage in Italy. The Lateran Pacts were then included in the new Constitution of the Italian Republic in 1947. They have continued to govern relations between the Italian State and the Church since the end of World War II, and were modernised in a new Concordat in 1984.

1328	Failure of the intervention in Italy by the Emperor Ludwig of Bavaria.
1378–1418	The **Great Schism of the West** (anti-popes in Pisa and Avignon) is brought to an end by the Council of Constance (1414–18).
1402	Last German intervention in Italy (the Lombard militia defeats the emperor).
1442	Alfonso V, King of **Aragon**, becomes King of the Two Sicilies.
1453	Constantinople, capital of the Christian Eastern territories, falls to the Turks.
1492	Death of **Lorenzo de' Medici. Christopher Columbus** discovers America.
1494	French King Charles VIII intervenes for Ludovico Il Moro.

ECONOMIC AND CULTURAL GOLDEN AGE (15C, EARLY 16C)

Trade transformed the north and centre of the peninsula, while the south kept its feudal structures. The economic importance of Italy derived from the large-scale production of consumer goods (cloth, leather, glass, ceramics, arms, etc.), as well as commerce. Merchants and bankers who settled in countries throughout Europe spread their civilisation, which bloomed brightest at the Italian courts. Wealthy patrons vied to support artists and commission splendid palaces. Foremost among them ranked the Medici of Florence, the Sforza of Milan, the Montefeltro of Urbino, the Este of Ferrara, the Gonzaga of Mantova and the popes in Rome (Julius II, Leo X).

Decline set in as trade shifted towards the Atlantic, crippling the maritime republics that prospered during the Middle Ages. **Genova** soon faced ruin, **Pisa** was taken over by its age-old rival Florence, and **Amalfi** and **Venice** were in serious trouble as the Turks advanced westwards. Additionally, political fragmentation made Italy a target for Europe's powerful nation-states.

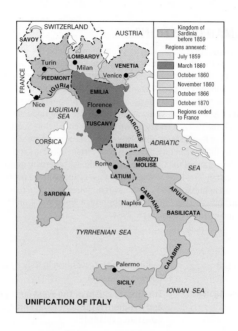

UNIFICATION OF ITALY

FROM THE 16C TO THE NAPOLEONIC ERA

France and Spain faced off in military campaigns. Rome was sacked. The Church responded to the Protestant Reformation. The Savoy family expanded its power to the South. Napoleon declared himself Emperor of Rome.

16C	France and Spain struggle for the supremacy of Europe.
1515–26	François I, victor at Marignano, vanquished at Pavia, is forced to give up the Italian heritage.
1527	Capture and **sack of Rome** by the troops of the Constable of Bourbon, in the service of Charles V.
1545–63	The Church attempts to re-establish its authority and credibility, damaged by the Protestant Reformation, with the Council of Trent.
1559	Treaty of Cateau-Cambrèsis: Spanish domination over Naples, Milan, Sicily and Sardinia until early-18C.
17C	Savoy becomes northern Italy's most powerful state.
1713	Victor-Amadeus II of Savoy acquires Sicily and the title of king. The Duke of Savoy swaps Sicily for Sardinia (1720).
1796	**Napoleon's campaign** in Italy. Creation of Cispadan Republic.
1797	Battle of Rivoli. Treaty of Campo-Formio. Cisalpine and Ligurian republics created.
1798	Proclamation of the Roman Republic. The French occupy Rome. Pope goes into exile.

1799	**Parthenopaean (Naples) Republic** declared.
1801	The Cisalpine Republic becomes the **Italian Republic**.
1805	Napoleon transforms the Italian Republic into a kingdom, and assumes the crown of the Lombard kings.
1808	Rome occupied by French troops. Murat becomes King of Naples.
1809	The Papal States are attached to the French Empire.
1812	Pius VII is taken to France as a prisoner.
1814	Collapse of the Napoleonic regime. Pius VII returns to Rome.

TOWARDS ITALIAN UNITY (1815–70)

Niccolò Machiavelli dreamed of a united Italy in the 16C, but no action unfolded for centuries. After the 1815 Congress of Vienna, many revolts by the "Carbonari" – patriots opposed to the Austrian occupation – were crushed. In 1831 **Giuseppe Mazzini** founded the Young Italy movement. This period, known as the **Risorgimento**, inspired the **First War of Independence** against Austria, led by Charles Albert of Savoy, King of Sardinia. Initial Italian successes were followed by a violent Austrian counter-attack, the abdication of Charles Albert in 1849 and the accession of **Victor Emmanuel II** to the throne. Europe finally took notice, thanks to the skilful campaigning of his minister **Camillo Cavour**, an ardent advocate of Italian liberty, and the participation of Piemonte in the Crimean War as France's ally. The Plombières agreement signed by Cavour and Napoleon III in 1858 led to the outbreak of the **Second War of Independence**, with combined Franco-Piedmontese victories in Magenta and Solferino.

Following popular uprisings in central and northern Italy, the Kingdom of Sardinia annexed Lombardy, Emilia Romagna and Tuscany. In 1860, after **Garibaldi** liberated Sicily and southern Italy from the Bourbons, the emerging State added southern Italy, the Marches and Umbria. On 17 March 1861, the Kingdom of Italy was proclaimed with Turin as the capital and Victor Emmanuel as king. In 1866 the capital moved to Florence.

In the same year, the **Third War of Independence** – with the Prussians as allies against Austria – led to the annexation of Veneto. Four years later, General Cadorna's troops entered Rome through Porta Pia. Rome joined Italy and became capital in 1871.

FROM 1882 TO THE PRESENT DAY

Italy occupied part of the Horn of Africa, then at home became theatre of action for two World Wars. Italy struggled to rebuild, facing terrorism at home, despite a 1980s boom in industry. By 2014, Italy had become encumbered by debt with businesses struggling or closing nationwide.

1882	Italy, Germany and Austria sign the **Triple Alliance**.
1882–5	Italians gain a footing in Eritrea and the Somali Coast.

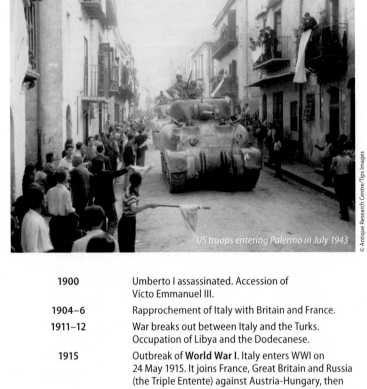

US troops entering Palermo in July 1943

© Antique Research Centre/Tips Images

1900	Umberto I assassinated. Accession of Victo Emmanuel III.
1904–6	Rapprochement of Italy with Britain and France.
1911–12	War breaks out between Italy and the Turks. Occupation of Libya and the Dodecanese.
1915	Outbreak of **World War I**. Italy enters WWI on 24 May 1915. It joins France, Great Britain and Russia (the Triple Entente) against Austria-Hungary, then Germany (28 August 1916).
4 November 1918	The Battle of Vittorio Veneto marks the end of WWI for Italy.
1919	Treaty of St-Germain-en-Laye: Istria and the Trentino are attached to Italy.
1920–21	Social disturbances fomented by the Fascist Party led by **Benito Mussolini**.
1922–6	Mussolini's squads terrorise opponents, then march on Rome. He becomes prime minister, then Il Duce.
1929	**Lateran Treaty** concluded between the Italian Government and the Papacy. This defined the relationship between Church and State and brought to an end the age-old "Roman Question".
1936	Italy occupies Ethiopia. Rome–Berlin Axis formed.
1939	**World War II** erupts.
1940	Italy enters World War II allied with Germany.
1943–10 July	The Allies land in Sicily. 25 July: Overthrow and arrest of Mussolini. 8 September: Armistice. German occupation in much of the country. 12 September: Mussolini is freed by the Germans and sets up the **Italian Socialist Republic** in the north.

1944–5	The Allies slowly reconquer Italy. The country is liberated (25 April 1945) and the war ends. Mussolini is arrested while trying to flee into Switzerland, tried and shot.
1946	Victor Emmanuel III abdicates. Accession of Umberto II. Proclamation of **The Republic** after a referendum.
1947	**Treaty of Paris**: Italy loses its colonies as well as Albania, Istria, Dalmatia and the Dodecanese. Frontier redefined to the benefit of France.
1948	**1 January**: New Constitution comes into effect.
1954	Trieste is attached to Italy.
1957	Treaty of Rome institutes the European Economic Community (now the EU): Italy is one of six founding members.
1960	Rome hosts Olympic Games.
1962	The Second Vatican Council reforms Church policy.
1963–8	Strikes and protests over the socioeconomic system: *autunno caldo*. Prime Minister Aldo Moro tries to unite the socialists and conservatives.
1970	Regional system instituted.
1970–80	Riots due to political unrest. The "Years of Lead".
1978	A left-wing terrorist group (the **Red Brigades**) kidnaps and assassinates Aldo Moro.
1980	Bologna station bombing.
1981	Attack on Pope John Paul II in St Peter's Square by Turkish terrorist Mehmet Alì Agca.
1982	Prefect of Palermo, Alberto Dalla Chiesa killed.
1991	Italian Communist Party (PCI) splits into two new parties, the Democratic Party of the Left (PDS) and the Communist Refoundation (RC). First wave of Albanian refugees arrives in Puglia.
1992	Operation to fight economic and political corruption in Italy commences, leading to the collapse of the Republic ruling classes. Two judges, Giovanni Falcone and Paolo Borsellino, are assassinated in Sicily.
1994	The centre-right led by **Silvio Berlusconi** wins the first political election under the new majority electoral system. Second Republic begins.
1996	Teatro La Fenice destroyed by fire in Venice. Electoral victory of the Ulivo alliance. The left governs for the first time in the Republic's history.
1997	Earthquakes in Umbria damage the Basilica of St Francis of Assisi.
27 March 1998	Italy signs up to the single European currency.
13 May 1999	Carlo Azeglio Ciampi, Governor of the Bank of Italy, becomes the 10th President of the Italian Republic.
13 May 2001	Electoral victory for the central-right and Berlusconi.
1 January 2002	Italy adopts the euro.

2002	Prices rise and the economy dips. Fiat plans to lay off 20 percent of its workforce.
2003	Berlusconi on trial for corruption relating to dealings in the 1980s. Protests against Iraq involvement intensify.
2004	Berlusconi's trial resumes. He is cleared of corruption.
2005	Pope John Paul II dies and German cardinal Joseph Ratzinger becomes Pope Benedict XVI. Voters throw out Berlusconi's coalition. He resigns, forms a new government and resumes rule.
2006	Giorgio Napolitano, a former Communist Party member, becomes Italy's 11th post-war president. Romano Prodi becomes prime minister.
2007	Romano Prodi resigns after a defeat on a foreign policy vote.
2008	Berlusconi wins a third term as prime minister. Venice suffers extensive flooding.
2009	Italy plunges into a recession. Berlusconi chooses young attractive women as candidates for the European election. His wife files for divorce.
6 April 2009	A 6.3 magnitude earthquake rocks Abruzzo.
2 November 2009	British student Meredith Kercher found dead in her Perugia home. American student Amanda Knox is among those accused of the crime.
2011	Berlusconi is on trial again in a controversy known as "ruby gate", where he was accused of paying an underage prostitute for sex, as well as ongoing financial scandals. Berlusconi resigns. Mario Monti, an economist and technocrat becomes PM.
2012	Cruise ship *Costa Concordia* partially sinks off the coast of the Island of Giglio, resulting in 32 deaths. An earthquake causes major damage in Emilia Romagna.
2013	In a controversial and unexpected move that sends shock waves through the Catholic Church and beyond, Pope Benedict XVI resigns the papacy. Jorge Mario Bergoglio is elected Pope on the 13th March, taking the name of **Francis**. Enrico Letta becomes Prime Minister and heads a coalition government. Berlusconi is convicted of tax fraud and expelled from government.
2014	Matteo Renzi, member of the Democratic Party and Mayor of Florence, becomes Prime Minister.
2015	The Universal Exposition (Expo), "Feeding the Planet, Energy for Life", in Milan. Beginning of the celebrations of the Extraordinary Jubilee of Mercy.

Pope Francis blesses the faithful in St. Peter's Square

"YOU ARE PETER AND ON THIS ROCK I WILL BUILD MY CHURCH" (MATTHEW 16: 18)

The title of "Pope", derived from the Greek *pápas* meaning "father", was originally used for patriarchs and bishops from the Orient. From the 5C on, it became widely used in the West, where with the increasing importance of the Roman See, it was eventually reserved for the Bishop of Rome alone. The Bishop of Rome maintained that his See in the traditional capital of the Empire had been founded by the Apostles, Peter and Paul, and therefore claimed first place in the ecclesiastical hierarchy. The Pope was initially chosen by both the people and the clergy, until the Conclave of the Cardinals was established in 1059. Strict regulations regarding this method of election were set out by Gregory X in the 13C.

Nowadays the cardinals meet in conclave in the Sistine Chapel and a vote is held twice a day; after each inconclusive vote the papers are burned so as to produce dark smoke. A majority of two-thirds plus one is required for an election to be valid; then a plume of white smoke appears above the Vatican. The senior cardinal appears at the window in the façade of St Peter's from which Papal blessings are given and announces the election in the Latin formula: *Annuntio vobis gaudium magnum: habemus papam* (I announce to you with great joy: we have a Pope). Over the centuries the Pope gradually assumed greater political power so that the history of the Papacy is inevitably linked with that of the relationship between the Church and the main political powers of the time. After the Unification of Italy, the Lateran Pacts of 1929 defined the present configuration of the Vatican City, which constitutes a separate State within the Italian State, of which the Pope is the sovereign ruler. The Holy Father is the undisputed leader of the Roman Catholic Church and exercises absolute infallibility over all ecclesiastical dogma, as set out in the first Vatican Council in 1870. Through the figure of the Pope, the spiritual influence of the Roman Catholic Church can be felt throughout the world.

Italian Art and Culture

Art and culture are not a mere part of special occasions, they are intertwined with daily life. Major city or small town, one can hardly avoid it, from ancient relics to architectural marvels, design and fashion, to an impromptu aria sung on a narrow street.

"Itinerant Vendors on The Forum," National Archeological Museum, Naples
© Samuel Magal / age fotostock

Evolution of Style

S tyle is never static in Italy, a major crossroads for evolution and trends in
 design. The Etruscan rage for Greek pottery, the Egyptomania craze in
Ancient Rome, Baroque piazzas and fountains – all elegantly blend form and
function. Classic to futuristic, style in Italy is always 'page one' news.

CONTEXT

A tour of Italy's art and architectural treasures can be disorientating, given the country's huge contributions to culture over the centuries. From saints and symbols to glistening mosaics, Italy boasts an impressive array of imagery. Historical context is vital to properly appreciate Italian art in all its diversity and richness. The rightful heir of the Greek, Etruscan and Roman civilisations, Italian art has adopted essential principles and characteristics from each period.

Italy has always been open to foreign influences. This melting pot was fuelled in part by its extensive geographical area, stretching from the Alps in the north to Sicily. After the fall of the Western Roman Empire, Byzantium held sway and greatly influenced the northern Adriatic shores for several centuries. Invaders – including the Ostrogoths, Lombards, Franks, Arabs and Normans – all left their imprint on conquered territory in southern Italy. The extraordinarily malleable Italian character absorbed these varied and exotic influences. One after another, the cities of Florence, Siena, Verona, Ferrara, Milan, Rome, Venice, Naples, Genova – and many other centres of minor or major importance – became cradles of artistic movements.

By the 12C, Italian artists were already beginning to show certain common characteristics: in particular, a shared taste for **harmony and solidity of form**, and an innate sense of space inherited from the Classical world. This restrained style tried to depict the rational and intelligible order of things. The Italians

Terraced gardens of Villa Rufolo, Ravello

© Arco Digital Images/Tips Images

rejected the naturalistic art popular with northern schools, and tempered the abstraction and decoration of Oriental artists. Slowly a representational technique evolved that reflected the artist's emotions. Idealisation – greatly prized in antiquity – continued to play a role as well.

In spite of this scholarly and well-mastered image, Italian art had a strong social component. Parallel to the artist's intellectual attempt to impose order on reality, art gradually developed a feeling for naturalism, influenced by Classical models. A good example of this was the medieval square, or "piazza". Following in the tradition of the Roman Forum, it contained the main public buildings, such as the church, baptistery, town hall or princely seat. Law courts, a hospital or a fountain were sometimes added.

Often designed to look like stage scenery, with extensive embellishment and ornamentation, the piazza was the social theatre for business, local markets, meetings, political decision-making and other important events. A typical Italian **piazza** is usually the result of centuries of construction. As a record of aesthetic influences and social moods, it can be used to interpret history. Scholars examine how certain elements were reused, ornamental motifs copied and styles mingled or superimposed. Aspiring architects, sculptors and painters could best exercise and promote their talents in this public arena.

Italy's excellent town planners, however, retained a **harmonious relationship with nature**. From Roman times onward, they embellished the countryside with sumptuous **villas and splendid terraced gardens**, skilfully designed to create shade and please the eye. Fountains, springs and follies invited the passerby to rest, meditate or simply enjoy nature's beauty. Thus the Italian architects and landscape gardeners, often indifferent to the solemn grandeur of French Classicism, have created many places that capture an architectural rapport with nature.

These range from Hadrian's Villa near Rome, to the flower-bedecked terraces of the Borromean Islands, including the Oriental charm of the Villa Rufolo in Ravello. This harmony also echoes through the elegant buildings of the Florentine countryside, the fantastic Mannerist creations of Rome, Tivoli or Bomarzo, the urban and regional projects designed by Juvarra in Piemonte, and Palladio's work on the delightful mansions of the Brenta Riviera.

Greeks and Etruscans

Etruscans and Greeks traded back and forth in Italy. Etruscans especially admired Greek pottery, tried to copy it and imported Greeks artists to set up famous workshops. Fine, delicate Etruscan gold filigree was highly prized in the Mediterranean. Their religions even shared gods, like Hercules.

GREEK
Cities

Territory in the Greek settlements was roughly divided into three different areas from the 8C BC onwards, when the first colonists arrived in Italy: places of worship, public spaces and residential areas. Generally the city was laid out in an octagonal grid – designed by **Hippodamus of Miletus**, a Greek philosopher and town planner who lived in Asia Minor in the 5C BC – organised around two main axes, the **cardo** (*stenopos* in Greek), which ran from north to south, and the **decumanus** (*plateia* in Greek), running from east to west. The road network was completed with minor *cardi* and *decumani*, which formed blocks. A number of public areas and buildings were situated within the town, such as the *agorà*, the main, central square where much of public life took place, the *ekklesiastérion*, a public building used for the meeting of the public assembly *(ekklesìa)*, and the *bouleutérion*, which housed meetings of the citizens' council (the *boulé*).

The temples, sometimes built outside the city limits, were often surrounded by other sacred buildings.

The monumental structures included porticoes, gymnasia, theatres and votive monuments.

The city itself was usually protected by fortifications, outside of which lay the agricultural land, subdivided into family plots, and the area used for burials.

Sculpture

The scarcity of marble and the particular Italian taste for pictorial and chiaroscuro effects resulted in the predomi-

GREEK MYTHOLOGY

The shores of Sicily and southern Italy held a sort of fascination for the ancient Greeks, who regarded them as the limits of the inhabited earth. Many mythological scenes unfold there: the Phlegrean Fields, near Naples, hid the entrance to the Kingdom of Hades; Zeus routed the Titans, with the help of Hercules, on Etna, where the Cyclops lived and Hephaestus, the god of fire, had his forges; Kore, the daughter of Demeter, was kidnapped by Hades, who had emerged from the River Tartara near Enna. In the *Odyssey*, Homer (9C BC) relates the adventures of Ulysses (Odysseus) after the siege of Troy, sailing between Scylla and Charybdis in the Straits of Messina and resisting the temptations of the Sirens in the Gulf of Sorrento. Pindar (5C BC) describes these mysterious shores, to which Virgil (1C BC) also refers in the *Aeneid*.

nant use of limestone and sandstone as raw materials. Clay was widely used in the pediments and acroteria of the temples, as well as for votive statues. The colonies employed the Ionic style from the end of the 6C BC. This introduced a greater individualisation of features, an increasingly dramatic sense of pathos and the use of softer shapes. The main artistic centres were Taranto, Naples, Paestum, Agrigento and Syracusae.

Painting and ceramics

Painting was considered by the Greeks to be the most noble and eloquent form of art; unfortunately, the perishable nature of the pigments used means that little remains of this art. The only surviving examples are inside tombs or on the façades of *hypogea* (underground chambers).

Vases with black figures painted against a red or yellow background date from the Archaic and beginning of the Classical periods. The detail on the figures was obtained by simply engraving the black varnish with a steel tip. Mythological subjects or scenes depicting daily life were the most common designs. Red figure vases appeared in southern Italy towards the end of the 5C BC. The black varnish, previously only for figures, now infused the background, with the figures "reserved" in the natural brick red clay and painted with touches of black and white. This reversal, which gave artists a greater freedom of expression, constituted a revolutionary discovery and allowed artists to produce more subtle designs. The themes used remained much the same. From the 3C BC the art of the native Italian peoples and of Magna Graecia became more decorative in style.

ETRUSCAN
Art

The Etruscan towns, built on elevated sites with walls of huge stones, show an advanced sense of town planning, often based on Greek models. Near the towns are vast burial grounds. These necropolises – cities of the dead – mimicked the streets, blocks, houses and furnishings of everyday life, often carved into the soft tufa.

Etruscan art is strongly influenced by the Orient and especially by Greece from the 6C BC onwards. It has a marked individuality sustained by realism and expressive movement. Vivid frescoes adorn the tombs at Tarquinia; the scenes range from the saucy to the sublime. These mysterious artists were also accomplished sculptors, architects, engineers and gold- and iron-workers.

Figurative arts

Sculpture makes up the main body of Etruscan art. The great period is the 6C BC, when large groups of statuary adorned the pediments of temples: the famous *Apollo of Veii* (in the Villa Giulia museum in Rome), of obvious Greek influence, belongs to this period. Some portrait busts are more original in their striking realism, intensity of expression and stylised features: their large prominent eyes and enigmatic smiles are typical of the Etruscan style.

The same applies to the famous groups of semi-recumbent figures on the sarcophagi, many of which are portraits. They also excelled in bronze sculpture, as demonstrated by the *Arezzo Chimera* (in Florence's Archaeological Museum) and elongated votive figurines.

The only surviving **paintings** are in burial chambers (Cerveteri, Veii and especially Tarquinia). These frescoes were supposed to remind the dead of the pleasures of life: banquets, games, plays, music, dancing, hunting, etc. These colourful and delicate wall paintings show amazing powers of observation and form a good record of Etruscan habits and customs.

Pottery and Goldwork

The Etruscans were artisans of genius. In pottery they used the little-known **bucchero** technique, producing black earthenware with figures in relief. Initially decorated with motifs in *pointillé*, the vases developed more elaborate shapes with a more complicated ornamentation, although in general these were not of the same quality as the earlier work.

In the 7C BC they modelled beautiful burial urns, *canopae*, in animal or human shapes. Both men and women wore heavy – often solid gold – ornaments that often showcased exceptional skill in the filigree and granulation techniques.

Ancient Art

Peripteral temple

Peristyle

Opisthodomos

Pronaos

Statue of the divinity
to whom the temple
was dedicated

Naos (cella)

Elevation of a Corinthian order temple

Pediment

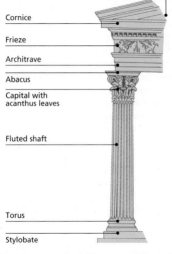

The section comprising
the architrave, frieze
and cornice is known
as the **entablature**

Cornice

Frieze

Architrave

Abacus

Capital with
acanthus leaves

Fluted shaft

Torus

Stylobate

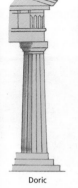

| Doric | Tuscan | Ionic | Corinthian | Composite |

H. Choimet/MICHELIN

Romans

Romans, like Etruscans and Greeks, loved colour. New were coloured marbles, brought in from around the empire. New engineering methods constructed roads, bridges, and aqueducts. Posh residences, grand theatres, baths, and spectacles doubled as meeting places in addition to the forum.

ROMAN TOWNS

Roman towns often had military roots. Walled in periods of trouble, they were generally divided into four quarters by two main streets, the *decumanus* and the *cardo*, intersecting at right angles and ending in gateways. Other parallel streets created a grid. The **streets** were edged with footpaths, sometimes 50cm/20in high, and lined with porticoes to shelter pedestrians. Large flagstones, which fitted together perfectly, paved the roads. Stepping-stones crossed the right-of-way, but grooves allowed horses and cartwheels to pass.

A ROMAN HOUSE

Excavations at Herculaneum, Pompeii and especially Ostia have uncovered two main types of houses. An *insula* was a dwelling of several storeys divided into apartments, often with shops open to the street. A *domus* was a luxurious, single-family mansion with an *atrium*, which had evolved from the earlier Greek model.

The latter had a modest external appearance owing to bare walls and few windows. But the interior – adorned with mosaics, statues, paintings and marbles and sometimes including private baths and a fish pond – revealed the riches of its owner. A vestibule overlooked by the porter's lodge led to the *atrium*.

The *atrium*, originally the *domus'* heart, later referred to the internal courtyard around the *impluvium*, a basin which caught rainwater.

The bedrooms *(cubiculae)* opened off the *atrium*, which was the only part of the house where strangers were usually

Ruins of the temple of Neptune, Parco Nazionale del Cilento, Campania © René Mattes / hemis.fr

admitted. At the far end was the *tabli-num*, or the living and dining room. The *atrium* and adjoining rooms constituted the oldest form of the Roman house, later inhabited by less wealthy citizens. The *peristyle* was a central court surrounded by a portico. Reserved for the family, it generally featured a garden with fountains, statues and mosaic-lined basins. The living quarters opened onto it. The *cubiculae* were simple sleeping chambers with a stone platform built against the wall or a movable bed. There were mattresses, cushions and blankets but no sheets. The dining room, or *triclinium*, takes its name from the three couches for the guests. Adopting a Greek custom, Romans ate reclined on cushions and leaning on one elbow. Slaves attended the central table.

Lastly, there was the great hall or *oecus*, which was sometimes embellished with a colonnade. The outbuildings included the kitchen with a sink and drain, and built-in stove and oven; baths, which were like the public baths on a smaller scale; and the slaves' quarters, barns, cellars, stables, etc. The latrines were usually in a kitchen corner to simplify drainage systems.

THE FORUM

Roman life revolved around the forum, each town's centre of politics, leisure and commerce. Originally a market, the large square usually stood at a major intersection and was often surrounded by a portico during the Imperial period. Government offices also flanked a forum. These included the *curia* or headquarters of local government; the voting hall for elections; the public tribune where candidates harangued crowds; the "basilica of finance" or exchange *(argentaria)*; the municipal treasury; the public granaries; the "basilica of justice" or law courts; the prison; temples and many commemorative monuments.

As they became less content with the forum, ancient Roman emperors built auxiliary centres nearby. Trajan, Nerva and Augustus all constructed opulent additions, now collectively known as the Fori Imperiali.

THE TOMBS

Roman cemeteries lined major roads at some distance from town. The tombs were marked by an altar, simple stela (a slab or pillar), or even a mausoleum for the most important families. Less affluent Romans rested in a *columbarium*,

a vault with niches for funerary urns, named for its resemblance to a dove-cote. The most famous cemetery is on the Via Appia Antica, south of Rome. Directly after death, the body was exhibited on a funeral couch surrounded with candlesticks and wreaths. Then the family buried or cremated the remains. The deceased was provided with objects thought useful in the afterlife: clothes, arms and tools for men, toys for children, and jewellery and toilet articles for women.

ARCHITECTURE

The Romans borrowed elements from Greek architecture, but created their own art. Innovations included softer, more flexible curved shapes, such as the arch, dome and vault.

Walls and pilasters replaced columns, the foundation of the Greek trilithic system. **Concrete**, thrown into moulds, allowed huge covered spaces like the Pantheon, the world's largest unreinforced solid concrete dome at 43.4m/ 142 ft in diameter. Also noteworthy were the Romans' many public civil engineering projects: bridges, aqueducts, roads, tunnels, sewers, baths, theatres, amphitheatres, stadia, circuses, basilicas, *nymphaea*, gymnasia, colonnades, triumphal arches and both public and private monuments (often rivals in terms of size and splendour).

TEMPLES

Temples honoured gods or emperors, raised to divine status from the time of Augustus. The Roman version, again inspired by the Greek, consists of a closed chamber, the *cella*, containing the image of the god, and an open vestibule. The building is surrounded, partly or completely, by a colonnade and is built on a podium. Romans also imported circular temple-plans. The most stunning example remains the Pantheon, dedicated to all the gods. This engineering marvel has an eye *(oculus)* in its grand concrete dome. Originally built in 27 BC, it has been a place of worship for over 2 000 years and this Catholic church now contains the tombs of the artist Raphael and Italian royalty.

TRIUMPHAL ARCHES

In Rome these commemorated the victories by generals or emperors. The low reliefs on the arches recorded their feats of arms. In the provinces, such as Aosta, Benevento and Ancona, there are municipal arches commemorating important events or erected in honour of some member of the Imperial family. Again, Rome has a concentration of superb structures, including the Roman Forum's AD 203 Arch of Septimius Severus, the worn AD 81 Arch of Titus, which commemorates the capture of Jerusalem (and thus is shunned by many Jews) and the pollution-scarred, AD 315 Arch of Constantine, which the dictator Benito Mussolini further damaged in a megalomaniac desire for a triumphal procession.

AQUEDUCTS

Nowhere is the Roman arch better employed than these waterways, many of which stand today (though an argument could perhaps be made for the Colosseum). These stone streambeds stride across the countryside and plunge underground. Rome alone built 11 between 312 BC and AD 206, which funnelled more than a million cubic metres a day into the city (35 million cu ft). Three ancient aqueducts continue to supply the capital's fountains and streetside taps.

BATHS

The Roman baths doubled as fitness centres, casinos, social clubs, libraries, lecture halls and meeting-places. The free amenities explain the amount of time people spent there. Decoration in these great buildings was lavish: mosaic ornaments, coloured marble facings, columns and statues.

The bather followed a medically prescribed circuit. From the gymnasium *(palestra)*, he entered a lukewarm room *(tepidarium)* to prepare for the hot baths *(caldarium)*. He then returned to a lukewarm room before plunging

Baths of the Villa Romana del Casale (3-4C A.D.)

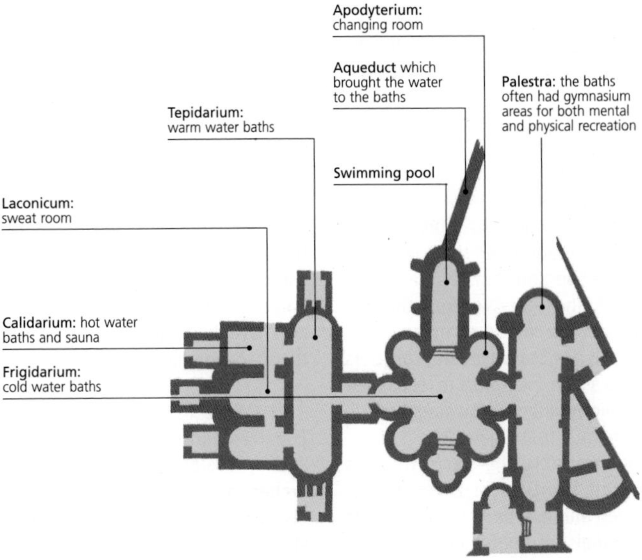

Apodyterium:
changing room

Aqueduct which
brought the water
to the baths

Palestra: the baths
often had gymnasium
areas for both mental
and physical recreation

Tepidarium:
warm water baths

Swimming pool

Laconicum:
sweat room

Calidarium: hot water
baths and sauna

Frigidarium:
cold water baths

Colosseum (1C AD)

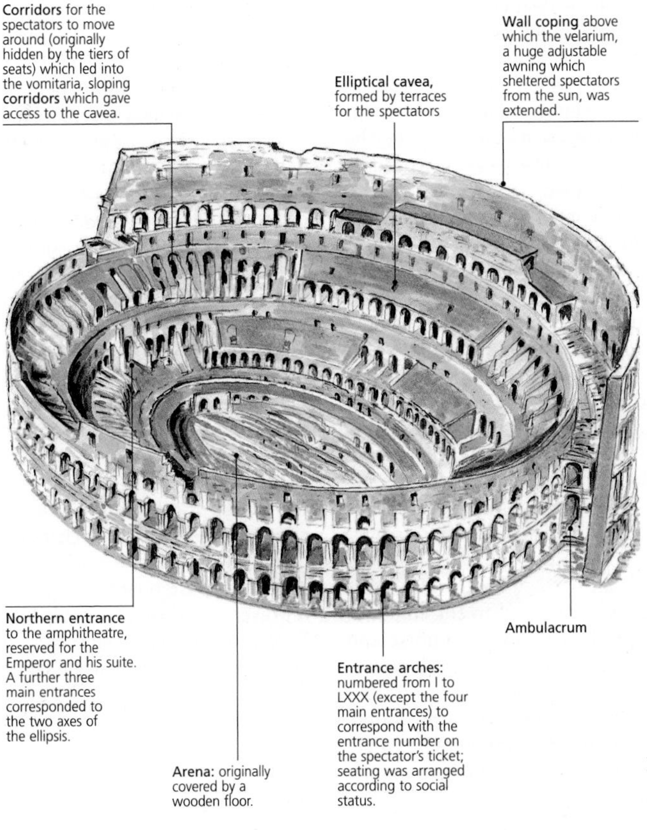

Corridors for the
spectators to move
around (originally
hidden by the tiers of
seats) which led into
the vomitaria, sloping
corridors which gave
access to the cavea.

Elliptical cavea,
formed by terraces
for the spectators

Wall coping above
which the velarium,
a huge adjustable
awning which
sheltered spectators
from the sun, was
extended.

Northern entrance
to the amphitheatre,
reserved for the
Emperor and his suite.
A further three
main entrances
corresponded to
the two axes of
the ellipsis.

Ambulacrum

Entrance arches:
numbered from I to
LXXX (except the four
main entrances) to
correspond with the
entrance number on
the spectator's ticket;
seating was arranged
according to social
status.

Arena: originally
covered by a
wooden floor.

R. Corbel

99

into the cold baths *(frigidarium)* to tone the skin. Underground furnaces (hypocausts) heated the water and air, which also circulated inside the walls and floors.

AMPHITHEATRES

This typical Roman structure, several storeys high, encircles an elliptical arena with seats. A huge adjustable awning, the *velarium*, sheltered the spectators from the sun and rain. Inside, a wall protected the front rows from the wild animals in the ring. A complex of circular galleries, staircases and corridors enabled all the spectators to reach their seats quickly without crowding through the *vomitaria* (passageways).

Always popular, the performances included fighting of three kinds: between animals, between gladiators and animals, and between gladiators. In principle, a human duel always ended in the death of one opponent. The public could ask for a gladiator's life to be spared and the President of the Games would indicate a reprieve by turning up his thumb. The victorious gladiator received a sum of money if he was a professional; a slave or a prisoner would be freed.

In some amphitheatres the stage could be flooded for naval spectacles *(naumachia)*, where actors battled in flat-bottomed boats.

Naturally, the Colosseum is the star of this genre. Three tiers high, it covers about 2.5ha/6 acres of drained marshland in Rome's heart. More than 50 000 people could squash onto the marble and tufa benches with standing room at the top. Known as the Flavian Amphitheatre until the 8C, the Colosseum is the model for modern sports stadiums.

CIRCUS

Usually connected to the Imperial palace, the circus hosted horse and chariot races. Its shape was long and narrow, with a short curved side and a straight side, where the races started. Spectators sat on the terraces, while the competitors whipped around the track. In the later Roman Empire, many different types of games took place here. The circus resembled the smaller **stadium**, which was copied from the Greek model. The Circus Maximus, near Rome's Forum, is among the most famous examples. However, the landmark Piazza Navona also began as a chariot track: the AD 86 circus known as *domitianus* or *agonalis* (from the ancient Greek for "games", which was corrupted into the modern name). Baroque churches, fountains and palaces have since encrusted the ruins, but the shape remains evident.

THEATRES

Theatres had rows of seats, usually ending in colonnades, a central area or **orchestra** for performance or elevating distinguished spectators, and a raised **stage**. Action unfolded before a wall – the building's finest part, which imitated a palace façade: decoration included several tiers of columns, niches containing statues, mosaics and marble facings. The perfect acoustics were generally due to a combination of sophisticated devices. The scenery was either fixed or mobile and there was an ingenious array of machinery either in the wings or below stage. Special effects were also impressive, including smoke, lightning, thunder and the sudden appearance of gods – the famous *deus ex machina* – or heroes.

Comedies and tragedies were the theatre's chief function; however, the space also hosted competitions, lottery draws and the distribution of bread or money.

Until the end of the 2C BC, all actors wore wigs of different shapes and colours, according to their character's nature. After that date, they adopted distinctive pasteboard masks, often represented in theatre sculptures. Tragic actors, to make themselves more impressive, wore buskins or sandals with thick cork soles.

Byzantines

E astern influences played a visible role, from the shift of the Empire to the stylised figures in art. Emphasis was less on realism and more on bold symbols and mystical moods, enhanced by interplays of light.

Barbarian invasions triggered the decline of the late Roman Imperial tradition and encouraged the popular and narrative early Christian art, which later formed the basis of the Romanesque style.

Honorius and his sister Galla Placidia chose Ravenna as the capital of the Empire. After the death of Theodoric and the Gothic invasions, the town came under direct Byzantine rule in the reign of Justinian (AD 527–65). The Byzantine emperors ruled the region of Ravenna and Venezia Giulia only until the 8C, but they held sway in Sicily and part of southern Italy until the 11C. Byzantine art inherited a legacy of naturalism and sense of space from the Greek and Latin artistic traditions, and a rich decorative style from its Oriental roots.

The vault and dome from the late Roman period developed the style's potential, often with extraordinary results, culminating in the Basilica of San Vitale in Ravenna. Simpler structures were also built, combining plain, sober exteriors with dazzling interior decoration in mosaic and marble. The bas-reliefs on sarcophagi, chancel parcloses, ambos and pulpits assume an essentially decorative character.

PAINTING

Animals and figures became stylised and symbolic. Byzantine paintings often have a "**cartoon**" quality to the modern eye. Flat, stiff figures – with large eyes – appear to float. Rich hues were frequently paired with gold-leaf backgrounds. Scenes are simple, so illiterate viewers could easily learn religious lessons.

MOSAICS

Byzantine artists excelled at this sumptuous form. Precious materials made mosaic the perfect technique for portraying Bible characters or courtly figures. The tiles *(tesserae)* were fragments of hard stone or glass that were glazed and irregularly cut to catch the light. They covered oven vaults, walls and cupolas, where their gold highlights could sparkle in the mysterious semi-darkness. Enigmatic, grandiose figures stood out against midnight blue backgrounds and landscapes filled with trees, plants and animals. The mosaics of Ravenna (5C–6C) are perhaps the most famous examples of the period. However, the Byzantine style continued to prevail during the 11C–12C at St Mark's in Venice, in Sicily (Cefalù, Palermo, Monreale) and in various forms up to the 13C in Rome.

© Corbis/hemis.fr

Façade St Mark's in Venice

Romanesque and Gothic (11–14C)

The Italian predilection for harmony and monumental ensembles meant that architecture did not reach the sublime heights of the great Gothic achievements of northern Europe.

ROMANESQUE PERIOD

Round Roman arches – based on thick, heavy basilica walls – grounded an 11C architectural renaissance. New cathedrals and Benedictine monasteries drew on Carolingian and Ottonian traditions, as well as regional influences. Alternating columns and pilasters provided buildings with rhythm, space and depth. These continued into the roof structure, where archivolts and ribs support the square vaults. In Romanesque style, the structural function of architectural features is always visible. The most flourishing school was initially in northern Italy. Here, master masons included the **Maestri Comacini**, who created exceptional stone buildings in the mountains and brick edifices in the valleys. The **Maestri Campionesi** hailed from the Lugano region and the Lombard lakes. The regions of central Italy were influenced by other cultural models and produced quite different styles. Florence's highly original Medieval style is characterised by delicate colours and a subtle intellectual character. Rome, however, drew on the early Christian tradition of the magnificent Constantinian basilicas. In Tuscany – especially in Pisa, Lucca and Pistoia – the Romanesque style shows strong Lombard and Classical Florentine influences, embellished by decorative details. Typical features include tiers of arcades with a multitude of small columns on the façades,

Civil architecture

Castel del Monte (13C)

Built by Frederick II, probably as a leisure residence, the castle is dominated by the number eight: the ground plan is octagonal, there are eight octagonal towers and eight rooms on each floor.

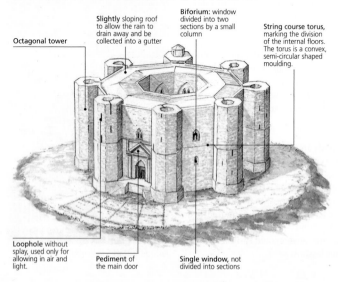

Slightly sloping roof to allow the rain to drain away and be collected into a gutter

Biforium: window divided into two sections by a small column

String course torus, marking the division of the internal floors. The torus is a convex, semi-circular shaped moulding.

Octagonal tower

Loophole without splay, used only for allowing in air and light.

Pediment of the main door

Single window, not divided into sections

Religious architecture

Plan of Parma cathedral (12-14C)

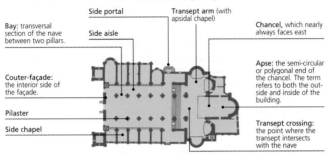

Bay: transversal section of the nave between two pillars.

Side portal

Side aisle

Transept arm (with apsidal chapel)

Chancel, which nearly always faces east

Couter-façade: the interior side of the façade.

Apse: the semi-circular or polygonal end of the chancel. The term refers to both the out-side and inside of the building.

Pilaster

Side chapel

Transept crossing: the point where the transept intersects with the nave

Cross-section of a church

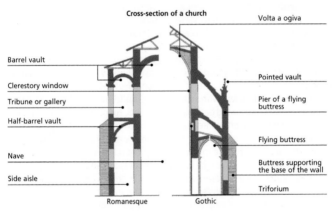

Volta a ogiva

Barrel vault

Clerestory window

Tribune or gallery

Half-barrel vault

Nave

Side aisle

Pointed vault

Pier of a flying buttress

Flying buttress

Buttress supporting the base of the wall

Triforium

Romanesque   Gothic

ROMANESQUE ARCHITECTURE
Milano – Basilica di Sant' Ambrogio (11-12C.)

A masterpiece of harmony and balance, Sant'Ambrogio is striking for the apparent simplicity of its composi-tion and for the juxtaposition between the light and the building materials used..

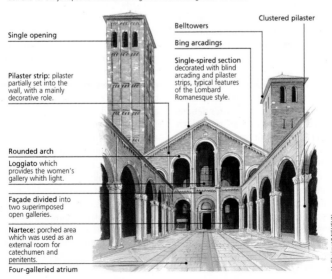

Single opening

Belltowers

Bing arcadings

Clustered pilaster

Pilaster strip: pilaster partially set into the wall, with a mainly decorative role.

Single-spired section decorated with blind arcading and pilaster strips, typical features of the Lombard Romanesque style.

Rounded arch

Loggiato which provides the women's gallery whith light.

Façade divided into two superimposed open galleries.

Nartece: porched area which was used as an external room for catechumen and penitents.

Four-galleried atrium

H. Chotmet/MICHELIN

tall blind arcades on the side walls and east end, decorative lozenges and different coloured marble encrustations. The **Maestri Cosmati**, a Roman guild of mosaic and marble workers, held sway in 12C–13C Latium. They specialised in assembling fragments of multicoloured marble (pavings, episcopal thrones, ambos or pulpits and candelabra) and the encrustation of columns and friezes in the cloisters with enamel mosaics. Finally, southern Italy and Sicily show a mixture of Lombard, Saracen, Byzantine and Norman influences, the result of which was the monumental and noble **Sicilian-Norman style** (see SICILY). This style also displays Oriental influence in its highly decorative façades, and Classical influence in the perfectly poised rhythm of its colonnades.

Sculpture was closely linked with architecture. Low reliefs presented both biblical and secular stories, often intended to educate.

Painting bloomed alongside mosaics in the large cathedrals, where the vast walls and vaults were covered with colour. The bare, austere walls seen in many churches today are almost always the result of the ravages of time or restoration work. Originally, bright and imaginative frescoes illustrated stories from the Bible, mixing new experimental artistic forms with old Byzantine influences. Finally, this period saw the rise of illustrated manuscripts, another learning aid.

GOTHIC PERIOD

"Then arose new architects who after the manner of their barbarous nations erected buildings in that style which we call Gothic *(dei Gotthi)*," complained Florentine historiographer Giorgio Vasari (1511–74). The style has since earned respect and even adoration, but the pejorative label – evoking barbarian hordes – stuck.

These ambitious builders wanted to push stone steeples closer to God. Romanesque barrel and groin vaults were better suited to squat, solid and dark structures. From the 11C, experiments began with pointed arches, stone ribs and flying buttresses, which propped up constructions with bridge-like arches. Interiors opened out and larger windows poured "divine" light inside.

The **pointed arch** allowed more height above the transept. Tall, spectacular pilasters – formed by bands of columns – supported the weight. Storey upon storey drew the gaze to the vault's highest point, symbolising Christians' yearning for heaven.

No longer bearing the entire load, the walls could be pierced with glass panels. While the solid structure of the building and the omnipresent Classical heritage remained vital, light became an important element. Lavish **stained-glass** scenes were common, as well as rose windows, which most famously adorn Notre-Dame in Paris.

The buildings reached unimagined heights, supported externally by a mass of buttresses and **flying buttresses**. These were hidden from sight inside the church, accentuating the impression of space and vertical movement.

The Cistercians introduced Gothic architecture into Italy, but its widespread adoption was due to the many new religious orders, especially the Franciscans and Dominicans. These groups often used the traditional model of the early Christian basilica, so practical and economical, and adapted it to current trends. The era's civil architecture showed more originality. Numerous prosperous towns displayed their civic pride with municipal palaces and loggias. The Venetian-Gothic style relieved bare façades with windows and loggias, and persisted until the late-15C.

The **Pisano** family from Pisa combined ancient traditions, seen through the Classicism championed by Frederick II (**Nicola**, 1215–c.80), and their vigorously expressive realism, explicitly Gothic in tone (**Giovanni**, 1248–after 1314).

These masters and the architect and sculptor **Arnolfo di Cambio** (c.1245–1302) introduced new iconography and ambitious projects for pulpits and funerary monuments. All exhibited the new humanism.

GOTHIC
Milano – Cathedral apse (14-15C)

Milano cathedral is a unique and extraordinary example of the late-Gothic style in Italy. It was started in 1386 and was not finished until the façade was completed in the 19C. The building, commissioned by Gian Galeazzo Visconti, clearly demonstrates a transalpine cultural influence far removed from contemporary Tuscan architecture.

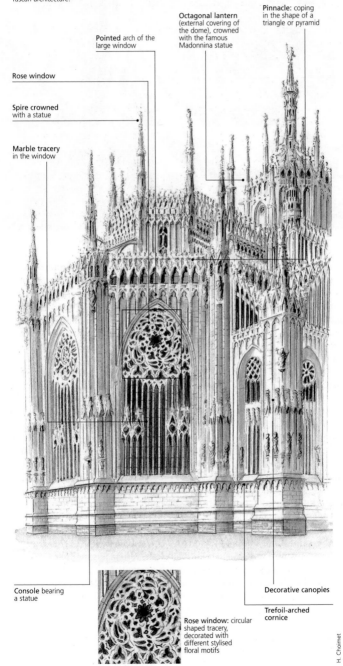

Pointed arch of the large window

Octagonal lantern (external covering of the dome), crowned with the famous Madonnina statue

Pinnacle: coping in the shape of a triangle or pyramid

Rose window

Spire crowned with a statue

Marble tracery in the window

Console bearing a statue

Rose window: circular shaped tracery, decorated with different stylised floral motifs

Decorative canopies

Trefoil-arched cornice

H. Choimet

13C frescoes, Battistero, Parma

© Serafiicus/iStockphoto.com

The painted Crucifixes in relief that appeared in the 12C were the first specimens of Italian painting. The rigidness inherited from Byzantine art gradually melted away. In the 13C a Roman, **Pietro Cavallini** (1273–1321), executed frescoes and mosaics with a greater breadth of style, reminiscent of Antique art. His Florentine contemporary, **Cimabue** (1240–1302), adorned the Upper Basilica of Assisi with frescoes displaying a new sense of pathos. This inspired **Giotto** (1266–1337), who added naturalism to the mix. Movement, depth and atmosphere were indicated or suggested.

Emotion flickered across his frescoes in Assisi, Padova and Florence. Giotto's masterful works influenced all successive painting, including that of Masaccio and Michelangelo.

At the same time in Siena, **Duccio di Buoninsegna** (c.1255–1318) still showed a strong Byzantine influence. He founded the **Siena school**, which explored a graceful linear technique and much decorative colour. Exponents of this delicate school included **Simone Martini** (c.1284–1344) and the brothers **Pietro** (c.1280–1348) and **Ambrogio Lorenzetti** (1285–1348).

The masters of the Florentine Trecento period (14C) developed a mystical and realistic style far removed from the lively work of Giotto. They stressed harmonies of line and colour, and a great refinement in the decorative elements. At the same time the **International Gothic** style, developed in the courts of Europe, was practised by artists from central and northern Italy and perfected in the frescoes painted by Simone Martini and Matteo Giovannetti (nd–1367) in Avignon. Other exponents of this refined, stately and occasionally decadent artistic movement, which lasted until the 15C, include **Stefano da Zevio** (c.1379–after 1438) from Verona, **Pisanello** (c.1380–1455), a portraitist, animal painter and distinguished medallist, and **Gentile da Fabriano** (c.1370–1427).

Quattrocento (15C)

Artists, scholars and poets flourished during this era, characterised by a passion for Antiquity, well-organised city-states governed by a noble or princely patron, and a new vision of man's place at the centre of the universe. The Medici city of Florence was the epicentre of this cultural movement, much later designated the Renaissance (Rebirth).

ARCHITECTURE

A new art concept was introduced by Florentine sculptor and architect **Filippo Brunelleschi** (1377–1446), an enthusiastic admirer of Antiquity. His strong personality transformed the practical approach of the medieval master builder into the creative role of the architect who designed on the drawing board. Brunelleschi was both an artist and an intellectual. His invention of geometrical perspective allowed him to plan harmonious and rationally designed buildings. His intuitive reproduction of three-dimensional objects on two-dimensional canvas provided the foundation for all future painting. His intellectual abilities and the abstract character of his architectural creations were imitated and made commonplace by his followers, but were never fully understood. **Leon Battista Alberti** (1406–72) also used his knowledge of ancient art to create a new expressive style. His vision was based on an emotional relationship between objects and space, which most likely inspired the architect Donato Bramante.

SCULPTURE

The magnificent doors of Florence's Baptistery, designed by **Lorenzo Ghiberti** (1378–1455), show the influence of Gothic tradition and ancient art. However, the most powerful sculptor of the period was undoubtedly **Donatello** (1386–1466), who eschewed intellectual speculation. His focus was on interpreting Classical forms with a free and innovative spirit, breathing dynamism into his work and bringing it to the height of expressive power. After Padova, where he created works that set a standard for all of northern Italy, Donatello returned to Florence.

Here, in the changing climate of the second half of the century, he explored the idea that humanity is acquired through suffering, presaging the crisis of the century's end. His contemporary, **Luca della Robbia** (1400–82), specialised in coloured and glazed terra-cotta works, while **Agostino di Duccio** (c.1418–81), **Desiderio da Settignano** (c.1430–64) and **Mino da Fiesole** (1429–84) continued in the Donatello tradition, at the same time moving away from the extremes of his intense dramatic style.

PAINTING

The third major figure of the 15C was the painter **Masaccio** (1401–28). He applied Brunelleschi's laws of perspective and added light. For the first time in centuries, figures cast a shadow, creating perspective and the notion of space. His substantial characters thus acquired a certain realism and a solidity that lent them a moral dignity. **Paolo Uccello** (c.1397–1475) took another tack: perspective based on two vanishing points. Uccello also demonstrated that more than one method exists for reproducing reality, with the philosophical implications all this entails.

At the same time, the Dominican friar **Fra Angelico** (1387–1455), who remained very attached to Gothic tradition, was attracted to the new theories of the Renaissance, while **Benozzo Gozzoli** (1420–97) adapted his style to the portrayal of brilliant secular festivities. **Andrea del Castagno** (1419–57) emphasised modelling and monu-

THE RENAISSANCE
Rimini – Tempio Malatestiano (Leon Battista Alberti, 15C)

Built in honour of Sigismondo Malatesta, this church is a celebration of classical cultures and civilisations, from which many of its structural and decorative features are taken, re-interpreted and adapted to the religious role of the building.

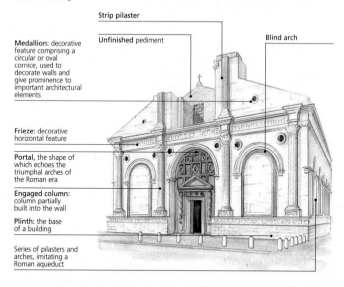

Strip pilaster

Medallion: decorative feature comprising a circular or oval cornice, used to decorate walls and give prominence to important architectural elements

Unfinished pediment

Blind arch

Frieze: decorative horizontal feature

Portal, the shape of which echoes the triumphal arches of the Roman era

Engaged column: column partially built into the wall

Plinth: the base of a building

Series of pilasters and arches, imitating a Roman aqueduct

Firenze – The interior of the Cappella dei Pazzi (Filippo Brunelleschi, 1430-1445)

The harmony of the proportions and the elegant play on colours between the grey of the *pietra serena* stone (which emphasises the architectural features) and the white of the plaster create an atmosphere of dignified and austere simplicity.

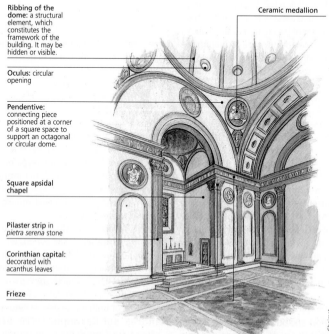

Ribbing of the dome: a structural element, which constitutes the framework of the building. It may be hidden or visible.

Ceramic medallion

Oculus: circular opening

Pendentive: connecting piece positioned at a corner of a square space to support an octagonal or circular dome.

Square apsidal chapel

Pilaster strip in *pietra serena* stone

Corinthian capital: decorated with acanthus leaves

Frieze

H. Choimet

Firenze – Palazzo Rucellai (Leon Battista Alberti, 1446-1451)

The palace is composed of three superimposed levels of the three classical orders (Doric, Ionic and Corinthian) and presents a pattern of vertical (the pilasters) and horizontal (the cornices) lines.

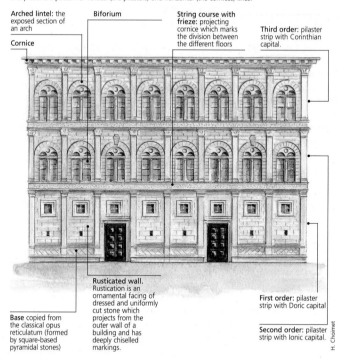

Arched lintel: the exposed section of an arch

Biforium

String course with frieze: projecting cornice which marks the division between the different floors

Third order: pilaster strip with Corinthian capital.

Cornice

Rusticated wall. Rustication is an ornamental facing of dressed and uniformly cut stone which projects from the outer wall of a building and has deeply chiselled markings.

First order: pilaster strip with Doric capital

Base copied from the classical opus reticulatum (formed by square-based pyramidal stones)

Second order: pilaster strip with Ionic capital.

H. Choimet

mental qualities (*see FLORENCE, p535*). **Sandro Botticelli** (1444–1510) produced a miraculous purity of line, giving a graceful and almost unreal fragility to his figures and a deep sense of mystery to his allegorical scenes. At the turn of the century, amid the crisis in humanist values, he created dazzling figures of sharp lines and muted colours.

Domenico Ghirlandaio (1449–94) revealed a gift for narrative painting in monumental frescoes that depicted the ruling class of Florence in an atmosphere of stately serenity.

The work of **Piero della Francesca** (1415–92) from Sansepolcro is a supreme example of Tuscan-Renaissance art. Here, he displays faultless harmony and draughtsmanship with his use of form, colour and light (*see AREZZO, p596*).

At the Gonzaga court in Mantova, **Andrea Mantegna** (1431–1506) painted scenes full of grandeur and vigour, using ancient models to create Renaissance paintings of strong and inscrutable heroes.

In the esoteric, astrological and alchemical atmosphere of the court of Ferrara, **Cosmè (Cosimo) Tura** (1430–95) created original and challenging compositions in which men and objects are hurled together in a mix of colours that resemble sharp metals and semiprecious stones.

The second major centre of art at this time was Venice, where **Giovanni Bellini** (1432–1516) created a sense of optical and empirical space in his paintings. He did this by using colour and tones, in contrast to the geometric, intellectual and anti-naturalist painting of Florence. Bellini was much influenced by the work of **Antonello da Messina** (1430–79) in the 1470s, who had in turn drawn on the work of the Flemish masters and his knowledge of Piero della Francesca.

Cinquecento (16C)

The 16C saw the development of the previous century's sensibility, infused even more with Antiquity, mythology and the discovery of humanity. The artistic centre of the Renaissance moved from Florence to Rome, where the popes rivalled one another in embellishing palaces and churches. Artists became more independent, acquiring social prestige. The canons of Renaissance art were already being exported and put into practice elsewhere in Europe. However, this golden age of poets and humanists was disrupted by political and religious upheavals in Europe, many linked to Lutheranism.

ARCHITECTURE

The century began with the return of **Donato Bramante** (1444–1514) from Milan to Rome, where he laid the foundations for the new Basilica of St Peter's, later completed by Michelangelo. Despite appearances, Bramante's architectural style was not completely Classical in tone; he made use of *trompe l'œil* effects (such as the false chancel created in Milan's San Satiro Church) that feigned depth. As a result, architecture became more than a rational representation of what exists. This development would find perfect expression in the later Baroque style.

Michelangelo, partly inspired by Bramante's ideas, attempted to give moulded form to large architectural structures – treating them as sculptures. **Giacomo da Vignola** (1507–73) also worked in Rome, while **Andrea Palladio** (1508–80) designed a number of buildings in Vicenza (see VICENZA, p463). In his important works on architecture, he advocated the Classicism of ancient art and was himself responsible for many churches, palaces and luxury villas in Venetia.

SCULPTURE

Michelangelo (1475–1564) did most of his life's work in either Florence or Rome. He was the most outstanding character of the century, owing to his creative, idealistic and even troubled genius, which found expression in masterpieces of unsurpassed vitality. His art explored questions like divine revelation, the human longing for something beyond its dissatisfying earthly existence, the soul trying to release itself from the prison of the body, and the struggle between faith and the intellect. He drew inspiration from ancient art and the work of Donatello, which he reinterpreted with impressive moral tension. Michelangelo towered above his contemporaries, including the elegant and refined **Benvenuto Cellini** (1500–71), a skilled goldsmith and sculptor known for his *Perseus* (now in Florence), and the powerful sculptor **Giambologna** (or Jean Boulogne) (1529–1608), who followed the dictates of a stately and courtly art.

PAINTING

The 16C was an important period for painting. Numerous outstanding artists produced works in the new humanist vein. Rome and later Venice replaced Florence as artistic centres. The century began with exceptional, but complementary, masters. **Leonardo da Vinci** (1452–1519) was the archetype of the new enquiring mind. He is famous for his *sfumato* (literally translated as "mist"), an impalpable, luminous veil effect that created an impression of distance between persons and objects or surroundings. His insatiable desire for knowledge, interest in mechanics

Ceiling of the Sistine Chapel, by Michelangelo

© lexan/iStockphoto.com

and attempt to form observations into a coherent system make him a precursor of modern scientists. His reflections on the soul – interpreted in paintings such as *The Last Supper* in Milan – had a lasting effect on future painters.

Raphael (1483–1520) was not only a prodigious portraitist and painter of gently drawn madonnas, but also a highly inventive decorator with an exceptional mastery of composition, given free rein in the Stanze of the Vatican. His style is Classical in the fullest sense. He communicated the most intellectual and sophisticated ideas in logical, fascinating and deceptively simple paintings.

Michelangelo (1475–1564), the last of the three great men, was primarily a sculptor, yet famously frescoed the ceiling of the Sistine Chapel. Here, his skill with relief and power were triumphant. The master's paintings portray a magnificent and heroic humanity, which appears devastated by the message of God. The bright optimism of contemporary Humanist Classicism was thus shattered and future artists were forced to choose between the divine Raphael or the terrifying Michelangelo.

The 16C Venetian school produced many great colourists. **Giorgione** (1478–1510) explored the relationship between man and nature by creating a wonderful sense of landscape and atmosphere. **Titian** (c.1490–1576), a disciple of Bellini, was influenced as a youth by Giorgione and imbued with his skill for both mythological and religious compositions. He was also a fine portraitist and was commissioned by numerous Italian princes and European sovereigns. His later work, characterised by bold compositions and densely coloured brushwork, is the impressive and personal document of one of the greatest artists of the century. **Tintoretto** (1518–94) added a tormented violence to his predecessors' luminosity, and ably exploited this in dramatic religious compositions. **Paolo Veronese** (1528–88) was foremost a decorator in love with luxury and sumptuous schemes. He delighted in crowd scenes with grandiose architectural backgrounds. In contrast, **Jacopo Bassano** (1518–92) handled rustic and nocturnal scenes, heightened with a new sense of reality and a freedom of touch and composition.

The Unsettled Years

Mannersim, in a world out of balance, stepped beyond realism in favour of the element of surprise, elongating a limb or exaggerating an element, or in the case of architecture, slipping it into another position.

The end of the 15C was a time of crisis: the invasion of Italy by foreign armies, with the resulting loss of liberty for many states, the increase in religious tensions, leading to the Lutheran Protestant movement, the sack of Rome and the Counter-Reformation all had a dramatic effect on artists. In northern Italy, **Lorenzo Lotto** (1480–1556) interpreted the spiritual anxieties of the provincial aristocracy and bourgeoisie with sharp psychological insight. In Brescia, following Foppa, artists explored reality and morality. **Romanino** (1484–1559) exploded with expressive violence. **Giovanni Girolamo Savoldo** (c.1480–1548) demonstrated a deep, lyrical intensity, while the paintings of **Alessandro Moretto** (1498–1554) were humble in their touching spirit of faith. But the most obvious examples of the anti-Classical crisis were in Florence, where **Jacopo Pontormo** (1494–1556) influenced by Raphael and Michelangelo, veered from the harmony of the Renaissance to a troubled tension, sharp colours and unreal sense of space.

MANNERISM

The art of the Counter-Reformation – which often tweaked the canon in an exaggerated or "mannered" way – marked the transition between Renaissance and Baroque. It attempted to voice the preoccupations of the previous generation. This refined genre pursued ideals of supreme and artificial beauty by copying the stylistic solutions of Raphael and Michelangelo. Mannerist art involved complex compositions of muscular and elongated figures. The period is generally considered to be one of technical accomplishment, but also of formulaic, theatrical and over-stylised work. A typical exponent of this style was **Giorgio Vasari** (1511–74), author of the *Lives of the Artists*, who had a strong influence on historical and critical judgement up to the present day. While Mannerism was widely adopted throughout Europe, it was countered in Italy by the Roman Catholic Church, which, following the Council of Trent, proposed that religious art be subjected to greater doctrinal clarity.

Part of the "Christ-Vine and the Legend of Saint Barbara," 1524, by Lorenzo Lotto

Naturalism, Classicism and Baroque: the 17C

N atural and classic forms were a swing back away from the unsettling aspects of Mannerism. The Baroque intensified drama and movement, both in tragedy as well as in sheer exuberance and joy.

PAINTING

Reacting against Mannerism, a group of Bolognese artists founded the **Accademia degli Incamminati** (Academy of the Eclectic), under the leadership of the **Carracci** family (**Annibale**, the most original, **Lodovico** and **Agostino**). They proposed a less artificial style that was truer to nature and paved the way for future artistic trends.

Classicism evolved first in Bologna and Rome, and later throughout Italy, following the premises laid down by the Carracci. One of the basic concepts is that certain forms – used in ancient art and by Raphael – constitute models of perfection and should be paradigms for any creation of high spiritual content. The vault of Palazzo Farnese in Rome, painted by Annibale Carracci, presages the Baroque style with its overwhelming dynamics and *trompe l'œil*.

Fanciful and dramatic, the Baroque style introduced a sense of movement, broken perspectives, scrolls and false reliefs. Painting paired with architecture to create disturbing visions of impressive verisimilitude. A good example is the ceiling of the Gesù church in Rome, where **Baciccia** (1639–1709) created a credible illusion of the sky in the physical architectural space of the ceiling.

The swashbuckling **Michelangelo Merisi** or **Caravaggio** (1573–1610) overthrew several centuries of Italian idealism. His intense and often cruel realism, inspired by the artistic traditions of Lombardy and Brescia, drew inspiration from everyday life in Rome. Contrasting light and shadow gave a dramatic visual impact to his work and often highlighted the moral reasons behind human actions and sentiments. He was widely imitated in Italy, France and the Netherlands – and was without doubt the most influential artist in 17C Europe.

ARCHITECTURE AND SCULPTURE

Unlike Mannerist architecture – static and intellectual – Baroque sought spatial dynamism. Spectators were amazed and confused by scenic devices, the continual intermingling of exterior and interior, curved and broken lines, and the role of light as a vehicle of divine intervention.

The true Baroque style, which is structural and found mainly in Rome, is often the creation of artists who worked as architects, painters, sculptors and scenographers. The transformation of St Peter's Basilica by **Gian Lorenzo Bernini** (1598–1680) offers typical examples: the famous colonnade solves the problem of the inharmonious extension of the church and makes the monumental but static façade the background to a dynamic piazza. The square then turns towards Rome and opens its arms to welcome the faithful.

Inside the cathedral, the flooding light and the immense bulk of the baldaquin compensate for the loss of centrality. The extension of the nave is transformed into an extraordinary tunnel of perspective of increasing tension.

An interesting variation of Baroque architecture can also be seen in Puglia (especially Lecce) and in Sicily, with ornate and imaginative decoration.

BAROQUE
Lecce – Basilica di Santa Croce (15-17C)

The Baroque style of Lecce is influenced both by Roman and Spanish architecture. The exuberant, highly-worked decoration evokes the Spanish Plateresque style (15-16C), in which façades were decorated with the precise detail of a goldsmith (platero in Spanish).

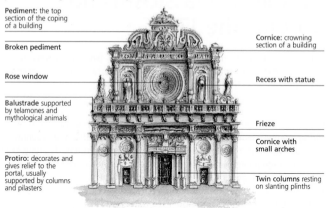

Pediment: the top section of the coping of a building

Broken pediment

Rose window

Balustrade supported by telamones and mythological animals

Protiro: decorates and gives relief to the portal, usually supported by columns and pilasters

Cornice: crowning section of a building

Recess with statue

Frieze

Cornice with small arches

Twin columns resting on slanting plinths

Roma – Interior of St John Lateran (4-17C)

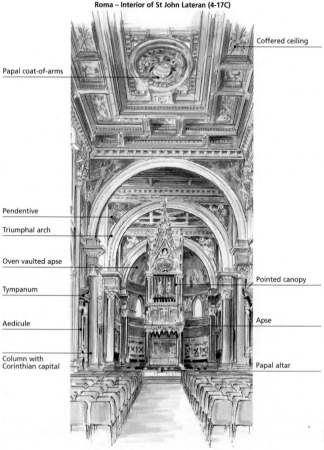

Papal coat-of-arms

Pendentive

Triumphal arch

Oven vaulted apse

Tympanum

Aedicule

Column with Corinthian capital

Coffered ceiling

Pointed canopy

Apse

Papal altar

H. Choimet

Settecento (18C)

Baroque drama took on a lighter tone and architecture played with space in rational ways, too. Herculaneum and Pompeii were discovered. The Grand Tour was the vogue and the "it" place in Europe was Naples.

The deep cultural changes of the new century, with its emphasis on rational and enlightened thinking, were reflected in art. Now, the Baroque style, exhausted of its most intimate religious content, became even more secular and decorative in tone. Art was departing from symbolic significance and becoming more autonomous. It was more inclined to entertain rather than to educate – a trend that began in France, where the style was known as *rocaille*.

Italy had by now relinquished its leading role, although the peninsula still produced some important artistic figures, especially in Piemonte. The era's most extraordinary project was the urban revival of Turin, which raised the city to the status of a European capital. Here, **Filippo Juvarra** (1678–1736) moved beyond the drama of his predecessor **Guarino Guarini** (1624–83). Instead, he designed a town plan (long tree-lined-avenues surrounding the buildings) of grandiose theatricality: the perfect backdrop for the fine costumes of the Court of Savoy. Art took another important step away from a mere representation of physical objects with the Venetian painter **Giovanni Battista (Giambattista) Tiepolo** (1696–1770), who created *trompe l'œil* perspectives for pure visual pleasure and no real regard for verisimilitude or the content of the stories represented: art was now being valued for its artistic qualities alone.

In architecture, **Luigi Vanvitelli** began construction on the Reggia di Caserta in 1752, developed on a scale to rival Versailles, in a project that would take over 20 years. In Rome Valadier brought rational space to **Piazza del Popolo** and a magnificent staircase to **Palazzo Braschi**, while Neapolitan architect Filippo Raguzzini created a flirtacious interplay of palaces in **Piazza Sant'Ignazio**.

Reggia di Caserta

Ottocento (19C)

The century begins with the Neoclassicism of Canova, a favourite of Napoleon, then radically shifts toward the Impressionistic examination of light, a fascination with machines, and the introduction of photography.

In the late-18C and early-19C, the vogue for all things Classical spread throughout Italy and Europe, following the excavations of Herculaneum and Pompeii. The style's sober, simple and harmonious lines – modelled on the Antiquity – contrast starkly with the exuberant, irregular Baroque fashion. The Italian Neoclassical style is exemplified by the sculptor **Antonio Canova** (1757–1822), whose works follow perfectly the "noble simplicity and quiet grandeur" of Greek art as described by Winckelmann (and only really observed through Roman copies). In his most famous sculpture, *The Three Graces* (in the Victoria and Albert Museum, London), the extreme formal perfection is transformed into an ambiguous sensuality that resonates with nostalgia for a perfect world lost forever. It is a subtle allusion to the impalpable screen between life and death that characterises all of his work, as well as the period's poetry.

Neoclassicism also infiltrated architecture, alongside the eclectic style. This free-for-all lasted throughout the century, often with erratic results. An exception is **Alessandro Antonelli** (1798–1888), who enlivened the idiom with new engineering principles, binding the academic tradition to the boldest experiments in Europe.

In painting, the often academic tone of **Francesco Hayez** (1791–1882) demonstrates the Romantic style, which existed alongside the Neoclassical tradition. This friend of Canova created paintings of medieval history, highly sentimental in tone, of the contemporary events of the Risorgimento. The **Macchiaioli** group, founded in

1855, started a revolt against academicism that lasted about 20 years. Also known as the "spotters", the painters were in some ways the precursors of the Impressionists; they frequently worked outdoors, using colour and simple lines, and drawing inspiration from nature. The main figures of the group included **Giovanni Fattori** (1825–1908), **Silvestro Lega** (1826–95) and **Telemaco Signorini** (1835–1901). Some artists worked with the Impressionists in Paris, and their influence had an indirect, but powerful, effect on Italian art.

At the end of the 19C, in parallel with the growth of a flowing and sketch-like style of painting, **Giovanni Segantini** (1858–99), **Pellizza da Volpedo** (1868–1907) and **Gaetano Previati** (1852–1920) developed the Divisionist school. This art reflected the theories of the French post-impressionists; on the one hand developing a deeper analysis of reality, with strong connotations of a social character, while at the same time lending itself to allegorical and symbolist themes. This was in line with artistic developments in the rest of Europe, and their solutions were of fundamental importance for the avant-garde trends of the 20C.

The coming of the Industrial Age also ushered in a fascination with machines, workers, and the changing cityscapes that result in an urban context. A counterpoint appears in *plein air* painting, where painters take their easels outdoors and capture rural sights and ruins. Photographers set up studios in major cities. Early motion pictures came to Italy in 1896 when the Lumière brothers projected early film in Rome, Milan, Naples and other cities.

Torino – Palazzo Carignano (Guarino Guarini, 1679-1681)

The façade is striking for the juxtaposition of its straight and curved lines, while the use of brick is a reminder of the Emilian origins of the architect.

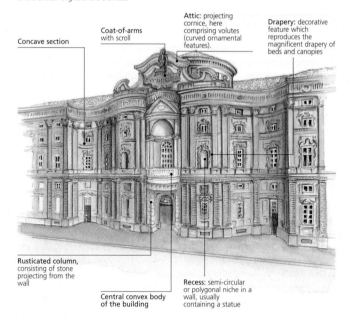

Coat-of-arms with scroll

Concave section

Attic: projecting cornice, here comprising volutes (curved ornamental features).

Drapery: decorative feature which reproduces the magnificent drapery of beds and canopies

Rusticated column, consisting of stone projecting from the wall

Central convex body of the building

Recess: semi-circular or polygonal niche in a wall, usually containing a statue

Milano – Teatro alla Scala (Giuseppe Piermarini, 1776-1778)

The sober and measured simplicity of the façade of this famous Milanese theatre contrasts with the rich decor of the interior. The theatre soon became a model for future neo-Classical theatres.

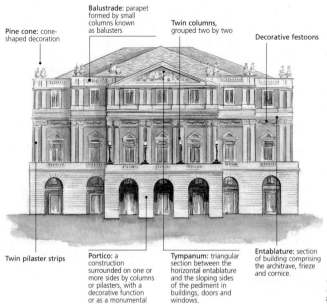

Pine cone: cone-shaped decoration

Balustrade: parapet formed by small columns known as balusters

Twin columns, grouped two by two

Decorative festoons

Twin pilaster strips

Portico: a construction surrounded on one or more sides by columns or pilasters, with a decorative function or as a monumental entrance.

Tympanum: triangular section between the horizontal entablature and the sloping sides of the pediment in buildings, doors and windows.

Entablature: section of building comprising the architrave, frieze and cornice.

H. Choimet

117

Novecento (20C)

Futurism embraced the modern world and machines, interpreting its dynamism in a variety of ways. Two World Wars subdued some of the enthusiasm for machines, leading others to naturalism and Expressionism.

The 20C began in an explosive manner with the sensational and anti-aesthetic style of the **Futurists**. Under the leadership of the poet **Filippo Tommaso Marinetti** (1876–1944), the movement's theorist, they celebrated speed, crowds and machinery. This was an explicit and anarchic reaction to bourgeois traditionalist values, which were attacked with vehemence and a sometimes superficial vitality. The movement soon adopted a nationalist tone, which in some cases developed into a sympathy for the Fascists. The Futurists tried to render the dynamism of the modern world, often with fragmented forms similar to Cubism's. However, they differed in their marked sense of rebellion, which was influenced both by contemporary philosophers such as Bergson, and by the violent and impassioned disharmony of the Expressionist movement.

The members of this avant-garde movement were **Umberto Boccioni** (1882–1916), **Giacomo Balla** (1871–1958), **Gino Severini** (1883–1966), **Carlo Carrà** (1881–1966) and the architect **Antonio Sant'Elia** (1888–1916). **Giorgio de Chirico** (1888–1978), together with Carrà, created metaphysical painting, a disturbing form where objects are placed in unlikely but credible positions in an ambiguous and enigmatic atmosphere. Giorgio Morandi was inspired by some of the same ideas. His still-lifes of everyday objects invite meditation on history and the meaning of the painting.

After World War I, the return to peace revived artistic activity both in Italy and abroad. This included the founding of the Novecento group, which developed naturalistic premises through Magical Realism, interpreted through a re-reading of metaphysics and of Italian Medieval and Classical art. The results were often highly poetic and stylised. Most of the painters, sculptors and architects in Italy either belonged to, or were influenced by this group, especially when the political regime declared itself in favour of this stylistic trend in the 1920s, opposing any relationship with contemporary European art. A few isolated voices, often criticised by the authorities, were raised in explicit or tacit opposition to these trends and in favour of a less provincial approach. Some of the most important forces were involved in the **Corrente** group from Milan, the **Scuola romana**, and the **Sei di Torino**.

These groups shared a common interest in Expressionism, which often gave their art a highly dramatic realism, a social tension and a deeply humane content. A good example is the painter **Renato Guttuso** (1912–87), with his personal interpretation of post-Cubist art, combined with explicitly anti-fascist material. Even in the general post-war crisis, he nearly always managed to avoid the risks of Socialist Realism, thanks to his openness to different cultural influences. One of the most important contemporary sculptors was **Giacomo Manzù** (1908–91), who succeeded in breathing new life into Christian art. A clear and luminous sensitivity gave his works, especially the low reliefs, an almost Donatellian vitality. As such, Manzù succeeded in making a sorrowful and humane statement against violence.

The Post-War Period

Trends moved away from established, traditional forms and toward new modes of expression. Artists selected new materials or used traditional materials in innovative ways, while others chose to work with found objects.

The tragedy of war always makes an indelible impression. Artists query the significance of creation in a world where all moral values have been brutally set aside. The phrase "the death of art" also surfaced in the new consumer society of the 1950s and 60s. The Classical artistic language was no longer understood as a system of signs able to give form to the aesthetic experience of reality. New expression was therefore anti-aesthetic and mirrored trends which previously had no influence.

Canvases were sometimes tossed aside or much abused. Alberto Burri (1915–95), who came to painting later in life, avoided the traditional academic circles. By pasting old torn bags onto his canvas, Burri's intention was not to represent ideas or objects, but to exhibit a fragment of reality. **Lucio Fontana** (1899–1968) also stretched the physical limits inherent in the traditional method of creating art. He cut canvases, seeking new solutions to the old problem of space, which can be created, but not represented. His "gesture" and action puts the here and now in contact with the other world of the canvas and destroys the Classical pretence of space. Other artists belonged to the movement known as **Arte Povera**, which opposed the "rich" world. Their break with the Classical method of creating and understanding art was complete. The apex was the artist's radical refusal to develop a role; something he believes to be a hoax, dominated by the system against which he is struggling.

Architecture took on bold new forms in the 21C in a break with the past. **Zaha Hadid** won international awards for her MAXXI museum (2011) in Rome, also home to **Renzo Piano**'s Auditorium, **Richard Meier**'s Ara Pacis museum, and **Santiago Calatrava**'s bridge, who built one other in Venice.

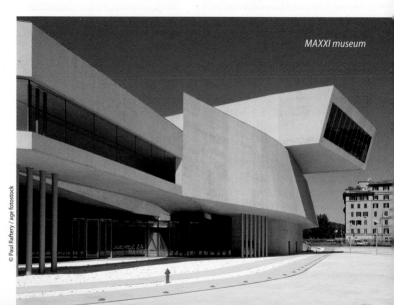

MAXXI museum

© Paul Raftery / age fotostock

Architectural Terms

Some of the terms given below are further explained by the illustrations on the Art and Culture pages.

Altarpiece (or **ancona**): a large painting or sculpture for an altar.
Ambulatory: extension of the aisles around the chancel for processions.
Apse: semicircular or polygonal end of a church behind the altar.
Architrave: the lowermost horizontal division of a Classical entablature sitting directly on the column capital and supporting the frieze.
Archivolt: arch moulding over an arcade or upper section of a doorway.
Atlantes (or **telamones**): male figures used as supporting columns.
Atrium (or **four-sided portico**): a court enclosed by colonnades in front of the entrance to an early Christian or Romanesque church.
Bastion: in military architecture, a polygonal defensive structure projecting from the ramparts.
Buttress: external support of a wall, which counterbalances the thrust of the vaults and arches.
Caisson (or **lacunar**): decorative square panel sunk into a flat roof or vaulted stonework.
Cappella: chapel.
Cathedra: high-backed throne in Gothic style.
Ciborium: a canopy (baldaquin) over an altar.
Corinthian: *see Order.*
Cortile: interior courtyard of a palace.
Counter-façade: internal wall of church façade.
Cross (church plan): usually a **Greek cross**, with four arms of equal length, or a **Latin cross**, with one arm longer than the other three in a church.
Crypt: underground chamber or vault usually beneath a church, often used as a mortuary, burial place or for displaying holy relics. Sometimes it was a small chapel or church in its own right.

Diptych: *see Polyptych.*
Doric: *see Order.*
Duomo: cathedral.
Entablature: the top of a colonnade consisting of three parts: the architrave (flat section resting on the capitals of a colonnade), the frieze (decorated with carvings) and the cornice (projecting top section).
Exedra: section in the back of Roman basilicas containing seats; curved niche or semicircular recess outside.
Fresco: mural paint applied onto a fresh undercoat of plaster.
Ghimberga: a triangular Gothic pediment adorning a portal.
Grotesque: a human, animal and plant forms are distorted and mixed.
High relief: sculpture or carved work projecting more than one half of its true proportions from the background (halfway between low relief and in-the-round figures).
Ionic: *see Order.*
Jamb (or **pier**): pillar flanking a doorway or window and supporting the arch above.
Lantern: turret with windows on top of a dome.
Lesene (or **Lombard strips**): decorative band of pilasters joined at the top by an arched frieze.
Low relief: bas-relief, carved figures slightly projecting from their background.
Merlon: part of a crowning parapet between two crenellations.
Modillion: small console supporting a cornice.
Moulding: an ornamental shaped band which projects from the wall.
Narthex: interior vestibule of a church.
Nave: the area between the entrance and chancel of a church, with or without aisles.

Oculus: round window.

Ogee arch: a pointed arch of double curvature: Cyma Recta where the lower curve is convex and the upper curve concave; Cyma Reversa where the reverse is true.

Order: system in Classical architecture ensuring a unity of style characterised by its columns (base, shaft, capital) and entablature. The orders used in Tuscany are: Doric (capitals with mouldings – the Tuscan Doric order is a simplified version of this), Ionic (capitals with volutes), Corinthian (capitals with acanthus leaves) and the Composite, derived from the Corinthian but more complex.

Pala: Italian term for altarpiece or reredos.

Palazzo: a town house usually of a noble family; derived from "Palatine" residences of the caesars.

Pediment: ornament in Classical architecture (usually triangular or semicircular) above a door or window.

Pendentive: connecting piece positioned at a corner of a square space to support an octagonal or circular dome.

Piano nobile: the principal floor of a palazzo raised one storey above ground level.

Pieve: Romanesque parish church.

Peristyle: the range of columns surrounding a Classical building or courtyard.

Pilaster strip: structural column partially set into a wall.

Pluteus: decorated balustrade made from various materials, separating the chancel from the rest of the church.

Polyptych: a painted or carved work consisting of more than three folding leaves or panels (diptych: 2 panels; triptych: 3 panels).

Portico: an open gallery facing the nave in early Christian churches; it later became a decorative feature of the external part of the church.

Predella: base of an altarpiece, divided into small panels.

Pronaos: the space in front of the *cella* or *naos* in Greek temples; later the columned portico in front of the entrance to a church or palace.

Pulpit: an elevated dais from which sermons were preached in the nave of a church.

Pyx: cylindrical box made of ivory or glazed copper for jewels or the Eucharistic host.

Retable: large and ornate altarpiece divided into several painted or carved panels, especially common in Spain after the 14C.

Rose window: A circular window usually inserted into the front elevation of a church, often filled with stained glass, and decorated with tracery arranged symmetrically about its centre.

Splay: a surface of a wall that forms an oblique angle to the main surface of a doorway or window opening.

Tambour: a circular or polygonal structure supporting a dome.

Tempera: a painting technique in which pigments are ground down and bound usually by means of an egg-based preparation. The technique was replaced by oil.

Tondo: a circular picture, fashionable in Italy in the mid-15C.

Triforium: an open gallery above the arcade of the nave, comprising mainly three-light windows.

Triptych: *see Polyptych*.

Trompe l'œil: two-dimensional painted decoration giving the three-dimensional illusion of relief and perspective.

Tympanum: the section above a door (or window) between the lintel and archivolt.

Vault: arched structure forming a roof or ceiling; **barrel vault**: produced by a continuous rounded arch; **cross vault**: formed by the intersection of two barrel vaults; **oven vault**: semicircular, usually over apsidal chapels, the termination of a barrel-vaulted nave.

Volute: architectural ornament in the form of a spiral scroll.

Literature

I taly is a country that still reads and that has managed to keep a good number of bookstores, from large chains to small independent shops. The literary tradition dates back to at least the 13C, and publishing is still active, from Torino, Bologna and Florence to Rome and Naples.

BIRTH OF ITALIAN LITERATURE

The Italian language acquired a literary form in the 13C. At Assisi **St Francis** (1182–1226) wrote his moving *Canticle of the Creatures* in the vernacular instead of the traditional Latin, so that the people could read the word of God. The 13C also gave rise to the **Sicilian school**, which, at the court of Frederick II, developed a language of love inspired by traditional ballads from Provence. The most famous of the 13C poetical trends was, however, that of the *dolce stil nuovo* ("sweet new style"): followers included Guinezzelli and Cavalcanti. The term was appropriated by **Dante Alighieri** (1265–1321), author of

Vita Nuova (New Life), *Convivio (The Banquet)* and *De Vulgari Eloquentia* (Concerning Vernacular Eloquence), to indicate the lyrical quality of this poetry which would celebrate a spiritual and edifying love for an angel-like woman in verse. It was with this new tool that he wrote one of the most powerful masterpieces of Italian literature: the *Divine Comedy* is the account of a lively, enquiring and impassioned visitor to Inferno, Purgatory and Paradise *(Inferno, Purgatorio, Paradiso)*. It is also an epic account of the Christianised Western world and the height of spiritual knowledge of the period. During the 14C **Petrarch** (1304–74), the precursor of humanism and the greatest

Detail of the "La Madonna del Magnificat", 1481, by Sandro Botticelli.

© dea / A. Dagli Orti / De Agostini Editore / age fotostock

Italian lyrical poet, and his friend **Giovanni Boccaccio** (1313–75), the astonishing storyteller who seems almost modern at times (🔆 *see SAN GIMIGNANO: Certaldo*), continued in the tradition of Dante. Each enriched the Italian language in his own way.

HUMANISM AND RENAISSANCE

Florentine humanism reinterpreted the ancient heritage and invented a scholarly poetry in which the tension of the words and images reflected the aspiration of the soul to attain an ideal. **Politian, Lorenzo de' Medici** (1449–92) and especially **Michelangelo** were exponents of the neo-Platonic notion of ideal poetry. However the Florentine Renaissance also favoured the development of other quite different lines of thought: scientific with Leonardo da Vinci, theorist with Leon Battista Alberti, philosophical with Marsile Fincin and encyclopaedic with the fascinating personality of Pico della Mirandola. Later Giorgio Vasari (🔆 *see FLORENCE*) became the first-ever art historian.

In the 16C writers and poets perfected the Italian language to a height of refinement and elegance rarely attained, and all this in the service of princes whom they counselled or entertained. The most famous was **Niccolò Machiavelli** (1469–1527), the statesman and political theorist whose name now symbolises cunning and duplicity. In his work entitled *The Prince* he defined with clarity and intelligence the processes which control society, and the moral and political consequences of these relationships.

At the court in Ferrara, **Matteo Maria Boiardo** (1441–94) fused the epic poetry of the Carolingian cycles with the courtly poetry of the Breton cycles in the poem celebrating chivalry, *Orlando Innamorato (Roland in Love)*. **Ludovico Ariosto** (1475–1533) and **Torquato Tasso** (1544–95) provided an element of intellectual brilliance. The former wrote *Orlando Furioso (Roland the Mad)*, an epic poem in episodes which enjoyed an extraordinary vogue, and Tasso, his successor at court in this genre, published his *Jerusalem Delivered (Gerusalemme Liberata)*.

At Urbino, **Baldassare Castiglione** (1478–1529) was the author of one of the great works of the period *The Courtier (Il Cortegiano)*, which was read throughout Europe. In Venice, **Aretino** (1492–1556) sketched the unsentimental portrait of his contemporaries *(Letters)* while in Padova, **Ruzzante** (1502–42) favoured realism in the local dialect.

COUNTER-REFORMATION AND BAROQUE PERIOD

After the discovery of America in 1492, an event which affected the Mediterranean economy adversely, and the spread of Lutheran Protestantism, the 17C to the early 18C marked a period of decadence for Italian literature. The exception was **Galileo** (1564–1642), a scientist, who, taking Archimedes as his point of reference rather than Aristotle, made a distinction between scientific methods and those applicable to theology and philosophy. He was implacably opposed by the Church in an attempt to reassert its influence under the onslaught of the Reformation. The fear of the Inquisition hampered original thought and favoured the development of Baroque poetical concepts in a quest for fantasy.

THE AGE OF ENLIGHTENMENT AND ROMANTICISM

The early 18C was marked by Arcadia, a literary academy which preached "good taste" inspired by the purity of Classical bucolic poetry, in opposition to the "bad taste" of the Baroque period.

The philosopher **Giambattista Vico** (1668–1744) elaborated the theory of the ebb and flow of history based on three stages (sense, imagination and reason). The dramatist **Pietro Metastasio** (1698–1783) was also a leading figure of the period whose biting yet well-thought-out vision advanced scientific and philosophical thought.

In Venice, the 18C was dominated by the dramatist **Carlo Goldoni** (1707–93), known as the Italian Molière, who peo-

ITALIAN-BORN NOBEL PRIZE WINNERS

Literature – Dario Fo (1997); Eugenio Montale (1975); Salvatore Quasimodo (1959); Luigi Pirandello (1934); Grazia Deledda (1929); Giosuè Carducci (1906).
Physics – Riccardo Giacconi (discovery of cosmic X-ray sources, 2002); Carlo Rubbia (discovery of the sub-atomic W and Z particles, 1984); Emilio Segrè (discovery of the antiproton, 1959); Enrico Fermi (nuclear reactions produced by the actions of slow neutrons and the resulting fission of uranium, 1938); Guglielmo Marconi (wireless telegraphy, 1909).
Chemistry – Giulio Natta (polymer structures and technology, 1963).
Medicine and Physiology – Mario Capecci (discovery of principles for introducing specific gene modifications, 2007); Rita Levi-Montalcini (growth mechanisms of nerve cells, 1986); Renato Dulbecco (discovery of the interaction between tumoral viruses and the genetic material of cells, 1975); Salvador Edward Luria (mechanisms of genetic repetition and structure of viruses and bacteria, 1969); Camillo Goigi (structure of the nervous system, 1906).
Economics – Franco Modigliani (analysis of saving cycles and the financial markets, 1985). **Peace** – Ernesto Teodoro Moneta (1907).

pled his plays in an amusing, alert and subtle manner with the stock characters and situations of the *Commedia dell'Arte* (&see BERGAMO), an art form which was then highly popular in Venice.

From the end of the 18C writers began to express a new national spirit (consciousness which developed until the upheaval of the Risorgimento).

Giuseppe Parini (1729–99), a didactic writer, and **Vittorio Alfieri** (1749–1803), who became known for his tragedies on the themes of liberty and opposition to tyranny, were the precursors of the violent and tormented **Ugo Foscolo** (1778–1827), whose patriotic pride is given full vent in *Of the Sepulchres*.

Giacomo Leopardi (1798–1837) in some of the finest poems expresses the growing gulf between the old faith and a fear of the unknown future.

The Milanese author **Alessandro Manzoni** (1785–1873) wrote one of the most important novels of 19C Italian literature, *The Betrothed (I Promessi Sposi)*, a grandiose epic of ordinary folk based on the notion of providence in human existence.

Realism and Decadence

The Sicilian **Giovanni Verga** (1840–1922) assured the transition between the 19C and 20C with his novels. He was one of the most important members of the Italian Realist *(Verismo)* school of novelists which took its inspiration from the French Naturalist movement. In his extravagant fiction series entitled *Vinti* he presents his pessimistic vision of the world and his compassion for the disinherited.

In the field of lyrical poetry in the second half of the 19C **Giosuè Carducci** (1835–1907), a Nobel Prize winner in 1906, drew inspiration from Classical poetry. He was a melancholy figure who criticised the sentimentality of the romantic movement. **Gabriele d'Annunzio** (1863–1938) adopted a refined and precious style to express his sensual love of language. The complex and anxious voice of the poet **Giovanni Pascoli** (1855–1912) filled the early years of the 20C. His nostalgic poetry recalls the age of innocence and a sense of wonder.

AUTHORS MODERN AND CONTEMPORARY

In the early-20C magazines devoted to political, cultural, moral and literary themes were published. Giuseppe Prezzolini (1882–1982) and Giovanni Papini (1881–1956) were among the contributors.

Futurism, which influenced other forms of artistic expression, was the most important of the contemporary literary movements. In his *Manifesto* (1909) **Filippo Tommaso Marinetti** (1876–1944), the leader and theoretician of the movement, exalted the attractions of speed, machines, war and "feverish insomnia", ideas which were echoed by the disjointed syntax, punctuation and words employed in this literary style.

In line with the European sensibility expressed by Musil, Proust and Joyce, Italian letters favoured the theme of discovery which was influenced by studies on repression and the unconscious in the early years of psychoanalysis. In *Zeno's Conscience*, **Italo Svevo** (1861–1928) examines the alienation of the main protagonist as past and present unfold in a long internal monologue. The Sicilian dramatist **Luigi Pirandello** (1867–1936) also analyses man's tragic solitude and the way in which the identity of the individual is eclipsed by the perceptions of the different persons with whom he associates. The only escape is madness.

Traces of realism and the influence of D'Annunzio can be detected in the work of **Grazia Deledda** (1871–1936), who shrouds her portrayals of Sardinian society in mythology. Her tales are dominated by passionate emotions and a deep religious sense of life and death. The **Hermetic movement**, which developed after World War I, celebrated the essential nature of words, liberated from the burden of a grandiloquent and commemorative tradition. The poetry of **Giuseppe Ungaretti** (1888–1970) is evocative and intense, while another leading figure of this movement, **Salvatore Quasimodo** (1901–68), produced successful translations of Greek and Latin Classical literature and of Shakespeare. The poetry of **Eugenio Montale** (1896–1981) relates with sharp and incisive eloquence the anguish which afflicts human nature. **Umberto Saba** (1883–1957), whose native Trieste was strongly marked by central European culture, uses both noble language and everyday vocabulary in his intensely lyrical and autobiographical work.

After World War II, **neo-Realism** – which was ideally suited to the cinema with its popular appeal – gave a graphic account of the life and misery of the working class, of peasants and street children.

The recurring themes in the works of **Cesare Pavese** (1908–50) are the loneliness and difficulty of existence, described with anguish in his diary, which was published posthumously with the title *This Business of Living*.

During recent decades the Italian novel has shown a strong vitality with such diverse personalities as Pratolini *(A Tale of Poor Lovers)*, Guido Piovene *(Pietà contro Pietà)*, Ignazio Silone *(Fontarama)*, Mario Soldati *(A Cena col Commendatore)*, Carlo Levi *(Christ Stopped at Eboli)* and Elsa Morante *(Arthur's Island)*.

In the 20C a handful of Italian authors have achieved international fame: **Alberto Moravia** (1907–90) is regarded as a significant narrator of modern Italy, identifying the importance of such issues as sex and money. His book *The Time of Indifference* recounts the decline and forbearance of a bourgeois Roman family. Another well-known neo-Realist author was **Italo Calvino** (1923–85), who experimented with the mechanisms of language and who wrote short stories tinged with subtle irony.

Leonardo Sciascia (1921–89) concentrated on revealing some of the ills of Italian society, such as the Mafia. He wrote essays, detective stories, historical memoirs and romantic surveys. **Carlo Emilio Gadda**, known as the "engineer", experimented with language and portrayed the hypocrisy, follies and obscure ills of contemporary society. **Pier Paolo Pasolini** (1922–75) provoked and contested the received ideas of his time, contrasting Marxist ideology with Christian spirituality and peasant values.

Dino Buzzati (1906–72), an original figure, was a poet, writer, illustrator and journalist. His penchant for fantasy and surrealism is tinged with scepticism and is reminiscent of Kafka and Poe.

The 1980s saw the huge success of *The Name of the Rose* (1980), a Gothic thriller written by the semiologist and essayist **Umberto Eco** (b.1932). The 1997 Nobel Prize for literature went to the playwright and actor **Dario Fo** (b.1926), whose plays attack the powerful and defend the oppressed.

Music

I taly played a significant role in the evolution of music with the invention of the musical scale and the development of the violin. It is the birthplace of Vivaldi, who inspired Bach and who was surprisingly neglected until the beginning of the 20C, and of Verdi, who created operatic works to celebrate the Risorgimento in the 19C.

EARLY MUSICAL COMPOSITION AND RELIGIOUS MUSIC

As early as the end of the 10C, a Benedictine monk, **Guido** of Arezzo (997–c.1050), invented the scale, naming the notes with the initial syllables of the first six lines of John the Baptist's hymn *"Ut queant laxis / Resonare fibris / Mira gestorum / Famuli tuorum / Solve polluti / Labii reatum Sancte Johannes"*. The "Si" formed by the initials of *Sancte Johannes* was added to these and the Ut was changed to Do in the 17C.

In the 16C the golden age of vocal polyphony, which was then very popular, was marked by **Giovanni Pierluigi da Palestrina** (c.1525–94), a prolific composer of essentially religious music (105 masses). During that period, **Andrea Gabrieli** (c.1510–86) and his nephew **Giovanni** (c.1557–1612), who were the organists at St Mark's in Venice were masters of sacred and secular polyphonic music. The latter composed the first violin sonatas.

FROM THE BAROQUE PERIOD TO THE 18C

It was only in the 17C and 18C that a proper musical school (for operatic as well as instrumental works) was born in Italy, characterised by charm and freshness of inspiration and melodic talent. The old and new musical forms evolved with the expressive and stylistic innovations of **Girolamo Frescobaldi** (1583–1643) for the organ and harpsichord, Corelli (1653–1713) for the violin and **Domenico Scarlatti** (1685–1757) for the harpsichord. The talented Venetian **Antonio Vivaldi** (1675–1741) composed a wealth of lively music greatly admired by Bach, particularly his concertos

Massimo Theatre, Palermo

©Marzolino/iStockphoto.com

THE VIOLIN

The violin was created as a new and improved model of the *viola da braccio*. Nowadays its fame is so closely linked to that of the old stringed instrument workshops (second half of the 16C – beginning of the 18C), almost all of which were based in Cremona, that the manufacturer's name (Gasparo da Salò, Amati, Guarneri, Stradivari, etc.) is almost synonymous with that of the instrument and is often mentioned on concert programmes. The most important composers for the violin include Arcangelo Corelli (1653–1713), who wrote a number of sonatas for the violin and *basso continuo* (the bass part over which the solo instrument plays the melody), including the well-known *La Follia*; Giuseppe Torelli (1658–1709), the composer of many *concerti grossi* (compositions for an orchestra and a group of soloists); Giuseppe Tartini (1692–1770), who wrote the anguished sonatas *The Devil's Trill* and *Dido Abandoned*; Pietro Locatelli (1695–1764), who perfected violin techniques in his *capricci* and *sonate*; Giovanni Battista Viotti; and the incomparable Niccolò Paganini. The violin museum in Cremona, restored in 2013, offers an opportunity to briefly hear the antique violins played. Shops there still repair and construct violins.

divided into three parts, *allegro/adagio/allegro*, and with descriptive interludes as in the *Four Seasons*. **Baldassare Galuppi** (1706–85), a native of Burano near Venice, composed the music for the librettos of Goldoni as well as sonatas for harpsichord with a lively tempo. Although Venice was in its final period of glory, her musical reputation grew with the **Marcello** brothers, **Benedetto** (1686–1739) and **Alessandro** (1684–1750). The latter composed a famous concerto for oboe, stringed instruments and organ with a splendid adagio. The instrumental compositions of **Tomaso Albinoni** (1671–1750) are reminiscent of Vivaldi's masterpieces.

In the 18C important Italian composers worked outside Italy. In the field of chamber music, **Luigi Boccherini** (1743–1805), a native of Lucca working in Spain, was famous for his melodies and minuets. He also wrote a powerful symphony, *The House of the Devil*.

Antonio Salieri (1750–1825) from the Veneto was an active composer and a famous teacher who taught Beethoven, Schubert and Liszt. Towards the end of his life, he became mentally disturbed and blamed himself for Mozart's death. This is the theme of the film *Amadeus* by Miloš Forman (1984). The Piedmontese **Giovanni Battista Viotti** (1755–1824), Salieri's contemporary, enriched the violin repertory with 29 fine violin concertos. He lived in Paris and London; he died when his wine business failed.

Although not a musician, **Lorenzo Da Ponte** deserves a mention for his poetic contribution to great musical works. His love of adventure took him not only to New York where he died, but also

THE PIANO

The piano was invented by Bartolomeo Cristofori (1655–1732), who modified the harpsichord by replacing the plectra, which "plucked" the strings, with hammers, which struck them. The first Italian to introduce this new instrument to the rest of Europe was Muzio Clementi (1752–1832), a rival of Mozart. He wrote a hundred studies for the piano, including *Gradus ad Parnassum*, and *Six Sonatas*, which were influenced by the work of both Mozart and Beethoven. The piano's wide range of tones and notes made it the ideal instrument for the Romantics, who composed a number of melancholic and passionate pieces for it. In more recent times some of Bach's compositions were adapted for the piano by Ferruccio Busoni (1866–1924).

Portrait of Claudio Monteverdi, Gallerie dell'Accademia, Venice

©World Illustrated/Photoshot

to Vienna, Europe's musical capital at that time. He collaborated with Mozart and wrote librettos for *The Marriage of Figaro*, *Don Giovanni* and *Così Fan Tutte*, which won him great fame. This great period ended with the Romantic movement, which is wonderfully celebrated by the great violinist **Niccolò Paganini** (1782–1840) although by that time the piano had become more popular than the violin. His adventurous life, genius of interpretation and legendary virtuosity as well as his slim, tall build turned him into a demonic figure. His most famous works include 24 **capricci** and six concertos; the finale of the second concerto is the well-known *Campanella*.

GIUSEPPE SINOPOLI

When he died in Berlin during a performance of *Aida* that he was conducting on 20 April 2001, this great Italian conductor was only 54 years old. Not only was he an accomplished musician and scholar of Wagner but he was passionate about psychiatry and archaeology and achieved professional qualifications in both these fields. A theatre hall within Rome's new Auditorium is dedicated to him.

Opera

Modern opera originated with **Claudio Monteverdi** (1567–1643) from Cremona whose masterpiece was *Orfeo*. Monteverdi heralded this musical idiom combining words and music, which was immediately very successful and became a popular pursuit influencing the whole cultural scene in Italy.

At the end of the 17C, Neapolitan opera with **Alessandro Scarlatti** established the distinction between arias, which highlight virtuoso singing and recitatives, which are essential for the development of the action. In the 18C **Giovan Battista Pergolese**, **Domenico Cimarosa** and **Giovanni Paisiello** were the leading composers of comic opera *(opera buffa)*.

In the 19C there were few great composers of instrumental music apart from Paganini, as lyrical art was made to reflect the intense passions of the Risorgimento. **Gioacchino Rossini** (1782–1868) marked the transition from the Classical to the Romantic period (*Othello*, *William Tell* and the comic operas *The Italian Girl in Algiers*, *The Thieving Magpie* and *The Barber of Seville*). **Vincenzo Bellini** (1801–35) composed undistinguished orchestral music but admirable melodies and arias *(La Somnambula, Norma)*. His rival **Gaetano Donizetti** (1797–1848) wrote several melodramas *(Lucia di Lammermoor)* where the action takes second place to the singing, as well as some charming comic operas: *L'Elisir d'Amore*, *Don Pasquale*. **Amilcare Ponchielli** (1834–86) is remembered mainly for his successful opera *La Gioconda*.

The greatest composer of the genre during the fight for independence from Austria was **Giuseppe Verdi** (1813–1901) with his dramatic, romantic works: *Nabucco*, *Rigoletto*, *Il Trovatore*, *La Traviata*, *Aida*, etc; he also wrote an admirable *Requiem*. The Realist movement *(Verismo)* then became popular, with Mascagni *(Cavalleria Rusticana)*, Leoncavallo *(I Pagliacci)*, and especially **Giacomo Puccini** (1858–1924) whose *Tosca*, *Madame Butterfly* and *La Bohème* crowned the era.

Teatro alla Scala, Milan

© Fototeca ENIT

Modern music

In reaction, the next generation concentrated on orchestral music; it included **Ottorino Respighi** (1879–1937), who composed symphonic poems *(The Fountains of Rome, The Pines of Rome, Roman festivals)*. 20C composers include Petrassi, who explored all musical forms and **Dallapiccola** (1904–75), the leader of the Dodecaphonic movement (the 12 notes of the scale are used) in Italy. The passionate **Luigi Nono** (1924–90) used serial music to express his political and liberating message; he wrote instrumental, orchestral and vocal works.

Venues and artists

The only relatively recent unification of the country accounts for the numerous and famous opera houses and concert halls: the prestigious La Scala in Milan, for which Visconti created marvellous sets, the Rome Opera House, the San Carlo Theatre in Naples, the Poncielli in Cremona, the Politeama in Palermo, the Fenice in Venice (destroyed by fire in January 1996 and rebuilt), the Carlo Fenice in Genova, and the Regio and the modern Lingotto in Turin. Florence is scheduled to inaugurate a new opera house in May 2014 and ever year hosts a renowned music festival. In summer splendid performances are held in the amphitheatre at Verona and in Cara-

calla's Baths in Rome. Rome's newest grand musical venue is Auditorium Parco della Musica designed by architect Renzo Piano.

Among the great orchestras and chamber music groups, the Orchestra of the Accademia di Santa Cecilia in Rome, the Filarmonica of La Scala in Milan, the Solisti Veniti and the Orchestra of Padova and the Veneto are note-worthy.

Among the great Italian conductors, Arturo Toscanini was renowned for the verve and originality of his interpretations. Other famous names include Victor De Sabata and nowadays, Claudio Abbado, Carlo Maria Giulini and Riccardo Muti, who perform all over the world. Artists of international reputation include the violinists Accardo and Ughi, the pianists Campanella, Ciccolini, Lucchesini and Maria Tipo, the cellists Brunello and Filippini and the ballet dancers Carla Fracci, Luciana Savignano and Alessandra Ferri.

The famous singers Cecilia Bartoli, Renato Bruson, Fiorenza Cossotto, Cecilia Gasdia, Katia Ricciarelli, Renata Scotto, Lucia Valentini Terrani as well as Ruggiero Raimondi and the late Luciano Pavarotti are worthy successors to La Malibran, Renata Tebaldi, Maria Callas, Caruso and Beniamino Gigli.

Cinema

Italians lost no time jumping into the new world of cinema, where even during the realm of silent movies they made superb films. Not so for recent decades, with doldrums due in part to a spoils system that locks out new talent and to a persistence in dubbing foreign films.

THE EARLY YEARS AND NEO-REALISM

The Italian cinema industry was born in Turin at the beginning of the 20C and grew rapidly (50 production companies in 1914) with great successes on the international scene. Film-makers specialised first in historical epics, then in the 1910s they turned to adventure films and in the 1930s to propaganda and escapist films subsidised by the State, which distracted spectators temporarily from the reality of the Fascist State.

In 1935 the Cinecittà studios and the experimental cinematographic centre which numbered Rossellini and De Santis among its pupils were founded in Rome. During the years of Fascist rule the cinema had become divorced from real life, and to bridge the gap film directors advocated a return to realism and close observation of daily life. The first major theme of **neo-Realism** was the war and its aftermath.

Roberto Rossellini denounced Nazi and Fascist oppression in *Rome, Open City* and *Germany Year Zero*. **Vittorio De Sica**'s *Sciuscia* (1946) and *Bicycle Thieves* (1948) depicted the unemployment and misery of the post-war years. In *Bitter Rice* (1949) and *Bloody Easter* (1950) **De Santis** portrays the working class divided between the prevailing ideology and revolutionary ambitions. Neo-Realism ended in the early 1950s as it no longer satisfied the public, who wanted to forget this bleak period, but its influence was still felt by future generations of film-makers.

1960S TO THE PRESENT DAY

In the 1960s, Italian cinema flourished and a large number of films (over 200 a year), generally of very high quality, was made with the support of a strong industrial infrastructure. Three great directors dominated this period. **Federico Fellini** (1920–93) shot the successful *La Strada (The Street)* in 1954 and

Roberto Rossellini

AWARDS AND OSCARS

Oscar Academy Awards

La grande Bellezza (The Great Beauty) Paolo Sorrentino – Best Foreign Language Film, 2014

La Vita è Bella (Life Is Beautiful) by Roberto Benigni – three Oscars, including Best Foreign Film, 1997

Mediterraneo by Gabriele Salvatores – Best Foreign Film, 1992

Cinema Paradiso by Giuseppe Tornatore – Best Foreign Film, 1990

The Last Emperor by Bernardo Bertolucci – nine Oscars, including Best Film and Best Director, 1988

Amarcord by Federico Fellini – Best Foreign Film, 1975

Il Giardino dei Finzi-Contini by Vittorio De Sica – Best Foreign Film, 1972

Indagine di un Cittadino al di Sopra di Ogni Sospetto by Elio Petri – Best Foreign Film, 1971

Ieri, Oggi, Domani by Vittorio De Sica – Best Foreign Film, 1965

Eight and a Half by Federico Fellini – Best Foreign Film, 1964

Le Notti di Cabiria by Federico Fellini – Best Foreign Film, 1958

La Strada by Federico Fellini – Best Foreign Film, 1957

Cannes Film Festival

La Stanza del Figlio by Nanni Moretti, 2001

L'Albero degli Zoccoli (The Tree of Wooden Clogs) by Ermanno Olmi, 1978

Padre Padrone by Paolo and Vittorio Taviani, 1977

Il Caso Mattei by Francesco Rosi and *La Classe Operaia Va in Paradiso* by Elio Petri, 1972

Signore e Signori by Pietro Germi, 1966

Il Gattopardo (The Leopard) by Luchino Visconti, 1963

La Dolce Vita by Federico Fellini, 1960

Due Soldi di Speranza by Renato Castellani, 1952

Miracolo a Milano by Vittorio De Sica, 1951

Venice Film Festival

Così Ridevano by Gianni Amelio, 1998

La Leggenda del Santo Bevitore by Ermanno Olmi, 1988

La Battaglia di Algeri by Gillo Pontecorvo, 1966

Vaghe Stelle dell'Orsa by Luchino Visconti, 1965

Deserto Rosso by Michelangelo Antonioni, 1964

Le Mani sulla Città by Francesco Rosi, 1963

Il Generale della Rovere by Roberto Rossellini and *La Grande Guerra* by Mario Monicelli, 1959

Giulietta e Romeo by Renato Castellani, 1954

Berlin Film Festival

La Casa del Sorriso by Marco Ferreri, 1991

The Canterbury Tales by Pier Paolo Pasolini, 1972

Il Giardino dei Finzi-Contini by Vittorio De Sica, 1971

Il Diavolo by Luigi Polidoro, 1963

La Notte by Michelangelo Antonioni, 1961

La Dolce Vita in 1960. His fantasy world is reflected in the original camerawork. **Michelangelo Antonioni** (1912–2007) made his debut in 1959 with *L'Avventura*, and his work (*The Red Desert*, 1960 and *Blow Up*, 1967) underlines the ultimate isolation of the individual. **Luchino Visconti** (1906–76) made *Rocco and His Brothers* in 1960 and *The Leopard* in 1963. His films, characterised by opulence and beauty, examine closely the themes of impermanence, degradation and death.

During the same period a new generation of film-makers made a political and social statement: **Pier Paolo Pasolini**, **Ermanno Olmi**, Rosi, Bertolucci and the Taviani brothers.

Bernardo Bertolucci and Marlon Brando filming "The Last Tango in Paris"

Italian cinema won great international success with several masterpieces until the mid-1970s: *Death in Venice* (1970) and *Ludwig* (1972) by Visconti; *Casanova* (1976) by Fellini, *The Passenger* (1974) by Antonioni; *L'Affare Mattei* (1971) by **Francesco Rosi** and *The Last Tango in Paris* by **Bernardo Bertolucci**. Since the late-1970s the industry has been in a state of crisis, as it faces competition from television and the collapse of the market. However, some films made by famous directors have won acclaim: *The Night of San Lorenzo* (1982) by the **Taviani brothers**, *The Ball* (1983) by **Ettore Scola**, *The Last Emperor* (1987) by Bertolucci and *Cinema Paradiso* (1989) by **Giuseppe Tornatore**.

An introduction to Italian cinema would be incomplete without the "Italian comedies", which include masterpieces such as *Guardie e Ladri* (1951), *I Soliti Ignoti* (1958), *La Grande Guerra* (1959), *L'Armata Brancaleone* (1966) and *Amici Miei* (1975) by **Mario Monicelli** and *Divorzio all'Italiana* (1962) by **Pietro Germi**.

The younger generation of film-makers embraced realism and their protagonists are engaged in the social struggle. The most interesting films include *Bianca* (1984), *La Messa È Finita* (1985) and *Caro Diario* (1993) by **Nanni Moretti**; *Il Portaborse* (1990) and *La Scuola* (1995) by **Daniele Luchetti**; *Regalo di Natale* (1986) by **Pupi Avati**; *Mery per Sempre* (1989), *Ragazzi Fuori* (1989) and *Il Muro di Gomma* (1991) by **Marco Risi**; and *Notte Italiana* (1987); *Vesna Va Veloce* (1996) by **Carlo Mazzacurati**; *Pane e Tulipani* (2000) by **Silvio Soldini**. Italian comedies exported abroad include *Ricomincio da Tre* (1981), *Non Ci Resta Che Piangere* (1984), *Le Vie del Signore Sono Finite* and *The Postman* (1994) by **Massimo Troisi**; *Un Sacco Bello* (1980), *Compagni di Scuola* (1988) and *Maledetto il Giorno Che Ti Ho Incontrato* (1992) by **Carlo Verdone**; *Il Ciclone* (1996) by **Leonardo Pieraccioni**; and *Il Piccolo Diavolo* (1988), *Johnny Stecchino* (1991) and *Il Mostro* (1994) by **Roberto Benigni**, and the Oscar-winning masterpiece *Life Is Beautiful* (1997).

The success of Italian cinema is above all due to its famous stars, such as Vittorio Gasmann, Gina Lollobrigida, Sophia Loren, Anna Magnani, Giulietta Masina, Marcello Mastroianni, Alberto Sordi, Ugo Tognazzi, Totò and many others.

Film today is in part held back by dubbing, which is often more lucrative for actors than acting, by poor sound and visual quality, and by over-acting, which gives a dated look to many new films. Recent exceptions were *Io Sono Li* and *Cesare deve Morire* (2012).

Fashion

The term "costume" dates back to the 16C. Its meaning, "way of dressing", had traditional and lasting connotations. "Fashion" is a 17C term which refers to novelty in dress codes and implied something short-lived. Bargains aren't easy to find, but fortunately quality is.

COSTUME OR FASHION?

"Fashion" is now synonymous with Italy, but its connotations – of status, grandstanding and conspicuous consumption – have their roots in late medieval Europe and the early Renaissance.

A trend towards greater extravagance started in the 11C and gathered momentum in the 14C, sweeping away the austerity of past centuries and the idea of "costume", with its traditional and lasting connotations, as a way of dressing. In Italy this move towards increased consumption flourished due to the importance of fine fabric production and importation to the northern Italian economy.

Merchants and manufacturers who made huge fortunes in the Florentine and Venetian city republics sought to buy the status they coveted, funding art and architecture and dressing ostentatiously to make statements of wealth and social standing.

By the 16C, this competition in dress had gained another aspect to it – that of the idea of "fashion".

Ever mindful of their desire to establish a new social hierarchy, rich Italians began to fit fabrics together in complex and highly stylised ways. This gave clothing a recognisable "cut" that could be embraced or discarded, according to whim. Clothing now had a novel, transitory value and a built-in obsolescence, where it could go "out of fashion" long before it wore out. Thus the imperative to continually update one's wardrobe was born, and with it new social status based on the ability to finance it. This new order was powerful enough to challenge even the inherited entitlement of nobility, who fought back valiantly with various sumptuary laws until the mid-16C, but to no real avail – fashion as a force and an expression had arrived in Europe, and was there to stay.

16th century scene in Venice showing attire

© Retrograph Collection / Mary Evans Picture Library / Photononstop

FADS AND TRENDS

Flamboyance and confidence characterised the Italian approach to fashion from the 13C onwards. Two new developments that were of great influence were **buttons** and **glasses** (Cardinale Ugo di Provenza is depicted wearing spectacles in a 1352 fresco in Treviso's Capitolo di San Nicolò, a first in the history of art). Hair also became longer and more carefully styled, while cosmetics gained in popularity. For nobles and the rich, personal expression became more important than conformity. This partly accounted for extremes of style, such as heels as high as 60cm/2ft. In Venice, it was said that, "such was the height of the heels they wore, the Venetian ladies passing through Piazza San Marco looked like dwarfs dressed up as giants". From the early Renaissance on, hats became a key part of the Italian man's wardrobe. The beret originated in Renaissance Italy as a piece of cloth on an embroidered band, with a string inside to adjust the fit to any head. Women also began to wear earrings again, something that had previously been denounced as unbecoming, as it was a Moorish influence. In the 18C black veils, masks, fans and three-cornered hats were the height of fashion in Venice. By the 19C jackets and coats were worn long and straight with a high waistline, and clothing was under the spell of Romanticism. Huge puffed sleeves were in vogue for women, as were corsets designed to make the waist as small as possible (creating the *vitino di vespa* or wasp waist). Next followed the popular crinoline, worn over ornately decorated undergarments.

COLOUR, AN ESSENTIAL ELEMENT

The trend for **colour** was particularly evident during the Renaissance, but tastes changed from century to century. Until the 13C, fashion favoured the dark blue of the Byzantine mosaics at San Vitale (Ravenna), giving way to a vogue for two-tone clothes. Pink was all the rage in the Quattrocento; in the 16C the fashion for gold, silver and black gave clothes a more solemn air (as exemplified in portraits by Titian). Pale colours were popular in the late-16C and 17C. So too was "slashing" on sleeves, doublets and hose to expose bright linings. This circumvented laws that commoners only wear clothes of one colour.

The 18C progressed to a preference for white and pastel shades, while the last word in 19C fashion was black and white – a monochromatic look that continued to be popular into the early 20C.

TODAY, AS IN THE PAST

Italy continues to influence global fashion, most notably from the haute couture fashion capital of Milan. Its twice-yearly Fashion Weeks, showing the new collections, rank beside those of Paris and New York for industry importance.

Away from the catwalks, looking good in Italy is a democratic art. Italians take immense pride in their appearance. Many seem to have inherently good taste: opting for classic, well-made clothes, rather than experimental, disposable fashion. The style imperative applies as much to those who can afford to shop in Via Monte Napoleone (Milan) or Via dei Condotti (Rome) as the locals who go to the market. And there is no off-duty; for Italians, dressing casually is no excuse for shabby, slovenly attire.

THE BIG NAMES

Italy is home to some of fashion's biggest names, and the "Italian look" is a phrase that now means many things. The most iconic fashion houses include: **Giorgio Armani**, whose signature style is understated elegance, and who believes that clothes are made to be worn, not just seen. For quintessential Italian chic, an Armani suit lasts many seasons, and his diffusion line, Emporio Armani, is good for quality separates and accessories *(www.giorgioarmani.com)*. **Laura Biagiotti** is known for clean lines and elegant separates. She has made a particular name in cashmere *(www.laurabiagiotti.it)*.

King of 1960s haute couture, designer **Pierre Cardin** was born in Italy to French parents. He introduced geomet-

Galleria Vittorio Emanuele, Milan

© Anshar73/iStockphoto.com

ric designs and experimented with the unisex style *(www.pierrecardin.com)*.

The designs of **Dolce & Gabbana** celebrate the female form. Renowned for their show-stopping evening wear, the duo fashions day wear that is equally confident, with an emphasis on corseting, figure-sculpting pencil skirts and décolletage. The diffusion line, D&G, is good for well-cut jeans *(www.dolce gabbana.it)*.

Luxury brand **Fendi** is best known for its leatherwork and furs; for style kudos, look for bags, wallets and shoes with the classic Fendi logo *(www.fendi.com)*.

Gianfranco Ferré focuses on "quality, comfort, individuality and simplicity". Trademark pieces include crisply cut white shirts, stylish eyewear and women's trouser suits (www.gianfrancoferre.com).

Gucci has reigned for some as the must-have label for the fashion faithful. Its look is sexy, streetwise and expensive. A Gucci bag is a key investment: still considered shorthand for style in A-list circles *(www.gucci.com)*.

The family-owned label **Missoni** is best known for sumptuous knitwear in colourful stripes. Its distinctive swimwear is popular with chic sunbathers on Mediterranean beaches *(www.missoni.com)*.

The **Moschino** style has remained true to the ethos of the late designer. The Cheap and Chic line is always full of surprising designs, with bright colours and quirky detailing *(www.moschino.it)*.

Miuccia Prada designs grown-up, stylish clothes fashioned from fine materials, which frequently dictate the next fashion trends. Her understated bags and shoes are global bestsellers *(www.prada.com)*.

Trussardi favours simple lines and a focus on high-quality tailoring and finishing *(www.trussardi.com)*.

The designer **Valentino** recognised that women should cultivate their own style to enhance their self-confidence. His label's designs lean towards elegant and classical, many incorporating the famous "V" logo *(www.valentino.com)*.

After her brother Gianni's murder in 1997, Donatella **Versace** has taken the family business to new heights. The Versace label is adored by rock and film stars, with a signature style that is glamorous and glitzy, with colourful prints, sequins, attitude and plenty of suntanned skin on show *(www.versace.com)*.

Florence has not only Gucci, but also **Pucci** for bright prints often geometric in pattern, while those seeking edgier and modern but still elegant fashion head for **Save the Queen**.

Nature

In a country where cuisine, wine, art and design often get top billing, nature almost becomes an afterthought. That's too bad, because an excursion outdoors might be just the antidote to the Stendhal syndrome from too much art. The beauty is still there, from the coastline of Sicily, Tuscany, or the Veneto, to the craggy alps of the North or the rounded mountains and sweeping meadows of Gran Sasso in Abruzzo. In Umbria it's easy to spot the lavenders and blues of Perugino early or late in the day, layered upon the hills. For drama, there's nothing like seeing a volcano erupt, which is easy at night by looking at Stromboli from the sea or even from Calabria. Etna, too, erupts every few years or even several times in a year. Marshy coastal areas can be paradises for birders in migratory season, while the parks of Abruzzo can offer the opportunity to see the rare Marsicano bear.

The boot of Italy, which stretches 1 300km/808mi from north to south, juts out into the Mediterranean between Greece and Spain. The country's relief rises from great swathes of plain that cover about a quarter of its total area of 301 262sq km/ 116 287sq mi. Its coastline (almost 7 500km/4 660mi long) is washed by four inner seas: the Ligurian, Tyrrhenian, Ionian and Adriatic.

Geography

Narrow and long, Italy's geography is bisected by mountains and surrounded by sea. The rest of the land is mostly undulating hills, with some areas, especially toward the northeast, which are flat. No two areas are alike, from the silver lagoon of Venice to the choppy Straights of Messina.

GEOGRAPHY

The **Alps**, which were created as the Earth's crust folded in the Tertiary Era, form a gigantic barrier with northern Europe and are a formidable source of hydroelectric power. Several passes and tunnels cross the Alps, which peak at Mont Blanc (4 810m/15 781ft), to link Italy with France and northern Europe. On the southern side of the Alps between the fertile Po Valley and the foothills there are several lakes of glacial origin.

The **Apennines**, a range of limestone hills formed by a more recent Tertiary geological movement, extend from Genoa down into Sicily, dividing the country into two zones. The peaks of this limestone chain are generally lower than those of the Alps. The Corno Grande at 2 914m/9 560ft is the highest mountain of the chain's tallest massif, the Gran Sasso. The section between Naples and Sicily is subject to tectonic plate movements resulting in earthquakes, volcanoes and marked changes in sea level. Such activity has altered the relief of this southern part of the peninsula. Even these mountains offer skiing, but they also offer unique environments like Carrara, which is streaked with marble and still very active for quarrying and stonecutting.

This thermal activity manifests itself in other ways, including thermal waters. Every locations is said to have different therapeutic properties. If you are looking for thermal baths and pools, look for *bagni* and *piscina* if you want more than just a glass of water to drink.

Flatter areas, such as Emilia Romagna, can make for good bicycle touring for all ages.

The sea and coastal areas remain the biggest draw for Italians for their holidays, which can range from densely developed around Rimini to secluded and wild in many other areas.

Monte Argentario, Tuscany
© Buffy1982 / iStockphoto.com

Flora and Fauna

F lora in Italy ranges from Mediterranean scrub along the coast to wild orchids in the forests, alpine trees, island cacti and palms. Bird diversity is great, especially during migratory periods. While in Tuscany or Campania it's not unusual for a winemaker to find that overnight a wild boar has chomped on precious grapes or forest truffles.

FLORA

Italy's botanical life is the most varied in Europe, ranging from firs and cypresses to palm trees and olive groves. Approximately four distinct vegetation regions make up Italy's landscape. In the north, the small **Alpine Zone** consists of cypress, oak and chestnut trees in the valleys followed by larches, firs, and pines at 1 000m–2 000m/3 281ft–6 562ft and wildflowers, dwarf pines, moss and lichen found above 2 000m/6 562ft and up to the snow line. The **Appenine Zone**, Italy's spine from Liguria to as far south as Calabria, is made up of dense forests of holm oak and beech trees in the upper elevations. While, at the lower reaches, pastures of heather, oleander and sunflowers give way to olive and mastic trees as well as swathes of iconic Italian cypress trees and umbrella pines. The **Po River Delta**, which stretches from Turin in the west to the Adriatic, contains Italy's largest wetlands, which are slowly being restored through land reclamation projects. Heavy industrialisation and centuries of inhabitation in the Po River region, Italy's agriculture hub, has meant the loss of some forests and native vegetation, though woods of poplar, chestnut and willow trees are common. Italy's **Mediterranean-Vegetation Zone** includes coastal plains along the Tyrrhenian and Adriatic as well as Sicily and Sardinia. It is characterised by dense pockets of evergreen shrubs (*macchia*), such as myrtle and juniper, scrubland and palm trees, of which the stocky canary date palm is the most common variety. Fruit trees, including lemon, orange, olive, fig and pomegranate, thrive in the Mediterranean Zone, especially from Campania and southwards.

FAUNA

Centuries of hunting and urban development have reduced the indigenous animal population in Italy, in both num-

Source of the Po river

© ATL Cuneo

ber and diversity. Among the native mammals are the ibex and marmot – whose habitat is in the Alps – foxes, grey wolves and red deer. Wild boar roam the central woodlands, especially in Tuscany and Umbria. And the Marsicano bear, a smaller relative of the grizzly though highly endangered, has been seen in Abruzzo. Italy is on the migratory route for hundreds of birds from northern and central Europe and there are several bird sanctuaries in the country, notably along the Tuscan Coast and in the Po River valley. In the Po Delta alone at least 300 different species, including the goldfinch, nightingale, night heron, great egret, magpie and kingfisher. In Sicily even flamingoes take a holiday break. Other avifauna include kite, harrier, falcon, grouse, quail, woodcock and partridge. The Moorish gecko, green lizard and Italian tree frog are common varieties of reptiles and amphibians, found mostly in the dry southern climes. Snakes include the western whip and the poisonous asp.

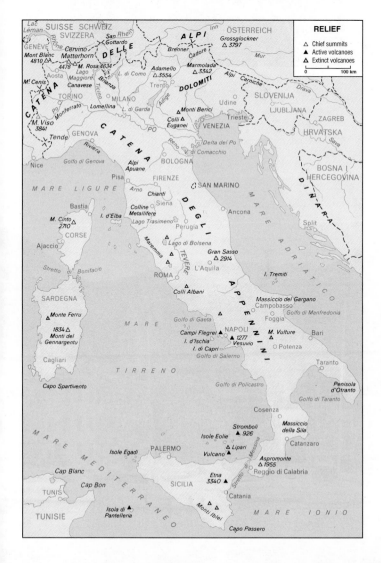

Discovering
Italy

Southern Italy

Fontana di Trevi, Rome
© S. Greg Panosian/iStockphoto.com

Southern Italy

The Eternal City overlooks southern Italy as it spreads eastward through the dark mountainous forests in Abruzzo and Molise to the bright aquamarine waters of the Adriatic Sea and southward, with untouched Calabria, Basilicata and Apulia forming the foot of the boot. Sun-kissed Sicily – the largest island in the Mediterranean – sits like a football being kicked by the toe, with Sardinia lying 305km/190mi from the mainland. With the exception of Lazio, these regions comprise the Mezzogiorno, so-called for the strength of the midday sun as it casts a golden glow upon this delightful corner of the bel paese.

Highlights

1 Discover 12 000 years of history in the Eternal City (p149)

2 Visit **UNESCO World Heritage** Sites, like Naples' chaotic historical centre (p201) and the Sassi caves in Matera (p280).

3 Experience the view from the **Amalfi Coast** and explore hidden bays, caves and grottoes (p244)

4 Dine on an authentic southern Italian meal, particularly in **Puglia, Calabria** or **Sicily** (p256, 274, 295)

5 Hike through Italy's largest national parks in **Abruzzo** and **Molise** (p190, 199)

Nostalgic Authenticity

Southern Italy is untamed and wild by northern standards and epitomises the Old World charm and Mediterranean lifestyle for which Italy is famous. Locals still take time to enjoy long lunches with their families; good friends and fun are appreciated more than timeliness or efficiency. Barring Italy's capital city and parts of Campania, the south is less-visited and often less touristy than other parts of the country. Adventurous travellers wanting an authentic glimpse into the Italian lifestyle will enjoy heading east of Rome into Abruzzo or Molise or south of Naples into Basilicata, Calabria or Puglia.

Global Influences

Greeks, Romans, Arabs, Normans, Spanish and the French are just a sampling of the nationalities that conquered this area and each left their unique footprint on the land. Remnants of the Greek language remain in villages throughout the south, namely Bova and Amendola in Calabria and parts of Grecia Salentina, the Sorrentine Peninsula, in Puglia. Albanian villages like Civita and Frascineto in Calabria still use their native language, have signs and menus in both Albanian and Italian and teach Albanian to their children in the classrooms; while Catalan thrives in Alghero on the island of Sardinia.

Majestic Greek ruins, such as those in Cumae and Paestum in Campania and Syracuse, Segesta and Agrigento in Sicily are scattered throughout the south. Byzantine treasures can be found in churches from Sulmona in Abruzzo, where a Byzantine relief of the Madonna is housed, to the proto-Christian frescoes in Massafra, Puglia to Castel San Vincenzo in Molise, home to the only completed 8C Byzantine fresco cycle painted in Europe.

Norman fortresses in Melfi and Lagopesole in Basilicata and Termoli in Molise are rivaled by the Aragonese castles in places like Taranto in Puglia, Le Castella in Calabria and Gaeta in Lazio.

When they first settled the area known as Magna Graecia in 8C BC, the Greeks brought their produce – figs, citrus, olives and grapes – all now staples in a southern Italian diet and found rampantly throughout the south. Sicilian cuisine was highly influenced by the Arab invasion that brought with it almonds, nutmeg, clove and cinnamon and inspired desserts such as marzipan with candied fruits. The Normans introduced rotisserie cooking and the Spanish brought chillies and sweet peppers. Even Sicily's North African neighbour's influences are seen by the use of couscous, found in dishes such as Couscous alla Trapanese in northwestern Sicily.

Southern Cuisine

Pasta is king in southern Italy, where the olive plantations, vineyards and citrus groves are among the greatest producers of these national specialities. Sicily's wine production is rivalled only by that of Puglia, each of which produce almost 17 percent of the nation's wine. Puglia is the world's leading producer of olive oil and together with neighbouring Calabria generate more than 65 percent of the nation's oil. Naples gave birth to pizza and Campania created mozzarella di bufala cheese and limoncello digestive liquor. Sardinia produces an impressive 80 percent of the nation's pecorino cheeses and fresh tuna, swordfish, anchovies and sardines are found in coastal areas throughout the south.

City and Rural Culture

With this complex history of conquests and invasions where prehistoric treasures meet Homeric mythology, southern Italy's landscape, culture and sights are widespread. Big cities like Rome, Naples and Palermo sit in sharp contrast to almost-abandoned hillside towns and villages. Ancient stone megalithic nuraghi tower over hills of ancient civilization in Sardinia just a few hours from where jet-setters launch their million-euro yachts. The Parco Nazionale d'Abruzzo features a landscape of peaks, valleys and forests and is intersected by a coastal plain. Baroque Lecce, sometimes called "The Florence of the South", is just a few hours from the whimsical trulli villas in the Terra dei Trulli. Ancient ruins rise from the sea set with a backdrop of a snow-topped, smoking mountain. Three national parks form the spine of Calabria, where locals and travellers are never further than 50km/30mi from the sea. Tropical beaches, emerald caves and secret bays are hidden beneath steep mountains and limestone cliffs. Some of the world's choicest islands like Capri in Campania, the Aeolian Islands in Sicily or Sardinia's La Maddalena archipelago are overshadowed by the world's fiercest volcanoes, such as Mt. Vesuvius and Mt. Etna.

Churches, monasteries and sanctuaries dot the land where locals still fear the malocchio (the evil eye) and display solemn paintings of their favourite saint above their beds. When they aren't on the roads or grabbing a coffee in a bar, southern Italians like to take life slowly. They don't rush off to meetings, they don't fret over a long coffee break and they don't watch the clock to ensure they open the office, museum or church when the sign says they should.

Southern Italy is the final frontier. Its less-trekked roads allow visitors to step back in time and enjoy a cinematic view of 1950s Italy. It is here, amidst this array of untamed landscape and southern hospitality, where a true Italian experience awaits for those who seek it.

Foro Romano

Rome and Lazio

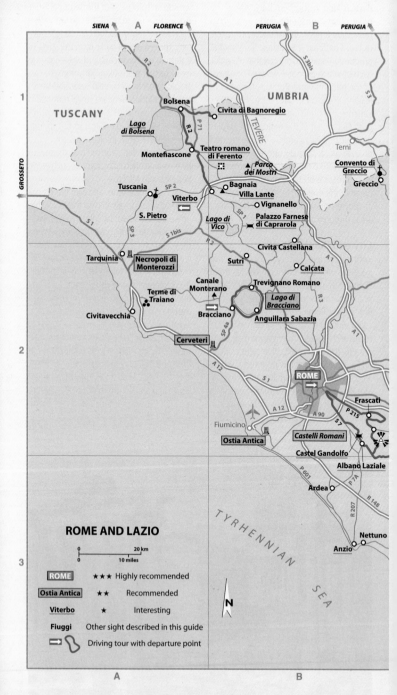

ROME AND LAZIO

| | 20 km |
| 0 | 10 miles |

ROME ★★★ Highly recommended

Ostia Antica ★★ Recommended

Viterbo ★ Interesting

Fiuggi Other sight described in this guide

⇨ Driving tour with departure point

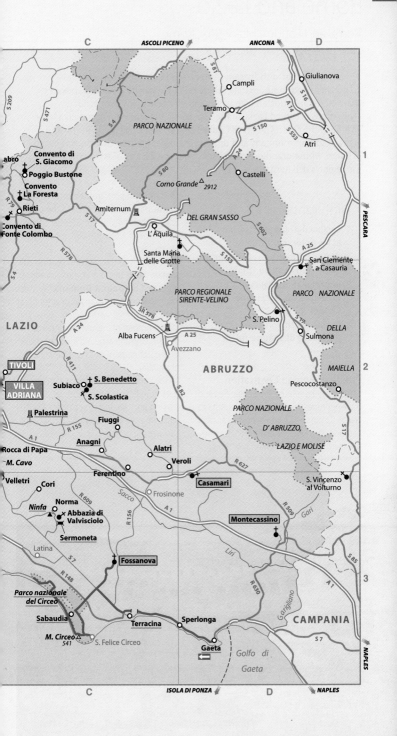

C   D

Giulianova

Campli

Teramo

S 150   Atri

PARCO   NAZIONALE

abro   Convento di
         S. Giacomo
    Poggio Bustone   Castelli
    Convento   Corno Grande △ 2912
    La Foresta
    Rieti   Amiternum   DEL GRAN SASSO
    Convento di   L'Àquila   San Clemente
Fonte Colombo   Santa Maria   a Casauria
               delle Grotte   PARCO   NAZIONALE

LAZIO   PARCO REGIONALE   DELLA
         SIRENTE-VELINO   S. Pelino   Sulmona
    Alba Fucens   A 25   MAIELLA
         Avezzano   Pescocostanzo
TIVOLI   ABRUZZO
**VILLA   S. Benedetto
ADRIANA**   Subiaco
    S. Scolastica   PARCO NAZIONALE
    Palestrina   Fiuggi   D' ABRUZZO,
Rocca di Papa   Anagni   LAZIO E MOLISE
M. Cavo   Alatri
    Ferentino   Veroli   S. Vincenzo
Velletri   Cori   al Volturno
    Norma   Frosinone   **Casamari**
Ninfa   Abbazia di
    Valvisciolo   **Montecassino**
    Sermoneta
Latina   **Fossanova**
Parco nazionale
del Circeo
Sabaudia   Sperlonga   CAMPANIA
M. Circeo △   Terracina
541   S. Felice Circeo   Gaeta   Golfo di
                        Gaeta

C   D

Rome and Lazio

Roma and Latium. Major City: Rome
Official Website: www.turislazio.it

Sharing a border with Tuscany, Abruzzo and Campania, Lazio bridges northern and southern Italy, where rolling hills of olives and grapevines share landscapes dotted with palms and umbrella pines. Two major civilisations occupied Lazio. In the 13C–6C BC, the Etruscans occupied a large swathe of the central peninsula, called *Etruria*, which included Viterbo and areas of southern Tuscany and Umbria. The other great civilisation was based in Rome, whose grandiose monuments and epic history outshine the rest of the region's rich heritage.

Highlights

1 Explore the gladiators' realm at the **Colosseum** (p155)
2 Walk in the footsteps of emperors at the **Foro Romano** (p155)
3 Inspect Michelangelo's masterpiece in the **Sistine Chapel** (p163)
4 People-watch from the steps of the **Piazza di Spagna** (p166)

Cradle of Roman Civilisation

Lazio lies between the Tyrrhenian Sea and the Apennines, from Tuscan Maremma to Gaeta. Its sandy coast once hosted ancient harbours, such as Ostia at the Tiber's mouth, now silted. Civitavecchia today is the principal modern port. In the centre of Lazio, **Rome**, the capital and seat of the Catholic Church, is mainly a residential city and epicentre of both public and religious organisations.

Volcanic hills to the east and north cradle solitary lakes in their craters, overlooking the **Campagna Romana**. Writers and painters have rhapsodised its great expanses, dotted with ancient ruins. This former hotbed of malaria has become fertile farmland and acquired industry, thanks to the drainage of the Pontine Marches, near Latina.

To the south the **Ciociaria** was name for traditional farm shoes *(ciocie)*. Montecassino and Anzio attract history buffs, while on the coast Sabaudia attracts chic sun-worshippers.

Inside the Colosseum, Rome

Rome★★★

Roma

The "Eternal City" is rich in monuments of its ancient history, which justify its renown. Today it's no longer the marble city left behind by Augustus and the emperors, nor is it the opulent court of the Papal era: since 1870, the year when it was proclaimed capital of Italy. Rome has seen a widespread and, especially after World War II, uncontrolled urban expansion. But the city measured from the Janiculum Hill in the golden light still beckons with its domes and towers. Seen up close, Rome's piazzas and streets are the social networks that they have been for millennia, bursting with news as well as fountains. Her monuments – famous the world over – continue to delight tourists: the Pantheon and Roman Forum, the majestic Colosseum, St Peter's, Castel Sant'Angelo, Piazza Navona, the Spanish Steps, the Trevi Fountain and the Villa Borghese. The Roman countryside remains almost intact with its cypresses, olives and pines. Its sky extends a luminous atmosphere that marvellously surrounds the Rome that you can still see today.

No other city in the world has managed to combine so successfully such a diverse heritage of Classical antiquities, medieval buildings, Renaissance palaces and Baroque churches. Far from being discordant, they constitute a logical continuity where revivals, influences and contrasts are evidence of the ingenuity of Roman architects and builders. Of course, the ruins no longer present the splendour of the Empire, when they were faced with marble. And even the city more recently acclaimed by Goethe and Stendhal has changed, due to the damage caused by heavy traffic and the modernisation of a busy capital city. Rome still impresses, as both the

- ▶ **Population:** 3 700 000
- **Michelin Map:** 563 Q 19; Michelin map of Rome 38 – see also *The Green Guide Rome.*
- **Info:** Via Parigi 5, 00185 Roma. ✆06 48 89 91, 06 06 06 08. Aeroporto di Fiumicino, International Arrival Hall. ✆06 65 95 1. www.turismoroma.it or www.060608.it
- **Location:** "All roads lead to Rome", so they say. In fact, Rome lies at the hub of a complicated motorway network with the traffic from the A 1, A 12 and A 24 all converging on the very busy Raccordo Anulare (ring road).
- **Parking:** There are few private car parks in Rome and they are extremely expensive, also access to the city centre by car is restricted (a permit is required). There are two underground car parks in the centre near Via Veneto: under the Villa Borghese gardens, and Parking Ludovisi, Via Ludovisi 60.
- **Don't Miss:** The Roman Forum, Colosseum, Pantheon, Trevi Fountain, the views from the Janiculum (Gianicolo) and Aventine (Aventino) belvederes, and the Pincio Hills.
- **Timing:** Allow at least three days.
- **Kids:** Bikes and pedal cars in the Pincio, row boats at the Villa Borghese, Ostia and the Ostia Lido.

great centre of ancient civilisation and a lively urban core. The best overall views of this complex – sprawling over the seven hills – are from the belvederes with the numerous domes and bell towers in the distance. Rome is the city of

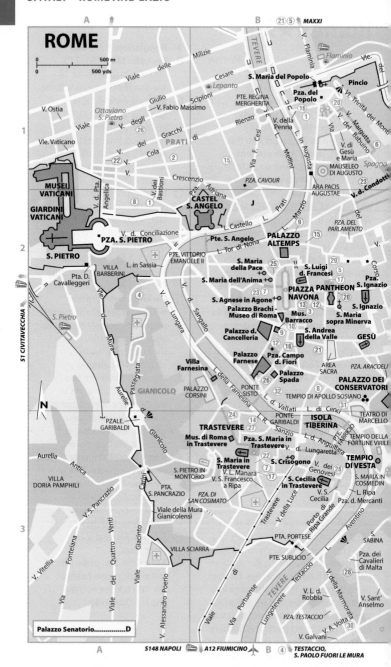

ROME

churches with over 300 edifices – some even side by side, many rich with decoration and the ingenious use of *trompe l'œil*. Interiors often are astonishing contrasts of dark and light, of inventiveness, of reverence and audacity. Luxury shops and quaint boutiques are on small streets near the Pantheon and Piazza Navona, as well as near famous Piazza di Spagna. Via Veneto – lined

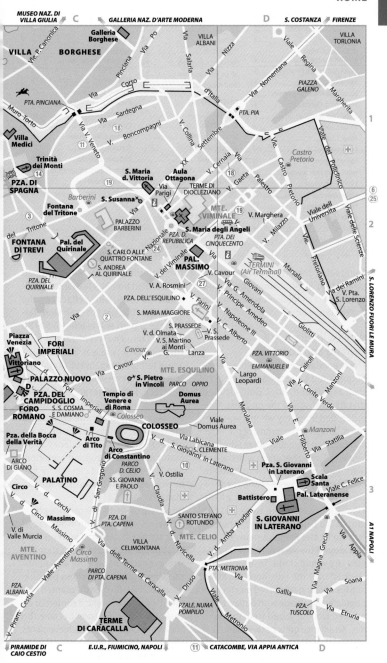

with caffès and luxurious hotels – once was centre of *La Dolce Vita* and remains a tourist centre. Piazza Navona is a fashionable meeting-place. Campo de' Fiori attracts for its market as well as night life. Antique shops dot Via dei Coronari. Across the river **Trastevere**, once home to artisans, is popular with foreigners but remains a favourite dining spot for Romans. And, of course, a visit to the

Fountain of Trevi is required. Legend claims that a coin thrown backward over the left shoulder ensures a return to the Eternal City.

A BIT OF HISTORY
Legend and Location

The legendary origins of Rome were perpetuated by historians and poets, such as Livy and Virgil. Both claimed that Aeneas, son of the goddess Aphrodite, fled from Troy when it was captured, landed at the mouth of the Tiber, and founded Lavinium. Rhea Silvia the Vestal, following her union with the god Mars, gave birth to the twins Romulus and Remus, who were abandoned.

Transported by the current of the Tiber, the twins came to rest at the foot of the Palatine, and were nursed by a wolf. Later Romulus marked a furrow around the sacred area where the new city would stand. Testing, Remus stepped over the line; Romulus killed him for violating the sacred precinct. He populated his village with outlaws who married women seized from the Sabines. An alliance grew between the two peoples, ruled by a succession of kings, alternately Sabine, Latin and Etruscan. But beyond legend, modern historians emphasise the strategic location of Rome's seven hills, especially the Palatine, which was a staging-post on the Salt Road (Via Salaria) and was first settled in the 8C BC.

Two centuries later the Etruscans had transformed Iron Age huts into a well-organised town, with a citadel on the Capitoline. The last Etruscan king, Tarquin the Superb, was ejected in 509 BC and the Consulate was instituted.

The Republican era was an ambitious one of territorial expansion. During the 2C and 1C BC, civil war tore the regime to pieces. **Julius Caesar** (101–44 BC) emerged as leader because of his audacious strategies (he conquered the whole of Gaul in 51 BC), his grasp of political affairs, his talents as an orator and his unbounded ambition. Appointed consul and dictator for life, he was assassinated on the Ides of March, 15 March 44 BC.

He was succeeded by his great-nephew, **Octavian**, a young man who was of delicate health and had won no military glory. Octavian was to demonstrate tenacity of purpose and political genius, ably vanquishing possible rivals. In 27 BC the Senate granted him the title **Augustus**, which conferred an aura of holiness. He soon became the first Roman emperor. His achievements were considerable: he extended Roman government and restored peace to the whole of the Mediterranean basin.

Among Augustus' successors were those driven by madness and cruelty (Caligula, Nero and Domitian). Others continued the work of Roman civilisation: the good administrator, Vespasian;

GETTING THERE

BY CAR – Driving in Rome is not advisable as parking in the city can be a major problem (visitors should note that most of the hotels in the city centre do not have private garages or parking). The few private car parks that do exist are extremely expensive and access to the city centre by car is severely restricted (a special permit is required). Two large underground car parks in central Rome are near Via Veneto: under the Villa Borghese gardens near Porta Pinciana, and Parking Ludovisi, Via Ludovisi 60. Most city traffic makes use of two ring roads: the outer ring road (Grande Raccordo Anulare) lies on the outskirts of the city at a junction of main national roads as well as the A 1, A 2, A 24 and A 18 motorways; the second ring road is the Tangenziale Est, which forms part of the traffic network within the city. It connects the Olympic Stadium to Piazza San Giovanni in Laterano, passing through the eastern quarters of the city (Nomentano, Tiburtino, Prenestino).

BY TRAIN – The mainline national and international trains arrive at Stazione Termini or Tiburtina, which are linked to the city centre on both Metro lines A and B. For information contact &89 20 21, or consult the website www.trenitalia.com.

BY AIR – The main airport is Leonardo da Vinci, at Fiumicino (26km/16.2mi SW of Rome; www.adr.it). It is linked to the centre by train, with services from Stazione Termini (14€), and from the stations at Tiburtina, Tuscolana and Ostiense (treno regionale FL1). A night-bus service departs from Stazione Tiburtina or Termini to the airport (1h).

GETTING AROUND

BY TAXI – Radiotaxi telephone numbers are: &06 66 45, 06 49 94, 06 55 51, 06 35 70, 06 88 22. Use only the official metered taxis, usually painted white.

BY BUS, TRAM OR UNDERGROUND – City route maps are on sale in bookshops and kiosks; the Rete dei Trasporti Urbani di Roma map published by ATAC (Azienda Tramvie e Autobus del Comune di Roma, &06 57 003), but are easier to find online (www.atac.roma.it). Tickets should be purchased before the beginning of the journey and punched in the machine in the bus and on the underground to be validated. Various ticket options include the BIT (valid for 100min; 1.50€). Tickets are also available for two-day (7€), four-day (12.50€) and weekly periods (24€).

SIGHTSEEING

The city of Rome has information booths located at strategic points of the city centre: Stazione Tiburtina, Via dei Fori Imperiali, Piazza Cinque Lune, Via Nazionale, the corner of Via Minghetti (near Fontana di Trevi) and many others. Enquire about all cultural and tourist events in the capital. Generally open from 9.30am to 7pm.

INTERNET – visit the city's official website: www.turismoroma.it.

COMBINED TICKETS – The Roma Archeologia Card (23€, valid 7 days) includes entrance to the following museums and monuments: Museo Nazionale Romano (Palazzo Massimo, Terme di Diocleziano, Palazzo Altemps and Crypta Balbi), the Colosseum, Foro Romano, Palatino, Terme di Caracalla, Tomba di Cecilia Metella and Villa dei Quintili. The card can be purchased at the relevant sites. The Roma Pass offers free entrance to a list of museums and reduced fees for all the other museums, and includes bus and metro fare (36€, valid 3 days). Visit the website www.romapass.it

Under the dome of the Pantheon – built by Hadrian

© Dale Halbur/iStockphoto.com

Titus, who was known as the love and delight of the human race; Trajan, the "best of emperors" and a great builder; and Hadrian, an indefatigable traveller.

Christianity

The old order passed away, undermined within by economic misery and the concentration of authority in the hands of one man, and from without by barbarian attacks. A new force – Christianity – began to emerge. The religion of Jesus of Nazareth originated in Palestine and Syria, and first reached Rome in the reign of Augustus. During the last years of the 1C and the early years of the 2C, the Christian Church became organised, but transgressed the law from the beginning because the emperor embodied religious power. It was not until the **Edict of Milan** (313), which allowed Christians to practise their religion openly, and the conversion of **Constantine** (314), that the Church could come out into the open.

From the first days of Christianity, the bishop was Christ's representative on Earth. Gradually the name "Pope", once used for all pontiffs, was reserved for the Bishop of the Empire's capital alone. For 19 centuries, these leaders have influenced the history of Christianity and given the Eternal City its character. In the 11C **Gregory VII** restored order to the Christian Church, which had by then an appalling reputation. He dealt with two scourges: the buying and selling of Church property, and the marriage of the clergy. In so doing he started the **Investiture Controversy**, which set in opposition the Sovereign Pontiff and the Holy Roman Emperor.

During the Renaissance, popes waged war and patronised the arts, bringing to their court such artists as Raphael and Michelangelo, whose genius embellished the capital. They included Pius II, Sixtus IV (who built the Sistine Chapel and Santa Maria del Popolo), Julius II (who commissioned Michelangelo to decorate the ceiling of the Sistine Chapel), Leo X (who had a great personal fortune and nominated Raphael as superintendent of the arts), Clement VII, Sixtus V (a great builder) and Paul III, who built the Farnese Palace.

The French, Spanish and Austrians ruled, prior to the Unification of Italy in 1871. Giuseppe Garibaldi led the revolt that led to the new State. Rome was – and still is – its capital. The world wars and the rise of Fascist dictator Benito Mussolini brought hardship and horrors to Rome. The climate of fear continued during the 1970s and 80s, as communists and conservatives vied for power, often employing terrorist tactics. Recent decades have seen calm and safety once again restored to this magnificent city.

MAIN SIGHTS

No other city in the world has such a wealth of Classical antiquities, medieval buildings, Renaissance palaces and Baroque churches. With this in mind, a minimum stay of two or three days is recommended. The following paragraphs give general information on some 20 of the best-known sights.

ANCIENT ROME

Explore over 1 000 years of ancient Rome, from the Palatine's Iron Age huts to splendid temples, residences, theatres and early Christian sights.

Colosseo★★★ (Colosseum)

&. Open daily 8.30am–1hr before dusk. Closed 1 Jan, 25 Dec. 12€ including Foro Romano and Palatino. Book in advance to bypass the crowds or summer evening tours. ℘06 39 96 77 00. www.coopculture.it.

This amphitheatre, inaugurated in AD 80, is known as the Flavian Amphitheatre after its initiator, Vespasian, first of the Flavian emperors. The name "Colosseum" probably originates from the colossal gilded bronze statue of Nero that once stood nearby, which was 36m/118ft high (its position is marked by a few slabs of stone on the ground near the beginning of Via dei Fori Imperiali), or from its own colossal dimensions (527m/576yds in circumference and 57m/187ft high). Three superimposed Classical orders (Doric, Ionic and Corinthian) crown this masterpiece of Classical architecture. The projections at the top supported wooden poles put through holes in the upper cornice, which with ropes manipulated a linen awning that could be extended over the amphitheatre to protect the spectators from sun or rain.

Some 50 000 spectators could watch fights between men and beasts, gladiatorial contests, races and perhaps mock naval battles that took place in the arena. In 2010 areas newly opened to the public: the hypogeum (underground warren where the wild animals waited before being brought to the surface by a system of pulleys and lifts); and the upper levels, more than doubling the area that visitors can tour. Adjacent to the Colosseum, the **Arco di Costantino★★★** is an arch erected to commemorate Constantine's victory over Maxentius in AD 315. The more sophisticated bas-reliefs were removed from other 2C monuments..

Domus Aurea★★

Entrance on Viale Domus Aurea, below the gardens of Colle Oppio. Closed for repairs at the time of writing. ℘06 39 96 77 00. www.coopculture.it.

The Golden House was the luxurious residence erected by Nero after the fire of AD 64. The grotto-like underground rooms are decorated with geometric designs, grapes, faces and animals. These "grotesques" inspired many Renaissance artists.

▶ From the Colosseum, follow Via dei Fori Imperiali to Foro Romano at Largo della Salaria Vecchia 5/6.

Foro Romano★★★

&.Open daily 8.30am–1hr before dusk. Closed 1 Jan, 25 Dec, 1 May, 2 Jun 13.30-19.15, ve Santo 8.30-14. 12€ including Colosseo and Palatino. Summer eve tours. ℘06 39 96 77 00. www.coopculture.it.

The remains of the Roman Forum, the religious, political and commercial centre of ancient Rome, reflect the 12 centuries of history that created Roman civilisation. The forum was excavated in the 19C and 20C.

The **Basilica Emilia** was the second basilica to be built in Rome (170 BC). Take the Sacred Way, **Via Sacra★**, along which victorious generals marched in triumph to the **Curia★★**, rebuilt in the 3C by Diocletian and more recently in 1937. Senate meetings were held here; nowadays it houses the **Plutei di Traiano★★**, sculpted bas-relief panels depicting scenes from the life of the Emperor Trajan, and sacrificial animals.

After the Romans attacked *Antium* (modern Anzio) in 338 BC and captured the prows (*rostra*) of the enemy ships, which they fixed to the **orators'** platform★, this then became known as the Rostra.

Nearby rises an imposing Triumphal Arch, **Arco di Settimio Severo★★**, built in AD 203 to commemorate the emperor's victories over the Parthians. At the foot of the Capitol stood some remarkable monuments: the late-1C **Tempio di Vespasiano★★** (Temple of Vespasian), of which only three elegant Corinthian columns remain; the **Tempio di Saturno★★★** (Temple of Saturn), which retains eight 4C columns; and the **Portico degli Dei Consentis★**, a colonnade with Corinthian columns dating back to restoration work of AD 367 – dedicated to the 12 principal Roman deities. The **Colonna di Foca★** (Column of Phocas) was erected in AD 608 in honour of the Byzantine Emperor Phocas, who presented the Pantheon to Pope Boniface IV. The **Basilica Giulia★★**, which has five aisles, was built by Julius Caesar and completed by Augustus. It served as a law court and exchange.

Three beautiful columns with Corinthian capitals remain of the **Tempio di Castore e Polluce★★★** (Temple of Castor and Pollux). The circular **Tempio di Vesta★★★** (Temple of Vesta) stands near the **Casa delle Vestalia★★** (House of the Vestal Virgins).

Foro Romano

© Bildagentur RM/Tips/ Photononstop

The **Regia** was held to have been the residence of King Numa Pompilius, who succeeded Romulus and organised the state religion.

The **Tempio di Antonino e Faustina★★** (Temple of Antoninus and Faustina) was dedicated to the Emperor Antoninus Pius and his wife (note the fresco of grotesques and candelabra). The temple now houses the church of San Lorenzo in Miranda, rebuilt in the 17C.

The **Tempio di Romolo** (the Romulus who was the son of Emperor Maxentius who died in 307) includes the concave façade and the bronze doors between two porphyry columns.

The grandiose **Basilica di Massenzio★★** (Basilica of Maxentius) was completed by Emperor Constantine. The **Arco di Tito★★** (Triumphal Arch of Titus), erected in 81, commemorates the capture of Jerusalem by this emperor. Next to the church of **Santa Francesca Romana★★**, the **Tempio di Venere e di Roma★★** (Temple of Venus and Rome) was erected by Hadrian between 121 and 136.

One of the Urbs' largest (110m by 53m/361ft by 174ft), it is distinctive for its two *cellas* with attached apses: the west side dedicated to goddess Rome looks toward the Forum; the east, dedicated to Venus, looks toward the Colosseum.

Palatino★★★

Access from Via San Gregorio 30.
&Open daily 9am–1hr before dusk; Good Friday 8.30am-14pm, 2 Jun 13.30-19.15. Closed 1 Jan, 25 Dec, 1 May.
€12 combined ticket with Colosseum and Forum. ✆06 39 96 77 00. www.coopculture.it.

The **Palatine Hill**, where Romulus and Remus were discovered by the wolf, was chosen by Domitian as the site for the Imperial Palace. The **Domus Flavia★** (or official State apartments) was made up of three main areas: the basilica, where the emperor dispensed justice, the throne room and the *lararium*, the emperor's private chapel. Also of note were the peristyle courtyard and the dining room or *triclinium*, which opened onto two small leisure rooms, *nymphaea*. The rooms in the **Domus Augustana★★** (private Imperial apartments) are arranged around two peristyles on two floors. Then there was the **Stadium★**, designed to stage private games and spectacles for the emperor.

The **Casa di Livia★★** (House of Livia) *(temporarily closed to public)* probably belonged to Augustus (fine vestiges of paintings). The **Orti Farnesiani** (Farnese Gardens), laid out in the 16C on the site of Tiberius' palace, afford **views★★** of the Roman Forum and town. *The view of Circus Maximus to Farnese Gardens is a beautiful walk.*

Fori Imperiali★★★

The visitor centre on Via dei Fori Imperiali offers guided tours of the sites, and has informative displays. Open daily 9am–7pm. Closed 1 Jan, 2 Jun, 25 Dec. ℰ06 06 08. www.sovraintendenzaroma.it/i_luoghi/roma_antica/aree_archeologiche/fori_imperiali.

Caesar, Augustus, Trajan, Nerva and Vespasian built these forums, though hardly any remains of the latter two's efforts. The Via dei Fori Imperiali, laid out in 1932 by Mussolini, divides the Imperial forums.

The **Mercati Traianei★★** (Via IV Novembre 94; open 9.30am–7.30pm; closed public hols afternoons, 1 Jan, 1 May, 25 Dec; €14; Torre delle Milizie: ⊶not presently open to visitors; ℰ06 06 08; www.mercatiditraiano.it), which have kept their semicircular façade, were a distribution and supply centre as well as a retail market. The dominant feature, they comprised about 150 shops.

The **Torre delle Milizie★** (Tower of the Militia) is part of a 13C fortress. All that remains of the finest of the Imperial forums, **Foro di Traiano★★★** (Trajan's Forum), is the **Colonna Traiana★★★** (Trajan's Column), which depicts in basrelief over 100 scenes, episodes of the war waged by Trajan against the Dacians. Attributed to Apollodorus of Damascus, it is an unrivalled masterpiece.

Of the Augustan Forum, **Foro di Augusto★★** *(view from Via Alessandrina)*, a few columns remain from the Temple of Mars the Avenger. Behind them are vestiges of the stairway and of the wall that enclosed the forum.

Above the forum is the House of the Knights of Rhodes (Casa dei Cavalieri di Rodi), built in the Middle Ages and rebuilt in the 15C amid the ancient ruins. At Caesar's Forum, the **Foro di Cesare★★** *(across Via dei Fori Imperiali, view from Via del Tulliano)*, there remain three lovely columns from the Temple of Venus Genitrix.

Campidoglio★★★

On the hill that symbolised the power of ancient Rome, there now stand the city's administrative offices, the church of Santa Maria d'Aracoeli, Piazza del Campidoglio and its palaces, and pleasant gardens. The Capitoline was known as the *caput mundi* in ancient times. *The view★★★ is superb.*

Chiesa di Santa Maria d'Aracoeli★★

The church has a lovely staircase built as a votive offering after the plague of 1346, and a beautiful, austere façade. It was built in 1250 on the spot where the Sibyl of Tibur (Tivoli) announced the coming of Christ to Augustus. In the first chapel on the right are **frescoes★** painted by **Pinturicchio** in about 1485.

Piazza del Campidoglio★★★

Michelangelo masterminded the exquisite square – framed by three palaces and a balustrade with statues of the Heavenly Twins or Dioscuri – from 1536 onwards. Its crowning glory is an equestrian statue of the Emperor Marcus Aurelius, celebrated on Italy's version of the 0.50€ coin. The Capitoline Museums now house the original sculpture. The **Palazzo Senatorio★★★**, constructed in the 12C and modified 1582 to 1602 by Giacomo della Porta and Girolamo Rainaldi, today is occupied by the mayor of Rome and houses the Tabularium. The **Palazzo dei Conservatori★★★** *(south)* and **Palazzo Nuovo★★★** *(north)* together form the Capitoline Museums (&see below).

Musei Capitolini★★★

& Open 9.30am–7.30pm (ticket office closes 6.30pm), 24 and 31 Dec 9.30am-2pm. Closed 1 Jan, 1 May, 25 Dec. 16€ including Centrale Montemartini (valid 7 days). &06 06 08. www.museicapitolini.org.

The museums are housed in the **Palazzo Nuovo** (New Palace), built in 1655 by Girolamo Rainaldi, in the **Palazzo Senatorio**, City Hall since 1144, remodelled between 1582 and 1602 by Giacomo della Porta and Girolamo Rainaldi, and in the **Palazzo dei Conservatori**.

Part of the collection, particularly Roman sculpture, is housed in the **Centrale Montemartini★★** (&open Tue–Sun 9am–6.30pm; 24 and 31 Dec 9am-2pm; closed 1 Jan, 1 May, 25 Dec; 7.50€; &06 06 08, www.centralemontemartini.org), at Via Ostiense 106.

Among the highlights in the Palazzo Nuovo are the **Dying Gladiator** (formerly Gaul)★★★, a Roman sculpture based on a bronze of the Pergamum school (3C–2C BC); the **Sala degli Imperatori★★** (Emperors' Room) with portraits of all the emperors; the **Capitoline Venus★★**, a Roman work inspired by the Venus of Cnidus by Praxiteles; and the **Mosaic of the Doves★★** from Hadrian's Villa at Tivoli.

The Palazzo dei Conservatori, built in the 15C and remodelled in 1568 by Giacomo della Porta, houses an **equestrian statue of Marcus Aurelius★★** (late-2C), the **She-Wolf★★★** (6C–5C BC), the **Boy Extracting a Thorn★★**, a Greek original or a very good copy dating to the 1C BC, and a **Bust of Junius Brutus★★**, a remarkable head dating from the 3C BC placed on a bust in the Renaissance period.

The picture gallery or **pinacoteca★** (2nd floor) displays mainly 14C to 17C paintings (Titian, Caravaggio, Rubens, Guercino, Reni).

The Tabularium, the Roman Public Records Office, under Palazzo Senatorio, dates to 78 BC with a stunning **view★★★** of the Roman Forum. The

caffè in Palazzo Caffarelli (behind the Palazzo dei Conservatori) unfurls a vista toward the Tiber River and is accessible without a ticket.

PIAZZA VENEZIA

A short walk around Piazza Venezia introduces you to major figures from the pages of history. Victor Emmanuel II, Napoleon, Mussolini and Ignatius Loyola each make appearances between this square and the Chiesa del Gesù.

Piazza Venezia★

This piazza in the centre of Rome is lined with palaces: Palazzo Venezia, Palazzo Bonaparte, where Napoleon's mother died in 1836, and the early-20C Palazzo delle Assicurazioni Generali di Venezia.

Palazzo Venezia★

& Open Tue–Sun 8.30am–7.30pm. 5€. &06 67 80 131.

The **Basilica di San Marco**, which was incorporated within the palace in the 15C, has a fine Renaissance **façade★** overlooking Piazza di San Marco.

This palace, built by Pope Paul II (1464–71), is one of the first Renaissance buildings. A **museum**, on the first floor, presents primarily medieval to Baroque art with ivories, enamels, paintings, gold- and silver-work, ceramics and small bronzes of the 15–17C. Its impressive Renaissance armour is not on display. The palazzo has a lovely hidden garden.

Monumento a Vittorio Emanuele II (Vittoriano)

Open daily 9.30am–5.30pm (winter 4.30pm). &06 678 0664.

This much-criticised memorial begun by Giuseppe Sacconi in 1885 in honour of the first king of a united Italy, Victor Emanuel II, overshadows the other monuments of Rome by its sheer size and dazzling white colour. The **view★★** of the Eternal City from the top is not to be missed.

Chiesa del Gesù★★★

The mother-church of the Jesuits in Rome, built by Vignola in 1568, is a typical building of the Counter-Reformation. On the outside, the engaged pillars replace the flat pilasters of the Renaissance, with light and shade effects and recesses. The spacious interior astounds the eye with its lavish abundance of Baroque gold. Inside the dome, the **Baciccia frescoes★★** illustrate the *Triumph of the Name of Jesus* (1679); the **Cappella di Sant'Ignazio★★★** *(north transept)*, a chapel where the remains of St Ignatius Loyola rest, is the work (1696–1700) of the Jesuit Brother Andrea del Pozzo and master goldsmiths.

Basilica di San Clemente★★

Dedicated to St Clement, one of the early successors to St Peter, founded in the 4C in a Christian's home is one of the most ancient Roman basilicas. Badly damaged in 1084, it was reconstructed following the plan of a 12C basilica divided into three naves.

The upper basilica – The courtyard and its 6C cloister lead to the interior. Don't miss the mosaics in the apse made by a 12C master whose brilliant Tree of Life is resplendent with images from nature, from flowers to peacocks and rivers. The Renaissance chapel painted in fresco by Masolino (1383–1447) and Masaccio (1401–28) shows St Catherine of Alexandria.

The lower basilica – &Open 9am–12.30pm and 3–6pm, hols 12–6pm. Closed 25 Dec. 5€. The descent into the lower levels takes you from the 12C, to the 4C, to the 1C and finally to a gurgling spring. As you descend, barely visible are the frescoes of Sisinius, 11C prefect of Rome. Towards the bottom is the foundation of a Roman house and a 1C **mithraeum**, where the monotheistic cult of Mithra was worshipped.

Piazza della Bocca della Verità★

Along the Tiber was a bustling cattle market *(forum boarium)* since the 6C BC near the Palatine. Here are two temples (the round one 2C BC dedicated to Hercules Victor and the other 1C BC to Portunus), a Romanesque church, an 18C fountain with two tritons, and some umbrella pines. The square's name – "Mouth of Truth" – refers to the ancient Roman medallion of a marine deity mounted on a portico wall of Santa Maria in Cosmedin. Legend warns that a liar who inserts his hand inside risks having it bitten off, so only those with a clear conscience should approach. The bell tower (12C) is one of Rome's loveliest. Inside, the geometric tile floor was crafted by the Cosmati, famous for Cosmatesque floors.

Circo Massimo

The Circus Maximus was probably the oldest of the Rome circuses (6C BC) and the largest, reaching its full splendour under Augustus. Situated in the Murcia Valley between the Palatine and Aventine, it featured races with chariots led by teams of two, three or four horses. The racetracks, more than 500m/550yds, ended at the southeast side where a triumphant arch once stood. The tribune was seated on the northwest side, where the race master presided. Emperors and power elite sat on the Palatine slope. Considered the largest stadium of all time, this circus held about 300 000 spectators, five to six times the crowds of the Colosseum. The obelisk originally positioned inside is now in Piazza del Popolo.

Terme di Caracalla★★★ (Baths of Caracalla)

&Open daily 9am–1hr before dusk. Tours with archaeologist Sun 3pm in Italian; book in advance for English. Closed Mon afternoon, 1 Jan, 1 May, 25 Dec. 7€. ℘06 39 96 77 00. www.coopculture.it.

These baths built by Caracalla in AD 212 extend over more than 11ha/27 acres and could take 1 600 bathers at a time. The main rooms (*caldarium, tepidarium* and *frigidarium*) occupy the middle part of the central section; the secondary rooms (vestibule, *palaestra* and *laconicum*) are symmetrically positioned at the sides. The circular *caldarium* for the very hot bath (34m/112ft in diameter) forms a backdrop for operatic performances in summer.

Next to the baths *(viale delle Terme di Caracalla 28)*, the church of **Santi Nereo** e **Achilleo** has magnificent 9C mosaics, while the 16C frescoes add bloody Counter-Reformation battle scenes.

San Pietro in Vincoli

Consecrated in the 5C for Pope Sixtus III (432–40), the church of St Peter in Chains has the famous chains of Peter: tradition holds that two sets of chains imprisoned the apostle, one in Jerusalem, the other in Rome, miraculously forged together after they arrived here. Of special interest here is the grand funerary monument that Michelangelo designed for Julius II. Scaled back from a much larger plan, slaves that were to be added are now in Paris and Florence.

THE VATICAN – CASTEL SANT'ANGELO

The Vatican treasures are so vast it would take years to see them all. Even so, a visit in one day offers a rich tapestry of lasting impressions, that culminates in a visit to the Sistine Chapel.

The Vatican★★★

The Vatican City is bounded by a wall, overlooking Viale Vaticano, and to the east by the colonnade of St Peter's Square. This makes up the greater part of the Vatican State as laid down in 1929 in the Lateran Treaty. The Vatican City, now reduced to only 44ha/109 acres and with 829 inhabitants, stems from the Papal States, a donation made in the 8C by Pepin the Short to Pope Stephen II, and lost in 1870 when Italy was united with Rome as its capital.

The Vatican State, with the Pope as ruler, has its own flag and anthem and prints its own stamps. In 1970 Pope Paul VI dissolved the armed forces, retaining only the Swiss Guard, who wear a colourful uniform said to have been designed by Michelangelo.

The Pope, who is the Head of State, is also the Supreme Head of the Universal Church, and from this very small state, the spiritual influence of the Church radiates throughout the world through the person of the Sovereign Pontiff. When the Pope is in residence, he grants **public audiences** on Wednesdays.

Religious ceremonies – Good Friday: Stations of the Cross take place in the evening between the Colosseum and the Palatine. **Easter**: midday the Pope gives the *Urbi et Orbi* benediction. **29 June**: Rome celebrates the feast day of Sts Peter and Paul.

Giardini Vaticani★★★

Reservations required at Vatican Museums. Closed Wed and Sun. 32€.
℘06 69 88 46 76.
www.museivaticani.va.

The vast, magnificent gardens are adorned with fountains and statues, gifts from various countries.

Piazza San Pietro★★★

This architectural masterpiece was begun in 1656 by Bernini. Two semicircles form the colonnades that adorn the square and frame the façade of the basilica, an ensemble of remarkable sobriety and majesty. At the centre of the square stands a 1C BC obelisk that Caligula ordered to be brought from Heliopolis in AD 37 for his circus. It was moved here in 1585 on the initiative of Sixtus V by Domenico Fontana. At the top is a relic of the Holy Cross.

The efficient Vatican Post has an office on the piazza's south side.

Basilica di San Pietro★★★

Constantine, the first Christian emperor, decided in AD 324 to build a basilica on the site where St Peter was buried after he had been martyred in Caligula's circus. By the 15C it was obvious that the structure needed rebuilding.

For two centuries, the plan of the new basilica was constantly revised. The plan, of a Greek cross surmounted by a dome designed by Bramante and adopted by Michelangelo, was altered to a Latin cross at the behest of Paul V in 1606, when he instructed Carlo Maderno to add two bays and a façade to Michelangelo's square plan. From 1629 onwards, the basilica was decorated in a sumptuous Baroque style by Bernini.

The **façade** (115m/377ft long and 45m/148ft high) was completed in 1614 by Carlo Maderno; it is surmounted by colossal figures. In the centre is the balcony from which the Sovereign Pontiff gives his benediction *Urbi et Orbi* (to the City and the World).

Under the **portico**, the first door on the left has bronze panels carved by Giacomo Manzù (1964); the bronze central door dates from the Renaissance (1455); the door on the right, or Holy Door, is opened and closed by the Pope to mark the beginning and end of a Jubilee Year. Inside, it is customary to first approach the stoups in the nave, which at first glance appear of normal size but are in fact huge. Such size emphasises the gigantic dimensions of the basilica, otherwise not apparent because of the harmony of its proportions. Compare the length of St Peter's to that of other great basilicas by finding the markers inlaid in the central nave's floor.

The first chapel on the right displays the **Pietà★★★**, the moving and powerful masterpiece carved by young Michelangelo in 1499–1500, which shows his early genius.

In the right aisle, adjoining the Cappella del S.S. Sacramento, **Gregory XIII's Monument★** is adorned with bas-reliefs illustrating the institution of the Gregorian calendar devised by that Pope. Immediately beyond the right transept, **Clement XIII's Monument★★★** is a fine Neoclassical design by Canova dating from 1792. The apse is dominated by the **Cattedra di San Pietro★★★** (St Peter's Throne) by Bernini

(1666), a great carved throne in bronze encasing a 4C episcopal chair, attributed to St Peter.

The 13C bronze **Statue of St Peter★★** overlooking the nave is attributed to Arnolfo di Cambio and is greatly venerated by pilgrims, who come to kiss its feet, shiny from being touched. **Innocent VIII's Monument★★★** *(between the second and third bays in the left aisle)* is a Renaissance work (1498) by Antonio del Pollaiuolo.

In the chancel on the right is **Urban VIII's Monument★★★**, again by Bernini (1647), a masterpiece of funerary art. On the left stands **Paul III's Monument★★★** by Guglielmo della Porta (16C), a disciple of Michelangelo.

St Leo the Great's Altar *(chapel to the left of the chancel)* has a fine Baroque **altarpiece★** carved in high relief by Algardi. Nearby, Alexander VII's Monumenta, characterised by extreme exuberance, is a late work by Bernini (1678) assisted by his pupils. The **baldacin★★★** by young Bernini that crowns the pontifical altar and is 29m/95ft tall (the height of the Farnese Palace) was strongly criticised: partly because the bronze had been taken from the Pantheon and partly because it was thought to be too theatrical and in bad taste.

The **dome★★★** designed by Michelangelo, which he himself built as far as the lantern, was completed in 1593 by Giacomo della Porta and Domenico Fontana. From the **summit** *(leave the basilica by the right aisle for access)*, the terrace affords a **view★★★** of St Peter's Square, the Vatican City and Rome from the Jan-

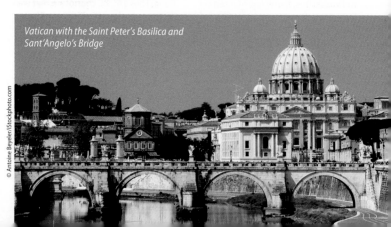

Vatican with the Saint Peter's Basilica and Sant'Angelo's Bridge

Staircase in Musei Vaticani

© M. Gaspar/MICHELIN

iculum to Monte Mario. You can go up to the lantern by climbing the steps in the narrow space between the inner and outer walls of the dome. Open daily Apr–Sept 7am–7pm; Oct–Mar 7am–6.30pm. 8€ in lift to roof level, then 320 steps; 6€ to take the stairs (551 steps). ℘06 69 88 37 31.

The **Museo Storico★** (St Peter's Treasury) *(entrance in the left aisle, opposite the Stuart Monument)* has many treasured items from St Peter's. ℘06 69 88 37 31.

Musei Vaticani★★★

Entrance in Viale Vaticano. ♿ Open Mon–Sat 9am–4pm. 8€ ticket includes visit to Cappella Sistina. Audio guides in various languages (7€), guided tours (Ville Pontificie, Giardini Vaticani, archaeological areas, " Arte e Fede" itinerary, Wed and Sat. visits for visitors with disabilities, family tour). Closed Sun (except last Sun of month, 9am-12.30, free), 1 Jan, 6 Jan, 11 Feb, 19 Mar, Easter, Easter Mon, 1 May, 29 Jun, 15 Aug, 8 Dec, 25–26 Dec. 16€. Bars, coffee shop, bookshops and self-service facilities. ℘06 69 88 46 76.

www.museivaticani.va.

The museums of the Vatican occupy part of the palaces built by the popes from the 13C onwards, which have been extended and embellished to the present day. These include on the first floor the **Museo Pio-Clementino★★★** (Greek and Roman antiquities) with its masterpieces: the **Belvedere Torso★★★** (1C BC), greatly admired by Michelangelo; the **Venus of Cnidus★★**, a Roman copy of Praxiteles' Venus; the **Laocoon Group★★★**, a 1C BC Hellenistic work; the **Apollo Belvedere★★★**, a 2C Roman copy; **Perseus★★**, a Neoclassical work by Canova, which was purchased by Pius VII; **Hermes★★★**, a 2C Roman work inspired by the work of Praxiteles; and the **Apoxyomenos★★★**, the athlete scraping his skin with a strigil after taking exercise, a 1C Roman copy of the Greek original by Lysippus.

The **Museo Etrusco★**, on the second floor, has a remar able 7C BC gold **fibula★★**adorned with lions and ducklings *(Room II)* and the **Mars★★** found at Todi, a rare example of a large bronze statue from the 5C BC *(Room III)*.

Room I has a 6C BC **chariot★★** that was restored in the 19C. The four **Stanze di Rafaello★★★** (Raphael Rooms), the private apartments of Julius II, were decorated by Raphael and his pupils from 1508 to 1524. The frescoes are remarkable: *The Borgo Fire*, *The School of Athens*, *Parnassus*, *The Expulsion of Heliodorus from the Temple*, *The Miracle of the Bolsena Mass* and *St Peter Delivered from Prison*. The **Collezione d'Arte Moderna Religiosa★★** is displayed in the Borgia apartment of Pope Alexander VI.

On the first floor is the **Cappella Sistina★★★ (Sistine Chapel)**; its splendid vault, painted by **Michelangelo** from 1508 to 1512, illustrates episodes from the Bible with the Creation, the Flood, the Creation of Man. Above the altar, *The Last Judgement* was painted by the artist in 1534. The upper sections of the long walls were decorated by Perugino, Pinturicchio and Botticelli. The **Pinacoteca★★★** (Picture Gallery) has five **compositions★★★** by **Raphael** including *The Coronation of the Virgin*, *The Madonna of Foligno* and *The Transfiguration* – Room VIII; **St Jerome★★** by Leonardo da Vinci (Room IX) and a **Descent from the Cross★★** by Caravaggio (Room XII).

Castel Sant'Angelo★★★

Open Tue–Sun Mon 9am–7.30pm. Closed 1 Jan, 25 Dec. 10.50€. ✆06 32 810. www.castelsantangelo.com.
The imposing fortress was built in AD 128–139 as a mausoleum for the Emperor Hadrian and his family. In the 6C Gregory the Great erected a chapel on top of the mausoleum to commemorate the apparition of Archangel Michael, who, by inserting his sword in its sheath, announced the end of a plague. In the 15C Nicholas V added a brick storey to the ancient building and corner towers to the surrounding wall. Alexander VI (1492–1503) added octagonal bastions. In 1527, during the sack of Rome, Clement VII took refuge in the castle and installed an apartment that was later embellished by Paul III; the **Popes' Apartment★** stands isolated at the summit of the fortress.
A fine spiral ramp dating from Antiquity leads to the seven castle levels. From a terrace at the summit there is a splendid **panorama★★★** of the whole town. The Castel Sant'Angelo is linked to the east bank of the Tiber by the graceful **Ponte Sant'Angelo★**, which is adorned with copies of Baroque angels by **Bernini** and with statues of St Peter and St Paul (16C). A long passageway (Il Passetto) links the fortress to the Vatican palaces.

1️⃣ THE PANTHEON AND CAMPO DE' FIORI

The most popular area with tourists in Rome is also the most fascinating. Here is the perfect union of art with history. From the Pantheon to the masterpieces by Caravaggio, to Romans' banter as they peruse market produce in Campo de' Fiori, this area is abuzz with locals surrounded by Antiquity.

Piazza della Rotunda

The small square that slopes down to the Pantheon makes a theatrical approach to the harmonious and majestic sight of the ancient temple that looms ahead. Tourists pause to relax by the fountain or take refreshment in one of the pleasant caffès.

© D. Chapuis/MICHELIN

Castel Sant'Angelo

Pantheon★★★

Open Mon–Sat 9am–7.30pm, Sun
9am–6pm, hols 9am–1pm. Closed 1 Jan,
1 May, 25 Dec. ♿ ☎347 82 05 204.
The Pantheon, an ancient temple beautifully preserved, founded by Agrippa in
27 BC and rebuilt by Hadrian (118–125),
was converted to a church in 608.
Access is through a portico supported
by 16 monolithic granite columns, all
ancient except for three on the left. The
doors are the original ones. The **interior★★★**, a masterpiece of harmony and
majesty, is dominated by the **ancient
dome★★★**, the diameter of which is
equal to its height. The side chapels,
adorned with alternately curved and
triangular pediments, contain the tombs
of the kings of Italy and of Raphael *(on
the left)*.
☉ *Piazza della Minerva. A 6C BC
obelisk from a temple to Isis sits atop an
elephant attributed to Bernini.*

Santa Maria sopra Minerva★★

Constructed above the foundation of a
temple to Minerva, Santa Maria sopra
Minerva was founded in the 8C and
reconstructed in Gothic style in the 13C.
Major changes in the 15C–17C brought
the simplicity of the rectangular façade.
The right transept has the 15C **Carafa
Chapel★** with beautiful frescoes painted
in part by **Filippino Lippi**.
To the left of the main altar, a 1521 marble sculpture of Christ the Redeemer
is attributed to Michelangelo. Behind
it on the floor is the marble tomb of
Dominican painter **Fra Angelico**, who
died in 1455.

Palazzo e Galleria Doria Pamphilj★★

Via del Corso 305. Open 9am–7pm (last
entry 6pm). Closed 1 Jan, Easter, 25 Dec.
12€ (with audioguide). ☎06 67 97 323.
www.dopart.it.
Galleria Doria Pamphilj★★ holds one
of Rome's richest art collections. Among
the highlights are **Flight into Egypt★★**
by Annibale Carracci, **Portrait of Innocent X Pamphilj★★★** by Velázquez, **Rest
after the Flight into Egypt★★★** and

John the Baptist★★★ by Caravaggio,
and the bust of **Olimpia Maidalchini
Pamphilj★★** by Algardi.

Piazza e Chiesa di Sant'Ignazio★★

This theatrical square is a stage set
enclosed by curvaceous buildings that
date to the 1730s designed by Raguzzini.
They form a lively delicate contrast to
the austere façade of the church. Upon
entering Sant'Ignazio, in the centre
nave eyes turn up towards the ceiling
vault, with dramatic perspective in the
frescoes★★ by **Andrea del Pozzo** that
makes the figures seem ready to drop
down from the heavens; the artist also
painted the false dome (1684) in *trompe
l'œil*, a remarkable trick, which he used
to compensate for lack of funds to complete the church with a real dome.
Via Burro, the street that winds behind
the piazza, is named for Napoleon's
administrative offices *(bureaux)*, and
leads to Piazza di Pietra. La **Borsa**, the
Stock Exchange and 18C customs seat,
is built into what was Hadrian's Temple.
Via dei Pastini leads to Piazza della
Rotonda, dominated in the centre by
Giacomo della Porta's fountain (1578).
Albergo del Sole, number 63 on the
square, is one of Rome's oldest hotels
(15C). The poet Ariosto (1474–1533) was
probably an early lodger.

♟ San Luigi dei Francesi★★

Piazza di San Luigi dei Francesi.
Open 10am–12.30pm, Thu 3–7pm,
closed Thu pm. ☎06 68 82 71.
The French church in Rome (Mass is
always given in French), dedicated to St
Louis, was first commissioned in 1518
by Cardinal Giulio de' Medici and completed in 1589.
The interior has frescoes by **Domenichino**, but the real draw is the Contarelli
Chapel with its three **Caravaggio★★★**
paintings that illustrate episodes from
the life of St Matthew.
Via della Dogana Vecchia leads to Piazza
Sant'Eustachio. From here there is a
lovely **view★★** of the spiral dome that
crowns **Sant'Ivo alla Sapienza**. On the
south side **Palazzo Maccarani** (1521),

designed by Giulio Romano (1499–1546), hosts the famous **Sant'Eustachio Il Caffè** (⚫*see Addresses, p174 onwards*).

⚫ Entrance to Sant'Ivo is through Palazzo della Sapienza on Corso Rinascimento 40.

Palazzo della Sapienza
In this palazzo, the National Archives has records of Rome and of the Pontifical State in the 9C-19C. The elegant courtyard leads to graceful **Sant'Ivo alla Sapienza★** by **Borromini**.

Piazza Navona★★★
Built on the site of Domitian's stadium (AD 86), one of Rome's largest squares retains its elliptical shape. Pleasant and lively, it has three Baroque fountains with Bernini's masterpiece in the centre, the **Fontana dei Fiumi★★★** (Fountain of the Four Rivers), completed in 1651. The statues represent the four rivers – Danube, Ganges, Rio de la Plata and Nile – symbolising the four known continents of the time.
Among the caffès, churches and palaces lining the square are **Sant'Agnese in Agone★★** with a Baroque façade by Borromini and attractive **interior★** on the plan of a Greek cross, and the adjoining 17C **Palazzo Pamphilj** (now the Brazilian Embassy).
👥 *A December market brings Befana, the Christmas witch; February brings Carneval performers*.

Museo Napoleonico★
Piazza Ponte Umberto I. ♿ Open Tue–Sun 10am–6pm. Free. 📞06 68 80 62 86.
Founded by Giuseppe Primoli (Princess Charlotte Bonaparte's son) and Count Pietro Primoli, who bequeathed the city his art collection after his death in 1927, this interesting glimpse into the Imperial family's home includes paintings, sculpture, furniture and clothing.

Palazzo Altemps – Museo Nazionale Romano★★★
Piazza di Sant'Apollinare 44. ♿Open Tue–Sun 9am–7pm. Closed 1 Jan, 25 Dec. 7€ , includes Palazzo Massimo,

Crypta Balbi and Terme Diocleziano (valid 8 days). 📞 06 39 96 77 00.
This magnificent palace begun in the 15C, and recently restored, now hosts the Ludovisi-Boncompagni collection. Cardinal Ludovico Ludovisi, in 1621–3, began collecting ancient and contemporary statues by the most renowned artists of their time (inevitably some by Bernini as well as by Algardi). Ancient masterpieces emerged such as the **Ludovisi Throne★★★**, a Greek sculpture of the Birth of Aphrodite from the Classic period (5C BC).
Across the street, Via di Tor Sanguigna, are the remains of Domitian's Stadium that are still visible.
Via dell'Anima leads to **Santa Maria dell'Anima**, Rome's German-language church. On the street behind it, Via della Pace, is the church **Santa Maria della Pace★** (17C façade by Pietro da Cortona), which was constructed on a very unusual plan with a short rectangular base covered by an octagonal dome. The four Sybils were painted in 1514 by Raphael. Its cloisters are one of the first works in Rome by **Bramante** (1444–1514). Already evident is the architect's curiosity about the vocabulary and technique of ancient architecture.
Also on Via della Pace is **Antico Caffè della Pace**, the atmospheric 1891 Victorian bar. Via di Parione leads to Via del Governo Vecchio; turn left to Piazza di Pasquino and its celebrated "talking" statue.
The statue of **Pasquino** was the spokesperson or message board for everyone and everything: written notes with news, vindications, critiques, protests and slander, often left in the dead of night for all to see the next day.

Palazzo Braschi – Museo di Roma★
Piazza Navona and Piazza Braschi. ♿ Open Tue–Sun 10am–6pm, 24 and 31 Dec 10am–1pm. Closed 1 Jan, 1 May, 25 Dec. 11€. 📞06 06 08.
www.museodiroma.it.
The last great palace built in Rome (18C) for Papal families, rebuilt 1802, today is home to Museo di Roma. This is a vibrant

tribute to the beauty of Rome, its pageants, and the history of those who shaped its destiny. Rooms are organised by theme (history, places, culture).

▶ From Palazzo Braschi, take Corso Vittorio Emanuele II (to 166a).

Museo Barracco

Open Tue–Sun 10am–3.30pm (Jun-Sept 1pm-6.30pm). Closed 1 Jan, 1 May, 25 Dec. Free.
The small Renaissance Palazzo della Farnesina ai Baullari begun in 1523 is attributed to Antonio da Sangallo. Now it houses a group of ancient sculptures (Assyrian, Egyptian, Cypriot, Phoenician, Etruscan, Greek, Roman).

▶ Continue on Corso Vittorio Emanuele II to Piazza Sant'Andrea della Valle.

The busy piazza has a **fountain attributed to Carlo Maderno**, who built the church **Sant'Andrea della Valle★★** 1608–23. Begun 1591 by Giacomo della Porta, the façade modified 1656–65 by Carlo Rainaldi is one of the Baroque's most elegant. Inside, the dome rises above a Latin cross plan with adjoining chapels, which creates a heightened impression of volume (the dome is second in size in Rome after St Peter's). The frescoes were painted by Giovanni **Lanfranco**. The effect of depth is striking, the perfect set for Puccini's opening act of the opera *Tosca*.
The street that housed bodice makers leads to where majestic Pompey's Theatre (1C BC) stood, the shape of which you can trace on the semicircle of buildings on Via di Grotta Pinta.

▶ Cross Via dei Giubbonari and proceed to Piazza del Monte di Pietà. Take Via dell'Arco del Monte, then turn right to Piazza Capo di Ferro.

Palazzo Spada★

Built in the 16C for Cardinal Gerolamo Capodiferro, then acquired by art dealer/collector Cardinal Bernardino Spada, this lovely palace has a Manneristic façade

and figures of Antiquity. Note the fine frieze in the courtyard★★. Don't miss the **perspective★★★** by **Borromini** (behind the library best seen from the inner courtyard). This architectural *trompe l'œil* is no longer than 9m/30ft!
Galleria Spada★ – *Inside Palazzo Spada.* This collection is noteworthy not only for the art, but for the savvy collectors. Spada protected and launched the careers of Guercino and Guido Reni (open Wed–Mon 8.30am–7.30pm; closed 1 May, 25 Dec; 5€).

Palazzo Farnese★★

Most beautiful of the Roman palaces, named for Alessandro Farnese (Pope Paul III, 1534), since 1635 this has been the French Embassy in Italy (officially since 1875), designed in part by Michelangelo in 1546.
Frescoes were painted (1593–1603) by **Annibale Carracci** with the assistance of his brother Agostino and pupils Domenichino and Lanfranco. The interior courtyard by Sangallo, Vignola and Michelangelo reflects Renaissance elegance (tours Mon, Wed, Fri, 3pm, 4pm, 5pm; reservation required 1 week in advance on www.inventer rome.com). If you can't visit, walk around the palace to Via Giulia to glimpse the garden.
The **Passeto Farnese**, that spans Via Giulia, connects the palace to Santa Maria della Morte. The street fountain, **Fontana del Mascherone** (1626), was made from an ancient Roman mask and granite tub.

Campo de' Fiori★★

This square, one of Rome's liveliest, begins the day as a picturesque fruit and vegetable market. Not always so bucolic for centuries it was the site of public executions, most famous of which was that of **Giordano Bruno**, a monk charged with heresy and burned at the stake here *(17 Feb 1600)*, during the Counter-Reformation.
Now Bruno often serves as a meeting-point, especially for evening revellers when the Campo can stay busy to the wee hours.

Piazza di Spagna

© J. Aparicio/AGE FOTOSTOCK

2 PIAZZA DI SPAGNA – PIAZZA DEL POPOLO – PINCIO

The square takes its name from the Spanish Embassy to the Holy See, but it's the elegant 18C staircase designed by De Sanctis and Specchi that descends from Trinità dei Monti that immortalises this quarter.

Piazza di Spagna★★★

This popular square was so named in the 17C after the Spanish Embassy occupied the Palazzo di Spagna. It is dominated by the majestic **Spanish Steps**, the **Scalinata della Trinità dei Monti★★★**, built in the 18C by the architects De Sanctis and Specchi, who employed Baroque perspective and _trompe l'œil_. At the foot of the stairway are the **Fontana della Barcaccia★** (Boat Fountain) by Bernini's father, Pietro (17C), and Keats-Shelley House, where Keats died in 1821. At the top of the stairs, the church of the **Trinità dei Monti★** is the French church, built in the 16C and restored in the 19C. It contains a **Deposition from the Cross★** _(2nd chapel on the left)_ dating from 1541 by Daniele da Volterra, a great admirer of Michelangelo. The French Academy at **Villa Medici★★**, built for the powerful Florentine Medici family as a power base in Rome, now houses French artists and scholars. The public can enjoy exhibits, films and concerts (in the garden in summer), and garden tours.

Leading west from Piazza di Spagna is **Via dei Condotti** lined with elegant shops and home to the famous Caffè Greco _(☞ see Addresses, p174)_ which was opened in 1760 and was a favourite of, among others, Goethe and Wagner. A quiet side street north, Via Margutta, was full of artists' studios and was home to Federico Fellini.

Piazza del Popolo★★

The **Piazza del Popolo** was designed by Giuseppe Valadier (1762–1839). The **Porta del Popolo★** was pierced in the Aurelian wall in the 3C, and adorned with an external façade.

The Renaissance church of **Santa Maria del Popolo★★** was remodelled in the Baroque period. It contains 15C **frescoes★** by Pinturicchio _(first chapel on the right)_; two **tombs★** by Andrea Sansovino _(in the chancel)_; two **paintings★★★** by **Caravaggio**: the _Crucifixion of St Peter_ and the _Conversion of St Paul (first chapel to the left of the chancel)_; and the **Cappella Chigi★** _(2nd on the left)_, a chapel designed by Raphael. Leading off the Piazza del Popolo is the main street (and former racetrack) of central Rome, **Via del Corso**, lined with handsome Renaissance palaces and shops.

MAXXI – Museo Nazionale delle Arti del XXI Secolo★★

2 Via G. Reni. Open Tue–Sun 11am–7pm, Sat to 10pm. 10€. ☎06 32 01 954. www.fondazionemaxxi.it.

The National Museum of 21st-Century Arts opened in 2010 to showcase contemporary art and architecture. Zaha Hadid's innovative design won the Stirling Prize from the Royal Institute of British Architects and World Building of the Year. Airy and sculptural, it's become a

Artisans' Workshops

Rome is a city that is full of artisans. The Via Giulia area has a tailor that makes shirts, an artist that paints trompe l'œil, a stationer, and the church of the goldsmiths, who throughout the centre can be seen creating their latest pieces. The Via di Monserrato area has luthiers that make and repair violins, furniture restorers, upholsterers and picture framers. Even regal Piazza Farnese has mattress makers. Stroll slowly!

meeting-place for locals. Bar, restaurant and bookshop.

Pincio

This fine public park was laid out in the 19C by Giuseppe Valadier. It is bordered by the gardens of the Villa Borghese and affords a magnificent **view★★★**, particularly at dusk when the golden glow so typical of Rome is at its mellow best.
♙♙ *Bike, rowboat and pedal-cart rentals in the Villa Borghese.*

Villa Borghese – Parco dei Musei

Here, 'villa' refers to public parks and this is one of Rome's largest (more than 80ha/4 acres).
Equipped for horse shows, the grounds have small temples, woods, ponds, umbrella pines, gardens adorned with ancient statues, a zoo, museums, a cinema and its crown jewel, Galleria Borghese, a pleasure villa later modified in design in 1814 by Valadier.

♙♙ Galleria Borghese
Piazzale Scipione Borghese 5. Open Tue–Sun 8.30am–7pm. Closed 1 Jan, 25 Dec. 11€. Reservations required on www.tosc.it. ☏ 06 32 810. www.galleriaborghese.it.
This early 17C pleasure villa was constructed to house the art collection of Cardinal Scipione Borghese (1579–1633), later Pope (1605–21). The collection was expanded throughout the centuries, until the beginning of the 19C. Camillo Borghese, married to Pauline, Napoleon's sister, was forced to sell a number of the ancient statues to Napoleon, but it still retains some of the best work of the most important 16C and 17C artists. On the ground floor is **Pauline Bonaparte★★★** sculpted by Canova; sculptures by **Bernini★★★** include **David**, **Apollo and Daphne** and **Abduction of Persephone**; **Sleeping Hermaphrodite**; and six masterpieces painted by **Caravaggio★★★** (room VIII). Masterpieces painted by **Raphael**, **Correggio**, **Domenichino**, **Carracci**, **Bellini**, **Titian**, **Lucas Cranach** and **Veronese** round out a collection unique in the world.

Museo Nazionale Etrusco di Villa Giulia
Piazzale di Villa Giulia 9. Open Tue–Sun 8.30am–6.30pm. 8€. ☏ 06 32 26 571.
Dedicated entirely to the ancient Etruscan civilisation, this museum is in the former summer villa of Julius III (constructed 16C by Vignola).
Artefacts from jewellery to bas-reliefs, and sarcophagi illustrate Italy's first great indigenous civilisation. Most objects were excavated in Latium necropoli, including the enigmatic terracotta sarcophagus **The Couple★★★** from Cerveteri. Other celebrated works, from Veio, are the Veii (**sculptures of deities**)**★★★**, **Ficoroni Cists★★★** and a **Chigi wine vessel★★**.

Galleria Nazionale d'Arte Moderna (GNAM)
Viale delle Belle Arti 131. Open Tue–Sat 8.30am–7.30pm, Sun 2-7.30pm. 8€.
☏ 06 32 29 81. Closed 1 Jan, 1 May, 25 Dec.
Constructed in 1911, this lovely gallery is primarily dedicated to painting and sculpture of the 19C and 20C, including sections on Futurism and on the innovative perspectives of **Metaphysical Painting** by Giorgio De Chirico, Modigliani and Morandi. Works by international artists include Klimt, Cézanne, Van Gogh and Degas. The lovely caffè attracts Romans.

3 FONTANA DI TREVI – VIA VENETO – QUIRINALE

Italy's president resides in the former Papal palace *(visits on Sun mornings)* on the Quirinale Hill. Its former stables, Scuderie, now host major exhibitions.

Fontana di Trevi★★★

A late Baroque creation and the largest Baroque fountain in Rome, the stunning Trevi Fountain was designed by **Nicola Salvi** in 1732, as commissioned by Pope Clement XIII. The central figure, the Ocean, rides in a chariot drawn by seahorses and tritons.

Tourists continue the tradition of throwing two coins over their shoulders into the fountain – one coin to ensure their return to Rome and the other for the fulfilment of a wish. *Watch your wallet in the thick crowds.*

Fontana del Tritone★

Bernini's Triton Fountain dominates Piazza Barberini. Note the bees, the Barberini heraldic symbol. In 1627 Urban VIII (Maffeo Barberini) commissioned Palazzo Barberini★★, on which both **Borromini** and **Bernini** worked, completing the palace begun by **Carlo Maderno**. Its art collection is stunning.

Santa Susanna★★

Rebuilt in the 9C by Leon III, the church reflects the hand of **Carlo Maderno** (1556–1629) on the façade★★ built 1595–1603. Strongly influenced by the Gesù, it follows Counter-Reformation style, with its austerity interrupted by the columns and by the play of light on the niches and ornamentation.

Santa Maria della Vittoria★★

Maderno built Santa Maria della Vittoria 20 years after Santa Susanna. The façade's lack of pomp reflects Counter-Reformation ideology: simplicity and austerity. The interior plan followed that simplicity with its single nave and wide transept crowned at the intersection by a dome. However, 17C Baroque additions brought elaborate ornamentation throughout, including the dome completely covered with a *trompe l'œil* painting, *The Triumph of the Virgin*.

This exuberance culminates with the sculptural group that features **The Ecstasy of St Teresa of Avila★★★** in the **Cornaro Chapel** *(left side)*. This **Bernini 1646 work** is often cited as the epitome of Baroque sculpture for its drama and theatricality. Struck by the divine arrow of the angel, Teresa dies voluptuously in the arms of God, as Zola noted in *Les Trois Villes, Rome*. The sculpture's mystical eroticism has elicited a wide range of responses.

Santa Maria degli Angeli★★

Constructed above part of the massive Baths of Diocletian, Michelangelo at age 86 was put in charge. The interior's unifying aspect is credited with 18C modifications by Neapolitan architect Luigi Vanvitelli. The outer façade, demolished in the 20C, reveals part of the baths' ancient *caldarium*, where hot thermal baths once were taken.

More ruins are in a room behind the transept that leads to a small courtyard. In the south transept, don't miss the 1702 meridian designed by Francesco Bianchini, by which all Rome clocks were once set and which was officially used to set the date for Easter after the spring equinox.

Aula Ottagona

Via Romita 8. ♿ Open during temporary exhibitions. ✆06 06 08.

This recently restored octagonal hall was probably part of a hall or frigidarium (for cold baths). Ancient Roman sculptures that once adorned thermal baths are placed around the room, including **The Boxer at Rest★★★** or the Hellenistic **Prince★★★**, two rare examples of bronze statues that are remarkably well preserved (c.3C BC).

Palazzo Massimo alle Terme★★★

Via di Villa Peretti 1. ♿ Open Tue–Sun 9am–7pm. Closed 1 Jan, 25 Dec. 7€ (including Palazzo Altemps, Crypya Balbi, Terme di Dioclezioano, valid 8 days). ✆06 39 96 77 00.

Constructed in 1883 as a Jesuit College by Prince Massimiliano Massimo, today this building houses once of the most important museums of Roman Antiquity. Four floors of collections hold artefacts, a **numismatic collection★★**, ancient sculptures, frescoes and mosaics. Among its many treasures (⟨●⟩*see THE MICHELIN GREEN GUIDE ROME*) are **Room of the Three Arches★★★**, where Emperor Augustus wears the High Priest's toga. Other sculptures are the Wounded **Niobe★★★** (Room VII), who is one of the early female nudes (440 BC), the **Young Girl from Anzio★★**, the Crouching **Aphrodite★★★** at her bath that replicates a Greek original 3C BC, and the **Discus Thrower★★★**, copied two centuries after the original 5C BC work.

The floor mosaics are masterpieces. Don't miss the summer dining room or **triclinium of Livia's Villa★★★** painted with realistic nature scenes on black background, as well as the stucco and paintings from the **Villa della Farnesina★★★**.

▶ Follow Via XX Settembre.

After passing **Fontana dell'Acqua Felice**, with its monumental Moses flanked by lions, designed in the 16C by Domenico Fontana, Piazza di San Bernardo has the round church **San Bernardo alle Terme** (the dome inside is especially graceful); you arrive to the intersection of **Via delle Quattro Fontane**. Commissioned by Sixtus V (1585–90), on each corner Domenico Fontana sculpted the Tiber, Arno and Juno, while Pietro da Cortona completed Diana.

Basilica di Santa Maria Maggiore★★★

One of the four major basilicas in Rome. Built by Pope Sixtus III (AD 432–40) and dedicated to St Mary Major, the basilica has since undergone extensive restoration. The campanile (bell tower), erected in 1377, is the highest in Rome. The **loggia** is decorated with **mosaics★** by Filippo Rusuti (end-13C).

The **interior★★★** contains remarkable **mosaics★★★**: in the nave, those above the entablature are among Rome's most ancient Christian mosaics (5C).

The coffered **ceiling★** is said to have been gilded with the first gold brought from Peru. The floor, the work of the **Maestri Cosmati** (12C), was subject to much restoration in the 18C. The **Cappella di Sisto V** *(south aisle)* and the **Cappella Paolina** *(north aisle)* were both built in the form of a Greek cross and surmounted by a cupola.

Another chapel was added at the end of the 16C and one in the 17C: they were richly decorated in the Baroque style. Popes Sixtus V, Pius V, Clement VIII and Paul V are buried here.

▶ Leave the church by the door at the far end of the south aisle.

From **Piazza dell'Esquilino**, with its Egyptian obelisk, there is a **view★★** of the church's imposing 17C façade.

San Carlo alle Quattro Fontane

This first known work by Borromini (1638) was also his last, with the unfinished concave–convex façade that he added 30 years later. The **interior★★** is an undulating geometric play on the elliptical form, even to the dome and lantern. The **cloister★** is exquisitely proportioned.

Basilica di Santa Maria Maggiore.

© T. Bognar / Photononstop

Sant'Andrea al Quirinale★★

One of Bernini's favourite works, Sant'Andrea al Quirinale is one of his most important churches. Its proximity to that of his rival Borromini undoubtedly pushed him towards innovation and technical complexity. Often, as he did here, Bernini imbued a small space with grandeur. Commissioned in 1658 by Camillo Pamphilj, newly Innocent X, the church was completed 20 years later. Its elliptical plan is oriented along the axis defined by the choir. Coloured marble and stucco, masterfully placed, enrich the effect.

Palazzo della Consulta

The Constitutional Court has a façade★ (18C) by Ferdinando Fuga that shows various Baroque motifs.

Palazzo del Quirinale★★

The former Papal palace now serves as the president's. The palace, square and hill owe their names to Quirinus, an Archaic Era god who, along with Mars and Jupiter, formed a triad symbolic of three aspects of society.

TRASTEVERE

"Across the Tiber" is the etymology of Trastevere, one of the most popular and colourful neighbourhoods of Rome,.

San Crisogono

The early foundations of this church, visible from the stairway by the sacristy, date to the 5C. The bell tower was added in the 12C, and the elevated façade in the 17C by Giovanni Battista Soria. The interior, divided into three naves, is a blend of Mannerist–Baroque. The ancient columns were crowned with stucco capitals, and the coffered ceiling shows the arms of Cardinal Borghese.

Santa Cecilia in Trastevere★

This tranquil complex occupies the spot where St Cecilia (3C AD) was martyred, and where Pascal I (817–24) built this church. Sentenced to death by suffocation, when Cecilia miraculously survived, the prefect ordered her decapitated.

The centuries here are clearly visible: the lower level has the foundations of an ancient Roman dwelling; the interior has a 9C mosaic that Pascal commissioned for the apse; and the bell tower dates to the 12C. The statue of St Cecilia★ (below the altar), by Stefano Maderno (1576–1636), is considered one of the foremost Baroque sculptures.

In the convent, the choir has The Final Judgement★★★ painted c.1293 by Pietro Cavallini (c.1250–c.1340), a contemporary of Giotto. It remains one of the masterpieces of Roman painting in the Middle Ages, unfortunately partly damaged.

Piazza di Santa Maria in Trastevere★★

This charming square, a favourite Trastevere gathering place, has a fountain built by Bramante that was modified by Bernini, a Medieval basilica, and lively caffès and restaurants.

Basilica di Santa Maria in Trastevere★★

Built as a 3C sanctuary, then a 4C basilica, and finally this 12C basilica commissioned by Innocent II, this may be the first church dedicated to the Virgin Mary. The interior columns are from ancient Roman buildings.

Mosaics in the choir★★★ – Prophets Isaiah and Jeremiah are joined by symbols of the Evangelists, Mary and other saints in 12C mosaics. Between the windows and at the base of the chancel, the 13C mosaics by Pietro Cavallini are a masterpiece, depicting scenes from the life of the Virgin.

Museo di Roma in Trastevere

Open Tue–Sun 10am–8pm (last entry 7pm). Closed 1 Jan, 1 May, 25 Dec. 8.50€. This ancient convent of Sant'Egidio converted to a city museum now displays paintings, prints, photos and ceramics, especially scenes that depict working-class life in 18C and 19C Rome. Temporary exhibits reflect similar themes.

Villa Farnesina

Via della Lungara 230. Open Mon–Sat 9am–2pm. 6€. English guide tour Sat 10am. ℘06 68 02 72 68. www.villafarnesina.it.

Built on the Tiber for wealthy banker Agostino Chigi (1465–1520), this sub-urban pleasure villa was built on the plans of Baldassare Peruzzi, with two wings perpendicular to its façade. Talent was supplied by the best architects and painters of the Renaissance. Of special note is the **Galatea Room**, with frescoes painted by Baldassare Peruzzi, Sebastiano del Piombo and Raphael (*The Triumph of Galatea*); *The Wedding of Alexander and Roxanne* was attributed to Giovanni Antonio Bazzi, called Sodoma, but may have been by a later artist.

ADDITIONAL SIGHTS
Basilica di San Giovanni in Laterano★★★

One of the four major basilicas in Rome. St John Lateran, the Cathedral of Rome, was the first basilica founded by Constantine prior to St Peter's in the Vatican. It was rebuilt in the Baroque era by Borromini and again in the 18C.

The 18C façade has central doors with bronze panels that originally belonged to the *curia* of the Roman Forum. The grandiose interior has a 16C **ceiling★★**, while the nave has **Statues of the Apostles★** by pupils of Bernini standing in niches. The transept **ceiling★★** dates from the end of the 16C.

The **Cappella del Santissimo Sacramento** (Chapel of the Blessed Sacrament – *north transept*) has fine ancient **columns★** in gilded bronze. The pretty **cloisters★** are by the Vassalletto (13C), marble-masons who were associates of the Cosmati. The 4C **baptistery★** has 5C and 7C mosaics and frescoes.

In **Piazza di San Giovanni in Laterano** rises a 15C BC Egyptian obelisk, the tallest in Rome.

The **Palazzo Lateranense** (Lateran Palace), rebuilt in 1586, was the Papal palace until the Papal court returned from Avignon. The staircase, **Scala Sancta**, is a precious vestige from the medieval Papal palace and is traditionally identified as the one Christ used in the palace of Pontius Pilate. Worshippers climb the stairs on their knees. At the top is the Papal chapel, called the Sancta Sanctorum, with its many precious relics.

Basilica di San Paolo Fuori Le Mura★★

One of the four major basilicas in Rome. St Paul's "Outside the Walls" was built by Constantine in the 4C on the site of St Paul's tomb. Rebuilt in the 19C after its destruction by fire in 1823, it follows an early Christian basilica plan.

The impressive **interior★★★** contains an 11C bronze door cast in Constantinople; and a Gothic **ciborium★★★** (1285) by Arnolfo di Cambio, placed on the high altar, with a marble plaque dated 4C inscribed with the name Paul. The **Cappella del Santissimo Sacramento★** has the **paschal candelabrum★★**, a 12C Romanesque work by Vassalletto. The **cloisters★** are also attributed to this family of artists.

Catacombe★★★

The Archeobus departs from Piazza dei Cinquecento and circles 14 major sites (also Catacombe di San Callisto and Catacombe di San Sebastiano).

🚲 Cycle along the traffic-free Via Appia on Sun. Rental shops in Via Appia Antica 58/60 or 175 or in Largo Tacchi Venturi.

There are numerous underground Christian cemeteries alongside the Via **Appia Antica★★**. In use from the 2C they were rediscovered in the 16C and 19C. They consist of long galleries radiating from an underground burial chamber (hypogeum) which belonged to a noble Roman family of the Christian faith. The decorations of the catacombs (carvings or paintings of symbolic motifs) are precious examples of early Christian art.

The visitor with little time should prioritise the following catacombs:

Catacombe di San Callisto★★★ (Via Appia Antica 110; 9am–noon and 2–5pm. Closed Wed and Feb; ℘06 51 30 151, www.catacombe.roma.it), **Catacombe di San Sebastiano★★★** (Via Appia Antica 136; Mon-Sat 10am-4.30pm. Closed Dec. ℘06 78 50 350, www.catacombe.org), **Catacombe di Domitilla★★★** (Via delle

Sette Chiese 282; ℘06 51 10 342). Guided tours only (40min), available in several languages. 8€.

EXCURSIONS
Castelli Romani★★

Castelli Romani, or Roman Castles, is the name given to the Alban Hills (Colli Albani), to the southeast of Rome. Each of these villages was set on the outer rim of an immense crater, itself pitted with secondary craters, some of which now contain lakes (Albano and Nemi). Romans leave the capital in summer for the "Castelli" where they find walking trails and country inns, with fewer crowds than at the beach.

Tour of the Castelli

◗ 122km/76mi. Allow half a day.

Leave Rome by the Via Appia in the direction of **Castel Gandolfo★**, now the Pope's summer residence. Perhaps Castel Gandolfo was built on the site of ancient Alba Longa, while **Albano Laziale★** was built on the site of Domitian's villa. Today the town boasts an attractive church, **Santa Maria della Rotonda★**, which has a Romanesque campanile, and **Villa Comunale★**, once a villa belonging to Pompey (106–48 BC). Close to Borgo Garibaldi is the **tomb of the Horatios and the Curiaces★**. **Velletri** is a prosperous town lying south of the Alban Hills in the heart of a wine-producing region.

◗ Take Via dei Laghi out of Velletri.

This scenic road winds through groves of chestnut and oak trees to reach **Nemi**, a small village in a charming **setting★★** on the slopes of the lake sacred to Diana. The road then climbs to **Monte Cavo** (949m/3 114ft), which was crowned by the Temple of Jupiter. A monastery, then a hotel have occupied the buildings. From the esplanade there is a fine **view★** of the Castelli region with Rome on the horizon. Beyond the attractively set **Rocca di Papa**, facing the Alban lakes, the road passes through **Grottaferrata** with its 11C **abbey★**. **Tusculo** was the fief of the powerful Counts of Tusculum, who governed the Castelli region. Next comes **Frascati** pleasantly situated on the slopes facing Rome. It is known for its 16C and 17C villas, particularly the **Villa Aldobrandini★** set above its terraced gardens (Entrance Via Cardinal G. Massaia 18; gardens, nymphaeum and terrace freely accessible Mon-Fri 9am-6pm; for info contact the Frascati Point; ℘06 94 01 53 78; www. aldobrandini.it). The road back to Rome passes **Cinecittà**, film studios of the Italian Hollywood.

Ostia Antica★★

Excavations Allow at least half a day. Open Tue–Sun Apr-Oct 8.30-6pm; Nov–Mar 8.30am–4pm. Occasional summer evening performances. Closed 1 Jan, 1 May, 25 Dec. 10€. ℘06 56 35 02 15. www.ostiaantica.beniculturali.it. The train from Stazione Ostiense (Metro Pyramide) is the easiest option. Ostia's roads can grow crowded and intense.

Ostia, at the mouth of the Tiber, takes its name from the Latin word *ostium* meaning "mouth". According to Virgil, Aeneas landed here but in reality its foundation dates back to the 4C BC when Rome embarked on her conquest of the Mediterranean.

Ostia's development was as a military port during the period of expansion, later a commercial port, and by the IC BC Ostia had become a real town. Like Rome, Ostia began to decline in the 4C. Slowly the harbour silted up and malaria decimated the population.

The **Porta Romana** opens to the **Decumanus Maximus**, the east–west axis of all Roman towns. Ostia was paved with slabs and lined with porticoed houses and shops. Discover a variety of interesting remains: taverns; marine mosaics; theatre (offers summer evening concerts); warehouses *(horrea)*; baths; sanctuaries; dwelling-houses, the *domus* built around its *atrium* or courtyard; and the blocks of flats, several storeys high *(insula)*. The forum was the political and social hub. See also the **Thermopolium★★** bar and **Casa di Diana★**. The **Museo★** displays objects found in Ostia and has a small caffè.

å‼ Children enjoy this ghost town, and the beach – Ostia Lido – nearby.

Cerveteri★★

The ancient *Caere* was a powerful Etruscan centre. Within the fortress, Palazzo Ruspoli houses the Museo Archeologico Nazionale. ♿ Open Tue–Sun 8.30am–6.30pm. Closed 1 Jan, 25 Dec. 8€. ℘06 99 41 354. www.etruriameridionale.beni-culturali.it. In the 4C BC *Caere* began to decline. It was only at the beginning of the 20C that excavation work began on this site.

Most of the finds are now displayed in the Villa Giulia in Rome (*See THE GREEN GUIDE ROME*). *Another outstanding Etruscan site is TARQUINIA.*

Necropoli della Banditaccia★★★

◐ 2km/1.2mi N of Cerveteri and signposted from the main piazza. Open Tue–Sun 8.30am–1h before dusk. Closed 1 Jan, 25 Dec. 8€. ℘06 99 40 001.

The splendid necropolis is an important testimonial to Etruscan burial cults. Laid out like a city with numerous tumuli lining a main street, the tombs underneath generally date from the 7C BC. A vestibule leads into the burial chambers, which often contain two funeral beds placed side by side. One of the tombs without a tumulus is the **Tomba delle Rilievi★★** with its bas-relief stuccoes giving a picture of Etruscan life.

Tombs are opened in rotations. Highlights include the Tomba Bella, Tomb dei Letti Funebri, Tomba delle Rilievi and Tomba dei Capitelli.

Tour around Lake Bracciano★★

◐ From Cerveteri go 18km/11.2mi N to Bracciano. The lake is good for a swim or rowboat. (*See GREEN GUIDE ROME*). **Bracciano** is dominated by **Castello Orsini Odescalchi★★★** (14C–15C). **The interior** has lovely frescoed rooms. The jewel of this palace is the enchanting **Central Courtyard★**. Closed Mon except in Aug. 8.50€; for information on opening times, call ℘06 99 80 43 48; www.odescalchi.it).

Clinging to the promontory, the medieval village of **Anguillara Sabazia★** offers magnificent lake views. **Trevignano Romano** is a medieval village with fishermen's houses arranged in a herringbone pattern.

ADDRESSES

⌂ STAY

A hotel tax is levied in Rome, adding €1–3 per person per night.

RELIGIOUS STAYS

Accommodation in convents and monasteries appeals to pilgrims as well as the budget-minded. Keep in mind that some have curfews or may separate men and women guests. Contact the Peregrinatio ad Petri Sedem, **Piazza Pio XII 4** (Vaticano–San Pietro district), ℘06 69 88 48 96; Fax 06 69 88 56 17 or **CITS** (Centro Italiano Turismo Sociale), Via della Pigna 13/a, ℘06 48 73 145 or 06 47 43 811; Fax 06 47 404 432, www.citsnet.it.

SELECTING A DISTRICT

A good selection of *pensioni* and hotels can be found in the **historic centre**, where the atmosphere and high concentration of tourist sights and shops make it particularly popular with visitors; however, many of these establishments have limited capacity and as a result are often full. The attractive village-like quarter of **Trastevere**, with its lively nightlife, is also a pleasant area in which to stay, although accommodation options here are somewhat limited.

The **Prati** district by the **Vatican** is close to the centre and quieter and more reasonably priced than the historic centre and Trastevere, with a good choice of hotels. The choice of accommodation around **Via Cavour** (near the Rione Monti district), between **Termini Station** and the Fori Imperiali, is also good for mid-range hotels.

Many of the cheaper *pensioni* and smaller hotels are concentrated around Termini Station. Many of the city's luxury hotels can be found on the **Via Veneto** and in the area around **Villa Borghese**.

AVENTINO

⊖⊖⊖⊖ **Sant'Anselmo** – Piazza Sant'Anselmo 2. ☎06 57 00 57. www.aventinohotels.com. 34 rooms. Far from city traffic, in green residential Aventino, three residential villas have lovely gardens and rooms with antique furnishings. Breakfast in the courtyard.

CAMPO DE' FIORI

⊖⊖⊖⊖ **Hotel Teatro di Pompeo** – Largo del Pallaro 8. ☎06 68 72 812. www.hotelteatrodipompeo.it. 13 rooms. Visitors smitten with ancient Rome enjoy the breakfast room that shows foundations from Pompey's Theatre. Comfortable rooms have wood-beamed ceilings, some with views.

⊖⊖⊖⊖ **Residenza Farnese** – Via del Mascherone 59. ☎06 68 21 09 80. www.residenzafarneseroma.it. 31 rooms. On a quiet street next to Palazzo Farnese (French Embassy), gracious touches include nicely appointed rooms (some with frescoes), billiards room, delicious breakfast buffet and roof terrace.

COLOSSEO

⊖⊖ **Hotel Lancelot** – Via Capo d'Africa 47. ☎06 70 45 06 15. www.lancelothotel.com. 60 rooms. Restaurant⊖. This family-run economical hotel has lovely Oriental carpets. Some rooms have views of the Colosseum

GIANICOLO

⊖⊖⊖⊖ **Gran Meliá Rome Villa Agrippina** – Via del Gianicolo 3. ☎06 925 901. www.melia.com. 116 rooms. Restaurant⊖⊖⊖⊖. Just across the Tiber River, this stunning urban resort opened in 2012 with luxury spa and swimming pool. Its gourmet restaurant Viva Voce is run by Alfonso Iaccarino.

PANTHEON

⊖⊖ **Hotel Mimosa** – Via Santa Chiara 61 (2nd floor, no lift). ☎06 68 80 17 53. www.hotelmimosa.net. 11 rooms. Behind the Pantheon, this modest pensione has clean, simple but somewhat worn rooms, not all with private bath.

⊖⊖ **Pantheon View B&B** – Via del Seminario 87. ☎06 69 90 294. www.pantheonview.it. 3 rooms. This small building has comfortable rooms with a view of the Pantheon. Book in advance.

⊖⊖ **Pensione Barrett** – Largo di Torre Argentina 47. ☎06 68 68 481. www.pensionebarrett.com. 20 rooms. A pleasant hotel with some rooms that face the ancient temples on Largo Argentina. Comfort touches include shower, Jacuzzi and foot hydromassage.

⊖⊖⊖ **Hotel Portoghesi** – Via dei Portoghesi 1. ☎06 68 64 231. www.hotelportoghesiroma.it. 27 rooms. Facing the legendary "Monkey Tower", this hotel has pleasant rooms with antiques. The terrace has views of the rooftops of old Rome.

PIAZZA NAVONA

⊖⊖⊖ **Hotel Due Torri** – Vicolo del Leonetto 23. ☎06 68 80 69 56. www.hotelduetorriroma.com. 26 rooms. Once the residence of high prelates, this delightful centrally located hotel is situated in a quiet, attractive street. Each room has unique decor with a parquet floor and high-quality furniture, including some genuine antiques. One of our favourite addresses in Rome.

⊖⊖⊖ **Hotel Navona** – Via dei Sediari 8. ☎06 68 30 12 52. www.hotelnavona.com. 30 rooms. ⊇. This delightful hotel has cool, attractive rooms decorated in classic style. The hotel is located in a 16C palazzo which was built on top of much older foundations.

⊖⊖⊖⊖ **Raphael** – Largo Febo 2. ☎06 68 28 31. www.raphaelhotel.com. One of Rome's most romantic hotels, from the ivy-covered palazzo in the quiet piazza, to superb rooftop dining with breathtaking views. Choose classic or modern on the two floors designed by Richard Meier.

PIAZZA DI SPAGNA

⊖⊖ **Eva's Rooms** – Via dei Due Macelli 31. ☎06 69 19 00 78. www.evasrooms.com. 12 rooms. Good quality-price value for this well-situated guesthouse.

⊖⊖ **Pensione Panda** – Via della Croce 35. ☎06 67 80 179. www.hotelpanda.it. 28 rooms. This well-kept *pensione* in a 17C palazzo not far from the Spanish Steps has quiet, simply furnished rooms, some with shared bathroom. It lacks charm, but is recommended for its excellent location and reasonable rates.

⊖⊖⊖ **Hotel Pensione Suisse** – Via Gregoriana 54 (3rd floor, lift). ☎06 67 83 649. www.hotelssuisserome.com. 12 rooms.

In a residential building, this polyglot family extends a warm welcome. Tasteful rooms, most situated around an interior courtyard. Guests must return by 2am. Breakfast served in room.

Hotel Art – Via Margutta 56. 06 32 87 11. www.hotelart.it. 46 rooms. The latest word in high-tech with vibrant Warholian colours in the nave of an age-old convent.

PORTA PIA

Hotel Virginia – Via Montebello 94. 06 49 77 48 74. www.hotelvirginia roma.com. 30 rooms. Situated in a residential area near the train station. Clean, comfortable rooms. Good value.

TERMINI (TRAIN STATION)

M&J Place – Via Solferino 9. 06 44 62 802. www.mejplacehostel.com. Restaurant. Comfortable dormitories or single rooms in colourful modern style in this lively youth hostel with restaurant.

58 Le Real de Luxe – Via Cavour 58. 06 48 23 566. 8 rooms. This B&B has cosy rooms. Suites have Jacuzzi. In the heart of town.

Quirinale Via Nazionale 7. 06 47 07. www.hotelquirinale.it. Pleasantly large rooms, near Piazza della Repubblica, and secret passageway to Teatro dell'Opera.

TRASTEVERE

Hotel Cisterna – Viale della Cisterna 7/8/9. 06 58 17 212. www. hotelcisternarome.it. 20 rooms. In a small 18C building on a narrow street with an original fountain – 'Cisterna' – this hotel has rooms with wood-beamed ceilings. A room on the top floor has a terrace.

Hotel Trastevere – Via Luciano Manara, 24a/25. 06 58 14 713. www. hoteltrastevere.net. 9 rooms. Near charming Piazza di Santa Maria in Trastevere, this hotel has rooms with modern decor and conveniences, most facing Piazza San Cosimato.

VATICAN/PRATI

Atlante Star Hotel – Via Vitelleschi 34. 06 68 63 86 www.atlante hotels.com. 70 rooms, 15 suites. Restaurant. Choose from antique-filled rooms with whimsical retro touches, or modern style, some with stunning views of St Peter's. Free airport transportation.

Colors Hotel & Hostel – Via Boezio 31. 06 68 74 030. www.colorshotel.com. 21 rooms. In this magnificently renovated building, five dormitories have varying prices (with or without bath). Kitchen, sitting room. An original hybrid between hotel and hostel.

Pensione Ottaviano – Via Ottaviano 6. 06 39 73 81 38. www.pensioneottaviano. com. 25 rooms. Popular with young foreign visitors, this cheerful *pensione* offers single rooms or dormitories (4–6 people). No breakfast.

Hotel della Conciliazone – Borgo Pio 163/166. 06 68 75 400. Well situated, 200m/650ft from Piazza di San Pietro on a historic medieval street, this hotel is furnished with antiques. Dependable since it opened in 1974.

VILLA BORGHESE/VALLE GIULIA

Hotel Aldrovandi Palace – Via Ulisse Aldrovandi 15. 06 32 23 993. www.aldrovandi.com. 108 rooms. Restaurant. On the western edge of Villa Borghese, this elegant hotel has a beautifully landscaped garden with swimming pool and spacious rooms. Oliver Glowing offers gourmet cuisine.

NEAR ROME

Hotel Louis – Via Montegrappa 33, Ciampino. 06 79 18 095. www.hotel-louis.it. 31 rooms. Cosy hotel next to Ciampino Airport iideal for an early flight.

EAT

CAMPO DE' FIORI

Forno di Campo de' Fiori – Campo de' Fiori 22. 06 68 80 66 62. www.forno campodefiori.com. The legendary bread bakery also sells pizza by the slice. No chairs or tables.

Zoc – Via delle Zoccolette 22. 06 68 19 25 15. www.zoc22.it. On a forgotten backstreet near the Tiber, the pleasantly eclectic salon leads to an inner courtyard. Creative cuisine for lunch, dinner, breakfast or snacks.

Ditirambo – Piazza della Cancelleria 74. Closed Mon lunch and Aug. This small restaurant has delicious dishes, including homemade breads, pastas and desserts.

LARGO ARGENTINA/GHETTO

Da Gino e Antonio – Piazza Costaguti 15. 06 68 30 94 20. Closed Mon dinner and Sun. Gino knows his wines and Antonio cooks casseroles and procures meats and cheeses. Cosy and friendly.

Vecchia Roma – Piazza Campitelli 18. 06 68 64 604. Closed Wed. Chef Raffaella has brought renewed vigor to solid Roman tradition. Her good-value lovely antipasti lunch buffet attracts locals. Outdoor seating is splendid and indoor rooms are soothing and tranquil.

MONTECITORIO (PARLIAMENT)

Trattoria dal Cavalier Gino – Vicolo Rosini 4. 06 68 73 434. Closed Sun and Aug. A friendly atmosphere with good Roman specialities like *gricia*, oxtails and *involtini* at affordable prices. This small trattoria is popular with local office workers, at lunchtime best to arrive early or late.

PANTHEON

Da Fortunato – Via del Pantheon 55. 06 67 92 788. www.ristorantefortunato.it. Open 12.30–11.30pm. This bastion of Roman tradition attracts businessmen for traditional Roman cuisine like pasta (especially with porcini mushrooms), meat and artichokes. A very few outside tables have a view of the Pantheon.

Enoteca Casa Bleve – Via Teatro Valle 48/49. 06 68 65 970. www.casableve.it. Closed Sun. This upmarket wine bar serves soufflés, roulades, salads and cheeses, but best is their excellent wine selection.

La Rosetta – Via della Rosetta 8. 06 68 61 002. www.larosetta.com. Closed 1 week Jan and 2 weeks Aug. Reservation required. This restaurant fluctuates wildly according to how patrons are assessed, which means the sophisticated can dine sublimely, while tourists may be treated to both indifferent food and service. Whether fish is marinated, smoked, raw or cooked, it can be perfection itself.

PIAZZA DEL POPOLO

La Penna d'Oca – Via della Penna 53. 06 32 02 898. www.lapennadoca.com. Closed 10 days in Jan and 20 days in Aug. Reservation recommended. Near Piazza del Popolo, this charming restaurant serves traditional cuisine, innovative fish and seafood dishes, savoury pies and soups.

In summer its pleasant veranda offers a glimpse of the Roman street scene.

All'Oro – Via del Vantaggio 14. 06 97 99 69 07. www.ristorantealloro.it. Closed lunch and Sun. Superb creative Mediterranean cuisine and lovely presentations are prepared by Ricardo di Giacinto, who relocated near Piazza del Popolo in 2012. Gracious and elegant, very welcoming. The rooftop summer bar serves more simple cuisine and fresh cocktails along with its lovely panoramic view of the centre.

Margutta Vegeteriano RistorArte – Via Margutta 118. 06 32 65 05 77. www.ilmargutta.bio. Open 12–3.30pm and 7–11.30pm. Reservation for dinner. Around the corner from Fellini's home, this friendly restaurant that doubles as art gallery serves creative vegetarian cuisine. The good-value lunch buffet attracts local business clientele.

PIAZZA NAVONA

Boulangerie MP – Via di Panico 6. Open 10am–7pm, to 4pm Sun, closed Mon. 06 93 57 72 30. This Rome bread bakery opened in 2013. Matteo bakes Roman and creative breads, pizza, biscuits, French croissants and baguettes. Delicious sandwiches and lunch specials lure everyone from labourers to senators.

Pizzeria Baffetto – Via del Governo Vecchio, 114. 06 68 61 617. www.pizzeria baffetto.it. Excellent classic thin-crusty traditional pizza going since the 1960s. Expect to queue. Service is swift and notoriously brusque.

Da Francesco – Piazza del Fico 29. 06 68 64 009. www.dafrancesco.it. Casual, boisterous, and crowded, the service is brusque but the draw is economical traditional Roman cuisine. Some outside tables.

PRATI/VATICAN

L'Arcangelo – Via G.G. Belli 59. 06 32 10 992. www.larcangelo.com. Closed Sun and Sat lunch. A tranquil atmosphere attracts savvy business clientele for traditional Roman fare that has been given a sophisticated update.

Romeo Chef & Baker – V ia di Silla 26/a .9am to midnight. 06 32 110 120. www.romeo.roma.it. Surrounded by contemporary design, chef Cristina

Bowerman and Roscioli bakers offer a range of inventive modern cuisine.

TERMINI/SAN LORENZO/MONTI

Da Franco Ar Vicoletto – Via dei Falisci 1a. *06 4470 4958. Closed Mon. Fish and seafood at lower prices. The quality is a bit rustic, but portions are large in this big friendly dining hall.

Pommidoro – Piazza dei Sanniti 46. *06 44 52 652. Closed Sun and Aug. This superb Roman trattoria offers excellent pasta, game, meat and grilled fish. Frequented by politicians and artists.

Asino d'Oro – Via del Boschetto 73. *06 48 91 382. Closed Sun and Mon lunch, 2 weeks in Aug. Creative cuisine with delightfully unusual combinations is prepared using top international ingredients.

TESTACCIO

Trattoria Perilli – Via Marmorata 39. *06 57 55 100. Closed Wed. Dated decor and delicious Roman tradition: pasta alla carbonara or amatriciana; roast pork or lamb, osso buco, or offal; vignarola or artichokes.

Checchino dal 1887 – Via Monte Testaccio 30. *06 57 46 318. www.checchino-dal-1887.com. Closed Sun dinner and Mon, 24 Dec–2 Jan and Aug. Booking recommended. A Roman tradition for meats and offal, accompanied by the best Italian wines. Specialities include *rigatoni all pajata*, sweetbreads and oxtail.

TRASTEVERE

Pizzeria Dar Poeta – Vicolo del Bologna 45. *06 58 80 516. www.dar poeta.com. A lively spot, rustic ambience, where pizzas and *bruschette* attract students, locals, and tourists.

Trattoria Augusto – Piazza de' Renzi 15. *06 58 03 798. Closed Sat dinner and Sun. Simple food, family run, tables that face the square.

Trattoria Da Enzo – Via dei Vascellari 29. *06 58 12 260. www.daenzoal29.com. Closed Sun and 15 days in Aug. Savour generous dishes like cannelloni, and lamb.

Paris in Trastevere – Piazza San Callisto 7a. *06 58 15 378. www.ristorante paris.it. Closed Mon lunch and Aug. Delicious Jewish-Roman cuisine, served in a simple but cosy dining room or outside facing the small square.

Glass Hostaria – Vicolo del Cinque 58. *06 58 33 59 03 . www.glass-restaurant.it. Closed Mon and July. Dinner only. Bold contemporary minimalist design sets off Cristina Bowerman's cuisine inspired by tradition but full of creativity and surprises, always emphasising freshness.

VIA VENETO/PORTA PIA/PARIOLI

Giuda Ballerino Ostaria & Ristorante – Piazza Barberini 23. *06 42 01 04 69. www.giudaballerino.com. Ostaria lunch and dinner. Ristorante dinner only, closed Sun. This restaurant has an unusual dual function – on one side the Osteria has a rustic feel and serves regional fare, while on the other a small, modern dining room focuses on creative, gourmet cuisine. Chef Andrea Fusco's superb creative cuisine and Romolo's wine pairings are enlivened by their passion for comics displayed everywhere.

Lo Stil Novo – Via Sicilia 66b. *06 43 41 18 10. www.ristorantelostilnovo.it. Closed Sat lunch and Sun. Creative menu and good cuisine. Nice wines, good service, very good value.

Doney – Via Vittorio Veneto 141. *06 47 08 2783. www.restaurantdoney.com. Freshly updated décor inside greets diners to this longstanding fixture in the Via Veneto. Patrons savour juniper-flavored grilled veal tagliata, a selection of fish or other inventive dishes. The lengthy sidewalk set-up is ideal for alfresco dining or pre-dinner cocktails.

Metamorfosi – Via G. Antonelli 30. *06 807 6839. www.metamorfosiroma.it. Closed Sun and Sat lunch. Roy Caceres lures even other top chefs to Parioli for his creative cuisine and high standards for a memorable meal.

TAKING A BREAK

Antico Caffè della Pace – Via della Pace 5, Piazza Navona district. *06 68 61 216. www.caffedellapace.it. Closed Mon morning. Victorian decor, but patrons more bohemian than prim.

Antico Caffè Greco – Via dei Condotti 86, Piazza di Spagna district. *06 67 91 700. Founded in 1760, it's still lovely and evocative.

Caffè Capitolino – Piazzale Caffarelli 4, Campidoglio district. *06 691 90 564. Open 9am–8pm. Closed Mon. The terrace caffè of Palazzo Caffarelli has an exceptional view over the rooftops of Rome.

Caffè Rosati – Piazza del Popolo 4. ☎06 322 5859. www.barrosati.com. Open 7.30am–11.30pm. A pretty sidewalk caffè facing the piazza.

Hotel de Russie – Via del Babuino 9, Piazza del Popolo district. ☎06 32 88 81. The terrace and bar lure fashionable Romans, for caffè or cocktails.

I Dolci di Nonna Vincenza – Via Arco del Monte 98a/b. ☎06 92 59 43 22. Open 8am–9pm, Fri–Sat 8am-12pm. Delicous Sicilian pastries and cakes. For breakfast, don't miss a brioche smeared with pistachio granita (ice).

La Casa del Caffè Tazza d'Oro – Via degli Orfani 84. ☎06 678 9792. Open 7am–8pm, Sun 10.30am-7.15pm. A rival bar for best coffee. In summer, *granita di caffè*: coffee ice with whipped cream.

Pasticceria Boccione (no sign) – Via Portico d'Ottavia, 1 Ghetto. ☎06 68 78 637. Closed Sat. Not-to-miss Jewish sweets, like *torta di ricotta* (cheesecake).

Sant'Eustachio Il Caffè – Piazza S. Eustachio 82, Pantheon district. ☎06 68 80 20 48. Open 8.30am–1am, Sat 8.30am–2am. Many Romans swear here is the city's best coffee.

ICE CREAM

Caffè Ciampini – Piazza San Lorenzo in Lucina 29. ☎06 68 76 606. Excellent ice creams on one of Rome's most beautiful squares.

Fassi Palazzo del Freddo – Via Principe Eugenio 65. ☎06 44 64 740. Open noon–midnight. Ice in Rome since 1880; old-fashioned parlour and still good quality.

Gelateria Corona – Largo Arenula 27. ☎06 68808054. Closed Sun. Tiny family-run gelateria near Largo Argentina tram tracks has delicious seasonal flavours.

Gelateria del Teatro – Via dei Coronari 65/66. ☎06 4547 48 80 One of Rome's best *gelaterie*, with classic or creative flavours.

Sora Maria – Corner of Trionfale and Via Telesio. Open 5pm–2am. A *grattachecca* that offers shaved ice with fresh fruit.

Sora Mirella – Corner of Lungotevere degli Anguillara and Ponte Cestio. Hand-shaved ice, mixed with syrup or fresh fruit, a Roman tradition.

GOING OUT

Nightlife in Rome is mainly concentrated in three areas. The districts around **Campo de' Fiori**, **Piazza Navona** and **Trastevere** have a wide choice of pubs and bars, drawing a mix of young students, foreign tourists and the theatre crowd. Nightclubs are concentrated in the Testaccio district.

SHOPPING

FASHION

Luxury stores with best-known names in the Italian fashion world (Armani, Gucci, Prada, Missoni and Valentino) are located in **Via Condotti** and **Piazza di Spagna**, and streets that fan off those like Via Frattina, Via Borgognona and Via Bocca di Leone. Rome is full of goldsmiths, the most famous being **Bulgari**, but there are many fine workshops to explore. Quality on **Via del Corso** has dropped, but a few fine boutiques remain. More exciting are the small streets that radiate from the Pantheon, Piazza Navona and Campo de' Fiori.

MARKETS

Borgo Parioli – Via Tirso 14 (Via Salaria). Open Sat–Sun 10am–8pm. Closed 4th Sun of the month. A big flea market with wide variety of goods.

Campo de' Fiori – 7am-2pm, closed Sun. Fruit and vegetable market every morning.

Castroni – Via Cola di Rienzo 196. ☎06 68 74 383. Closed Sun. International food specialities.

Franchi – Via Cola di Rienzo 204. ☎06 68 74 651. www.franchi.it. Closed Sun. Meats, cheeses and hot dishes.

La Bottega del Cioccolato – Via Leonina 82. ☎06 48 21 473. www.labottegadel cioccolato.it. Open 10am–7.30pm. Closed Sun. Exclusively for chocolate lovers. More than 50 varieties.

Mercato di Piazza di San Cosimato – Every morning except Sun. Lively food market in Trastevere.

Mercato di Testaccio – Via Galvani. Large food market with many quality choices.

Mercato di Via Sannio – Via Sannio, San Giovanni in Laterano district. Open 7.30am–2pm. Closed Sun. New and second-hand clothes.

Porta Portese – Trastevere district. Open Sun to 2pm. Rome's largest flea market, Via Portuense. Beware pickpockets.

Volpetti – Via Marmorata 47. ☎06 57 42 352. www.volpetti.com. Closed Sun. Cured meats, cheeses, savoury pies, delicacies and wines.

Tivoli★★★

The villas testify to Tivoli's importance as a holiday resort from the Roman period through the Renaissance. Tivoli or *Tibur* in Antiquity came under Roman control in the 4C BC. The poet Virgil described it as "proud Tivoli ... making every kind of weapon with 1 000 anvils." Legend claims a Sibyl prophesied the coming of Jesus Christ to the Emperor Augustus there. Famous for its two contrasting gardens, its true glory is the Imperial Villa Adriana (Hadrian's Villa).

▶ **Population:** 56 531
ⓖ **Michelin Map:** 563 Q 20 – Lazio.
🛈 **Info:** Piazza Garibaldi, 00019 Tivoli (RM). ✆0774 33 45 22. www.tibursuperbum.it.
▶ **Location:** Tivoli, a small town on the lower slopes of the Apennines where the River Aniene plunges in cascades into the Roman plain, lies off the SS 5, the Via Tiburtina, 36km/22.4mi from Rome.
▶ **Train:** Tivoli (Roma 47mins).
👁 **Don't Miss:** Villa Adriana and Villa d'Este.
🕐 **Timing:** Allow a day for Tivoli and excursions.

VILLA ADRIANA★★★

▶ 6km/3.7mi SW of Tivoli.
Before visiting the villa, visitors are advised to buy a detailed map of the site (on sale at the ticket office). Open daily 9am–1hr before dusk (last admission 1hr 30min before closing). Closed 1 Jan, 1 May, 25 Dec. 8€, Apr-Oct 11€, free first Sun of the month. ✆06 39 96 79 00. www.villaadriana.beniculturali.it

This was probably the richest building project in Antiquity and was designed by the Emperor **Hadrian** (AD 76–138), who had visited every part of the Roman Empire. He wished to re-create monuments and sites he had visited during his travels. In AD 134 the villa was almost finished, but Hadrian, ill and grief-stricken by the death of his young favourite Antinoüs, was to die four years later. Although later emperors continued to visit, Tivoli soon fell into ruin. The site was explored from the 15C to the 19C, when works were dispersed to various museums and private collections. Only in 1870 did the Italian government organise the excavation.

Pecile★★ – The water-filled Pecile takes its name from a portico in Athens. Its rectangular form with portico and curved ends was oriented to keep one side always in the shade. The apsidal chamber called the **Sala dei Filosofi** (Philosophers' Room) was perhaps a reading room.

Teatro Marittimo★★★ – The circular construction consists of a portico and a central building surrounded by a canal. It provided an ideal retreat for the misanthropic Hadrian. Bear south to the remains of a **nymphaeum** *(ninfeo)* and the great columns which belonged to a building comprising three semicircular rooms round a courtyard *(cortile)*.

Terme★★ – The Small Baths and then the Great Baths with an apse show the high architectural standards.

Canopo★★★ – Beyond the **museum** is a complex which evokes the Egyptian town of Canope with its famous Temple of Serapis. The route to Canope from Alexandria consisted of a canal lined with temples and gardens. Having reached the ruins overlooking the *nymphaeum*, turn right before skirting the **fishpond** and portico.

Palazzo imperiale – The palace complex extended from Piazza d'Oro to the Libraries. The rectangular **Piazza d'Oro★★** was surrounded by a double portico and was an aesthetic indulgence. On the far side are traces of an octagonal chamber and a domed chamber opposite.

Sala dei Pilastri Dorici★★ – The hall is named for the surrounding portico, composed of pilasters with Doric bases and capitals.

Caserma dei Vigili (firemen's barracks) show remains of a summer dining room and a *nymphaeum*. These buildings connect to the **library court** by a *cryptoporticus* (underground passage).

The suite of 10 rooms along one side of the library court was an infirmary. Note the fine mosaic **paving★**. According to custom the **library** was divided in two for a Greek section and a Latin section. The route to the **Terrazza di Tempe** goes past rooms paved with mosaic that belonged to a dining room.

The path runs through the trees on the slope above the valley past a **round temple** attributed to the goddess Venus, and skirts the site of a **theatre**, on the left.

Villa d'Este

©Davide Romanini/Dreamstime.com

VILLA D'ESTE★★★

Head to the centre of Tivoli and park in the car park in Piazzale Matteotti, near the Rocca Pia. Entrance on Piazza Trento. ♿(reservation requested for special assistance to visitors with a disability). Open Tue–Sun, 8.30am–1hr before dusk. Closed 1 Jan, 1 May, 25 Dec. 8€, free first Sun of the month. ℘0774 31 20 70 or 199 76 61 66. www.villadestetivoli.info.

In 1550 Cardinal Ippolito II d'Este – raised to great honours by François I of France but disgraced when the king's son Henri II succeeded to the throne – decided to retire to Tivoli, where he converted the former Benedictine convent. The simple architecture of the villa contrasts with the elaborate terraced gardens. The statues, pools and fountains enhance the natural beauty with all the grace of the Mannerist style. Small wonder UNESCO added this watery spectacle to its World Heritage List.

To the left of the main entrance stands the old abbey church of **Santa Maria Maggiore** with its attractive Gothic façade and a 17C bell tower.

Palace and gardens★★★ – Walk through the elaborately decorated Old Apartments. A double flight of stairs leads to the upper garden walk. The shell-shaped Fontana del Bicchierone is attributed to Bernini. A splendid avenue lined with fountains, **Viale delle Cento Fontane★★★**, leads to the Oval Foun-

tain, **Fontana dell'Ovato★★★**, dominated by a statue of the Sibyl.

The Organ Fountain, **Fontana dell'Organo★★★**, has a concealed water-powered organ that still plays music *(every 2hrs)*. At the bottom of the garden, **Fontana della Natura** has a statue of Diana of Ephesus.

On the central avenue admire the **Fontana dei Draghi**, built in 1572 in honour of Pope Gregory XIII. The Bird Fountain, **Fontana della Civetta**, plays birdsongs *(from 10am every 2hrs)*.

VILLA GREGORIANA★

Enter from Piazza Tempio di Vesta or Largo Sant'Angelo. Open Tue–Sun Mar and 16 Oct–Nov 10am–2.30pm; Apr–Oct 10am–6.30pm;. 5€. ℘06 39 96 77 01. www.coopculture.it.

This wooded park's tangle of paths winds down the steeply wooded slopes to the River Aniene where it cascades through the ravine, plunging down at the **Grande Cascata★★**, disappearing at the **Grotta della Sirena** and bursting from the rock-face in **Grotta di Nettuno**. Visit the **Tempio della Sibilla**, an elegant Corinthian-style structure dating from the end of the Republic. An Ionic temple stands alongside.

EXCURSIONS
Palestrina★

◐ 23km/14.3mi SE.

With its panoramic position overlooking the Prenestini Mountains, a historic centre and the remains of the celebrated Temple of Fortuna Primigenia, Palestrina makes for an extremely pleasant excursion. This splendid town flourished from the 8C to 7C BC; after various vicissitudes it submitted to Roman domination. The cult of the goddess Fortuna prospered until the 4C AD when the medieval city was born on its remains.

Palazzo Barberini★ and Museo Archeologico Prenestino★

♿ Open daily 9am–8pm (last entrance 7pm). 5€. ☏06 95 38 100.

Artefacts from necropoli and the Barberini collection are displayed. The museum's masterpiece is the Nile mosaic★★, which portrays Egypt with the Nile flooding.

Tempio della Fortuna Primigenia★

This magnificent sanctuary, some of the finest Hellenic architecture in Italy,. dates from the 2C–1C BC. In the Lower Sanctuary the Basilical Room remains as well as two side buildings, a grotto and the Apse Room. The Upper Sanctuary was built on the temple's fourth esplanade (now Piazza della Cortina). The 11C Palazzo Colonna-Barberini houses the archaeological museum. From the terrace there is a fine view★ of the town

ADDRESSES

🍽 STAY

🛏 **B&B La Panoramica** – Viale Arnaldi 45. ☏0774 33 57 00. www.villadestetivoli.it. 🖚. 3 rooms. This pleasant early 19C villa in Tivoli is 200 m/220 yds from Villa d'Este and has a panoramic view.

Tarquinia★

Tarquinia crowns a rocky platform, facing the sea, in a barley- and corn-growing region interspersed with olive groves. As D.H. Lawrence noted in 1932 travelogue *Etruscan Places*: "**Tarquinia, its towers pricking up like antennae on the side of a low bluff of a hill, is some few miles inland from the sea. And this was once the metropolis of *Etruria*, chief city of the great Etruscan League."** All that remains of this ancient civilisation are the necropolis and its frescoes, column stubs on the acropolis and artwork in museums.

▶ **Population:** 16 630
⚲ **Michelin Map:** 563 P 17.
🛈 **Info:** Barriera San Giusto. ☏0766 84 92 82. www.tarquinia.net.
◐ **Location:** Tarquinia is located off the S 1 (the Via Aurelia) in northern Lazio.
◐ **Train:** Tarquinia (Roma 1hr 19mins)
⊚ **Don't Miss:** The Necropoli di Monterozzi and Museo Nazionale Tarquiniese.
⊕ **Timing:** Allow a day.
👥 **Kids:** Watch ships at the Civitavecchia port.

A BIT OF HISTORY

According to legend, the town was founded in the 12C or 13C BC. Archaeologists have found 9C BC vestiges of the Villanovian civilisation, which derived its name from the village of Villanova near Bologna, and developed around the year 1000 BC in the Po Plain, in Tuscany and in the northern part of Latium, where the Etruscans later settled. Standing on the banks of the River Marta, Tarquinia was a busy port and in the 6C BC ruled the coast of *Etruria*.

Under Roman rule, Tarquinia was decimated by malaria in the 4C BC and was sacked by the Lombards in the 7C AD. The inhabitants then moved about 2km/1.2mi northeast.

ETRUSCAN TARQUINIA
Necropoli di Monterozzi★★

◑ 4km/2.5mi SE. Open Tue–Sun 8.30am–1hr before dusk. Closed 1 Jan, 25 Dec. 6€; 8€ including Museo Nazionale. ℘0766 85 63 08. www.necropoliditarquinia.it.

The burial ground extends over an area 5km/3mi long and 1km/0.6mile wide. It contains 6 000 tombs dating from the 6C–1C BC. There are remarkable **paintings★★★** in the burial chambers. The most important tombs include: the **Tomba del Barone**, dating from the 6C BC; the 5C BC **Tomba del Leopardi**, in which are depicted leopards and scenes of a banquet and dancing; the 6C BC **Tomba dei Tori** with its erotic paintings; the **Tomba delle Leonesse** dating from around 530–520 BC; the 4C BC **Tomba Gigliogi** decorated with *trompe l'œil* paintings; and the late-6C BC **Tomba delle Caccia e della Pesca**.

Museo Nazionale Tarquiniense★

Piazza Cavour 1. ♿ Open 8am–9pm, Sat 8am–7pm, Sun 8am–1pm. Closed 1 Jan, 25 Dec. 6€; 8€ including Necropoli di Monterozzi. ℘0766 85 60 36.

The National Museum is housed in the **Palazzo Vitelleschi★**, built in 1439. It contains a most remarkable collection of Etruscan Antiquities originating from the excavations in the necropolis. Note especially the two admirable **winged horses★★★** in terra-cotta.
After visiting Palazzo Vitelleschi (Piazza Cavour), you can proceed to **Palazzo Comunale** and discover the lovely **Piazza Trento e Trieste** with its *fontana monumentale*. End your walk at the belvedere with a view of the countryside. Via Mazzini takes you to Porta Castello and its 12C Romanesque church, **Santa Maria in Castello★** *(contact the houses to the left of the church; donation).*

EXCURSIONS
Civitavecchia

◑ 20km/12.4mi S. www.civitavecchia.com.

Civitavecchia, the Roman *Centumcellae*, has been the port of Rome since the reign of Trajan. The port is guarded by the Fort of Michelangelo, completed by Michelangelo in 1557.

Terme di Traiano
(or Terme Taurine)

◑ 3km/1.8mi NE. Open 9.30am–1pm. 8€. The two groups of baths date from both the Republican period and the time of Emperor Hadrian.

Tuscania★

◑ 25km/15.5mi N.

Tuscania was a powerful Etruscan town, a Roman *municipium* and an important medieval centre. Vestiges of its wall remain and two superb churches, situated just outside town. The 1971 earthquake considerably damaged its artistic heritage. The charming *borgo* is ringed with churches, ancient *palazzi*, alleys and towers. The Torre di Lavello garden offers a beautiful **view★** of **San Pietro**, the façade of which stands on the site of the Etruscan acropolis. The **crypt★★** is a forest of columns of various periods.

Chiesa di Santa Maria Maggiore★

This 12C church, dedicated to St Mary Major, is modelled on St Peter's. The **13C Romanesque doorways★★** are decorated with sculptures. The interior is formed of 8C, 9C and 12C fragments. Below the triumphal arch is a 14C fresco.

ADDRESSES

🛌 STAY

🛏 **Locanda di Mirandolina** – Via del Pozzo Bianco 40/42, Tuscania. ℘0761 43 65 95. www.mirandolina.it. 5 rooms. Restaurant 🍽🍽. This B&B is in the heart of the ancient medieval *borgo* of Tuscania. The façade is covered with jasmine. Excellent regional specialities.

Viterbo★

Viterbo has kept its medieval aspect, notably in the San Pellegrino quarter★★, that houses many craftsmen, with its vaulted passageways, towers and external staircases. The city also is known for its thermal baths.

▶ **Population:** 63 597
⚐ **Michelin Map:** 563 O 18.
🄸 **Info:** Via Ascenzi 4. ℘0761 32 59 92. www.comune.viterbo.it.
◖ **Location:** 20km/12.4mi southeast of Lago di Bolsena. Access to the A 1 is by dual carriageway.
◖ **Train:** Viterbo (Roma 1hr 35mins).
◉ **Don't Miss:** Piazza San Lorenzo, Villa Lante di Bagnaia and the Palazzo Farnese di Caprarola.
🄰🄸 **Kids:** The 16C theme park of Bomarzo; boating on Lago di Bolsena; or a swim in Viterbo's thermal baths.

SIGHTS

Piazza San Lorenzo★★

This medieval square, former site of the Etruscan acropolis, has a 13C house on Etruscan foundations, an 1192 cathedral adorned with a fine Gothic campanile, and a 13C Papal palace, **Palazzo dei Papi★★**. From Piazza Martiri d'Ungheria see the lovely view of the piazza.

Museo Civico

Piazza Crispi. ⚐ Open Tue–Sun Apr–Oct 9am–7pm; Nov–Mar 9am–6pm. Closed 1 Jan, 1 May, 4 Sept, 25 Dec. 3.10€. ℘0761 34 08 10.
Etruscan and Roman objects discovered in area tombs are here. The picture gallery has a terra-cotta by the della Robbia as well as works by Salvator Rosa and Sebastiano del Piombo.

EXCURSIONS

Teatro Romano di Ferento★

◖ 9km/5.6mi N. ⚐ ℘0761 32 59 29. www.teatroferento.it.
The 1C Roman theatre of Ancient Ferentium has a brick back wall, portico of blocks without mortar, and 13 tiers of seats. The site hosts summer shows.

Villa Lante di Bagnaia★

◖ 5km/3mi NE. Via Jacopo Barozzi 71. ⚐ Open Tue–Sun 8.30am–1h before dusk. Closed 1 Jan, 1 May, 25 Dec. 5€, free first Sun of the month. ℘0761 28 80 08.
This elegant 16C villa by Vignola, residence of several popes, features lovely Italian terraced gardens with geometric motifs and numerous fountains. Mannerist highlights include a grotto, the cardinal's table and a crayfish-shaped waterfall. Sacheverell Sitwell –

the eccentric English art historian – praised it as "the most lovely place of the physical beauty of nature in all Italy or in all the world".

🄰🄸 Sacro Bosco di Bomarzo★★

◖ 21km/13mi NE by the S 204. Park open Apr–Ago 8.30am–7pm; Sept–Mar 8.30am–dusk. 10€. ℘0761 92 40 29. www.sacrobosco.it.
Parco dei Mostri or **Sacro Bosco** (Monster Park/Sacred Wood) is a Mannerist creation that Vicino Orsini adorned with fantastically shaped **sculptures★**. This 16C theme park includes whales, dragons, harpies and nymphs.

Lago di Vico★

◖ 18km/11.2mi SE by the Via Santa Maria di Gradi.
This solitary but charming lake occupies a forested crater.

Palazzo Farnese di Caprarola★

◖ 18km/11.2mi SE. Open 8.30am–6.45pm. For guided tours: ℘0761 64 79 41. Closed Mon, 1 Jan, 1 May, 25 Dec. 5€. ℘0761 64 60 52. www.caprarola.com.
Palace highlights include a delightful circular courtyard, Vignola's **spiral staircase★★** of 30 paired Doric columns, and paintings by the Zuccaro brothers,

Taddeo (1529–66) and Federico (c.1540–1609) as well as Bertoja (1544–74).

Civita Castellana

◗ 36km/22.4mi SE.

Here the Etruscan city *Falerii Veteres* was destroyed by the Romans in 241 BC, but rebuilt in the 8C or 9C. The **Duomo's portico★** was built in 1210. The late-15C **Rocca** (castle), built by Sangallo the Elder, became Cesare Borgia's residence.

🚗 DRIVING TOUR

LAGO DI BOLSENA★

Round trip. 80km/49.7mi. Allow 1 day.

◗ From Viterbo take the S 2 NW to Bolsena (28km/17.4mi). Return by Civita di Bagnoregio.

Montefiascone

13km/8mi NW of Viterbo.

Montefiascone vineyards produce a variety of wines. Inside the Church of **San Flaviano★** is the funerary plaque of a German bishop who died from drinking too much of the good local Est! Est!! Est!!! (*sic*) wine on his way to Rome c.1111.

Bolsena

15km/9.3mi NW of Montefiascone.

Bolsena, the ancient Etruscan city of *Volsinii*, is on Italy's largest **lake★** of volcanic origin. There is a good view from the S 2, the Viterbo–Siena road. *Book boat trips from Capodimonte (www. navigabolsena.com).*

Chiesa di Santa Cristina★

Catacombs: 10am–noon and 4–6pm (winter 3.30–5pm). 4€. ℘0761 79 90 67. www.basilicasantacristina.it.

Pilgrims visit this 11C church dedicated to the 3C martyr for the **Chapel of the Miracle of Bolsena**.

◗ From Bolsena, go towards Orvieto, then, at the crossroad for the S 71, take the road SE to Bagnoregio (about 12km/7.4mi). Civita is a further extension of this.

Civita di Bagnoregio★

Set on a plateau of volcanic rock above the Tiber River Valley, the *paese che muore* (dying town) suffered severe damage after an 18C earthquake and subsequent erosion. Only in the 1960s was it linked to Bagnoregio, by means of a pedestrian bridge that spans a white sea of *calanchi*.

Rieti

Rieti is the geographical centre of Italy, and a good centre from which to follow in the footsteps of St Francis of Assisi, who preached locally.

SIGHTS

Piazza Cesare Battisti

This is the centre of the town, where the most important buildings are to be found. Take the gateway by the 16C–17C Palazzo del Governo to reach the **public garden★**, from where there is a lovely view of the tow

Duomo

This cathedral has a 15C portico and a lovely Romanesque campanile dating

▶ **Population:** 47 774
⚅ **Michelin Map:** 563 O 20.
🛈 **Info:** ℘0746 48 85 37. www.comune.rieti.it.
◗ **Location:** At the foot of Mount Terminillo, the main access roads are the SS 4, the Via Salaria, which links the town to L'Aquila, the A 1, and the SS 79, which goes to Terni.
⊛ **Don't Miss:** The Convento di Fonte Colombo and the caves of St Francis.
🕐 **Timing:** Allow a day.
◗ **Train:** Rieti (Terni 35mins).

from 1252. The fresco of Madonna dates from 1494 while the **crypt** is 12C.

Palazzo Vescovile

This 13C episcopal building has heavily ribbed **vaulting★** over the two naves.

EXCURSIONS
Convento di Fonte Colombo

▶ 5km/3mi SW. Take the Contigliano road and after 3km/1.8mi turn left.
It was in the old monastery that **St Francis** had an eye operation. He dictated the Franciscan Rule in the grotto, having fasted for 40 days. Note the 12C Chapel of St Mary Magdalene adorned with frescoes, the Cross designed by St Francis, the grotto and the tree-trunk in which Jesus appeared to him.

Convento di Greccio★

▶ 15km/9.3mi NW. Take the road via Contigliano to Greccio and continue for 2km/1.2mi. Park on the esplanade.
This 13C monastery clings to a rocky overhang. It was here that St Francis celebrated Christmas in 1223 and said Mass at a manger *(presepio)* between an ox and an ass, thus starting the custom of Nativity scenes. There's access to the areas where St Francis and his companions lived.

Convento di Poggio Bustone

▶ 10km/6.2mi N by the Terni road. Open daily 8.30am–12.30 and 3–7pm; (winter 6pm). ℘0746 68 89 16.
Perched at 818m/2 684ft, the monastery consists of a 14C church, with its 15C to 17C frescoes, 15C–16C cloisters, a 14C refectory and two caves in which St Francis is said to have lived.

Convento La Foresta

▶ 5km/3mi N. Guided tours only, daily 8.30am–noon and 2–6.30pm. ℘0746 20 00 85.
St Francis wrote *Canticle of the Creatures* here and performed the miracle of the vine.

Anagni★

Anagni, a small medieval town east-southeast of Rome in the Ciociaria, is the birthplace of several popes, including the infamous Boniface VIII (1235–1303). In 1303, after years of conflict, the French king, Philip the Fair, who had been excommunicated by the Pope, sent a delegation to Anagni to assess its administration and to evaluate accusations of heresy and corruption. Boniface VIII was ignobly humiliated and this is what gave birth to the legend which became known as the "Slap (or Outrage) of Anagni".

SIGHTS
Cathedral★★

Open 9am–1pm and 3–7pm (winter 6pm). To visit the crypt see www.cattedraledianagni.it for details. 9€. ℘0775 72 83 74.

▶ **Population:** 21 705
⚲ **Michelin Map:** 563 Q 21 – Lazio.
🛈 **Info:** Piazza Innocenzo III Papa. ℘0775 72 78 52.
▶ **Location:** Situated on a rocky spur that overlooks the Sacco Valley, Anagni is not far from the A 1, 30km/18.6mi from Frosinone.
▶ **Train:** Anagni fiuggi (Roma 49 mins)
🚇 **Don't Miss:** The cathedral, Abbazia di Casamari and Monastero di San Benedetto.
🕐 **Timing:** Allow two days to explore the town and surrounding area.

The town's most important building stands on the site of the former acropolis. This Romanesque cathedral was built in

Fresco in the crypt of the cathedral depicting Galen and Hippocrates

the 11C and 12C and remodelled in the 13C with Gothic additions. Walk around the outside to admire the three Romanesque apses with Lombard mouldings and arcades, the 14C statue of Boniface VIII over the loggia on the north side and the Romanesque campanile. Inside, the 13C **paving★** was the work of the Cosmati. The high altar is surmounted by a Romanesque *ciborium* or canopy. The **paschal candelabrum** is adorned with multicoloured encrustations; it rests on two sphinxes and is crowned by an infant holding a cup. The work, like the nearby **episcopal throne**, is by Pietro Vassaleto. The **crypt★★★** also has magnificent 13C **frescoes** depicting the Old Testament and the lives of the saints and men of science such as Galen and Hippocrates.

Medieval Quarter★

This quarter consists almost entirely of 13C buildings and is particularly evocative. The façade of **Boniface VIII's Palace** has two pierced galleries one above the other. One has wide round-headed arches while the other consists of twinned windows. In Piazza Cavour is the 12C–13C **Palazzo Comunale** with a great **vault★** at ground level.

EXCURSIONS
Alatri★

◗ 22km/13.7mi E of Anagni on the SP 24. This important city, which was built in the 6C BC, retains several of its cyclo-

pean walls (4C BC). The **acropolis★** can be reached on foot from the Porta di Città and is laid out on a trapezoidal plan. One of the best-preserved examples in Italy, it affords a fine **view★★**. The city is a maze of steep stairways and alleyways lined with Gothic houses. The **Palazzo Gottifredi** (at the crossroads of the three major town roads) is 13C and the church of **Santa Maria Maggiore★** (in the piazza of the same name) in the transitional Romanesque-Gothic style has a façade with three porticos. Inside there is 12C–15C **carved woodwork★**

Abbazia di Casamari★★

◗ 35km/21.8mi SE of Anagni on the S 6 and S 214. For opening hours see the website. Donations welcome.
☎0775 28 23 71. www.casamari.it.
The abbey occupies a lonely site, originally a Benedictine foundation. It was consecrated in 1217 by Pope Honorius III, and later taken over by the Cistercians, who rebuilt the abbey in accordance with the order's rules of austerity and self-sufficiency.
A lovely example of early Italian-Gothic architecture, above the entrance porch of the abbey church is a gallery of twinned openings which served as the abbots' lodging. The simplicity of the façade is Burgundian with a round-headed doorway, the rose window, and the Cistercian transept tower.
The interior is spacious, austere and solemn. Built to a Latin cruciform plan, it has a nave and two aisles separated by massive cruciform piers with engaged columns supporting the lofty pointed vaulting. On the south side of the church are the cloisters, a well and a flower garden. On the east side is the chapter house with ribbed, pointed vaulting.

Subiaco

◗ 38.5km/23.9mi N of Alagni on the SS 155 and SS 411 (scenic route).
St Benedict, founder of the Benedictine Order, and his twin sister Scolastica retired to this spot at the end of the 5C and built 12 little monasteries before moving to Monte Cassino.

◗ Access to the monasteries of Santa Scolastica and San Benedetto is 3km/1.8mi before Subiaco, shortly after the Aniene Bridge.

Monastero di Santa Scolastica

Guided tours only, 9.30am–12.15pm and 3.30–6.15pm. Donations welcome. ✆0774 82 421. www.benedettini-subiaco.it.

Standing on a fine site overlooking the Aniene Gorges, the monastery has preserved a majestic 11C campanile, and its remodelled 18C church has three cloisters. The third, the work of the Cosmati, is admirable in its simplicity.

Monastero di San Benedetto★

Open 9am–12.30pm and 3–6pm. Donations welcome. Book in advance. ✆0774 85 039.

This 14C monastery clings to the rock-face above an earlier one. The **upper church** has frescoes of the 14C Sienese school and 15C Umbrian school.

The **lower church** is frescoed by Magister Consolus, of the 13C Roman school. Visitors are admitted to the Sacred Cave (Sacro Speco) where St Benedict lived as a hermit for three years.

A spiral staircase then leads up to a chapel, which contains the earliest portrait of St Francis (without Stigmata or halo). The Holy Staircase (Scala Santa) leads down to the Chapel of the Virgin, the Shepherd's Cave and the rose garden where St Benedict threw himself into brambles to resist temptation.

Gaeta★

Gaeta is a former fortress, still partly walled. The last bastion of the Bourbons, it now hosts a Nato base. A handsome castle crowns the medieval quarter. South of Gaeta, Serapo Beach is a pleasant stretch of sugar-fine sand.

SIGHTS
Duomo

The cathedral has a 10C and 15C Romanesque Moorish campanile adorned with glazed earthenware. The late-13C **paschal candelabrum★** has 48 bas-reliefs. A medieval quarter lies near the cathedral.

Castello

The 8C castle, altered many times, has a lower castle built by the Angevins.

Monte Orlando

Info Point: Sede del Parco della Riviera di Ulisse, Piazza della Breccia 5. ✆0771 74 30 70. www.parks.it/parco.monte.orlando.

Legends claim that this sea-cliff split when Jesus died.

▶ **Population:** 21 500
♿ **Michelin Map:** 563 S 22.
🛈 **Info:** ProLoco: Piazza Traniello 18. ✆320 03 804 13. www.prolocogaeta.it.
◗ **Location:** Gaeta is in the south of Lazio, on the point of a promontory bounding a beautiful **bay★**. The coastal road affords magnificent views.
😊 **Don't Miss:** A tour along the coast of the Archipelago Ponziano, pretty Sperlonga beaches, and the Abbazia di Fossanova.
🕐 **Timing:** Allow a day.

🚗 DRIVING TOUR

GOLFO DI GAETA TO AGRO PONTINO

55km/34.2mi, plus a stop to visit the Abbazia di Fossanova. Allow 1 day.

◗ Follow the SS 213 towards **Terracina**.

Grotta di Tiberio and Museo Archeologico★

♿Open daily 8.30am–7.30pm. Closed 1 Jan, 1 May, 25 Dec. 5€. ☎0771 54 80 28. This cave (*grotta*), with a large ornamental pool, is where Emperor Tiberius narrowly escaped death when part of the roof crumbled. The superb museum has 4C–2C BC statues and realistic theatrical masks. A colossal group depicts Ulysses punishing Cyclops Polyphemus.

A pleasant sandy beach – dotted with bars – stretches between the grotto and Sperlonga. Purchase tickets at the museum: the grotto is fenced off.

The village of **Sperlonga**⚓ stands on a rocky spur, pitted with caves, between the sea and the Aurunci mountains.

▶ Head W 18km/11.2mi on the SS 213.

At the foot of Monti Ausoni, the seaside town of **Terracina**⚓ has been popular since Roman times, with its dramatic clifftop Temple of Jupiter. The 1075 **Duomo★** overlooks Piazza del Municipio.

Tempio di Giove Anxur – 3km/1.8mi E of the historic centre of Terracina (allow 45min to climb from Piazza Municipio up the Via Anxur on foot). Open 9-12pm (Oct-May 9am-dusk). Several guided tours. ☎06 88 522 480 or 348 81 85 541. www.tempiodigioveanxur.it

Although there are few remains other than the foundations, a vaulted gallery and an underground passage (*cryptoporticus*), it is worth visiting the site of the Temple of Jupiter for the extensive **panorama★★** of the town, the canals and port, Monte Circeo and the Pontine marshes, Fondi with its lakes, and the coast as far as Gaeta.

▶ Continue along the coast to San Felice Circeo.

Parco Nazionale del Circeo★

Behind the local museum, a road winds up to the summit and ancient temple. 🛈Via C. Alberto 107, Sabaudia. ☎0773 51 22 40. www.parcocirceo.it.

This nature reserve covers a narrow coastal strip between Anzio and Terracina. **Monte Circeo** was the refuge of the witch Circe who transformed Ulysses' companions into a herd of pigs. **Lago di Sabaudia** is a lake linked by bridge from the town of **Sabaudia**⚓.

▶ Head NE from Sabaudia (inland) 23km/14.3mi.

Abbazia di Fossanova★★

Open Apr–Oct 8am–7.30 (5.30pm Nov–Mar). Guided tours by appointment: ☎340 32 89 592. ☎0773 93 90 61. www.abbaziadifossanova.it.

The oldest abbey of the Cistersian Order in Italy (1133) was built in the Burgundian style. Picturesque cloisters combine Romanesque and pre-Gothic styles.

EXCURSIONS

Arcipelago Ponziano★

For information on ferries contact: ☎199 123 199; from mobile or from abroad 081 31 72 999. Agenzia Regine ☎0771 80 565; Libera Navigazione Mazzella: www.navlib.it. ☎081 552 07 63.

This volcanic island, lying beyond the Gulf of Gaeta, has a verdant ridge and blue-grey cliffs, bordered by narrow beaches. The village of **Ponza★★** has gaily painted houses around a small harbour, busy with fishing boats and ferries, and also a popular spot with divers.

Abbazia di Montecassino★★

Open daily 8.30am–12.30pm and 3.30–6pm (winter 5pm). Museum: in winter opens only on Sun. ☎0776 31 15 29. www.abbazie.com/montecassino

The road's hairpin bends afford wonderful valley views. The majestic abbey rises above the summit of Monte Cassino, one of the holiest places of Roman Catholicism, seat of the Benedictines. Founded in 529 by **St Benedict** (d.547), he drew up a complete, precise set of rules. Cloisters lead to the abbey. The basilica **interior★★** is sumptuous with marble, stucco, mosaics and gild, both dazzling and austere.

☺ *Don't miss St Benedict's tomb.*

Abruzzo and Molise

Major City: L'Aquila

Official Websites: www.abruzzoturismo.it;
www.regione.molise.it/turismo

The regions of Abruzzo and Molise were collectively known as "Abruzzi" when they were administered as one territory as part of the Kingdom of Two Sicilies. In 1963 they were divided into their present day configurations. Among the most under-populated and under-visited areas in Italy, the regions attract active tourists with hiking, skiing and caving in the Abruzzo and Maiella national parks.

Highlights

1 Hike the nature trails in the **Parco Nazionale d'Abruzzo** (p191)

2 Inspect four centuries of art in Sulmona's **Palazzo dell'Annunziata** (p194)

3 Stroll through the Samnite/ Roman settlement of **Altilia Saepinum** (p199)

Abruzzo

This part of the Apennines most suggests a country of high mountains, grand and wild, with its **Gran Sasso** and **Maiella massifs**. The **Parco Nazionale d'Abruzzo**, where the highly endangered Marsican Brown Bear still roams, is the doyen of the Italian national parks and was established in the Upper Sangro Valley in 1923. In basins sheltered from the wind are vineyards, almond and olive groves; industry is concentrated in the Chieti-Pescara zone and areas such as Vasto (glass-making), Sulmona (car factories), L'Aquila (steelworks) and Avezzano (textile and food industries). The tourism industry is important for the coastal regions and the winter resorts of the Gran Sasso massif.

Molise

Molise extends south of Abruzzo, with which it shares several features: a mountainous relief, dark valleys and wild forests where wolves still hunt. The region comprises two provinces: Isernia, bordered to the west by the Maiella Mountains, and Campobasso, which houses the regional capital of the same name and borders the Adriatic. The main industrial area, where automotive and textile factories operate, can be found on the outskirts of Termoli, which is also a seaside resort and site of several buildings from the Middle Ages. Agriculture still forms the basis of the local economy, the main crops being wheat, oats, maize, potatoes and vines.

Santo Stefano di Sessanio, L'Aquila,
Parco Nazionale del Gran Sasso

© imagebroker/hemis.fr

Abruzzo

The splendours of Abruzzo lie in the grandeur and diversity of the wild and rugged terrain it occupies: stark karst formations give way to lush woodland, and barren plateaus to fertile pastures. Enclosed by three national parks – the long-established Parco Nazionale d'Abruzzo, the Parco Nazionale del Gran Sasso and the Parco Nazionale della Maiella – the region offers plenty of variety, in both summer and winter. Other attractions include the seaside resorts of Alba Adriatica, Giulianova Lido, Roseto degli Abruzzi, Silvi Marina and Vasto.

- **Michelin Map:** 563 N–R 21–26
- **Info:** Corso Vittorio Emanuele II, 301, 65122 Pescara. ℘085 42 900 212. www.abruzzoturismo.it.
- **Location:** The Abruzzo is easily accessible from Rome, taking the A 24, and the Adriatic coast, taking the A 25. The main access routes are Bisegna, Barrea and Forca d'Acero.
- **Don't Miss:** The Parco Nazionale d'Abruzzo and Gran Sasso.
- **Timing:** Allow at least four days for the region.

A BIT OF HISTORY

Various Italic populations dominated the region until the 3C BC when Rome overtook the area. After the fall of the Roman Empire the region became a Lombard, then a Frankish territory. In the 12C it became part of the Kingdom of Naples, until the Unification of Italy in 1861.

In the Middle Ages the diffusion of Benedictine rule from the neighbouring abbey at Monte Cassino (♦see Abbazia di Montecassino, p189) led to the construction of cathedrals, abbeys and churches whose ornate *ciboria* and pulpits constitute the glory of Abruzzi art. In the 15C–16C the finest examples of Renaissance art were those of painter and architect **Cola dell'Amatrice**, the painter **Andrea de Litio**, the sculptor **Silvestro dell'Aquila** and the goldsmith **Nicola da Guardiagrele**.

Notable figures of the region include Ovid (Publius Ovidius Naso, 43 BC–AD 17), and Gabriele D'Annunzio (1863–1938), Benedetto Croce (1866–1952) and novelist Ignazio Silone (1900–78).

PARCO NAZIONALE D'ABRUZZO, LAZIO E MOLISE★★★

Visitors should call the park for opening times. By car the main routes are Bisegna in the north, Barrea to the east and Forca d'Acero in the west.

P The park is best seen on foot. Car park areas are at the bottom of the valley.

For information on park activities contact Centro Operativo Accoglienza Turisti (CAOT) or local offices at Villetta Barrea, Civitella Alfedena and Villavallelonga. The main office is temporarily situated in Pescasseroli, Viale Santa Lucia. ℘0863 91 131. www.parcoabruzzo.it.

A nature reserve was founded in 1923 to protect the region's fauna, flora and landscapes. The park extends over

Parco Nazionale d'Abruzzo, Lazio e Molise

© De Agostini Picture Library/Fototeca ENIT

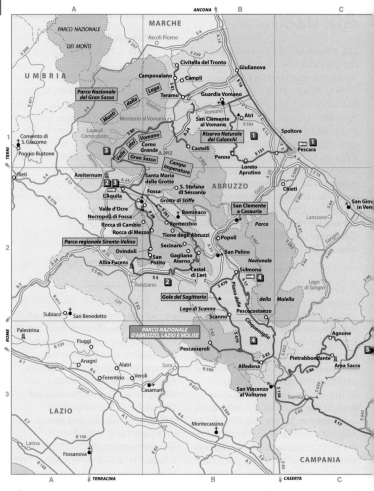

40 000ha/100 000 acres, not including the 4 500ha/11 119 acres of the Mainarde territory (in the Molise region), and is surrounded by an external protected area of 60 000ha/150 000 acres. Two-thirds of the park is forest area that offers the last refuge for animals that once lived in the Apennine range: brown bears, Apennine wolves, Abruzzi chamois, wild cats and royal eagles. **Pescasseroli** is the principal town in the Sangro Valley.

L'AQUILA★
Airport: L'Aquila–Preturo. ⓘVia Carlo I d'Angiò 23. ℘0862 196 09 97. www.comune.laquila.gov.it, www.abruzzoturismo.it.

Overlooked by Gran Sasso, the highest massif in Abruzzo, this town had until recently a wealth of artistic treasures. Tragically, on 6 April 2009, the region was shaken by a 6.3 degree magnitude earthquake with L'Aquila near the epicentre.

Nearly 300 people died in the quake and much of the city's cultural heritage, including some of the sights listed here, were reduced to rubble.

😊 *It is unclear at the time of publishing whether restoring L'Aquila's treasures will be possible. A number of companies and countries have pledged support to help rebuild important sights. In light of the ongoing rebuilding process, we have chosen to retain sight descriptions.*

ADRIATIC SEA

MOLISE

Vasto

Termoli

Madonna di Canteto

Lago del Liscione

PUGLIA

Lago di Occhito

Campobasso

Lucera

Altilia Saepinum

Troia

BENEVENTO

Some of the following sights have either full or limited closures.

A BIT OF HISTORY

According to legend, L'Aquila was founded in the 13C when the inhabitants of 99 castles in the valley at the foot of the Gran Sasso joined forces to form a city in which each castle had a corresponding church, square and fountain. Caught up in the vicissitudes of the Kingdom of Naples, L'Aquila was besieged, destroyed and rebuilt several times until the 15C when it became the second most important city of the Kingdom. Rich in splendid monuments, it also had a resurgence thanks to the commerce all over Europe of saffron, "red gold",

which grows on the plateaux of Navelli. This was the period in which St Bernardino of Siena (who died in L'Aquila in 1444) resided in the city; the initials IHS (Iesus Hominum Salvator – Jesus Saviour of Mankind), marked on several doorways, bear witness to his presence.

Basilica di Santa Maria di Collemaggio★★

Rebuilding in process. Partially reopen daily 9am–1pm. ℘0862 40 41 67. www.basilicacollemaggio.it.

Begun in 1287, the basilica was constructed in the Romanesque style on the initiative of Pietro da Morrone, the future Pope **Celestine V**, who was crowned there in 1294.

The ample, horizontally crenellated **façade★★**, adorned with geometrical patterns in white and pink stone, is pierced with rose windows. Porta Santa, an ornate Romanesque doorway, is on the left side and the interior houses the 16C Lombard-Renaissance-style tomb of Pope St Celestine V.

Chiesa di San Bernardino★★

Reopened in 2015. To visit call ℘0862 20 03 90. www.basilicasanbernardino.it.

This church, a masterpiece of **Cola dell'Amatrice** (1527), has a majestic and rich **façade★★** which is articulated by entablatures that give definition to the three orders of double columns (Ionic, Doric and Corinthian).

The spacious interior, in the form of a Latin cross, contains the **mausoleum of St Bernardino★**, adorned with figures by local sculptor Silvestro dell'Aquila, as is the **tomb★** of Maria Pereira.

Castello★

Closed. Exterior rebuilding in progress.

Built in the 16C by Pirro Luigi Escribà, who also designed Castel Sant'Elmo in Naples, this square castle is a good example of 16C military architecture. The great rooms now house the **Museo Nazionale d'Abruzzo★★**. On the ground floor are the **Archidiskodon Meridionalis Vestinus**, the fossil remains of an ancestor of the elephant that lived one

Abdication

Pietro da Morrone (1215–96), hermit and founder of the Celestine order of the Morronese Abbey near Sulmona, was elected Pope in September 1294. Overwhelmed by the intrigues and plots of the pontifical court, Pope Celestine V abdicated after only a few months and was banished to the castle of Fumone by his successor, Boniface VIII. He died there shortly afterwards and in 1313 was canonised by Pope Clement V.

million years ago, and some interesting exhibits from Roman times, including the **Calendario Amiterno**. On the first floor the section on **Sacred Art** (12C–17C) is the core of the museum and displays significant examples of painting, sculpture and decorative arts from Abruzzi. Note the polychrome wooden sculptures; the **Croce processionale★**, a masterpiece of workmanship in gold; and the statue of St Sebastian by Silvestro d'Aquila.

SULMONA★

Train: Sulmona (L'Aquila 1hr). ☑ Corso Ovidio 208, 67039 Sulmona (AQ). ℰ0864 21 02 16. www.comune.sulmona.aq.it. Sulmona lies at the head of a fertile basin framed by majestic mountains. It was the birthplace of the Roman poet Ovid, who immortalised his origins in the verse *Sulmo Mihi Patria Est* (hence the acronym SMPE on the town's emblem).

Porta Napoli★
Southern town gateway.
This Gothic gate has 14C historiated capitals. The exterior is adorned with gilded bosses, Angevin coats of arms and Roman low reliefs. **Corso Ovidio**, which cuts through the medieval heart of the city, starts here.

Piazza Garibaldi
The square is bordered by the pointed arches of the 13C **aqueduct★**, the Baroque corner of Santa Chiara and the Gothic doorway of San Filippo. At Easter, the feast of the *Madonna che scappa in piazza* is celebrated when a statue of the Virgin is rushed to a meeting with the Risen Christ.
This square hosts a large, colourful market on Wednesdays and Saturdays.

Chiesa di San Francesco della Scarpa
This church was erected in the 13C by Franciscan monks who wore shoes (hence its name, *scarpa*, the Italian word for "shoe"). It has a Romanesque **doorway★** on Corso Ovidio.

Palazzo dell'Annunziata★★
Built by a Brotherhood of Penitents from 1415, the palace constitutes a synthesis of Gothic (the doorway with statues of the Virgin and St Michael, the ornate **trefoil openings★** and statues of four Doctors of the Church), Renaissance (the middle doorway, the right portal and the twin openings) and Baroque art (the theatrical façade of the adjacent church). There is a carved **frieze★** halfway up the façade. Inside is the **Museo Civico** (access only

---

Colourful Little Delicacies

From the windows of Corso Ovidio colourful and unusual bunches of flowers peep out: these are the famous confetti, Sulmona sweets which were created at the end of the 15C. A taste of these confetti will hold some pleasant surprises in store: a glacé of pure sugar hides Sicilian almonds, hazelnuts, chocolate, candied fruit and rosolio. To find out more, go to the small museum, Museo dell'Arte e della Tecnologia confettiera, at the Pelino factory in Via Introdacqua 55. *Via Stazione Introdacqua 55.* Tours only, Mon–Sat 8.30am–12.30pm and 3–7pm. Closed public hols. ℰ0864 21 00 47. http://confettimariopelino.com.

to archeologic section, roman area;Tue–Sun 9am–1pm, Thu 9am–1pm and 3.30–6.30pm; free; www.comune.sulmona.aq.it).

Basilica di San Pelino★

13km/8mi NW, near the village of Corfinio. Open daily. Donation recommended. ℘0864 72 81 20.
This bishop's seat was erected in the 11C and 12C. The rear of the basilica offers a good view of the **apse complex★**. The interior houses a 12C **ambo**.

🚗 DRIVING TOURS

1 BEACHES AND BAYS

From Pescara. Approximately 140km/87mi. Allow 1 day.

▶ From **Pescara**, take the S 165 W for 5km/3mi to Spoltore.

The village of **Spoltore** is perched on a plain that dominates the valley of Pescara. As well as beautiful views, the 16C and 17C Palazzo Castiglioni, with its impressive entrance, is worth a visit.

▶ Leaving Spoltore, drive 12km/7.4mi; turn right onto the S 16b. Take the SR 151 towards Cappelle sul Tavo.

Formerly known as Castrum Laureti, the village of **Loreto Aprutino** spills down the hill surrounded by olive trees producing the Olio Extravergine d'Oliva Aprutino Pescarese. Via del Baio is flanked by 19C palaces, specifically the Palazzo Casamarte, housing one of the most important private libraries in Abruzzo, and the Amorotti Castelletto, a Gothic palazzo home to the Museo dell'Olio.

▶ Follow the SR 151 9km/5.6mi W of Loreto Aprutino until you reach Penne.

The historic centre of **Penne** is characterised by brick streets and houses. The 12C church of Santa Maria in Colleromano has medieval arches and important frescoes and paintings. The 10C Duomo

houses the Diocesan Museum and an 8C crypt.

▶ Take the S 81 17km/10.6mi N, then follow signs on the SP 31 and SP 553 to Atri.

Atri

The ancient settlement of *Hatria-Picena*, founded by an Italic people and later becoming a Roman colony, has a beautiful hillside setting overlooking the Adriatic Sea. The historic centre has splendid medieval, Renaissance and Baroque buildings as well as scenic vistas.

Cathedral★ – Open 7am–12.30pm and 3.30–7pm. ℘085 87 0000. www.cattedraleatri.it Built in the 13C–14C on the foundations of a Roman edifice, the cathedral is a fine example of the transitional Romanesque-Gothic style, with a series of sculpted **doorways★** that became a model for later work. The **interior** has tall Gothic arches and, in the apse, **frescoes★★** by Abruzzi artist **Andrea de Litio** (1450–73) that depict scenes from the life of Joachim and Mary.

The adjoining cloisters lead to the Roman cistern and the **Chapter Museum** with its collection of Abruzzi ceramics.

☺ *In Piazza Duomo traces of the ancient Roman city are visible.*

▶ Turn right on the SP 553 and drive 2km/1.2mi N of Atri on the S 353.

Riserva Naturale dei Calanchi★★

Calanchi, known locally as *scrimoini* (streaks), are the result of the natural phenomenon that occurred in the Tertiary Era when a plateau was eroded by water. Comparable to scenes from Dante's *Inferno*, this lunar landscape is characterised by precipices descending for hundreds of metres, sparse vegetation and white sediment. This is a good spot for a guided hike, which must be reserved with a park ranger (www.riservacalanchidiatri.it).

▶ Take the S 150 5km/3mi NW until you reach San Clemente al Vomano.

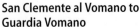

San Clemente al Vomano to Guardia Vomano

To visit, send an e-mail to:
info@sanclementealvomano.it.
Via San Clemente 10.
www.sanclementealvomano.it.
This 9C church has been rebuilt several times over the years. The Classical 12C portal opens into a surprisingly simple interior. Sadly, little remains of the frescoes that once covered the walls and apse, but bits of their former glory make surprise appearances throughout the church. The altar is enriched with Oriental motifs and inlaid terra-cotta.

Giulianova

This 16C city dominates this part of the Adriatic coastline and is a popular holiday destination.

2 PARCO REGIONALE SIRENTE-VELINO★★

From L'Aquila. 140km/87mi. Allow 1 day to explore the valley and park.

The park was created in 1989 and has 50 000 ha/123 548 acres of diverse landscape, from the limestone mountains of Velino (2 487m/ 8 160ft) to hills and rivers, each with its unique type of fauna and vegetation. The Rocche Plateau and Aterno River separate the two massifs – the Velino and Sirente – and are marked by caves, gorges and canyons. The Sirente crater, a 140m/460ft lake that was formed in the 4C by a meteor impact, is interesting. Castelvecchio Subequo is the heart of Parco Sirente-Velino and is a nice place from which to explore the area. For excursions and outdoor sporting activities, visit the tourist office in L'Aquila (see p192).

▷ Take the SR 5bis to the S 37 for 10km/6.2mi and follow signs to Valle d'Ocre.

This is a scenic drive along the S 5a through the **Valle d'Ocre** area. The ruins of the village and fortified castle are on a hill overlooking the Aterno Valley and create a magnificent landscape.

▷ Leaving Valle d'Ocre, drive 5km/3mi on the S 5b.

The charming village of **Fossa** suffered major damage from the 2009 earthquake and is best known for the little church **Santa Maria ad Cryptas★**, whose walls are decorated in beautiful 13C and 14C frescoes. At the **Necropoli di Fossa★** 500 graves were discovered in a 2 000sq m/2 390sq yd necropolis that dates to the Iron Age.

▷ From Fossa, drive S 70km/43.5mi. Follow signs to the A 24, then take the A 25/E 80.

Alba Fucens★ are the **excavations** of a Roman colony founded in 303 BC. Amid the foundations are the remains of a basilica, the forum, baths, a covered market complete with paved streets, wells, latrines and an **amphitheatre**. Above the ruins rises the 12C **church of San Pietro★**, erected on the remains of a 3C BC temple of Apollo. The **interior** houses two notable examples of **Cosmati** work, unusual in Romanesque Abruzzi buildings: the **ambo★★** and the **iconostasis★★** of the 13C. Daily from dawn to dusk. Free. ℘0863 44 96 42 or 339 44 58 783 (mobile). www.albafucens.info.

▷ Drive 15km/9.3mi NE of Alba Fucens.

Bominaco★

Churches: open daily 9am–1pm and 2–7pm (winter 4pm). ℘0862 93 764.. Donations welcome.

Two Romanesque churches stand 500m/1 640ft above the hamlet of Bominaco, and are all that remain of a Benedictine monastery that was destroyed in the 15C. The church of **San Pellegrino★** is a 13C oratory decorated with contemporary **frescoes★** portraying the Life of Christ and St Pellegrino. Two elegant 10C *plutei* demarcate the chancel whose central wall is decorated with the **Calendario Bominacense**, depicting courtly scenes that were influenced by French tradition. The **Church of Santa Maria Assunta★** (11C and 12C) has beautiful ornamented apses. The interior, with its Benedictine imprint, has a graceful Romanesque colonnade. Note the striking 12C **ambo**★.

▶ Leaving Bominaco, drive 4km/2.5mi to San Demetrio ne' Vestini on the SP 40 and SR 261.

Grotte di Stiffe★

Open daily 10am–1pm and 3–6pm. 10€. ✆0862 86 142. www.grottestiffe.it. One of the most impressive karst landscapes in the region. The waterfall is spectacular.

③ GRAN SASSO★★

From L'Aquila to Civitella del Tronto. 160km/99.4mi. Allow half a day, excluding tour of L'Aquila and the surrounding area.

Gran Sasso is the highest massif in the Abruzzi and its main peak is **Corno Grande** (2 912m/9 554ft). On the northern side, spines with many gullies slope away gently, while on the southern face Gran Sasso drops to the great glacial plateaux edged by deep valleys.

L'Aquila★

↪See L'Aquila, p192.

Campo Imperatore★★

↪Access by cablecar (funivia) Fonte Cerreto Assergi. Open daily 8.30am–dusk (Sun and public hols open 8am). Closed a period in Jun and Oct. 10€ (15€ Sun and public hols) return ticket (round trip). ✆0862 60 61 43 (winter) or 0862 40 00 07. Access also by car on the S 17 (closed winter).
The road passes through velvety rounded mountains and craggy peaks up to a vast meadow grazed by sheep and horses. Mussolini escaped from here in 1943 in a daring raid by German airmen.

▶ Return to Fonte Cerreto Assergi, follow signs for the Valico delle Capannelle road (open May–Nov); then take the S 80 to Montorio al Vomano.

The road then skirts the lower slopes of the Gran Sasso, as it follows the long green valley, **Valle del Vomano**★★, before entering the magnificent gorges with their striking stratified rock walls.

▶ Leave Montorio and turn right on the S 491. At Isola del Gran Sasso follow signs for Castelli.

Castelli★, at the foot of Monte Camicia, has been famous since the 13C for its ceramics, of which the 17C **ceiling**★ in the **Church of San Donato** is a fine example. Just outside town, the 17C ex-Franciscan convent housed the **Museo delle Ceramiche** . The convent closed after the earthquake and the museum is temporarily housed in the Palazzo Municipale dell'Artigianato, open 10am–1pm Sat–Sun also 3–6pm. Closed Mon. ✆0861 97 91 42.

▶ Drive 40km/24.8mi N of Castelli. Take the A 24 exit at Teramo.

Twenty kilometres from the Adriatic Sea on the slopes of the Gran Sasso, **Teramo**★ is on a plateau between the Tordino and Vezzoli rivers. A number of interesting ruins were discovered here, most importantly, the Amphitheatre, built in the second half of the 1C BC, and Augustus' theatre. The 12C Cattedrale di San Bernado has a modern relief sculpture on the **façade**★ and a Romanesque-Gothic portal.

▶ Drive 15km/9.3mi N of Teramo on the S 81, then take the S 262 (first right).

Campli's★ main square is filled with beautiful buildings. The 14C **Collegiata di Santa Maria in Platea**★★ has a stunning 18C painted ceiling. Two steps beneath the arches of a former Franciscan convent is the **Museo Archeologico Nazionale** (Piazza San Francesco I; open Tue–Sun 9am–8pm; 2€), which holds protohistoric finds from the town's necropolis. The **Chiesa di San Giovanni Battista** is worth the detour, particularly for its **holy staircase**★.

🚗 Drive 7km/4.3mi N of Campli.

Some of the 600 graves from the necropolis are visible from the **Campovalano** Plains at the foot of Mount dei Fiori.

▶ Take the first route on the right.

The village of **Civitella del Tronto**★ on a travertine mountain sits 645m/2 116ft above the sea and enjoys a splendid **setting**★★. Its winding streets are lined with religious and civic architecture from the 16C–17C.

4 GREAT PLATEAUX

Round trip from Sulmona. 140km/87mi. Allow 1 day excluding tour of Sulmona.

Sulmona★
🖝 *See Sulmona, p194.*

Piano delle Cinquemiglia

Beyond Sulmona, part of the road has nice views and eventually reaches the **Piano delle Cinquemiglia**, the largest plateau between Sulmona and Castel di Sangro. With an average altitude of 1 200m/3 937ft, the plateau was the obligatory stagecoach route to Naples.

▶ Take the S 84 to the left.

Pescocostanzo★ is a flourishing craft village specialising in wrought-iron work, gold, woodwork and lace. The **Collegiate Church of Santa Maria del Colle** was built to a Renaissance plan but has Romanesque features and Baroque additions *(organ loft and grille)*. 8am–noon, 4.30–6pm (summer 7pm). Donations welcome. 𝒫0864 641 430. The houses of the small town of **Alfedena**★ are grouped about the ruined castle. Paths lead to the ancient city of Alfedena with its cyclopean walls. A town of 2 000 people, **Pescasseroli** is a popular winter resort (1 167m/3 829ft) and is surrounded by forests.

Scanno★ overlooks the lovely **Lago di Scanno**★. The steep streets are lined with old houses and churches. Towards Anversa degli Abruzzi the road is hollowed out of the rock, skirts deep gorges (**Gole del Sagittario**★★) and affords 10km/6.2mi of spectacular nature.

ADDITIONAL SIGHTS
Chieti
🖝 63km/39.2mi E of L'Aquila.
Train: Chieti (Sulmona 55 mins).

Chieti is built on an olive-tree covered hill and is enclosed by mountains. Due to its panoramic position it is known as "Abruzzo's balcony". **Corso Marrucino**, bordered by elegant arcades, is the town's principal street.

The **Museo Archeologico Nazionale d'Abruzzo**★★ (open Tue–Suat 9am–8pm, Sun and public hols open 10.30am; last admission 30min before closing; 4€; 𝒫0871 33 16 68) is in the Neoclassical town hall (**Villa Comunale**). It is set in lovely **gardens**★ and has an important collection of Abruzzi artefacts. Statues and portraits (note the **Seated Hercules** discovered at Alba Fucens) relate local history.

An interesting coin display formed by the Sulmonese **Giovanni Pansa** (ex-votos, domestic objects and bronze figures such as the **Venafro Hercules**) and the stunning bone **bier**★ (1C BC–1C AD) complete the selection. The 6C BC **Warrior of Capestrano**★★ symbolises the Abruzzi, the most notable artefact of Picenum civilisation.

Abbazia di San Clemente a Casauria★★
🖝 30km/18.6mi SW of Chieti on the SS 5. Open 9am–1.30pm. 𝒫085 88 85 162. www.sanclementeacesauria. beniculturali.it.

This 9C abbey was founded for Emperor Ludovic II. After Saracen attacks it was restored in the 12C by Cistercian monks in a Romanesque-Gothic style. Inside, note the **paschal candelabrum**★ and 12C **pulpit**★★★; these are two of the best examples of Romanesque style in Abruzzi. The altar consists of an early Christian tomb (5C) and is surmounted by a Romanesque **ciborium**★★★.

Abbazia di San Giovanni in Venere

⬤ 35km/21.8mi SE of Pescara on the S 16. Call for opening times ℰ0872 60 132. www.sangiovanninvenere.it.
This 8C abbey is on the site of a temple dedicated to Venus and was remodelled in the 13C. It has a panoramic **setting★**. On the façade, note the 13C **Portale della Luna★** with reliefs depicting sacred and profane subjects.

Molise

Molise is a land of passage for movement of cattle, armies and travellers. Mountains dominate and inhabitants have looked to them as a refuge: strongholds, fortified castles and villages nestle on hillsides.

🚗 DRIVING TOUR

⑤ TOUR OF MOLISE

Round trip. 240km/150mi. Allow 2 days.

Termoli★ is the departure point for the Tremiti Islands. It has a 13C **castle** and alleys that wind to the **cathedral★★**.

⬤ W on the S 16 for Salvo Marina; turn left on the S 650 for Roccavivara.

Santa Maria di Canneto is an 8C monastery and an expression of Lombard-Cassinese culture, including an 8C **pulpit★** and a 10C **altarpiece★**.

⬤ Continue on the S 650 towards Castelveriino/Agnone.

The village of **Agnone** is home to the 10C **Fonderia Pontificia Marinelli**, the oldest bell factory in the world (complete with bell tuner), that now houses the **Museo Internazionale della Campana** (♿guided visits only, noon and 4pm, Aug also 11am and 5pm; closed Sun pm, Easter, 25 Dec. ℰ0865 78 235; www.campanemarinelli.com).

⬤ Take the S 86 and turn left.

- ♿ **Michelin Map:** 564 A–C 24–27.
- 🅸 **Info:** Castello Monforte, 86100 Campobasso. ℰ0874 98 397. www.regione.molise.it.
- ⬤ **Location:** Molise is shaped like a wedge between the Apennines, the sea and Abruzzo and Puglia. The main access road is the A 14.
- ⬤ **Train:** Termoli (Foggia airport 45 mins).

The **Sanctuary of Pietrabbondante★** (open Tue–Sun 10am–3.30pm. ℰ0865 76 129) was a sacred site for the Samnites and a stunning theatre with ergonomically designed seats.

⬤ Follow directions to Isernia.

San Vincenzo al Volturno
Beautiful views of the Mainarde Mountains and ongoing excavations.
www.sanvincenzoalvolturno.it.

⬤ S 158 in the direction of Isernia, then S 17 towards Bojano.

Altilia Saepinum★
Access free. ℰ0874 79 02 07.
The ruins of *Saepinum* rise in the middle of the town founded by Samnites. Enter Porta di Terravecchia gateway south of *cardo*, the city's main street. The **Porta di Boiano rises east★**. The **theatre★** is against the inner face of the wall.

Naples and Campania

Napoli and Campania. Major City: Naples

Official Website: www.incampania.com

Campania owes its rich heritage to several civilisations. Colonised by the ancient Greeks and Romans, the region has also come under the jurisdiction of the French/Spanish Bourbons, who, as rulers of the Kingdom of Naples, constructed a spectacular Baroque palace at Caserta. Other palaces, or *palazzi*, built during the Bourbon era are sprinkled throughout the city of Naples, a chaotic but cultured metropolis in the shadow of Mount Vesuvius. Many visitors to sunny Campania brave the frenzy of Italy's third-largest city for a short while before heading off to more subdued settings such as the Island of Capri or the hilltop village of Ravello on the Amalfi Coast. The sombre ruins at Pompeii, approximately 25km/15mi from Naples, draw some of the largest crowds in Italy.

Highlights

1 Taste Naples' contribution to world cuisine – **pizza** (p217)

2 Hike the slopes of **Mount Vesuvius** (p223)

3 Tour eerie Roman ruins at **Pompeii** (p231)

4 Mingle with the jet set on the **Island of Capri** (p240)

5 Linger in the lavish gardens of the **Royal Palace of Caserta** (p253)

Fertile Volcanic Landscapes

Campania forms a fertile crescent around the **Bay of Naples**. The charm and mystery once stirred the imagination of the ancients. The area is dominated by **Mount Vesuvius**. The still-active volcano, which last erupted in 1944, is responsible for the demise of several settlements during Roman times, evidence of which is visible at **Pompeii** and **Herculaneum**.

It is Campania's volcanic soil, however, that accounts for the lush countryside and the bountiful growth of hemp, tobacco, cereals, olive groves, lemon trees and vineyards.

Although the coast is struggling to retain its charm through all of the new building developments, the **Sorrento Peninsula** and the **Island of Capri** are two notable beauty spots.

Naples and the Mount Vesuvius

© C. Bowman/age fotostock

Naples★★★

Napoli

Naples is a universe of its own, imbued with fantasy and fatalism, superstition and splendour. It is a city of a thousand faces: chaotic and heaving with traffic, yet rich with history, art and culture, ready to surrender its mysteries to anyone who scratches the surface.
Then there is the lovely bay with its horizon bounded by Posillipo, the islands, the Sorrento Peninsula and lofty Vesuvius; it is one of the most beautiful in the world. Cradled within, its charms and architectural splendours have been praised by poets and writers. UNESCO included the historic centre of the city in its 1995 World Heritage List.

NAPLES TODAY

While other Italian cities are defined by their great buildings, Naples lives forever in the shadow of Mount Vesuvius, the volcano that destroyed Pompeii and the surrounding Roman enclaves more than 2 000 years ago. The still-active mountain, framed by the blue waters of the Bay of Naples, makes for a stunning backdrop as well as a metaphor for the city's hot-blooded energy.
From the loud, zooming traffic crowding Naples' streets to the fast-talking denizens, Naples moves at a hurried pace – perhaps the legacy of living on the edge of a cauldron. It is no wonder, then, that pizza – a food that one can easily eat on the go – originated and was perfected in this vibrant city.

A BIT OF HISTORY

According to legend, the siren Parthenope gave her name to a town which had sprung up round her tomb, which is why Naples is called the Parthenopaean City. Naples was named *Neapolis*, conquered by the Romans in the 4C BC. Inhabitants of Rome such as Virgil, Augustus and Tiberius used to winter there, but the Neapolitans retained the Greek

▶ **Population:** 1 000 000
⟡ **Michelin Map:**
564 E 24 –San Campania.
🛈 **Info:** Via San Carlo 9. ℘081 40 23 94. Piazza del Gesù. ℘081 55 12 701. www.inaples.it.
◐ **Location:** The main access roads to Naples include the A 1, Autostrada del Sole, the A 3 for those arriving from the south and the A 16, linking Naples to the Adriatic.
🅿 **Parking:** Proceed on foot and public transport, as Naples' traffic is among Italy's – and possibly the world's – fiercest.
👁 **Don't Miss:** Spaccanapoli, the treasures of the Museo Archeologico Nazionale and the Galleria Nazionale di Capodimonte, the Carthusian monastery of Certosa di San Martino, Piazza del Plebiscito and the Porto di Santa Lucia and the pretty port and views of Mergellina.
🕐 **Timing:** Dedicate at least three days to exploring the city. Allow around half a day for the Spaccanapoli and the Decumanus Maximus alone.
👪 **Kids:** The Bible illustrations in a nutshell at Chiesa di San Lorenzo Maggiore, the collections of cribs at the museum at Certosa di San Martino and the door knockers at Palazzo Reale.

customs until the Empire's decline. Since the 12C, seven princely dynasties have reigned over Naples. The Normans, Hohenstaufens, Angevins, Aragonese, Spanish and Bourbons ruled until the end of the 18C.
The French Revolution of 1789 brought in French troops, and in 1799 a **Parthenopaean Republic** was set up, followed

GETTING AROUND

It is preferable to get to Naples by train or plane as traffic in the city is chaotic and few hotels have garages. Capodichino Airport, 𝄞081 78 96 767; www.gesac.it/en (for general information), is 6km/3.7mi away from the city. Buses to Naples include no.14 (the terminus is in Piazza Garibaldi where the railway station is) and no. 3 S, which stops at the station and at Molo Beverello.

Naples has a generally good network of public transport although overground transport does fall prey to traffic, which can be chock-a-block.

⊘Information listed is intended for guidance only; for details check transport maps available from tourist offices.

BY TRAIN – The Cumana and Circumflegrea trains (terminus in Piazza Montesanto) connect Naples to Bagnoli and the Campi Flegrei district. The Circumvesuviana train (terminus in Corso Garibaldi) has swift connections to Herculaneum, Pompeii, Castellammare, Vico Equense and Sorrento.

BY UNDERGROUND – The Metropolitana FS crosses the city vertically from Piazza Garibaldi to Pozzuoli, while the Metropolitana collinare from Piazza Vanvitelli goes up to Piscinola/Secondigliano. The new link goes from Piazza Vanvitelli to the Museo Archeologico.

BY FUNICULAR RAILWAY – Three routes connect to the Vomero: the Funicolare centrale (Via Toledo–Piazza Fuga), the Funicolare di Chiaia (Via del Parco Margherita–Via Cimarosa) and the Funicolare di Montesanto (Piazza Montesanto–Via Morghen).

The Funicolare di Mergellina links Via Mergellina to Via Manzoni.

TICKETS – "TIC" tickets allow travel on buses, trams, the funicular railway and the underground (both the Metropolitana FS and the Metropolitana collinare). There are many types of ticket: one-run tickets (1€), 90min tickets (1.50€), 1-day tickets (4.50€), weekly tickets (15.80€) and monthly passes (42€). Visit www.unicocampania.it.

BY RADIOTAXI – Free: 𝄞081 55 15 151, Partenope: 𝄞081 55 60 202 and Consortaxi: 𝄞081 551 53 35.

SEA CONNECTIONS – Ferry and hovercraft crossings to Capri, Ischia, Procida, the Amalfi Coast and Sorrento leave from Molo Beverello and Mergellina port. Boats depart from Molo Angioino for Sardinia and Sicily.

Tirrenia (to Cagliari and Palermo): 𝄞892 123. www.tirrenia.it.

Alilauro (to Ischia Porto, Forio, Capri, Sorrento, Isole Eolie). 𝄞081 49 72 206. www.alilauro.it. Aliscafi SNAV: to Ischia, Procida, Capri, Palermo and Isole Eolie. 𝄞081 42 85 555. www.snav.it. **Navigazione Libera del Golfo** (to Capri, Sorrento, Amalfi Coast and Isole Pontine): **Molo Beverello**, Napoli. 𝄞081 55 20 763. www.navlib.it.

SIGHTSEEING

The Campania Artecard is available for 3 *(21€)* or 7 days *(34€)*, and gives free or discounted entry into many of the principal museums and archaeological sites in Naples and the Campania region, and discounts on other events and attractions. The card includes three days of free public transport. www.campaniaartecard.it.

by a French kingdom (1806–15) under Bonaparte (Napoleon's brother) and afterwards Joachim Murat (Napoleon's brother-in-law), who promoted excellent reforms. From 1815 to 1860 the Bourbons remained in power despite two serious revolts.

ART IN NAPLES
A Royal Patron of the Arts

Under the princes of the House of Anjou, Naples was endowed with many ecclesiastical buildings, influenced by the French-Gothic style. "**Robert the Wise**" of Anjou (1309–43) attracted

A Lot of Rubbish

Naples' recent foray into the international spotlight has not been flattering. A rubbish problem that had been building for years developed into a crisis in 2007, when municipal workers refused to collect waste to protest the city's overflowing landfills. Since then thousands of tonnes of rubbish has built up on Naples' streets, creating an unsightly, smelly mess and a public health hazard. Residents blame their politicians for the disaster, but many believe the Camorra, Naples' powerful organised crime syndicate which amassed millions in the waste disposal business, is pulling the strings. The city is still plagued by garbage, despite warnings of EU sanctions. In 2011 the mayor agreed to adopt a zero-waste strategy, although unrecycled waste is shipped to the Netherlands.

poets, scholars and artists from regions of Italy to his court in Naples. Boccaccio spent part of his youth in Naples where he fell in love with Fiammetta, whom some believe to have been the king's own daughter. His friend Petrarch also spent time in this city. In 1324 Robert the Wise brought the Sienese sculptor **Tino di Camaino** to adorn many of the churches with his monumental tombs. Other churches were embellished with frescoes by the Roman artist Pietro Cavallini, and later by Giotto whose works have unfortunately disappeared.

The Neapolitan School of Painting (17C–early-18C)

The busiest period in Neapolitan painting was the 17C, which began with the arrival in Naples in 1607 of the great innovator in painting **Caravaggio**. The master's style was bold and realistic: he often used real people as models for his crowd scenes. He used chiaroscuro with dramatic effect with light playing a fundamental part. So a new school of painting flourished, its members greatly inspired by the master.

The principal followers were Artemisia Gentileschi, the Spaniard **José de Ribera** alias Spagnoletto, **Giovanni Battista Caracciolo** and the Calabrian Mattia Preti. One pupil who differed greatly from the others was **Luca Giordano** whose spirited compositions were full of light. His decorative work heralds the painting of the 18C. **Francesco Solimena** perpetuated Giordano's style but he was also influenced by the more sombre style

of Mattia Preti and by Classicism. His paintings are characterised by chiaroscuro effects which lend a strong balance to the use of space.

The Baroque Period

Numerous architects built fine Baroque buildings in Naples and the surrounding area. **Ferdinando Sanfelice** (1675–1748) had a highly inventive and theatrical approach to staircases, which he placed at the far end of the courtyard where they became the palace's most important decorative feature. It was, however, **Luigi Vanvitelli** (1700–73) who was the greatest Neapolitan architect of the 18C.

The Bourbon King Charles III entrusted Vanvitelli with the project to build another Versailles at Caserta (&see Reggia di CASERTA). It was in the 17C that Naples began to specialise in the marvellous **Christmas mangers** (presepi).

WALKING TOUR

Chiesa di Sant'Anna dei Lombardi

Piazza Monteoliveto 3. Open Mon–Sat 9am–1pm and 4–6pm. &081 55 13 333. This Renaissance church, to St Anne of the Lombards, is rich in contemporary Florentine **sculpture★**.

Piazza del Gesù Nuovo

In the centre of the piazza stands a monument dedicated to the Immaculate Conception that pays tribute to

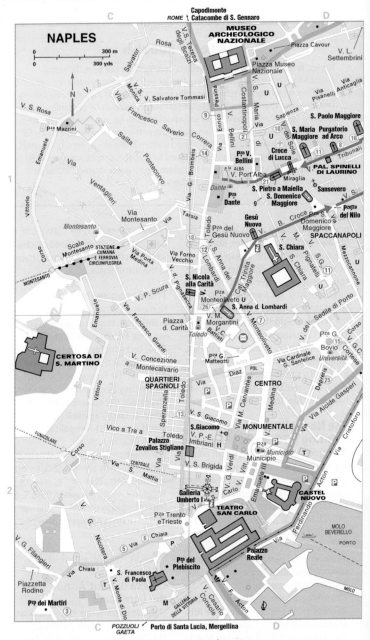

NAPLES

Capodimonte
ROME \ Catacombe di S. Gennaro

MUSEO
ARCHEOLOGICO
NAZIONALE

0   300 m
0   300 yds

N

the victims of the plague of 1656. On the north is the church of Gesù Nuovo, whose beautiful façade is from the original 15C palazzo. Inside is *The Expulsion of Heliodorus from the Temple* (1725), a Baroque masterpiece by Solimena. Enter via Benedetto Croce.

Chiesa di Santa Chiara★

Open 7.30am–1pm and 4.30–8pm.
📞081 79 71 231. Museum: Open
9.30am–5.30pm, Sun and public
hols 10am–2.30pm. 6€.
📞081 55 16 673.
www.monasterodisantachiara.com.

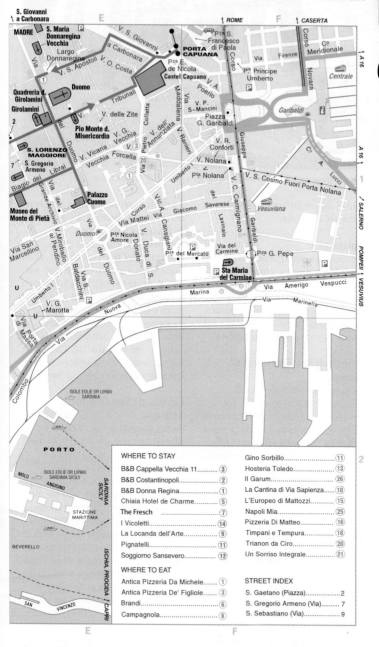

Sancia of Majorca, the wife of Robert the Wise of Anjou, had this Church of the Poor Clares built in the Provençal Gothic style. The interior was destroyed in the 1943 bombing and then rebuilt in its original form. A lofty nave, lit by narrow twin windows, opens onto nine chapels. At the end, memorials to the Anjou dynasty line the wall: including the **tomb★★** of Robert the Wise and on the right the tomb of Charles of Anjou, attributed to **Tino di Camaino**, who is also responsible for the **tomb★** of Marie de Valois *(near the south wall)*. To the

Detail of the majorca decoration in the cloisters, Chiesa di Santa Chiara

right of the presbytery a vestibule leads to the 14C **chancel**★.

Cloisters★★

The current layout is the work of Domenico Antonio Vaccaro, who, in the 18C, transformed the interior of the cloisters into a garden. He was also responsible for embellishing the wall of the portico, the seats and the columns that line the avenues with **majolica decoration**★.

Chiesa di San Domenico Maggiore

Piazza San Domenico Maggiore 8. Open daily. ℘081 45 92 98.
The interior of this church has both Gothic (**caryatids** by Tino di Camaino support a huge paschal candelabrum) and Baroque features. In the right side aisle, the second **chapel**★ has frescoes by Pietro Cavallini (1309). The 18C **sacristy**★ contains coffins of members of the court of Aragon *(in the balustrade)*.

Cappella Sansevero

Open 9.30am–6.30pm, Sun/holydays 9.30am–2pm, closed Tue. 7€. ℘081 55 18 470. www.museosansevero.it.
This 16C chapel was completely restored in the 18C by Raimondo de Sangro, an eccentric whose passion for alchemy and scientific study gave rise to a certain notoriety. There are even two skeletons complete with "petrified" circulatory system *(in an underground chamber, access from the south aisle)*.
In the chapel there are fine marble **sculptures**★: on either side of the choir are *Chastity* (the veiled woman) and *Despair* (symbolised by a man struggling with

a net); the central one depicts **Christ covered by a shroud**★, a masterpiece by **Giuseppe Sammartino**.
Just before Via S. Biagio dei Librai is **Piazzetta del Nilo**, which derives its name from a statue of the Nile. Further along, to the left, is Via S. Gregorio Armeno, lined with shops and workshops where the figurines for the Nativity scenes *(presepio)* are produced. The skills have been handed down from father to son since the 19C. These days the statuettes include modern figures. The area is charming around Christmas.

Chiesa di San Gregorio Armeno

Via San Gregorio Armeno 1. Open 9am–noon, Sat, Sun/holidays 9am–1pm. Cloyster: daily 9am–noon. Donation recommended. ℘081 55 20 186.
This church is dedicated to St Gregory. A spacious *atrium* leads into the **interior**★ of the church, which is opulently Baroque in style. The frescoes along the nave and in the cupola are the work of Luca Giordano. At the end of the nave are two huge Baroque **organs**. Of particular interest in the presbytery is the high altar with intarsia work in polychrome marble and, to the right, the *comunichino*, a brass screen from behind which the nuns followed Mass.
The **cloisters** *(access via the steps in the monastery)* have a splendid fountain *(centre)* decorated with statues of Christ and the Samaritan woman (late-18C).
At the end of Via San Gregorio Armeno is Via dei Tribunali, which runs into the Decumanus Maximus that dates back to ancient Rome.

Palazzo Como★

Via Duomo 288.
Museum open Tue–Sat 9am–6pm.
℘081 20 31 75.

This late-15C palace contains the **Museo Civico Filangieri**, which displays collections of armour, ceramics and porcelain, furniture and paintings.

Pio Monte della Misericordia★

Via Tribunali 253. Open 9am–2pm.
Closed Wed, Easter Sun, 25 Dec .7€.
℘081 44 69 44. www.piomontedella misericordia.it.

Founded in the 17C by seven noblemen from Naples, the Brotherhood of Mercy maintains six altarpieces whose subject relates to the charity of the institution. The Baroque church is adorned with *The Liberation of St Peter (La Liberazione di San Pietro)* by Caracciolo and **The Seven Works of Misericordoia** *(Le Sette Opere di Misericordia)*★★★, a stunning painting by Caravaggio. Upstairs, the gallery showcases an important series of paintings of Naples-born artist Francesco de Mura (1696–1782).

Castel Capuano

Via Concezio Muzii. Open Mon–Fri 9am–6.30pm. Free entrance.

The oldest castle in Naples inherited its name from Porta Capuana, one of four entrances to this ancient city.
The Norman fortress was built in 1165 and later revised by the House of Anjou. It was an Aragon residence before being turned into a prison, then a courthouse.

Porta Capuana★

This is one of the fortified gateways built in 1484 to the plans of Giuliano da Maiano. The nearby **Castel Capuano** was the former residence of Norman princes and the Hohenstaufens.

Chiesa di San Giovanni a Carbonara★

Via Carbonara 5. ℘081 29 58 73.
This 14C church holds the tomb of Ladislas of Anjou (15C) and a Crucifixion by Giorgio Vasari. From both sides of the choir, the Caracciolo del Sole Chapel with its blue majolica tile and the Caracciolo di Vico chapel are worth noting.

MADRE (Museo d'Arte Contemporanea DonnaREgina)

Via Settembrini 79. Open 10am–7.30pm, Sun 10am–8pm. Closed Tue. 7€; free entrance on Mon. ℘081 193 13 016. www.madrenapoli.it.

Transformed into a contemporary art museum by the Portuguese architect Alvaro Siza, this former palace opened as a museum in December 2005. The ground floor houses temporary exhibitions while the upper floors hold a collection of work from local and international artists, including Horn, Rauschenberg, Warhol, Klein and Koons.

Chiesa di Santa Maria Donnaregina Vecchia★

Vico Donnaregina 25. ℘081 44 67 99.
The cloisters are adorned with 18C faience. A Baroque church of the same name precedes the 14C Gothic church. Inside is the **tomb★** of the founder, Mary of Hungary, widow of Charles II of Anjou, by **Tino di Camaino**. The chancel is decorated with 14C **frescoes★**. The church holds exhibitions from MADRE.

Duomo★

Via Duomo 147. Open Mon–Sat 8.30am–1.30pm and 2.30–7.30pm, Sun 8am–1pm and 4.30–7.30pm.
℘081 44 90 97.

Built in the 14C, the Santa Maria Assunta cathedral was altered at a later date. Held in great veneration by the people, the **Tesoro di San Gennaro★** (Chapel of St Januarius), in a Baroque style, is preceded by a remarkable 17C bronze grille: behind the high altar are two glass phials containing the saint's blood which is supposed to liquefy, failing which disaster will befall the town. The Feast of the **Miracle of St Januarius** is held twice annually on the first Sunday in May and on 19 September. The dome is decorated with a Lanfranco fresco showing an admirable sense of movement.
The south transept houses an **Assumption** by Perugino and the Gothic **Minu-**

tolo Chapel, which has a beautiful 13C mosaic floor. The **succorpo** (crypt) is an elegant Renaissance structure.

A door in the north aisle gives access to the 4C **Basilica di Santa Restituta**, which was transformed in the Gothic period and again in the 17C. At the far end of the nave, the 5C **Baptistery of San Giovanni** is a fine structure containing **mosaics★★** of the same period. The apse on the left offers access to spectacular archaeological finds from the Greek, Roman and Middle Ages.

Museo del Tesoro di San Gennaro★

Via Duomo 149. Open 9am–5pm. 5€.
&081 29 49 80.
www.museosangennaro.it.

This museum holds documents, ex-voto, sculptures and paintings that were part of the treasure of San Gennaro, including the famous portrait of the saint by Solimena (1702). At the entrance are two vials containing the blood of the saint. Beautiful frescoes by Luca Giordano adorn the sacristy.

Monumento Nazionale dei Girolamini

Entrance from Via Duomo 142.
&081 229 45 71. Open Mon–Fri 8.30am–2pm. 7€. &081 22 94 571.
www.polomusealenapoli.beniculturali.
it/museo_gi/museo_gi.html

On the first floor of a convent, this collection has a considerable body of work from the Neapolitan, Roman and Florentine schools of the 16C–18C. These include paintings by Luca Giordano, G.B. Caracciolo, José de Ribera (**Apostles**), Guido Reni and Francesco Solimena (**Prophets**). The convent also houses a library with a splendid **18C room★**. The **Chiesa dei Girolamini** has works of art by Pietro Bernini (father of Lorenzo), Pietro da Cortona, Luca Giordano and Francesco Solimena.

A little further on is the church of **San Paolo Maggiore**, whose sacristy houses fine **frescoes★** by Solimena: *The Fall of Simon Magus and the Conversion of St Paul (on the side walls) are among this artist's masterpieces.* Further along,

to the right, is the church of **Purgatorio ad Arco** with its tiny underground cemetery *(cimitero sotterraneo)* where, until recently, the widespread practice of cleaning the bones was carried out for the purposes of receiving grace.

At no. 362 is **Palazzo Spinelli di Laurino** with an elliptical courtyard embellished by one of Sanfelice's staircases.

On the parvis of the church of **Santa Maria Maggiore**, also known as Pietrasanta, with its beautiful brick and majolica flooring (1764), rise the Renaissance chapel, Cappella Pontano, and, to the right, a fine 11C campanile.

Beyond **Croce di Lucca**, a 17C church with coffered ceiling of gilded wood, is the church of **San Pietro a Maiella**.

The tour ends in Piazza Bellini, which is a pleasant place to spend the evening. In the centre are the ruined Greek walls. A little further on is **Piazza Dante**, overlooked by a range of buildings, the work of Vanvitelli. *The beautiful Baptistery mosaics are worth visiting.*

Chiesa di San Lorenzo Maggiore★

Via Tribunali 316. Open 9.30am–5.30pm, Sun and public hols 9.30am–1.30pm. &081 21 10 860.
www.sanlorenzomaggiorenapoli.it.

The church of St Lawrence was built in the 14C over an early Christian church, the remains of which include the perimeter walls and columns from the nave. It is built on the plan of a Latin cross with an elegant **arch★** that spans the transept crossing. The nave, a simple, austere rectangular space (except for a chapel on the west wall which has kept its splendid Baroque additions), is a testament to the Franciscan influence. The **polygonal apse★** is an interesting specimen of French-Gothic architecture in southern Italy. It is surmounted by elegant arches crowned by twin bays and terminates in an ambulatory onto which open chapels with frescoes by disciples of Giotto. The north transept houses a large chapel dedicated to St Anthony and, on the altar, a painting of the saint surrounded by angels (1438), on a gold background. To the right of the high altar is the remarkable **tomb★** of Catherine of Austria, attributed to Tino di Camaino. From the cloisters of the church make for the 👥 **chapter house**, which houses a unique "illustrated Bible" – terra-cotta figurines placed inside nutshells which date from the 1950s. Access to the **ruins** is also from the cloisters. The ruins reveal a crucial part of Naples' Greco-Roman history: along with the forum there are traces of the treasury, bakery and *macellum* (large covered market).

Ruins (♿entrance from Vico dei Maiorani; Mon–Sat 9.30am–5.30 pm; Sun and public hols 9.30am–1.30pm).

Napoli Sotterranea★★

Associazione Napolisotterranea, Piazza San Gaetano 68. Guided tours in English daily 10am, noon, 2pm and 4pm, 6pm. 😐 Tour not recommended for people who suffer from claustrophobia. Info: 📞081 29 69 44.

www.napolisotterranea.org.

121 stairs lead 40m/131ft into the depths of the Naples' underground. It was from these caves that the Greeks scooped the tufa they would use to build the walls to surround the city. The remains of these 4C BC walls can be found in Piazza Bellini and on Via Foria. The Romans continued to build the underground during the Augustean Era by constructing an aqueduct (5m/16ft deep) along with underground tunnels that served as the city's streets.

From there the path leads through a narrow passage to several private cisterns built by the Greeks, which was transformed into a wine cellar and used until 1952 by the cloister San Gregorio Armeno.

The tour ends with the 6000-seat Roman theatre (1C–2C), discovered in 2002. Part of the ruins can be reached by a *basso* (modest living room ground floor). You can also see two arches of the monument along Via Anticaglia.

Continuing along the major *decumanus* (Via Tribunali), beyond Via San Gregorio Armeno on the right, the church of **Santa Maria delle Anime del Purgatorio ad Arco**, literally "St Mary of Souls-of-Purgatory"(Via Tribunali 39; church,

museum and tomb open Mon–Fri 9am–2pm, Sat 10am–5pm, tomb and museum only guided tours. 📞081 44 04 38) is rich in macabre symbols. It was once the headquarters of a fraternity responsible for celebrating Mass for the souls in purgatory and contains numerous bones.

Palazzo Spinelli di Laurino★

Via Tribunali 362.

This 18C Renaissance palace was created by architect Ferdinando Sanfelice and was commissioned by Trojano Spinelli VIII, Duke of Laurini. It is situated in an elliptical courtyard that is adorned with statues representing the eight virtues and medallions in bas-relief depicting mythological and pastoral scenes. Nearby the church of Santa Maria Maggiore (also known as "La Pietrasanta") has beautiful brick pavement and majolica (1764). The Renaissance **Cappella Pontano** (Via Tribunali 16, open Mon–Sat 9am–1pm) is on the left and on the right is the beautiful 11C red-brick tower from the original church.

Piazza Bellini

One of the most enjoyable spots in the historic centre, Piazza Bellini is the gathering place for Fine Arts students and the literary crowd. Remains of the town's Greek walls (4C BC) are still visible from the centre of square. The Palazzo Firrao has a façade with statues that represent Kings of Spain, in the 15C–17C.

Piazza Dante

This large semicircular square was modified in the 18C for the wife of the King of Naples by architect Luigi Vanvitelli and was called "Foro Carolino". After the unification of Italy, the name was changed to honour the poet Dante and a monument by Tito Angelini was erected in his honour. Today the piazza serves as a bridge between the old centre and the Spanish Quarter and is a noisy passage where many of Naples' youth play ball under the stern gaze of Dante.

CITY CENTRE★★

Europe's largest historic centre is a world of contradictions. Glamorous palm-tree-lined boulevards hide dingy houses while ornate palaces rise above trash-filled streets. This blend of chaos, glamour and grunge create an atmosphere that is uniquely Neapolitan. Piazza vendors peddle their creations from stalls as people rush through the alleyways, dashing on their scooters between Baroque churches and Renaissance palaces.

Chiesa di San Nicola alla Carità

Via Toledo 337. Open daily. ℘081 55 25 733. www.sannicolaallacarita.it.
Designed by Solimena, this Baroque church (17C–18C) is home to some beautiful frescoes by Paolo de Matteis of Salerno (1662–1728), including *The Glory of St Nicolas* and *The Passage of St Nicolas*, located at the altar. Nearby Via Pignasecca leads to the Pignasecca market *(open daily)*, a food market area in the heart of Montesanto.

Quartieri Spagnoli

Built in the 16C to house the Spanish troops of the Viceroy Don Pedro de Toledo, Naples' Spanish Quarter is guarded by the proud Certosa di San Martino. Every street from this labyrinth-like maze opens into a church and the neighbourhood has to be explored in bits to appreciate it.
The Spanish Quarter has a rough reputation and the Neapolitans will advise you to avoid it at night. However, taking a few precautions such as not walking alone at night, keeping your purse or wallet out of sight and not drawing attention to yourself will reduce the chance of unpleasant surprises. The Spanish Quarter is one of the most exciting places in Naples and it would be a shame to miss this intriguing area.

Galleria di Palazzo Zevallos Stigliano★

Via Toledo 185. Open Tue–Fri 10am–6pm, Sat–Sun 10am–8pm. 5€. ℘800 454 229. www.gallerieditaliacom.
This magnificent palace, easily recognised by its ornate entrance, was constructed in the late-16C and rebuilt in

1637 by Cosimo Fanzago. The covered courtyard was beautifully transformed with bay windows and balconies. Climb up two floors and you'll find the masterpiece: the magnificent **Martirio di Sant'Orsola★** (*Martyrdom of St Ursula*), painted by Caravaggio in 1610, weeks before his death.

Galleria Umberto I★

Via San Carlo.
This gallery, with its mosaic pavement and marble reliefs, was inaugurated in 1890 and is reminiscent of the Galleria Vittorio Emanuele II in Milan. Housing some of the best shops of the city, the gallery opens onto busy Via Toledo and is opposite the San Carlo Theatre. In the centre, the glass and wrought-iron dome is supported by elegant female figures. The Galleria Umberto is the setting for the 1947 novel *The Gallery*, by American writer John Horne Burnes

Teatro San Carlo★★

Guided hourly tours,10.30am–12.30pm, 2.30–4.30pm, Sun morning only (depending on rehearsal times). 6€. ℘081 79 72 468. www.teatrosancarlo.it.
The theatre was built under Charles of Bourbon in 1737 and rebuilt in 1816 in the Neoclassical style. It is an institution in the Italian music world.
The auditorium, with boxes on six levels and a large stage, is built of wood and stucco to achieve perfect acoustics.

Piazza Trento e Trieste

This irregularly shaped square is enclosed by the San Carlo Theatre, one side of the Royal Palace and the famous Gran Caffè Gambrinus. The Baroque church of San Ferdinando is also in the piazza. Via Chiaia begins here.

Piazza del Plebiscito★

This semicircular "square" (19C) is enclosed by the royal palace and the Neoclassical façade of the church of San Francesco di Paola, built on the model of the Pantheon in Rome. The equestrian statues of Ferdinand I and Charles III of Bourbon are by Canova.

Palazzo Reale★

Piazza del Plebiscito 1. ♿Open Thu–Tue 9am– 7pm. Closed public hols. 4€. ℘081 40 05 47. www.palazzorealenapoli.it.

The palace was built in the early-17C by the architect Domenico Fontana and has been remodelled several times.

The façade retains more or less its original appearance. Since the late-19C the niches on the façade have contained eight statues of the most famous Kings of Naples.

A huge staircase with twin ramps and crowned by a coffered dome leads to the apartments★ and the sumptuously decorated chapel. The richly ornamented rooms have retained their numerous works of art, tapestries, paintings, furniture and fine porcelain. Of particular interest are the splendid ♔♔door knockers★ made of wood: putti, nymphs and animals are set off against a gilded background.

Piazza del Municipio

Facing the lungomare, the Piazza Municipio is located on the site of an old Roman port. During the building of the subway system, remains, including those of two Roman ships, were excavated. They are now on display in the subway station (♿see box p215).

Castel Nuovo (or Maschio Angioino)★

Piazza Municipio. ♿Open Mon–Sat 9am–7pm (ticket office closes 6pm). Closed public hols. 6€. ℘081 795 77 13.

This imposing castle, surrounded by deep moats, was built in 1282 by Pierre de Chaulnes and Pierre d'Agincourt, the architects of Charles I of Anjou. It was modelled on the castle at Angers. A remarkable triumphal arch★★ embellishes the entrance on the town side. This masterpiece bearing sculptures to the glory of the House of Aragon, was built to designs by Francesco Laurana in 1467. Access to the Sala dei Baroni is via the staircase in the inner courtyard. The fine vaulting is star shaped, formed by the tufa groins intersecting with other architectural features. The panoramic terrace offers beautiful views, with the

Royal Lunching

Built with funds provided by Neapolitan nobility, San Carlo Theatre, named for the Bourbon King Charles III, was built in record time near the royal palace. It was not only open at night for performances, but, with the king's permission, would open during the day so royal families could lunch, arrange meetings and get together to discuss the latest news.

port and rooftops of Spaccanapoli in the background.

PORT AND MARKET QUARTER

Founded by the Greeks who landed here in the 8C BC, the port is one of the most important harbours in Italy and the busiest passenger port in the country. The Angioino port was built in the early-14C by the House of Anjou and is home to the maritime station (1936). Fascists stripped the façade to welcome passengers from Sicily and Sardinia. The last tram runs from the port to the Santa Maria del Carmine church and beyond.

Chiesa di Santa Maria del Carmine

Piazza del Carmine 2. Open Mon–Tue and Thu–Sat 6.30am–12.30pm and 4–6.30pm, Wed, Sun 6.30am–1pm. ℘081 20 11 96. www.santuariocarminemaggiore.it

The market area is highlighted by the church's tower that faces the docks and is adorned with 16C majolica tiles. The single-nave church was built in the late-13C and has a gilded coffered ceiling and a bas-relief of the Madonna and Child. It is also worth noting the beautiful organ pipes that are located near the altar. The church is home to the venerated Byzantine icon Madonna della Bruna, around which the Carmine festival is celebrated every year on 16 July. Opposite the square was the scene in the 17C revolt led by Masaniello. Just steps away, the Piazza del Mercato, in a semicircle, was built in the 18C following a fire that ravaged the neighbourhood. It is dominated by the façade of Santa Croce. Market: open daily 7am–3pm.

CHIAIA AND IL LUNGOMARE★

The *lungomare* runs from the port of Santa Lucia to the little cove of Mergellina. On Sundays this area is filled with locals who gather for a *passeggiata* – a popular Italian pastime enjoyed with friends and family members. Young lovers take refuge in the shady pine trees of the Villa Comunale. Piazza Sannazzaro is busy from late evening through to the early morning and is a popular spot.

Porto di Santa Lucia★★

See map of the built-up area on Michelin Map 431.

Santa Lucia is the name of the small suburb that juts out towards the sea. It is best known as the name of a tiny port, immortalised by a famous Neapolitan song, nestling between a rocky islet and the jetty. **Castel dell'Ovo** (Via Eldorado 3; open Mon–Sat 9am–6pm, Sun 10am–2pm; free entrance; ℘081 795 45 93) is a severe edifice built by the Normans and remodelled by the Angevins in 1274. Legend has it that Virgil hid a magic egg *(uovo)* within its walls and that the destruction of the egg would destroy the castle. The first castle in the city, this was a residence of the House of Anjou. It is now a museum that occasionally hosts arts events. It has stunning views from its terrace.

From the jetty there is a splendid **view★★** of Vesuvius on the one hand and of the western side of the bay on the other. In the evening, go further along to Piazza Vittoria, which offers a **view★★★** of the suburbs on the Vomero and Posillipo hillsides, brightly lit up by a myriad of twinkling lights.

Via Partenope

Via Partenope is at the beginning of the seafront path at Castel dell'Ovo. Great hotels, trendy bars and trattorias line the sunny avenue. The quays, lined with restaurants on stilts and the Borgo Marinaro

(sea village), set up a picturesque kingdom on which the severe Castel dell'Ovo is guarded by Vesuvius.

Piazza dei Martiri

This pleasant piazza in the neighbourhood of Chiaia is highlighted by a memorial column of the martyrs (1866), which pays tribute to the people who fell during the revolt against the Bourbons. Reach the Villa Comunale via the tiny Calabritto, where the biggest names in Italian and French fashion are found.

Villa Comunale

Main entrance is at Piazza Vittoria. Open May–Oct 7am–midnight; rest of the year 7am–10pm.

Vanvitelli laid out these public gardens along the waterfront in 1780. Stretching for almost 1km/0.5mi they are popular with Neapolitans for an evening stroll. At the centre of the gardens is the **Aquarium** (closed at time of writing; ℘081 58 33 111). www.szn.it.

Museo Principe di Aragona Pignatelli Cortes

Riviera di Chiaja 200, opposite the Villa Comunale. Open Wed–Mon 8.30am–2pm. Closed 1 Jan, 1 May, 25 Dec. 2€. ℘081 76 12 356 or 081 66 96 75.

The ground floor of the summer residence of the Princess Pignatelli (she lived here until the 1950s) is open to visitors. The stables house a collection of English, French and Italian carriages.

Mergellina★

Mergellina, at the foot of the Posillipo hillside, affords a splendid bay **view★★**: the Vomero hillside, crowned by Castel Sant'Elmo, slopes down towards the Santa Lucia headland, with Castel dell'Ovo and Vesuvius in the distance.

VOMERO★

Whether by foot or cablecar, the best views of the city and the Gulf of Naples are from Vomero. The stepped alleyways and lush, green parks are a relaxing contrast to the historic centre. In the centre of Vomero, the Piazza Vanvitelli is dedicated to the great architect Luigi

Vanvitelli. The main avenues, filled with the big fashion names, radiate around the square. Vomero is a haven of peace overlooking the city and is just a few meters above the lively Spanish area.

Certosa di San Martino★★

Largo San Martino 5. Visit: 1hr. ♿ Open Thu–Tue 8.30am–7.30pm. Closed 1 Jan, 25 Dec. 6€. ℘081 22 94 503.
This 14C Carthusian monastery founded by the Anjou dynasty is situated on the Vomero hill. The **Castel Sant'Elmo** was rebuilt by the Spaniards in the 16C and used as a prison. From the drill square (access on foot or by lift) there is a wonderful view over the city and the bay.

Church

The **interior★★** is lavishly Baroque and adorned with paintings by Caracciolo, Guido Reni and Simon Vouet. Beyond the sacristy is the treasury decorated with frescoes by Luca Giordano and a painting by Ribera, La Pietà.
The **great cloisters** is the work of the architect-sculptor Cosimo Fanzago.

Museum★

The section devoted to festivals and costumes contains an exceptional collection of figurines and Neapolitan **cribs★★** (presepi) in polychrome terra-cotta from the 18C and 19C. The tour concludes with a large, impressive crib from the late-19C.

Villa Floridiana★

Via Cimarosa 77, W of Naples. Open Sun 10am–noon, Mon, Wed–Sat 9am–1pm. 2€. ℘081 57 88 418. www.beniculturali.it.
This graceful small white palace (palazzina) in the Neoclassical style stands high up on the Vomero hillside. The façade overlooks the gardens, which afford a splendid **panorama★★**. The villa houses the **Museo Nazionale di Ceramica Duca di Martina★**, with fine displays of faience and porcelain.

RIONE SANITÀ★

Lodged between two noble Neapolitan institutions, the National Archaeological Museum and the Royal Palace of Capodimonte, this popular suburb is a tangle of winding streets built on both sides of the Corso Amedeo di Savoia. It is home to three catacombs whose residents were decimated by recurrent epidemics that ravaged Naples until the 19C. The neighbourhood is considered a stronghold of the Camorra but during the day is relatively safe. For guided tours of the neighbourhood contact the Cooperativa sociale "La Paranza", a group from Rione Sanità dedicated to promoting their neighbourhood. Via Tondo di Capodimonte 13. ℘081 744 37 14. www.catacombedinapoli.it.

Catacombe di San Gennaro★★

North of the city. Guided tours only (40min), hourly Mon–Sat 10am–5pm, Sun 10am–1pm. 25 Dec and 1 Jan only by reservation. 8€. ℘Same as above.
The catacombs dug in the volcanic rock extend over two floors. The tomb of St Januarius, whose remains were transferred here in the 6C, is decorated with frescoes of the saint. There are beautiful paintings in the niches (3C–10C). The upper section and the atrium vault is adorned with early Christian work and portraits adorning family tombs.

Cimitero delle Fontanelle★★

Via Fontanelle 80. Daily 10am–5pm. ℘081 197 03 197.
www.cimiterofontanelle.com
At the end of the winding Via Fontanelle, the old Greco-Roman quarry houses the bones of thousands of victims from the deadliest century in Naples' history. The 1600s were defined by three revolts, three famines, three earthquakes, five eruptions of Vesuvius and three epidemics, including the plague of 1656 that killed three-quarters of the inhabitants of Naples (some estimate 300 000 people died). Wanting to bury the victims outside the city, the government chose this once-isolated area. Made famous by the Rossellini film Italian Journey (1953), the vast cellar consists of three long aisles lined with skulls and is home to an altar made of bones and wood. The rest of the bones are in-ground, up to 70m/230ft deep. Open

The Captain's Head

A famous tale to arise from the bones at Fontanelle is that of the "Captain's Head". According to legend, a young woman dreamed the skull she had "adopted" belonged to a captain and she prayed he would help her find a husband. On her wedding day, a mysterious guest appeared dressed as a captain. The groom was overcome with jealousy and hit the captain, causing a dent in his skull.

to the public in the 19C, like other parts of the city (the church of Santa Maria delle Anime del Purgatorio ad Arco, for example), the cemetery was the object of worship for abandoned souls.

It was this spontaneous devotion to the unknown dead in which the faithful "adopted" a skull they regularly visited and prayed for that led the Archbishop of Naples to close the cemetery in 1969. Since 2002 the cemetery has gone through bouts of openings and closures for a variety of reasons.

MUSEO ARCHEOLOGICO NAZIONALE★★★

Piazza Museo Nazionale 19. Visit: 2hrs. ⑤ Open Wed–Mon 9am–7.30pm. Closed 1 Jan, 1 May, 25 Dec. 8€. ℘081 44 22 149. www.coopculture.it.

The National Archaeological Museum collections comprise art belonging to the Farnese family and treasures discovered at Pompeii and Herculaneum. It is one of the world's richest museums for Greco-Roman Antiquities. *Look for the Tazza Farnese, blue vase and Temple of Isis.*

GROUND FLOOR
Greco-Roman Sculpture★★★

The large *atrium* displays sculptures from Pompeii and Herculaneum. At the front of the room a staircase on the right leads to the section in the basement dedicated to the **epigraphy section** (ancient inscriptions) and the **Egyptian collection**.

Galleria dei Tirannicidi – *Turn right on entering the atrium.* The Tyrant-Slayers' Gallery is devoted to Archaic art. The **Aphrodite Sosandra** with a fine, proud face and elegantly draped robe is a splendid copy of a Greek bronze (5C BC), while the powerful marble group of the **Tyrant-Slayers**, a copy of a Greek bronze, represents Harmodios and Aristogiton, who delivered Athens from the tyrant, Hipparchus, in the 6C BC.

Galleria dei Grandi Maestri – *Access from the Galleria dei Tirannicidi.* The Great Masters' Gallery contains the statue of the Farnese Pallas (Athena), Orpheus and Eurydice bidding each other farewell, a low relief copied from an original by Phidias (5C BC), and the **Doryphorus**, the spear-bearer, a copy of the famous bronze by Polyclitus.

At the end of the Galleria dei Tirannicidi, to the left, is a gallery displaying the famous **Callipygian Aphrodite** (callipige signifies "with lovely buttocks", 1C) and the statue of **Artemis of Ephesus** (2C) in alabaster and bronze, representing the deity venerated at the temple by the Aegean Sea. She is represented by numerous breasts.

Galleria del Toro Farnese – *Access from the preceding gallery.* This recently renovated gallery houses the monumental sculptural groups found at the Baths of Caracalla in Rome in the 16C. In the centre is the colossal *Flora farnese.* In the last room is the impressive sculptured group called the **Farnese Bull** depicting the death of Dirce, a legendary queen of Thebes. It was carved from a single block of marble. It is a 2C Roman copy, which like many works in the Farnese collection, has undergone much restoration. In the right wing is the **Farnese Hercules**. Visit the room dedicated to **engraved gemstones** that includes a great masterpiece, the **Tazza Farnese★★★**, an enormous cameo in the shape of a cup made in Alexandria in the 2C BC.

Mosaics★★

To the left on the mezzanine.
Although most of these come from Pompeii, Herculaneum and Stabia, they offer a wide variety of styles and subject

matter. There are two small works *(Visit to a Fortune-Teller and Roving Musicians)* by Dioscurides of Samos along with the Actors on stage in the Room of the Tragic Poet *(Room LIX)*.

Mosaics including a frieze with masks and the splendid mosaic of the Battle of Alexander and Darius *(Room LXI)*, which paved the floor of the House of the Faun at Pompeii, are found in Rooms LX and LXI. The collection includes examples of *opus sectile*.

FIRST FLOOR
Works from Villa di Pisone and dei Papiri★★★

At the beginning of the Salone della Meridiana, on the right.

The villa, which was discovered at Herculaneum in the 18C but was later reburied, is thought to have belonged to L. Calpurnius Pison, who was Julius Caesar's father-in-law. The owner had turned the house into a museum. The documents and splendid works of art from his collections are priceless. The Sala dei Papiri *(Room CXIV)* contains photographs of some of the 800 papyri from the library. In Room CXVI are exhibited **bronze statues** that adorned the peristyle of the villa: the **Drunken Faun** lost in euphoria, a **Sleeping Satyr** with a beautiful face in repose; the two **Wrestlers** are inspired from Lysippus (4C BC); the **Dancers from Herculaneum** are probably water-carriers; *Hermes at Rest* reflects Lysippus' ideal.

Silver, Ivory, Terra-cotta and Glass Gallery★

At the beginning of the Salone della Meridiana, on the left.

These rooms are mostly devoted to finds brought back from Pompeii and Herculaneum. Exhibits include silver from the House of Menander, ivory ornaments, weapons, glass; note the stunning **blue vase★★** decorated with *putti* and harvest scenes. From here, head to the room with a **model of Pompeii**.

Sale del Tempio di Iside★★★

After the room above.

This room features objects and pictures from the Temple of Isis discovered behind the Great Theatre at Pompeii. Three areas have been partially reconstructed to evoke the original structure: the portico, the *ekklesiasterion* (the assembly room where the worshippers met) and the *sacrarium* (sanctuary). The frescoes illustrate a still life (figs, grapes, geese and doves are elements linked to the worship of this Egyptian goddess). Of particular interest are the large panels illustrating the myths of Isis.

Sale degli Affreschi★★★

At the far end of the Salone della Meridiana, on the left, or after the Sale del Tempio di Iside.

The collection includes some frescoes from Pompeii, Herculaneum and Stabia in particular. The diversity of style and colour is a testament to the richness of this art practised by the Romans *(🄲see POMPEII)*. Exhibits include beautiful

---

The Port of Neapolis Underground

A few meters below the Archaeological Museum at the Museo underground stop designed by architect Gae Aulenti, is an archaeological exhibit, Stazione di Neapolis, derived from years of construction of Naples' underground railway system. The corriodor that connects with the museum houses archaeological remains uncovered during the construction of Metro Line 1 of Naples' subway. In addition to amphorae, ceramics and coins, two wooden boats were discovered in Piazza Municipio and provide important archaeological information on the ancient port of Neapolis. The sea then extended from the Piazza Municipio in the Piazza Bovio, forming a bay that was protected by two headlands. Notice wooden spoons and traces of a Neolithic till from Via Diaz.

paintings with mythological subjects such as Heracles, Ariadne, and Medea and Iphigenia, and epic poems including episodes from the Trojan War that are inserted in architectural perspectives, friezes of cupids, satyrs and maenads.

PALAZZO AND GALLERIA NAZIONALE DI CAPODIMONTE★★

Via Milano 2, North of the city. Visit: 2hrs. &Open Thu–Tue 8.30am–7.30pm (office closes 6.30pm). Closed 1 Jan, 1 May, 25 Dec. 7.50€ (6.50€ after 2pm). ℘081 74 99 111. www.museocapodimonte. beniculturali.it.

This former **royal estate★** includes a palace, a park, the remains of the 18C porcelain factory and an art gallery.

Pinacoteca★★

The nucleus is the Farnese Collection, inherited by the Bourbons, enriched subsequently and tracing main trends in the evolution of Italian painting.

The collections open with the Farnese Gallery, which displays famous portraits of the most important members of the Farnese family. Note the portrait of **Paolo III with his nephews★★**, a masterpiece by Titian.

In the **Crucifixion★★★** by Masaccio, Mary Magdalene in a red dress with arms stretched towards the cross is a fine example of perspective that made Masaccio a key figure in the revolution of the Renaissance.

Renaissance painting is represented by the works of Botticelli *(Madonna and Child with Saints)*, Filippino Lippi and Raphael. A fine example of the Venetian school is the **Transfiguration★★** by Giovanni Bellini.

In the Venetian section note the celebrated **Portrait of Fra Luca Pacioli**, possibly by a Spanish artist. Among the main exponents of Mannerism are Sebastiano del Piombo (**Portrait of Clement VII★**), Pontormo and Rosso Fiorentino. Titian's study of light is exemplified in the sensual **Danae** and in the works of his pupil El Greco. Serenity and tenderness are evoked in a small canvas, *The Mystic*

Marriage of St Catherine, by Correggio and in the Holy Family by Parmigianino, which stresses the essential role of the mother. Also note the Lucrezia and the **Antea★**. The section devoted to Flemish artists includes fine works by Peter Bruegel the Elder (*The Misanthrope* and **The Parable of the Blind★★**).

The second floor houses the "Neapolitan Gallery", a collection formed by Gioacchino Marat of works acquired from suppressed monastic orders. Masterpieces include *St Ludovic of Toulouse* by Simone Martini, *St Jerome in his studio* by Colantonio and the **Flagellation★★** by Caravaggio. The third floor is devoted to contemporary art.

Royal Apartments

The rooms on the first floor have fine furnishings. Of note is the **room★** with walls decorated with chinoiserie flowers. Also on view is a fine porcelain collection.

ADDITIONAL SIGHTS
Decumanus Maximus★★

Broadly takes the course of the Via Tribunali. Tour of Decumanus monuments daily 9am–1.30pm.

Turn right to get to the 17C **Pio Monte della Misericordia**, which houses six panels; the themes are linked to the charitable works carried out by the institute. Of particular interest are *St Peter Freed from Prison* by Caracciolo and **The Seven Works of Mercy★★★** by Caravaggio.

Spaccanapoli★★

Enter Via Benedetto Croce. To ensure access to all of the buildings, set out in the morning.

The main axis of old Naples, formed by the Via S. Benedetto Croce, Via S. Biagio dei Librai and Via Vicaria Vecchia is nicknamed "Spaccanapoli", or rather, "Split Naples", because that is what it does. Spaccanapoli follows the course of a main road through ancient Naples, the **Decumanus Maximus**, which now traces the Via Tribunali. In Piazza del Gesù Nuovo is the church of **Gesù Nuovo**, whose façade is decorated inside with Solimena's *Expulsion of Heliodorus from the Temple*.

ADDRESSES

🛏 STAY

🛏 **I Vicoletti** – Via San Domenico Soriano 46, 80135 Napoli. ☎081 54 49 179. www.ivicoletti.it. 3 rooms. ⌑. The main attraction here is the vast terrace with views over the Castel Capuano. Other strong points include the spacious rooms, and the friendly staff. Situated in the historic centre, this hotel exudes a Mediterranean atmosphere. Shared bathrooms and lots of stairs.

🛏 **La Locanda dell'Arte** – Via Enrico Pessina 66. ☎081 544 43 15. www.bbnapoli.org. 6 rooms. These simple, elegant rooms are decorated with dark wood furniture and have large windows overlooking a pedestrian street in the historic centre. A delicious smell of orange blossoms are a nice touch to this B&B that is housed in a palace from the early 19C. Opposite is the Academy of Fine Arts.

🛏🛏 **B&B Cappella Vecchia 11** – Via Santa Maria a Cappella Vecchia 11. ☎081 24 05 117. www.cappellavecchia11.it. 6 rooms. ⌑. Close to Piazza dei Martiri, this bright and cheerful B&B combines minimalist style with a great central location. Price includes internet connection.

🛏🛏 **B&B Costantinopoli** – Via Santa Maria di Costantinopoli 27. ☎081 44 67 99. www.discovernaples.net. 2 rooms. A superb apartment on the top floor of an old building, this B&B will delight art lovers of all ages. The hearty breakfast is served in the kitchen that is covered with majolica tiles. Spacious rooms decorated with antiques. Private bathroom is outside the room.

🛏🛏 **B&B Donna Regina** – Via Luigi Settembrini 80. ☎081 44 67 99. www.discovernaples.net. 6 rooms. This B&B is located in a 13C monastery. It has a grand Bohemian salon with high walls covered with paintings. The terrace opens to the old cloister. The owner is in love with his city and is also an independent guide.

🛏🛏 **The Fresh** – Via Donnalbina 7. ☎081 02 02 255. www.the-fresh.it. 6 rooms. A nice B&B close to the Via Monteoliveto. Comfortable rooms with original furniture design. Competitive prices.

🛏 **Pignatelli** – Via San Giovanni Maggiore Pignatelli 16. ☎081 65 84 950. www.hotelpignatellinapoli.com. 5 rooms. In the heart of the historic centre, just steps from the Piazza San Domenico Maggiore, these apartments were the home of the Marquis Pignatelli. Spacious and bright rooms.

🛏🛏 **Soggiorno Sansevero** – Via Foria 42. ☎347 564 71 17. www.sanseveronaples.it. 5 rooms. The Sansevero group of hotels offers stylish accommodation in three 18C *palazzi*. Good-sized rooms have been attractively decorated. Cheerful, sunny atmosphere makes for a pleasant stay. The prices are reasonable. It is worth noting that the rooms with shared bathrooms are cheaper.

🛏🛏🛏 **Chiaia Hotel de Charme** – Via Chiaia 216. ☎081 41 55 55. www.chiaiahotel.com. 27 rooms. ⌑. The hotel is located inside the former apartment of the Marquis Nicola Lecaldano Sasso La Terza, on the first floor of a 17C noble palace. The rooms are tasteful and equipped with modern comforts.

🍴 EAT

🍴 **Antica Pizzeria Da Michele** – Via Cesare Sersale 1/3. ☎081 55 39 204. www.damichele.net. Closed Sun and 3 weeks Aug. A very popular pizzeria, the tile decor is unpretentious and the main attraction is the excellent pizza. Come armed with bags of patience – queuing is part of the experience.

🍴 **Antica Pizzeria De' Figliole** – Via Giudecca Vecchia 39. ☎081 28 67 21. Closed Sun. 🍴. Located at the heart of Spaccanapoli, this crowded pizzeria is a great place to try Naples' fried pizza.

🍴 **Gino Sorbillo** – Via dei Tribunali 32. ☎081 44 66 43. www.sorbillo.it. Closed Sun and 3 weeks Aug. 10 percent service charge. One of the best pizzerias in town. Proprietor Gino comes from a long line of *pizzaioli* – there are 21 of them in all. Great ambience and fantastic pizzas.

🍴 **Brandi** – Salita di S. Anna di Palazzo 1/2. ☎081 41 69 28. www.brandi.it. Closed Tue. 🍴. Here on 11 June 1889 the legendary pizza margherita, named in honour of the queen, was born. Brandi is a well-loved institution in Naples, although a bit touristy.

☺ **Campagnola** – Via Tribunali 47.
📞081 45 90 34. Closed Sun in winter
and Tue in summer. A clean, simple
osteria with daily specials listed on the
blackboard. Nice wine cellar.

☺ **Cicciotto** – Calata Ponticello a
Marechiaro 32. 📞081 575 11 65. www.
trattoriadacicciotto.it. Reservations
recommended. A romantic tavern where
you can enjoy excellent fish-based
cuisine and authentic local dishes

☺ **Hosteria Toledo** – Vico Giardinetto 78a.
📞081 42 12 57. www.hosteriatoledo.it.
Closed Tue. In the heart of the Spanish
Quarter, this *hosteria* celebrates the
flavours of Naples. Great selection of
ingredients.

☺ **Pizzeria Di Matteo** – Via Tribunali 94.
📞081 45 52 62. www.pizzeriadimatteo.com.
Closed Sun.🚭. Celebrities from Bill Clinton
to great Mastroianni have enjoyed this
pizza. Unbeatable prices and service.

☺ **Timpani e Tempera** – Vico della
Quercia 17 (enter through Via Toledo and
Piazza del Gesù Nuovo). 📞081 55 12 280.
Closed Sun afternoon, Mon and Aug.
Cheese, prosciutto and *antipasti* are
essential starters. Southern Italian
flavours in this tiny shop.

☺ **Trianon da Ciro** – Via Pietro
Colletta 44/46. 📞081 55 39 426. www.
pizzeriatrianon.it. Closed 1 Jan, 25 Dec.
Decorated in 1920s style with yellow-
ochre walls, this establishment
is rich in history.

☺☺ **'A Tiella** – Riviera di Chiaia 98.
📞081 76 18 688. Closed Wed. Fish
dishes and homemade pasta, a good
choice after a walk on the beach. Sit
outside, where the lemon and ivy is
complemented by old photographs.

☺☺ **Il Garum** – Piazza Monteoliveto 2a.
📞081 54 23 228.www.ristoranteilgarum.it.
Open daily. A short distance away from
Spaccanapoli, in the Monteoliveto
Piazza, this property is always full.
Professional staff serve delicious
regional cuisine. Excellent fish.

☺☺ **La Cantina di via Sapienza** – Via
Sapienza 40/41. 📞081 45 90 78. Closed Sun
evenings.🚭. This trattoria is frequented
by students and doctors from the
nearby hospital. Excellent value for
veggie-based cuisine.

☺☺ **L'Europeo di Mattozzi** –
Via Marchese Campodisola 4. 📞081 55 21
323. Closed Sun dinner and 2 weeks Aug. 12
percent service charge. Authentic home
cooking inspired by seasonal ingredients
which are super-fresh. Friendly staff
combine great courtesy with infectious
love for food.

☺☺ **Napoli Mia** – Riviera di Chiaia 269.
📞081 55 22 266. www.ristorantenapoli
mia.it. Closed Mon. Small, friendly family-
run. Nice service proffers authentic
cuisine and local dishes.

☺☺ **Un Sorriso Integrale** – Vico S.
Pietro a Maiella 6. 📞081 45 50 26.
www.sorrisointegrale.com. Open daily.
A nice vegetarian restaurant located in a
courtyard. Broccoli with lemon, cabbage
meatballs, pancakes with ricotta and
spinach, all organic products, are worth
a taste.

TAKING A BREAK

Caffè Mexico – Piazza Dante 86.
📞081 54 99 330. A Naples institution.
Coffee is served sweet.

Gran Caffè Gambrinus – Via Chiaia 1/2.
📞081 41 75 82. www.grancaffegambrinus.
com. Open daily 7am–1am. The most
famous of all the Neapolitan caffès, it
exudes an air of historical importance.
Its sumptuously decorated rooms
have witnessed 150 years of the most
important events of Neapolitan history.

ENTERTAINMENT

Bourbon Street Club – Via Bellini 52/53.
📞338 82 53 756 (mobile). www.bourbon
streetjazzclub.com. Open at 8pm. Closed
Mon. At the corner of Piazza Dante,
this is a great meeting-place for jazz
lovers. Soft lighting and comfortable
booths.

Intra Moenia – Piazza Bellini 70. 📞081
45 16 52. www.intramoenia.it. This bar/
bookshop is also the headquarters of
a publishing house.

Teatro San Carlo – Via San Carlo 98.
📞081 79 72 331. www.teatrosancarlo.it.
Opera season: Dec–May. Box office:
10am–5.30pm (Sun 10am–2pm). With its
permanent opera company, the San
Carlo is one of the best opera houses in
the world.

SHOPPING

The figurines from the Nativity scenes (head for Via San Gregorio Armeno) make lovely souvenirs and presents. Cameos and coral pieces are made especially in Torre del Greco.

Augustus – Via Toledo 147. ☎081 55 13 540. One of the best caterers in Naples sits on the edge of the Spanish Quarter.

👥 **Ferrigno** – Via S. Gregorio Armeno 8. ☎081 55 23 148. www.arteferrigno.it. A boutique shop known for its figurines.

Gay Odin – Via Toledo 214 and 427. ☎081 40 00 63 and 081 551 34 91. www. gay-odin.it. Closed Sun and 3 weeks Aug. These masters of Neapolitan chocolate have been delighting patrons since 1894, some of Italy's best. In summer, the Via Benedetto Croce 61 shop adds gelato or in winter, hot chocolate.

Il Mercato in Via Pignasecca – Open every morning. Fresh fruits, vegetables, fish, shellfish and Campania's famous mozzarella di bufala are displayed in colourful stalls of the Pignasecca Street market. It is Naples at its best!

Librerie Antiquarie Luigi Regina – Via Santa Maria di Costantinopoli 51 and 103. ☎081 45 99 83. www.libreriaregina.it. Closed 3 weeks Aug. A charming bookshop founded in 1881 at no. 51, sells prints and watercolours.

Marinella – Riviera di Chiaia 287. ☎081 245 11 82. www.marinellanapoli.it. The most famous tie shop in Italy.

👥 **Ospedale delle Bambole** – Via San Biagio dei Librai 81. ☎081 20 30 67. A historic site where doll-makers cure broken dolls and stuffed animals.

EVENTS AND FESTIVALS

Great ceremony is evident in religious festivals including Madonna di Piedigrotta (8 Sept), Santa Maria del Carmine (16 Jul) and especially the Feast of the Miracle of St Januarius (1st Sun in May and 9 Sept). At Christmas churches are decorated with Nativity scenes.

Bay of Naples★★★

Golfo di Napoli

The Bay of Naples, from *Cumae* to Sorrento, is one of the most beautiful bays in Italy. Here, in close proximity, you will find isolated areas conducive to meditation, such as the archaeological sites, the bare slopes of Vesuvius, the Sibyl's Cave or Lake Averno, and others bustling with activity and crowded with traffic. Its legendary beauty is somewhat marred by the sprawl of industrial development that has reached the outskirts. However, its islands and mountains are as lovely as they were 2 000 years ago.

🚗 DRIVING TOURS

Below are four itineraries (the first two departing from Naples), each of them a natural progression from the

- 🦽 **Michelin Map:** 564 E–F 24–26 – Campania.
- **Info:** Centro Direzionale, Napoli, ☎081 79 68 814. www.incampania.com. Via Luigi de Maio 35, Sorrento, ☎081 807 40 33, www.sorrentotourism.com. Via Campi Flegrei 3, Pozzuoli. ☎081 52 62 419. www.infocampiflegrei.it
- **Location:** The main access roads are the A 1, the Autostrada del Sole, the A 3 if you are arriving from the south and the A 16.
- **Don't Miss:** Campi Flegrei, Vesuvius, Sorrento and the Penisola Sorrentina.
- **Timing:** 4–5 days.
- 👥 **Kids:** The eerie vapours at Solfatara or Planetarium.

previous one. For itinerary 5, 🦽*see the AMALFI COAST.*

1 CAMPI FLEGREI★★

From Naples to Lago d'Averno.
45km/28mi. Allow 6hrs.

This volcanic area, the Phlegrean Fields, received its name from the ancients (*phlegrean* is derived from a Greek word meaning "to blaze"), and extends along the Gulf of Pozzuoli. Hot springs, steam-jets and sulphurous gases rise from the ground and sea, due to underground activity. Lakes have formed in the volcanic craters.

Naples★★★
See NAPLES.

Posillipo★

This famous hill forms a promontory and separates the Bay of Naples from the Gulf of Pozzuoli. Posillipo, dotted with villas, lovely gardens and modern buildings, is Naples' main residential area. It affords splendid bay views.

Marechiaro★

This small fishermen's village built high above the sea was made famous by a Neapolitan song, *Marechiare.*

Parco Virgiliano★

Also called the **Garden of Remembrance,** the park has splendid **views★★** over the Bay of Naples, from Cape Miseno to the Sorrento Peninsula, and the islands of Procida, Ischia and Capri.

Città della Scienza at Bagnoli★

For opening hours see the website or call ✆081 73 52 424. 8€. Guided tour and workshops by reservation. www.cittadellascienza.it.
A fine industrial building from the mid-19C houses the innovative Science Centre, divided up into sections – each with a different theme (physics, classical world, nature, evolution, communications). Most areas including the Planetarium are temporarily closed. New exhibits scheduled to open are on the human brain and on dinosaurs. ♟ **Officina dei Piccoli** is directed at children from one to ten years of age.

Pozzuoli★

Train from Napoli Montesanto to Pozzuoli Solfatara 32 mins.
www.comune.pozzuoli.na.it.
Pozzuoli, which is of Greek origin, became an active trading port under

GETTING AROUND

Ticket UnicoCampania3T – www.unicocampania.it. This ticket allows three days of use of public transport, including boats to Ischia and Procida (20€). **Ticket Unico Costiera** allows to use the public transport in 20 municipalities of the coast. The cost of the ticket varies according duration (45 min., 90 min, one day or 3 days) **Campi Flegrei** – www.eavsrl.it. ✆800 211 388. From Naples Montesanto, a line of Sepsa Metro goes to Torregaveta, passing through Bagnoli and Pozzuoli. Train lines and Cumana Circumflegrea also serve other stations in the area. You can make the round trip in one day.
Archeobus Flegreo – ✆800 00 16 16. Fri–Sun and public hols. Service from Pozzuoli to the Phlegrean

archaeological fields (Baia, Bacoli, Fusaro, Cuma). **Metrodelmare** – www.metrodelmare.it. Boats to Capri, Amalfi, Sorrento and Ischia.

MUSEUMS

Campania Artecard – Campania Artecard, available for three (32€) or seven days (34€), entitles its holder to free or reduced admission in most museums, archaeological sites, castles and other attractions in and around Naples. It also allows three days of public transport in Naples and Campi Flegrei. ✆06 39 96 76 50. www.campaniaartecard.it.
Combination Tickets – Five site tickets *(11€)* that are valid for three days can be used at Pompeii, Herculaneum, Boscoreale, Stabiae and Oplontis. www.coopculture.it.

Pompei

the Romans. As the town is at the centre of the volcanic area known as the Phlegrean Fields and is constantly affected by changes in the ground level that occur in this region, the town centre has been evacuated. The town's name derives from the word *pozzolana*, a volcanic ash with a high silica content, which is used in the production of certain kinds of cement.

Anfiteatro Flavio★★

Via Terracciano 75. ⼤ Open 9am–2pm Closed Tue, 1 Jan, 25 Dec. 4€. ℘06 399 67 050.
This amphitheatre is one of the largest in Italy and dates from the reign of Vespasian, the founder of the Flavian dynasty. It could accommodate 40 000 spectators. Built of brick and stone, it is relatively well preserved: note the outer walls, the entrances and the particularly well-preserved **basements★★**.

Tempio di Serapide★

Set back from Via Roma.
The temple, dedicated to Serapis, which is situated near the sea, was really the ancient marketplace and was lined with shops. There is a sort of apse in the end wall that contained the statue of Serapis, the protecting god of traders. The central edifice shows the effects of variations in ground level: the columns reveal signs of marine erosion.

Tempio di Augusto★

The temple, dedicated to Augustus, dated from early Empire and was con-

verted into a Christian church in the 11C. A recent fire has revealed a grandiose marble colonnade.

Solfatara★★

Via Solfatara 161. ⼤Open daily Apr–Oct 8.30am–7pm; Nov–Mar 8.30am–4.30pm. 7€. ℘081 52 62 341. www.solfatara.it.
Although extinct, this crater still has some of the features of an active volcano such as jets of steam charged with sulphurous fumes, strong-smelling and with traces of yellow, miniature volcanoes spitting hot mud, and bubbling jets of sand. The ground gives a hollow sound and the surface is hot.
The sulphurous vapours have been used for medicinal purposes since Roman times. ♣♣ *The excitement of mild volcanic activity is fun for children.*

Lago Lucrino

In Antiquity, oyster farming was practised here on the lake and the banks were lined with villas. One of these belonged to Cicero; another was the scene of Agrippina's murder.

Bacoli

www.comune.bacoli.na.it.
In the old town rises the **Cento Camerelle★** (Via Cento Camerelle, to the right of the church; closed to public at the time of writing; ℘081 52 35 968.).
This huge reservoir, which belonged to a private villa, is built on two levels: the grandiose upper level built in the 1C has four sections and immense arches; the lower part, built much earlier, has a net-

work of narrow galleries forming a cross, which emerge high above sea level. The famous **Piscina Mirabile** (at the church take the road to the left, Via Ambrogio Greco, and then Via Piscina Mirabile to the right; ✆081 52 35 968) was an immense cistern designed to supply water to the Roman fleet in the port of Miseno. It is 70m long, 25m wide and nearly 15m high (230ft x 82ft x 49ft) and is divided into 5 sections with 48 pillars supporting the roof. There are remarkable light effects.

Miseno

This name is given to a lake, a port, a promontory, a cape and a village. Lake Miseno, a former volcanic crater, was believed by the ancients to be the Styx, across which Charon ferried the souls of the dead. Under the Emperor Augustus it was linked by a canal to the port of Miseno, the base of the Roman fleet. The village of Miseno is dominated by Monte Miseno, on which Misenus, the companion of Aeneas, is said to have been buried. The slopes of the promontory were studded with villas, including the one where in AD 37 the Emperor Tiberius choked to death.

Baia★

Train: Capolinea Torregaveta (Napoli Montesanto 35 mins).
This Greek colony was in Roman times a fashionable beach resort, as well as a thermal spa *(terme)* with the most complete equipment in the world for hydrotherapy. The Roman emperors and patricians had immense villas, all of which disappeared under the sea after a change in ground level. An underwater archaeological park has recently been opened to allow visitors to explore these ruins. For underwater visits, call ✆081 52 48 169. www.baiasommersa.it.

Parco Archeologico★★

Open Tue–Sun 9am–1hr before dusk. 4€. ✆06 399 67 050. www.coopculture.it.
Ruins of famous baths remain on the hilltop overlooking the sea. Facing the hill, these include, from left to right, the baths of Venus, Sosandra and Mercury. The archaeological area also includes

ruins of the Imperial palace of Baia and a late-Republican period villa.

Castello di Baia

Open Tue–Sun. 9am–2.30pm. 4€, combined ticket with other sites. ✆06 399 67 050. www.coopculture.it.
Built in the 15C over the remains of a villa traditionally thought to belong to Caesar, this castle is now home to the **Museo Archeologico dei Campi Flegrei**.

Lago del Fusaro

A lagoon with a small island on which Vanvitelli built a hunting lodge for King Ferdinand IV of Bourbon in 1782.

Cuma★

Cumae, one of the oldest Greek colonies, was founded in the 8C BC. The city soon dominated the whole Phlegrean area including Naples, leaving an important Hellenic heritage. Its splendour was at its height under the tyrant Aristodemus. After its capture by the Romans in 334 BC, decline set in and continued until AD 915 when it was pillaged by the Saracens. The ancient city of *Cumae* stands in a serene and solemn setting near the sea. Visitors have access to the ruins of the acropolis, the upper town where most of the temples stood. In the lower town, excavations have revealed the remains of an amphitheatre, a temple dedicated to the Capitoline Triad (Jupiter, Juno and Minerva) and baths.

Parco Archeologico★★

Open daily, 9am–1hr before dusk. Closed 1 Jan, 1 May, 25 Dec. 4€ combined ticket with other sites (valid 2 days). ✆06 399 67 050 or 848 800 288 (free-phone). www.coopculture.it.
The acropolis is built on a hill of volcanic material (lava and tufa) in a lonely site and is reached by an alley lined with laurels. After the vaulted passageway, the path to the left leads to the Sibyl's Cave, **Antro della Sibilla★**, one of the most venerated places of Antiquity. Here the Sibyl delivered her oracles. The cave was hollowed out of the rock by the Greeks in the 6C or 5C BC and it is rectangular in shape with three small niches.

The Cumaean Sibyl

In Antiquity the Sibyls were virgin priestesses who were dedicated to the cult of Apollo and deemed to be semi-divine creatures with powers of divination. The Sibyl from *Cumae* (one of the main centres of Greek civilisation in Italy) was a famous prophetess. She is reputed to have sold the Sibylline Books, collections of Sibyls' prophecies, to the Etruscan King of Rome, Tarquin the Elder or Tarquin the Superb (6C BC). The oracles were later used by the rulers to answer their subjects' petitions and expectations.

Take the stairway up to the Sacred Way (Via Sacra). From the belvedere there is a nice **view★** of the sea. Some finds from the excavations are on display. On the right are the remains of the **Tempio di Apollo** (Temple of Apollo), which was later transformed into a Christian church. Further on is the **Tempio di Giove** (Temple of Jupiter), which was also converted by the early Christians. In the centre stands a large font and there are several Christian tombs near the sanctuary.

Arco Felice★

The minor road in the direction of Naples leads to this triumphal arch which was erected on the Via Domitiana.

Monte Nuovo

This hill is in fact the youngest mountain in Europe. It was formed from the volcanic eruption of 1538 that was preceded by numerous earthquakes that led to the depopulation of Pozzuoli. The natural oasis of Monte Nuovo is an interesting excursion. Open 9am–1hr before dusk, Sun and public holidays 9am–1pm. ☒ III Traversa Virgilio. ✆081 80 41 462.

Lago d'Averno★

The lake lies below the Cumae–Naples road: the belvedere on the right is 1km/0.6mi beyond Arco Felice.
This lake within a crater is dark, still and silent and wrapped in an atmosphere of mystery, which was all the more intense in Antiquity as birds flying overhead were overcome by fumes and dropped into it. Virgil regarded it as the entrance to the Underworld. Under the Roman

Empire, Agrippa, a captain in the service of the Emperor Augustus, developed it as a naval base and linked it by canal with Lake Lucrino (♦*see above*), which in turn was linked to the open sea. An underground gallery 1km/0.6mi long, known as **Grotta di Cocceio** (Cocceio's Cave), connected *Avernus* with *Cumae*, and was used by chariots.

② VESUVIUS★★★

From Naples to Torre Annunziata. 45km/28mi. Allow 1 day.

The coastal road relieves the Salerno motorway across a densely populated industrial zone and was once a favoured resort of the Neapolitan aristocracy (18C–19C). There are two important sites located a short distance from the road.

Portici

www.comune.portici.na.it.
The road crosses the courtyard of the **royal palace** built in 1738 for the Bourbon King Charles III. Today the palace buildings are the home of the Naples Faculty of Agronomy. In his opera *The Mute Girl of Portici (Muette de Portici)*, the French composer Auber features the 17C revolt against the Spaniards, instigated by **Masaniello**.

Herculaneum★★
♦*See HERCULANEUM.*

Vesuvius★★★

Train: Ercolano Scavi (Napoli 20 mins).
The outline of Vesuvius, one of the few still-active volcanoes in Europe, is an intrinsic feature of the Neapolitan

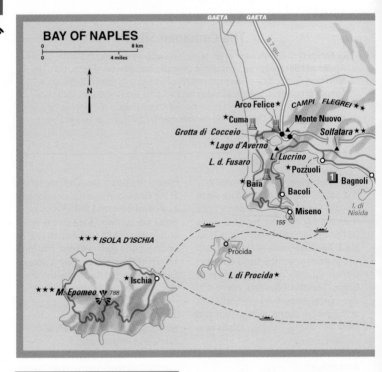

BAY OF NAPLES

GAETA   GAETA

Arco Felice ★
CAMPI   FLEGREI ★ ★
★Cuma
Monte Nuovo
Grotta di Cocceio
Solfatara ★ ★
★Lago d'Averno
L. Lucrino
L. d. Fusaro
★Pozzuoli
★Baia
Bacoli
Bagnoli
Miseno
I. di Nisida
155
★★★ ISOLA D'ISCHIA
Procida
I. di Procida ★
★Ischia
★★★ M. Epomeo ▲ 788

The Eruptions of Vesuvius

Until the earthquake of AD 62 and the eruption of AD 79 which buried Herculaneum and Pompeii, Vesuvius seemed extinct; its slopes were clothed with famous vines and woods. By 1139, seven eruptions had been recorded. Then came a period of calm during which the slopes of the mountains were cultivated. On 16 December 1631 Vesuvius had a terrible awakening, destroying all the settlements at its foot: 3 000 people perished. The eruption of 1794 devastated Torre del Greco. The volcano had minor eruptions in 1858, 1871, 1872, from 1895 to 1899, 1900, 1903, 1904, a major eruption in 1906, 1929 and one in 1944 which altered the shape of the crater. Since then, apart from brief activity linked with the 1980 earthquake, Vesuvius has emitted only a plume of smoke.

landscape. It has two summits: to the north **Monte Somma** (1 132m/3 714ft) and to the south Vesuvius proper (1 277m/ 4 190ft). Over time the volcanic materials on the lower slopes have become fertile soil with orchards and vines producing the famous *Lacryma Christi* wine.

Climbing the Volcano

From Herculaneum and Via Torre del Greco: 27km/16.8mi plus 20min on foot each way. Wear good walking shoes. Paid parking, on the street or in Herculaneum; bus service from railway station, Circumvesuviana Line. 10€. ℘081 86 53 911. www.parconazionalevesuvio.it.

A good road leads to a junction in the midst of lava flows. Take the left fork *(car park a few kilometres further on)*. The path is an easy but most impressive climb up the volcano, scattered with cinders and lapilli.

From the summit there is an immense **panorama★★★** over the Bay of Naples with the Sorrento Peninsula in the south

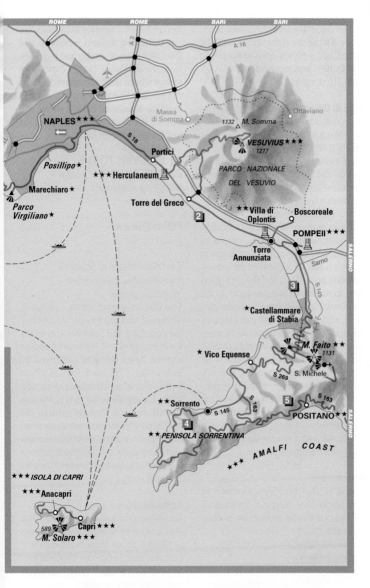

and Cape Miseno in the north. Beyond is the Gulf of Gaeta.

The crater affords an unforgettable sight for its sheer size and the sense of desolation on the slopes of the jagged walls, for the great yawning crater, which takes on a pink colour in the sun, and for the spouting steam-jets.

Torre del Greco

This rather rough and tumble town, which has been repeatedly destroyed by the eruptions of Vesuvius, is well known for its ornaments made of coral and volcanic stone.

Torre Annunziata

www.comune.torreannunziata.na.it.
This town is the centre of the famous Neapolitan pasta industry. It has been

buried under the lava of Vesuvius seven times. It is the site of the sumptuous Villa di Oplontis, which is open to the public and in 1997 was included in UNESCO's World Heritage List.

Villa di Oplontis★★

Open daily Apr–Oct 8.30am–7.30pm; Nov–Mar 8.30am–5pm (last entry 90min before closing). Closed 1 Jan, 25 Dec. 5.50€ inclusive (valid 1 day) for Oplonti, Stabiae and Boscoreale; 20€ for Pompeii, Herculaneum, Oplonti, Stabiae and Boscoreale (valid 3 days). ℘06 399 67 850. www.coopculture.it.

This fine example of a Roman suburban villa is thought to have belonged to Poppea, wife of Nero. The vast building, in which can be identified the slaves' quarters (to the east) and the area given over to the Imperial apartments (to the west), has many well-preserved examples of beautiful original **wall paintings**. In particular, there are landscape scenes featuring architectural elements, portrait medallions and still-life paintings. Of the various animals depicted, the peacock appears so frequently as to have supported the theory that the name of the villa was derived from it. Within the villa, the kitchens are easily identified (with ovens and sink), as are the latrines, which represent a drainage system.

Boscoreale

In the 1C the territory was home to 30 villae rusticae, a type of agricultural home used for the production of olive and wine.

Antiquarium★

Via Settetermini 15. Open Apr–Oct 8.30am–7.30pm, Nov–Mar 8.30am–5pm (last entry 90 min before closing). 5.50€, combined ticket good for admission to Oplontis and Stabiae (valid 1 day). 20€ combined ticket including Pompeii, Herculaneum, Oplonti, Stabiae (valid 3 days). ℘06 399 67 850. www.coopculture.it.

The antiquarium was established near the ruins of Villa Regina, a winery that dates back to the 1C BC. It provides a glimpse into the rural economy of the Roman era, before the famous erup-

tion of AD 79. The main activities were concentrated around livestock and the cultivation of cereals and legumes. Note the dormouse cage, a mouse-like rodent whose meat was appreciated by the Romans. The visit ends at the villa, a building discovered in 1977, where you can see the ruins of 18 terra-cotta tubs half buried in the ground.

3 VESUVIUS TO THE PENINSOLA SORRENTINA★★

From Torre Annunziata. 70km/43.5mi. Allow 1 day.

POMPEII★★★

See POMPEII.

Castellammare di Stabia⚓

www.comune.castellammare -di-stabia.napoli.it.

This was an ancient Roman spa town. Occupied successively by the Oscans, the Etruscans, the Samnites and finally the Romans in the 4C BC, *Stabiae* rebelled against Rome but was destroyed by Sulla in the 1C BC. The town was rebuilt in the form of small clusters of houses, while luxury villas for rich patricians spread over the high ground. In the AD 79 eruption of Vesuvius the new town was wiped out along with Herculaneum and Pompeii. In the 18C the Bourbons undertook excavations, repaired the port and built shipyards.

Antiquarium★

Via Passeggiata Archeologica (Villa di S. Marco). Same admission times and charges as Villa di Oplontis. www.coopculture.it
Finds from excavations are displayed here and include a series of **mural paintings** from villas and **low reliefs**.

◗ Drive 2km/1.2mi E. From the N take the S 145 and follow directions for Agerola-Amalfi, then take the flyover. After the tunnel, turn left.

Roman villas

Same admission times and charges as Villa di Oplontis.
Villa di Arianna was one of the luxurious villas facing the sea with an incomparable

view of the bay and Vesuvius. The architectural refinement of **Villa San Marco** with its two storeys was enhanced by gardens and swimming pools.

Monte Faito★★

Access is from Vico Equense via a scenic route; alternatively, there is a cablecar that departs from Circumvesuviana station in Castellammare di Stabia. The cableway (10min) operates Apr–Oct, departures every 20–30min, 9.35am–4.25pm; Jun–Aug 7.25am–7.15pm. ✆081 87 00 121.

Monte Faito is part of the **Lattari Range**, a headland which separates the Bay of Naples from the Gulf of Salerno and forms the Sorrento Peninsula. Its name is derived from the beech trees (*fagus* in Latin). From Belvedere dei Capi there is a splendid **panorama★★★** of the Bay of Naples. From there the road continues up to a chapel, **Cappella San Michele**, which affords an especially enchanting **panorama★★★** – the wild landscape of the Lattari Mountains contrasts strongly with the smiling scenery of the Bay of Naples and the Sarno Plain.

Vico Equense★

This is a small health and seaside resort on a picturesque rocky site. In the historic **centre★** you will find the cathedral, a rare example of a Gothic church in the region, and the Angevin castle that rises above the sea and is surrounded by a beautiful garden. Do not miss the **Marina di Equa★** or the Spiaggia della Tartaruga (Turtle Beach), located north of the town.

④ SORRENTO AND THE PENISOLA SORRENTINA★★

30km/18.6mi. Allow half a day.

The innumerable bends on this road afford constantly changing views of enchanting landscapes, wild, fantastically shaped rocks plunging vertically into a crystal-clear sea, deep gorges spanned by dizzy bridges and Saracen towers perched on jagged rock stacks. The Amalfi Coast, with its wild and rugged landscape, is formed by the jagged fringe of the Lattari Mountains, a deeply eroded limestone range. Contrasting with these awe-inspiring scenes are the more charming views of fishing villages and the luxuriant vegetation, a mixture of orange, lemon, olive and almond trees, vines and all the Mediterranean flora. The region is popular with artists. A significant part of the attraction is the local cuisine with abundant seafood, and the local mozzarella cheese washed down with the red Gragnano or white Ravello and Positano wines.

Sorrento★★

Train: Sorrento (Napoli 52 mins).

This important resort, known for its many beautiful gardens, overlooks the bay of the same name. Orange and lemon groves are found in the surrounding countryside and even encroach on the town. Local craftsmen produce various marquetry objects. The poet **Torquato Tasso** (🖙 *see FERRARA*) was born in Sorrento in 1544.

Museo Correale di Terranova★

Via Correale 50. Open Tue–Sat 9.30am–6.30pm, Sun 9.30am–1.30pm. Closed Mon. 8€. ✆081 87 81 846. www.museocorreale.it.

Housed in an 18C palace, the museum has some splendid examples of local intarsia work (**secretaire**, 1910), a small archaeological section and, on the first floor, a collection of 17C and 18C furniture as well as an interesting collection of 17C–18C Neapolitan paintings. Two rooms are devoted to the landscape painters of the **Posillipo school**, which flourished in the 1830s, including the main exponent of this school, **Giacinto Gigante** (1806–76). On the second floor is a collection of porcelain and ceramics. From the terrace there is a fine **view★★** over the Gulf of Sorrento.

The Historic Centre★

Via San Cesareo, the *decumanus* of the Roman city, leads to the **Sedile Dominova**, seat of city administration in the Angevin period. It consists of a loggia decorated with frescoes surmounted by a 17C ceramic dome. The steeply sloping street, Via San Giuliani, leads to the church of San Francesco. This Baroque

Sorrento street

© Gino Cianci/Fototeca ENIT

church has a bulbous campanile and is flanked by delightful 13C **cloisters**★ whose vegetable-motif capitals sustain interlaced arcades in Sicilian-Arab style. The nearby public gardens, **Villa Comunale**, offer a splendid **view**★★ of the Bay of Naples.

◐ Leave Sorrento to the W by the S 145 and at the junction take the road to the right to Massa Lubrense.

Penisola Sorrentina★★

This winding road skirts the Sorrento Peninsula and affords fine views of the hillsides covered with olive groves, orange and lemon trees and vines.

From the headland (**Punta del Capo di Sorrento**) *(footpath: from the church in the village of Capo di Sorrento take the road to the right and after the college the paved path, 1hr round trip)* there is a superb **view**★★ of Sorrento.

At **Sant'Agata sui Due Golfi**, perched on a crest dominating the Gulf of Salerno and the Bay of Naples, the **Belvedere del Deserto** (a Benedictine monastery situated 1.5km/1mi west of the town) affords a splendid **panorama**★★. Visit 10am–noon and 5pm–7pm (Oct–Mar to 5pm).

Beyond Sant'Agata, the road which descends steeply to Colli di San Pietro is spectacular. From here you could return to Sorrento by the S 163, which offers superb **views**★★ over the Bay of Naples, or you could head for Positano (◐*see itinerary 5 described in AMALFI COAST).*

ADDRESSES

🏨 STAY

⊖ **Villa Oteri** – Via Miliscola 18, Bacoli. ℘081 52 34 985. www.villaoteri.it. **P**. 9 rooms. This early-19C villa is elegant and refined. Its rooms are decorated with beautiful felt fabrics. Ask for a room facing Lake Bacoli.

⊖ **Camping Il Vulcano Solfatara** – Via Solfatara 161, Pozzuoli. ℘0815 26 23 41. www.solfatara.it. 112 pitches. A campsite located in the crater of a volcano. Shaded, close to the sea and comfortable with hot water, washing machines and a swimming pool. The cosy cabins are equipped with a bathroom – with shower – and the kitchen has a refrigerator. Visits to the crater are free for guests.

⊖⊖ **La Ginestra** – Via Tessa 2, loc. Santa Maria del Castello. 10km/6.2mi SE of Vico Equense in the direction of Moiano. ℘081 80 23 211. www.laginestra.org. 7 rooms. Located at 600m/1970ft on the slopes of Monte Faito, this farmhouse dates from the 17C and has nice terraces and a playground. Spacious tidy rooms hold up to six people. Organic farm products.

🍴 EAT

⊖⊖ **Abraxas** – Via Scalandrone 15, loc. Lucrino, Pozzuoli. ℘081 85 49 347. www.abraxasosteria.it. Closed Sun evening and Tue. A restaurant/wine bar with a beautiful panoramic location. Delicate cuisine and wine by the glass.

⊖⊖ **Ludovico** – Via Roma 15/19, Pozzuoli. ℘081 52 68 255. A pleasant restaurant overlooking the port, serving simply prepared fish dishes that highlight the fresh quality of the ingredients used. The raw fish dishes, pasta and fish soup are highly recommended.

⊖⊖ **Taverna del Capitano** – Piazza delle Sirene 10/11, Marina del Cantone, Massalubrense, 8km/5mi SW of Sant'Agata sui Due Golfi. ℘081 80 81 028. www.taverna delcapitano.com. Closed Mon–Tue (Oct–May), Mon (summer), closed also a period between Jan and Mar. Sober and elegant, with huge windows overlooking the sea, the dishes in this pretty restaurant are Mediterranean style, some of which are based on raw fish. Good taste characterises the adjoining rooms.

Herculaneum★★

Erculano

Herculaneum was founded, according to tradition, by Hercules. Like Pompeii the Roman town was buried during the AD 79 eruption of Vesuvius. Many craftsmen and rich and cultured patricians were drawn to Herculaneum because of its beautiful setting, overlooking the Bay of Naples. Herculaneum is a UNESCO World Heritage Site.

▶ **Population:** 57 638
🖈 **Michelin Map:** 564 E 25 – *see also the local map in BAY OF NAPLES.*
🛈 **Info:** Corso Resina 1, Ercolano (NA). ℘081 85 75 347. www.pompeiisites.org.
◗ **Location:** Herculaneum lies at the foot of Vesuvius, off the A 3, the Naples–Salerno road
◗ **Train:** Ercolano Scavi (Napoli 25 mins).
🚠 **Don't Miss:** The baths, Casa del Mosaico di Nettuno e Anfitrite and the Casa dei Cervi.
◷ **Timing:** Avoid visiting Herculaneum in the midday sun, as there is very little shade in the ruins.

VISIT

Entrance at Corso Resina. Access from Porta Marina (Via Villa dei Misteri or Piazza Esedra) or from Piazza Anfiteatro. NB: Some of the houses listed below may be closed for maintenance and restoration. Open Apr–Oct 8.30am–7.30pm (last entry 6pm); Nov–Mar 8.30am–5pm (last entry 3.30pm). Closed 1 Jan, 25 Dec. 11€; 22€ combined ticket for Pompeii, Herculaneum, Oplontis, Stabiae and Boscoreale (valid 3 days).

Herculaneum is broadly divided into four sections, delineated by the two main streets *(decumani)* and three other thoroughfares *(cardi)*. All timber structures (frameworks, beams, doors, stairs and partitions) were preserved by a hard shell of solidified mud, whereas at Pompeii they were consumed by fire. Most of the houses were empty, but many inhabitants died as they tried to flee the city or make for the sea.

◗ The following itinerary starts at the bottom of Cardo III.

The **Casa dell'Albergo** was about to be converted into apartments for letting, hence its name. This vast patrician villa was one of the most badly damaged by the eruption.

The **Casa dell'Atrio a Mosaico★★** takes its name from the chequered mosaic on the floor in the *atrium*. There is a garden, bedrooms and a pleasant *triclinium* (dining room). The terrace, flanked by two small rest rooms, offers an attractive view of the sea.

In the **Casa a Graticcio★★** the framework *(graticcio)* of the walls was formed by a wooden trellis. It is a unique example of this type of house from Antiquity. With a remarkably well-preserved façade, the **Casa del Tramezzo carbonizzato★** is an example of a patrician dwelling that housed several families. The *atrium* was separated from the *tablinium* (living room) by a wooden partition.

Next door is the **Bottega del Tintore (A)**, the dyer's shop, which contains an interesting wooden clothes press.

The **Casa Sannitica★★** was built on the very simple plan typical of the Samnites (an Italic people of the Sabine race). The **atrium** is surrounded by a gallery with Ionic columns.

The **baths★★★** of Herculaneum, which are in excellent condition, were built at the time of Augustus and show a remarkable degree of practical planning. In the **men's baths** visit the *palestra*, the cloakroom, the *frigidarium* with frescoes on the ceiling, the *tepidarium* and the *caldarium*. The **women's baths** include the waiting-room, the cloakroom *(apodyte-*

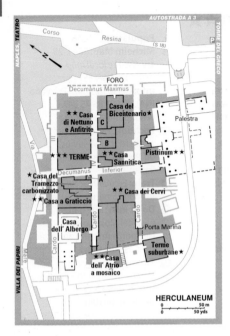

rium), adorned with a mosaic pavement depicting the sea god Triton, the *tepidarium* with a fine floor mosaic representing a labyrinth, and the *caldarium*.

The **Casa del Mobilio carbonizzato★ (B)** has the remains of a charred *(carbonizzato)* bed in one room.

The **Casa del Mosaico di Nettuno e Anfitrite★★** is equipped with a **shop★**; its counter opened onto the street. Mosaics depicting Neptune and Amphitrite adorn the *nymphaeum*.

Nearby is one of the most original houses in Herculaneum, the **Casa del Bel Cortile★ (C)**, with its courtyard *(cortile)*, stone staircase and balcony.

The **Casa del Bicentenario★** was unearthed in 1938, 200 years after digging officially started. The house has fresco decorations and a small cross incorporated in a stucco panel. This is one of the oldest Christian relics brought to light in the Roman Empire.

An inscription states that the **Pistrinum★★** (bakery) belonged to Sextus Patulus Felix. In the shop are flour mills, storage jars and a large oven.

The **Casa dei Cervi★★** was probably the most grandiose patrician villa overlooking the bay. It is adorned by works of art, including a sculptured group of stags *(cervi)* being attacked by dogs.

The tour concludes with a visit to the **Terme suburbane★**, elegantly decorated baths, and the **teatro★** *(entrance Via Mare 123)*.

Villa dei Papiri

Approximately 250m/275yds W of the archaeological area, below the modern town. Visits by appointment only, Sat–Sun 9am–noon. ☎081 732 43 11. 2€.

This large country villa takes its name from the collection of 1 000 Greek papyrus manuscripts that were discovered here. Although excavation work is still taking place, visitors are admitted to the frescoed lower floor and the upper floor, with its *atrium* and mosaics, *natatium* and *nymphaeum* – and to other ruins to the northwest of the site.

♣♣ MAV – Museo Archeologico Virtuale

Via IV Novembre 44 – 500m/ 550yds NW of the archaeological site. ♿ *Mar–May: 9am–5.30pm; Jun–Sept: 10am–6.30pm; Oct–Feb: Tue–Sun 10am–4pm. 7.50€.* ☎081 19 80 65 11. www.museomav.com.

Local archaeological finds are housed in the MAV, a centre that is 5 000sq m/ 54 000sq ft spread over three levels. Through an interactive virtual tour, visitors can travel into Herculaneum's past, until just before the eruption of Mount Vesuvius in AD 79.

Mosaic of Triton in the women's baths at Herculaneum

© Carri Keill/iStockphoto.com

Pompeii★★★

Pompeii, the opulent town that was buried in AD 79 in one of the most disastrous volcanic eruptions in history, provides evidence of the ancient way of life. The extensive and varied ruins of the dead city, in its attractive setting, movingly evoke on a grand scale a Roman city at the time of the Empire. Pompeii was included in UNESCO's World Heritage List in 1997.

A BIT OF HISTORY

Pompeii was founded in the 8C BC by the Oscans, but by the 6C BC a Greek influence was already prevalent in the city from its neighbour *Cumae*, then a powerful Greek colony. From the end of the 5C BC, when it came under Samnite rule, to the beginning of the 1C AD, the city knew great prosperity; town planning and art flourished. In the year 80 BC, the town fell under Roman domination and soon became a favourite resort of rich Romans. Roman families settled there. Pompeii adopted Roman organisation, language, lifestyle, building methods and decoration. When the eruption of Vesuvius struck, Pompeii was a booming town with a population of about 25 000. The town was situated in a fertile region, trade flourished and there was even some industrial activity; it also had a port. The numerous shops and workshops that have been uncovered, its wide streets and the deep ruts made in the cobblestones by chariot wheels are evidence of the intense activity that went on in the town.

The people had a lively interest in spectacles, games and active politics, as can be seen in a fresco housed at the Archaeological Museum in Naples. In AD 59, after a fight between rival supporters, the amphitheatre was closed for 10 years and reopened after Nero's wife Poppea interceded. In the year AD 62, an earthquake extensively damaged the town but before it could be put to rights, Vesuvius erupted (August AD 79) and also destroyed

- ⚐ **Michelin Map:** 564 E 25 – Campania.
- ⚑ **Info:** ☎081 85 75 347. www.pompeiisites.org.
- ◖ **Location:** Pompeii is situated at the foot of Vesuvius, the volcano to which it owes its fame. The main access road is the A3.
- ◖ **Train:** Pompei Scavi VM (Napoli 40 mins).
- ⚐ **Don't Miss:** The Foro (forum), Terme Stabiane (baths) and the fresco at the Villa del Misteri.
- ⚐ **Timing:** The site is extensive so allow a day to see it all.

Herculaneum and *Stabiae*. In two days Pompeii was buried under a layer of ash 6m–7m/20ft–23ft deep. Bulwer-Lytton describes events in his novel *The Last Days of Pompeii*. It was only in the 18C, under the reign of Charles of Bourbon, that systematic excavations began.

VISIT

Access from Porta Marina (Via Villa dei Misteri or Piazza Esedra) or from Piazza Anfiteatro. Allow 1 day. ⚐ Open daily Apr–Oct 8.30am–7.30pm (last entry 6pm); Nov–Mar 9am–5pm (last entry 3.30pm). Closed 1 Jan, 25 Dec. 11€; 20€ combined ticket for Pompeii, Herculaneum, Oplonti, Stabiae and Boscoreale (valid 3 days). ☎06 399 67 850. www.coopculture.it.
⚐ Some of the houses listed may be closed for cleaning and maintenance.

Porta Marina

The road passed through this gateway down to the sea, with separate gates for animals and pedestrians.

Streets

The streets are straight and intersect at right angles. They are sunk between raised pavements and are interrupted at intervals by blocks of stone to enable pedestrians to cross when the roadway was awash with rain.

Foro★★★

The forum was the centre of the town and the setting for most of the large buildings. In this area, religious ceremonies were held, trade was carried out and justice was dispensed. The immense square, closed to traffic, was paved with large marble flagstones and adorned with statues of past emperors. A portico enclosed it on three sides.

The **basilica★★** is the largest building (67m by 25m/220ft by 82ft) in Pompeii and is where judicial affairs were conducted. The **Tempio di Apollo★★** is a temple dedicated to Apollo, built before the Roman occupation, which stood against the background of Vesuvius. The altar was placed in front of the steps leading to the shrine *(cella)*. Facing each other are copies of the statues of Apollo and Diana found on the spot (the originals are in the Naples Museum).

The **Tempio di Giove★★**, in keeping with tradition, has pride of place. Dedicated to the Capitoline Triad (Jupiter, Juno and Minerva), it is flanked by two triumphal arches, once marble.

The **Macellum** was a market lined with shops. A kiosk crowned by a dome contained a basin for cleaning fish.

The **Tempio di Vespasiano**, dedicated to the Emperor Vespasian, contained an altar adorned with a sacrificial scene.

A fine **doorway★** with a marble frame decorated with carvings gives access to the **Edificio di Eumachia** (Building of Eumachia), built by the priestess Eumachia for the guild of the *fullones* (fullers), of which she was the patron.

Foro Triangolare★

There are several Ionic columns of a majestic *propylaeum* that preceded the Triangular Forum. A few vestiges of its **Doric temple** provide evidence of the town's existence in the 6C BC.

Teatro Grande★

The Great Theatre was built in the 5C BC, remodelled in the Hellenistic period (200–150 BC) and again by the Romans in the 1C AD. It was an open-air theatre that could hold 5 000 spectators.

Caserma dei Gladiatori

The Gladiators' Barracks has an esplanade bounded by a gateway, originally used as a foyer for the theatres.

Odeon★★

Odeums, or covered theatres, were used for concerts, oratorical displays and ballets. This held only 800 spectators. It dates from early Roman colonisation.

Tempio d'Iside★

The cult of the Egyptian goddess Isis spread in the Hellenistic period thanks to contact with the Orient and Egypt. The small building stands in the middle of an arcaded courtyard. To its left is the *purgatorium*, a site set aside for purification ceremonies that contained water from the Nile. The pictorial decorations of the temple are housed in the Archaeological Museum in Naples.

Casa di Lucius Ceius Secundus

This interesting house has a façade faced with stucco in imitation of stone.

Casa di Menandro★★

This large patrician villa named after Menander, was richly decorated with paintings (fourth style) and mosaics and had its own baths. In the *atrium* is a *lararium* (shrine to the household gods) arranged as a miniature temple.

The house opens onto **Via dell'Abbondanza★★**, a commercial street, evocative with its shops and houses.

Casa del Criptoportico

After passing through the peristyle (note the painting in the *lararium: Mercury with a Peacock, Snakes and Foliage*), go down to the Cryptoporticus, a wide underground passage surmounted by a fine barrel vault and lit by small windows. This type of corridor, popular in Roman villas during the Empire, was used as a passage and for exercise.

Fullonica Stephani★★

This is an example of a dwelling-house converted into workshops. The clothing industry flourished in Roman times

ARCHITECTURE AND DECORATION

Building Methods

Pompeii was destroyed before a degree of uniformity in building methods had been achieved and it presents examples of the diverse methods and materials used: *opus quadratum* (large blocks of freestone piled on top of one another, without mortar of any kind); *opus incertum* (irregularly shaped blocks of tufa or lava bonded with mortar); *opus reticulatum* (small square blocks of limestone or tufa arranged diagonally to form a decorative pattern); and *opus testaceum* (walls are faced with triangular bricks laid flat with the pointed end turned inwards). Sometimes the walls were faced with plaster or marble. There are several types of dwelling in Pompeii: the sober and austere house of the Samnites, which became larger and more richly decorated through Greek influence. With the arrival of the Romans and the problems arising from a growing population, a new kind of house evolved in which limited space is compensated for by rich decoration.

Pompeiian Painting

A large number of paintings, which adorned the walls of the dwellings, have been transferred to the Archaeological Museum in Naples. However, a visit to the dead city gives a good idea of the pictorial decoration of the period. There are **four different styles**. The first style by means of relief and light touches of colour imitates marble. The second style is by far the most attractive: walls are divided into large panels by false pillars surmounted by pediments or crowned by a small shrine, with false doors all designed to create an illusion of perspective.

The artists show a partiality for Pompeiian red, cinnabar obtained from mercury sulphide, and a dazzling black. The third style abandoned *trompe l'œil* in favour of scenes and landscapes painted in pastel colours. Most of the frescoes uncovered at Pompeii belong to the fourth style.

© Risamay / iStockphoto.com

as the full, draped costume required a lot of material. In the *fullonicae*, new fabrics were finished and clothes were laundered. Several of these workshops have been uncovered in Pompeii. The *fullones* cleaned the cloths by trampling them with their feet in vats that were filled with water and soda or urine.

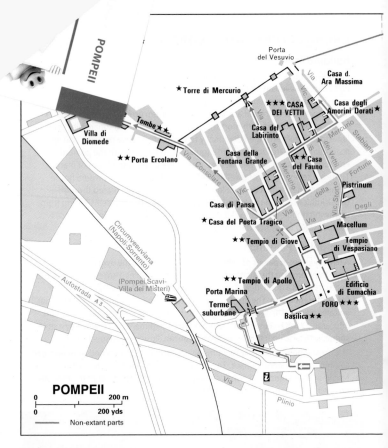

POMPEII

Porta
del Vesuvio

★ Torre di Mercurio

Casa d.
Ara Massima

★★★ CASA
DEI VETTII

Casa degli
Amorini Dorati ★

Tombe ★★

Casa del
Labirinto

Villa di
Diomede

★★ Porta Ercolano

Casa della
Fontana Grande

★★ Casa
del Fauno

Pistrinum

Casa di Pansa

★ Casa del Poeta Tragico

Macellum

★★ Tempio di Giove

Tempio
di Vespasiano

★★ Tempio di Apollo

Porta Marina

Edificio
di Eumachia

Terme
suburbane

FORO ★★★

Basilica ★★

Circumvesuviana
(Napoli-Sorrento)

(Pompei Scavi-
Villa dei Misteri)

Autostrada A3

Via Consolare

Via

di

Mercurio

della

Vic. Storto

Fortuna

Degli

Via

Via del Vesuvio

Mercurio

Stabiana

Via

Plinio

POMPEII

0 — 200 m
0 — 200 yds
—— Non-extant parts

Termopolio di Asellina

This was a bar which also sold pre-cooked dishes *(thermopolium)*. A stone counter giving directly onto the street formed the shopfront; jars embedded in the counter contained food for sale.

Termopolio Grande★

This bar, which is similar to the previous one, has a painted *lararium*.

Casa di Trebius Valens

The inscriptions on the wall are electoral slogans.

Casa di Loreius Tiburtinus★

This was a rich dwelling, judging from the fine marble *impluvium*, the triclinium adorned with frescoes and the **decoration**★ against a white background of one of the rooms, which is among the best

examples of the fourth Pompeian style. But its most luxurious feature was the splendid **garden**★, which was laid out for water displays.

Villa di Giulia Felice★

Built just within the town boundary, it has three main parts: the dwelling, the baths, which the owner opened to the public, and a section for letting, including an inn and shops. The large garden is bounded by a fine **portico**★.

Anfiteatro★

This is the oldest Roman amphitheatre known (80 BC). It was built away from the city centre to enable easy access. On hot days spectators were protected from the sun by a linen drape held up by wooden poles. Alongside is the **palestra**, a training ground for athletes.

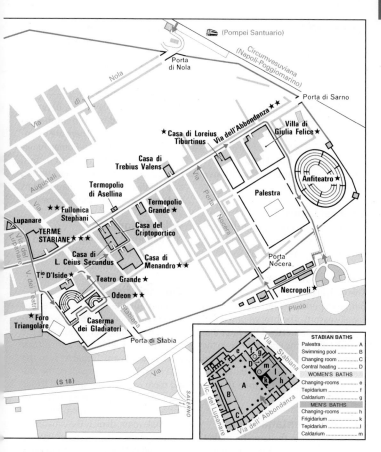

Necropoli Fuori Porta Nocera★

Tombs line one of the roads leading out of town, via the Nocera Gate.

▶ Take Via Porta Nocera to return to the Via dell'Abbondanza, then turn left.

Terme Stabiane★★★

These are the oldest baths in Pompeii (2C BC). The entrance is through the gymnasium *(palestra)*; to the left are changing-rooms *(spogliatoio)*, and a swimming pool *(piscina)*.

The **women's baths** begin at the far end on the right, with changing-rooms and lockers, a *tepidarium* (lukewarm bath) and a *caldarium* (hot bath). The men's baths have changing-rooms, a *frigidarium* (cold bath), a *tepidarium* and a *caldarium*. There is stucco decoration on the coffered ceiling.

Lupanare

The official brothel of Pompeii is decorated with licentious subject matter, illustrating the "specialities" of the prostitutes. Wall graffiti provides customers' opinions on services received.

Pistrinum

The baker's oven and flourmills.

Casa dei Vettii★★★

The Vettii brothers were rich merchants. Their dwelling, the most lavishly decorated in the town, is the finest example of a faithfully restored house and garden. The reroofed *atrium* opens onto the peristyle surrounding a garden with statues, basins and fountains.

Frescoes in the *triclinium* depict mythological scenes and friezes of cupids.

Casa degli Amorini Dorati★

This house shows the refinement of the owner, who probably lived during the reign of Nero, and his taste for the theatre. The glass and gilt medallions depicting cupids (amorini) have deteriorated but the building as a whole, with its peristyle with one wing raised like a stage, is well preserved.

Casa dell'Ara Massima

There are well-preserved **paintings★** (one in trompe l'œil).

Casa del Labirinto

One of the rooms opening onto the peristyle has a mosaic of the Labyrinth with Theseus killing the Minotaur.

Casa del Fauno★★

This vast, luxurious house had two atriums, two peristyles and dining rooms for all seasons. The bronze original of the famous statuette of the faun that adorned one of the impluviums is in the Naples Museum. The rooms contained admirable mosaics including the famous Battle of Alexander and Darius (Naples Museum).

Casa della Fontana Grande

Its main feature is the large **fountain★** (fontana) shaped as a niche decorated with mosaics and fragments of coloured glass in the Egyptian style.

Torre di Mercurio★

A tower on the town wall, dedicated to the god Mercury, now affords an interesting **view★★** of the excavations.

Casa del Poeta Tragico★

This house takes its name from a mosaic now in the Naples Museum. A mosaic of a watchdog at the threshold bears the inscription Cave Canem (Beware of the Dog).

Casa di Pansa

A spacious house, partly converted for letting.

Porta Ercolano★★

The Herculaneum Gate was the main gateway of Pompeii, with two gates for pedestrians and one for vehicles.

Via delle Tombe★★

A great melancholy feeling pervades this street lined with monumental tombs and cypresses. There are examples of all forms of Greco-Roman funerary architecture: tombs with niches, round or square temples, altars resting on a plinth, drum-shaped mausoleums and simple semicircular seats or exedrae.

Villa di Diomede

This important dwelling dedicated to Diomedes has a loggia overlooking the garden and swimming pool.

Villa dei Misteri★★★

Located outside the city centre, this ancient patrician villa comprises a luxurious residential part (west) and the eastern half reserved for agricultural work and servants' quarters. In the area inhabited by the owners, the dining room contains the splendid **fresco** from which the villa derives its renown and name. This composition, which fills the whole room, depicts the initiation of a young bride to the mysteries (misteri) of the cult of Dionysus. The mistress of this house was probably a priestess of the Cult of Dionysus, which was then very popular in southern Italy. There is a fine peristyle and underground passage (criptoportico).

ADDRESSES

TAKING A BREAK

Snack Wine's Todisco – Piazza Schettini 19, Pompeii. ☎081 85 05 051. This simple caffè, near the Sanctuary, is a nice spot to stop and relax. Shaded by a perfumed citrus grove, it serves simple food at reasonable prices.

Viva Lo Re Osteria – Corso Resina 261, Ercolano. ☎081 73 90 207. www.vivalore.it. Closed Mon and Sun Ev. Near the entrance to Herculaneum, this inviting wine bar also serves food.

Isola
d'Ischia★★★

Ischia, known as the Emerald Island because of its luxuriant vegetation, is the largest island in the Bay of Naples and one of its major attractions. A clear, sparkling light plays over a varied landscape: a coast covered with pinewoods, indented with bays and creeks sheltering villages with their colourful cubic houses; the slopes covered with olive trees and vineyards (producing the white or red Epomeo wine); and an occasional crumbling tower. The cottages, sometimes roofed with a dome and with an outside staircase, often have vine-swathed walls.

A BIT OF HISTORY

The island rose out of the sea during the Tertiary Era at the time of a volcanic eruption. The soil is volcanic and there are many hot springs with various medicinal properties.

Celebrities from Michelangelo to Elizabeth Taylor have sought refuge here. Norwegian playwright Henrik Ibsen once pottered about in Casamicciola, the town where Giuseppe Garibaldi recovered from his war wounds.

▶ **Population:** 17 883
◔ **Michelin Map:**
564 E 23 – Campania.
Info: ℰ081 33 33 220 or 33 33 221. www.comuneischia.it.
◯ **Location:** Capri's neighbour in the Bay of Naples.
Parking: Only pedestrians, mules and mopeds are allowed in Sant'Angelo. Park and walk in.
◕ **Timing:** A few hours to tour the island.

Gods and mythological heroes rested on Ischia too. Ulysses visited the king on Castiglione Hill, while Aphrodite soaked in the thermal waters.

Aeneas beached his boat in Lacco Ameno and the archangel Michael gave the picturesque fishing village of Sant'Angelo its name.

🚗 DRIVING TOUR

40km/24.8mi. Follow the itinerary on the map. The narrow road offers numerous viewpoints of the coast. ⊘From late-Mar–30 Sept, non-residents may not bring cars onto the Island of Ischia.

GETTING THERE

Ischia and Procida can be reached from Naples, Capri and Pozzuoli. For Ischia: from Naples there are daily ferry crossings (1hr 25min); from Capri there are daily hovercraft crossings (40min) from April to October; from Pozzuoli there are daily ferry crossings (1hr); from Procida there are daily ferry crossings (30min) and hovercraft crossings (15min). For Procida: from Naples there are daily ferry crossings (1hr) and hovercraft crossings (35min); from Ischia there are daily ferry crossings (25min); from Pozzuoli there

are daily ferry crossings (30min) and hovercraft crossings (15min).
Caremar (Naples and Pozzuoli to Ischia and Casamicciola), ℰ081 18 96 66 90; www.caremar.it.
Alilauro Volaviamare (Naples, Sorrento, Capri and locations on the Amalfi Coast to Ischia and Forio), ℰ081 497 22 22; www.volaviamare.it.
Medmar (Naples and Pozzuoli to Ischia and Casamicciola), ℰ081 333 44 11; www.medmargroup.it.
SNAV (Naples and Procida for Casamicciola), ℰ081 42 85 555; www.snav.it.

ISCHIA★

The capital is divided into two settlements, **Ischia Porto** and **Ischia Ponte**. The Corso Vittoria Colonna, an avenue lined with caffès and smart shops, links the port, in a former crater, and Ischia Ponte. The latter owes its name to the dike built by the Aragonese to link the coast with the rocky islet on the summit of which stands the **Castello Aragonese★★**, a beautiful group of buildings comprising a castle and several churches. Open daily 9am–dusk. 10€. ℘081 99 19 59. www.castelloaragonese.it. There is an enchanting **view★★** from the terrace of the bar of the same name. On the outskirts are a large pinewood and a fine sandy beach.

TOUR OF THE ISLAND

25km/ 15.5mi. Follow the map.

Barano d'Ischia

The Barano territory extends over the hillside to the beautiful **Marina dei Maronti★** (Maronti Beach).

Monte Epomeo★★★

Access is by a path which branches off in a bend of the road once level with the public gardens. 1hr 30min on foot round trip.

The dramatic landscape was the cinematic backdrop for *The Talented Mr Ripley*. Cliffs swoop down to sandy beaches, with Mount Epomeo towering 788m/2 585ft above. Its name means "To see from a height panoramically" – and visitors can do just that after a steep hike. Footsore tourists may prefer to rent a mule in Fontana. From the summit of this tufa peak there is a vast panorama of the entire island and the Bay of Naples.

Serrara Fontana

Not far from this settlement a belvedere offers a plunging **view★★** of the site of Sant'Angelo with its beach and peninsula.

Sant'Angelo★

This peaceful fishing village clusters around a small harbour. Artists flocked there in the 1950s, and painter Werner Gilles declared it "the most beautiful place in the world".

A narrow isthmus stretches to one of the Tyrrhenian Sea's most distinctive landmarks. The *Roja* – otherwise known as the **Isolotto di Sant'Angelo** – is a volcanic cone, capped with the remains of a tower and Benedictine monastery

Ischia Ponte viewed from the Castello Aragonese

(both destroyed when Nelson's English fleet shelled the area in 1809).

Visitors can clamber onto the islet's eroded lower slopes or catch a water taxi on the isthmus. The Maronti Beach *fumarole* (steam plume) and the ancient Roman baths at Cava Scura are popular destinations *(access by footpaths)*.

🅿 Only pedestrians, mules and mopeds are allowed inside the village. Park and stroll – or catch an "ape", a three-wheeled minicab.

Spiaggia di Citara★

This fine beach is sheltered by the majestic headland, Punta Imperatore.

Forio and La Mortella

Via F. Calise 39, Forio. Open April–Oct Tue, Thu and Sat–Sun 9am–7pm. 12€; concert tickets 20€ (includes visit to the garden). ☏081 98 62 20. www.lamortella.org.

Landscaper Russell Page transformed a rough valley, dismissed as a quarry, into a tropical paradise. Built by the British composer William Walton, La Mortella (meaning "Myrtle") includes a small museum housing photographs, many snapped by scene-setter Cecil Beaton.

Lacco Ameno and Museo Archeologico di Pithecusae

Corso Angelo Rizzoli, Lacco Ameno. Open Tue–Sun 9.30am–1pm. ☏081 99 61 03. www.pithecusae.it.

In 770 BC the Greeks established their first colony in the West here, called *Pithecusa*. Scholars once thought the name was connected to *pithêkos* (monkey), but now believe it derives from *pithos* (pitcher).

The **Pithecusae Archaeological Museum** in Lacco Ameno houses artefacts, including the Cup of Nestor. It is

now a holiday resort. The church of Santa Restituta (Piazza Santa Restituta) was built on the remains of an early Christian basilica and a necropolis. There is a small archaeological museum. The tour of the island ends with the important thermal spa of **Casamicciola Terme**.

BOAT TRIP
Procida★

Procida is a 15/30min boat ride from Ischia (🔵 see Getting There, p237).

Procida was formed by craters levelled by erosion and remains the wildest island in the Bay of Naples. The fishermen, gardeners and winegrowers live in a setting of colourful houses with domes, arcades and terraces.

ADDRESSES

🏨 STAY

hotel is run by a family of artists. There is a private, rocky beach.

♈️ EAT

🍴 **Pizzeria Il Califfo** – Via San Montano 37, ℘081 98 60 68. Lacco Ameno. Typical family pizzeria with wood-fired oven.

😋 **Damiano** – Via Variante Esterna SS 270. ℘081 98 30 32. Dinner only. This spacious, rustically furnished hall overlooks Ischia. The cuisine features some simple traditional fish specialities and is famous for its signature rabbit dish.

😋 **Gorgonia** – Marina Corricella, Procida. ℘081 81 01 060. An great place to taste the catch of the day. Dishes are served on the quay of the fishing port.

😋 **La Corricella** – Via Marina Corricella 88, Procida. ℘081 89 67 575. www.hotel corricella.it. 9 rooms. This hotel is an old fisherman's house that holds a panoramic position on the Corricella Marina and Chiaia Beach.

😋 **Scarabeo** – Via Salette 10, Ciraccio. ℘081 89 69 918. Closed Sept–Jun lunch and Nov–20 Dec. Situated in a beautiful pergola of lemon trees, specialities are from the land and the sea.

😋 **Trattoria da Peppina di Renato** – Via Montecorvo 42, Forio. ℘081 99 83 12. www.trattoriadapeppina.it. Closed Wed and 15 Nov-15 Feb. Once you ascend the narrow, winding streets, you'll be rewarded with spectacular views of the sea. Sit in the shade of a pergola on their interesting wrought-iron sofas (made from antique headboards) and enjoy delicious home-style cooking.

😋/😋 **Caracalè** – Località Marina Corricella 62, Procida. ℘081 081 89 69 192. In a former boat-house or, in summer, outdoors, a few metres from the water. Simple but fragrant fish dishes.

Isola di Capri★★★

This island's enchantment owes much to its ideal position off the Sorrento Peninsula, beautiful rugged landscape, mild climate and luxuriant vegetation. It has captivated everyone from Roman emperors Augustus and Tiberius to luminaries such as D.H. Lawrence, George Bernard Shaw and Lenin, and today the swathes of tourists that wander the fashionable lanes of Capri town.

CAPRI★★★

Capri is like a stage-setting for an operetta with its small squares, little white houses and Moorish-looking alleyways. Here wild and lonely spots can still be found near crowded and lively scenes. *Capri is expensive; expect big-city prices, especially in outdoor bars.*

Piazza Umberto I★

This famous *piazzetta* is the centre of town. The narrow side streets, such as **Via Le Botteghe★**, are lined with souvenir shops and boutiques.

▶ **Population:** 7 200

🜨 **Michelin Map:** 564 F 24 – Campania.

🅸 **Info:** Piazzetta Cerio 11, 80073 Capri (NA). ℘081 83 75 308, Fax 081 83 70 918. www.capritourism.com.

🜨 **Location:** Capri can be reached by ferry from Naples, Sorrento and other towns along the Amalfi Coast. **Marina Grande★** is the main port where boats arrive on the northern side of the isle. A funicular railway connects Marina Grande to Capri, where there is a bus service to Anacapri.

🅿 **Parking:** Much of Capri Town is pedestrianised.

🜨 **Don't Miss:** The blue waters of Grotta Azzurra.

🕐 **Timing:** A couple of days.

👪 **Kids:** The Marina Grande–Capri funicular.

Belvedere Cannone★★

To reach the belvedere take **Via Madre Serafina★**. The promenade presents the mysterious aspect of Capri with its covered and winding stepped alleys.

Belvedere di Tragara★★

Access by Via Camerelle and Via Tragara. From here there is an splendid view of the *Faraglioni* (sea stacks).

Certosa di San Giacomo e Giardini d'Augusto

Daily 9am–2pm and 5–8pm, closed Mon (Certosa), 9am–7pm (Giardini). 4€.
This 14C Carthusian Monastery has two cloisters, with Roman statues taken from the Blue Grotto on one. From Augustus' Gardens there is a beautiful **view★★** of Punta di Tragara and the *Faraglioni* (sea stacks).
Lower down, **Via Krupp★**, clinging to the rock-face, leads to Marina Piccola.

Marina Piccola★

At the foot of Monte Solaro is a fishing harbour and beautiful small beaches.

Villa Jovis★★

The steep walk from Piazza Umberto – along Via Botteghe and Via Tiberio – takes 30–40min. Open 10am–2pm. Closed Tue. 2€. ✆081 83 75 308.
Jupiter's Villa was the residence of the Emperor Tiberius. Excavations have uncovered servants' quarters, the cisterns and the Imperial apartments.
From the esplanade there is a **panorama★★** of the whole island. Take the stairway behind the church for **Tiberius' Leap★** (Salto di Tiberio), from which his victims were allegedly thrown.

Arco Naturale★

A 25min walk from Capri, along Via Sopramonte and Via Croce.
Coastal erosion created this gigantic natural rock arch. Lower down is the **Grotta di Matermania**, a cave where the Romans venerated the fertility goddess Mater Magna (Great Mother).

ANACAPRI★★★

Take Via Roma to reach Anacapri, a delightful village with shady streets and fewer crowds than Capri.

Villa San Michele★★

Access from Piazza della Vittoria. Open daily 9am–1hr before dusk. 7€. ✆081 83 71 401. www.sanmichele.org.
The villa was built at the end of the 19C for the Swedish doctor-writer Axel Munthe (d.1949), who lived here up to 1910 and described the atmosphere of the island in his *Story of San Michele*. The house contains 17C and 18C furniture and Roman sculptures. The pergola at the end of the **garden** provides a splendid **panorama★★★** of

Faraglioni, Capri

©Alexandre Fagundes De Fagundes/Dreamstime.com

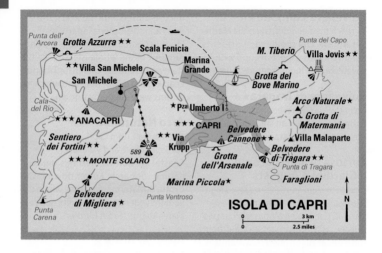

ISOLA DI CAPRI

Capri, Marina Grande, Mount Tiberius and the *Faraglioni*.

Just below the villa is a stairway, **Scala Fenicia**, of nearly 800 steps down to the harbour. For a long time, this was the only link between the town and its port.

Chiesa di San Michele

Piazza San Nicola. Call for opening times. ℰ081 83 72 396.

From the organ gallery note the majolica **floor★** (1761) representing the Garden of Eden.

Monte Solaro★★★

The chairlift operates 9.30am–3.30pm, (to 4pm Mar–Apr, to 5pm May–Oct).10€. ℰ081 83 71 438. www.capriseggiovia.it. The chairlift swings above gardens and terraces brimming with luxuriant vegetation. From the summit there is an unforgettable **panorama★★★** of the Bay of Naples as far as the island of Ponza, the Apennines and the mountains of Calabria to the south.

Belvedere di Migliara★

1hr on foot round trip. Pass under the chairlift to take Via Caposcuro.

There is a remarkable **view★** of the lighthouse on the headland, Punta Carena.

Sentiero dei Fortini★★

About 4hrs. Return via bus or taxi.

Directions available at the tourist office. This trail takes you along the western side of Capri and connects the Punta Carena and Punta dell'Arcera. The course offers views of the Tombosiello, Pino and Mesola Orrico forts.

BOAT TRIPS
Grotta Azzurra★★

Boats leave from Marina Grande. It is also possible to go by road (8km/5mi from Capri). Boat trip and visit to the cave all year, daily (except at high tide and when the sea is rough), 9am–1pm dusk. Duration: 1hr. 14€ + entrance 13€. Excursion from Marina Grande with the following companies: Laser Capri (ℰ081 83 75 208; info@lasercapri.com, www.lasercapri.com); Motoscafisti Capri (ℰ081 83 75 646; www. motoscafisticapri.com); includes trip by fast or small boat and grotto. The **Blue Grotto** is the most famous of Capri's caves. The light enters not directly, but by refraction through the water, giving it a beautiful blue colour.

Around the Island★★★

Leave from Marina Grande. Boat trip all year (except when the sea is rough), departing from Marina Grande at regular intervals with the following companies: Motoscafisti Capri (ℰ081 83 75 646;

www.motoscafisticapri.com); Laser Capri (℘081 83 75 208; www.lasercapri. com). Duration: about 2hrs. 18€ + 13€ to the Grotta Azzurra. Ⓖ Visitors are not permitted to swim in the cave.

Visitors will discover a rugged coastline, pierced with caves and peaceful creeks, fringed with fantastically shaped reefs and lined with cliffs dipping vertically into the sea. The island is barely 6km/4mi long and 3km/2mi wide with a particularly mild climate favouring the growth of a varied flora. The boats travel clockwise and the first sight is the **Grotta del Bove Marino** (Sea Ox Cave), which derives its name from the roar of the sea rushing into the cave in stormy weather.

Beyond the headland (Punta del Capo) is dominated by Mount Tiberius (Monte Tiberio). Once past the impressive cliff known as Tiberius' Leap (Ⓖ*see above*), the headland to the south, Punta di Tragara, is fringed by the famous **Faraglioni**; rocky islets eroded into fantastic shapes by the waves.

The **Grotta dell'Arsenale** (Arsenal Cave) was used as a *nymphaeum* during the reign of Tiberius. Continue past the port of Marina Piccola to reach the more gentle west coast. The last part of the trip covers the north coast and includes the visit to the Blue Grotto.

ADDRESSES

🛏 STAY

⊜⊜ **Da Giorgio** – Via Roma 34, 80073 Capri. ℘081 83 75 777. www.dagiorgio capri.com. Restaurant ⊜⊜. A pleasant, unpretentious hotel-restaurant with a wonderful veranda and huge windows with splendid views over the Gulf of Capri.

⊜⊜ **Hotel Florida** – Via Fuorlovado 34, 80073 Capri. ℘081 83 70 710. ⛶. A small hotel, centrally located. 1950s-style, simple interior with a lacquer finish. Breakfast is served on the terrace in the garden.

⊜⊜⊜ **Albergo Villa Sarah** – Via Tiberio 3a. ℘081 83 77 817. www.villasarah.it. 20 rooms. Spacious villa with bright rooms,

some overlooking the Mediterranean Sea and others looking into a citrus orchard. Very charming.

🍴 EAT

⊜ **Pulalli Wine Bar** – Piazza Umberto I, 80073 Capri. ℘081 83 74 108. Closed Tue. A pleasant wine bar near the tourist office. Head for the much-sought-after tables on the terrace where there is a good view over the piazza. Excellent wine list.

⊜⊜⊜ **Da Paolino** – Via Palazzo a Mare 11, 80073 Marina Grande. ℘081 83 76 102. www.paolinocapri.com. Open Easter–middle Oct. This restaurant is best described as the Mediterranean equivalent of the Garden of Eden, deliciously scented with the aroma of lemons. Warm, friendly ambience. The wrought-iron tables are a nice touch.

⊜⊜⊜ **Mammà** – Via Madre Serafina 6/11, ℘081 83 77 472, www. ristorantemamma.com. Just a stone's throw from the famous piazzetta, this charming restaurant decorated in Mediterranean colours bears the mark of Michelin-starred chef Gennaro Esposito. The focus is on the flavours of the Campania region while also paying tribute to traditional dishes from Capri. Enjoy Pizza Napoletana and a selection of fried dishes at the typical 17C vaulted restaurant next door.

⊜⊜⊜⊜ **L'Altro Vissani Capri** – Via Longano 3, ℘081 18 99 05 75. www. laltrovissanicapri.it. Closed Nov, Jan and Feb. High quality ingredients for excellent traditional cuisine. Unexpected view on the gulf!

TAKING A BREAK

Pasticceria rosticceria Buonocore – Via Vittorio Emanuele 35, Capri. ℘081 83 76 151. This is a good place to taste the sweet specialities of the region, like *torta caprese* made with dark chocolate and almonds.

SHOPPING

Carthusia–I profumi di Capri – Viale Matteotti 2d, Capri. ℘081 83 70 368. www.carthusia.com. The legendary scent of Capri is made here by combining local fragrances such as lemon, rosemary, rose and carnation.

Amalfi Coast★★★

Costiera Amalfitana

With its charming fishing villages and luxuriant vegetation – a mixture of orange, lemon, olive and almond trees, as well as vines and bougainvillea – the Amalfi Coast has long been popular with travellers and artists. The wild and rugged landscape contrasts with its glamorous reputation. The international jet set of the 1950s and 60s came aboard fabulous yachts in search of *La Dolce Vita*, and although these days the "Costiera" attracts tourists from all walks of life, it maintains its reputation as a hot-spot for the rich and famous.

♿ **Michelin Map:** 564 F 25 – Campania.

🛈 **Info:** Via delle Repubbliche Marinare 27, 84011 Amalfi (Salerno). ℘089 87 11 07. www.amalfitouristoffice.it www.amalficoastweb.com.

▶ **Location:** Arguably the most stunning coastline in Italy, the Amalfi Coast runs between Sorrento and Salerno. The beauty of this area earned it a place in UNESCO's 1997 World Heritage List.

🅿 **Parking:** There is plenty of parking by the beach at Amalfi. Visitors to Salerno can park in the car park at Via Alveraz.

👁 **Don't Miss:** Jaunty Amalfi or Ravello's dramatic stairways and roof passages.

🕐 **Timing:** Allow a day for a leisurely coastal drive.

👪 **Kids:** Grotta dello Smeraldo, or fun on the beach at Amalfi.

♿ **Also See:** The first four itineraries are included in Bay of NAPLES, which is the ideal start for this tour.

🚗 DRIVING TOUR

5 ALONG THE COAST

80km/49.7mi. Allow 1 day. The route below constitutes the continuation of itinerary 4, as described in Bay of NAPLES. For exploring the "Costiera" alone, the best point of departure is Positano.

Positano★★

🛈Via Regina Giovanna 13. ℘089 87 50 67. www.aziendaturismopositano.it.
The white cubic houses of this old fishing village reveal a strong Moorish influence; lush gardens dotted on terraced slopes go down to the sea. Positano is "the only place in the world designed on a vertical axis" (Paul Klee).
Much loved and frequented in the past by artists and intellectuals (Picasso, Cocteau and Steinbeck) and by the trend setters of *La Dolce Vita* who used to meet up at the *Buca di Bacco* nightclub, today Positano is one of the most popular resorts of the Amalfi Coast. "Positano fashion" was born here in the 1950s, with its brightly coloured materials and famous sandals.

Vettica Maggiore

Its houses are scattered over the slopes. From the esplanade there is a fine view★★ of the coast and sea.

Praiano

This Moorish-looking town has houses that are sprinkled along the slopes of Monte Sant'Angelo and features the lovely **Marina di Praia★**, an attractive hidden beach. It can be accessed at the marina by a path that passes by the **Asciola Torre** *(free)*, built during the Saracen invasions. The painter and ceramicist Paolo Sandulli lived here, devoted to capturing local village life.

Positano

© S. Vidler/Travelpix/age fotostock

Vallone di Furore★★

The Furore Valley, between two road tunnels, is the most impressive section of the coast owing to the dark depths of its steep, rocky walls and, in stormy weather, the thunder of wild, rough seas. A fishermen's village has, nevertheless, been built where a small torrent gushes into the sea. The houses cling to the slopes and vividly coloured boats are drawn up on the shore. Those who wish to explore the spot on foot should take the path that goes along one side of the gorge. Note the "**Art walls**" *(Muri d'autore)*, contemporary paintings and sculptures.

Grotta dello Smeraldo★★

Access to cave by lift from street above 9am–4pm. 5€. Visit also possible by boat from harbour, 10€ round trip (admission not included). ℘089 87 11 07. www.amalfitouristoffice.it.

The exceptionally clear water of this marine cave is illuminated indirectly by rays of light which give it a beautiful emerald *(smeraldo)* colour. The bottom looks quite near, though the water is 10m/33ft deep. Fine stalactites add to the interest of the trip. The cave became submerged as a result of variations in ground level caused by the volcanic activity that affects the whole region.

Amalfi★★

Set in a steep valley, Amalfi is centred on the beach. The main street, Via Genova, leads to a wild gorge with mill-ruins.

🅿 By the beach. 🛈 Via delle Repubbliche Marinare 27. ℘089 87 11 07. www.amalfitouristoffice.it.

Amalfi is a Spanish-looking little town with tall white houses built on slopes facing the sea in a wonderful **setting★★★**. Amalfi enjoys a mild climate, making it a popular holiday resort.

Starting at Piazza Duomo, Via Genova, Via Capuano (its continuation) and **Via dei Mercanti** (parallel on the right) make up the **historic centre★** and business heart of the city with its picturesque variety of façades, flowering balconies and niches. The Islamic-looking layout of the town is characterised by winding alleyways, staircases and vaulted passages which open out onto little squares. Famous for its lemons, Amalfi produces a sweet-and-sour liqueur called *limoncello*.

Duomo di Sant'Andrea★

Open 7.30am–10am; and 5.30pm–7pm. Chiostro del Paradiso and Museo Diocesano 9am–6pm, 3€. ℘089 87 13 24. Founded in the 9C, the cathedral is an example of the Oriental splendour

Amalfi's Prosperous Past

Amalfi is Italy's oldest republic, founded in 840; by the end of the 9C it came under the rule of a *doge*. It enjoyed its greatest prosperity in the 11C, when shipping in the Mediterranean was regulated by the Tavole Amalfitane (Amalfi Codex), the oldest maritime code in the world. Amalfi traded regularly with the Orient, in particular Constantinople, and the Republic had an **arsenal** *(to the left of Porta della Marina)* where many large galleys were built. This fleet of galleys played a large part in carrying Crusaders to the Levant.

favoured by maritime cities. The façade, rebuilt in the 19C, is the focal point, with striking geometrical designs in multicoloured stone. The campanile, on the left, is all that remains of the original church. A beautiful 11C bronze **door★**, cast in Constantinople, opens onto the vast *atrium* that precedes the church.

The *atrium* leads into the **Cloisters of Paradise★★** (Chiostro del Paradiso), which date from 1268 where the architecture combines Romanesque austerity and Arab fantasy. The Museo Diocesano is housed in the **Basilica del Crocefisso**. From the basilica make for the crypt,

which holds the relics of St Andrew the Apostle, brought to Amalfi from Constantinople in 1206.

Atrani★

This pleasant fishermen's village at the mouth of the Dragon Valley (Valle del Dragone) has two old churches: Santa Maria Maddalena and San Salvatore. The latter was founded in the 10C and has a fine bronze door similar to the one in Amalfi Cathedral. The road winds up the narrow valley, planted with vines and olive groves, to Ravello.

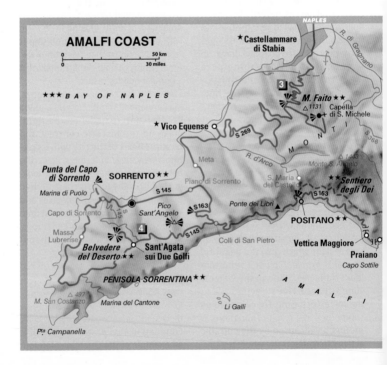

Ravello★★★

Most attractions cluster around the Piazza Vescovado. 🅰 The Villa Rufolo and Villa **Cimbrone**. 🅱 Via Roma 18. ☎089 85 70 96. www.ravellotime.it.

Ravello's stairways and roofed passages cling to the steep slopes of the Dragon Hill. The **site★★★**, suspended between sea and sky, is unforgettable. The town's aristocratic restraint has, over the centuries, beguiled artists, musicians and writers such as members of the Bloomsbury Group led by Virginia and Leonard Woolf (🅲 see Villa Cimbrone, p248), D.H. Lawrence, Graham Greene, Gore Vidal, Hans Escher and Joan Miró.

Villa Rufolo★★★

Piazza Vescovado, next to the Duomo. Open daily 9am–8pm (winter 9–dusk). Closed 1 Jan, 25 Dec. 5€. ☎089 85 76 21.

The villa was built in the 13C by the rich Rufolo family of Ravello (cited in Boccaccio's *Decameron*) and was the residence of several popes, Charles of Anjou and more recently, in 1880, of **Richard Wagner**. When the German composer, in search of inspiration for *Parsifal*, laid eyes on the villa's splendid garden he exclaimed, "the garden of Klingsor is found". A well-shaded avenue leads to a Gothic entrance tower. Beyond is a Moorish-style courtyard with sharply pointed arches in the Sicilian-Norman style.

From the terraces there is a splendid **panorama★★★** of the jagged peaks as far as Cape Orso, the Bay of Maiori and the Gulf of Salerno. Summer **concerts** *(Ravello Concert Society;* ☎089 84 24 082; fax 089 85 82 49; www.ravelloarts.org) in the gardens are held against a backdrop of trees, flowers and sea.

Duomo

Open daily 9–noon and 5.30–7pm. Museum 9am–7pm (winter 6pm), closed 27 Jul, 3€ (museum). ☎089 85 83 11. www.chiesaravello.com.

The cathedral, founded in 1086, was remodelled in the 18C, the campanile is 13C. The splendid **bronze door★** with its panels of reliefs was cast in 1179 by Barisanus da Trani. The mosaic-covered

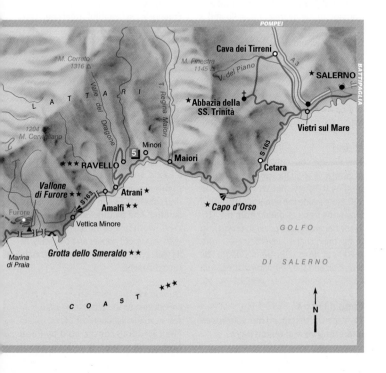

pulpit★★ features a variety of motifs and fantastic animals (1272). On the left is a 12C **ambo** adorned with green mosaics representing Jonah and the Whale. The small **museum** in the crypt has mosaics and a silver head-reliquary containing the relics of St Barbara.

To the left of the Duomo, the Cameo Factory houses a tiny **coral museum** displaying some prized pieces.

Chiesa di San Giovanni del Toro

Open 9am–1pm and 4pm–6.30pm. ℘089 85 71 60.

Via San Giovanni del Toro, with its stunning **belvedere★★**, leads to this 11C church with its 11C **pulpit★**, a Roman sarcophagus (south aisle) and 14C frescoes in the apses and the crypt.

Villa Cimbrone★★

Via Santa Chiara 26. For guided tours call: ℘089 85 74 59 or visit the website www.villacimbrone.com.

A charming **alley★** leads from Piazza Vescovado to the 19C villa, passing through the Gothic porch of the convent of St Francis. Villa Cimbrone is a homage to the history of Ravello and a point of reference for the **Bloomsbury Group** for whom the garden embodied the ideal aesthetic of clarity, order and harmony. A wide alley leads through the garden to the belvedere, adorned with marble busts. There is an immense **panorama★★★** over the terraced hillsides, Maiori, Cape Orso and the Gulf of Salerno.

Maiori

This village conceals the cave church of **Santa Maria Olearia★**, an ancient medieval abbey that was built in the 10C. Note inside the remains of beautiful Byzantine frescoes dating from the 11C. Three haloed figures cover the crypt and in the main chapel, several scenes from the life of Jesus (The Annunciation, The Visitation and the Adoration of the Magi). Call for opening times ℘089 81 42 09.

Capo d'Orso★

The cape with its jagged rocks affords an interesting view of **Maiori Bay★**.

Cetara

A little fishing village twinned with Sète and loved by windsurfers. The beach, **Marina de Cetara**, is peaceful.

Vietri sul Mare

At the eastern end of this stretch of coastline, this pretty town is known for its ceramic ware. It affords magnificent **views★★** of the Amalfi Coast.

Abbazia della Santissima Trinità★

Cava de' Tirreni, 5km/3mi N of Vietri sul Mare. Guided tours 8.30am–noon, call ℘089 46 39 22 or visit the website www.badiadicava.it.

This Benedictine abbey was founded in the 11C and was one of the most powerful in southern Italy during the Middle Ages. The church, rebuilt in the 18C, has a fine pulpit and paschal candelabra. The tour includes the halls of the monastery, the cloister, cemetery and museum.

Cava dei Tirreni

This pleasant city is nestled in a valley and is marked at its entrance by a medieval bridge with six arches. Corso Vittorio Emanuele is a beautiful street lined with arcades and stucco façades.

Salerno★

The medieval quarter starts at Corso Vittorio Emanuele and stretches along Via dei Mercanti. **P** The largest car park is on Via Alvarez. **🛈** Lungomare Trieste 7/9. ℘089 23 14 32. www.aziendaturismo.sa.it.

Salerno, lying along the graceful curve of its gulf, has retained a medieval quarter on the slopes of a hill crowned by a castle. From the Lungomare Trieste, planted with palm trees and tamarinds, there is a wide view of the Gulf of Salerno. The picturesque Via dei Mercanti, which crosses the old town, is lined with shops, old houses and oratories. At its west end stands an 8C Lombard arch, Arco di Arechi.

Duomo★★

For opening times: ℘089 23 13 87, www.cattedraledisalerno.it 2€.

The cathedral, consecrated by Pope Gregory VII in 1085, is dedicated to St

Matthew the Evangelist, who is buried in the crypt. The Norman-style building was remodelled in the 18C and was damaged in the 1980 earthquake. The church is preceded by an *atrium* of multicoloured stone with ancient columns. The square tower to the right is from the 12C. The central doorway has 11C **bronze doors★**. The interior contains two **ambos★★** encrusted with decorative mosaics and on columns with carved capitals, along with the paschal candelabrum and the elegant iconostasis. The Crusaders' Chapel at the end of the south aisle is where the Crusaders had their arms blessed. Under the altar is the tomb of Pope Gregory VII, who died in exile at Salerno (1085).

Museo Archeologico

Via San Benedetto 28.
& Open 9am–7.30pm, closed Mon.
*℘*089 23 11 35.
Housed in the attractive St Benedict monastery complex, the museum has artefacts dating from prehistory to the late Imperial era. Of particular note is the **bronze Head of Apollo★** (1C BC) and a fine collection of pre-Roman amber.

ADDRESSES

🏠 STAY

⊖ **B&B Villa Avenia** – Via Torquato Tasso 83, Salerno. *℘*089 25 22 81. www.villaavenia.com. 3 rooms. A B&B set in a magnificent villa overlooking the historic centre and the harbour. Wide panoramic gardens.

⊖⊜ **Antica Repubblica** – Vico dei Pastai 2, Amalfi. *℘*089 87 36 310. www.anticarepubblica.it. 7 rooms. This former palace has vaulted ceilings. It is cosy, well kept and has modern comforts. There is a beautiful roof terrace to admire the bell tower from.

⊖⊜ **La Fenice** – Via G. Marconi 4. 1km/0.6mi E of Positano. *℘*089 87 55 13. www.lafenicepositano.com. 12 rooms. Two 19C–20C villas surrounded by lush vegetation. Rooms are simple and pleasant. A panoramic swimming pool is fed by seawater.

⊖⊜ **La Maliosa d'Arienzo** – Via Arienzo 74. *℘*089 81 18 73. www.lamaliosa.it. 10 rooms. This beautiful B&B is just outside Positano and is surrounded by Mediterranean olives, lemon and orange blossoms. Comfortable rooms.

⊖⊜⊜ **Villa San Michele** – Via Carusiello 2, Ravello. Castiglione di Ravello, 5km/3mi S of Ravello. *℘*/Fax 089 87 22 37. www.hotel-villasanmichele.it. Closed Nov–Feb. 12 rooms. Situated at the top of the cliff-face, the hotel boasts fine views over the Gulf and the Capo d'Orso. Delightful setting with its luscious garden and the steps down to the beach. Decorated with tiled floors, the rooms are sunny.

🍴 EAT

⊖ **Hostaria Il Brigante** – Via Fratelli Linguiti 4, Salerno. *℘*089226592. Closed Mon. Authentic traditions served with a twist. In the heart of the city, just steps away from the Duomo.

⊖⊜ **A' Paranza** – Traversa Dragone 1, Atrani. *℘*089 87 18 40. www.ristorante paranza.com. Closed Tue. Steps from the village's main square, this restaurant offers authentic cuisine that celebrates local flavours.

⊖⊜ **Da Memé** – Salita Marino Sebaste 8, Amalfi. *℘*089 83 04 549. Closed Mon. A trattoria-pizzeria in a former Benedictine monastery. Fresh, homemade pasta and fish soup are some of the specialities.

⊖⊜ **Giardiniello** – Corso Vittorio Emanuele 17, 84010 Minori 5km/3mi NE of Amalfi on the S 163. *℘*089 87 70 50. www.ristorantegiardiniello.com. Closed Wed except in summer. Situated in the heart of the village with a large airy dining room. Specialising in fish. Pizzas served in the evening.

⊖⊜ **Il Ritrovo** – Via Montepertuso 77, loc. Montepertuso. 4km/2.5mi N of Positano. *℘*089 81 20 05. www.ilritrovo.com. Closed 7 Jan–middle Mar. Located a few miles above Positano, this restaurant serves traditional fish and meat dishes. Outdoor dining in summer.

⊖⊜ **Saraceno d'Oro** – Via Pasitea 254, Positano. *℘*089 81 20 50. www.saraceno doro.it. Closed Dec–Feb except at Christmas. Traditional cuisine, pizza and good takeaway.

Parco Nazionale
del Cilento★

The Cilento nature reserve was founded in 1991 and is on UNESCO's World Nature Reserve List. This superlative Mediterranean park is situated at the crossroads of the most diverse cultural influences, from the basin of the Mediterranean to the Apennines, and has some gorgeous coastline with lovely beaches, interesting caves and rocky outcrops.

A BIT OF HISTORY

The vast variety of landscapes is the result of the twofold nature of the rocks. The flysch variety of the Cilento is to be found in the western part of the park and along the coast (Stella and Gelbison mountains) with its gentle landscape and Mediterranean vegetation.

The calcareous rock of the interior (Alburni Mountains and Mount Cerviati) and the southern coast (from Cape Palinuro to Scario) produces a barren landscape with karst formations.

The most interesting floral species is the Palinuro primrose, the park's symbol, while fauna includes otters, wolves and royal eagles.

🚗 DRIVING TOUR

Itinerary which descends from Vella towards the coast and then up to the NW. 170km/106mi. Allow at least 1 day.

Velia★

40km/25mi SE of Paestum on the S 18 and S 267. www.velia.it.

This colony was founded in 535 BC by Phoenician Greek refugees who had been expelled by the Persians. A prosperous port, Velia (known as *Elea* to the Greeks) became a Roman territory in 88 BC. The city was famous for its Eleatic school of philosophy in the 6C–5C BC, including Parmenides and his pupil Zeno.

🕭 **Michelin Map:** 564 F–G 26–28 – Campania.

🛈 **Info:** Tenuta Montesani, 84078 Vallo della Lucania. ℘0974 71 99 11, 0974 71 99 200. www.parks.it/parconazionale.cilento/ www.cilentoediano.it

⬭ **Location:** The nature reserve extends from the Tyrrhenian Coast to the Diano Valley. It lies off the A 3 south of Salerno.

⬭ **Train:** Vallo della Lucania (Salerno 55 mins).

⬭ **Don't Miss:** The natural wonders of the Oasi WWF di Persano.

🕐 **Timing:** Enjoy the beaches in the mornings and visit shady caves in the hot afternoon.

👫 **Kids:** Room of Sponges at the Grotte di Pertosa.

⬭ Pass under the railway line to reach the ruins.

Ruins

Open daily 9am–1hr before dusk. Closed 1 Jan, 1 May, 25 Dec. 3€, 11€, combined ticket with Museum and Archeologic Area of Paestum (valid 3 days). ℘0974 97 23 96. From the entrance there is an interesting view of the archaeological site of the **città bassa** (lower town) with its lighthouse, 4C BC city wall, the south sea-gateway and Roman baths from the Imperial era (mosaic and marble floor remains). From the baths, Via di Porta Rosa borders the marketplace and climbs up to the ancient gateway (6C BC) and the **Porta Rosa★** (4C BC), a fine example of a cuneiform arch and the most important Greek civic monument in *Magna Graecia*. The **acropolis** on the promontory above the lower town has remains of the medieval castle erected on the foundations of a Greek temple, and the Palatine Chapel, which houses epigraphic material. Slightly below are the remains of the Greek theatre, remodelled in the Roman era.

♁♙ Capo Palinuro★★

30km/18.6mi SE of Velia on the S 447. ℘0974 93 81 44 (Pro Loco). ♁♙Boat trip to the Grotta Azzurra: Open daily 9am–6pm (20min round trip). ℘0974 93 16 04. www.capopalinuro.it.

Aeneas' mythical steersman Painuro was killed here. Boat trips to the Grotta Azzurra★ and other caves on the promontory. From the S 562 head towards the beautiful beaches on the coast.

▶ Drive 66km/41mi NE on the SS 562, SS 447 (pass through Poderia and follow signs for Policastro Busentino), then take the SS 517 and SS 19.

Certosa di Padula★

Open Wed–Mon, 9am–7pm. 4€. ℘0975 77 745.

The charterhouse of San Lorenzo, founded in 1306, is one of the largest architectural complexes in southern Italy. The Baroque church houses the Padri★. The Great Cloisters (104m by 149m/341ft by 488ft) are surrounded by monks' cells, while the left arcade leads to a dramatic 18C staircase★.

▶ Go 35km/21.8mi NW on the SS 19.

♁♙ Grotte di Pertosa★

⚿ Guided tours only, different tours avaliable, ticket from 13€. Closed Mon, 25 Dec, 7Jan–12 Feb. 10–15€. ℘0975 39 70 37. www.grottedipertosa.it.

These caves, which extend over an area of about 2.5km/1.5mi, lie in the natural amphitheatre of the Alburni Mountains and are reached via a small lake. Inhabited since Neolithic times, the caves have fine concretions; the most interesting area is the ♁♙Room of Sponges (Sala delle Spugne). The S 166 leads up to the Sentinella Pass (932m/3 057ft) crossing landscapes★ dotted with yellow broom.

▶ Drive 42km/26.1mi NE on the SS 19.

Oasi WWF di Persano

⚿ Guided tours only (2hrs), (book in advance). 6€ (guided tour 10€). ℘0828 97 46 84. www.wwf.it.

The "oasis" extends over 110ha/272 acres of alluvial plains interesting flora in the marshland, a refuge of the otter.

Paestum★★★

One of Italy's most important archaeological sites, Paestum was discovered by chance around 1750, when the Bourbons started to build the road that crosses the area today. The initial settlement was an ancient Greek colony founded around 600 BC under the name of *Poseidonia* by colonists from Sybaris.
Around the year 400 BC the city fell to a local tribe, the Lucanians. It became Roman in the year 273 BC, but began to decline towards the end of the Empire due to malaria, which eventually drove out its inhabitants.
The yellow limestone temples stand amid the ruins of dwellings, sheltered by cypresses and oleanders.

- ⚲ **Michelin Map:** 564 F 26–27 – Campania.
- ▤ **Info:** Via Magna Grecia 887, 84047 Capaccio-Paestum (SA). ℘0828 81 10 16. www.infopaestum.it.
- ▶ **Location:** Paestum is on the coast, close to the S 18, 48km/ 29.8mi south of Salerno.
- ▶ **Train:** Paestum (Napoli 1hr 28 mins).
- ◉ **Don't Miss:** The Tempio di Nettuno. The metopes and Tomba del Tuffatore in the Museo.
- ◷ **Timing:** Allow half a day.

VISIT

The suggested itinerary (2hrs) proceeds from south to north. Those wishing to visit the museum first should start from the north. Open daily 8.45am–1hr before dusk; 7€ including museum; Unico ticket 11€, including museum and Archeological Area of Velia). ℘0828 81 10 16 and 0828 72 26 54. www.infopaestum.it.

Take the Porta della Giustizia through the 5km/3mi-long city wall, **Cinta Muraria★**, and follow the **Via Sacra**, the principal street of the ancient city.

Basilica★★

The rear of the "Basilica" stands to the right of the Via Sacra. This mid-6C BC temple, the oldest in the city, was dedicated to Hera, sister and bride of Zeus. The swelling at the centre of the columns (*entasis*) and the squashed *echini* (moulding above the capital) of the columns convey the way in which architectural structures were considered living entities that swell and squash when submitted to pressure. The porch (*pronaos*) leads into the central chamber divided into two aisles, indicating that two cults were practised here.

Tempio di Nettuno★★★

When Paestum was first discovered this well-preserved Doric temple was thought to have been dedicated to Neptune (or Poseidon in Greek, hence the town's name *Poseidonia*), but it has since been proved that it was dedicated to Hera. Dating from the mid-5C BC, one of the most impressive structural devices is the convexity (2cm/1in) of the horizontal lines, which makes the numerous columns look straight. For this same reason the fluting on the corner columns veers slightly inwards.

In the centre of the city stands the **forum**, surrounded by a portico and shops, and overlooked by the **curia**, the adjacent *macellum* (covered market) and the *comitium* (3C BC), the most important public building where magistrates were elected. To the left of the *comitium* stands the **Temple of Peace** (2C–1C BC) constructed on a north–south plan according to Italic custom.

To the east of the forum stands the **amphitheatre**, constructed between the Republican and Imperial ages and divided by the main road. Unusually it is not located outside the city centre, a measure that was adopted to enable a flow of people to the amphitheatre.

The *gimnasium* (c.3C BC) was probably a sanctuary with a pool. During ritualistic celebrations the statue of the divinity was immersed in the pool and then placed on a platform. The pool was buried in the 1C AD and the structure subsequently housed the gymnasium.

The **Tempietto Sotterraneo** (small underground temple, 6C BC) has been interpreted as being a *heroon*, a kind of cenotaph devoted to the cult of the city's founder, who was made a hero after his death. Some bronze vases with traces of honey were also found here; these are housed at the museum.

Tempio di Cerere★★

Originally erected in the late-6C BC in honour of Athena, the Temple of Ceres combines an interesting mix of styles. Near the entrance of the temple, on the east side, is the sacrificial altar, the **ara**.

Museo★★

&. Open 8.30am–7.30pm. Closed 1st and 3rd Mon of the month, 1 Jan, 1 May, 25 Dec. 4€ (only when Scavi are closed); 7€ including archaeological site. ℘0828 81 10 23. www.museopaestum. beniculturali.it.

The masterpieces in this museum include the famous **metopes★★**, 6C BC low reliefs in the Doric style that adorned both the *Thesauròs*, or temple of Hera (scenes from the life of Heracles and the Trojan Wars), and the High Temple (Dancing Girls) of the Sanctuary of Hera at Sele (10km/6.2mi N near the mouth of the River Sele) as well as the Tomb of the Diver. The **Tomba del Tuffatore★★** constitutes a rare example of Greek funerary painting with banquet scenes and the dive, symbol of the passage from life to death. The museum also houses **vases★** (6C BC) from the underground temple, a true masterpiece of bronze sculpture, the painted Lucanian tombs (4C BC) and the representations of Hera Argiva with a pomegranate (symbol of fertility), and the flower-woman in terra-cotta, used as an incense burner.

Reggia di Caserta★★

Charles III of Bourbon chose Caserta, far from the vulnerable Neapolitan Coast, to host a magnificent edifice that could compete with other European courts. The Royal Palace of Caserta was included in UNESCO's World Heritage List in 1997.

SIGHTS

Palazzo

Vanvitelli's masterpiece staircase.
Open Wed–Mon 8.30am–6.45pm. Closed 1 Jan, 1 May, 25 Dec. Apartments: 9€ (only when park is closed); park and apartments: 12€. 0823 44 80 84 or 0823 27 71 11. www.reggiadicaserta. beniculturali.it.

In 1752 Charles III of Bourbon commissioned the architect **Luigi Vanvitelli** to erect a palace (*reggia*). Compared to the grand royal residences of the period, Caserta has a more geometric layout. If its purity of line seems to anticipate the Neoclassical style, the theatrical interior is still typically Rococo.

The building consists of a vast rectangle (249m/273yds long and 190m/208yds wide) containing four internal courtyards interconnected by a magnificent **entrance hall★**. The façade is adorned by a projecting colonnade and a double row of windows supported by a rusticated base. Facing the garden this

Sculpture depicting hounds attacking a stag at the foot of the great cascade

- **Michelin Map:**
  564 D 25 – Campania.
- **Info:** Piazza Vanvitelli 64, 81100 Caserta. 0823 27 32 89 or 840 00 18 17. www.comune.caserta.it.
- **Location:** Off the A 1 (exit Caserta Nord), about 20km/12mi from Naples.
- **Train:** Caserta (Napoli 24 mins).
- **Don't Miss:** The palazzo and the treasures of the Museo Archeologico dell'Antica Capua.
- **Timing:** Allow half a day to see all the major sights.
- **Kids:** The Roman amphitheatre at Santa Maria Capua Vetere.

motif is embellished with pilaster strips. The **grand staircase★★** (*scalone d'onore*) leads to the Palatine Chapel (closed to visitors) and to the royal apartments decorated in the Neoclassical style. The **Eighteenth Century Apartment** (*Appartamento Settecentesco*) has vaulted frescoed ceilings depicting the seasons and views of ports by J.P. Hackert. The **Queen's Apartment** (*Apartamento della Regina*) has some curious pieces including a chandelier adorned with little tomatoes and a cage containing a clock and a stuffed bird. In the Sala Ellittica, there is an 18C Neapolitan **crib★** (*presepe*).

©Giuseppe Masci/iStockphoto.com

253

Park

Epitomising the ideal grand Baroque garden, its seemingly infinite expanse is arranged around a central canal. This ambitious work spans five mountains and three valleys with a total length of 40km/25mi. Notable mythological sculptures include the group of *Diana and Actaeon* which stands at the foot of the great **cascade★★** (78m/256ft high). To the right of the cascade lies a picturesque **English garden★★** *(giardino inglese)* created for Maria-Carolina of Austria.

EXCURSIONS
Caserta Vecchia★

◯ 10km/6.2mi N.

This small town has a charm with its narrow alleyways lined by old buildings with brown tufa walls. Dominated by the ruins of its 9C castle (castle toursby reservation, ℘333 981 46 68 or 0823 27 32 89), there is also a 12C **cathedral** which combines Sicilian-Arab, Apulian and Lombard motifs.

Basilica di Sant'Angelo in Formis★★

◯ 15km/9.3mi NW of Caserta Vecchia (take the SS 87 to S. Iorio). Open Mon–Tue and Thu–Fri 9am–6.30pm.
℘0823 96 08 17.

One of the most beautiful medieval buildings in Campania. Erected in the 11C by Desiderio, the interior is covered in **frescoes**: the Last Judgement *(east wall)*, the Life of Christ *(nave)*, the Old Testament *(north and south aisle)* and Maestà *(apse)*. They show a strong Byzantine influence.

Capua

◯ 6km/3.7mi SW of S. Angelo in Formis. www.comunedicapua.it. ℘0823 56 03 07.

This walled city is the native town of Ettore Fieramosca, captain of the 13 Italian knights who vanquished the French in the Defeat of Barletta (1503, ◷ *see page 258*).
Duomo – Open daily 8.30am–noon and 3–6pm. ℘0823 96 10 81. The cathedral, which dates from the 9C, has been rebuilt. The columns of the *atrium* have 3C **Corinthian capitals**.

Museo Campano★ – At the corner of Via Duomo and Via Roma. ✇ The earth–goddess figurines. ♿ Open Tue–Sat 9am–1.30pm, Tue and Thu also 3pm–6pm, Sun 9am–1pm. Closed Mon. 6€. ℘0823 62 00 76. www.museocampano.it.

Housed in a 15C building with a fine lava stone Catalan **doorway**, the archaeological section has an astonishing collection of 6C–1C BC **Matres Matutae**, Italic earth goddesses holding their newborn children; and a gateway built by the Emperor Frederick II of Hohenstaufen around 1239. Note the female head known as *Capua Fidelis*.

Southeast of the museum is an area with interesting Lombard churches (San Giovanni a Corte, San Salvatore Maggiore a Corte, San Marcello).

♟♟ Santa Maria Capua Vetere

◯ 5km/3mi SE of Capua. The second-largest Roman amphitheatre, where Spartacus revolted.

This is the famous Roman Capua where the downfall of Hannibal was brought about. One of the most opulent cities of the Roman Empire, after Saracen attacks in the 9C, the inhabitants of the city moved to the banks of the River Volturno where they founded the present Capua.

The **Anfiteatro Campano★**, restored in the 2C AD, was the seat of the famous gladiator school in which the revolt headed by Spartacus erupted in 73 BC. Open Tue–Sun 9am–1 hr before dusk. Closed 1 Jan, 1 May, 25 Dec. 2.50€ including the Mitreo and the Museo dell'Antica Capua. ℘0823 84 42 06. 9–7.30pm. www.cir.campania.beniculturali.it.

The **Mitreo** (2C AD) is an underground chamber boasting a rare **fresco★** of the Persian god Mithras sacrificing a bull.

The **Museo Archeologico dell'Antica Capua** (Via R. d'Angiò) has artefacts relating to local history from the Bronze Age to the Imperial Age. ♿ Open Tue–Sun, 9am–7pm. Closed 1 Jan, 1 May, 25 Dec. 2.50€ including the Anfiteatro and the Mitreo. ℘082384 42 06. www.archeosa.beniculturali.it

Benevento

This was the ancient capital of the Samnites, who hindered the Roman expansion for some time. In 321 BC they trapped the Roman army in a defile known as the Caudine Forks (Forche Caudine) between Capua and ancient Beneventum. The Romans occupied the town following the defeat in 275 BC of Pyrrhus and his Samnite allies. During the reign of Trajan, the town was designated as the starting point for the Appian Trajan Way (Via Appia Traiana) leading to Brindisi. Under Lombard rule it became the seat of a duchy in 571 and later a powerful principality. Following the Battle of Benevento in 1266, Charles of Anjou, supported by Pope Urban IV, claimed the kingship.

▸ **Population:** 63 000
◔ **Michelin Map:**
   564 D 26 – Campania.
🛈 **Info:** Via Nicola Sala 31.
   ℰ 0824 31 99 11.
   www.eptbenevento.it.
   www.comune.benevento.it.
◖ **Location:** To get to Benevento take the S 88, which links the town with Isernia, and the A 16, which goes to Caserta.
◖ **Train:** Benevento (Caserta 52 mins).
◉ **Don't Miss:** Performances at the Teatro Romano.
◍ **Timing:** Allow half a day to explore this compact town.

VISIT

Teatro Romano

Access from Via Port'Arsa, left of S. Maria della Verità church. ♿ Open daily 9am–1hr before dusk. Closed 1 Jan, 1 May, 25 Dec. 2€. ℰ 0824 47 213. www.archeosa.beniculturali.it.
One of the largest Roman theatres still in existence, it was built in the 2C by the Emperor Hadrian and enlarged by the Emperor Caracalla. In summer it hosts performances.
From Piazza Duomo turn into Corso Garibaldi, lined with the city's most significant buildings. Note the Egyptian obelisk from Isis' Temple (AD 88).

Arco di Traiano★★

From Corso Garibaldi, left on Via Traiano. The "Porta Aurea", erected in AD 114 to commemorate the emperor who turned Benevento into an obligatory stopover on the journey to Puglia, is Italy's best-preserved triumphal arch. Its low reliefs depict scenes of peace on the side facing the city and scenes of war facing the countryside.

Chiesa di Santa Sofia

Piazza Matteotti.
An 8C building, rebuilt in the 17C. The interior hexagon is enclosed by a decagonal structure. The 12C **cloisters★**, with their Moorish-style arches, lead to the **Museo del Sannioa** housing an important archaeological collection.

The Witches of Egypt

In the 1C AD, Benevento was one of the principal centres of the cult of the Egyptian goddess Isis, which flourished until the 6C. With the invasion of the Lombards, the practice of magic and mystic rites was considered incompatible with Christianity. Believers continued to conduct rites outside the city walls, near a walnut tree, in the valley of the River Sabato. This gave rise to the myth of witches' Sabbaths and the witches of Benevento. According to legend, St Barbato ended these activities in the 7C by cutting down the trunk. The myth lives on, however, in the famous bright yellow liqueur *Strega* (witch), created in 1861 by Giuseppe Alberti in a secret recipe using dozens of herbs. The Società Strega now finances the prestigious literary prize that bears this name.

Puglia

Major Cities: Bari, Brindisi, Lecce
Official Website: http://viaggiareinpuglia.it

Forming the heel of the boot, Puglia enjoys a long coastline that skirts the Adriatic, the Strait of Otranto, separating it from Albania, and the Gulf of Taranto. Puglia's white sandy beaches have helped to transform its mostly agrarian economy into one that relies on tourism. Other attractions in the region include Lecce, a city of Baroque splendour, and Alberobello, whose conical "Trulli" dwellings are a World Heritage Site. The small town of San Giovanni Rotondo, in the Gargano Mountains, has also become a place of pilgrimage; it is where Padre Pio, canonised in 2002, once preached. The elevation of the Gargano Promontory, otherwise known as the "boot's spur", is distinctive and is home to the Gargano National Park.

Highlights

1 Drive the coastal road between **Bari and Barletta** (p258)

2 Embark on a boat trip around the **Tremiti Islands** (p262)

3 Tour the land of curious conical houses in the **Terra dei Trulli** (p265)

4 Stroll the Baroque historic centre of **Lecce** (p267)

5 Explore Greek and Roman artefacts at Taranto's **Museo Nazionale** (p272)

Geography

This region is made up of mostly broad flat plains and low-lying hills. The spectacular limestone Gargano Promontory in the north of Puglia, jutting out into the Adriatic Sea, is the only mountainous terrain in the region.
Bari, the capital of Puglia, is a busy port, which still enjoys numerous trading links with the Middle East.

Agriculture

Puglia has many assets. Cereals are grown between Foggia and Manfredonia and in the plains of Bari, Taranto, Lecce and Brindisi.
Vines flourish almost everywhere, often alongside almonds and olive trees. In fact, Puglian olive oil accounts for approximately one-third of Italian production. Other crops that thrive in this region are peppers, figs, broad beans and citrus.

A Bit of History

In the late-8C BC, Greeks founded the Puglian towns of *Gallipoli, Otranto* and *Taranto*. Between the 5C and 4C BC, *Taranto* was the most prosperous town in *Magna Graecia*. In the 3C BC, however, these cities came under Roman rule. *Taranto* declined as *Brindisi*, a trading post facing the eastern Mediterranean, flourished. The latter was linked to Rome when the Appian Way was extended. The area was occupied successively by the Byzantines, Lombards and Arabs before Puglia sought help in the 11C from the Normans who then dominated the entire area. Puglia greatly increased its trade and its architectural heritage thanks to the early Crusades, most of which embarked from the Puglian ports.

It was under the Emperor Frederick II of Hohenstaufen that the region had a golden period in the first half of the 13C. His son Manfred continued his work but had to submit to Charles of Anjou in 1266. The French lost interest in the region and it began to lose its prestige. Puglia then passed to the Aragon dynasty, who, by isolating the region, contributed to its decline. After a period of Austrian domination, the Bourbons of Naples improved to some small extent the stagnation.

During the 20C Puglia has achieved a certain vigour and now claims two thriving industrial towns, Taranto and Lecce, a trade fair in Bari and several universities.

Bari★

An agricultural and industrial centre, Bari is first and foremost a port. The Levantine Fair *(Fiera del Levante)*, held in September, is an important trade fair, which was inaugurated in 1930 to encourage trade with other Mediterranean countries. Bari comprises the old town, clustered on its promontory, and the modern town with wide avenues, laid out on a grid plan in the 19C.

SIGHTS

Basilica di San Nicola★★

The basilica in the heart of the old town *(città vecchia)*, also known as the "Nicholas stronghold" *(citadella)*, was begun in 1087 and consecrated in 1197 to St Nicholas, Bishop of Myra in Asia Minor, who achieved fame by resurrecting three children, whom a butcher had cut up and put in brine. The building is one of the most remarkable examples of Romanesque architecture and the model for many local churches.

On the north side there is the richly decorated 12C Lions' Doorway. Inside, the nave and two aisles with a triforium were re-roofed in the 17C with a coffered ceiling. A 12C *ciborium* (canopy) surmounts the high altar behind which is an 11C marble **episcopal throne★**. The tomb of St Nicholas lies in the crypt.

Cattedrale★

This 11C–12C Romanesque cathedral was added to and then altered at a later date. The works of art include a pulpit made up of 11C and 12C fragments, and a baldachin rebuilt from 13C fragments. A copy of the **Exultet** is displayed in the north aisle (the original is kept in the sacristy just outside the church), a precious 11C Byzantine parchment scroll in Beneventan script, typical of medieval southern Italy. The illustrations are on the reverse side so that the congregation could see them as the parchment was unrolled.

▶ **Population:** 328 458

♾ **Michelin Map:**
564 D 32 – Puglia.

🕊 **Info:** Piazza Aldo Moro 32a.
℮080 52 42 244.

◎ **Location:** The capital of Puglia, Bari overlooks the Adriatic. To get there, take either the A 14 or the S 16 motorway.

🔁 **Don't Miss:** A wander through the treasures of the Basilica di San Nicola and Cattedrale.

⏱ **Timing:** The old town can be enjoyed in half a day, or allow a day to explore the modern town as well.

Castello★

Open daily 8.30am–7.30pm, last entry 1h before closing. 3€. ℮080 52 86 261. www.puglia.beniculturali.it.
The Emperor Frederick II of Hohenstaufen built the castle in 1233 over the foundations of earlier Byzantine and Norman buildings. The irregular courtyard and two towers date from the Swabian period.

Pinacoteca

Lungomare Nazario Sauro. ♿ Open Tue–Sat 9–7pm, Sun 9am–1pm. Closed public hols. 3€. ℮080 54 12 422. www.pinacotecabari.it.

Byzantium's Capital

Legend has it that Bari was founded by the Illiri and then colonised by the Greeks. Between the 9C and 11C Bari was the capital of Byzantium's domain in Italy. In its role as a pilgrimage centre to St Nicholas' shrine and as a port of embarkation for the Crusades, Bari was a very prosperous city in the Middle Ages. It declined under the Sforza of Milan and Spanish rule in the 16C.

The Barletta Challenge

In 1503 the town, which was held by the Spanish, was besieged by French troops. The Italians, accused of cowardice by a French prisoner, issued a challenge, following which 13 Italian knights led by **Ettore Fieramosca** met and defeated 13 French knights in single combat. In the 19C this deed was deemed a fine example of patriotism and Ettore Fieramosca became a heroic figure. In 1833 the author Massimo d'Azeglio based a novel on this event, *Ettore Fieramosca or the Tournament of Barletta (Ettore Fieramosca o la disfida di Barletta)*. Visit the 17C Palazzo della Marra; its façade is richly decorated in the Baroque style.

The gallery, on the fourth floor *(lift)* of the Palazzo della Provincia, comprises Byzantine works of art (sculpture and paintings), a 12C–13C painted wood statue of **Christ★**, *The Martyrdom of St Peter* by Giovanni Bellini and canvases by the 17C–18C Neapolitan school.

Museo Archeologico
Largo Monsignor Tommaso M. Ruffo 73.
Open Tue–Sun 8.30am–6.30pm.
℘080 54 12 596.
The archaeological museum displays Greco-Roman collections from excavations made throughout Puglia.

COAST EXCURSION
The road from Bari to Barletta passes through many attractive coastal towns that were fortified against invasion by the Saracens during the Middle Ages and the Turks at the end of the 15C. These include **Giovinazzo** with its small 12C cathedral dominating the fishing harbour; **Molfetta** pinpointed by the square towers of its Puglian Romanesque cathedral; and **Bisceglie**, a picturesque fishing village.

Barletta★
In the 12C and 13C Barletta was an embarkation port for the Crusades and many military or hospitaller Orders chose this as the site for an institution. Now a commercial and agricultural centre, the town has a fine historic nucleus comprising medieval religious and secular buildings. The symbol of the town is the **Colosso★★** or Statua di Eraclio, a gigantic statue over 4.5m/15ft tall of a Byzantine emperor whose identity is uncertain. Probably 4C, this work marks the transition from decadent Roman to early Christian art. The figure's stiffness is offset by its intense expression.
The statue stands in front of the basilica of **San Sepolcro**, which dates from the 12C–14C and has a fine **reliquary★**, with Limoges enamels on the base.
The **Castello★**, an imposing fortress built by the Emperor Frederick II of Hohenstaufen, houses a pinacoteca exhibiting a **collection★** of paintings by the local artist Giuseppe de Nittis (1846–84).
In Via Cialdini, the ground floor of the 14C Palazzo di Don Diego de Mendoza is where the Barletta challenge, **la Disfida di Barletta**, was issued.

Trani
This wine growing town has an ancient port and an 11C–13C Romanesque **cathedral★★** dedicated to St Nicholas the Pilgrim, a Greek shepherd who arrived in Trani on the back of a dolphin. It has a fine 12C **bronze door★** and a nave and aisles built over two immense crypts. From the **public gardens★**, east of the port, there is a view of the old town.

EXCURSIONS
Ruvo di Puglia
❯ 34km/21.1mi W of Bari.
On the edge of the Murge Hills, Ruvo has a Puglian-style Romanesque **cathedral★**. The **Museo Archeologico Jatta** has a fine collection of Attic, Italic and Apulian **vases★**.

Of these the **Crater of Talos★★**, a red-figured vase with a black background, is particularly notable. &Open daily 8.30am–1.30pm, Thu and Sat to 7.30pm . ☎080 36 12 848. www.palazzojatta.org.

Gioia del Colle

In the centre of the town stands the massive **Norman castle** built on the site of a Byzantine fortress. The ground floor houses the Archaeological Museum (note the fine 4C BC Apulian red-figure bowl depicting a burial temple at the centre), as well as the old bakery and prison. On the upper storey is the **throne room** (&open daily 8.30am–7.30pm; closed 1 Jan, 1 May, 25 Dec; 2.50€; ☎080 34 81 305; www.archeopuglia.beniculturali.it).

Bitonto

◗ 17km/10.6mi SW of Bari.
www.comune.bitonto.ba.it.
Set amid olive groves, this small town has a fine **Duomo★** that resembles those in Trani and Bari. The pulpit dates from 1229.

Brindisi

⌚See p266.

Canosa di Puglia

◗ 23km/14.3mi SW of Barletta.
The inhabitants of this Greek, then Roman, city were known for their ceramic vases (*askoi*). The 11C Romanesque **Duomo**, which shows

Byzantine influence, was remodelled in the 17C following an earthquake. The façade is 19C. Inside note the 11C episcopal throne and the **tomb★** of Bohemond, Prince of Antioch (d.1111), the son of Robert Guiscard (1015–85), a Norman adventurer who campaigned in southern Italy.

In the Via Cadorna there are three 4C BC *hypogea*, the **Ipogei Lagrasta**, and to the right of the Andria road, the remains of the palaeo-Christian basilica of **San Leucio**, built on the site of a Roman temple. Ipogei: Mar–Oct Tue–Sun 9am–1pm and 4–6pm, Nov–Feb 8am–2pm. ☎0883 66 40 43. www.pugliaimperiale.com.

Canne della Battaglia

◗ 12km/7.4mi SW of Barletta.
The strategic importance of the site in late Antiquity is evidenced by a battle in AD 216 when the Carthaginians led by Hannibal won a victory over the Roman army under Scipio. There are ruins of a medieval necropolis and of a Puglian village; and on the opposite slope, a stronghold where the main Roman axis, the *decumanus*, intersected by streets (*cardi*) is still visible, as well as the remains of a medieval basilica and of a Norman castle.

Castel del Monte★★

◗ 29km/18mi S of Barletta. &Open daily Apr–Sept 10.15am–7.30pm; rest of the year 9am–6.30pm. Closed 1 Jan, 25 Dec. www.casteldelmonte.beniculturali.it.

Frederick's Castles

A cultivated and eclectic man, **Frederick II of Hohenstaufen** (1194–1250) had numerous castles and fortresses built in Puglia, and was closely involved in their construction. Their basic plan is the square, deriving from the Roman *castrum* as well as symbolising the number four, which was considered a magical number in the Middle Ages. The square and the circle were considered symbols of the Earth and the sky, Man and God. This magical and practical synthesis reached a peak in the octagonal plan of Castel del Monte. The octagon was considered a perfect balance between the circle and the square, the form that blended and united the human and the divine. Eight is the number which comes up almost obsessively in this building: the castle is eight-sided, there are eight towers and each floor has eight rooms. Among Frederick's memorable castles in Puglia are those in Bari, Barletta, Brindisi, Castel del Monte, Manfredonia (erected by Frederick's son Manfred) and Trani.

⚘The last section of road is closed to vehicles; car park.

Frederick II built this castle c.1240 on the summit of one of the Murge Hills. Its octagonal plan makes Castel del Monte the exception in 200 quadrilateral fortresses built by this sovereign on his return from the Crusades.

Grotte di Castellana★★★

◗ 40km/24.8mi SE of Bari at Castellana-Grotte. Guided tours only, for information visit the website. 15€. ✆080 49 98 221. www.grottedicastellana.it.

These vast chambers have richly coloured stalactites and stalagmites. They climax at the White Cave, **Grotta Bianca★★★**, which glistens with calcite crystals. ⚘ *Tour not recommended for visitors with heart conditions.* ♣♣ *Caves are enchanting for older children.*

Promontorio del
Gargano★★★

Gargano Promontory

The Gargano Promontory is one of Italy's most attractive natural regions, with its wide horizons, mysterious forests and rugged coastline. This sun and sea paradise is marred by one drawback: most of the beaches and bays belong to campsites and hotels, and are not easily accessible.

A BIT OF GEOGRAPHY

Geologically, Gargano is independent from the Apennine Mountains; it is a limestone plateau fissured with crevices. Originally an island, Gargano was connected to the mainland by accumulated deposits brought down by the rivers from the Apennines.

Today the massif is riven by high-altitude valleys and heavily forested in

Altamura

◗ 42km/26mi SW of Bari.

This market town has an old hilltop quarter. The 13C **Duomo** has a façade that is pierced by a 13C **rose window★** and a sculptured 14C–15C **doorway★**.

ADDRESSES

✎ STAY

⚬ **Pensione Giulia** – Via Crisanzio 12. ✆080 52 16 630. www.hotelpensione giulia.it. 11 rooms. Small inn near the railway station and Piazza Aldo Moro.

♈ EAT

⚬⚬ **Al Sorso Preferito** – Via Vito Nicola De Nicolò 40. ✆080 52 35 747. www.ristorantealsorsopreferito.it. Closed Mon. A popular restaurant that is surprisingly good value. Menu includes regional specialities.

⚓ **Michelin Map:** 564 B–C 28–30 – Puglia.

🛈 **Info:** Parco Nazionale del Gargano, Via Sant' Antonio Abate 121, 71037 Monte Sant'Angelo. ✆0884 56 89 11. www.parcogargano.gov.it.

◗ **Location:** The Gargano Promontory projects like a spur from the "boot" of Italy. The nearest main road is the A 14.

◗ **Train:** Foggia (Bari Centrale 1hr 4mins).

⚘ **Don't Miss:** Foresta Umbra, views from Monte Sant'Angelo.

◷ **Timing:** The promontory is a good place to stay for a few days' holiday, but for a short visit allow a day.

---

the east. The plateau supports sheep, goats and black pigs. The Tremiti Islands belong to the same geological formation.

GETTING THERE

You can reach the Tremiti Islands year-round by ferry, fast boat or hydrofoil from Abruzzo (Pescara, Ortona, Vasto), Molise (Termoli) and the Gargano (Manfredonia, Vieste, Peschici and Rodi Garganico). The best connections are from the port of Termoli (ferry 1hr 40min; fast boats about 1hr).

Companies: **Navigazione Libera del Golfo** – ☎0875 70 48 59. www.navlib.it.
Tirrenia – ☎892 123. www.tirrenia.it. From the Foggia Eliporto Alidaunia helicopters depart regularly for the Tremiti Islands (20min trip). ☎0881 024 024. www.alidaunia.it.

🚗DRIVING TOURS

1 THE COAST AND GARGANO PROMONTORY

Round trip from Manfredonia. Approx. 160km/99mi. Allow 1 day.

Manfredonia ⚐

www.comune.manfredonia.fg.it.
Manfred, the son of the Emperor Frederick II of Hohenstaufen, founded the port in the 13C. It is guarded by a 13C castle. The **Church of Santa Maria di Siponto★** *(3km/1.8mi s on the S 89)* is an 11C building in the Romanesque style which shows Oriental (square plan and terraced roof hiding the dome) and Pisan (blind arcades with columns enclosing lozenges) influences. The late-11C church of **San Leonardo** *(beyond the church of Santa Maria, take the Foggia road to the right)* has a fine delicately sculptured 13C **doorway★**.

▶ Leaving Manfredonia drive 15km/9.3mi left on the S 89 and follow signs for Mattinata.

Mattinata

www.comune.mattinata.fg.it.
From the road to Mattinata there is a fine **view★★** of the market town, encircled by olive groves and mountains.

▶ From Mattinata, take the SS 28 to the SP 53 for 38km/23.6mi into Vieste. There is a series of sharp turns and bends on part of the SP 53.

Vieste ⚐

www.comune.vieste.it.
This town, dominated by its 13C cathedral, has an interesting shell museum, **Museo Malacologico.** ♿Open Mon–Sun 9.30am–12.30pm and 2pm–8pm. Free. ☎0884 70 76 88, www.museomalacologicovieste.it. To the south is a vast beach with a limestone sea-stack, **Faraglione di Pizzomunno**. Between Vieste and Mattinata is a nice **scenic stretch★★**

Baia delle Zagare

of road. The square tower in **Testa del Gargano** marks the massif's eastern-most extremity. There's a pretty **view★** of the inlet, **Cala di San Felice**. Beyond the resort of **Pugnochiuso** lies the **Baia delle Zagare★** (Bay of Zagare).

▶ Take the SS 89 to the SP 52 for 21km/13mi.

Peschici★

www.peschicisole.it.
Well situated on a spur jutting out into the sea, this fishing town is now a sea-side resort.

▶ From Peschici, drive 28km/ 17.4ml on the S 89.

Foresta Umbra★★

www.forestaumbra.com.
Forests are rare in Puglia and this vast expanse of beeches, elders, oaks and ancient yews, covers over 11 000ha/ 27 000 acres. The forest is equipped with recreational facilities. Shortly after Vieste there is a forestry lodge, which is now a **visitor centre**.

TREMITI ISLANDS – MARINE RESERVE★

Access from Termoli, Vasto, Pescara, Ortona, Vieste, Manfredonia, Peschici and Rodi Garganico (see Getting There). Allow 2 days. For guided tours contact Iris Società Cooperativa, ☎0808 91 07 77.

The Tremiti Islands (pop. 370) lie off-shore from the Gargano Promontory and belong to the same geological for-mation. This tiny archipelago, the only one on the Adriatic Coast, comprises two main islands, San Nicola and San Domino, as well as two uninhabited isles, Capraia and Pianosa.
The boat trip from Manfredonia offers unforgettable **views★★★** of the coast. As the boat rounds the promontory there are also good **views★★★** of the coastal towns.

San Nicola★

🔖 Isola di San Nicola. ☎0882 46 30 02.
On the clifftop stands the **Abbazia di Santa Maria al Mare** (open daily, ☎0882 46 30 63), a 9C Benedictine abbey. Of interest are the remains of an 11C mosaic pavement, a 15C Gothic polyptych and a 13C Byzantine Crucifix.

San Domino★

A boat trip round this island reveals its rugged coasts. Above Cala Matano is the home of Lucio Dalla, a famous Italian singer who organises a festival and free concert in the courtyard of the Abbazia di Santa Maria al Mare in San Nicola every June.

② PIANA DEL TAVOLIERE

From Monte Sant'Angelo. Approx. 150km/93mi. Allow 2 days.

Street in Vieste

© Poike/iStockphoto.com

Monte Sant'Angelo★

www.turismomontesantangelo.it.
Monte Sant'Angelo stands in a wonderful **site★★**. The town is built on a spur (803m/2 634ft) dominated by its castle and overlooks both the Gargano Promontory and the sea. It was in a nearby cave between 490 and 493 that the Archangel Michael appeared three times to the Bishop of Siponto. After another 8C apparition, an abbey was founded. During the Middle Ages Crusaders prayed to the Archangel before embarking at Manfredonia. On 29 September the annual feast day includes the procession of the Archangel's Sword.

GARGANO

Santuario di San Michele★★

www.santuariosanmichele.it
The church dedicated to St Michael, designed in the transitional Romanesque-Gothic style, is flanked by a detached 13C octagonal campanile. Opposite the entrance a stairway leads to the 11C **bronze door★**.
It gives access to the nave with pointed vaulting, which opens onto the cave *(to the right)* in which St Michael is said to have appeared. The marble statue of the saint is by Andrea Sansovino (16C) and the 11C episcopal throne is decorated in characteristic Apulian style.

Tomba di Rotari★

Go down the stairs opposite the campanile.
Open 9am–1pm and 2.30–6pm.
The tomb is on the left of the apse in the ruined church of San Pietro. Inside, the tower rises through a square, an octagon and finally a triangle to the dome. The tomb was thought to contain the remains of Rotharis, a 7C Lombard king, but is really a 12C baptistery.

Chiesa di Santa Maria Maggiore

Right of Tomba di Rotari.
This church in the Puglian-Romanesque style boasts a fine doorway. Inside there are traces of Byzantine frescoes.

▷ Drive 15km/9.3mi W of Monte Sant'Angelo on the S 272.

San Giovanni Rotondo

www.sangiovannirotondo.it.
This is a site of pilgrimage dear to devotees of **Padre Pio** (1887–1968). The Capuchin monk from **Pietrelcina**, near Benevento, was ordained and lived here. In 1918 stigmata appeared on his body, disappearing on his death. He was canonised in 2002.

▷ Continue driving W on the S 272 for 10km/6.2mi past San Giovanni.

San Marco in Lamis

This village is perched on the Gargano Promontory and is known for the procession of *fracchie*, gigantic torches that are set ablaze each year on the evening of Good Friday. The tradition dates back to the last century when farmers were chased through the darkness waving bundles of twigs above their heads.

▷ Return to the S272 and continue W for 23km/14.3mi.

San Severo★

www.comune.san-severo.fg.it.
Severely shaken by an earthquake in 1627, the city developed during the Middle Ages and was rebuilt in the 17C. Its cobbled streets, flanked by Baroque

buildings, make this city a promenade of great beauty. The historic **centre★** is built around the Palazzo di Città and is a good starting point for exploring the town.

▶ Drive 22km/13.7mi S on the S 160.

Lucera

Important in Roman times, Lucera was ceded by Emperor Frederick II to the Saracens of Sicily, who were expelled by Charles II of Anjou. Lucera has an imposing 13C Angevin **fortress★** with a fine **panorama★** of the Tavoliere Plain. The historic centre is dominated by the 14C **Duomo**. Nearby a palace, unfortunately in poor condition, houses the **Museo Civico G. Fiorelli**, which displays a marble **Venus★**, a Roman replica of a model by the School of Praxiteles (Via De Nicastri 74; Tue–Sun 9am–1pm and 3–7pm (hours are subject to change). ✆800 767 606). A short distance from the centre is a well-preserved Roman **amphitheatre★**.

▶ Take the SP 109 and SS 160 for 20km/12.4mi to Troia.

Troia

This market town overlooks the Tavoliere Plain.

▶ Take the SP 115 and turn left on the SS 90 to Foggia.

Foggia

Town map in the Michelin Atlas Italy. Foggia is in the heart of a vast cereal-growing plain, the Tavoliere. Its **Duomo** incorporates parts of an earlier building (13C), notably the lower walls with some blind arcading. This earlier structure, destroyed by the 1731 earthquake, has been rebuilt.

ADDRESSES

🏠 STAY

ISOLE SAN DOMINO

⊜⊜⊜ **Hotel San Domino** – ✆0882 46 34 04. www.hotelsandomino.com. 25 rooms. The hotel is located on the

beach and has simple, comfortable rooms and warm service.

MONTE SANT'ANGELO

⊜⊜⊜ **Palace Hotel San Michele** – Via Madonna degli Angeli. ✆0884 56 56 53. www.palacehotelsanmichele.it. ⚓. 55 rooms. This hotel is one of the few that is open in winter and is on a rocky outcrop overlooking Monte Sant'Angelo.

PESCHICI

⊜ **Hotel Peschici** – Via San Martino 31, 71010 Peschici. ✆0884 96 41 95. www.hotel peschici.it. Open Easter–Sept. 13 rooms. ⚓. This *pensione* is situated in the heart of the village overlooking the sea. Rooms are simple and clean. Family-style guesthouse with a warm welcome.

⊜⊜ **Park Hotel Paglianza e Paradiso** – Loc. Manacore, 10.5km/6.5mi E of Peschici. ✆0884 91 10 11. www.hotelpaglianza.it. Closed 15 Oct–Mar. 140 rooms. ⚓. Just a few minutes' walk from the sea, deep in a forest, it is nice for those wanting a comfortable hotel with sporting facilities.

⊜⊜⊜ **Masseria La Chiusa** – 71010 Peschici. Località Padula, Gargano S.S. 89. ✆3470 57 72 72 . www.lachiusadellemore.it. 64 rooms. ⚓. Is a charming Apulian farmhouse set 500 metres from the sea. It offers rooms with independent entrance, free mountain bikes, and panoramic views of the hills and countryside. La Chiusa Delle More's rooms feature wrought-iron beds and fine high-quality linens. Breakfast at the Masseria includes homemade cakes, pies and pastries, freshly squeezed orange juice and fresh ricotta cheese. Masseria La Chiusa it is 1.5 km from the centre of Peschici, and a 10-minute walk from the sea.

VIESTE

⊜⊜ **Hotel Svevo** – Via Fratelli Bandiera 10, 71019 Vieste. ✆0884 70 88 30. www.hotelsvevo.com. Closed Oct–Mar. ⚓. 30 rooms. ⚓. A charming hotel not far from the castle. Rooms are simple but well maintained. Wonderful terrace-solarium with swimming pool. Fantastic panorama.

🍴 EAT

MONTE SANT'ANGELO

⊜⊜ **Medioevo** – Via Castello 21, 71037 Monte Sant'Angelo. ✆0884 56 53 56. www.ristorantemedioevo.it. Closed Mon except summer. Closed also 2 weeks in Nov. Diners are given a warm welcome in this little trattoria which is tucked away up in the heart of the historic centre. Simple, modern-style dining room with a vaulted ceiling. Regional cuisine with some personal touches, dishes are lovingly prepared using the freshest ingredients – wonderful aromas.

PESCHICI

⊖⊖ **La Collinetta** – Loc. Madonna di Loreto, Peschici, 2km/1.2mi SE of Peschici. ℘0884 96 41 51. www.lacollinettagargano.com. Closed lunch and Oct–15 Mar. Reservation recommended. Wonderful views over the coast from the terrace and excellent seafood dishes (prepared with super-fresh ingredients). Overnight stays possible – pleasant room.

⊖⊖ **Da Mimi Ristorante Altrabucco** – Loc. Punta San Nicola Peschici. ℘0884 96 25 56. www.altrabucco.it. Lunch; dinner Apr–Oct. Reservation recommended.

Rustic wooden tables on an enchanting spindly fishing pier overlooking the water. Specialities are fresh fish and seafood, Puglia wines and artisinal beer.

SAN SEVERO

⊖⊖ **La Fossa del Grano** – Via Minuziano 63. ℘0882 24 11 22. www.lafossadelgrano.com. Closed Sun evening and Mon and 2 weeks Aug. A great place for fans of traditional family recipes and authentic Puglian cuisine.

VIESTE

⊖⊖ **Taverna al Cantinone** – Via Mafrolla 26, 71019 Vieste. ℘0884 70 77 53. Open Easter–Oct. Simple, cheerful trattoria in the centre. Traditional home cooking with fresh, local produce, good value for money.

Terra dei Trulli★★★

This region between Fassano, Ostuni, Martina Franca and Alberobello takes its name from the curious buildings, the trulli, found in this part of Puglia. These square structures have conical roofs covered with chiancarelle, grey-limestone roof slabs. Originally built without using mortar, the walls and the edges of the roof are whitewashed. They are crowned by differently shaped pinnacles, each with a magical significance. Each dome corresponds to a room, some abodes comprise three or four trulli.

SIGHTS
Alberobello★★★
Train: Alberobello (Bari 1hr 21 mins).
Visit the Trullo Museo Casa Pezzolla. This town has an entire district of trulli (about 1 400), spread over the hillside to the south of the town (Zona Monu-

Michelin Map: 564 F 35 – Puglia.

Info: Piazza Sacramento 10, Alberobello. ℘080 432 6030. www.alberobellonline.it.

Location: La Terra dei Trulli is located in central Puglia and stretches across the provinces of Bari, Brindisi and Taranto.

Train: Brindisi (Bari Centrale 1hr).

Kids: ZooSafari.

mentale, Rioni Monti and Aia Piccola). The hilltop church of **Sant'Antonio** is also a trullo (Via Monte Sant'Angelo). It is possible to visit these strange dwellings. A good example is at the **Museo del Territorio Casa Pezzolla ★** (in Piazza XXVII Maggio; www.alberobellocultura.it), a large 18C trullo, now used for exhibitions. Trullo Sovrano is another large **Trullo complex** in Alberobello. For places to stay in Trullo, Trullidea features some nice options (www.trullidea.it; ℘080 43 23 860).

Locorotondo

www.comune.locorotondo.ba.it.

This town is named for its alleyways that wind in circles (*loco rotondo*: round place) around the hill. In the **historic centre★** is the Neoclassical church of San Giorgio. The road from Locorotondo to Martina Franca follows the **Valle d'Itria★★**, a vast plain dotted with *trulli*.

Martina Franca★

www.comunemartinafranca.gov.it.

This white city in the Murge Hills has an old town, girdled by ramparts. **Piazza Roma** is bordered by the 17C Palazzo Ducale. Head towards Corso Vittorio Emanuele and Piazza del Plebiscito. The adjacent Piazza Maria Immacolata leads to **Via Cavour★**.

Ostuni★

This large market town spreads over several hills. At the centre, with its white alleyways and Aragonese ramparts, is the 15C **Cattedrale**. The **façade★** features a pattern of concave and convex lines. In the centre is a beautiful **rose window★** with complex symbolism relating to the passage of time: 24 external arcs, representing 24 hours in a day, 12 internal ones, for the months, while Christ, in the centre, is surrounded by seven angels, representing the days of the week. Nearby the church of San Vito has an **archaeological museum**, that displays the plaster cast of **Delia**, a young pregnant woman who lived 25 000 years ago (her skeleton shows the foetus' tiny bones). &Open daily 10am–2pm and 6–10pm. 5€ (includes guided tour). ✆0831 307 510.

EXCURSIONS
Brindisi

◗ 35km/21.7mi E of Ostuni. Via C. Colombo 88. ✆0831 56 21 26. www.pugliaturismo.com.

This important naval and trading port (pop. 87 935) lies on the Adriatic Sea and is accessible by car on the S 379. The main reason visitors come today is for the ferries for Greece. Trajan replaced the old Appian Way beyond Benevento with the new Via Traiana, increasing Brindisi's importance from AD 109 onwards. After the Norman conquest, the town became a port for Crusades to the Holy Land, in particular the Sixth Crusade (1228).

The centre contains the most interesting monuments. Principal access to the old city is through the 13C **Porta Mesagne**. The 13C **Swabian Castle** was built for Frederick II and today houses the Navy. The two marble **Roman columns** on the cape probably denoted the end of the Appian Way.

Piazza Duomo

The square is overlooked by the 14C **Balsamo Loggia**, the 14C Portico of the Knights Templar and the 18C Romanesque Duomo. The piazza also houses the **Museo Archeologico F. Ribezzo**. ⊘ Note the collection of Puglian, Messapici and Attic vases. 9.30am–1.30pm Tue–Sat, and Tue 3.30–6.30pm. Closed public hols. Free. ✆0831 56 55 01. www.provincia.brindisi.it.

Chiese

The historic centre has many churches. The 11C church of **San Giovanni al Sepolcro** is a Templar church and the Romanesque church of **Santa Lucia** has 13C fresco remains in its interior.

Chiesa di Santa Maria del Casale★

◗ Approx. 5km/3mi N. www.santamariadelcasale.net.

This 14C Romanesque-Gothic church was built by Philip d'Anjou and his wife Catherine of Flanders. The exterior features bi-coloured geometric patterns and has a porch crowned by an embellishment consisting of Lombard arches. The interior has an interesting cycle of Byzantine frescoes from the same period.

ADDRESSES

ACTIVITIES

👥 **ZooSafari** – Via dello Zoosafari, 72015 Fasano. ✆080 44 14 455. www.zoosafari.it. Italy's largest wild safari park.

Lecce★★

Nicknamed "the Baroque Florence", the town boasts a profusion of incredibly decorative buildings. At night, decked in lights, it resembles a sumptuous theatrical set. Lecce was in Roman times the prosperous town of Lupiae. The Normans greatly favoured the town and made it the capital of the region known as Terra d'Otranto. From the 16C to the 18C, Lecce knew a period of great splendour during which it was embellished with Renaissance, Rococo and Baroque monuments. The local finely grained limestone was particularly easy to work, and the town's numerous Baroque buildings are remarkable for the abundance of decorative work. The most inventive artists came from the Zimbalo family: their work is to be found in both churches and palaces and is widespread throughout the Salentina Peninsula.

- ▶ **Population:** 83 137
- 🖥 **Michelin Map:** 564 F 36 – Puglia.
- 🅱 **Info:** Castello Carlo V, Viale XXV luglio. ✆0832 24 65 17. www.comune.lecce.it.
- ◖ **Location:** Lecce is set in the very heart of the Salento region, off the S 613.
- ◖ **Train:** Lecce (Brindisi 30 mins).
- 👁 **Don't Miss:** The historic Baroque centre and the sumptuous decoration of the Basilica di Santa Croce.
- 🕐 **Timing:** Allow a day for the town and excursions.

BAROQUE LECCE★★

The historic centre, once surrounded by ramparts (16C), of which only traces remain, and a **castle** (built by Charles V on an existing Angevin fort), is now delineated by a ring of avenues. The heart of the city is the lively **Piazza Sant'Oronzo**, which is dominated by a statue of the patron saint on top of one of the two columns that mark the end of the Appian Way, the other being in Brindisi (◖*see opposite*).

To the south side of the square, parts of a **Roman amphitheatre** (2C), originally double tiered, have been unearthed. Also in the piazza are the small church of **San Marco**, attributed to Gabriele Riccardi and built by the Venetian colony, and the very old **palazzo del Seggio**, which temporarily houses a

Intricate façade of Basilica di Santa Croce

APT Puglia/Fototeca ENIT

papier mâché statue of San Giuseppe Patriarca (19C).

Basilica di Santa Croce★★

Several architects worked on this basilica in the 16C and 17C and it constitutes the best example of the Baroque style of Lecce. The façade is sumptuously decorated without being overbearing (the lower part is Renaissance in structure). The upper storey is almost without doubt the work of Zimbalo and is richly ornamented. The two storeys are linked by a long balcony held up by animal atlantes and caryatids while the parapet is adorned with cherubs holding mitres and books.

The central rose window above seems as if it were fashioned by an expert lacemaker. The **interior** is light and airy and reminiscent of the Florentine-Renaissance idiom. There is also abundant Baroque decoration of great delicacy. The side chapel at the end of the north aisle contains a fine **high altar** with low reliefs by Francesco Antonio Zimbalo and depicts scenes from the life of Francesco da Paola.

Palazzo del Governo

Adjoining the basilica the Governor's residence, a former Celestine monastery, has a rusticated façade with a frieze above and intricately decorated window surrounds, especially at first-floor level, designed by Zimbalo (ground floor) and Cino.

Chiesa del Gesù (or del Buon Consiglio)

The austere style of this church, built by the Jesuits (1575–79), makes a stark contrast to the other churches in Lecce. Inside is an ornate **Baroque altar★**.

Chiesa di Sant'Irene

Built by Francesco Grimaldi for the Theatine monks, this church has lavish **Baroque altars** that are attributed to Francesco Antonio Zimbalo.

Piazza del Duomo★★

Enclosed in a homogeneous body of Baroque buildings and heralded by an arch facing Corso Vittorio Emanuele, this is one of the most remarkable squares in southern Italy. To the left, the **campanile** (1661–82) and the adjacent **Duomo** (1659–82) are by Giuseppe Zimbalo, the 17C **Palazzo Vescovile** and the **Seminario**, dating from 1709, by Giuseppe Cino. In the courtyard of the latter there is an ornately decorated **well★** by the same sculptor.

Duomo

The first sighting of the Duomo is in fact of the north side. It is the most ornate façade of the church with its imposing entrance and arcade with a statue of St Oronzo. The main façade (visible from the square) is more restrained. Inside, the **crypt**, rebuilt in the 16C on an existing medieval structure, is held up by 92 columns with capitals adorned by figures of animals.

Chiesa del Rosario (or di San Giovanni Battista)★

This church was Giuseppe Zimbalo's last work and the façade features an abundance of decoration.

The **interior★** is adorned with richly embellished Baroque altars and some fine 17C altarpieces.

Via Palmieri

Several elegant buildings border this street; particularly noteworthy are the ones at Piazza Falconieri, Palazzo Marrese and Palazzo Palmieri (18C). At the end of the street, **Porta Napoli** (or Arco di Trionfo) was built in the 16C in honour of Charles V.

Chiesa di Sant'Angelo

Although unfinished, this façade is typical of Zimbalo's style (1663), with garlands, cherubs and angels.

Chiesa di San Matteo★

This church with its harmonious façade by Achille Carducci (1667–1700) shows the distinct influence of Borromini and his Roman work, the church of San Carlo alle Quattro Fontane.

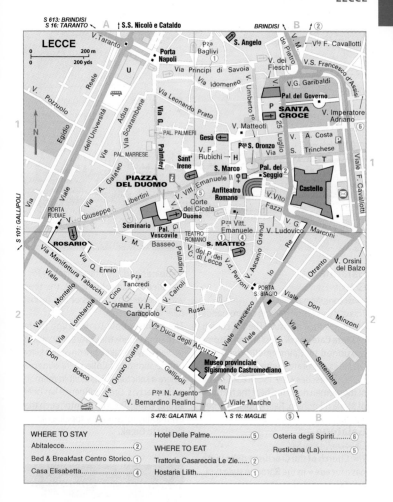

LECCE

ADDITIONAL SIGHT
Museo Provinciale Sigismondo Castromediano★

Viale Gallipoli 28. & Open Mon–Sat 9am–1.30pm and 2.30–7.30pm, Sun and public hols mornings. ℘0832 68 35 03. www.comune.lecce.it.

Housed in a modern building, the museum has a rich archaeological section *(ground floor)* and important **ceramics collection★★** *(first floor)*.

Of particular interest are the Attic vases decorated with red figures. There is also a collection of epigraphs and two beautiful bronze statues (a figure of a woman and a priest). An art gallery is on the third floor.

EXCURSIONS
Abbazia di Santa Maria di Cerrate★

◐ 14km/8.7mi N on the road to Brindisi. & For opening times visit the website. Closed 1 Jan, 25 Dec. ℘0832 36 11 76. www.visitfai.it.

This enchanting 12C Benedictine abbey has an isolated country setting. The **church★** north side 13C portico has capitals embellished with figurative scenes and a doorway vault with New Testament scenes. The interior retains part of the frescoes that probably once covered its entire surface. Some fresco fragments are conserved in the **Museo delle Tradizioni Popolari**.

Old Town of Gallipoli

© Polke/iStockphoto.com

Galatina

▶ 21km/13mi S.

www.comune.galatina.le.it.

This craft and wine making centre stands on the Salento Peninsula. The 14C church of **Santa Caterina di Alessandria★**, commissioned by Raimondello del Balzo Orsini, is decorated with a marvellous cycle of **frescoes★** by 15C artists. Many of the women depicted bear the features of Maria d'Enghien, Raimondello's wife.

Galatone

▶ 24km/14.9mi SW.

The **Church of the Crocifisso della Pietà** has a **façade★** in the Baroque style typical of the Lecce area.

Gallipoli★

▶ 40km/24.8mi SW. Train: Gallipoli (Lecce 1hr 2mins).

The old town with its small port is set on an island and linked to the modern town by a bridge. Note the imposing 16C **castle** and **cathedral** with a Baroque façade (the interior contains paintings of the 17C and 18C). Along the Riviera, which follows the old city wall, stands the **Church della Purità**; the **interior★** has a remarkable ceramic floor.

Otranto

▶ 45km/28mi SE.

This fishing port was once capital of "Terra d'Otranto", the last remaining Byzantine stronghold that resisted the Lombards and then the Normans for a considerable time. In the 15C the town was besieged by troops of the Turkish ruler Mohammed II.

The townspeople took refuge in the cathedral where they were massacred. Survivors were taken prisoner and killed on the summit of Colle della Minerva, where a sanctuary was built in memory of the martyrs. Greek influence has been strong in the "Terra d'Otranto", such that even today inhabitants speak a dialect similar to Greek.

Painting inside the Gallipoli cathedral

© APT Puglia/Fototeca ENIT

Città Vecchia

The northeast pier offers a good view of the old town; to the left is the 15C **Castello Aragonese**. To reach it pass through the Porta di Terra and the 15C Porta Alfonsina.

Cattedrale★

This 12C cathedral was altered in the late-15C. The interior has a stunning mosaic **floor**, built between 1163 and 1165 by Pantaleone, a priest. The central nave shows the Tree of Life, held up by two Indian elephants. The tree's branches embrace biblical scenes, creatures from a medieval bestiary, poem heroes, mythological images and the cycle of months and astrological signs. At the end of the aisles are two other trees and representations of Paradise and Hell. The **crypt** is sustained by ancient capitals.

Chiesetta di San Pietro

This 9C church has frescoes of the same period; sadly in poor condition.

🚗 DRIVING TOUR

THE COAST TO THE SOUTH★

Between Otranto and **Santa Maria di Leuca** *(51km/31.7mi)* the road offers fine views of the coastline. At the head of an inlet is a cave, **Grotta Zinzulusa**, with salt water and freshwater lakes (guided tours only; 20min, when sea is calm; www.viaggiareinpuglia.it).

▶ Take Via De Gaspari to reach Piazza Matteotti, flanked by palaces and medieval ruins.

The market town of **Trola** overlooks the Tavoliere Plain. The Romanesque **cathedral** is embellished with a lovely **rose window★** and 12C **bronze door★**.

Taranto★

🕮 *see Taranto.*

Isole Tremiti★

🕮 *see Isole Tremiti.*

ADDRESSES

🛏 STAY

🛏 **B&B Centro Storico** – Via Andrea Vignes 2. ☏0832 24 27 27. www.centrostoricolecce.it. In the historic centre. Rooms are sometimes dark, but they have high ceilings. Beautiful terrace.

🛏🍴 **Antico Belvedere** – Via Andrea Vignes 15. ☏0832 30 70 52. www.beb-lecce.com. 13 rooms. Located in a beautiful villa with Spanish decorations. A quiet location in the historic centre.

Nuvole Barocche B&B – Piazzetta Brizio De Santis 3. ☏0832 16 92 758. www.nuvolebarocche.com/it/. 2 rooms. Is located less than a 5-minute walk from the Basilica di Santa Croce cathedral. The rooms have a white-themed décor and refined light-wood furnishings. An Italian breakfast at the B&B Nuvole Barocche includes sweet pastries, while savoury options are available on advance request.

🛏🍴🍷 **Hotel Delle Palme** – Via Leuca 90. ☏/Fax 0832 34 71 71. www.hoteldellepalmelecce.it. 🅿 96 rooms. Restaurant 🛏🍴🍷. Near the historic centre. The wood and leather decorations offer a Spanish flair.

🍴 EAT

🛏 **La Rusticana** – Via del Delfino, 3. ☏0832 24 94 19. Also lunch, www.larusticalecce.it. Good pasta, pizza, crêpes and *rustici* (stuffed puff pastry). Ideal for a quick bite. Cheap.

🛏🍴 **Hostaria Lilith** – Via Principi di Savoia 39. ☏0832 33 14 80. Closed Mon. Near Santa Croce, this trattoria serves regional seafood and meat. Good wine list.

🛏🍴 **Osteria degli Spiriti** – Via Cesare Battisti 4. ☏0832 24 62 74. www.osteriadeglispiriti.it. Closed Sun evening and 15 days in Sept. Close to the public gardens, this rustic trattoria offers good Puglian cooking.

🛏🍴 **Trattoria Casareccia Le Zie** – Via Costadura 19. ☏0832 24 51 78. www.lezietrattoria.com. Closed Sun and Mon evenings 30 Aug–15 Sept and 24 Dec–6 Jan. Historic trattoria with a culinary tradition of over sixty years. Delicious homemade recipes are prepared to order. Competitively priced.

Taranto★

Taranto is a naval base, closed at the seaward end by two fortified islands. Founded in the 7C BC, it was an important colony of *Magna Graecia*. During Holy Week many impressive ceremonies take place in the town, including several processions between Thursday and Saturday, one lasting 12 hours and another 14 hours, which go from church to church at a very slow pace.

▶ **Population:** 199 012
☀ **Michelin Map:** 564 F 33; town map in the Michelin Atlas Italy – Puglia.
🗊 **Info:** Corso Umberto 113. ℘099 45 32 392. www.pugliaturismo. com/apt-taranto/.
◖ **Location:** Tucked away behind the "heel", Taranto lies off the S 106 (if you are travelling from Calabria), S 7, Via Appia and S 172.
◖ **Train:** Taranto (Brindisi 1hr).
👁 **Don't Miss:** During Holy Week many processions take place.
🕐 **Timing:** Allow half a day.

SIGHTS

Museo Nazionale Archeologico di Taranto★★

Via Cavour 10. ᵭ Open daily 8.30am–7pm. 5€. ℘099 45 32 112. www.museotaranto.org.
This museum houses a good collection of local archaeological finds. The exhibit follows the history of Taranto from Prehistory, to the Greek and Roman eras, up to medieval times. On the ground floor are reconstructed Greek and Roman "towns" where are displayed the highlights of the museum, including a **Poseidon★★** discovered at Ugento, a **collection of ceramics★★** and Hellenic **gold jewellery★★★** (4C and 3C BC).

Lungomare Vittorio Emanuelea★

This is a long promenade planted with palm trees and oleanders.

La Città Vecchia★

The old city is an island connected to the mainland by two bridges, one of which is a revolving bridge. At the eastern extremity of the island stands the **Aragon Castle**, which today is the Naval seat.

Duomo

The 11C–12C cathedral with a Baroque façade has been greatly remodelled. The nave and two aisles are separated by ancient columns with Romanesque or Byzantine capitals and the ceiling is 17C. The chapel of **San Cataldo★** was faced with polychrome marble and embellished with statues in the 18C.

Chiesa di San Domenico Maggiore

This 14C church was remodelled in the Baroque era. There is a fine, if damaged, façade with an ogival portal surmounted by a rose window.

Cathedral of San Cataldo, main navata

© Francesco Cantone/iStockphoto.com

Calabria and Basilicata

Major Cities: Matera, Reggio Calabria,
Official Websites: www.turiscalabria.it; www.aptbasilicata.it

Hot and mountainous describe Calabria and Basilicata, the two southernmost regions of the Italian peninsula. Here is where the Apennines make their final appearance, such as in the Pollino National Park and along the sea at Tropea, where buildings cling to limestone cliffs. The scorching heat caused the ancient people of Matera to seek shelter in the Sassi, or cave dwellings, which are World Heritage Sites. Lined with beaches – another respite from the heat – is Reggio Calabria, the largest city, facing Sicily across the Strait of Messina.

Rocky and Fertile Contrasts

Basilicata, known as **Lucania** during Roman times, and Calabria comprise very different types of country; the rocky corniche from the Gulf of Policastro to Reggio; the vast, green mountains of the **Sila Massif** with its extensive mountain pastures and wide horizons; and at the southern extremity of the peninsula between two inner seas, lies the **Aspromonte Massif** clad with pine, beech and chestnut forests. Between Basilicata and Calabria is Italy's largest national park, **Parco Nazionale del Pollino** (inaugurated in 1990), which is covered in pine forests. Formed by the Pollino Massif, it boasts an interesting array of fauna (red kite, Apennine wolf) and flora (Bosnian pine, various medicinal herbs). There are also several natural history museums in the area. Basilicata has a small coastline on the Gulf of Taranto and a narrow outlet to the Tyrrhenian Sea.

Highlights

1 Gaze at Sicily and Mt Etna from Reggio's **Lungomare** (p276)

2 See the **Riace Warriors** in the **Museo Nazionale Archeologico** (p276)

3 Explore Matera's ancient **Sassi cave dwellings** (p280)

Inland, the region is characterised by mountains, particularly Monte Pollino and **Monte Vulture**, a dormant volcano. Calabria, with the southern Apennine massifs forming its spine, is itself a peninsula, and includes beaches recalled in tales by Homer.

Both regions were part of *Magna Graecia* and many of the artefacts recovered from that time are on display at the Museo Nazionale Archeologico in Reggio Calabria.

Town of Matera overlooks the rock dwellings—Sassi, Basilicata

©Giuseppe Bevacqua/Fotolia.com

Calabria

Greeks colonised the southernmost tip of Italy over 2 800 years ago. The coast rivalled Athens as a cosmopolitan centre in 8 BC; the mystic philosopher Pythagoras preached vegetarianism there alongside the decadent Sybarites and Homer set part of *The Odyssey* on Calabria's coastline.

Invaders plundered this land throughout history; Byzantines, Germanic warriors, Saracens, Normans, Turks and Bourbons. Once infamous for bandits and 'Ndrangheta bloodshed, Calabria also has a gentle side. The sea – often purple-hued between Gioia Tauro and Villa San Giovanni – washes the base of this craggy coast. Ionian ruins and Roman mosaics dot the farmland, rich with agritourism B&Bs. High in the crumbling mountains, five villages retain vestiges of ancient Greek culture. In season, mushroom hunters search the slopes here among the ski chalets.

The backbone of Calabria is formed by the Pollino Massif (the Pollino Mountains have an altitude of 2 248m/7 375ft) and by the Sila and Aspromonte massifs, all of which are national parks. Here, the olive groves produce excellent oil – Rossano's has a very low level of acidity – and the citrus harvest includes clementines and blond and bergamot oranges.

Michelin Map: 564 G–N 28–33.

Info: Parco Nazionale del Pollino: Complesso Monumentale Santa Maria della Consolazione, 85048 Rotonda (Potenza). ℘0973 66 93 11. www.parcopollino.it.
Parco Nazionale dell'Aspromonte: Via Aurora, 89057 Gambarie di Santo Stefano. ℘0965 74 30 60. www.parcoaspromonte.gov.it.
Parco Nazionale della Sila: Via Nazionale, 87055 Lorica. ℘0984 53 71 09. www.parcosila.it.

Location: Calabria is in the extreme south and covers the narrow stretch of land between the Gulfs of Policastro and Taranto. The main access road is the A 3, Salerno–Reggio Calabria motorway.

Train: Reggio Calabria, Tropea (1hr 38mins), Palmi (Reggio Calabria 48 mins), Scilla (Reggio Calabria 28 mins).

Don't Miss: The mythology of the town of Scilla.

Timing: Allow a day to explore the Tyrrhenian Coast and two days for the "Toe" and Ionian Coast.

Kids: Wolf and deer enclosures at Parco Nazionale della Sila.

A BIT OF HISTORY

The first colonies on the Ionian Coast were founded by the Greeks in the 8C BC and they, together with the Byzantines and Basilian monks (St Basil, father of the Greek Church, lived in c.AD 330–79), shaped the early art and history of this region. In the 3C BC Rome undertook the conquest of southern Italy, but did not establish a complete and peaceful domination until Sulla reorganised the administration of these provinces in the 1C BC. After the fall of the Roman Empire, Calabria and the neighbouring regions fell under the sway of the Lombards, Saracens and Byzantines before being reunited with the Norman Kingdom of the Two Sicilies and finally becoming part of a unified Italy in 1860. Natural disasters, such as the powerful earthquakes which struck in 1783 and 1908, and famine, poverty, banditry, social and emigration problems have plagued Calabria, which, thanks to agrarian reform and commitment to tourism and cultural activities, finally has occasion to hope for a real rebirth.

VISIT
Massiccio della Sila★★
www.parcosila.it.

Sila has an ancient name which signifies "primordial forest": the Greek version of the word is *hyla*, the Latin *silva*. This plateau measures 1 700sq km/656sq mi, alternating prairies and forests of larch pine and beech trees.

On the Sila Grande are the two towns of Camigliatello and Lorica. About 10km/6mi away from Camigliatello is the visitor centre of the **Parco Nazionale della Calabria**. Fauna enclosures display deer and wolves in their natural habitat, viewed from wooden hides with windows. The centre also offers botanical and geological walks for visitors. The wooden houses that dot the landscape contribute to the northern-country atmosphere, particularly along the lakes, Cecita, **Arvo★** and Ampolino.

Aspromonte★
The Aspromonte Massif forms Calabria's southern tip and culminates in a peak of 1 955m/6 414ft. Fabled mushrooms sprout on this misty crag, known as "the Cloud Gatherer" or the "harsh mountain" and was celebrated by Homer: "piercing the sky, with storm cloud round the peak dissolving never ... No mortal man could scale it, nor as much land there, not with twenty hands and feet, so sheer are the cliffs." The park protects chestnut trees, oaks and beeches and is home to wolves, Peregrine falcons and eagle owls. The massif serves as a catchment area from which radiate deep valleys eroded by fast-flowing torrents *(fiumare)*.

The wide riverbeds are dry in summer but may fill up rapidly and the waters can become destructive. The S 183 between the S 112 and Melito di Porto Salvo runs through attractive scenery and affords numerous and often spectacular **panoramas★★★**.

Watch out for shattered asphalt roads and hairpin turns in Parco Nazionale dell'Aspromonte (0965 74 30 60; www.parcoaspromonte.gov.it).

TYRRHENIAN COAST
Paola
St Francis of Paola was born here around 1416. A **monastery** *(santuario)* visited by numerous pilgrims stands 2km/1.2mi away up the hillside. This large group of buildings includes the basilica with a lovely Baroque exterior that enshrines the relics of the saint, cloisters and a hermitage hewn out of the rock, which contains striking votive offerings. Open daily 6.30am–7pm (winter 6.30am–6pm, Jul–Aug 6.30am–8pm). 0982 58 25 18. www.santuariopaola.it.

Tropea★★
www.tropea.biz.

Tropea is built on a sandy cliff top. Opposite stands the solitary church of

Tropea–aquamarine waters of the Tyrrhenian Coast

A City Rebuilt

Founded as a *Rhegion* by Greek settlers in the 8C BC, Reggio Calabria has been destroyed by nature and rebuilt by man several times over the centuries. The worst earthquakes came in 1783 and on 28 December 1908. The latter quake was the most devastating and remains the worst on record in modern Western European history. Some 80 percent of all buildings in Reggio collapsed and thousands were killed. It took Reggio a generation to fully recover.

Santa Maria dell'Isola, which clings to a rock. The most evocative reference to the past is the Romanesque-Norman **cathedral** and its original façade. The Swabian portico, grafted onto it, links the church to the bishop's residence. Toward Palmi, Nicotera is a wonderful spot to watch the sunset over the Stromboli volcano, with lava activity visible as darkness falls.

Palmi★

Palmi town perched high above the sea has a fishing harbour and lovely sandy beaches. The SS18 descends to Palmi Lido. For a delightful swim at more rugged unspoiled beach with good restaurant and camping facilities, between the Lido and Gioia Tauro, Palmi Contrada Scinà is worth a detour.

Scilla★★

This town, like a perfect cameo carved from the rock, has a bloody mythology. Here Ulysses confronted the monster Scylla, a woman with dog-headed tentacles, who ate six of his sailors, as well as the Sirens "on their sweet meadow lolling… bones of dead men rotting in a pile beside them and flayed skins shrivel around the spot". Opposite Scilla, near Messina, lurked Charybdis, whom Jupiter turned into a sea monster for her voracity. Three times daily she engulfed the surrounding waves. Subsequently

Charybdis spurted the water out, creating a dangerous current. Ulysses' vessel rowed past her once. During their second encounter, he narrowly escaped her clutches by grabbing a fig tree at the entrance of the monster's grotto. The fisherman's district, the Chinalèa, comprises an intricate maze of houses and alleys leading to the water's edge. Higher up, Ruffo Castle (1255) gazes nobly over the town, while the waters around Scilla, like the waters of nearby Bagnara Calabra, contain numerous swordfish. Scuba divers enjoy the diversity of fish brought in by the currents.

THE MESSINA STRAIT
Reggio Calabria

Via Fata Morgana 13, 89125 Reggio Calabria. ℘0965 36 22 344 or 0965 36 222 69. http://turismo.reggiocal.it.
This pleasant regional capital backs against the Aspromonte Massif, was rebuilt after the earthquake of 1908. Reggio sits across the Messina Strait from the city of Messina (◔see MESSINA) in Sicily. The city is surrounded by groves of olives, vines, orange and lemon trees, and fields of flowers used for making perfume; half the world's production of bergamot (a citrus fruit) comes from here.
An elegant seafront **Lungomare★** *(promenade)* lined with palm trees affords lovely views of the Sicilian coastline and Etna. Join locals at dusk for a stroll along this favoured spot.

Museo Nazionale Archeologico★★

⌖ Open 9am–8pm. Closed Mon. 5€.
℘0965 81 22 55.
Although most visitors come to this museum wanting to see the mysterious bronze warriors it would be a pity not to have a look at other exhibits, including the **pinakes★**, terra-cotta low reliefs used in Locri as ex-votos in the 5C BC. They were dedicated to Persephone, bride of Hades who carried her off to the Underworld while she was picking flowers. The lower floor is "home" to the two stunning bronze **Riace Warriors★★★**, discovered in the sea near Riace in 1972.

The City of Bronzes

Made in Greece in the 5C BC, the **Riace Warrior** bronze statues are 1.98m/6.5ft and 2m/6.6ft tall respectively. Cleaned of marine sediment and hollow inside, they each weigh 250kg/550lb. Their "names" – A and B – are clinical in the extreme but their expressions are anything but anonymous. Their eyes (B is missing one) have ivory and limestone irises and pupils made from a vitreous paste; the eyelashes are silver, as are the teeth, which are revealed only through the lips of A. Both hold on their left arms the holding straps of shields and in their right hands a lance. But each warrior seems troubled by different thoughts and feelings: A seems aggressive and indomitable and has been captured while thrusting his left leg forward. He has just turned his head and seems about to speak. B has a frightened and tentative expression; the position of his shoulders suggests he is reluctant to progress.

Statue B of Bronzi di Riace (c.450 BC)

©World Illustrated/Photoshot

AROUND THE "TOE" AND ALONG THE IONIAN COAST

The Graecanico mountain villages, as their ancient Greek-Italian culture is fading quickly.

Pentedattilo★

Pentedattilo is a striking ghost town, totally abandoned by its inhabitants. Once the site of a grisly ambush in the 17C, the bloody handprints of the slaughtered Alberti family are said to be visible, pressed in stone.

Legend has it that the menacing rock resembling a hand that stands above it (in Greek *pentedaktylos* signifies "five fingers") put an end to men's violence. There is some truth to this: no voices have echoed in the narrow alleyways of the town since the mid-1960s as the crumbling rock was deemed unsafe.

Gerace

Gerace rises up on a hill of 480m/1 575ft. The Graecanico town has a more commercial veneer – the vast 11C Romanesque cathedral, crowned by Greek domes, courtyards and ornate pillars (pirated from ancient buildings), charges admission, which destroys the remote aura. Byzantines and Normans lived there together, and it was subjected to invasions by the Swabians, French and Aragonese. At one time Gerace had so many churches it was known as "the city of a hundred bells". In the Largo delle Tre Chiese (Square of Three Churches) the **Church of San Francesco** has a polychrome marble **high altar★**. www.comune.gerace.rc.it.

Stilo

The native town of philosopher **Tommaso Campanella** (1568–1639), filled with hermitages and Basilian monasteries, clings to a mountain at an altitude of 400m/1 312ft. Further up, almost camouflaged, is the Byzantine jewel of a church, **La Cattolica★**. This 10C structure has a square plan and is roofed with five cylindrical domes. The external decoration consists of brickwork, central dome and roof tiles. Inside, the Greek cross has nine domed and barrel-vaulted sections, each held up by four marble columns. From here is a stunning view across mountain forests to the sea. & Open daily 8am–6pm (summer 8am–8pm). Free. ℘0964 77 60 06. www.comune.stilo.rc.it.

Le Castella

Le Castella engulfs a tiny island of the same name on the Isola di Capo Rizzuto. While the origins are debated, legend links the fortress to mythical Ogygia, the island where the sea goddess Calypso held Ulysses in Homer's *The Odyssey*.

The Protected Marine Area of Capo Rizzuto also has a diving centre. www. lecastella.info.

Capo Colonna

This cape was once called *Capo Lacinio*. From the last decades of the 8C BC, one of *Magna Graecia*'s most famous temples, that of Hera Lacinia, stood here. It had a golden age in the 5C BC, but began to decline in 173 BC, when part of the marble roof was removed. It was plundered by pirates and became a quarry for the Aragonese foundations of Crotone. The temple was finally destroyed by an earthquake in 1683. Now only one of the original 48 columns remains of this Doric temple. In 1964 Pier Paolo Pasolini (1922–75) shot some scenes of his film *The Gospel According to St Matthew* here.

Crotone

The ancient town of *Kroton* was an Achaean colony of *Magna Graecia*, founded in 710 BC. It was celebrated in Antiquity for its riches, the beauty of its women and the prowess of athletes such as Milo of Croton. Around 532 BC Pythagoras founded several religious communities devoted to the study of mathematics. The rival city of *Locris* defeated *Kroton* in the mid-6C BC, which in turn defeated its other rival, *Sybaris*. The city welcomed Hannibal during the Second Punic War, before being conquered by Rome.

Today *Crotone* is a prosperous seaport and industrial centre. The town also houses an archaeological museum. Open Tue–Sun 9am–7pm. 2€. ℘0962 90 56 25.

Rossano

The town spreads over a hillside clad in olive groves. In the Middle Ages Rossano was the capital of Greek monasticism in the West, where expelled or persecuted Basilian monks came for refuge, living in cells that can still be seen today. The little church of San Marco dates from this period. The flat east end has three projecting semicircular apses with graceful openings. To the right of the cathedral, the **Museo Diocesano** has a valuable **Purpureus Codex★**, a 6C evangelistary with brightly coloured illuminations. Open mid–Sept–Jun Tue–Sat 9.30am–12.30pm and 3–6pm, Sun and public hols 10am–noon and 4–6pm; Jul–mid–Sept daily 9.30am–1pm and 4.30–9pm. ℘0983 52 52 63. The town's oldest licorice factory runs a museum. Visits by reservation, ℘0983 511 219, www. museodellaliquirizia.it.

Citrons for Sukkot

The **Feast of the Tabernacles**, *Sukkot,* is the Jewish Festival of Tents, commemorating Exodus, when the Jews slept in the wilderness. The citron is traditionally used for this feast and is chosen with painstaking care. Each summer rabbis come to Santa Maria del Cedro (which has ideal growing conditions for this fruit) in the province of Cosenza, to select citrons for their communities all over the world.

Leviticus 23, 39–40: On the fifteenth day of the seventh month, when you have gathered up the produce of the land, you shall keep the festival of the Lord, lasting seven days; a complete rest on the first day, and a complete rest on the eighth day. On the first day you shall take the fruit of majestic trees, branches of palm trees, boughs of leafy trees, and willows of the brook: and you shall rejoice before the Lord your God for seven days.

HEART OF CALABRIA
Cosenza★
Town map in the Michelin Atlas Italy.
The modern town is overlooked by the old town, where streets and palaces recall the prosperity of the Angevin and Aragonese periods. Cosenza a university town, was the artistic and religious capital of Calabria. The 12C–13C **cathedral** *(duomo)* has recently been restored to its original aspect. It has a **mausoleum** that contains the heart of Isabella of Aragon, wife of Philip III, King of France who died in 1271 outside Cosenza on the way back from Tunis.

Altomonte
The large market town is dominated by an imposing 14C Angevin cathedral dedicated to Santa Maria della Consolazione, which boasts a fine rose window. Inside there are no aisles and the east end is flat. The fine **tomb★** is that of Filippa Sangineto. The small *museo civico* beside the church has several precious works of art in addition to a statue of **St Ladislas★** attributed to Simone Martini. Open daily. 3€. ℘0981 94 88 04. www.iresudcalabria.it.

Serra San Bruno
Between the Sila and Aspromonte massifs, amid the Calabrian mountains covered with oak and **pine forests★**, this small market town grew up around a hermitage founded by St Bruno, who died in 1101.

ADDRESSES

🛏 STAY
🍴🛏 **Hotel Aquila-Edelweiss** – Viale Stazione 15, 87052 Camigliatello Silano, 31km/19.3mi NE of Cosenza on the S 107. ℘0984 57 80 44. www.hotelaquila edelweiss.com. Closed Nov–Dec. 48 rooms. ⛄. Restaurant🍴🛏. This comfortable wood-panelled hotel provides a warm and friendly atmosphere tucked away in the conifer woods up in La Sila; it offers great views. The restaurant's Calabrian specialities but call ahead.

🍴🛏 **Hotel Villa Aurora** – Via Volandrino, 88841 Le Castella, Isola di Capo Rizzuto. ℘0962 79 51 37. www.hotelvillaaurora.it. 18 rooms. Charming rustic-style hotel near the centre of Le Castella. Walking distance to the beaches and castle. Guests can dine in beautiful garden during warm-winter months.

🍴🛏 **Residenza il Barone** – Largo Barone, 89861 Tropea. ℘0963 60 71 81. www.residenzailbarone.it. 6 rooms. ⛄. This beautiful family-owned B&B has six suites in the heart of Tropea's historic centre. On warm days breakfast is served from their top-floor terrace that offers stunning views of the sea.

🍴 EAT
🍴 **Hostaria de Mendoza** – Piazza degli Eroi 3, 87036 Rende, 10km/6.2mi NW of Cosenza. ℘0984 44 40 22. Closed Tue. Reservation recommended. A rustic ambience, heavy wooden furnishings and a multitude of objects hang from the walls. Genuine home cooking. In summer, meals are served under a large wooden gazebo.

🍴 **Il Normanno** – Via Real Badia, 89852 Mileto, 30km/18.6mi SE of Tropea on the S18. ℘0963 33 63 98. www.ilnormanno. com. Closed Mon. Attractive trattoria in the centre of Mileto with a rustic-style interior. The small terraced area is nice for dining in summer. They have good, traditional home cooking.

🍴 **Trattoria del Sole** – Via Piave 14bis, 87075 Trebisacce, 15km/9.3mi N of Sibari on the S 106. ℘0981 51 797. Closed Mon. This simple eatery is tucked away in a maze of little streets in the historic centre. A warm and friendly atmosphere and a nice selection of seafood dishes. Summer meals are served on the outdoor terrace.

🍴🍴 **Gambero Rosso** – Via Montezemolo 65, 89046 Marina di Gioiosa Ionica, 10km/6.2mi N of Locri on the S 106. ℘0964 41 58 06. www.gamberorosso.net. Closed Mon. A traditional restaurant on the main thoroughfare. A good selection of *antipasti* that is laid out on a large table in the entrance of the main dining room. Variety of delicious fish dishes, prepared with super-fresh ingredients.

Basilicata, Matera★★★

Matera overlooks a ravine separating it from the Murge Hills in Puglia. This provincial capital stands in the heart of a region dissected by deeply eroded gorges – a desolate landscape with wide horizons. In modern Matera, the town's centre of activity overlooks the lower town with its Sassi rock dwellings, now mostly abandoned. In the town and surrounding area there are some 130 churches hewn out of the rock. These date back to the 8C BC and the arrival of non-Latin monastic communities who settled locally. They were adept in this form of underground architecture, which shows a Byzantine influence.

▶ **Population:** 59 144
✿ **Michelin Map:** 564 E 31 – Basilicata.
▤ **Info:** Via Don Minzoni 11. ✆0835 33 43 13. www.comune.matera.it or www.sassiweb.it.
▶ **Location:** Matera lies in Basilicata, on the S 7, Via Appia.
▶ **Train:** Matera (Bari 1hr 23 mins).
☺ **Don't Miss:** A stroll down the panoramic Strada dei Sassi.
◔ **Timing:** Allow half a day.

VISIT

The Sassi★★★

The two main cave-like quarters are on either side of the rock crowned by the cathedral. The roofs on some houses serve as walkways while the lower storeys are hewn out of the rock. Lime-washed houses and stairways overhang one another in a labyrinth.

Strada dei Sassi★★

This panoramic street skirts the wild gorge and runs around the cathedral rock. The rock walls are riddled with both natural and man-made caves.

Duomo★

The cathedral was built in the 13C Apulian-Romanesque style; the façade has a lovely rose window and a projecting gallery above the single doorway. The walls are embellished with blind arcades. On the south side are two richly sculpted doorways. The interior was remodelled in the 17C and 18C. The Byzantine fresco portraying the Madonna dates from the 12C–13C and the Neapolitan crib is 16C. The **Chapel of the Annunciation★** has a beautiful Renaissance decoration.

Chiesa di San Pietro Caveoso★★

Open during celebration: winter Mon–Sat 6.30pm, Sun 9am and 11am; summer Mon–Sat 7pm, Sun 11am (except Jul and Aug), 7pm. www.visitmatera.it.
This Baroque church is at the foot of Monte Errone where several rock-hewn churches are decorated with frescoes.

Museo Nazionale Ridola

& Open 2pm–8pm. 2.50€. ✆0835 31 00 58.
This museum in a former monastery has an interesting collection of local archaeological finds. ☺There are views of **Matera★★** from the two belvederes (4km/2.5mi on the Altamura road, then take the Taranto road, turn right and follow the *"chiese rupestri"* (rock churches) signpost).

ADDRESSES

☞ STAY

➾**Le Monacelle** – Via Riscatto 9/10. ✆0835 34 40 97. 12 rooms. Located near the Duomo in the Sassi district, the building was constructed in 1594 as a conservatory of Santa Maria della Pietà. It has views of the gorge that borders the city. There are spacious social areas, private bedrooms, two dormitories and a chapel all set in a simple, tranquil ambience.

Sardinia

Sardegna. Major City: Cagliari

Official Website: www.sardegnaturismo.it.

Sardinia offers an almost primeval landscape of rocks sculpted by the wind and sea, forests of holm and cork oaks, oleander, aromatic plants and shrubs, the clear blue waters of the Mediterranean and the silence of an earlier age broken only by the sounds of nature.

Sardinia Today

Sardinia, the Mediterranean's second-largest island, owes its modern role as a tourism hot-spot to two foreign entities. After World War II, the Rockefeller Foundation helped the island eliminate mosquitoes. With malaria gone, Sardinia was ripe for development. In 1961 Aga Khan IV invested in a tourist complex on the northeastern coast. This development, the **Costa Smeralda** (Emerald Coast), is today a playground of the jet set. Tourism to Sardinia's beaches as well as its wild interior is a major component of the island's economy. The military industrial complex also contributes to Sardinia's coffers.

Although Sardinia has undergone a long period of "Italianisation", it is by definition one of the autonomous regions of Italy, which is evident in the island's culture and language. People of the island still speak a variety of dialects, including **Catalàn**, a result of Spanish influence, and Gallurese, a language akin to Corsican. Sardinia is also known among Italians for its rebellious streak. The phenomenon of banditry

Highlights

1 Enjoying the high life on **The Emerald Coast** (p284)

2 Descending the stairs to the fantastical **Grotta di Nettuno** (p288)

3 The vibrant atmosphere of the island's capital **Cagliari** (p293)

Info: Palazzo Civico, Via Roma 145, 09124 Cagliari. ℘070 67 78 173. www.sardegnaturismo.it.

Location: Sardinia is surrounded by the Tyrrhenian Sea to the east and south, the Mediterranean Sea to the west and the Straits of Bonifacio, which divide it from Corsica, to the north.

Don't Miss: Alghero, the Nuraghi Su Nuraxi and the Costa Smeralda.

Timing: Allow four days, or preferably a week.

Typical mural

© S. Bedessi /FOTOTECA ENIT

still exists, particularly in the mountainous **Barbagia** region. In **Orgosolo**, a collection of political murals depict the struggles the natives have endured at the hands of the Italian government and fellow islanders.

Earliest Inhabitants

Sardinia has traces of human settlement dating back to prehistoric times – *domus de janas* (fairies' houses) with their dis-

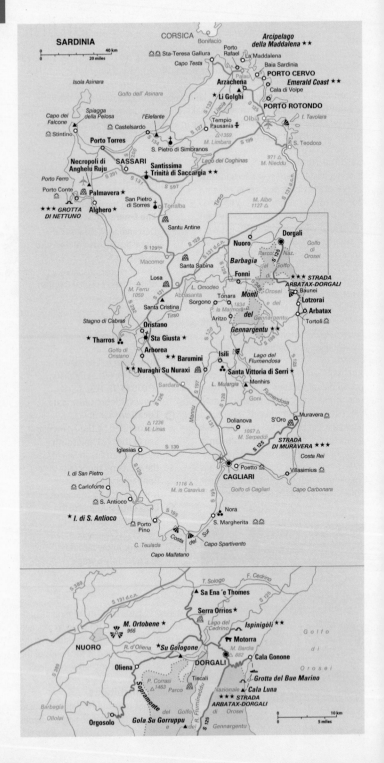

SARDINIA

40 km
20 miles

CORSICA

Arcipelago della Maddalena ★★

Sta-Teresa Gallura
Capo Testa
Porto Rafael
Palau
La Maddalena
Baia Sardinia
PORTO CERVO
Cala di Volpe
Emerald Coast ★★
Arzachena
★ **Li Golghi**
PORTO ROTONDO
Olbia
I. Tavolara

Isola Asinara
Golfo dell' Asinara
l'Elefante
Tempio Pausania †
△-1359 M. Limbara
S. Teodoro
Capo del Falcone
Spiaggia della Pelosa
Castelsardo
Stintino
S. Pietro di Simbranos
Porto Torres
Lago del Coghinas
M. Nieddu 971 △
Necropoli di Anghelu Ruju
SASSARI
Santissima Trinità di Saccargia ★★
Porto Ferro
Porto Conte
Palmavera ★
San Pietro di Sorres
Torralba
M. Albo 1127 △
★★★ *GROTTA DI NETTUNO*
Alghero ★
Santu Antine
Nuoro
Dorgali
Golfo di Orosei
Barbagia
Macomer
Santa Sabina
Fonni
★★★ *STRADA ARBATAX-DORGALI*
Losa
L. Omodeo
Baunei
M. Ferru 1050 △
Abbasanta
Tonara
Monti
Lotzorai
Arbatax
Santa Cristina
Sorgono
Aritzo
del
1834 △ P. la Marmora
Tortoli
Stagno di Cabras
Oristano
Gennargentu ★★
★ **Tharros**
★ **Sta Giusta** ★
Arborea
Isili
Lago del Flumendosa
Barumini
★★ **Nuraghi Su Nuraxi**
Santa Vittoria di Serri ★
Golfo di Oristano
Sardara
Menhirs
L. Mulargia
Goni
Flumendosa
△ 1236 M. Linas
Mannu
Dolianova
1067 △ M. Serpeddi
S'Oro
Muravera
STRADA DI MURAVERA ★★★
Iglesias
Costa Rei
I. di San Pietro
Poetto
Villasimius
Carloforte
1116 △ M. is Caravius
CAGLIARI
Golfo di Cagliari
Capo Carbonara
S. Antioco
Nora
★ *I. di S. Antioco*
S. Margherita
Porto Pino
Costa
Sur
del
C. Teulada
Capo Spartivento
Capo Malfatano

T. Sologo
F. Cedrino
▲ **Sa Ena 'e Thomes**
Serra Orrios ★
Lago del Cedrino
Ispinigòli ★★
★ *M. Ortobene* 955
Motorra
Golfo
NUORO
R. d'Oliena
Su Gologone
M. Bardia 882 △
di
DORGALI
Cala Gonone
Orosei
Oliena
P. Corrasi 1463 △ Parco
Tiscali
Grotta del Bue Marino ★★★
Sopramonte
Nazionale ▲ **Cala Luna**
del
★★★ *STRADA ARBATAX-DORGALI*
Orgosolo
Gola Su Gorruppu ★
Gennargentu

10 km
5 miles

GETTING THERE

Ferries leave from Civitavecchia, Genova, La Spezia, Livorno, Palermo and Trapani for the ports of Cagliari, Golfo Aranci, Olbia, Porto Torres, Santa Teresa di Gallura and Arbatax (*see Planning Your Trip*). Visitors are advised to book in advance if travelling in the summer season. Sardinia can also be reached by **air**, with airports in Alghero, Cagliari, Olbia and Sassari.

SIGHTSEEING

Sardinia offers endless opportunities with its rugged scenery, views of the sea and megalithic remains. Allow at least a week to see the island fully. When exploring the east side of the island it is advisable to leave with a full tank of petrol, as petrol stations are few and far between.

SHOPPING

Sardinia is well known for its cottage industries, which produce a range of products including goldwork, ceramics, leather, wood and cork, tapestries and basketware.

WHAT TO EAT AND DRINK

The traditional recipes of Sardinia are simple but tasty, flavoured with the many aromatic plants and herbs that grow on the island. Bread is often the crunchy *carasau*, known as *carta da musica* in the rest of Italy. *Gnocchetti sardi*, a type of pasta shell which has nothing to do with the traditional Italian gnocchi, are also known as *malloreddus*, and are often served with a sausage and tomato sauce. Meat lovers should try the suckling pig (*porchetto da latte*) roasted on a spit. The island has many different varieties of cheese, including goat's cheese, Sardinian *fiore* and Sardinian *pecorino*. Local desserts include the rhomboid-shaped *papassinos*, which are often covered with icing and sprinkled with small coloured sugar balls, and *sebadas*, round doughnuts which are fried and covered with honey. The best-known local wines are the Anghelu Ruju and Cannonau; *mirto* is an excellent local myrtle berry liqueur.

turbing human-like features, dolmens standing alone in the middle of fields and ancient *nuraghi*.

The Nuraghic civilisation lasted from 1800 to 500 BC; its golden age is considered to have been from 1200 to 900 BC.

The island has over 7 000 **nuraghi** or fortified tower-houses, structures in the form of a truncated covered cone. The name comes from the root *nur*, which means both "mass" and "cavity". The *nuraghi* were built of huge blocks of stone without any mortar, possibly using an inclined plane along which they would have been pushed or rolled. They were used as dwellings, as watchtowers and, when built together as a group, as fortresses.

Other structures remain from this prehistoric period, including dolmens and Giants' Tombs (*see EMERALD COAST*).

As water was a rare commodity on the island, it played an important part in the Nuraghic religion. The god who lived in the wells and rivers and who had the power to overcome periods of drought was represented by the bull, often pictured throughout the island.

Successive Invasions

Sardinia has been invaded throughout history. The first to arrive were the Phoenicians in the 8C BC, followed by the Romans in 238 BC, the Vandals in AD 455 and the Byzantines in AD 534. The Saracens arrived in the 7C and after the year 1000 the island was fought over by the Pisans and Genovese. It then fell to the Spanish in 1295 and later, during the War of Succession, to the Austrian Empire in 1713.

The Kingdom of Sardinia was created in 1718 by Vittorio Amedeo II of Savoy and the island was annexed to the new united Italy in 1861. Sardinia was made an autonomous region in 1948.

Emerald Coast★★

Costa Smeralda

This wild and undulating region is a succession of pink-granite headlands, covered with maquis scrub overlooking the sea, which is a clear emerald green. Once a region of farmers and shepherds, it was discovered in 1962 by the international jet set. The development of the Emerald Coast was promoted by a consortium originally presided over by the Aga Khan. This peninsula of the Gallura region now offers tourist facilities, including windsurfing, sailing, golf and tennis. The main beach resorts are Porto Cervo⌂⌂⌂, Cala di Volpe and Baia Sardinia⌂.

ARCIPELAGO DI LA MADDALENA★★

www.lamaddalena.com.
The Maddalena Archipelago consists of the islands of Maddalena, Caprera, Santo Stefano, Spargi, Budelli, Razzoli, Santa Maria and other islets in the **Straits of Bonifacio**. These isolated islands, occasionally frequented by Corsican shepherds, were annexed to the Kingdom of Sardinia in 1767. Maddalena then became a military base. The archipelago was made a **national park** in 1996.

- ⏱ **Michelin Map:** 566 D 10.
- 🏠 **Info:** Pro Loco La Maddalena
  ☎0789 73 63 21.
  Ente Parco Nazionale
  Arcipelago di La Maddalena
  ☎0789 79 02 11.
  www.lamaddalenapark.it
- ▶ **Location:** The Costa Smeralda lies towards the northeast of the island. Arzachena is on the S 125.
- 😊 **Don't Miss:** The Maddalena Archipelago.
- 🕐 **Timing:** Allow a couple of days.

Maddalena★★

A lovely scenic route *(20km/12.4mi)* follows the coastline of this small island.

Caprera★

This island was once the home of Garibaldi and is connected to Maddalena by the Passo della Moneta causeway. It now houses a sailing centre.

Casa di Garibaldi★

♿ Open Tue–Sun 9am–1.30pm and 2–8pm (last entry 7.15pm). In winter opening and closing times can vary. Closed 1 Jan, 25 Dec. 6€. ☎0789 72 71 62. www.compendiogaribaldino.it.
The tree planted by Garibaldi (1807–82) on the birth of his daughter Clelia (1867) can be seen in the garden of his one-time home, where he is also buried.

Isole di Spargi, Archipelago di La Maddalena

©matteo barili/iStockphoto.com

INLAND
Arzachena
www.turismoarzachenacostasmeralda.it.
Once an agricultural market town, Arzachena owes its fame to its position in the heart of the Costa Smeralda hinterland at the foot of a mushroom-shaped rock (Fungo).

Tomba dei Giganti di Li Muri

Megalithic Stones
The remains of a **Giants' Tomb** (Tomba dei Giganti di Li Muri) and a necropolis can be seen from near town, on the Arzachena–Luogosanto road.
Popular tradition gave the name Giants' Tomb to these tombs dating from the Nuraghic period. The funeral chambers lined and roofed with megalithic slabs (like a dolmen) were preceded by an arc forming the *exedra* or area of ritual. The front of the structure is formed by a central stela with fascia in relief, which leads to the corridor of stones. This "false door" may have symbolised the connection with the afterlife.

ADDRESSES

 STAY

⊖ **Centro Vacanze Isuledda** – 07020 Cannigione, 6.5km/4mi NE of Arzachena. ℘0789 86 003. www.campingisuledda.com. Great position overlooking the

Gallura

This region in the northeast of Sardinia is justly famous for the stunning white-sand beaches and rugged coves of the Costa Smeralda (Emerald Coast). However, a short trip inland reveals a harsh and desolate landscape. Dominating the area is the Monte Limbara granite mountain range, the highest peak of which is Punta Balistreri (1 359m/4 459ft).

Maddalena Archipelago with accommodation to suit the most and least adventurous travellers: there are tents, bungalows, rooms, mobile homes and *tukul*. Other facilities include supermarkets, shops and various essential services. Lively atmosphere.

⊖ **Hotel Citti** – Viale Costa Smeralda 197, 07021 Arzachena. ℘0789 82 662. www.hotelcitti.com. Closed 23 Dec–6 Jan. 50 rooms. ⌷. One of the main attractions of this establishment is that it offers excellent value for money, making it a good base for exploring the entire Costa Smeralda. The street on which it is situated may be slightly busy but the rooms are spacious and comfortable and there is a lovely sun lounge with a pool at the back.

⊖⊖ **Hotel Da Cecco** – Via Po 3, 07028 Santa Teresa di Gallura, 17km/10.6mi W of Palau on the S 133b. ℘0789 75 42 20. www.hoteldacecco.com. Closed 1 Dec–20 Mar. 32 rooms. ⌷. From the rooms and the sun lounge there is a magnificent view over the Straits of Bonifacio beyond the Saracen Tower. This is a small, modern hotel which would suit visitors looking for a relaxing holiday and the best of Sardinian hospitality.

⊖⊖ **Hotel Selis** – Loc. Santa Teresina, 07021 Arzachena, Strada provinciale (in the direction of Porto Cervo). ℘0789 98 630. www.selishotel.com. 18 rooms. ⌷. The splendid stone building which houses this hotel is off the beaten track. The good-sized rooms are light and airy, with tiled floors and wrought-iron beds: some have a small garden-terrace which makes a lovely children's play area or a sunbathing place (and would also suit anyone travelling with their dog).

⊟⊟⊟ **Hotel Villa Gemella** – Baia Sardinia, 07020 Baia Sardinia. ℘0789 99 303. www.hotelvillagemella.com. 26 rooms. ⊟. One of the main attractions of this hotel is the lovely flower-filled garden, which is a great spot for relaxation. There is also a swimming pool … not to mention the sea (the Bay of Sardinia) nearby. The rooms, which are light and airy, have been tastefully furnished; some have a terrace and a view (ask when booking).

⊟⊟⊟ **Residence Hotel Riva Azzurra** – Loc. Banchina, 07020 Cannigione, 6.5km/4mi NE of Arzachena. ℘0789 89 20 05. www.residence rivaazzurra.it. Closed 12 Oct–24 Apr. 29 apartments for 4 people. Attractive pastel-coloured, Mediterranean-style hotel which blends in well with the setting. The comfortable, two-roomed apartments are laid out in an arc around a lovely garden, a stone's throw from the beach. Friendly, welcoming atmosphere.

⬚ EAT

⊖ **La Terrazza** – Via Villa Glori 6, 07024 La Maddalena. ℘0789 73 53 05. www. ristorantelamaddalena.com. Closed Sun in Oct–Apr. Having fallen in love with Sardinia, the dynamic owners (originally from Bologna) have adopted the island's delicious gastronomy as their own. The varied menu focuses on fish – always of the best quality – and includes regional specialities. Meals are served on the terrace, which boasts a wonderful panoramic view.

⊖ **La Vecchia Costa** – 07021 Arzachena, 5km/3mi SW of Porto Cervo (in the direction of Arzachena). ℘0789 98 688. www.lavecchiacosta.it. If you want good pizza, this is the place. Made with the flat crunchy bread, called *carasau*, that is peculiar to Sardinia, the pizzas are deliciously thin and crispy, as well as vast! Very reasonable prices, unusual in this area.

⊖ **Panino Giusto** – Via della Marina Nuova , 07020 Porto Cervo. ℘0789 91 259. Situated at the entrance to Porto Cervo marina, overlooking the yachting harbour, this establishment would suit anyone looking for a snack or a light meal but who does not want to stray far from the beach. Open all day, it serves simple meals, salads and sandwiches. You can eat outside looking out over the boats moored in the harbour, or inside where there is a pub-style dining area.

⊖ **Pinocchio** – Loc. Cascioni, 07021 Arzachena, Strada provinciale (in the direction of Porto Cervo). ℘0789 98 886. A traditional establishment which specialises in fish, the dishes inspired by traditional recipes of the area. Also serves excellent pizzas cooked in a wood-fired oven. Reasonably priced accommodation available: simple, comfortable rooms with private access from the garden. Not far from the Costa Smeralda.

⊖⊟⊟ **Madai** – Promenade du Port-via del Porto Vecchio 1, 07020 Porto Cervo. ℘0789 91 056. www.eliosironi.it. Situated at the end of Porto Cervo's elegant promenade dotted with famous boutiques, this restaurant focuses on simple, yet delicious dishes with a Mediterranean flavour. The delightful terrace overlooking the port is perfect for a romantic dinner (booking recommended).

OFF THE BEATEN TRACK

⊖ **Terza Spiaggia** – Loc. Terza Spiaggia, 07020 Golfo Aranci, 44km/27.3mi SE of Arzachena. ℘0789 46 485. www.terza spiaggia.com. Closed Oct–Mar. What could be better than relaxing on the beach next to the crystal-clear sea and with a wonderful view of the Golfo degli Aranci, while tucking into a delicious sandwich? Or maybe you would prefer a simple fish dish (prepared with fish caught by the owners themselves earlier that day). Meals are served inside (simple beach-style caffè interior).

⊖⊟⊟ **S'Ollastu** – Loc. Costa Corallina, 07026 Olbia. ℘0789 36 744, www.ollastu.it. This restaurant features cuisine based on regional flavours with the occasional imaginative twist. Dishes are served either on the lovely summer terrace or in the quiet, welcoming dining rooms.

Sassari

Sassari is the second-largest town in Sardinia. Its airy modern quarters contrast with its medieval nucleus, around the cathedral. The busiest thoroughfares are the Piazza d'Italia and the Corso Vittorio Emanuele II.

VISIT
Museo Nazionale Sanna★

Via Roma 64. Open Tue–Sat 9am–8pm, Sun and public hols 9am–2pm. Closed 1 Jan, 1 May, 25 Dec. 3€. ℘079 27 22 003. www.museosannasassari.beniculturali.it. The museum contains archaeological finds, including a section devoted to Sardinian ethnography and a small picture gallery.

Duomo

The cathedral is built in many styles and has a 13C campanile with a 17C upper storey, a late-17C Spanish-Baroque façade★ and a Gothic interior.

EXCURSIONS
Santissima Trinità di Saccargia★★

◐ 17km/10.6mi SE by the Cagliari road, S 131, and then the Olbia road, S 597. This former 12C Camaldulian abbey church was built in courses of black and

- **Population:** 124 929
- **Michelin Map:** 566 E 7; town map in the Michelin Atlas Italy.
- **Info:** Palazzo di Città, Via Satta 13. ℘079 20 08 072. www.comune.sassari.it.
- **Train:** Sassari (Olbia Viale Aldo Moro 2hr 9min).
- **Location:** Sassari is situated about 20km/12mi from the Golfo dell'Asinara. The main access roads are the S 131, S 291 and S 597.

white stone, typical of the Pisan style. The elegant façade includes a porch added in the 13C and is flanked by a campanile. Inside, the apse is adorned with fine 13C frescoes depicting scenes of the Passion.

The Symbol of Sassari

This is the Fontana di Rosello, the huge fountain near the church of the Holy Trinity. It is a rather grand and elaborate Renaissance structure which was erected by the Genoese in 1605, although records show that there has been a fountain on this spot since the end of the 13C.

Santissima Trinità di Saccargia

Alghero★

Coral divers operate from the port of Alghero, which is the main town on the Riviera del Corallo. In 1354 Alghero was occupied by the Catalans; the town still has a Catalan-Gothic centre and its inhabitants still speak Catalan. Its Spanish air has earned it the nickname "Barcelonetta of Sardinia". The beach extends 5km/3mi to the north of the village.

OLD TOWN★ (CITTÀ VECCHIA)

The fortifications encircle a network of narrow streets in the old town. The **Duomo** (*Via Roma*) has a beautiful doorway and a campanile in the Catalan-Gothic style. The 14C–15C church of **San Francesco** has **cloisters** in golden-coloured tufa. The fishing harbour is the embarkation point for the boat trips to the **Grotta di Nettuno★★★** (see below).

EXCURSIONS
Grotta di Nettuno★★★

◯ 27km/16.8mi W; also possible by boat. Call for times. ℘079 97 9054. www.grottedinettuno.it.

The road out to the headland, Capo Caccia, offers splendid **views★★** of the rocky coast. Neptune's Cave is on the point. A stairway (*654 steps*) leads down the cliff-face. There are small

Narrow stairway to Grotta di Nettuno
©sabrina del nobili/iStockphoto.com

▶ **Population:** 40 257
⟡ **Michelin Map:** 566 F 6.
▣ **Info:** Piazza Porta Terra 9, 07041 Alghero (SS). ℘079 97 90 54. www.comune.alghero.ss.it.
◗ **Location:** Alghero is located 35km/21.7mi southwest of Sassari and is served by the Alghero-Fertilia Airport (www.aeroportodialghero.com).
⊛ **Don't Miss:** The Grotta di Nettuno.
◷ **Timing:** Allow a day, with a visit to the Grotta di Nettuno.

inner lakes, a forest of columns, and concretions in the form of organ pipes.

Nuraghe Palmavera★

◗ 10km/6.2mi on SS127 Porto Conte road km42. Open daily Apr–Oct 9am–7pm; Nov–Feb 10am–2pm, Mar 9.30am–4pm. 3€. ℘079 99 44 394. www.smuovi.com.

This *nuraghe* is surrounded by the remains of a prehistoric village, formed by approximately 50 individual dwellings crowded closely together.

ADDRESSES

▨ STAY

◔◔ **Hotel Al Gabbiano** – Viale Mediterraneo 5, 08013 Bosa Marina, 45km/28mi S of Alghero on the coastal road. ℘0785 37 41 23. Fax 0785 37 41 09. www.hotelalgabbiano.it. 30 rooms. ▱. Simple and courteous with a private beach, a pizzeria, a traditional restaurant and Art Nouveau-style apartments.

℗ EAT

◔ **La Muraglia** – Bastioni Marco Polo, 07041 Alghero. ℘079 97 55 77. Closed Wed. Marvellous situation, housed within the fortifications. The view from the top floor, which takes in the harbour and stretches as far as the Capo Caccia promontory, is breathtaking. Excellent cooking to boot. You will need to book in advance to get a table.

Nuoro

Nuoro lies at the foot of Monte Ortobene, the summit of which affords good viewpoints★. The customs and folklore in this large central town bordering the Barbagia region have remained unchanged since ancient times – including the splendid Sagra del Redentore (Feast of the Redeemer), an annual costumed procession through the town. The author Grazia Deledda, a native of Nuoro, won the Nobel Prize for Literature in 1926 for her descriptions of Sardinian life.

▶ **Population:** 36 678
Ⓒ **Michelin Map:** 566 G 9–10.
Ⓘ **Info:** Piazza Italia 19.
  ☎0784 30 083.
◐ **Location:** Nuoro is situated off the S 131.
Ⓐ **Don't Miss:** Views from Monte Ortobene.
Ⓣ **Timing:** Allow a couple of hours.

SIGHT
Museo della Vita e delle Tradizioni Popolari Sarde
Via A. Mereu 56. ♿Tue–Sun mid-Mar–Sept 9am–1pm, 3–6pm; Oct–mid-Mar

10am–1pm and 3–5pm. 1€.
☎0784 25 70 35 or 0784 24 29 00.
www.isresardegna.it.
The small museum of Sardinian life and popular traditions has a lovely collection of Sardinian costumes. It also exhibits traditional carnival masks.

Barbagia

Wild and evocative, this area is full of steep ravines, known only to local shepherds, and has a wide variety of flora (holm oak, chestnut, hazelnut, thyme and yew) and fauna (golden and bonelli eagle, peregrine falcon, golden kite, wild boar, fox and moufflon). The **Monti del Gennargentu★** and Supramonte, a limestone plateau in the Orgosolo, Oliena and Dorgali areas, are also situated in this region.

Ⓒ **Michelin Map:** 566 G–H 9–10.
◐ **Location:** This region of Sardinia lies behind the immense Gennargentu Massif.
Ⓐ **Don't Miss:** Grotta di Ispinigòli.
👪 **Kids:** The stalagmites at Grotta di Ispinigòli.

🚗DRIVING TOUR

WILD LANDSCAPES, HISTORY AND THE SEA

Ⓒ Circuit in green on map on p282. 160km/99.4mi. Allow a couple of days.

Arbatax
www.arbatax.com.
This isolated port is situated in a beautiful mountain setting overlooking the Tortolì Sea. A secluded bay can be found at Cala Moresca (follow the signs).
The magnificent stretch of **road between Arbatax and Dorgali★★★** (70km/43.5mi) skirts impressive gorges.

Tortolì ≜
Tortolì is the main town of **Ogliastra**, a wild region characterised by cone-like rocks known as 'Tacchi' ('Shoe Heels'). The sea is calm along this coastline, especially at Gairo, where the pebbles are called *coccorocci* (coconut rocks).

SS 125 at Baunei with a view towards Arbatax

© Sandro Bedessi/Fototeca ENIT

Between Lotzorai and Baunei

The SS 125 road **from Arbatax to Dorgali★★★** passes through an increasingly atmospheric landscape as it runs further into the Barbagia region.

Stop at the road's highest point (1 000m/3 281ft) to admire the view.

Dorgali

www.enjoydorgali.it.

The main resort in the Barbagia, Dorgali lies in the bay of Cala Gonone and is the cultural, culinary and craftwork centre of the region. Its main street, Via Lamarmora, offers traditional shops selling local rugs made with a distinctive knot. The local *cannonau* grape has been producing excellent wine for 2 000 years. The Nuraghic village of **Serra Orrios★** lies not far from Dorgali on the road leading to the S 129, while the Giants' Tomb **Sa Ena 'e Thomes** is situated on the Lula road. This tomb has the traditional layout of a Giants' Tomb. The funerary chamber, a passage roofed with large slabs, is preceded by stones forming the arc of a circle.

Domus de Janas

The attractively named *hypogea* (*domus de janas* means "house of fairies") typical to Sardinia were built in the Chalcolithic and Bronze Age.

They are constructed from sandstone, granite, limestone and basaltic rock and some are decorated with drawings of oxen and goats.

Cala Gonone

A winding **road★★** leads to this resort built in an attractive bay. Boat trips leave from the harbour to **Cala Luna**, whose sandy beach is lapped by calm water and backed by oleanders.

There are a number of caves around the bay, including **Grotta del Bue Marino** (arrive by boat from various ports in Golfo di Orosei; www.sardegnaturismo.it). The *bue marino* or "sea ox" refers to the monk seal that occupied this cave until the end of the 1970s.

▶ Head north. After a bend in the road, at the 207km/128mi point on the S 125, a sign marks the path to the dolmen.

Dolmen Mottorra

The dolmen is situated in the middle of a field. It consists of an almost circular slab of schist supported by seven upright stones and dates from the third millennium BC.

Grotta di Ispinigòli★★

The road to the cave is approximately 7km/4mi from Dorgali on the SS 125. Open Apr–Oct 9am–1pm and 3–6pm. 7€. ☎0784 92 72 00.

www.sardegnaturismo.it.

On entering the cave, the visitor realises that the cave is formed by an immense cavity and not by a tunnel. The eye is caught by a **stalagmite column** (38m/125ft), the second tallest in the world. The cave is now a fossil, as there is no more water to form concretions, which are lamellar (in the shape of knives or drapes) or cauliflower (formed underwater, like coral) in form.

The abundant flow of water in the past quickly built up deposits on the floor of the cave; as a result the stalagmites are much larger than the stalactites.

Phoenician jewellery and human bones have been found in the cave, suggesting that it was perhaps used for sacrificial purposes or as a burial chamber.

👥 Children will gaze in wonder at the world's second-tallest stalagmite.

Su Gologone★

20km/12.4mi to the SE of Nuoro,
on the Oliena–Dorgali road.
The town of **Oliena** stands at the foot
of a steep slope of the Sopramonte.

▶ Just beyond Oliena take a local
road to the right for about 6km/4mi.

The lovely spring at Su Gologone
gushes at 300 litres/79gal per second.
Not far from Supramonte di Dorgali a
cave open to the sky hides the **Nuraghic
village of Tiscali**.

Orgosolo

20km/12.4mi S.
This market town is notorious for having been the stronghold of bandits
and outlaws in the not-so-long-ago
past (popularised by the Italian film
producer Vittorio de Seta in his film
Banditi a Orgosolo made in 1961). Today
it is a pleasant town with bright Cubist-inspired murals.

ADDRESSES

🏨 STAY

😊😊 **Hotel L'Oasi** – Via Garcia Lorca 13,
08022 Cala Gonone. ☎0784 93 111.
www.loasihotel.it. Open Easter–9 Oct.
30 rooms. ☲. A small hotel which offers
good-sized rooms and apartments,
attractively furnished. The main
attraction is the building that houses
the restaurant: perched on the cliff
overlooking the sea with a splendid
view of the bay.

🍴 EAT

😊😊 **Colibrì** – Via Gramsci corner via
Floris, 08022 Dorgali. ☎078 49 60 54. This
restaurant offers home-style cooking,
which is faithful to the flavours and
traditions of Dorgali, as well as a warm
welcome from the friendly hosts. One
of the most tempting dishes on the
menu is the suckling lamb stew, known
as saccaju in Sardinian.

Oristano

Oristano is the main town on the west
coast and was founded in 1070 by the
inhabitants of nearby Tharros.

SIGHTS
Piazza Roma

The crenellated tower, Torre di San
Cristoforo, was originally part of the
13C town wall. Off Piazza Roma is **Corso
Umberto**, the main shopping street.

Chiesa di San Francesco

Via Duomo 10. ☎0783 78 275.
The church has some interesting **works
of art★** including a wooden statue of
Christ by the 14C Rhenish school and a
statue of *St Basil* by Nino Pisano (14C).

EXCURSIONS
Basilica di Santa Giusta★

▶ 3km/1.8mi S.
This church, built between 1135 and
1145, stands in the town of the same

▶ **Population:** 32 781
🕐 **Michelin Map:** 566 H 7.
🅸 **Info:** Piazza Eleonora 18.
☎0783 36 831.
www.gooristano.com.
▶ **Location:** The main
access road is the S 131.
▶ **Train:** Oristano (Cagliari 2hr).
🅰 **Don't Miss:** Tharros.
🕐 **Timing:** Allow one day,
with excursions.

name. The sober elegance is characteristic of all Sardinian churches with Pisan
and Lombard influences.

Tharros★

▶ On Capo San Marco, on the northern
side of the gulf. www.tharros.info.
The Phoenicians founded Tharros in the
8C–7C BC. It was a depot on the Marseilles–Carthage trading route, before
it was conquered by Rome c.3C BC.

Zona Archeologica di Tharros

Open 9am–1pm, 4–8pm (winter 7pm). Closed Mon Nov–Mar. ℘0783 290636. www.comunedicabras.it.

The excavation site lies near a hill crowned by a Spanish tower (Torre di San Giovanni). Here are remains of Punic fortifications, tanks, baths, a Punic temple with Doric half-columns and, on the hilltop, a *tophet* (◔ *see Isola di SANT'ANTIOCO*).

Arborea

◉ 18km/11.2mi S.

This town was laid out in 1928 by the Fascist government, following the draining of the marshes and the extermination of the malaria mosquito.

ADDRESSES

🏨 STAY

◔◔◔ **Hotel La Caletta** – Loc. Torre dei Corsari, 09031 Marina di Arbus, 20km/12.4mi S of Arborea through Stagno di Marceddi. ℘070 97 71 33. www.lacaletta.it. Open Easter–Sept. 32 rooms. ⌷. Restaurant. The hotel may not be in keeping with the landscape, but it boasts a magnificent cliff top location with views over the sea.

Barumini★★

The town of Barumini is surrounded by numerous traces of the earliest period of Sardinian history.

NURAGHI SU NURAXI★★

◉ 2km/1.2mi W, on the left-hand side of the Tuili road. Only guided tour. Open daily 9am–7pm, winter to 4pm. 10€ (ruins and Casa Zapata). ℘070 93 61 039. www.fondazionebarumini.it.

The oldest part of Su Nuraxi dates from the 15C BC. The fortress was consolidated due to the threat posed by the Phoenician invaders between the 8C and 7C BC and was taken by the Carthaginians between the 5C and 4C BC and abandoned in the 3C with the arrival of the Romans.

- ▶ **Population:** 1 395
- ◔ **Michelin Map:** 566 H 9.
- 🅱 **Info:** www.sardegnaturismo.it.
- ◉ **Location:** Barumini is in the heartland of Sardinia, 10km/6.2mi N of Villanovaforru, off the S 197.
- ◔ **Timing:** Allow an hour.

SANTA VITTORIA DI SERRI★

38km/23.6mi E by the Nuoro road and a road to the right in Nurallao. Tue–Sun 9am–5pm. www.sardegnaturismo.it.

There are remains of a prehistoric religious centre. On the way out, the road passes through the crafts village of **Isili** (furniture-making and weaving).

Nuraghi

©Card76/iStockphoto.com

View of Cagliari

©Natale Matteo/Dreamstime.com

Cagliari

Cagliari is the capital of the island. It is a modern town with a busy harbour and old nucleus surrounded by fortifications, built by the Pisans in the 13C. Before becoming Roman it was a Carthaginian city called *Karalis*. The Terrazza Umberto 10 affords a fine view★★ of the town, harbour and bay.

SIGHTS
Cattedrale
Open 8am–noon (Sun 1pm) and 4–8pm (Sun 4.30–8.30pm). ℘070 66 38 37. www.duomodicagliari.it.
Built in the 13C, the cathedral was remodelled in the 17C. Inside are 12C **pulpits★★** by Guglielmo of Pisa. A door on the right of the choir leads to the **Santuario**, a crypt containing the remains of 292 Christian martyrs placed in urns along the walls. The chapel contains the tomb of Marie-Louise of Savoy, the wife of King Louis XVIII of France and sister of the King of Sardinia.

Museo Archeologico Nazionale★
Piazza arsenale. & Open Tue–Sun 9am–7.15pm. 5€. ℘070 65 59 11. www.archeocaor.beniculturali.it
The National Archaeological Museum has a large collection of arms, pottery

- ▶ **Population:** 161 465
- ⚐ **Michelin Map:** 566 J 9.
- ▤ **Info:** Palazzo Civico, Via Roma 145, ℘070 67 78 173. www.cagliariturismo.it.
- ◖ **Location:** Cagliari is located in the south of the island, overlooking the Golfo di Cagliari. The road network that converges on the town includes the S 195, S 130, S 131, S 125 and the coastal road to Villasimius..
- ⊘ **Don't Miss:** Strada di Muravera.
- ◷ **Timing:** Allow a day.

and small **bronzes★★★**, grave artefacts from the earliest period of Sardinian history.
Phoenician, Punic and Roman art are in the other rooms.

Torre dell'Elefante and Torre San Pancrazioa
Via Santa Croce and Piazza Indipendenza. ℘070 40 92 306.
The 14C Elephant and St Pancras towers were part of the Pisan fortifications.

Anfiteatro Romano
This amphitheatre is the most important Roman monument in Sardinia. It is the largest Roman ruin on the island.

Despite its state of decay, you can still see the trenches for the animals, the underground passages and several rows of seats. There are open air concerts here in the summer, and tickets are sold in the ticket office.

Isola di
Sant'Antioco★

This volcanic island is the largest of the Sulcis Archipelago. It has a hilly terrain with high cliffs on the west coast. The chief town, also called Sant'Antioco, is linked to the mainland by a road. Catacombs, some of which have been transformed from Punic *hypogea*, can be seen under the Sant'Antioco church. They date from the 6C–7C.

VESTIGIA DI SULCIS★

  Open daily 9am–7pm. Closed hols. 13€. ℘0781 80 05 96. www.archeotur.it.
Named after the ancient town of *Sulci*, founded by the Phoenicians in the 8C BC, the archaeological area comprises the Phoenician-Punic *topheta*, once believed to be where the first-born male child was sacrificed, but now understood to be a cemetery for children who died in infancy.
The archaeological museum includes a fine collection of **stelae★**.

EXCURSION
Strada di Muravera★★★

Some 30km/19mi from Cagliari, the SS 125 road enters wild gorges with reddish walls of porphyritic granite, dotted with oleander and prickly pear cacti.

▸ **Population:** 11 756
  Michelin Map: 566 J–K 7.
  Info: Piazza Repubblica 41, ℘0781 84 05 92. www.prolocosantantioco.it.
  Location: Off Sardinia's southwest coast. The main access road is the S 126.

EXCURSION
Monte Sirai

▸ 19km/11.8mi from Sant'Antioco. Summer Tue–Sun 10am–7pm, winter Wed–Sun 10am–3pm. ℘0781 63 512 or 320 57 18 454 (mobile). www.comune.carbonia.ci.it.
Traces of a Phoenician-Punic settlement remain on this hill. The Phoenicians arrived here in 750 BC. Their city was destroyed in 520 BC by the Carthaginians, who built a new fortress, in turn destroyed by the Romans in 238 BC.

Vestigia di Sulcis

©Tommaso Di Girolamo/Photoshot

Sicily

Sicilia. Major Cities: Catania, Palermo
Official Website: www.regione.sicilia.it

From sun-scorched earth in the summer, the land turns a brilliant green as soon as the spring rain arrives. With its mountainous terrain at the heart of the island, and glorious coastline, Sicily has much to offer. Visitors who come to relax by the sea or marvel at the island's rich artistic heritage and traditional way of life are rewarded with a marvellous collage of colourful images and sensations inherited from diverse continents and civilisations.

A Bit of History

Sicily has been a constant pawn for marauding forces in the Mediterranean because of its strategic location. First came Phoenicians, then Greeks in the 8C BC who discovered an island divided between two ethnic groups: the **Sicani**, the oldest inhabitants, and the **Siculi** (Sicels), who came from the mainland.

The Carthaginians were for several centuries the main rivals of the Greeks. They were finally pushed back to the western part of the island, where they remained until the siege of Motya by Dionysius I of Syracuse in 397 BC. The 5C BC was the apogee of Greek rule in Sicily *(Magna Graecia)*.

By 241 BC, at the end of the First Punic War, the whole of Sicily had been conquered by the Romans, who coveted the island for the richness of its soil.

In 535 the island passed to the Byzantines and in the 9C the Muslims of the Aghlabid

Highlights

1 Explore Agrigento's **Valle dei Templi** (p314)

2 Marvel at mosaics at the **Villa Romana del Casale** (p317)

3 Scale the slopes of **Mount Etna** (p326)

4 Take a boat tour of the **Aeolian Islands** (p332)

Info: Via Notarbartolo 9, 90141 Palermo.
☎091 707 82 76.

Location: Sicily, the largest of the Mediterranean islands, has an area of 25 709sq km/9 927sq mi. It is triangular and was named Trinacria ("three points") under Greek rule. The island is generally mountainous and reaches at its highest point, Mount Etna (an active volcano), an altitude of 3 340m/10 958ft.

Don't Miss: The Valley of the Temples at Agrigento, the splendour of Mount Etna, the Eolie and Egadi Islands, visits to Palermo, Siracusa and Taormina.

Timing: Allow 3–4 days to explore the island, preferably a week.

Greek temple in Agrigento

© anzeletti/iStockphoto.com

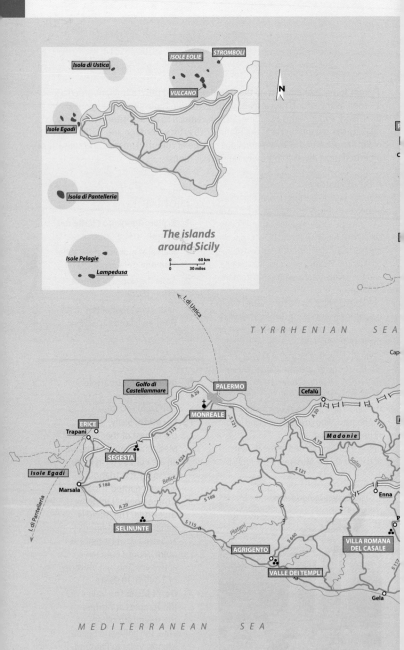

The islands around Sicily

0 — 60 km
0 — 30 miles

Isola di Ustica

ISOLE EOLIE   STROMBOLI

VULCANO

Isole Egadi

Isola di Pantelleria

Isole Pelagie

Lampedusa

I. di Ustica

TYRRHENIAN   SEA

Cap·

Golfo di Castellammare   PALERMO   Cefalù

ERICE   MONREALE
Trapani

Madonie

SEGESTA

Isole Egadi

I. di Pantelleria

Marsala

Belice

Enna

SELINUNTE   Platani

AGRIGENTO   VILLA ROMANA DEL CASALE

VALLE DEI TEMPLI   Gela

MEDITERRANEAN   SEA

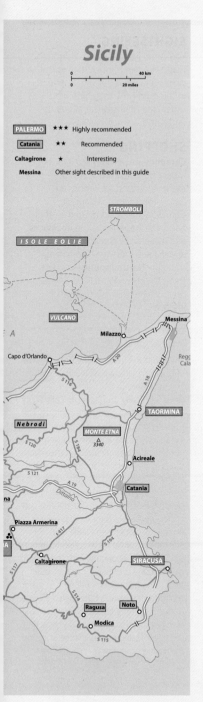

Sicily

PALERMO ★★★	Highly recommended
Catania ★★	Recommended
Caltagirone ★	Interesting
Messina	Other sight described in this guide

dynasty (Tur...
expelled by th...
The son of the G...
Roger II (1095-...
man Kingdom...
his court at Pal... ...ng his reign
the island enjoyed a prosperous period
of considerable political power and cultural influence.

The Hohenstaufen Emperor Frederick
II dominated the reign of this Swabian
dynasty. The house of Anjou followed
in 1266; however, Charles of Anjou was
expelled following the Palermo revolt
of 1282. Power passed to the Aragon
dynasty; Alfonso V the Magnanimous
reunited Naples and Sicily, taking the title
of King of the Two Sicilies (1442).

The island passed to the Bourbons of
Naples by marriage until they were over-
thrown by the Expedition of Garibaldi
and the Thousand (1860). World War II left
its mark on Licata and Siracusa: in 1943
the Anglo-American landings ended in
the abandonment of the island by the
Germans.

Architecture

The Greeks built admirable Doric temples
and also splendid theatres. During the
brief Normans domination of the island,
Sicily's economic prosperity brought prolific construction that blended Moorish
and Byzantine influences. Known vari-
ously as Sicilian Norman or Arab Norman,
this style can be seen at Palermo, Monreale, Cefalù and Messina.

The Renaissance left few traces on the
island, with some outstanding exceptions
by **Antonello da Messina**. But the Sicilians adopted the Spanish-influenced
Baroque style with great fervour in the
late-18C, notably in Noto, Ragusa, Catania
and Palermo.

Literature

Sicilian literature is particularly rich. In
the 19C **Giovanni Verga** created a new
form of Italian novel, and Luigi Pirandello,
plays. Among 20C writers are Elio Vit-
torini (1908–66) and Leonardo Sciascia

GETTING AROUND

BY BOAT: The main connections to Sicily by boat leave from Cagliari, Genova, Livorno, Naples, Salerno (great for direct access to Catania), Reggio Calabria and Villa San Giovanni.

BY AIR: By air, you will arrive at either Palermo or Catania, the island's two main airports. There are also airports at Trapani, Pantelleria and Lampedusa with connecting flights to these airports at busy times of the year (Easter and in summer). Another possibility is the airport at Reggio Calabria, which, although not in Sicily itself, is very near the Straits of Messina. See the Practical Points section at the beginning of the guide for further details.

SIGHTSEEING

You could just about get around the island in a week. In addition to the places and areas that are described in this guide, the map highlights other areas of interest and beauty (indicated in small, black type).

SHOPPING

Ceramics are perhaps the island's most celebrated artisanal trade: the most important centres are Caltagirone, Santo Stefano di Camastra and Sciacca. On the other hand, the Trapani area has **necklaces** and other objects made out of coral, and in Erice there is a rug-making tradition. **Natural sponges** are the thing to buy on Pantelleria, and in Syracuse the papyrus may be of interest.

(1921–89). Other writers include Gesualdo Bufalino (1920–96), Salvatore Quasimodo (1901–68) and Giuseppe Tomasi di Lampedusa (1896–1957), whose epic *The Leopard* is set in Sicily during the Risorgimento.

Sicily Today

The long period of foreign domination in Sicily has left its imprint not only on the art, culture and literature of the island but also on its economy. Following the Arab invasions, the island's economy was neglected by its foreign rulers, with the exception of the Normans and Swabians. Forests were cleared, the locals exploited, and the island was prevented from developing.

Today Sicily survives on an assisted economy, a long-term result of the *Cassa per il Mezzogiorno*, Italy's development fund for the South created in 1950. In theory, the fund was for new development projects that would stem the emigration of Sicily's young people and restore former glory. Unfortunately, many projects have not been realised, as corrupt officials squander or mismanage the monies or the funds have fallen into the hands of the **Cosa Nostra**, the Sicilian mafia, whose reach extends far beyond Palermo.

Geographically and economically Sicily can be divided into three regions. The first region comprises the provinces of Catania, Siracusa and the southern part of Messina. The agriculture of the region tends to be intensive and of high quality. Palermo, Trapani and the north of Messina have a highly developed services sector and building industry. Finally, the poorest part of Sicily consists of the interior provinces of Agrigento, Caltanissetta and Enna.

The fishing industry is still of prime importance to local economy, with the annual **mattanza** – a massive catch of bluefin tuna using giant nets – bringing in major profits for the island's fishermen. As world demand for tuna increases, however, the Mediterranean supply is rapidly depleting, thereby threatening this ancient ritual and the fishing economy.

Palermo★★★

Palermo, the capital and chief seaport of Sicily, is built at the head of a wide bay enclosed to the north by Monte Pellegrino and to the south by Capo Zafferano. It lies on the edge of a fertile plain bounded by hills and nicknamed the "Conca d'Oro" (Golden Basin), where lemon and orange groves flourish.

A BIT OF HISTORY

Palermo was founded by the Phoenicians, conquered by the Romans and later came under Byzantine rule. From 831 to 1072 it was under the sway of the Saracens, who gave the city its special atmosphere suggested today by the luxuriance of its gardens and the shape of the domes on some buildings. Conquered by the Normans in 1072, Palermo became the capital under Roger II, who took the title of King of Sicily. This great builder succeeded in blending Norman architectural styles with the decorative traditions of the Saracens and Byzantines: his reign was the golden age of art in Palermo. Later the Hohenstaufen and Angevin kings introduced the Gothic style (13C). After three centuries of Spanish rule, the Bourbons gave Palermo its Baroque finery.

The Sicilian Vespers

Since 1266 the brother of Louis IX of France, Charles I of Anjou, supported by the Pope, had held the town. But his rule was unpopular. The Sicilians had nicknamed the French, who spoke Italian badly, the *tartaglioni* or 'stammerers'. On the Monday or Tuesday after Easter 1282, as the bells were ringing for vespers, some Frenchmen insulted a young woman of Palermo in the church of Santo Spirito. Insurrection broke out, and all Frenchmen who could not pronounce the world *cicero* (chickpea) correctly were massacred.

▶ **Population:** 682 000
⚲ **Michelin Map:** 432 M 21-22 (including built-up area).
🛈 **Info:** Via Principe di Belmonte 92, 90141 Palermo. ℘091 58 51 72. www.provincia.palermo.it/turismo/.
◗ **Location:** Situated on the northern coast. The main access road is the A 19.
◗ **Train:** Palermo Centrale.
🅿 **Parking:** Traffic is congested and parking is difficult. Walk or use public transport. Car parks can be found on the city outskirts.
☺ **Don't Miss:** Cappella Palatina, Galleria Regionale della Sicilia, Catacombe dei Cappuccini or Monreale.
🕐 **Timing:** Allow two days to see Palermo and one more for the surrounding area.
👪 **Kids:** Puppets at the Museo Internazionale delle Marionette.

🐾WALKING TOURS

1 THE HISTORIC QUARTER

🖑Circuit in green on map on p302. Allow 4hrs.

Palazzo dei Normanni (Reale)★★

Open Mon–Sat 8.15am–5.40pm (last admission 5pm), Sun and hols 8.15am–1pm (last admission 12.15am). Closed 1 Jan, 25 Dec. 8.50€ Fri–Mon; 8.50€ Tue–Sat. ℘091 62 62 833. www.fondazionefedericosecondo.it.
Only the central part and the Pisan Tower are of the Norman period, built on the site of an earlier Moorish fortress.

Cappella Palatina★★★

First floor of Palazzo dei Normanni.
Built in the reign of Roger II from 1130 to 1140, this is a wonderful example of

Piazza Pretoria

©savoia/iStockphoto.com

Arab-Norman decoration. The upper walls, dome and apses are covered with dazzling **mosaics**★★★ which, along with those of Constantinople and Ravenna, are the finest in Europe. This decoration is complemented by the carved stalactite ceiling, marble paving, ornate pulpit and paschal candelabrum. On the second floor the old royal apartments, **Antichi Appartamenti Reali**★★, house the 12C King Roger's chamber, **Sala di Re Ruggero** (guided tours only).

Chiesa di San Giovanni degli Eremiti★★

Open Tue–Sat 9am–7pm, Mon, Sun and public hols 9am–1.30pm. 6€. 𝒫091 65 15 019.

Close to the Palazzo dei Normanni, this church, with its surrounding gardens, is a green oasis. The church was built with the aid of Arab architects in 1132 and is crowned with pink domes. Beside it is a tropical garden with 13C **cloisters**★. The attractive gardens, **Villa Bonanno**★, boast superb palm trees.

Cattedrale★

Open Mon–Sat 7am–7pm, Sun 8am–1pm and 4pm–7pm. Donation suggested. 𝒫091 33 43 73. www.cattedrale.palermo.it.

Founded at the end of the 12C, the cathedral is built in the Sicilian-Norman style but has often been modified. The **apses**★ of the east end have retained their Sicilian-Norman decoration. In the interior, which was modified in the 18C in the Neoclassical style, note the tombs of the Emperor Frederick II and other members of the Hohenstaufen dynasty as well as of Angevin and Aragonese rulers. The **Treasury** (Tesoro) (2€; open Mon–Sat 9am–5.30pm; 𝒫091 33 43 73) displays the **Imperial crown**★ that belonged to Constance of Aragon. Other areas to tour include the crypt and the roof. Finish your tour at **Chiesa del Santissimo Salvatore**★, a 17C oval-shaped church today used as an auditorium.

② THE QUATTRO CANTI TO THE ALBERGHERIA

♿Circuit in green on map on p302. Allow 1.5hrs.

I "Quattro Canti"★★

Two main streets, Via Vittorio Emanuele and Via Maqueda, intersect to form this busy crossroads decorated with statues and fountains. The mid-17C church of **San Matteo** has an astonishingly decorative interior.

Piazza Pretoria★★

The square has a spectacular **fountain**★★ surmounted by numerous marble statues, the work of a 16C Florentine artist. The **Palazzo Pretorio** (♿ open Mon–Sat 9am–1pm and 3pm–6pm; 𝒫091 74 0 2216; www.comune.palermo.it), now the town hall, occupies one side of this square.

GETTING THERE

The easiest and quickest way to get to Palermo is by **air**. The city airport, Falcone-Borsellino (www.gesap.it) (formerly known as Punta-Raisi), is situated 30km/18.6mi north of Palermo,off the A 29 dual carriageway. It is served by various airlines including Alitalia, Alpi Eagles, Air Sicilia, Med Airlines, Meridiana and Air Europe, from 5am until the arrival of the last flight of the day, buses stopping in Via Libertà, Via Amari (in front of Politeama Hotel, another stop at port), and the main railway station. The journey takes 50 minutes and costs 6.30€. For information, contact Prestia e Comandè, www.prestiaecomande.it; ℘091 58 04 57. Palermo can also be reached by **ferry** from **Genova**, **Livorno** and **Naples**: **Grandi Navi Veloci**, ℘010 209 45 91, www1.gnv.it. **Tirrenia** ℘892 123, www.tirrenia.it. **SNAV**, ℘081 42 85 555; www.snav.it.

GETTING AROUND

It is best to avoid driving in Palermo because of traffic congestion and the difficulty of finding somewhere to park. Large car parks can be found on the outskirts of the city (marked by a **P** on the map). There is also a free car park in Piazza Maggiore, 300m/328yds from the Botanical Gardens. Other parking facilities (for which there is a charge) include Piazza Giulio Cesare 43, Porto; Via Guardione 81, Porto and Via Stabile 10. However, by far the best way to see the city is by public transport and taxi for longer distances and on foot once in the old town.

BY BUS – There are several types of ticket: tickets valid for 90 minutes *(1.40€)*, the daily tickets – which expire at midnight – *(3.50€)*, the 2-days tickets *(5.70€)*, the 3-days ticket *(8€)*. www.amat.pa.it.

BY TAXI – Autoradio Taxi Palermo ℘091 51 33 11 and Radio Taxi Trinacria ℘091 68 78.

La Martorana★★

Open Mon–Sat 9.30am–1pm and 3.30–5pm, Sun and public hols 9.15–10.30am. 2€. ℘345 828 8231.

The real name of this church is Santa Maria dell'Ammiraglio (St Mary of the Admiral). It was founded in 1143 by the Admiral of the Fleet to King Roger II and altered in the 16C and 17C by the addition of a Baroque façade on the north side. Pass under the 12C belfry-porch to enter the original church, newly restored in 2013, decorated with Byzantine **mosaics★★** depicting scenes from the New Testament and, in the cupola, the imposing figure of Christ Pantocrator (Christ as Ruler of All).

At the very end of the two side aisles note the two panels depicting *Roger II Crowned by Christ (right)*, and *Admiral George of Antioch Kneeling before the Virgin (left)*.

San Cataldo★★

Open Mar–Oct Mon–Sat 9am–1pm and 3.30–6.30pm, Nov–Feb daily 9am-1pm, ℘091 348 728.

This splendid church, founded in the 12C, recalls Moorish architecture with its severe square shape, its domes and the traceried openings of the façade. The two churches face each other on the small Piazza Bellini. The Moorish and Norman features of the square are particularly evident in the three rose-coloured cupolas of San Cataldo. The church is bordered by **San Giuseppe ai Teatini,** an eye-catching Baroque church with a theatrical **interior★**.

Continue your tour by dropping into **Palazzo Comitini** *(open Mon–Fri 9.30am–12.30pm, 3.30–5.30pm (Tue and Thu to 4.45pm); closed public hols; ℘091 66 28 251)* built for the Prince of Gravina in the late-18C. **Sala Martorana★**, now the seat of the Provincial Council, is lined with wood-panelling inlaid with mirrors.

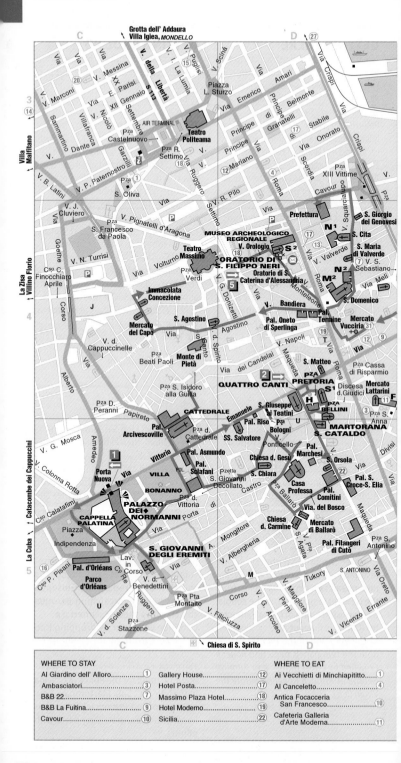

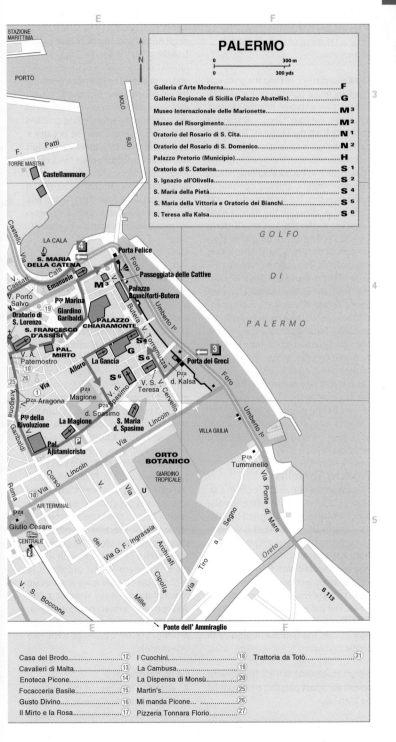

PALERMO

0   300 m
0   300 yds

Galleria d'Arte Moderna .... **F**
Galleria Regionale di Sicilia (Palazzo Abatellis) .... **G**
Museo Internazionale delle Marionette .... **M³**
Museo del Risorgimento .... **M²**
Oratorio del Rosario di S. Cita .... **N¹**
Oratorio del Rosario di S. Domenico .... **N²**
Palazzo Pretorio (Municipio) .... **H**
Oratorio di S. Caterina .... **S¹**
S. Ignazio all'Olivella .... **S²**
S. Maria della Pietà .... **S⁴**
S. Maria della Vittoria o Oratorio dei Bianchi .... **S⁵**
S. Teresa alla Kalsa .... **S⁶**

GOLFO

DI

PALERMO

STAZIONE MARITTIMA
PORTO
F. Patti
TORRE MASTRA
Castellammare
LA CALA
S. MARIA DELLA CATENA
Porta Felice
Passeggiata delle Cattive
Emanuele
M³
Palazzo Branciforti-Butera
V. Cassari
Castello Via
V. Porto Salvo
Oratorio di S. Lorenzo
P.za Marina
Giardino Garibaldi
PALAZZO CHIARAMONTE
S. FRANCESCO D'ASSISI
PAL. MIRTO
V. A. Paternostro
Alloro
La Gancia
G
S⁶
Porta dei Greci
Via
P.za Aragona
S⁵
V. d. Spasimo
P.za Magione
V. S. Teresa
P.za d. Kalsa
Cervello
P.za della Rivoluzione
La Magione
P.za d. Spasimo
S. Maria d. Spasimo
Lincoln
VILLA GIULIA
Pal. Ajutamicristo
Lincoln
Corso
Via
U
ORTO BOTANICO
GIARDINO TROPICALE
P.za Tumminello
Roma
Via
AIR TERMINAL
P.za Giulio Cesare
CENTRALE
dei
Via G. F. Ingrassia
Archirafi
Cipolla
Mille
V. S. Boccone
Via Tiro a Segno
Oreto
Via Ponte di Mare
S 113
Ponte dell' Ammiraglio

Molo Sud
Foro
Butera
V. Torremuzza
Umberto I°
Foro
Umberto I°

③ LA KALSA AND VIA ALLORO

Circuit in green on map on p302.
Allow 4hrs.

The **Kalsa district**, behind the port, was razed by Allied bombing raids in 1943. The ruins were thrown into the sea and, as a result, the Foro Italico now stands a little way from the seafront. This fascinating district is currently under major reconstruction, with the creation of new squares such as **Piazza Magione**, *palazzi* and monuments, and the opening of cultural centres. The focal point is Piazza della Kalsa, although the district itself stretches all the way to Corso Vittorio Emanuele, and contains a high proportion of the city's most interesting monuments. The main entrance to the quarter is the **Porta dei Greci** beyond which lies the piazza and the church of **Santa Teresa alla Kalsa**, a monumental Baroque church built between 1686 and 1706. Turning onto Via Torremuzza, note the beautiful stone-framed Noviziato dei Crociferi at number 20 and, farther along on the opposite side of the street, **Santa Maria della Pietà**. Throughout the Middle Ages, **Via Alloro** served as the quarter's main street. Today, most of the elegant *palazzi* that once lined the thoroughfare have fallen into disrepair.

Palazzo Abatellis★

This magnificent palazzo, built in Catalan-Gothic style with some Renaissance features, was designed by Matteo Carnelivari, who worked in Palermo towards the end of the 15C. Its elegant front has a great square central doorway ornamented with fasces (bundles of rods, an ancient symbol of authority), and a series of two- and three-light windows. The palazzo is arranged around an attractive square courtyard and now houses the **Galleria Regionale di Sicilia** (Via Alloro 4, Tue–Fri 9am–6pm, Sat–Sun and public hols 9am–1.30pm; 8€; ☎091 6230011, 091 62 30 047) with an extraordinary painting by Antonello da Messina.

La Gancia

The church dedicated to **Santa Maria degli Angeli** was originally built by the Franciscans in the late-15C. The exterior retains from the original its square profile and rustication. The **interior★** gives the impression of being Baroque although elements date from several different periods. The wooden ceiling painted with stars, the magnificent **organ★★** by Raffaele della Valle, the marble **pulpit** and Antonello Gagini's relief tondi of the *Annunciation (on either side of the altar)* date from the 16C. Most of the superficial decoration dates from the 17C and fine original details survive, including a **novice monk★** peeping out over a cornice.

▶ Cross Piazza Magione.

Santa Maria dello Spasimo★

The church and convent were built inside the walls of the Kalsa in 1506 and to mark the occasion **Raphael** was commissioned to paint a picture of the anguish of the Madonna before the Cross (now in the Prado in Madrid). Building work on the church was not yet completed when the Turkish threat made it necessary to build a new bastion just behind the church. In turn the complex was transformed into a fortress, a theatre, a hospice for plague victims (1624) then, later, for the poor (1835) and finally a hospital; it was eventually abandoned in 1986. The church and old hospital have been transformed into venues for cultural events (the church houses the Scuola Europea di Music Jazz). The section around the 16C cloisters is accessible to the public.
The **church★** beyond is the only example of Northern-Gothic architecture in Sicily; the slender nave reaches up towards the open sky without a roof and ends with a lovely polygonal **apse**, while the original entrance is given prominence by a *pronaos* with two side chapels.

La Magione

An attractive little avenue of palm trees leads up to the Romanesque church, which was founded in the 12C by Matteo d'Ajello, a prominent official in the service of the Norman sovereigns. The **front elevation**★ rises through three tiers of pointed arches, elegantly ornamented at the lower levels. The church has fine **cloisters** from the original Cistercian monastery. Vestiges of pre-existing constructions, including a 10C Arab tower, are visible from the cloisters.

Via della Magione runs along the side of **Palazzo Ajutamicristo**, an imposing building that was designed by **Matteo Carnelivari** in the 15C.

◗ Go back towards Via Roma and follow it to the square.

Piazza Sant'Anna

In the heart of the ancient **Lattarini market**, this very lively little square is home to the church of Sant'Anna (17C–18C) and the adjoining **Galleria d'Arte Moderna**, which is housed in a former monastery.

Piazza della Rivoluzione

This square is where the anti-Bourbon rebellion of 1848 was ignited. In the centre is a fountain depicting a king feeding a serpent and symbolising the city.

◗ Head back to Via Alloro. The walk continues with the monuments located to the north of Via Alloro.

San Francesco d'Assisi★

The church was built in the 13C. After its destruction during World War II it was rebuilt in the original style. Particularly noteworthy are the **portal**★ (original) and the rose window on the façade.

Oratorio di San Lorenzo★★★

Chiesa di San Francesco d'Assisi.
Open daily 10am–6pm, 2.50€.
℘091 61 18 168.
A late work and masterpiece of **Giacomo Serpotta** decorated with stuccowork is an imaginative riot of *putti*.

Palazzo Chiaramonte★

This fine Gothic palace (1307) served as a model for many buildings in Sicily. In the gardens, **Giardino Garibaldi**, opposite,

there are two spectacular **magnolia-fig trees**★★ *(Ficus magnolioides)*.

④ THE OLD HARBOUR TO THE VUCCIRIA

Circuit in green on map on p302.
Allow 3hrs.

The old harbour is known as the *cala*, once enclosed by chains, now in the **Santa Maria della Catena**★.

The design of the church is attributed to Matteo Carnelivari. Its elevation is dominated by the broad square portico with three arches; behind these are doorways set with low reliefs by Vincenzo Gagini.

Oratorio del Rosario di San Domenico★★★

Open Mon–Sat 9am–1.30pm. 3€.
The stucco decor of this church was the work of **Giacomo Serpotta**, an important artist of the Baroque period.

Santa Cita★★★

Open Mon–Sat 9am–1pm. 5€.
℘091 33 27 79.
This church is considered to be the masterpiece of **Giacomo Serpotta**, who worked on it between 1686 and 1718. Panels depicting the Mysteries are framed by rejoicing angels.

⑤ FROM VIA ROMA TO THE CAPO QUARTER

Circuit in green on map p302. Allow 3hrs.

This tour takes you from Sant'Ignazio all'Olivella, a Baroque church, to Chiesa di Sant'Agnostino, a splendid 13C church with a duotone geometric decorated **front**★.

CITTÀ NUOVA

At the beginning of the 19C, the city underwent a period of expansion. The wealthy merchant bourgeoisie chose the northwest side of the city to build fine residences lavishly decorated with wrought-iron work, glass and floral panels.

Teatro Massimo★

Open daily 9.30am–6pm, guided tours by reservation, 8€. Visita alla terrazza con vista su Palermo su prenotazione, 20€ ℘091 605 32 67.
www.teatromassimo.it.
This opera house is a Neoclassical structure modelled on the *pronaos* of an ancient temple. The initial design was completed by Giovanni Battista Basile in 1875; building work was concluded by his son Ernesto.

HISTORIC CENTRE

Galleria Regionale della Sicilia★★

Open Tue–Sat 9am–6pm. 8€.
℘091 62 30 011.
This museum and gallery is housed in the attractive 15C **Palazzo Abatellis★**. It includes a medieval art section and a picture gallery featuring works from the 11–18C.
Outstanding works include the dramatic fresco of **Death Triumphant★★★** from Palazzo Sclafani and a very fine **bust of Eleonora of Aragon★★** by Francesco Laurana. Paintings of note include the **Annunciation★★** by Antonello da Messina and a triptych, the **Malvagna Altarolo★★**, by the Flemish artist Mabuse.

Palazzo Mirto★

Via Merlo 2. Open Mon–Sun 9am–7pm. 4€. ℘091 61 67 541.
The main residence of the Lanza-Filangieri princes contains its original 18–19C furnishings. Outside, the 19C **stables★** are of interest. The *piano nobile (first floor)* is open to visitors.
The splendid **Salottino Cinese** (Chinese Room) has leather flooring and silk wall coverings depicting scenes from everyday life, while the walls in the **Smoking Room★** are decorated with engraved leather. Exhibits of note include a 19C Neapolitan dinner service (in the passageway facing the Chinese Room).

Museo Internazionale delle Marionette★★

Piazzetta Antonio Pasqualino 5 (entrance Via Butera 1). Open Mon–Sat 9am–1pm and 2.30–6.30pm. Closed public hols. 5€. ℘091 32 80 60.
www.museomarionettepalermo.it.
This museum is a testament to the tradition of puppet *(marionette)* shows in Sicily. Shows concentrated on chivalric themes, in particular the adventures of two heroes, Rinaldo and Orlando. The museum houses a splendid collection of Sicilian puppets. The delicate features of Gaspare Canino's puppets are admirable: these puppets are among the oldest in the collection (19C). The second part of the museum is dedicated to European and non-European craftsmanship with puppets from Asia and Africa. ♣♣ *See the puppet collection in action in a chivalric show.*

Museo Archeologico Regionale★

Via Bara all'Olivella 24. Exhibition spaces can be partially closed. ℘091 61 16 806.
Etruscan art is shown at the Real Albergo delle Povere, Corso Calatafimi, ℘091 422 314. www.regione.sicilia.it/beniculturali.
The archaeological museum, which is housed in a 16C convent, contains the finds from excavations in Sicily. On the ground floor are displayed two Phoenician sarcophagi, an Egyptian inscription known as the Palermo Stone and pieces from Selinus.
These last include a fine series of twin stelae and the reconstruction of a temple pediment *(Sala Gabrici)* and the **metopes★★** from the temples (6C and 5C BC). On the first floor are displayed bronzes including **Heracles with Stag★** and the famous **Ram★★**, a Hellenistic work from Syracuse, and marble statues, notably **Satyr★**, a copy of an original by Praxiteles. On the second floor are two fine mosaics (3C BC), *Orpheus with Animals* and the *Mosaic of the Seasons*.

MODERN CITY
Villa Malfitano★★

Off the map. Follow Via Dante. Open
Mon–Sat 9am–1pm. 6€. ℘091 68 20 522.
www.fondazionewhitaker.it

Surrounded by beautiful **gardens★★**,
this Liberty-style villa has retained
many Oriental furnishings.

Particularly worthy of note is the
decoration of the **Sala d'estate** (Summer Room) by Ettore de Maria Bergler;
the *trompe l'œil* effect transforms the
room into a cool veranda surrounded
by greenery.

Orto Botanico★★

Mon–Sun 9am–1hr before dusk. 5€.
℘091 23 89 12 36. www.ortobotanico.
unipa.it or www.ortobotanicoitalia.it.

A garden with a fine collection of exotic
flora, including magnificent **magnolia-
fig trees★★** *(Ficus magnolioides).*

BEYOND THE CITY GATES
Catacombe dei Cappuccini★★

Access by Via dei Cappuccini, at the
bottom of Corso Vittorio Emanuele.
Open daily 9am–1pm and 3–6pm.
Closed Sun afternoon Nov–Mar. 3€.
℘091 21 21 17.

These Capuchin catacombs are an
impressive sight. About 8 000 mummies were placed here from the 17C to
the 19C, preserved by the very dry air.

Castello della Zisa★

& Open Mon–Sat 9am–6.30pm, Sun
and public hols 9am–1pm. 6€. ℘091
65 20 269. www.regione.sicilia.it/
beniculturali.

This magnificent palace now houses a
collection of Islamic art from the Mame-
luke and Ottoman periods.

Parco della Favorita

3km/1.8mi N along Via Diana.

This 18C park was laid out for the
Bourbons. Beside the Chinese Pavilion
(Palazzina Cinese) is a museum, the
Museo Etnografico Pitrè, which dis-
plays traditional Sicilian objects. Closed
at time of writing. ℘091 74 04 893.

EXCURSIONS
Monreale★★★

◗ 8km/5mi SW.

The town, dominating the Conca
d'Oro (Golden Basin) of Palermo, grew
up around the 12C Benedictine abbey
founded by the Norman King William II.

Duomo★★★

Open daily Mon–Sat 8.30am–12.45pm
and 2.30pm–5pm; public hols.
8am–10am and 2.30pm–5.30pm. 3€.
℘091 64 04 413.

The central doorway of the cathedral
has beautiful **bronze doors★★** (1185),
which were carved by Bonanno Pisano.
The Byzantine north **doorway★** is the
work of Barisano da Trani (12C). The
decoration of the **chevet★★** blends
Moorish and Norman styles.

The cathedral has a basilical plan. The
interior is dazzling with multicoloured
marbles, paintings, and especially the
12C and 13C **mosaics★★★**.

A gigantic **Christ Pantocrator** (Ruler
of All) is enthroned in the central apse.
Above the episcopal throne, in the choir,
a mosaic represents King William II
offering the cathedral to the Virgin.

A mosaic opposite shows King William
receiving his crown from Christ. From
the **terraces★★★** there are magnificent
views★★ over the fertile plain of the
Conca d'Oro.

Chiostro★★★

& Open Mon–Sat 9am–1.30pm and
2pm–6.30pm, Sun and public hols
9am–1pm. 6€. ℘091 64 04 403.

The cloisters to the right of the church
are as famous as the mosaics. On the
south side there is a fountain that was
used as a lavabo by the monks.

Riserva Naturale
Monte Pellegrino

◗ 14km/8.7mi N.

The road out of the city affords splendid
glimpses★★★ of the Conca d'Oro.

Golfo di Castellammare★★★

◗ 25.7km/16mi W.

This splendid gulf is characterized by
soft hills, dominated to the west by the

imposing size of the **Mount Còfano**, best seen from the promontory on **Capo San Vito**. In addition to the splendid coastal landscapes, the region offers castles, tuna fisheries and archaeological zones.

Castellammare del Golfo

Set in the beautiful bay of the same name, this town, now a popular seaside resort, was once the main port and principal trading post for the ancient cities of Segesta and Erice. In the centre of the town stands the **medieval castle**. After Castellammare del Golfo, a road to Scopello winds its way up a ruggedly bleak mountainside with **views★**.

Rovine di Solunto★

● 19km/11.8mi E. Open 9am–6pm, Sun and public hols 9am–1pm. 4€. ℘338 78 45 140.

Soluntum has a splendid site overlooking a headland, Capo Zafferano. The site (**zona archeologica**) includes ruins of the baths, forum and theatre. Take Via Ippodamo da Mileto to the summit for a lovely **view★★**.

ADDRESSES

🏨 STAY

🛏 **Albergo Cavour** – Via A. Manzoni 11 (5th floor with lift). ℘/Fax 091 61 62 759. www.albergocavour.com. 8 rooms. Hotel on the fifth floor of an old palazzo conveniently located near the railway station has light, airy rooms with high ceilings and functional furnishings.

🛏 **B&B La Fuitina** – Via Garraffello 6. ℘091 976 65 01. This little B&B is a stone's throw from the Vucciria market and offers cosy rooms and a generous breakfast. It lacks a lift, but offers a plunging view over the rooftops of Palermo.

🛏 **Hotel Moderno** – Via Roma 276 (3rd floor with lift). ℘091 58 86 83. www.hotelmodernopa.com. 38 rooms. A welcoming friendly, family-run hotel with fair-sized rooms with simple, functional furnishings.

🛏🛏 **Al Giardino dell'Alloro** – Vicolo San Carlo 8. ℘091 61 76 904 or 338 224 35 41

(mobile). www.giardinodellalloro.it. 5 rooms. Located in an alley in Kalsa, this guesthouse offers comfortable rooms with a mixture of contemporary style and traditional decor. Copious breakfast and a friendly welcome.

🛏🛏 **B&B 22** – Largo Cavalieri di Malta 22. ℘091 32 62 14 or 335 79 08 733 (mobile). 7 rooms. In a little street in the historic centre is this charming, impeccably renovated house. Bright rooms mixing modern design. Suites face onto a garden.

🛏🛏 **Ambasciatori** – Via Roma 111 (5th & 6th floors with lift). ℘091 61 66 881. www.ambasciatorihotelpalermo.net. 12 rooms. A welcoming hotel boasting spacious rooms with street or courtyard views and good facilities. Breakfast is served on a roof terrace with views over the city and the port.

🛏🛏 **Hotel Posta** – Via A. Gagini 77. ℘091 58 73 38. www.hotelpostapalermo.it. 30 rooms. Behind the busy Via Roma, this family-run hotel with 27 simple, but comfortable rooms. Popular with Teatro Massimo actors.

🛏🛏🛏 **Gallery House** – Via M. Stabile 136. ℘091 61 24 758. Fax 091 61 24 779. www.hotelgalleryhouse.com. 10 rooms. Very cosy and particularly pleasant, with rooms on the luxurious side and efficient, attentive staff.

🛏🛏🛏 **Massimo Plaza Hotel** – Via Maqueda 437. ℘091 32 56 57. www.massimoplazahotel.com. 11 rooms. Situated opposite the Neo-classical Teatro Massimo, offers excellent service and comfortable rooms with parquet floors and tasteful furnishings.

🛏🛏🛏 **Sicilia** – Via Divisi 99 (1st floor). ℘091 61 68 460. 15 rooms. Opposite Palazzo Comitini, a simple friendly hotel offers bright, fresh rooms.

🍴 EAT

SICILIAN FAST FOOD

Local specialities include snacks such as *u sfinciuni* or *sfincione* (a type of pizza topped with tomato, anchovies, onion and breadcrumbs), *pani ca' meusa* or *panino con la milza* (roll filled with charcoal-grilled pork offal), *panelle* (fried chickpea flour pancakes) and *babbaluci* (marinated snails sold in paper cornets). Sold from stalls in the markets.

🍽️ **Antica Focacceria San Francesco** – Via Alessandro Paternostro 58. ☎091 320 264. www.anticafocacceria.it. Opposite San Francesco, this historic (1834) family caffè has marble tables and serves traditional *focaccia con la milza* from an antique cast-iron stove. The *focaccia farcita* (flat, thick pizza dough baked with various fillings); *arancini* (a Sicilian staple – deep-fried rice balls stuffed with various fillings from vegetables to meat sauce, cheese and nuts), and *torte salate* (Sicilian savoury "tarts").

🍽️ **Cafeteria Galleria d'Arte Moderna** – Via Sant'Anna 21. ☎091 84 31 605. 9.30am–6.30pm. Closed Mon. The bright modern art museum cafeteria serves snacks, salads and a few hot dishes.

🍽️ **Enoteca Picone** – Via G. Marconi 36. ☎091 33 13 00. www.enotecapicone.it. Closed Sun afternoon. A vast wine selection (over 4 000 labels) in this family *enoteca* since 1946 has made an art of wine selling.

🍽️ **Focacceria Basile** – Via Bara all'Olivella 76, Quartiere Massimo. ☎091 33 56 28. Closed Sun. This trattoria-cum-*rosticceria* offers takeaway pizza and *focaccie*, prepares fast-cooked meals and has two somewhat plain dining rooms.

🍽️ **Gusto Divino** – Corso Pisani 30. ☎091 64 57 001. Closed Sun evening and some public hols. Near Palazzo d'Orléans, locals enjoy inventive cuisine inspired by local produce, such as filet of john dory with pistachios or spaghetti with cuttlefish shavings. Good wine cellar.

🍽️ **I Cuochini** – Via R. Settimo 68. ☎091 58 11 58. www.icuochini.com. Mon–Fri 8.30am–2.30pm, Sat 8.30am–2.30pm and 4.30pm–7.30pm. For 170 years this tiny shop has occupied the courtyard of Palazzo del Barone di Stefano, selling an irresistible range of Sicilian specialities, such as pizza, *panzerotti* (fried pastries) and *arancini*. Not to be missed!

🍽️ **Santandrea** – Piazza Sant'Andrea 4. ☎091 33 49 99. Wood and stone in view in a welcoming oasis in the chaotic, colourful Vucciria market; the traditional regional dishes reflect the style of the locality.

🍽️ **Pizzeria Tonnara Florio** – Discesa Tonnara 4, Arenella/Parco della Favorita district. ☎392 11 88 613. www.tonnaraflorio.com. Closed Mon evening in winter. A pretty Art Nouveau building with a pleasant garden. Formerly a *tonnara* (tuna fishing centre), it contains a pizzeria and a nightclub.

🍽️ **Trattoria da Totò** – Via Coltellieri 5. ☎333 31 57 558 (mobile). Three generations of this fishing family have offered delicious fresh fish dishes in the Vucciria quarter.

🍽️ **Ai Vecchietti di Minchiapititto** – Piazza San Oliva 10. ☎091 58 56 06. www.aivecchiettidiminchiapititto.com. This restaurant with a separate pizzeria is housed in a 19C building. Atmospheric, rustic-style dining rooms have vaulted ceilings and brick arches. Or in summer dine outside in a small garden.

🍽️ **Al Canceletto** – Via Ottavio d'Aragona 34. ☎091 58 30 69. Closed Sun. This family trattoria is humble, but serves ultra-fresh cuisine. Buffet of *antipasti*, homemade pasta and delicious meat dishes. Quality food at good prices.

🍽️ **Casa del Brodo** – Corso Vittorio Emanuele 175. ☎091 32 16 55. www.casadelbrodo.it. Closed Sun in summer and Tue in winter. Founded in 1890, the ambience is elegant. A copious *antipasti* buffet. Excellent Sicilian cuisine focuses on fish specialities. Good value.

🍽️ **Cavalieri di Malta** – Vicolo Pantelleria 30. ☎091 58 65 95. Closed Wed. This *osteria* behind San Domenico offers wines with a generous plate, or specialities such as stuffed squid and spaghetti with sea urchins.

🍽️ **Il Mirto e la Rosa** – Via Principe di Granatelli 30. ☎091 32 43 53. www.ilmirtoelarosa.com. Closed Sun. Primarily vegetarian dishes, such as *caponatina di melanzane* – a sweet and sour aubergine stew – served with pistachio couscous. Very welcoming.

🍽️ **La Cambusa** – Piazza Marina 16. ☎091 58 45 74. www.lacambusa.it. Closed Wed in winter. Overlooking Piazza Marina, this elegant, quiet restaurant specialises in fish dishes. Excellent *antipasti* buffet.

Segesta★★★

Splendidly situated against the hillside, its ochre colours in pleasant contrast with the vast expanse of green, the archaeological park is dominated by a fine Doric temple standing in an isolated site. Probably founded, like Erice, by the Elimi, Segesta soon became one of the main cities in the Mediterranean under Greek influence.

ARCHAEOLOGICAL SITE

Open 9am–7pm, winter to 5pm. 6€. A regular shuttle service operates to the theatre (1.50€). ℘0924 95 23 56. www.segestawelcome.com

Tempio★★★

The temple of Segesta stands alone, encircled by a deep ravine, in a landscape of receding horizons. The Doric building (430 BC), pure and graceful, is girt by a peristyle of 36 columns in golden-coloured limestone. The road

- **Michelin Map:** 565 N 20.
- **Info:** www.regione.sicilia.it/turismo.
- **Location:** Segesta is 35km/21.7mi southeast of Trapani.

leading up to the theatre *(2km/1.2mi; shuttle bus available)* affords a magnificent **view★★** of the temple.

Teatro★

This Hellenistic theatre (63m/207ft in diameter) is built into the rocky hillside. The tiers of seats are oriented towards the hills, behind which, to the right, is the Gulf of Castellammare.

Sanctuary of the Elymians

This site is only accessible by a hike uphill towards Contrado Magno. Now an overgrown and partially excavated area, it was once a site of some religious significance to the Elymians (c.6C BC).

Tempio

© Rndrpgqr/iStockphoto.com

View from Giardino del Balio

Erice★★★

Occupying a unique and beautiful setting★★★, this ancient Phoenician and Greek city presents two faces. During the hot summers, it is bright and sunny and the sun-drenched streets of the village, strategically located, offer splendid views★★ over the valley. In winter Erice is wreathed in mist and seems a place lost in time. In Antiquity this area was a religious centre famous for its temple consecrated to Astarte, then to Aphrodite and finally Venus, who was venerated by mariners of old.

▸ **Population:** 29 000
ⓒ **Michelin Map:** 565 M 19.
🏠 **Info:** Piazza della Loggia 3, 91016 Erice (TP).
    ☎0923 50 21 11.
    www.comune.erice.tp.it.
◉ **Location:** Erice, rising almost vertically (750m/2 461ft) above the sea, lies about 14km/9mi from Trapani, on the western side of the island.
🔎 **Don't Miss:** Views from Castello di Venere.
🕐 **Timing:** Allow a couple of hours.

SIGHTS

Castello di Venere

5€. ☎366 671 28 32. For times information: www.comune.erice.tp.it.
This castle, built by the Normans in the 12C, crowns an isolated rock on Monte Erice, on the site of the Temple of Venus (Venere). From here and the nearby gardens (Giardino del Balio) there are admirable **views★★**: in clear weather the Tunisian coast can be seen in the distance.

Chiesa Matrice★

This church was built in the 14C using stones quarried from the Temple of Venus. The porch was added in the 15C and flanked by the square-battlemented bell tower (13C).

ADDRESSES

🏨 STAY

🍴🍴🍴 **Azienda Agrituristica Tenuta Pizzolungo** – Contrada San Cusumano.

☎0923 56 37 10. www.pizzolungo.it. 10 apartments. A rustic and romantic 19C farmhouse surrounded by a luxuriant garden is a few metres from the sea. Apartments, of various sizes, each equipped with a kitchen.

🍴🍴🍴🍴 **Hotel Baglio Santacroce** – Contrada Ragosia (2km/1.2mi E of Valderice on the SS 187. ☎0923 89 11 11. www.bagliosantacroce.it. 67 rooms. ⬜. This 17C farmhouse is a delightful small hotel in a bucolic setting with magnificent views of the Golfo di Cornino. The small rooms have wood-beamed ceilings and tiled floors.

🍴 EAT

🍴🍴🍴 **Monte San Giuliano** – Vicolo San Rocco 7. ☎0923 86 95 95. www.monte sangiuliano.it. Booking recommended. This fine restaurant located in the heart of Erice specialises in local cuisine. Wide-ranging menu, meals served in pleasant, rustic dining rooms or under a pretty arbour in a cool inner courtyard.

© Sandro Bedessi/Fototeca ENIT

Trapani★

Situated within sight of the Egadi Islands, Trapani has windmills and a sheltered port, which is important to the salt trade.

SIGHTS
Santuario dell'Annunziata★

Open 7am–noon (public hols 1.30pm) and 4pm–7pm (8pm in summer). Donations welcome. ☎0923 53 91 84.
Built in the 14C, the church was remodelled and enlarged in the 17C. On the north side the **Cappella dei Marinai** (Renaissance Sailors' Chapel) is crowned with a dome. Inside, access to the **Cappella della Madonna★** is through a 16C Renaissance arch; the chapel contains the statue of the Virgin (14C) known as the **Madonna di Trapani** and attributed to Nino Pisano.

Museo Pepoli★

Open Mon–Sat 9am–1.30pm and 3pm–7.30pm, Sun and public hols 9am–12.30pm. 6€. ☎0923 55 32 69.
⊘ Poor lighting in the museum means that it is best to visit early in the day.
The Pepoli Museum is located in the former Carmelite convent which adjoins the Annunziata. The works include sculpture (by the Gagini) and paintings, such as the 15C Trapani polyptych, a **Pietà★** by Roberto di Oderisio.

Centro Storico★

The old town is built on the promontory, with the Villa Margherita to the east.

EXCURSIONS
Salt Flats

◗ 30km/18.6mi from Trapani to Marsala. Allow one day, including boat to Mozia.
The coastal road which leads from Trapani to **Marsala** is lined with salt flats (saline) and open **views★★**; the water is divided into a multicoloured grid by strips of land. In places there are windmills, a reminder of times gone by when they pumped water for the salt. The view is even more evocative in the summer when the rose-coloured

---

▸ **Population:** 68 000
⚙ **Michelin Map:** 565 M 19.
🈯 **Info:** Piazza Saturno. ☎0923 544 533. www.apt.trapani.it.
◗ **Location:** Trapani is at the westernmost point of the island. The main access roads are the A 29 and S 113.
◗ **Train:** Trapani (Palermo Palazzo Reale-Orleans 2hr 53 mins).
☻ **Don't Miss:** Museo del Sale, Isola di Mozia.
🕑 **Timing:** Allow half a day.
👪 **Kids:** The restored windmill near Mozia.

---

tint of the water is more intense (the colour changes as the saline content increases) and the shimmering pools of water inland are drying in the sun. At Nubia there is the small, but interesting **Museo del Sale**.
♿ Open daily 9.30am–7pm. Guided tours available (only italian, 40min). 2.50€. ☎0923 8670 61. www.museodelsale.it. Wind permitting, the windmill operates upon request. 3.50€. Saline Ettore and Infersa. www.salineettoreinfersa.com
👪 A restored **mill** can be visited not far from Mozia (◖see below).

Isola di Mozia★

◗ 14km/8.7mi S of Trapani.
Leave the car at the jetty; fishermen provide a ferry service to the island. This ancient Phoenician colony was founded in the 8C BC on one of the four islands of the **Laguna dello Stagnone**. Visitors can explore the ruins by following the path around the island (about 1hr 30min; counter-clockwise direction recommended). A small **museum** houses exhibits found on the island, including the magnificent **Ephebe of Mozia★★**, a noble figure of rather haughty bearing clothed in a long, pleated cloak which shows an obvious Greek influence.
♿ Access to the island and museum 9am–1.30pm, 2.30–6.30pm. 3€ ferry;

9€museum. ℘0923 71 25 98. www.
marsalaturismo.com.

Marsala

Marsala, the ancient *Lilybaeum* on Capo
Lilibeo, the westernmost point of the
island, owes its name to the Saracens,
who destroyed then rebuilt the city,
calling it Marsah el Ali (Port of Allah).
It is known for its sweet Marsala wine,
which an English merchant, John Wood-
house, rediscovered in the 18C. **Piazza
della Repubblica** is the hub of city life,
lined by the cathedral and Palazzo
Senatorio. A former wine cellar, near the
sea, now houses a museum, the **Museo
Archeologico di Baglio Anselmi** *(Via
Boeo)*: the exhibits include the wreck
of a **warship★** that fought in the Punic
War and was found off the coast near
Mozia. ⚐ Open Mon 9am–1.30pm, Tue–
Sun 9am–8pm. 4€. ℘0923 95 25 35.

Selinunte★★★

Selinus was founded in the mid-7C
BC by people from the east-coast
city of *Megara Hyblaea* and destroyed
twice, in 409 BC and 250 BC, by the
Carthaginians. The huge ruins of
its temples with their enormous
platforms are impressive.

⚐ **Michelin Map:** 565 O 20.
🛈 **Info:** www.selinunte.net.
▶ **Location:** Selinunte is
situated on the south coast.
The main access roads are
the S 115 and S 115d.

ARCHAEOLOGICAL SITE

⚐Open 9am–5pm. 6€. ℘0924 46 277.
Visitors to the site first reach an esplanade around which are grouped the
remains of three **temples**. The first to
come into view is **Temple E** (5C BC),
which was reconstructed in 1958. To
the right stands **Temple F**, completely
in ruins. The last of the three, **Temple G**
was one of the largest in the ancient
world. It was over 100m/330ft long;
its columns were built of blocks, each
weighing several tonnes.

Cross the depression, Gorgo Cot-
tone, to reach the **acropolis**. The site
is dominated by the partially reconstructed (1925) columns of **Temple
C** (6C BC). This, the earliest surviving
temple at Selinus (initiated early-6C
BC), was probably dedicated to Apollo
or Heracles. There are four more ruined
temples nearby. To the west, across
the River Modione are the remains of a
sanctuary to Demeter Malophoros (the
dispenser of pomegranates).

Temple E

Agrigento and La Valle dei Templi★★★

Agrigento, the Greek city of Akragas, is attractively set on a hillside facing the sea. The Greek poet Pindar referred to Agrigento as "man's finest town". It includes a medieval quarter on the upper slopes above the modern town, and impressive ancient ruins strung out along a ridge below, erroneously called the Valley of the Temples (a UNESCO World Heritage Site).

▶ **Population:** 55 000
🜨 **Michelin Map:** 565 P 22.
🛈 **Info:** Via Cesare Battisti 15.
  ☎0922 20 454.
  ☎0922 59 02 46.
  www.comune.agrigento.it.
▷ **Location:** Agrigento is linked to Palermo by the S 189 and the north coast of the island by the S 640 and A 19.
▷ **Train:** Agrigento Centrale (Palermo Centrale 2hr 5 mins).
👁 **Don't Miss:** Giardino della Kolymbetra, Tempio della Concordia and the fine exhibits at the Museo Archeologico Regionale.
🕐 **Timing:** Allow at least half a day for the Valley of the Temples.

👣WALKING TOUR

Tour: half a day. Archaeological site: Open daily 9am–7pm (the site often stays open until 11pm in summer). 10€. Museo Archeologico: Open Tue–Sat 9am–7pm, Sun–Mon and public hols 9am–1pm. 8€. 13.50€ combined ticket. ☎0922 62 16 11. www.parcovalledeitempli.it.

Valle dei Templi (Valley of the Temples)★★★

The monuments in the Valley of the Temples are grouped in two areas: the first includes the actual temples, the Giardino della Kolymbetra, the antiquaria and the paleo-Christian necropolises. The second comprises the archaeological museum, the Chiesa di San Nicola, the Oratorio di Falaride and the Greco-Roman quarter. To walk from one area to the other, visitors may follow either the very busy main road or the quiet road within the park. Car parks are located near to the Temple of Zeus and the archaeological museum.
Of the many temples from the late-6C to the late-5C BC, parts of nine are still visible. The destruction of the temples was long thought to have been caused by earthquakes but is now also attributed to the anti-pagan activities of the early Christians. Only the Temple of Concord was spared when it became a church in the late-6C AD.

Tempio di Zeus Olimpio★

Had this now-ruined temple been completed, its size (113m/371ft long by 56m/184ft wide) would have made it one of the largest in the ancient world. The entablature of the Temple of Olympian Zeus (Roman Jupiter) was supported by 20m/66ft-tall columns, between which stood **telamones** (columns in the form of male figures). One of these colossal statues, standing 7.5m/25ft high, has been reconstructed and is now on view in the Archaeological Museum (👁see next page).

Tempio dei Dioscuri★★

Of the hexastyle temple of Castor and Pollux, only four columns supporting part of the entablature remain.
Alongside is a **sacred area** dedicated to Demeter and Persephone: there are two sacrificial altars, one with a holy well.

Giardino della Kolymbetra★

Open daily Apr–May 10am–6pm; Jun–Sept 10am–7pm; Feb–Nov 10am–2pm, Mar–Oct 10am–5pm. 4€. ☎335 12 29 042 (mobile).
This 5ha/12-acre "basin" has developed over the centuries into a fertile grove

of fruit and citrus trees. After years of neglect, the Kolymbetra, now restored and managed by the FAI, is planted out with olive trees, prickly pear, poplar, willow, mulberry, orange, lemon and mandarin trees. Paths laid out in the garden make this a pleasant area for a stroll.

▶ Return to the square and take Via dei Templi.

Tempio di Eracle★★
Dating from the late-6C, the Temple of Hercules is probably the oldest of the Agrigento temples and is built in the ancient Doric style. Eight of its columns have been raised.
South of the temple can be seen the mistakenly named **Tomba di Terone**. The monument was not the tomb of the tyrant Theron; in fact, it honours Roman soldiers killed during the Second Punic War. Made of tufa, it is slightly pyramidal and probably once had a pointed roof. The high base supports a second order with false doors and Ionic columns at the corners. Continuing along the path, observe the cartwheel **ruts**, eroded deep into the mud by water.

Tempio della Concordia★★★
The Temple of Concord is the most massive, majestic and best preserved of the Doric temples in Sicily. It has a peristyle of 34 tufa limestone columns, the original stucco facing having disappeared. The internal arrangement dates from the Christian period (mid-5C).

Tempio di Hera Lacinia★★
Set on the edge of the ridge, this temple, dedicated to Hera (Roman Juno), conserves part of its colonnade. On the east side there is a sacrificial altar and behind the temple an ancient cistern. From the Antiquarium di Casa Pace a small road leads up the Collina di San Nicola, crossing fields of prickly pears, pistachio and olive trees.

▶ As you approach the top of the hill, continue straight on. This path leads to the Greco-Roman Quarter.

©Diego Barucco/Dreamstime.com

Tempio della Concordia

The **Greco-Roman quarter★** is an extensive urban complex of ruined houses, some adorned with mosaics.

Chiesa di San Nicola
Variable hours. Donations welcome.
This church contains a magnificent Roman **sarcophagus★** on which the death of Phaedra is portrayed. From the terrace there is a fine temple **view★**.

Oratorio di Falaride
Legend has it that the palace of Phalaris, the first tyrant of Agrigento, was in the vicinity. The building is in fact a Roman-Hellenistic temple transformed during the Norman period.

Tyrants, Philosophers and Writers

The town was founded in 580 BC by people from Gela who originated from Rhodes. Of the governing "tyrants", the cruellest in the 6C was Phalaris, while Theron (5C) was renowned as a great builder. The 5C philosopher Empedocles was a native of Agrigento, as was Luigi Pirandello (1867–1936), winner of the Nobel Prize for Literature in 1934 and innovator in modern Italian drama (*Six Characters in Search of an Author*), whose plays were woven around the themes of incomprehension and absurdity.

Museo Archeologico Regionale★★

The museum contains a fine collection of **Greek vases**★ including the Dionysius Cup and the Perseus and Andromeda Cup on a white background. One room is devoted to the **telamones**★ from the Temple of Zeus. There are also the 5C BC marble statue of a youth, the **Ephebe of Agrigento**★★ *(Room 10)* and the **Gela Cup**★★ *(Room 15)*, which illustrates a centaur and the battle between the Greeks and the Amazons.

TOWN CENTRE

The centre of the town is concentrated around the **Piazzale Aldo Moro**, which leads into the **Via Atenea**, a busy shopping street. On the way back down to Piazzale Aldo Moro visit a small abbey church, **Abbaziale di Santo Spirito**★, which has four **high reliefs**★ in stucco attributed to Giacomo Serpotta.

Casa di Pirandello

6km/3.7mi W by the Porto Empedocle road, S 115. Turn left shortly after the Morandi viaduct. ♿ Open daily 9am–7pm. 4€. ☎0922 51 18 26. www.lavalledeitempli.it.

This small house was the birthplace of Luigi Pirandello, buried under a nearby pine tree. The rooms contain material pertaining to the writer and Marta Abba, the actress to whom he became close late in his life.

Enna★

Situated on a beautiful plateau in the centre of the island, Enna is called the "lookout of Sicily" and is the highest capital of an Italian province at 948m/3 110ft. One of the oldest towns on the island, it was founded by the Sicani, long before the Greeks. The town's main attractions are the 13C Lombard Castle, built by Frederick II, and a plethora of churches.

▸ **Population:** 28 424
◔ **Michelin Map:** 565 O 24.
🛈 **Info:** Via Roma 413. ☎0935 50 23 62. www.provincia.enna.it.
▶ **Location:** At the centre of the island, Enna rises to 942m/3 091ft. The main access road is the A 19.
👁 **Don't Miss:** The view from the Castello di Lombardia.
🕐 **Timing:** Allow half a day.

VISIT

Castello di Lombardia★★

Open daily 9am–dusk.
This medieval castle has 6 of its original 20 towers. From the top of the tallest there is an exceptional **panorama**★★★ of the hilltop village of Calascibetta, Mount Etna and most of the Sicilian mountain peaks. Beyond the castle, the **belvedere**, once the site of a temple to Demeter, offers a fine **view**★ of Calascibetta and of Enna itself.

Duomo

Open daily 8am–1pm and 4–7pm.
The cathedral was rebuilt in the Baroque style in the 16C and 17C and has a carved coffered **ceiling**★ with winged creatures at the end of each beam.

Torre di Federico★

At the far end of Via Roma opposite the castle.
Because of the town's strategic, defensive function, in the past Enna could have been described as the city of towers.

Caltagirone★

Caltagirone is famous for its pottery, which is displayed in profusion in the local shops and on bridges, balustrades, balconies (notably 18C Casa Ventimiglia), and the façades of palaces lining Via Roma in the town centre.

▶ **Population:** 37 475
🕐 **Michelin Map:** 565 P 25.
🖪 **Info:** Via Duomo 15.
    𝒫 335 579 59 45.
    www.comune.caltagirone.ct.it.
▶ **Location:** Caltagirone lies just off the S 417, which links Catania with Gela.
🕅 **Don't Miss:** A history of local ceramics at the Museo della Ceramica.
🕓 **Timing:** Allow a couple of hours.

SIGHTS

Santa Scala di Santa Maria del Monte★

The stairway built in the 17C to join the old and new town has 142 steps in volcanic stone; the risers are decorated with polychrome ceramic tiles with geometric, floral and other decorative motifs.

Villa Comunale★

This beautiful garden was designed in the mid-19C by Basile as an English garden. The side flanking Via Roma is bounded by a balustrade adorned with majolica vases. On an esplanade stands the delightful Arab-style **palchetto della musica** (bandstand) decorated with ceramics.

Museo della Ceramica

Via Roma, Teatrino del Bonaiuto. ♿Open 9am–6.30pm. 4€. 𝒫 0933 58 418.
The **Teatrino**, a curious little 18C theatre decorated with ceramics, houses an interesting museum that traces the history of local ceramics from prehistory to the early 20C. There is a fine 5C **cup★** depicting a potter at his wheel.

Villa Romana del Casale★★★

This immense 3C or 4C Roman villa (3 500sq m/37 680sq ft) probably belonged to some dignitary and is important for its mosaic pavements, which cover almost the entire floor space. These picturesque mosaics, in a wide range of colours, were probably the work of African craftsmen and portray scenes from mythology, daily life, and events such as hunts or circus games. UNESCO declared the Villa Romana del Casale a World Heritage Site in 1997.

🕐 **Michelin Map:** 565 O 25.
🖪 **Info:** Piazza Amerina (EN).
    𝒫 0935 68 00 36.
    www.villaromanadelcasale.it.
▶ **Location:** The villa is situated near Piazza Armerina, off the S 117b.
🕅 **Don't Miss:** The mosaics in the Sala della Piccola Caccia, Ambulacro della Grande Caccia and the *triclinium*.

VISIT

Villa Mosaics★★★

Open summer 9am–6pm, winter to 4pm. 10€. Free the first Sun of the month.

𝒫 0935 68 00 36.
www.villaromanadelcasale.it.
Noteworthy mosaics portray **cupids ★★** fishing or playing with dolphins, a hunting scene in the **Sala della Piccola Caccia★★★**, the capturing and selling of wild animals for circus use in the **Ambulacro della Grande Caccia★★★**

Roman mosaics

and sports practised by young girls who appear to be wearing modern swim-wear in the **Sala delle Dieci Ragazze★★**. Finally, the interesting mosaics of the **triclinium★★★** portray the **Labours of Hercules**.

EXCURSION
Piazza Armerina★
⬤ 5km/3mi SW.
The **medieval centre★** of Piazza Armerina huddles near its Baroque **cathedral** on the green slopes of a valley.

Siracusa★★★

Syracuse

Syracuse is superbly situated at the head of a beautiful bay. It was one of Sicily's, if not *Magna Graecia's*, most prestigious cities and at the height of its splendour rivalled Athens.

A BIT OF HISTORY
Greek Colony
Syracuse was colonised in the mid-8C BC by Greeks from Corinth who settled on the island of Ortigia. It soon fell under the yoke of the tyrants, and it developed and prospered. In the 5C–4C BC the town had 300 000 inhabitants. Captured by the Romans during the Second Punic War (212 BC), it was occupied by the barbarians, Byzantines (6C), Arabs (9C) and Normans.

Tyrants and Intellectuals
In the Greek world, dictators called tyrants (from the Greek word *turannos*) exercised unlimited power over certain cities, in particular Syracuse. Already in 485 BC **Gelon**, the tyrant of Gela, had become master of Syracuse. His brother **Hiero**, an altogether more unpleasant person, nonetheless patronised poets and welcomed to his court **Pindar** and **Æschylus**, who died in Gela in 456.

▶ **Population:** 124 083
♿ **Michelin Map:** 565 P 27.
🛈 **Info:** Via Roma 31, Siracusa.
   ✆ 800 055 500.
   www.siracusaturismo.net.
⬤ **Location:** Syracuse is situated on the east coast, overlooking the Ionian Sea. The main access roads are the S 114 (from Catania) and the S 115 (from the south).
⬤ **Train:** Siracusa Centrale (Catania Centrale 1hr 10mins).
👁 **Don't Miss:** Ortygia and the Museo Archeologico Regionale Paolo Orsi.
👥 **Kids:** Testing the echoes at the Orecchio di Dionisio.

Dionysius the Elder (405–367 BC) was the most famous but even he lived in constant fear. He had a sword suspended by a horsehair above the head of Damocles, a jealous courtier, to demonstrate to him the many dangers which threatened a ruler. He rarely left the safety of his castle on Ortigia, wore a shirt of mail under his clothing and changed his room every night. He had Plato expelled from the city when he came to study the political habits of the people under his dictatorship.

Archimedes, the famous geometrician born at Syracuse in 287 BC, was so absent-minded that he would forget to eat and drink. In his bath he discovered his famous principle: any body immersed in water loses weight equivalent to that of the water it displaces. Delighted, he jumped out of the bath and ran naked through the streets shouting "Eureka!" (I have found it!). When defending Syracuse against the Romans, Archimedes devised a system of mirrors and lenses to set fire to the enemy fleet by focusing the Sun's rays. But when the Romans entered the town by surprise, Archimedes, deep in his calculations, did not hear them, and a Roman soldier ran him through.

PARCO ARCHEOLOGICO DELLA NEAPOLIS★★★

Access by Via Rizzo or Via Paradiso. 2hrs on foot. &. Open daily 9am–1 hour before dusk. 10€. ℘0931 66 206. www.siracusaturismo.net.

Teatro Greco★★★

The Greek theatre dates from the 5C BC and is one of the largest of the ancient world. The tiers of seats are hewn out of the rock. The first performance of *The Persians* by Æschylus was held here. Behind the theatre stretches the road of the tombs, **Via dei Sepolcri**.

Latomia del Paradiso★★

This former quarry, now an orange grove, dates from ancient times. Part of its roof fell in during the 1693 earthquake.
The **Orecchio di Dionisio★★★** (Ear of Dionysius) is an artificial grotto in the form of an earlobe. The grotto was named in 1608 by Caravaggio as a reminder of the legend recounting how the exceptional echo enabled the tyrant Dionysius to overhear the talk of the prisoners he confined below.
👥 Children will love testing the echo in the Orecchio di Dionisio. The park tour concludes with the **Ara di Ierone II**, a rock-hewn altar (c.200m/656ft long) used for public sacrifices.

Ara di Ierone II

This enormous altar, 200m/650ft partly carved out of the rock, was commissioned by the tyrant Hieron II in the 3C BC for public sacrifices. Originally, a large rectangular area may have stretched out in front, probably with a portico and a central pool.

Piazza Duomo★★

The attractive irregular square precedes the cathedral, curving at one end to accommodate its majestic front elevation. The open space becomes especially dramatic when the cathedral façade is caught by the setting sun or floodlit after nightfall. The other fine Baroque buildings enclosing the square include the **Palazzo Beneventano del Bosco**, which conceals a lovely courtyard, and opposite, **Palazzo del Senato**, whose inner courtyard displays an 18C senator's carriage; at the far end stands the Church of **Santa Lucia**.
Next to Santa Lucia, the former convent and Church of Montevergini houses the Galleria Civica di Arte Contemporanea.

Tomba di Archimede

Visible from the outside from the corner of Via Romagnoli and Via Teracati.
At the eastern end of Latomia Intagliatella is the **Grotticelli Necropolis**. Among the cavities hollowed out of the rock, one is ornamented with Doric columns *(now badly damaged)*, pediment and tympanum. This "Tomb of Archimedes" actually conceals a Roman *columbarium* (a chamber lined with niches for funerary urns).

MUSEO ARCHEOLOGICO REGIONALE★★

Viale Teocrito 66. &. Open Tue–Sat 9am–6pm, Sun and public hols 9am–1pm. 8€. ℘0931 48 95 14. www.siracusaturismo.net
The **Villa Landolina** museum features local geology and early fauna, and Greek colonisation (mid-8C BC onwards); a (marble *kouros*)and a statue of the **goddess-mother★**, and small replicas of the great sanctuaries of Ortigia. The **Venus Anadiomede★**,

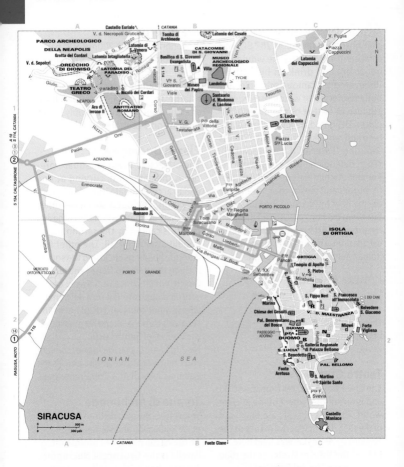

SIRACUSA

a Roman copy of a Greek statue by Praxiteles, is on temporary display. Part is devoted to the various Syracusan colonies.

Ortigia

© S. Bedessi /FOTOTECA ENIT

CATACOMBE DI SAN GIOVANNI★★

Via San Giovanni alle Catacombe 1. Open Tue–Sun 9.30am–12.30pm and 2.30–5.30pm. Only guided tours. 8€. ℘0931 64 694. www.siracusaturismo.net. After the catacombs in Rome, these are the finest examples in Italy. Big enough to hold up to seven tombs, they consist of a main gallery off which branch galleries ending in rotundas.

ORTIGIA (ORTYGIA)★★★

Visit: 45min. The island of Ortigia, the most ancient area of settlement, is linked to the mainland by the Ponte Nuovo. Ortigia boasts numerous medieval and Baroque palaces, the latter mainly in **Via della**

Maestranza★. The **Piazza Duomo★** is particularly attractive, lined by palaces adorned with wrought-iron balconies and the monumental façade of the **Duomo★**. It was built in the 7C on the foundations of a temple dedicated to Athena, some columns of which were reused in the Christian building.

Fonte Arethusa★

This is the legendary cradle of the city. The nymph Arethusa, pursued by the river-god Alpheus, took refuge on the island of Ortigia, where she was changed into a spring (*fonte*) by Artemis. The **Passaggio Adorno**, a favourite walk for the Syracusans, starts below.

Galleria Regionale di Palazzo Bellomo★

Via Capodieci 14. Open Tue–Sat 9am–7pm and the first Sun of the month. 8€. ℘0931 69 511. www.siracusaturismo.net. Housed in a beautiful 13C palace, the art gallery has an admirable **Annunciation★** (damaged) by Antonello da Messina and The **Burial of St Lucy★**, Siracusa's patron saint, by Caravaggio.Other works by goldsmiths, Sicilian cribs, liturgical objects and furniture.

EXCURSIONS
Fiume Ciane★★

▶ Traversa Testa Pisima. 8km/5mi SE. Walk or reserve boat excursions. ℘0931 65201, 0931 464255, or 0931 462452. www.siracusaturismo.net
The River Ciane, which almost merges with the River Anapo, is the main link with the internal area of Pantalica. Its mouth is a favourite starting point for **boat trips★★**. A splendid view of the Grand Harbour of Siracusa opens out. The boat continues through lush vegetation, enters a narrow gorge and emerges in a papyrus grove. Here, in the myth Ovid tells (*Metamorphoses: The Rape of Proserpine*), Cyane the water nymph tried to obstruct Pluto from abducting Persephone and was transformed into a spring.

Castello Eurialo★

9km/5.6mi NW along Via Epipoli, in the Belvedere district. Open daily summer 9am–6.30pm, winter closing varies. 4€. ℘0931 71 17 73. www.siracusaturismo.net.
This was one of the greatest fortresses of the Greek period; it was built by Dionysius the Elder. Fine **panorama★**.

ADDRESSES

🛏 STAY
🍽🍽 **Agriturismo La Perciata** – Via Spinagallo 77, 14km/8.7mi SW of Siracusa on P 14 (from Maremonti, head to Canicattini, then take the turn-off to Floridia). ℘0931 71 73 66. www.perciata.it. 11 rooms, 3 villas. 🚗. Restaurant 🍽🍽. Mediterranean farm holiday stay offers tennis, horse riding and massage.

🍽🍽 **B&B Dolce Casa** – Via Lido Sacramento 4, loc. Isola (S 115 towards Noto, then turn left to loc. Isola). ℘0931 72 11 35. www.bbdolcecasa.it. 10 rooms. 🚗. Situated halfway between Siracusa and the sea, this friendly B&B has light, spacious rooms and a beautiful garden.

🍽🍽🍽 **Albergo Domus Mariae** – Via Vittorio Veneto 76, Siracusa. ℘0931 24 854. www.sistemia.it/domusmariae 16 rooms. Elegant rooms and terrace with ocean views. Run by Ursuline nuns.

🍴 EAT
🍽🍽 **Castello Fiorentino** – Via del Crocifisso 6, Ortigia. ℘0931 21 097. Closed Mon. A popular noisy trattoria-pizzeria with a large, slightly down-at-heel dining room.

🍽🍽🍽 **Darsena da Jannuzzo** – Riva Garibaldi 6, Ortigia. ℘0931 61 522. Closed Mon. Simple but delicious seafood to enjoy in dining room or on the veranda, with its view of the canal.

FESTIVAL
Festa di Santa Lucia – The festival of the patron saint of Siracusa, St Lucy, is celebrated on 13 December.

Noto★★

Noto, dating from the time of the Siculi, was destroyed by the earthquake of 1693. It was rebuilt on a new site 10km/6.2mi from the original town. Lining the streets, laid out on a grid plan, are palaces and churches in local white limestone. Several Sicilian architects worked on this project, including Rosario Gagliardi.

▶ **Population:** 22 971
◐ **Michelin Map:** 565 Q 27.
▯ **Info:** Via Gioberti 13, 96017 Noto (SR). ℘0931 83 65 03. www.pronoto.it. www.regione.sicilia.it/ turismo.
◖ **Location:** Noto is situated in the south of the island. The main access road is the S 115.
◉ **Don't Miss:** The Baroque centre.
◷ **Timing:** Allow two hours.

THE BAROQUE CENTRE★★

The hub of the town is **Corso Vittorio Emanuele**, which widens into three squares overlooked by the monumental façades of churches designed in an imposing but flexible Baroque style: **San Francesco all'Immacolata** and the **cathedral★★** (the cupola and much of the central nave collapsed in 1996) in the attractive **Piazza Municipio★**, and **San Domenico★**. To the right of San Domenico is **Via Corrado Nicolaci★**, a gently sloping street which offers an enchanting vista with the church of Montevergine as focal point. It is lined with palaces sporting splendid balconies; the most notable is **Palazzo Nicolaci di Villadorata** with exuberantly fanciful balconies★★★.

Ragusa★★

Ragusa, partly rebuilt following the 1693 earthquake, boasts a splendid setting on a plateau between deep ravines. The modern town lies to the west while the old town, Ragusa Ibla, clusters on an outlying hill, Monti Iblei, to the east. The Syracuse road offers magnificent views★★ of the old town.

▶ **Population:** 72 755
◐ **Michelin Map:** 565 Q 26.
▯ **Info:** Piazza San Giovanni, 97100 Ragusa Ibla. ℘0932 68 47 80. www.comune. ragusa.gov.it.
◖ **Location:** Ragusa is situated at the southernmost point of the island. The main access road is the S 115.
◉ **Don't Miss:** A walk in Ragusa Ibla and a visit to pretty Modica.
◷ **Timing:** Allow a day, or two days including the surrounding region.

SIGHTS
Ragusa Ibla★★

The medieval area is a maze of streets, but much of the old town was rebuilt in the Baroque style. The hub of the town is Piazza del Duomo, where the elegant Baroque church of **San Giorgio★★** stands. The church was designed by Rosario Gagliardi, who also worked in Noto.
The nearby church of **San Giuseppe★** shares certain similarities with San Giorgio and may be by the same architect.

Città Nuova

The new town is laid out in a grid pattern around the 18C cathedral of **San Giovanni**, which is fronted by a wide terrace. Not far away, the **Museo Archeologico Ibleo** (Palazzo Mediterraneo, Via Natalelli) contains the finds from excavations undertaken locally, notably from the ancient Greek city of *Camarina*. Open 9am–6.30pm, closed Sun and public hols. ℰ0932 62 29 63.

EXCURSION
Modica★
◐ 15km/9.3mi S.

This village, known for its Mexican-style chocolate, situated in a narrow valley, has retained many of its magnificent Baroque buildings, the most impressive of which is the majestic church of **San Giorgio**, preceded by a long flight of stairs.

Catania★★

Catania is a busy seaport and industrial town that has developed considerably in recent years, despite being destroyed several times by the eruptions of Mount Etna. This fine city has wide, regular streets overlooked by numerous Baroque buildings by the architect Vaccarini, who rebuilt Catania after the 1693 earthquake. Natives of the town include the musician Vicenzo Bellini (1801–35), composer of the opera *Norma*, and the novelist Giovanni Verga.

SIGHTS
Piazza del Duomo★
This square is the centre of town and is surrounded by a Baroque ensemble designed by Vaccarini which includes the **Fontana dell'Elefante** (Elephant Fountain) dating from 1735, the **Palazzo Senatorio or degli Elefanti** (town hall) with its well-balanced façade, and the **Duomo★** (cathedral) dedicated to St Agatha, the town's patron saint.

The cathedral, built at the end of the 11C by the Norman, Roger I, was remodelled after the 1693 earthquake and has an elegant **façade★** by Vaccarini. To the left of the cathedral, the beautiful abbey church **Badia di Sant'Agata★** contributes to the harmony of the square. Not far from here, in Via Museo Biscari, stands **Palazzo Biscari**, one of the most beautiful examples of civil architecture in the city. The , , 95121 Cataniasouth side of the mansion has a decorated **façade★★** with figures, cherubs and scrolls.

▶ **Population:** 296 469
◉ **Michelin Map:** 565 O 27.
▤ **Info:** Minoriti Palace, Via Etnea 63/65, 95121 Catania. ℰ095 40 14 070. www.turismo.provincia.ct.it.
◐ **Location:** Catania is situated on the east coast, overlooking the Ionian Sea. The main access roads are the A 18 (from Messina), A 19 (from Enna) and S 114, which links the town with Syracuse.
◐ **Train:** Catania Centrale.
◉ **Don't Miss:** The elegant Piazza del Duomo and Palazzo Biscaria and Castello Ursino.
◔ **Timing:** Catania gets very hot in summer, with searing temperatures. Explore early in the day if possible.
▲▲ **Kids:** The Circumetnea railway that circles Mount Etna from Catania.

Via Etnea★
Catania's best shops and boutiques flank this 3km/1.8mi thoroughfare, which runs through Piazza del Duomo, Piazza dell'Università and Piazza Stesicoro, before arriving in front of Villa Bellini, Catania's flower-filled public gardens.

Quartiere Occidentale
This district to the west of the town runs through Via Vittorio Emanuele II, along which the old theatre, **Teatro**

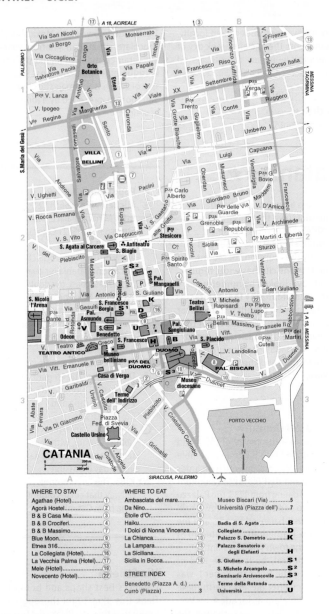

CATANIA

WHERE TO STAY	WHERE TO EAT	
Agathae (Hotel)................①	Ambasciata del mare..............①	Museo Biscari (Via) 5
Agorà Hostel...................②	Da Nino..............................④	Università (Piazza dell') 7
B & B Casa Mia.................③	Étoile d'Or..........................⑤	
B & B Crociferi.................④	Haiku.................................⑦	Badia di S. Agata ....B
B & B Massimo.................⑦	I Dolci di Nonna Vincenza...⑧	Collegiata ....D
Blue Moon.......................⑨	La Chianca.........................⑩	Palazzo S. Demetrio ....K
Etnea 316........................⑬	La Lampara........................⑬	Palazzo Senatorio o
La Collegiata (Hotel).........⑯	La Siciliana.........................⑯	degli Elefanti ....H
La Vecchia Palma (Hotel)....⑰	Sicilia in Bocca....................⑱	S. Giuliano ....S¹
Mele (Hotel).....................⑲		S. Michele Arcangelo ....S²
Novecento (Hotel)............㉒	STREET INDEX	Seminario Arcivescovile ......S³
	Benedetto (Piazza A. d.) 1	Terme della Rotonda V
	Currò (Piazza) 3	Università ....U

Antico, can be seen. It is crossed by **Via Crociferi★**, one of the best examples of Baroque architecture in Catania.

Castello Ursino

𝄢 095 34 58 30.

This bare, grim castle, fortified by four towers, was built in the 13C by the Emperor Frederick II of Hohenstaufen.

EXCURSION
Acireale★

▶ 17km/10.6mi N.

The route passes through **Aci Castello**, with its **castle★** built from black volcanic rock, and **Aci Trezza**, a small fishing village. Offshore, the **Faraglioni dei Ciclopia** (Cyclops' Reefs) emerge from the sea. These are supposed to be the rocks hurled by the Cyclops Polyphemus after Ulysses had blinded him by thrusting a blazing stake into his single eye. The road leads to **Acireale**, a modern town with numerous Baroque buildings which include those of the **Piazza del Duomo★** with the Basilica of St Peter and St Paul and the town hall, as well as the church of **San Sebastiano** with its harmonious **façade★** embellished with columns, niches and friezes.

ADDRESSES

🏠 STAY

🛏 **Agorà Hostel** – Piazza Currò 6. 📞095 72 33 010. www.agorahostel.com. 🛏 🍴. This reasonably priced hostel is situated in a 19C building fronting an old square close to the fish market. It offers two doubles, rooms with bunk beds and a number of communal areas.

🛏 **B&B Massimo** – Via Etnea 290. 📞095 31 13 43. www.massimobedandbreakfast.it. 🛏 6 rooms. 🍴. Opposite Villa Bellini, this small, charming guesthouse is well kept and welcoming. Plain, spacious, peaceful rooms, with a few parking spaces in the courtyard.

🛏 **Blue Moon** – Via Collegiata 11. 📞095 327 787.www.bluemooncatania.com. 🛏 6 rooms 🍴. A very central place, where you will be welcomed with a smile. Choose between three rooms with a shared shower on the landing, or three other more expensive but brand new rooms with private bathrooms and air conditioning.

🛏 **Hotel Mele** – Via Leonardi 24. 📞095 31 22 58. www.hotelmele.it. 🛏 8 rooms. 🍴. You have to pass the entrance to a goth/punk pub to access this modest *pensione* on the first floor run by a friendly mamma. The place is clean and very floral, if a little decrepit. Only one room has a private shower; the rest share bathrooms. Noisy weekend evenings.

🛏🛏 **B&B Crociferi** – Via Crociferi 81. 📞095 71 52 266. www.bbcrociferi.it. 3 rooms. 🍴. Huge, bright rooms in a very attractive 18C palazzo. One of them, which can sleep four, has a remarkable painted Art Nouveau

ceiling. Two others enjoy a charming view over Piazza San Baggio. Free transfer from the airport if you stay more than two nights.

🛏🛏 **Duomo Bed & Breakfast** – Via Etnea 4, Porta Uzeda, 95124 Catania. 📞095 09 36 454. www.duomobb.com 5 rooms. 🍴. Set inside the historical Porta Uzeda monument, Duomo Bed & Breakfast offers accommodation in Catania. Certain rooms include charming views of the garden or city. Piazza Duomo is a few steps from B&B, while Catania Cathedral is 100 metres away.

🛏🛏 **Etnea 316** – Via Etnea 316. 📞095 25 03 076. www.hoteletnea316catania.com. 12 rooms. 🍴. You will find a warm welcome and honest prices at this hotel just opposite the Villa Bellini. The rooms are large, tastefully decorated and comfortable. Naturally, those facing the courtyard are quieter. A popular spot, so book well in advance. Parking on the square or side streets.

🛏🛏 **Hotel La Collegiata** – Via Vasta 10 (on the corner of Via Etnea). 📞095 31 52 56. www.lacollegiata.com. 🅿 12 rooms. 🍴. In the heart of the historic centre, this welcoming hotel offers small but pleasant rooms with slightly theatrical decor dominated by red velvet.

🛏🛏🛏 **Hotel Agathae** – Via Etnea 229. 📞095 25 00 436. www.hotelagathae.it. 15 rooms. 🍴. This recent three-star hotel takes advantage of its elegantly decorated Art Nouveau-style building, The rear faces the park of Villa Bellini; breakfast amid the greenery on the splendid terrace. Well equipped with high-tech electronics, lift, parking.

🛏🛏🛏 **Hotel Novecento** – Via Monsignore Ventimiglia 37. 📞095 31 04 88. www.hotelnovecentocatania.com. 17 rooms. 🍴. Not far from the station and the Teatro Massimo Bellini, this is a cosy, quiet, friendly hotel. The communal areas are inviting, and the rooms, although fairly small, all come with fitted carpets

🍴 EAT

Midday options include the city centre bars, which sell sandwiches and one-course lunches, and the trattorias near the fish market (behind Piazza Duomo).

😔 **I Dolci di Nonna Vincenza** – Piazza San Placido 7 (Palazzo Biscari). ☎095 71 51 844. www.dolcinonnavincenza.it. A deliciously array of Sicilian pastries and cakes, from a brioche to smear with granita (ice) to the Cassatelle (breasts) of St. Agatha, Catania's patron saint. Also, almond paste and liqueurs.

😔🍽 **Da Nino** – Via Biondi 19. ☎095 31 13 19. Closed Sun. The decor lacks warmth, but it's all about the food: regulars enjoy the tasty antipasti, fish of the day and ripe fruit for dessert.

😔🍽 **Étoile d'Or** – Via Dusmet 7/9. ☎095 34 01 35. Near the market, this very popular *tavola calda* cooks up a vast array of appetising dishes: stuffed aubergines, *arancini* (deep-fried balls of rice with meat), marinated pork chops, beef stew, spaghetti with clams.

😔🍽🍽 **Haiku** – Via Quintino Sella 28. ☎095 53 03 77. www.haiku-ct.it. Closed Mon dinner. This haven of peace and greenery in the city is well worth the walk! Tasty, generously portioned organic dishes that revisit the repertoire of Italian classics. Enjoy them under the fig trees in the large garden. Try the luscious pistachio tiramisu.

😔🍽🍽 **La Chianca** – Piazza Duca di Genova 21. ☎095 32 70 22. Closed Mon and lunch. A wine bar with a good reputation on a quiet little square with an inviting, trendy atmosphere. Good Sicilian wine list. Jazz musicians some evenings.

😔🍽🍽 **La Lampara** – Via Pasubio 49. ☎095 38 32 37. Closed Wed. A simple, family-run restaurant, where the son is the chef and the father serves. The cuisine here is traditional, based on fresh fish and seafood.

😔🍽🍽 **La Siciliana** – Viale Marco Polo 52a. ☎095 37 64 00. www.lasiciliana.it. Closed Sun evening, Mon and evenings of public hols. This renowned local restaurant is well worth a visit for its traditional Sicilian cuisine served in a rustic setting. The patio is superb to sit out on in summer.

😔🍽🍽 **Sicilia in Bocca** – Via Dusmet 35. ☎095 25 00 208. www.siciliainbocca.it. Closed Tue lunch. Nice, rustic dining room under a basalt stone vaulted ceiling, attracting a varied clientele, from families to young, artistic types. An eclectic menu combines traditional seafood cuisine with more inventive dishes according to the chef's mood.

😔🍽🍽🍽 **Ambasciata del mare** – Piazza del Duomo 6. ☎095 34 10 03. www.ambasciatadelmare.it. Closed Mon. "The" fish restaurant in Catania, located just by the market. People come in family groups to enjoy a delicious meal in refined surroundings.

Etna★★★

At 3 340m/10 958ft (although this varies with summit eruptions) Etna is the highest point in the island. An imposing sight that dominates the eastern side of Sicily, Etna remains snow-capped for most of the year. The volcano is still active and is the largest and one of the most famous in Europe. Etna was born of undersea eruptions that also formed the Plain of Catania, formerly covered by the sea.

A BIT OF GEOGRAPHY
In 1987 the Parco dell'Etna was created, covering an area of 59 000ha/145 790

🕭 **Michelin Map:** 565 N–O 26–27.

🗊 **Info:** Parco dell'Etna, Via del Convento 45, Monastero di San Nicolo La Rena, 90035 Nicolosi (CT). ☎095 82 11 11. www.parcoetna.it.

▶ **Location:** Etna dominates the Ionic coastline between Catania and Taormina.

👁 **Don't Miss:** An ascent of Mount Etna.

🕓 **Timing:** Allow a day.

👪 **Kids:** Older children will enjoy scaling a volcano.

The Giant Awakes

Etna's eruptions were frequent in ancient times: 135 are recorded. But the greatest disaster occurred in 1669, when the flow of lava reached the sea, largely devastating Catania as it passed. The worst eruptions in recent times occurred in 1910, when 23 new craters appeared, 1917, when a jet of lava squirted up to 800m/2 625ft above its base, and 1923, when the lava ejected remained hot 18 months after the eruption. Stirrings of Etna have been numerous. In 2001, on the southeast side, eruptions swept away the lifts and the funicular platform, threatening the Sapienza Refuge and the town of Nicolosi. Activity in that area was intense again in 2011-2012, with activity subsiding to moderate levels in 2013.

acres; in the centre of the park, the mountain has the appearance of a huge, black, distorted cone which can be seen from a distance of 250km/155mi.

On its lower slopes, which are extremely fertile, orange, mandarin, lemon and olive trees flourish as well as vines which produce the delicious Etna wines. Chestnut trees grow above the 500m/1 640ft level and give way higher up to oak, beech, birch and pine.

Above 2 100m/6 900ft is the barren zone, where only a few clumps of *Astralagus siculus* (a kind of vetch) will be seen scattered on the slopes of secondary craters, among the clinker and volcanic rock.

ASCENT OF THE VOLCANO★★★

By the south face from Catania via Nicolosi, or by the northeast face from Taormina via Linguaglossa. xAs the volcano may erupt at any time, tourist facilities (roads, paths, cablecars and refuge huts) may be closed, moved or withdrawn. Excursions may be cancelled in the case of bad weather (fog) or volcanic activity. The best time for the ascent is early morning. Wear warm clothing even in summer (anorak, thick pullover) and strong shoes (the stony terrain of the paths through the lava can cause injuries, particularly to ankles). Wear sunglasses to avoid the glare.

South Face

Depending on snow conditions, excursions take place all-year-round. Duration and cost depend upon the tour and include insurance and guide. For further information, contact Funivia dell'Etna, Piazzale Rifugio Sapienza, Nicolosi. ✆095 91 41 41. www.funiviaetna.com. For mountain treks on the south side, contact Gruppo Guide Alpine Etna Sud, Piazza V. Emanuele 43, Nicolosi. ✆095 79 14 755. www.etnaguide.com.

The ascent depends on the conditions on the volcano and stops close to the grandiose valley, Valle del Bove, which is hemmed in by walls of lava (1 200m/

Etna

3 900ft high) and pierced with potholes and crevasses belching smoke.

Northeast Face

May–Oct, 9am–4pm. Excursions leave from Piano Provenzana. Duration: approx. 2hr round trip. 60€ including alpine guide. STAR, Via Santangelo Fulci 40. ℘095 91 41 41 or 347 49 57 091. The road goes through Linguaglossa, a lovely pinewood, and the winter-sports resort of Villaggio Mareneve.

Messina

Despite having been destroyed numerous times throughout the centuries, including weathering a devastating earthquake in 1908, Messina – the ancient *Zancle* **of the Greeks – is today a thriving market town.**

SIGHTS

Museo Regionale★

North of the town at the end of the Viale della Libertà. &Open Tue–Sat, 9am–7pm, Sun and hols 9am–1pm. 8€. ℘090 36 12 92. www.regione.sicilia.it/beniculturali. The museum comprises painting, sculpture and decorative arts section. The painting section displays a **polyptych of St Gregory** (1473) by Antonello da Messina, a remarkable composition that

---

Antonello da Messina

Born in Messina in 1430, he studied in Naples where he was influenced by the then-popular Flemish art. Later, he was attracted by the innovations of Tuscan painting which emphasised volume and architectural details. His works show a complete mastery of his art: forms and colours, skilfully balanced, enhance an inner vision which greatly influenced the Venetian painters of the Renaissance, notably Carpaccio and Giovanni Bellini. Antonello died on his native island around 1479.

The surfaced road ends at Piano Provenzana (1 800m/5 900ft). There is a magnificent **view★★** from the area around the new observatory. The climb ends amid an extraordinary landscape of lava, which still smokes at times.

Circumetnea

This road runs around Etna, offering varied views of the volcano and passing through a number of interesting villages and vineyards.

▶ **Population:** 243 381
& **Michelin Map:** 565 M 28 (including town plan).
🛈 **Info:** Via Calabria, isol 301 bis, 98122 Messina. ℘090 67 42 36. www.comune.messina.it.
◐ **Location:** Messina overlooks the stretch of sea that separates Sicily from the mainland.
◐ **Train:** Messina Centrale (Taormina Giardini 44 mins).
◉ **Don't Miss:** The Museo Regionale and the Duomo.
◕ **Timing:** Allow half a day.

---

combines the Tuscan idiom with the earliest Flemish influences, a remarkable **Descent from the Cross** by the Flemish artist Colin van Coter (15C); and two Caravaggios, **Adoration of the Shepherds** and **Resurrection of Lazarus**, both painted towards the end of his life from 1608 to 1610. The **Berlina del Senato★** painted in 1742 is worthy of note.

Duomo

Open daily 7.30am–12.30pm and 4pm–8pm. ℘090 67 51 75.
To the left of the campanile (60m/197ft tall) is an **astronomical clock★** made in Strasbourg in 1933 and believed to be the world's largest. At noon daily the clock "comes alive" with a mechanical presentation of the moving parts and Ave Maria solemnly playing.

Santissima Annunziata dei Catalani

Take the Via Cesare Battisti from the south side of the cathedral.

The church was built in 1100 during the Norman reign and altered in the 13C; it takes its name from the Catalan merchants who owned it. The apse★ is characteristic of the composite Norman style, which blends Romanesque (small columns supporting blind arcades), Moorish (geometric motifs and polychrome stonework) and Byzantine (dome on a drum) influences.

EXCURSION
Tindari★

▶ 62km/38.5mi W.

The ancient Greek *Tyndaris*, founded in 396 BC, is perched on the cape of the same name. The **ruins** *(rovine)* are essentially those of the city **ramparts**, the **theatre** and the so-called **Basilica**, an arcaded Roman building. Open daily 9am–7pm. 6€. ✆0941 36 90 23. www.regione.sicilia.it.

Taormina★★★

Taormina stands in a wonderful site★★★ at an altitude of 250m/820ft and forms a balcony overlooking the sea and facing Etna. It is renowned for its peaceful atmosphere and its beautiful monuments and gardens. The nearby seaside resort of Giardini Naxos also hosts cultural events.

SIGHTS
Teatro Greco★★★

♿ Open daily 9am, closing time can vary. 10€. ✆0942 23 220. www.regione.sicilia.it/turismo. Performances www.taoarte.it.

The Greek theatre is 3C but was remodelled by the Romans who used it as an arena for their contests. The upper tiers afford an admirable view★★★ between the stage columns of the coastline and Etna, a remarkable backdrop.

Corso Umberto★

The main street of Taormina has three gateways: Porta Catania; Porta di Mezzo, with the Torre dell'Orologio (Clock Tower); and Porta Messina. The Piazza del Duomo hosts the Gothic **cathedral**. **Piazza 9 Aprile★** forms a terrace, which affords a splendid **panorama★★** of the gulf. Piazza Vittorio Emanuele was laid out on the site of the forum and is overlooked by the 15C **Palazzo Corvaja**.

▶ **Population:** 11 096

♿ **Michelin Map:** 565 N 27; town map in the Michelin Atlas Italy.

🗊 **Info:** Piazza Santa Caterina (Palazzo Corvaja), Taormina (ME). ✆0942 23 243. www.comune.taormina.me.it.

▶ **Location:** Taormina is situated on the east coast, overlooking the Ionion Sea. The main access road is the A 18.

▶ **Train:** Taormina Giardini (Catania Centrale 41 mins).

👁 **Don't Miss:** Teatro Greco and the waterfalls at Gole dell'Alcantara.

🕐 **Timing:** Allow a day.

Giardino di Villa Comunale★★

From these terraced public gardens there are views of the coast and sea.

EXCURSIONS
Castello di Tauro

▶ 4km/2.5mi NW by the Castelmola road, and then a road to the right. www.regione.sicilia.it/beniculturali. 1hr walk there and back. Avoid walking in the midday sun or at the height of summer.

The castle was built in the medieval period on the summit of Monte Tauro (390m/1 280ft), on the remains of the

Taormina, Teatro greco with Etna in the background

© Antonino Gitto/iStockphoto.com

former acropolis. There are splendid **views★★** of Taormina.

Castelmola★

◐ 5km/3mi NW.
This tiny village strategically located near Taormina enjoys a splendid **site★** and fine **views★** of Etna. The focus of the village is the Piazzetta del Duomo.

Gole dell'Alcantara★

◐ 17km/10.6mi W. Open daily 8am–7pm. 10-13€, plus rental of boots and overalls. ℘0942 98 50 10. www.golealcantara.it.
The volcanic walls of these gorges are formed by irregular geometrical shapes, turning the waterfalls that cascade down the rock into prisms of light.

ADDRESSES

🛏 STAY

⊜⊜ **B&B Villa Regina** – Punta San Giorgio, Castelmola, 5km/3mi from Taormina. ℘0942 28 228. www.villareginataormina.com. 12 rooms. ⌁. This simple guesthouse has a cool, shady garden and a delightful view of Taormina and the coast. Ideal for a peaceful break.

⊜⊜⊜ **Hotel Villa Sonia** – Via Porta Mola 9, Castelmola, 5km/3mi from Taormina. ℘0942 28 082. www.hotelvillasonia.com. Closed Nov–Mar. ♿. 44 rooms. ⌁. Situated at the charming village of Castelmola, this attractive villa

is tastefully decorated with period items and Sicilian handicrafts. Standard and luxury rooms, excellent standards of comfort and service. Exorbitant prices.

🍴 EAT

⊜ **Porta Messina** – Largo Giove Serapide 4. ℘0942 23 953. www.ristoranteportamessina.it. The list of pizzas in this friendly restaurant is endless, with some unusual options.

⊜⊜ **Al Grappolo d'Uva** – Via Bagnoli Croci 6/8. ℘0942 62 58 74. www.algrappoloduva.net. This little rustic wine bar has a few little tables, some made from barrels, for sampling wines from Etna and throughout Sicily. Prosciutto, antipasti, bruschetta, grilled vegetables.

⊜⊜⊜ **Al Saraceno** – Via Madonna della Rocca 18, Taormina. ℘0942 63 20 15. www.alsaraceno.it. Closed Mon, except Jun-Sept. The splendid view from the terrace extends to the Straits of Messina.

TAKING A BREAK

Bar San Giorgio – Piazza Sant'Antonio 1, 98030 Castelmola, 5km/3mi from Taormina. ℘0942 28 228. www.barsangiorgio.com. This early 20C traditional caffè has a wonderful location in quiet Piazza Sant'Antonio, with superb views of Taormina and the sea. Try the local *vino alla mandorla* (almond liqueur).

FESTIVAL

Festa del costume e del carretto siciliani – In April and May, this festival celebrates Sicilian carts and costume.

Cefalù★★

Cefalù is a small fishing town in a fine setting★★, hemmed in between the sea and a rocky promontory. It boasts a Romanesque cathedral.

DUOMO★★

Open Apr-Oct 8am–6pm, Nov–Mar 8am–1pm and 3.30am–5pm. ℘0921 92 20 21. www.cattedraledicefalu.com

Built of a golden-tinted stone that blends in with the cliff behind, this cathedral was erected to fulfil a vow made by the Norman King Roger II (12C), when in danger of shipwreck. The church (1131–1240) has well-marked Norman features in its tall main apse flanked by two slightly projecting smaller ones and abutted by the two square towers.

The portico was rebuilt in the 15C by a Lombard master. The timber ceiling of the two aisles and the transept galleries are also Norman. The columns are crowned with splendid **capitals★★** in the Sicilian-Norman style.

The presbytery is covered with beautiful **mosaics★★** on a gilded background, displaying a surprising variety of colour and forming an admirable expression of Byzantine art. Above is Christ Pantocrator (Ruler of All) with underneath, on three different levels, the Virgin with four archangels and the 12 Apostles. In the choir, the angels on the vaulting

▶ **Population:** 13 771
♿ **Michelin Map:** 565 M 24.
ℹ **Info:** Corso Ruggero 77, 900 15 Cefalù (PA). ℘0921 42 10 50. www.comune.cefalu.pa.it.
◑ **Location:** Cefalù is situated on the north coast, overlooking the Tyrrhenian Sea. The main access roads are the A 20 (from Palermo) and the S 113 (from Messina).
◑ **Train:** Cefalù (Palermo Centrale 52 mins).
◷ **Timing:** Allow two hours.

and the prophets on the side walls date from the 13C. Note the episcopal throne *(south side)* and the royal throne *(north side)*, both in marble and mosaic.

↪ It is worth visiting **Museo Mandralisca** (home of **Portrait of an Unknown Man★** by Antonello da Messina).

EXCURSIONS

The **Nebrodi Mountains★★** are home to Sicily's largest and most important woodland (50 000ha/123 500 acres) as well as shepherding highlands. The **Madonie National Park★★** has gentle rolling hills, rivers and a wild variety of flora and fauna. Both regions offer great driving tour and hiking possibilities.

Beach of Cefalù

Isole
Eolie★★★

Aeolian or Lipari Islands

The Aeolian Islands, also known as the Lipari Islands, are so called because the ancients thought Aeolus, the God of the Winds, lived there. The archipelago comprises seven main islands, Lipari, Vulcano, Stromboli, Salina, Filicudi, Alicudi and Panarea, all of exceptional interest for their volcanic nature, their beauty, their light and their climate. Deep, blue, warm, clear waters, ideal for underwater fishing, harbour interesting marine creatures including flying fish, swordfish, turtles, seahorses and hammerhead sharks. Boat trips provide good views of the beautiful indented coastlines and hidden coves and bays. The inhabitants of the islands fish, grow vines and quarry pumice stone.

- ▶ **Population:** 12 000
- ⓑ **Michelin Map:** 565 L 25–27 and K 27.
- 🄸 **Info:** Corso Vittorio Emanuele 202, Lipari. ℰ090 98 80 095. Porto di Levante, Vulcano. ℰ090 98 52 028.
- ◐ **Location:** The Aeolian Islands lie off the coast near Milazzo, in the Tyrrhenian Sea.
- 🅐 **Don't Miss:** A glass of local Malvasia wine, Stromboli and the Great Crater on Vulcano.
- 🕓 **Timing:** Allow 3–4 days to explore the islands.
- 👥 **Kids:** Beaches at Cave di Pomice a Porticello and Canneto.

SIGHTS

Lipari★

www.comunelipari.gov.it.

This, the largest island in the archipelago, is formed of volcanic rock dipping vertically into the sea. In ancient times Lipari was a source of obsidian, a glassy black volcanic rock from which pumice stone was quarried on the east coast (the industry is now in decline). The islanders fish and grow cereals and capers. Two bays (Marina Lunga, with its beach, and Marina Corta) frame the town of Lipari, dominated by its old quarter encircled by 13C–14C walls. Inside is the castle rebuilt by the Spaniards in the 16C on the site of a Norman building. The castle houses the **Museo Archeologico Eoliano★★**, which exhibits a re-creation of Bronze Age necropoli, a lovely collection of red-figure **kraters★**, **amphorae★** and terra-cotta theatrical **masks★★**. ⓑ Open 9am–7.30pm, Sun and public hols 9am–1.30pm. 6€. ℰ090 98 80 174. www.regione.sicilia.it.

GETTING AROUND

The Aeolian Islands are linked to the mainland by hydrofoil *(aliscafo)* and ferry *(traghetto)*. On average, the hydrofoil (foot-passengers only) costs twice as much and takes half the time.

Ferries run regularly from **Milazzo** on the main island (1hr 30min–4hrs) and are operated by Siremar; the same agency also runs a hydrofoil service (40min–2hrs 45min). Ferries (14hrs; twice a week) and hydrofoils (4hrs, Jun–Sept) also leave from Naples. The former are operated by Siremar and the latter by SNAV. For information and reservations, contact: **Siremar** (Gruppo Tirrenia); ℰ091 74 93 315, www.siremar.it. **SNAV**, Stazione Marittima, Naples; ℰ081 42 85 555; www.snav.it. For information on additional services, contact N.G.I, ℰ0800 25 00 00 or 090 92 84 091; www.ngi-spa.it.

Island of Vulcano seen from Lipari, Isole Eolie

© Michał Krakowiak/iStockphoto.com

There are **boat trips★★** leaving from Marina Corta which take the visitor round the very rugged southwest coast of the island. When making a tour of the island by car, stop at Canneto and Campo Bianco to visit the pumice stone quarries. The splendid **view★★** from the Puntazze Headland includes five of the islands: Alicudi, Filicudi, Salina, Panarea and Stromboli. However, it is the belvedere at Quattrocchi which affords one of the finest **panoramas★★★** of the whole archipelago.

Vulcano★★★

This 21sq-km/8sq-mi island is in reality four volcanoes. According to mythology it is here that Vulcan, the god of fire, had his forges – whence the term "volcanism". Although there has been no eruption on the island since 1890 there are still important signs of activity: fumaroles (smoke-holes), spouting steam-jets often underwater, and hot sulphurous mud flows greatly appreciated for their therapeutic properties. The island has a wild but forbidding beauty, with its rugged rocky shores, desolate areas and strangely coloured soils due to the presence of sulphur,

iron oxides and alum. The island's main centre, Porto di Levantee, stands below the great crater. The beach is known for its particularly warm water due to the underwater spouting steam-jets. Excursions to the **Great Crater★★★** (about 2hrs on foot there and back) are interesting for the impressive views they afford of the crater and of the archipelago. The headland Capo Grillo affords a view of several islands.

A tour of the island by boat (starting from Porto Ponente) offers the visitor many curious views, especially along the northwestern coast, which is fringed with impressive basalt reefs.

Don't miss the impressive views from Great Crater.

Stromboli★★★

The volcano of Stromboli, with its plume of smoke, has a sombre beauty and is a wild island with steep slopes. There are very few roads and such soil as can be cultivated is covered with vines yielding a delicious golden-coloured Malvasia wine. Visit the little square, with its white houses that are markedly Moorish in style.

The **crater★★★**, in the form of a 924m/ 3 032ft cone, has frequent minor eruptions with noisy explosions and accompanying flows of lava. To see the **spectacle★★★** climb up to the crater (about 5hrs on foot there and back, difficult climb, ⊘ visitors are advised to make the ascent in the company of a guide) **or watch from a boat the famous flow of lava along the crevasse named Sciara del Fuoco towards the sea.** Excursions: Authorised CAI–AGAI guides, Piazza San Vincenzo, Stromboli. ℘/Fax 090 98 62 11, 090 98 62 63. Visitors are recommended to book authorised guides only.

Salina★

The island is formed by six extinct volcanoes of which two have retained their characteristic outline. The highest crater, Monte Fossa delle Felci (962m/3 156ft), dominates the archipelago. There is a pleasant panoramic road around the island. Caper bushes and vines grow on the lower terraced slopes. The latter yield the delicious golden Malvasia wine.

ADDRESSES

🏠 STAY

⊜🍴 **Hotel La Canna** – Contrada Rosa, Filicudi. ℘090 98 89 956. www. lacannahotel.it. 14 rooms. ⊊10€. This typical hotel, built in keeping with its surroundings, enjoys an excellent location overlooking the port and the sea. The two rooms both have small sun terraces, and offer the perfect romantic hideaway for newlyweds. Facilities here include an attractive pool and sun terrace.

⊜🍴 **Hotel Ericusa** – Via Regina Elena, Alicudi. ℘090 98 89 902. www.alicudihotel.it. Closed Oct–May. 21 rooms. ⊊. The only restaurant and accommodation option on the island, this small, simple hotel is situated right on the beach. Ideal for visitors in search of sun, sea and solitude, the rooms at the Ericusa each have their own private entrance. The restaurant serves freshly caught fish, accompanied by simple salads.

⊜🍴 **Hotel Poseidon** – Via Ausonia 7, Lipari. ℘090 98 12 876. www.hotelposeidon lipari.com. Closed Nov–Feb. 18 rooms. ⊊. This central hotel is built in typical Mediterranean style with vivid blue and white tones. The fully equipped rooms are spotless, with modern, practical furnishings. Service is polite and there's a pleasant sun terrace.

⊜🍴 **Locanda del Barbablù** – Via Vittorio Emanuele 17, Stromboli. ℘090 98 61 18. www.barbablu.it. Closed Nov–Feb lunch. 6 rooms. ⊊. Restaurant ⊜🍴. This inn has six pleasant rooms, decorated in a successful fusion of modern, Arte Povera and period styles. The menu offers a wide selection of typical Aeolian dishes.

🍴EAT

⊜🍴 **Filippino** – Piazza Mazzini, Lipari. ℘090 98 11 002. www.filippino.it. Closed Oct–May Mon and mid-Nov–mid-Dec. ⊐. Compulsory 12 percent service charge. This century-old restaurant is renowned throughout the Sicily region for its wonderful fish, which is prepared according to traditional recipes. It has a relaxed atmosphere, friendly service and a delightful view of Piazza della Rocca.

⊜🍴 **Punta Lena** – Via Marina, loc. Ficogrande, Stromboli. ℘090 98 62 04. Closed Nov–Apr. The Punta Lena is renowned for its high-quality fresh fish and delicious seafood specialities served under an arbour with magnificent sea views.

⊜🍴 **E Pulera** – Via Isabella Conti Eller Vanicher, Lipari. ℘090 98 11 158. www.pulera.it. Closed lunch and Nov–May. Booking recommended. Compulsory 12 percent service charge. E Pulera has a garden for dining. In July and August, a menu of typical Aeolian dishes is accompanied by folk dancing.

Isole **Egadi**★

Egadi Islands

The islands are popular for their wild aspect, clear blue sea and beautiful coastlines. It is here in 241 BC that the treaty ending the First Punic War was concluded, in which Carthage surrendered Sicily to Rome.

VISIT

Favignana★★

The island covers an area of 20sq km/ 7.7 sq mi and is butterfly shaped. www.isoladifavignana.com.

The **Montagna Grossa** culminating at 302m/991ft runs right across the island and ends as an indented coastline. The islanders were masters in the art of tuna fishing, which took place for about 50 days between May and June.

Having captured the tuna in a series of nets, they would perform a dangerous manoeuvre and pull in the fish towards the shore where they were harpooned. The main town of the group of islands, **Favignana**, is guarded by the fort of Santa Caterina, a former Saracen look-out tower, which was rebuilt by the Norman King Roger II, and served as a prison under the Bourbons.

To the east of the harbour are the former **tufa quarries**★, now drowned by the sea. Boat trips take visitors to the various caves (contact the fishermen at the harbour), including the **Grotta Azzurra**★, which is situated on the west coast.

▲▲ *Take a boat trip to Grotta Azzurra.*

Levanzo★

This tiny island is only 6sq km/2.3sq mi in size. In 1950 traces of life in prehistoric times were found in the **Grotta del Genovese**★, which is reached on foot or by boat from Cala Dogana. To visit, contact ℘0923 92 40 32 or 339 74 18 800 (mobile).

Marettimo★

Off the beaten tourist track, Marettimo with its attractive **harbour** (no landing stage, rowing boats take visitors to the

▶ **Population:** 4 358
⚭ **Michelin Map:** 565 M–N 18–19.
🛈 **Info:** Palazzo Florio, Via Florio, Favignana (TP). ℘0923 925443. www.welcometoegadi.it.
◖ **Location:** The three islands – Favignana, Levanzo and Marettimo – which make up this small archipelago lie offshore from Trapani.
⊙ **Don't Miss:** The Grotta Azzurra at Favignana, the Grotta del Genovese on Levanzo and the caves around Marettimo.
◐ **Timing:** Allow a day to explore the caves on the islands.
▲▲ **Kids:** A boat trip to the Grotta Azzurra.

GETTING AROUND

Several hydrofoil and ferry services operate every day out of Trapani. For information contact: **Siremar**, ℘091 74 93 315 or 081 497 29 99; www.siremar.it; or **Ustica Lines**, Trapani; ℘0923 87 38 13; www. usticalines.it.

quay) has several restaurants but no hotels. Take a **trip**★★ around the island in a boat (contact the fishermen at the harbour) to discover the numerous caves that riddle the cliff-faces.

ADDRESSES

☞ STAY

⊜⊜ **Hotel Egadi** – Via Colombo 17, Favignana. ℘0923 92 12 32. www. albergoegadi.it. Closed Nov–Mar. 11 rooms. ⊊. This hotel has become something of an institution on the island, such is the level of hospitality and courtesy. The rooms are simple but spotlessly clean. In the evening there is a selection of imaginative dishes, carefully put together and prepared with good-quality ingredients.

⊜⊜🍽 **Hotel Aegusa** – Via Garibaldi 11/17, Favignana. ✆0923 92 24 30. www.aegusahotel.it. Closed end Oct–Mar. 28 rooms. ⌸. Restaurant⊜⊜🍽.

This hotel has a real holiday feel about it. Inviting (and reasonably priced) menu with a good selection of fish and other traditional dishes. Meals served in the lovely courtyard garden.

Isola di
Pantelleria★★

Pantelleria Island

Known as the "Black Pearl of the Mediterranean", the island is full of character with its indented coastline, steep slopes covered with terraces under cultivation, and its Moorish-looking cubic houses *(dammusi)*. **The highest point of this volcanic island is Montagna Grande (836m/2 743ft). The vineyards grow Zibibbo grapes used in wines such as Passito di Pantelleria. Capers are also grown here. Pantelleria has remains of prehistoric settlements and, like Sicily, later suffered invasions by the Phoenicians, Carthaginians, Greeks, Romans, Vandals, Byzantines, Moors and Normans who in 1123 united the island with Sicily.**

▶ **Population:** 7 000
⚅ **Michelin Map:** 565 Q 17–18.
🚹 **Info:** Lungomare Borsellino, 91017 Pantelleria (TP). ✆334 39 09 360. www.prolocopantelleria.it.
◗ **Location:** The island of Pantelleria is only 84km/52.2mi away from Tunisia. It is the westernmost island.
🕐 **Timing:** Allow half a day.

GETTING THERE

The quickest way to reach the island is by air with connecting flights from Trapani and Palermo. There are also direct flights from Rome and Milan via **Alitalia** ✆89 20 10 (from Italy), ✆06 65 649 (from abroad), www.alitalia.com. Hydrofoils *(2hrs 30min)* leave from Trapani via **Ustica Lines** ✆0923 87 38 13, www.usticalines.it.

ISLAND TOUR★★

About 40km/25mi: Allow 3hrs.
The picturesque coastal road gives the visitor a chance to discover the beauty of the indented coastline, thermal springs and lakes. Driving south from Pantelleria, road signs indicate a Neolithic village, where the **sese grande★**, an elliptic funerary monument, can be seen. Further along the road, the village of **Scauri★** boasts a lovely site. On the south coast towards **Dietro Isola** the corniche road affords plunging **views★★** of this coastal area. The cape, **Punta dell'Arco★**, is terminated by a natural rock arch known as the **Arco dell'Elefante★** (Elephant Arch). On the northeast coast the inlet **Cala dei Cinque Denti★** and the rest of the coastline further north make a lovely volcanic landscape. From here, you can go on to visit the **Specchio di Venere★** (Venus' Mirror), a beautiful green lake.

MONTAGNA GRANDE★★

13km/8mi SE of Pantelleria.
From the summit of this peak there is a splendid **panorama★★** of the island, as far as Sicily and Tunisia.

Clear water around Ustica

©Roberto Rinaldi/Tips Images

Ustica★★

This tiny volcanic island boasts an indented coastline which hides magnificent caves, inlets and bays. It has been a marine reserve since 1987.

- ▶ **Population:** 1 335
- 🖒 **Michelin Map:** 565 K 21.
- 🚩 **Info:** Piazza Umberto I, 90010 Ustica (PA). www.comune.ustica.pa.it.
- ◖ **Location:** Ustica is situated off the coast around Palermo. There are regular ferry departures from Palermo. During the summer months there is also a hydrofoil service (route: Trapani–Favignana–Ustica–Naples).

VISIT

The village of **Ustica★** is built overlooking the bay. A **prehistoric village★** dating from the Bronze Age has been discovered in the Colombaia district. The coastline is dotted with rocky inlets, such as the **piscina naturale★**, known as the natural swimming pool.

Riserva Marina

℘091 84 48 124, www.ampustica.it.
This marine reserve was established in 1987 to protect the natural marine environment around Ustica, where the sea is particularly free of pollution (Ustica is located in the middle of the Atlantic current). The reserve organises guided tours to caves around the island and snorkelling trips. Experienced divers can enjoy a spectacular **underwater show★★** near **Scoglio del Medico**.

Northern Italy

Passo di Pordoi, the Dolomites
©Antonio Scarpi/Bigstockphoto.com

Northern Italy

Stretching from France in the west to Slovenia in the east and touching on Austria and Switzerland in between, northern Italy is very much an area characterised by its borders. San Marino is also here, entirely surrounded by Italian territory on the southern edge of Emilia Romagna and into Marche.

Highlights

1 Experience aristocratic traditions and modern design in **Turin** (p343)

2 Discover the picturesque villages of **Cinque Terre in Liguria** (p382, 384)

3 Explore the canals and piazzas of timeless **Venice** (p435)

4 Winter skiing and summer walking in the beautiful **Dolomites** (p487)

5 Enjoy delicious dinners everywhere, especially **Bologna,** a gastronomic capital (p497)

Bilingual Culture

Such a mosaic of different cultures makes for a colourful melange, with cross-border traditions and bilingualism well rooted and actively encouraged in several regions. Valle d'Aosta, for example, has road signs in French as well as Italian; in Trentino-Alto Adige German is used widely, as well as the minority language of Ladino in some areas, while the eastern part of Friuli-Venezia Giulia, which only became definitively Italian in November 1975 when disputes with Yugoslavia were finally resolved, has a substantial percentage of Slovenian speakers. Elsewhere in the area, and throughout Italy as a whole, local dialects are still spoken by many Italians. They're less frequent in the major cities perhaps but far from extinct even there and in some cases people from one town or valley can have difficulty fully understanding the dialect of another close by.

Landscape of Contrasts

There's huge variety in the geographical aspect of northern Italy too. The Alps are a noble presence, forming a wide band across the far north, with Europe's highest mountain, Monte Bianco, or Mont Blanc (4 810m/15 780ft), divided between Italian and French territory. Winter-sports resorts that welcome visitors with typically Italian hospitality have excellent standards throughout the Alps as well as in many parts of the Apennines, the mountain range which forms Italy's backbone. In contrast with the mountainous areas, northern Italy also has vast expanses of plains, most notably the Padania Plain or Val Padana, which covers large parts of Piemonte, Lombardy, Veneto and Emilia Romagna. It's crossed by Italy's longest river, the Po (652km/405mi), which then flows into the Adriatic Sea through a wide delta, now an area of natural beauty much frequented by ornithologists.

Between the starkly contrasting mountainous and flat regions, the terrain of northern Italy is largely made up of attractively undulating hills. Southern Piemonte, famous for its excellent wines, and the Colli Euganei near Padova, where the spa centres are among Europe's best, are two of the most appealing hilly areas.

Sun-seeking Holidaymakers

Italy being a peninsula, the coastal areas are important although they make up a lesser proportion of the territory here than in the rest of the country. Right from the northernmost corners, the difference between the western and eastern coastlines is evident. In the west the Ligurian Sea, which becomes the Tyrrhenian farther south in Tuscany, is wild and rocky in many places, a beautiful coastline which contrasts with the calm, sandy expanses of the beaches of the Adriatic on the east coast. Both are exceedingly popular among holidaymakers.

Wheat field in Lombardy

© Matteo_Parma/iStockphoto.com

Further inland, the territory includes several magnificent lakes, which also make alternative destinations for lovers of beaches and watersports. Surrounded by stunning mountain landscapes and generally benefiting from mild climates, the lakes of northern Italy have, with good reason, attracted visitors, including numerous well-known writers and artists, since tourism first started to become widespread.

Cultural Highlights

The splendours of northern Italy's many cities of art are another long-standing draw for tourists. The unique city of Venice, stunning Verona and spiritual Padova are all in Veneto, while the awe-inspiring Byzantine mosaics of Ravenna are in Emilia Romagna and the list doesn't stop there. In terms of more recent culture, cities such as Turin and Milan are among the world's best when it comes to design and fashion.

Industrial Hotspots

Most of Italy's industry is grouped together in the north, around the industrial poles around Milan, Turin and Venice. Historic home to the Fiat group, Turin is also famous for the automobile industry, a theme that's continued on a more exclusive scale in Emilia Romagna's so-called Motor Valley where Ferrari, Lamborghini and Maserati make their cars and where motorcycle manufacturers Ducati are also based.

Despite such a concentration of industry and densely populated cities, northern Italy is also highly developed when it comes to agriculture. The flat expanses of the Padania Plain are ideal for crops, the watery areas close to the River Po itself being perfect for rice, which is grown in abundance. Fruit trees and vines are in evidence throughout the area with excellent wines produced from the alpine regions of the north down to Emilia Romagna and Liguria.

Experimental Gastronomy

When it comes to gastronomy, excellence is a constant in Italy and specialities vary considerably from one place to another. The zero-km foodie philosophy is growing fast in Italy and themed travel is becoming increasingly popular. Well-planned wine and food routes allow visitors to meet producers and taste at source for a genuine behind-the-scenes experience.

Valle d'Aosta and Piemonte

Aosta Valley and Piedmont. Major City: Turin

Official Websites: www.lovevda.it; www.piemonteitalia.eu

The smallest and least populous region in Italy, the Valle d'Aosta shares an alpine geography and a decidedly French flavour with its neighbours France and Switzerland. Its tallest mountain – Mont Blanc – is also Italy's highest peak. Conversely, Piemonte, which borders Valle d'Aosta to the south, is one of Italy's largest regions, in both area and inhabitants. Turin, the capital, was the first seat of the Kingdom of Italy, established in 1861.

Highlights

1 Behold the mystery of the Holy Shroud in Turin's **Duomo** (p347)
2 Examine Egyptian antiquities at the **Museo Egizio** (p349)
3 Explore the world of film at the **Museo del Cinema** (p350)
4 Sample Piemonte's exquisite wines in **Monferrato** (p358)
5 Ski alpine pistes in **Courmayeur** (p363)

Valle d'Aosta (Aosta Valley)

This wide valley between the highest mountains in Europe is watered by the Dora Baltea River, whose tributaries run along picturesque lateral valleys: the Valtournenche, Val di Gressoney, Val d'Ayas and Val Grisenche. The **Parco Nazionale del Gran Paradiso** is found in the southwest of the region.

Aosta, well placed at the centre of the valley, is the regional capital and has enjoyed a degree of administrative autonomy since 1947. In addition to the pastoral activities of the mountain people, the valley's economy depends primarily on tourism which has developed as a result of the Great St Bernard and Mont Blanc tunnels and the hydroelectric and iron and steel industries. From Pont-St-Martin to Courmayeur the towns and villages have retained French names; many of the local inhabitants still speak French or other varied dialects.

Piemonte (Piedmont)

Piemonte, at the foot of the mountain range, is a varied region with the plains of the Po River Valley, hilly wine-making areas to the south and the mountains of the Alps and Apennines on three sides. The fertile plains feature are ideal for rice growing (three-fifths of the Italian rice production is concentrated in the districts of Vercelli and Novara). The many rivers which cross the region (the Ticino, Sesia, Dora Baltea and Riparia, Tanaro, Bormida and Scrivia) are all tributaries of the **River Po**, which has its source at Pian del Re on Monviso (approximately 100km/62mi southwest of Turin), and which flows for 652km/405mi before joining the Adriatic through a wide-reaching delta. Numerous hydroelectric power stations supply electricity to local industry: textile factories in Biella and metal, engineering and chemical works in Turin. Agriculture plays an important role in the economy and landscape of Piemonte. The region produces world-renowned wines, including Barolo and Barbaresco, and it's home to over 30 000 wineries, with a concentration of vineyards in the south, particularly in Le Langhe. White truffles, found near Alba, are a precious commodity. The international Slow Food Movement, which promotes high-quality traditional local food and wine, is headquartered in the town of Bra.

Courmayeur
©abras/Fotolia.com

Turin★★★

Torino

The city of Turin has a complex character and it takes time to capture the profound contrasts that comprise its soul and charm. On two occasions Turin has cleverly reinvented itself as a capital: first of the newly created Kingdom of Italy and in more recent history of the automobile industry. Now the city has managed to shake off the role of "factory-city" and become an important centre for culture and design. The aristocratic rulers of the Savoy dynasty gave Turin an elegant, rather Parisian look which can be seen in the wide boulevards and the grandiose architecture. For centuries the city has jealously guarded the Turin Shroud, at the same time cherishing a vocation for the esoteric that has attracted personalities such as Paracelsus, Nostradamus and Cagliostro. Nietzsche lived his last years in Turin where he wrote his major works. He claimed that "Turin is the first place where I am possible."

THE CITY TODAY

Turin was given a massive facelift in view of the 2006 **Winter Olympic Games**, held here. Numerous cultural and infrastructure projects have made what was considered a northern factory town into a highly fashionable place at the forefront of Italian culture and innovation. Projects included a new driverless subway system, high-speed rail links between the city and Milan and improvements to tourist and convention facilities. With the Olympic revellers long gone, the Torinesi are anxiously monitoring the travails of Fiat, which forged an alliance with American carmaker Chrysler in January 2009 in order to ensure its survival in the midst of the global economic downturn. Turin hopes that its rebirth as a cultural centre will see it through the crisis.

- ▶ **Population:** 909 538
- **Michelin Map:** 561 G 4–5.
- **Info:** Piazza Castello, 10100 Torino. ℘011 53 51 81. Piazza Carlo Felice. www.turismotorino.org.
- **Location:** Situated at the foot of the Alps, against a backdrop of wonderful alpine scenery, Turin lies at the hub of a motorway network which takes in the A 4, as well as the A 5 (to the Valle d'Aosta), A 32 (to the Val di Susa) and A 32 (to Moncenisio), A 21 (to Piacenza) and A 6 (to Cuneo).
- **Train:** Turin (Torino GTT Dora 19mins).
- **Parking:** If arriving by car, park and explore the city on foot or on the extensive public transport system.
- **Don't Miss:** The Holy Shroud, the Galleria Sabauda, Museo del Cinema and the Museo Egizio.
- **Timing:** Turin is a good weekend destination and two days is the minimum to see the city – allow three to four days for a more thorough exploration.
- **Kids:** The Mole Antonelliana panoramic lift.

ECONOMY

Intense activity of local industries has made it the capital of Italian engineering. It was here that the **Italian motor industry** was born with Fiat, founded in 1899 by Giovanni Agnelli, and Lancia, created in 1906 by Vincenzo Lancia and taken over by the Fiat group in 1969. The famous **Lingotto** Fiat factory built in 1920 with such innovative technical features as the spectacular test ramp on the roof, was defined by Le Corbusier as "one of the most striking spectacles provided by industry". When production

Mole Antonelliana with a view to the Alps

©Nicola Destefano/iStockphoto.com

A BIT OF HISTORY

During the 1C the capital of the Celtic Taurini tribe was transformed by the Romans into a military colony with the name of Augusta Taurinorum. Converted to Christianity, it became the seat of a bishopric in the early-5C and a century later a Lombard duchy before passing under Frankish rule. From the 11C onwards and for nearly 900 years the city's destiny was linked to the **House of Savoy** (Italy's reigning royal family from 1861 to 1946). Skilful rulers, they often sided with the Pope rather than the emperor, and played France off against the Dukes of Milan. In the early-18C, Charles Emmanuel II and Victor Amadeus II embellished the city with buildings by Guarini and Juvarra.

Charles Emmanuel III increased the city's importance during his long reign (1732–73) by reorganising the Kingdom's administration and establishing formal etiquette at court similar to Versailles.

In 1798 Charles Emmanuel IV was expelled from Turin by French troops who wanted to impose a regime based on the revolutionary principles of 1789. On the fall of Napoleon Bonaparte, Victor Emmanuel I was restored to power and promoted a policy against foreign interference. Turin became the centre of the struggle against the Austrians, and for the unification of Italy. Following the reorganisation of Piemonte by Camillo Cavour, the Franco-Piemontese alliance against Austria and the victories at Solferino and Magenta (1859), Victor Emmanuel

ceased, the building was transformed by **Renzo Piano** into an avant-garde conference and exhibition centre with an auditorium and a commercial area. Top tyre manufacturers and well-known coach-builders (including the famous Pininfarina) have contributed to the prosperity of Turin's motor industry.

Turin also boasts some other very solid traditions. There are numerous publishing companies such as Bollati Boringhieri, Einaudi, Lattes, Loescher, Paravia, SEI and UTET as well as one of the major national newspapers, *La Stampa*, founded in 1895. Music also thrives in Turin thanks to the presence of the RAI National Symphony Orchestra and the prestigious *Teatro Regio*. Two prestigious festivals are *Settembre Musica* and the *Torino Film Festival*.

Not Just Fiat

For many Turin is synonymous with Fiat but numerous companies known all over the world were born here or have their central offices in or around the city. Among these are: Lavazza, Cinzano, Martini & Rossi, Gancia, Caffarel and Peyrano in the food and drink sector; the textile group GFT, producers of the Armani, Valentino, Cerruti and Ungaro brands; the Istituto Bancario San Paolo and the Cassa di Risparmio di Torino (the second-largest bank in Italy) in the banking sector; SAI, Toro and Reale Mutua Assicurazioni in the insurance sector; STET-Telecom Italia in the telecommunications sector; Robe di Kappa, Superga and Invicta in the sports clothing sector and De Fonseca in the shoe manufacturing industry; without forgetting Michelin, naturally, who opened their first factory outside France in 1906 in the famous building on Via Livorno.

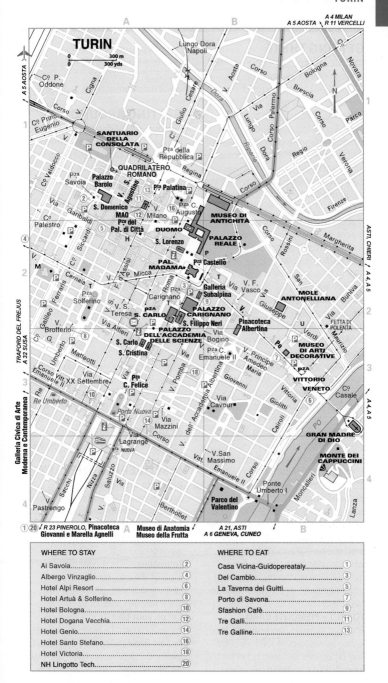

A 4 MILAN
A 5 AOSTA / R 11 VERCELLI

WHERE TO STAY		WHERE TO EAT	
Ai Savoia	②	Casa Vicina-Guidopereataly	①
Albergo Vinzaglio	④	Del Cambio	③
Hotel Alpi Resort	⑥	La Taverna dei Guitti	⑤
Hotel Artuà & Solferino	⑧	Porto di Savona	⑦
Hotel Bologna	⑩	Sfashion Cafè	⑨
Hotel Dogana Vecchia	⑫	Tre Galli	⑪
Hotel Genio	⑭	Tre Galline	⑬
Hotel Santo Stefano	⑯		
Hotel Victoria	⑱		
NH Lingotto Tech	⑳		

II was proclaimed the first King of Italy and Turin became the seat of the Italian government, to be replaced by Florence in 1865 and then Rome. The House of Savoy reigned over Italy until the proclamation of an Italian Republic in 1946.

GETTING THERE

BY CAR – In spite of its decentralised position (the city is only about 100km/62mi from the French border) there is a good network of motorways linking Turin to various cities. Furthermore, thanks to its famous octagonal plan and wide 19C avenues, traffic, although heavy at times, is manageable and it is easier to travel in and around Turin by car than it is in many other Italian cities.

BY BUS – The intercity bus terminal is at Corso Vittorio Emanuele 131H (intersection with Corso Ferrucci), www.autostazionetorino.it.

BY TRAIN – For train info: ℘06 68 47 54 75. The main railway stations in the city are:

Porta Nuova, Corso Vittorio Emanuele II 53.

Porta Susa, Piazza XVIII Dicembre 8.

BY AIR – Turin's international airport is situated 11km/6.8mi north of the city in Caselle. It is served by national and international airline companies (www.aeroportoditorino.it).

Buses operated by Sadem ensure regular connections between the airport and the city, taking 45min, from 6.10am to midnight (depart from the airport, arrivals floor) and from the city from 5.15am to 11pm (depart from Porta Nuova – Corso Vittorio Emanuele II 57a – and Porta Susa – Corso Bolzano 42). Tickets can be purchased at the airport from the tourist office and automatic ticket machine on the arrivals floor and, when leaving from the city, from the bars close to the bus stop. For a small surcharge (1€) they can also be bought on board.

TORINO + PIEMONTE CARD

The card includes free entrance for 2, 3 or 5 days to over 180 museums and other sites, reduced ticket for the touristic bus City SightSeeing and other touristic services, discounts for concerts and various other events. The card costs 35/42/51€ (an additional fee allows to travel for free on public transports). For information contact Turismo Torino, ℘011 53 51 81, www.turismotorino.org.

GETTING AROUND

The best way of discovering the city is by walking. The historic centre is compact and can be covered on foot; pedestrians are protected from inclement weather by the arcades lining the main streets.

BY PUBLIC TRANSPORT – GTT (City transport company) gives information on public transport, ℘800 01 91 52 (freephone), for information on car parking or traffic: www.gtt.to.it. Visit www.5t. torino.it Tickets can be purchased at tobacconists, newspaper stands and authorised bars. There are various types of tickets: the biglietto ordinario urbano (1.50€) is valid for 90mins, a biglietto giornaliero (5€) allows unlimited travel all day, or for two (7.50€) or three days (10€); the shopping ticket (3€) is valid for four hours from when it is stamped, from 9am–8pm.

BY TAXI – Pronto Taxi: ℘011 57 37. Radio Taxi: ℘011 57 30 or 011 33 99.

DISCOVERING THE CITY

Boat trips on the Po – With new boats since 2011, there's more choice with hop-on/hop-offs available and evening trips with dinner. Departures are from Murazzi: ℘800 01 91 52. www.gtt.to.it.

Touristbus – This service operates tours of the city, the hills and the Savoy residences: ℘011 53 51 81, www.turismotorino.org.

Get on your bike – Cycle through the magnificent La Mandria Park at Venaria Reale (1 340 ha/3 311 acres of parkland 15km/9.3mi NW of the city centre); bicycles can be rented. The park also offers excursions in horse-drawn carriages and touristic train, and nature walks: ℘011 49 93 381, www.parchireali.gov.it.

HISTORIC CENTRE
Piazza San Carlo★★
This is a typical example of Turin's graceful town planning. The churches of **San Carlo** and **Santa Cristina**, symmetrically placed on the south side, frame Via Roma. The curious façade of Santa Cristina *(on the left)*, surmounted by candelabra, was designed by the famous Sicilian-Turinese architect Juvarra, who was responsible for many of Turin's lovely buildings. In the centre of the square stands the famous "bronze horse" by C. Marocchetti (1838), an equestrian monument to Emanuele Filiberto of Savoy, who, after defeating the French at the Battle of San Quintino in 1557, salvaged his states after 25 years of French occupation (Treaty of Cateau-Cambrésis).

Palazzo dell'Accademia delle Scienze
This 17C palace by Guarini now houses two major Italian museums.

Palazzo Carignano★★
Victor Emmanuel II (1820–78), responsible for the Unification of Italy and the country's first king (1861), was born in this beautiful Baroque palace by **Guarini**. The palace is now home to the **Museo del Risorgimento Italiano**.

Piazza Castello
The political and religious heart of the city, this square was designed by the architect Ascanio Vitozzi (1539–1615). The main city streets lead off this square and it is bordered by the Royal Palace and the arcades of the **Teatro Regio**, inaugurated in 1740.
Severely damaged by bombardments in World War II, it was rebuilt and opened to the public in 1973. In the theatre's *atrium* there is a gateway designed by the artist Umberto Mastroianni entitled **Musical Odyssey**. In the centre of the square stands the imposing castle from which it derives its name. The castle was later named Palazzo Madama.

Palazzo Madama★
The palace derives its name from the two "Madame Reali" who stayed here in the 17C–18C: Maria Cristina of France, widow of Victor Amadeus I and Giovanna of Savoia-Nemours, widow of Charles Emmanuel II. The castle was erected in the 14C and 15C on the remains of the Roman gateway, Porta Pretoria, which formed part of the Augustan ramparts, while the west façade was designed in the 18C by Juvarra. The palace is now home to the **Museo di Arte Antica** (&see p351).

Palazzo Reale★
The Princes of the House of Savoy lived in this imposing building until 1865. The façade was designed by Amedeo di Castellamonte in the 17C. The sumptuous **apartments** (**appartamenti**) are accessed by a fine staircase, **Scala delle Forbici**, designed by Filippo Juvarra and are decorated in the Baroque, Rococo and Neoclassical styles. & Open Tue–Sun 8.30am–6pm. 12€. ℘011 43 61 455. www.ilpalazzorealeditorino.it.
The Royal Armoury, **Armeria Reale★**, contains a splendid collection of arms and armour and military memorabilia dating from the 13C to the 20C. Open Tue–Sun 9am–6pm. 12€. ℘011 56 41 729. www.artito.arti.beniculturali.it.
To the left of the palace stands the **church of San Lorenzo** to which the architect Guarini added a dome and rather daring crenellations.

Duomo★
☺ *The* **Shroud of Turin**.
This Renaissance cathedral, dedicated to St John, Turin's patron saint, was built at the end of the 15C for Cardinal Della Rovere. The façade has three carved doorways; the crown of the campanile was designed by Juvarra.
Inside, behind the high altar surmounted by a dome, a Baroque masterpiece by Guarini, is the **Cappella della Santa Sindone** (Chapel of the Holy Shroud), which enshrined the precious but much-contested **Holy Shroud★★★** in which Christ is said to have been wrapped after the Descent from the Cross. In 1997 a

raging fire caused grave damage to Guarini's dome (temporarily replaced by a *trompe l'œil*) but fortunately the urn containing the precious relic was saved for posterity.

Archaeological Area

There are some interesting Roman remains near the cathedral: remains of a 2C AD theatre and the **Porta Palatina** (1C AD), a fine Roman city gateway.
Via IV Marzo crosses the oldest part of the city and leads to the harmonious, elegant Piazza del Palazzo di Città, dominated by the 17C Town Hall which was erected by Francesco Lanfranchi.
Nearby (turn right onto Via Milano) stands **San Domenico** (14C), the city's only Gothic church, which has a beautiful cycle of 14C frescoes.

Museo di Antichità★

Via XX Settembre 86 (ticket office in Palazzo Reale). Open Tue–Sat 9am–6.30pm, Sun 2–6.30pm. Closed 1 Jan, 1 May, 25 Dec. 12€ (includes Palazzo Reale, Armeria Reale, Galleria Sabauda. ℘011 52 11 106).

The museum is divided into three sections: the historic collections of the Dukes of Savoy; the Piemontese archaeological collections in the new building, which begin with the Middle Ages and then go backwards in time to the prehistoric era; and the rooms facing onto the ruins of the Roman theatre, which are dedicated to the ancient history of the city itself.

ROMAN QUARTER

Wine bars, pubs and restaurants of all descriptions draw people each evening to the narrow streets of this fashionable area. Sample **Barolo** and Barbera wines, some of Italy's great reds. Piemonte also is renowned for its cheeses.

Palazzo Barolo★

Via delle Orfane 7. Open Mon–Fri 10am–12.30pm and 3–5.30pm, Sat 3–5.30pm, Sun 3–6.30pm. 4€. ℘011 26 36 111. www.palazzobarolo.it.
Splendid example of a late-17C nobleman's palazzo, with a sumptuous stair-

case and handsome rooms decorated with frescoes. The writer Silvio Pellico, who served as librarian to the Marquesa di Barolo, lived here until his death in 1854. It was also in the cellars here that the renowned Barolo wine was made for the very first time.

◗ Continue along Via delle Orfane, or take noisier parallel street, Via della Consolata.

Santuario della Consolata★

The current building was built by Guarino Guarini on the site of an earlier church, of which the Romanesque belltower survives, but Filippo Juvarra was the architect responsible for the elliptical presbytery and the main altar, with its venerated icon of the Virgin.
On the square of the same name stands the charming little **Caffè Al Bicerin** with its adjoining *pasticceria*, as well as the attractive herbalist's shop Rosa Sarafino, founded in 1875.
Skirting the apse of the church, you'll reach Piazza Emanuele Filiberto, and then further to the right, you'll get to **Piazza della Repubblica**, where the city's largest market is held every morning except Sundays. Look at the sculpted medallions below the roof line of the buildings surrounding the square. Piazza Emanuele Filiberto is the starting point of Via Sant'Agostino with its succession of fashionable boutiques and restaurants (*see Addresses*).

◗ From Piazza della Repubblica, take Via Milano.

At nos. 11, 13 and 18 on Via Milano take a look at the animal decoration adorning the buildings.

San Domenico★

Dating from the 14C, this is the city's only Gothic church, and contains a precious cycle of 14C frescoes, as well as works by Defendente Ferrari and Giovanni Martino Spanzotti.

MAO
(Museo d'Arte Orientale)

Via San Domenico 11. Open Tue–Fri
10am–6pm, Sat 11am–8pm,
Sun 11am–7pm. Last entry 1h before
closing. 10€. ☎011 44 36 927.
www.maotorino.it.

You will find the museum of Oriental
art close to the church of San Domenico in the Baroque Palazzo Mazzonis.
The collections are arranged by region
or culture: Gandhara, India, South-East
Asia, China, Japan, the Himalayas and
Islam.

Via Garibaldi

This street laid out in 1775 links Palazzo
Madama to Piazza Statuto and for many
years was the longest pedestrianised
street in Europe. It remains one of the
city's most animated thoroughfares
with a great concentration of shops.
Also worth a visit is the **Cappella
della Congregazione dei Mercanti e
Banchieri** (chapel of the congregation
of merchants and bankers), dating
from 1662.

Museo di Arti Decorative★

Via Po 55.

The museum houses the collection of
mainly 18C furniture, paintings and porcelain amassed throughout his life by
the owner of the palazzo, Pietro Accorsi.
♿🍴☕Guided tours Tue–Sun 10am–1pm
and 2–6pm (Sat–Sun to 7pm). 10€. ☎011
83 76 883. www.fondazioneaccorsi-
ometto.it.

FROM PIAZZA CASTELLO
TO THE PO
Via Po★

This beautiful street was created
between the 17C and the 18C to connect the historic centre to the River Po
and is bordered by palaces and arcades.
Nearby stands the **Pinacoteca Albertina**, a gallery with collections of Piemontese, Lombard and Venetian paintings, a section on Flemish and Dutch
paintings, and a group of **cartoons★** by
Gaudenzio Ferrari and his school. Open
10am–6pm, closed Wed. 5€. ☎011 089
73 70. www.accademialbertina.torino.it.

Mole Antonelliana★

This unusual structure, towering at
167m/548ft, is the symbol of Turin.
Its daring design was the work of the
architect Alessandro Antonelli (1798–
1888). Originally destined to be a temple
for the Jewish community, it was ceded
to the city in 1877. The summit affords a
vast **panorama★★** of Turin. Lift operates
9am–8pm, Sat 10am–11pm, last entry
1h before closing. Tue closed. 7€; 14€
combined ticket with Museo del Cinema
housed here. ☎011 81 38 560. www.
museonazionaledelcinema.it.

Piazza Vittorio Veneto

This large 19C square affords a wonderful **view★★** of the hills and dips down
towards the river. Beyond the Victor
Emmanuel I bridge, erected by Napoleon, stands the church of the Gran
Madre. To the right of the church, Monte
dei Cappuccini (284m/932ft) affords an
exceptional **panorama★★★** of the city.

Parco del Valentino★★

This wooded park extends along the
Po for about 1.5km/1mi and affords a
pleasant walk along the river. To the
north stands the **Castello del Valentino**,
erected in the first half of the 17C for
Duchess Marie Christine of France. There
is also the Palazzo delle Esposizioni
(Exhibition Hall), the Teatro Nuovo and
the **Borgo Medievale★**, an interesting
reconstruction of a medieval town and
Fénis Castle. Open 9am–7pm (Borgo summer 8pm). Closed Mon (fortress). Free for
Borgo; 6€ for fortress. ☎011 44 31 701.
www.borgomedioevaletorino.it.

SIGHTS
Museo Egizio★★★

Via Accademia delle Scienze 6. ♿Open
Mon 9am–2pm, Tue–Sun 9am–6.30pm.
13€. ☎011 56 17 776.
www.museoegizio.org.

The Egyptian Museum is one of the
richest collections of Egyptian antiquities in the world. The basement houses
the finds from the excavations carried
out in 1911 by two Italian archaeologists, Schiaparelli and Farina. On the
ground floor is the section on statuary

4 May 1949

Heavy rain and fog over Turin. An aeroplane flies over Superga with its illustrious passengers: 18 players from Grande Torino, the legendary football team who won five championships in a row and provided Italy's national team with 10 players. They were on their way back from Lisbon where they had played a friendly and were accompanied by technicians, executives and journalists. With zero visibility, at 5.05pm the plane loses radio contact and plunges down, its left wing hitting the basilica, finally crashing to the ground. The city of Turin is paralysed with grief, the Grande Torino team dies and its memory is imbued with a sense of nostalgia and the desire to make the sport live forever.

art with 20 seated or standing figures of the lion-headed goddess Sekhmet from Karnak, and an important series of statues of Pharaohs of the New Kingdom (1580–1100 BC), Egypt's Golden Age. The collections on the first floor represent all aspects of Egyptian civilisation, in particular: the sarcophagi – simple examples dating from the Middle Kingdom (2100–1580 BC) and sculpted ones during the New Kingdom; and an important number of mummies and copies of funerary papyri rolls known as the Book of the Dead. In addition to re-created funeral chambers (*mastabas*, Giza 2500 BC), there is an exceptional collection of funerary stelae dating from the Middle and New Kingdoms. Jewellery and pottery from the pre-dynastic civilisations, known as Nagadian, date from 4000–3000 BC. The influence of the Greek world made itself felt from the 4C BC following the conquest by Alexander the Great (masks and statuettes), followed by the Romans from 30 BC (bronze vases). The current layout is set to change drastically in 2013 with large-scale refurbishment.

Galleria Sabauda★★★

Via XX Settembre 86 (ticket office in Palazzo Reale). Open Tue–Sun 9am–6.30pm (ticket office closes 6pm). 12€ including Palazzo Reale, Armeria Reale and Museo Antichità. ℰ011 56 41 729. www.artito.arti.beniculturali.it.
The gallery houses the collections of the House of Savoy and is divided into thematic and chronological sections. On the second floor, the section on 14C to 16C **Piemontese painting★** has works

by Martino Spanzotti (1455–1528), the principal exponent of the Late Gothic Piemontese school, his pupil Defendente Ferrari (1510–31), Macrino d'Alba (1495–1528) and Gaudenzio Ferrari (1475–1546). One of his masterpieces is the **Crucifixion★**. The **Prince Eugene Collection** has both Italian and European painting including a collection of **Dutch and Flemish paintings ★★**. One of the richest in Italy, it includes the *Stigmata of St Francis* by Van Eyck (1390–1441), *Scenes from the Passion of Christ* by Hans Memling (c.1435–94), the *Old Man Sleeping* by Rembrandt (1606–69) and enchanting **landscapes** by Jan Brueghel (1568–1625).
On the third floor the **Dynastic Collections**, divided into three sections presented in chronological order, includes fine examples of Italian and European painting from the 15C to the 18C. Some of the most notable works include the **Visitation★** by the Flemish artist Van der Weyden (1400–64), the **Meal at the House of Simon★**, the **Assumption★★** by Orazio Gentileschi (1563–1639), the **Sons of Charles I of England★**, a fine portrait by Van Dyck (1599–1641), and the beautiful **views★** by the Venetian painter Bellotto (1720–80). The fine **Gualino Collection** includes works from the fine and decorative arts of various nationalities, among which is some fine Chinese sculpture.

Museo del Cinema★★★

&. Open 9am–8pm, Sat 9am–11pm, closed Tue. 10€; 14€ museum and panoramic lift. ℰ011 81 38 560. www.museonazionaledelcinema.it.

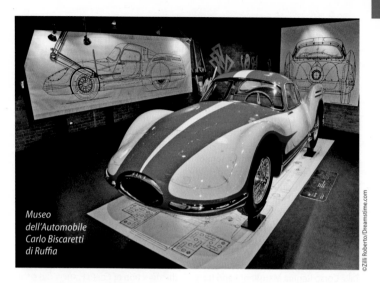

Museo
dell'Automobile
Carlo Biscaretti
di Ruffia

©Zilli Roberto/Dreamstime.com

In the unique context of the Mole Antonelliana, this vast collection of film-sets, documents and other items relating to the history of cinema spirals up through the many floors of the building. Exciting exhibits and film projections make it a fun experience for all.

Museo dell'Automobile Carlo Biscaretti di Ruffia★★★

Corso Unità d'Italia 40, 10126 Torino (Lingotto area). ♿Open Mon 10am–2pm, Tue 2–7pm, Wed–Thu and Sun 10am–7pm, Fri–Sat 10am–9pm (last entry 1hr before closing). 12€.
✆011 67 76 66. www.museoauto.it.
A vast modern building houses an extensive collection of cars, chassis and engines, as well as graphic documents outlining the history of the auto from its beginnings to the last 20 years.
After large-scale refurbishment, the museum now has a new look and an inspiring section focusing on cult vehicles and how they attained that status.

Museo di Arte Antica★★

Palazzo Madama, Piazza Castello. Open 10am–6pm, Sun 10am–7pm (last entry 1h before closing). Closed Tue. 10€.
✆011 44 33 501.
www. palazzomadamatorino.it.
The museum of ancient art is on the ground floor. Exhibits include Gothic

carvings, work by the 15C–16C Piemontese school (Gian Martino Spanzotti, Macrino d'Alba, Defendente and Gaudenzio Ferrari), a *Portrait of a Man* (1475) by Antonello da Messina and a 14C *Madonna* by Barnaba da Modena.

Museo Nazionale del Risorgimento Italiano★★

Via Accademia delle Scienze 5/ Piazza Carlo Alberto 8. Open Tue–Sun 10am–6pm (last entry 5pm). 10€.
✆011 56 21 147. www.museo risorgimentotorino.it.
After receiving a recent major overhaul, this museum, set in the graceful Palazzo Carignano, has become highly user-friendly. The displays based on the period of Italy's unification are well presented. The museum includes the **Sala del Parlamento Subalpino★**, where speakers included Cavour, Garibaldi, Verdi and Manzoni.

GAM – Galleria Civica di Arte Moderna e Contemporanea★★

Via Magenta 31. ♿ Open Tue–Sun 10am–7.30pm (last entry 6.30pm). 12€.
✆011 44 29 518. www.gamtorino.it.
This ample collection of fine art gives a good overview of Italian art and its main exponents, focusing on the 19C and 20C Piemontese schools. The sec-

ond floor, devoted to 19C art, has the largest body of work by the Reggio artist Antonio Fontanesi (1818–82).

The first floor, devoted to the 20C, shows the development of Italian and European art through the work of the more significant artists and movements: Balla, Casorati, Martini, the Milanese Novecento group, the Ferrara metaphysical paintings (Carlo Carrà, Giorgio de Chirico), the Roman school (Scipione, Mafai), Turin's *Gruppo dei Sei* (Jessie Boswell, Gigi Chessa, Nicola Galante, Carlo Levi, Francesco Menzio and Enrico Paolucci), examples of Informal Art and Arte Povera from the 1960s.

HILLS AROUND TURIN★

▶ 50km/31mi.

Take Corso Regina Margherita and turn left into Corso Casale after crossing the River Po. Take the next right onto the Circuito della Maddalena.

Basilica di Superga★

Basilica: Open Mon–Fri 9am–noon and 3–5pm (Apr–Oct 6pm), Sat–Sun 9am–noon and 3–6pm (Apr–Oct 7pm). 3€ (cupola), 5€ (apt, tombs). ✆011 89 97 456. www.turismotorino.org.

This masterpiece was built by Juvarra from 1717 to 1731 on a hill (670m/ 2 198ft high). The basilica is circular in plan with a monumental façade and roofed with a marvellous cupola from where you can see the Alps. The chapel dedicated to the Virgin, in the chancel, is a pilgrimage centre. To reach the basilica you can take an unusual historic tram from Stazione Sassi.

Tombe dei Reali

The royal tombs in the crypt include that of Victor Amadeus II, who built the basilica to fulfil a vow made when his capital was being besieged by a French and Spanish army in 1706. Alongside are the tombs of Charles-Albert and other Princes of the House of Savoy. From the esplanade there is a fine view★★★ of Turin, the Po Plain and the Alps. Tours of royal tombs 4€.

Colle della Maddalena★

From Superga take the scenic route via Pino Torinese, which affords good views ★★ of Turin.

From Pino Torinese continue to the hilltop, Colle della Maddalena, and the Parco della Rimembranza, commemorating those who died in World War I. On the way down there are more lovely views★. The Parco Europa at Cavoretto overlooks the southern part of the town.

🚗 DRIVING TOUR

VAL DI SUSA★★

150km/93.2mi. Allow 1 day.

▶ From Turin take the west exit in the direction of Corso Francia. Take the S 25. From the S 25 follow the turn-off 6km/3.7mi after Rivoli.

Abbazia di Sant'Antonio di Ranverso★

Open Tue–Sun 9am–12.30pm and 1–5.30pm. 2.60€. ✆011 93 67 450.

This abbey was a pilgrims' resting place and a centre for curing "St Anthony's Fire" (egotism). Founded in the 12C, the church has three 15C doorways adorned with Gothic pediments and pinnacles. The interior has frescoes★by Giacomo Jaquerio (1401–53).

Avigliana

Until the 15C this town was one of the Savoy family's favourite residences. The heart of the historic centre is the Piazza Conte Rosso, dominated by the ruins of a castle (15C). Southeast stands the church of San Pietro★(10C–11C) which has a fine cycle of frescoes (mainly 14C–15C). Other interesting medieval frescoes can be seen in the church of San Giovanni.

A scenic road skirts the two lakes of Avigliana, eventually leading up to the abbey of San Michele. (13.5km/8.4mi).

Sacra di San Michele★★★

See website for opening hours. 5€. ✆011 93 91 30. www.sacradi sanmichele.com.

Sacra di San Michele

© C. Labonne/MICHELIN

This Benedictine abbey, perched on a rocky site (962m/3 156ft), was a powerful establishment in the 13C. It was built at the end of the 10C by Hughes de Mont-boissier from Auvergne. Climb the great staircase leading to the Zodiac Door; its pilasters and capitals were decorated by the famous Master Nicolò (1135). The Romanesque-Gothic church built on top of the rocky eminence has 16C **frescoes**. From the esplanade there is a lovely **view★★★**of the Alps.

◗ Head back along the S 25 or A 32 through the Fréjus Tunnel.

Susa★

Situated at the foot of an impressive mountain range dominated by the Rocciamelone (3 538m/11 608ft) stands Susa, also known as "Italy's gateway" because it lies at a junction of two roads which lead to France. The symbol of the city is the **Savoy Door★**, which dates from the late-3C to early-4C AD when the ramparts were built. Next to the door stands the **cathedral**, founded in the years 1027–29 with Gothic additions made in the 14C. To the south side of the church Piazza San Giusto is dominated by the **Romanesque campanile★★**. In a delightful corner stands the elegant **Arco di Augusto★**, the oldest monument in the city (8 BC).

◗ Head 8km/5mi NE towards Novalesa on the SP 210 Via Susa.

Abbazia della Novalesa

Open mid-Sept–Jun Sat–Sun 9.30am–12.30pm and 2–4pm; Jul–mid-Sept 9.30am–12.30pm and 2–5.30pm, closed Thu. Guided tours of Cappella Sant'Eldrado and other chapels. Donation recommended. www.abbazianovalesa.org. This powerful Benedictine abbey was founded in the 8C and destroyed by Saracens in the 10C. The real jewel of this abbey are the **frescoes★★**in the **Cappella Sant'Eldrado** (12C). Parking is 500m/550yds away and access is on foot (10min).

ADDRESSES

⊚STAY

⊛ *It is worth noting that during trade fairs hotels tend to put their prices up.*

⊝ **Albergo Vinzaglio** – Corso Vinzaglio 12. ℰ011 56 13 793. Fax 011 56 13 894. www. albergovinzaglio.it. Closed Aug. 14 rooms. A small, bright hotel in an old building 20 minutes' walk from the centre. The rooms – some without a bathroom – are functional and well kept. A good-value choice.

⊖⊟ **Ai Savoia** – Via del Carmine 1/h. ☏339 12 57 711 (mobile). www.aisavoia.it. Closed Aug. Elegant B&B located in the Palazzo Saluzzo Paesana, in the city's fashionable and artistic centre. The aristocratic rooms are named after the Queens of the House of Savoy.

⊖⊟ **Hotel Alpi Resort** – Via Bonafous, 5. ☏011 81 29 677. Fax 011 81 34 973. www. hotelalpiresort.it. 29 rooms. A pleasant hotel near Piazza Vittorio Veneto. Comfortable, well-furnished rooms.

⊖⊟ **Hotel Artuà & Solferino** –Via Brofferio 1–3 (4th floor with lift). ☏011 51 75 301. www.hotelartuasolferino.it. 20 rooms. In a pretty building located in the quiet district around Piazza Solferino, this hotel offers plain but comfortable rooms. Prices vary according to the comfort of the room. Least expensive rooms do not include breakfast.

⊖⊟ **Hotel Bologna** – Corso Vittorio Emanuele II 60. ☏011 56 20 193. www. hotelbolognasrl.it. 45 rooms. In a late-19C building near Porta Nuova station, this hotel offers carefully presented, comfortable rooms.

⊖⊟ **Hotel Dogana Vecchia** – Via Corte d'Appello 4. ☏011 43 66 752. Fax 011 43 67 194. www.hoteldoganavecchia.com. **P** 50 rooms. The hotel was built in the late-18C as a coaching house. Illustrious guests to have passed through include the likes of Mozart, Napoleon and Verdi. Period-style or more functional modern rooms, in the heart of the city.

⊖⊟⊟ **Hotel Genio** – Corso Vittorio Emanuele II 47. ☏011 65 05 771. Fax 011 65 08 264. www.hotelgenio.it. 120 rooms. The Genio is close to Porta Nuova station and offers elegant, cosy rooms. Prices are higher in the week but very good value at the weekend.

⊖⊟⊟⊟ **Hotel Santo Stefano** – Via Porta Palatina 19. ☏011 52 23 311. www. nh-hotels.com. 125 rooms. A recently opened designer hotel occupying an excellent location between the Duomo, the Palatine Towers, the Quadrilatero Romano and the Royal Palace. The exterior looks like a medieval tower, whereas the interior combines natural materials and high-tech features. Turkish baths open to all.

⊖⊟⊟⊟ **Hotel Victoria** – Via Nino Costa 4. ☏011 56 11 909. Fax 011 56 11 806. www.hotelvictoria-torino.com. 106 rooms. A charming, classy hotel with extremely refined rooms decorated with period furniture and lavish drapery.

⊖⊟⊟⊟ **NH Lingotto Tech** – Via Nizza 230. ☏011 66 42 000. www. nh-hotels.it. 140 rooms. This creation by the architect Renzo Piano will appeal to well-heeled lovers of contemporary design. Rooms boast superb views.

ⵏ/ EAT

⊖⊟ **Porto di Savona** – Piazza Vittorio Veneto 2. ☏011 81 73 500. www.food andcompany.com. This historic trattoria dates from 1863 and serves a good selection of traditional, regional dishes such as *agnolotti* (filled pasta).

⊖⊟ **Sfashion Cafè** – Via Cesare Battisti 13. ☏011 51 60 085. www. foodandcompany.com. After the F. lli La Cozza pizzeria at Corso Regio Parco 39 (☏011 85 99 00). Created by the comedian Piero Chiambretti: bar, traditional restaurant and pizzeria with unusual decor.

⊖⊟ **Tre Galli** – Via Sant'Agostino 25. ☏011 52 16 027. www.3galli.com. Closed Sun. A pleasant restaurant-cum-wine bar sheltered from the traffic in the heart of the city's fashionable nightlife district. The kitchen serves up food to match the wines, with a good selection of cured meats and cheese. Terrace in summertime.

⊖⊟ **Tre Galline** – Via Bellezia 37. ☏011 43 66 553. Closed Mon–Fri lunch and Sun. www.3galline.it. A traditional restaurant operated by the same owner as the Tre Galli, where you can try the most typically Piemontese dishes. Don't miss out on the *bolliti* (stewed meat) in season.

⊖⊟⊟⊟ **Casa Vicina-Guidopereataly** – Via Nizza 224. ☏011 19 50 68 40. www. casavicina.com. Closed Sun evening and Mon. As part of Eataly (☾*see Taking a Break*), this restaurant offers creative and very tasty dishes in a minimalist atmosphere.

⊖⊟⊟⊟ **Del Cambio** – Piazza Carignano 2. ☏011 54 66 90. www. delcambio.it. Closed Mon. Reservation recommended. Dating from 1757 this historic and extremely classy restaurant has valuable works of art, Baroque mirrors and gilded stuccowork. Excellent cuisine.

TAKING A BREAK

Al Bicerin – Piazza della Consolata 5. ☎011 43 69 325. www.bicerin.it. This caffè was founded in 1763, where Cavour came to forget about the tribulations of politics.

Baratti & Milano – Piazza Castello 29. ☎011 44 07 138. www.barattiemilano.it. Closed Mon. Founded in 1875, this was originally a sweet shop. With its Art Nouveau rooms the caffè was a favourite with Turin's high society.

Caffè San Carlo – Piazza San Carlo 156. ☎011 53 25 86. An opulent caffè that first opened in 1822 and was one of the patriot strongholds during the Risorgimento, later becoming the meeting-place for the city's artists.

Caffè Torino – Piazza San Carlo 204. ☎011 54 51 18. www.caffe-torino.it. Open 8am–1am. Another of Turin's many historic caffès, this one was frequented by actors such as James Stewart, Ava Gardner and Brigitte Bardot.

Eataly – Via Nizza 230. ☎011 19 506 801. www.eatalytorino.it. This giant, contemporary space located in the former Carpano vermouth factory, brings together the cream of Italian gastronomy: wines, cheeses, specialities … You can do your shopping, go to tastings or take courses. This is a showcase for the pleasures of the table, with maturing cellars, spice sacks, meat slicers, wine cellars, etc.

Fiorio – Via Po 8. ☎011 81 73 225. www.fioriocaffegelateria.com. Open Tue–Sun 8am–1am. Founded in 1780, this was the place for aristocrats and intellectuals to meet. Great ice cream!

Grom – Piazza Paleocapa 1d; Via Accademia delle Scienze 4; Via Garibaldi, 11; Piazza Santa Rita 6 (Corso Orbassano). www.grom.it. A chain of ice-cream parlours that originated in Turin in 2003, before opening outposts all over the world. The quality of the ingredients has helped to build its reputation.

Mulassano – Piazza Castello 15. ☎011 54 79 90. www.caffemulassano.com. An intimate, charming caffè founded in 1907, with lavish decoration in marble, bronze, wood and leather. It was once frequented by members of the House of Savoy and performers from the nearby Teatro Regio.

Platti –Corso Vittorio Emanuele II 72. ☎011 50 69 056. www.platti.it. This liqueur merchant's shop became a caffè over the years, frequented mainly by intellectuals and writers, including Cesare Pavese. It now contains a restaurant.

Stratta – Piazza San Carlo 191. ☎011 54 79 20. www.stratta1836.it. This *pasticceria* dates to 1836. It is famous for its multicoloured sweets.

GOING OUT

Docks Dora – Via Valprato 68. A former railway depot dating from the early-20C has been converted into a cultural "container" hosting exhibitions and events staged by avant-garde groups.

Murazzi – Along the River Po and around Piazza Vittorio, this is where the fashionable night-time crowd hang out.

Parco del Valentino – Numerous riverside discos.

Quadrilatère romain – Between Via Sant'Agostino and Via delle Orfane. The streets of this area are teeming with restaurants, literary caffès and wine bars.

ENTERTAINMENT

There are several prestigious concert halls in Turin including the **Auditorium Giovanni Agnelli del Lingotto**, Via Nizza 280, ☎011 66 77 415, www.lingottomusica.it (classical music) and the **Conservatorio Giuseppe Verdi**, Via Mazzini 11, ☎011 88 84 70 or 011 81 78 458, www.conservatoriotorino.eu. Without forgetting the **Teatro Regio**, in Piazza Castello 215, ☎011 88 15 241, www.teatroregio.torino.it.

SHOPPING

There are 18km/11.2mi of arcades in the historic centre. On **Via Roma**, which the architect Piacentini modernised in the 1930s, there are luxurious shops and the elegant San Federico gallery.

Art and antique lovers should head for the nearby **Via Cavour**, **Via Maria Vittoria** and **Via San Tommaso**. Most antiquarian bookshops are concentrated around **Via Po**, **Via Accademia Albertina** and **Piazza San Carlo**, while **Via Lagrange** is a gourmet's paradise. Turin specialities. King of red wines is **Barolo**, but also Barberesco Barbera, Dolcetto di Diano d'Alba, and Gavi. Cheese, agnolotti pasta, bagna cauda, and chocolate. Enjoy local wines or vermouth, first created in Turin in the late-18C.

Two streets lead off **Piazza Castello**: Via Po and Via Garibaldi, one of the longest pedestrian streets in Europe. Every Saturday morning and all day on the second Sunday of the month is the Balôn in Borgo Dora, Turin's traditional flea market, in existence since 1856.

ACTIVITIES
CONTEMPORARY ART
Turin is a mecca for contemporary art with many exhibition spaces – www.contemporarytorinopiemonte.it.

EVENTS
Salone internazionale del Gusto e Terra Madre – Lingotto Fiere. www.salonedelgusto.com. Oct. This fair brings together farmers and artists, university culture and chefs, novices and the great figures of the world of food and wine.

Salone Internazionale del Libro – www.salonelibro.it. May. The most important book fair in Italy.

Vercelli★

In the heart of the misty Piemontese paddy fields, which turn from tender green to gold as the season progresses, amid farms founded by monastic orders and elegant castles, stands the city of Vercelli. In the 13C Vercelli enjoyed a period of great prosperity, which is still reflected today in the city's essentially medieval layout.

- ▸ **Population:** 46 967
- ⚅ **Michelin Map:** 561 G7.
- **Info:** Viale Garibaldi 90, 13100 Vercelli. ✆0161 58 002. www.atlvalsesiavercelli.it.
- **Location:** Vercelli is approximately halfway between Turin and Milan.
- **Train:** Vercelli (Torino Porta Susa 40 mins).
- **Timing:** Allow half a day for visiting central Vercelli.
- **Kids:** The paths between the rice fields are ideal for an easy bicycle ride.

SIGHTS
Basilica di Sant'Andrea★★
Piazza Bicheri (opposite the station). This superb basilica was built during the city's golden age in 1220 and combines the Italian-Gothic style (as seen in the verticality of the towers and the octagonal bell tower) with the characteristic style of the Po Plain (exemplified by the triangular gable, the arches and the use of brick).

The façade, flanked by its two soaring towers, is enlivened by the contrasting colours of its marble and stone, and adorned with three doorways. The decoration in the tympana above the doors is attributed to the sculptor Benedetto Antelami. The stockier bell tower, to the right, dates from the 15C. The austere interior is divided into a nave and two aisles, and contains choir stalls in inlaid wood and the 14C tomb of Tommaso Gallo, the basilica's first abbot (2nd chapel in the right transept). The left-hand aisle gives access to the abbey buildings and the **cloister**, which offers a good view over the complex. From the basilica, take Via G. Ferrari (where you will find the arched porch of the former hospital of Sant'Andrea, dating from the 13C). This will take you to Piazza Cavour, a square that dates back to the Middle Ages. You will come to the very lively Corso Libertà, lined with churches, *palazzi* and shops.

Europe's Rice Province

When rice cultivation was introduced to the Vercelli region in the 15C, it changed the lifestyle and the landscape of this unassuming corner of Italy. Work was undertaken to improve and irrigate the land and a specific type of rectangular farm and accommodation complex developed. This type of settlement was known as the *cascina a corte chiusa*. The paddy fields around Vercelli stretch for miles, defining the seasons by their different colours and different activities. Today, farming is entirely mechanised, but the landscape retains a sense of nostalgia for the harsh but romantic existence of the *mondine*. The story of these women who worked in the paddy fields is wonderfully evoked in Giuseppe De Santis' 1949 film *Bitter Rice*, which was filmed at the Cascina Veneria in Lignana. Over 100 varieties of rice are grown around Vercelli, including Baldo, Arborio, Nuovo Maratelli, Sant'Andrea, Carnaroli and Balilla.

San Cristoforo

This church built in the 16C then renovated in the 18C contains a magnificent cycle of frescoes, painted between 1529 and 1534 by Gaudenzio Ferrari. The paintings depict episodes from the life of Mary Magdalene (to the right) and the Virgin Mary (to the left). The Crucifixion and the Ascension are among the finest paintings by Ferrari, whose work adorns the Sacro Monte of Varallo, and who also painted the fine *Madonna degli Aranci* in the apse.

Museo Borgogna★

Via Antonio Borgogna 4/6. Open
Tue–Fri 3–5.30pm, Sat 10am–12.30pm
(Mar–mid-May also 2–6pm),
Sun 10am–12.30pm and 2–6pm. 10€.
☎0161 25 27 76. www.museoborgogna.it.
Piemonte's largest collection outside of Turin's Galleria Sabauda contains works from the Italian and northern schools dating from the 15C to the 19C. The frescoes from churches around the region and the Piemontese Renaissance works (Martino Spanzotti, Il Sodoma, Defendente Ferrari, Gaudenzio Ferrari and Bernardino Lanino) are of interest.

Sinagoga

Via E. Foa, 56/58. Guided tours, hours vary, for information ☎339 25 79 283 (mobile).
The synagogue is located in the former ghetto and was built in the 1870s in the Moorish style by Giuseppe Locarni.

EXCURSIONS

Novara

❍ 22km/13.7mi NE of Vercelli.
Novara, an industrial and commercial centre, is also of interest. The 16C–17C **Basilica di San Gaudenzio★** is crowned with a slender **dome★★** (1844–78), an audacious addition by a local architect, A. Antonelli. Inside are several interesting works of art, including paintings by Morazzone (17C) and Gaudenzio Ferrari (16C), and the silver **sarcophagus★** of the city's patron saint (St Gaudentius). The Neoclassical **Duomo** by Antonelli has a 6C–7C paleo-Christian baptistery. The chancel is adorned with a black-and-white Byzantine-style mosaic **floor★**.

Biella

❍ 42km/26.1mi NW via the SS 230.
Piazza Vittorio Veneto 3. ☎015 35 11 28.
www.atl.biella.it.
The town of Biella is the main centre of Italy's textile industry and is composed of two distinct parts connected by a funicular railway. Biella Piano is the lower, more modern part of town, but boasts a remarkable 11C baptistery, decorated with 14C frescoes. Not far away stands the C16 church of San Sebastiano, where you can admire artworks and the handsome cloister.
Piazzo, the older, upper town, is arranged around the pretty Piazza della Cisterna, which is lined with historic buildings such as the medieval Casa dei Teccio. The Fondazione

Pistoletto on Via Serralunga (no. 27) is a contemporary art centre (open Tue–Fri 10am–1pm, Sat–Sun 11am–7pm; ℘015 28 400; www.cittadellarte.it). The town is surrounded by protected natural areas, like the **Parco della Burcina Felice Piacenza** (in Pollone, 7km/4.3mi to the NE) – the best time to visit is May and June when the rhododendrons are in flower. Another option is the **Oasi Zegna**, between Trivero and Rosazza, which is crossed by a panoramic road.

Santuario di Oropa

◗ Alt. 1 180 m/3 871ft, 13km/8mi NE of Biella on the SS 144.

A miraculous black figure of the Virgin has been venerated here since the 13C. Construction of this mountainside sanctuary began in the 17C, but was finished in 1960 with the completion of the new church. The complex contains 19 chapels.

Ricetto di Candelo★

◗ 5km/3mi SE of Biella.

Ricetti are a common feature of the Piemontese landscape. These rural strongholds were designed to protect stores of grain and wine, and also served as a refuge in times of danger. The medieval *ricetto* in Candelo (13C–14C) is covered in flowers in April and May.

ADDRESSES

SHOPPING

Try *bicciolani*, the local spiced biscuits. One of the best places to try them is **Pasticceria Follis** (Corso Libertà 164, 13100 Vercelli; ℘0161 25 11 91, www.follis.it).

The Langhe and Monferrato★★

The vineyards of the Langhe and Monferrato produce some world-class wines, and this verdant enclave stretching up to the Ligurian Alps is also a gourmet's paradise. The region used to be controlled by the Marquises of the Falletti family, and retains an interesting cultural heritage, as well as hosting some enjoyable festivals.

- ⊙ **Michelin Map:** 561 G7.
- ⊟ **Info:** (*Langhe*) Via Risorgimento 2, 12051 Alba. ℘0173 35 833. www.langheroero.it. (*Monferrato*) Piazza Alfieri 34, 14100 Asti. ℘0141 53 03 57. www.astiturismo.it.
- ◗ **Location:** To the south and southeast of Turin.
- ◷ **Timing:** Allow at least two days to explore the area.
- ♚♛ **Kids:** Barolo Castle's Wine Museum has plenty to appeal to all ages.

SIGHTS

Langhe★★

◗ From Bra to Alba, a 90km/56mi itinerary. www.langhe.it.

The rivers Tanaro and Bormida di Spigno mark the borders of this region. The vineyards here produce prized wines such as **Barolo** and **Nebbiolo**. This route passes through La Morra, Monforte, Dogliani, Belvedere Langhe, Bossolasco, Serralunga d'Alba and Grinzane Cavour, before reaching **Alba★**.

The Wine Museum (℘0173 38 66 97; www.wimubarolo.it) in Barolo's imposing Falletti castle provides a memorable experience which appeals to all

Grinzane Cavour, the Langhe

© Stefano Pezzolato/iStockphoto.com

the senses. The landscape affords panoramic **views★**. Alba is a gourmet centre famous for its delicious **tartufi bianchi** or white truffles and its wines.

Monferrato★★

An attractive region, famous for its fine wines. The valley of Villafranca d'Asti and the lower part of the River Tarano divide the area into Lower and Upper Monferrato.

Asti★

▶ 38km/23.6mi SE on the S 458.
Asti, home of the famous sparkling wine, Asti Spumante, is the scene of an annual horse race *(palio)*, which is preceded by a procession with over 1 000 participants in 14C and 15C costume. The 12C **baptistery of San Pietro★**, the 15C church of San Pietro and the Gothic cloisters form an attractive group.

Strada dei Castelli dell'Alto Monferrato★

From Acqui Terme to Gavi (24km/14.9mi to Ovada on the S 456 and 24km/14.9mi to Gavi on minor roads) this scenic route follows the crest of the hillsides covered with vineyards. **Acqui Terme♨♨**, famous in Roman times for its spa water, is a pleasant town with hot springs.

Castello di Rivoli and Museo d'Arte Contemporanea★★

Victor Amadeus II commissioned Juvarra to build a grandiose residence (18C) in the Baroque style. The château now houses the **Museo d'Arte Contemporanea★★**. ♿ Open Tue–Fri 10am–5pm, weekends 10am–7pm. Closed 1 Jan, 1 May, 25 Dec. 6.50€. ℘011 95 65 222. www.castellodirivoli.org.

Palazzina di Caccia di Stupinigi★

Return to the ring road and follow signs to Savona/Alessandria. Exit at Stupinigi. Open Tue–Fri 10am–5.30pm, Sat–Sun 10am–6.30pm. Last entry 30min before closing. 12€ ℘011 62 00 634.
This huge building was a hunting lodge built by Juvarra for Victor Amadeus II of Savoy. Napoleon stayed here before assuming the crown of Italy. The palace now houses a **Museo d'Arte e del Mobilio** (Fine Arts and Furniture Museum). The apartments are decorated in the Rococo style of the 18C. A magnificent park surrounds the *palazzina*.

Cuneo

Due to its strategic position at the confluence of the Gesso and Stura rivers, ownership of Cuneo was disputed by France and Italy for centuries. Today, the peaceful capital of the "Provincia Granda" is a good base for explorations of southern Piemonte.

▶ **Population:** 55 464
⚫ **Michelin Map:** 561 F - I
▤ **Info:** Via Vittorio Amedeo 8, 12100 Cuneo ✆0171 690 217. www.comune.gov.it. www.cuneoholiday.com.
◗ **Location:** Cuneo is about 100km/62mi south of Turin.
◗ **Train:** Cuneo (Torino Porta Nuova 1hr 11mins).
🕐 **Timing:** Allow a day.

SIGHTS

The vast, elegant **Piazza Galimberti★** takes its name from Duccio Galimberti, the Resistance hero born in Cuneo in 1906. The square is the starting point for **Via Roma**, the central thoroughfare of the historic centre. Immediately to the right stands the **cathedral** (17C–19C), where you will find an altarpiece by Andrea Pozzo in the apse. Next take a right turn into Via Mondovì, which leads to the **Contrada Mondovì★**.

Returning to Via Roma, you will find the old Torre Comunale and, opposite, the 17C town hall (Municipio). A little farther along on the right is the 18C church of **Sant'Ambrogio** with its ornately decorated interior. Behind the town hall, the Jesuit church of **Santa Maria** contains works by Andrea Pozzo and Lanfranco. In Via Santa Maria, the former church of San Francesco houses the Museo Civico in its cloister. Next door, the 18C church of **Santa Croce**, with its fine concave façade, contains major artworks.

EXCURSIONS

Vallées de Cuneo

To the northwest, the Valle Grana, is the home of Castelmagno cheese. The valley of the Stura di Demonte separates the Cottian Alps from the Maritime Alps. To the southwest, the Gesso Valley takes you into the Parco delle Alpi Marittimea (AB4), Piemonte's largest natural park. The highest peak in this former hunting reserve is Monte Argentera (3 297m/10 817ft). The park is criss-crossed by trails, offering views over the dozens of lakes. The Vermenagna Valley climbs up to the main ski resort of the Maritime Alps, and the Tende Pass (1 908 m/6 260ft).

To the east, the Pesio Valley leads to the **Certosa di Pesio★**, a Carthusian monastery complex founded in the 12C.

Mondovì★

◗ 26km/16.2mi E on the SS 564.
This small town is divided into two parts: Breo and Piazza at an altitude of 550m/1 804ft overlooking the Ellero Valley. In Breo, the church of Santi Pietro e Paolo (15C–17C) stands on the Piazza San Pietro. Behind Chiesa della Missione's façade is a set of Baroque **frescoes★★**. On Piazza Maggiore is the 18C cathedral, with its monumental façade and lavish decor. Gardens with fine **views★**.

Santuario di Vicoforte

◗6km/3.7mi SE of Mondovì on the SS 28.
This imposing sanctuary was built in the late-16C. Its elliptical **dome★** (one of the largest in the world) was built in the 18C by Francesco Gallo and is covered in fresco decoration.

Grotta di Bossea à Frabosa Soprana★

◗20km/12.4mi S of Mondovì. ✆0174 34 92 40. www.grottadibossea.com. Closed 1 Jan, 25 Dec. 11€.
This cave contains spectacular karst formations, pools and fossils.

Vernante

◗23km/14.3mi S of Cuneo on the SP 21.
Pinocchio's adventures are illustrated in 130 murals on the building façades. The paintings are based on those of Attilio Mussino (1878–1954), who lived here.

Saluzzo★

This pretty medieval hillside town has an imposing castle. A prosperous centre of art and culture, it is also the birthplace of the patriot and writer Silvio Pellico (1789–1854), author of *My Prisons*.

▶ **Population:** 16 877
Ⓖ **Michelin Map:**
  561 I 4 – Piemonte.
🛈 **Info:** Piazza Risorgimento 1,
  12037 Saluzzo (CN).
  ☏0175 46 710.
  www.saluzzoturistica.it.
◖ **Location:** Saluzzo is situated
  between Cuneo and Turin.
☺ **Don't Miss:** Casa Cavassa.
🕒 **Timing:** Allow two days.

SIGHTS

Casa Cavassa★

Open Oct–Mar Tue–Fri 2.30–5pm, Sat–Sun 10am–12.30pm and 2.30–5pm; Apr-Sept Tue, Thu, Sat, Sun 10am–1pm and 3–6pm, Fri 3–6pm. 5€; 6€ including Torre Civica and Antico Palazzo Comunale. ☏0175 41 455. www.casacavassa.it.

The Renaissance portal of this elegant 15C house is surmounted by the motto *droit quoy qu'il soit* (forward at all costs) and by the emblem of the Cavassa family, a fish swimming upstream. The gallery of the panoramic loggia has a *grisaille* decoration depicting the *Labours of Hercules* by the Flemish-Burgundian artist Hans Clemer. Note his altarpiece, **Madonna della Misericordia★** in one of the rooms opening onto the loggia.

Chiesa di San Giovanni

Open daily 8am–noon and 2.30–6.30pm. ☏0175 46 710. www.saluzzoturistica.it.

The austere façade of this 14C church conceals a fine cycle of 15C **frescoes★**. The masterpiece of the church is the extraordinary **apse★★**, a jewel of Burgundian-Gothic art. The 15C **Torre Civica** has magnificent **views★**.

EXCURSIONS

Castello della Manta

◖4km/2.5mi S of Saluzzo on the S 589. Open Tue–Sun Mar–Sept 10am–6pm; Oct–Nov 10am–5pm. 7€. ☏0175 87 822. www.fondoambiente.it.

This 12C stronghold was turned into an aristocratic residence in the 15C. The **frescoes★★★** in the Baronial Room depict the scenes from the courtly poem *The Wandering Knight*, by Tommaso III.

Savigliano

◖13km/8mi E on the SS 662. 🛈Corso Roma 36. ☏0172 71 02 47.

Piazza Santarosa, the main square of this charming town, dates from the 12C. The 13C Torre Civica and a triumphal arch (1560) dedicated to the House of Savoy are here along with other medieval and Renaissance buildings. Via Sant'Andrea, which winds through the town's aristocratic quarter, is flanked by the Baroque church of Sant'Andrea and, opposite, the 17C Palazzo Taffini d'Acceglio, with its elegant main courtyard. In Via Jerusalem stands the Palazzo Muratori Cravetta, where painting, sculpture and architecture combine to form a harmonious whole. Going back across Piazza Santarosa, you'll come to the 19C Teatro Milanollo, boasting an elegant interior.

Castello di Racconigi★★

◖14km/8.7mi N of Savigliano on the SS 20. ☏0172 84 005. www.ilcastello diracconigi.it. Castle: Guided tours Tue–Sun 9am–7pm, Nov–Mar closed also Tue and Thu. 5€. Grounds: Tue–Sun Apr–Oct 10am–7pm; Nov–Mar 10am–6pm. 2€.

The military fortress of the Marquises of Saluzzo was acquired in the 17C by the Savoy–Carignano family, who transformed it into a summer residence. Originally designed by Guarino Guarini, the façade was added by Giovanni Battista Borra in 1755. A lavishly decorated first floor contrasts significantly with the simpler second floor, where the family

Priceless Mushrooms

Truffles grow in symbiosis with roots of oaks, willows or poplars in damp soil that has little exposure to the sun. They are hunted out by *trifolai* (dialect for truffle hunters), accompanied by highly trained pigs or dogs who must find the truffles without damaging them. Most prized are white, but black are heavenly too. Avoid truffle oil, though, which may be fake.

lived until the end of World War II. The most remarkable parts are the **Salone d'Ercole** and **Sala di Diana** rooms, the Chinese apartments, the **Gabinetto Etrusco** and the kitchens.

The Margaria, a model farm built in the Gothic Revival style in 1852, lies in the castle's vast grounds.

& Drive around the edge of the grounds to reach the Centro Cicogne, set up in 1985 to promote the reintroduction of the white stork *(for information ℘0172 83 457; www.cicogneracconigi.it).*

Abbazia di Staffarda★

⊙ 10km/6.2mi NW on the S 589. Open Tue–Sun 9am–12.30pm and 1.30–5pm (Mar–Oct 6pm). 6.50€. ℘0175 27 32 15. www.ordinemauriziano.it.

This imposing Romanesque-Gothic Cistercian monastery was built in the 12C–13C. Visit the guest quarters with their Gothic refectory, and the 13C *loggia del mercato*, the covered market. The **cloister** is reached via the long building where the lay brothers lived. At the end is the **church**, fronted by a portico.

To the south, 9km/5.6mi away is **Revello** (A3), the summer residence of Margaret of Foix and Ludovico II, Marquis of Saluzzo, who built the Cappella Marchionale (inside the town hall), a late Gothic masterpiece entirely decorated in frescoes. To visit, ask at the municipality ℘0175 25 71 71. Nearby is the **collegiate church**. The fine marble doorway dating from 1534 leads into an interior containing precious 16C works.

Valle d'Aosta★

Aosta Valley

With its castles and villages of balconied houses roofed with flat stone slabs *(lauzes)*, the Valle d'Aosta is one of Italy's most attractive tourist areas. This region comprising the Dora Baltea and adjacent valleys is surrounded by alpine peaks: Mont Blanc, the Matterhorn (Cervino), Monte Rosa, Grand Combin, Dent d'Hérens, Gran Paradiso and Grande Sassière. Since 1948 the Valle d'Aosta has been an autonomous region: inhabitants speak a Franco-Provençal dialect and public documents are published in Italian and French.

⚖ **Michelin Map:** 561 E 3–4.

🛈 **Info:** Piazza Porta Praetoria 3, 11100 Aosta. ℘0165 23 66 27. www.lovevda.it.

⊙ **Location:** Flanked by France and Switzerland, the Valle d'Aosta covers the northwest corner of Italy.

😊 **Don't Miss:** Skiing in Courmayeur and the beautiful Parco Nazionale del Gran Paradiso.

🕐 **Timing:** Three days to explore the region.

& **Kids:** This area is famous for its wooden toys.

FACILITIES

Owing to its marvellous position the Valle d'Aosta offers splendid **viewpoints★★★**. It is also a ski lover's paradise (resorts at **Breuil-Cervinia★★**, **Courmayeur★★**, **La Thuile**, **Gressoney**, **Champoluc** and **Cogne★**).
The slopes wind through breathtaking landscapes, woods and glaciers.

PARCO NAZIONALE DEL GRAN PARADISO★★

The Gran Paradiso National Park Department organises outings with park guides. For information, contact the Segreteria Turistica del Parco in Turin: Open Mon–Fri 9am–noon, ℘011 86 06 233, www.pngp.it or the info points including: Loc. Cheriettes, Aymavilles (Aosta) ℘0165 90 26 93, Chanavey, Rhêmes Notre-Dame (Aosta) ℘0165 93 61 93, Valsavarenche ℘0165 90 00 55. www.grand-paradis.it.

This national park (70 000ha/270sq mi) includes an area previously preserved as a royal hunting ground. It can be reached by the Rhêmes, Savarenche, Cogne and Locana valleys or the Nivolet Pass road. The park is rich in wildlife and important as a reserve.

Val di Rhêmes and Val Savarenche

These valleys are reached via Introd, a pretty town that overlooks the Dora di Rhêmes river gorge.
The bright, open and well-organised **Val di Rhêmes** is an excellent starting point to explore the Gran Paradiso national park. The attractive village **Rhêmes-St-**

Georges★ has old stone houses, gardens and peaceful streets. In **Rhêmes-Notre-Dame**, the park office has information on the local flora and fauna. From here, you can reach the Grande-Rousse Massif (3 607m/11 834ft). The road ends at the Benevolo refuge.

Val di Cogne★★

The road passes numerous villages on the way to **Cogne★**, the heart of the park, at the foot of a vast valley dominated by the glaciers of the Gran Paradiso (4 061 m/13 323ft). Popular for winter sports, this former mining settlement now lives by tourism and crafts.

4km/2.5mi from Cogne is the **Lillaz waterfall**, just beyond the hamlet of the same name. For a slightly longer walk (round trip about 2.5hrs), head towards the waterfall and follow the signed path on the right for **Lago di Loie★**. After a steep climb, you'll reach this delightful mountain lake (alt. 2 396m/7 861ft), an ideal spot for picnics, with spectacular views. From **Valnontey**, you can visit the **Giardino Alpino Paradisia**, which is in full bloom during July. This alpine botanical garden (alt. 1 700m/5 577ft) was created in 1955 and contains over 1 000 varieties of plant. There is a butterfly garden. Open mid-Jun–mid-Sep 10am–5.30pm. 3€. ℘0165 75 301. www.pngp.it.

🚗 DRIVING TOUR

COURMAYEUR TO IVREA
160km/99.4mi. Allow 1 day.

Courmayeur★★
Maps in the Michelin Atlas Italy.
This well-known mountaineering and winter-sports resort is a good for excursions. Take a cablecar to the Cresta d'Arp and across the Mont Blanc Massif and make a short detour into France (🄲see *THE GREEN GUIDE FRENCH ALPS*). By car you can explore the following valleys: Veny, Ferret or Testa d'Arpi and the road to the Little St Bernard Pass, used by the Romans. Once through St-Pierre and past the road for the Cogne Valley, is

Gran Paradiso National Park
© Anze_Bizjan/iStockphoto.com

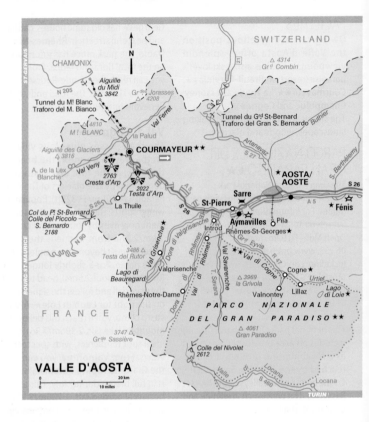

VALLE D'AOSTA

Castello di Sarre, the summer residence of the Counts of Savoy.

Val Grisenche★

This isolated, majestic valley offers fine walks in lovely natural surroundings. Alongside grey-stone and slate buildings, the village of **Valgrisenche** has the pretty church of **St-Grat★**, dedicated to the 5C Bishop of Aosta.

Just after the hamlet of Le Perret, the **Lago di Beauregard** extends over some 4km/2.5mi (alt. 1 770m/5 807ft). To find the tourist route around the lake, go past the dam. On foot or by car, this circular route offers views over the lake and the glaciers of the Testa del Rutor (3 486m/11 437ft).

St-Pierre

The sturdy **Castello Sarriod de la Tour** stands over the River Stura. The castle (10C–12C) originally built around a square tower protected by a perimeter wall underwent extensive alterations until the 18C. There are fine **frescoes★** dating from 1250 in the chapel. The ceiling beams in the **sala delle teste★** are decorated with 171 carvings (15C). Open Thu–Tue 10am–12.30pm and 1.30–5pm (open later in summer). 3€. ℘0165 90 46 89. www.lovevda.it.

Castello di Saint-Pierre/Museo regionale di Scienze Naturali – This 11C castle towers over the village, which also has a Romanesque bell tower, and an interesting museum of the local flora, fauna and minerals. ⊶Closed for renovation at time of writing ℘0165 18 45 115. www.museoscienze.it.

Aosta★

Train: Aosta (Torino Porta Susa 2hr 19mins).

Aosta, capital of the region, has retained the geometric plan of a military camp

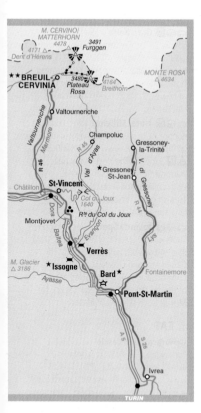

(castrum), a picturesque centre and some interesting ancient Roman monuments. An active religious centre in the Middle Ages, this was the birthplace of theologian St Anselm, who became Archbishop of Canterbury.

Roman Monuments★

These are grouped in the centre of Aosta and include the **Porta Pretoria**, a majestic 1C BC arch, **Arco di Augusto**, a **Roman bridge**, a **theatre** and the ruins of an **amphitheatre**.

Complesso Ursino – The church has some lovely carved 15C **stalls** and a Baroque rood screen. Beside the 11C **crypt★** a doorway opens onto Romanesque cloisters with historiated **capitals★★**. **Priorato di Sant'Orso★★** is a Renaissance-style priory with elegant **windows★**. For opening times, visit the website or call. ℘0165 26 20 26. www.lovevda.it.

Pila

A lovely excursion from Aosta is to Pila, a small resort at 1 800m/5 905ft by either car (18km/11.2mi, via Gressan or Charvensod) or cablecar – the terminus is close to the centre (www.pila.it). From the top, there's a 360° **view★★★**. Excellent skiing in winter.

Castello di Fénis★

Open 10am–6pm, closed Tue. Times may vary. Closed 1 Jan, 1 May, 25 Dec. 5€.
℘0165 76 42 63. www.lovevda.it.
This fortress contains carved furniture in the local style.

Breuil-Cervinia★★

This winter-sports resort is situated at 2 050m/6 726ft. Cablecars link it to the Rosa Plateau (Plan Rosa) and the Furggen Pass at 3 491m/11 453ft.

St-Vincent

The famous Casino de la Vallée is set in a fine park. It's close to Castello di Montjovet and **Castello di Verrès**.

Castello d'Issogne★

Open 10am–6pm. Times may vary
Closed Wed in winter. 5€. ℘0125 92 93 73. www.lovevda.it.
A 15C castle featuring a wrought-iron pomegranate tree in the courtyard.

Fortezza di Bard★

The fortress commands the upper **Dora Baltea Valley**.

Pont-St-Martin

A village named after the Roman bridge that was guarded by a chapel dedicated to St John Nepomuk.

Val di Gressoney

From Pont-St-Martin, continue along the Val di Gressoney (33km/20.5mi to Gressoney-la-Trinité on the R 44) to **Gressoney-St-Jean★** (1 385 m/4 544ft) where French and Swiss-German dialects are spoken. The village offers walking trails or cross-country skiing among the pine trees. In winter, skiers can take a shuttle to **Gressoney-la-Trinité** (1 637m/5 371ft) and access the valleys of the Monte Rosa ski area via the Jolanda chairlift. This vast area, with 180km/112mi of slopes, covers the Ayas Champoluc, Gressoney and Valsesia valleys.

Ivrea

This town stands at the mouth of the Valle d'Aosta. To the east of Ivrea is the largest moraine in Europe, the Serra d'Ivrea.

ADDRESSES

🛏 STAY

😊 **Agriturismo Lo Mayen** – Loc. Bien 1. (4km/2.5mi from Valsavarenche). ✆0165 90 57 35. 🅿 8 rooms. A pleasant *agriturismo* (farmstay) with quiet, simply decorated and very clean attic rooms. The owners are cheese makers.

😊 **Hotel Tourist** – Via Roma 32, 11028 Valtournenche. 8km/5mi S of Cervinia. ✆0166 92 070. www.hotel-tourist.it. Closed Oct. 🦽🅿 34 rooms. Bright, welcoming decor, spacious rooms, wood furniture. Restaurant serves local food. Free minibus to ski slopes.

😊😊 **Albergo dei Camosci** – Fraz. La Saxe 7, 11013 Courmayeur. ✆0165 84 23 38. www.hoteldeicamosci.com. Closed May–mid-Jun and Oct–Nov. 🦽🅿 24 rooms. 🍽. Classic mountain-style hotel. Great views of Mont Blanc. Cooking focuses on regional specialities.

😊😊 **Albergo Granta Parey** – Loc. Chanavey, 11010 Rhêmes-Notre-Dame. 1.5km/0.9mi N of Rhêmes-Notre-Dame. ✆0165 93 61 04. www.rhemesgrantaparey. com. Closed Oct–Nov. 🅿 33 rooms. 🍽. Children are particularly welcome. Family-run hotel situated very near the ski lifts. Spacious rooms, pine furniture and mountain views. Gym, sauna, Turkish bath.

😊😊 **Hotel La Barme** – Loc. Valnontey, 11012 Cogne. 4km/2.5mi SE of Cogne. ✆0165 74 91 77. www.hotellabarme.com. Closed May and Nov. 🦽🅿 15 rooms. 🍽. A small, family-run hotel ideally situated for excursions into the Parco del Gran Paradiso. Stone and wooden structure and pale furnishings. Restaurant, garden and a sauna.

😊😊😊 **Gran Baita** – Strada Castello Savoia, 26 loc. Gressmatten, 5min walk from Gressoney-St-Jean. ✆0125 35 55 35. www. hotelgranbaita.it. 12 rooms. A charming hotel located in an 18C *baita*, with views of Monte Rosa. Relaxing with sauna. Half-board.

😊😊😊 **Hotel Milleluci** – Loc. Porossan Roppoz 15, 1km/0.6mi from Aosta, 11100 Aosta. ✆0165 23 52 78. www.hotelmilleluci.com. 🦽🅿 5 rooms. The bedrooms have panoramic views. Solar-heated swimming pool, Jacuzzi, sauna and Turkish bath. Welcoming with very large and tasty breakfasts.

😊😊😊 **Jolanda Sport** – Loc. Edelboden Superiore 31. Gressoney-la-Trinité. ✆0125 36 61 40. www.hoteljolandasport.com. Closed May and Oct–Nov. 32 rooms. A comfortable family-run hotel at the foot of the ski slope. A practical choice for Monte Rosa ski area. Half-board.

🍽 EAT

😊😊 **Ristorante Casale** – Frazione Condemine 1, 11020 S-Christophe. 4km/2.5mi NE of Aosta. ✆0165 54 12 72. www.hotelristorantecasale.it. Closed Sun evening and Mon. Good food – features local traditions. Welcoming, family atmosphere. Lovely terrace.

😊😊 **Vecchia Aosta** – Via Porta Pretoriana 4, 11100 Aosta. ✆0165 36 11 86. www.vecchiaaosta.it. Closed Tue and Wed lunch. Booking recommended. Very good restaurant choice in town, with several dining rooms set in an old building. Specialises in cured meats and pasta with fontina cheese. Pleasant terrace and charming service.

TAKING A BREAK

La Bottega degli Antichi Sapori – Via Porta Praetoria 63. ✆0165 26 38 42. Open Mon–Sat 8am–1pm and 3–7.30pm. Cheeses, hams, wines, various pastas and delicious sauces.

Old Distillery Pub – Via Prés-Fossés 7. ✆0165 23 95 11. Live music and a lively crowd at this English-style pub. Open late.

Liguria

Major City: Genova
Official Website: www.turismoinliguria.it

Clinging to the coast above the Ligurian Sea, the crescent-shaped region of Liguria stretches from a border with France in the west to Tuscany in the south and east. Hemmed in by the Alps, Apennines and the sea, Liguria is a region of dramatic land- and cityscapes, chief among them the dazzling Portofino Promontory, with its fine harbour, and the Cinque Terre, five pastel-hued villages crowning the rocky coast between La Spezia and Genova, the regional capital. Between the 11C and the 18C, Genova was a powerful independent city-state and its importance as a maritime hub continues to this day.

Remnants of an Empire

Liguria, furrowed by deep, narrow valleys at right angles to the coast, had a maritime civilisation before the Roman era. The steep slopes of the inner valleys are dotted with poor hilltop villages, watching over groves of chestnut or olive trees and cultivated terraces. The rocky, indented coastline has few fish to offer but has enjoyed heavy coastal traffic since the time of the Ligurians, facilitated by many small deep-water ports. The Roman Empire gave its appearance to the country, with olive groves and vineyards, now complemented by vegetables, fruit (melons and peaches) and flowers grown on an industrial scale.

The **Riviera di Ponente** (Western Riviera) west of Genova is sunnier and more sheltered than the **Riviera di Levante** (Eastern Riviera), but the latter has a more luxuriant vegetation. The chief towns are Imperia, Savona and **Genova** (shipyards, steel production, oil terminal and thermal power station) and La Spezia (naval base, commercial port, thermal power station and arms manufacture).

Highlights

1 Embark on a whale-watching excursion from Genova's **Port** (p369)
2 Interact with marine life at the **Acquario** (p369)
3 Glimpse historic *palazzi* along the **Strada Nuova** (p371)
4 Unwind at a waterfront caffè in **Portofino** (p377)
5 Visit the villages of **Cinque Terre** (p382)

Manarola, Cinque Terre

© Borut Trdina/iStockphoto.com

Genova★★★

Genoa

The capital of Liguria, Italy's greatest seaport and the birthplace of Christopher Colombus, Genova "la Superba" boasts a spectacular location★★. Stretched across the slopes of steeply tiered hillside, the port is overlooked by the colourful façades of a host of buildings. It is a city full of character and contrasts, where splendid palaces stand alongside the humblest alleyways.

A BIT OF HISTORY

By the 11C the Genovese fleet ruled supreme over the Tyrrhenian Sea, having vanquished the Saracens. With around 70 ships, all built in the city's dockyards, Genova was a formidable sea power much coveted by foreign rulers.

In the Crusades Genova established trading posts on the shores of the eastern Mediterranean and following the creation of the Republic of St George in 1100, seamen, merchants, bankers and moneylenders worked together to keep Genova a notch above the rest.

Previously allied with Pisa against the Saracens (11C), the two cities fought over Corsica (13C) and in the 14C Genova entered rivalry with Venice, for trading rights of the Mediterranean.

In the 14C Genova's trade with the Orient flourished and the Bank of St George was founded in 1408. The merchants became ingenious moneylenders and instituted such modern methods as bills of credit, cheques and insurance.

Continual struggles between rival families led to the decision (1339) to elect a *doge* for life. In the 15C foreign protection was sought.

The great admiral **Andrea Doria** (1466–1560) gave Genova its aristocratic constitution and status of mercantile republic in 1528. Enterprising and independent, Andrea Doria distinguished himself against the Turks in 1519 and, while serving François I, by covering the French retreat after their defeat at Pavia

- ▶ **Population:** 609 746
- ◔ **Michelin Map:** 561 I8.
- **Info:** Via Garibaldi 12r. ℘010 55 72 903. Via al Porto Antico 2. www.visitgenoa.it.
- ▶ **Location:** The city is enclosed by a mountain range curving around 30km/18.6mi of coastline. The historic centre around the port is a maze of alleyways *(carruggi)*; the modern part of the city is crossed by wide avenues.
- ▶ **Train:** Genova Principe.
- **Parking:** Pay for parking in Piazza della Vittoria or at the Porto Antico.
- **Don't Miss:** The lively Porto Antico area, the Baroque palaces of Strada Nuova, Galleria di Palazzo Spinola and the Palazzo del Principe.
- **Timing:** Two to three days.
- **Kids:** The Acquario, and Città dei Bambini at Antichi Magazzini del Cotone.

(1525). In 1528, indignant at François I's unjust treatment of him, he entered the service of Charles V, who plied him with honours and favours. Following his death and the development of ports on the Atlantic coast, Genova declined and it was Louis XIV who destroyed the harbour in 1684. In 1768, by the Treaty of Versailles, Genova surrendered Corsica to France. In 1848, under Giuseppe Mazzini, it became one of the cradles of the Risorgimento.

Fine Arts in Genova – As happened elsewhere the decline of Genova's commercial prosperity in the 16C–17C coincided with intense artistic activity. This can be seen in the new *palazzi* built and in the arrival of foreign artists, especially Flemish. In 1607 Rubens published a work on the *Palazzi di Genova* and in 1621–27 Van Dyck painted the city's nobility. Puget lived at Genova (1661–67), working for the Doria, Spinola and other patrician families.

Porto Antico, Genova

©Peeter Viisimaa/iStockphoto.com

The Genovese School, characterised by dramatic intensity and muted colours, includes such artists as Luca Cambiaso (16C), Bernardo Strozzi (1581–1644), the fine engraver Castiglione, and especially **Alessandro Magnasco** (1667–1749), whose sharp and colourful brushwork marks him out as a precursor of modern art. In the field of architecture, Galeazzo Alessi (1512–72), at his best, was the equal of Sansovino and Palladio in the nobility and ingenuity of his designs.

PORT★★★

Boat tours: 70min tour of port daily, from Aquarium; 1day excursions to San Fruttuoso, Portofino, Cinque Terre; 1 day whale-watching cruises ℘010 26 57 12, www.liguriaviamare.it.
The historic **Porto Antico** has been delightfully restructured and includes a marina, bars and restaurants and the famous aquarium. The **Bigo**, an unusual structure with a lift, was designed by **Renzo Piano** and has an excellent **bird's-eye view★**.
To the west, the entrance to Genova's Porto Nuovo is marked by **La Lanterna** lighthouse, symbol of the city (open Sat–Sun and public hols 2.30–6.30pm; the panoramic terrace is temporarily closed to the public. 6€; ℘349 28 09 485; www.lanternadigenova.it).

♁♁ Acquario★★★

♿ Open Jul–Aug 8.30am–10.30pm; rest of the year 9 or 9.30am–8pm (Sat–Sun 9pm) (last entry 2hr before closing). 24€. ℘010 23 45 678. www.acquariodigenova.it.
Genova's vast, well-organised aquarium has illuminated information panels (also in English), state-of-the-art displays, interactive sections and reconstructions of underwater environments from around the world. The tank with species that can be touched holds great appeal; so do behind-the-scenes visits.

Palazzo San Giorgio

This imposing 13C palazzo, restructured in the 16C, faces the Porto Antico and was the headquarters of the Bank of St George. Behind the building on **Piazza Banchi** is the Loggia dei Mercanti, where markets were held and which now houses temporary exhibitions.

Museo Nazionale dell'Antartide

Open Tue–Sun 10am–6pm. 6€.
℘010 23 451. www.portoantico.it.
Housed in Palazzina Millo, at the Porto Antico, the museum's aim is to raise awareness of the fascinating but relatively unknown continent of Antarctica. Continuing along Via del Molo, you reach Porta Siberia, the city gate designed by Alessi in 1553, which houses Museo Luzzati, with works by local artist and children's book illustrator Emanuele Luzzati (1921–2007). Workshops for children are held. Open Tue–Sun 10am–1pm and 2–6pm. 5€. ℘010 25 30 328. www.museoluzzati.it.

GETTING AROUND
Information

📞010 55 81 14; www.amt.genova.it. Genova's well-organised public transport includes buses, an underground line, funiculars, lifts and a ferry service. **GenovaPass** permits free travel on all forms of public transport (except Navebus and Volabus). 4.50€ for a 24hr pass. **Volabus** – This bus links the airport with the city centre stopping at both Brignole and Piazza Principe railway stations, departing every hour (6€ allows up to 1hr on all public transport, 📞848 000 030; www.amt.genova.it).

Tours

A day out by train – This is one of the locals' favourite Sunday outings. A trip into the country on a historic narrow-gauge railway that runs up into the hills between Genova and Casella making frequent stops at villages on the way. The train is ideal for walkers and there's plenty of info on footpaths and features on the railway's website. There are frequent departures daily from Genova Piazza Manin station; while trip takes around an hour (📞848 000 030 or 010 55 82 414; www.ferroviagenovacasella.it).

Card Musei – Includes entry to 21 museums in Genova as well as discounts on certain attractions including the Acquario and exhibitions at the Palazzo Ducale. 12€ for a 24hr pass/13.50€ including use of public transport; 16€ for a 48hr pass /20€ including use of public transport; www.visitgenoa.it.

SIGHTSEEING

Genova City Tour – Daily departures from Piazza Caricamento (in front of the Acquario) every 30min (Apr–Nov). 15€. 60min. 📞335 54 17 825; www.genova.city-sightseeing.it.

Magazzini del Cotone

Built in the 19C, the former cotton warehouse was restored by Renzo Piano to mark the celebrations honouring Christopher Columbus. On the first floor is the **👥 Città dei Bambini e dei Ragazzi★**, devoted to children aged 2–12. Through a series of interactive games, young visitors are encouraged to explore their senses, the natural world, basic technological and scientific principles and to develop their social skills. Open Tue–Sun 10am–6pm. Closed 3 weeks in Sept. 5€/7€. 📞010 24 85 790. www.portoantico.it.

Galata Museo del Mare★

Porto Antico. Open Mar–Oct daily 10am–7.30pm; Nov–Feb Tue–Fri 10am–6pm, Sat–Sun and hols 10am–7.30pm (last entry 1hr before closing). 12€. 📞010 23 45 655. www.galatamuseodelmare.it. One of several maritime museums in Genova, this has interesting interactive displays giving an overview of the city's maritime trading traditions.

👣WALKING TOURS

1 THE GOLDEN AGE★★

Circuit in green on town map on p373. Allow half a day with the museum visits. Start from Piazza Matteotti.

Palazzo Ducale★

Piazza Matteotti 9. 📞010 81 71 663. www.palazzoducale.genova.it. Temporary exhibitions and occasional tours. Behind the monumental façade of **Palazzo Ducale** (1778) the interior includes a lovely **chapel★** with frescoes by G.B. Carlone illustrating scenes from the city's history.

Chiesa del Gesù (or dei Santi Andrea e Ambrogio)

Built by Tibaldi in 1597, the church houses in its sumptuous interior *The Assumption* by Guido Reni and two paintings by **Rubens★★**: *The Circumcision* and *The Healing by St Ignatius*. Another painting not to be missed is Simon Vouet's splendid *Crucifixion*.

Take Via Cardinale to Piazza de Ferrari, where the selection of grand buildings includes **Teatro Carlo Felice** and the Ligurian Academy of Fine Arts. This area was developed in the 19C–20C when churches and convents were demolished to make way for the new Via Roma (1870), to connect the centre with the new residential areas in the hills. The street still contains examples of the Art Nouveau style, as does Via XX Settembre. Also from this period is **Galleria Mazzini**, a shopping arcade.

▷ Walk through the peaceful Galleria Mazzini, parallel to Via Roma.

Palazzo Doria Spinola

This square-shaped palazzo built 1541–3 originally had two storeys. The first floor, with loggia, is decorated with a stucco frieze. Inside, the 16C frescoes by L. Cambiaso depict Italian and foreign cities and include a fine view of Genova. The building is now occupied by the city's prefecture.

▷ Take Salita Santa Caterina to Piazza Fontane Marose, which is the starting point of Via Garibaldi (ⓒ*see below*).

Via Interiano will take you to Piazza Portello, where you can take a lift up to **Castelletto** and the Belvedere Montaldo, which has fabulous **views★★**.

Strada Nuova (Via Garibaldi)★★★

In the mid-16C a number of patrician families built their residences on this street away from the historic centre. It is one of the loveliest streets in Italy and a UNESCO World Heritage Site. Three of the most significant palazzi now form a single museum: Palazzo Rosso, Palazzo Bianco and Palazzo Tursi. Open Tue–Fri 9am–7pm (winter 6pm), Sat–Sun 9.30am–7pm (winter 6.30pm). 9€. ℘010 55 74 972. www.museidigenova.it.

Palazzo Tursi★★ – The palazzo (no. 9) was commissioned by Nicolo Grimaldi, banker to King Philip II of Spain, and

boasts a lengthy façade and terraced gardens. Acquired by Giovanni Andrea Doria in 1596, it went to the Savoy family in 1820 and was finally purchased by the city of Genova in 1848.

Palazzo Bianco – No. 11, this houses an art gallery with paintings by Caravaggio, Veronese, Rubens and Van Dyck.

Palazzo Rosso – This palazzo (no. 18) was commissioned by the Brignole Sale brothers and designed as a double residence around a courtyard. The sumptuous interior also hosts art collections including works by Van Dyck, Dürer and Veronese.

Several of the other buildings in the street are now occupied by banks, including:

No. 1 – Palazzo Agostino Pallavicini (Banco Popolare di Brescia); **no. 2 – Palazzo Pantaleo Spinola** (Banco di Chiavari e della Riviera Ligure) – the sober façade belies a magnificent interior with 17C frescoes; **no. 5 – Palazzo Angelo Giovanni Spinola** (Deutsche Bank). Among the other buildings are **Palazzo Tobia Pallavicino (no. 4)** with a delightful entrance hall decorated with grotesques and a dazzling gilded Rococo **gallery★**; **no. 6 – Palazzo Doria**, owned by the Doria family since 1723 – in the entrance hall you can see a lamp with an eagle, which is the family's symbol.

Take a small detour to see the church of **Santa Maria Maddalena**, the **interior★** of which is one of the most characteristic examples of the local Baroque style.

▷ Return to Via Garibaldi.

Palazzo Lomellino★ (no. 7) is open to the public on the first Saturday of each month (10am–6pm; 8€). The ornate façade of this palazzo (1565–7) hides a fine **nymphaeum★** that opens onto a courtyard. Fine frescoes by Strozzi decorate the interior.

Nos. 8–10 – Palazzo Cattaneo Adorno – Here there are two main entrances, one for each wing: the west wing, which has belonged to the Adorno family for three centuries and contains frescoes by Lazzaro Tavarone, and the east wing, which has belonged to the Cattaneo family since the late-19C.

Nos. 14–16 – Palazzo delle Torrette – This was built in 1716 in order to conceal medieval houses from view.

▶ Follow Via Cairoli and then turn left at Via San Siro and walk in the direction of the church.

The highlight of the church of **San Siro** is its **interior★**, decorated with 17C frescoes by G.B. Carlone. The high altar, in marble and bronze, is the work of P. Puget (1670).

Take the Salita San Siro, followed by Via Lomellini, a small street off to the right: no. 11, the house where Giuseppe Mazzini was born, is now home to the **Museo del Risorgimento** (open Tue, Fri 9am–1pm, Wed 9am–6pm, Sat 9.30am–6.30pm; closed Thu, Sun (except 1st of the month, 9.30am–6.30pm), Mon, public hols; 5€; ℘010 24 65 843; www.museidigenova.it).

Via Balbi★

This street is lined with palaces. The **Palazzo Reale** (Royal Palace) is at no. 10 (⌖see below). The imposing 17C university building, **Palazzo dell'Università★**, at no. 5 has a beautiful courtyard and a majestic staircase.

Palazzo Reale (Balbi-Durazzo)★★

♿Open Tue–Sat 9am–7pm, Sun and public hols 1.30pm–7pm. 4€; 6.50€ with Palazzo Spinola. ℘010 27 10 286. www.palazzorealegenova.beniculturali.it.

Built (1643–50) by the Balbi family, then enlarged by the Durazzo family, the building has stunning frescoes and decorations together with works of art by Tintoretto, Van Dyck and Guercino among others. Among the frescoes are some by Domenico Parodi (1668–1740), who also designed the stunning **Mirrored Gallery★** styled on the Gallery in the Doria Pamphilj palace in Rome and the more famous one at Versailles. Beyond the sumptuous throne room, in the audience room is the portrait of *Caterina Balbi Durazzo* by Van Dyck.

▶ At the end of the street, turn left into the Salita San Giovanni.

Chiesa e Commenda San Giovanni di Prè★

This Romanesque church is made up of two levels, one on top of the other, and was founded in 1180 by the Knights of Malta. The bell tower, one of the few to have survived from that period, is topped by a stone steeple. The adjoining building served as a hospital providing accommodation for pilgrims en route for the Holy Land. It now houses one of the city's maritime museums.

② OLD TOWN★★

Allow 3hrs. Start at Piazza San Lorenzo.

Heading east out of Porto Antico you wind your way up charming, narrow alleyways.

Cattedrale di San Lorenzo★★

The cathedral, originally built in the 12C, with additions made through to the 16C, has a splendid Gothic **façade★★**, typical of the Genovese style. French influence appears in the placing of the 13C doorways and the large rose window. The carving on the central doorway represents a Tree of Jesse and scenes from the Life of Christ *(on the piers)* and the Martyrdom of St Lawrence and Christ between the Symbols of the Evangelists *(on the tympanum)*. The severe and majestic **interior★** has marble columns in the nave and a false gallery above. The **Chapel of St John the Baptist★** *(at the end of the north aisle)* once held the remains of St John.

Museo del Tesoro di San Lorenzo★

Open Mon–Sat 9am–noon and 3–6pm. 4.50€; 6€ with Museo Diocesano. ℘010 24 71 831. www.museidigenova.it. Access from the left.

The treasury museum includes the 9C Sacro Catino, a hexagonal cup in emerald-green blown glass, which, according to legend, is said to be the Holy Grail.

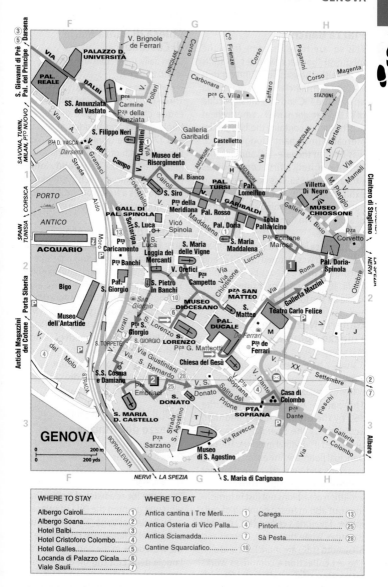

GENOVA

WHERE TO STAY

Albergo Cairoli.....................①
Albergo Soana.......................②
Hotel Balbi.............................③
Hotel Cristoforo Colombo....④
Hotel Galles...........................⑤
Locanda di Palazzo Cicala.....⑥
Viale Sauli..............................⑦

WHERE TO EAT

Antica cantina i Tre Merli......①
Antica Osteria di Vico Palla....④
Antica Sciamadda..................⑦
Cantine Squarciafico.............⑩

Carega..................................⑬
Pintori...................................㉕
Sà Pesta................................㉘

Museo Diocesano★

Via Tommaso Reggio 20r. & Open
Mon–Sat 3–7pm. 6€. ℘010 24 75 127.
www.museodiocesanogenova.it.
This museum is housed in the beautiful **cloisters★** of the Cathedral Canons'
residence (12C). It has finds from the
Domus Romana (1C BC) and a collection of sculptures and paintings, many
of which are by Genovese artists.

◗ Take Via di Scurreria then turn right
into the Vico San Matteo.

Piazza San Matteo★

In the city centre, this small but harmonious square is lined with 13C–15C
palaces that belonged to the Doria
family. No. 17 is a Renaissance building
presented to Andrea Doria by a grateful
republic. The **church of San Matteo** has
a Genovese-style façade.

Piazza Banchi

This square takes its name from the medieval "bankers" who set up stalls outside the houses surrounding it. It was the commercial centre of Genova up until the 19C and also the site of one of its three major markets, where wheat was traded. It contains the **Loggia dei Mercanti** (merchant's loggia), which was built in the late-16C and became the site of Italy's first commodities exchange in 1855. It is now used as an exhibition space. The square is dominated by the astonishing raised church of **San Pietro in Banchi** with its *trompe l'œil* façade.

Via San Luca leads to the church of San Luca, which was restored in the 17C and decorated with frescoes by Domenico Piola. It also contains a fine *Nativity* scene by the local artist Grechetto.

Galleria Nazionale di Palazzo Spinola★★

Piazza Pellicceria 1. ♿ Open Tue–Sat, 8.30am–7.30pm, Sun 1.30–7.30pm. 4€; 6.50€ with Palazzo Reale. ℰ010 27 05 300. www.palazzospinola.beniculturali.it.
This palace, built at the end of the 16C by the Grimaldi family and then acquired by the Spinola family, has preserved its original interiors. The two principal floors are fine examples of 17C (first floor) and 18C (second floor) interior styles. It is thus possible to identify the evolution of fashions not just in furnishings but also in fresco painting of **ceilings★**. Tavarone's ceiling (17C) is richly Baroque, while those by L. Ferrari and S. Galeotti (18C) are more light and airy. The **art collection★** comprises works by painters of the Italian and Flemish Renaissance, among them an enchanting **Portrait of Ansaldo Pallavicino** by Van Dyck, a *Portrait of a Nun* by the Genovese painter Strozzi, *Sacred and Profane Love* by Guido Reni and, on the third floor, a moving **Ecce Homo★** by Antonello da Messina.

Chiesa di Santa Maria di Castello★

Open daily 10am–1pm and 3–6pm. ℰ010 86 03 690. www.santamariadicastello.it.
Three cloisters surround this Romanesque church, the nave of which is flanked by chapels added in the 15C and 17C. In the Grimaldi chapel, note the polyptych of The *Annunciation* by Mazzone (1469). The second cloister (15C), the loggia of which overlooks the port, houses a fresco of The *Annunciation* by Giusto di Ravensburg.

Chiesa di San Donato★

Built in the 12C and 13C, this church has its original doorway and a delightful Romanesque octagonal **campanile★**. The Romanesque interior is also alluring: note the sumptuous **Adoration of the Magi★★** polyptych by Joos Van Cleve. Via San Donato leads into Piazza delle Erbe, where the youth of Genova gather in the evening. The Salita del Priore leads to **Porta Soprana**, one of the oldest entrances to the city (12C), characterised by twin towers.

ADDITIONAL SIGHTS
Palazzo del Principe★

Piazza Principe 4.
Open daily, 10am–6pm (last entry 5.15pm). 9€. ♿ ℰ010 25 55 09. www.doriapamphilj.it.
This is the 16C residence of Andrea Doria who was granted the title of prince in 1531. **Perin del Vaga** (1501–47), a pupil of Raphael in Rome, was responsible for the **frescoes★** in the entrance hall, the Loggia degli Eroi and the symmetrical apartments of the prince and his wife, accessible from the loggia. The fresco in the Salone della Caduta dei Giganti (which takes its name from the subject) is particularly well preserved and contains a **Portrait of Andrea Doria★** by **Sebastiano del Piombo** (1526) and another portrait of Doria at 92.

Museo di Sant'Agostino

Piazza Sarzano 35r. &Open Tue–Fri 9am–7pm (winter 6pm), Sat–Sun 9.30am–7pm (winter 6.30pm). Closed public hols. 5€ (under-18s free). ✆010 25 11 263. www.museidigenova.it.
The convent and adjoining 13C church (now the auditorium) contain the Museum of Ligurian Architecture and Sculpture, where you will find fragments and sculptures from religious buildings that have been demolished and from private houses. Highlights include the 13C tombstone of Simonetta and Percivalle Lercari, which looks like a stone version of a page from an illuminated manuscript, and the 14C Monument to Margaret of Brabant by Giovanni Pisano; on the second floor, you will find sculptures by Pierre Puget *(The Abduction of Helen)* and Antonio Canova *(The Penitent Magdalene)*.

Villetta di Negro-Museo Chiossone★

Piazzale Mazzini 4. Open Tue–Fri 9am–7pm (winter 6pm), Sat–Sun 9.30am–7pm (winter 6.30pm). 5€. ✆010 54 22 85. www.museidigenova.it.
On higher ground to the northwest of Piazza Corvetto, this is a sort of belvedere-labyrinth with palm trees, cascades and artificial grottoes.
From the terrace there is a lovely **view★** over the town and the sea. Standing on the summit is the Museo Chiossone di Arti Orientali, which houses the collection of the Genovese engraver Chiossone, who was passionate about Oriental art after living in Japan for 23 years. The collection includes sculptures, Buddhas, *objets d'art*, armoury and a remarkable assortment of prints, ivories and lacquerwork.

Chiesa di Santo Stefano

From its elevation on the Via XX Settembre, the church overlooks the town's arterial road, flanked by elegant, Art Nouveau-style buildings. The Romanesque church has a fine Lombardy-style apse. Inside note the splendid painting by Giulio Romano, the Martyrdom of St Stephen★ (c.1524).

Chiesa di Santa Maria di Carignano

Via Ravasco.
This vast church was built in the 16C to plans by Alessi. Inside, there is a fine statue of St Sebastiana by Puget.

EXCURSIONS
Cimitero di Staglieno★

❯ 1.5km/0.9mi N. From Piazza Corvetto take Via Assarotti (off the map) and then turn left into Via Montaldo.
In this curious cemetery there are ornate tombs and simple clay tumuli.

Albora

❯ 34km/21mi E..
This is the location of the lido, which has been built around avenues shaded with trees and is flanked by elegant buildings. Albara has been a holiday resort since the end of the 14C and it retains some fine 16C villas, including the **villa Cambiaso Giustiniania**, designed by Alessi. **Corso Italia**, where the locals head for their early evening *passeggiata*, is flanked by Art Nouveau-style villas. The little **Porto di Boccadasse★**, overlooked by the multicoloured fishermen's houses, has retained its charm. From the top of Santa Chiara is a wonderful **view★★** over the Riviera as far as Portofino.

Pegli

❯ 15km/9.3mi W of Genova.
This neighbourhood contains the most beautiful **park★** in Genova. It was designed around the middle of the 19C by Michele Canzio, the set designer at the Carlo Felice theatre. He arranged the garden in a series of theatrical scenes marked by little buildings, lakes, grottoes and waterfalls. Parco Durazzo Pallavicini: Via Pallavicini 11 (next to the railway station). &Park: only guided tours by reservation, ✆329 533 21 67 (10€); botanical garden open Wed–Fri 9am–1pm, Sat–Sun 10am–12.45pm and 3–4.45pm. Call for other opening hours. 3.50€. ✆010 40 76 473.

ADDRESSES

🏠 STAY

🕙 During international events, hotels tend to raise their prices.

🛏️ **Albergo Cairoli** – Via Cairoli 14/4. ☎010 24 61 454. www.hotelcairoligenova.com. 12 rooms. Rooms aren't large but there's a good terrace and a small gym plus a handy location in the historic centre.

🛏️ **Albergo Soana** – Via XX Settembre 23/8 (4th floor), 16121 Genova. ☎010 56 28 14. www.hotelsoana.it. 19 rooms. Another centrally located no-frills hotel. Wifi.

🛏️ **Hotel Balbi** – Via Balbi 21/3. ☎010 27 59 288. www.hotelbalbigenova.it. 13 rooms. Spacious bedrooms with frescoed ceilings at this family-run hotel.

🛏️ **Hotel Cristoforo Colombo** – Via di Porta Soprana 27. ☎010 25 13 643. www.hotelcolombo.it. 18 rooms. A characterful central hotel with a curious display of assorted items. Breakfast terrace.

🛏️ **Hotel Galles** – Via Bersaglieri d'Italia 13. ☎010 24 62 820. www.hotelgallesgenova.com. 21 rooms. 🍽️ Between the station and the port, comfortable rooms and wooden floors.

🛏️ **Locanda di Palazzo Cicala** – Piazza S. Lorenzo 16. ☎010 25 18 824. www.palazzocicala.it. 10 rooms. A combination of historic and contemporary styles, in a prestigious palazzo.

🍴 EAT

Ligurian specialities such as focaccia and pesto are served widely and quality is generally high. Good choice of restaurants and bars with view – even a microbrewery at Porto Antico.

🕙 FRIGGITORIE

At these fry-shops you can stock up on fried fish, veg and polenta and try local specialities such as *farinata* (soft pancake-style chick pea flour disc).

Antica Sciamadda – Via San Giorgio 14r. ☎010 24 68 516.

Carega – Via Sottoripa 113r. ☎010 24 70 617.

La Farinata dei Teatri – Piazza Marsala 5r (N of Piazza Corvetto).

🛏️ **I Tre Merli** – Calata Cattaneo 17. ☎010 246 44 16. www.itremerli.it. A historic wine bar with a varied menu including plenty of fish and traditional *focaccie* and *farinate*.

🛏️ **Antica Osteria di Vico Palla** – Vico Palla 15. ☎010 24 66 575. www.vicopalla.it. Reservation reccomended. A rustic place serving delicious Ligurian specialities.

🛏️ **Cantine Squarciafico** – Piazza Invrea 3r. ☎010 24 70 823. www.cantinesquarciafico.it. A charming eatery in a 16C palazzo. Authentic local cuisine.

🛏️ **Pintori** – Via S. Bernardo 68r. ☎010 27 57 507. www.pintori.net. Closed Sun–Mon. A well-established family-run restaurant specialising in Sardinian cuisine.

🛏️ **Sà Pesta** – Via Giustiniani 16r. ☎010 24 68 336. www.sapesta.it. Closed Sun. 🍽️. Authentic Ligurian cuisine with informal service.

TAKING A BREAK

F. lli Klainguti – Piazza Soziglia 98. Founded 1828, this bar-*pasticceria* has period interiors and tasty specialities.

Gelateria Box Cream – Via degli Orefici 59r. Making mouthwatering creations since the 1960s.

Mangini – Piazza Corvetto 3. A famous 19C caffè where politicians meet.

Panificio Grissineria Claretta – Via della Posta Vecchia 12r. Try the focaccia at this historic bakery.

SHOPPING

Antica Drogheria Torielli – Via San Bernardo 32r. A prestigious historic shop selling spices, chocolate and teas.

Casa del Cioccolato Paganini – Via di Porta Soprana 45r. Wonderful hand-made chocolates.

Libreria Ducale – The bookshop within Palazzo Ducale specialises in books and maps of Genova.

Romanengo – Via Soziglia 74/76r. A feast for the eyes – and tastebuds – at this 18C confectionery shop.

EVENT

International Boat Show – This top-level show held each October started out in 1962. *www.salonenautico.com.*

Promontorio di
Portofino★★★

Portofino Promontory

This rocky, rugged promontory offers one of the most attractive landscapes on the Italian Riviera. The coastline is dotted with villages in sheltered bays, among these some of Italy's most glamorous resorts which, along with the glitz, retain the age-old appeal of simple fishing ports. Part of the peninsula has been designated a nature reserve *(parco naturale)* to protect the fauna and flora. Numerous footpaths crisscross over the headland – ideal for discovering the secret charms of this region.

PORTOFINO★★★

Access by sea: From Santa Margherita, Rapallo and San Fruttuoso. From 6.50€/8€/8.50€ (one way) and 9.50€/11.50€/12€ (round trip). ☎0185 28 46 70. www.traghettiportofino.it. From Camogli to San Fruttuoso: 9€ (one way) and 13€ (round trip). ☎0185 77 20 91. www.golfoparadiso.it.

To reach the delightful village of Portofino, famously frequented by the international jet set, drive through **Santa Margherita Ligure★★** *(5km/3mi)*, another elegant seaside resort and popular watersports centre.

From here the **Strada Panoramica★★** has lovely views of the rocky coast. From the picturesque portside piazza of Portofino, take the steps up to the church of San Giorgio and on along the footpath past **Castello Brown** (formerly di San Giorgio) and the **walk to the lighthouse★★★** *(1hr on foot there and back)* through olives and pines for breathtakingly lovely **views★★★** of Portofino and the Gulf of Rapallo. It's particularly lovely at dusk to watch the sun setting over the sea. Continue along the pathway to the lighthouse, from where the view extends as far as La Spezia.

Michelin Map:
561 J 9 – Liguria.

Info: Via Roma 35, Portofino. ☎0185 26 90 24. www.terrediportofino.eu. Pro Loco Camogli: Via XX Settembre 33, Camogli ☎0185 77 10 66. www.camogliturismo.it.

Location: The promontory is 40km/24.8mi from Genova, off the S 1.

Train: Santa Margherita Ligure (Genova Brignole 34 mins).

Don't Miss: Glamorous Portofino; secluded San Fruttuoso and walking the headland's footpaths.

Timing: Allow a day for Portofino; another one or two for excursions to the surrounding area.

Parco Naturale Regionale di Portofino

Ente Parco Portofino, Viale Rainusso 1, Santa Margherita Ligure. ☎0185 28 94 79. www.parcoportofino.com.
The whole of the Portofino Promontory is a regional park. Over 3km/1.8mi long

Portofino

©Isabelle Barthe/Fotolia.com

and 610m/2 001ft at its highest point, it separates the Golfo Paradiso to the west from the Golfo del Tigullio to the east and incorporates Camogli, Portofino and Santa Margherita Ligure. Explore the dense network of trails to discover this unique natural environment with its combination of Apennine and Mediterranean vegetation – chestnuts grow alongside olives. The underwater panorama is also fascinating with numerous dive sites.

🚶 HIKE
San Fruttuoso★★

🚩 Footpaths from Portofino, Portofino Vetta, Camogli and Santa Margherita Ligure. www.sanfruttuoso.eu. Boat services operate from many places along the coast including Rapallo, Portofino and Camogli. www.traghettiportofino.it. www.golfoparadiso.it.

This tiny village at the head of a narrow cove can only be reached on foot or by sea. There is a beautiful 13C–14C abbey, Abbazia di San Fruttuoso, and an underwater statue of Christ in the bay.

🚗 DRIVING TOUR

FROM PORTOFINO TO CAMOGLI★★
20km/12.4mi. Allow half a day at least.

▶ Drive 10km/6.2mi N of Portofino.

Chiesa di San Lorenzo della Costa

At Santa Margherita Ligure take the scenic **road**★★ for lovely views over the Gulf of Rapallo. The church of San Lorenzo contains a **triptych**★ (1499) by an artist from Bruges.

Portofino Vetta★★

Lovely coastal views from the hilltop (450m/1 476ft).

Belvedere di San Rocco★★

More wide panoramas from the church terrace, this time to Camogli and the western coast as far as Genova. A path leads to **Punta Chiappa**★★★ (1h15 each way by steps and footpath to the right of the church). Unforgettable views from here.

Camogli★★

Tall houses crowd around a small harbour in this picturesque fishing village.

ADDRESSES

🛏 STAY

🍽🛏 **Agriturismo Villa Gnocchi** – Via Romana 53, 16038 San Lorenzo della Costa. 3km/1.8mi W of Santa Margherita Ligure. ☎0185 28 34 31. www.villa gnocchi.it. 12 rooms. Wonderful setting with magnificent views from the lovely terrace garden. A friendly place where it's easy to feel at home.

🍽🛏 **Albergo La Camogliese** – Via Garibaldi 55, 16032 Camogli. ☎0185 77 14 02. www.lacamogliese.it. 21 rooms. A comfortable family-run hotel close to the sea – some rooms have sea views.

🍴 EAT

🍽🛏 **La Cucina di Nonna Nina** – Via Molfino 126, San Rocco (6km/3.7mi from Camogli). ☎0185 77 38 35. www. ristorantelacucinadinonnanina.com. Closed Wed, 2 weeks in late Jan and 3 weeks in Nov. Appealing decor, delicious traditional cuisine and a lovely summer terrace.

Riviera Ligure★

Ligurian Riviera

The enchanting Italian or Ligurian Riviera is, like the French Riviera, a tourist paradise. The mild climate makes it popular all year round. The coast is dotted with popular resorts with good amenities and a wide range of hotels. The hinterland is marvellous for walkers.

🚗 DRIVING TOURS

1 RIVIERA DI PONENTE★

Entimiglia to Genova
175km/109mi. Allow a day.

The busy, winding main road of the riviera, **Via Aurelia** (parallel to the A 10 motorway), is of Roman origin and has some remarkable coastal viewpoints. It passes through resorts with villas and luxuriant gardens. Thanks to its climate and position, the riviera specialises in the flower industry.

Ventimiglia
Train: Ventimiglia (Nice Ville, France, 47 mins).
Ventimiglia, near the French border, has an old centre with narrow alleys, an 11C–12C *duomo*, and other monuments. The spectacular **Giardini Hanbury**★★ (Hanbury Gardens) at Mortola *(6km/3.7mi W towards the French border)* have varied and exotic vegetation, in terraces overlooking the sea. ⚙ Open Mar–Oct daily 9.30am–dusk; Nov–Feb Tue–Sun 9.30am–dusk. Jul–Mar 7.50€; Mar–Jun 9€. ☎0184 22 95 07. www.giardinihanbury.com.

Dolceacqua
A charming little medieval town dominated by the 14C Castello dei Doria, and crossed by a 15C bridge.

Apricale (8km/5mi further N) also dates back to the Middle Ages and is known as the "village of the artists" due to the murals decorating its historic centre.

Info box

⚙ **Michelin Map:**
561 I–K 4–12 – Liguria.

🛈 **Info:** Via Garibaldi 12r, Genova. ☎010 55 72 903. www.turismoinliguria.it.

▶ **Location:** From Ventimiglia to the Gulf of La Spezia, the coast is backed by the slopes of the Alps and the Ligurian Apennines. Coastal roads include the A 10, A 12 and S 1.

🅿 **Parking:** Parking is difficult along the Cinque Terre. It is best to visit the villages on foot via the coastal path or by public transport.

⊘ **Don't Miss:** The Cinque Terre, Portofino, Sanremo.

🕐 **Timing:** Allow four days for the riviera (excluding Genova).

👫 **Kids:** Grotte di Toirano.

Return to the SP 64 and continue to **Pigna** *(11km/6.8mi)*, another medieval settlement. The 15C church of San Michele has a splendid rose window by Giovanni Gagini and a fine 16C **polyptych**★ by Giovanni Canavesio.

▶ Head back towards the coast.

Bordighera★★
The villas and hotels of this resort are scattered among flower gardens. The old town still has fortified gateways.

Sanremo★★
Train: Sanremo (Genova Principe 1hr 5mins).
The capital of the Riviera di Ponente boasts coastal Liguria's longest hours of sunshine and has spas, a marina and frequent cultural events. Sanremo is the main Italian flower market, exporting all sorts of blooms worldwide.

Corso Imperatrice – A promenade known for its Canary palms.
⊙ *Sanremo hosts Italy's most famous popular music festival in late February.*

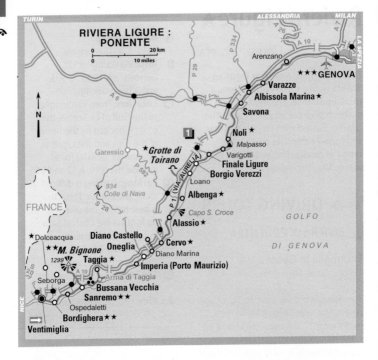

RIVIERA LIGURE : PONENTE

La Pigna★ – La Pigna has a medieval aspect, its winding alleys lined with narrow houses. From Piazza Castello climb up to the church of the Madonna della Costa, for bay **views★**.

13km/8mi north, **views** from **Monte Bignone★★** (1 299m/4 262ft) stretch to Cannes.

Bussana Vecchia

The medieval village destroyed by an earthquake in 1887 was deserted until the 1960s, when artists began restoring it, opening shops to sell their work.

Taggia★

Set amid vineyards and olive groves, dominating the Argentina Valley, this 15C–16C centre for the arts has a fine collection of **works★** by Louis Bréa (Virgin of Pity and the Baptism of Christ) in the church of **San Domenico**.

Imperia

The town is made up of two distinct parts, separated by the River Impero: **Oneglia** is more recent and industrial whereas Porto Maurizio is the maritime

district. Parisio, perched on a promontory, is particularly attractive.

In Oneglia see the **Olive Museum** run by well-known olive oil producer Fratelli Carli. Via Garessio 11, behind the station. Open Mon–Sat 9am–1pm and 2–7pm. Times may vary. ✆0183 29 57 62. www.museodellolivo.com.

Diano Marina

Visit the fortified village of Diano Castello and 12C Chapel of the Knights of Malta (Cappella dei Cavalieri di Malta).

Cervo★

A gorgeous village clinging to the coast. Piazza dei Corallini has the **San Giovanni Battista** church with a Baroque **façade★**, where a prestigious festival of chamber music is held each summer. From Marina di Andora, head inland to **Andora Castello**, an isolated site with castle ruins and the medieval church of **Santi Giacomo e Filippo**.

Albenga★

Train: Albenga (Genova Principe 1hr 7mins).

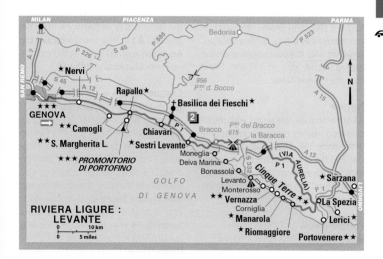

RIVIERA LIGURE : LEVANTE

A short distance inland, with a medieval **old town★** clustered round the **cattedrale**. The octagonal 5C baptistery has a paleo-Christian mosaic.

👥🧒 Grotte di Toirano★

Guided tours only, Jul–Aug 9.30am–12.30pm and 2–5pm. Closed 10 days in Jan. 12€ (includes Museo Etnografico di Toirano). ✆0182 98 062. www.toiranogrotte.it.
The caves, which have striking stalagmites and stalactites, were inhabited in the late Neolithic period. Footprints, torch-marks and bearprints remain.

Borgio Verezzi

A spectacular winding road leads from the Via Aurelia to Verezzi. The pretty medieval village high above the sea, hosts a well-known drama festival in summer. www.festivalverezzi.it.

Finale Ligure

Made up of four villages including **Finale Marina** with a decorative Baroque basilica façade; **Finalpia**'s abbey has an elegant late-13C campanile and **Finalborgo★**, 2km/1.2mi inland, has old town walls and the church of San Biagio.
Walk from Via del Municipio to **Castel San Giovanni** (1hr there and back), for fine **views★**.

Noli★

A fishing village with traditional houses, 13C towers and a Romanesque church with a huge wooden statue of Christ.

Savona

Renaissance palaces and a 16C *duomo* and fortress, **Fortezza Priamar**, where Giuseppe Mazzini was imprisoned.

Albissola Marina★

The tradition of ceramics production dates back to the 13C. The 18C **Villa Faraggiana** set in a lovely **park★**, has extravagant interiors including a superb **ballroom★** with stucco and fresco decoration. Guided tours only, mid-Mar–Sept Tue–Sun 3–7pm (last tour 6.15pm). 8€ (guided tour only); garden only 4€. ✆019 48 06 22. www.villafaraggiana.it.

Varazze

This seaside resort has a long history of shipbuilding.

Genova★★★

👁See GENOVA.

2 RIVIERA DI LEVANTE★★★

Genova to La Sarzana

173km/108mi. Allow 1 day.

This stretch of coast has more character and is wilder than the Riviera di Ponente.

Rugged cliffs and promontories, sheltered coves and tiny fishing villages, together with the pinewoods and olive groves inland, all lend it charm. Don't miss the Cinque Terre.

Nervi★

An attractive seaside resort with multicoloured houses that was fashionable in the early-20C. The *passeggiata* **Anita Garibaldi★** is a pleasant coastal walk with fine views from the Alpi Marittimi to Portofino. The gardens of three villas make up the **public parks**.

Portofino★★★

See PROMONTORIO DI PORTOFINO.

Rapallo★

Train: Rapallo (Genova Brignole 36 mins). A sophisticated seaside resort on a bay east of the Portofino Peninsula. Lungomare Vittorio Veneto is a palm-shaded seafront **promenade★**.

Chiavari

A popular resort with a vast beach and marina. In San Salvatore, 2km/1.2mi to the northeast, is the 13C **Basilica dei Fieschi★** of black-and-white marble.

Sestri Levante★

Busy shipyards, but also a seaside resort with a peninsula running along

the famous **Bay of Silence★** (Baia del Silenzio). In May, Sestri organises the Andersen Festival (www.andersenfestival.it), dedicated to childhood.

Cinque Terre★★

Limited parking. Proceed on foot or by train or boat. www.cinqueterre.it.

The spectacular beauty of the Cinque Terre (Five Lands – Riomaggiore, Manarola, Corniglia, Vernazza and Monterosso) is a combination of natural and man-made features: the coastline and countryside together with vineyards and fishing villages. A **panoramic footpath★★** links the villages. The area is a UNESCO World Heritage Site.

Vernazza★★ – Train: Vernazza (Genova Brignole 1hr 35min). The most attractive, with colourful houses, church and tower clustered around a well-sheltered cove.

Manarola★ – A fishing village with a small 14C church set in a landscape of terraced vineyards.

Riomaggiore★ – Picturesque houses and boats lie around a narrow inlet.

Corniglia – The only one of the five to be set up the cliff, away from the water.

Monterosso – The largest of the villages and the only one allowing traffic.

Portovenere★★

A lovely little seaside town with picturesque seafront houses and views over the water to Palmaria Island *(boat trips available)*. The church of San Pietro dates back to the 6C. From here there are fine **views★★** of the **Bay of Poets**, so named as Byron and Shelley spent time here.

La Spezia

Town map in the Michelin Atlas Italy. Viale Mazzini 47. www.laspezia.net. Italy's largest naval dockyard also specialises in the manufacture of arms. Housed in a restored 17C monastery, the collection at **Museo Lia★★** (open Tue–Sun 10am–6pm; 7€. 0187 73 11 00). includes works of art from Roman times to the 18C with important sections on ivory, enamels, illuminated manuscripts (mostly Italian 14C–16C) and paintings (13C–18C). Significant pieces include an Umbrian *Virgin and Child* in polychrome

Manarola

©Agenzia Regionale In Liguria

wood (13C), an **amethyst head**, probably one of Caligula's sisters, and a 13C Limoges cross (516). Paintings include **Pontormo**'s self-portrait and Venetian landscapes and portraits. *See naval items at Museo Navale.*

Lerici★

An attractive port and resort dominated by an imposing medieval castle.

Sarzana★

The busy town of Sarzana was once a base of the Republic of Genova, and the numerous historic buildings bear witness to its past importance. The **Cattedrale** has a marble **altarpiece★** (1432) by Riccomani and a **Crucifixion★** (1138) by Guglielmo.

The **Fortezza di Sarzanello★** (1322), built by Castruccio Castracani, is a curious example of military architecture with moats and curtain walls guarded by round towers. Apr–Jun 10.30am–12.30pm, Sat–Sun also 4–6.30pm; Jul–Aug daily 10am–1pm and 5.30–7.30pm; Sept daily 10.30am–12.30 and 3.30–6.30pm; Oct 10.30am–12.30pm, Mon, Fri–Sun also 2.30–5.30pm; Nov–Mar Sat–Sun 10.30am–1pm and 2–5pm. 3.50€. ✆0187 62 20 80. www.fortezzadisarzanello.com.

ADDRESSES

🏠STAY

⊝ **Albergo Rosita** – Via Mànie 71, Finale Ligure (3km/1.8mi NE). ✆019 60 24 37. www.hotelrosita.it. 11 rooms. ⊡. Restaurant ⊝⊜. Splendid clifftop with sea views and a good seafood restaurant with panoramic terrace.

⊝⊜ **Agriturismo Villanova** – Villanova, 1.5km/0.9mi E of Levanto. ✆0187 80 25 17. www.agriturismovillanova.it. Closed Jan. 11 rooms and apartments. A splendid farm property with attractive accommodation and a lovely garden.

⊝⊜ **B&B Le Terrazze** – Via Fieschi 102, Corniglia. ✆0187 81 20 96. www.eterasse.it. This old family home perched up on the cliffs has been very tastefully transformed into a bed and breakfast.

⊝⊜ **Bel Soggiorno** – Corso Matuzia 41, Sanremo. ✆0184 66 76 31. www.bel soggiorno.net. 36 rooms. Bright, renovated rooms close to the seafront.

⊝⊜ **Da Ö Vittorio** – Via Roma 160, Recco. ✆0185 74 029. www.daovittorio.it. 29 rooms. A former coaching inn with a good restaurant serving local dishes.

⊝⊜ **Hotel Ca' d'Andrean** – Via Discovolo 101, Manarola. ✆0187 92 00 40. www.cadandrean.it. 10 rooms. ⊡7€. A small, charming hotel in the upper village. Free wifi and a lovely garden.

⊝⊜ **Hotel Due Gemelli** – Via Litoranea 1, Riomaggiore. 4.5km/2.8mi E of Riomaggiore. ✆0187 92 06 78. www.duegemelli.it. 🅿. 13 rooms. ⊡. Simple place with splendid panoramic views from balconies and terrace restaurant.

⊝⊜ **Hotel Ines** – Via Cavour 10, Varazze. ✆019 97 302. www.hotelinesvarazze.it. 12 rooms. A pretty villa in the centre of Varazze, near the sea. Comfortable rooms and a terrace.

⊝⊜ **Hotel Suisse** – Via Mazzini 119, Alassio. ✆0182 64 01 92. www.suisse.it. 49 rooms. A central Art Nouveau hotel with private beach and use of bicycles.

⊝⊜ **Hotel Villa Beatrice** – Via Sant'Erasmo 6 (Via Aurelia), Loano. ✆019 66 82 44. www.panozzohotels.it. 30 rooms. Near the port and old town, set in a luxuriant garden with pool, gym.

⊝⊜ **Pensione Miramare** – Via Fiascherino 22, Tellaro (4km/2.5mi from Lerici). ✆0187 96 75 89. www.miramaretellaro.com. 🅿 22 rooms. A welcoming family-run guesthouse, views of Bay of Poets, good terrace.

⊝⊜ **Villa Argentina** – Via Torrente San Lorenzo 2, Moneglia. ✆0185 49 228. www.villa-argentina.it. 18 rooms. An early-20C villa with bright airy rooms and garden.

⊝⊜⊜ **Hotel e Residenza Beau Rivage** – Lungomare Roma 82, Alassio. ✆0182 64 05 85. www.hotelbeaurivage.it. Painter Richard West stayed and worked here 1885–1905. Pleasant rooms, apts.

⅄/EAT

⊝ **Ristorante Ines** – Via Vignolo 1, Noli. ✆019 74 80 86. www.ristoranteines.com. Good seafood.

⊝⊜ **Beppa** – Via Antonio Mosto 89, Carasco. 7km/4.3mi from Chiavari. ✆0185 38

07 25. Closed Tue. This trattoria prepares delicious local dishes.

⊖⊖ **Da Casetta** – Via XX Settembre 12, Borgio Verezzi. ☎019 61 01 66. A lovely place built into the rock, serving excellent versions of local dishes. Extra-fresh home-grown veg.

⊖⊖ **Enoteca internazionale** – Via Roma 62, Monterosso. ☎0187 81 72 78. www.enotecainternazionale.com. A well-established wine shop and wine bar also serving snacks.

⊖⊖ **Il Ristorantino di Bayon** – Via Felice Cavallotti 23, La Spezia. ☎0187 73 22 09. Closed Sun. An elegant restaurant near the theatre. Seafood specialities.

⊖⊖ **La Favorita** – Strada San Pietro 1, Apricale. ☎0184 20 81 86. www.lafavorita apricale.com. Reservation recommended. A welcoming restaurant serving fresh dishes. Also rooms.

⊖⊖ **La Giara** – Via Bertoloni 35, Sarzana. ☎0187 61 00 73. www.lagiarasarzana.com. Closed Sat and Sun lunch. A welcoming restaurant in the centre of town. Seasonal local specialities.

⊖⊖ **Luchin** – Via Bighetti 53, Chiavari. ☎0185 30 10 63. www.luchin.it. Closed Sun. A traditional, informal eatery dating back to 1907 with a reputation for Ligurian cooking.

⊖⊖ **Maggiorino** – Via Roma 183, Sanremo. ☎0184 50 43 38. Closed Sun. An ideal place to sample a *farinata*, a vegetable tart or a focaccia.

⊖⊖ **Magiargè Vini e Cucina** – Piazza Giacomo Viale, Bordighera. ☎0184 26 29 46. www.magiarge.it. Friendly and relaxed with good food – lots of seafood – wine and an open-air terrace.

⊖⊖ **Osteria Mezzaluna** – Vico Berno 6, Alassio. ☎0182 64 03 87. www.mezzalunaalassio.it. Attractive decor with tiles and naval items. Menu includes tasty cold meats and cheeses. Good wines.

⊖⊖ **Puppo** – Via Torlaro 20, Albenga. ☎0182 51 853. www.dapuppo.it. Closed Sun and Mon; open Jun–Sept evenings only, also Sun. Simple, tasty food such as *farinata* and pizza.

⊖⊖ **Quintilio** – Via Gramsci 23, Altare. 12km/7.4mi from Savona. ☎019 58 000. www.ristorantequintilio.it. Closed Sun evening and Mon. Both decor and dishes combine the elegant and rustic. Menu is seasonal. Rooms available.

⊖⊖ **Sotto la Scala** – Via Cerisola 7, Rapallo. ☎0185 53 630. Closed Sat–Sun lunch and Tue. A relaxed atmosphere and tasty pizzas (evenings) as well as a traditional menu.

⊖⊖ **Vino e Farinata** – Via Pia 15, Savona. Closed Sun–Mon. A historic place specialised in *farinata*.

TAKING A BREAK

Cafè SMS – Via Chiesa 1, Albisola Capo. ☎019 48 32 83. Caffè also serving food with a terrace on the seafront promenade.

Pasticceria-Focacceria Scalvini – Via Colombo 3, Noli. ☎019 74 82 01. Founded in 1820, specialities include *torta di mandorla* (almond tart) and tasty breads.

SHOPPING

A Bütiega – Via Fieschi 142, Corniglia. ☎0187 81 22 92. A tiny grocery stocked with local and organic produce: oils, honey, pesto and fresh fruit for walkers.

Olioteca Bansigo – Via Capellini 70, Portovenere. ☎0187 79 10 54. www.olioteca bansigo.it. Taste olive oils and buy some of the favourites. Jars and kitchen items also on sale.

ACTIVITIES

BOAT TRIPS

A wide range of excursions and ferry services are available.

Consorzio Marittimo Turistico 5 Terre – Via Don Minzoni 13, La Spezia. ☎0187 73 29 87. www.navigazionegolfodeipoeti.it. Serves the area between Portofino and Tuscany.

Cooperativa Battellieri del Porto di Genova – Calata Zingari, Genova. ☎010 25 31 041. www.battellierigenova.it. Runs whale-watching trips and night excursions.

WALKING IN THE CINQUE TERRE

Footpath no.2 links the five villages. The stretch between Riomaggiore and Manarola ('Via dell'Amore', 1km/0.6mi) is suitable for all. Via dei Santuari, higher up the cliff, links chapels. Trails can be challenging so proper footwear is essential. www.parconazionale5terre.it.

Ⓐ A **Cinque Terre Card** covers certain sight entrance fees, public transport costs and excursions. Choose from several different versions. Details at tourist information offices.

Lombardy and the Lake Region

Lombardia. Major City: Milan
Official Website: www.turismo.regione.lombardia.it

Lombardy is among the peninsula's largest regions and one of its wealthiest. Diverse industries, including fashion, agriculture and publishing, drive the region's economic engine, accounting for approximately one-quarter of Italy's GDP. The capital Milan holds about 10 percent of the country's wealth, a fact that's visible along the city's ritzy shopping streets. The Regione dei Laghi, a collection of tidy lakeside villages centred around Lakes Como, Lugano and Maggiore, is another affluent enclave. Lombardy also has a rich artistic tradition. Stendhal called the historic centre of Bergamo "the most beautiful place on Earth" and Leonardo da Vinci lived for some time in Milan, where he painted his superb *Last Supper*.

Centre of Enterprise

Lombardy's emphasis on commercial activity is mainly due to its favourable geographical location in the green Po Delta between the Ticino and the Mincio, which together with the Adda feed lakes Maggiore, Como and Garda.

To the north the great lake valleys give access to the alpine passes. Lombardy, with the mulberry bushes of the **Brianza** district, takes first place in the production of silk. The permanent grazing and grasslands are used by modern dairy farming and processing industries. In the **Lomellina** district, large areas are given over to rice growing. The many towns, scattered throughout the countryside, were important banking and trading centres in medieval and Renaissance times and spread the name of the Lombards all over Europe. Today Como is the centre of the silk industry, Brescia has steel, chemical and engineering industries, Bergamo textile and engineering works, Mantova petrochemicals and plastics, Cremona is the agricultural focus and Pavia the seat of an important university.

Highlights

1 Get a bird's-eye view of Milan from the roof of the **Duomo** (p388)
2 Window-shop along Milan's fashionable **Via della Spiga** (p395)
3 Be awed by Leonardo's *Last Supper* at **Cenacolo** (p400)
4 See a **Commedia dell'Arte** performance in **Bergamo** (p406)
5 Explore lakeside villages by boat on the **Lago di Como** (p426)

It is Milan, the economic capital of Italy, that has the highest density of population and businesses. This town with its modern architecture and numerous commercial enterprises and cultural institutions has an outer ring of industrial suburbs which are the home base of textile, oil, chemical, steel and food industries.

Bergamo

Milan★★★

Milano

Milan is Italy's second city in terms of population, politics and cultural affairs. But the real spirit of Lombardy's capital lies in its commercial, industrial and banking activities, which have made Milan, set in the heart of northern Italy at the foot of the Alps, the country's financial heartland. The enterprising spirit of its people has built upon the city's history to make Milan one of the country's most dynamic towns.

THE CITY TODAY

Milan prides itself on its knack for innovation. This is, after all, the design capital of Italy, home to mega-brands such as Gucci, Versace and Giorgio Armani, among the biggest trendsetting fashion houses in the world. Though the public's taste for luxury goods may be on the wane in light of the economic downturn, Milan is planning for the future with numerous urban renewal projects involving high-profile international architects. One successfully completed projected is MiCo – a new 18 000-seat convention centre, the largest trade show space in Europe (www.micmilano.it).

In addition to these endeavours are sustainability projects, which include the reclamation of an Alfa Romeo industrial area for an urban park, expansion and renovation of Teatro alla Scala and the European Library of Information and Culture (www.beic.it), which is making use of an abandoned railway station. All of these projects are in preparation for 2015, when Milan hosts the Universal Exposition (Expo), with the theme of "Feeding the Planet, Energy for Life".

A BIT OF HISTORY

Milan is probably Gallic (Celtic) in origin, but it was the Romans who subdued the city of Mediolanum in 222 BC and ensured its expansion. At the end of the 3C Diocletian made Milan the seat

▶ **Population:** 1 307 495
🚗 **Michelin Map:** 561 F 9 and the Michelin City Map 46 of Milan.
🖪 **Info:** Galleria Vittorio Emanuele. ✆02 88 45 55 55. www.visitamilano.it.
◗ **Location:** Milan lies at the heart of a network of motorways that includes the A 4 (Turin–Venice), A 7 (Milan–Genova), A 1 (Milan–Reggio Calabria) and A 8–A 9 (the Lake District). The town is bounded by two concentric boulevards: the shorter, enclosing the medieval centre; the outer, marking the town's expansion during the Renaissance.
🅿 **Parking:** Parking in the city and access to the central limited traffic zone is by payment.
☺ **Don't Miss:** The Duomo, *The Last Supper* by Leonardo da Vinci in the Cenacolo, the Pinacoteca di Brera, Cappella Portinari and the Museo della Scienza e della Technologia Leonardo da Vinci.
🕐 **Timing:** Allow two days to see the city.
👤👤 **Kids:** Models of the gadgets of Leonardo da Vinci at the Museo della Scienza e della Technologia Leonardo da Vinci.

of the rulers of the Western Empire, and in 313 Constantine published the **Edict of Milan**, which gave freedom of worship to the Christians. In 375 **St Ambrose** (340–96), a doctor of the Church, became bishop of the town, thus adding to its prestige.

The barbarian invasions of the 5C and 6C were followed by the creation of a Lombard kingdom with Pavia as capital. In 756 Pepin, King of the Franks, conquered

GETTING THERE

BY CAR AND TRAIN – A good
network of motorways serves
the city (A 4 Turin–Venice, A 8/A 9
Milan–Lakes, A 7 Milan–Genova, A 1
Autostrada del Sole, which heads
south).

BY TRAIN – Milan's majestic central
railway station has good metro links.

BY AIR – **Linate Airport**, 7km/4.3mi
from the centre, has regular bus links
to Piazza San Babila (bus 73,
journey time 30min, 1.50€) and
Stazione Centrale (Air Bus, journey
time 25min, 5€).

Malpensa Airport is 45km/28mi out
of town and is connected by train
(journey time 40min, ✆02 72 49 49
49, www.malpensaexpress.it, 12€)
and by bus (journey time 50min,
✆02 58 58 31 85, www.malpensa
shuttle.it, 10€).

Note that taxis from Malpensa can be
rather expensive and liable to delays
caused by heavy traffic.

Orio al Serio Airport is 50km/31mi
from Milan, at Bergamo. There
are direct bus links to central
Milan (journey time 50 min, www.
orioshuttle.com, www.autostradale.it,
5€; or www.terravision.eu; 5€).

GETTING AROUND

BY PUBLIC TRANSPORT – It is highly
advisable to use public transport:
in general it is punctual and quick
(especially the underground lines).
It also avoids problems like getting
stuck in heavy traffic, getting lost
in one-way systems and lengthy
searches for parking spaces.

BY CAR – From Mon to Fri 7.30am–
7.30pm (Thu to 6pm) central Milan
becomes a limited traffic zone and
access is regulated by **Ecopass**
permits, which can be bought by
the day or for longer periods. For
information and activation: ✆02 02
02 ("Area C"), www.comune.milano.it
(link "Area C" and "ZTL").

Parking is by payment throughout
the city. Yellow lines indicate parking
for residents only; blue lines allow
parking for a limited length of time
(check signs) with a prepaid scratch-
card *(gratta e sosta)* displayed. These
can be bought from tobacconists
and newsagents.

BY TAXI – Taxis can be picked up at
a taxi rank or by calling one of the
following numbers: ✆02 53 53/02 85
85/02 40 40 or 02 69 69.

BY BICYCLE – BikeMi, the city's bike-
sharing project, allows for day- and
week-long subscriptions as well as
longer-term season tickets.
For information: ✆02 48 607 607,
www.bikemi.com or visit the ATM
points around town, including at the
Duomo and the main railway station.

the area, and his son Charlemagne was
to wear the Iron Crown of the Kings of
Lombardy from 774. In 962 Milan again
became Italy's capital.

In the 12C Milan allied itself to other cities to form the Lombard League (1167)
to thwart the attempts of the Emperor
Frederick Barbarossa to conquer the
region. With victory at **Legnano** the
cities of the league achieved independence. In the 13C the **Visconti**, Ghibellines and leaders of the local aristocracy
seized power. The most famous member
was **Gian Galeazzo** (1347–1402), a man
of letters, assassin and pious builder of
Milan's cathedral and the Monastery of
Pavia. His daughter, Valentina, married
Louis, Duke of Orleans, the grandfather
of Louis XII of France. This family connection was the reason for later French
expeditions into Italy.

After the death of the last Visconti,
Filippo-Maria (d.1447), the Sforza took
over the rule of Milan. The most famous
figure in the **Sforza** family, **Ludovico il
Moro** (1452–1508) made Milan a new
Athens by attracting to his court the
geniuses of the time, Leonardo da

Vinci and Bramante. However, Louis XII of France proclaimed himself the legitimate heir to the Duchy of Milan and set out to conquer the territory in 1500. His successor François I renewed the offensive but was thwarted at Pavia by the troops of the Emperor Charles V. From 1535 to 1713 Milan was under Spanish rule. During the plague, from 1576 to 1630, members of the Borromeo family, St Charles (1538–84) and Cardinal Federico (1564–1631) distinguished themselves by their humanitarian work. Under Napoleon, Milan became the capital of the Cisalpine Republic (1797) and later of the Kingdom of Italy (1805). In 1815 Milan assumed the role of capital of the Venetian-Lombard Kingdom.

ART AND ARCHITECTURE

The cathedral (Duomo) marks the climax of architecture of the Gothic period. Prominent architects during the Renaissance were the Florentine Michelozzo (1396–1472) and especially **Donato Bramante** (1444–1514), master mason of Ludovico il Moro before he left for Rome. An admirer of Classical art, he invented the **rhythmic articulation** (a façade with alternating bays, pilasters and niches), which imparted harmony to Renaissance façades.

The Lombard school of painting sought beauty and grace above all else. Its principal exponents were Vincenzo Foppa (c.1427–1515), Bergognone (1450–1523) and Bramantino (between 1450 and 1465–1536).

The works of Andrea Solario (c.1473–1520), Boltraffio (1467–1516) and especially the delicate canvases of **Bernardino Luini** (c.1480–1532) attest to the influence of **Leonardo da Vinci**, who stayed in Milan for some time.

Today Milan is Italy's publishing capital and an important centre, with numerous contemporary art galleries.

◗◖WALKING TOURS

1 THE DUOMO TO CASTELLO SFORZESCO

Duomo★★★
Exterior

This Gothic marvel of white marble, bristling with belfries, gables, pinnacles and statues, stands at one end of an esplanade teeming with pigeons – largely responsible for the building's deterioration. The Duomo's recent restoration was a lengthy, technical process, and it should ideally be seen by the light of

Duomo

© Massimo Merlini/iStockphoto.com

the setting sun. Building began in 1386 on the orders of Gian Galeazzo Visconti, continued in the 15C and 16C under Italian, French and German master masons and finished between 1805 and 1809, on Napoleon's orders.

Walk round the cathedral to view the **east end** with three bays of curved and counter-curved tracery and wonderful rose windows. The design is the work of a French architect, Nicolas de Bonaventure, and of a Modenese architect, Filippino degli Organi.

From the Rinascente store *(7th floor)* in Corso Vittorio Emanuele there is a close-up view of the architectural and sculptural features of the roofs.

Interior

The imposing nave and aisles are separated by 52 high pillars (148m/486ft). The mausoleum of Gian Giacomo Medici in the south arm of the transept is a fine work by Leoni (16C). In the north arm is the curious statue of St Bartholomew (who was flayed alive), by the sculptor Marco d'Agrate. Meanwhile, in the crypt *(cripta)* and treasury *(tesoro)* the silver urn containing the remains of St Charles Borromeo, Bishop of Milan, who died in 1584, is on display.

On the way out, you can see the entrance to the early Christian baptistery *(battistero)* and the 4C basilica of Santa Tecla, whose outline has been marked out on the parvis. Cathedral: open daily 8am–8pm. 2€. Baptistery: Open daily 8am–8pm. 6€. ☎02 72 02 26 56. www.duomo milano.it.

Visit to the Roof★★★

Open daily 9am–8pm. Lift 13€; on foot 8€. ☎02 72 02 26 56. www.duomomilano.it.
Don't miss a walk on the roof among the numerous pinnacles and multiple white-marble statues (2 245 in all). The Tiburio or central tower (108m/354ft), is topped by a gilt statue, the Madonnina (1774).

Museo del Duomo★★

Mon 2.30pm–7.30pm, Tue–Sun 9.30am–7.30pm. ☎02 72 02 26 56. www.museo.duomomilano.it.

Housed in the royal palace built in the 18C by Piermarini, the museum shows the various stages in the building and restoration of the cathedral.

Also of note are the splendid **Aribert Crucifix★** (1040), the original support for the Madonnina (1772–3), and the wooden **model★** of the cathedral made to a scale of 1:20 in the 16C–19C.

Museo del Novecento★★

Via Marconi 1. Open Mon 2.30–7.30pm, Tue, Wed, Fri and Sun 9.30am–7.30pm, Thu and Sat 9.30am–10.30pm; last admission 1hr before closing. 5€ (entrance is free during the last two hours prior to closing). 02 88 44 40 61. www.museodelnovecento.org.

Located in the Arengario, an interesting modern building constructed in the 1930s, the museum displays a range of 20C artwork. The exhibits are organized chronologically, giving visitors an overview of Italian art movements from the beginning of the 1900s to the 1980s, and include works by Boccioni, Balla, Carrà, de Chirico, Burri, Fontana and Kounellis, as well as Giuseppe Pellizza da Volpedo's "The Fourth Estate." The world's largest collection of Futurist art is also on display. The large windowed façade offers a beautiful view over Piazza Duomo.

Palazzo Reale

Hours vary according to individual exhibitions. 02 87 56 72.

Located on Piazza Duomo opposite the entrance to Galleria Vittorio Emanuele, Palazzo Reale was renovated and redesigned halfway through the 18C by

Detail of Basket of Fruit *(1595–1596)* by Caravaggio, Pinacoteca Ambrosiana

© VWPics/Photoshot

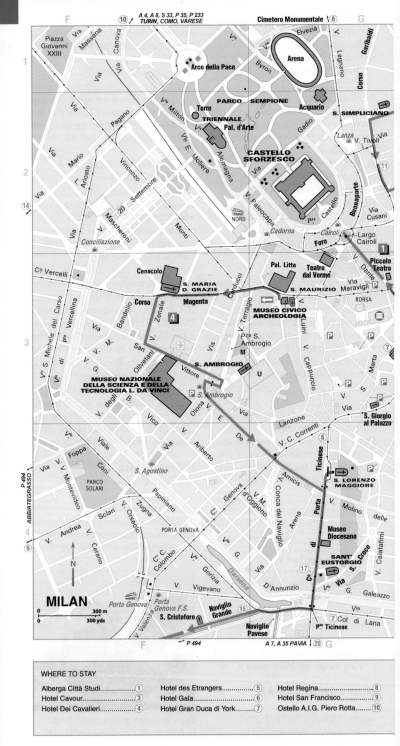

MILAN

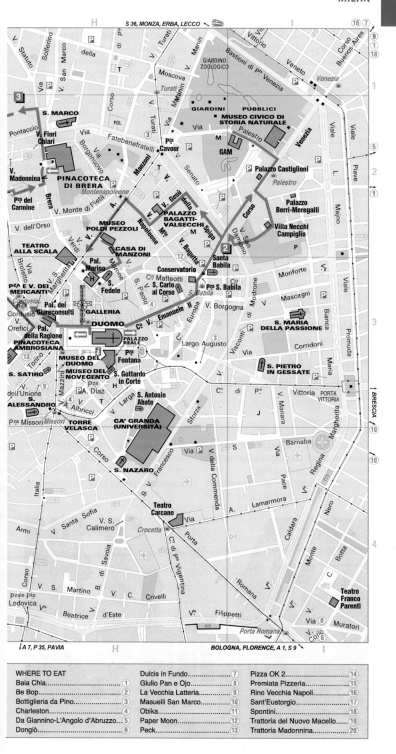

WHERE TO EAT		
Baia Chia.................................①	Dulcis in Fundo...................⑦	Pizza OK 2...........................⑭
Be Bop..................................②	Giulio Pan e Ojo..................⑧	Premiata Pizzeria.................⑮
Bottiglieria da Pino...............③	La Vecchia Latteria..............⑨	Rino Vecchia Napoli.............⑯
Charleston............................④	Masuelli San Marco.............⑩	Sant'Eustorgio.....................⑰
Da Giannino-L'Angolo d'Abruzzo⑤	Obika...................................⑪	Spontini...............................⑱
Dongiò..................................⑥	Paper Moon.........................⑫	Trattoria del Nuovo Macello...⑲
	Peck....................................⑬	Trattoria Madonnina............⑳

Piermarini (1743-1808) at the behest of the Austrian court. Originally home to the city's municipal offices, today the building is used as a cultural center and exhibition space, and hosts most of Milan's most important temporary exhibitions.

Cross over to the **Galleria Vittorio Emanuele II★**, laid out in 1877. The far end opens onto Piazza della Scala.

Via and Piazza dei Mercanti★

In Via Mercanti stands the Palace of Jurisconsults (Palazzo dei Giureconsulti), built in 1564 with a statue of St Ambrose teaching on the façade. The Piazza dei Mercanti is quiet and picturesque.

The charming Loggia degli Osii (1316) is decorated with heraldic shields, statues of saints and the balcony from which penal sentences were proclaimed. Opposite is the town hall, the **Palazzo della Ragione** or Broletto Nuovo, built in the 13C and extended in the 18C.

Pinacoteca Ambrosiana★★

Open Tue–Sun 10am–6pm. Closed 1 Jan, Easter, 25 Dec. 15€. Booking recommended. ✆02 80 69 21. www.ambrosiana.eu.

This 17C palace, erected for Cardinal Federico Borromeo, was one of the first public libraries, and boasts Leonardo's **Codice Atlantico** drawings.

The gallery opens with an original body of work donated by the cardinal, and other acquisitions of the same period (15C and 16C). Note the delightful **Infant Jesus and the Lamb★★** by Bernardino Luini. One of the most notable paintings of the Lombard School is the **Sacra Conversazione** by Bergognone (1453–1523), with its Madonna dominating the composition.

The **Musician★★** by Leonardo da Vinci has an unusually dark background for the artist who tended to create a strong relationship between the dominant figures and their surrounding space. In Room 3 the **Madonna Enthroned with Saints★** by Bramantino is striking for the huge toad at the feet of St Michael (symbolising the dragon slain by the saint) contrasting with the grotesque swollen figure of Arius. The **Nativity**, a copy from Barocci, is pervaded by a glowing light which irradiates from the child. The splendid preparatory **cartoons★★★** for Raphael's *School of Athens* (the fresco was painted in the Vatican *stanze* in Rome) are the only surviving example of their kind. In Caravaggio's **Basket of Fruit ★★★** shrivelled leaves and rotten fruit render idea of life's transitory nature. The cardinal's collection includes Flemish Jan Brueghel's remarkable **Mouse with a Rose★**, painted on copper. Other rooms are mainly focused on painting from Lombardy. Of particular note are four **portraits★** by Francesco Hayez.

Castello Sforzesco

© M. Borgese/HEMIS.FR

Castello Sforzesco★★★

Open daily 7am–7.30pm (winter 6pm), Thu to 10.30 pm. Museums open Tue–Sun 9am–7pm. Closed 1 Jan, Easter Mon, 1 May, 25 Dec. 3€. 📞02 88 46 37 03. www.milanocastello.it.

This huge brick quadrilateral building was the seat of the Sforza, Dukes of Milan. The **municipal art collections** are now on display in the castle.

Museo di Scultura★★

The minimalist layout displays Romanesque, Gothic and Renaissance works by Lombard sculptors, including the **tomb of Bernabò Visconti★★** (14C), and the **reclining figure of Gaston de Foix** and **statues★★** (1523) by Bambaia, as well as the unfinished **Rondanini Pietà★★★** by Michelangelo.

Pinacoteca★

The gallery displays works by Mantegna, Giovanni Bellini, Crivelli, Bergognone, Luini, Moretto, Moroni, Magnasco, Tiepolo, Guardi, Lotto, etc.

Museo degli Strumenti Musicali★

An extensive collection of stringed and wind instruments and keyboards.

Museo Civico di Archeologico

In the vault under Rochetta courtyard. The museum includes prehistory, Egyptian art and lapidary collections. Another section of the museum is housed in the San Maurizio monastery (🕮 see p397).

Parco Sempione

In this park, both Luigi Canonica's Arena (G1) and the Arco della Pace (F1), the triumphal arch built for Napoleon I by Luigi Cagnola (1752–1833), take their inspiration from Classical Antiquity. The Palazzo d'Arte (F2), designed by the architect Giovanni Muzio (1893–1982), is the home of the Triennale, an exhibition space and cultural centre that is particularly active in the areas of architecture, urban planning, design and communication.

👥 **Triennale Design Museum★** (F2) – Open daily 10am–10pm. 📞02 72 43 41. 12€. www.triennaledesignmuseum.it. This museum takes a scientific but fun approach to Italian design and changes its themed presentation each year. The museum will be enjoyed by adults and children alike.

Torre Branca (F2) – Built in the 1930s by Gio Ponti and Cesare Chiodi for the fifth Triennale, this slender metal structure stands 104m high and offers a magnificent panorama of the city.

Arco della Pace – Located at the northwesternmost limit of the park, the Arco della Pace was designed by Luigi Cagnola but only completed in 1838, after his death. Napoleon ordered the arch built here to provide a triumphal greeting upon the French ruler's arrival from Paris, but when Austrian rule returned to the city the construction was dedicated to peace. The arch stands in a broad pedestrian amphitheater surrounded by popular bars and restaurants. Although you can stop here for a drink or bite to eat any time of the day, this corner of the city truly comes alive in the evenings, when the bars and cafés fill up for Milan's traditional aperitivo hour. The bronze statues atop the arch include a Minerva by Abbondio Sangiorgio, and the four horsemen of victory by Giovanni Putti.

Arena Civica – Designed by neoclassical architect Luigi Canonica, the Arena Civica is a Roman-style amphitheater that is now used for athletic events and concerts.

👥 **Acquario civico** (G1–2) – ♿Open Tue–Sun 9am–7pm. 5€, free Tue after 2pm. 📞02 88 46 57 50. www.acquariocivicomilano.eu. This small but very enjoyable aquarium is housed in an Art Nouveau-style pavilion from the 1906 Universal Exhibition. Various activities are organised for children.

② CORSO VENEZIA AND FASHION QUARTER

Corso Vittorio Emanuele II

This pedestrian thoroughfare is home to a succession of boutiques, caffès and restaurants. Almost at the end, on the left, stands the Neoclassical church of

San Carlo al Corso, dating from 1839, which is dedicated to Carlo Borromeo. Corso Vittorio Emanuele ends at **Piazza Babila**, where you will find the church of the same name, dedicated to the Bishop of Antioch. It was founded in the 11C but underwent extensive restoration in the early 20C. Opposite the church stands the **Conservatorio**.

Corso Venezia

This broad boulevard is an extension of Corso Vittorio Emanuele II, lined by imposing buildings, including several examples of the Art Nouveau style in vogue in Milan in the early 20C, which is known in Italy as the Liberty-style . At no. 47, near the Palestro metro station, Palazzo Castiglioni is considered to be Italy's finest example of a Liberty style building, due to its size and the relationship between its architecture and sculpture. It was built between 1900 and 1903 by the architect Giuseppe Sommaruga and the sculptor Ernesto Bazzaro.

The *corso* leads to the 17ha/42-acre Giardini Pubblici (public gardens), which also contain two museums.

Museo Civico di Storia Naturale★

Corso Venezia 55. Open Tue–Sun 9am–7pm. Closed 1 Jan, 1 May, 25 Dec. 5€. ✆02 88 46 33 37. www.comune.milano.it/museostorianaturale.

Interesting natural history collections, covering geology, palaeontology and zoology. The educational presentation is brought to life with the help of numerous three-dimensional models, which will appeal to children.

Galleria d'Arte Moderna★★

Via Palestro 16. Open Tue–Sun 9am–7pm. Closed Mon, 1 Jan, 25 Dec. 5€, free Tue after 2pm. ✆02 88 44 59 47. www.gam-milano.com.

The Modern Art Gallery has been hosted in the 18C Villa Belgiojoso since 1921. Set in a delightful **English garden★** it also hosts the **Carlo Grassi Collection** including impressive artworks by Gaspare Van Wittel, Pietro Longhi,

Cézanne, Van Gogh, Manet, Gauguin, Sisley and Toulouse-Lautrec. The **Contemporary Art Pavilion** (Via Palestro 14) has temporary exhibitions. ✆*Make a visit to the* **Ca' Granda-Ex Ospedale Maggiore★★** (University), *p402.*

Villa Necchi Campiglio

Via Mozart 14. ♿ Open Wed–Sun 10am–6pm. 9€ villa and gardens. ✆02 76 34 01 21. www.fondoambiente.it.

Built between 1932 and 1935 to a design by the Milanese architect Piero Portaluppi (1888–1967), with additions by Tommaso Buzzi, this villa stands discreetly on the elegant Via Mozart. Its rationalist architecture draws on decorative features that are inspired by Art Deco, but at the same time highly personal. The exterior, however, does not prepare you for the taste, restraint and modernity of the building as a whole, which includes a garden with a heated swimming pool and a tennis court.

Visitors will discover the lifestyle of a well-heeled, cultivated Milanese family, who were able to successfully combine functionality with good taste (dumb waiter, lift, intercom, wardrobe with automatic lighting, etc.). The house retains its very handsome furniture and an extensive art collection (taking in Sironi, De Pisis, Carrà, Casorati, Martini, Marino Marini, Marussig, Casorati, Morandi, De Chirico and Savinio as well as works by Canaletto, Rosalba Carriera and Tiepolo).

○ Continue along Via Mozart and turn right into Via San Damiano then left into Corso Venezia to return to Via della Spiga.

Fashion Quarter

The square marked out by **Via Monte Napoleone**, **Via Gesù** and **Via della Spiga** is the heartland of Milanese fashion. This is where the most famous Italian designer brands have their storefronts: Armani, Dolce & Gabbana, Versace, Prada, Gucci… Only the wealthy elite come to shop, but it is still very pleasant to stroll through the narrow streets. The succession of seductive window displays (nothing can stop you from dreaming…) lead into stores oozing luxury and design, and the area also contains some beautiful homes. At the corner of Via Monte Napoleone and Via Sant'Andrea, food lovers will make a beeline for the Pasticceria Cova, founded in 1817.

Palazzo Bagatti Valsecchi★★

Via Gesù 5. Open Tue–Sun 1–5.45pm. Closed public hols and Aug. 9€. ☏ 02 76 00 61 32. www.museobagattivalsecchi.org.

The palazzo stands opposite the current residence of the Bagatti Valsecchi family, of which you can see the attractive inner courtyard. Its façade is in two parts, linked by a loggia *(1st floor)* with a terrace above.

The museum – A staircase with a fine wrought-iron banister takes you up to the *piano nobile* (first floor) of the home of Fausto and Giuseppe Bagatti Valsecchi. At the end of the 19C, the brothers decided to decorate the interior of their home in the Renaissance style, in keeping with contemporary tastes, mixing genuine pieces and high-quality replicas. You can visit their two private apartments and the reception rooms. Fausto's apartment is made up of the **fresco room** (named after the fresco of the *Virgin of Mercy*, dating from 1496), the **library**, with its two magnificent 16C leather globes and antiques such as the 17C German roulette wheel, and the **bedroom**, with its splendid bed carved with Christ's Ascent to Calvary and battle scenes; in the bathroom, the bathtub is part of a Renaissance niche. The **labyrinth passage** (look up at the ceiling to see the reason for its name) leads to the **dome gallery**, which links the different areas of this floor. The **Valtelline stove room** (Sala della stufa valtellinese) leads into Giuseppe's apartment. The inviting atmosphere here is created by the fine woodwork adorned with a sculpted frieze of anthropomorphic figures, animals and plant motifs. The **red bedroom**, which belonged to Giuseppe and his

wife Carolina Borromeo, contains children's furniture and a fine 17C Sicilian bed, whereas Giuseppe's room is decorated in green and boasts a sculpted ceiling.

Returning to the dome gallery, you can move on to the reception rooms: a large **drawing room** with an imposing fireplace, the **arms gallery** (with its close-combat weapons) and the **dining room** (17C ceramic ware), in which the walls are hung with a combination of 14C Flemish tapestries and paintings.

▶ Coming out of the palazzo, turn right onto Via Gesù. In Via Monte Napoleone, turn right and walk to Via Manzoni, where you should turn left.

Museo Poldi Pezzoli★★

Open Wed–Mon 10am–6pm. Closed public hols. 10€. ☏ 02 79 48 89. www.museopoldipezzoli.it.

Attractively set out in an old mansion, the museum displays collections of weapons, fabrics, paintings, **clocks★** and bronzes. Among the paintings are works by the Lombard school, **portraits★★** of Luther and his wife by Lucas Cranach and the famous **Portrait of a Woman★★★** by Piero del Pollaiolo, a **Descent from the Cross** and a **Madonna and Child★★** by Botticelli, and a **Dead Christ★** full of pathos by Giovanni Bellini. The other rooms are hung with works by Pinturicchio, Palma il Vecchio, Francesco Guardi, Canaletto, Tiepolo, Perugino and Lotto.

Casa di Manzoni★

Via Gerolamo Morone 1. Open Tue–Fri 9am–noon and 2–4pm. Closed public hols, 25 Dec–6 Jan. Free. ☏ 02 86 46 04 03. www.casadelmanzoni.mi.it.

Alessandro Manzoni lived in this mansion for 60 years. On the ground floor is the library and the writer's books and desk. On the first floor are memorabilia and illustrations of his most famous novel, **The Betrothed**. The bedroom where he died has its original furniture.

Teatro alla Scala★★

Traditionally recognised as being the most famous opera house in the world, La Scala surprises people seeing it for the first time because of the simplicity of its exterior, which gives no hint of the magnificence of its auditorium. Built from 1776 to 1778 with six levels of boxes, it can seat 2 000 people.

The **Museo Teatrale alla Scala★** presents Toscanini and Verdi memorabilia. From the museum, you can visit boxes and see the auditorium. Open daily 9am–12.30pm and 1.30–5.30pm. Closed public hols, 7 Dec, 24 Dec afternoon. 7€. ℰ02 88 79 74 73. www.teatroalla scala.org.

Teatro alla Scala

© E. Grund/AGE FOTOSTOCK

③ BRERA

Allow half a day.

Pinacoteca di Brera★★★

Open Tue–Sun 8.30am–7.15pm (last entry 6.40pm), Sat to 11pm (last entry 10.40pm. Closed 1 Jan, 1 May, 25 Dec. 10€. ℰ02 72 26 32 64.
www.brera.beniculturali.it.

Forms part of a series of institutes – the Accademia di Belle Arti (Fine Arts Academy), the biblioteca (library), the Osservatorio Astronomico (observatory) and the Istituto Lombardo di Scienze, Lettere ed Arti (The Lombardy Institute of Science, Arts and Letters) – all housed in a fine 17C building. In the courtyard a statue of Napoleon (1809) by Canova depicts him as a victorious Roman emperor.

The tour of the gallery starts with the Jesi collection, which introduces the main artistic movements of the first half of the 20C: note the sense of movement and dynamism of the Futurist painters (Boccioni's **La Rissa**) and the clean geometry of the metaphysical works by Carrà (**The Metaphysical Muse**) and Morandi (**Still Life**). The sculpture collection is dominated by three artists: Medardo Rosso, Arturo Marini and Marino Marini. Along the passage to the left, it is possible to admire the Maria Theresa Room and the library, Biblioteca Braidense.

The Cappella Mocchirolo gives a brief review of Italian painting from the 13C to the 15C (*Polyptych of Valle Romita* by Gentile da Fabriano).

Brera's collection of **Venetian paintings** is the largest and most important outside Venice. Masterpieces include the **Pietà★★** by Giovanni Bellini and the famous **Dead Christ★★★** by Mantegna, a meditation on death with a realism given added pathos by the artist's skill in foreshortening. In the Napoleon Rooms hang major works by Tintoretto (**Miracle of St Mark★**), Veronese (**Dinner at the House of Simon**) and Giovanni and Gentile Bellini *(St Mark Preaching at Alexandria in Egypt)*.

The **Lombard school** is well represented and pride of place is given to a **Polyptych with Madonna and Saints★** by Vicenzo Foppa and Mantegna in particular, and the Leonardesque **Madonna of the Rose Garden★★** by Bernardino Luini.

One room contains two Renaissance masterpieces from **central Italy**: the **Montefeltro altarpiece★★★** by Piero della Francesca, in which the ostrich egg symbolises both the Immaculate Conception and the abstract and geometrical perfection of form sought by the artist, and the **Marriage of the Virgin★★★** by Raphael, in which the graceful, delicate figures merge in the background with the circular Bramante-style building. Farther along, Caravaggio's magnificent **Meal at**

Courtyard, Pinacoteca di Brera

© C. Labonne/MICHELIN

Emmaus★★★ is a fine example of the artist's use of strong contrast and of his realism.

The 18C Venetian room has **Rebecca at the Well**★★ by Piazzetta, an exquisite portrayal of the girl's gaze of astonishment and innocence, while the last rooms are dedicated to 19C–20C painting, including **The Kiss** by Hayez.

Chiesa di San Marco★

Rebuilt in 1286 over much older foundations, this church has an interesting black-and-white fresco by the Leonardo da Vinci school *(north aisle)* of a **Madonna and Child with St John the Baptist** that was discovered in 1975.

Basilica di San Simpliciano★

Built in AD 385 for St Ambrose, Bishop of Milan with additions built in the early Middle Ages and Romanesque period. The apse vaulting has a **Coronation of the Virgin** by Bergognone (1481–1522). *Both churches host good concerts.*

4 SANTA MARIA DELLE GRAZIE TO NAVIGLI QUARTER

Chiesa di San Maurizio Monastero Maggiore★

This monastery church built in the Lombard-Renaissance style (early -16C) has a bare façade, which often goes unnoticed on Corso Magenta, concealing an interior entirely decorated with **frescoes**★ by Bernardino Luini.

Museo Civico Archeologico★

Open Tue–Sun 9am–5.30pm. Closed Mon, 1 Jan, 25 Dec. 5€, free Tue after 2pm. ✆02 88 44 52 08. www.poliarcheo.it. www.comune.milano.it/museoarcheologico/

The museum housed in the extant buildings of the Benedictine monastery is divided into Roman and barbarian art on the ground floor and Greek, Etruscan and Indian (Gandhara) art in the basement. The most outstanding exhibits are the 4C **Trivulzio Cup**★ cut from one piece of glass, and the **silver platter from Parabiago**★ (4C) featuring the festival of the goddess Cybele. Opposite stands **Palazzo Litta**.

Chiesa di Santa Maria delle Grazie★★

This Renaissance church erected by the Dominicans from 1465 to 1490 was finished by Bramante. The interior (restored) is adorned with frescoes by Gaudenzio Ferrari in the fourth chapel on the right, and with the impressive **dome**★, gallery and cloisters all by Bramante. The best view of the **east end**★ is to be had from Via Caradosso.

Cenacolo

Open Tue–Sun 8.15am–7pm, by reservation only (at least two months in advance). Closed 1 Jan, 1 May, 25 Dec. 6.50€ + 1.50€ reservation. ✆02 92 80 03 60. www.cenacolovinciano.net.

In the former refectory of the monastery is **The Last Supper**★★★ by Leon-

A CITY OF ART AND DESIGN

The City in History

Although Milan's origins are probably Gaulish, the development of Mediolanum, as it was then called, followed the Roman conquest in 222 BC. At the end of the 3C AD, the Emperor Diocletian declared Milan the capital of the Western Roman Empire, and it was here in AD 313 that Constantine issued the Edict of Milan granting Christians freedom of worship. In 375 St Ambrose (340–96), an amazingly eloquent orator and one of the Doctors of the Church, became Bishop of Milan, helping to build the city's prestige.

From the Lombard Kingdom to the Ghibellines

In the 5C and 6C barbarian invasions swept through the region, before the Lombards founded a kingdom with Pavia as its capital. The city was taken in 756 by Pepin the Short, King of the Franks, whose son Charlemagne was crowned with the Iron Crown of Lombardy in 774. Milan only regained the status of capital in the year 962.

In the 12C Milan joined forces with neighbouring cities to form the Lombard League in order to counter attempts by the Holy Roman Emperor Frederick Barbarossa to take control of the region, and went on to win autonomy at the Battle of Legnano. In the 13C the Ghibelline Viscontis took control of the city. The most famous member of this important noble family, Gian Galezzo (1351–1402), was a cunning military strategist and a cultivated man of letters, a murderer and a devout Christian. He obtained the title of Duke of Milan in 1395, and built the Duomo and the Certosa di Pavia. His daugher Valentina married the grandfather of Louis XII of France, laying the foundations for the dynastic dispute that underpinned the Italian Wars.

The Rise of the Sforza Family

After the death of the last Visconti duke, Filippo Maria, the people proclaimed the Ambrosian Republic. Before long, however, the Sforzas were brought to power by Filippo Maria's brother-in-law, Francesco Sforza, son of a simple peasant who had become a *condottiere*. The most illustrious Sforza was Ludovico Il Moro (1452–1508), who transformed Milan into the "new Athens" and attracted brilliant figures such as Leonardo da Vinci and Bramante. In 1500, however, the city was conquered by Louis XII of France, who claimed to be the legitimate heir to the Duchy of Milan. France attempted to gain control again under Francis I, but his dream of conquering the Empire was stopped short in Pavia by the determined forces of the Holy Roman Emperor Charles V.

From Spain to the Kingdom of Italy

From 1535 to 1713, Milan was under Spanish control. During this time, two great religious figures left their mark on the city: Carlo Borromeo (1538–84) and Federico Borromeo (1564–1631), both of whom distinguished themselves through their humanitarian work when the city was ravaged by the plague in 1576 and 1630.

Under Napoleon, Milan became the capital of the Cisalpine Republic in 1797 and the Kingdom of Italy in 1805. In 1815 it became the capital of the Kingdom of Lombardy-Venetia.

After joining the Kingdom of Italy, Milan became a major economic, financial and cultural force within the country and a renowned European metropolis.

The Fine Arts

Even though Milan is a Romanesque city in spirit and in terms of the history of art, due to the extraordinary basilicas founded by St Ambrose, its architectural reputation is based on the Duomo. The cathedral marks the culmination of the Lombard take on the Flamboyant-Gothic style and reveals significant Romanesque influences.

In the Renaissance, the most popular architects were the Florentine Michelozzo (1396–1472) and Donato Bramante (1444–1514), who was Ludovico Il Moro's leading architect before he moved to Rome. Bramante was an admirer of Classical Antiquity but also an imaginative figure, who invented the rhythmic style characterised by an alternation of bays, pilasters and niches that gives so many Renaissance façades their harmonious feel. In painting, the Lombard school's overriding concern was to achieve "beauty and grace": its most famous exponents are Vincenzo Foppa (c.1427–1515), Bergognone (1450–1523) and Bramantino (between 1450 and 1465–1536). The paintings of Andrea Solario (c.1473–1520), Boltraffio (1467–1516), Il Sodoma (1477–1549) and above all the delicate works of Bernardino Luini (c.1480–1532) demonstrate the decisive influence of Leonardo da Vinci, who lived for a time in the city.

Milan's 16C architecture is dominated by Pellegrino Tibaldi (1527–96), who worked under Carlo Borromeo, while the leading 17C figure was Richini (1584–1658). Next came the Neoclassical period, with Piermarini (1734–1808), followed by the eclecticism of the second half of the 19C (as exemplified by the Galleria Vittorio Emanuele II, Piazza della Scala and the monumental cemetery). The Liberty style then developed, with elegant buildings in the residential districts, followed by modernism and finally, the contemporary creations of masters of design Ettore Sottsass (1917–2007), Gae Aulenti (Piazza Cadorna), Vittorio Gregotti (Teatro degli Arcimboldi and the Bicocca district), Renzo Piano (headquarters of the newspaper *Il Sole 24 Ore*) and Fuksas (the Rho-Pero Fiera).

The Present and the Future, after the Universal Exhibition of 2015

Stimulated by Expo 2015, the city is currently undergoing a major architectural transition with large-scale projects, including the restoration of the central station (Stazione Centrale), built 1912–34, and the Museo del Novecento (Museum of the 20th Century) in one of the two marble buildings that make up the Arengario Palace (1939–56) on Piazza Duomo. On March 2015 the Mudec (Museo delle Culture) opened its venue in the formerly Ansaldo industrial plant to display the municipal collections of ethnographic material, and the following month the new canal port of the Darsena– navigable again–was re-opened with its new pedestrian area and a new market. The calendar of 2015 openings included the new Fondazione Prada venue. Conceived by architecture firm OMA—led by Rem Koolhaas—, this amazing space devoted to contemporary art has an architectural configuration that combines seven existing buildings of a distillery dating back to the 1910s with three new structures.

CityLife, the project devised by the architects Hadid, Isozaki and Libeskind, is under construction on the site of the former exhibition centre. The plan includes a museum of contemporary art, a park and a cultural centre. The development plan for the Garibaldi-Porta Nuova district has already produced the Palazzo Lombardia, a park and a centre for culture, leisure, fashion and business. Fulcrum of the district is the elevated Piazza Gae Aulenti crowned with arched highrises, amongst these the Banca Unicredit tower designed by architect Cesar Pelli, the tallest building in Italy (231 meters).

For more information, visit the websites www.expo2015.org, www.city-life.it, www.museodelnovecento.org, www.mudec.it, www.fondazioneprada.org

ardo da Vinci, painted 14957 at the request of Ludovico il Moro. A skilful composition, it creates the illusion that the painted space is a continuation of the room itself.

Christ is depicted at the moment of the institution of the Eucharist: his half-open mouth suggests that he has just finished speaking. Around him there is a tangible sense of shock and premonition of imminent disaster with its intimation of Judas' betrayal. The technique used (Leonardo chose egg tempera, possibly mixed with oil, and placed the image on the coldest wall in the room), dust, WWII bomb damage and, more recently, smog have all contributed to the need for considerable restoration work (it's been restored 10 times). In fact the condition was already compromised in 1517. In May 1999, after 21 years of restoration work, the Cenacolo was finally unveiled to show its original colours and use of chiaroscuro.

Opposite is a Crucifixion★ (1495) by Montorfano, somewhat overshadowed by The Last Supper.

Museo Nazionale della Scienza e della Technologia Leonardo da Vinci★★

&. Open Tue–Fri 9.30am–7pm, Sat–Sun 9.30am–9pm. Closed 1 Jan, 25 Dec. 10€. ☏02 48 55 55 58. www.museoscienza.org.

This vast museum exhibits interesting documents. In the Leonardo da Vinci Gallery are models of the artist's inventions. Other sections deal with acoustics, chemistry, telecommunications and astronomy. Large pavilions have displays relating to railways, aircraft and shipping.

▲▲ Look out for the models of Leonardo da Vinci's gadgets.

Basilica di Sant'Ambrogio★★★

The basilica, founded at the end of the 4C by St Ambrose, is a magnificent example of 11–12C Lombard-Romanesque style with its pure lines and fine atrium★ adorned with capitals. The façade pierced by arcading is flanked

by a 9C campanile to the right and a 12C one to the left. The doorway has 9C bronze panels. In the crypt, behind the chancel, lie the remains of St Ambrose, St Gervase and St Protase. Inside the basilica there is a magnificent Byzantine-Romanesque ambo★ (12C) to the left of the nave, and a precious gold-plated altar front★★, a masterpiece of the Carolingian period (9C). In the chapel of San Vittore in Ciel d'Oro (at the end of the south transept) there are remarkable 5C mosaics★. Access to Bramante's portico is from the end of the north transept.

Basilica di San Lorenzo Maggiore★★

Founded in the 4C and rebuilt in the 12C and 16C the basilica has kept its original octagonal plan. In front of the façade is a majestic portico★ of 16 columns, all that remains of the Roman town of Mediolanum.

The Byzantine-Romanesque interior has galleries exclusively reserved for women. From the south atrium go through the 1C Roman doorway to the 4C Cappella di Sant'Aquilino★, which has paleo-Christian mosaics (Cappella: open Mon–Sat 7.30am–6.45pm, Sun 7am–7pm; 2€; ☏02 89 40 41 29; www.sanlorenzomaggiore.com). Further on, the Porta Ticinese, a vestige of the 14C ramparts, leads to the artists' quarter, the Naviglio Grande.

Corso di Porta Ticinese

This road leads down to the Navigli canal district and is lined with independent stores selling up-to-the-minute and unusual fashions. Lively bars.

Museo Diocesano

Corso di Porta Ticinese 95.
Open Tue–Sun 10am–6pm. Closed 1 Jan, 1 May, 25–26 Dec. 8€ (Tue 4€).
☏02 89 42 00 19.
www.museodiocesano.it.

This museum inaugurated in 2001 has a very contemporary design. Displays include liturgical items, and artworks.

Mosaics, Basilica di Sant'Ambrogio

Chiesa di Sant'Eustorgio★

This church was used by the Inquisition prior to moving to Santa Maria delle Grazie, and is dedicated to St Peter Martyr, the inquisitor, murdered in 1252.

Cappella Portinari★★

&Open daily 10am–6pm. ℘02 89 40 05 89. www.santeustorgio.it.

This chapel, a Lombard-Renaissance jewel, houses the finest cycle of paintings by the Milanese artist **Vincenzo Foppa** (c.1427–1515). Near the entrance are the *Annunciation* and *Assumption*. St Peter, preaching is on the right, next to a scene of the devil assuming the guise of the Madonna and Child. Other scenes include the saint healing a boy's foot and within the Barlassina woods where Peter's earthly story reaches its conclusion. The **Museo Diocesano** houses works belonging to the diocese. Open Tue–Sun 10am–6pm. Closed 1 Jan, 25–26 Dec. 8€. ℘02 89 40 47 14. www. museodiocesano.it.

Navigli

Porta Ticinese stands on the line of the old 14C fortifications. To the right of the square is the Darsena, Milan's former harbour, and from here, two canals extend almost at right angles: **Naviglio Grande** (50km/31mi) and Naviglio Pavese (33km/20.5mi).

Alzaia Naviglio Grande runs alongside the first of the two canals. It has colourful houses, picturesque bridges and an old wash-house, beyond which is **San Cristoforo**, a charming complex of two brick churches, of the 12C and

14C–15C. This appealing district is now one of Milan's fashionable areas, with a plethora of restaurants and bars. It is popular with people who work in fashion and design, who have moved into the area. An antiques market is held on the last Sunday of every month.

ADDITIONAL SIGHTS

Santa Maria della Passione★★

Via Vincenzo Bellini 2.

One of Milan's largest churches after the Duomo. It stands on a pretty square next to the Conservatorio. The church was built in 1482, and its Baroque façade was added in the 18C. Inside, you will find many works of art, including a very fine Last Supper by Gaudenzio Ferrari in the left transept, along with works by Daniele Crespi, Bernardino Luini and Bergognone, who also painted the splendid sacristy frescoes.

Santa Maria presso San Satiro★

Via Torino 9.

With the exception of its 9C bell tower and façade dating from 1871, both the church and the baptistery are the work of Bramante, who resolved the issue posed by the church's lack of space with an entirely Classical vocabulary: with clever *trompe l'œil* decor in gilded stucco, he created a marvellous false choir. The dome is another remarkable feature, and the basilica also includes a small eastern-style chapel built on a Greek cross plan, a 15C Descent from the Cross in painted terra-cotta and 9C–12C fresco fragments.

Ca' Granda-Ex Ospedale Maggiore (Università)★★

Now occupied by the university, this was originally a hospital, built in 1456 for Francesco Sforza to a design by Filarete. Modified several times since, notably by Guiniforte Solari, it has a lengthy brick façade adorned with pairs of windows, arches and sculpted busts in medallions. Inner courtyard designed by Richini.

San Nazaro★

Near Ca' Granda, on the corner of Corso Romana and Via Francesco Sforza.
This Romanesque basilica dates from the 12C, but the tower housing the Mausoleo Trivulzio was added by Bramantino for Marshal Gian Giacomo Trivulzio (who occupied Milan for King Louis XII of France) and his family. Inside, the Chapel of San Lino contains 12C and 15C frescoes.

Sant'Antonio Abate

Via Sant'Antonio 5, near the university.
Open Mon–Sat 10am–6pm.
The façade may not attract much attention, but the interior is a typical example of early Milanese Baroque. The pretty cloister features Renaissance terra-cotta arcades.

Torre Velasca★★

This pink skyscraper was erected in 1956 and has become an emblem of Milan. It was designed by Belgioioso, Peresutti and Rogers. The top nine floors project outwards, giving the reinforced concrete tower its distinctive mushroom shape.

Sant'Alessandro★

Open daily 7am–noon and 4–7pm.
℘02 86 45 30 65.
A magnificent example of Milanese Baroque (17C) with marble, gilding and frescoes as well as an interesting pulpit and main altar. Paintings by 18C Milanese masters.

San Pietro in Gessate

Opposite the law courts. For opening times contact ℘02 54 10 74 24.

This 15C church contains the Grifi Chapel with attractive frescoes of the life of St Ambrose.

Cimitero Monumentale★

Piazzale Cimitero Monumentale. Open 8am–6pm. Closed Mon except holidays. 02 88 46 56 00. www.comune.milano.it/monumentale
This vast cemetary is the final resting place for many famous Italians, including writer Alessandro Manzoni, conductor Arturo Toscanini and painter Francesco Hayez. The cemetary's primary neogothic façade was designed by Carlo Machiachini and built during the second half of the 19C. Countless funereal artworks make the cemetary a sort of open air museum, where visitors can view works by Mosè Bianchi, Medardo Rosso, Francesco Messina, Pietro Cascella, Giacomo Manzù and others.

EXCURSIONS

Abbazia di Chiaravalle★★

◗ 7km/4.3mi SE. Leave by Porta Romana and head towards San Donato. Consult the map of the built-up area on Michelin map 561. Open Tue–Sat 9am–noon and 3–5pm, Sun 3–5pm. Closed Mon, public hols. 5€. ℘02 57 40 34 04 or 02 84 93 04 32. www.monasterochiaravalle.it.
The early Gothic abbey, founded by St Bernard of Clairvaux in 1135, is dominated by a polygonal bell tower★. Visit the delightful cloisters.

Monza★

◗ 21km/13mi N.
Monza is a textile town on the edge of the hilly Brianza area dotted with lakes, villas and gardens.

Duomo★

This 13C4C cathedral has a white, green and black marble Lombard façade★★ (1390–6), by Matteo da Campione, one of the Maestri Campionesi, who spread the Lombard style throughout Italy. Highlights of the interior★ include a 14C silver gilt altar front★, 15C frescoes★ in the Chapel of the Queen of the Longobards and the treasury★ (tesoro) with a splendid 5CC Iron Crown★★ of the Kings of Lombardy, presented by Pope Gregory I the Great to the queen. Museum: Open Tue–Sun 9am–6pm, Mon 3–6pm. 8€. Reservation required for Iron Crown and Teodolinda Chapel, 8€. Combined ticket Museum, Iron Crown and Teodolinda Chapel 14€. ℘039 32 63 83. www.museoduomomonza.it.

Parco di Villa Reale★★

This Neoclassical royal villa was the residence of Eugène de Beauharnais (Napoleon's stepson) and Umberto I of Italy, who was assassinated at Monza in 1900. In the northern part of the park is the Monza racing circuit, the venue for the Grand Prix Formula One race.

ADDRESSES

🏠 STAY

As most hotels put their prices up during the frequent trade fairs and exhibitions, budget travellers could try outside the city (&see PAVIA, p419).

⊖ **Ostello A.I.G. Piero Rotta** – Via Salmoiraghi 1. ℘02 39 26 70 95. www. ostellomilano.it. &. Basic but good value; 15 minutes from the centre by metro.

⊖⊖ **Albergo Città Studi** – Via Saldini 24, zona Città Studi. ℘02 74 46 66. www. hotelcittastudi.it. 45 rooms. ⊆. In the busy university area, a quiet, simple hotel, with adequate facilities.

⊖⊖ **Hotel Gala** – Viale Zara 89. ℘02 668 08 91. 22 rooms. ⊆. Family-run, easy access to the centre by car, quiet with lovely garden.

⊖⊖ **Hotel San Francisco** – Viale Lombardia 55. ℘02 23 60 302. www. hotel-sanfrancisco.it. 🅿 28 rooms. Simple accommodation and a pretty garden, not far from the centre.

⊖⊖⊜ **Hotel des Etrangers** – Via Sirte 9. ℘02 48 95 53 25. www. hoteldesetrangers.it. 94 rooms. ⊆. Near the trade fair district and good for public transport. Comfortable rooms.

⊖⊖⊜ **Hotel Regina** – Via Correnti 13. ℘02 58 10 69 13. www.hotelregina.it. 43 rooms. ⊆. Grand and elegant hotel with a glass-covered courtyard lobby.

⊖⊜⊜ **Hotel Cavour** – Via Fatebenefratelli 21. ℘02 62 00 01. www.hotelcavour.it. 125 rooms. ⊆. Understated elegance, run by one of Milan's oldest families of hoteliers.

⊖⊜⊜ **Hotel Dei Cavalieri** – Piazza Missori 1. ℘02 88 571. www.hoteldei cavalieri.com. 177 rooms. ⊆. On lively Piazza Missori. Contemporary decor and a pleasant atmosphere. Restaurant with panoramic terrace.

⊖⊜⊜ **Hotel Gran Duca di York** – Via Moneta 1a. ℘02 87 48 63. www. ducadiyork.it. 33 rooms. ⊆. Lovely rooms and atmosphere in an elegant 18C palazzo in the city's historic heart.

♈/EAT

Local specialities include *cotoletta alla milanese* (fillet of veal fried in breadcrumbs with cheese), *ossobuco* (a knuckle of veal with the marrowbone) and *risotto alla milanese* (saffron risotto). Among the good regional wines are sparkling Franciacorta, red Valtellina, and Oltrepò Pavese.

⊖ **Bottiglieria da Pino** – Via Cerva 14. ℘02 76 00 05 32. Closed Sun. A down-to-earth trattoria with home cooking and decent prices. Lunch only.

⊖⊖ **Baia Chia** – Via Bazzini 37. ℘02 23 61 131. www.ristorante sardobaiachia.it. Closed Mon lunch, Sun and 3 weeks Aug. Booking advised. Charming. Sardinian specialities, fish and seafood.

⊖⊖ **Be Bop** – Viale Col di Lana 4. ℘02 83 76 972. www.ristorantebebop.com. Restaurant and pizzeria with gluten-free and soya options.

⊖⊖ **Charleston** – Piazza Liberty 8. ℘02 79 86 31. www.ristorantecharleston.it. Popular with shoppers thanks to its central location.

⊖⊖ **Da Giannino-L'Angolo d'Abruzzo** – Via Pilo 20. ℘02 29 40 65 26. www.dagianninolangolodabruzzo.it. Booking advised. A family-run trattoria serving hearty specialities from the Abruzzo region.

⊖⊖ **Dongiò** – Via Corio 3. ℘02 55 11 372. www.ristorante-dongio.it. Closed Sat lunch, Sun, 2 weeks Aug. Booking advised.

Simple and authentic place serving tasty Calabrian specialities.

Dulcis in Fundo – Via Zuretti 55. 02 66 71 25 03. www.dulcisinfundo.it. Open Tue–Fri lunch, Thu dinner, Sat brunch (booking advised). Post-Modern meets 1970s in an old industrial building. Sweet and savoury snacks, unusual mains.

Giulio Pane e Ojo – Via Muratori 10. 02 54 56 189. www.giuliopaneojo.com. A friendly place specialising in Roman cuisine.

La Vecchia Latteria – Via dell'Unione 6. 02 87 44 01. Good vegetarian food and shared tables at this busy lunch place in central Milan.

Masuelli San Marco – Viale Umbria 80. 02 55 18 41 38. www. masuellitrattoria.com. Closed Mon lunch, Sun. Booking advised. Family-run restaurant, dates from 1921. The seasonal local dishes vary by the day.

Obikà – Via Mercato 28 Brera district. 02 86 45 05 68. www.obica.com. Designer mozzarella di bufala. On the top floor of La Rinascente in Piazza del Duomo.

Paper Moon – Via Bagutta 1. 02 76 02 22 97. A traditional, elegant choice in Milan's fashion district.

Peck – Via Spadari 9. 02 80 23 161. www.peck.it. Open Tue–Sat lunch, Sun brunch. A historic fine foods store with a coffee and snack bar upstairs.

Pizza OK 2 – Via San Siro 9. 02 48 01 71 32. Closed. Huge, tasty, thin-crust pizzas – a busy place.

Premiata Pizzeria – Via De Amicis 22. 327 28 76 197. www.premiata pizzeriamilano.it. Great pizzas; attractive and busy restaurant; set in the Navigli district.

Rino Vecchia Napoli – Via Giorgio Chavez 4. 02 26 19 056. www. pizzeriavecchianapoli.it. Closed Mon and Sun lunch. Excellent pizzas and speedy service at this highly popular pizzeria. Best to book.

Sant'Eustorgio – Piazza Sant'Eustorgio 6. 02 58 10 13 96. www.sant-eustorgio.it. Italian classics – traditional and pleasant.

Spontini – Via Spontini 4. 02 20 47 444. Considered by some to serve the best pizza by the slice in town.

Trattoria del Nuovo Macello – Via Cesare Lombroso 20. 02 59 90 21 22. www.trattoriadelnuovomacello.it. Closed Sun and Sat lunch. Booking advised. This welcoming trattoria offers creative cuisine based on local produce.

Trattoria Madonnina – Via Gentilino 6. 02 89 40 90 89. Closed Sun, Mon–Wed evenings. Typical, informal trattoria.

TAKING A BREAK

Shockolat-Maggi – Via Boccaccio 9. A contemporary ice-cream parlour close to Santa Maria delle Grazie specialising in chocolate flavour.

Gelateria Marghera – Via Marghera 33. 02 46 86 41. Open 10am–midnight. By the National Theatre and the exhibition centre. Deliciously creamy ice creams.

Il Massimo del Gelato – Via Castelvetro 18. www.ilmassimodelgelato.it. Closed Mon and 25 Dec-2nd Sat of Feb. Ice-cream parlour in the Sempione district with inventive flavours.

Luini Panzerotti – Via Santa Radegonda 16. www.luini.it. A local institution serving *panzerotti* a Southern Italy filled dough snack.

Panarello – Via Speronari 3 and Piazza San Nazaro in Brolo 15, corner of Corso di Porta Romana. These two Milanese stalwarts have been open since 1930.

Rigoletto – Via San Siro, corner of Via Sanzio. www.gelateriarigoletto.it. A little ice-cream parlour near Teatro Nazionale, especially good fruit-based flavours.

Riva Reno – Viale Col di Lana 8, and Via Mercato 20, www.rivareno.com/ita/. A *gelateria* with branches in the Ticinese district and in Brera, serving delicious and imaginative flavours. Try the pine-nut, chocolate and puffed rice ice cream.

A DRINK

Bar Basso – Via Plinio 39, zona Stazione Centrale. 02 29 40 05 80. www.barbasso. com. Closed Tue. The "wrong" Negroni cocktail was invented here, using champagne instead of gin.

Bar della Crocetta – Corso di Porta Romana 67. ☎02 54 50 228. www.crocetta.com. Fantastic panini at all hours of the day.

Bar Jamaica – Via Brera 32. ☎02 87 67 23. www.jamaicabar.it. The Jamaica is one of those bars with a story to tell. Opened in June 1921, between World War II and the 1960s it became a hang-out for an extraordinary generation of artists, writers and photographers, such as Piero Manzoni and Lucio Fontana, many of whose work can be seen in the Museo del Novecento.

Bar Magenta – Via Carducci 13, Sant'Ambrogio district. ☎02 805 38 08. Open 7am. Well known bar with a wide-ranging clientele, serving drinks to match. Lunches and snacks also available.

Cafè Trussardi – Piazza della Scala 5. www.cafetrussardi.it. Part of the modern Palazzo Trussardi, by the prestigious opera house. Refined and very busy at *aperitivo* time.

Cova – Via Monte Napoleone 8. www.pasticceriacova.it. Historic caffè in the heart of Milan, perfect for a coffee. Cakes look like works of art.

Gattullo – Piazzale Porta Lodovica 2. www.gattullo.it. For warm brioches and a good cappuccino.

Hôtel Bulgari – Via Fratelli Gabba 7b. A hyper-trendy atmosphere in the Brera-Montenapoleone district.

La Hora Feliz – Via San Vito 5, behind the Basilica of San Lorenzo. A bit of Cuba in Milan, with a wide choice of cocktails and a generous selection of bar snacks.

Radetzky Caffè – Corso Garibaldi 105. www.radetzky.it. A Milan classic in the Mittel Europa style. Informal, good for a snack or for brunch.

GOING OUT

The villagey Brera district with its street artists and galleries is a good spot for the evening, while Navigli, Milan's canal district, is also a haven for artists. The range of bars and restaurants of different styles is amazing – the area buzzes each evening.

Blue Note – Via Pietro Borsieri 37, district Garibaldi-Isola. ☎02 69 01 68 88.

www.bluenotemilano.com. Little brother of the famous New York club hosting jazz concerts.

ENTERTAINMENT

Milan has a very lively cultural and artistic scene. The city hosts a number of musical events – classical, jazz, rock – where some of the world's most famous stars come to perform. There are also a number of theatres.

MUSIC

Auditorium di Milano – Largo Gustav Mahler. ☎02 83 38 94 01. www.laverdi.org. Performances of classical, jazz and other types of music. Also hosts literary evenings, events for children as well as audiences with well-known artistes.

La Scala – Piazza Scala. ☎02 86 07 75. www.teatroallascala.org. Stages opera and ballet. The season traditionally starts on St Ambrose's Day (7 Dec), the city's patron.

Teatro Dal Verme – Via San Giovanni sul Muro 5. ☎02 87 905. www.dalverme.org. Mainly classical concerts but also some drama staged here.

DRAMA

Piccolo Teatro – The Piccolo Teatro di Strehler comprises three theatres, all of which are centrally located: Teatro Strehler, Largo Greppi; Teatro Grassi, Via Rovello 2; Teatro Studio, Via Rivoli 6. ☎02 42 41 18 89 (from abroad), 848 800 304 (from Italy). www.piccoloteatro.org.

Teatro Carcano – Corso di Porta Romana 63. ☎02 55 18 13 77. www.teatrocarcano.com.

Teatro Franco Parenti – Via Pier Lombardo 14. ☎02 59 99 52 06. www.teatrofrancoparenti.com.

Teatro Manzoni – Via Manzoni 42, zona Centro Storico. ☎02 76 36 901. www.teatromanzoni.it.

SHOPPING

City life focuses around Piazza del Duomo and the adjacent shopping areas by day. Corso Vittorio Emanuele II has all the high-street names while the Golden Quad around Via Monte Napoleone is the realm of top designers. Trendy independent shops are to be found on Corso di Porta Ticinese.

Bergamo★★

Bergamo is on the northern edge of the Lombardy Plain at the confluence of the Brembana and Seriana valleys. It has a strong artistic heritage, and is also a thriving industrial centre. The lower town is modern in contrast to the delightfully historic upper town.

A BIT OF HISTORY

The Gauls seized the settlement in 550 BC and called it *Berghem*. The Romans renamed it Bergomum when they took over in 196 BC. The city was destroyed by the barbarians, before enjoying a period of peace under the Lombards and, in particular, Queen Theodolinda. An independent 11–13C commune, it then joined the Lombard League.

The town suffered during the struggles between the Guelphs (followers of the Pope) and the Ghibellines (followers of the emperor). Under the rule of **Bartolomeo Colleoni** (1400–75), the town fell first to the Visconti family from Milan and then to the Republic of Venice, which the mercenary leader served successively. Bergamo came under Austrian rule in 1814 and was liberated by Garibaldi in 1859.

Artists both local (including Previtali, Baschenis and Fra Galgario) and from elsewhere, namely **Lorenzo Lotto**, Giovanni da Campione and Amadeo, worked here. Bergamo was home to composer Donizetti (1797–1848). Local musical folklore includes the lively Bergamasque, a pipe-dance.

👤👤 The **Commedia dell'Arte** originated in Bergamo in the 16C. The comedy consists of an improvisation *(imbroglio)* based on a pre-arranged theme *(scenario)*, with gags *(lazzi)* uttered by masked actors. The stock characters are the valet (Harlequin), a stubborn but wily peasant from the Brembana Valley, the braggart (Pulcinella), the lady's maid (Columbine), the lover (Pierrot), the knave (Scapino), the old fox (Scaramouch), the clown (Pantaloon) and the musician (Mezzetino).

▶ **Population:** 118 019
♿ **Michelin Map:** 561 E 10–11 – Lombardy.
🔲 **Info:** Via Gombito 13, Città Alta. ☏035 24 22 26. www.visitbergamo.net.
◑ **Location:** Bergamo is crowned by the old town of Bergamo Alta. The town is 50km/31mi from Milan.
◑ **Train:** Bergamo (Brescia 54mins). Milan via bus to Sesto San Giovanni station.
🅿 **Parking:** Park outside the walls of the Città Alta.
👁 **Don't Miss:** Piazza Vecchia in the Città Alta.
🕐 **Timing:** Allow a day. It is also an ideal base for excursions into mountain valleys nearby and visits to lakes Como, d'Iseo and Garda.
👤👤 **Kids:** Nativity scenes at the Museo del Presepio and *Commedia dell'Arte*.

CITTÀ ALTA★★★
🅿 Outside the walls.

The road to the upper city is steep so it may be better to drive or take the funicular *(station in Viale Vittorio Emanuele II)*, which ends in **Piazza del Mercato delle Scarpe** (Square of the Shoe Market).

Piazza Vecchia★

Stendhal once called this historic centre "the most beautiful place on Earth". **Palazzo della Ragione**, Italy's oldest town hall, dates from 1199, but was rebuilt in the 16C. It has graceful arcades and a Lion of St Mark over a central balcony symbolising Venetian rule. A covered stairway leads to the majestic 12C tower *(campanone)* with its 15C clock (open Apr–Oct Tue-Fri 9.30am–6pm; Sat–Sun 9.30am–8pm, Nov-Mar Tue-Fri 9.30am-1pm and 2.30- 6pm, Sat and Sun 9.30am-6pm. Closed Mon; 3€; ☏035 24 71 16; www.bergamoestoria.it). **Palladian**-style **Palazzo Scamozziano** is opposite.

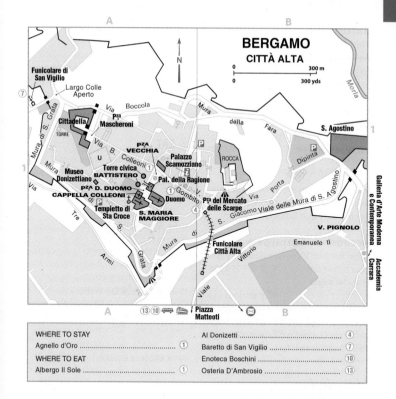

BERGAMO
CITTÀ ALTA

WHERE TO STAY	
Agnello d'Oro .... ①	
WHERE TO EAT	
Albergo Il Sole .... ①	

Al Donizetti .... ④	
Baretto di San Vigilio .... ⑦	
Enoteca Boschini .... ⑩	
Osteria D'Ambrosio .... ⑬	

◗ Through Palazzo della Ragione head towards Piazza del Duomo, bordered by the chief monuments of the upper town.

Cappella Colleoni★★

Open Tue–Sun Mar–Oct 9am–12.30pm and 2–6.30pm; Nov–Feb 9am–12.30pm and 2–4.30pm. Donations welcome. ℘035 21 00 61. www.lombardiabeniculturali.it
Amadeo, who built Pavia's Carthusian monastery, designed the chapel (1470–6), a jewel of Lombard-Renaissance architecture. As Bartolomeo Colleoni wanted, his mausoleum opens onto the Basilica of St Mary Major. The elegant **façade** features multicoloured marble and delicate sculptures while the **interior** is sumptuously decorated with bas-reliefs, frescoes by Tiepolo and Renaissance stalls.
Amadeo's **Colleoni Monument** has a gilt statue of Colleoni on horseback.

Basilica di Santa Maria Maggiore★

Open daily 9am–12.30pm and 2.30–6pm (winter 5pm). Donations welcome. ℘035 22 33 27. www.lombardiabeniculturali.it.
The church dates from the 12C although the lovely north and south **porches** – with Lombard-Romanesque loggias – were added in the 14C by Giovanni da Campione. The interior contains nine Florentine **tapestries**★★ (1580–6), based on cartoons by Alessandro Allori, relating the life of the Virgin. A sumptuous Flemish tapestry depicting the **Crucifixion**★★ hangs on the west wall. The tapestry was woven in Antwerp (1696–8) after cartoons by L. Van Schoor. The church also contains Donizetti's tomb (1797–1848) and some superb 16C **intarsia work**★★ depicting Old Testament scenes.

◗ Exit onto Piazza Santa Maria Maggiore door.

Battistero★

This charming octagonal baptistery encircled by a red Verona marble gallery and 14C statues of the Virtues was originally inside St Mary Major but it was demolished in 1660 and rebuilt in 1898. ⊛ Make sure you also see the **Duomo** (*Via Bartolomeo Colleoni, Luogo Pio Colleoni*) and visit the Rocca for excellant **views**★.

CITTÀ BASSA★

Piazza Matteotti is central to the business and shopping area. Market days are Monday and Saturday.

Accademia Carrara★★

Open Tue-Sun 10am-7pm (last entry one hour before closing). 10€. ☎035 23 43 96. www.lacarrara.it.

A collection of 15C–18C paintings in a Neoclassical palace. Highlights include portaits of **Giuliano de'Medici** by Botticelli and of **Lionello d'Este** by Pisanello, 16C Venetian masters, Titian and Tintoretto.

ld Quarter★

The main street, **Via Pignolo**★, winds among 16C–19C *palazzi* and churches such as the **church of San Bernardino**, which has a **Virgin Enthroned and Saints**★ (1521) by Lorenzo Lotto.

Piazza Matteotti★

This huge square, flanked by the **Sentierone**, is popular for a stroll. The **Donizetti Theatre** and **Church of San Bartolomeo**, with the **Martinengo Altarpiece** by Lorenzo Lotto, are here.

EXCURSIONS

San Pellegrino Terme⚓⚓

◗ 25km/15.5mi N of Bergamo; SS 470.

A traditional spa town (alt. 350m/1 148ft) with lots of early 20C architecture.

Dalmine

◗ 11km/6.8mi S.

Over 800 nativity scenes of all sizes can be seen at the 👥 **Museo del Presepio**★. The largest measures 80sq m/861sq ft. **Via XXV Aprile 179.** Open Thu–Sun 2–6pm. 3.50€. www.museodelpresepio.com.

ADDRESSES

🛏 STAY

☺☺ **Agnello d'Oro** – Via Gombito 22. ☎035 24 98 83. www.agnellodoro.it. 20 rooms. Simple but comfortable rooms on four floors (with lift). Inviting restaurant, good local cuisine.

🍴 EAT

☺☺ **Al Donizetti** – Via Gombito 17. ☎035 24 26 61. www.donizetti.it. Quality food and good service with hanging hams, a pleasant terrace and a rustic interior.

☺☺ **Albergo Il Sole** – Via Bartolomeo Colleoni 1. ☎035 21 82 38. www.ilsole bergamo.com. This pizzeria in the centre of the upper town has eclectic decor inside and a small garden.

☺☺ **Baretto di San Vigilio** – Via Castello 1. ☎035 25 31 91. www.baretto.it. A stylish restaurant serving local and creative dishes. Sit outside in summer for wonderful views over the town.

☺☺ **Enoteca Boschini** – Via T. Tasso, 96. ☎035 22 21 81. Closed Sun evening and Mon. Large windows and a courtyard garden; great food and wines.

☺☺ **Osteria D'Ambrosio** – Via Broseta 58a. ☎035 40 29 26. Closed Sat lunch and Sun. Reservation recommended. An authentic, rustic *osteria*. Come for a warm welcome and genuine local dishes.

TAKING A BREAK

Caffè della Funicolare – Via Porta Dipinta 3. www.caffedellafunicolare.it. This bar at the funicular stop is ideal for a drink or snack. Fantastic views from the terrace.

SHOPPING

Angelo Mangili – Via Colleoni 7. ☎035 24 87 74. A high-class food shop and a feast for the eyes with a tempting array of jars, cured meats and wines.

EVENTS

Festival pianistico internazionale – ☎391 46 19 293. www.festivalpianistico.it. Prestigious piano festival held at the Donizetti Theatre each May–June, with concerts also in Brescia. The city hosts a **Jazz festival** in March.

Brescia★

The important industrial town of Brescia lies at the foot of the Lombard Pre-Alps, and has retained the regular street plan of the Roman camp *(castrum)* of Brixia. The town is dominated to the north by a medieval castle (Castello) and its bustling historic centre has many fine buildings from all periods: Antiquity, Romanesque, Renaissance and Baroque. In 2011 Brescia's Santa Giulia complex was granted World Heritage status by UNESCO. Local vineyards produce Franciacorta, Italy's sparkling wine, as a response to France's Champagne.

SIGHTS
Piazza della Loggia★
The **Loggia**, now the town hall, dates from the end of the 15C to the beginning of the 16C. Sansovino and Palladio were among those involved in building the upper storey.
👥 The **clock tower** opposite the Loggia is topped by two clockwork figures (Jacks) that strike the hours. On the square's south side stand the palaces, **Monte di Pietà Vecchio** (1484) and **Monte di Pietà Nuovo** (1497).

Piazza Vittoria
This square dominated by the white marble post office building with its tall arcade was laid out in the 1930s as part of a modernisation plan for the city centre, and illustrates the tendencies in urban planning under the Fascist regime.

Piazza Paolo VI
The 17C Duomo Nuovo (New Cathedral) in white marble seems to crush the Duomo Vecchio (Old Cathedral), a late 11C Romanesque building that succeeded an earlier sanctuary, known as the rotunda after its shape. Inside, there is a magnificent sarcophagus in rose-coloured marble, and in the chancel paintings by local artists, Moretto and Romanino.

▶ **Population:** 191 618
🚗 **Michelin Map:**
  561 2 – Lombardy.
🅘 **Info:** Via Trieste 1.
  ☎030 24 00 357.
  www.bresciatourism.it.
◖ **Location:** Brescia lies on the A 4, not far from Lake Garda. By train, it takes 45 minutes from Verona and a couple of hours from Venice.
◖ **Train:** Brescia (Verona Porta Nuova 35 mins).
👁 **Don't Miss:** The Roman section at the Santa Giulia museum.
🕐 **Timing:** Allow a day.
👥 **Kids:** The charming clockwork figures on the clock tower opposite the Loggia and collections of armour at the Museo delle Armi Luigi Marzoli.

Via dei Musei★
This picturesque street has some interesting sites: the ruins of the **Capitoline Temple★** (AD 73), with the remains of the cells, the tribunal and the adjacent Roman theatre (**Teatro Romano**). Beyond the remains of the forum is a monastery founded in AD 753 by Ansa, the wife of the last King of the Lombards, Desiderio. Legend has it that Desiderio's daughter, Ermengarda, wife of Charlemagne (who later repudiated her), died here. Included in the monastery complex were the basilica of San Salvatore, the Romanesque church of Santa Maria in Solario and the church of Santa Giulia, now part of the city museum.

◖ Before reaching the Santa Giulia museum take the steps on the left to the Corpus Christi church.

Chiesa del Santissimo Corpo di Cristo★
This church forms part of a convent complex founded in 1467, which also includes two cloisters. Behind the sim-

ple façade in the Lombard-Gothic style, you will find a barrel-vaulted nave with no side aisles, which is entirely covered in painted decoration. The volume of the interior, the ceiling divided into sections, the walls entirely covered with frescoes and the dominant motif of the Last Judgement on the triumphal arch have led to the church being nicknamed Brescia's "Sistine Chapel". On the right-hand side, three chapels were added in 1620 by the architect Bagnatore.

Santa Giulia – Museo della Città★★

Via Musei 81bis. Open Tue–Sun middle Jun–Sept 10.30am–6pm; rest of the year 9.30am–4.30pm. 10€. ℘030 29 77 834. www.bresciamusei.com.

The magnificent city museum is housed in monastery buildings founded in 753 by the last Lombard king, Desiderius, and his wife Ansa. According to the famous writer Alessandro Manzoni, it is the resting place of Desiderius' daughter Ermengarda.

Over the centuries, the monastery was expanded with the addition of the Lombard basilica of San Salvatore, the Romanesque church of Santa Maria in Solario and the Renaissance church of Santa Giulia, which has a dome decorated with a fresco of God the Father giving his blessing against a star-studded sky and **Desiderio's Cross★★** (8C–9C), also part of the museum. As the building was built on an old Roman district, discoveries made during excavations can be seen inside the museum itself. These include two **Roman houses**, still decorated with very fine mosaics, which have been uncovered in the basement. The museum integrates a presentation of the history of the monastery itself with a chronological presentation of archaeological and architectural artefacts and artworks from the city and the surrounding area, dating from the prehistoric period to the 19C. In all, there are 12,000 items on display over a floor area of 14 000sq m/150 700sq ft!

You begin your visit in the Benedictine monastery of San Salvatore and Santa Giulia, then continue to the cloisters and the monastery churches. The **basilica and the crypt of San Salvatore** contain wonderful capitals from the Ravennate-Byzantine period and Romanino's cycle of frescoes on the life of Sant'Obizio. The Romanesque oratory of **Santa Maria in Solario**, with its frescoes by Ferramola and a ceiling decorated with a starry night sky, contains the monastery treasure: the large **cross of Desiderius** dating from the late-8C, which is inlaid with precious stones and cameos, and the **Lipsanoteca**, a magnificent ivory reliquary from the second half of the 4C. On the first floor, the **Coro delle monache** (nuns' choir) dates from the Renaissance period. This part of the complex allowed the nuns to follow the ceremonies held at San Salvatore through openings in the east wall. The choir contains a very fine cycle of frescoes, including a **Crucifixion by Ferramola**.

Pinacoteca Tosio Martinengo★

o—¬ Closed for restoration at time of publication. www.bresciamusei.com.

The art gallery displays works of the **Brescia school**, characterised by richness of colour and well-balanced composition: religious scenes and portraits by Moretto, more sumptuous religious scenes in the Venetian manner by Romanino and other works including canvases by Vincenzo Foppa and Savoldo. The works of Clouet, Raphael, the Master of Utrecht, Lorenzo Lotto and Tintoretto are also on view.

Castello

Built in 1343 for the Visconti over the remains of a Roman temple, this castle now houses the **Museo delle Armi Luigi Marzoli**, a collection of 14C–18C arms and armour, and Museo del Risorgimento where Roman remains can be seen inside. Open middle Jun–Sept Fri–Sun 11am–6.30pm; Oct–middle Jun Thu and Fri 9am–3.30pm, Sat and Sun 10am–4.30pm. Closed 24, 25, 31 Dec. 5€. ℘030 29 77 834. www.bresciamusei.com.

WHERE TO STAY	WHERE TO EAT	
Impero .... ①	La Campagnola .... ①	Trattoria Briscola .... ④

CHURCHES

Brescia boasts several Romanesque, Renaissance and Baroque churches, with interesting artworks, particularly by members of the Brescia school. The 13C church of **San Francesco★** contains Moretto's **Three Saints**, a *Pietà* by a follower of Giotto (14C) and a Virgin and Child altarpiece by Romanino. **Santa Maria dei Miracoli** dates from the 15C–16C and has a fine marble **façade★**. **San Nazaro-San Celso** contains a masterpiece by Moretto, the **Coronation of the Virgin★**, and a polyptych by Titian; **Sant'Alessandro** contains a 15C Annunciation by Jacopo Bellini and a **Deposition from the Cross★** by Civerchio. **Sant'Agata**, with its lavishly decorated interior, contains a 16C polyptych of the Virgin of Mercy by an artist of the Brescia school, and the **Madonna of the Coral★**, a delightful 16C fresco.

Also worth a mention is **San Giovanni Evangelista** for its works by Moretto and Romanino, the church of the **Madonna delle Grazie** for its Baroque interior, and the eastern-looking **Madonna del Carmine**.

ADDRESSES

🏠 STAY

⊖⊜ **Impero** – Via Triumplina 6. ☎030 38 14 83. www.hotelimpero.it. This cosy, family-run hotel has been fully restored and also has a pizzeria.

🍴/EAT

⊖⊜ **La Campagnola** – Via Val Daone 25. ☎030 30 06 78. www.trattorialacampagnola brescia.it. Closed Mon evening–Tue. An authentic trattoria serving rustic food.

⊖⊜ **Trattoria Briscola** – Via Costalunga 18g. ☎030 39 52 32. Closed Wed lunch. From its location on a green hillside, this typical trattoria boasts a fine city view.

EVENT

Festival pianistico internazionale – ☎030 29 30 22. www.festivalpianistico.it. Prestigious piano festival at the Teatro Grande each May–June.

Mantova★★

Mantua

Mantova is set in a flat fertile plain, which was formerly marshland, on the southeastern border of Lombardy. It is encircled to the north by three lakes formed by the slow-flowing River Mincio. This active and prosperous town has important mechanical and petrochemical industries. This region is also the number-one hosiery producer worldwide.

▶ **Population:** 48 324

🦯 **Michelin Map:**
561 or 562 G 14.

🅱 **Info:** Piazza Andrea Mantegna 6. ✆0376 43 24 32. www.turismo. mantova.it.

◗ **Location:** Mantova lies at the southeast corner of Lombardy. The main access roads are the A 22 and S 236 from Brescia.

◗ **Train:** Mantova (Verona Porta Nuova 45 mins).

😊 **Don't Miss:** The lavish apartments of Palazzo Ducale and the dramatic Palazzo Te.

🕐 **Timing:** Allow a day.

A BIT OF HISTORY

Although, according to a legend quoted by Virgil, Mantova was founded by Monto, daughter of Tiresias, its origins would seem to be Etruscan, dating back to the 6C or 5C BC. It passed to the Gauls before becoming Roman in the 3C BC. In 70 BC **Virgil** (Publius Virgilius Maro), the great poet and author, was born in the Mantova area. Author of the *Aeneid*, in which he recounts the wanderings of Aeneas, the Trojan prince, and the foundation of the earliest settlement from which Rome was to spring, Virgil describes his beloved Mantovan countryside, with its soft, misty light, and the pleasures of rural life in his harmonious but melancholy style in the *Eclogues* or *Bucolica* and in the *Georgics*.

In the Middle Ages Mantova was the theatre for many struggles between factions that successively sacked the town, before it became an independent commune in the 13C and finally the domain of Luigi Gonzaga, nominated Captain General of the People. Under the **Gonzaga** family, who were enlightened rulers and patrons of the arts and letters, Mantova became an important intellectual and artistic centre in northern Italy of the 15C and 16C. Thus Gian Francesco Gonzaga (ruled 1407–44) placed his children in the charge of the famous humanist Vittorio da Feltre (1379–1446) and commissioned the Veronese artist **Pisanello** (1395–1455) to decorate his Ducal Palace. His son Ludovico III (1444–78), a mer-

cenary army leader by profession, was a typical Renaissance patron: he gave land to the poor, built bridges and favoured artists. The Sienese humanist Politian (1454–94), the Florentine architect Leon Battista Alberti (1404–72) and the Padovan painter **Andrea Mantegna** (1431–1506) all belonged to his court. Francesco II (1484–1519) married Isabella d'Este, a beautiful and wise woman who contributed to the fame of Mantova. Their son Federico II was made duke by the Emperor Charles V in 1530 and he commissioned the architect and artist **Giulio Romano** (1499–1546), Raphael's pupil, to embellish his native town; the artist worked on the Ducal Palace and cathedral and the Palazzo Te.

In 1627 Vicenzo II died without heirs and the succession passed to the Gonzaga-Nevers family, the cadet line. The Habsburg Emperor Ferdinand II opposed the French succession, and in 1630 sent an army which sacked the town and then deserted it following a plague which decimated Milan and Lombardy (the background to these dramatic events is described in the novel *I Promessi Sposi* by Manzoni).

The Gonzaga-Nevers restored the fortunes of the town until 1707 when they were deposed. Mantova became part of

Palazzo Ducale

the Austrian Empire, which ruled until 1866, except for a period under Napoleonic rule (1787–1814), when it joined the Kingdom of Italy.

PALAZZO DUCALE★★★

Allow 1hr 30min. Open Tue–Sun 8.15am–7.15pm (last entry 6.20pm). Tour Corte Vecchia or Tour Castello di San Giorgio with Camera degli Sposi. Booking advised for Tour Castello di San Giorgio. Closed 1 Jan, 1 May, 25 Dec. 6.50€ tour Corte Vecchia with Isabella d'Este Apartment; 12€ combined ticket. ℰ 0376 22 48 32. www.mantovaducale.beniculturali.it

The imposing Ducal Palace comprises buildings from various periods: the Magna Domus and the Palazzo del Capitano erected in the late-13C by the Bonacolsi, Lords of Mantova from 1272 to 1328; the Castello di San Giorgio, a 14C fortress; and other inner sections built by the Gonzaga in the 15C6C, including the 15C Palatine chapel of Santa Barbara.

Apartments★★★

Start from the 17C Ducal Stairway, which gives access to the first floor. One of the first rooms displays *The Expulsion of the Bonacolsi and the Triumph of the Gonzaga on 16 August 1328* by Domenico Morone (1442–1517). The painting shows the medieval aspect of Piazza Sordello with the old façade of the cathedral. The **Pisanello rooms** on the first floor have fragments of frescoes and remarkable **sinopie**★★ (preparatory sketches using a red-earth pigment), that were discovered in 1969 and are a good example of the refined and penetrating work of Pisanello. These lyrical scenes draw inspiration from the feats of the Knights of the Round Table and the fantastic and timeless world of medieval chivalry. The **Tapestry Room** (*Appartamento degli Arazzi*), formerly known as the **Green Apartment** (*Appartamento Verde*), in the Neoclassical style, is hung with nine splendid Brussels tapestries after Raphael. The **Room of the Zodiac** (*Camera dello Zodiaco*) leads to the **Room of the Moors** (*Stanzino dei Mori*), in the Venetian style, and to the **Hall of the Rivers** (*Sala dei Fiumi*), which overlooks the **Hanging Garden** (*Giardino Pensile*). The giants depicted on the walls represents the rivers of Mantova. The **Corridor of the Moors** (*Corridoio dei Mori*) leads into the famous **Hall of Mirrors** (*Sala degli Specchi*) used for dancing and music. In the elegant **Room of the Archers** (*Sala degli Arcieri*), the antechamber to the Ducal Apartments, hang paintings by Rubens and Domenico Fetti.

The **Ducal Apartments** (*Appartamento Ducale*) comprise a suite of rooms remodelled for Vincenzi I in the early-17C by Antonio Maria Viani, and including the Paradise Room (*Appartamento del Paradiso*) and the tiny Room of the Dwarfs (*Appartamento dei Nani*). The building known as the **Rustica** and the **Equestrian Court** (*Cortile della Cavallerizza*) are by Giulio Romano; the courtyard is lined by a **gallery**, Galleria della Mostra, built in the late-16C by Antonio Maria Viani for Vicenzo I's art collection, and by the **Hall of the Months** (*Galleria dei Mesi*) erected by Giulio Romano.

In the **Castello di San Giorgio** you can see the **Room of the Spouses**★★★ (Camera degli Sposi) – so-called because this is where marriages were recorded – executed from 1465 to 1474 by **Andrea Mantegna**. The walls are covered with a celebrated cycle of frescoes that glorify

413

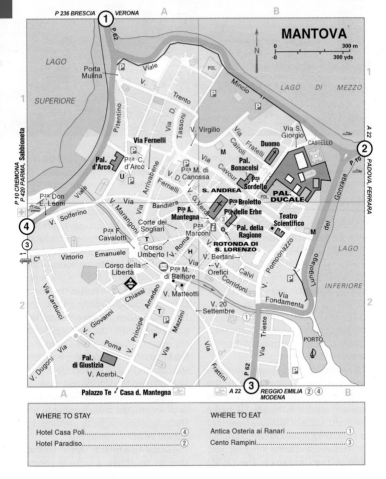

WHERE TO STAY		WHERE TO EAT	
Hotel Casa Poli...............................④		Antica Osteria ai Ranari ....①	
Hotel Paradiso...............................②		Cento Rampini..③	

the superb and refined world of the Gonzaga court. Mantegna creates an illusion of space with his knowledge of foreshortening and perspective and his skilful use of volume and materials.

The painted *trompe l'œil* and carved stucco decorations and garlands of foliage and fruits are also admirable. On the north wall look for Ludovico II turned towards his secretary, and his wife Barbara seated full-face. The children cluster around their parents, as do other members of the court, including an enigmatic dwarf.

On the west wall the fresco presents Ludovico with his son, Cardinal Francesco, against the background of a town with splendid monuments, which could well be Rome as imagined by Mantegna.

Mantegna has portrayed himself as the figure in purple which can be glimpsed on the right of the dedication. His great mastery of *trompe l'œil* culminates in the ceiling oculus from which gaze cupids and servants. This invention introduces a note of wry humour to this otherwise rather solemn ensemble.

SIGHTS
Piazza Sordello★

This square, which was the centre of old Mantova, has retained its medieval aspect. To the west is the 13C Palazzo Bonacolsi – the tall Tower of the Cage (Torre della Gabbia) still bears on its façade the cage *(gabbia)* in which wrongdoers were exhibited – and the 18C Palazzo Vescovile, where telamones adorn the 18C façade. To the east are the oldest buildings of the Palazzo Ducale: the Magna Domus and the crenellated Palazzo del Capitano.

On the north side stands the **cathedral** *(duomo)*, which features varied elements and styles: the Neoclassical façade, the late Gothic right wing and a Romanesque campanile. The 16C interior was designed by Giulio Romano.

Piazza Broletto

This was the centre of public life at the time of the commune (13C), when the Palazzo Broletto, a 13C communal palace, was also built. On its façade it has a seated statue of Virgil (1225). At the right corner rises the Torre Comunale, a tower that was later converted into a prison.

Piazza delle Erbe★

The piazza derives its name from a fruit and vegetable market. It is lined to the north by the rear façade of the Palazzo Broletto and to the east by the 13C Palazzo della Ragione, flanked by the 15C clock tower and the Romanesque church, the **Rotonda di San Lorenzo★**. Sober and elegant, this circular building has a colonnaded ambulatory with a loggia above and a dome crowning all. ♿Open Mon–Fri 10am–1pm and 3–9pm (winter 2–6pm), Sat–Sun 10am–6pm. Donation recommended. ☎0376 32 22 97.

Basilica di Sant'Andrea★

The basilica dedicated to St Andrew, built in the 15C to the plans of Alberti, is a masterpiece of the Italian Renaissance. The façade retains Classical architectural features: the tympanum, the triumphal arch, the niches between the pilasters. The **interior** has a single nave. The barrel vaulting and walls are painted in *trompe l'œil*. The first chapel on the left contains the tomb of Mantegna. In the crypt two urns housed in a reliquary contain a relic of the Blood of Christ.

Teatro Accademico

♿Open Tue–Fri 10am–1pm and 3–6pm; Sat, Sun and public hols 10am–6pm. 2€. ☎0376 32 76 53.
www.turismo.mantova.it.

This pretty 18C theatre by Bibiena has a stage set in imitation marble with four architectural orders in pasteboard and a monochrome decor. It welcomed the 13-year-old Mozart on 13 December 1769, and is still used for concerts.

Palazzo d'Arco

Open Sat and Sun 9.30am–1pm and 2.30–6pm; May–Sept Tue–Fri 10am–1pm and 3–6pm; middle Mar–Apr and Oct–Nov Tue–Fri 10am–1pm and 2.30–5.30pm. Closed 1 Jan, Easter, 15 Aug, 25–26 Dec. 5€. ☎0376 32 22 42.
This Neoclassical palace in the Palladian tradition *(see VICENZA)* contains interesting collections of 18C and 19C furniture, paintings and ceramics.

Palazzo di Giustizia

The monumental façade of the Law Courts with caryatids is early-17C. At no. 18 in this street is Giulio Romano's house built in 1544 to his own designs.

Casa del Mantegna

47 Via Acerbi.
This rather severe-looking brick building was probably built to designs by Mantegna himself in 1476. It has a delightful courtyard.

Palazzo Te★★

♿ Open Mon 1–6pm, Tue–Sun 9am–6pm (last entry 1h before closing). Closed 25 Dec. 8€. ☎0376 32 32 66. www.palazzote.it.

This large country mansion was built on the plan of a Roman house by Giulio Romano for Federico II from 1525 to 1535. It combines Classical features and melodramatic invention, such as the amazing "broken" entablature in the main courtyard, and is a major achievement of the Mannerist style.

The **interior** was ornately decorated by Giulio Romano and his pupils. In the **Room of the Horses** *(Salone dei Cavalli)*, used for receptions, some of the finest horses from the Gonzaga stables are depicted. In the **Room of Psyche** *(Sala di Psiche)*, used for banquets, the sensual and lively style of Giulio Romano is the best illustration of the hedonistic character of the palace. The frescoes in the **Room of the Giants** *(Sala dei Giganti)*, which is the most celebrated room of the palace, depict the wrath of Jupiter against the Titans.

The overall decoration that covers the walls and vaulted ceiling creates an indefinite spatial illusion and the dome above a sense of artificiality in sharp contrast to the effect sought by Mantegna in the Camera degli Sposi in the Palazzo Ducale.

EXCURSION
Sabbioneta★

▶ 34km/21.1mi SW of Mantova. Guided tours daily. For information on opening times for the Palazzo del Giardino, Chiesa dell'Incoronata, Teatro and Palazzo Ducale contact the tourist office. ✆0375 52 039. www.iatsabbioneta.org.

The town was built from 1558 by Vespasiano Gonzaga (1531–91), a mercenary leader in the service of Philip II of Spain who conferred on his loyal servants the glorious order of The Golden Fleece. The order was created in 1429 by Philip the Good, Duke of Burgundy. Vespasiano was a cultured man and he wanted to take personal charge of the construction of his ideal town. Its hexagonal walls and star plan and monuments make Sabbioneta a jewel of Italian Mannerism.

The **Garden Palace** (Palazzo del Giardino) was designed for festivities and its walls and ceilings were richly painted with frescoes by Bernardino Campi (1522–91) and his school. The great **Galleria** (96m/315ft long) is one of the longest Renaissance galleries.

The **Olympic Theatre** (Teatro Olimpico), a masterpiece by Vicentino Scamozzi (1552–1616), was built from 1588 to 1590 and is one of the oldest covered theatres in Europe. The interior is decorated with frescoes by the school of Veronese.

The **Ducal Palace** (Palazzo Ducale) has finely carved wooden and coffered ceilings. There are interesting equestrian statues of the Gonzaga family. The Galleria degli Antenati is also noteworthy. Vespasiano Gonzaga is buried in the **church of the Incoronata** with its octag-

onal plan and dome. Vespasiano's mausoleum is adorned with a bronze statue by Leone Leoni (1509–90); he is depicted as Marcus Aurelius.

The **Museo d'Arte Sacra** displays the order of the **Golden Fleece** discovered in 1988 in Vespasiano's tomb *(⟲see above)* in the church.

The 19C **synagogue** *(sinagoga)* traces the story of the town's Jewish community, whose legacy was the elegant printworks also used by Vespasiano.

ADDRESSES

🛏️STAY

🍴EAT

TAKING A BREAK

Caffè Modì – Via San Giorgio 4. Designer caffè behind the Ducal Palace. An ideal spot for a glass of wine with a plate of cured meats or cheeses. Music and cultural events are held.

EVENTS AND FESTIVALS

Each September, Mantova hosts a Festival of Literature with audiences with authors, conferences, performances, workshops and literary studies. www.festivaletteratura.it.

Cremona★

The original Gallic settlement became a Latin city before emerging as an independent commune in the Middle Ages when it suffered from the Guelph and Ghibelline troubles. In 1334 the town came under Visconti rule and was united with the Duchy of Milan in the 15C. During the Renaissance the town was the centre of a brilliant artistic movement. In the 18C and 19C the French and Austrians fought for supremacy over Cremona until the Risorgimento. Cremona is the birthplace of Claudio Monteverdi (1567–1643), who created modern opera. Cremona is famous for its violin-making heritage and for its *torrone* a deliciously sticky winter holiday sweet.

▶ **Population:** 72 248
◔ **Michelin Map:** 561 or 562 G 11/12 – Lombardy.
🛈 **Info:** Piazza del Comune 5, 26100 Cremona. ✆0372 40 63 91. www.turismocremona.it.
◑ **Location:** Cremona is an important agricultural market town in the Pianura Padana, on the banks of the River Po. Near the A 21, which links Brescia with Piacenza.
◑ **Train:** Cremona.
✦ **Don't Miss:** Zodiac illustrations in the Torrazzo's tower and the Duomo, and its violins.
◔ **Timing:** Allow half a day.
👪 **Kids:** Torrone candy factories; contact the tourist office (see above).

SIGHTS
Torrazzo★★★

Open daily 10am–1pm and 2.30–6pm (last entry 30min before closing). Closed Easter, 25 Dec, 15 Aug. 5€. ✆0372 49 50 29.

The remarkable late-13C campanile is linked to the cathedral by a Renaissance gallery. Its massive form is elegantly crowned by an octagonal 14C storey. From the top (112m/367ft), there is a lovely **view**★ over the town. The astronomical clock (1471) has undergone a number of alterations in its history, the last being in the 1970s. It is notable for its illustrations of the stars and the constellations of the Zodiac.

Duomo★★

This magnificent Lombard cathedral was begun in the Romanesque and completed in the Gothic style (1107–1332). The richly decorated white-marble façade is preceded by a porch. Later decorative features include the frieze by the followers of Antelami, the large 13C rose window and the four statue-columns of the central doorway.

Torrazzo and Duomo

© Vito Arcomano/Fototeca ENIT

The spacious **interior** is decorated with **frescoes**★ by the Cremona School (Boccaccino, the Campi, the Bembo, Romanino da Brescia, Pordenone and Gatti). At the entrance to the chancel, are the **high reliefs**★★ by Amadeo, the architect–sculptor of the Carthusian Monastery at Pavia.

The Violins of Cremona

From the late-16C the stringed-instrument makers of Cremona gained a reputation as violin and cello makers. The town was the birthplace of the greatest violin makers of all time and their instruments are still highly sought after by famous violinists today. The sound they produce is quite extraordinary, almost supernatural in tone and incredibly close to the human voice. The International School of Violin Making carries on this tradition. The first of the famous violin makers of Cremona was Andrea Amati, from whom King Charles IX of France commissioned instruments in the 16C. His work was continued by his sons and his nephew, Nicolò, master of Andrea Guarneri and the most famous of all of them, **Antonio Stradivarius** (c.1644–1737), who made more than 1 000 instruments including the "Cremonese"made in 1715. **Andrea Guarneri** was the first of another renowned dynasty in which the most skilled violin maker of them all was **Giuseppe Guarneri** (1698–1744), better known as Guarneri del Gesù because of the three letters IHS (Jesus, Saviour of Mankind) inscribed on all his violins. Knowledgeable music lovers find it easy to distinguish between the crystal-clear tones of a Stradivarius and the deeper, powerful tones of a Guarneri del Gesù. **Niccolò Paganini** (1782–1840), the violinist whose genius of interpretation, virtuosity and pyrotechnics were legendary. Paganini played a number of violins made in Cremona and these include the Guarneri (1743), known as 'Il Cannone', now owned by the Comune of Genova. Its displays were renovated in 2013. Musicians are appointed to play the violins – inquire at the tourist office to hear them; some workshops allow visitors.

Battistero★

This harmonious octagonal baptistery, preceded by a Lombard porch and decorated with a gallery, was remodelled during the Renaissance.

Palazzo Comunale

&. Open Mon–Sat 9am–6pm, Sun and public hols 10am–5pm. Closed 1 Jan, 1 May, 25 Dec. Free. ℘0372 40 72 91. www.turismocremona.it.
This 13C palace was later remodelled. Inside are displayed the most famous violins in the world: the Charles IX of France (Amati), the Hammerle (Amati), the Quarestani (Guarneri), the Cremonese 1715 (Antonio Stradivarius) and the Stauffer (Guarneri del Gesù). To the left of the palace is the lovely 13C **Loggia dei Militi**.

Museo Civico Ala Ponzone

&. Open Tue–Sun and public hols 10am–5pm. Closed 1 Jan, 1 May, 25 Dec. 7€. ℘0372 40 77 70. www.musei.comune.cremona.it.
A 16C palace hosts the municipal museum's **picture gallery**, with works of the Cremona school. Note the dramatic **St Frances in Meditation** by **Caravaggio**, and the *Vegetable Gardener* by **Arcimboldo**.

Museo del Violino

Piazza Marconi. &. Open Tue–Sun 10am–6pm. Closed 1 Jan, 25 Dec. 10€. ℘0372 80 18 01
www.museodelviolino.org.
This museum (renovated in 2013) displays wooden models and tools belonging to Stradivarius, as well as stringed instruments from the 17–20C.

ADDRESSES

ℙ/ EAT

◒◙ **Alba** – Via Persico 40. ℘0372 43 37 00. Closed Sun–Mon. Reservations recommended. Typical trattoria with a family atmosphere. Hearty regional home cooking, tradition at its best during the winter months. The *cotechino* (pork sausage) baked in a bread crust is particularly good.

Pavia★

This proud city is rich in Romanesque and Renaissance buildings. An important military camp under the Romans, it later became capital of the Lombard kings, an intellectual and artistic centre during the 14C under the Visconti, a fortified town in the 16C and an active centre of the 19C independence movement.

▶ **Population:** 71 184
⚙ **Michelin Map:**
  561 G 9 – Lombardy.
▮ **Info:** Palazzo del Broletto, Piazza della Vittoria. ℘0382 59 70 01. www.provincia.pv.it.
◖ **Location:** On the River Ticino, Pavia is 38km/23.6mi from Milan (A 7 and SS 35).
◖ **Train:** Pavia (Milano Rogoredo 17 mins).
⚄ **Don't Miss:** The Pinacoteca, Chiesa di San Michele and Certosa di Pavia.
🕐 **Timing:** Allow half a day.

SIGHTS

Castello Visconteo★

Open Tue–Sun Jul–Aug and Dec–Jan 9am–1.30pm; Sept–Nov and Feb–Jun 10am–5.50pm. Last entry 45 min before closing. 6€ museums; courtyard free. ℘0382 399 770. www.museicivici.pavia.it.
This impressive brick castle built by the Visconti houses the **Musei Civici★**. The collections include archaeological finds, Medieval and Renaissance sculpture and paintings. The **Pinacoteca★** has numerous masterpieces.

Duomo★

This vast cathedral, with one of Italy's largest domes, dates from 1488; both Bramante and Leonardo da Vinci are said to have worked on the plan. The façade is 19C. The 11C municipal tower, to the left, collapsed in March 1989. The 16C Bishop's Palace is opposite while the adjoining Piazza Vittoria is overlooked by the 12C **Broletto**, or town hall.

Chiesa di San Michele★★

This Romanesque church has a sandstone **façade★** and an impressive Romanesque door lintel showing Christ giving a papyrus to St Paul and the Keys of the Church to St Peter. The attractive interior has a 15C **fresco★** of the *Coronation of the Virgin* in the apse.

Chiesa di San Pietro in Ciel d'Oro★

This Lombard-Romanesque church (1132) has a richly decorated west **door★**. The Arca di Sant'Agostino (Tomb of St Augustine – 354–430) in the chancel is by the Maestri Campionesi.

Chiesa di San Lanfranco

◖ 2km/1.2mi W.
In the chancel is a **cenotaph★** (late-15C) by Amadeo that commemorates Lanfranc, who was born in Pavia and became Archbishop of Canterbury, where he is buried (d.1098).

EXCURSIONS

Certosa di Pavia★★★

◖ 10km/6.2mi N. Open Tue–Sun 9–11.30am and 2.30–6pm (earlier in winter). Guided tours available. Donations. ℘0382 92 56 13. www.certosadipavia.com.
The 14C "Gratiarum Cartusia" (Charterhouse of the Graces) is a remarkable example of Lombard art and home to a community of Cistercian monks.
Façade – The ornate lower part (1473–99) is by the Mantegazza brothers; Amadeo, who worked also in Bergamo, and his pupil, Briosco, while the upper part (1560) is by Cristoforo Lombardo. The façade is adorned with multicoloured marble sculptures and statues of saints. Bible scenes and episodes of Gian Galeazzo Visconti's life surround Amadeo's famous windows and bas-reliefs around the main door are by Briosco.
Interior and cloisters – The grand

Certosa di Pavia

© Gim42/iStockphoto.com

interior is essentially Gothic, but with Renaissance hints. Features include a painted Carthusian monk above the south chapels. **Bergognone**'s *Virgin and Child* (1481–1522) is in the south transept and his *Madonna del Tappeto* is above the entrance of the **small cloisters**, with their Lombard terra-cottas. The ceiling of the **refectory** *(adjacent)* is decorated with Bergognone's *Madonna del Latte*. The atmospheric **large cloisters** are vast; from here the chimneys of the 24 monks' cells, inhabited until 1968, can be seen. Back in the church, on the right altar of the transept, note the *Virgin Enthroned* receiving the charterhouse from Gian Galeazzo Visconti. The latter's tomb dates from the late-15C. A *Madonna del Garofano (Virgin with Carnation)* by Bernardino Luini (c.1480–1532) is in the **lavatorium**. The transept is separated from the chancel by a marble partition with inlaid choir stalls by Bergognone.

The **old sacristy** has a **triptych** by Baldassare degli Embriachi (late-14C), made from ivory and hippopotamus teeth, with scenes from the lives of the Virgin and Christ. In the middle of the sacristy, the *Virgin and Child*, a recurring theme which attests to the profound gratitude of Gian Galeazzo's wife Catherine to the Virgin.

In the north transept is Bergognone's *Ecce Homo*, as well as the cenotaph of Ludovico il Moro and Beatrice d'Este, by Cristoforo Solari (1497).Perugino's *Eternal Father* (c.1445–1523) is in the second chapel.

La Lomellina

Italy's rice-growing area lies between the Ticino and Po rivers. Towns of interest are: **Lomello** *(32km/19.9mi SW of Pavia)*; **Mortara** *(15km/9.3mi N of Lomello on the S 211)* with its 14C church of San Lorenzo (paintings by Gaudenzio Ferrari) and **Vigevano** *(12km/7.4mi NE of Mortara on the S 494)*. Bramante's tower dominates the square (possibly designed by Leonardo da Vinci).

Novara is also of interest; in particular the 16C–17C **Basilica di San Gaudenzio★** with its slender **dome★★** (1844–78). Inside is the silver **sarcophagus★** of the city's patron saint (St Gaudentius). The Neoclassical **Duomo** by Antonelli has a 6C–7C paleo-Christian baptistery and the chancel has a black-and-white Byzantine-style mosaic **floor★**.

ADDRESSES

🏠 STAY

🍴🛏 **Agriturismo Tenuta Camillo** – 27010 Bascapé. 23km/14.3mi N of Pavia. ☎0382 66 509. www.tenutacamillo.it. 6 rooms. Between rice fields and rows of poplars this farmstay offers simple but attractive rooms and good food.

🍴 EAT

🍴🍴 **Osteria della Madonna** – Via dei Liguri 28 (in the heart of the city, near the Duomo). ☎0382 30 28 33. http://lnx.osteria dellamadonna.it. Closed Mon and Tue-Fri lunch. Reservation recommended. Delicious regional cuisine served in a rustic setting.

The Lakes★★★

Regione dei Laghi

Narrow and long, these lakes are all of glacial origin and their banks are covered with luxuriant vegetation that flourishes in the particularly mild climate. A fairy-tale land of blue waters with a spectacular mountain backdrop, the area has always been a favourite haunt of artists and travellers. The charm of the lakes is due to the contrast between alpine and Mediterranean scenery, the numerous villas with lakeside gardens, the great variety of flowers throughout the year and the small lakeside villages, where fresh fish is the speciality, along with delightful local wines. Each lake has its own specific character, quite different from its neighbour.

- **Michelin Map:** 561 and 562 D–F 7–14, Piemonte – Lombardy – Trentino-Alto Adige – Veneto.
- **Info:** See individual lake entries for details.
- **Location:** The Lake District extends from Piemonte to Veneto and from Switzerland to Trentino in the north.
- **Don't Miss:** Lago Maggiore, Isole Borromee, Lago di Como, Bellagio, Lago di Garda and vast panoramas from Limone and the Tremosine Plateau.
- **Timing:** Allow two to three days to explore the Lake District.
- **Kids:** The Doll Museum (Museo della Bambola) at Angera, the puppet theatre on Isole Borromee, **Villa Pallavicino**'s wildlife park and the funicular to the top of Monte Baldo.

LAGO MAGGIORE★★★

Piazzale Duca d'Aosta, Arona. ☎0322 24 36 01. www.illagomaggiore.com.

Lake Maggiore is the most famous of the Italian lakes, in part for its legendary beauty, majestic and wild, and also for the Borromean Islands. It is fed by the River Ticino, which flows from Switzerland, and its waters change from a jade green in the north to a deep blue in the south.

The mountains of the Alps and Pre-Alps shelter the lake, which enjoys a mild climate, in which a luxuriant and exotic vegetation flourishes.

Angera★

This wonderful holiday resort stands in the shadow of the **Rocca Borromeo**, a castle with sweeping panoramic views best seen from the **Torre Castellana** tower. Known since the days of the Lombards (8C), the Rocca still has Law Courts decorated with admirable 14C **frescoes★★** depicting the life of Archbishop Ottone Visconti. The fortress also houses the **Museo della Bambola e del Giocattolo★** (open mid-Mar– mid-Oct daily 9am–5.30pm; 9€; ☎0331 93 13 00; www.isoleborromee.it), with over a thousand exhibits detailing doll design since the 18C. In 2013, a section opened with doll houses.

Arona

The chief town on Lago Maggiore is overlooked by a gigantic statue, **il San Carlone★**, of **St Charles Borromeo**, the Cardinal Archbishop of Milan who distinguished himself by the authority he showed in re-establishing discipline in the Church and by his heroic conduct during the plague of 1576.

Walk up the hill from Arona and climb up inside the statue for fantastic views. Open end Mar–Sept daily 9am–12.20pm and 2–6.15pm; Oct Sat–Sun 9am–12.30pm and 2–6.15pm; Nov Sat–Sun 9am–12.30pm and 2–4.30pm (Dec Sun). Closed 25–26 Dec. 5€. ☎0322 24 96 69. www.statuasancarlo.it.

GETTING THERE

One of the most pleasant ways to get around the lakes is is to take a boat trip.

LAGO MAGGIORE – Various excursions available including from Arona to Locarno (middle Mar–middle Oct only), lunch available on board, from Stresa for the Isole Borromee and Villa Taranto (middle Mar–middle Oct only). Car ferry between Laveno and Intra. Night cruises only middle Aug and 31 Dec. *℘0322 23 32 00. www.navigazionelaghi.it.*
The delightful **Borromee Islands** are situated in the middle of the lake. All-day ticket valid for the islands *20.50€ 2 islands; 24€ 2 islands and Rocca di Angera. ℘0323 30 046. www.borromeoturismo.it.*

LAGO D'ORTA – Regular departures from Orta to Isola San Giulio. *Duration 5min. 3.15€ return; Omegna-Orta-Isola San Giulio 7.35€ roundtrip; Orta-Isola San Giulio-Pella roundtrip 4.90€. ℘345 51 70 005. www.navigazionelagodorta.it.*

LAGO DI LUGANO – The wide choice of lake cruises includes lunch and dinner cruises and a panoramic cruise *(daily from Apr to Oct, departing from Lugano)*. Restaurant on board. *℘0041 91 97 15 223. www.lakelugano.ch.*

LAGO DI COMO – Boats run from Como to Colico, Tremezzo, Bellagio or Menaggio. From Tremezzo to Dongo, Domaso and Colico. Hydrofoil from Como to Tremezzo, Bellagio and Menaggio. Car ferries: between Bellagio, Varenna, Menaggio and Cadenabbia. Various lake cruises available, more in summer including evening cruises. *℘031 57 92 11. www.navigazionelaghi.it.*

LAGO D'ISEO – Tours of the lake's three islands available in summer; 1hr 30min from Iseo *(7.50€)*; 1hr from Sulzano *(6.50€)*. Regular ferries all year round to Monte Isola. *℘035 97 14 83. www.navigazionelagoiseo.it.*

LAGO DI GARDA – Excursions include from Desenzano to Sirmione and Gardone with generous stops at each and Peschiera to Garda and Gardone with optional tour of Il Vittoriale. Some boats can provide lunch on board. *℘030 91 49 511. www.navigazionelaghi.it.*

For general information regarding all lakes call *℘800 551 801.*

At the summit of the old town the church of Santa Maria contains a **polyptych★** (1511) by Gaudenzio Ferrari. From the Rocca, the ruined castle, there is a view of Lake Maggiore, Angera and its mountain setting.

Baveno★

This quiet holiday resort, once visited by Queen Victoria, has a Romanesque church and an octagonal Renaissance baptistery.

Isole Borromee★★★

Town map in the Michelin Atlas Italy, under Stresa. www.isoleborromee.it.

A large area of the lake was given to the princely Borromeo family in the 15C, but only gradually did they purchase all the islands in the tiny archipelago. In the 17C Charles III established a residence on **Isola Bella**, named after his wife, Isabella. The Lombard-Baroque palace has several state rooms – medals room, state hall, music room, Napoleon's room, ballroom and Hall of Mirrors. The most unusual feature is the caves where palace residents could find cooler air on hot days. There's an amphitheatre in the exotic gardens which form an amazing Baroque composition, a truncated pyramid of 10 terraces ornamented with statues, basins, fountains and architectural perspectives like stage sets.

Boat trips are available to Isola dei Pescatori, which has retained its original charm, and **Isola Madre**, an island totally covered with a splendid garden of flowers and rare or exotic plants. In the palazzo here there is a **👥 Puppet Museum** (open Mar–Oct daily 9am–5.30pm; 10€; 🖉0323 30 556) with items dating from the 17C and three puppet theatres.

Cannero Riviera★★

The houses of this resort rise in tiers above the lake amid olive trees, vineyards and orange and lemon groves.

Cannobio★

www.cannobio.net.
Cannobio is a small resort near the Swiss border with a Renaissance church of the Madonna della Pietà. Out of town (on the Malesco road) is the **Orrido di Sant'Anna★**, a precipice formed by the torrent.

Cerro★

This peaceful lakeside village has a fishing port and a **ceramics museum**.

Laveno Mombello

A cablecar climbs to the summit of **Sasso del Ferro★★** for a fine **panorama**. 🖉0332 66 80 12. www.funiviedellago-maggiore.it.

Pallanza★★

This wonderful flower-filled resort has **quays★★** sheltered by magnolias and oleanders with lovely views of the lake. On the outskirts of the town on the Intra road is the **Villa Taranto★★** with its gardens of azaleas, heather, rhododendrons, camellias and maples. ♿Open daily 8.30am–6.30pm; Oct–Nov 9am–4pm. 10€. 🖉0323 55 66 67. www.villataranto.it.

Eremo di Santa Caterina del Sasso★

About 500m/550yds from Leggiuno.
Open daily 9am–noon and 2–6pm (winter 5pm), Nov–Feb only Sat–Sun

and public hols. Donation welcome. 🖉0332 64 71 72. www.santacaterina delsasso.com. www.eremodisanta caterina.it.
This 13C hermitage was founded by an anchorite, Alberto Besozzo, and clings to a rock overlooking the lake.

Stresa★★

Train: Stresa (Milano Centrale 58min).
This pleasant resort, which has always attracted artists and writers, has an idyllic location on the west bank of Lago Maggiore facing the Isole Borromee. It's a delightful all-year-round resort. The ski slopes are on **Mottarone★★★** (take the Armeno road: 29km/18mi; the scenic toll road from Alpino: 18km/11.2mi; or the cablecar), with a magnificent panorama of the lake, Alps and Monte Rosa Massif and a botanical garden. (Funivia Stresa–Alpino–Mottarone closed at the time of writing; www.stresa-mottarone.it; town map in the Michelin Atlas Italy).
On the outskirts of the town sits the **👥 Villa Pallavicino★** and its wildlife park (♿open middle Mar–Oct daily 9am–7pm, last entry 5pm; 9.50€; www. parcozoopallavicino.it).

▶ 8km/12.8mi SW from Stresa.

Museo dell'Ombrello e del Parasole

▶ 8km/5mi SW. ♿ Open Apr–Oct Tue–Sun 10am–noon and 3–6pm. 2.50€. 🖉0323 89 622. www.gignese.it/museo/ombrello.
At **Gignese**, this interesting museum illustrates the history of the umbrella, particularly around Lago Maggiore with its celebrated umbrella-making tradition.

LAGO D'ORTA★★

www.illagomaggiore.com.
Lake Orta, one of the smallest Italian lakes, is separated from Lake Maggiore by the peak "Il Mottarone" in the northeast. It is delightful, with wooded hills and an islet, Isola San Giulio. The lakesides have been inhabited since earliest times and in the 4C the people were converted to Christianity by St Julius.

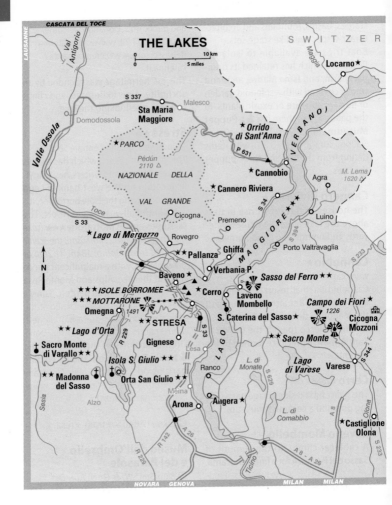

Chiesa della Madonna dal Sasso★★

From the church terrace there is a magnificent view of the lake in its verdant mountain setting.

Orta San Giulio★★

This small resort on the tip of a peninsula has alleyways lined with old houses adorned with elegant wrought-iron balconies. The **Palazzotto**★ or 16C town hall is decorated with frescoes.

Sacro Monte d'Orta★

◯ 1.5km/0.9mi from Orta.
This sanctuary dedicated to St Francis of Assisi and set on a hilltop comprises 20

chapels, decorated in the Baroque style, with frescoes that serve as background to lifelike terra-cotta statues.

Isola San Giulio★★

Boats leave from Orta.
On this jewel of an island, 300m/330yds long and 160m/175yds wide, stands the **Basilica di San Giulio** (open 9.30am–12.15pm and 2–6pm, winter to 7pm) ℘0322 90 56 14), said to date from the 4C, when St Julius came to the island. Inside there is a lovely 12C ambo decorated with frescoes by the school of Gaudenzio Ferrari (16C). Note also the shrine containing relics of St Julius.

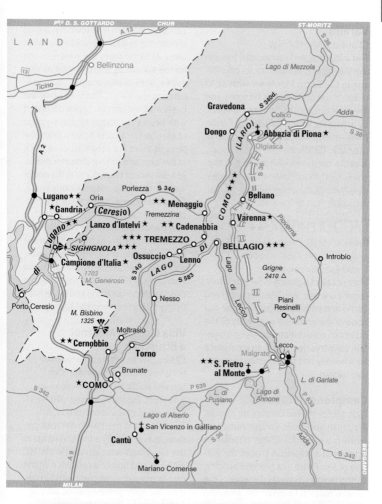

P50 D. S. GOTTARDO — A 13 — CHUR — ST-MORITZ

LAND

Bellinzona

Ticino

Lago di Mezzola

Gravedona

Dongo

Colico

Adda

Abbazia di Piona ★

Olgiasca

S 38

S 36

Porlezza — S 340

Lugano ★★ — Oria

★ Gandria — (Ceresio)

★★ Menaggio

Tremezzina

Lanzo d'Intelvi ★

★★ Cadenabbia

Bellano

Varenna ★

Proverna

★★★ TREMEZZO

SIGHIGNOLA ★

Ossuccio — Lenno

Campione d'Italia ★

1703

M. Generoso

BELLAGIO ★★★

Introbio

Grigne 2410 △

Porto Ceresio

Nesso

Piani Resinelli

M. Bisbino 1325

Moltrasio

★★ Cernobbio

Torno

Brunate

Lecco

Malgrate

★★ S. Pietro al Monte

L. di Garlate

★ COMO

S 342

P 639

L. di Pusiano

Lago di Annone

P 639

Lago di Alserio

San Vicenzo in Galliano

Cantù

Mariano Comense

S 36

Adda

S 342

BERGAMO

MILAN

Isola San Giulio, Lago d'Orta

Varallo

◉ About 20km/12.4mi W.

This industrial and commercial town in the Val Sesia is famous for its pilgrimage to the **Sacro Monte★★** with its 43 chapels decorated with frescoes and life-size terracotta figures (16–18C), by artists including Gaudenzio Ferrari (1480–1546), a local painter, a pupil of Leonardo da Vinci.

A cable car takes visitors to the top. www.sacromontedivarallo.it (⌖ open daily 9am–6pm, winter to 5pm, Sat, Sun and public hols to 7pm). 4€.

LAGO DI LUGANO★★

🏛 Riva Albertolli, Palazzo Civico 6900 Lugano. ✆0041 (0)58 86 66 600. www.luganoturismo.ch.

Most of **Lake Lugano** is in Swiss territory. Lugano is wilder than lakes Maggiore and Como and with its irregular outline has none of the grandeur or majesty of the others. Its mild climate and steep mountain countryside make it an ideal place for a holiday and for its famous summer jazz festival.

Campione d'Italia★

Train: Melide (Milano Centrale 1hr 13mins).
An Italian enclave in Switzerland, Campione is a colourful village, popular on account of its casino. A chapel, the oratory of San Pietro, is a graceful building dating from 1326. It was the work of the famous **Maestri Campionesi**, who vied with the Maestri Comacini in spreading the Lombard style throughout Italy (⌖see Visual Arts p102).

Lanzo d'Intelvi★

Set in the heart of a pine and larch forest, this resort (907m/2 976ft) is also a ski centre in winter. Some 6km/3.7mi away is the **Belvedere di Sighignola★★★**, also known as the "balcony of Italy" because of its extensive view of Lugano, the Alps as far as Monte Rosa and, on a clear day, Mont Blanc.

Varese

◉ 13km/8mi SW of Porto Ceresio.
Town map in the Michelin Atlas Italy. www.varesecittagiardino.it.

This busy modern lake town has a mild climate due to its proximity to the Italian lakes. At 8km/5mi to the west rises the hilltop known as **Sacro Monte di Varese★★**, with its pilgrimage church dedicated to the Virgin. The road up to the basilica is lined with 14 chapels decorated with frescoes in *trompe l'œil* and groups of life-size terra-cotta figures. From the summit there is a magnificent view★★ of the lakes and surrounding mountains. At a distance of 10km/6.2mi to the northwest is the long mountainous ridge, **Campo dei Fiori★**, which raises its forest-clad slopes above the plain. There is a vast **panorama★★** of the Lake District. About 10km/6.2mi to the south, on the road to Tradate, is **Castiglione Olona★**, with fine **frescoes★** by **Masolino da Panicale** (c.1383–1440) in the *collegiata* (*Story of the Virgin Mary*) and in the baptistery (*Story of St John the Baptist*).

Villa Cicogna Mozzoni a Bisuschio

◉ 8km/5mi NE of Varese on the road to Porto Ceresio. ⌖ Open Apr–Oct Sun and public hols 9.30am–noon and 2.30–7pm. Guided tours only. ✆0332 47 11 34. www.villacicognamozzoni.it.

The villa, set in fine Italian terraced gardens, was originally a hunting lodge in the 15C, which was extended in the 16C with the addition of a residence. In the first-floor rooms, complete with furnishings, the ceilings are adorned with fine frescoes in the Renaissance style.

LAGO DI COMO★★★

www.lakecomo.it.

Set entirely within Lombardy, **Lake Como**, of all the Italian lakes, has the most variety. Pretty villages, ports, villas in exotic gardens and mountain views.

Bellagio★★★

Bellagio occupies a magnificent site on a promontory dividing Lake Lecco from the southern arm of Lake Como.

The gracious resort town has a worldwide reputation for friendliness and excellent amenities. The splendid lakeside **gardens★★** of **Villa Serbelloni** (1hr 30mins guided tours middle Mar–Oct

Tue–Sun 11am and 3.30pm (winter 2.30pm) - from Uff. Promobellagio, Piazza della Chiesa 14; 9€; ℘031 95 15 55; www.bellagio lakecomo.com) and Villa Melzi (&open Apr–Oct daily 9.30am–6.30pm; 6.50€; ℘339 45 73 838, www.giardinivilla melzi.it), with their fragrant and luxuriant vegetation, are the main sights to visit in Bellagio.

Bellano

This small industrial town stands on the River Pioverna at the mouth of the valley (Valsassina), with the Grigne towering behind. The attractive 14C church with a façade by Giovanni da Campione is in the Lombard-Gothic style.

Cadenabbia★★

This delightful resort occupies an admirable site opposite Bellagio. A handsome avenue of plane trees, Via del Paradiso, links the resort with the Villa Carlotta and Tremezzo. From a chapel, **Capella di San Martino** *(1hr 30min on foot there and back)*, there is a good **view★★** of Bellagio, lakes Como and Lecco and of the Grigne.

Cernobbio★★

This location is famous for the **Villa d'Este**, the opulent 16C residence now transformed into a hotel and surrounded by fine parkland *(access to both the villa and the park is limited to hotel guests)*. The best view of the villa (from the ground) is from Piazza del Risorgimento, near the landing stage.

Chiavenna

Train: Chiavenna (Milano Centrale 3hr).
Ancient Chiavenna owes its name to its key *(clavis* in Latin) position in the Splügen and Maloja transalpine passes between Italy and Switzerland. Chiavenna is also famous for its **crotti**, restaurants housed in natural caves and serving local specialities (found only in Valtellina) such as *pizzoccheri* (buckwheat pasta served with melted cheese) and *bresaola* (dried meat).

Nearby, above the Palazzo Balbini (15C), is **Il Paradiso**, a rock that was once a fortified site and is now a pleasant garden, the **Giardino botanico e archeologico** (open

Tue–Sun 10am–noon and 2–6pm (winter to 5pm); 3€; ℘0343 33 795); www.valchi-avenna.com). See also the strange frescoes on the exterior of the Palazzo Pretorio and the doorways in the Via Dolzino on which the inscriptions date back to the days of the Reformation.

Collegiata di San Lorenzo

& Open Jun–Sept Tue–Sun 9am–noon and 2–6pm (Mar–May Sat–Sun only 5pm, Oct Sat only). Treasury open afternoons (Sat also morning). ℘0343 33 442.

The Collegiate Church of St Lawrence, built during the Romanesque period and reconstructed in the 16C after a fire, contains two paintings, one by Pietro Ligari (1738) *(second chapel on the right)* and one by Giuseppe Nuvoloni (1657) *(first chapel on the left)*.

The **Baptistery** has a Romanesque **font★** (1156) in *ollare* stone: the name of the stone being a reference to its being used to make *olle* (urns and vases). The low reliefs illustrate a baptismal scene depicting various social classes (nobleman hunting with his falcon, soldier and craftsman), a child with his godfather, a priest and acolyte, and members of the clergy. The inscription reveals the sponsors of the work.

The treasury houses a wonderful 12C binding for an evangelistary.

Strada del Passo dello Spluga★★

▶ 30km/18.6mi from Chiavenna to the pass.

The Splügen Pass Road is one of the boldest and most spectacular in the Alps. The **Campodolcino–Pianazzo section★★★** is grandiose as it climbs the mountainside in hairpin bends.

Como★

Train: Como (Milano Centrale 35mins).
Already prosperous under the Romans, the town was the birthplace of naturalist Pliny the Elder and his nephew, the writer Pliny the Younger. Como reached its zenith in the 11C. It was destroyed by the Milanese in 1127, rebuilt by Emperor Frederick Barbarossa and from 1355 shared the fortunes of Milan. The **Maes-**

Lago di Como at Varenna

© E. Zane/MICHELIN

tri **Comacini**, known as early as the 7C, were masons, builders and sculptors who spread the Lombard style *(see Visual Arts p102)* throughout Italy and Europe.

Duomo★★

Begun in the late-14C the cathedral was completed during the Renaissance and crowned in the 18C with an elegant dome by Juvarra. It has a remarkable **façade★★** that was richly decorated from 1484 onwards by the **Rodari brothers**, who also worked on the **north door**, known as the "Porta della Rana" as a frog *(rana)* is carved on one of the pillars, and the exquisitely delicate **south door**.

The **interior★**, full of solemn splendour, combines Gothic architecture and Renaissance decoration. In addition to the curious banners, hung between the pillars, and the magnificent 16C–17C **tapestries★**, there are canvases by B. Luini (**Adoration of the Magi, Virgin and Child with Saints★**), and G. Ferrari (**Flight into Egypt**), in the south aisle as well as a **Descent from the Cross★** (1489) carved by Tommaso Rodari in the north aisle. Note the organ in five parts, comprising 96 registers and 6 000 pipes. Various 17C artists were involved in its construction although its current form is by organ makers Balbiani and Vegezzi-Bossi. Adjoining the façade is the **Broletto★★**, or 13C town hall, with a lovely storey of triple-arched windows.

Chiesa di San Fedele★

In the heart of the old quarter lies this church in the Romanesque-Lombard style. The nave and two aisles are terminated by a polygonal Romanesque **chancel★** with radiating chapels.

Basilica di Sant'Abbondio★

This masterpiece of Romanesque-Lombard architecture was consecrated in 1093. The noble **façade★** has a lovely doorway. The remarkable 14C **frescoes★** evoke the Life of Christ.

Villa Olmo

◐ 3km/1.8mi N by the S 35 and then the S 340 to the right. Via Cantoni 1. Open Mon–Sat 9am–12.30pm and 2–5pm. ℘031 25 23 52. www.lakecomo.it.

This large Neoclassical building hosts large art exhibitions. The gardens contain a small theatre and a lovely **view★** of Como in its lakeside setting.

Dongo

It was in this village that Mussolini and his mistress, Clara Petacci, were captured on 27 April 1945.

Gravedona

This fishing village has an attractive Romanesque church, **Santa Maria del Tiglio★**. The 5C baptistery was remodelled in the Lombard style in the 12C.

Menaggio★★

Favoured by a cool summer breeze, this is one of the lake's smart resorts.

Abbazia di Piona★

▶ 2km/1.2mi from Olgiasca. This monastery adopted Cistercian Orders under St Bernard of Clairvaux (1090–1153) and features Lombard-Romanesque **cloisters★** (1252).

Torno

On the outskirts of this attractive port, the 14C church of San Giovanni has a fine Lombard-Renaissance **doorway★**.

Tremezzo★★★

A mild climate and a beautiful site combine to make Tremezzo a favourite place for a stay. The terraced gardens, **Parco Comunale★**, are peaceful. The 18C **Villa Carlotta★★★** *(entrance beside the Grand Hotel Tremezzo)* occupies an admirable site facing the Grigne Massif. Open daily Apr–Oct 9am–6.30pm; two weeks in Mar and two in Oct 10am–5.30pm; gardens remain open 30 min later then the museum. 9€. ℘0344 40 405. www.villacarlotta.it. Statues include a copy by Tadolini of the famous group of *Cupid and Psyche* by Canova. The main attraction is, however, the beautiful terraced **garden**.

Santuario della Madonna di Tirano

▶ 69km/42.9mi E of Colico, at the northernmost point of the lake.
The church of the **Madonna di Tirano** was built from 1505 onwards on the spot where the Virgin Mary had appeared in a vision. It has a nave and side aisles. The west front dates from 1676 and is enhanced with highly ornate Baroque decoration, including frescoes by Cipriano Valorsa di Grosio (1575–8), nicknamed the "Raphael of La Valtellina" *(nave)*, a fresco of the

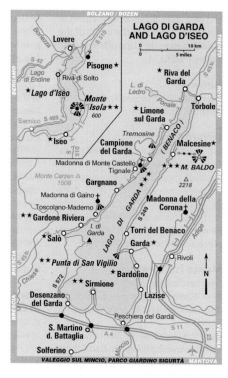

Apparition dating from 1513 *(left, above the confessional)*, paintings by a pupil of Morazzone *(chancel)* and a highly ornate, grandiose 17C organ. The loft was made by Giuseppe Bulgarini and the panels on the gallery representing the Birth of the Infant Jesus, The Adoration of the Magi and The Circumcision were painted by Giuseppe Bulgarini Salmoiraghi (1638).

Varenna★

Train: Varenna Esino (Milano Centrale 56mins).
This town with its many gardens stands on a promontory. The 16C Villa Monastero also has beautiful **gardens★★**.
Villa open Jun–Sept 9.30am–7pm, closed Mon except Aug; Oct Thu 1pm–6pm, Fri–Sun 9.30am–6pm. 8€; gardens only 5€ Mar–Oct 9.30am–6pm. ℘0341 29 54 50. www.villamonastero.eu.

LAGO D'ISEO★

Though Lake Iseo is not very well known, its wild scenery, high mountain backdrop and peaceful villages all lend charm to this small lake. From the midst of the waters emerges the island of **Monte Isola** (600m/1 970ft).

Iseo★

The church, Pieve di Sant'Andrea, faces a charming square.

Lovere

In this small industrial town, the **Galleria Tadini** (open May–Sept Tue–Sat 3–7pm, Sun 10am–noon and 3–7pm, Apr and Oct Sat 3–7pm, Sun 10am–noon and 3–7pm; 7€; & ℘035 96 27 80; www.accade miatadini.it) has a collection of arms, paintings (Bellini and Parmigianino), porcelain and sculpture by Canova.

Monte Isola★★

From Iseo, Sulzano, Sale Marasino. ℘035 97 14 83. www.navigazionelagoiseo.it (frequent connections). 3.60€ or 5.30€ round trip.
From the church of the Madonna della Ceriola, crowning this green island, there is a vast **panorama★★** of the lake and the Alps near Bergamo.

Pisogne★

This small port has an attractive lakeside setting. The church of **Santa Maria della Neve** is adorned with 16C **frescoes★** by Romanino.

Valcamonica

The Valcamonica follows the River Oglio as far as Lago d'Iseo. The main access road from Bergamo is the S 42. The valley, which stretches from Lovere to Edolo, and is linked to the Valtellina by the **Passo di Gavia**, may have much industry at lower level, but the higher you climb the more picturesque it is, dotted with castle ruins. Over a stretch of 60km/37.3mi are UNESCO World Heritage prehistoric and early Roman rock carvings.

Rock Carvings★★

Access from Capo di Ponte. Open Tue–Sun Mar–Oct 8.30am–7.30pm, Sun and public hols 8.30 am–1.30pm. ℘0364 42 140. 6€. www.invallecamonica.it.

Eroded by the alpine glaciers, the rocks of the Valcamonica became a highly polished surface, which lent itself to figurative engravings. Created by tapping or scratching away at the stone, the carvings are a testament to the daily life of the people who lived here. Having been hunters during the Palaeolithic era (c.8000–5000 BC), they adopted farming methods during the Neolithic era and then metallurgy during the Bronze Age (from 1800 BC) and Iron Age (from 900 BC). There are four basic types of representation: deer (hunting scenes); ploughs and other agricultural machinery; weaponry and warriors; religious representations: prayers, symbols, idols. The carvings can be seen in the Parco Nazionale delle Incisioni Rupestri di Naquane.

Riserva Naturale Regionale di Ceto

& Open daily 9am–5.30pm (winter 4pm). 3€ with entry to the Museo di Nadro. ℘0364 43 34 465. www.invallecamonica.it. Models of Iron Age huts, 6,000-year old rock drawings, and nature walks.

LAGO DI GARDA★★★

www.visitgarda.com.
Lake Garda, the largest lake, is also considered one of the most beautiful. Its many assets include low-lying banks in the south, steep slopes on the west bank, and the mountain chain of Monte Baldo to the east.
The Dolomites to the north shelter the lake from the cold winds, creating a very mild climate which had already earned it the name of the "beneficent lake" (*Il Benaco*) in ancient times. It had both strategic and commercial importance and throughout history has been coveted by neighbouring powers.
Artistically, the region was influenced by the Venetian Republic, which ruled in the 15C–18C. Even in Roman times the lakes were popular for holidays, and today there are many resorts to choose from.

Bardolino★

This village, famous for its red wine, has an elegant 11C Romanesque church★ dedicated to St Severinus.

Campione del Garda

The bishops of Trent, Brescia and Verona met here to bless the lake.

Desenzano del Garda

Train: Desenzano del Garda/Sirmione (Milan Centrale 1hr 6mins).

The old port, picturesque Piazza Malvezzi and the neighbouring old quarter are all good places for a stroll. The 16C parish church, the **Parrocchiale Santa Maria Maddalena**, has an intense **Last Supper★** by Tiepolo. To the north of the town in Via Scavi Romani, the **Villa Romana** boasts remarkable multicoloured Roman **mosaics★** (&open Tue–Sun 8.30am–7.30pm; Nov–Feb Archeologic Area closes at 5pm. Closed 1 Jan, 1 May, 25 Dec; 2€; ℘030 91 43 547).

San Martino della Battaglia

◐ 8km/5mi from Desenzano. &Open middle Mar–midde Oct Mon–Sat 9am–12.30pm and 2.30–7pm, Sun 9am–7pm; middle Oct–middle Mar 9am–12.30 and 2–5.30pm. 5€ (museum and tower), chapel free. ℘030 99 10 370. An ossuary chapel, a museum and a tower commemorate the battle of 24 June 1859 at Solferino (◐see Solferino, p432), and the wars waged by the Italians for independence from Austria.

Garda★

This popular resort which gave its name to the lake shows a strong Venetian influence. Both the Palazzo dei Capitani and the Palazzo Fregoso are 15C.

Gardone Riviera★★

A small resort with long hours of sunshine and a wide choice of hotels. At 1km/0.6mi from the town is the **Vittoriale★** estate, which belonged to the poet **Gabriele D'Annunzio** (1863–1938), buried here. The Neoclassical villa, La Priora, is full of the curious atmosphere that this writer aesthete so cultivated. The museum and park display mementoes of his turbulent life. Open Apr–Sept, 8.30am–8pm (Mon museum 10am–3.45pm); Oct–Mar 9am–5pm (museum closed Mon). Closed 1 Jan, 24–25 Dec. 8€ (gardens); 16€ villa, museum and gardens. ℘0365 29 65 11. www.vittoriale.it.

Gargnano

This charming resort is famous for its lemon trees. The church of **San Francesco** has 15C cloisters with curious Moorish-style galleries featuring capitals carved with oranges and lemons, recalling the fact that it was probably the Franciscan monks who introduced citrus fruits to the area. The lakeside promenade leads to **Villa Feltrinelli** (now a hotel) that served as Mussolini's headquarters during the Fascist Republic (1943–5).

Limone sul Garda★

This is one of the lake's most attractive villages. Terraced lemon groves stretch along the shores. From Limone a **panoramic route★★** climbs up to the Tremosine Plateau before descending to Tignale, offering walkers superb lake **views★★★**.

Malcesine★

This attractive town stands on a promontory at the foot of Monte Baldo and is dominated by the crenellated outline of the Castello Scaligero.

This 13C–14C castle belonged to the Scalider family of Verona. The 15C Palazzo dei Capitani in the Venetian style stands on the edge of the lake. From the summit of Monte Baldo (cablecar) there is a splendid **panorama★★★** of the lake and the Brenta and Adamello massifs. ♣♣ Take a ride on the funicular. Open Apr–Oct 8.30am–6pm, each 30min. 20€ round trip. ℘045 74 00 206. www.funiviedelbaldo.it.

Punta di San Vigilio★★

This headland is in a romantic setting. Sanmicheli planned this 16C Villa Guarienti (o—▪ not open to the public) for the Veronese humanist Agostino Brenzoni.

Riva del Garda★

Once a busy trading centre, today the **old town★** is a maze of shopping streets.

Salò★

This was the seat of the Venetian Captain under the Venetian Empire. Inside the 15C **Duomo** are a large gilt **polyptych★** (1510) and works by Moretto da Brescia and Romanino.

Sirmione★★

This important resort spa is said to be particularly effective in the treatment of respiratory disorders.

The houses cluster around the 13C castle, **Rocca Scaligera★★**, at the tip of the Sirmione Peninsula, as it stretches out into the lake (open Tue–Sat 8.30am–7pm, Sun 8.30am–1pm; 4€; ℘030 91 64 68). On the peninsula tip are the remains of a vast Roman villa belonging to the poet Catullus, the **Grotte di Catullo★★** (&open winter Tue–Sat 8.30am–5pm archeologic area, 8.30am–7.30 museum; Sun 8.30–2pm; summer Tue–Sat 8.30am–7.30pm, Sun 9.30am–6.30pm. Closed 1 Jan, 1 May, 25 Dec; 6€; ℘030 91 61 57). www.grottedi catullo.beniculturali.it.

Solferino

An ossuary chapel and a **museum** recall the battle of 24 June 1859 (the field of battle extended to San Martino, &see p431) when the French and Piemontese troops defeated the Austrians and brought about Italy's independence. The heavy casualties led to the founding of the **Red Cross** by Henri Dunant. Museum: &Open middle Mar–middle Oct Tue–Sun 9am–12.30pm and 2.30–7pm; winter only groups by reservation. 2.50€. ℘0376 85 40 19.

Torbole

Coloured houses hug the bay of this pleasant resort on the eastern bank of Lake Garda. Torbole is popular with windsurfing and sailing enthusiasts.

Valeggio sul Mincio

Carlo **Sigurtà** (1898–1983), an industrial pharmacist, spent 40 years working on the properties of thermal springs and completely transformed the 17C villa, Napoleon III's headquarters in 1859. The beautifully maintained **Parco Giardino Sigurtà★★** (50ha/123 acres) on the magnificent Mincio, offers a wonderful range of Mediterranean flora, grassy swards, architectural and natural features, and, in certain areas classical music. 10km/6.2mi S of Peschiera. Car parks along the approach route. & Open Mar–Oct daily 9am–7pm (last entry 6pm; Mar and Oct closes 6pm). 12€. Park can be visited by mini-train, bike rental available. ℘045 63 71 033. www.sigurta.it.

ADDRESSES

🏠 STAY

😊😊 **Agriturismo Il Bagnolo** – Loc. Bagnolo di Serniga, 25087 Salò (L. di Garda). ℘0365 20 290. www.ilbagnolo.it. Reservation recommended. 16 rooms. This farm guesthouse has a wonderful setting and serves excellent food.

😊😊 **Hotel Il Chiostro** – Via F.lli Cervi 14, 28921 Verbania Intra (L. Maggiore). ℘032340 40 77. www.chiostrovb.it. 100 rooms. ⌧. A converted 17C convent, this hotel retains its calm. Frescoed reading room, charming cloisters and simple rooms.

😊😊 **Albergo Silvio** – Via Carcano 10/12, 22021 Bellagio (L. di Como), 2km/1.2mi SW of Bellagio. ℘031 95 03 22. www.bellagio silvio.com. 21 rooms. ⌧. Family run since 1919, this charming place has a stunning location, excellent restaurant with a lovely summer terrace, and fish caught by the owner.

😊😊 **Hotel Cangrande** – Corso Cangrande 16, 37017 Lazise (L. di Garda), 5km/3mi S of Bardolino on the N 249. ℘045 64 70 410. www.cangrandehotel.it. 17 rooms. ⌧ **P**. Charming with simple, attractive rooms, one incorporated into the medieval stone walls.

😊😊 **Hotel Desirée** – Via San Pietro 2, 25019 Sirmione (L. di Garda). ℘030 99 05 244. www.hotel-desiree.it. Closed Nov–mid -Mar. 18 rooms. ⌧. An unpretentious hotel in a quiet location near the beach and the thermal baths. Standard rooms all have balconies

😊😊 **Hotel Garni La Contrada dei Monti** – Via Contrada dei Monti 10, 28016 Orta San Giulio (L. d'Orta). ℘0322 90 51 14. www.lacontradadeimonti.it. 17 rooms. A charming hotel in a beautifully restored palazzo; great attention to detail in the rooms.

⊖⊜ **Hotel La Fontana** – Via Sempione Nord 1, 28838 Stresa (L. Maggiore). ℘0323 32 707. www.lafontanahotel.com. 19 rooms. ☒. A 1940s villa hotel – some rooms have lake views and retro decor. Reasonable rates.

⊖⊜ **Hotel Miravalle** – Via Monte Oro 9, 38066 Riva del Garda. ℘0464 55 23 35. www.hotelvillamiravalle.com. 28 rooms. ☒. A central location, lovely garden and swimming pool. Simple yet stylish rooms.

⊖⊜ **Hotel Palazzina** – Via Libertà 10, 25084 Gargnano (L. di Garda). ℘0365 71 118. www.hotelpalazzina.it. Closed Oct–mid-Apr. 25 rooms. ☒. There's a relaxed atmosphere at this hotel, which boasts two large panoramic terraces and an open-air swimming pool.

⊖⊜ **Hotel Rigoli** – Via Piave 48, 28831 Baveno (L. Maggiore). ℘0323 92 47 56. www.hotelrigoli.com. 31 rooms. ☒ **P**. The rooms are spacious and the public areas are sunny and pleasant. There's a lakeside terrace garden with lovely views over the Isole Borromee.

♀/EAT

⊖ **Al Porto** – Via Zanitello 3, 28922 Verbania Pallanza (L. Maggiore). ℘0323 55 71 24. Closed lunch, Mon and Nov. Rustic – like an old sailing ship. Open late for drinks, simple homemade snacks and meals. Lake views.

⊖⊜ **Villa Aurora** – Via Ciucani 1, 25080 Soiano del Lago (L. di Garda). 10km/6.2mi N of Desenzano on the S 572. ℘0365 67 41 01. Closed Wed. Good food at decent prices - a rarity for restaurants specialising in fish dishes. A good choice.

⊖ **Caffè delle Rose** – Via Ruga 36, 28922 Verbania Pallanza (L. Maggiore). ℘0323 55 81 01. Closed Mon–Tue. Atmospheric surroundings, good music and a reasonably priced bistrot menu.

⊖ **Italia** – Via Ugo Ara 58, Isola dei Pescatori (L. Maggiore). ℘0323 30 456. www.ristoranteitalia-isolapescatori.it. A simple trattoria and bar with a wisteria-canopied terrace over the lake. The restaurant boat will ferry you to or from Stresa if you call. Lake fish specialities.

⊖ **Ristoro Antico** – Via Bottelli 46, 28041 Arona (L. Maggiore). ℘0322 46 482. Reservation recommended. A family-run restaurant with genuine and tasty home cooking.

⊖ **Agriturismo Il Monterosso** – Loc. Cima Monterosso, 28922 Verbania Pallanza (L. Maggiore), 6km/3.7mi from Pallanza. ℘0323 55 65 10. www.ilmonterosso.it. 15 rooms. ☒. This farmhouse situated at the top of Colle Monterosso has a stunning setting surrounded by chestnut, pine- and beech woods and with breathtaking views over the lakes below and Monte Rosa. Simple decor and authentic home cooking.

⊖⊜ **Gatto Nero** – Via Monte Santo 69, 22012 Cernobbio (L. di Como). ℘031 51 20 42. www.ristorantegattonero.com. Closed Mon–Fri lunch. Reservation recommended. Stylish yet cosy with welcoming atmosphere. Fantastic views from the summer terrace.

⊖⊜⊜ **Amélie** – Via I Maggio 17, Baveno (L. Maggiore). ℘0323 92 44 96 or 339 87 52 621 (mobile). www.ristoranteamelie.it. Tue–Sat. Reservation 24 hours before. Few tables, smart interior and excellent cuisine.

TAKING A BREAK

Caffè Retrò – Piazza del Popolo 24, 28041 Arona (L. Maggiore). ℘0322 46 640. Open Tue–Sun 8am–2am. One of the loveliest outdoor terraces in Arona with a view of the piazza, a small church and the blue lake. Try a fruity cocktail.

Gardesana – Piazza Calderini 5, 37010 Torri del Benaco (L. di Garda). ℘045 72 25 411. www.hotel-gardesana.com. Closed Mon and middle Oct–middle Mar. Elegant hotel restaurant and terrace caffè, a lovely location beside the tower and overlooking the port.

Gelateria Cremeria Fantasy – Via Principessa Margherita 38, 28838 Stresa (L. Maggiore). ℘0323 33 227. Closed Nov–Jan except public hols. Delicious homemade ice creams.

LEISURE

Garda Yachting Charter – Lungolago Zanardelli, 25088 Maderno (L. di Garda). ℘0365 54 83 47. www.gyc.it. Open daily Mar–Nov 9am–6pm. Motorboats (with or without a licence) and yachts for hire.

Veneto, Friuli-Venezia Giulia

Major Cities: Trieste, Venice, Verona, Vicenza

Official Websites: www.veneto.to; www.turismofvg.it

The Veneto and Friuli-Venezia Giulia regions have strong maritime histories. Veneto's capital Venice was once the seat of the powerful Venetian Republic, which ruled large swathes of territories in the Adriatic and Mediterranean for more than 1 000 years and developed new trade routes to the Far East thanks to the exploration of Marco Polo. Trieste, Italy's easternmost city and the capital of Friuli-Venezia Giulia, was once part of the Austrian Habsburg's domain and the gateway to the East for the countries of central Europe. Both regions are also known for their refinement, ranging from Palladian villas to excellent wines, from delicate to robust. Shakespeare's great love story between Romeo and Juliet was set in the splendid city of Verona.

Highlights

1 Tour the canals of Venice in a **gondola** (p436)
2 Wonder at the marvel of **Piazza San Marco** (p438)
3 Study Palladio's architectural style in **Vicenza** (p463)
4 Attend an outdoor opera at **Verona's Arena** (p467)
5 Sample Italo-Slavic culture in **Trieste** (p474)

Northern Veneto

The western massifs of the Dolomites and the Venetian Pre-Alps dominate the landscape of northern Veneto and make this area a prime skiing destination. In the Tofane range, in northwestern Belluno Province, peaks reach as high as 2 980m/9 777ft. The rivers Ardo and Piave converge in the town of Belluno.

Central Veneto

Rolling hills and wide open plains make up the central part of the Veneto region, which stretches from the eastern coast of Lake Garda to the Adriatic coast and the Po Delta. The area is home to stunning cities of art such as Verona, Padova and Vicenza, close to which are the Berici Hills. Nearer Padova, the appealing slopes of the **Euganean Hills** are home to picturesque villages and a number of thermal springs which draw visitors to the various excellent spa centres.

Venice and the Coast

The **Po Delta** covers a wide stretch of coastline between Ravenna and Venice. Much of the area is reclaimed land which survives thanks to continual pumping stations. The delta has emerged from an impoverished past as an attractive area of natural beauty where age-old traditions survive and an extraordinarily rich birdlife draws ornithologists from all over the world.

Agriculture is fundamental to the local economy, as is fishing, particularly clam-fishing in the various lagoons and inlets which are numerous in the area. The vast area of the **Venice** lagoon also includes a great deal of industry: oil refineries, smelting works and chemical plants are concentrated around Mestre and Marghera.

Friuli-Venezia Giulia

This region extends east from Veneto to the Italian boundary with Austria and Slovenia. Its people are in fact largely of Germanic or Slavic heritage and the area enjoys a large degree of autonomy in administrative affairs. In the north is the schistose massif of the **Carnic Alps** with conifer forests and alpine pastures. Friuli-Venezia Giulia has an important history of silk making.

There is significant farming and industry, particularly around Udine and Pordenone, while the stately city of **Trieste**, the region's capital, was a major Austrian port – a "little Vienna" on the Adriatic.

Venice★★★

Venezia

Venice is a legendary city, presiding regally over the lagoon for more than a thousand years. "La Serenissima" – "the most serene" – has a multitude of moods: labyrinthine streets, lively wine bars *(bacari)*, lavish ballrooms, and broody landscapes à la *Death in Venice*. Painting has flourished here, alongside the exquisite glass art of Murano Island. Yet the true attraction is always Venice itself, which Lord Byron dubbed "a fairy city of the heart".

▶ **Populati**

Michelin
– **See a**
GUIDE VEN

Info: San M
℘ 041 52 98 711.
www.turismovenezia.it.

Location: The main road to Venice is the A 4. It is linked to Mestre by the Ponte della Libertà. The Grand Canal – 4km/2.5mi –divides central Venice.

Don't Miss: Piazza San Marco, Ponte di Rialto and the islands of Murano and Burano.

Timing: A week offers a real feel for the place, time to stroll the narrow streets and explore the lagoon islands. Spring and autumn are ideal times to visit.

Kids: A ride in a gondola or gondola ferry *(traghetto)*.

THE CITY TODAY

The sea is the source of Venice's fortunes and grief. In recent years, however, the water has become the city's primary foe. December 2008 saw the *acqua alta* (high water) peak above 1.5m/5ft, flooding buildings and *piazze*, halting transport and scaring away tourists. The **MOSE project**, which would create a system of mechanised gates to defend against the rising tides, has been controversial since its commencement in 2003, with opponents claiming that the barriers will damage the fragile ecosystem of the Venetian Lagoon. In addition to MOSE, which installed and tested gates in 2013, a number of charities, including Save Venice *(www.savevenice.org)*, have been established to help preserve Venice's artistic heritage. It is often said that the charm of Venice is more at risk from the tourist tidal wave than from sinking

Gondolas with a view of
Isola di San Giorgio Maggiore

Gwen Cannon/MICHELIN

GETTING AROUND

It goes without saying that in Venice all public transport is water-borne. It is important to bear in mind that heavy traffic on the Grand Canal and the fact that stops do not always take one "door to door" mean that walking can sometimes be quicker. However, the experience of travelling along the Grand Canal by boat, however crowded, is a terrific way to begin a stay in Venice – and it also saves on struggling over bridges with heavy luggage.

The famous Venetian water-boats, the **vaporetti**, have a well-organised and frequent timetable of lines. Here are two of the most useful routes:

Line 1 leaves from Piazzale Roma, stopping all along the Grand Canal, including Ponte di Rialto and San Marco before terminating at the Lido.

Lines 4.1/4.2 run between Piazzale Roma and Murano, stopping at Giudecca and San Zaccaria (adjacent to San Marco) on the way.

A single ticket costs 7.50€ (75min). 24hr (20€) and multiple day – up to 7 days (60€) – tickets can also be purchased; these need be stamped only on the initial journey.

GONDOLAS

The unique experience of a gondola ride is justifiably costly (a 40 min journey without a musical accompaniment costs 80€). Rides – and costs – can be divided among six people sharing a gondola. (Each 20min after the initial 50min costs 40€.) A tour in a gondola by night is unforgettable and costs rather more (from 8pm to 8am a 40min journey costs 100€, each 20min thereafter costs 50€). For more information contact the Istituzione per la Conservazione della Gondola e la Tutela del Gondoliere, ℘041 52 85 075. For a budget gondola experience hop on a *traghetto* (gondola ferry).

These take passengers across the Grand Canal for just 2€ and are available at various points along the Grand Canal (San Marcuola, Santa Sofia, al Carbon, San Tomà, San Samuele, Santa Maria del Giglio and Dogana). Due to the limited number of bridges crossing the Grand Canal (Scalzi, Rialto, Accademia and Costituzione) the *traghetti* are a fundamental means of transport for Venetian citizens.

VENEZIA UNICA CITY PASS

This card allows to access public transport, cultural and tourism offers within the city, and many other useful services. You can buy the pass online on www.veneziaunica.it, receiving by email a voucher accompanied by a reservation code (PNR) with which you will be able to collect your tickets at one of the ACTV automatic ticket machines or by presenting the PNR at one of the many Venezia Unica ticket counters. For information call ℘041 24 24 or see the website www.veneziaunica.it, also to see the selling-points around the city.

FOR YOUNG VISITORS

For young people aged between 14 and 29, the **Rolling Venice** card (6€) offers a varied range of discounts for ACTV public transport and the transfer from ant to Marco Polo airport. It also includes discounts for restaurants, discos, museums, concerts, shops taking part in this scheme. These are all listed in www.veneziaunica.it.

Cards, which are valid 1 year, can be purchased online or in one of the Venezia Unica selling-points around the city (see the website www.veneziaunica.it) with proof of identity. For information call ℘041 24 24.

into the sea. The city is keen to incentivise longer-stay visitors rather than day-trippers, who contribute little to the local economy.

A BIT OF HISTORY

Venice is built on 117 islands; it has 150 canals and 400 bridges. A canal is called a *rio*, a square a *campo*, a street a *calle* or *salizzada*, a quay a *riva* or *fondamenta*, a filled-in canal *rio terrà*, a passageway a *sottoportego*, a courtyard a *corte* and a small square a *campiello*.

Gondolas – For centuries gondolas have been the traditional means of transport in Venice. The gondola is an austere and sober craft except for its typical iron hook, which acts as a counterweight to the gondolier. The curved fin is said to echo the *doge's corno* (horn-shaped hat) and the prongs to represent the *sestieri* or districts of the city. The prong on the back of the stern symbolises the Giudecca.

The Venetians – The Venetians are both proud and fiercely traditional, known for their commercial and practical skills. The **bautta** (black velvet mask) and **domino** (a wide hooded cape), once very popular with the locals and still worn in Venice at Carnival time, add to their elusiveness. Skilled courtesans, diplomats and spies have given Venice a reputation for intrigue. Venetian is a very lively dialect which is used in place of Italian.

Venice was founded in AD 811 by the inhabitants of Malamocco, near the Lido, fleeing from the Franks. They settled on the Rivo Alto, known today as the Rialto. In that year the first *doge* – a name derived from the Latin *dux* (leader) – Agnello Partecipazio, was elected and thus started the adventures of the Venetian Republic, known as "La Serenissima", which lasted 1 000 years. In 828 the relics of St Mark the Evangelist were brought from Alexandria; he became the town protector.

The Venetian Empire – From the 9C to the 13C Venice grew steadily richer as it exploited its position between East and West. With its maritime and commercial power it conquered important markets in Istria and Dalmatia.

The guile of Doge Dandolo and the assistance of the crusaders helped the Venetians capture Constantinople in 1204. The spoils from the sack of Constantinople flowed to Venice, while trade in spices, fabrics and precious stones from markets established in the East grew apace. **Marco Polo** (1254–1324) returned from China with fabulous riches. The 14C war with Venice's rival Genova ended in victory for the Venetians in 1381.

The first half of the 15C saw Venetian power at its peak: the Turks were defeated at Gallipoli in 1416 and the Venetians held the kingdoms of Morea, Cyprus and Candia (Crete) in the Levant. In mainland Italy, from 1414 to 1428, they captured Verona, Vicenza, Padova, Udine, and then Brescia and Bergamo. The Adriatic became the Venetian Sea from Corfu to the Po.

The capture of Constantinople by the Turks in 1453 started the decay. The discovery of America caused a shift in the patterns of trade and Venice had to keep up an exhausting struggle with the Turks, who were defeated in 1571 in the naval **Battle of Lepanto**, in which the Venetians played an important part. Their decline, however, was confirmed in the 17C when the Turks captured Candia (Crete) after a 25-year siege.

The "Most Serene Republic" came to an end in 1797. Napoleon Bonaparte entered Venice and abolished a thousand-year-old constitution. Then, by the **Treaty of Campoformio**, he ceded the city to Austria. Venice and the Veneto were united with Italy in 1866.

The government of the Republic was, from the earliest, organised to avoid the rise to power of any one man. The role of *doge* was supervised by several councils: the Grand Council drew up the laws; the Senate was responsible for foreign affairs, military and economic matters; the Council of Ten was responsible for security and kept a network of secret police and informers that ensured control of all aspects of city life.

VENETIAN PAINTING

The Venetian school of painting is characterised by the predominance of colour over draughtsmanship. Art historians have often noted the contrast between the scholarly and idealistic art of the Florentines and the freer, more spontaneous work of the Venetians, which later influenced the Impressionists.

The real beginnings of Venetian painting are exemplified by the **Bellini** family: Jacopo, the father, and Gentile (1429–1507) and **Giovanni** (or **Giambellino**, 1432–1516), his sons. The latter, the younger son, was one of the first Renaissance artists to integrate landscape and figure compositions harmoniously. In parallel, their pupil **Carpaccio** (1455–1525) recorded Venetian life with his usual care for detail while **Giorgione** remained an influence. His pupil, **Lorenzo Lotto**, was also influenced by the realism of northern artists.

The Renaissance came to a glorious conclusion with three artists: Titian (c.1490–1576), who painted dramatic scenes where dynamic movement is offset by light effects; Paolo **Veronese** (1528–88), whose rich colours reflected the splendour of La Serenissima; and **Tintoretto** (1518–94), whose dramatic technique reflects an inner anxiety.

The artists of the 18C captured Venice and its peculiar light; grey-blue, iridescent and slightly misty: **Canaletto** (1697–1768), whose works won favour with English Grand Tourists, and his pupil Bellotto (1720–80) were both inspired by townscapes; Francesco **Guardi** (1712–93), who painted in luminous touches; Pietro Longhi (1702–58), the artist of intimate scenes; **Giovanni Battista (Giambattista) Tiepolo** (1696–1770), a decorator who painted frescoes of light and movement.

Spontaneity and colour are also found in Venice's musicians; the best known is **Antonio Vivaldi** (1678–1741), who was master of violin and viola at a hospice, Ospedale della Pietà. (Hospices were also academies of music and drama.)

SAN MARCO, THE DRAWING ROOM OF VENICE

Piazza San Marco★★★

St Mark's Square is the heart of Venice, where the covered galleries of the **Procuratie** (procuratorships) shelter famous caffès (Florian, Quadri), and luxury shops. The square opens onto the Grand Canal through the **Piazzetta San Marco**. The two granite columns crowned by "Marco" and "Todaro" (St Mark and St Theodore) were brought from the East in 1172.

Basilica★★★

St Mark's combines the Byzantine and Western styles. Building was carried out throughout the 11C and when the basilica was consecrated in 1094, the body of St Mark, stolen from Alexandria in 828, had been miraculously recovered. Built on the plan of a Greek cross, the basilica is crowned by a bulbous dome flanked by four smaller domes of unequal height placed on the cross.

Façade

This is pierced by five large doorways adorned with sculptures. Above the central doorway are copies of the four **bronze horses** (the originals are in the gallery of the basilica).

On the first arch on the left is depicted the Translation of the Body of St Mark. On the south side near the Doges' Palace stands the porphyry group, known as the **Tetrarchs★** (4C). At the corner is the proclamation stone (pietra del bando).

Atrium

As an introduction to the stories told by mosaics inside the basilica, those in the atrium depict Old Testament scenes.

Interior

The dazzling decoration of St Mark's combines the mosaics (1071) by artists from Constantinople and a 12C pavement decorated with animal and geometric motifs. An iconostasis separates the raised presbytery (sanctuary) from the nave. Beyond, a ciborium raised on **alabaster columns★★** precedes the

Façade, Basilica di San Marco

©Roberto Vannucci/Bigstockphoto.com

Pala d'Oro★★ (Golden Altarpiece), a masterpiece of Gothic art dating from the early-10C. The relics of St Mark rest under the high altar (Pala d'Oro: open Nov-Easter Mon–Sat 9.45am–4pm, Sun and public hols 2pm–4pm; Easter–Oct 9.45am–5pm, Sun and public hols 2p–5pm; 2€; ☎041 27 08 311; www.basilicasanmarco.it). The mosaic decoration depicts the New Testament, starting with the dome of the apse with Christ as Pantocrator (Ruler of All) and ending with the Last Judgement in the area above the *atrium*. Near the entrance, the Arch of the Apocalypse illustrates the visions described in the gospel of St John. As one approaches the central dome, the west arch presents a synthesis of the *Passion and Death of Christ*. The south arch opening onto the south transept depicts the *Temptation of Christ* and *His Entry into Jerusalem*, the *Last Supper* and the *Washing of the Feet*. In the centre is the Dome of the Ascension depicting the Apostles, the Virgin, the Virtues and the Beatitudes. *Christ in Benediction* dominates the scene. The mosaics on the north arch giving onto the north transept are after cartoons by Tintoretto and Veronese. The Dome of St John the Evangelist in the left transept illustrates the *Sermon on the Mount* and the *Life of St John the Evangelist*.

The south transept gives access to the **treasury★**. ♿open Nov-Easter Mon–Sat 9.45am–4pm, Sun and public hols 2pm–4pm; Easter–Oct 9.45am–5pm, Sun and public hols 2p–5pm. 3€. ☎041 27 08 311 www.basilicasanmarco.it. The famous **gilded bronze horses★★**, the originals of those to be seen on the gallery of the basilica, are on display at **Museo di San Marco**. Open daily 9.45am–4.30pm. 5€. ☎041 27 08 311. www.museosanmarco.it.

Campanile★★
Open daily Easter–Jun and Oct 9am–7pm; Jul–Sept 9am–9pm; Nov–Easter 9.30am–3.45pm; 8€. ☎041 27 08 311. www.basilicasanmarco.it.
A symbol of Venice, the bell tower (99m/325ft high) is a reconstruction of the 15C campanile, which collapsed in 1902. The **panorama★★** from the top extends to the Grand Canal. At the base is the **Loggetta Sansoviniana** with statues of Minerva, Apollo, Mercury and Peace.

Palazzo Ducale★★★
♿Open daily Apr–Oct 8.30am–7pm (last entry 6pm); Nov–Mar 8.30am–5.30pm (last entry 4.30pm). Closed 1 Jan, 25 Dec. 18€ (Museum Card for all museums in Piazza San Marco). ☎041 27 15 911. www.visitmuve.it.
The palace was a symbol of Venetian power and glory, residence of the *doges* and seat of government and the law courts as well as being a prison. It was built in the 12C but was transformed between the 13C and the 16C.
A pretty, geometric pattern in white-and-pink marble lends great charm to the two **façades**. The groups at the corners of the palace represent, from left to right, the **Judgement of Solomon** (probably by Bartolomeo Bon), *Adam and*

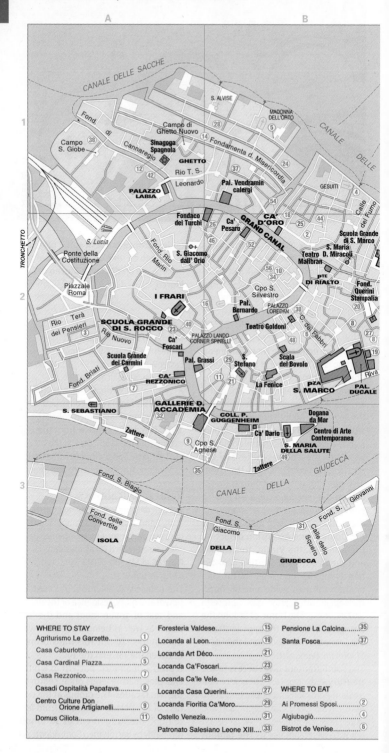

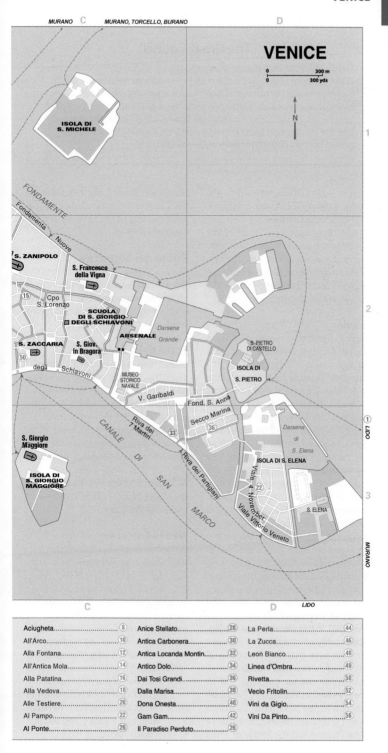

VENICE

ISOLA DI S. MICHELE

FONDAMENTE

Fondamenta Nuove

S. ZANIPOLO

S. Francesco della Vigna

15   Cpo S. Lorenzo

SCUOLA DI S. GIORGIO DEGLI SCHIAVONI

ARSENALE

Darsena Grande

S. PIETRO DI CASTELLO

ISOLA DI S. PIETRO

S. ZACCARIA

50

S. Giov. in Bragora

degli   Schiavoni

MUSEO STORICO NAVALE

V. Garibaldi

Fond. S. Anna

Secco Marina

33

36

Darsena di S. Elena

LIDO ①

S. Giorgio Maggiore

ISOLA DI S. GIORGIO MAGGIORE

CANALE DI SAN MARCO

Riva dei 7 Martiri

Riva dei Partigiani

ISOLA DI S. ELENA

Viale 4 November

Viale Vittorio Veneto

S. ELENA

MURANO

MURANO C

MURANO, TORCELLO, BURANO

D

0   300 m
0   300 yds

N

1

2

3

C

D   LIDO

The Great Council

This was the most important institution governing the Republic, which covered all the functions of state, passed laws and appointed the most important figures in Venice. The hall in the Doge's Palace where it sat would have offered an amazing spectacle during the meetings: the *doge* presided over the council from his seat on the raised platform, also known as the Bancale di San Marco, whereas the members of the aristocracy sat on seats along the walls and on parallel benches running the full length of the room.

Eve and **Noah's Drunkenness** (14C–15C Gothic sculptures). The main entrance is the **Porta della Carta★★**.

It has on its tympanum a Lion of St Mark before which kneels Doge Foscari (19C copy). The gateway leads into the Porticato Foscari; opposite is the **Scala dei Giganti** (Giants' Staircase) dominated by statues of Mars and Neptune.

Interior

Start at the top of Sansovino's **Scala d'Oro** (Golden Staircase) and pass through a suite of rooms as follows: the **Sala delle Quattro Porte** (Room of the Four Doors), where the ambassadors awaited audience with the *doge*; an antechamber, **Sala dell'Antecollegio**, for diplomatic missions and delegations; **Sala del Collegio**, where the *doge* presided over meetings; the Senate Chamber, **Sala del Senato** or "dei Pregadi", where the members of the Senate submitted their written request to participate in the meetings. **Sala del Consiglio dei Dieci** (Chamber of the Council of Ten) is where the council met the powerful magistrates who used the secret police and spies to safeguard the institutions.

Beyond **Sala della Bussola**, the waiting-room for those awaiting interrogation, and the armoury (armeria) is **Sala del Maggior Consiglio** (Grand Council Chamber). In this vast room sat the legislative body which appointed all public officials; here also the constitutional election of the new *doge* was conducted. In the chamber hang portraits of 76 *doges* as well as Tintoretto's **Paradise**. Proceed to the **Sala dello Scrutinio** (Ballot Chamber); the **Prigione Nuove** (New Prisons) and the Bridge of Sighs (Ponte dei Sospiri). Further along are the Censors' Chamber (**Sala dei Censori**), the seat of the judiciary and the Sala dell'Avogaria.

Ponte dei Sospiri★★

The 16C Bridge of Sighs connects the Doges' Palace with the prisons and is so named as prisoners had their final enchanting glimpse of Venice from the window.

Torre dell'Orologio

Guided tours only, Mon–Wed 10am and 11am, Thu–Sun 2pm and 3pm (in English). Book ahead. Closed 1 Jan, 25 Dec. The tour starts from the Museo Correr ticket counter 5 mins before the departure time. 12€ including Museo Correr, Museo Archeologico Nazionale and Sale Monumentali della Biblioteca Marciana. ☎041 24 05 211. www.visitmuve.it.
At the top of the late-15C Clock Tower are the Moors (Mori), a pair of bronze jacks that strike the hours.

Museo Correr★★

&Open daily Apr–Oct 10am–7pm (last entry 6pm); Nov–Mar 10am–5pm (last entry 4pm). Closed 1 Jan, 25 Dec. 18€ (Museum Card for all Piazza San Marco museums) &See Torre dell'Orologio, above. ☎041 24 05 211. www.visitmuve.it.
Interesting paintings and artefacts. The museum is named after Teodoro Correr (1750–1830), the nobleman who left this large collection of mainly Venetian history and art to the city. It is divided into departments, which lead from the Napoleonic wing to the library, and through the Procuratie Nuove.

© Philip Coblentz/Brand X Pictures

Ponte di Rialto

GRAND CANAL (CANAL GRANDE)★★★

The Grand Canal (3.8km/2.4mi long, between 30m and 70m/100ft–230ft wide and 5.5m/18ft deep) is an inverted "S" and affords the best view of the palazzi.

LEFT BANK

Palazzo Labia★★

By the Riva di Biasio vaporetto stop. The Labia family were Spanish merchants, and their elegant residence dates from the late-17C.

Palazzo Vendramin Calergi★

An early 16C mansion, residence of the Codussi, where Wagner lived and died.

Ca' d'Oro★★★

Although it has lost the gilded decoration which gave it its name, the mansion retains an elegant façade in the ornate Gothic style. It houses the **Galleria Franchetti**, which displays a fine **St Sebastian★** by Mantegna. *Gallery:* &Open 8.15am–7.15pm. Mon to 2pm. Closed 1 Jan, 1 May, 25 Dec. 15€ (includes Palazzo Grimani). ✆ 041 52 00 345. www.cadoro.org.

Ponte di Rialto★★

Today's Rialto Bridge, the sixth version and the first in stone, was built by Antonio da Ponte (1591). Classic views of the Grand Canal.

Palazzo Grassi★

Built in the 18C by Giorgio Massari, this was the last great Venetian palace to be constructed before the fall of the Republic. It now hosts major exhibitions.

Palazzo Cavalli Franchetti★

After the Accademia vaporetto stop (& see map p440, B2–3).

A palazzo dating from the second half of the 15C. Its grand façade contains five-light windows embellished with interlacing arches and four-lobed motifs.

Palazzo Corner della Ca'Granda

Between the Giglio and Accademia vaporetto stops (& see map p440, B2–3). A Renaissance palazzo designed by Sansovino, now housing the city's prefecture. The ground floor, with its rusticated stonework, contains three monumental archways, while the round-arched windows of the upper floors alternate with pairs of columns.

RIGHT BANK

Fondaco dei Turchi

Dating from the 13C, this former warehouse for Turkish Merchants is among the city's oldest Veneto-Byzantine buildings. Merchandise was sold directly to boats that moored by the ground floor portico. Nowadays, the building houses Venice's natural history museum.

Ca' Pesaro★

The palace built by Longhena is the home of the **Museo d'Arte Orientale** (Museum of Oriental Art) and the **Galleria Internazionale di Arte Moderna** (International Gallery of Modern Art), which in 2013 inaugurated a new layout. Museo d'Arte Orientale: &Open Tue–Sun Apr–Oct 10am–6pm, last entry 5pm; Nov–Mar 10am–5pm (last entry 4pm). Closed 1 Jan, 1 May, 25 Dec. 10€. ✆041 72 11 27. www.visitmuve.it.

Linee di naviga

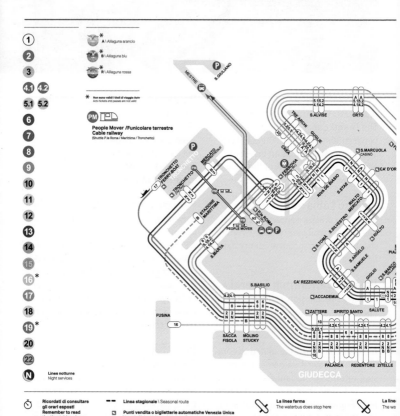

Presso i punti vendita Venezia Unica puoi trovare anche: biglietti per eventi, musei, mostre e teatri // guide e mappe
At the Venezia Unica ticket points you can also find: tickets for events, museums, exhibitions and theaters // guides and maps /

Info call center Hellovenezia +39 0412424 \ www.veneziaunica.it

Pescherìa
Rialto Mercato vaporetto stop.
The arcades of this early-20C Gothic-Revival building are taken over each morning by the stalls of the fish market.

Palazzo Bernardo
Attractive Gothic building (1442) with particularly interesting window architecture.

Ca' Foscari★
San Tomà vaporetto stop. www.unive.it
This 15C palazzo has a perfectly symmetrical façade, with three superimposed groups of windows with multiple lights, creating a harmonious rhythm with the single-light windows and the stretches of stonework. The building is currently the main seat of Venice's university, hosting occasional exhibitions.

azione \ Waterborne routes

www.actv.it

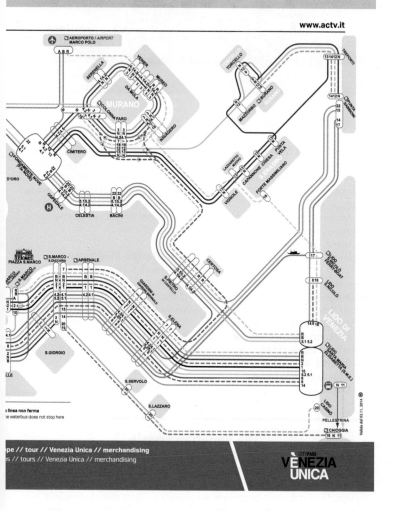

pe // tour // Venezia Unica // merchandising
s // tours // Venezia Unica // merchandising

VENEZIA UNICA
CITYPASS

Ca' Rezzonico★★
The last palace designed by Longhena now houses the **Museo del Settecento Veneziano** (Museum of 18C Venice), full of period furnishings as well as art. A memorable spot for periodic concerts.
⛱ Open Wed–Mon Apr–Oct 10am–6pm; Nov–Mar 10am–5pm. Last entry 1h before closing. Closed 1 Jan, 1 May, 25 Dec. 10€.
☎041 72 11 27. www.visitmuve.it.

Ca' Dario★
The late-15C palazzo has gained a sinister reputation owing to the suspicious deaths of several of its owners.

Santa Maria della Salute

© Risphoto2/iStockphoto.com

VENICE ON CANVAS

GALLERIE DELL'ACCADEMIA★★★

Open 8.15am–7.15pm. Closed Mon afternoon, 1 Jan, 1 May, 25 Dec. 15€ (includes Palazzo Grimani). ℘041 52 00 345. www.gallerieaccademia.org.

The Academy presents the most important collection of Venetian art from the 14C to the 18C. Masterpieces include a **Madonna Enthroned** and the **Virgin and Child between St Catherine and Mary Magdalene** by Giovanni Bellini; **St George** by Andrea Mantegna; **The Tempest** by Giorgione; a **Portrait of a Young Gentleman in His Study** by Lorenzo Lotto; a sinister **Pietà** by Titian; **Christ in the House of Levi** by Veronese; and the cycle of the **Miracles of the Relics of the True Cross** by Gentile Bellini and Carpaccio.

CHURCHES

Santa Maria della Salute★★

Built to mark the end of a plague epidemic (1630), this church is a landmark with its modillions and concentric volutes. In the sacristy hangs a **Wedding at Cana** by Tintoretto in which the artist included himself as the first Apostle on the left.

San Giorgio Maggiore★

The church on the island of San Giorgio was designed by Palladio. The top of the tall **campanile** affords the finest **view★★★** of Venice. In the presbytery hang two large paintings by Tintoretto, the *Last Supper* and the *Harvest of Manna*. Campanile: Ascent 9.30am–6.30pm (dusk Oct–Apr); Sun 8.30–11am and 2.30–6.30pm (dusk Oct–Apr). 5€ with lift. ℘041 52 27 827.

The Venetian Scuole

Instituted during the Middle Ages, the *scuole* (literally meaning "schools") were lay guilds drawn from the middle classes which were active in all aspects of life, be it devotional, charitable or professional, until the fall of the Republic. Each school had its own patron saint and *mariegola*, a rule book and constitution of the guild. In the 15C the *scuole* were housed in magnificent palaces with their interiors decorated by famous artists. To appreciate the rich artistic heritage of the guilds, visit the **Scuola di San Rocco★★★**, decorated with scenes from the Old and New Testaments by Tintoretto. After 15 years, the restoration of its Grande Cantoria was completed in 2013. The **Scuola di San Giorgio degli Schiavoni★★★** is a perfect setting for exquisite paintings by Carpaccio.

San Rocco: ♿ Daily 9.30am–5.30pm. Closed 1 Jan, 25 Dec. 10€. ℘041 52 34 864. www.scuolagrandesanrocco.org. **San Giorgio degli Schiavoni:** ♿ Open Tue–Sun 9.15am–1pm and 2.45–6pm, Mon 2.45–6pm. Closed Sun afternoon. 5€. Occasionally closed for Confraternity meetings. ℘041 52 28 828.

San Zanipolo★★

The square boasts an **equestrian statue★★** of the mercenary leader Bartolomeo **Colleoni** by Verrocchio and contains the **Scuola Grande di San Marco★** and the imposing Gothic church of Santi Giovanni e Paolo (contracted in Venetian dialect to Zanipolo), burial place for the *doges*.

I Frari★★★

Open Mon–Sat 9am–6pm, Sun 1–6pm. 3€. ℘041 272 86 11. www.basilicadeifrari.it.
This great Franciscan church recalls San Zanipolo on account of its imposing appearance and funerary monuments. The focal point of the perspective is an **Assumption of the Virgin** by Titian.

San Zaccaria★★

The interior of the Renaissance-Gothic Church of St Zachary is covered with paintings; the most important is Giovanni Bellini's **Sacra Conversazione**.

OTHER AREAS AND MUSEUMS OF VENICE

Arsenale★

Venice's dockyard dates at least from 1104 when the Crusades stimulated shipbuilding. The land gateway to the Arsenal is guarded by ancient Greek lions, and the watergate has two towers.

Ghetto★★

The Jewish quarter *(ghetto)*, in the Cannaregio district, was the first to be differentiated as such in Western Europe.

Island of Murano from the lagoon

©Luke Daniek/iStockphoto.com

In the Venetian dialect the term *geto* referred to a mortar foundry.
The g, pronounced soft (as in George), was hardened by the first Jews who came from Germany. The Museo Ebraico and synagogues are open to visitors.

Giudecca

Giudecca Island offers a glorious view of Venice and the Palladian church of **Il Redentore★** *(Fondamenta S. Giacomo)*.

Collezione Peggy Guggenheim★

Open Wed–Mon 10am–6pm. Closed 25 Dec. 15€. ℘041 24 05 411. www.guggenheim-venice.it.
An 18C palazzo where the American Peggy Guggenheim lived until her death, is the setting for an interesting collection of 20C art.

EXCURSIONS

Lido★

Venice's lively seaside resort has a casino, and hosts a prestigious annual film festival.

Murano★★

By the end of the 13C, the threat of fire was constant in Venice with its wooden buildings, so the Grand Council moved the glassworks to Murano. This glassmaking island has a museum, **Museo del Vetro★**, with displays of exquisite glassware. The apse of the basilica, **Santi Maria e Donato★★**, is a masterpiece of 12C Veneto-Byzantine art and the **mosaic floor★★** recalls that of St Mark's. Museo del Vetro: Open daily Apr–Oct 10am–6pm; Nov–Mar 10am–5pm. Last entry 1h before closing. Closed 1 Jan, 1 May, 25 Dec. 10€. ℘041 52 74 718. www.visitmuve.it.

Burano★★

Boldly coloured houses and a rich lacemaking tradition render the island impressively picturesque.

Torcello★★

Despite being scarcely populated today, remnants from times when the island was more powerful than Venice include the lovely Cattedrale di Santa Assunta.

Burano

D. Pics/GraphicObsession

ADDRESSES

The hub of daytime life is Piazza San Marco, which pulses with people – and pigeons – at all times of year. Orchestras provide classical music from the terraces of the caffès – ideal spots for letting the beauty of the place sink in. The Florian is the most celebrated of Venice's historic caffès; founded in 1720 it counts Byron, Goethe, George Sand, and Wagner among former clients. I Quadri (one Michelin star) is the most celebrated for its cuisine. The shops in and around St Mark's have sumptuous window displays of lace, jewellery, mirrors and the famous glassware from Murano. The area around the Rialto Bridge is a must, with its vibrant fish market *(Pescheria)*, fruit and veg markets *(erberie)* and numerous atmospheric bars.

🏠STAY

The accommodation listed includes details of religious orders which offer reasonably priced rooms to visitors. Possible drawbacks with these are that guests are usually expected to be back in the evening by a specified hour and they usually need to be pay cash.

HOSTELS, RELIGIOUS INSTITUTES, HOLIDAY HOMES

☞ **Casa Cardinal Piazza** – Palazzo Contarini Minelli, Sestiere Cannaregio, 3539a. ☎041 72 13 88. 24 rooms.

☞ **Casa di Ospitalità Papafava** – Ponte della Guerra 5402, Castello. ☎041 52 25 352. 14 rooms. A popular choice for families.

☞ **Ostello Venezia** – Fondamenta Zitelle 86, Giudecca. ☎041 877 82 88. www.hostelvenice.org. ♿☞. 260 beds. A member of the international youth hostelling federation with an idyllic

waterfront location on the island of Giudecca. Dormitory accommodation only.

☞ **Santa Fosca** – Fondamenta Canal 2372, Cannaregio. ☎041 71 57 75. www.cpuvenezia.it. ☞. 100 beds. Accommodation for students and tourists between the station and the Rialto Bridge.

☞☞ **Casa Caburlotto** – Fondamenta Rizzi 316, Santa Croce. ☎041 71 08 77. www.sangiuseppecaburlotto.com. ☞. 64 rooms. A simple, mid-priced choice.

☞☞ **Centro Culturale Don Orione Artigianelli** – Zattere 909a, Dorsoduro. ☎041 52 24 077. www.donorione-venezia.it. 76 rooms. Spacious and pleasant with an on-site restaurant.

☞☞ **Foresteria Valdese** – Castello 5170. www.foresteriavenezia.it. 48 rooms. ☞. Pleasant rooms, some with frescoes or canal views.

☞☞ **Patronato Salesiano Leone XIII** – Castello 1281. ☎041 52 30 796. www. salesianivenezia.it. ☞. 35 rooms. A quiet location near the Biennale Gardens.

☞☞☞ **Domus Ciliota** – Calle delle Muneghe, San Marco 2976. ☎041 52 04 888. www.ciliota.it. A fully restored former Augustinian monastery offering comfortable, pleasant accommodation.

HOTELS

☞☞ **Agriturismo Le Garzette** – Lungomare Alberoni 32, Lido. ☎041 73 10 78. 5 rooms. In a countryside location at the quiet end of Lido Island, this *agriturismo* (farmstay) is ideal for families. Home cooking using own-grown produce.

☞☞ **Locanda al Leon** – Calle degli Albanesi 4270, Castello. ☎041 27 70 393. www.hotelalleon.com. 12 rooms. Just round the corner from St Mark's, this small guesthouse has rooms furnished in Venetian style.

Locanda Ca' Foscari – Calle della Frescada 3887, Dorsoduro. 041 71 04 01. www.locandacafoscari.com. 11 rooms. A simple but pleasant establishment with light, airy rooms and a family atmosphere. Extremely good value for money – a rare thing in Venice.

Casa Rezzonico – Fondamenta Gherardini 2813, Dorsoduro. 041 27 70 653. www.casarezzonico.it. 6 rooms. Quiet and peaceful despite being close to lively Campo Santa Margherita. Well-maintained interiors, canal views and a pleasant garden.

Locanda Art Déco – Calle delle Botteghe 2966, San Marco. 041 27 70 558. www.locandaartdeco.com. 8 rooms. Beamed ceilings and wooden furniture make for cosy rooms. A central location in a pleasant area.

Locanda Ca'le Vele – Calle delle Vele 3969, Cannaregio. 041 24 13 960. www.locandalevele.com. 6 rooms. Small guesthouse with a typically Venetian atmosphere in a 16C palazzo.

Locanda Casa Querini – Campo San Giovanni Novo 4388, Castello. 041 24 11 294. www.locandaquerini.com. 6 rooms. A small 16C palazzo offering comfortable, mid-sized rooms.

Locanda Fiorita Ca'Moro – Campiello Novo 3457, San Marco. 041 52 34 754. www.locandafiorita.com. 10 rooms. A delightful hotel in a charming, flower-filled square. Rooms have 18C furniture with matching – but newer – upholstery.

Pensione La Calcina – Fondamenta Zattere ai Gesuati 780, Dorsoduro. 041 52 06 466. www.lacalcina.com. 27 rooms. The only reminder of the *locanda* where Ruskin stayed in 1876 is a photograph in the lobby, but the hotel stands on the same site as the old guesthouse. A very pleasant choice thanks to its excellent location on the Giudecca Canal and a light-filled interior.

/EAT

Lunch or dinner at a trattoria is one of the pleasures of Venetian life. Seafood is of course a speciality and many chefs shop at the Rialto market each morning

so produce is generally ultra-fresh. Try the squid, cuttlefish, crabs, clams and other local shellfish. Although not a local fish, cod (baccalà) is another Venetian speciality and so is fegato alla veneziana (calf's liver fried with onions). Light and sparkling white **Prosecco** is a popular local wine; others to try from the region include Soave, Valpolicella and Amarone. For lighter meals go to a bacaro (Venetian wine bar) for a selection of traditional local snacks – cicheti.

GRAND CANAL

Ai Promessi Sposi – Calle dell'Oca 4367, Cannaregio. 041 24 12 747. Closed Mon and Wed. Fish specialities at this *bacaro* near Campo Sant'Apostoli. Pleasant garden.

Alla Vedova – Calle del Pistor 3912 (following on from the Ca' d'Oro vaporetto pier, beyond the Strada Nuova), Cannaregio. 041 52 85 324. Closed Sun lunch and Thu. This *bacaro* is often packed, so you would do well to book; retro ambience and tasty local cuisine. Ask for recommendations.

Antica Carbonera – Calle Bembo 4648 (first left after the Goldoni Theatre), San Marco. 041 52 25 479. www.anticacarbonera.it. Closed Tue. In a dining room decorated with items and furniture from the yacht that belonged to Archduke Rudolph, you can enjoy classic Venetian cuisine, either seafood- or meat-based.

Osteria Leon Bianco – Salizada San Luca 4153, San Marco. 041 52 21 180. www.osterialeonbianco.com. Closed Sun. Quick snacks at the bar or hot meals in the restaurant.

Vini da Gigio – Fondamenta San Felice 3628a, Cannaregio. 041 52 85 140. www.vinidagigio.com. Closed Mon–Tue and 3 weeks Aug. The rustic ambience and informal service in this *osteria* is popular with locals. Fish is prepared in a variety of ways, including marinated and grilled choices. Also meat dishes and a good wine list.

Alle Testiere – Calle del Mondo Novo 5801, Castello. 041 52 27 220. www.osterialletestiere.it. Closed Sun–Mon. Reservation recommended. A small place that maintains a relaxed and inviting atmosphere while serving top-quality food. Local specialities – particularly fish – made with seasonal ingredients sourced locally.

☺☺☺ **Bistrot de Venise** – Calle dei Fabbri, 4685 San Marco. ☎041 52 36 651. www.bistrotdevenise.com. Lunch and dinner menu includes historic Venetian dishes. Excellent and vast wine selection, also by the glass. Lively readings, exhibits, and wine tasting with winemakers.

SCHIAVONI-ARSENALE

☺☺ **Aciugheta** – Campo Santi Filippo e Giacomo 4357, Castello. ☎041 52 24 292. www.aciugheta.com. Anchovies are the stars of the menu. Dine outside in the often packed terrace or inside in the simple, busy *trattoria*-ambience.

☺☺ **Rivetta** – Salizada San Provolo 4625, Castello, between Piazza San Marco and Campo San Zaccaria. ☎041 52 87 302. A wide choice of *cicheti* right by San Zaccaria.

RIALTO-FRARI-SAN ROCCO

☺☺ **Al Ponte** – Ponte del Megio 1666 (corner of Calle Larga leading to Campo San Giacomo dell'Orio), Santa Croce. ☎041 71 97 77. Closed Sat evening and Sun. At the end of the "millet bridge", in the area once occupied by millet and wheat warehouses, this trattoria serves excellent fish specialities.

☺☺ **Alla Patatina** – Calle Saoneri 2741a, San Polo. ☎041 52 37 238. www.lapatatina.it. Reservation recommended. A friendly and popular trattoria with rustic decor. Good food, with plenty of fish.

☺☺ **All'Arco** – Calle dell'Occhialer 436 (from Ruga San Giovanni take Sottoportego dei Do Mori), San Polo. ☎041 52 05 666. Open Mon–Sat 8am–2.30pm. This tiny place is always packed when the market is in full flow. Known for its *crostini* and excellent choice of wines.

☺☺ **Antico Dolo** – Ruga Rialto 778, San Polo. ☎041 52 26 546. A small *osteria* with walls panelled in red wood. Tripe, *crostini*, polenta and *baccalà mantecato*, plus a tasting menu at lunch- and dinnertime. Wine and *cicheti* are served all day.

☺☺ **Dona Onesta** – Ponte de la Dona Onesta 3922 (not far from Ca' Foscari), Dorsoduro. ☎041 71 05 86. www.dona onesta.com. Closed Sun. An excellent

trattoria: the *sarde in saor* are exemplary and the grilled fish is remarkable. Diligent, friendly service.

☺☺ **La Zucca** – Ramo del Megio 1762, Santa Croce. ☎041 52 41 570. www. lazucca.it. Closed Sun. Reservation recommended. If you're in the mood for more varied and slightly exotic dishes, prepared with a lightness of touch, this is the place to go. A simple trattoria, with wood-panelled walls, it offers a good selection of vegetable dishes – it's named after a pumpkin *(zucca)*.

☺☺ **Vecio Fritolin** – Calle della Regina 2262 (behind Campo San Cassiano), Santa Croce. ☎041 52 22 881. www.veciofritolin.it. Closed Mon and Tue lunch. This good little place has a reputation based on fried fish and fresh market produce. Also try the swordfish tartare with olives and lemon and delicious homemade pasta.

☺☺ **Vini Da Pinto** – Campo delle Beccarie 367, San Polo. ☎041 52 24 599. www.ristorantevinidapinto.it. Closed Sun evening and Mon. A glass of wine and a few *cicheti* during a trip to the Rialto fish market or for a meal later.

ACCADEMIA-SALUTE

☺☺ **Antica Locanda Montin** – Fondamenta di Borgo 1147, Dorsoduro. ☎041 52 27 151. www.locandamontin.com This famous trattoria on a peaceful canalside walkway has a nice shady courtyard area where scenes from the film *The Anonymous Venetian* were shot. Accommodation available too.

☺☺ **Linea d'Ombra** – Dorsoduro (Punta della Dogana) 19, La Salute. ☎041 24 11 881. www.ristorantelineadombra.com. Closed Dic.–Feb and Tue (except May–Sept). Contemporary interiors that shout "style" and a menu of creative cuisine, all stemming from local traditions, makes this place a treat for all the senses. The location is unique too – at Punta della Dogana with unbeatable views from the terrace tables over to central Venice.

CANNAREGIO-GHETTO

☺☺ **Algiubagiò** – Fondamenta Nuove 5039, Cannaregio. ☎041 52 36 084. www. algiubagio.net. This rustic tavern turned stylish restaurant has a view of the lagoon and is well worth a visit. Ideal before catching a boat for the islands as it's close to the stop.

⊖⊖ **Alla Fontana** – Fondamenta Cannaregio 1102, Cannaregio. ☎041 71 50 77. Closed Sun evening and Mon. This wine bar frequented by a very local clientele also has a little restaurant serving tasty food. Tables on the canalside when the weather is good.

⊖⊖ **All'Antica Mola** – Fondamenta Ormesini, 2800 Cannaregio. ☎041 71 74 92. Closed Wed. This place set beside a small canal, a stone's throw from the Ghetto, serves up unpretentious but very tasty Venetian cuisine.

⊖⊖ **Anice Stellato** – Fondamenta de la Sensa 3272, Cannaregio. ☎041 72 07 44. www.osterianicestellato.com. Closed Mon and Tue lunch. A simple, modern place with a good choice of fish at decent prices.

⊖⊖ **Dalla Marisa** – Ponte dei Tre Archi 652b, Cannaregio. ☎041 72 02 11. Closed Mon evening and Tue evening. Carnivores take note! This is one of the few specialist meat restaurants in Venice, and with good reason, as it is run by a family of butchers. Excellent food in generous portions.

⊖⊖ **Gam Gam** – Ghetto Vecchio 1122. ☎366 250 4505. www.gamgamkosher.com. Reservation reccomended. Popular kosher restaurant, one of several in the historic Ghetto area. Delicious, interesting dishes in a cosmopolitan, canalside environment.

⊖⊖ **La Perla** – Rio Terrà di Franceschi 4615, Cannaregio. ☎041 52 85 175. www.laperlavenezia.com. Pizza enthusiasts will find around 150 to choose from, including some unusual options – at this simple pizzeria where film posters line the walls.

SANT'ELENA-SAN PIETRO

⊖⊖ **Al Pampo** – Calle Chinotto 24, Island of Sant'Elena. ☎041 52 08 419. www.osteriadapampo.it. Closed Tue. A trattoria serving up traditional cuisine that is particularly popular in summer when the tables are set up outside. A favourite among artists and exhibitors at the Biennale.

⊖⊖ **Dai Tosi Grandi** – Secco Marina 768, Castello. ☎041 241 14 72. www.trattoriadaitosigrandi.it. An ideal solution if you have worked up an appetite walking round the Biennale exhibitions. A wide choice of pizzas and incomparable home made pasta.

TAKING A BREAK

Ai Nomboli – Calle dei Nomboli 2717, San Polo. ☎041 523 09 95. A snack bar with a huge array of *tramezzini* – the sliced-bread sandwiches which are highly popular in Venice.

Ai Rusteghi – Corte del Tentor, 5513, San Marco. ☎041 52 32 205. www.osteriarusteghi.com. Closed Sun. A wide choice of panini, accompanied by a very good selection of wine.

Caffè Florian – Piazza San Marco 57. ☎041 52 05 641. www.caffeflorian.com. Dating from 1720, this famous caffè is almost a museum piece. Antique interiors with streaked mirrors and frescoes exude a timeless atmosphere. Or from the open-air terrace, enjoy the beauty of St Mark's, while the orchestra plays music and sip a (costly) coffee.

Caffè Quadri – Piazza San Marco 121. ☎041 52 22 105. For a break from all that sightseeing, this is the spot to treat yourself to a Michelin-starred gourmet meal. Or simply enoy a top-quality cup of coffee (in the 1830s, this was one of the first caffès in Venice to serve Turkish coffee) on the square.

Gran Caffè Lavena – Piazza San Marco 133–134. ☎041 52 24 070. www.lavena.it. In the same spirit as the two previous places, this little caffè with its age-yellowed mirrors also dates from the mid-18C.

Harry's Bar – Calle Vallaresso 1323, San Marco. ☎041 52 85 777. www.harrysbarvenezia.com. Near Piazza San Marco the legendary Harry's Bar, a national heritage site, was inaugurated in 1931 by Giuseppe Cipriani. Birthplace of the Bellini cocktail made with sparkling Prosecco and white peach juice. Come just for a drink or for the delicious food; variety of local and international dishes.

Il Caffè (Caffè Rosso) – Campo Santa Margherita 2963, Dorsoduro. ☎041 528 79 98. Closed Sun. This caffè with a reggae vibe gets busy at *aperitivo* time and after dinner.

Marchini – Campo San Luca 4589, San Marco. ☎041 24 13 087. Smart *pasticceria* caffè with cakes and pastries.

Pasticceria Dal Mas Cioccolateria – Lista di Spagna 149/150A, Cannaregio. ☎041 71 51 01. www.dalmaspasticceria.it.

A chocolate-lovers' delight, also excellent pastries. Near St. Lucia train station.

Pasticceria Italo Didovich – Campo di Santa Marina 5909, Castello. ☎041 523 00 17. Well-known cake shop and bar.

Pasticceria Pitteri – Cannaregio 3843. ☎041 522 2687. Dense and delicious traditional Venetian green pistachio cakes. Near Ca' d"Oro, also serves coffee.

Rosa Salva – Calle Fiubera 950, San Marco. ☎041 52 10 544. www.rosasalva.it. Quality cakes. Delicious cappuccino too.

Torrefazione Cannaregio – Rio Terrà San Leonardo, Cannaregio 1337. ☎041 716 371. Probably Venice's best coffee, roasted on the premises since 1930. Small bar.

GOING OUT

Al Gatto Nero – Fondamenta Giudecca 88, Burano, ☎041 73 01 20, www.gattonero. com, closed Mon. The best of the lagoon, prepared by chef Ruggero Bovo: polenta with shrimp, cuttlefish risotto and vegetables grown on neighboring islands. Make sure you try the *risotto di gò*.

Al Volto – Calle Cavalli 4081, San Marco, near Campo Manin. ☎041 52 28 945. www. alvoltoenoteca.com. A cosy, inviting wine bar that is always packed and offers wine buffs plenty of scope for new discoveries.

Busa alla Torre – Campo Santo Stefano 3, Murano, ☎041 73 96 62, closed evenings. Seafood cuisine and Venetian specialties served on a pretty terrace set back from the busy wharf. Very warm welcome.

Devil's Forest – Calle degli Stagneri 5185, San Marco. ☎041 52 00 623. www.devilforestpub.com. Open daily 11am–1am. A lively English-style pub. TV sports events are shown. Free wifi

Il Paradiso Perduto – Fondamenta della Misericordia 2540, Cannaregio. ☎041 72 05 81. Closed Tue and Wed. Live music, art shows and good food served up in a friendly and stimulating environment.

The Irish Pub – 3487 Corte dei Pali, Cannaregio. ☎041 09 90 196. Open 11am–2am. Formerly The Fiddler's Elbow, this lively bar stays open late with live music and good beer. Sports also shown.

ENTERTAINMENT

☺ Music and theatre have always played an integral part of Venetian life in its 18C heyday hosting more than 20 theatres. Today concerts are held in venues that include churches La Pietà, I Frari and Santo Stefano. Find city events in the local newspaper, the *Gazzettino*.

Gran Teatro La Fenice – Campo San Fantin 1965, San Marco. ☎041 78 65 11. www.teatrolafenice.it. World famous opera.

Teatro A l'Avogaria – Corte Zappa 1617, Dorsoduro. ☎041 099 19 67. www.teatro-avogaria.it.

Teatro Fondamenta Nuove – Fondamenta Nuove 5013, Cannaregio. ☎41 52 24 498. www.teatrofondamentanuove.it. On the Fondamenta Nuove, near Sacca della Misericordia. Plays, concerts and dance.

Teatro Goldoni – Calle Goldoni 4650b, San Marco. ☎041 24 02 014. www.teatro stabileveneto.it. Plays and concerts.

Venice Jazz Club – Behind Campo Santa Margherita (Dorsoduro 3102). ☎041 52 32 056. www.venicejazzclub.weebly.com. Open Mon–Wed and Fri–Sat with concerts from 9pm; food from 7.30 only for those who stay for the concert. Closed Aug. The resident quartet, frequently joined by special guests from the international circuit, plays traditional tunes and more up-to-date sounds.

SIGHTSEEING

Combined tickets – The **Museum Pass** includes one entry to each museum: Palazzo Ducale, Palazzo Correr, Museo Archeologico, Biblioteca Nazionale Marciana, Casa di Goldoni, Ca' Rezzonico, Ca' Pesaro, Palazzo Mocenigo, Museo di Storia Naturale, the Museo del Vetro on Murano and the Museo del Merletto on Burano (24€, valid for 6 months). ☎848 08 20 00 (from Italy) or 041 427 30 892. www.visitmuve.it.

EVENTS

Each year in early September, the Lido hosts the world-famous Venice Film Festival: **Mostra del Cinema di Venezia**. Every other year, the six-month long **Biennale** art exhibition is held in the Arsenal and Giardini districts. www.labiennale.org.

Laguna Veneta★★

Venetian Lagoon

The Laguna Veneta is the largest in Italy. It was formed at the end of the Ice Age by the convergence of flooded rivers, swollen by melted snow from the Alps and Apennines.

A BIT OF HISTORY

In the 12C Europe enjoyed a long period of mild weather followed by a noticeable rise in temperature; then came torrential rains that caused high tides and flooding. The River Brenta broke its banks and water flooded a large part of the lagoon, depositing silt, mud and detritus. Malaria broke out.

The Republic of Venice tried to defend itself by placing palisades along the coast, diverting the course of the rivers and building great dykes, but the lagoon continued to pose a threat. Over the ensuing centuries (15C–17C), major drainage programmes were implemented, affecting the Brenta, Piave, Livenza and Sile rivers. In 1896 the operation aimed at diverting the waters of the Brenta was finally completed, channelling them into the mouth of the Bacchiglione. Despite these measures, as water levels continue to rise and fall, the sand deposited into the lagoon by the rivers is buffeted back inland by the sea and the wind forming sandbanks. Caught between marine erosion and the rebuilding action of the rivers, Venice itself is at risk: it is slowly sinking.

NATURE OF THE LAGOON

The Laguna Veneta survives thanks to a subtle balance between excessive sedimentation (leading to the emergence of new land) and erosion (in which the deposits carried by the sea and rivers are so scarce that a stretch of lagoon can become sea). This is the risk currently threatening the lagoon.

⚅ **Michelin Map:** 562 E, F, G 18–22. ⚅ See also *VENICE* and *THE GREEN GUIDE VENICE*.

🗊 **Info:** Palazzo Ravagnan, Riva Vena 895, 30015 Chioggia. ☏ 041 89 42 110. 041 40 10 68. www.veneziaturismo.it. www.chioggiavenezia.it

▶ **Location:** The Laguna Veneta is bordered to the south by Chioggia and to the north by Trieste. The main access road is the A 4.

❀ **Don't Miss:** The Basilica at Aquileia.

🕐 **Timing:** Allow a day to explore the area.

👪 **Kids:** The Parco Zoo Punta Verde and family-friendly beaches at Lignano.

The Tide, Lifeblood of the Lagoon

Tidal changes occur every six hours, fluctuating between two high points per day. Seawater is drawn into the lagoon through the three ports, flushing new water in and old water out – assisted by a current from the rivers on the opposite side. Parts affected by these tides are thereby known as the **laguna viva** (living lagoon), whereas the sections little affected by this lifeline are referred to as the **laguna morta** (dead lagoon). These outlying parts tend towards marsh, channelled with canals, fishing banks and dyked lakes built by and for the fishing industry.

The Tide, Destroyer of the Lagoon

The health of the lagoon is totally dependent upon the influx of "new" water brought by the tides; however, the inflow of fresh water provided by the rivers that once maintained saline levels has been greatly reduced as the rivers have progressively been diverted. This has also reduced the strength of current across the lagoon and allowed vast quantities of polluting material to be deposited.

In the 20C the problem was exacerbated by the growth of industrial sites and petrol-tankers around Mestre and Porto Marghera threatening the environment of the lagoon, while the decrease in oxygenated water flowing through the canals of Venice is compromising plant and marine life.

Tidal Flooding

The tide along these coasts can fluctuate wildly; for it to be classified as tidal flooding its level has to reach or exceed 1.10m/3ft 6in. The last such occurrence happened on 4 November 1966 when consequences were felt way beyond the shores of Venice – the Arno overflowed in Florence with tragic results. That year an alarming prediction was rumoured that Venice might possibly disappear – fortunately, radical action against further subsidence, including the closure of artesian wells on the mainland, have proved the prophecy false. Similar crises of this kind are documented as far back as 589. Contemporary personal accounts are terrifying. **Paolo Diacono** (c.720–99) wrote of the first flood tide: *"non in terra neque in aqua sumus viventes"* ("neither on earth nor in water were we alive"). Records from 1410 state that "almost one thousand people coming from the fair at Mestre and other places drowned". Since the 17C the water level of the Laguna Veneta has dropped by 60cm/24in. In past centuries, once every five years, the tide would rise above the damp-proof foundations made of Istrian stone that were built to protect the houses against salt deposits. Nowadays, in the lower areas, these foundations are immersed in water more than 40 times in a single year and the buildings can do very little to stall the degradation.

Flora and Fauna

Fish are the lagoon's real treasure, in their distinctive shoals around the sandbanks. At the lower end of the food chain are a variety of molluscs and at the other end is man, seeking to exploit such rich resources.

Crab and **clams** are central to the fishing industry and to Venetian cuisine. The seafood attracts a variety of seabirds, including **wild duck** (mallard and teal), and many **coots**, **herons** and **marsh harriers**. The little **egret** is another common local resident, recognisable by its elegant carriage and bright white feathers with which ladies adorned themselves in the early-20C.

The sandbanks are abundantly cloaked in vegetation: **glasswort**, **sea lavender** and **asters** turn the mounds first green, then red, then blue, then grey. Rooted in the water are various **reeds** and **rushes** with long stalks and colourful spiky flowers.

🚗 DRIVING TOUR

FROM GRADO TO CHIOGGIA
Follow the coastline from Grado to Chioggia. 220km/137mi.

Grado★

At the time of the barbarian invasions the inhabitants of Aquileia founded Grado, which was, from the 5C to the 9C, the residence of the Patriarchs of Aquileia. Today Grado is a busy little fishing port and seaside resort with a growing reputation and wonderful old town with cobbled streets.

Quartiere Vecchio★

The picturesque old town has a network of narrow alleys *(calli)* running between the canal port and the cathedral. The Duomo di Santa Eufemia (6C) has marble columns with Byzantine capitals, a 6C mosaic pavement, a 10C ambo and a valuable 14C Venetian silver-gilt **altarpiece★**. Beside the cathedral a row of sarcophagi and tombs leads to the 6C basilica of Santa Maria delle Grazie, which has some original mosaics.

Aquileia★

While the town site was being outlined with a plough (181 BC), according to Roman custom, an eagle *(aquila)* hovered overhead: hence its name. Aquileia was a flourishing market and the general headquarters of Augustus during his conquest of Germanic tribes, becoming one

Laguna Veneta

© StrenghtOfFrame/iStockphoto.com

of Italy's most important patriarchates (554–1751), ruled by bishops.

Basilica★★

Open Apr–Sept 9am–7pm, Mar and Oct 9am–6pm, Nov–Feb 10am–4pm; Sut, Sun and public hols 9am–5pm; bell tower Apr–Oct 9.30am–1.30pm and 3.30pm–6.30pm; Sat and Sun 10am–5pm. Crypts 4€; bell tower 2€. ℘0431 91 97 19. www.basilicadiaquileia.it.

The Romanesque church was built in the 11C on the foundations of a 4C building and restored in the 14C. Preceded by a porch, it is flanked by a campanile.

The interior with its nave and two aisles is in the form of a Latin cross. The splendid 4C mosaic **paving★★**, which is one of the largest and richest in Western Christendom, depicts religious scenes. The timber ceiling and the arcades are both 14C, the capitals are Romanesque and the decoration of the transept Renaissance. The 9C Carolingian crypt known as **Cripta degli Affreschi** is decorated with fine Romanesque **frescoes★★**.

The **Cripta degli Scavi** is reached from the north aisle. Finds from the excavations are assembled here, notably admirable 4C mosaic **paving★★**.

Aree Archeologiche★

&. Open 8.30am–7pm, closed Mon. Free. ℘0431 91 016. 4€. (Museo Paleocristiano: Loc. Monastrero, open Thu 8.30am–1.45pm. Free. ℘0431 91 131). www.museoarcheologicoaquileia. beniculturali.it.

Excavations have uncovered the remains of Roman Aquileia: behind the basilica, the Via Sacra leading to the river port, houses and the forum. The **Musei Archeologico e Paleocristiano** (Archaeological and Early-Christian Museums) contain some important finds from local excavations.

▶ Head N out of Aquileia and turn left onto the S 14, towards Portogruaro. After about 25km/15.5mi, turn left onto the S 354 towards Lignano.

Lignano

Stretching E from the mouth of the Tagliamento, it closes off part of the Marano Lagoon, an angling reserve.

Lignano, the largest seaside resort on the coastline of Friuli, lies on a long, sandy peninsula covered with pinewoods. Its ≗ **beach★★**, facing Grado, the Trieste Gulf and the coastline of Istria (which is often visible), is popular for its 8km/5mi of fine, golden sand. A good holiday resort for families with children. **Lignano Riviera** gets its name from the nearby Tagliamento. Inland, holidaymakers can enjoy the 18-hole golf course and visit the zoo, the ≗ **Parco Zoo Punta Verde**, which presents animals from all over the world. &. For opening times visit the website. 13€. ℘0431 42 87 75. www. parcozoopuntaverde.it.

Venezia★★★

&See VENICE.

Chioggia

Strictly speaking, Chioggia is not one of the lagoon islands, resting as it does on two parallel islands, linked to terra firma by a long bridge. The realm of fisherman and the fish market, the Chioggia's wee hours are lively with returning boats and market preparations.

La Città

The main street, **Corso del Popolo**, runs parallel to Canale della Vena – the Fossa Clodia of ancient times – rendered colourful and lively by its fish market, ending in Piazzetta Vigo. The column bearing a winged lion marks the end of the Fossa Clodia. Cross the canal, over the stone bridge, Ponte Vigo, built 1685. Along the corso is the 11C **Duomo★**, dedicated to Santa Maria Assunta, and several other churches. The **Isola di San Domenico** (promontory) extends at the far end of Chioggia and is reached by Calle di San Croce. The church houses a *St Paul* painted by Carpaccio.

Museo Civico della Laguna Sud – Just before the town gate, Campo Marconi. Open Sept–middle Jun Tue–Wed 9am–1pm, Thu–Sat 9am–1pm and 3–6pm; middle Jun–Aug Tue–Wed 9am–1pm, Thu–Sun 9am–1pm and 9–11pm. Closed 1 Jan, Easter, 25 Dec. ☎041 55 00 911. www.chioggia.org. 4€. The museum's three floors offer a chronological presentation of Chioggia's maritime history with the help of archaeological finds from the region. The ground-floor room is devoted to water technology and trade in Roman times; on the first floor covers the period from the Middle Ages to the 16C; the second floor takes you from the 17C to modern times and examines fishing and boatbuilding techniques, with a specific focus on Chioggia's distinctive *bragozzo* fishing boats.

La lagune★ – *Information from Chioggia tourist office.* With their location between the Laguna Veneta and the Po Delta, Chioggia, Sottomarina and Isola Verde make ideal starting points for exploring the region's watery landscape, which can be more easily appreciated from flat-bottomed boats or by bicycle. A few kilometres south east of the port of Chioggia is the Adriatic's largest expanse of the sea-bed phenomena known as "Tegnùe". These reefs at depths of 17m–25m/56ft–82ft have been formed over nearly 4 000 years by coralline red algae. They are alive with flora and fauna and have been a protected area since 2002.

ADDRESSES

🛏 STAY

😑😑 **Hotel Park** – Lungomare Adriatico 74, 30019 Lido di Sottomarina, 10km/6.2mi E of Chioggia. ☎041 49 07 40. www.hotel parkchioggia.it. 40 rooms. ☲. A family-run establishment situated opposite the beach. Spacious, simple rooms.

😑😑 **Park Spiaggia** – Via Mazzini 1, 34073 Grado. ☎0431 82 366. www.hotel parkspiaggia.it. A simple, traditional hotel in pedestrianised Grado.

😑😑 **Sole** – Via Mediterraneo 9, 30019 Sottomarina, Chioggia. ☎041 49 15 05. www.hotel-sole.com. ☲. Closed Oct–Mar. Clean and comfortable rooms, private beach and pool.

♟/EAT

😑 **Ristorante Da Franco** – Strada Romea 364/a, 30015 Sant'Anna di Chioggia, 8km/5mi S of Chioggia on the S 309 Romea. 041 49 50 301. Welcoming (mostly) fish restaurant. Good list of wines and whiskeys.

😑 **Da Luigi** – Via Dante 25, 30020 Torre di Fine, 40km/24.8mi NE of Venice. ☎0421 23 74 07. www.daluigiristorante.it. Closed Wed in winter. This trattoria is renowned for its quality home cooking. The grilled seafood dishes are particularly good.

😑 **La Colombara** – Via Zilli 34, 33051 Aquileia, 2km/1.2mi NW of Aquileia. ☎0431 91 513. www.lacolombara.com. Closed Mon. Worth seeking out, this fish restaurant serves carefully prepared dishes made with fresh ingredients. Rustic decor and a pleasant outside dining area.

ACTIVITIES

To discover the lagoon at your own pace, you could rent a houseboat. Via Roma 1445, Sottomarina. ☎041 55 10 400. www.rendez-vous-fantasia.com.

Riviera del
Brenta★★

The Riviera del Brenta is a bucolic strip of land favoured by the Venetian nobility for summer residences. For visitors to the area, these grandiose villas★ – their reflections sparkling in the river that meanders from Padova to the lagoon – exude an aristocratic quality.

VISIT
Strà

The **Villa Pisani★** has a majestic garden with a delightful vista. The spacious **apartments★** of this 18C palace were decorated by artists, including Giovanni Battista Tiepolo, who painted his masterpiece, **The Apotheosis of the Pisani Family★★**. Open Tue–Sun Apr–Sept 9am–7pm; Oct–Mar 9am–4pm. Closed 1 Jan, 25 Dec. Park 7.50€; park and villa 10€. ℘049 50 20 74. www.villapisani.beniculturali.it.

Mira

The **Palazzo Foscarini** and **Villa Widmann-Foscari** are both 18C. The **ballroom★** of the latter is entirely decorated with frescoes. *Villa Widmann:* Open Tue–

- ⚲ **Michelin Map:** 562 F 18 – 35km/21.8mi east of Padova – Veneto.
- **Info:** Via Mazzini 76, 30031 Dolo. ℘041 51 02 341. www.rivieradelbrenta turismo.com.
- ⟳ **Location:** The Riviera del Brenta runs along the ancient course of a river linking Padova to Venice. Standing alongside the Brenta Canal between Strà and Fusina are numerous Classical villas by Palladio (⚲*see Index*). By car take the road that follows the Brenta passing through Strà, Dolo, Mira and Malcontenta.
- ⚲ **Don't Miss:** A walk around the stunning gardens at Villa Pisani.
- 🕐 **Timing:** The length of visit will depend on the method of getting to the Riviera (car or boat) and villas visited. For a first visit two days are recommended.

Villa Pisani

A River Trip with a Difference ...

Experience life on the Burchiello in the 18C – if only for a day. A modern boat follows the old 18C transport route. &(If accompanied). The Burchiello excursion runs from Mar to Oct. Departure from Padova (Pontile del Portello) on Wed, Fri and Sun at 8am and arrival in Venice (Pontile della Pietà, Riva degli Schiavoni) at 5.30pm approx., including visits to Villa Pisani, Villa Widmann and Villa Foscari (known as "La Malcontenta"). Departure from Venice (Pontile della Pietà, Riva degli Schiavoni) on Tue, Thu and Sat at 9am; same programme but visits in reverse order. Arrival in Padova 7pm approx. 99€, 65€ (half tour). Reservation required – contact Il Burchiello ℘049 87 60 233. www.ilburchiello.it.

Sun 10am–1pm and 1.30–4.30pm. Closed 1 Jan, 25 Dec. 5.50€. ℘041 56 00 690.

Malcontenta

Palladio built Villa Foscari (1574) and Giovanni Battista Zelotti and Battista Franco painted the frescoes. The villa's nickname, "Malcontenta" ("Unhappy") is for a Foscari wife, displeased at being sent here. Open May–Oct Tue and Sat 9am–noon. 10€. ℘041 54 70 012. www.lamalcontenta.com.

Padova★★

Padua

An art and pilgrimage centre, Padova revolves around historic Piazza Cavour. Caffè Pedrocchi, a meeting-place of the liberal elite in the Romantic period, is close by.

A BIT OF HISTORY

Few traces exist of ancient *Patavium*, one of the most prosperous Roman cities in Veneto during the 1C BC owing to its river trade, agriculture and the sale of horses. In the 7C Padova was destroyed by the Lombards, and from the 11C to the 13C it became an independent city-state. The city underwent its greatest period of prosperity under the enlightened rule of the Lords of Carrara (1337–1405). In 1405 Padova came under the sway of the Venetian Republic and remained a loyal subject until 1797 when Napoleon abolished the Venetian Constitution.

The City of St Anthony the Hermit – This Franciscan monk, born in 1195, died aged 36 near Padova. He was a forceful

- ▶ **Population:** 212 989
- ◔ **Michelin Map:** 562 F 17 – Veneto.
- ℹ **Info:** Galleria Pedrocchi, railway station, Piazza del Senato. ℘049 201 00 80. www.turismopadova.it.
- ◖ **Location:** Padova is off the A 4, 40km/24.8mi from Venice. It is linked to Bologna by the A 13.
- ◖ **Train:** Padova (Venezia Santa Lucia 25mins).
- ◕ **Don't Miss:** Giotto's frescoes in the Scrovegni Chapel, the Basilica del Santo and mud treatments at Abano Terme.
- ◔ **Timing:** Allow one day to explore the town.

preacher and is generally represented holding a book and a lily.
A famous university – The University of Padova, founded 1222, is the second oldest in Italy after Bologna. Galileo was a professor and students included Copernicus and the poet Tasso.

Art in Padova – In 1304 **Giotto** came to Padova to decorate the Scrovegni Chapel, with a superlative cycle of frescoes.

In the 15C the Renaissance in Padova was marked by **Donatello**, another Florentine, who stayed in the city from 1444 to 1453. Also in the 15C, Padovan art flourished under the Padovan artist **Andrea Mantegna** (1431–1506), a powerful painter and an innovator in the field of perspective.

SIGHTS

Frescoes by Giotto in the Scrovegni Chapel★★★

&. Open daily 9am–7pm. Closed 1 Jan, 25–26 Dec. 13€ including Museo Civico agli Eremitani and Palazzo Zuckermann; 8€ Mon (Museo Ermitani closed). ℰ049 20 100 20. www.cappelladegliscrovegni.it. The cycle of 39 frescoes was painted c.1305–10 by Giotto on the walls of the **Cappella degli Scrovegni.** The chapel, built in 1303, illustrates the lives of Joachim and Anna (the parents of the Virgin), Mary and Jesus: the *Flight into Egypt*, *Judas' Kiss* and the *Entombment* are among the most famous.

On the lower register, the powerful monochrome figures depict the Vices *(left)* and Virtues *(right)*. The *Last Judgement* on the west wall completes the cycle. On the altar stands a **Virgin★** by the Tuscan sculptor Giovanni Pisano.
⊘*Don't let Giotto's frescoes overshadow* **Pisano's Virgin★** *on the altar.*

Frescoes in the Chiesa degli Eremitani★★

In the Cappella Ovetari of the 13C Church of the Hermits *(the second on the right of the Cappella Maggiore)* are fragments of frescoes by **Mantegna.** The Lady Chapel (Cappella Maggiore) has splendid frescoes by **Guariento,** Giotto's pupil.

Museo Civico agli Eremitani★

&.Open Tue–Sun 9am–7pm. Closed 1 Jan, 1 May, 25–26 Dec. 13€/10€ with/without Cappella degli Scrovegni. Ticket includes Palazzo Zuckermann. ℰ049 82 04 551. www.cappelladegliscrovegni.it.

The museum in the Hermitage of St Augustine comprises archaeology (Egyptian, Etruscan, Roman and pre-Roman), coins (Bottacin Bequest) and 15C–18C Venetian and Flemish paintings. The museum contains the former art gallery's collection including **paintings★★**, mostly the Venetian school (14C–18C). Note works by Giotto.

Basilica di Sant'Antonio★★

This important pilgrimage church overlooks the square in which Donatello erected an **equestrian statue★★** of the Venetian leader **Gattamelata** (nicknamed "Erasmo di Nardi"). The basilica was built from 1232 to 1300 in the transitional Romanesque-Gothic style. The **interior★★** contains the **Cappella del Santo★★**, location of the tomb/altar of St Anthony (Arca di Sant'Antonio) by Tiziano Aspetti (1594). On the walls are 16C **high reliefs★★**. In the chancel the **high altar★★** has bronze panels (1450) by Donatello. The third chapel has **frescoes★** by Altichiero (14C), a Veronese artist. There is a fine **view★** of the building from the cloisters, to the south.

Oratorio di San Giorgio and Scuola del Santo★

&. Open daily 9am–12.30pm and 2.30–5pm (7pm Summer). Closed 1 Jan, Easter, 25 Dec. 5€. ℰ049 82 25 652. www.arciconfraternitasantantonio.org. St George's Oratory is decorated with 21 **frescoes★** (1377) by Altichiero. In the adjacent Scuola del Santo are 18 16C **frescoes★** relating the life of St Anthony including four by Titian.

Palazzo della Ragione★

&. Open Tue–Sun Feb–Oct 9am–7pm; Nov–Jan 9am–6pm. Closed 1 Jan, 1 May, 25 Dec. 4€. ℰ049 82 05 006. www.padovanet.it.

The Law Courts, between two **squares★**, the Piazza della Frutta and the Piazza delle Erbe, are remarkable for their roof in the form of an upturned ship's keel. The **salone★★** is adorned with 15C frescoes depicting the *Labours of the Months*, the *Liberal Arts*, the *Trades* and the *Signs of the Zodiac.*

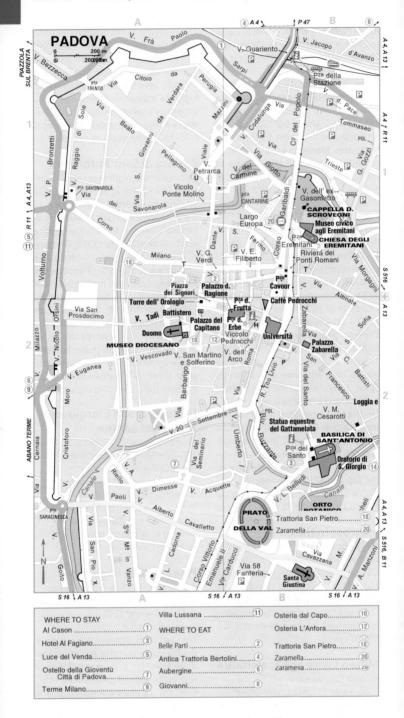

PADOVA

WHERE TO STAY		Villa Lussana	.... (11)	Osteria dal Capo	.... (10)
Al Cason	.... (1)	WHERE TO EAT		Osteria L'Anfora	.... (12)
Hotel Al Fagiano	.... (3)				
Luce del Venda	.... (5)	Belle Parti	.... (2)	Trattoria San Pietro	.... (18)
Ostello della Gioventù Città di Padova	.... (7)	Antica Trattoria Bertolini	.... (4)	Zaramella	.... (20)
		Aubergine	.... (6)	Zaramella	.... (20)
Terme Milano	.... (9)	Giovanni	.... (8)		

Piazza dei Signori
This square is overlooked by the Clock Tower, **Torre dell'Orologio★**.

Duomo
Michelangelo contributed to the construction of the cathedral (16C7C), which is on the site of older churches.

Battistero★★
The 12C baptistery adjoining the cathedral contains frescoes covering the entire scriptures, painted 1376–1378 by **Giusto de' Menabuoi**. The sequence runs from the creation of the world at the top of the dome to the final Apocalypse.

Museo Diocesano★★
Piazza Duomo 12. Open Thu–Sat 2–6pm, Sun and public hols 10am–6pm. Closed Easter, 25 Dec. 5€; 7€ with baptistery. ℘049 87 61 924.
www.museodiocesanopadova.it.
The vast **bishops' hall★** in the Palazzo Vescovile (Bishop's Palace) has a loggia painted with *trompe l'œil* of all the Bishops of Padova. Bartolomeo Montagna started work on this in the late-15C, and the *trompe l'œil* work, with its false marble and perspective views, is particularly elegant.
The chapel of Santa Maria degli Angeli (1495) is also here and the museum continues with a series of rooms charting the history of the diocese, one of Italy's largest and oldest. The numerous artworks include a 14C *Virgin and Child* attributed to Paolo Veneziano and an 18C depiction of San Francesco di Paola by Tiepolo.

Università
Palazzo Bo has housed the university since the 15C. It has retained a lovely 16C courtyard and an anatomy theatre, **Teatro Anatomico** (1594). Guided tours only. Closed Sun, 1 May, 2 Jun, 13 Jun, public hols. 5€. ℘049 82 75 111. www.unipd.it.

Caffè Pedrocchi
This historic caffè (1831) hosts numerous cultural events as well as the Museo del Risorgimento on the first floor. Open Tue–Sun 9.30am–12.30pm and 3.30–6pm. Closed 1 Jan, 1 May, 25–26 Dec. 4€. ℘049 87 81 231. www.caffepedrocchi.it.

Palazzo Zabarella
Via San Francesco 27. Contact for information. ℘049 87 53 100.
www.zabarella.it.
This privately owned palazzo regularly hosts major exhibitions.

Chiesa Santa Giustina
A 16C church dedicated to St Justina with an **altarpiece★** by Veronese.

Orto Botanico
Open daily Apr–Sept 9am–7pm, Oct 9am–6pm, Nov–Mar 9am–5pm. Closed Mon (except Apr–May), 25 Dec, 1 Jan. 12€. ℘049 20 10 222.
www.ortobotanico.unipd.it.
The Botanical Gardens, laid out in 1545, contain many exotic species.

EXCURSIONS
Montagnana★
47km/29.2mi SW.
Enclosed by 14C **ramparts★★**, the town also has a **Duomo**, by Sansovino, with a *Transfiguration* painted by Veronese.

Abano Terme⫪⫪⫪
This attractive spa town in the Euganean Hills is one of Italy's most famous.

Montegrotto Terme⫪⫪
Another pleasant town in the Euganean Hills with outstanding spa facilities.

Monselice★
This town was an ancient Roman mining community. The upper terrace of Villa Balbi affords a lovely **view★**.

Arquà Petrarca★
6.5km/4mi NW of Monselice.
The poet **Petrarch** (1304–74) lived and died here. **Petrarch's house★** has a collection of memorabilia and autographs. Open Tue–Sun Mar–Oct 9am–12.30pm and 3–7pm; Nov–Feb 9am–noon and 2.30–5.30pm. Closed 1 Jan, 1 May, 25–26 Dec. 4€. ℘0429 71 82 94. www.arqua petrarca.com.

ADDRESSES

🏠 STAY

☺ Ostello della Gioventù Città di Padova – Via Aleardo Aleardi 30. ℘049 87 52 219. www.ostellopadova.it. 🅿 ♿. A centrally located youth hostel with simple accommodation suitable for all kinds of visitors, including families.

☺☺ Al Cason – Via Frà Paolo Sarpi 40. ℘049 66 26 36. www.hotelalcason.com. 🅿 48 rooms. A little out of the centre but close to the railway station. Family run with fairly basic facilities and simple but high-quality cooking.

☺☺ Hotel Al Fagiano – Via Locatelli 45. ℘049 87 50 073. www.alfagiano.com. 40 rooms. ☒. Only 100m/110yds from the Basilica di Sant'Antonio, a pleasant hotel with attractively furnished rooms.

☺☺ Luce del Venda – Via Monte Venda 1194. Vò, loc. Boccon, 26km/16.2mi SW of Padova. ℘049 9941243. 🅿 5 rooms. A peaceful country home with a lovely garden and a wine cellar with 4 000 bottles. Kitchen facilities for guests.

☺☺ Terme Milano – Viale delle Terme 169, 35031 Abano Terme, 13km/8mi SW of Padova. ℘049 86 69 444. www.termemilano.it. 🅿 89 rooms. In the pedestrianised area of Abano, this hotel offers indoor and outdoor pools to help you make the most of the thermal waters. Gym and tennis court.

☺☺ Villa Lussana – Via Chiesa 1, 35037 Teolo, 21km/13mi SW of Padova. ℘049 99 25 530. www.villalussana.com. Closed 3 weeks Jan. 🅿 11 rooms. An attractive hotel in an Art Nouveau villa with fine views over the Colli Euganei.

🍴 EAT

☺☺ Antica Trattoria Bertolini – Via Altichiero 162, Altichiero, 5km/3mi N of Padova. ℘049 60 03 57. www.bertolini1849.it. Closed Fri evening, Sat and 3 weeks Aug. 🅿 14 rooms. Just outside Padova, this long-standing restaurant serves good traditional dishes. Close to the motorway, it's also a good place to stay for travellers.

☺☺ Aubergine – Via Ghislandi 5, Abano Terme, 13km/8mi SW of Padova. ℘049 86 69 910. www.aubergine.it. Closed Tue. A good choice if you are staying in Albano for the spa. Pizzas are also served.

☺☺ Belle Parti – Via Belle Parti 11. 049 87 51 822. www.ristorantebelleparti.it. A very elegant setting for a seasonal menu of tasty meat and fish dishes.

☺☺ Giovanni – Via Maroncelli 22. ℘049 77 26 20. www.ristorantedagiovannipd.it. Closed Sat lunch, Sun, Aug and 24 Dec–2 Jan. 🅿. A historic restaurant that's worth seeking out for good homemade pasta and tasty stews.

☺☺ Osteria dal Capo – Via degli Obizzi 2. ℘049 66 31 05. www.osteriadalcapo.it. Closed Mon lunch and Sun. A traditional trattoria just a stone's throw from the cathedral. Specialities from Padova and the Veneto.

☺☺ Osteria L'Anfora – Via del Soncino 13. ℘049 65 66 29. Closed Sun. Good for just a drink or a meal in an attractive, informal setting at the heart of the ghetto.

☺☺ Per Bacco – Piazzale Ponte Corvo 10. ℘049 87 52 883. www.per-bacco.it. Closed Sun. 🅿. A good wine cellar and delicious local cuisine.

☺☺ Trattoria San Pietro – Via San Pietro 95. ℘049 87 60 330. Closed Sun and public hols. 🅿. A renowned trattoria in the historic centre, with elegant, carefully presented decor. Tables are limited, so reservations are essential.

☺☺ Zaramella – Largo Europa 10. ℘049 87 60 868. www.ristorantezaramella.it. Closed Sat lunchtime and Sun. This restaurant's origins date back to the 19C. Delicious cuisine focusing on classic Italian fare and traditional specialities from the Veneto, as well as attentive and friendly service are just some of its attractions.

ACTIVITIES

👤👤 Boat – A trip on the water to visit the villas of the Riviera del Brenta (*♿See Riviera del BRENTA, p457*) or for a shorter trip around Padova is an experience not to be missed. ℘049 80 33 069. www.padovanavigazione.it.

Padova Card – www.padovacard.it. 16€ for 48 hrs; 21€ for 72 hours. This card gives free or 10–40 percent discounted access to most of Padova's museums. The card also provides discounts on numerous attractions and allows visitors to the urban transit buses for free.

Vicenza★★

Strategically located at the crossroads of the routes that link the Veneto with the Trentino, the proud and noble city of Vicenza is now a busy commercial and industrial centre. In addition to its traditional textile industry, and newer mechanical and chemical industries, Vicenza has a reputation as a gold-working centre. The gastronomic speciality of Vicenza is *baccalà alla Vicentina*, salt cod with a sauce served with slices of polenta (maize semolina), which is best with wine from the Berici Mountains (Barbarano, Gambellara and Breganze).

▶ **Population:** 115 550
- **Michelin Map:** 562 F 16. Town map in the Michelin Atlas Italy – Veneto.
- **Info:** Piazza Matteotti 12. ℘0444 32 08 54. www.visitvicenza.org
- **Location:** Vicenza is in central Veneto, at the foot of the Berici Mountains. The main access road is the A 4.
- **Train:** Vicenza (Venezia Santa Lucia 43mins).
- **Don't Miss:** Splendid frescoes by Giovanni Battista at Villa Valmarana ai Nani.
- **Timing:** Allow a day.

A BIT OF HISTORY

The ancient Roman town of *Vicetia* became an independent city-state in the 12C. After several conflicts with the neighbouring cities of Padova and Verona, Vicenza sought Venetian protection at the beginning of the 15C. This was a period of great prosperity, when Vicenza counted many rich and generous art patrons among its citizens and it was embellished with an amazing number of palaces.

Andrea Palladio

Vicenza was given the nickname of "Venice on terra firma" due to an exceptionally gifted man, Andrea di Pietro, known as Palladio, who spent many years in Vicenza. The last great architect of the Renaissance, Palladio was born at Padova in 1508 and died at Vicenza in 1580. He succeeded in combining, in a supremely harmonious idiom, the precepts of ancient art with the contemporary preoccupations. Encouraged by the humanist Trissino, he made several visits to Rome to study her monuments and the work of Vitruvius, a Roman architect of the time of Augustus. He perfected the Palladian style and in 1570 published his **Treatise on Architecture**, in four volumes, which made his work famous throughout Europe.

The **Palladian style** is characterised by rigorous plans where simple and symmetrical forms predominate and by harmonious façades which combine pediments and porticoes, as at San Giorgio Maggiore in Venice (*see VENICE*). Palladio was often commissioned by wealthy Venetians to build residences in the countryside around Venice. He combined architectural rhythm, noble design and, in the case of the country mansions, a great sense of situation, decoration and height, so that the villas seemed to rise like a series of new temples on the banks of the Brenta (*see Riviera del BRENTA)* or the slopes of the Berici Mountains. His pupil, Vicenzo Scamozzi (1552–1616), completed several of his master's works and carried on his style.

SIGHTS
Piazza dei Signori★★

Like St Mark's Square in Venice, it is an open-air meeting-place recalling the forum of Antiquity. As in the Piazzetta in Venice, there are two columns, here bearing effigies of the Lion of St Mark and the Redeemer.

With the lofty **Torre Bissara★**, a 12C belfry, the **Basilica★★** (1549–1617) occupies one whole side of the square. The elevation is one of Palladio's masterpieces, with two superimposed galleries in the Doric and Ionic orders, admirable for their power, proportion and purity of line. The great keel-shaped roof, destroyed by bombing, has been rebuilt. The building was not a church but a meeting-place for the Vicenzan notables. For opening times see the website. 3€. ℘0444 22 28 11. www.museicivici vicenza.it.

The 15C **Monte di Pietà** opposite, its buildings framing the Baroque façade of the church of San Vincenzo, is adorned with frescoes. The **Loggia del Capitano**★, formerly the residence of the Venetian governor, which stands to the left, at the corner of the Contrà del Monte, was begun to the plans of Palladio in 1571 and left unfinished. It is characterised by its colossal orders with composite capitals and its statues and stuccoes commemorating the naval victory of Lepanto (*see Venice, p437*).

Teatro Olimpico★★

Open Tue–Sun 9am–5pm (summer 10am–6pm). Closed 1 Jan, 25 Dec. 11€ (15€ Unico Museum Card valid for Vicenza's Musei Civici). ℘0444 22 28 00. www.museicivicivicenza.it.

This splendid building in wood and stucco was designed by Palladio in 1580 on the model of the theatres of Antiquity. The tiers of seats are laid out in a hemicycle and surmounted by a lovely **colonnade** with a balustrade crowned with statues. The **stage**★★★ is one of the finest in existence with its superimposed niches, columns and statues and its amazing perspectives painted in trompe l'œil by Scamozzi, who completed the work.

Corso Andrea Palladio★

This, the main street of Vicenza, and several neighbouring streets are embellished by many palaces designed by Palladio and his pupils. At the beginning is the **Palazzo Chiericati**, an imposing work by Palladio; at no. 147 the 15C **Palazzo Da Schio** in the Venetian-Gothic style was formerly known as the Ca' d'Oro (Golden House) because it was covered with frescoes with gilded backgrounds. The west front of **Palazzo Thiene** overlooking Contrà San Gaetano Thiene was by Palladio, while the entrance front at no. 12 Contrà Porti is Renaissance, dating from the late-15C. The **Palazzo Porto-Barbaran** opposite is also by Palladio. At no. 98 the **Palazzo Trissino** (1592) is one of Scamozzi's most successful works. Next is the Corso Fogazzaro, where the **Palazzo Valamarana** (1566) at no. 16 is another work by Palladio.

Museo Civico★

On the first floor of Palazzo Chiericati. Open Tue–Sun 9am–5pm (summer 10am–6pm). 5€ (15€ Unico Museum Card valid for Vicenza's Musei Civici). ℘0444 22 28 11. www.museicivicivicenza.it.

The collection of paintings includes Venetian Primitives (*The Dormition of the Virgin* by Paolo Veneziano); a **Crucifixion**★★ by Hans Memling; and canvases by Bartolomeo Montagna (pupil of Giovanni Bellini), Mantegna and Carpaccio, one of the most active artists in Vicenza. There are Venetian works by Lorenzo Lotto, Veronese, Bassano, Piazzetta, Tiepolo and Tintoretto as well as Flemish works by Brueghel the Elder and Van Dyck.

Chiesa della Santa Corona

Opposite Santa Corona.

The church was built in the 13C in honour of a Holy Thorn presented by St Louis, King Louis IX of France, to the Bishop of Vicenza. Works of art include a **Baptism of Christ**★★ by Giovanni Bellini *(fifth altar on the left)* and an **Adoration of the Magi**★★ (1573) by Veronese *(third chapel on the right)*. The fourth chapel on the right has a coffered **ceiling**★, adorned with gilded stucco, and a *Mary Magdalene and Saints* by Bartolomeo Montagna.

Duomo

The cathedral, built between the 14C and the 16C, has an attractively colourful Gothic façade and a Renaissance east end. Inside, the lovely **polyptych**★ (1356) is by Lorenzo Veneziano.

Giardino Salvi

This garden is attractively adorned with statues and fountains. Canals run along two sides of the garden.

EXCURSIONS

Villa Valmarana ai Nani★★

❍ 2km/1.2mi S by the Este road, then the first road to the right. Open Tue–Fri 10am–12.30pm and 3–6pm, Sat–Sun and public hols 10am–6pm. 10€. ☎0444 32 18 03. www.villavalmarana.com.

The villa dates from the 17C. Both the Palazzina and the Forestiera buildings were adorned with splendid frescoes★★★ by Giovanni Battista (Giambattista) Tiepolo and his son.

La Rotonda★

❍ 2km/1.2mi SE by the Este road, then the second road to the right. Open Tue–Sun (interior Wed and Sat only) Apr–Oct 10am–noon and 3–6pm; Nov–Mar 10am–12.30 and 2.30–5pm. 10€; 5€ garden only. www.villalarotonda.it.

Villa La Rotonda is one of Palladio's most famous creations. The gracefully proportioned square building is roofed with a dome and fronted on each side by a pedimented portico, making it look like an ancient temple.

Basilica di Monte Berico and Monti Berici★

❍ 2km/1.2mi S by Viale Venezia, then Viale X Giugno.

As the road climbs uphill, it is lined with an 18C portico and chapels. On the summit is the Baroque basilica roofed with a dome. From the esplanade there is a wide panorama★★ of Vicenza, the Venetian Plain and the Alps. Inside, is a *Pietà* (1500) by Bartolomeo Montagna.

Montecchio Maggiore

❍ 13km/8mi SW by the S 11.

The ruins of these two castles brings to mind *Romeo and Juliet*. There are good views★ of the Po Plain and Vicenza.

On the outskirts of Montecchio on the Tavernelle road the Villa Cordellina-Lombardi has one room entirely covered with frescoes★ by Tiepolo. ♿ Open Apr–Oct Tue and Fri 9am–1pm,

La Rotonda
© Flavio Vallenari/iStockphoto.com

Wed–Thu and Sat–Sun 9am–1pm and 3–6pm; Nov–Mar only by reservation (min. 20 pers.). 3€. ☎0444 90 81 12. www.provincia.vicenza.it.

ADDRESSES

🛏 STAY

⊜⊜ **Hotel Victoria** – Strada Padana (in the direction of Padova) 52, 7km/4.3mi E of Vicenza on the SS 11. ☎0444 91 22 99. www.hotelvictoriavicenza.com. 123 rooms. 🏊. Reasonable prices and comfortable surroundings. Offers good-sized rooms and apartments. In summer guests can use the open-air pool. Not far from the motorway and yet a few minutes from the centre.

⊜⊜⊜ **G Boutique Hotel** – Via Giuriolo 10. ☎0444 32 64 58. www.gboutiquehotel.com. 17 rooms. 🏊. Behind a classic exterior lie super-stylish rooms that don't cut on comfort. Location close to the Teatro Olimpico.

🍴 EAT

⊜ **Al Pestello** – Contrà Santo Stefano 3. ☎0444 32 37 21. www.ristorantealpestello.it. Closed Tue; also lunch Mon, Wed, Thu. Specialising in local cusine, there is also a lovely outdoor area.

⊜⊜ **Antica Osteria da Penacio** – Via Soghe 62, Arcugnano, 10km/6.2mi S of Vicenza on the S 247. ☎0444 27 30 81. www.penacio.it. Closed Thu lunch and Wed. Creative cuisine using local ingredients and lovely presentation. The family has presided for several generations. Warm, welcoming, elegant-rustic décor.

Bassano del Grappa ★

Bassano del Grappa has grown up on the banks of the lovely River Brenta. It's an attractive place with painted houses and squares bordered by arcades. The main square is Piazza Garibaldi while the most famous sight is an attractive 13C covered bridge. Although the town is named after the majestic mountain, Monte Grappa, which looms nearby, Bassano is a well-known centre for the production of grappa.

▸ **Population:** 43 015
⚲ **Michelin Map:** 562 E 17 – Veneto.
🛈 **Info:** Largo Corona d'Italia 35. ℘0424 52 43 51. www.bassano.eu.
◗ **Location:** On the S 47 linking Bassano del Grappa with Padova.
◗ **Train:** Bassano del Grappa (Venezia Santa Lucia 1hr 27mins).
⊛ **Don't Miss:** Views from Monte Grappa; taste of grappa.
◷ **Timing:** Half a day.

SIGHTS

Museo Civico★ – Open Tue–Sat 9am–7pm, Sun 10.30am–1pm and 3–6pm. Closed 1 Jan, Easter, 25 Dec. 5€; 7€ with other sights. ℘0424 51 99 01. www.museibassano.it. The Municipal Museum, housed in a monastery, has works by Jacopo da Ponte, aka **Jacopo Bassano** (1510–92), whose works, including **St Valentine Baptising St Lucilla**, show remarkable realism with dramatic contrasts of light.

Piazza Garibaldi – The square has the 13C **Torre di Ezzelino**, and the church of San Francesco (12C–14C) with an elegant porch (1306) and a 14C Christ by Guariento.

EXCURSIONS

Monte Grappa★★★

◗ 32km/19.9mi N (alt. 1 775m/5 823ft). The road heads up through forests and mountain pastures to the summit, from where there is a magnificent **panorama** out to Venice and Trieste.

Asolo★

◗ 14km/9mi E.
The attractive little town, dominated by its castle, is lined with frescoed palazzi. Robert Browning spent time here. Eleonora Duse, the Italian actress, is buried in the Sant'Anna cemetery.

Marostica★

◗ 7km/4.3mi W.
Piazza Castello★, the main square of this charming medieval town, serves as a giant chessboard for an unusual game of chess held in Sept every other year. www.marosticascacchi.it.

Cittadella

◗ 13km/8mi S.
A 12C Padovan stronghold with splendid city walls★.

Possagno

◗ 18km/11.2mi NW.
This is the birthplace of Neoclassical sculptor **Antonio Canova** (1757–1822). ♿Open Tue–Sun 9.30am–6pm. Closed 1 Jan, Easter, 25 Dec. 10€. ℘0423 54 43 23. www.museocanova.it.

The impressive **Tempio Canoviano**, designed by Canova, contains his tomb and last sculpture, a **Descent from the Cross★**. Open Tue–Sun 9am–noon and 3–7pm (winter 2–6pm). Ask the custodian for access to the dome. ℘0423 54 43 23, or mobile 339 6548000.

Castelfranco Veneto★

◗ 26km/16.2mi SE.
This pleasant, moated town has a splendid **Madonna and Child with Saints★★** by Giorgione (1478–1510) in the cathedral. The artist's birthplace is open to the public. Open Tue–Sun 9.30am–12.30pm, Fri–Sun also 2.30–6.30pm. 5€. ℘0423 73 56 26. www.museocasagiorgione.it.

Verona★★★

Verona stands on the banks of the Adige against a hilly backdrop. With such a rich artistic and historical heritage, it comes a close second within the region to Venice in terms of culture.

A BIT OF HISTORY

A major Roman colony in ancient times, Verona reached its peak under the Scaligers who governed for the Holy Roman Emperor (1260–1387). It then passed first to Milan and then Venice from 1405. Occupied by Austria in 1814, Verona became a part of Italy in 1866.

Artists of the Veronese school, influenced by northern art, developed a Gothic style with combined flowing lines with a meticulous detail. **Antonio Pisanello** (c.1395–c.1450), traveller, painter, medal-maker and draughtsman, was the greatest exponent. His detailed works had soft colours and flowing lines, marking the transition between medieval and Renaissance art.

●●WALKING TOUR

The route starts in Piazza Bra, the heart of the city and site of the stunning Roman amphitheatre.

Arena★★

& Open daily 8.30am–7.30pm (Mon opens 1.30pm). 6€. ℘045 800 32 04. www.turismoverona.eu.
Verona's famous pink-marble amphitheatre, still used for opera, was among the largest in Roman Italy, seating 25 000. From the top level there is a **panorama★★** of the town, surrounding hills and, on a clear day, to the Alps.

Castelvecchio and Ponte Scaligero★★

This splendid castle built by Cangrande II Scaliger (1354), is divided into two parts guarded by a keep. The castle contains the **Museo d'Arte★★**, which shows the development of Veronese art from the

- ▶ **Population:** 264 475
- **Michelin Map:** 561, 562 F 14–15. Town map in the Michelin Atlas Italy.
- **Info:** Piazza Bra. ℘045 80 68 680. www.tourism.verona.it.
- **Location:** Verona is very well situated with easy access to Venice (take the A 4) and the Brenner transalpine pass (take the A 22). Also nearby are Lake Garda and the wine-growing areas of Soave and Valpolicella.
- **Train:** Verona Porta Nuova (Venezia Santa Lucia 1hr 9 mins).
- **Don't Miss:** Castelvecchio and Ponte Scaligero, theatrical performances at Teatro Romano and Chiesa di San Zeno Maggiore.
- **Kids:** Roman amphitheatre, and the Tomb of Juliet.

12C to the 16C with canvases by Pisanello, Giambono, Carlo Crivelli, Mantegna and Carpaccio as well as the Bellinis.
On the upper floor there are also Veronese-Renaissance works and by Venetians Tintoretto, Tiepolo and Longhi. Open Mon 1.30–7.30pm, Tue–Sun 8.30am–7.30pm. 6€. ℘045 80 62 640. www.comune.verona.it.

 Take Corso Cavour. After Vicolo Calcina on the left, look out for the church of San Lorenzo, also on the left.

San Lorenzo

Open Mon–Sat 10am–6pm, Sun 1–6pm. ℘045 59 28 13.
Built (1117) on a Latin cross plan, the basilica has an unusual façade with external staircase towers leading to raised galleries. Inside, features include 13C frescoes.

 Follow Corso Cavour, home to the church of San Lorenzo, then continue to Porta dei Borsari (1C). Continue the tour along Corso Porta Borsari.

Arena

© RnDmS/iStockphoto.com

Piazza delle Erbe★★

This lively, attractive square, nowadays lined with bars and market stalls, is on the site of the Roman forum. A fountain, a Roman statue representing the town and columns, including a Venetian column topped by the winged Lion of St Mark (1523), are in the centre of the square. Attractive historic *palazzi*, some with frescoes, are here too, including the Baroque **Palazzo Maffei**.

In Via Cappello (no. 23) is **Casa di Giulietta** (Juliet's House); in reality a Gothic palace thought to have belonged to the Capulet family. The famous, much-photographed balcony is in the courtyard. Open Mon 1.30–7.30pm, Tue–Sun 8.30am–7.30pm. 6€. ℘045 80 34 303.

Piazza dei Signori★★

Go under Arco della Costa – where a huge bone, supposedly a whale rib, has hung for centuries, giving rise to legends. The elegant piazza, almost an open-air drawing room, contains imposing buildings including the 12C **Palazzo del Comune** (town hall), dominated by the **Torre dei Lamberti** tower, and **Palazzo dei Tribunali**. The **Loggia del Consiglio** on the opposite side is an

elegant Venetian-Renaissance edifice. Tower: Open daily 11am–7pm. 8€. ℘045 92 73 027. At the far end of the square, the late-13C **Palazzo del Governo** with its machicolations and fine Classical doorway (1533) by Sammicheli was initially a Scaliger residence before it became that of the Venetian governors.

Arche Scaligere★★

The Scaligers built their elegant Gothic tombs between their palace and church. They are decorated with the family coat-of-arms that includes a ladder *(scala)* and with carvings of religious scenes and statues of saints. Over the door of the Romanesque **Santa Maria Antica** church is the tomb of the popular Cangrande I (d.1329).

Chiesa di Sant'Anastasia★

Open daily Mar–Oct 9am–6pm (Sun opens 1pm); Nov–Feb 10am–1pm and 1.30–5pm (Sun opens 1pm). 2.50€; 6€ with other churches. ℘045 59 28 13. www.chieseverona.it.

Built between the 13C and the 15C, the church has a remarkable campanile and 14C double doorway with frescoes and sculpture.

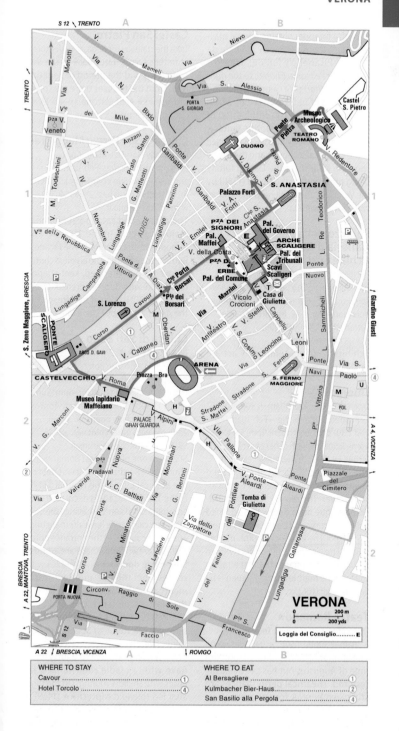

S 12 ↘ TRENTO

↙ TRENTO

Castel
S. Pietro

Museo
Archeologico

TEATRO
ROMANO

V. Redentore

PORTA
S. GIORGIO

Ponte
Pietra

DUOMO

V. Duomo

S. ANASTASIA

Palazzo Forti

PZA DEI
SIGNORI

Pal.
Maffei

Pal.
del Governo

ARCHE
SCALIGERE

Pal. dei
Tribunali

PZA D.
ERBE

Scavi
Scaligeri

Pal. del Comune

Marzini

Casa di
Giulietta

S. Lorenzo

Pta dei
Borsari

Cso Porta
Borsari

Ponte
Nuovo

↗ Giardino Giusti

PONTE
SCALIGERO

ARCO D. GAVI

ARENA

S. FERMO
MAGGIORE

CASTELVECCHIO

Piazza Bra

↗ A 4, VICENZA

Museo lapidario
Maffeiano

PALACE
GRAN GUARDIA

Pta
Pradaval

Tomba di
Giulietta

PORTA NUOVA

VERONA

| 0 | 200 m |
| 0 | 200 yds |

Loggia del Consiglio...........E

↙ BRESCIA, VICENZA   ↓ ROVIGO

WHERE TO STAY		WHERE TO EAT	
Cavour	①	Al Bersagliere	①
Hotel Torcolo	④	Kulmbacher Bier-Haus	②
		San Basilio alla Pergola	④

The lofty interior contains several masterpieces: the Apostles by Michele da Verona; Pisanello's famous **fresco**★ *(above the Pellegrini Chapel, to the right of the high altar)* of St George delivering the Princess of Trebizonda (1436), which has an almost surreal combination of realistic precision and Gothic fantasy; **17 terra-cottas**★ by Michele da Firenze in the Cappella Pellegrini; and the fresco showing Knights of the Cavalli family being presented to the Virgin (1380) by the Veronese artist Altichero *(first chapel in the south transept).*

Palazzo della Ragione – Galleria d'Arte Moderna Achille Forti

Cortile del Mercato Vecchio 6. Open Jun–Sept Tue–Sun 11am–7pm; Oct–May Tue–Fri 10am–6pm, Sat–Sun and public hols 11am–7pm. 4€, 8€ with Torre dei Lamberti. ℘045 80 01 903. www.comune.verona.it.
Exhibitions of contemporary art are held here.

Duomo★

Open daily Mar–Oct 10am–5.30pm (Sun opens 1.30pm); Nov–Feb 10am–1pm and 1.30–5pm (Sun opens 1pm; Sat closes 4pm). 2.50€; 6€ with other churches. ℘045 59 28 13. www.chieseverona.it.
The cathedral has a 12C Romanesque chancel, a Gothic nave and a Classical-style tower. The remarkable Lombard-Romanesque main doorway is adorned with sculptures and bas-reliefs by Maestro Nicolò. The interior has pink-marble pillars. The altarpiece decorated with an *Assumption* by Titian is the first altar on the left. The marble chancel screen is by Sammicheli (16C).

Teatro Romano★

Open Mon 1.30–7.30pm, Tue–Sun 8.30am–7.30pm. 4.50€. ℘045 80 00 360. The Roman Theatre dates from the time of Augustus but has been heavily restored. Theatrical performances are still given here. A former monastery, **Convento di San Girolamo** *(access by lift),* has a small **Museo Archeologico** and there is a lovely view over the town.

Castel San Pietro

Take the stairway off Regaste Redentore. St Peter's Castle dates back to the Visconti (14C) and the period of Venetian rule. From the terraces there are splendid **views**★★ of Verona (⚲ interior closed to the public).

Chiesa di San Fermo Maggiore★

Open daily Mar–Oct 10am–6pm (Sun opens 1pm); Nov–Feb 10am–1pm and 1.30–5pm (Sun opens 1pm). 2.50€; 6€ with other churches. ℘045 59 28 13. www.chieseverona.it.
The church, dedicated to St Firmanus Major, was built in the 11C–12C and remodelled at a later date. The façade is Romanesque Gothic. The aisleless church is covered by a stepped, keel-shaped roof. By the west door the Brenzoni Mausoleum (1430) is framed by a **fresco**★ of the *Annunciation* by Pisanello.

Chiesa di San Zeno Maggiore★★

Access via Largo Don Bosco. TMap of the built-up area in the Michelin Atlas Italy. Open daily Mar–Oct 8.30am–6pm (Sun opens 12.30pm); Nov–Feb 10am–1pm and 1.30–5pm (Sun opens 12.30pm). 2.50€; 6€ with other churches. ℘045 59 28 13. www.chieseverona.it.
St Zeno is one of the finest Romanesque churches in northern Italy. It was built on the basilical plan in the Lombard style in the 12C. The façade is decorated with Lombard bands and arcading; the side walls and campanile have alternate brick and stone courses. In the entrance porch resting on two lions, there are admirable bronze **doors**★★★ (11C–12C) with scenes from the Old and New Testaments. On either side are low reliefs by the master sculptors Nicolò and Guglielmo (12C). On the tympanum of the doorway is a statue of St Zeno, patron saint of Verona.
The imposing interior has a lofty, bare nave with a cradle roof flanked by aisles with shallow roofing. On the high altar is a splendid **triptych**★★ (1459), a good example of Mantegna's style characterised by precise draughtsmanship and rich ornamentation. There are 14C

statues on the chancel screen and a curious polychrome statue of St Zeno laughing in the north apse.

Tomba di Giulietta

Open Mon 1.30–7.30pm, Tue–Sun 8.30am–7.30pm. 4.50€. ℘045 80 00 361. www.tourism.verona.it.
Juliet's tomb is in the crypt of the former San Francesco al Corso monastery, where, it is said, Romeo and Juliet were married. Medieval to Renaissance frescoes are on display in the same building together with sculptures from the 19C to the present day.

ADDRESSES

🏠 STAY

It is worth noting that during trade fairs and exhibitions the hotels tend to put their prices up so it's worth checking before booking a trip. Otherwise good accommodation can be found at reasonable prices outside the city.

⊖⊖ **Cavour** – Vicolo Chiodo 4. ℘045 59 01 66. www.hotelcavourverona.it. Closed 7 Jan–12 Feb, two weeks in Nov and 1 week in Dec. 21 rooms. 🚇. The main benefit of this hotel is its quiet, central location between Castelvecchio and Piazza Bra. Simply furnished rooms.

⊖⊖ **Hotel Torcolo** – Vicolo Listone 3. ℘045 80 07 512. www.hoteltorcolo.it. Closed 2 weeks Jan. 19 rooms. 🚇14€. Simple but pleasant rooms, each decorated in a slightly different style. Wifi available.

🍽 EAT

⊖ **Al Bersagliere** – Via Dietro Pallone 1. ℘045 80 04 824. www.trattoriaal bersagliere.it. Closed Sun and Mon. A typical little trattoria, where you can eat in the cellar dining room or at tables outside.

⊖ **Kulmbacher Bier-Haus** – Via Marconi 72. ℘045 59 75 17. www.kbh.it. Closed Sat lunch. This Bavarian tavern offers generous servings of tasty food in a convivial atmosphere.

⊖⊖ **San Basilio alla Pergola** – Via Pisano 9. ℘045 52 04 75. www.trattoria sanbasilio.it. Closed Sun. With its rustic-style dining rooms and splendid wooden floors, there is a pleasant, country feel to this restaurant. Complementing the ambience is the chef's traditional but imaginative cooking.

SHOPPING

Il Pandoro – This tall melt-in-the-mouth cake topped with a snowy dusting of icing sugar is a Veronese speciality associated with Christmas.

WINE

Cantine Bertani – Via Asiago 1, Grezzana. Open Mon–Fri 8.30am–6.30pm, Sat 8am– noon. ℘045 86 58 461. www.bertani.net. Contact Bertani to arrange a tour of the lovely **Villa Novare** at the centre of historic vineyards.

Soave – This delicious crisp white wine is also made near Verona. For information on visits, tastings and lots more, contact the producers' association: ℘045 76 81 407. www.stradadelvinosoave.it.

Valpolicella and Amarone – The Valpolicella wine-making area is close to Verona. You can tour the area, visit the vineyards where the robust red is made and even stay, or at least have a meal, at some of them. For information: ℘045 686 1192, www.valpolicellatourism.it or www.stradadelvalpolicella.com.

ACTIVITIES

Horse riding, walking – The Lessinia natural park offers numerous possibilities to explore on foot, by bicycle or on horseback. For horse-riding trips: Basalovo Trekking – ℘045 90 75 41 or 347 76 52 884 (mobile). www.basalovo.it.

EVENTS AND FESTIVALS

From June to the end of August, the opera season at the Arena attracts opera, ballet, and music lovers from all over the world. Information from the **Fondazione Arena di Verona** – ℘045 800 51 51. www.arena.it. Other annual summer music festivals in Verona include the **Verona Jazz Festival** and the Concerti Scaligeri (world music).

Treviso★

Treviso, close to Venice, has a charming historic centre laced with canals. The fortunes of the two cities have been linked since the 14C.

A BIT OF HISTORY

Treviso flourished under Carolingian rule in the early Middle Ages. In 1164 Emperor Frederick I recognised the city as a free commune; Treviso extended its domain and held lively feasts, earning the name of "Joyous and harmonious March". In 1237, however, the city fell to tyrant Ezzelino da Romano and over a century of torment and civil war ensued. Treviso made a pact with Venice in 1389 and enjoyed a long period of prosperity with much building in the Venetian-Gothic style. From 1509 the city was important to Venice's defence and gained new fortifications. In 1797 Treviso and Venice fell to Napoleon, remaining under Austrian rule until freed by Italians in 1866. American bombings in 1944 caused heavy losses.

SIGHTS
Piazza dei Signori★

This central piazza has impressive monuments: Palazzo del Podestà, **Palazzo dei Trecento★** (1207) and the Renaissance Palazzo Pretorio. In Piazza del Monte di Pietà is the Chapel of the Rectors (Cappella dei Reggitori). In Piazza San Vito there are two adjoining churches, **San Vito** and **Santa Lucia**; the latter has 14C frescoes★ by Tommaso da Modena.

Chiesa di San Nicolò★

A large Romanesque-Gothic church with frescoes inside. The Onigo Chapel has portraits of local citizens by Lorenzo Lotto (16C). The *Virgin in Majesty* in the chancel is by Savoldo (16C). The adjoining **monastery** has portraits of Dominicans by Tommaso da Modena.

Musei Civici ★

Piazzetta Botter 1. Tue–Sun 9am– 12.30pm and 2.30–6pm. Closed public hols. 3€.
℘0422 65 84 42.
www.museicivicitreviso.it.

Recently moved to the Santa Caterina complex, the museum includes an archaeological section, medieval and Renaissance art and frescoes.

Duomo

The 15C–16C cathedral has seven domes, a Neoclassical façade and a Romanesque crypt with an 11C–12C baptistery nearby. The Chapel of the Annunciation has Mannerist frescoes by Pordenone and Titian's *Annunciation*.

Chiesa di San Francesco

Viale Sant'Antonio da Padova.
This transitional Romanesque-Gothic church holds the tombs of Petrarch's daughter and one of Dante's sons.

EXCURSIONS
Maser

◗ 29km/18mi NW by the S 348.
An agricultural town with a famous Palladian **villa★★★** (1560) built for Daniele Barbaro, Patriarch of Aquileia, and his brother the Venetian ambassador, Marcantonio. Inside is a splendid cycle of **frescoes★★★** by Veronese (1566–68). The villa is at the centre of a working vineyard; tastings and light lunch available and footpaths in the grounds. Also here is Palladio's **Tempietto**. Open Sat–Sun 11am–6pm (winter to 5pm), Apr–Oct also Tue–Fri 10am–6pm; Mar Tue, Thu and Sat 10.30am–6pm, Sun 11am–6pm. Times and days may vary. Closed Easter,

▸ **Population:** 82 208
✦ **Michelin Map:** 562 E–F 18. Town map in the Michelin Atlas Italy – Veneto.
▯ **Info:** Via Fiumicelli 30. ℘0422 54 76 32. www.turismo.provincia.treviso.it.
◗ **Location:** Treviso is close to Venice, linked by the S 13.
◗ **Train:** Treviso Centrale (Venezia Santa Lucia 31mins).
◉ **Don't Miss:** Chiesa di San Nicolò and the villa at Maser.
◕ **Timing:** Allow a day.

9 Dec–131Jan. 9€. ℘0423 92 30 04. www.
villadimaser.it.

Conegliano

◗ 28km/17.4mi N.

Conegliano is surrounded by vineyards
making excellent **Prosecco** white wine.
Cima da Conegliano (1459–1518), the
colourist, was born here. His **Sacra Con-
versazione★** is in the **Duomo** (open daily
7am–noon and 3.15–7pm; ℘0422 18 48
904). The **castello** houses art and archaeology and has a lovely **panorama★** of
the town (open Tue–Sun 10am–12.30pm
and 3–6.30pm (Nov–Mar 2.30–6pm);
2.50€; ℘0438 21 230). The **Scuola dei
Battuti** has 15–16C **frescoes★**.

Vittorio Veneto

◗ 41km/25.5mi N.

Named after Vittorio Emanuele II, Italy's
first king, the Italian victory over Austria
in 1918 is documented in the **Museo della**

Battaglia (open Tue–Fri 9.30am–12.30pm,
Sat–Sun 10am–1pm and 3–6pm; 5€;
℘0438 57 695; www.museobattaglia.it).
In charming Serravalle the church of
San Giovanni has interesting **frescoes★**
attributed to Jacobello del Fiore and Gentile da Fabriano (15C).

Portogruaro★

◗ 56km/34.8mi E.

This riverside town dates from the 11C.
Medieval and Renaissance Venetian-style
palazzi and porticoes flank the river. On
Corso Martiri della Libertà★★ near the
leaning Romanesque campanile, is a 14C
late Gothic **Palazzo Municipale★**. Don't
miss two 15C watermills and a 17C fishermen's chapel with its own landing stage.
In Concordia Sagittaria (3km/1.8mi S),
Museo Nazionale Concordiese has
Roman artefacts from a Roman colony
founded here in 40 BC. Open 8.30am–
7.30pm. 3€. ℘0421 72 674.

Belluno★

A pleasant town standing at the
confluence of two rivers – Piave and
Ardo – Belluno is surrounded by
mountains. An independent commune
in the Middle Ages, Belluno went to
the Venetian Republic in 1404.

●●WALKING TOUR

Walk along Via Rialto through the Porta
Dojona, across **Piazza del Mercato★**,
bordered with arcaded Renaissance
houses, along Via Mezzaterra and Via
Santa Croce to Porta Rugo. Via del Piave
has great **views★** of the Piave Valley.
Buildings on **Piazza Duomo★** include
the late-15C Venetian-style **Rectors'
Palace★** (Palazzo dei Rettori), the
Episcopal Palace (Palazzo dei Vescovi)
and the 16C **cathedral** (Duomo) with
a Baroque campanile by Juvarra. In the
crypt there is a 15C **polyptych★** by the
Rimini school. The Palazzo dei Giuristi
houses the Museo Civico. Open 9am–
12pm; Tue, Fri also 3–6pm; Closed public

▶ **Population:** 36 618
◔ **Michelin Map:** 562 D 18 –
Veneto.
🗊 **Info:** Piazza Duomo 2.
℘0437 94 00 83.
◗ **Location:** On A 27 to Venice.
◗ **Train:** Belluno (Venezia
Santa Lucia 2hr 6mins).
◉ **Don't Miss:** Feltre.
◷ **Timing:** Leave half a day.

hols, 31 Dec. 5€. ℘0437 91 32 82. http://
museo.comune.belluno.it.

EXCURSION
Feltre

◗ 31km/19.3mi SW.

Centred around a castle, Feltre has frescoed buildings in **Via Mezzaterra★** and
lovely **Piazza Maggiore★** with elegant
buildings, arcades and stairways. The
Municipal Museum has works by local
artist **Lorenzo Luzzo**. ♿Open Sat–Sun
10.30am–1pm and 2.30–7pm. 4€. ℘0439
88 52 41. http://musei.comune.feltre.bl.it.

Trieste★

Close to the Slovenian border and with historic links with Austria, Trieste is very much a Mittel-European city. The cultural mix brings a vibrancy to Trieste, which takes the best from all three heritages. While yachting is a popular pastime, the well-developed port and shipyards have always played a large role in the local economy and, thanks to stunning scenery, so does tourism.

▶ **Population:** 205 523
◔ **Michelin Map:** 562 F 23 – Friuli-Venezia Giulia.
▣ **Info:** Piazza dell'Unità d'Italia. ✆040 34 78 312. www.turismofvg.it.
◖ **Location:** Trieste stands at the head of a bay of the same name and at the foot of the Carso Plateau.
⊛ **Don't Miss:** Colle di San Giusto and the Grotta Gigante.
◷ **Timing:** Allow one day.

A BIT OF HISTORY

Ancient Trieste was fought over by the Celts and Illyrians before it became an important trading centre, *Tergeste*, under the Romans. It was fundamental in defending the eastern frontiers of the Empire. In the Middle Ages the Patriarch of Aquileia took over, then, in 1202, Venice. In 1382 Trieste rebelled and chose the protection of Austria, becoming mediator between the two powers until the 15C. In 1719 Charles VI declared it a free port. Trieste then enjoyed a new period of prosperity and was embellished by numerous fine buildings. Many political exiles sought refuge here. In 1919, after fierce fighting, Trieste united with the Kingdom of Italy. In the early 20C Trieste was an active literary centre. James Joyce lived in the town for some years until 1914.

SIGHTS

Colle di San Giusto★★

This hilltop was the site of the ancient city and in **Piazza della Cattedrale★** there are ruins of a Roman basilica, a 15C–16C castle, a 1560 Venetian column, the altar of the Third Army (1929) and the Basilica of San Giusto.

Basilica di San Giusto★

Although founded in the 5C on a Roman site, the present structure is largely 14C. The massive campanile has fragments of Roman columns built into its lowest storey. **Views★** from the top over Trieste. The **interior★** has a magnificent 12C **mosaic★★** in the north apse showing the Virgin in Majesty, Archangels Michael and Gabriel and the Apostles.

Castello di San Giusto

Open Tue–Sun 10am–7pm. 1€ (only Castle), 6€ (with museum). ✆040 30 93 62. www.castellodisangiustotrieste.it. Interesting interiors and ramparts with fabulous views.

Museo di Storia e d'Arte

Open Tue–Sun 10am–7pm (winter 6pm). Closed 1 Jan, 25 Dec. 5€. ✆040 30 86 86. www.museostoriaeartetrieste.it. The Museum of History and Art contains a remarkable collection of **Greek vases★** and charming **small bronzes★** dating from the Roman Archaic period.

Teatro Romano

The remains of a 2C Roman theatre lie at the foot of the Colle di San Giusto.

Piazza dell'Unità d'Italia★

This vast and majestic square opens onto the sea and contains the City Hall and other elegant *palazzi*.

Civico Museo del Mare★

Via Campo Marzio 5. Open daily except Wed 9am–1.30pm. 4.50€. ✆040 30 48 85. www.museodelmaretrieste.it. The history of sea-faring is traced from its beginnings to the 18C. Interesting fishing section★★.

EXCURSIONS
Santuario del Monte Grisa
▶ 10km/6.2mi N. Leave by Piazza della Libertà for Prosecco, then Villa Opicina and follow the signposts to "Monte Grisa". www.montegrisa.org.
There is a splendid **panorama**★★ of Trieste from the terrace of this mid-20C temple.

Villa Opicina
▶ 9km/5.6mi N. Funicular runs daily 7am–8pm. ℘800 01 66 75. www.tramdeopcina.it.
Take the historic funicular from Trieste up to this village on the edge of the Carso Plateau (348m/1 142ft Magnificent **views**★★ over Trieste and its bay.

Grotta Gigante★
▶ 13km/8mi N. Follow the above directions to Villa Opicina, then turn left to Borgo Grotta Gigante. Guided tours only, 1hr approx, regularly 10am–6pm (Oct–Mar 4pm). Closed Mon (except summer), 1 Jan, 25 Dec. 12€. ℘040 32 73 12. www.grottagigante.it.
This vast cave has some impressive formations.

Castello di Miramare★★
▶ 8km/5mi NW by coast road. Open daily 9am–7pm (winter to 4pm). 8€. ♿℘040 27 70 470. www.castello-miramare.it.
Standing on a headland, this striking white mid-19C castle has delightful terraced **gardens**.

ADDRESSES

🏠 STAY
🛏🍴 **Hotel Abbazia** – Via della Geppa 20. ℘040 36 94 64. www.albergoabbazia.com. 21 rooms. 🍽. Centrally located with simple but comfortable rooms. Opened in 1855.

🍴 EAT
🛏🍴 **Ai Fiori** – Piazza Hortis 7. ℘040 30 06 33. www.aifiori.com. Closed Sun lunch and Mon. Good food, particularly fish, and a wide choice of local wines.

TAKING A BREAK
Of the many historic caffès in Trieste these two are particularly atmospheric: **Caffè San Marco** (Via Cesare Battisti 18; ℘040 36 35 38) and **Caffè Tommaseo** (Riva 3 Novembre 5; ℘040 36 26 66; www.caffetommaseo.com).

Udine★

This attractive town was the seat of the Patriarchs of Aquilea (1238–1420). Udine nestles around a hill encircled by a picturesque lane, Vicolo Sottomonte, and with a castle on its summit. The centre has charming secluded squares and narrow streets, many with arcades. The town was badly damaged, like most of Friuli, by the 1976 earthquake.

▶ **Population:** 99 439
🍂 **Michelin Map:** 562 D 21. Town map in the Michelin Atlas Italy – Friuli-Venezia Giulia.
🅸 **Info:** Palazzo Morpurgo, Via Savorgnana 12 ℘0432 414 717. www.udinecultura.it.
▶ **Location:** Udine is connected to the A 4 by the A 23.
▶ **Train:** Trieste Centrale (Venezia Santa Lucia 2hr 5mins).

SIGHTS
Piazza della Libertà★★
This harmonious Renaissance piazza is home to the former town hall – the Venetian-Gothic **Loggia del Lionello** (1457), with white- and rose-coloured stonework. Opposite is the 16C **Loggia di San Giovanni**, a Renaissance portico surmounted by a 16C clock tower, with jacks (Mori) to strike the hour, similar to the ones in Venice. At the centre of the square is a 16C fountain, statues of Hercules and Cacus and the columns of Justice and St Mark.

Castello

Open Tue–Sun 10.30am–7pm (5pm Oct–Apr). 5€. ℘0432 27 15 91.

This imposing early-16C castle of the Venetian rulers, is in a panoramic position and houses the civic museums. Alongside is the 13C church of **Santa Maria del Castello**. Inside, there is a 13C fresco of the *Descent from the Cross*.

Duomo

Pass through the striking Gothic doorway of the 14C cathedral to see the attractive **Baroque decoration★**. Tiepolo painted the *trompe l'œil* frescoes in the Chapel of the Holy Sacrament. **Oratorio della Purità**, to the right of the cathedral, has a remarkable *Assumption* (1757) by Tiepolo on the ceiling. Open 7am–noon and 4–6.45 pm. Donation recommended. ℘0432 50 68 30.

Palazzo Patriarcale

Open Wed–Mon 10am–1pm and 3–6pm. 7€. ℘0432 25 003.

This historic palazzo now hosts the Museo Diocesano e Gallerie del Tiepolo with delightful **frescoes★** by Tiepolo including the *Fall of the Rebel Angels*.

Piazza Matteotti

A square with arcades and market.

EXCURSIONS

Villa Manin★★

◗ 30km/18.6mi SW, in Passariano.
&Exhibitions: hours vary; villa open Sun 10am–7pm. 12€. ℘347 25 222 (mobile). www.villamanin-eventi.it.

This majestic 17C villa was the summer residence of the Manin family, counterpart of their palazzo on the Grand Canal. Napoleon stayed here prior to the Treaty of Campoformio, which marked the end of the Venetian Republic. Hosts temporary exhibitions.

Cividale del Friuli★

◗ 16km/10mi W. www.cividale.net.
This historic town was the first duchy of the Lombards, who came from Scandinavia (6C). From the 15C onwards it belonged to Venice.

Duomo

The Duomo **Museo Cristiano** museum of Lombard art includes the octagonal baptismal font of the Patriarch Callisto and the 8C "altar" of Duke Ratchis. Open Wed–Sun 10am–1pm and 3–6pm. 4€. ℘0432 73 04 03. www.mucris.it.

Museo Archeologico Nazionale★★

&Open Mon 9am–2pm, Tue–Sun 8.30am–7.30pm. 4€. ℘0432 70 07 00. www.museoarcheologicocividale. beniculturali.it.

Housed in a 16C palazzo, attributed to Palladio. Exhibits range from a reused Roman sarcophagus to Lombard jewellery and weapons.

Tempietto Longobardo★★

Open Mon–Fri 10am–1pm and 3–6pm (Oct–Mar 2–5pm); Sat–Sun and public hols 10am–6pm (Oct–Mar 5pm). 4€ with Monastero di Santa Maria in Valle. ℘0432 70 08 67. www.tempiettolongobardo.it.

A UNESCO heritage site with magnificent 8C Lombard friezes.

ADDRESSES

🛏 STAY

🍴🍴 **Hotel Clocchiatti** – Via Cividale 29. ℘0432 50 50 47. www.hotelclocchiatti.it. 27 rooms. ☲. A choice of classic or stylish rooms, an open-air pool for guests' use in summer and use of bicycles.

🍽EAT

🍴🍴 **Al Vecchio Stallo** – Via Viola 7. ℘0432 21 296. Closed Wed. 🎫. A real find indeed: a good rustic-style eatery which has been in the same family for generations.

🍴🍴 **Alla Vedova** – Via Tavagnacco 9. ℘0432 47 02 91. www.allavedova.it. Closed Sun evening and Mon. An authentic atmosphere plus delicious flavours make this historic trattoria memorable.

SHOPPING

Dry-cured ham, San Daniele, is the speciality from San Daniele del Friuli, near Udine.

Trentino-Alto Adige/Südtirol

Major Cities: Bolzano, Trento

Official Websites: www.visittrentino.it; www.suedtirol.info

Trentino-Alto Adige/Südtirol consists of two autonomous provinces: the southern portion, Trentino, whose capital is Trento, and Alto Adige/Südtirol, also known as Südtirol, as it was once a part of the Austrian region of the same name. These cultural and geographic divisions have lasted at least since the end of the Roman Empire when the lands were ceded to invading Germanic tribes. The entire region is dominated by massifs of the Dolomite mountain range, making it a popular winter holiday destination.

Germanic–Italian Culture

This is one of five Italian regions to enjoy special autonomy. The people are partly of Germanic culture and German-speaking owing to the fact that this region was once part of Austria-Hungary until its annexation by Italy in 1919 as part of the Treaty of St Germain. Trentino-Alto Adige/Südtirol is also referred to as Trentino-Südtirol (South Tyrol), its German name.

The area includes the Adige and Isarco valleys and the surrounding mountains. The **Adige Valley**, at the southern exit from Austria of the Brenner Pass, has always been easily accessible and much used by traffic. Though deep, it opens out towards the sunny south and is very fertile. Cereals are grown on the flatter valley bottom, with vines and fruit trees on the lower slopes and pastures above. Avelengo in the vicinity of Merano is known for its breed of horses.

Highlights

1 Marvel over prehistoric Ötzi at the **Museo Archeologico dell'Alto Adige** (p482)
2 Survey the snowy serenity from a cablecar above the **Dolomites** (p487)
3 Drive the hairpin bends and enjoy the views from the **Passo di Sella** (p488)

The highly eroded limestone massif of the **Dolomites** extends across the Veneto and Trentino-Alto Adige /Südtirol. These include the Tre Cime di Lavaredo (Three Peaks), one of the Dolomites' best-known mountain groups because of its iconic crags, a challenge to mountaineers since the mid-19C.

Santa Magdalena, Alto Adige/Südtirol

© walli/iStockphoto.com

Trento★

Trent

Austrian and Italian influences meet at this agricultural and industrial centre which is located at a major intersection of routes from the Brenner Pass, Brescia and Venice.

A BIT OF HISTORY

This former Roman colony became an episcopal see in the 4C. Occupied successively by the Ostrogoths under Theodoric and by the Lombards in the 6C, it was united to the Holy Roman Empire in the late-10C.

From 1004 to 1801 the town was governed by a succession of prince-bishops. The Council of Trent (1545–63) was called here by Pope Paul III to study methods of combating Protestantism. These important deliberations led to the Counter-Reformation and to major changes in the character of the Church. The main decisions which aimed at the re-establishment of ecclesiastical credibility and authority, concerned compulsory residence for bishops and the abolition of the sale of indulgences.

After a period of Napoleonic rule in the 19C, Trento was ceded to the Austrians (1814). In 1918 the town was liberated, after a long hard struggle, by Italian troops. The Valle dei Mocehni to the east has some excellent grappa distilleries.

▶ **Population:** 115 511

⚬ **Michelin Map:** 562 D 15. Town map in the Michelin Atlas Italy – Trentino-Alto Adige /Südtirol.

▪ **Info:** Via Manci 2, 38122 Trento. ☎0461 21 60 00. www.discovertrento.it.

◖ **Location:** Trento, capital of Trentino, stands on the Adige not far from the Brenta Massif and is encircled by rocky peaks and valleys. The town lies off the A 22, the Brenner transalpine pass.

◖ **Train:** Trento (Verona Porta Nuova 59 mins).

⊛ **Don't Miss:** The Castello del Buonconsiglio. Tasting grappa at distilleries

◷ **Timing:** Allow half a day.

VISIT

PIAZZA DEL DUOMO★

Trento's cobbled main square is the setting for the cathedral, Palazzo Pretorio (13C, restored), the belfry and the 16C frescoed Rella houses.

Duomo★

Features of the Lombard-Romanesque 12C–13C cathedral include a window representing the Wheel of Fortune and,

Piazza del Duomo

© Krasnevsky/iStockphoto.com

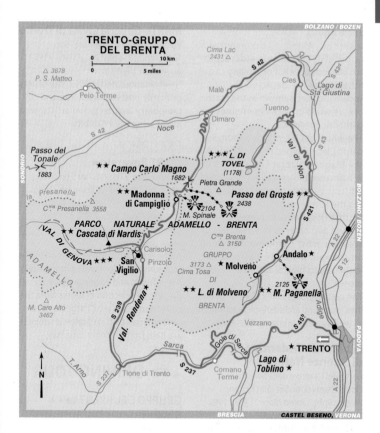

in the 17C Chapel of the Crucifix (Cappella del Crocifisso), a wooden Christ in front of which decrees of the Council of Trent were proclaimed.

The tomb of Venetian mercenary leader Sanseverino, killed in 1486, is in the south transept while beneath the chancel lie the remains of a 5C early Christian basilica, **Basilica Paleocristiana★**. Open Mon–Sat 10am–noon and 2.30–5.30pm. 1.50€; 5€ combined ticket with Museo Diocesano. ℘0461 23 44 19. www.museodiocesanotridentino.it.

Museo Diocesano★

♿ Open 9.30am–12.30pm and 2.30–6pm (winter 2–5.30pm), Sun 10am–1pm and 2–6pm (winter also Sat). Closed Tue. 5€ (includes Basilica Paleocristiana). ℘0461 23 44 19. www.museodiocesanotridentino.it. The Diocesan Museum in Palazzo Pretorio displays carved **wooden panels★**,

altarpiece★ and eight early-16C **tapestries★**, woven in Brussels by Pieter Van Aelst, from the cathedral's treasury.

Via Belenzani

This street is lined with Venetian-style palaces. The frescoed houses opposite the 16C town hall (Palazzo Comunale).

Via Manci

Venetian (loggias and frescoes) and mountain (overhanging roofs) styles intermingle along the street.

Castello del Buon Consiglio★★

Open Tue–Sun 10am–6pm (winter 9.30am–5pm). 10€. ℘0461 23 37 70. www.buonconsiglio.it. This castle was the residence of Trento's prince-bishops (13C to early-14C). Castelvecchio (Old Castle) is the oldest part of the castle and incorporates the

Torre Aquila (audioguide tours of the tower every 45 min; 2€), decorated with Gothic-style Bohemian frescoes depicting the **months★★**. For January castle inhabitants are depicted throwing snowballs; May is shown as the season of love while in December figures are gathering firewood.

The influential 16C prince-bishop, Bernardo Cles, enlarged the castle adding the Magno Palazzo. Cles was a true Renaissance prince, calling renowned artists to decorate his residence including the Ferrarese painters Dosso and Battista Dossi, who decorated the Sala Grande and other rooms. Frescoes by Brescian artist Gerolamo Romanino on the vaulting and lunettes of the **loggia** depict biblical and mythological scenes.

The castle houses collections of paintings, coins and archaeological artefacts as well as a Risorgimento Museum.

♁♁ Museo Tridentino di Scienze Naturali

Corso del Lavoro e della Scienza 3. Open 10am–6pm, Sat–Sun to 7pm, Wed to 9pm. Closed Mon, 25 Dec. 10€. ℘0461 27 03 11. www.muse.it. Interactive exhibits and activities abound at this museum which combine nature, science and play.

Palazzo Tabarelli★

This remarkable Venetian-Renaissance building features pilasters, pink-marble columns and medallions.

Chiesa di Santa Maria Maggiore

The Council of Trent met at this Renaissance church dedicated to St Mary Major. There's a Romanesque campanile, an elegant marble organ loft (1534) in the chancel by Vincenzo and Girolamo Grandi and a 16C altarpiece of the *Madonna and Saints* by Moroni.

Chiesa di Sant'Apollinare

A Romanesque church on the west bank of the Adige with a pointed roof covering two Gothic domed vaults.

MART – Galleria Civica di Trento

Via Belenzani 44. Open Tue–Sun 10am–1pm, 2–6pm. 2€. ℘0461 9855 11. www.mart.trento.it.

Newly inaugurated in 2013, the gallery primarily hosts works of 20C and contemporary architects and artists, with major temporary exhibits.

EXCURSION

MART Rovereto★

◗ Rovereto, 22km/13.7mi S on the A22. Corso Bettini 43, Rovereto. Open Tue–Thu and Sat–Sun 10am–6pm, Fri 10am–9pm. 11€. ℘800 39 77 60 (freephone within Italy). www.mart.trento.it.

Architect Mario Botta's extension to the Museum of Modern and Contemporary Art of Trento and Rovereto (&see above) presents a selection of works from the collections each year. Large-scale temporary shows featuring original subjects are held from December to May.

🚗 DRIVING TOUR

GRUPPO DEL BRENTA★★★

Round trip starting from Trento. 233km/145mi. Allow 2 days.

The striking Brenta Massif prolongs the Dolomites beyond the Adige Valley. Its characteristic features are deep valleys, lakes and eroded rocks.

Lago di Tovel

©canebisca/Fotolia.com

The map (☞see p479) locates the places described as well as other beauty spots, in small black type.

▶ Take the S 45b in the direction of Vezzano.

Lago di Toblino★

www.parks.it/biotopo.lago.toblino.
A charming rush-fringed lake overlooked by an attractive castle, once inhabited by the Bishops of Trent.

Val Rendena★

www.campigliodolomiti.it.
This fir-clad valley is dotted with charming villages and fresco-covered churches such as the remarkable *Dance of Death* (1539) on **San Vigilio** church near Pinzolo.

Val di Genova★★★

www.valgenova.com.
The road and footpaths which crisscross the river in this stunningly beautiful valley lead to a spectacular 100m/330ft waterfall, **Cascata di Nardis★★**.

Madonna di Campiglio★★

A resort popular for lovers of sport and relaxation. A wide range of walking trails start here.

Campo Carlo Magno★★

Named after Charlemagne, this place draws sports enthusiasts thanks to golf in summer and cross-country skiing in winter. From **Passo del Grosté★★** – *cablecar and then on foot* – there is a fine **panorama★★** of the Brenta Massif. *Cablecar:* ℘0465 44 77 44. www.funivie campiglio.it.

▶ Continue to Dimaro and Malè and at Cles turn right towards Tuenno.

Lago di Tovel★★★

www.pnab.it.
Located in a lovely woodland setting, this lake used to turn bright red in summer due to microscopic algae.

Andalo★

A small holiday resort in a majestic location near the Brenta Massif. From the summit of **Monte Paganella** *(cablecar)* at 2 125m/6 972ft there is a splendid **panorama★★** of the whole region, and as far as Lake Garda on clear days. Access for cableway or chairlift from mid-Jun to mid-Sept and from Dec to Apr. Access also possible from Fai della Paganella by chairlift. ℘0461 58 55 88. www.paganella.net.

Molveno★

This resort overlooks a **lake★★** that's famous for its transparent waters.

ADDRESSES

☜ STAY

⊖⊗ **Hotel America** – Via Torre Verde 52, Trento. ℘0461 98 30 10. www.hotel america.it. 67 rooms. ☕. A modern, centrally located hotel. Some rooms offer views over the town, Castello del Buonconsiglio and the mountains.

♈/ EAT

⊖ **Antica Trattoria Due Mori** – Via San Marco 11, Trento. ℘0461 98 42 51. www.ristoranteduemori.com. Closed Mon. Near the castle, this restaurant has vaulted ceilings and a menu based on seasonal local dishes.

⊖⊖ **Osteria a Le Due Spade** – Via Don Rizzi 11, Trento ℘0461 23 43 43. www. leduespade.com. Closed Mon lunch and Sun. Reservation recommended. A meal at this Michelin-starred restaurant, which dates from the 16C, is a culinary experience. Regional dishes with an innovative flair.

ACTIVITIES

Grappa distilleries – Fine grappa, a pomace brandy, is produced near Trento: Marzadro, Bertagnoll and Pisoni, among others, offer interesting tours.

Bike trips – The province of Trento has abundant hiking paths and mountainbike trails. Routes at Monte Baldo and in the Val Lagarina mountains can be accessed more easily by cablecar.

Bolzano★

Bozen

Nestling in a valley covered with orchards and vineyards, the industrial and commercial town of Bolzano is now also a busy tourist centre. The architecture of the town shows a marked Austrian influence, which was exercised between the 16C and 1918. At the centre of the town are Piazza Walther and the delightful Via dei Portici★.

SIGHTS

Duomo★

Construction work on the pink-sandstone cathedral was carried out in the 5C–13C. On the north side is the "Small Wine Portal" (Porticina del Vino) on which all the decorative features have a connection with grape harvesting. It indicates the privilege enjoyed by this church to sell wine at this doorway. Inside, there is a fine late Gothic sandstone **pulpit★** (1514).

Piazza Walther, Bolzano

©Richard Banary/Dreamstime.com

- ▶ **Population:** 103 135
- 🚲 **Michelin Map:** 562 C 15–16.
- ℹ **Info:** Piazza Walther 8, 39100 Bolzano. ℘0471 30 70 00. www.bolzano-bozen.it.
- ▷ **Location:** Capital of the Alto Adige, Bolzano lies on the A 22, the Brenner transalpine route, at the confluence of the Adige and the Isarco.
- ▷ **Train:** Bolzano (Verona Porta Nuova 1hr 34mins).
- ✦ **Don't Miss:** The Renon Plateau.
- ⏱ **Timing:** Allow a day, with half a day for the plateau.
- 👫 **Kids:** "Ötzi" at the museum.

Museo Archeologico dell'Alto Adige, "Il Museo di Ötzi"★

&. Open 10am–6pm (last entry 5.30pm). Closed 1 Jan, 1 May, 25 Dec. 9€. To avoid a long wait, book in advance. ℘0471 32 01 00. www.iceman.it. This museum illustrates the chronology of the Alto-Adige region from the last Ice Age (15000 BC) to the Carolingian Age (AD 800) and houses the "Iceman", known as "Ötzi", whose ice-preserved remains were found by German mountain climbers in the Ötzi Alps, in 1991. Ötzi lived in the Copper Age and is 5 300 years old. A study in 2001 concluded that his death at about 45 years old was due to an arrow wound.

Chiesa dei Francescani

Via Francescani 1. Open Mon–Sat 10am–noon and 2.30–6pm, Sun and public hols 3–6pm. Donations welcome. ℘0471 97 72 93. ✦ *The Nativity altar.*
Burned down in 1291, the Franciscan church was rebuilt in the 14C and the Gothic vaulting added in the 15C. The **Nativity altar★** is a remarkable wooden altarpiece carved by Hans Klocker (16C).

Vecchia Parrocchiale di Gries

Via Martin Knoller. Open Apr–Oct 10.30am–noon and 2.30–4pm, summer open only morning, ℘0471 28 30 89.

The original Romanesque building was replaced by a 15C Gothic parish church containing a side altar with an **altarpiece★** carved by Michael Pacher (1430–98), an Austrian sculptor, depicting the Crowning of the Virgin between Archangel Gabriel, about to strike the devil, and St Erasmus, holding a winch with which to tear out his guts.

EXCURSION
The Renon Plateau (Ritten)★
The Renon (*Ritten* in German) is the dazzlingly green fertile plateau that dominates the Isarco Valley (Eisacktal) between Bolzano and Ponte Gardena. It can be reached by car from Bolzano north or the funicular at Soprabolzano in Bolzano. Romantics may prefer to take the electric train from Maria Assunta (Maria Himmelfahrt) to Collalbo (Klobenstein). The Renon overlooks the Dolomites, best seen from the funicular to Corno del Renon. Parking is available at the bottom of the funicular. The plateau is full of charming villages and curious erosion caused by a natural phenomenon called "earth pillars" at Soprabolzano, Monte di Mezzo and Auna di Sotto.

ADDRESSES

🛏 STAY
☞ **Albergo Belvedere-Schönblick** – Pichl 15, 39050 San Genesio. ℘0471 35 41 27. Fax 0471 35 42 77. www.schoenblick-belvedere.com. 28 rooms. 🚐. A short drive from Bolzano, this hotel has fine views over the city. An oasis of calm with cheerful, Tyrolean-style interior decor. High standard of cooking; local fare.

🍽 EAT
☞☞ **Vögele** – Via Goethe 3. ℘0471 97 39 38. www.voegele.it. A historic rustic-style eatery, situated near Piazza delle Erbe. Warm and friendly atmosphere, and traditional regional cooking. Downstairs wooden tables, no tablecloths, with smarter, more stylish dining facilities on the first floor.

Merano★★

Meran

Merano is an important tourist centre and spa, whose thermal waters attract people seeking relief from respiratory problems, rheumatism and other conditions. Other attractions include the Gran Premio Ippico, the most famous steeplechase race in Italy. Cablecars and chairlifts rise up to Merano 2000, a winter-sports centre, also popular for summer excursions into the mountains.

SIGHTS
Passeggiate d'Inverno and d'Estate★★
These winter and summer promenades run along the Passirio River.

▶ **Population:** 37 673
⚲ **Michelin Map:** 562 B–C 15 – Trentino-Alto Adige/Südtirol.
🛈 **Info:** Corso della Libertà 45. ℘0473 27 20 00. www.meran.eu.
◗ **Location:** Merano lies at the start of the upper valley of the Adige, the Val Venosta. There is a motorway link with Bolzano.
👁 **Don't Miss:** Views from Passeggiata Tappeiner and a drive through the pretty Val Venosta.
🕐 **Timing:** Allow a day, and enjoy views and promenades along the Passeggiate d'Inverno and d'Estate at sunset.

The winter one, facing south, is lined with shops, caffès and terraces and is by far the busier. It is prolonged by the Passeggiata Gilf, which ends near a waterfall.

The summer promenade, on the opposite bank, meanders through a park planted with pines.

Passeggiata Tappeiner★★

This promenade (4km/2.5mi long) winds above Merano with views to the Tyrol.

Duomo di San Nicolò

This Gothic cathedral has a huge belfry and a west front with a crenellated gable. The interior, roofed with beautiful ribbed **Gothic vaulting★**, includes two 15C stained-glass windows and two painted wooden **Gothic polyptychs★**(16C) by Knoller, a native of the Tyrol.

In the neighbouring **Cappella di Santa Barbara** standing at the start of the old footpath leading to Tirolo is a 16C high relief of the Last Supper.

Via Portici (Laubengasse)★

This street is overlooked by houses with painted façades and oriel windows.

Castello Principesco★

& Open Apr–Dec Tue–Sat 10.30am–5pm, Sun 10.30am–1pm. Closed 25 Dec. 5€. ✆329 01 86 390 (mobile). www.comune.merano.bz.it.
This 15C castle was used by the Princes of Tyrol when they stayed in the town.

EXCURSIONS

Avelengo★

▶ 10km/6.2mi SE.
A scenic road leads to the Avelengo Plateau, dominating the Merano Valley.

Merano 2000✳

Access by cablecar. Open daily, hours vary. ✆0473 23 48 21. www.meran2000.net.
This plateau is a winter-sports centre. It also makes a good base for excursions into the mountains in summer.

Tirolo★

▶ 4km/2.5mi N. It can also be reached by chairlift from Merano.
This charming Tyrolean village is dominated by **Castel Tirolo**, built in the 12C by the Counts of Val Venosta. Open Tue–Sun 10am–5pm. Times may vary. 7€. ✆0473 22 02 21. www.schlosstirol.it.
Castel Fontana (also known as the **Brunnenburg**) is a strange set of 13C fortifications rebuilt at a later date. The American poet Ezra Pound worked on his *Cantos* here from 1958, when the accusation of Nazi collaboration, based on his radio programmes, was lifted.

VAL PASSIRIA★

▶ 50km/31mi to the Rombo Pass; 40km/24.8mi to the Monte Giovo Pass.
The road follows the Passiria Valley as far as the Tyrolean village of **San Leonard**. The steep **Rombo Pass Road★** (Timmelsjoch) offers impressive views of the mountain peaks on the frontier. The **Monte Giovo Pass Road★** (Jaufenpass) climbs amid conifers. On the way down, there are splendid **views★★** of the snow-capped summits of Austria.

VAL VENOSTA★

▶ From Merano, take the S 38 in the direction of Resia.
Covered in orchards, Venosta Valley is a long, sunny valley which gradually widens as it climbs towards the Resia Pass. It begins at Merano, just after the Birreria Forst. It is bordered by the Valtellina at the **Stelvio Pass**, Switzerland at the Tubre Mountain Pass and Austria at the Resia Pass.

Val Venosta's most famous inhabitant, Ötzi, lived 5 300 years ago and his body was preserved by the ice in the spot where he died, in Val Senales. *(Ötzi is now in the Archaeological Museum of Bolzano. &See BOLZANO.)*

Naturno

From Merano take the road towards Resia Pass for 15km/9.3mi. The road leads to Naturno at the crossroads of the Val Venosta and the Val Senales. This "junction" is dominated by the

13C **Juval Castle**, now owned by the mountain climber Reinhold Messner. Open late Mar–Jun and Sept–Oct Thu–Tue. Guided tours. 9€. ☏0471 63 12 64. www.messner-mountain-museum.it.
Before entering the town, the slightly hidden church of **San Procolo★**, surrounded by fruit orchards, can be seen. The structure houses the oldest frescoes in the German-speaking part of the Alto Adige (8C). The most notable fresco is the *Saint on a Swing*, thought to portray Procolo, the Bishop of Verona who fled the city. &.Open Tue–Sun 5 Apr–14 Oct 9.30am–noon and 2.30–5.30pm; 15 Oct–4 Nov 9.30am–noon and 2–5pm. Donations welcome. ☏0473 66 73 12 or 348 920 38 29. www.prokulus.org.

Sluderno

Sluderno's 13C **Coira Castle** has a renowned armoury. Open 20 Mar–Oct Tue–Sun 10am–noon and 2–4.30pm. Guided tours. 10€. ☏0473 61 52 41. www.churburg.com.

Glorenza

This old city counts fewer than 1 000 inhabitants. Glorenza was already documented in 1178 and is well worth a visit as it is the only fortified town in the Alto Adige where time has stood still.
Entirely surrounded by ramparts, it has the only arcading in the whole valley.

The parish church, situated outside the city walls, has a frescoed exterior (1496) depicting The Last Judgement.

Malles

Malles is home to a jewel of Romanesque architecture, the 9C **Church of San Benedetto★**. Note the frescoes that depict a Frankish nobleman holding a sword and an ecclesiastic holding a model of the church. For opening times call ☏0473 83 11 90. www.venosta.net.

Burgusio

Those en route to the Resia Pass cannot miss the huge white abbey of **Montemaria**. Even when it is snowing the sloping roof and the bulbous towers of the campanile are still visible.
The 12C Romanesque frescoes based on the Apocalypse, in the **crypt** *(accessible for prayer only)*, are a theme of the **Abbey Museum**. Open Mon–Sat 10am–5pm (winter hours vary). Closed public hols and Nov–mid-Mar (except 27 Dec–5 Jan). 5€. ☏0473 84 39 80. www.marienberg.it.

Lago di Resia

A bell tower mysteriously appears out of the waters of the lake: originally part of the church of Curono Vecchia, it was submerged by the waters of this artificial basin in 1950.

©yjm83/Fotolia.com

Lago di Resia

Vipiteno

Sterzing

Only 15km/9.3mi from the Austrian border, Vipiteno is a pretty town set around a single street lined with typical Tyrolean houses *(Erker)* and arcading. The first settlement here was in the Bronze Age; in Roman times it became Vipitenum and in 1180 the town was documented as Stercengum (from which Sterzing derives). Vipiteno flourished in the 15C–16C thanks to silver and lead mines in nearby valleys.

▶ **Population:** 6 306
⟐ **Michelin Map:** 562 B 16 – Trentino-Alto Adige/Südtirol.
▤ **Info:** Piazza Città 3. ☎0472 76 53 25. www.sterzing.net.
◗ **Location:** Vipiteno is the last exit of the A 22 before the Brenner pass.
◖ **Train:** Vipiteno/ Sterzing (Verona Porta Nuova: 2hr 46mins).
◉ **Don't Miss:** Cascate.
◷ **Timing:** Allow a couple of hours for the town, and a day for excursions.

WALKING ABOUT

The 15C tower, Torre dei Dodici, divides the street, the more picturesque **Città Nuova★** (New City) street lying to the south and the **Città Vecchia** (Old City) street to the north. The 16C town hall is on Via Città Nuova while the church of the Holy Spirit (Chiesa dello Spirito Santo), richly decorated with 15C frescoes, is in the square where the two streets converge.

EXCURSIONS

Cascate di Stanghe

◗ Road to Racines; follow Stanghe signs. Open daily May–Oct 9.30am–5.30pm (Jul–Aug 9am–6pm). 3.50€. ☎0472 76 06 08. www.ratschings.info.
This waterfall descends a narrow gorge. Passageways and small wooden bridges help walkers on the winding paths. The pleasant walk through the ravine and wood near the town can be done uphill or downhill. You can also descend via the waterfall leaving the car at the top where there is a cafeteria and a small chapel, and return via panoramic footpath no. 13. Both routes take about one hour up and 45 minutes down.

♟♟ Il Mondo delle Miniere★

◗15km/9.3mi W towards Ridanna on the SP 36. ♿ Open Tue–Sun 9.30am–4.30pm (Aug open daily). 10–35€. Reservation required. ☎0472 65 63 64. www.bergbaumuseum.it.

The **mines of Schneeberg** stand at an altitude of 2 000m–2 650m/6 560ft–8 700ft (guided tours ♿1.5hrs to 10hrs, including several hours underground). Silver, lead and zinc extraction began here in the 16C, with 1 000 miners working in 70 galleries. When the mine closed in 1985 there were 1 000 galleries.

Montecavallo

Along the Brennero road, just after Via Città Vecchia, there is a cablecar to Montecavallo (2 000m/6 560ft). On arrival there is a wide choice of footpaths and walks.

Vipiteno– typical of the colourful villages in the Valle Isarco

© E. Zane/MICHELIN

The Dolomites★★★

Dolomiti

Situated between the Veneto and Trentino-Alto Adige/Südtirol, the fan of so-called "Pale Mountains" *(Monti Pallidi)* take on red tints at sunset. Their harsh, rocky contours embrace crystalline lakes and mysteries, which have become the very stuff of numerous poetic legends. The Dolomites are Italy's winter playground and include the Dolomiti Superski, a network of 1 200km/3 937mi of ski slopes and more than 400 lift facilities. But with an average of 300 days of sunshine and some mountains reaching an altitude over 3 000m/9 840ft, it is possible to enjoy the slopes year-round. Val Gardena is a popular tourist centre and the village of Cortina d'Ampezzo, for years a favourite winter destination for the jet set, is one of the premier ski resorts in Europe.

A BIT OF HISTORY

The Dolomites are made of a white calcareous rock, dolomite, which takes its name from the French geologist Déodat de Dolomieu, who studied its composition in the 18C. Some 150 million years ago this land was submerged by the Tethys Sea. On its sandy depths coral reefs and limestone began to shape the "Pale Mountains".

About 70 million years ago, during the alpine orogenis (the corrugation of the Earth's crust), the layers were violently compressed and forced to the surface. The Dolomites were nearly completed in the Quaternary Era (about 2 million years ago) when glaciers softened and hollowed out the valleys.

The massifs – To the southeast rise the Pelmo (3 168m/10 393ft) and the Civetta (3 220m/10 564ft) massifs.

To the south, near the peak of the Vezzana, the Pale di San Martino, streaked by fissures, divide into three chains separated by a plateau. The Latemar (2 842m/9 324ft) and the Catinaccio

- **Michelin Map:** 562 C 16–19 – Veneto –Trentino-Alto Adige/Südtirol.
- **Info:** Ufficio Turistico di Belluno, Piazza Duomo 2, 32100 Belluno. ℘334 28 13 222. www.infodolomiti.it. Associazione Turistica Corvara, Strada Col Alt 36, 39033 Corvara. ℘0471 83 61 76. www.altabadia.org. Associazione Turistica Santa Cristina, Strada Chemun 9, 39047 Santa Cristina. ℘0471 77 78 00. www.valgardena.it. Val d'Ega Turismo, Via Dolomiti 4, 39056 Nova Levante. ℘0471 61 95 00. www.eggental.com. Associazione Turistica Alpe di Siusi, Compatsch 50, 39040 Alpe di Siusi. ℘0471 72 79 04. www.alpe-di-siusi.info.
- **Location:** The Dolomites are reached by the A 22 off the Brennero transalpine route. From the Veneto region take the A 27.
- **Parking:** Leave your car in the car park north of Chiusa if visiting the Convento di Sabiona.
- **Don't Miss:** Val Gardena and panoramas from Tofana di Mezzo.
  Time: Allow for three– four days of skiing or walking.
- **Kids:** Vigo di Fassa, and the funicular railway at Sesto.

(2 981m/9 780ft) massifs, together with the Torri del Vaiolet (Towers of Vaiolet), frame the Costalunga Pass. To the north of the pass rise the Sasso Lungo and the vast Sella Massif (Gruppo di Sella).

To the east, the chief summits in the Cortina Dolomites are the Tofane, the

Sorapiss and the Cristallo. Finally, in the heart of the range, stands the **Marmolada Massif** (Gruppo della Marmolada, 3 342m/10 964ft).

Between Cortina and the Piave Valley the wooded region of **Cadore** boasts the Antelao (3 263m/10 705ft) and the triple peak, Tre Cime di Lavaredo (Drei Zinnen), which it shares with the Parco delle Dolomiti di Sesto in Alto Adige.

Flora and fauna – The Dolomite landscape is coloured by coniferous forests, crocuses, edelweiss, rhododendrons, lilies and alpine bluebells.

Tourist activity drives away wild animals, but the Dolomites are still a refuge for many, including royal eagles and woodcock.

🚗 DRIVING TOURS

1 STRADA DELLE DOLOMITI★★★

Bolzano to Cortina. 210km/131mi. 2 days.

The great Dolomite Road, a world-famous example of road engineering.

Bolzano★
See BOLZANO.

Gola della Val d'Ega★
This narrow gorge, the Ega Valley, with pink-sandstone walls, is guarded by the **Castel Cornedo.**

Nova Levante★
This village with its onion-domed bell tower lies along a mountain river and is dominated by the Catinaccio (Rosengarten) Mountains.

Lago di Carezza★
This minuscule lake set in a dark sea of conifer woods is dominated in the background by the Latemar and Catinaccio mountains.

Passo di Costalunga★
From this pass on the Dolomite Road there is a **view★** over the Catinaccio on one side and the Latemar on the other.

👥 Vigo di Fassa★
Ski school and kinderpark for children. Piazza J.B. Massar 1, 38039 Vigo di Fassa. ℘0462 76 31 25.
Strada Rezia 10, 38039 Vigo di Fassa. ℘0462 60 97 00. www.fassa.com.
This resort, in a picturesque **site★** in the Val di Fassa, is a mountaineering centre in the Catinaccio Massif (cablecar).

Canazei★★
Piazza Marconi 5, 38032 Canazei. ℘0462 60 96 00. www.fassa.com.
Canazei lies in the heart of the massif, between the Catinaccio, the Towers of Vaiolet (Torri del Vaiolet), the Sella Massif and the Marmolada. This is the usual base for excursions in the Marmolada range.

▶ At Canazei turn right onto the S 641

This road affords very fine **views★★** of the Marmolada range and its glacier. As one comes out of a long tunnel a lake, **Lago di Fedaia★**, suddenly appears.

Marmolada★★★
www.marmolada.com.
This is the highest massif in the Dolomites, famous for its glacier and very fast ski runs. The **cablecar** from Malga Ciapela goes up to 3 265m/10 712ft offering admirable **panoramas★★★** of the Cortina peaks (Tofana and Cristallo), the Sasso Lungo, the enormous tabular mass of the Sella Massif and in the background the summits of the Austrian Alps including the Grossglockner.

▶ Return towards Canazei and turn left after 5.5km/3.4mi.

Passo di Sella★★★
Linking the Val di Fassa and Val Gardena this pass offers one of the most extensive **panoramas★★★** in the Dolomites, including the Sella, Sasso Lungo and Marmolada massifs.

Selva di Val Gardena

Val Gardena★★★

www.val-gardena.com.
One of the most famous valleys in the Dolomites for both its beauty and crowds of tourists. The inhabitants still speak a language which was born during the Roman occupation: the Ladin dialect.
Skilful local woodwork can be seen in shops in Selva (Wolkenstein), Santa Cristina and Ortisei (St Ulrich).
Selva di Val Gardena★★ – www.valgardena.it. This resort lies at the Sella Massif base and is a craft centre.
Ortisei★★ – www.valgardena.it. From Ortisei a cablecar climbs up to **Alpe di Siusi** (Seiser Alm), a 60sq km/23sq mi plateau in a delightful **setting★★** overlooking the Sasso Lungo and the Sciliar. This base for excursions suits all tastes and abilities.

Passo Pordoi★★★

The highest pass (2 239m/7 346ft) on the Dolomite Road lies between huge blocks of rock with sheer sides and tops.

Passo di Falzarego

Nearing Cortina the pass cuts through the Tofane and skirts the barren landscape of the Cinque Torri, which inspired Tolkien.

Cortina d'Ampezzo★★★

www.cortina.dolomiti.com.
Cortina, the capital of the Dolomites, is a winter-sports and summer resort with a worldwide reputation. It was the site of the 1956 Winter Olympic Games and served as a stunning backdrop for several films, including the James Bond thriller *For Your Eyes Only*.

The Legend of the Pale Mountains

Legend has it that a prince who lived at the foot of the Alps married the daughter of the King of the Moon. The young girl loved flowers and meadows but was disturbed by the dark colour of the rocks. She so desperately missed the pale mountains of her home that she felt compelled to return to the moon. Some dwarfs came to the disconsolate prince's aid and made some skeins of thread from the moon's rays, weaving them into nets which they placed on the mountains. The princess was thus able to return and the dwarfs were allowed to live in the kingdom.

At sunset, however, the **Monti Pallidi** were lit up by the fiery hues of the sun reflecting on the King of the Dwarfs' beautiful rose garden. One day, attracted by the rose garden, some foreign warriors arrived in the kingdom and imprisoned the king, who cursed the plant and ordered that the roses would never be seen again, by day or night. The curse did not, however, mention sunset, a moment suspended between day and night. Thus for those few minutes the **Catinaccio Mountain**, which the Germans refer to as **Rosengarten** (rose garden), is still inflamed and throws light onto every rock causing a stunning spectacle each evening.

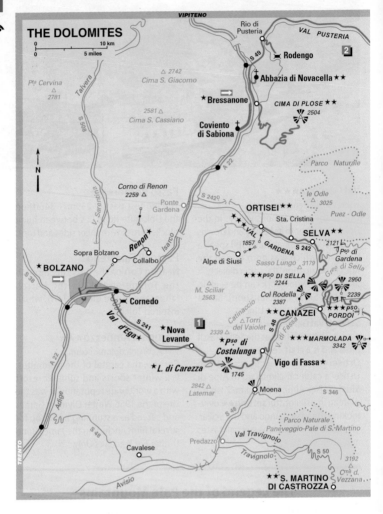

THE DOLOMITES

Set in the heart of the Dolomites at an altitude of 1 210m/3 970ft Cortina makes a good excursion centre for discovering the magnificent **mountain scenery★★★**.

Tondi di Faloria★★★

🚡Cablecar service to Monte Faloria from Via Ria de Zeto, Cortina d'Ampezzo and $chairlifts in summer and winter. ✆0436 25 17. www.cortinacube.com. From the summit a grand panorama may be enjoyed. Excellent ski slopes.

Tofana di Forcella Staunies – *Cablecar. You will need a vehicle from Cortina.* The cablecar takes you up to 2 930m/

9 613ft, where the refuge stands on a particularly spectacular site, with 360° views.

Tofana di Mezzo★★★ – *"Freccia del Cielo" cablecar* ✆0436 50 52. www. freccianelcielo.com. A cablecar climbs to 3 244m/10 643ft, for a superb panorama.

Belvedere Pocol★★ – *Regular bus service from Piazza Roma, Cortina.* For bus information call ✆0436 86 79 21. www. cortina.dolomiti.org. Lying to the south-west, this viewpoint affords a lovely sunset view of Cortina.

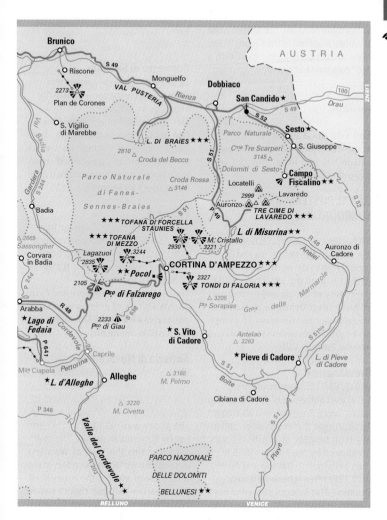

1 SOUTH OF CORTINA

Around 190km/118mi. Allow 1 day.

Valle del Cordevole★★
The road from Caprile to Belluno is lined with hilltop villages. **Alleghe** on the **lake★** is a good excursion centre.

San Martino di Castrozza★★
A good starting point for excursions, San Martino di Castrozza is a resort town with 45km/28mi of ski runs and, at the edge of the village on Pra' delle Nasse, three cross-country loop trails.

Pieve di Cadore★
The birthplace of the artist **Titian**, the town church holds one of his works and his family house is now a **museum**. Open by appointment only. Closed hols. 3€. ☎0435 32 262. www.magnifica comunitadicadore.it.

Cibiana di Cadore
Between Pieve di Cadore and Cortina, the road to Cibiana continues to the pass of the same name (6km/3.7mi from the main road). From there, the path to the summit will take 1.5 hours on foot *(shuttle service in summertime)*. There, you will find a small museum dedicated

to Reinhold Messner, the **Museo nelle Nuvole** ("Museum in the Clouds"). The main attraction is its location with a 360° panorama of the Alps. Open Jun–Sept 10am–1pm and 2–5pm (6pm Jul and Aug). 7€. ℘0435 89 09 96. www.messner-mountain-museum.it.

San Vito di Cadore★

At the foot of Monte Antelao, this pretty village has two little churches with steep shingle roofs.

② VAL PUSTERIA AND SURROUNDING AREA

Val Pusteria, or Pustertal, is bordered to the south by the Dolomites and by the central Alps to the north. From the end of the 13C until the 16C it belonged to the county of Gorizia and formed part of the Strada d'Alemagna, a road which linked Venice and Germany. This itinerary begins in Bressanone and continues into the Pusteria Valley.

Bressanone★

℘0472 83 64 01. www.brixen.org.
Set at the confluence of the Rienza and Isarco rivers, Bressanone is an elegant Tyrolean town that enjoys an exceptionally high number of sunshine hours. Conquered by the Romans in 15 BC, it then belonged to Bavaria and Austria, until 1919 when it became Italian.
Duomo – This Baroque cathedral has a Neoclassical west front, luminous interior decorated with gold leaf frescoes and Romanesque **cloisters★**.
Palazzo Vescovile – Commissioned by Prince-Bishop Bruno de Kirchberg after 1250, the palace underwent numerous alterations but retained its superb **courtyard★**. It now houses the vast **Museo Diocesano★** containing a wonderful set of polychrome **woodcarvings★★** (Romanesque and Gothic-Tyrolean), **altarpieces★** carved in the round dating from the Renaissance, the cathedral **treasure★** and **Nativity scenes★** dating from the 18C to the 20C. Open mid-Mar–Oct Tue–Sun 10am–5pm, end Nov–8 Jan daily 10am–5pm. 7€ combined ticket; in winter, only

Nativity Scenes, 4€. ℘0472 83 05 05. www.hofburg.it.

Convento di Sabiona

🅿 Leave the car in the car park N of Chiusa. To get to the convent from the village, go on foot (30min).
This convent, still inhabited by Benedictine nuns, is also known as the "Tyrolean Acropolis". It was built on the rock where the bishop's palace had stood, the palace having burned down after being struck by lightning in 1535.

Plose★★

SE. Alt. 2 446m/8 025ft. Cablecar: from Sant'Andrea, SE of Bressanone, cablecar to Valcroce (winter and Jul–Sept), then chairlift to Plose (winter only). 🚩℘0472 20 04 33. www.plose.org
The cablecars from Valcroce and Plose enable visitors to enjoy a wonderful **panorama★★★** of the Dolomites and the Austrian mountains.

Abbazia di Novacella★★

◗ 3km/1.8mi N. Guided tours Mon–Sat 10am, 11am, 2pm, 3pm, 4pm; other times by arrangement. Closed Mon in winter. 7€. ℘0472 83 61 89. www.abbazianovacella.it.
The abbey was founded in 1142 and run by Augustinian monks. The courtyard contains the **Well of Wonders** decorated with "eight" wonders of the world, one of which is the abbey itself. The Bavarian-Baroque **church** has an ornate interior and **Rococo** library of 76 000 rare books and manuscripts.
The first village encountered when arriving on the state road is Rio di Pusteria. Close by stands the **Castello di Rodengo**, decorated with the oldest cycle of Romanesque frescoes (13C) with a profane theme: the epic poem *Iwein* by Hartmann von Aue. Guided tours (1hr) Sun–Fri Jun–Nov 11.30am and 2.30pm (summer also 3.30pm). For more info call ℘0472 45 40 56. www.suedtirolerland.it.

Brunico

This is the main town in the Pusteria Valley. The interesting **Museum of Folk Traditions ★** (♿open Tue–Sat

The Ladin and Mòcheno Cultures

Ladin is a curious ancient language which has its roots in the Latin language and is spoken by around 30 000 people in and around the Dolomites. It had emerged by the 5C as a direct result of the earlier Roman expansion into the mountainous regions. At Ciastel de Tor, in San Martino in Badia, there is the Museumladina, which has an impressive exhibition on the Ladin culture. Open May–Oct, 10am–5pm, Sun 2–6pm, closed Mon ecxept Jul–Aug; rest of the year Thu–Sat 3–7pm only. Apr by reservation. Closed Nov, 1–25 Dec. 8€. ☎0474 52 40 20. www.museumladin.it. **Near Trento** in the **Valle dei Mòcheni** with its grappa distilleries, some 1,600 residents speak a Bavarian German that dates to the 13C.

10am–5pm (Jul–Aug 6pm),Sun and public hols 2–6pm (Aug also Mon); closed Nov–Easter; 7€; ☎0474 55 20 87; www.museo-etnografico.it) in **Teodone** covers an area of 3ha/7 acres, and includes various types of rural building: country manor, hayloft, farm, grain store, oven and mill.

Lago di Braies★★★

Alt. 1 495m/4 905ft. This shimmering lake (called Pragser Wildsee in German) can be circumnavigated in one hour. It is also the starting point of some rather arduous mountain footpaths.

Tre Cime di Lavaredo★★★

From the refuge at Auronzo the Lavaredo shelter is reached in half an hour. From there the Locatelli shelter is reached in an hour. This last stretch offers spectacular views of the Tre Cime range. The Tre Cime can also be reached from Sesto, along path 102, which leads to Locatelli in two and a half hours.

Lago di Misurina★★

Alt. 1 759m/5 770ft. This lake is set among a plantation of fir trees and is an excellent starting point for excursions to the surrounding mountains, from the Tre Cime di Lavaredo to the Cristallo.

Dobbiaco

www.altapusteria.info.
Dobbiaco (Toblach in German) was an important town in the Middle Ages as it was at a crossroads with the Strada dell'Alemagna.

San Candido★

www.altapusteria.info.
This pretty village, known as Innichen in German, has the most important Romanesque church in the Alto Adige. The **collegiata★** dates from the 13C. Most striking is the *Crucifixion*, a 13C wood sculptural group with Christ's feet resting on Adam's head. To visit call. ☎0474 913149.

Tre Cime di Lavaredo

© G. Cianci /Fototeca ENIT

Sesto★

www.altapusteria.info.

Sesto (Sexten) overlooks the Dolomites and offers a huge variety of footpaths and alpine excursions. The Monte Elmo funicular 🚡 makes distances shorter. For a peaceful walk, path 4D crosses the forest and high pastures and affords views of the Meridiana del Sesto.

ADDRESSES

🏠 STAY AND 🍴 EAT

🕙 Most accommodation in the mountains is based on half-board and full-board packages. Consequently, the hotels offer varied, traditional and/or creative menus and their restaurants are not necessarily restricted to their own guests. This makes it difficult to classify hotels and restaurants in separate sections and to allocate price categories for hotels, given that most of them only state half-board rates.

THE DOLOMITES ROAD

⊜🍴 **Concordia** – Via Roma 41, 39046 Ortisei. ℘0471 79 62 76. www.restaurant concordia.com. Closed mid-Apr–May and Nov. One of the few restaurants in the region that is worthy of the name, where you can enjoy delicious, carefully prepared traditional dishes served up in a convivial atmosphere.

⊜🍴 **Gérard** – Plan de Gralba 37, 39048 Selva di Val Gardena. ℘0471 79 52 74. www.chalet-gerard.com. Closed Apr, May, part of Oct and Nov. While the food served is traditional (polenta and local produce), the splendid view from this chalet perched at an altitude of 2 000m/6 560ft is unique: the panorama of the Stella Massif and Langkofel (Sassolungo) is literally enchanting. Accommodation available.

⊜🍴 **Hotel Cavallino d'Oro** – Piazza Kraus, 39040 Castelrotto, 26km/16.2mi NE of Bolzano. ℘0471 70 63 37. www. cavallino.it. Closed mid- Nov–mid-Dec. 18 rooms. ☲. Ideal if you're looking for a romantic, typically Tyrolean place to stay. Four-poster beds and elegant antique Tyrolean-style furniture. The dining area housed in the 17C wood-

panelled *Stuben* and the wellness facilities in the historic wine cellar add to the enjoyment.

⊜🍴 **Hotel Gran Ancëi** – 39030 San Cassiano, 26.5km/16.5mi W of Cortina d'Ampezzo. ℘0471 84 95 40. www.granancei.com. Closed mid-Apr–mid-Jun and Oct–Dec. 29 rooms. ☲. Surrounded by woodland and located near the ski slopes, this is very much a mountain-style hotel. Furniture and decor in the rooms and public areas are mostly in wood. Relaxing, peaceful ambience. Spacious and airy with wonderful views over the Dolomites.

⊜🍴🍴 **Hotel Colfosco-Kolfuschgerhof** – Via Rönn 7, 39030 Colfosco di Corvara, 2km/1.2mi E of Passo Gardena on the S 244. ℘0471 83 61 88. www.kolfuschgerhof.com. Closed mid-Apr–end May and Oct–Nov. ♿ 47 rooms. ☲. Situated near the lifts, this hotel appeals to both summer and winter mountain-sports enthusiasts. Facilities include squash courts, table-tennis tables, sauna, Turkish baths and massage rooms. The ambience is typically Tyrolean. Friendly atmosphere. Good if you're in search of some peace and quiet.

SOUTH OF CORTINA

⊜🍴 **Rifugio Alpe di Senes** – Loc. Senes, 32046 San Vito di Cadore, 9km/5.6mi S of Cortina d'Ampezzo on the S 51. ℘0436 94 76. Accessible by car, but that would mean missing out on a lovely, invigorating walk. This traditional mountain hut-cum-restaurant offers carefully prepared typical local cuisine in surroundings to match. Very good views.

THE VAL PUSTERIA AND AROUND

⊜🍴 **Hotel Erika** – Via Braies di Fuori 66, 39030 Braies, 5km/3mi N of Lago di Braies. ℘0474 74 86 84. www.hotelerika.net. Closed Apr–mid-May and mid-Oct–Nov. 29 rooms. ☲. Friendly and enthusiastic staff on hand to ensure you get the best out of your stay in the Dolomites – whatever the season. Comfortable rooms with chunky wooden furniture – the rooms on the third floor are particularly attractive. Rates for half-board and full-board accommodation.

⊖⊖ **Hotel Lavaredo** – Via Monte Piana 11, 32041 Misurina. ☎0435 39 227. www.lavaredohotel.it. Closed mid-Apr–May and Oct–Nov. 29 rooms. 🍽. Lakeside setting overlooked by the magnificent mountain peaks of the Cime di Lavaredo. Family-run hotel with comfortable rooms and spacious public areas (lots of wood!). Tennis courts, table tennis and sauna are among the facilities.

⊖⊖ **Hotel Masl** – Valles 44, Valles, 7km/4.3mi from Rio di Pusteria. ☎0472 54 71 87. www.hotel-masl.com. 🅿. 55 rooms. An elegant, friendly hotel occupying a large 17C house that is decked with flowers in summertime. The Messner family will take very good care of you.

⊖⊖⊖ **Monika Hotel** – Via del Parco 2, 39030 Sesto. ☎0474 71 03 84. www.monika.it. Closed mid-Apr–mid-May and 15 Oct–Nov. 57 rooms. 🍽. The rooms are simple but comfortable. In contrast, the dining room is more elegant. Stylish, spacious rooms, traditional-Tyrolean wood-panelled public areas and a well-equipped wellness centre make for a relaxing and refreshing holiday in gorgeous natural surroundings.

GOING OUT

Enoteca Cortina – Via Mercato 5, 32043 Cortina d'Ampezzo. ☎0436 86 20 40. www.enotecacortina.com. Open throughout the day in high season. A beautiful old door opens onto this lovely little wine bar with its wooden ceiling. A great place for tasting the local wines.

ACTIVITIES

MOUNTAIN FOOTPATHS

The Dolomites have a dense network of footpaths. Whether you are an expert climber or simply want to take a peaceful walk, there is a vast choice of routes for those wishing to get a better look at the Monti Pallidi. Maps and guides listing paths, mountain huts and bivouacs are on sale just about everywhere.

Some mountain pathways include:

No 2 (Bressanone–Feltre): This path crosses the Plose, the Puez Group, the Gardenaccia, the Sella and the Marmolada massifs.

No 3 (Villabassa–Longarone): This path winds its way through Val Pusteria, the Croda Rossa, Misurina, the Cristallo, the Sorapis and the Antelao.

No 4 (San Candido–Pieve di Cadore): This track goes through the Sesto Dolomites, the Cadini di Misurina and the Marmarole.

⚑ To be fully prepared for a mountain excursion it is advisable to contact the tourist offices listed above.

Gruppo Guide Alpine Scuola di Alpinismo – Corso Italia 69a, 32043 Cortina d'Ampezzo. ☎0436 86 85 05. www.guidecortina.com. Waterfalls, lakes, caves, routes with ropes (open to everybody) – a wide variety of organised excursions on offer in summer and lots of activities in winter too.

👥 **Fanes Nature Park** (Parco Naturale Fanes-Sennes-Braies) All the paths and trails begin at Dobbiaco, which is the departure point for walks, and will take you to altitudes of between 1 000m and 3 000m (3 280ft and 9 840ft). Certain paths are set up for winter outings. Dobbiaco is less well equipped for skiing and more family-oriented, offering numerous activities for children in summer.

Scuola di parapendio Icarus Flying Team – www.icarusfassa.it. No physical training is required before undertaking paragliding. For those brave enough the sensation is absolutely exhilarating.

SKI

The Dolomites have the largest area in Europe for cross-country skiing, with over 1 100km/680mi of groomed trails. Information can be found on www.dolomitinordicski.com.

Bologna and Emilia Romagna

Major Cities: Bologna, Modena, Parma

Official Website: www.emiliaromagnaturismo.it

The western part of the region derives its name from the Via Emilia, a straight Roman road that crosses from Piacenza to Rimini. The south eastern half of the region is Romagna, once governed over by Ravenna, an outpost of the Byzantine Empire. Emilia Romagna has long been a breadbasket for Italy and is considered the country's gastronomic heart. Prosciutto di Parma, Parmesan cheese and balsamic vinegar from Modena are among the region's most famous products. Mortadella sausage and tortellini, among other dishes, originated in Bologna, the culinary capital.

Highlights

1 Savour cuisine in Italy's gastronomic capital **Bologna** (p497)

2 Meander the medieval streets of **Ferrara** (p505)

3 Behold Byzantine mosaics in Ravenna's **Basilica di San Vitale** (p511)

4 Walk between the castles at the **Republic of San Marino** (p516)

5 Taste the world's most famous ham and cheese of **Parma** (p521)

Tracing the River

Emilia Romagna is neatly divided into north and south by the Via Emilia (SS 9), along which are most of the region's major cities.

To the north, the vast Po Plain (Pianura Padana), which also touches Lombardy and Veneto, stretches the length of **Emilia Romagna**, making it one of Italy's most productive agricultural regions. Large areas are given over to vines and fruit trees, kiwis, peaches and plums. South of the Via Emilia the slopes of the **Apennine Mountains** separate Emilia Romagna from Tuscany and Marche. These mountain ranges are home to wild boars and deer, which inhabit the thick beech, chestnut and conifer forests. The independent Republic of San Marino occupies a small perch of the Apennines at the border with Marche in a picturesque area.

The Po River runs into the sea in a wide delta between Ravenna and Venice (*see p509*), devoted in part to rice growing. Among the many lagoons are the **Valli di Comacchio**, well known for its eels. The Adriatic Coast also has long stretches of sandy beach. Around Rimini is most popular.

Mosaics inside Basilica di San Vitale, Ravenna

© Y. Kanazawa/MICHELIN

Bologna★★

The Emilian city of Bologna is often referred to as *dotta, grassa e rossa* (learned, fat and red). Wise it is indeed, thanks to its university, founded in 1088 and considered the world's oldest, and an intense cultural life; *fat* comes from the city's gastronomic opulence and traditionally rich style of cooking which has enshrined it as the country's food capital. Its "redness", which over time has acquired political connotations, refers to the colour of its masonry. The city centre, dotted with towers and an incredible 37km/23mi of arcades, buzzes with activity.

A BIT OF HISTORY

The Etruscan settlement of *Felsina* was conquered in the 4C BC by the Boïan Gauls, whom the Romans then drove out in 190 BC. Their settlement, *Bononia* fell under the sway of the barbarians until the 12C. In the subsequent century, the city enjoyed the status of an independent commune and developed rapidly. A fortified city was built, and the university flourished.

Against the Ghibellines and the emperor, Bologna supported the Guelphs, partisans of communal independence. The latter won, defeating the Imperial Army of Frederick II at Fossalta in 1249. The emperor's son, Enzo, was taken prisoner and remained at Bologna until his death 23 years later.

In the 15C, following violent clan struggles, the city fell to the **Bentivoglio** family whose rule continued until 1506. The city then remained under Papal control, until the arrival of Napoleon. The Austrians severely repressed several insurrections in the early-19C. Bologna was united with Piemonte in 1860.

Famous citizens include Pope Gregory XIII, who established our present Gregorian calendar (1582).

The **Bologna school of painting** was an artistic movement founded by the brothers Agostino (1557–1602) and

- ▶ **Population:** 374 500
- **Michelin Map:** 562 and 563 I 15–16 (together with town map) – Emilia Romagna.
- **Info:** Piazza Maggiore. ℰ051 23 96 60.
- **Location:** Bologna is well placed for access to the Adriatic and Tuscan coasts, as well as the Dolomites. Situated at an important motorway interchange, the city has access to the A 1, the A 14 to the Adriatic and the A 13. It is also near the beginning of the A 22, the Brenner transalpine route.
- **Parking:** Driving in Bologna can be difficult. Private traffic is forbidden in the centre 7am–8pm. There are car parks located near public transport interchanges or stations.
- **Don't Miss:** Piazza Maggiore, the Due Torri, Basilica di Santo Stefano and the **Maestà** by Cimabue in Santa Maria dei Servi.
- **Timing:** Scratch the surface of Bologna in a day, but allow two for a fuller experience.
- **Kids:** The city hosts the world's largest fair of children's books each April, so bookshops here are always well stocked. Families also enjoy the **Torri Pendenti**.

Annibale (1560–1609) with their cousin Ludovico (1555–1619) **Carracci**. They reacted against Mannerism with more "Classical" compositions that tried to express a simple spirituality.

Numerous artists – in particular the Bolognese painters **Francesco Albani**, **Guercino**, **Domenichino** and the celebrated **Guido Reni** – followed this movement, known as the **Accademia**

GETTING AROUND

BY CAR – Situated 100km/62mi from Florence, 200km/125mi from Milan and 150km/93mi from Venice, Bologna is at a key intersection of a busy motorway network.

P Those intending to stay in the city for a while should park and use public transport to get around.

BY TRAIN – The railway station is in Piazza Medaglie d'Oro, at the end of Via dell'Indipendenza. Buses nos. 25 and 30 go to Piazza Maggiore.

BY PLANE – Guglielmo Marconi Airport is situated 6km/3.7mi NW of the city in Borgo Panigale. It is served by major national and international airline companies, which connect it to Italian and European cities.

THE AEROBUS – The Aerobus offers a fast connection between the airport and the city centre and the railway station. Services reach the trade fair *(fiera)* district when events are on. Journey time between the railway station and airport is about 20min. It runs from 5.30am to midnight. (Departures every 15min, costs 6€: Price includes luggage transport.)

Purchase tickets at TPER points, automated machines or on board. For information contact ℘051 29 02 90. www.tper.it.

PUBLIC TRANSPORT – Bologna has a wide network of public transport. For information call ℘051 29 02 90. Purchase tickets at TPER points, authorised vendors and automated machines. There are various types of tickets: the City pass *(12€)* provides 10 journeys, no more than 75min long in the daytime, and can be used by one or more people at the same time; one-day tickets (5€) are valid 24h; ordinary tickets (1.30€) are valid for 75min in the daytime.

TAXIS – CO.TA.BO. (Cooperativa Taxisti Bolognesi) radiotaxi ℘051 37 27 27 and C.A.T. (Consorzio Autonomo Taxisti) radiotaxi ℘051 45 90.

VISITING

Girotp City Tour – ℘051 35 08 53. www.cityredbus.com. 13€. An open-top tourist bus that covers the city's main highlights In around 1 hour. A quick and easy way to get your bearings in Bologna.

Piazza Maggiore with Palazzo del Podestà

degli Incamminati (Academy of the Eclectic), focusing on the study of nature. In 1595 Annibale Carracci moved to Rome to work on a commission for the Farnese family. His frescoes at Palazzo Farnese veer towards an illusionism that heralds Baroque art.

CITY CENTRE★★★

The two adjoining squares, **Piazza Maggiore** and **Piazza del Nettuno★★★**, a harmonious ensemble, form the heart of Bologna together with **Piazza di Porta Ravegnana★★** nearby.

Fontana del Nettuno★★

This vigorous fountain is the work of Flemish sculptor Giambologna (1529–1608). The gigantic muscular bronze Neptune is surrounded by four sirens spouting water from their breasts.

Palazzo Comunale★

The façade of the town hall is composed of 13–16C buildings and is surmounted by a statue of Pope Gregory XIII. Above and to the left of the doorway is a statue of the *Virgin and Child* (1478) in terracotta by Niccolò dell'Arca. At the far end of the courtyard under a gallery rises a great ramp, the so-called *Scala dei Cavalli*, built in such a way that horses could use it, leading to the first-floor. Opening off the Farnese Gallery, which has 17C frescoes, are the splendid former rooms of Cardinal Legato, now housing the **Collezioni Comunali d'Arte**, the town's art collections. There are sections on furniture, the decorative arts and a selection of Emilian **paintings★** (14–19C). The **Museo Morandi★**, which boasts the largest collection of works by the painter and engraver from Bologna, as well as a reconstruction of his studio, is temporarily housed in MAMBO.
Collezioni Comunali: &Open Tues–Fri 9am–6.30pm, Sat–Sun 10am–6.30pm. Closed 1 Jan, 1 May, 25 Dec. 5€. ℘051 21 93 998. www.comune.bologna.it/iperbole/MuseiCivici. **Museo Morandi:** &Open Tues–Sun Noon–6pm, Thu, Sat–Sun to 8pm. Closed 1 Jan, 1 May, 25 Dec. 6€. ℘051 64 966 11. www.mambo-bologna.org/museomorandi.

Fontana del Nettuno

© V. Arcomano /Fototeca ENIT

Basilica di San Petronio★★

Building on the basilica, dedicated to St Petronius, began in 1390 to the plans of Antonio di Vincenzo (1340–1402) and ended in the 17C. The unfinished façade is remarkable chiefly for the expressive reliefs over the **doorway★★** created by Jacopo della Quercia.

The **interior** is immense and has many **works of art★** including frescoes by Giovanni da Modena (15C) in the first and the fourth chapels. Particularly striking is the fourth chapel, the right wall of which depicts the *Journey of the Kings* and the left wall an impressive *Inferno* and *Paradise*. Additional works include a *Martyrdom of St Sebastian* by the late-15C Ferrara school in the fifth chapel and the tomb of Elisa Baciocchi, Napoleon's sister, in the seventh chapel.

Near the basilica is the Museo Civico Archeologico (&*see below and map*) and the 16C Palazzo dell'Archiginnasio, home of an extensive library (10 000 manuscripts) and the 17C–18C Anatomy Theatre (Teatro Anatomico). &Open Mon–Fri 10am–6, Sat to 7pm, Sun and public hols 10am–2pm. 3€. ℘051 27 68 11. www.archiginnasio.it. In the nearby **Santa Maria della Vita**, note the dramatic **Mourning of Christ★**, a stunning 15C terracotta group of sculptures by Niccolò dell'Arca.

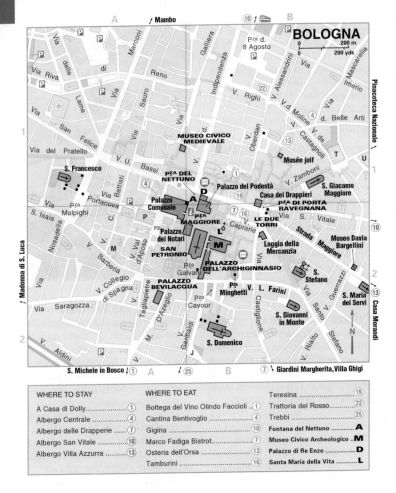

Museo Civico Archeologico★★

Via dell'Archiginnasio 2. ♿ Open Tue–Thu 9am–6.30pm, Fri 9am–10pm, Sat–Sun: 10am–6.30pm. From Jul 2016 Tue–Fri 9am–3pm, Sat–Sun 10am–6.30pm. Closed 1 Jan, 1 May, 25 Dec. 5€. ☏051 27 57 211. www.iperbole.bologna.it/museoarcheologico.

The *atrium* and courtyard house a stonework collection, and the adjoining wing contains the collection of plaster casts. On the first floor are ornate funerary items (7C BC) from the tombs of the Verucchio necropolis near Rimini, which was a great centre of the Villanovan culture. Another relic from this civilisation is the Askos Benacci, a container probably used for oils and perfumes.

The museum also includes prehistoric, Egyptian, Greco-Roman and Etrusco-Italic sections, with a fine Roman copy of the head of Phidias' *Athena Lemnia*.

Palazzo del Podestà and Palazzo di Re Enzo★

Palazzo del Podestà and Palazzo di Re Enzo are only open for special events and exhibitions. ☏051 23 96 60.

The Renaissance façade facing onto Piazza Maggiore consists of an arcade on the ground floor formed by arches interspersed with Corinthian columns and topped by a balustrade; the floor above is adorned with pilasters, and the attic floor contains small round windows known as oculi. Adjoining the Palazzo del Podestà is the 13C **Palace of King Enzo**, with its fine inner courtyard and a magnificent staircase leading up to a gallery, to the left of which is a courtyard overlooked by the Arengo tower. The staircase also leads to the great hall known as the Salone del Podestà.

Le Due Torri★★

These two leaning towers in Piazza di Porta Ravegnana belonged to noble families and are symbols of the continual conflict between the rival Guelphs and Ghibellines in the Middle Ages. The taller, **Torre degli Asinelli**, nearly 100m/330ft high, dates from 1109. It is worth climbing the 486 steps that lead to the top in order to admire a **panorama★★** of the city. The second, **Torre Garisenda**, is 50m/164ft high and has a tilt of over 3m/10ft. Torre degli Asinelli: Open daily summer 9am–6pm; rest of the year 9am–5pm. 3€. www.bologna welcome.com.

The handsome 14C Palazzo della Mercanzia or Merchants' House, in the next square, bears the coats of arms of the various guilds and now houses the Chamber of Commerce.

OUTSIDE THE CENTRE
Chiesa di San Giacomo Maggiore★

Open daily 7.30am–12.30pm and 3.30–6.30pm, Sat–Sun opens 8.30am. Donations welcome. ✆051 22 59 70. ♿Cappella Bentivoglio.

The church, dedicated to St James the Greater, was founded in 1267. On the north side is a fine Renaissance portico. Inside is the magnificent **Cappella Bentivoglio★**. Its frescoes depict *The Triumph of Fame and Death* and the beautiful *Madonna Enthroned with the Bentivoglio Family*, both by the Ferrarese painter Lorenzo Costa. The chapel also houses a masterpiece of Francesco Francia, the *Madonna Enthroned and Saints* (c.1494). Opposite the chapel, in the ambulatory, stands the **tomb★** (c.1433) of the jurist Antonio Bentivoglio, by Jacopo della Quercia.

St Cecilia's Chapel (entrance on Via Zamboni 15) is a small church, founded in the 13C with additions made in the 15C. Inside there are remarkable **frescoes★** depicting St Cecilia (1506) by F. Francia, L. Costa and A. Aspertini.

Strada Maggiore★

Along this elegant street, lined with some fine palaces (note Casa Isolani at no. 19, a rare example of 13C architecture with a wooden portico), is the **Museo d'Arte industriale e Galleria Davia Bargellini**, housed in an attractive palace dating from 1658 (at no. 44), which has collections of "industrial art" (applied and decorative arts) and paintings from the 14C–18C. Open Tue–Sat 9am–2pm, Sun 9am–1pm. Closed 1 Jan, 1 May, 25 Dec. Free. ✆051 23 67 08.

A little further down, on the right, is the church of **Santa Maria dei Servi** (founded in the 14C), which is heralded by a Renaissance quadrisection **portico★**. Inside, in the third chapel on the right, there is a **Maestà★★** by Cimabue.

Basilica di Santo Stefano★

Open daily 8am–7pm. Donations welcome. ✆051 64 80 611. www.bolognawelcome.com.

The basilica comprises a group of buildings (originally seven) overlooking the square with its Renaissance mansions. Entrance is through the **Church of the Crucifix** (Crocifisso), an old Lombard cathedral restored in the 11C and remodelled in the 19C.

Turning left make for the atmospheric 12C **Church of the Holy Sepulchre** (Santo Sepolcro) and the shrine of Bologna's patron saint, St Petronius. The black cipolin marble columns were originally part of the ancient Temple of Isis (AD 100), which was turned into a baptistery and later into a church. The font, originally consecrated with water from the Nile, was reconsecrated with water from Jordan. Go through the Church of the Holy Sepulchre to reach the charming **Court of Pilate** (11C–12C) and, from there, through to the **Church of the Trinity** (Trinità), 13C, the old *Martyrium* (4C–5C) where the bodies of martyrs were brought.

The Lord's Dogs

St Dominic was born in Spain in 1170. His mother was Blessed Joan de Aza de Guzmán, who, when pregnant, had a vision that her unborn child was a dog bearing a torch, symbolising truth and the flame of faith. In 1216 St Dominic founded the Order of Preachers, more commonly known as the Dominicans. This name came from the Latin name for the legend (*Domini canes*, the Lord's dogs), and the dog and torch sometimes appear in representations of St Dominic. He established a friary in Bologna and died there in 1221.

San Giovanni in Monte

On the square of the same name, almost at the intersection of Via Santo Stefano and Via Luigi Farini.

The church was built in 1286 and its façade was completed in 1474, but the real attraction is the interior: in a chapel to the left you will find Guercino's marvellous St Francis of Assisi (1647), and further along, an image of the Holy Family (1753) attributed to Antonio Crespi. A 16C fresco decorates the ceiling and the lunettes of the chapel of St Ubaldo.

Chiesa di San Domenico★

The church, dedicated to St Dominic, was built at the beginning of the 13C and remodelled in the 18C. It houses the beautiful **tomb★★★** *(arca)*: the fine sarcophagus is by Nicola Pisano (1267), while the arch with statues (1468–73) crowning it was executed by Niccolò da Bari, who was afterwards known as Niccolò dell'Arca, and completed by Michelangelo in 1494 with the two missing saints (St Procolo and St Petronius) and the angel on the right. The finial by Niccolò celebrates the creation, symbolised by *putti* (sky), garlands (earth) and dolphins (sea).The chapel to the right of the presbytery has a fine painting by Filippino Lippi, the **Mystic Marriage of St Catherine** (1501). In Via D'Azeglio is **Palazzo Bevilacqua★**, a Renaissance palace.

Chiesa di San Francesco★

This church was erected in the 13C and is one of the first examples of Gothic architecture in Italy. Inside, at the high altar, is a marble **altarpiece★** (1392), by the Venetian sculptor Paolo dalle Masegne. The Museo Civico Medievale is nearby (⌖*see below*).

ADDITIONAL SIGHTS
Pinacoteca Nazionale★★

Via Belle Arti 56. 🏛 **St Cecilia** by Raphael and the **Carracci Room**. ♿ Open Tue–Wed 9am–1.30pm, Thu–Sun 2–7pm. 4€. 📞051 42 09 411. www. pinacotecabologna.beniculturali.it.

An important collection, predominantly of the Bolognese school (13C–18C). Among the works are the energetic **St George and the Dragon★** by Vitale da Bologna and Giotto's *Madonna Enthroned and Child*. The section on Renaissance painting boasts Perugino's **Virgin and Child★** – a profound influence on the Bolognese school – and **St Cecilia★★** by Raphael, who portrays renunciation with symbolic instruments abandoned on the ground. The **Carracci Room★★** contains numerous masterpieces by Ludovico, one of the great interpreters of the new spirituality of the Counter-Reformation with his blend of quiet intimacy and high emotion: the graceful *Annunciation*, the *Bargellini Madonna*, the *Madonna degli Scalzi* and the dramatic *Conversion of St Paul*, which heralds Baroque painting. Of Agostino Carracci note the *Communion of St Jerome* and of Annibale Carracci's work, the *Assumption of the Virgin*, a masterpiece and early example of Baroque painting. The **Guido Reni Room** houses some stunning work by this painter. In the famous **Massacre of the Innocents**, the eternal moment is captured in the balance of architecture and figures forming a reversed triangle.

Madonna di San Luca

The intense *Portrait of a Widow*, generally thought to be a portrait of the artist's mother, is considered one of the finest portraits in Italian 17C painting. In the **Baroque corridor** is **St William★**, an early masterpiece of Baroque art by Guercino. Of 18C painting note the works by Giuseppe Maria Crespi, one of the major painters of 18C Italy including the **Courtyard Scene★**.

Museo Civico Medievale

&Open Tue–Fri 9am–3pm, Sat–Sun 10am–6.30pm. Closed 1 Jan, 1 May, 25 Dec. 5€. ℘051 21 93 930. www.museibologna.it.

The Medieval Civic Museum is housed in the **Palazzo Fava-Ghisilardia** (late-15C) which stands on the site of the Imperial Roman palace. The collections relate the development of art in Bologna from the Middle Ages to the Renaissance.

EXCURSION
Madonna di San Luca

◗ 5km/3mi SW. Leave the city centre by Via Saragozza.

The 18C hilltop church is linked to the city by the world's longest arcaded pavement or **portico★** (4km/2.5mi long) of 666 arches. In the chancel is the Madonna of St Luke, a painting in the 12C Byzantine style. There is a lovely **view★** of Bologna and the Apennines.

ADDRESSES

🛏STAY

Many of the hotels raise their prices during trade fairs so best to check dates and costs before booking.

⊜⊜ **A Casa di Dolly** – Via della Libertà 9 (entrance on Via Mura di Porta d'Azeglio). ℘051 33 19 37. 3 rooms. This second-floor B&B located 10 minutes' walk from Piazza Maggiore offers a friendly welcome and an ideal location from which to explore the city.

⊜⊜ **Albergo Centrale** – Via della Zecca 2. ℘051 22 51 14. www.albergo centralebologna.it. 25 rooms. Housed in a historic building in the centre of town, with pleasantly simple rooms.

⊜⊜ **Albergo delle Drapperie** – Via delle Drapperie 5. ℘051 22 39 55. www.albergodrapperie.com. 20 rooms. Beautifully renovated rooms, each one individually decorated. Good value.

⊜⊜ **Albergo San Vitale** – Via San Vitale 94. ℘051 22 59 66. www.albergo sanvitale.com. 17 rooms. A pleasant hotel with simple rooms, hospitable service and free wifi.

⊜⊜ **Hotel Villa Azzurra** – Viale Felsina 49. ℘051 53 54 60. www.hotelvilla azzurra.com. 15 rooms. This is a peaceful hotel located in an attractive 19C villa with a pretty garden. Not central but handy for drivers.

♿/EAT

🍽 **Bottega del Vino Olindo Faccioli** – Via Altabella 15b. ☎349 300 29 39. A family *enoteca* since 1924 offers 500 wines from all over the country. Atmosphere and a concise menu of quality bites.

🍽 **Tamburini** – Via Caprarie 1. ☎051 23 47 26. www.tamburini.com. A historic delicatessen famous for its tortellini. Well worth queuing for a delicious lunch at the self-service section.

🍽🍽 **Cantina Bentivoglio** – Via Mascarella 4b. ☎051 26 5416. www.cantinabentivoglio.it. Live jazz every night, featuring international musicians, a great menu and wonderful wines. Come for an evening to remember.

🍽🍽 **Gigina** – Via Henri Beyle Stendhal 1. ☎051 32 23 00. www.trattoriagigina.it. Just outside the centre, this family-run trattoria has a good reputation for homey traditional Bolognese specialities. The atmosphere is cosy.

🍽🍽 **Marco Fadiga Bistrot** – Via Rialto 23c. ☎051 23 21 04. www.marcofadiga bistrot.it. Fish restaurant. Creative cooking plus an oyster bar make this an intriguing place to dine.

🍽🍽 **Osteria dell'Orsa** – Via Mentana 1. ☎051 23 15 76. www.osteriadellorsa.com. An institution among staff and students from the nearby university. Authentic local dishes and stays open late.

🍽🍽 **Teresina** Via Oberdan 4, 41026 Bologna. ☎051 22 89 85. www.ristorante teresinabologna.it. Reservation recommended. A busy trattoria close to the main sights of the centre; local food plus dishes of the day.

🍽🍽 **Trattoria del Rosso** – Via Righi 30. ☎051 23 67 30. www.trattoriadelrosso.com. Good traditional food and rock bottom prices make this centrally located informal trattoria a popular place!

🍽🍽 **Trebbi** – Via Solferino 40b. ☎051 58 37 13. www.trattoria-trebbi.com. Reservation recommended. Since 1946, this unpretentious trattoria tucked into a backstreet near the law courts has been serving an interesting menu of good food, appreciated by locals and business travellers alike. Very good buffet of fresh vegetable dishes.

TAKING A BREAK

Gelateria Gianni – Via Montegrappa 11; www.gelateriagianni.com. A must for lovers of quality ice cream with a wide range of classic and imaginative flavours.

Enoteca Regionale Emilia-Romagna – Piazza Rocca Sforzesca, Dozza, 29km/18mi SE of Bologna. ☎0542 36 77 00. www.enotecaemiliaromagna.it. This statuesque medieval castle is set in picturesque hilltop Dozza, which is also famous for the murals by international artists painted all around the village during a biennial festival. The castle cellars house all the best-quality wines produced in the region. They have to be approved each year and are sold here at honest prices. Well worth the trip!

Paolo Atti & Figli – Via Caprarie 7. ☎051 22 04 25. www.paoloatti.com. Gastro tours by reservation ☎051 23 33 49. This well-known bakery and delicatessen, founded in 1880 and frequented by Giosuè Carducci and the painter Morandi among others, still has original interiors. Specialities include tortellini and Bologna's rich *certosino* cake traditionally made for Christmas.

GOING OUT

Enoteca des Arts – Via San Felice 9a. ☎051 23 64 22. Open Mon–Sat 5pm–3am. An informal wine bar with vaulted ceilings and a collection of old bottles.

Il Circolo Pickwick – Via San Felice 77a. ☎051 55 51 04. Set in an old pharmacy, this place has plenty of atmosphere. Serves a mix of Italian wines, English beer and Cuban cocktails.

Le Stanze – Via Borgo San Pietro 1. ☎051 22 87 67. Closed Mon lunch and Thu. A unique location for an evening to remember. This former chapel close to the lively university area, features original 17C frescoes and contemporary design elements. Events are held frequently.

Ferrara★★

The whole of Ferrara's stunning historic centre is a UNESCO World Heritage Site, one of many in Italy. Already important in the Middle Ages, the city came into its own as a thriving cultural centre during the Renaissance. It's a tranquil place with a leisurely feel to it; bicycles are a popular way to get around, widely used by locals, and everywhere is easily accessible on foot. With prestigious galleries and numerous events, Ferrara continues to be one of the major artistic and cultural centres in Italy.

A BIT OF HISTORY
Patrons of the Arts

Initially an independent commune, Ferrara belonged to the **Este** family from 1208 to 1598, and despite numerous family dramas, often bloody, the Estes embellished their native city with fine buildings and patronised both men of letters and artists.

NiccolòIII (1393–1441) murdered his wife Parisina and her lover but he begat **Lionello** and **Borso**, moulding them into efficient administrators and enlightened patrons. **Ercole I** (1431–1505), who was responsible for his nephew's murder, encouraged artists, as did his two famous daughters, Beatrice and Isabella d'Este. **Alfonso I** (1475–1534), the son of Ercole, became the third husband of Lucrezia Borgia, and **Ercole II** (1508–59) married Renée of France, the protector of the Calvinists. After the demise of **AlfonsoII** (1533–97), who left no heirs, Ferrara came under the rule of the Papacy and the Estes retired to the Duchy of Modena.

The arts flourished with the secular university (founded in 1391) and the patronage of the Este dynasty. Three poets benefited from the Estes' largesse: **Matteo Maria Boiardo** (1441–94), **Ludovico Ariosto** and **Torquato Tasso** (1544–95).

▶ **Population:** 134 967
🖰 **Michelin Map:** 562 H 16 – Emilia Romagna.
🛈 **Info:** Castello Estense, 44100 Ferrara. ✆0532 20 93 70. www.ferrarainfo.com. www.artecultura.fe.it.
◖ **Location:** Near the Po Delta, off the A 13, which links Bologna with Padova.
◖ **Train:** Ferrara (Bologna Centrale 27mins).
◈ **Don't Miss:** The cathedral, Corso Ercole I d'Este, the salons of Palazzo Schifanoia and Rosetti works in Palazzo dei Diamanti.
◷ **Timing:** Allow two days for the whole city.

The Ferrarese School

The leader of the Ferrarese school of painting (known as the Officina Ferrarese) was **Cosmè (Cosimo) Tura** (c.1430–95); the school's main characteristic was a meticulous realism, borrowed from the northern schools. The main members were **Francesco del Cossa** (1435–77), whose free and luminous style is evocative of Piero della Francesca; **Ercole de' Roberti** (1450–96), who conversely adopted Tura's strong modelling tradition; and **Lorenzo Costa** (1460–1535), who moved his studio to Bologna where the dark tones of the Umbrian and Tuscan schools prevailed. In the 16C the colourist **Dosso Dossi** (c.1490–1542) and **Benvenuto Garofalo** (1481–1559) favoured a greater harmony of colour in line with the Venetian style and allied themselves to the

GETTING THERE

BY CAR: The centre of Ferrara is out of bounds for unauthorised vehicles, but hotel guests can obtain a temporary parking permit. **FREE PARKING:** EX-MOF – *via Darsena, south of the town.*

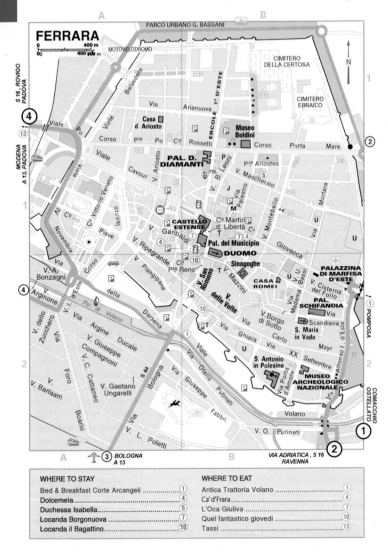

Classical tradition of Raphael and the Roman school.

OLD TOWN
Castello Estense★

  Open Mon–Sun (Jan–Feb–Jul–Aug closed Mon) 9.30am–5.30pm (7pm Jun–Aug). 8€. ℘0532 29 92 33. www.castelloestense.it.
This imposing castle, guarded by moats and four fortified gateways with drawbridges, was the seat of the Este family. The ground floor houses the spartan prison where Parisina and her lover were

locked away. On the *piano nobile*, where the orangery is, visitors may view the Ducal Chapel collection and the apartments decorated with frescoes by the Filippi, active in Ferrara in the second half of the 16C. Temporary exhibitions are also held.

Duomo★★

The cathedral was built in the 12C in the Romanesque-Gothic Lombard style and presents a triple **façade★★** with a splendid porch. On the tympanum is depicted the Last Judgement.

The Jewish Community of Ferrara

The Jewish community flourished in the 14C and 15C owing to the policy of the Estes, who welcomed Jews from Rome, Spain and Germany. The ghetto was instituted under Papal rule in 1624: five gates closed at dusk sealing off the area bounded by Via Mazzini, Vignatagliata and Vittoria. The gates were taken down under the new Italian Kingdom in 1859. The Jewish community of Ferrara is portrayed in the novel *Garden of the Finzi-Contini* by Giorgio Bassani, which was turned into an Oscar-winning film in 1970 by Vittorio De Sica.

In the lunette above the central door, the sculpture of St George is by Nicholaus, an artist of the school led by the Romanesque master Wiligelmo, who was responsible for the carved decoration of Modena Cathedral. On the south side there are two tiers of galleries on the upper section; below is the Loggia dei Merciai, a portico occupied by shops in the 15C. Here stood the Portal of the Months; the panels are now in the cathedral museum.

The unfinished bell tower was designed by Leon Battista Alberti. In the south arm of the transept note *The Martyrdom of St Lawrence* by Guercino and two 15C bronze statues (St Maurelius and St George) and *The Last Judgement* by Bastianino on the vaulting in the apse.

Museo della Cattedrale

Housed in the old church and monastery of San Romano, in the street of the same name. Open Tue–Sun 9am–1pm and 3–6pm. 6€. &0532 24 49 49. The museum contains two statues by Jacopo della Quercia, the **panels★★** of an organ painted by **Cosmè Tura** representing *St George Slaying the Dragon* and *The Annunciation* and the admirable 12C **sculptures★** from the Portal of the Months, admirable in their immediacy and close observation of reality. The 13C town hall, **Palazzo del Municipio**, facing the cathedral, was once the ducal palace.

Medieval Streets

Via San Romano, which is still a commercial artery, linked the market square (Piazza Trento e Trieste) and the port (now Via Ripagrande). It is lined with several houses with porticoes, an unusual feature in Ferrara. **Via delle Volte** has become one of the symbols of the town. Covered alleyways *(volte)* linked the houses of the merchants and their warehouses.

Along Via Mazzini are the **Sinagoghe** (synagogue complex and museum), which comprise three temples for different rites: the Italian and German traditions and that from Fano in the Marches. The synagogue complex and the museum are closed due to the damages caused by 2012 earthquake. &0532 21 02 28. www.comune.fe.it/museoebraico.

Casa Romei★

Open Sun–Wed 8.30am–2pm, Thu–Sat 2–7.30. 3€. &0532 23 41 30.
This rare example of a 15C bourgeois residence combines late Gothic decorative features (Room of the Sibyls) and Renaissance elements such as the courtyard portico.

Palazzina di Marfisa d'Este★

Open Tues–Sun 9am–1pm and 3–6pm. Closed 1 Jan, 6 Jan, Easter Sun, 1 Nov, 25–26 Dec. 4€. &0532 24 49 49. www.artecultura.fe.it.
This elegant single-storey residence (1559) is where Marfisa d'Este entertained her friends, among them the poet Tasso. The interior is remarkable for the ornate ceiling decoration including grotesques, and elegant 16C–17C furniture. Pass into the garden to visit the Orangery (Loggia degli Aranci); the vault features a mock pergola complete with vine shoots and animals.

Palazzo Schifanoia★

Due to the 2012 earthquake the Palazzo is partially closed. Public is allowed only to Salone dei Mesi and Sala delle Virtù. Open Tue–Sun 9.30am–6pm. 3€. ℘0532 24 49 49. www.artecultura.fe.it

This 14C palace is where the Estes used to come to relax (*schifanoia* means "away with boredom"). There are splendid frescoes in the Room of the Months (**Salone dei Mesi★★**). This complex cycle to the glory of Borso d'Este retains only some of the 12 months. The three levels illustrate themes of everyday life at court, astrology and mythology. The frescoes attest to Ferrara's Renaissance cultural achievements. The palace museum, the **Museo Civico di Arte Antica**, has archaeological collections, medals, bronzes and marquetry. The museum houses the **Lapidario**.

Monastero di Sant'Antonio in Polesine

Open Mon–Fri 9.30–11.30am and 3.15–5pm, Sat 9.30–11.30am and 3.15–4.30pm. Donations welcome. ℘0532 64 068.

The convent founded in 1257 by Beatrice II d'Este stands in an isolated and peaceful setting. The **church** has three chapels decorated with fine 14C–16C **frescoes★** by the Giotto and Emilian schools.

RENAISSANCE TOWN

In 1490 Ercole I d'Este commissioned **Biagio Rossetti** to extend the town to the north. The extension (**Addizione Erculea**) built around two main axes – Corso Ercole I d'Este and Corso Porta Pia, Bragio Rossetti and Porta Mare – is a great Renaissance town featuring parks and gardens. With this grandiose town-planning scheme Ferrara became the first modern city in Europe, according to the art historian Jacob Burckhardt, and in 1995 was included in UNESCO's World Heritage List.

Corso Ercole I d'Este★

The street lined with splendid Renaissance palaces but lacking any shops retains its original residential aspect. The focal point is the **Quadrivio degli Angeli**, emphasised by three palaces with a rich angular decoration, including the Palazzo dei Diamanti.

Palazzo dei Diamanti★★

Palazzo dei Diamanti, Corso Ercole I d'Este 21. ♿. Temporary exhibits open daily 9am–7pm. About 10€. www.palazzodiamanti.it.

The most distinctive of all the works by **Biagio Rossetti**, the palace takes its name from the marble façade of 8 500 diamond bosses; the different angles at which they have been placed creates a curious optical effect. The palace was designed for a diagonal view: the central feature is therefore the corner embellished with pilasters and a balcony. This palace regularly hosts some of Italy's most prestigious temporary art exhibits. On the first floor is the art gallery (*see below: Pinacoteca*).

Pinacoteca Nazionale★

Open 9am–2pm (Thu closes 7pm). Closed Mon. 4€. ℘0532 24 49 49. www.ferraraterraeacqua.it.

The gallery displays paintings showing the development of the Ferrarese, Emilian and Venetian schools in the 13–8C.

Museo Archeologico Nazionale

Via XX Settembre 124. ♿ Open Tue–Sun 9.30am–5pm. 5€. ℘0532 66 299. www.archeoferrara.beniculturali.it.

The Palazzo Costabili, designed in the 15C by Biagio Rossetti, houses the archaeological museum. An important collection of 5C–4C BC Attic **vases★** and burial accoutrements found at Spina, once one of the most important commercial ports in the Mediterranean.

ADDRESSES

⌂ STAY

⊖⊜ **Dolcemela** – Via della Sacca 35. ℘0532 76 96 24. www.dolcemela.it. Closed 5–20 Aug. 6 rooms; 1 apartment. City-centre B&B in summer, breakfast, including homemade cakes and biscuits, is outside on the patio.

Locanda Borgonuovo – Via Cairoli 29. 0532 21 11 00. www.borgonuovo.com. 4 rooms. A delightful B&B in the heart of the historic centre. Free wifi and use of bicycles. Apartments available.

Locanda il Bagattino – Corso Porta Reno 24. 0532 24 18 87. www.ilbagattino.it. 6 rooms. An attractive guesthouse in the old town with comfortable and welcoming rooms.

Bed & Breakfast Corte Arcangeli – Via Pontegradella 503, Pontegradella, 3km/1.8mi NE. 348 44 35 041. www.locandacortearcangeli.it. 6 rooms. A lovely place with beams and stone walls in the beautifully decorated rooms. Swimming pools and an excellent fish restaurant.

3C Duchessa Isabella – Via Palestro 70. 0532 20 21 21. www.duchessaisabella.it. 27 rooms. Ferrara's most elegant hotel; fine furnishings in all the rooms. Lovely restaurant with traditional and creative cuisine is popular well-heeled locals. Bicycles.

ƴ/EAT

Tassi – Viale Repubblica 23, Bondeno, 20km/12.4mi NW of Ferrara on the S 496. 0532 89 30 30. Closed Sun evening and Mon. Long established restaurant specialising in local meat dishes.

Ca' d'Frara – Via del Gambero 4. 0532 20 50 57. www.ristorantecadfrara.it. Don't be taken in by the modern decor, this Ferrarese house is a bastion of tradition: hung hams, pasticcio di maccheroni, and salama da sugo with mashed potato.

Antica Trattoria Volano – Viale Volano 20. 0532 76 14 21. www.anticatrattoriavolano.it. Closed Thu. An appealing old-style trattoria serving authentic local dishes, including eel. Delicious homemade pasta.

L'Oca Giuliva – Via Boccacanale di Santo Stefano 38. 0532 20 76 28. www.ristorantelocagiuliva.it. Closed Mon and Tue lunchtime. An elegant, refined restaurant, where you can savour the local cuisine. Magnificent choice of wines.

Quel fantastico giovedì – Via Castelnuovo 9. 0532 76 05 70. Closed Wed. Contemporary decor and a young team serving imaginative, creative takes on traditional dishes.

Delta del Po★

Po Delta

This outstanding area of natural beauty, now an important nature reserve, providing an ideal habitat for a wide range of flora and fauna, has a far less appealing past. Less than a century ago it was a depressed malaria-infested marshy district. Since then, land reclamation and drainage have turned it into a fertile agricultural area and nature reserve which draws experts, birdwatchers in particular, from all over the world. The Chioggia to Ravenna road (90km/56mi) traverses flat, watery expanses interspersed with clumps of trees and grassy banks, built-up to protect from flooding.

Michelin Map: 562 H 18 – Emilia Romagna, Veneto.

Info: Parco Delta del Po, Via Mazzini, 44022 Comacchio (FE) 0533 31 40 03. www.parcodeltapo.it.

Location: The Po Delta covers the coastal area between Venice and Ravenna, taking in parts of the provinces of Rovigo and Ferrara.

Don't Miss: Charming Comacchio and the striking Abbazia di Pomposa.

Timing: Allow half a day for Comacchio; another day for exploring the area.

Many of these have cycle and footpaths along the top. Eel fishing is traditional in the canals, while clams are a common shellfish crop on the coast.

VISIT

Comacchio

Comacchio Tourist Information, Via Agatopisto 3. ℘0533 31 41 54. www.comune.comacchio.fe.it.
Laced with canals and picturesque bridges, such as the famous Trepponti, Three-Legged Bridge, Comacchio holds considerable charm. The traditional activity of eel fishing is celebrated with a lively annual festival each October.

Abbazia di Pomposa★★

Open 8.30am–7.30pm. Tue–Sat 5€; Sun: entry to church free; other areas 3€. ℘0533 71 91 19.
This Benedictine abbey was founded in the 6C and enjoyed fame in the Middle Ages when it was distinguished by its abbot, St Guy (Guido) of Ravenna, and by another monk, **Guido d'Arezzo**, the inventor of the musical scale and note system. In July and August the abbey hosts classical music concerts.
The fine pre-Romanesque **church** in the style typical of Ravenna is preceded by a narthex whose decoration exemplifies the Byzantine style. The nave has some magnificent **mosaic flooring** and two holy water stoups, one in the Romanesque style and the other in the Byzantine style. The walls bear an exceptional cycle of 14C **frescoes** based on the illuminator's art. From right to left the upper band is devoted to the Old Testament while the lower band has scenes from the life of Christ; the corner pieces of the arches depict the *Apocalypse*. On the west wall are a *Last Judgement* and in the apsidal chapel *Christ in Majesty*. Opposite the church stands the Palazzo della Ragione, where the abbot dispensed justice.

ADDRESSES

🛏STAY

🍽🛏 **Hotel Villa Belfiore** – Via Pioppa 27, Ostellato, 27km/16.8mi W of Comacchio. ℘0533 68 11 64. www.villabelfiore.com. 18 rooms. ⌧. A delightful country residence with large rooms and a lovely garden complete with swimming pool surrounded by fruit trees. Free cookery lessons for guests and a restaurant serving genuine dishes.

♀/EAT

🍽🛏 **La Capanna** – Via per le Venezie 21, 44021 Codigoro, 6km/3.7mi W of the Abbazia di Pomposa. ℘0533 71 21 54. Closed Wed evening and Thu. A typical *osteria* with straw-seated chairs and rustic-style interior. Place settings and attentive service lend the place a certain style. Hearty, home cooking. Specialises in fish, and game in winter. The eel *arost in umad* (roasted) and *schille* (prawns) come recommended.

Traditional fishing house at Comacchio Valley

© Lelepado/iStockphoto.com

Ravenna★★★

In the peaceful provincial-looking town of Ravenna, the sober exteriors of its buildings belie the wealth of riches accumulated initially when Ravenna was the capital of the Western Empire and later when it was an Exarchate of Byzantium. The mosaics that adorn the city's ecclesiastical buildings are breathtakingly beautiful in the brightness of their colours and powerful symbolism.

▶ **Population:** 157 459
🚲 **Michelin Map:** 562, 563 I 18.
🗲 **Info:** Piazza Caduti per la Libertà. ☎0544 35 755. www.turismo.ra.it.
▶ **Location:** Ravenna lies just south of the Po Delta.
▶ **Train:** Ravenna (Bologna Centrale: 1hr 18mins).
👁 **Don't Miss:** The mosaics in Cappella di Sant'Andrea, the Mausoleo di Galla Placidia, Basilica di Sant'Apollinare in Classe and Basilica di Sant'Apollinare Nuovo.
🕐 **Timing:** Allow one day.

A BIT OF HISTORY

After the division of the Empire in AD 395 by Theodosius, Rome, already in decline, was abandoned in AD 404 by the Emperor Honorius, who made Ravenna the capital of the Roman Empire. Honorius' sister, **Galla Placidia**, governed the Western Empire before the barbarian invasions brought the Ostrogoth kings Odoacer (476–93) and **Theodoric** (493–526) to Ravenna; they embellished Ravenna in their turn.

The strategic location of Ravenna's port, Classis, on the Adriatic Sea, inevitably led to trading with Byzantium, which had become the Imperial capital in 476. Ravenna came under Byzantine rule in 540 in the reign of the **Emperor Justinian** (482–565).

From then on it exercised considerable influence over much of the Italian peninsula.

THE MOSAICS

The oldest mosaics are in the Neonian Baptistery and the Tomb of Galla Placidia (5C). Next in chronological order are those adorning the Baptistery of the Arians, St Apollinaris the New, St Vitalis, and finally St Apollinaris in Classe (6C). The mosaic heritage of the city combines the two great schools of the ancient world: the Hellenic-Roman school, characterised by a realistic rendition of figure and landscape, and the Byzantine School, whose rarefied and stylised figures seem to be fixed on their gold background. In 1996 UNESCO recognised these early Christian monuments on the World Heritage List.

VISITING THE MOSAICS

Basilica di S. Vitale, Mausoleo di Galla Placidia: Open daily Mar and Oct 9am–5.30pm; Apr–Sept 9am–7pm; Nov–Feb 9.30am–5pm. **Battistero Neoniano, Museo Arcivescovile and Basilica di Sant'Apollinare Nuovo:** Open daily Mar and Oct 9.30am–5.30pm; Apr–Sept 9am–7pm; Nov–Feb 10am–5pm. 9.50€ combined ticket for entrance to all above-mentioned sites. ☎0544 54 16 88. www.ravennamosaici.it.
Museo Nazionale: ♿Open Tue–Sun 8.30am–7.30pm. 5€/8€/10€ only Museo Nazionale/with entrance to Mausoleo di Teodorico/also with Sant'Apollinare in Classe. ☎0544 21 56 18.
Sant'Apollinare in Classe: Open Mon–Sat 8.30am–7.30pm, Sun 1–7.30pm. 5€, 8€/10€ with Museo Nazionale/also with Mausoleo di Teodorico. ☎0544 47 35 69.

SIGHTS

Basilica di San Vitale★★★

Access to the basilica affords a view of the fine recomposed **fresco** by Pietro da Rimini (c.1320), originally in the Church of Santa Chiara. Consecrated in 547 by Archbishop Maximian, the basilica is an architectural masterpiece; the splendour, originality and light effects are

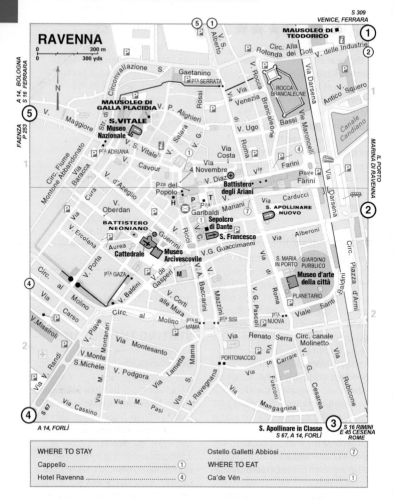

WHERE TO STAY		Ostello Galletti Abbiosi .... ⑦
Cappello .... ①		WHERE TO EAT
Hotel Ravenna .... ④		Ca'de Vén .... ①

typical features of the later period of Ancient art. The church, dedicated to St Vitalis, has an octagonal plan, two storeys of concave exedrae encircled by an ambulatory and a deep apse. The richly decorated interior is dazzling: precious marbles, splendidly carved Byzantine capitals, frescoes and especially the **mosaics** of the apse with their brilliant colours.

The chancel is adorned with sacrificial scenes from the Old Testament; on the side walls of the apse are wonderful groups representing the **Empress Theodora** with her retinue and the **Emperor Justinian** attended by his court. These works display the splendour, hieratic power and strong outlines which are typical of Byzantine art. On the ceiling **Christ in Majesty** is between St Vitalis and Bishop Ecclesio *(on the right)*, the church's founder.

Mausoleo di Galla Placidia★★★

This mid-5C mausoleum is embellished by mosaics. Serene scenes decorate the tympanum and pendentives. Note the *Good Shepherd*, on the west wall. The sarcophagi in the mausoleum were made to house Galla Placidia and her family. The Benedictine monastery adjacent to the basilica houses the **Museo Nazionale**, which has some fine displays, particularly late Roman and paleo-Christian artefacts, textiles, ivories and Cretan-Venetian icons.

Battistero Neoniano
(or degli Ortodossi)★

The baptistery, erected in the 5C by Bishop Neoni, is also known as the Orthodox Baptistery in contrast to the Arian baptistery erected by the Goth Theodoric. It has a vault that is covered in splendid mosaics: in the dome there is a portrayal of the **Baptism of Christ** accompanied by the Apostles; the lower section portrays eight small temples with altars and thrones surmounted by the cross, an Eastern iconography which refers to the preparation of the Almighty's throne for the Last Judgement.

Museo Arcivescovile

The Episcopal Palace museum displays a small lapidary collection and Archbishop Maximian's **throne★★** (6C), a masterpiece in carved ivory. The **Cappella di Sant'Andrea★** contains remarkable mosaics.

Battistero degli Ariani

The **Arians' Baptistery** was built by the Goth Theodoric in the 6C. The dome is decorated with **mosaics** that make use of the same iconography, if less elegantly, as the Neoniano Baptistery.

Basilica di
Sant'Apollinare Nuovo★★

Erected between 493 and 526 by Theodoric, probably as a Palatine church, St Apollinaris is divided into a nave and two aisles articulated by beautifully crafted columns in Greek marble with Corinthian capitals.

The north and south walls are decorated with a series of **mosaics** on a gold background distributed over three sections: the upper sections date from Theodoric's reign while the lower section was remodelled by Justinian, who eliminated any reference to Arianism. The lower registry on the south side shows a **Procession of martyrs** leaving Theodoric's palace led by St Martin making their way towards Christ the King. The opposite side shows a **Procession of Virgins** led by the Magi leaving the city of Ravenna and the port of Classis with its three anchored ships.

Basilica di Sant'Apollinare
in Classe★★

❯ 5km/3mi S. Leave Ravenna by the S 67.

The basilica stands in open country not far from the sea. The basilica was begun in 534 and consecrated in 549; a cylindrical campanile was added in the 11C. The majestic interior is composed of a nave and two aisles separated by arches on marble columns with Corinthian capitals. In the aisles lie Christian sarcophagi (5C–8C). The triumphal arch and apse feature 6C–7C **mosaics** with a lovely harmony of colour.

The triumphal arch shows Christ the Saviour surrounded by symbols representing the Evangelists; underneath there are two groups of six lambs (the Apostles) leaving two towered cities (Bethlehem and Jerusalem). The vaulting of the apse shows the Transfiguration: dominated by the hand of God. At the ends of the arms the Greek letters alpha and omega indicate that Christ is the beginning and the end.

Mausoleo di Teodorico★

Open daily 8.30am–7pm (winter 4.30pm). 4€, 8€/10€ with Museo Nazionale/also with Basilica di Sant'Apollinare in Classe. ℘0544 68 40 20. www.turismo.ra.it.

This curious mausoleum, erected by Theodoric around 520, is built of huge blocks of freestone assembled without mortar. The two-storey building is covered by a remarkable monolithic dome. Inside, the decoration includes

---

What is Arianism?

The spread of Arianism began in the 4C following the preaching of the Alexandrian priest Arius (280–336). The Arian heresy maintained that Christ was not fully divine. Condemned by the Council of Nicaea in 325, Arianism flourished in the East in the 4C and among Goths, Vandals and Lombards until the 6C.

a Romanesque porphyry basin that has been transformed into a sarcophagus.

Sepolcro di Dante

The writer Dante was exiled from the city of Florence and eventually took refuge at Ravenna, where he died in 1321. The Classical building in which the tomb now stands was erected in 1780.

Chiesa di San Francesco

This 10C Romanesque church is flanked by a campanile of the same period. Remodelled after World War II, it still retains some fine Greek marble columns, a 5C high altar and a 10C crypt.

ADDRESSES

⌂ STAY

🛏 **Hotel Ravenna** – Via Maroncelli 12. ☎0544 21 22 04. www.hotelravenna.ra.it. 25 rooms. Simple rooms that are uncluttered and comfortable.

🛏 **Ostello Galletti Abbiosi** – Via di Roma 140. ☎0544 31 313. www.palazzo gallettirabbiosi.it. ♿ 32 rooms. ⌷. Set in Ravenna's old town centre, this hotel offers spacious and comfortable accommodation.

🛏🍽🍽 **Cappello** – Via IV Novembre 41. ☎0544.21 98 13. www.albergocappello.it. 7 rooms. A distinguished hotel occupying in the centre. Elegant rooms, some with Renaissance frescoes, with evocative names and a charming atmosphere.

🍽 EAT

🛏 **Ca' de Vén** – Via Corrado Ricci 24. ☎0544 30 163. www.cadeven.it. Closed Mon. Reservation recommended. A rustic trattoria with a timeless atmosphere and long wooden tables. Famous for its *piadina* – the local speciality flatbread.

Rimini★★

A popular seaside resort with modern hotels and a great beach, Rimini's attractive historic centre has a completely different character testifying to an illustrious past. The picturesque Borgo San Giuliano district, a former fishermen's village, contrasts with both.

A BIT OF HISTORY

Rimini flourished during the Roman Empire. In the 13C, ruled by the **Malatesta** family, the town grew again. Dante immortalised the tragic story of lovers Paolo Malatesta and Francesca da Rimini, murdered by Gianni Malatesta (his brother and her husband). In the 16C Rimini became a Papal town. Giotto's work in Tempio Malatestiano sparked the **Riminese school** in the 14C. As birthplace of film director **Federico Fellini** (1920–93) Rimini shot to international fame in the 20C.

▶ **Population:** 141 505

⚙ **Michelin Map:** 562, 563 J 19. Town map in the Michelin Atlas Italy.

🛈 **Info:** Piazzale Cesare Battisti 1. ☎0541 51 331. www.riminiturismo.it. www.riviera.rimini.it.

◉ **Location:** On the Adriatic Coast. The main access roads are the A 14, S 9 (the Via Emilia) and the S 16.

◉ **Train:** Rimini.

◉ **Don't Miss:** Ponte di Tiberio, Borgo San Giuliano, Tempio Malatestiano.

◉ **Timing:** Allow half a day.

SIGHTS
Tempio Malatestiano★★

Via 4 Novembre 35. ♿Open Mon–Fri 8.30am–12pm and 3.30–6.30pm, Sat 8.30am–12.30pm and 3.30–7pm, Sun

Tempio Malatestiano

9am–12.30pm and 3.30–6.30pm.
℘0541 51 130.

Originally a 13C Franciscan church, it became the Malatesta mausoleum, modified (15C) by **Leon Battista Alberti** with Classical elements to house the tombs of Sigismondo and his beloved wife Isotta. The **interior** has an decoration by Agostino di Duccio with medieval, pagan and Classical elements (note the enchanting **childhood games**, second chapel, right). The south aisle houses Sigismondo's tomb and reliquary chapel with a portrait **Sigismondo Malatesta and St Sigismondo★★** by Piero della Francesca. Isotta's tomb rests on elephants holding Sigismondo's crest (SI). Behind the altar is Giotto's **painted 14C crucifix★★**.

Arco d'Augusto

Piazzale Giulio Cesare.
The majestic Arch of Augustus was built in 27 BC.

The Historic Centre

Piazza Cavour has the town hall, Palazzo dell'Arengo and Palazzo del Podestà, all 13C–14C. In Via Cairoli the **Church of Sant'Agostino** has some good examples of 14C Riminese painting.

Ponte di Tiberio

The bridge was begun under Augustus, completed under the Emperor Tiberius in AD 21, and built from blocks of Istrian limestone. Over the bridge is **Borgo San Giuliano**, with former fishermen's dwellings and a good choice of trattorias.

ADDRESSES

🛏 STAY

🛏 **Hotel Rondinella et Dependance Viola** – Via Neri 3. ℘0541 38 05 67. www.hotelrondinella.it. 🅿🛶 59 rooms. A modern hotel with impeccable service, a garden for breakfast and a private pool.

🛏🛏 **Hotel Diana** – Via Porto Palos 15, Viserbella, 8km/5mi N of Rimini. ℘0541 73 81 58. www.hoteldiana-rimini.com. Closed Oct–Feb. 38 rooms. 🛶🛶 Seafront hotel with swimming pools, fitness centre and plenty to do for kids.

🛏🛏 **Locanda Antiche Macine** – Via Provinciale Sogliano 1540, Montalbano, 18km/11.2mi W of Rimini, beyond Sant'Arcangelo di Romagna. ℘0541 62 71 61. www.antichemacine.it. 10 rooms. A 17C house with adjoining olive mill set in verdant countryside. Swimming pool and excellent local cuisine.

🛏🛏🛏🛏 **Grand Hotel** – Parco Fellini 1, Rimini. ℘0541 56 000. www.grandhotelrimini.com. 117 rooms. 🛶. Restaurant 🛏🛏🛏. An elegant, majestic hotel inextricably linked to Rimini-born film-maker Federico Fellini.

🍽 EAT

🛏🛏 **Dei Cantoni** – Via Santa Maria 19, Longiano, 22km/13mi NW. ℘0547 66 58 99. www.ristorantedeicantoni.it. Closed Wed. This lovely restaurant is situated in historic Longiano. Outside tables and seasonal regional cuisine.

🛏🛏 **La Baracca** – Via Marecchiese 373, Vergiano. 4.5km/2.8mi SW. ℘0541 72 74 83.

www.labaracca.com. Closed Wed. A simple restaurant with a friendly, family atmosphere.

🍷🍷 **Osteria De Borg** – Via Forzieri 12. 📞0541 56 074. www.osteriadeborg.it. Closed Jul–Aug lunch. Set in the characteristic San Giuliano district, serving hearty local food and wine.

SHOPPING

Stamperia Ruggine – Via Bertani 36. 📞0541 50 811. Open Tue–Sat 9am–1pm and 3.30–7.30pm. Watch craftsmen make traditional rust-printed fabrics.

ACTIVITIES

Delfinario – Lungomare Tintori 2. 📞0541 50 298. www.leonimarinirimini.it. Closed Oct–Mar. This dolphinarium has live shows daily.

👥 **La Riviera dei Parchi** – There are several theme parks around Rimini, including **Italia in Miniatura** at Viserba, **Fiabilandia** at Rivazzurra, and the **Acquarium** in Cattolica. Riccione has **Acquafan and Oltremare**. Consorzio La Riviera dei Parchi. www.larivieradeiparchi. it. At the Acquarium in Cattolica, visitors can experience a thrilling dive into the shark tank. Must be booked in advance. 📞0541 83 71. www.acquariodicattolica.it.

Répubblica di San Marino★

San Marino Republic

One of the smallest states in the world (61sq km/23sq mi), San Marino stands in an admirable site★★★ on the slopes of Monte Titano. This ancient republic still has its own postage stamps and police force. The system of government has changed little over the centuries, and the leading figures are still the two Captains Regent, who are chosen from among the 60 members of the Grand Council.

▶ **Population:** 31 000

📍 **Michelin Map:** 562, 563 K 19. Town map in the Michelin Atlas Italy.

ℹ️ **Info:** Contrada Omagnano20, Repubblica di San Marino. 📞0549 88 29 14. www.visitsanmarino.com.

▶ **Location:** San Marino is set back from the Adriatic Sea, 22km/13.7mi southwest of Rimini, on the S 72.

👁 **Don't Miss:** The panoramic views, the walk between the three fortresses.

🕐 **Timing:** Allow a day.

A BIT OF HISTORY

Officially founded in AD 301, the republic is considered the world's oldest. San Marino's inaccessible location and relative poverty helped it to maintain its independence, which was recognised in 1631 by the Papacy. Even during World War II this small state was able to remain neutral. San Marino was the world's smallest republic until Nauru gained independence in 1968.

SIGHTS
Palazzo Pubblico

Open daily summer 8am–8pm; rest of the year 9am–5pm. Closed

1 Jan, 25 Dec, 2 Nov (pm). 4€. 📞0549 88 31 52. www.museidistato.sm. Government House was rebuilt in the Gothic style in the late-19C. The Great Council Chamber and other rooms are open to visitors. Fescoes recount some of the history of the republic.

Basilica di San Marino

The basilica contains the relics of the saint while the nearby church of San Pietro has niches hewn into the rock where San Marino and his companion San Leo are said to have slept. A little out of the centre steps lead to a more substantial cave-like niche where Marino lived as a hermit.

Rocche (Guaita, Cesta and della Fratta, Montale)

These three peaks are crowned with three fortified buildings linked by a lovely panoramic footpath. There are splendid views★★★ of the Apennines, the plain, Rimini and the sea on clear days. Torre Cesta houses a museum of historic firearms, **Museo delle Armi Antiche.** Open daily summer 8am–8pm; rest of the year 9am–5pm. Closed 1 Jan, 2 Nov (pm), 25 Dec. 4€. ℘0549 99 12 95. www.museidistato.sm.

Museo-Pinacoteca di San Francesco

Open daily summer 8am–8pm; rest of the year 9am–5pm. Closed 1 Jan, 2 Nov (pm), 25 Dec. 4€. ℘0549 88 51 32. www.museidistato.sm.
Paintings of the 12C–17C and 20C, Etruscan pottery and funerary objects.

EXCURSIONS
San Leo★★
🚗 16km/10mi SW.
A steep winding road climbs to the summit of the huge limestone rock (639m/2 096ft) in a very impressive **setting★★**, made famous by Dante in his *Divine Comedy*, with the historic village of San Leo and its 15C **fortress★** designed by Francesco di Giorgio Martini. From the fortress, which houses a **museum**, there is an immense **panorama★★★**.
The cathedral, which is in the Lombard-Romanesque style (1173), and the pre-Romanesque parish church (restored) are noteworthy. The 16C Palazzo Mediceo *(Piazza Dante Alighieri 14)* houses the **Museo d'Arte Sacra**, with works of the 14C–18C. *Museums:* Open 9.30am–6.45pm. Fortezza: 9€; museo d'Arte Sacra: 3€. ℘0541 92 69 67. www.riviera.rimini.it.

ADDRESSES

🍴 EAT
🍽️ **Righi** – Piazza Libertà 10. ℘0549 99 11 96. www.ristoranterighi.com. A renowned eating establishment in San Marino's lovely main square. Elegant dining room with an interesting and varied menu. Downstairs is the informal *osteria,* with some outdoor tables.

Faenza

Having given its name to the faience ceramics *(ceramica di Faenza)*, Faenza is synonymous with its glazed and painted ceramics, produced here since the 15C.

VISIT
Pinacoteca Comunale★
Via Santa Maria dell'Angelo 9. Open Sat–Sun, Jun–Sept 10am–1pm and 3–7pm; Oct–May 10am–6pm. Free. ℘0546 68 02 51. www.racine.ra.it/pinacotecafaenza.
This important art collection includes works by Giovanni da Rimini, Palmezzano, Dosso Dossi and Rossellino.

- ▶ **Population:** 57 664
- **Michelin Map:** 562, 563, 430 J 17 – Emilia Romagna.
- **Info:** Voltone della Molinella 2. ℘0546 25 231. www.prolocofaenza.it.
- **Location:** Faenza is off the SS 9, the Via Emilia, linking Bologna with Rimini.
- **Train:** Faenza (Bologna Centrale 26 mins).
- **Don't Miss:** The Museo Internazionale delle Ceramiche.
- **Timing:** Set aside a day to see the town fully.

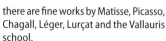

Museo Internazionale delle Ceramiche

Cattedrale
The 15C cathedral was built by Giuliano da Maiano but the façade is unfinished. It contains the tomb (1471) of Bishop St Savinus by Benedetto da Maiano.

Piazza del Popolo
The elongated square is bordered by the 12C Palazzo del Podestà (governor's house) and the 13C–15C Palazzo del Municipio (town hall).

MUSEUM
Museo Internazionale delle Ceramiche★★
Viale Baccarini 19. ♿ Open Tues–Sun, Apr–Sept 10am–7pm; Oct–Mar 10am–5.30pm (closes 1.30pm Tue–Fri). Closed 1 Jan, 1 May, 15 Aug, 25 Dec. 8€. ☎0546 69 73 11. www.micfaenza.org.
These vast collections present the development of ceramic work throughout the world. On the first floor is a collection of Italian-Renaissance majolica, examples of the local ware and an Oriental section. On the ground floor

---

Ceramics

In Italy faience is also known as majolica, because during the Renaissance Faenza potters were inspired by ceramics which were imported from Majorca in the Balearic Isles. Faenza ceramics feature fine clay, remarkable glaze, brilliant colours and a great variety of decoration. An international competition and biennial of art ceramics celebrate a vocation that is still strongly felt by artists and artisans.

---

there are fine works by Matisse, Picasso, Chagall, Léger, Lurçat and the Vallauris school.

EXCURSIONS
Cesena
▶ 20km/12.4mi SE of Forlì. Tourist Office, Piazza del Popolo 9. ☎0547 35 63 27. www.comune.cesena.fc.it.
The town lies at the foot of a hill on which stands the great 15C castle of the Malatestas. It contains the Renaissance library, **Biblioteca Malatestiana★** *(Piazza Bufalini)*. On display are valuable manuscripts, including some from the famous school of miniaturists at Ferrara. Guided tours by appt. Nov–Mar Mon 2–4pm, Tue–Sat 9am–4pm, Sun 10am–4pm; Apr–Oct Tue–Fri 9am–7pm, Sat 9am–1pm. 5€. ☎0547 61 08 92. www.malatestiana.it.

Forlì
▶ 17km/10.6mi SE.
Situated on the Via Emilia, Forlì was an independent commune ruled by an overlord in the 13C and 14C. The citadel was heroically defended against Cesare Borgia in 1500 by Caterina Sforza.
The **Basilica of San Mercuriale** *(Piazza Aurelio Saffi)* is dominated by an imposing Romanesque campanile. Numerous works of art inside include several paintings by Marco Palmezzano and the tomb of Barbara Manfredi by Francesco di Simone Ferrucci. Forli's **Pinacoteca** (art gallery) is located in the refurbished San Domenico museum complex and includes works by local 13–15C artists. Open Tue–Sun, 10am–6pm. 3€. ☎0543 71 26 59. www.turismoforlivese.it.

Bertinoro
▶ 12km/7.4mi W of Cesena. Piazza della Libertà 9. ☎0543 46 92 13. www.comune.bertinoro.fc.it.
This small town is famous for its panorama and its yellow wine (Albana). In the middle of the town is a "hospitality column" fitted with rings, each corresponding to a local house. The ring to which the traveller tethered his horse would determine which family should be his hosts. From the nearby terrace there is a wide **view★** of Romagna.

Modena★

Modena is a commercial and industrial centre; it is also home of the iconic Ferrari racing cars and one of the most important towns in Emilia Romagna, with an archbishopric and university. It remains a quiet town, however, with an old quarter around the cathedral. Look out for such gastronomic specialities as balsamic vinegar, *zamponi* (stuffed pigs' trotters) and Lambrusco, the sparkling red wine which is produced locally.

- ▶ **Population:** 183 114
- **Michelin Map:** 561, 562 or 563 I 14. Town map in the Michelin Atlas Italy – Emilia Romagna.
- **Info:** Piazza Grande 14, 41100 Modena. ℘059 20 32 660. www.visitmodena.it.
- ▶ **Location:** About 40km/ 25mi from Bologna.
- ▶ **Train:** Modena (Bologna Centrale 23 mins).
- **Don't Miss:** The Duomo and Galleria Estense.
- **Timing:** Allow a day.

VISIT
Duomo★★★
www.duomodimodena.it.

The cathedral, founded in 1099 and dedicated to St Geminiano, is one of the best examples of Romanesque architecture in Italy. Here Lombard architect **Lanfranco** gave vent to his sense of rhythm and proportion, the *Maestri Campionesi* adding the finishing touches. Most of the decoration is due to **Wiligelmo**, a 12C Lombard sculptor. The façade is divided into three parts, crowned by the Angel of Death carrying a fleur-de-lis, a work carried out by the Campionesi Masters. The central portal is enhanced by a porch supported by two lions by Wiligelmo. The remarkable south side, overlooking the square, has from left to right the Prince's Doorway by Wiligelmo, the Royal Entrance by the Campionesi Masters in the 13C and a 16C pulpit decorated with the symbols of the four Evangelists. To reach the other side of the church, walk under the Gothic arches linking the cathedral to the Romanesque campanile built of white marble (88m/289ft) known as **Ghirlandina** because of the bronze garland on its weather vane. The recessed orders of the arches are decorated with episodes from the Breton cycle.

The **interior** of the cathedral is Gothic Romanesque. In the north aisle beyond the 15C Altare delle Statuine is a 14C pulpit and a wooden seat said to have been used by the public executioner.

The **roodscreen★★★**, a Romanesque masterpiece, is supported by Lombardy lions and telamones and is by the Campionesi Masters (12C–13C). The atmospheric crypt has a terra-cotta sculpture group of the **Holy Family★** (15C) by Guido Mazzoni, and St Geminiano's tomb. In the south aisle is an exquisite 16C Nativity.

The **Museo del Duomo** contains the famous 12C **metopes★★**, low reliefs which used to surmount the flying buttresses. They represent wandering players or symbols incomprehensible today, but whose modelling, balance and style have an almost Classical air. ♿Open Tue–Sun 9.30am–12.30pm and 3.30–6.30pm. 4€. ℘059 43 96 969. www. duomodimodena.it.

Palazzo dei Musei
This 18C palace contains the two most important art collections gathered by the Este family.

Biblioteca Estense★
♿ Open Mon–Sat 8.30am–7.15pm (Fri closes 3.45pm, Sat closes 1.45pm). ℘059 22 22 48.

This is one of the richest libraries in Italy, containing 600 000 books and 15 000 manuscripts. The prize exhibit is the **Bible of Borso d'Este★★**. It has 1020 pages illuminated by 15C Ferrara artists, including Taddeo Crivelli.

Galleria Estense★

♿ Open Tue–Sat 8.30am–7pm, Sun–Mon 2–7pm. 4€. ✆059 43 95 711. www.galleriaestense.org.

This gallery opens with the **Marble bust of Francesco I d'Este** by Gian Lorenzo Bernini. The 15C Modena school is well represented; from the Ferrarese school is the powerfully modelled **St Anthony★** by Cosmè Tura. There is also a fine collection of Venetian masters, 16C Ferrarese painting and works linked to the Accademia degli Incamminati in Bologna. Foreign works include the **Portrait of Francesco I d'Este** by Velázquez. The gallery also has 15C–16C terra-cotta figures, ceramics and musical instruments; note the **Este harp** (1581).

Palazzo Ducale★

This noble and majestic building, the Ducal Palace, was begun in 1634 for Francesco I d'Este and has an elaborately elegant design. Today it is occupied by the Infantry and Cavalry schools.

EXCURSIONS

Abbazia di Nonantola

◐ 11km/6.8mi N. Open 10am–1pm, Sat and Sun also 2–6pm.
Hours are subject to change.
www.abbazia-nonantola.net.

The abbey was founded in the 8C and flourished during the Middle Ages. The 12C abbey church has some remarkable **Romanesque sculpture★** carved by Wiligelmo's assistants in 1121.

Carpi

◐ 18km/11mi N.

This attractive small town has a 16C Renaissance cathedral by Peruzzi, overlooking **Piazza dei Martiri★**. Frescoed rooms and a museum on the town's history can be seen at **Castello dei Pio★**. Open Thu, Sat–Sun 10am–1pm and 3–7pm, other days by request. 5€. ✆059 64 99 55. www.palazzodeipio.it. The 12–16C Church of Sagra has a Romanesque campanile, **Torre della Sagra.**

Reggio Emilia

◐ 25km/15.3mi W on the SS 9 (Via Emilia). http://turismo.comune.re.it.

This rich industrial and commercial centre on the Via Emilia was the birthplace of the poet Ariosto (1474–1533) and painter Antonio Fontanesi (1818–82). Like Modena and Ferrara, it belonged to the Este family (1409–1776).

The Historic Centre

Piazza Prampolini, the political, religious and economic centre of the town, is overlooked by the 15C cathedral, the Romanesque baptistery and the town hall with its 16C Bordello tower.

To the right of the cathedral is the lively Via Broletto, which leads into Piazza San Prospero. This square is dominated by the 18C façade of the San Prospero basilica, which has a cycle of frescoes in the apse by C. Procaccini and B. Campi.

Tempio della Beata Vergine della Ghiara★

Corso Garibaldi 44. Open 7.30am–noon and 4–5.30pm (Sun and public hols to 8.30pm. ✆0522 43 97 07.

This beautiful early-17C church was built following a miracle. The interior has splendid frescoes and an anthology of 17C Emilian painting; note the *Crucifixion* by Guercino.

ADDRESSES

⊕/EAT

⊖⊜ **Al Boschetto-da Loris** – Via Due Canali Nord 202. ✆059 25 17 59. Closed Sun eve. The historic Duca d'Este's shooting lodge (18C) among ancient trees serves good Modenese cooking.

⊖⊜ **Osteria Francescana** – Via Stella 22. ✆059 22 39 12. www.osteriafrancescana.it. Closed Sun and Mon, 2 weeks in Jan. Chef Massimo Bottura is legendary for his creative cuisine, great wines, first-rate ingredients, lovely presentations, and professional serivce. One of Italy's few restaurants to be awarded three Michelin stars.

Parma★★

Parma is an important market town with a rich musical heritage – the famous 20C conductor Arturo Toscanini was born here. The town has a refined charm and a gastronomic reputation that centres on two of the country's most prized culinary possessions: Parmesan cheese and dry-cured Parma ham. At the heart of the town is Piazza Garibaldi, a popular meeting-place.

A BIT OF HISTORY

A settlement was founded here by Etruscans in 525 BC and it became a Roman station on the Via Emilia in 183 BC. It declined but revived in the 6C under Ostrogoth King Theodoric. After having been an independent commune in the 11C–13C, it became a member of the Lombard League. After the fall of the commune's government in 1335, Parma was governed in turn by the Visconti, the Sforza and, later, the French before being annexed by the Papacy in 1513. In 1545 Pope Paul III, Alessandro Farnese, gave two Papal territories, Parma and Piacenza, having made them a duchy, to his son Pier Luigi Farnese, who was assassinated in 1547. However, the **Farnese** dynasty reigned until 1731 and several members of the house were patrons of the arts and letters, collectors and great builders.

When Parma passed to the Bourbons, the first sovereign was Charles, successively King of Naples then King of Spain. When Don Philip, son of Philip V of Spain and Elizabeth Farnese, married Louise Elizabeth, the favourite daughter of Louis XV, the town underwent a period of great French influence (1748–1801), echoes of which linger to this day. Numerous Frenchmen came to work in Parma while others like Stendhal chose to live here; he made Parma the setting of his well-known novel *The Charterhouse of Parma*. The Bourbons of Parma had their Versailles at Colorno, north of the town.

▶ **Population:** 184 467

⚹ **Michelin Map:** 561, 562 H 12–13 – Emilia Romagna.

🛈 **Info:** Piazza garibaldi 1, 43121 Parma. ℘0521 21 88 89. http://turismo. comune.parma.it.

▶ **Location:** Parma is situated near the A 1, between the Po and the Apennines.

▶ **Train:** Parma (Bologna Centrale 52 mins).

⊛ **Don't Miss:** The Episcopal Centre, the food museums (Musei del Cibo) and Castello di Torrechiara.

🕓 **Timing:** Allow two days to see Parma fully.

The Parma School

The school is represented by two main artists, Correggio and Il Parmigianino, whose works formed the transition between Renaissance and Baroque art. Antonio Allegri (1489–1534), known as **Correggio**, was a master of light and chiaroscuro; his work shows a gracefully sensual and optimistic vision which heralds 18C French art. Francesco Mazzola (1503–40), known as **Il Parmigianino**, was a more melancholy personality. His elongated forms and cold colours were characteristic of Mannerism. His canon of feminine beauty influenced the Fontainebleau school and the other 16C European Mannerists, through Niccolò dell'Abbate and Il Primaticcio.

🐾WALKING TOUR

This historic core of the city comprises the Romanesque **Episcopal Centre★★★** including the cathedral and baptistery, the Baroque church of San Giovanni and surrounding palaces as well as the Palazzo della Pilotta (16C–17C) and Correggio's Room.

Duomo★★

The Romanesque cathedral is flanked by an elegant Gothic campanile. The façade has a Lombard porch supported by lions and surmounted by a loggia and three tiers of galleries. Inside, the dome is decorated with the famous **frescoes** painted by Correggio (1522–30). The ascending rhythm of the *Assumption of the Virgin* with the central figure amid a swirling group of cherubim is remarkable. The artist's mastery of perspective and movement is expressed in an original and almost Baroque exuberant style. In the south transept the **Descent from the Cross** (1178) by sculptor Antelami clearly shows the influence of the Provençal school, although the solemnity of the figures distinguishes it.

In the nave, the frescoes are by Gambara (1530–74); those on the vaulting are by Bedoli (16C). The gilded copper *Angel* (1284) that was on the spire of the bell tower is now on the third pillar to the left of the nave.

Battistero★★★

This is Italy's most harmonious medieval monument. The octagonal baptistery in Verona rose-coloured marble dates from 1196 with 13C decoration. The baptistery is attributed to Antelami, who was also responsible for the sculptures; his signature appears on the lintel of the north door. The interior, a 16-sided polygon, has remarkable bas reliefs of the labours of the months with signs of the zodiac, admirable 13C Byzantine-style **frescoes** depicting scenes from the *Life of Christ* and the *Golden Legend*.

Chiesa di San Giovanni Evangelista

This Renaissance church, dedicated to St John the Evangelist, has a Baroque façade. Inside, the **frescoes on the dome★★**, by Correggio (1520–24), depict the *Vision of St John at Patmos* and the *Translation of St John the Evangelist*. Those on the arches of the chapels to the north *(first, second and fourth)* were executed by Parmigianino. In the monastery next door are the **Renaissance cloisters**. Church open 8.30am–11.45 and 3–5.30pm,

Sun only pm; monastery open 9–11.45am and 3–5pm, closed Thu and Sun. ℘0521 23 53 11.

Antica Spezieria di San Giovanni Evangelista

&. Open Tue–Sat 8.30am–2pm. 2€. ℘0521 50 85 32.
This 13C pharmacy was started by the Benedictine monks. The furnishings date from the 16C.

Camera di San Paolo★

&. Open Tue–Fri 8.30am–2pm, Sat 8.30am–6pm, Jul–Aug Sat 8.30am–2pm. 2€.
This was the dining room of the Abbess of St Paul's Convent. The light-filled ceiling frescoes depicting mythological scenes are Correggio's first major work (1519–20). Garlands of flowers, trelliswork and architectural detail reveal the influence of Mantegna, whom he met in his youth in Mantova (&*see MANTOVA)*.

Teatro Regio

www.teatroregioparma.org.
The Royal Theatre, built 1821–9 for Marie-Louise of Habsburg, has a Classical frontage and excellent acoustics. The first performance was Bellini's opera *Zaira*.

Chiesa di Madonna della Steccata

Open daily 9am–noon and 3–6pm. Donation recommended.
℘0521 23 49 37.
This 16C church, designed by Bernardino and Zaccagni, has fine **frescoes★** by Parmigianino representing *The Foolish and the Wise Virgins*, *Adam and Moses* and *Eve and Aaron*. The mausoleum of Neipperg, husband of the former French Empress Marie-Louise, who became Duchess of Parma, is on the left, and the tombs of the Farnese family and the Parma Bourbons are in the crypt.

Palazzo della Pilotta

The palace was so called because the game of fives *(pilotta)* was played in its courtyards. This austere building houses the Palatine Library, National Archaeological Museum, National Gallery and the Farnese Theatre (&see below).

Museo Archeologico Nazionale★
& Open Tue–Fri 9am–4.30pm, Sat–Sun 1–7pm, closed last Sun of the month. 4€. ☏0521 23 37 18. www.archeobo.arti. beniculturali.it.
Displays include pre-Roman and Roman artefacts with finds made in the excavation of Velleia, west of Parma.

Galleria Nazionale★★
& Open Tue–Sat 8.30am–7pm, Sun 8.30am–2pm. 6€ including Teatro Farnese. ☏0521 23 33 09. www.parmabeniartistici.beniculturali.it.
The gallery exhibits Emilian, Tuscan and Venetian paintings of the 14C–16C by Fra Angelico, Dosso Dossi, El Greco, Canaletto, Bellotto, Piazzetta and Tiepolo. Parmigianino is represented by his portrait *Turkish Slave*, and Correggio by one of his masterpieces, *The Virgin with St Jerome* (1528). The gallery also houses a sketch by Leonardo da Vinci (*La Scapigliata*).

Teatro Farnese★★
& Open Tue–Sat 8.30am–7pm, Sun 8.30am–2pm. 6€ including Galleria Nazionale. ☏0521 23 33 09. www.parmabeniartistici.beniculturali.it.
This imposing theatre was built in wood in 1619 by G. B. Aleotti, following the model of Palladio's Olympic Theatre in Vicenza (&see VICENZA). Inaugurated for the marriage of Margaret de' Medici and Odoardo Farnese, the theatre was almost totally destroyed in 1944 and was rebuilt exactly as before in the 1950s.

Palazzo del Giardino
The **Parco Ducale**★(Ducal Garden) was landscaped by the French architect Petitot and adorned with statues by another Frenchman, Boudard.

ADDITIONAL SIGHTS
Museo Glauco Lombardi★
& Open Tue–Sat 9.30am–4pm, Sun and public hols 9am–7pm (Jul–Aug to 2pm). 5€. ☏0521 23 37 27. www.museolombardi.it.

The museum focuses mainly on life in the Duchy of Parma and Piacenza in the 18C and 19C, with paintings and artefacts relating to Duchess Marie-Louise, whose capable rule lasted until 1847. The collections include works by numerous French painters, including La Tour, Boucher, Hubert Robert, Vigée-Lebrun, David and Millet.

Museo Casa Toscanini
Borgo Rodolfo Tanzi 13. & Open Tue 9am–1pm, Wed–Sat 9am–1pm and 2–6pm, Sun 10am–6pm. 2€. ☏0521 28 54 99. www.museotoscanini.it.
The birthplace of the famous conductor Toscanini (1867–1957) contains some interesting exhibits for those with a keen interest in music, including distinctions and decorations received by the conductor, sculptures and objects connected to the Toscanini family, as well as to the Verdi and Wagner families, letters from Mazzini, Garibaldi, D'Annunzio and Einstein, plus numerous mementoes of Toscanini's time in America. There is also an audiovisual presentation of the conductor's career.

Pinacoteca Stuard
Borgo Parmigianino 2. & Open Wed–Mon 10am–5pm, Sat–Sun 10.30–6.30pm. 4€. ☏0521 21 87 95.
In the former monastery of San Paolo, this collection contains works of the 14C–20C, including an extensive section devoted to 14C–15C Tuscan art. The exhibition area includes the *sacellum*, a former defensive structure later transformed into a belfry.

Museo dell'Opera
Piazzale San Francesco 1. & Open Thu–Fri 10am–2pm (afternoon by reservation), Sat and Sun 10am–6pm, Mon–Wed by reservation. Closed 1 Jan, 1 May, 25 Dec. 2€. ☏0521 03 11 70. www.operamuseo.parma.it.
The museum, which forms part of the Casa della Musica, an institution dedicated to musical research and documentation, offers an interactive presentation of the history of opera in Parma.

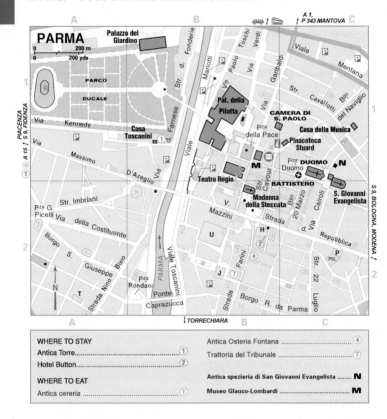

EXCURSIONS

Castello di Torrechiara★

🕒 17km/10.6mi S. ♿Open Mar–Oct Tue, Sun and hols 8.30am–7.30pm; Nov–Feb Tue–Fri 9am–4.30pm, Sat–Sun and hols 10am–5pm. 3€. ✆0521 35 52 55. www.castellidelducato.it.

This 15C fortress, built on a hilltop, is powerfully fortified by double ramparts, massive corner towers, a keep and machicolated curtain walls. The upper rooms (the Gaming and Gold rooms) have remarkable **frescoes★**. From the terrace there is a superb **view★** as far as the Apennines.

Castello di Canossa

🕒 32km/19.9mi SW of Parma. From Torrechiara (23km/14.3mi), take the SS 513 and follow for San Polo d'Enza. Open Oct–Mar Wed–Sun 9am–1pm and 1.30–4.30pm; Apr–Sept Tue–Sun 9am–12.30pm and 3–7pm. 3€. www.castellodicanossa.it.

Only the romantic ruins, perched on a rock, remain of the stronghold which belonged to the Countess of Tuscany, Matilda (1046–1115), who supported the Pope against the emperor for 30 years during the quarrel over the investiture of bishops and abbots.

Emperor Heinrich IV of Germany came barefoot and in his shirtsleeves through the snow, to make amends to Pope Gregory VII in 1077. He had to wait three days for his absolution. This is the origin of the expression "to go to Canossa"; that is, to humble oneself after a quarrel.

Fidenza

🕒 23km/14.3mi W on the SS 9.

This attractive agricultural town has a 11C Gothic-style **Duomo★** completed in the 13C. The sculpture of the **central porch★★** is most likely the work of the Parmesan sculptor Antelami. The three fine **Romanesque doors** are adorned with lions, a typically Emilian feature.

Fontanellato

◗ 19km/11.8mi NW then to Soragna.
The vast moat-encircled castle, **Rocca Sanvitale**, stands in the centre of the town of Fontanellato. The ceiling of one of the rooms is decorated with a **fresco★** depicting Diana and Actaeon by **Parmigianino.** ♿Open Apr–Oct Mon–Sat 9.30–11.30am and 3–6pm, Sun 9.30am–noon and 2.30–6pm; Nov–Feb Tue–Sat 10–11.30am and 2.30–4.30pm, Sun 10am–noon and 2.30–5pm, Mar Tue–Sat 9.30–11.30am and 3–5pm, Sun 9.30am–noon and 2.30–5pm. 4/7/8€ depending on the tour. ℘0521 82 90 55. www.castellidelducato.it.

Brescello

◗ 22km/13.7mi NW.
The town owes its name (originally *Brixellum*) to the Celts who settled on the Po Plain and who, as they had moved along the plain, had already founded the settlements of Bressanone *(Brixen)* and Brescia *(Brixia)*.
In spite of its ancient origins, Brescello nowadays is famous for being the setting of the films about Don Camillo and Peppone. The museum contains memorabilia and posters from the films as well as objects used during the filming such as bicycles, a motorcycle and sidecar and even a tank. ♿To visit, ask at tourist office. 4€ (ticket valid for three museums). ℘0522 48 25 64 or 0522 96 21 58. www.mondoguareschi.com.

ADDRESSES

🏠STAY

🛏Note that most hotels have higher tariffs when exhibitions and trade fairs are being held. It is advisable to check prices by telephone beforehand.

🍽🛏 **Antica Torre** – Via Case Bussandri 197, Cangelasio, 43039 Salsomaggiore Terme (from Salsomaggiore, head towards Cangelasio for 8km/5mi, then follow the signs for "Antica Torre"). ℘0524 57 54 25. www.anticatorre.it. Closed Dec–Feb. An ideal place to stay in the heart of the countryside, especially for families, on a farm that entirely encloses several hectares of land. Pleasant rooms with simple, rustic furnishings and friendly hosts. Guests can dine at the farm on delicious local cuisine.

🍽🛏 **Hotel Button** – Borgo della Salina 7. ℘0521 20 80 39. www.hotelbutton.it. 40 rooms. 🛏. Situated in the heart of the historic centre, between the Teatro Regio and Piazza del Duomo, this rather old-fashioned hotel is housed in a late-19C palazzo which incorporates various Art Nouveau features.

🍴EAT

🍽🍽 **Antica Cereria** – Borgo Rodolfo Tanzi 5. ℘0521 20 73 87. www.anticacereria.it. Closed lunch (except public hols). A very pleasant restaurant where customers choose their wine from the cellar. Local dishes with particularly good antipasti.

🍽🍽 **Antica Osteria Fontana** – Strada Farini 24. ℘0521 28 60 37. Closed Sun–Mon and Jul–Aug. At this *enoteca*-cum-restaurant, you can enjoy good wine to accompany cheeses, cured meats or more substantial dishes.

🍽🍽 **Trattoria del Tribunale** – Vicolo Politi 5. ℘0521 28 55 27. www.trattoriadeltribunale.it. A well-known local institution that takes its name from its location by the law court and combines the best of the local tradition with some appealing new ideas.

SHOPPING

Parma's world-class food products have fascinating dedicated museums – Musei del Cibo: www.museidelcibo.it.

Museo del Parmigiano Reggiano – Via Volta, Soragna (31km/19.3mi NW of Parma). ℘0524 59 61 29. Open Mar–8 Dec Sat–Sun and public hols 10am–1pm and 3–6pm. 5€ including taste.

Museo del Prosciutto – Via Bocchialini 7, Langhirano (23km/14.3mi S of Parma). ℘0521 86 43 24. Open Mar–8 Dec Sat–Sun and public hols 10am–6pm. 4€; 7€ including taste.

Museo del Salame di Felino – Castello di Felino (17km/10.6mi SW of Parma). ℘0521 83 18 09. Open Mar–8 Dec Sat–Sun and public hols 10am–1pm and 3–6pm. 4€ without taste.

Piacenza★

Piacenza was originally built by the Romans at the end of the Via Emilia on the south bank of the Po. It flourished in the Middle Ages and was a member of the Lombard League. In 1545 Pope Paul III, Alessandro Farnese, gave the Papal lands of Piacenza and its neighbour Parma to his son Pier Luigi along with a dukedom. After this the Farneses ruled Piacenza until 1731 when the dukedom passed to the Bourbons.

▪▪WALKING TOUR

The following is a walking excursion through Piacenza's historic centre. It is possible to break the tour into two days by ending one day at Chiesa di San Savino and beginning the next day at Palazzo Farnese. The walking tour takes about 2hrs altogether; visiting each sight requires extra time.

Piazza dei Cavalli★

The old political and economic centre of the city, this square derives its name from the equestrian statues★★ of Dukes Alessandro and Ranuccio I Farnese, a Baroque masterpiece by Francesco Mochi (1580–1654).

The square is dominated by the imposing "Gotico"★★, the old town hall, a masterpiece of 13C Lombard-Gothic architecture. The building is both severe and harmonious and displays a notable contrast between the marble lower part and the brick upper storeys, the great openings and the elegantly decorated windows.

To the left of the square is the façade of the 13C Church of San Francesco, an interesting example of Franciscan-Gothic architecture, embellished by a fine splayed doorway.

▶ Exit the piazza on its southern end (to the left of "Gotico") and head towards Piazzale Plebiscito. From there, turn left on Via Sopramura then

▶ **Population:** 102 687

▲ **Michelin Map:** 561 G 11. Town map in the Michelin Atlas Italy – Emilia Romagna.

▤ **Info:** Piazza Cavalli 10. ℘0523 49 20 01. www.provincia.pc.it/turismo.

▶ **Location:** Piacenza is situated on the banks of the River Po. It is the first city you reach as you enter Emilia from Lombardy on the A 1. The main road connecting it to Turin and Brescia is the A 21.

▶ **Train:** Piacenza (Milano Centrale 55mins).

▶ **Don't Miss:** The Duomo and the Musei Civici di Palazzo Farnese.

▶ **Timing:** The main sights can be seen in half a day.

right on Via Frasi. Walk down Via Frasi for about 100m/110yds until you reach Via Sant'Antonino. Turn right and the basilica is another 50m/55yds.

Basilica di Sant'Antonino

This former paleo-Christian basilica dedicated to St Anthony was remodelled in the 11C and has interesting features: an octagonal tower (40m/131ft high) and the north "Paradise" vestibule (1350) in the Gothic style.

▶ Return to Via Sant'Antonino and turn right. At Via Chiapponi, turn left and follow it straight until you reach Piazza del Duomo.

Duomo★

This remarkable Lombard-Romanesque cathedral dates to the 12C–13C. The façade is adorned with a rose window and a porch with three notable doorways. The two lateral doorways are influenced by the sculptural styles at Modena and Nonantola. The interior on the plan of a Latin cross is simple but enriched by the sweeping frescoes

(Guercino, Morazzone, 17C) which adorn the dome, and by the canvases in the chancel (Camillo Procaccini and Ludovico Carracci).

⊙ (The route from the Duomo to Chiesa di San Savino is about 0.5km/0.3mi long.) Exit Piazza del Duomo at Via Legnano. Follow this road for about 100m/110yds until you reach Via Roma. Turn right. Take Via Roma until Via Alberoni. Chiesa San Savino is located at Via Alberoni 35.

Chiesa di San Savino

This 12C church, with its pure architectural lines, contains priceless traces of the original construction, such as the fine capitals and the mosaic flooring★ in the chancel and in the crypt.

⊙ Return to Via Roma and follow it W for approximately 0.8km/0.5mi until it turns into Via Borghetto. Turn right on Via Cittadella. Palazzo Farnese is in Piazza Cittadella.

Palazzo Farnese

This imposing late Renaissance palace, built to designs by Vignola but never completed, now houses the Museo Civici★ (⊙see Additional Sight).

⊙ Take the NW exit and follow to Piazza Casali. Turn right onto Vicolo Angilberga then right again at Via San Sisto (about 5min).

Chiesa di San Sisto

This curious 16C building was designed by Alessio Tramello, an architect from Piacenza. The façade is preceded by a doorway, dated 1622, which opens onto a 16C atrium. The interior has an interesting Renaissance decoration and a splendid 16C wood chancel. Raphael painted the famous Sistine Madonna for this church, now replaced by a copy.

⊙ The walk from Chiesa di San Sisto to Chiesa della Madonna di Campagna is itself about 1km/0.6mi. Take Via San Sisto back to Vicolo Angilberga and turn right on Via Borghetto. At

Via Tomaso turn left, walking for about 5min to Via Campagna, where you should turn right. The Chiesa della Madonna di Campagna is about 0.5km/0.3mi down Via Campagna where it meets with Piazzale delle Crociate. The view of the church is worth the walk.

Chiesa della Madonna di Campagna★

This beautiful church, in the form of a Greek cross and built in the style of Bramante, is one of the most important Renaissance buildings in Italy. The interior contains splendid frescoes★ by Pordenone (1484–1539), an exponent of the Mannerist style.

ADDITIONAL SIGHT

Musei Civici di Palazzo Farnese★

Piazza Cittadella. ♿ Open 10am–1pm and 3–6pm (Fri–Sun to 7pm). Hours are subject to change. Closed public hols, 4 Jul. 6€. ☏0523 49 26 61. www. palazzofarnese.piacenza.it.

On the ground floor the sumptuous Fasti Farnesiani★ cycle of frescoes by Draghi and Ricci is richly framed in stuccowork. The images portray stories of Alessandro Farnese, who became Pope Paul III. There are also collections of ceramics and glass, frescoes from local churches (14C–15C) and a series of Romanesque sculptures of the "Piacenza school", which combine influences from both the contemporary French school and Wiligelmo (The Prophets David and Ezekiel, 12C).

Note also the bronze Etruscan Divining Liver★★, a soothsayer's device dating from the 2C to the 1C BC. The first floor houses collections of paintings from the 16C to the 19C Emilian, Lombard and Ligurian schools, a Virgin and Child with St John by Botticelli and the Fasti Farnesiani dedicated to Elisabetta Farnese. There is also a Carriage Museum and a Risorgimento Museum.

Central Italy

Lucca
© Marco Brivio / age fotostock

Central Italy

Framed by the Ligurian and Tyrrhenian seas to the west and by the Adriatic Sea to the east, central Italy is rich in artistic treasures, stunning landscapes, sports, medieval hill towns, culinary traditions and excellent wines.

Natural Beauty

The Apennine Mountains touch all three regions, but are more prevalent in Umbria. Thermal areas are a reminder of the volatile nature of the geography. From thermal baths to drinking water prescribed for a variety of ailments, each region has an abundance. With all the topological similarities, all regions have their own distinct characteristics. Even the colours change. The amber light of Tuscany casts an olive hue on the landscape. Umbria is drenched with the deep dense greens of its mountain forests, but above the hills the peculiar misty lavenders and blues of Raphael and Perugino are easy to observe. Le Marche's hills, an agricultural quilt, glow bright emerald green in patches.

Winter sports are on a small scale, but the Sibillini Mountains have simple ski runs that attract skiers from the region. The wide meadows of Castelluccio lead to an almost Shangri-La sensation when rounding the mountain pass. Sports facilities are ample in all regions, from riding paths for horses and bikes, to hiking, skiing, and swimming and boating along the coasts or soaking in thermal waters.

Power and Industry

The regions were all conquered by the Romans, but all have unique pre-Roman histories, from Etruscans to Picenes. All had medieval development, with a boom in church building as well as powerful families that built castles and controlled their own empires. The word "Renaissance" almost immediately conjures Florence, but Urbino was a major cultural and economical power too.

Tuscany on the west is the major force, more than double in size, population and economic power than Le Marche, which in turn has more than double the economy, about double the population, and is more than 13 percent larger than its neighbour Umbria. Tuscany's capital city Florence is the major draw, along with major art centres of Siena and Pisa. But its rich variety ranges from the Island of Elba to the Apuan Alps, and the dense Apennine forest on its border with Le Marche.

Agriculture is important to all regions, each with its own exquisite wines and cuisines. Tuscany has heavy industry like mining, quarrying and textiles, which are present to a much lesser extent in the other two. Le

Urbino

© FrancoDeriu/iStockphoto.com

Marche, like Tuscany, is famous for its shoe production, but instead of large factories, they tend to be mostly family-run small enterprises.

Tourist Attractions

The most glamorous is Tuscany, the region also most oriented to tourism, with excellent accommodation in cities as well as in the countryside. Not surprisingly, as a region it is first for tourists, who can choose from simple to deluxe, according to their needs and whims. Umbria, for centuries accustomed to religious pilgrims coming to Assisi to see the birthplace of St Francis, until recent decades was content to cater to their needs with modest facilities. Having awakened to Tuscany's success, it has increased its offerings to the worldly traveller, who may be more interested in art, cuisine and excellent wines rather than solely religious retreats. One of Italy's few landlocked regions, Umbria has central–southern Italy's largest lake, Trasimeno. Its capital city, Perugia, is a lively university town, also rich in artistic treasures. Le Marche has gentle rolling hills, broken only by the coastline or patches like the rugged Conero Promontory or Sibillini Mountains to the south. The most insular region of the three, Le Marche has been slowest to develop tourism, in part because of its historical isolation as a Papal state and also because its focus is on family industries that are its major economic force. Only recently have Marchigiani been converting some historic properties to sophisticated accommodation. As a general rule, prices in Tuscany are most expensive and as you go east, they drop, with some exceptions. Italians by far prefer the seaside for their holidays, which means that even during mid-August holiday peak, you'll find the hillside towns, full of treasures, a delight to explore if you seek tranquillity.

All these hillside towns, though, may be a bit difficult for the very young, the elderly or those with special needs. Consider choosing a flat area as a base from which to explore. That way, taking a stroll to go to dinner is easier on tired feet. In Tuscany or Le Marche, coastal towns are an option, and are economical off-season. In Umbria, a lovely valley town like Bevagna offers complete needs within a short stroll. Another option is to book into a spa town, like Chianciano Terme or Montecatini. There are a variety of treatments to sooth and renew vigour. Their peak season is relatively short, so there are some excellent-value hotels, if not always the most luxurious.

Cultural Treats

If you like theatre or concerts, keep an eye out for interesting venues. Le Marche, for example, is extremely rich in beautiful theatres from the 18C and 19C, some very intimate, with ceiling frescoes, stucco, fine balconies and enchanting details. Even some of the smallest towns in Umbria or Tuscany have their own too. Summer performances in archaeological sites, like Spoleto or Urbisaglia, use their Roman amphitheatres for performances. Opera festivals in Florence, Torre del Lago, Lucca, Spoleto, Pesaro and Macerata can keep an opera fan busy – and those are only the world-class venues. Many smaller, but quality productions are easy on the pocket. Performances are a chance to mingle away from the tourist crowds.

Food and Drink

In Italy, almost any activity concludes with a great meal. Certain pasta dishes and grilled meats you will find in all three regions, but each has its own seasonal specialities. From forest areas look for superb game in season, especially wild boar, truffles and mushrooms. Farm-raised Chianina beef is justifiably famous. Superb fish soups and other dishes are found along coastal areas, as well as inland. The most famous wines are Brunello di Montalcino, Chianti, and Vino Nobile di Montepulciano, but don't overlook others like Umbria's Sagraintino di Montefalco and unique wines in Le Marche. This is the place to experiement, where prices are much lower than in export countries. Even famous winemakers often have economical "base" wines, from a DOC like Rosso di Montalcino, to an IGT (Indicazione Geografica Tipica), which protects the geographic origin of the wine, like an Umbria Rosso. And to help all this digest, there is no lack of digestivo, from potions made in a monastery to those from commercial distilleries, often taken in a caffè corretto, an espresso "corrected" with liqueur.

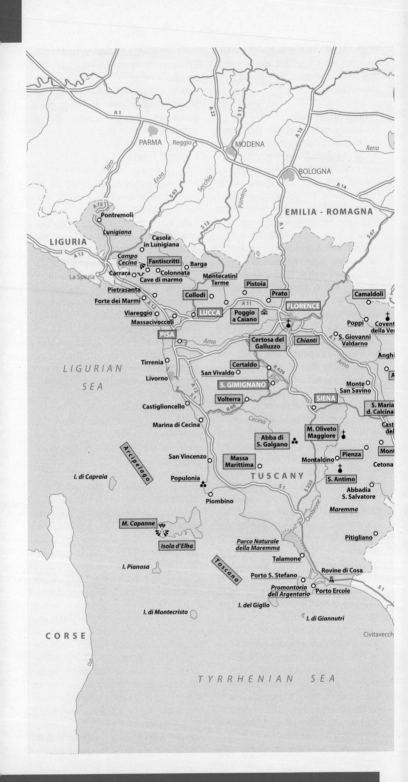

PARMA Reggio MODENA BOLOGNA Reno

Taro Enza Secchia Panaro A 1 A 13 A 14 S 67

EMILIA - ROMAGNA

Pontremoli

Lunigiana

LIGURIA

Casola
in Lunigiana

Campo
Cecina **Fantiscritti** Barga

La Spezia Carrara **Colonnata**
Cave di marmo

Pietrasanta Montecatini
Terme Pistoia

Forte dei Marmi **Collodi** Prato Camaldoli

Viareggio **LUCCA** **Poggio
a Caiano** **FLORENCE**

Massaciuccoli Poppi Coventi
della Ver

PISA Certosa del
Galluzzo *Chianti* S. Giovanni
Valdarno

Arno Arno Anghi

Tirrenia Certaldo Monte
San Savino

Livorno San Vivaldo A

S. GIMIGNANO S. Maria
d. Calcina

Volterra **SIENA**

Castiglioncello Cecina Cast
del

Marina di Cecina R 68

Abba di
S. Galgano M. Oliveto
Maggiore

San Vincenzo Massa
Marittima Pienza Mont

Populonia Montalcino Cetona

Piombino **S. Antimo**

TUSCANY S 1 S 223

Abbadia
S. Salvatore

Maremma

M. Capanne Pitigliano

Isola d'Elba *Parco Naturale
della Maremma*

I. Pianosa Talamone

Rovine di Cosa

Porto S. Stefano

*Promontorio
dell'Argentario* Porto Ercole

S 1

I. di Montecristo I. del Giglio

I. di Giannutri

Civitavecch

LIGURIAN
SEA

Arcipelago

I. di Capraia

Toscano

CORSE

TYRRHENIAN SEA

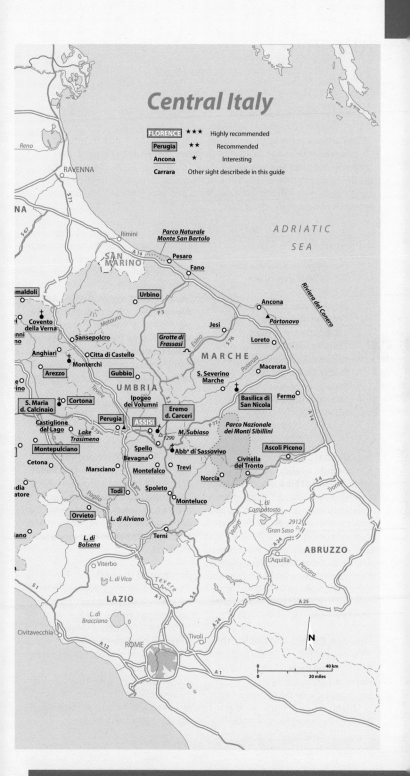

Central Italy

FLORENCE ★★★   Highly recommended

Perugia   ★★   Recommended

Ancona   ★   Interesting

Carrara   Other sight describede in this guide

RAVENNA

ADRIATIC SEA

Reno

Rimini

Parco Naturale Monte San Bartolo

SAN MARINO

Pesaro

Fano

Riviera del Conero

maldoli

Urbino

Ancona

Covento della Verna

Metauro

P 3

Jesi

Portonovo

Sansepolcro

Grotte di Frassasi

Loreto

Anghiari

Citta di Castello

Esino

MARCHE

Potenza

Macerata

Arezzo

Monterchi

S 76

Gubbio

UMBRIA

S. Severino Marche

Tevere

Ipogeo dei Volumni

Fermo

S. Maria d. Calcinaio

Cortona

Eremo d. Carceri

Basilica di San Nicola

A 14

Castiglione del Lago

Perugia

ASSISI

M. Subiaso

Parco Nazionale dei Monti Sibillini

Lake Trasimeno

S 3 bis

290

Montepulciano

Spello

Abbᵃ di Sassovivo

Ascoli Piceno

Cetona

Bevagna

Montefalco

Trevi

Civitella del Tronto

Marsciano

Norcia

S 4

dia atore

Todi

Spoleto

Paglia

S 3

Tronto

Orvieto

L. di Alviano

Monteluco

L. di Campotosto

2912 Gran Saso

L. di Bolsena

Terni

Velino

ABRUZZO

iano

Viterbo

L. di Vico

Tevere

L'Aquila

Pescara

S 1

L. di Bracciano

A 1

S 4

A 25

Civitavecchia

A 12

ROME

Tivoli

A 24

N

0   40 km

0   20 miles

Tuscany

Toscana. Major Cities: Florence, Pisa, Siena
Official Website: www.turismo.intoscana.it

See also The Green Guide Tuscany

The harmony of the beautiful Tuscan landscape of low-lying hills with graceful curves affording wide views of olive groves, vineyards and cypress trees reinforces the great aesthetic sense of the Tuscan people. This region has the greatest concentration of Italy's artistic treasures, particularly in Florence, the capital and a model Renaissance city. Siena and San Gimignano are stunning examples of medieval architecture.

Highlights

1 Encounter Renaissance art at the **Galleria degli Uffizi** (p544)

2 Bicycle around Lucca's car-free **Città Vecchia** (p558)

3 Climb to the top of Pisa's **Leaning Tower** (p569)

4 Regard the splendour of Siena's **Piazza del Campo** (p585)

5 Indulge in a glass of Montepulciano's **Vino Nobile** (p594)

Tuscan Coast

The Tuscan Archipelago, with the mountainous **Island of Elba** and its rich iron-bearing deposits, faces a shore which is sometimes rocky (south of Livorno, also known as the Etruscan Riviera for some of the ruins found strewn near the coast), and sometimes flat and sandy as in the Viareggio area, known as **Versilia**. **Pisa**, a former maritime power, now lies inland, a result of silt deposits from the River Arno, fluctuations that contributed to the leaning of the city's bell tower.

Florence, Chianti and the North

In the heart of Tuscany lies the fertile and beautiful **Arno Basin**, an ideal setting for **Florence**. Just beyond the art city's southern limits is the wine-cultivating sub-region of **Chianti**, which bridges the farmland between Florence, Siena, Arezzo, Pisa,

Pistoia and Prato. Vines and silvery olives alternate with fields of wheat, tobacco and maize. The old farms, with their distinctive grand architectural style, often stand alone on hilltops.

North of the Arno, the dramatic **Apuan Alps** (named for their resemblance to the real Alps) are quarried for marble (Carrara) which is famous the world over. **Montecatini Terme** and several other towns near Pistoia and Lucca have been known for centuries for their therapeutic hot springs.

Siena and the South

Southern Tuscany is a land of hills, soft and vine-clad in the **Sienese Chianti**, quiet and pastoral near Siena, dry and desolate round Monte Oliveto Maggiore, and massive and mysterious in the area of the **Colli Metalliferi** (metal-bearing hills) south of Volterra. Bordering Lazio, **Maremma**, with its melancholy beauty, was once a marshy district haunted by bandits, cowboys and shepherds. Much of the area has now been reclaimed.

Arezzo and the East

The terrain in eastern Tuscany rises to meet the Apennine Mountains and is particularly undulating at **Cortona**, a hill town with dramatic views of the Chiana Valley.

Arezzo, a significant Roman settlement known for its red ceramics, is notable today for its trade in gold.

Tuscan red wines, many based on Sangiovese grapes like Chianti, Nobile di Montepulciano, Brunello and Morellino di Scansano, are justly famous.

Florence★★★

Firenze

Acknowledged as one of Italy's most beautiful cities and one of the world's greatest artistic capitals, Florence is a testament to the Italian capacity for genius. The birthplace of Dante and the model for the Italian language, the city was the cradle of civilisation which nurtured the humanist movement and the Renaissance in the first half of the 15C.

▶ **Population:** 371 282

◈ **Michelin Map:** 563 K 15.

▤ **Info:** Via Cavour 1, 50129 Firenze. ℘055 29 08 32. 055 29 08 33. www.firenzeturismo.it

◑ **Location:** Florence lies at the foot of the Apennines in the Arno Valley. The city is situated where the A 1 and A 11 (Florence-coast route) meet.

ℙ **Parking:** A large car park is at Fortezza da Basso, www.firenzeparcheggi.it. There is also the pricier Santa Maria Novella station. Beware, some charge incrementally by the hour.

☺ **Don't Miss:** Piazza del Duomo, the Uffizi Gallery, Palazzo Vecchio, Museo del Bargello, Chiesa di San Lorenzo and the Medici tombs, Galleria Palatina in the Palazzo Pitti, Museo di San Marco, frescoes by Ghirlandaio in Chiesa di Santa Maria Novella.

◕ **Timing:** Allow at least four days to see all the main sights; many are clustered in the compact city centre, easily traversed on foot.

♟ **Kids:** Secret passages tours of Palazzo Vecchio, Giardino di Boboli, mummies at Museo Archeologico, climb Brunelleschi's dome.

THE CITY TODAY

Florence has long depended on its legacy as the birthplace of the Renaissance to market itself, particularly to the millions of foreign tourists who swarm its streets and fill its coffers year after year. But the city's dependence on tourism has also meant a reduction in the native population, who for the last decade have been relocating to the suburbs to escape the crowds and high costs. While tourism increased in 2010 and 2011, it declined slightly in 2012, but still remains key to the economy. Some days more English than Italian seems to be spoken in the centre. Florence, seeking to make the centre less congested, has closed major sights to car traffic (Duomo and Santa Maria Novella) and has set major exhibits in outlying areas like Fiesole, Bagno a Ripoli, Figline and Scandicci. Rather than being an inconvenience to the visitor, it's an opportunity to see less explored areas and to once again rub shoulders with Florentines.

A BIT OF HISTORY

Florence is without doubt the city where the Italian genius has flourished with the greatest display of brilliance and purity. For three centuries, from the 13C to the 16C, the city was the cradle of an exceptional artistic and intellectual activity from which evolved the precepts which were to dictate the appearance of Italy at that time and also the aspect of modern civilisation throughout Europe. The main characteristics of this movement, which was later to be known as the Renaissance, were partly a receptivity to the outside world, a dynamic open-minded attitude which encouraged inventors and men of science to base their research on the reinterpretation of the achievements of ancient Rome, and on the expansion of the known horizons. The desire to achieve universality

Brunelleschi's Santa Maria del Fiore and the view of Florence

resulted in a multiplication of the fields of interest.

Dante was not only a great poet but also a grammarian and historian who did much research on the origins and versatility of his own language. He was one of Florence's most active polemicists. **Giotto** was not only a painter but also an architect. **Lorenzo the Magnificent** was the prince who best incarnated the spirit of the Renaissance. An able diplomat, a realistic politician, a patron of the arts as well as a poet himself, he regularly attended the Platonic Academy in the Medici Villa at Careggi, where philosophers such as Marsilio Ficino and Pico della Mirandola and men of letters like Poliziano and others established the principles of a new humanism. This quest to achieve a balance between nature and order had its most brilliant exponent in **Michelangelo**, painter, architect, sculptor and scholar whose work typifies a purely Florentine preoccupation.

Florence is set in the heart of a serenely beautiful **countryside★★★** bathed by a soft, amber light. The low surrounding hills are clad with olive groves, vineyards and cypresses which appear to have been harmoniously landscaped to please the human eye. Florentine architects and artists have striven to re-create this natural harmony in their works, whether it be the campanile of La Badia by Arnolfo di Cambio, or that of the cathedral by Giotto, the façade of Santa Maria Novella by Alberti or the dome of Santa Maria del Fiore by Brunelleschi. The pure and elegant lines of all these works of art would seem to be a response to the beauty of the landscape and the intensity of the light. The Florentine preoccupation with perspective throughout the Quattrocento (15C) is in part the result of this fascination for the countryside and that other great concern of the period, the desire to re-create what the eye could see.

This communion of great minds, with their varied facets and fields of interest, expressed a common desire to push their knowledge to the limits, and found in the flourishing city of Florence an ideal centre for their artistic and intellectual development. The city's artists, merchants, able administrators and princely patrons of the arts, all contributed to the creation of just the right conditions for nurturing such an intellectual and artistic community, which for centuries was to influence human creativity.

In the Beginning…

The colony of *Florentia* was founded in the 1C BC by Julius Caesar on the north bank of the Arno at a spot level with the Ponte Vecchio. The veteran soldiers who garrisoned the colony controlled the Via Flaminia linking Rome to northern Italy and Gaul.

The Middle Ages

It was only in the early-11C that the city became an important Tuscan centre when Count Ugo, Marquis of Tuscany, took up residence here, and again towards the end of the same century when the Countess Matilda affirmed its independence. During the 12C Florence prospered under the influence of the new class of merchants who built such fine buildings as the baptistery and San Miniato. This period saw the rise of trades organised in powerful guilds (arti), which soon became the ruling class when Florence became an independent commune. In the 13C one-third of Florence's population was engaged in either the wool or the silk trade, both of which exported their products to the four corners of Europe and were responsible for a period of extraordinary prosperity. These tradesmen were ably supported by the Florentine money houses which succeeded the Lombard and Jewish institutions, and themselves acquired a great reputation by issuing the first-ever bills of exchange and the famous florin, struck with the Florentine coat of arms. The latter was replaced in the late-15C by the Venetian ducat. The main banking families were the Bardi-Peruzzi, who advanced huge sums to England at the beginning of the Hundred Years' War; they were soon to be joined in the forefront by the Pitti, Strozzi, Pazzi and of course the Medici.

The Guelph Cause

Despite its prosperity, Florence did not escape the internal strife between the Ghibellines who were partisans of the Holy Roman Emperor and the Guelphs who supported the Pope. The Guelphs at first had the advantage; but the Ghibellines on being driven out of Florence, having allied themselves with other enemies of Florence, notably Siena, regained power after the Battle of Montaperti in 1260. The Guelphs counter-attacked and retook Florence in 1266. Under their rule the physical aspect of the city changed considerably, notably with the destruction of the fortified tower houses built by the Ghibelline nobility. They created the system of government known as the signoria, which was made up of the priori (masters of the city's guilds). There then occurred a split between the Black Guelphs and the White Guelphs who opposed the Papacy.

During the split, Dante, who supported the White Guelphs, was exiled for life in 1302. In 1348 the Black Death killed more than half the population and put an end to the period of internal strife.

A Glorious Era (15C)

Among the numerous wealthy families in Florence, it was the **Medici** who gave the city several leaders who exercised their patronage in the spheres of both fine arts and finance. The founder of this illustrious dynasty was Giovanni di Bicci de'Medici, a wealthy banker who left his fortune in 1429 to his son **Cosimo the Elder**, who in turn transformed his heritage into the city's most flourishing business. He discreetly exercised his personal power through intermediaries, and astutely juggled his own personal interests with those of the city, which assured Florence a kind of peaceful hegemony. His chief quality was his ability to gather around him both scholars and artists, whom he commissioned for numerous projects. Cosimo the Elder was a passionate builder and Florence owes many of her great monuments to this "Father of the Land". His son, Piero II Gottoso (The Gouty), survived him by only five years and he in turn bequeathed all to his son **Lorenzo the Magnificent** (1449–92). Having escaped the Pazzi Conspiracy, Lorenzo reigned like a true Renaissance prince, although always unofficially. He distinguished himself by his skilful politics and managed to retain the prestige of Florence and to keep peace, but ultimately ruining the Medici financial empire. This humanist and man of great sensitivity was a great patron of the arts, and he gathered around him poets and philosophers, who all contributed to make Florence the capital of the early Renaissance.

A Turbulent Period

On Lorenzo's death, which had repercussions throughout Europe, the Dominican monk **Girolamo Savonarola**, taking advantage of a period of confusion, provoked the fall of the Medici. This fanatical and ascetic monk, who became the Prior of the Monastery of

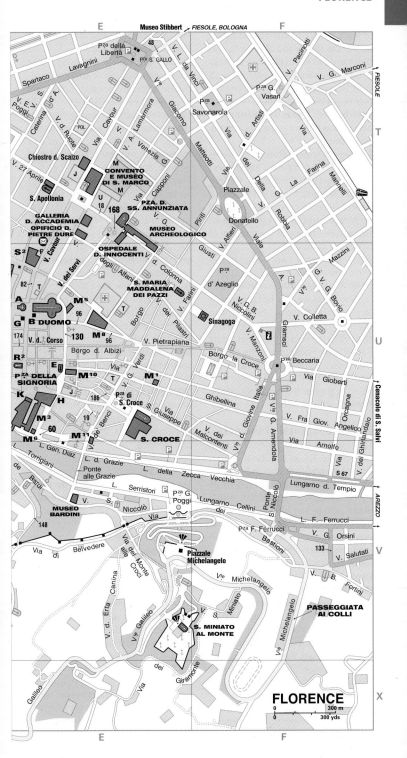

Museo Stibbert / *FIESOLE, BOLOGNA*

FIESOLE

AREZZO

Cenacolo di S. Salvi

FLORENCE

0   300 m
0   300 yds

St Mark, preached against the pleasures of the senses and of the arts, and drove the citizens of Florence to make a "bonfire of vanities" in 1497 in Piazza della Signoria, on which musical instruments, paintings and books of poetry were burned. A year later Savonarola himself was burned at the stake on the same spot.

The Medici family returned to power with the help of Emperor Charles V and they reigned until the mid-18C. **Cosimo I** (1519–74) brought some lost splendour back to Florence, conquered Siena and he himself became Grand Duke of Tuscany. He continued the tradition of patronage of the arts.

The 16C brought two Medici popes and a Rome power base. Francesco I's (1541–87) daughter Maria married Henri IV, King of France. The last prominent Medici was Ferdinand I (1549–1609), who married French Princess Christine de Lorraine. After the Medici, the Grand Duchy passed to the House of Lorraine, then to Napoleon Bonaparte until 1814, before returning to the House of Lorraine until 1859. As part of the Italian Kingdom, Florence was capital from 1865 to 1870.

Florence, Capital of the Arts

The relatively late emergence of Florence in the 11C as a cultural centre, and its insignificant Roman heritage, no doubt contributed to the growth of an independent art movement, which developed vigorously for several centuries. One of its principal characteristics was its preoccupation with clarity and harmony, which influenced writers as well as architects, painters and sculptors. **Dante Alighieri** (1265–1321) established the use of the Italian vernacular in several of his works, thus superseding Latin as the literary language. He made an admirable demonstration with his *New Life (Vita Nuova)*, recounting his meeting with a young girl, Beatrice, who was to be the inspiration for his **Divine Comedy** *(Divina Commedia)*, in which Dante, led by Virgil and then by Beatrice, visits the Inferno, Purgatory and Paradise. In the 14C Dante was responsible for creating a versatile literary language to which

Petrarch added his sense of lyricism and Boccaccio the art of irony.

Niccolò Machiavelli (1469–1527) was the statesman on whose account Machiavellism became a synonym for cunning. His essay, **The Prince** (*Il Principe* – 1513), on political science and government in which he counselled that in politics the end justifies the means, perhaps was modelled after Cesare, or his Pope father Rodrigo, Borgia.

Francesco Guicciardini (1483–1540) wrote an important history of Florence and Italy. Artist **Giorgio Vasari** (1511–74) wrote *The Lives of the Most Eminent Italian Architects, Painters and Sculptors*, a bestseller that also made him first Italian art historian. He studied and classified local schools of painting, tracing their development from the 13C.

The Florentine school had its origins in the work of **Cimabue** (1240–1302) and slowly it freed itself from the Byzantine tradition with its decorative convolutions, while **Giotto** (1266–1337) in his search for truth gave priority to movement and expression. Later **Masaccio** (1401–28) studied spatial dimension and modelling. From then on perspective became the principal preoccupation of Florentine painters, sculptors, architects and theorists.

The Quattrocento (15C) saw the emergence of a group of artists such as **Paolo Uccello** (1397–1475), **Andrea del Castagno** (1423–57), **Piero della Francesca**, a native of Le Marche, who were all ardent exponents in the matters of foreshortening and the geometrical construction of space; while others such as **Fra Angelico** (1387–1455), and later **Filippo Lippi** (1406–69) and **Benozzo Gozzoli** (1420–97), were imbued with the traditions of International Gothic and were more concerned with the visual effects of arabesques and luminous colours.

These opposing tendencies were reconciled in the harmonious balance of the work of **Sandro Botticelli** (1444–1510). Alongside Botticelli, the **Pollaiuolo** brothers, **Domenico Ghirlandaio** (1449–94) and **Filippino Lippi** (1457–1504) ensured the continuity and diversity of Florentine art.

The High Renaissance with its main centres in Rome and other northern towns reached Florence in the 16C. **Leonardo da Vinci**, **Michelangelo** and **Raphael**, all made their debut at Florence, and inspired younger Mannerist artists such as **Jacopo Pontormo**, **Rosso Fiorentino**, **Andrea del Sarto** (1486–1530) and the curious portraitist of the Medici, **Bronzino** (1503–72).

The emergence of a Florentine school of painting is, however, indivisible from the contemporary movement of the architects who were creating a style, also inspired by Antiquity, which united the Classical traditions of rhythm, a respect for proportion and geometric decoration. The constant preoccupation was with perspective in the arrangement of interiors and the design of façades. **Leon Battista Alberti** (1404–72) was the theorist and grand master of such a movement. However, it was **Filippo Brunelleschi** (1377–1446) who best represented the Florentine spirit, and he gave the city buildings which combined both rigour and grace, as in the magnificent dome of the cathedral of Santa Maria del Fiore.

Throughout the Quattrocento (15C), buildings were embellished with admirable sculptures. The doors of the baptistery were the object of a competition in which the very best took part. If **Lorenzo Ghiberti** (1378–1455) was finally victorious, **Donatello** (1386–1466) was later to provide ample demonstration of the genius of his art, so full of realism and style, as did **Luca della Robbia** (1400–82) and his dynasty, who specialised in glazed terra-cotta decoration, **Andrea del Verrocchio** (1435–88) and numerous other artists who adorned the ecclesiastical and secular buildings of Florence.

In the 16C **Michelangelo**, who was part of this tradition, confirmed his origins with his New Sacristy (1520–55) of San Lorenzo, which he both designed and decorated with sculpture. Later **Benvenuto Cellini** (1500–71), who also wrote a fascinating autobiography, and Giambologna or **Jean Boulogne** (1529–1608) and **Bartolomeo Ammannati** (1511–92) maintained this unity of style, which was responsible for the exceptional beauty of Florence.

PIAZZA DEL DUOMO★★★

In the city centre, the cathedral, campanile and baptistery form an admirable group, demonstrating the traditions of Florentine art from the Middle Ages to the Renaissance. The square is even more beautiful.

Duomo (Santa Maria del Fiore)★★★

Open 10am–4pm. Crypt 10am–4pm. Hours are frequently subject to change, visit the website. ℘055 23 02 885. www.operaduomo.firenze.it.

One of the largest cathedrals in the Christian world, the Duomo is a symbol of the city's 13C and 14C power and wealth. It was begun in 1296 by Arnolfo di Cambio and consecrated in 1436.

Exterior – Walk around the cathedral starting from the south side to admire the marble mosaic decoration and the sheer size of the **east end★★★**.

The harmonious **dome★★★** by Brunelleschi took 14 years to build. To counteract the excessive thrust he built two concentric domes, linked by props. The façade dates from the late-19C.

Top of the dome: Open 8.30am–6.20pm, Sat 8.30am–5pm, Sun noon–3pm. Hours are frequently subject to change, visit the website. Climb to the top of the dome, 463 steps. 15€ including five monuments. ℘055 23 02 885. www.operaduomo. firenze.it.

Interior – The bareness of the interior contrasts sharply with the exterior's sumptuous decoration. The great octagonal **chancel** under the dome is surrounded by a delicate 16C marble balustrade. The dome is painted with a huge fresco of the Last Judgement. The inner gallery offers an impressive view of the nave. Then climb to the top of the dome (463 steps) for a magnificent **panorama★★★** of Florence.

The sacristy doors adorned with pale blue terra-cottas by Luca della Robbia represent the Resurrection and the Ascension. In the new sacristy (left),

GETTING THERE

Amerigo Vespucci Airport (very small) serves major European capitals and is well connected by bus to the centre. ℘055 30 61 300. www.aeroporto.firenze.it.

GETTING AROUND

Walking is by far the best way to explore the city. Florence has an ancient urban structure with narrow streets full of innumerable scooters and cars driven by Florentines, who tend to be rather fast drivers.

The one-way systems can be daunting if one doesn't know the city, traffic is often restricted to residents only and some car parks are also open to residents only. A good car park is at Fortezza da Basso; Santa Maria Novella station is closer but costlier. Beware car parks with incremental price increases, www.firenzeparcheggi.it.

BUSES Lines 12 and 13 go to the Colli and Piazzale Michelangiolo. **Line 7** goes from the station to Fiesole. **Line 10** goes from the station to Settignano. **Line 17** goes from the station to the youth hostel. A tram serves outlying areas. (Tickets with 90min validity cost 1.20€ (2€ on board); a booklet of four tickets costs 4.70€. Tourist ticket: valid for 24hrs (5€), 3 days (12€) and 7 days (18€). The "carta agile" is valid for 10 journeys and costs 10€.)

For further information consult the ATAF website: www.ataf.net, ℘800 42 45 00 (toll-free), ℘199 10 42 45 (from a mobile).

TAXIS Dial either ℘055 42 42, 055 43 90, or ℘055 41 01 33.

CAR RENTAL Cars can be rented at the airport or at offices in the city:
AVIS, Borgo Ognissanti 128r, ℘055 21 36 29, www.avis.com.
EUROPCAR, Borgo Ognissanti 53r, ℘055 29 04 38, www.europecar.com.
HERTZ, Via Borgo Ognissanti 137/R, ℘055 23 98 205, www.hertz.com.

GETTING AROUND BY BICYCLE

Cycling is a quick way of getting around Florence, which is always beleaguered by traffic.

Some hotels rent out bicycles but there are also bicycles to rent at Via San Zanobi 54/r, called Florence by Bike (www.florencebybike.it). They also organise tours of the city by bike, with commentary by a tour leader.

SIGHTSEEING

To avoid the queues (of anything up to an hour) visitors are advised to book their tour of the Uffizi in advance. Booking office: ℘055 29 48 83 (booking fee: 4€), www.uffizi.firenze.it.

---

there are inlaid armorial bearings by the Maiano brothers (15C).

A dramatic episode of the **Pazzi Conspiracy** took place in the chancel. The Pazzi, who were rivals of the Medici, tried to assassinate Lorenzo the Magnificent on 26 April 1478, during the Elevation of the Host. Lorenzo, though wounded by two monks, managed to take refuge in a sacristy, but his brother Giuliano fell to their daggers.

Ghiberti's masterpiece, the sarcophagus of St Zanobi, shows the first Bishop of Florence. Frescoes in the north aisle show Dante explaining the *Divine Comedy* to the city of Florence (1465).

The **Crypt of Santa Reparata** *(3€)*, a Romanesque basilica demolished when the present cathedral was built, shows the 5C–6C remains, with traces of mosaic and Brunelleschi's tomb.

Campanile★★★

Open daily 8.15am–6.50pm (Sun 5.50pm). Hours are subject to change, visit the website. Closed 1 Jan, Easter, 25 Dec. 15€ including five monuments. ℘055 23 02 885. www.operaduomo.firenze.it.

The tall slender bell tower (82m/269ft) is the perfect complement to Brunelleschi's dome, the straight lines of the former balancing the curves of the latter. Giotto drew plans for it and began building in 1334, but died in 1337. The Gothic campanile was completed at the end of the 14C; its geometric decoration is unusual. The admirable bas-reliefs at the base of the campanile have been replaced by copies. The originals, designed by Giotto, are in the Cathedral Museum.

From the top of the campanile (414 steps) there is a fine **panorama★★★** of the cathedral and town.

Battistero★★★

& Open Mon–Sat 8.15–6.30pm, Sun and public hols 7.15am–12.30pm. Hours are subject to change, visit the website. Closed 1 Jan, Easter, 24–25 Dec. 15€ including five monuments. ☏055 23 02 885. www.operaduomo.firenze.it.

The baptistery is faced in white-and-green marble. The **bronze doors★★★** are world famous.

The south door *(entrance)* by Andrea Pisano (1330) is Gothic and portrays scenes from the life of St John the Baptist *(above)*, as well as the Theological Virtues (Faith, Hope, Charity) and the Cardinal Virtues *(below)*. The door frames are by Vittorio Ghiberti, son of the designer of the other doors.

The north door (1403–24) was the first done by Lorenzo Ghiberti. He was the winner of a competition in which Brunelleschi, Donatello and Jacopo della Quercia also took part.

The east door (1425–52), facing the cathedral, is the one that Michelangelo declared worthy to be the **Gate of Paradise**, the name by which it is known. In it Ghiberti recalled the Old Testament; prophets and sibyls adorn the niches. The artist portrayed himself, bald and cunning-looking, in one medallion.

Interior – With its 25m/82ft diameter, its green-and-white marble and its paving decorated with Oriental motifs, the interior is grand and majestic.

The dome is covered with magnificent 13C **mosaics★★★**. The Last Judgement is depicted on either side of a large picture of Christ the King; on the five concentric

Mosaics inside the dome, Battistero

© Y. Kanazawa/MICHELIN

bands that cover the other five panels of the dome, starting from the top towards the base, are the Heavenly Hierarchies, Genesis, the Life of Joseph, scenes from the Life of the Virgin and of Christ, and St John the Baptist.

On the right of the apse is the tomb of the anti-pope John XXIII, a work executed in 1427 by Donatello assisted by Michelozzo.

Museo dell'Opera di Santa Maria del Fiore (Duomo)★★

& Open 9am–7pm. Closed 1 Jan, Easter, 24–25 Dec. 15€ including five monuments. ☏055 23 02 885. www.operaduomo.firenze.it.

The museum exhibits works from the cathedral, campanile and baptistery. See models of Brunelleschi's dome. Michelangelo's famous **Pietà** stands unfinished. Donatello sculpted a repentant **Magdalene★** carved in wood, and the prophets Jeremiah and Habakkuk, the latter nicknamed "Zuccone" ("Squash Head"). The **Cantorie★★**, choristers' tribunes from the cathedral, are by Luca della Robbia and Donatello. A silver **altarpiece★★** depicts the life of St John the Baptist, a 14C–15C masterpiece. Note the admirable **bas-reliefs★★** from the campanile.

PIAZZA DELLA SIGNORIA★★★
Piazza★★★

The political stage of Florence, past and present, has a wonderful backdrop formed by the Palazzo Vecchio, the Loggia della Signoria and, in the wings, the Uffizi Museum. Its many statues form an open-air museum: near the centre of the square is the equestrian statue of *Cosimo I*, after Giambologna, and at the corner of the Palazzo Vecchio is the Fountain of Neptune (1576) by Ammannati. In front of the Palazzo Vecchio are copies of the proud *Marzocco* or *Lion of Florence* by Donatello and Michelangelo's *David*.

Loggia della Signoria★★

The Loggia, built at the end of the 14C, was the assembly hall and later the guard room of the *Lanzi* (foot soldiers) of Cosimo I. It contains ancient (Classical) and Renaissance statues: the *Rape of a Sabine* (1583), *Hercules and the Centaur Nessus* by Giambologna and the wonderful **Perseus** holding up the severed head of Medusa, a masterpiece executed by Benvenuto Cellini from 1545 to 1553.

Palazzo Vecchio★★★

♿ Open Oct–Mar 9am–7pm (Thu 9am–2pm), Apr–Sept 9am–11pm (Thu 9am–2pm). Closed 25 Dec. Cafeteria. Bookshop. 10€, tower 10€, combined ticket 14 €. ☎055 27 68 325. www.musefirenze.it.

The Old Palace's powerful mass is dominated by a lofty bell tower. Built from 1299 to 1314, probably to plans by Arnolfo di Cambio, it is in a severe Gothic style.

The refinement and splendour of the Renaissance interior is a complete contrast. The **courtyard★** was restored by Michelozzo in the 15C and decorated in the following century by Vasari.

Initially the seat of government (Palazzo della Signoria), the palace was taken over in the 16C by Cosimo I as his private residence. Most of Vasari's redecoration dates from this period. When Cosimo I abandoned it in favour of the Pitti Palace it was renamed Palazzo Vecchio.

The apartments were decorated with sculptures by Benedetto and Giuliano da Maiano (15C) and paintings by Vasari and Bronzino (16C).

On the first floor the great Sala dei Cinquecento, painted with frescoes by several artists including Vasari, contains a group carved by Michelangelo, *The Genius of Victory*. The walls of the magnificent **studiolo★★**, or study, of Francesco de' Medici, which was designed by Vasari, were painted by Bronzino, who was responsible for the portraits of Cosimo I and Eleanora of Toledo.

Cosimo I's apartments, known as the "Apartment of the Elements", were designed by Vasari.

Beyond these chambers are Eleonora of Toledo's apartments, again designed by Vasari. In the apartments of the *Priori*, the best-known chamber is the **Sala degli Gigli★** (Chamber of Lilies), which has a magnificent coffered ceiling by Guiliano da Maiano and the **Sala del Guardaroba★** lined with 16C maps.

Galleria degli Uffizi★★★

♿ Open Tue–Sun 8.15am–6.30pm. Closed 1 Jan, 1 May, 25 Dec. 8€. Book in advance to avoid the long queues. Booking office and information: ☎055 29 48 83. www.polomuseale.firenze.it.

One of the finest art museums in the world, with collections assembled by generations of Medici, follows the evolution of Italian art from its beginnings to the 17C.

Housed in the Renaissance palace, designed by Vasari in 1560, once this housed the offices *(uffizi)* of the Medici administration.

Galleries

The first gallery *(east)* is essentially dedicated to Florentine and Tuscan artists: there are works by Cimabue, Giotto, Duccio, Simone Martini (the *Annunciation*, a masterpiece of Gothic art), Paolo Uccello (*Battle of San Romano*) and Filippo Lippi.

The Botticelli Room★★★ houses the artist's major works: the allegories of the *Birth of Venus* and *Spring* and the *Madonna with Pomegranate*. Other exhibits in the gallery include the *Ado-*

Palazzo Vecchio, Piazza della Signoria

ration of the Magi, the *Annunciation* by Leonardo da Vinci and a series of Italian and foreign paintings from the 15C and 16C (Perugino, Cranach, Dürer, Bellini, Giorgione and Correggio).

The second gallery displays works from the Italian Cinquecento (16C): *Tondo Doni* by Michelangelo, *Madonna and the Goldfinch* and *Leo X* by Raphael, *Madonna and the Harpies* by Andrea del Sarto, *Urbino Venus* by Titian and *Leda and the Swan* by Tintoretto. The other rooms are dedicated to both Italian and foreign paintings from the 17C and 18C: included in the collection are *Isabella Brandt* by Rubens, **Caravaggio**'s *Adolescent Bacchus* and works by **Claude Lorrain** and **Rembrandt**.

Ponte Vecchio★★

As its name suggests, this is the oldest bridge in Florence. It has been rebuilt several times and spans the narrowest point of the Arno. Its original design includes a line of jewellers' shops and the **Corridoio Vasariano**, a passageway which was built by Vasari to link the Palazzo Vecchio to the Pitti Palace and which passes overhead.

Palazzo Pitti★★

This 15C Renaissance building, of rugged but imposing appearance, with pronounced rustication and many windows, was built to the plans of Brunelleschi for the Pitti family, the rivals of the Medici. It was Cosimo I's wife, Eleanora di Toledo, who enlarged the palace by the addition of two wings. The court moved to the palace in 1560.

Galleria Palatina★★★

& Open Tue–Sun 8.15am–6.30pm. Closed 1 Jan, 1 May, 25 Dec. 13€ (includes Galleria d'Arte Moderna). ☎055 29 48 83. www.polomuseale.firenze.it

This gallery houses a marvellous collection of paintings: **groups★★★** of works by Raphael (*Portrait of a Lady* or *La Velata, Madonna del Granduca* and *Madonna della Seggiola*) and Titian (*La Bella, The Aretino, The Concert* and the *Grey-Eyed Nobleman*).

On the first floor are the **Appartamenti Reali★** (State Apartments).

The building also houses the **Galleria d'Arte Moderna★**, which mainly displays Tuscan works from the 19C and 20C. The section devoted to the **Macchiaioli** movement is represented by an exceptional **series★★** by Fattori, Lega, Signorini and Cecioni. &Open daily 8.15am–6.30pm. Closed Mon, Jan, 1 May, 25 Dec. 13€ including Galleria Palatina. ☎055 29 48 83. www.polomuseale. firenze.it.

In the other wing is the Silver Museum (**Museo degli Argenti★★**) presenting Medici treasures and miniature portraits and Costume Gallery. 7€. ☎055 29 48 83. www.polomuseale.firenze.it.

Giardino di Boboli★

10€. 𝒫055 29 48 83.
www.polomuseale.firenze.it.
This Italian-style terraced garden,
behind the Pitti Palace, was designed
in 1549 by Tribolo. At one end of an avenue to the left of the palace is the **grotta
grande**, a grotto created in the main by
Buontalenti (1587–97). Cross the amphitheatre to reach the highest point, from
which, on the right, the **Viottolone★**,
an avenue of pines and cypresses, runs
down to **Piazzale dell'Isolotto★**, a circular pool with a small island with citrus
trees and a fountain by Giambologna. A
pavilion houses a Porcelain Museum, the
Museo delle Porcelane★.
The Forte del Belvedere, at the top of
the hill, affords a splendid **panorama★**.

Palazzo e Museo Nazionale del Bargello★★★

♿ Open daily 8.15am–1.40pm. Closed
1st, 3rd, and 5th Sun; 2nd and 4th Mon
of the month, 1 Jan, 1 May, 25 Dec. 4€.
𝒫055 29 48 83. www.polomuseale.
firenze.it.
Formerly the residence of the
magistrate *(podestà)*, then police
headquarters *(bargello)*, the palace's
fine 13C–14C medieval architecture
centres around its majestic
courtyard★★ with a portico and
loggia, and is now a museum of
sculpture and decorative arts. Among
the 16C Florentine works are *Brutus*
and the *Pitti Tondo* by **Michelangelo**;
bas-reliefs from the pedestal of the
Perseus bronze by Benvenuto Cellini.
Fine **sculpture★★★** by **Donatello**
includes *Marzocco* (the Florentine
heraldic lion), the bronze *David*, as
well as the low relief of *St George* from
Orsanmichele. Note **Verrocchio**'s
famous bronze of *David*.

Chiesa di San Lorenzo★★★

The Medici family parish church★★,
where most of the family were buried, was begun by Brunelleschi c.1420.
His great achievement is the **Old Sac-
risty★★**, which Donatello decorated
part of, as well as the two **pulpits★★** in
the nave.

Biblioteca Medicea Laurenziana★★

Entrance via a staircase from the upper
gallery of the cloisters. Open Mon, Wed,
Fri 8am–2pm, Tue and Thu to 5.30pm.
Closed 2 weeks Sept, public hols. 𝒫055
29 37 911. www.bml.firenze.sbn.it.
Cosimo the Elder's library was added to
by Lorenzo the Magnificent. Charming
15C **cloisters★**. The vestibule has a magnificent **staircase★★** built by Ammannati to Michelangelo's designs. The
library, also by Michelangelo, displays
10 000 manuscripts in rotation.

Cappelle Medicee★★

Entrance on Piazza Madonna degli
Aldobrandini. Open daily 8.15am–5pm.
Closed 1st, 3rd and 5th Mon of the
month, 2nd and 4th Sun of the month,
1 Jan, 1 May, 25 Dec. 6€. 𝒫055 29 48 83.
www.polomuseale.firenze.it.
The **Princes' Chapel** (17C–18C), grandiose but gloomy, is faced with semi-pre-
cious stones and is the funerary chapel
for Cosimo I and his descendants.
The **New Sacristy**, Michelangelo's first
architectural work, a funerary chapel,
was begun 1520, but left unfinished
when he departed Florence in 1534.
The famous **Medici tombs★★★** were
also the work of Michelangelo. Giuliano,
Action, surrounded by Day and Night;
and Lorenzo II, a Thinker with Dawn and
Dusk at his feet. For Lorenzo the Magnificent's tomb only the Madonna and
Child flanked by saints was completed.
In the plain tomb underneath lie Lorenzo the Magnificent and his brother
Giuliano. ✋*Don't miss the Medici tombs
by Michelangelo.*

Palazzo Medici-Ricardi★★

♿ Open Thu–Tue 9am–6.30pm. 7€.
𝒫055 27 60 340. www.palazzo-medici.it.
This noble but austere palace, begun
in 1444 by Michelozzo on the orders
of Cosimo the Elder, shows Florentine-
Renaissance mathematical plan and
rustication. A Medici residence 1459–
1540, Lorenzo the Magnificent held
court here. In the 17C the palace passed
to the Riccardi.

Cappella★★★

This tiny chapel was decorated with admirable **frescoes** (1459) by **Benozzo Gozzoli**. *The Procession of the Magi* is a vivid picture of Florentine life with portraits of the Medici and of famous dignitaries from the east who had assembled for the Council of Florence in 1439.

Sala di Luca Giordano★★

The 17C roof, splendidly decorated with gold stucco, carved panels and great painted mirrors, is covered by a brightly coloured Baroque fresco of the Apotheosis of the second Medici dynasty, by Luca Giordano in 1683.

Museo di San Marco★★

♿ Open Mon–Fri 8.15am–1.50pm, Sat–Sun and public hols 8.15am–4.50pm. Closed 1st, 3rd and 5th Sun of the month, 2nd and 4th Mon of the month, 1 Jan, 1 May, 25 Dec. 4€. ☎055 29 48 83. www.polomuseale.firenze.it.

The museum in a former Dominican monastery, rebuilt c.1436 in a very plain style by Michelozzo, is virtually the **Fra Angelico Museum★★★**. Fra Angelico took orders in Fiesole before coming to St Mark's, where he decorated the walls of the monks' cells with edifying scenes. The former guest hall, opening off the cloisters on the right, contains many of the artist's works on wood, especially the triptych depicting the *Descent from the Cross*, the famous *Last Judgement* and other religious scenes. The chapter house has a severe *Crucifixion* while the refectory contains an admirable *Last Supper* by Ghirlandaio.

The staircase leading to the first floor is dominated by Fra Angelico's masterpiece, the *Annunciation*. The monks' cells open off corridors, with lovely timber ceilings. Along the corridor to the left of the stairs are the *Apparition of Christ to the Penitent Magdalene (1st cell on the left)*, the *Transfiguration (6th cell on the left)* and the *Coronation of the Virgin (9th cell on the left)*. Off the corridor on the right is the **library★**, one of Michelozzo's finest achievements.

Galleria dell'Accademia★★

♿ Open Tue–Sun, 8.15am–6.50pm. Closed 1 Jan, 1 May, 25 Dec. 6.50€; during exhibitions 12.50€. ☎055 29 48 83. www.polomuseale.firenze.it.

Here the extraordinary personality of **Michelangelo** shows the conflict between the nature of his raw materials and his idealistic vision.

The **main gallery★★★** displays powerful figures of *Four Slaves* (1513–20) and *St Matthew* (all unfinished), who try to struggle free from the marble. The monumental figure of *David* (1501–4), the symbol of youthful but well-mastered force, perfectly shows the sculptor's humanism. The **picture gallery★** has works by 13C–15C Tuscan masters, including two Botticellis.

Chiesa di Santa Maria Novella★★

Open Mon–Thu 9am–5.30pm (Apr–Sept to 7pm), Fri 11am–5.30pm (Apr–Sept to 7pm), Sat 9am–5.30pm (summer to 6.30pm), Sun and public hols 1–5.30pm (summer noon–6.30pm). 5€. www.chiesasantamarianovella.it

The Church of Santa Maria Novella and the adjoining monastery were founded in the 13C by the Dominicans. Its square was the setting for chariot races.

Michelangelo's David, Galleria dell'Accademia

©Philip Coblentz/Brand X Pictures

The **church★★**, built 1279–1360, had its geometric marble **façade** designed by Alberti in the 15C.

The famous **fresco★★** of the Trinity with the Virgin, St John and the donors shows Masaccio's great mastery of perspective. The Strozzi di Mantora Chapel has **frescoes★** (1357) by the Florentine Nardo di Cione of the Last Judgement on a grand scale. The **polyptych★** on the altar is by Nardo's brother, Orcagna di Cione. The sacristy contains a fine **crucifix★** by Giotto and a delicate glazed terra-cotta **niche★** by Giovanni della Robbia.

In the Gondi Chapel, the **crucifix★★** by Brunelleschi so struck Donatello that upon first seeing it, he is said to have dropped the eggs he was carrying.

Admirable **frescoes★★★** by **Domenico Ghirlandaio** show the Lives of the Virgin and of St John the Baptist, a dazzling picture of Florentine life in the Renaissance era. The cloisters, **Chiostro Verde★** (Green Cloisters), have frescoes painted by Paolo Uccello and his school. The **Cappellone degli Spagnoli** (Spaniards' Chapel) has late-14C **frescoes★★** by **Andrea di Bonaiuto** (Andrea da Firenze). **Museum and cloisters**: ♿ Open Apr–Sept Mon–Thu 9am–7pm, Fri 11am–7pm, Oct–Mar Mon–Thu 9am– 5.30pm, Fri 11am–5.30pm; Sat 9am– 5.30pm (summer to 6.30pm); Sun and public hols summer noon–6.30pm, rest of year 1–6.30pm. Closed 1 Jan, Easter, 1 May, 15 Aug, 25 Dec. Guided tours available. 5€. 𝓟055 28 21 87. http://musei civicifiorentini.comune.fi.it.

Chiesa di Santa Croce★★

Mon–Sat 9.30am–5pm, Sun and public hols 2–5pm. 6€. (includes Cappella Pazzi and museum). 𝓟055 24 66 105. www.santacroceopera.it.

The church and cloisters of the 13C–14C Santa Croce look onto one of the town's oldest squares. The **interior** is vast (140m x 40m/460ft x 130ft) and is paved with 276 tombstones.

South aisle – By the first pillar, a *Virgin and Child* by Antonio Rossellino (15C); opposite, the tomb of Michelangelo (d.1564) by Vasari; opposite the second pillar, the funerary monument (19C) to Dante (d.1321, buried at Ravenna); by the third pillar, a fine **pulpit★** (1476) by Benedetto da Maiano and facing it the monument to V. Alfieri (d.1803) by Canova; opposite the fourth pillar, the 18C monument to Machiavelli (d.1527); facing the fifth pillar, a bas-relief of the **Annunciation★★** carved in stone and embellished with gold by Donatello; opposite the sixth pillar, the **tomb of Leonardo Bruni★★**, humanist and chancellor of the Republic (d.1444), by Bernardo Rossellino; and next to it the tomb of the composer Rossini (d.1868). The Baroncelli Chapel **frescoes★** (1338) depict the Life of the Virgin by Taddeo Gaddi and at the altar, the **polyptych★** of the Coronation of the Virgin from Giotto's studio.

The 14C **Sacristy★** has **frescoes★** including a Crucifixion by Taddeo Gaddi. The Medici Chapel (1434) built by Michelozzo, has an **altarpiece★** in glazed terra-cotta by Andrea della Robbia.

The chancel altar shows evocative **frescoes★★** (c.1320) by Giotto depicting the life of St Francis. The chancel is covered with **frescoes★** (1380) by Agnolo Gaddi. The famous **Crucifixion★★** is by Donatello.

The fine **monument to Carlo Marsuppini★** is by Desiderio da Settignano (15C); facing the fourth pillar, the tombstone of Lorenzo Ghiberti (d.1455); the last tomb (18C) is that of Galileo (d.1642).

Façade, Santa Maria Novella

© Y. Kanazawa/MICHELIN

Frescoes by Masaccio in Cappella Brancacci, Santa Maria del Carmine

Cappella dei Pazzi★★

♿ Open Mon–Sat 9.30am–5pm, Sun and public hols 2–5pm. 6€ combined ticket with church and museum.
☎ 055 24 66 105.
This chapel by Brunelleschi is a Florentine-Renaissance masterpiece, remarkable for the harmony of its decoration (glazed della Robbia terra-cotta).

Museo dell'Opera di Santa Croce

♿ Open Mon–Sat 9.30am–5pm, Sun and public hols 2–5pm. 6€ combined ticket with church and Cappella dei Pazzi.
☎ 055 24 66 105.
The museum contains a famous **Crucifixion★** by Cimabue that was seriously damaged by the 1966 floods.

ADDITIONAL SIGHTS
Passeggiata al viale dei Colli Colli★★

2hrs on foot or 1hr by car.
For a drive to the hills head east along the south bank of the Arno to the medieval tower in Piazza Giuseppe Poggi. Take the winding pedestrian street to Piazzale Michelangelo for a splendid city **view★★★**.
Uphill in the marvellous **setting★★** overlooking the town is the church of **San Miniato al Monte★★**, a remarkable example of Florentine-Romanesque architecture. The **Chapel of Cardinal James of Portugal★** is a fine Renaissance structure. The pulpit and chancel screen *(transenna)* form a remarkable **ensemble★★** inlaid with marble (early-13C). The **frescoes★** (1387) in the **sacristy** are by Spinello Aretino.

Santa Maria del Carmine★★★

Mon, Wed–Sat 10am–5pm; Sun and public hols opens 1pm, closed Tue. Guided tours available. 6€. ☎ 055 27 68 224. www.museicivicifiorentini. comune.fi.it.
Cappella Brancacci: fresco cycle (1427) by Masolino, **Masaccio** and Filippino Lippi depicting Original Sin and the Life of St Peter.

La Badia

The 10C church of a former abbey *(badia)* has an elegant **campanile★**. Inside are a coffered **ceiling★★** and Filippino Lippi's **Virgin Appearing to St Bernard**, a delicate **relief★★** sculpture in marble by Mino da Fiesole and the **tombs★** carved by the same artist.

Museo Archeologico★★

♿ Open Tue–Fri 8.30am–7pm, Sat–Mon 8.30am–2pm. Closed 1 Jan, 1 May, 25 Dec. 4€. ☎ 055 29 48 83. www.archeotoscana.beniculturali.it.
The museum has an important collection of Egyptian, Greek (**François Vase★★**), Etruscan (**Arezzo Chimera★★**) and Roman art and mummies.

Opificio delle Pietre Dure★

♿ Mon Sat 8.15am 2pm. 4€. ☎ 055 26 511. www.opificiodellepietredure.it.
Lorenzo the Magnificent revived finestone *(pietre dure)* crafts, now specialising in restoration from mosaic to sculpture, with a small **museum**.

Orsanmichele★

Orsanmichele, rebuilt in the 14C, has works by Donatello, Ghiberti and Verrocchio and a splendid Gothic **tabernacle★★** by Orcagna.

Palazzo Rucellai★★

By Leon Battista Alberti, the palace façade is the first cohesive example of the three ancient orders placed one on top of the other.

Palazzo Strozzi★★

www.palazzostrozzi.org.
This 15C building has rusticated stonework, cornice and arcaded courtyard with open access to the ground level bar. The palace hosts important temporary exhibits with a lively programs for families, including visitor kits in English.

Piazza della Santissima Annunziata★

This fine piazza is enhanced by Giambologna's statue of Ferdinando I de' Medici and two Baroque fountains.

Chiesa Santissima Annunziata

This 15C church has fine **frescoes★** by Rosso Fiorentino and Pontormo that were completed by Franciabigio. The vault displays the **Madonna with the Sack★** by Andrea del Sarto (16C).

Ospedale degli Innocenti★

Open Mon–Sat 9am–6.30pm. Closed public hols and 24 Jun, 25 Dec. 3€. ℘055 20 37 308. www.istitutodeglinnocenti.it.
Brunelleschi's **portico★★** has terra-cotta **medallions★★** by Andrea della Robbia. The Foundlings' Hospital houses a **gallery** of Florentine works.

Other sights worth visiting in Florence include: **Casa Buonarroti★**; Cenacolo di Sant'Apollonia (for the *Last Supper* by Andrea del Castagno); Cenacolo di San Salvia (**fresco★★** by Andrea del Sarto); **Santo Spirito★** (works of **art★**); Santa Trinità (for frescoes by Lorenzo Monaco and Ghirlandaio); **Loggia del Mercato Nuovo★**; Museo della Casa Fiorentina Antica★ and Museo di Storia della Scienza★.

ADDRESSES

🏠STAY

The accommodation listed below also includes information on religious orders (addresses with no description) which offer reasonably priced rooms to visitors.

Hotel Orchidea – Borgo degli Albizi 11. ℘055 24 80 346. www.hotelorchidea florence.it. 7 rooms. This little *pensione* is in a palazzo in the historic centre. The English owner offers a gracious atmosphere. Reasonably spacious cheerful pale pink rooms have high ceilings and antiques. Shared bathrooms.

Istituto Sette Santi Fondatori – Viale dei Mille 11. ℘055 50 48 452. http://eidinet.com/7santi. 65 rooms.

Residenza Johanna I – Via Bonifacio Lupi 14. ℘055 48 18 96. www.johanna.it. 11 rooms. Pleasant with great attention to detail and lovely antiques. A small breakfast buffet is set up in the cosy salon, that doubles as lounge. Near Piazza San Marco, with an inviting atmosphere and reasonable prices.

Albergo Scoti – Via De' Tornabuoni 7. ℘055 29 21 28. www.hotelscoti.com. 11 rooms. An eclectic residence in a Renaissance palazzo with its richly frescoed salon, creates a charming atmosphere of genteel aristocratic decline. Tiny, shared bathrooms.

Casa della Madonna del Rosario – Via Capo di Mondo 44. ℘055 67 96 21. Fax 055 67 71 33. 32 rooms.

Hotel Cimabue – Via Bonifacio Lupi 7. ℘055 47 56 01. www.hotel cimabue.it. 16 rooms. Some rooms have Art Nouveau frescoed ceilings, but all are spacious and tastefully furnished.

Brunelleschii – Via de' Calzaiuoli, Piazza Sanat Elisabetta 3. ℘055 27 370. www.hotelbrunelleschi.it. 70 rooms. Near Piazza della Repubblica in its own quiet piazza with Byzantine tower. Bright, spacious, modern rooms have beautiful design elements. Two delightful restaurants, traditional and creative gourmet.

Convitto Ecclesiastico della Calza – Piazza della Calza 6. ℘055 22 22 87. www.calza.it. 36 rooms.

⊜⊜⊟ **Hotel Cellai** – Via XXVII Aprile 14. ☎055 48 92 91. Fax 055 47 03 87. www. hotelcellai.it. ☕. Near San Marco and decorated with great flair, Cellai's gracious hospitality includes splendid lounges and rooms, candlelit breakfast, afternoon tea, free bikes, plus a savvy and helpful staff.

⊜⊜⊟ **Hotel La Scaletta** – Via Guicciardini 13. ☎055 28 30 28. www. hotellascaletta.it. 14 rooms. ☕. Warm colours and lovely antique furniture create a cosy feel. Wonderful roof terrace near Palazzo Pitti overlooks the historic centre. Rooms are bright and airy. Ample breakfast and free wifi.

⊜⊜⊟ **Locanda di Firenze** – Via Faenza 12. ☎055 28 43 40. 6 double rooms. ☕. Near San Lorenzo in an 18C palazzo, this hospitable ex-university professor's home is comfortable with good rates.

⊜⊜⊟ **Marignolle Relais** – Via di San Quirichino 16. ☎055 22 86 910. Fax 055 20 47 396. www.marignolle.com. 9 rooms. ☕. A beautifully decorated hilltop villa, 3km/1.8mi south of Porta Romana, with very attentive service. Swim in the pool, take a cooking course with Paola, play night tennis, or ask pro Lorenzo to book tee time in a local golf course.

⊜⊜⊟ **Relais Uffizi** – Chiasso de' Baroncelli-chiasso del Buco 16. ☎055 26 76 239. www.relaisuffizi.it. An elegant, convivial hotel in a 16C Florentine palazzo. Splendid lounge and breakfast area overlook Piazza della Signoria. Furnished in Tuscan style. Pets are welcome.

⊜⊜⊟ **Tornabuoni 1** – Via Tornabuoni 1. ☎055 26 58 161. www.tornabuoni1.com. 22 rooms. ☕. Warm beige tones in spacious rooms are inviting. The roof terrace overlooks the Arno and Duomo, lovely for buffet breakfast, or hot drinks. A lovely place.

⊻/EAT

In Florence, there is no shortage of bars selling sandwiches and ready-cooked food as well as restaurants catering for tourists – but few of them are good. The best places to head for are the little *trattorie* which serve traditional Florentine dishes including Chianina (prized local beef), tripe (*trippa*

and lampredotto), vegetable soup (*ribollita*), bread cooked with tomatoes (*pappa al pomodoro*), various pasta dishes including *rigatoni strascicati*, steak (*bistecca alla Fiorentina*), stewed meatloaf (*polpettone in umido*), sausages with beans (*salsiccia con i fagioli all'uccelletto*) and the sweetened loaf *schiacciata dolce fiorentina*. *Biscotti* with *vin santo* (biscuits with sweet wine).

⊜ **Cafaggi** – Via Guelf 35r. ☎055 29 49 89. www.ristorantecafaggi.it. Closed Sun. Vintage 1960s decor in this 1922 trattoria near San Marco that has reasonable food and wine prices. Excellent Tuscan fare like black cabbage soup, pappardelle with wild boar sauce, braised veal, fried brain with artichokes. For dessert, try Andrea's crème caramel.

⊜ **Cantinetta dei Verrazzano** – Via dei Tavolini 18/20r. ☎055 26 85 90. www.verrazzano.com. Open 8am–9pm, Sun 10am–4.30pm. Their wood-burning oven turns out good breads and pastries, but only Verrazzano wines are served here.

⊜ **Palle d'Oro** – Via Sant'Antonino 43/45r. ☎055 28 83 83. www.trattoriapalledoro firenze.com. Reservation recommended. Near the San Lorenzo market, in the early-20C, the great-grandfather set up a wine shop. Tuscan specialities and first courses. Sandwiches offered at the bar.

⊜ **Vini e Vecchi Sapori** – Via dei Magazzini 3r. ☎055 29 30 45. Closed Sun. Reservation recommended. Small and pleasant, tucked away behind the Palazzo Vecchio. Local specialities include vegetable soup (*ribollita*) and tripe (including the *lampredotto*), crostini, sliced ham and salami (*affettati*) and cheeses (*formaggi*). It can get very busy.

⊜⊜ **Accademia** – Piazza San Marco. ☎055 21 73 43. Across from San Marco, art professors, bankers and neighbours come for Aldo's specialities like mushroom strudel with Parmesan sauce, rabbit roll stuffed with artichokes, and lasagna with lamb *ragù*. Gianni matches with good wines.

⊜⊜ **Cibrèo Trattoria (il Cibrèino)** – Via dei Macci 122r. ☎055 23 41 100. Closed Mon. Reservation recommended. This wine bar adjacent to its sister restaurant is informal, friendly and trendy, but lower-priced. One of the city's most popular establishments, reliable for delicious food and quality wines.

Del Fagioli – Corso Tintori 47r. ✆055 24 42 85. Closed Sat–Sun. A perfect Chianina steakhouse and bastion of Florentine tradition, with fresh vegetables and good wines, perfect for a business lunch or leisurely meal.

Il Latini – Via dei Palchetti 6r. ✆055 21 09 16. www.illatini.com. Closed Mon. Wooden tables heaving with diners, dozens of prosciutti hanging overhead, a Florentine traditional menu, and witty banter make this a lively establishment. Wines are French and Italian.

Osteria de' Benci – Via de' Benci 11/13r. ✆055 23 44 923. Reservation recommended. Informal atmosphere, jazz soundtrack. Dishes range from traditional Tuscan to strawberry risotto. Tuscan wines only.

Trattoria 13 Gobbi – Via del Porcellana 9r. ✆055 28 40 15. Reservation recommended. A popular trattoria known for its authentic Tuscan cooking and cheerful atmosphere. Rustic decor and furnishings in the two dining rooms. Summer adds service in the lovely little courtyard.

Cibrèo – Via Andrea del Verrocchio 8r. ✆055 23 41 100. cibreo.fi@tin.it. Closed Mon. Reservation recommended. No pasta is served in this informal but very stylish establishment near the Sant'Ambrogio market. Chef Picchi passionately researches Tuscan traditions and ingredients, then does them his way, all beautifully presented. The service is attentive and excellent-quality wines are reasonably priced.

TAKING A BREAK

Caffè Ricchi e Ristorante – Piazza Santo Spirito 8/9r. ✆055 28 08 30. Open 7.30am–11pm. For drinks or gelato, with lovely outdoor summer terrace.

Gelateria Grom – Via del Campanile. ✆055 21 61 58. Open daily 10.30am–11pm. Florence's best *gelateria* is a Turin import, steps from the Duomo.

Teatro del Sale – Via de' Macci 111r. ✆055 20 01 492. This private Cibrèo club (low-cost membership) is theatre, shop, restaurant open for three meals a day – a quirky Florentine salon that the chef-owner frequents himself. Delicious food and wines.

Gelateria Carabè – Via Ricasoli 60r. ✆055 28 94 76. www.parcocarabe.it. Authentic Sicilian gelato and granita, handy to San Marco and the Accademia.

GOING OUT

Antico Caffè del Moro "Caffè des artistes" – Via del Moro 4r. ✆055 28 76 61. Closed Sun and three weeks Aug. Artists in the 1950s often paid with paintings, which now decorate the bar walls.

GranCaffè Giubbe Rosse – Piazza della Repubblica 13/14r. ✆055 21 22 80. www.giubberosse.it. The waiters wear their red jackets with great pride – this caffè popular with writers and artists, including the early Italian Futurist movement. Indoor and outdoor tables.

Il Rifrullo – Via San Niccolo 55r. ✆055 23 42 621. www.ilrifrullo.com. Off the beaten tourist track near Porta San Miniato, this bar is popular with Florence's late-night revellers, on the terrace, or in the back by the fireplace.

Jazz Club – Via Nuova dei Caccini 3. ✆055 527 18 15. Closed Mon. A jazz club showcasing primarily Italian musicians.

Nuova Tripperia Fiorentina – ✆055 238 17 65. San Lorenzo central market, open market hours. Legendary tripe sandwiches, the family business since the 19C.

CONCERTS AND THEATRE

La Nazione and *Firenze Spettacolo* have listings. **Box Office** – Via delle Vecchie Carceri 1 ✆055 21 08 04. www.boxofficetoscana.it. Sells tickets for various theatres.

Teatro della Pergola, Via della Pergola 12/32. www.teatrodellapergola.com.

Around Florence

Outside the busy centre, Renaissance artists and architects graced the landscape with stunning art and buildings. Many were agricultural power bases, secular or religious, such as the Certosa (Charterhouse) del Galluzzo. Medici villas and gardens today offer tranquillity and harmony, as does the Vallombrosa Abbey. Fiesole offers a glimpse of a town nestled in the Tuscan landscape. These stops, tours and detours make for leisurely visits.

▶ **Population:** 14 341
◔ **Michelin Map:** 563.
🚹 **Info:** Via Portigiani 3, Fiesole. ℘055 59 61 323, www.comune.fiesole.fi.it.
◐ **Location:** Fiesole is 7km/4.3mi from Florence. Bus 7 (Santa Maria Novella).
☺ **Don't Miss:** The view from San Francesco convent.
◔ **Timing:** Allow half a day.
👨‍👧 **Kids:** Explore Fiesole's archaeological area, then find tombs in the museum.

SOUTH OF FLORENCE

Galluzzo

Certosa del Galluzzo★★

6km/3.7mi S by Via Senese (SR2). Guided tours only, hourly Tue–Sat 9–11am and 3–5pm (Sun pm only, winter 4pm). Donations welcome. ℘055 20 49 226. www.cistercensi.info/certosadifirenze. The grandiose 14C Carthusian monastery has frescoes by Pontormo, a quiet garden, and a bar for coffee or to sample liqueurs from their distillery.

Scandicci

8km/5mi SW through Porta al Prato, or Tram 1/Resistenza stop.
Castello dell'Acciaiolo (Via Pantin 7) hosts Bistrot del Mondo, a pleasant Slow Food restaurant (℘055 73 51 620. www.acciaioloslow.it). Nearby abbeys to explore include Badia di San Salvatore a Settimo and San Martino a Gangalandi.

NORTH OF FLORENCE

The Medici Villas★

The Medici villas dot the hills north of Florence. Gardens are open; some also offer villa tours or an Etruscan museum. Admission to these is free.

Villa di Castello★

5km/3mi N of Castello. Garden open daily 8.15am–7.30pm Jul–Aug; other months closing time varies. Closed 2nd and 3rd Mon of the month, 1 Jan, 1 May, 25 Dec. Free. ℘055 45 26 91. www.polomuseale.firenze.it.
The villa (🔒 closed to the public) was acquired by Lorenzo and Giovanni de' Medici in 1477, while in 1538 Cosimo I had Tribolo plan the gardens.The statues, fountains and grottoes were all various symbols of power.

Villa La Petraia★

Near Villa di Castello, at the end of Via della Petraia. Open daily 8.15am–2hrs before dusk. Closed 2nd and 3rd Mon of the month, 1 Jan, 1 May, 25 Dec. Free. ℘055 45 26 91. www.polomuseale. firenze.it.
In 1575 Cardinal Ferdinand de' Medici commissioned Buontalenti to convert this castle into a villa. In the **garden**, there is a fine fountain by Tribolo. The villa's first floor has a statue of Venus by Giambologna. Both are open to the public.

Villa La Ferdinanda ◔See Prato.

🚗 DRIVING TOUR

Scenic Drive: Colli Alti★

26km/16.2mi to Sesto Fiorentino. From Florence drive N (SS/SR 65).

After Montorsoli, go le1ft to Monte Morello. The road *(Via dei Colli Alti)* winds

Villa Gamberaia, Settignano

©Mmoraru3/Dreamstime.com

up through woods to Piazzale Leonardo da Vinci, with a view of Florence, the Arno Valley, Chianti Hills and Prato Plain. After Gualdo, the road descends to Quinto Alto, with massive 7C BC Etruscan tombs, **Montagnola★** (Via Fratelli Rosselli 95; ☎055 44 891, or 055 449 6357), distinctive for their size, their circular rooms, and a dome of more than 5m/16ft.

Sesto Fiorentino★

The sixth (Sesto) mile west of Florence shed its medieval aspect to modern industry, primarily porcelain and ceramics. Richard Ginori Museo di Doccia *(closed to the public)* has porcelain from the factory founded in 1735.

Monte Senario★

🕒 Scenic drive to the N. 38km/23.6mi. Bus 25a or take the SS/SR 65 N from Florence. Drive towards Pratolino, stopping first in Parco Villa Demidoff (Via Fiorentina 276, Pratolino; free; ☎055 29 08 32; www.firenzeturismo.it).
Stroll through the vast Medici park to the Apennine Colossus, a giant sculpted by Giambologna (1579–1580). Continue towards Bivigliano, taking the first turn towards Convent of Monte Senarioa, founded in the 13C. Then go to Bivigliano, and loop back south on Via dei Condotti towards Pratolino and Florence.

EAST OF FLORENCE
Settignano★
Bus 10 (Santa Maria Novella).
Michelangelo spent his early years at the home (now Villa Michelangelo) of a stonecutter and his wife. Boccaccio set the beginning of *The Decameron* here, an area that lured Mark Twain, Eleonora

Duse, d'Annunzio and Bernard Berenson. Stroll through the sublime garden of **Villa Gamberaia★** (Via del Rossellino 72; ☎055 69 72 05; www.villagamberaia.com). They rent villas and some rooms (⊜⊜⊜⊜).

Fiesole★

🕒 8km/5mi NE of Florence. Bus 7.
Art and nature blend in harmony and afford a romantic **view★★★** of Florence, especially from San Francesco convent. Explore its archeological site and **Museo Civico Archaeologico** *(Via Portigiani 1; www.museidifiesole.it)*. Walk to Piazzale Leonardo, or even back down to Florence (1hr 40min).

Abbazia di Vallombrosa★

🕒 36km/22.4mi E of Florence.
The **abbey** *(www.abbazie.com/vallombrosa)* has a commanding view, luxuriant forest setting, art and pharmacy with herbal remedies. This is also a hotel, dining room and bar.

ADDRESSES

🍴 EAT

⊜⊜ **Bistrot del Mondo** – Castello dell'Acciaiolo, Via Pantin, Scandicci. ☎055 73 51 620. www.acciaioloslow.it. A friendly, rustic Tuscan slow-food restaurant. Occasional cooking courses and wine tastings.

⊜⊜ **Trattoria Bibe** – Via delle Bagnese 15, Galluzzo. ☎055 20 49 085. www.trattoriabibe.com. Superb small rustic restaurant in the same family since 1870. Cuisine ranges from traditional Tuscan to creative new twists. Fabio has good wines.

Montecatini Terme★

The spring water here has been famous for its medicinal properties for centuries and Montecatini is one of Italy's most popular spa resorts. With its parks, wide variety of entertainment and racecourse, this elegant spa town provides the ideal setting for an enjoyable break.

VISIT

In the 19C and 20C the town attracted luminaries from the worlds of art and literature, including Giuseppe Verdi, Luigi Pirandello and the English Romantic poets. Montecatini was at its height of fame in the early-20C, which is reflected in the spa town's Art Nouveau-style buildings and ornamentation, like Tettuccio Terme.

The spring water here is used to treat metabolic disorders, liver, stomach and intestinal complaints and rheumatism. The spas also offer a full range of beauty and wellness services, such as massage, facials and fitness programmes.

EXCURSIONS

Collodi★★

▶ 15km/9.3mi W.

Collodi was the pen-name adopted by Carlo Lorenzini, the author of *Pinocchio*, whose mother was born in the village. **Parco di Pinocchio** was laid out in the form of a maze on the banks of the River Pescia in 1956. ♿Open daily 9am–dusk (Sat–Sun opens 10am). 12€, 21€ with butterfly house. ☎0572 42 93 42. www.pinocchio.it.

Castello e Giardino Garzoni

Garden only. Open daily 9am–1hr before dusk (Sat–Sun opens 10am). 13€. For information call ☎0572 42 73 14. www.pinocchio.it.

Dating from the Renaissance-Baroque periods, the **gardens** offer vistas, pools, fountains, clipped trees, grottoes, sculpture and mazes, creating an imaginative spectacle.

▶ **Population:** 21 374
♿ **Michelin Map:** 563 K 14.
🛈 **Info:** Viale Verdi 66/68, 51016 Montecatini Terme. ☎0572 77 22 44. www.comune. montecatini-terme.pt.it. www.termemontecatini.it.
▶ **Location:** Montecatini Terme is situated between Florence and Lucca, off the motorway that links Florence to the coast.
▶ **Train:** Montecatini Terme (Firenze SMN 51 mins).
⊚ **Don't Miss:** A visit to a spa.
🕐 **Timing:** Allow half a day.
👫 **Kids:** Parco di Pinocchio.

ADDRESSES

🛏 STAY

🍴🛏 **Hotel La Pia** – Via Montebello 30. ☎0572 78 600. www.lapiahotel.it. Closed Nov–9 Apr. 37 rooms. ⬜. An extremely well-run establishment, with simple, well-maintained rooms, centrally located in a quiet part of town. The young proprietors are very thoughtful. Excellent food (guests only).

🍴 EAT

🍴🍴🍴 **La Torre** – Piazza Giusti 8/9, Montecatini Alto. 5km/3mi NE of Montecatini Terme. ☎0572 70 650. Closed Tue. Well-established restaurant situated in the main piazza of this charming village. Combines gastronomic cuisine with top-quality wines. Warm welcome. Has been in the same family for more than 40 years.

TAKING A BREAK

Caffè Giusti – Piazza Giuseppe Giusti 24, Montecatini Alto. 5km/3mi NE of Montecatini Terme. ☎0572 70 186. www.cafferistorantegiusti.it. Open Thu–Tue 9am–midnight. With tables set out in the little piazza and a good view of the medieval tower, what better place to sit and watch the world go by?

Montecatini Spa offers a wide range of treatments and varous waters attributed with specific healing properties. www.termemontecatini.it

Pistoia★★

Pistoia's historic centre is evidence of its importance in the 12C–14C. Both Lucca and Florence coveted Pistoia, but it was Florence that annexed it in 1530. The town has some wonderful examples of Medieval architecture and the streets are relatively free of tourists.

▶ **Population:** 90 288
⚅ **Michelin Map:** 563 K 14.
🈳 **Info:** Piazza dei Duomo 13.
  📞800 01 21 46.
  www.comune.pistoia.it.
▷ **Location:** Between Florence and the coast (36km/22.4mi from Florence).
▷ **Train:** Pistoia (Firenze SMN 35mins).
😊 **Don't Miss:** The birthplace of Leonardo da Vinci.
🕓 **Timing:** A day and a half.

VISIT
Piazza del Duomo★★
This is a most attractive and well-proportioned square lined with elegant secular and religious buildings.

Duomo (Cattedrale di San Zeno)★
Cappella di San Jacopo: Open 10am–12.30pm and 3–5.30pm, Sun 8–11.30am and 4–5.30pm. 3.60€. 📞0573 25 095.
Rebuilt in the 12C and 13C, the cathedral has a façade★ that is a harmonious blend of the Pisan-Romanesque style (tiers of colonnaded galleries) and the Florentine-Renaissance style (porch with slender columns added in the 14C). Inside is the altar of St James★★★, a 13C masterpiece of silversmith work.

Battistero★
Hours vary, phone Duomo or tourist office.
This Gothic baptistery dates from the 14C. The tympanum of the central doorway bears a statue of the Virgin and Child attributed to Nino and Tommaso Pisano.

Palazzo Pretorio
This palace was built in the 14C as the residence of the governing magistrate (podestà) and remodelled in the 19C.
Palazzo del Comune – The town hall was built from 1294 to 1385 and has a graceful arcaded façade★ with elegant paired windows or triple bays. The palace houses the **Museo Civico** with its collection of paintings and sculptures from the 13C–20C Tuscan school. ♿ Thu–Sun, holidays 10am–6pm. 3.50€. 📞0573 37 12 96. www.comune.pistoia.it.

Chiesa di Sant'Andrea★
St Andrew's Church is in the pure Pisan-Romanesque style. Its dramatic **pulpit★★** (1298–1308) is by Giovanni Pisano. The gilded wood **crucifix★** is also by Pisano.

Basilica della Madonna dell'Umiltà★
Via della Madonna Open Tue, Thu and Sat 9am–7pm, other days 9am–noon and 4–9pm. 📞0573 22 045.
The octagonal basilica, dedicated to the Virgin of Humility and its miraculous painting, has a dome Vasari designed, inspired by Brunelleschi's in Florence.

😊Additional sights include: Palazzo del Tau, Ospedale del Ceppo (**frieze★★** by Giovanni della Robbia), San Giovanni Forcivitas (**north façade★, pulpit★**, *Visitazione* by Luca della Robbia).

EXCURSION
Vinci★
▷ 24km/14.9mi S.
Leonardo da Vinci was born not far from this charming hilltop town. The **Museo Leonardiano★** in the castle exhibits models of Leonardo's inventions (♿open daily Mar–Oct 9.30am–7pm, Nov–Feb 9.30am–6pm; closed 1 Jan, 25 Dec; 10€; 📞0571 93 32 51).
The **house of Da Vinci's birth** lies 2km/1.2mi to the north in Anchiano. ♿Open 10am–5pm (Mar–Oct 7pm). 6€. 📞0571 93 32 48. www.museo leonardiano.it.

Prato★★

In 1351 Prato fell under the rule of its illustrious neighbour, Florence, until the 18C. Despite the peaceful, provincial air of the central districts, Prato is the fourth-largest city in central Italy, one of the most highly industrialised. Prato has the second-largest Chinese population after Milan, many employed in the garment industry.

VISIT
Duomo★
The 12C–13C cathedral blends Romanesque and Gothic styles. The façade has a graceful pulpit (15C) by Michelozzo and Donatello.
The **Capella del Sacro Cingolo** (Chapel of the Holy Girdle) is enclosed by delicately worked bronze **screens★** decorated with frescoes (1392–5) by Agnolo Gaddi. Giovanni Pisano sculpted a **Virgin and Child★** (1317). **Frescoes★★** by **Filippo Lippi** show the stunning *Banquet of Herod* and *Salome's Dance*. A marble **pulpit★** has the shape of a chalice, and in a niche is the moving *Virgin of the Olive Tree*, a terra-cotta statue (1480) by Benedetto da Maiano.

Palazzo Pretorio★
Galleria Comunale presents works by the 14C and 15C Tuscan school, notably important **polyptychs★**.

Castello dell'Imperatore
Frederick II commissioned this mighty **Imperial fortress** (c.1248).
Additional sights include: Santa Maria delle Carceri, San Francesco (**frescoes★**), Museo dell'Opera del Duomo (**panels★** carved by Donatello).

EXCURSIONS
Villa di Poggio a Caiano★★
▶ 17km/10.6mi N by the SS 66.
Open daily Mar and Oct 8.15am–5.30pm; Apr–May, Sept to 6.30pm; Jun–Aug to 7.30pm; Nov–Feb to 4.30pm. Closed 2nd and 3rd Mon of the month. Free. www.polomuseale.firenze.it.

▶ **Population:** 188 011
Michelin Map: 563 K 15.
Info: Piazza Buonamici 7, 59100 Prato. ℘0574 24 112. www.pratoturismo.it.
◐ **Location:** Prato is only 17km/10.6mi from Florence. The main access roads are the A 1 (Bologna–Florence) and the road that links Florence with the coast.
Don't Miss: Frescoes by Fra Filippo Lippi in the Duomo.
◐ **Timing:** Allow half a day.

Sangallo designed this villa for Lorenzo the Magnificent, with Pontormo **frescoes** of Vertumnus and Pomona, goddesses of orchards.
The **Museum of Still Life** requires advance booking: ℘055 87 70 12. www.polomuseale.firenze.it.

Artimino
Villa La Ferdinanda★★
◐ 26km/16.2mi W of Artimino. www.artimino.com.
Here is the chance to sleep in the grounds of a 16C Medici villa with Etruscan archaeology museums. *See also North of Florence, p553.*

ADDRESSES

🏠STAY
Borgo al Cornio – Via Convenevole da Prato 30. ℘0574 44 02 22. www.borgoalcornio.com. 6 rooms. Small, family hotel near the Duomo.

Hotel San Marco – Piazza San Marco 48. ℘0574 21 321. www.hotelsanmarcoprato.com. 40 rooms. Simple rooms close to the train station.

Bed & Breakfast Villa Rucellai – Via di Canneto 16. 4km/2.5mi N of Prato. ℘0574 46 03 92. www.villarucellai.it. 11 rooms. 16C mansion, set in parkland with a swimming pool. Old fashioned with a degree of elegance.

Lucca★★★

Situated in the centre of a fertile plain, Lucca has preserved within its girdle of ramparts a rich heritage of churches, palaces, squares and streets that give the town a charming air, unscathed by contemporary developments. The ramparts (4km/2.5mi long) extend all the way round the old town. They were built in the 16C and 17C and include 11 bastions, linked by curtain walls, and four gateways.

▶ **Population:** 84 928
- **Michelin Map:** 563 K 13.
- **Info:** Piazzale Verdi. ℘0583 58 31 50. www.turismo.lucca.it. www.comune.lucca.it.
- **Location:** 74km/46mi from Florence and 20km/12.4mi from Viareggio.
- **Train:** Lucca (Firenze SMN: 1hr 18mins).
- **Parking:** Lucca has a number of car parks located just inside the ramparts.
- **Don't Miss:** Stroll through old Lucca, to the Duomo and San Michele in Foro. Magnificent 17C gardens at Villa Reale di Marlia.
- **Timing:** Take half a day to explore Lucca, and a day to visit the villas.

A BIT OF HISTORY

Lucca was colonised by the Romans in the 2C BC and it has retained the plan of a Roman military camp, with the two principal streets perpendicular to one another. During the Middle Ages a complicated system of narrow alleys and oddly shaped squares was added to the original network. The town became an independent commune at the beginning of the 12C and flourished until the mid-14C with the silk trade. In the early-14C the town's prosperity and prestige grew under Castruccio Castracani (d.1328). Lucca's finest religious and secular buildings date from this period. Luccan architects adopted the Pisan style to which they added their characteristic refinement and fantasy. From 1550 onwards the town became an important agricultural centre and with this new prosperity came a renewed interest in building. The countryside was dotted with villas.

In the early-19C, Elisa Bonaparte ruled the city for a brief period from 1805 to 1813. Following Napoleon's Italian campaigns he bestowed the titles of Princess of Lucca and Piombino on his sister. Elisa showed a remarkable aptitude for public affairs and ruled her fief with wisdom and intelligence, encouraging the development of the town and the arts.

THE LEGEND OF THE HOLY CROSS

The Volto Santo (Holy Visage) is a miraculous Crucifix kept in the cathedral. It is said that after Christ had been taken down from the Cross, Nicodemus saw the image of his face on it. The fame of the Volto Santo, spread by merchants, gained Lucca a significant increase in visitors and commerce. In addition to its centre and villas, Lucca today attracts visitors for its lively arts scene with festivals of music, photography, and even comics.

WALKING TOUR

OLD TOWN
(Città Vecchia)

The atmospheric streets and squares of old Lucca have Gothic and Renaissance palaces, noble towers, old shops, sculptured doorways and coats of arms, wrought-iron railings and balconies. Starting from **Piazza San Michele**, follow Via Roma and Via Fillungo to **Piazza del Anfiteatro** situated inside the Roman amphitheatre.

Go towards Piazza San Pietro (12C–13C church) and then take Via Guinigi, where at no. 29 stands Casa dei Guinigi with its **tower** (**panorama**★ of the town from the top) crowned with trees. Continue to the Romanesque church of **Santa Maria Forisportam**. Via Santa Croce, Piazza dei Servi and Piazza dei Bernardin lead back to Piazza San Michele.

SIGHTS
Duomo★★

The cathedral, dedicated to St Martin, was rebuilt in the 11C, with changes in the 13C–15C. The green-and-white marble **façade**★★ is striking in its asymmetry. The upper section is the first example of the Pisan-Romanesque style (⌾ see PISA) as it developed in Lucca, with lighter, less rigid lines and inventive ornamentation. The campanile harmoniously combines the use of brick and marble, and the number of openings increases with height.

The portico shelters pillars with simply carved columns, arcading, friezes and a variety of scenes.

The Gothic interior has an unusual Romanesque sculpture of St Martin dividing his cloak, a style that heralds Nicola Pisano. The lovely shrine (tempietto) was built to house the Volto Santo. The great 12C **figure**★ of Christ in wood blackened through time shows a distinctly Oriental influence, said to be a copy of the legendary holy image.

Sienese artist Jacopo della Quercia (1406) sculpted the **tomb of Ilaria del Carretto**★★ in the early-15C, with the dog a symbol of fidelity.

See also the *Presentation of the Virgin in the Temple* by Bronzino and the large-scale **Last Supper**★ with its subtle lighting by Tintoretto.

Chiesa di San Michele in Foro★★

The white 12C–14C church on the site of the Roman forum has an exceptionally tall **façade**★★, a good example of Lucca-Pisan style. The simple Romanesque **interior** has a **Madonna**★ by Andrea della Robbia. The south transept has a lovely **painting**★ with brilliant colours by Filippino Lippi.

Chiesa di San Frediano★

This great church, dedicated to St Frigidian, was rebuilt in the original Lucca-Romanesque style in the 12C. The sober façade is faced with marble from the Roman amphitheatre.

The upper middle section, remodelled in the 13C, is dominated by a Byzantine-style mosaic of the Ascension by local artists. A curious Romanesque **font**★ (12C) with bas-reliefs depicts the story of Moses.

Pinacoteca Nazionale di Palazzo Mansi

♿ Open Tue–Sat 8.30am–7.30pm. Closed 1 Jan, 1 May, 25 Dec. 4€; 6.50€ combined ticket with Museo Nazionale di Villa Guinigi. ✆0583 55 570. www.luccamuseinazionali.it.

The apartments of this 17C palace have remarkable interior **decoration**★ (17C–18C). The Pinacoteca has works by 17C Italian artists (Salimbeni and Barocci) and foreign paintings.

Detail of the façade, Chiesa di San Michele in Foro

© O. Forir/MICHELIN

Giacomo Puccini's Birthplace Museum

Corte San Lorenzo 8. Open May–Sept 10am–7pm; Mar–Apr and Oct 10am–6pm (closed Tue); Nov–Feb 10am–1pm and 3–5pm (closed Tue). ✆0583 58 40 28. www.puccinimuseum.org.

An opera lover's pilgrimage, after years of restoration, Puccini's birthplace house reopened in 2011 to show his music, records, paintings, original furnishings, relics, letters, photos and his words.

Museo Nazionale di Villa Guinigi

Via della Quarquonia. Open Tue–Sat 8.30am–7.30pm. Closed 1 Jan, 1 May, 15 Aug, 25 Dec. 4€; 6.50€ combined ticket with Pinacoteca di Palazzo Mansi. ✆0583 49 60 33. www.luccamuseinazionali.it.

The villa exhibits archaeological finds, sculpture (Romanesque, Gothic and Renaissance) and painting (Lucca and Tuscany). Note the remarkable panels of intarsia work.

EXCURSIONS

Villa Reale di Marlia

▶ 8km/5mi N. ♿ Garden only. Mar–Oct 10am–6pm, Nov–Feb only Sun and public hols 10am–4pm. 8€.
For information call ✆0583 30 108. www.parcovillareale.it.

The Villa Reale is surrounded by 17C gardens★★ modified by Elisa Bonaparte. Unusual features include a lemon grove, a 17C *nymphaeum* and an open-air theatre.

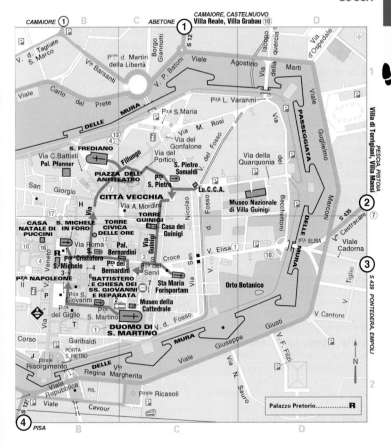

Villa Grabau

▶ Near the Villa Reale. ♿ Open Easter–
Jun and Sept–Nov 10am–1pm and
2–6pm; Jul–Aug 10am–1pm and 3–7pm;
Nov–Easter Sun and public hols only
11am–1pm and 2.30–5.30pm. Closed
Mon am, 24–26 Dec, 31 Dec, 1 Jan, 6 Jan.
Park and villa 6.50€; park only 5€.
℘0583 40 60 98. www.villagrabau.it.
The magnificent perspective draws the
eye from the villa entrance avenue to
the Italian garden, and beyond.
Fountains with bronze mascarons
and white-marble statues add to the
elegant appearance of the **park**★★, an
area of 9ha/22 acres, a real botanical
garden. The layout includes an outdoor
theatre, an informal English garden and
an Italian garden, decorated with old
18C and 19C lemon trees in their original containers.

Villa Mansi

▶ At Segromigno, 11km/6.8mi to the
NE. ♿ Garden open Apr–Sept Mon–Fri
9am–4.30pm, Sat–Sun 10am–1pm and
2–6pm; Nov–Mar daily 10am–1pm and
2–5pm. 5€. ℘0583 92 02 34.
www.villeepalazziluchhesi.it.
This 16C villa has a façade covered with
statues and a **park**★ where statue-lined
alleys lead to a lovely pool.

Villa di Torrigiani
(or di Camigliano)★

▶ 12km/7.4mi to the NE. ℘0583 92 80
41. www.villeepalazziluchhesi.it.
This 16C villa was converted in the 17C
into a summer residence by Marques
Nicolao Santini. The gardens, designed
by Le Nôtre, are adorned with fountains,
grottoes and nymphaea. The villa,
which has a delightful Rococo façade,
contains rooms adorned with frescoes.

ADDRESSES

🏠 STAY

Hotel Stipino – Via Romana 95. ☎0583 49 50 77. www.hotelstipino.com. 🅿 20 rooms. A well-run family hotel on the outskirts of town.

Lucca Elisa e Gentucca – Viale Diaz 71. ☎0583 051 962. www.luccainvilla.it. 🅿 6 rooms. By the entrance to the historic centre is this lovely Art Nouveau villa. Kitchen facilities, bicycle rental and tours.

Ostello San Frediano – Via della Cavallerizza 12. ☎0583 484 77. www.ostellolucca.it. ♿ 29 rooms. Adjacent to San Frediano are hotel comforts at guesthouse prices. Spacious public areas, plus a lovely garden.

Piccolo Hotel Puccini – Via di Poggio 9. ☎0583 55 421.www.hotelpuccini.com. 14 rooms. ☕3.50€. Near San Michele in Foro, this little hotel prides itself on its Puccini memorabilia.

Albergo San Martino – Via della Dogana 9. ☎0583 46 91 81. www.albergosanmartino.it. ♿ 9 rooms. ☕. Ideally situated near the Duomo. Spacious, airy rooms, modern amenities, and pleasant, modern furnishings.

Alla Corte degli Angeli – Via degli Angeli 23. ☎0583 46 92 04. www.allacortedegliangeli.com. 🅿 21 rooms. Steps from romantic Piazza dell'Anfiteatro, this charming hotel offers spacious rooms with decor inspired by colours and flowers.

🍴 EAT

Agli Orti di Via Elisa – Via Elisa 17. ☎0583 49 12 41. www.ristorantegliorti.it. Closed Thu lunch, Wed. Traditional and creative fare – grilled meats,huge salads, pizza (evening), daily specials, with a bistrot ambience.

Da Giulio in Pelleria – Via delle Conce 45, Piazza San Donato. ☎0583 55 948. Closed Sun. Reservation recommended. Large, historic trattoria offers regional cooking at reasonable prices. Very busy but pleasant.

Trattoria da Leo – Via Tegrimi 1. ☎0583 49 22 36. www.trattoriadaleo.it.. Steps from San Michele in Foro, lively with simple and abundant cuisine. Some outside tables.

Osteria Baralla – Via Anfiteatro 9. ☎0583 44 02 40. www.osteriabaralla.it. Closed Sun and mid-Jan–mid-Feb. Charming, in a medieval palazzo. One room has a vaulted ceiling, the other is more intimate. The daily menu features typical Tuscan dishes.

Antica Osteria – Via Santa Croce 55. ☎0583 44 02 75. www.anticaosteria.wix.com. Correct prices for this local cooking in attractive, atmospheric rooms.

Buca di Sant'Antonio – Via della Cervia 3. ☎0583 55 881. www.bucadisantantonio.com. Closed Sun evening, Mon, 13–21 Jan and 29 Jun–6 Jul. Founded in 1782, this rustic spot remains a favourite of Luccans for traditional cuisine at reasonable prices.

Ristorante Villa Bongi – Via di Cocombola 640, Montuolo. 6.5km/4mi from Lucca. ☎348 734 01 43. www.villabongi.it. Villa Bongi's two pretty rooms and splendid panoramic terrace are the setting or traditional and modern Tuscan cuisine. Large garden.

Puccini – Corte Lorenzo 1. ☎338 980 59 27. Close to the Puccini house, fish arrives daily from Versilia. They offer a good meat selection too.

Ristorante All'Olivo – Piazza San Quirico 1. ☎0583 49 62 64. www.ristoranteolivo.it. Closed Oct–Jan Wed and Feb. On a picturesque square, small refined restaurant has a terrace.

TAKING A BREAK

Gelateria Sergio Santini – Piazza Cittadella 1. www.gelateriasantini.it. Lucca's historic *gelateria* also makes *paciugo* and *panettone gelato*.

EVENTS AND FESTIVALS

Luminara di Santa Croce procession illuminates Lucca after dark. Fireworks on the banks of the river. (Sept)

Versilia★

Versilia is a district with a mild climate and contrasting landscapes lying between the sea coast and the mountains, which form a natural barrier against the north wind. The gently rolling hills give way to the lush coastal plain, which was formed in the Quaternary Era by the alluvium deposited by the streams tumbling down from the mountain peaks. Along the coast is a string of superb resorts boasting fine sandy beaches (up to 100m/110yds wide), which slope gently into the sea and are ideal for families with young children. In the distance one can see the Apuan Alps, which give Upper Versilia its natural resources of white-and-red marble and slate. In the hinterland and mountains, Nature has the upper hand. Traditional villages, surrounded by olive and chestnut trees, provide a contrast to the crowded coast. The Apuan Alps are a Parco Naturale, which includes Camaiore, Pietrasanta, Seravezza and Stazzema. The park is an ideal place for outdoor activities.

🚗 DRIVING TOUR

FROM QUARRY TO QUAYSIDE
50km/31mi. Allow half a day.

Cave di Carraracela
The wild countryside and gigantic nature of the quarrying operations afford a spectacular sight. The impressive quarries, **Cave dei Fantiscritti★★** (5km/3mi NE) and the **Cave di Colonnata★** (8.5km/5.3mi E), are both actively worked and regularly despatch quantities of marble (marmo) to the port of **Marina di Carrara** (7km/4.3mi SW).

Marina di Massa and Marina di Carrara
A deserted stretch of coast precedes these two resorts, the latter of which has a major marble shipping port.

- 🕙 **Michelin Map:** 563 J 12–K12/13.
- ℹ️ **Info:** Informazione Turistica della Versilia, Via Donizetti 14, 55044 Marina di Pietrasanta (LU). ℘0584 20 331. www.comune.pietrasanta.lu.it. Viale Carducci 10, 55049 Viareggio (LU). ℘0584 96 22 33.
- ◖ **Location:** Versilia is easily accessible from the motorways that link Genova to Livorno and Florence to the coast.
- ◖ **Train:** Camaiore Lido-Capezzano (Firenze SMN 1hr 35mins).
- 🚫 **Don't Miss:** Cave dei Fantiscritti and the Migliarino-San Rossore-Massaciuccoli Country Park.
- 👫 **Kids:** Sandy beaches at Marina di Pietrasanta.

Forte dei Marmi★
www.versilia-turismo.it.
Elegant and popular with the Italian jet set, artists, and Russian nouveau riche, this beach resort has regular rows of colourful little cabins. To the north, the mountains of Liguria turn west towards the coast and plunge into the sea, marking the end of the Versilian coastline.

👫 Marina di Pietrasanta★
The seaside resort has a long beach (over 5km/3mi), delightful paths through the pinewoods for walking or cycling, sports and active nightlife. On the outskirts, on the bank of the Fiumetto, is **Versiliana Park** (80ha/200 acres of woodland) with summer events. Don't forget to visit the beaches here.

Lido di Camaiore
www.toscanamare.com
Lido di Camaiore is more modern and more of a family resort than tonier Viareggio (🕙see page 564), but has the same fine sandy beach, the same pinewoods and a delightful esplanade.

Viareggio★

This fashionable seaside resort, on the Tyrrhenian Coast, has lovely beaches and plenty of amenities. Its late-1920s architecture blends Art Nouveau and Art Deco, like the splendid Gran Caffè Margherita. At **Torre del Lago Puccini** *(5km/3mi SE)* the composer Puccini wrote the majority of his operas. The **Villa Puccini** contains the tomb and mementoes of Puccini. See website for details. 7€. www.giacomopuccini.it.

▶ Take Via Aurelia (SS 1) N towards Viareggio; turn left to Torre del Lago.

Massaciuccoli★

Migliarino-San Rossore-Massaciuccoli Park has a shallow lake with turtles, and some 250 species of birds.

ADDRESSES

🛏 STAY

Hotel Byron – Viale E. Morin 46, 55042. Forte dei Marmi. ☎0584 78 70 52. www.hotelbyron.net. ♿ 29 rooms. 🛏. An Art Nouveau villa on the Lungomare, beautifully furnished, with swimming pool. La Magnolia restaurant has a superb chef who also cooks poolside in summer.

Carrara

Cited by Dante in his *Divine Comedy*, this region of the Apuan Alps, where the seer Aruns lived for centuries, is known for its "white marble" that Pliny considered almost as beautiful as that of the Greeks. It's still the capital of marble quarrying and of stonecutting, where marble and other stone is shipped from around the world to be cut here. Carrara's name perhaps derives from the ancient Ligurian *kar*, stone. Here Romans exploited the quarries and Michelangelo chose his blocks to release his masterpieces. In 1769 Maria-Teresa Cybo-Malaspina, the last descendant of the noble family that dominated Massa and Carrara, instituted an academy of fine arts that even today teaches technique and artistry.

SIGHTS
Duomo

The Roman-Gothic church (11C–14C) has a Pisan-style façade, a rose window and an elegant 13C campanile. The interior has interesting marble statues, including an *Annunciation* (14C). Next to the cathedral is a monumental 16C fountain.

▶ **Population:** 65 602
🚲 **Michelin Map:** 563 J 12.
ℹ **Info:** Ufficio Informazioni di Carrara, Viale XX Settembre, località Stadio Carrara (MS). ☎0585 84 41 36. www.turismomassacarrara.it.
▶ **Train:** Carrara (Avenza Firenze SMN 1hr 55mins).
🐾 **Don't miss:** Marble quarries and mammoth construction manoeuvres.
🕐 **Timing:** Allow a full day.
👪 **Kids:** Watch huge marble blocks being loaded onto ships.

Museo del Marmo★

♿ Open Oct–Apr Mon–Sat 9am–12.30pm; 2.30–5pm. Closed public hols. 4.50€. ☎0585 84 57 46. www.turismomassacarrara.it.
Marble from Antiquity to the present is exhibited in five sections: quarrying by Romans and archaeological finds; over 300 marble and granite slabs from the world's largest deposits; extraction methods from the 18C to the 20C; various uses of marble; and modern sculpture.

EXCURSIONS
Cave di Marmo★
(Marble Quarries)

The fierce landscape, mammoth white castoffs, and men working on a giant scale all offer an extraordinary spectacle. Along the route, small observation platforms allow you to follow the machines' various manoeuvres (during work hours). The "diamond wire", a steel cable bound by cylinders covered with diamond dust, severs marble blocks that are lifted towards the plain to be cut, then are sent off for further treatment.

Marina di Carrara

See also Versilia.

The main marble export centre has huge blocks of marble stacked and warehoused near the port.

Fantiscritti★★ (Marble Quarries)

▶ 4km–5km/2.5mi–3mi NW towards Miseglia.

This quarry is most impressive for its rugged site, its staging area, and its steep road to various levels. Access is through three viaducts, Ponti di Vara, built in the 19C for the mine railway.

Colonnata★ (Marble Quarries)

▶ 8km/5mi E towards Bedizzano or Carrara through the valley.

More accessible than those above, the level road leads to more cheerful surroundings offset by surrounding vegetation. Gourmets prize the *lardo* (fatback) cured in Colonnata caves.

Route de Campo Cecina★

▶ Scenic tour to Campo Cecina. From Carrara, 20km/12.4mi N on the SS 446.

Via Provinciale di Gragnana follows the western slopes of the Apuan Alps, climbing north over a wooded valley and through the villages of Gragnani and Castelpoggio, with a view of the sea to Marina di Carrara and Montemarcello Promontory. The road winds sharply west, then east on pine-covered slopes towards Campo Cecina (beware of marble trucks) with a view of Mount Pizzo. At Piazzale dell'Uccelliera, enjoy a superb view★★ across Torano to Marina di Massa and Montignoso, the islands of the Tuscan Archipelago and the peaks of the Southern Alps.

Massa

The provincial seat of Massa-Carrara, at the foot of the Apuan Alps, is only 4km/2.5mi from the coast, a modern town with ancient monuments. Squares, façades and fountains are adorned with white Carrara marble.

Ruled by the Malaspina in the 15C–18C, the city still has its 15C–16C castle, hidden in the half-ruined medieval fortress on the rocky hill overlooking the city, as well as the family's palace in Piazza Aranci. The Duomo has a *Pinturicchio Madonna* over the altar and the Malaspina tombs. Massa also has a botanical garden of plants indigenous to the Apuan Alps.

Fantiscritti

Garfagnana

Inhabited since prehistoric times, this mountainous region passes through Serchio Valley between the Apuan Alps and the green hills of the Apennines. Less frequented by tourists but not far from Lucca, it attracts nature lovers.

🚗 DRIVING TOUR

This tour along the east face of the Apuan Alps (50km/31mi) departs from Borgo a Mozzano and runs north to to Castelnuovo di Garfagnana. Two roads run parallel along the banks of the Serchio. The west branch of the SS 12 arrives at Borgo a Mozzano; the east branch at Bagni di Lucca.

Borgo a Mozzano

On the road to Abetone, the 12C bridge, **Ponte della Maddalena**, has five distinct arches that span the Serchio River. It is also called **Ponte del Diavolo**, because according to legend, the devil helped complete the bridge, in exchange for which he demanded the first soul to cross it. The builder avoided Inferno by letting a dog cross the bridge first.

▶ Go NW 16km/10mi on the SS 12 and SS 445, then right (E) on the SP 2.

Barga★

This picturesque medieval *borgo* has a *castello* constructed in the high part of town. Via del Pretorio leads to the Duomo, a 9C Romanesque cathedral dedicated to Sts Christopher and John. Inside are some fine sculptures, including a 12C polychrome wood St Christopher. The cloister leads to a terrace with a lovely **panorama★** of town rooftops and the Apuan Alps. Piazza del Comune has Renaissance palaces, as does Piazza Angelio.

Castelvecchio Pascoli

▶ 4km/2.5mi N of Barga.
The town has poet **Giovanni Pascoli**'s house where he lived 1895–1912 (📞0583 76 61 47).

▶ **Population:** 6 117 (Castelnuovo di Garfagnana)
🖐 **Michelin Map:** 563 J 13.
🔢 **Info:** www.castelnuovo garfagnana.org.
▶ **Location:** Garfagnana Valley lies between the Apuan Alps and Abetone. From Lucca go north on the SS 12; after Borgo a Mozzano, continue north to Barga and Castelnuovo di Garfagnana.
▶ **Train:** Castelnuovo di Garfagnana (Lucca 56 mins).
🕐 **Timing:** Allow one day, more if you go hiking.
👥 **Kids:** Grotta del Vento.

▶ Return towards Barga; continue SW 5km/3mi to Gallicano on the SP 20. Continue to Fornovolasco 9km/5.6mi on the SP 39 to "Wind Cave".

👥 Grotta del Vento

Guided tours only. 9€ 1hr; 14€ 2hrs; 20€ 3hrs. 📞0583 72 20 24. www.grottadelvento.com.
Explore stalactites and stalagmites, polychrome flowstone, alabaster draperies, crystal-brimmed lakes, underground water-courses and bizarre forms of erosion. Bring a light jacket or sweater; the temperature is 10.7°C (51.3°F).

▶ Return to Gallicano and go N on the SS 445 to Castelnuovo di Garfagnana.

Castelnuovo di Garfagnana

Located in the heart of the Apuan Alps near Parco Orechiella, the small industrial town has a nice hike up to the Rocca, residence of the Este family governors.

▶ Return to Borgo a Mozzano S by the SS 445.

Lunigiana★

This narrow, green woodland strip along the Magra River that borders Tuscany, Liguria and Emilia Romagna is dotted with castles and Romanesque churches called *Pieve*. The simple cuisine is based on olive oil, sheep's cheese, wild herbs and vegetables. Inhabited since Palaeolithic times, Lunigiana welcomed Etruscans and then Romans, who founded a colony of 2 000 inhabitants at Luni (now in Liguria), thus Lunigiana.

▶ **Population:** 1 042
Michelin Map: 563 I/J 11/12.
Info: www.comunevilla francainlunigiana.it.
▶ **Location:** Enter from the A 15 Parma-Mare *(exit Pontremoli and Aulla)*. The SS 62, called la Cisa, parallels the A 15, and runs along the Via Francigena, also called Romea. The SS 63, called Cerreto, passes from Aulla to Fivizzano.
▶ **Train:** Villafranca-Bagnone (Lucca 1hr 42mins).
Timing: Allow 1 day.
Kids: Museo Etnografico della Lunigiana.

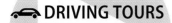

🚗 DRIVING TOURS

AULLA TO CASOLA IN LUNIGIANA
35km/21.8mi. Allow half a day.

Aulla
The fortress of **Brunella**, perhaps Medici, houses the **Museo di Storia Naturale** (Natural History Museum open Tue–Sun 9am–noon and 4–7pm (winter 9am–noon and 3–6pm); 3.50€; ✆0187 40 02 52), showcasing Lunigiana's natural world.

▶ Follow the SS 63 E to the SS 445, near Gragnola; go S towards Equi.

Equi Terme
The sulphuric thermal waters are used to treat respiratory, skin, bone and joint ailments. **Karstic caves, pool** (phone for details; some periods by reservation only; ✆0585 94 93 39, www.termediequi.it), rich in stalactites and stalagmites, had evidence of Palaeolithic and Neolithic man, and cave bears.

▶ Return to the SS 445. Go E towards Codiponte and Casola in Lunigiana (Aulella Valley).

Codiponte
The Romanesque church has Lombard Carolingian decorative motifs.

Casola in Lunigiana
A nice walk through town reveals 15C–16C buildings.

AULLA TO PONTREMOLI
22km/13.7mi. About half a day. From Aulla follow the SS 62 N towards Pontremoli, about 11km/6.8mi to Villafranca.

Villafranca in Lunigiana
The Museo Etnografico (open Tue–Sun 9am–noon and 4–7pm (winter 9am–noon and 3–6pm); 3€ ✆0187 49 34 17; www. terredilunigiana.com), housed in a 14C mill, documents peasant culture.

▶ Continue to Filattiera, 5km/ 3mi on the SS 62.

Filattiera
The Tuscan-Lombard **pieve de Sorano** has a lovely apse.

▶ Take the SS 62; continue 7km/ 4.3mi N to Pontremoli.

Pontremoli
Piagnaro, the 10C castle, houses the **Museo delle Statue Stele** (open 9am–12.30, 2.30–5.30pm, closed Mon; 5€ with castle. ✆0187 83 14 39, www.statuestele. org), which displays anthropomorphic sculptures of 2000 BC–5C BC.

Pisa★★★

Pisa's superb buildings reflect past splendours. More spacious than Florence and joyous with its yellow-, pink- or yellow-ochre houses, Pisa, like Florence, is bisected by the River Arno here in a majestic meander. Pisa's charm is reflected in its aristocratic air, genteel lifestyle, and special quality of the light, probably due to the proximity of the sea. Almost totally encircled by walls, Pisa is traversed by a main street lined with shops; on the south bank this is the Corso Italia and on the north bank a narrow street flanked by arcades, Borgo Stretto. The winding Via Santa Maria links Piazza del Duomo to the Arno, characteristically noble yet cheerful. These two streets flank the busiest district in the city, full of shops and restaurants.

- **Population:** 88 217
- **Michelin Map:** 563 K 13.
- **Info:** Piazza del Duomo, 56126 Pisa. ✆050 55 01 00. www.comune.pisa.it/turismo.
- **Location:** Pisa is near the mouth of the Arno. Parco Naturale di Migliarino-San Rossore-Massaciuccoli is between Pisa and the sea.
- **Train:** Pisa Centrale (Pisa airport 8 min).
- **Don't Miss:** The Torre Pendente (Leaning Tower), Duomo and Battistero.
- **Timing:** Allow one day.
- **Kids:** Trying to "hold up" the Leaning Tower of Pisa.

A BIT OF HISTORY

Sheltered from raiding pirates, Pisa was a Roman naval base and commercial port until the end of the Empire (5C). It became an independent maritime republic at the end of the 9C and continued to benefit from its geographical location. Pisa became the rival of Genova and Venice, and the Pisans waged war against the Saracens in the Mediterranean basin. It was in the 12C and the beginning of the 13C that Pisa reached the peak of its power and prosperity. This period was marked by the construction of fine buildings, including the famous leaning tower (begun in 1173) and the foundation of the university.

During the 13C there were struggles between the emperor and the Pope. Pisa supported the Ghibellines and opposed Genova on the seas and Lucca and Florence on land.

Piazza del Duomo

©Luciano Mortula/Dreamstime.com

In 1284 the Pisan fleet was defeated at the naval **Battle of Meloria**. Ruined by internal strife, Pisa's maritime empire foundered; Corsica and Sardinia, which she had ruled since the 11C, were ceded to Genova. Pisa herself passed under Florentine rule and the Medici took a special interest in the city, especially in the study of science there. Its most famous son was the astronomer and physicist **Galileo** (1564–1642). His patron was Cosimo II, Grand Duke of Tuscany. Nevertheless, Galileo had to defend his theory of the rotation of the Earth before the Inquisition and in fact renounced it.

The powerful maritime Pisan Republic from the 11C to the 13C fostered the development of a new art style, particularly in the fields of architecture and sculpture. The **Pisan-Romanesque style**, with the cathedral as the most rigorous example, is characterised by external decoration: the alternate use of different-coloured marbles to create geometric patterns, a play of light and shade due to the tiers of loggia with small columns on the upper parts of the façade, and intarsia decoration showing the strong influence of the Islamic world and of Christian countries of the Near East that had relations with the maritime Republic.

Alongside architects such as Buscheto, Rainaldo and Diotisalvi there were numerous sculptors to embellish the exteriors. Pisa became an important centre for Gothic sculpture in Italy, thanks to the work of **Nicola Pisano** (1220–c.80), originally from Puglia, and his son **Giovanni Pisano** (1250–c.1315).

SIGHTS

Piazza del Duomo (Campo dei Miracoli)★★★

For opening time of the monuments visit the website. Duomo: free; single monument: 5€; two monuments: 7€; three monuments (except Leaning Tower): 8€. ☎050 83 50 11. www.opapisa.it.

In and around this famous square, also known as "Campo dei Miracoli" (Field

GETTING THERE

AIRPORT: Pisa International Airport (Galileo Galilei) is served by a number of low-cost carriers (Ryanair, Easyjet, etc.) as well as Delta and major European carriers. Well connected by bus to Florence, Siena , Lucca, Viareggio and to central Pisa. www.pisa-airport.com.

of Miracles), are four buildings that form one of the finest architectural complexes in the world. It is advisable to approach on foot from the west through the Porta Santa Maria for the best view of the Leaning Tower.

Duomo★★

www.opapisa.it
Building of this splendid cathedral started in 1063 under Buscheto. Rainaldo designed the façade.

The light and graceful **west front★★★** has four tiers of small marble columns, its facing alternates light- and dark-coloured marble. The plan is a Latin cross. The **bronze doors★** cast in 1602 are by Giambologna. The south transept door has very fine Romanesque bronze **panels★★** (late-12C) by Bonanno Pisano, depicting the Life of Christ.

The **interior**, with its nave and four aisles, is impressive for its length (100m/330ft), its deep apse, its three-aisled transept and the forest of piers which offer an astonishing variety of perspectives. Note the beautiful 1302–11 **pulpit★★★** by **Giovanni Pisano**, supported by six porphyry columns and five pillars carved with religious and allegorical statues. Its eight panels recount the Life of Christ, full of personages and dramatic expressions. ☺Don't miss Galileo's lamp, which prompted his original theory about movement of the pendulum.

Torre Pendente★★★

For opening time visit the website. 18€. Book at least 15 days in advance. ☎050 83 50 11. www.opapisa.it.

Battistero

©Paul Topp/Dreamstime.com

The **Leaning Tower of Pisa** is both a bell tower and a belfry. This white-marble tower (58m/189ft high) was begun in 1173 in a pure Romanesque style by Bonanno Pisano and completed in 1350. Built, like the towers of Byzantium, as a cylinder, the tower has six storeys of galleries with columns which seem to wind round in a spiral because of the slope of the building. The lower level lozenges are specific to the architecture of Pisa. The tower slowly began leaning in 1178 and has continued to do so at a rate of between 1mm and 2mm a year (or half an inch over a typical decade). The movement is caused by the alluvial soil on which the tower is built; soil that is insufficiently resistant to bear the weight of the building. Architects tried in vain to correct the unfortunate "lean".

The tower was closed to the public in 1990 and a committee was formed to debate how best to find a long-term solution to the problem. In 1992 the tower was surrounded by two stainless-steel cables at first-floor level and, in 1993, the base was strengthened by a reinforced concrete "corset", which included 670 tons of lead to counterbalance the lean; progression of the lean was effectively stopped for several years.

Another restoration attempt in September 1995 ended in disaster when the tower shifted 2.5mm/1/8in in one night, double the annual rate. Engineers dumped lead on the base of the north side, and the tower was prevented from falling. In 1998 steel-cable "braces" were attached to the tower, then removed in 2001 when the tower had moved a further 40cm/16in towards the vertical, returning the tower its 1838 angle. The tower reopened to the public in 2001.

☺ Visiting the tower can be gruelling. There are 300 winding steps that lead to the top, especially challenging for visitors with health problems. Children under the age of eight are not allowed to visit, however, they love to admire the curious leaning tower.

Battistero★★★

The baptistery, begun in 1153, has two Pisan-Romanesque lower storeys, while the frontons and pinnacles above are Gothic. The majestic interior is full of light and has a diameter of 35m/115ft. The centre has a lovely octagonal **font★** (1246) by Guido Bigarelli. Its masterpiece is the admirable **pulpit★★** (1260) by Nicola Pisano, which depicts the Life of Christ, less ornate than that by his son for the cathedral.

Camposanto★★

This burial ground, begun in 1277, has one of the most famous 14C cycles, **The Triumph of Death★★★** and the **Last Judgement★★** and **Hell★**.

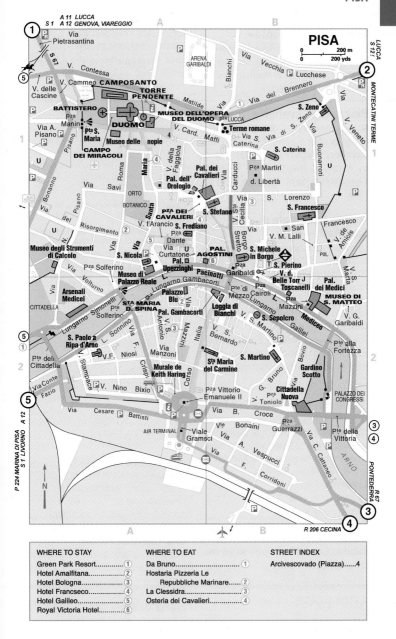

Museo dell'Opera del Duomo★★

The Cathedral Museum has 12C–16C sculptures (Romanesque period influenced by Islamic, Burgundian, Gothic and Renaissance styles), a stunning ivory *Madonna and Child* by Giovanni Pisano, silverware, 15C–18C paintings, sculpture and 12C–13C illuminated manuscripts.

Museo delle Sinopie★

Sketches in a reddish-brown pigment from Sinope (on the Black Sea) under frescoes reveal free draughtsmanship of the 13C–15C painters.

Piazza dei Cavalieri★

Named for Cavalieri di Santo Stefano (Knights of St Stephen), **Palazzo dei Cavalieri**'s façade★ was decorated by Vasari, as was the 1607 **Palazzo Gherardesca**. **Santo Stefano** dates to 1569.

Museo Nazionale di San Matteo★★

Open Tue–Sat 8.30am–7pm, Sun and hols 8.30am–1.30pm. 5€. ℘050 54 18 65. Works dating from 13C–15C by Nino Pisano and Masaccio.

Chiesa di Santa Maria della Spina★★

This 14C church, dedicated to St Mary of the Thorn, has pinnacles and statues by the Pisano and their workshop.

EXCURSIONS

Basilica di San Piero a Grado★

◗ 6km/3.7mi on SS224.

This Romanesque church occupies the spot on which St Peter is said to have landed when he came from Antioch.

Livorno

◗ 24km/14.9mi SW.
www.comune.livorno.it.

The Medici rebuilt Livorno's harbour in 1620. Piazza Micheli's statue is dedicated to Grand Duke Ferdinando, the last prominent Medici.

ADDRESSES

🏠STAY

⊖ **Hotel Galileo** – Via Santa Maria 12 (1st floor, no lift). ℘050 40 621. www. hotelgalileo.pisa.it. 9 rooms. In the centre, simple with large windows, reasonable rates. Most baths en suite.

⊖⊖ **Green Park Resort** – Via dei Tulipani 1, Calambrone. ℘050 31 35 711. www.greenparkresort.com. 148 rooms.

Set in a pine forest on the coast, enjoy spa treatments and fine dining options.

⊖⊖ **Hotel Amalfitana** – Via Roma 44. ℘050 29 000. www.hotelamalfitana.it. 21 rooms. This 15C palazzo near the university is small, comfortable, has courteous service and good rates.

⊖⊖⊖ **Hotel Bologna** – Via Mazzini 57. ℘050 50 21 20. Fax 050 43 070. www.hotel bologna.pisa.it. **P** Shuttle to Duomo or airport. 64 rooms. This tasteful historic residence offers all comforts in a lovely setting.

⊖⊖⊖ **Hotel Francesco** – Via Santa Maria 129. ℘050 55 54 53. www.hotel francescopisa.com. A quiet part of town, near the Leaning Tower, these comfortable rooms are modern and spacious. Breakfast al fresco in summer.

⊖⊖⊖ **Royal Victoria Hotel** – Lungarno Pacinotti 12. ℘050 94 01 11. www.royal victoria.it. **P** 48 rooms. Along the Arno, in a 14C palazzo, a double without bath is as low as 78€.

🍴 EAT

⊖ **La Clessidra** – Via del Castelletto 26/30. ℘050 54 01 60. www.ristorantela clessidra.net. Closed Sun; lunch only by reservation. Simple and pleasant, the Tuscan cuisine has innovative variations, in one of the smartest historic parts of town.

⊖⊖ **Hostaria Pizzeria Le Repubbliche Marinare** – Vicolo Del Ricciardi 8. ℘050 20 506. www.repubblichemarinare.eu. Closed Mon and Jan; Jul and Aug only dinner. A quiet oasis in Sant'Antonio with terrace, the speciality is fish.

⊖⊖ **Osteria dei Cavalieri** – Via San Frediano 16. ℘050 58 08 58. www.osteria cavalieri.pisa.it. Closed Sat lunch and Sun. A favourite of Pisans that serves traditional cuisine.

⊖⊖⊖ **Da Bruno** – Via Luigi Bianchi 12, Porta a Lucca. ℘050 56 08 18. www. anticatrattoriadabruno.it. Closed Wed lunch and Tue. One of the city's best restaurants. Pisan and Tuscan specialities.

TAKING A BREAK

Caffè dell'Ussero – Lungarno Pacinotti 27. ℘050 58 11 00. Closed Sat. Grand 18C caffè that overlooks the Arno River.

Estruscan Riviera

The Etruscan Riviera stretches between Livorno and Piombino. Etruscan sites, the clear sea, small medieval villages, and a countryside with wine roads and parks make for an enjoyable tour.

VISIT

Bounded by the sea and natural parks, dotted with medieval towns, here are Etruscan traces to explore, a metal industry that dates back to the Iron Age, and prestigious wines, all along a route easy to do on bicycle. Most of the route is on or near the SS 1 **Via Aurelia**.

🚗 DRIVING TOUR

160km/99.4mi round tour beginning and ending in Rosignano Marittimo Plombino. Allow 1 day.

Rosignano Marittimo Piombino has a hilltop medieval centre, and its castle with **Archaeological Museum** *(www.costadeglietruschi.it)* shows Etruscan to Renaissance artefacts, and rooms that reconstruct a Roman villa. Go south to **Cecina**, which in the 18C became a brick manufacturing centre. It has a working-class beach and its own **Museo Archeologica** with a stunning 8C funerary urn that has a banquet scene on its lid. **Marina di Castagneto-Donoratico** has a long sandy beach sheltered by a beautiful pine forest. Turn inland to **Marina di Castagneto Carducci**, renamed in the early-20C for the poet who evoked its beauty, especially its long avenue of cypress trees that leads to San Guido in **Bolgheri**. **Torre di Donoratico**, now in ruins, is the tower where Ugolino della Gherardesca, accused of treason after the Battle of Meloria for Pisa (1284), was locked in the tower to starve with his children in 1289; Ugolino was dubbed the "cannibal count" from Dante's depiction of their ambiguous fate.

▶ **Population:** 35 075 (Piombino)

Ⓖ **Michelin Map:** A 2–563 L/M 13.

🄑 **Info:** www.costadegli etruschi.it.

◐ **Location:** The Etruscan Riviera stretches along the coast from Piombino to Livorno.

◐ **Train:** Piombino (Pisa Centrale 1hr 21mins).

🕐 **Timing:** 1–2 days.

👫 **Kids:** Bolgheri bird sanctuary, mine train, swim on the coast.

Bolgheri is known for its two famous wines, Sassicaia, "the father of Super-Tuscans", made in lovely Tenuta San Guido; and Ornellai. If your budget is less than 100€ plus per bottle, do seek out the lesser-known wines from more than 60 smaller wineries that make Bolgheri DOC, Val di Cornia, and **Bibbona** wines. Campiglia's **Porta Fiorentina** has four emblems that symbolise Campiglia (greyhound), the cross of Pisa, the lily of Florence, and the star of Gherardesca, the family that built the monastery. In the **Church of San Giovanni**, see the bas-relief of Meleager's boar hunt, and the *pieve*, which holds an inscription on a mysterious magic square, which dates back to at least the beginning of the Christian era. The significance of the five words remains obscure, apparently a magic formula to ward off bad luck. **Parco Archeo-Minerario di San Silvestro** has a section on mining, with a ride on a mining car.

East on the coast, **Populonia★**, where Etruscans once controlled metal mining and shipping, has a fascinating Etruscan necropolis with cylindrical tombs and an enormous dome. The upper town has artisans' shops.

Piombino, a major mining area since Etruscan times, is worth a good walk around, heading through the centre to see its architecture and museums. Piombino has ferries to Isola d'Elba (Ⓖ *see Isola d'ELBA*).

ADDRESSES

🛏 STAY

🛏 **Podere La Cerreta** – Via Campagna, Loc. Pian delle Vigne, 57020 Sassetta. 📞0565 79 43 52. www.lacerreta.it. 9 rooms. Traditional style rooms. This farm grows organic products, makes wine, has horses and a thermal spa.

🛏🛏 **Albergo Miramare** – Via Marconi 8, 57012 Castiglioncello. 📞0586 75 24 35. Closed Oct–May. 47 rooms. This coral palazzo has hosted Churchill,Pirandello and has a garden and walk to the beach.

🛏🛏 **Casa Vacanze Il Chiostro** – Via del Crocifisso, Suvereto. 📞0565 82 70 67. www. vacanzeilchiostro.it. 15 apartments. Rustic apartments with kitchen. In the historic centre, lovely view of the valley.

🛏🛏 **Poggio ai Santi** – Via San Bartolo, 100 l, 57027 San Vincenzo. 📞0565 79 8032 . www.poggioaisanti.com. 12 suites, 1 villa. Gracious hosts, excellent Il Sale restaurant (also open to ourside guests).

🍽 EAT

🍽 **The Gramola** – Via Marconi 18, Castagneto Carducci. 📞0565 76 36 46. www.lagramola.it. Closed Nov–Feb. Breathtaking views, at sunset over the valley down to the sea. Pizzas, salads,traditional regional dishes.

🍽🍽 **Bagno Nettuno** – Via Costa 3, 57027 San Vincenzo. 📞0565 70 10 95. www.bagnoristorantenettuno.it. Set on the beach, enjoy fish overlooking the sea.

🍽🍽 **Gualdo del Re** – Piazza dei Giudici 1, 57028 Suvereto. 📞0565 82 99 47. www. osteriadisuvereto.it. A typical restaurant with a charming outdoor dining area in a stunning setting right in the historic centre. The regional cuisine is made from organic and local produce.

🍽🍽🍽🍽 **La Pineta** – Via dei Cavalleggeri Nord 27, Marina di Bibbona. 📞0586 60 016. www.lapinetadizazzeri.it. Closed Mon and Tue lunch (winter also dinner). Dubbed the "winemakers' mess" because they regularly dine in this fisherman-turned-chef restaurant.

Isola d'Elba★★

The Allied Governments exiled Napoleon Bonaparte here in 1814 to 1815. Though given the title "Emperor of Elba", he escaped after nine months and began the 100 Days Campaign – his last hurrah – in France. It's the largest island in the Tuscan Archipelago★★, which includes Pianosa, Capraia, Giglio, Giannutri and Montecristo. The capital is Portoferraio.

A BIT OF HISTORY

Elba, a mountainous island, has its highest peak on Monte Capanne. The jagged coastline has natural, well-sheltered coves with small beaches. Napoleon commanded a small court and initiated several public works projects from his homebase in Portoferraio (🔵 see below).

⚐ **Michelin Map:** 563 N 12/13.

🗊 **Info:** Calata Italia 44, 57037 Portoferraio (LI). 📞0565 91 46 71. www.visitelba.info. www.arcipelagodellatoscana. com. Ferries are operated by Moby Lines: Via Giuseppe Ninci 1, 57037 Portoferraio (LI). 📞199 30 30 40. www. moby.it. Toremar: Calata Italia 36, 57037 Portoferraio (LI). 📞0565 91 80 80. www.toremar.it.

🔵 **Location:** Elba has ferry crossings from Piombino (45–50min) to Portoferraio and Rio Marina.

☺ **Don't Miss:** The beach at Biodola and panorama at Monte Capanne.

🕐 **Timing:** Two days to tour the island.

🚗 DRIVING TOUR

WESTERN TOUR★

70km/43.5mi. Allow 5 hrs anticlockwise from Portoferraio, following the map.

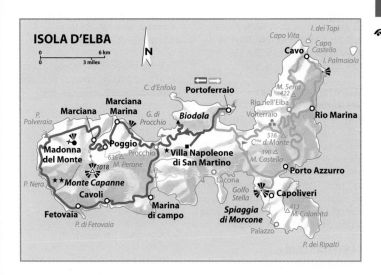

Portoferraio ⏋

The capital of the island lies on the shores of a beautiful bay. **Museo Nazionale della Palazzina dei Mulini** (Mill House), in the upper town, is where Napoleon lived during his brief period of sovereignty.

Museo Napoleonico has the officers' mess, Napoleon's library, his bedroom and the antechamber; downstairs are the WC, the servants' room, Napoleon's salon, his study and the door to the garden. Open Mon, Wed–Sat 8.30am–7pm, Sun and hols 8.30am–1pm. 5€; joint ticket with the Palazzina dei Mulini (valid 3 days) 8€. ☏0565 91 58 46. www.infoelba.com.

The **road★** west from Portoferraio to Marciana Marina affords lovely views of Procchio and Procchio Bay.

Biodola is a vast, beautiful sandy beach.

Marciana Marina ⏋⏋ holds the ruins of the Medici Tower *(Torre Medicea)*.

▷ W of Marciana Marina, the road climbs through the wooded northern slopes of Monte Capanne.

Poggio is a small resort perched on a spur of rock.

▷ The road climbs. On the outskirts of Marciana is the cablecar station to Monte Capanne.

Monte Capanne★★

20min by cablecar. Operates Easter–Oct daily 10am–1pm and 2.20–5pm. 18€ return. ☏0565 90 10 20. From the rocky summit *(15min on foot from the top station)*, the superb **panorama★★** overlooks the island of Elba, the coast of Tuscany and the east coast of Corsica.

Marciana – On the eastern slopes of Monte Giove, the village provides a wonderful **view★**. The small **Museo Archeologico** (Archaeological Museum) has artefacts from the Iron and Bronze Ages and Greek pottery. Open middle Jun–middle Sept 10am–1pm, and 4–7pm. 2€. ☏0565 90 12 15. www.comune.marciana.li.it.

Madonna del Monte

Alt. 627m/2 057ft. 45min there and back on foot from the road to the castle above Marciana.

A rocky path leads to panoramic views from the 16C chapel on the north slope of Monte Giove. The **view★** embraces Marciana Marina and Procchio Bay, and the villages of Marciana and Poggio. The road west passes the beaches of Sant'Andrea and **Fetovaia**. East of Fetovaia the road reaches **Cavoli**, a seaside resort with a sandy beach.

Marina di Campo is a superb beach, next to fishermen who enliven the harbour.

Take the road up to Galea Valle, which returns to Procchio, then go towards Portoferraio; at San Martino, turn right to Villa Napoleone.

Museo Nazionale di Villa San Martino★
Open Mon–Sat 8.30am–3pm, Sun and hols 8.30am–1pm. 5€ . Joint ticket with the Palazzina dei Mulini (valid 3 days) 8€. ℘0565 91 46 88. www.infoelba.com. Above the Neoclassical palace built by Prince Demidoff, stands the modest summer residence used by Napoleon; the interior decoration has been restored to Napoleon's occupation.

EASTERN TOUR★
68km/42.3mi. Allow 3hrs from Portoferraio, following the map.

Take the road S; after 3km/1.8mi turn left towards Porto Azzurro.

The road skirts the harbour, then crosses the Monte Calamita Peninsula.

Capoliveri
On the western outskirts the **Three Seas Panorama★★** offers views of three bays: Portoferraio, Stella and Porto Azzurro Bay; below is the beach at Morcone. Out to sea are the islands of Pianosa and Montecristo.
Porto Azzurro faces a delightful harbour commanded by a fortress. The road winds north across the slopes of Monte Castello and Cima del Monte.

Turn right to Rio Marina.

Rio Marina
This fine village and mining harbour has a small tower. The **coast road★** to Cavo affords views of the tiny rocky islands of Cerboli and Palmaiola, of Follonica Bay and of the mainland.

Cavo
This pretty harbour is protected by Cape Castello.

Take the road via Rio nell'Elba towards Porto Azzurro. At the crossroads, turn left and then first right.

The **Volterraio road★★** provides a number of breathtaking views of the ruins at Volterraio and Portoferraio Bay.

ADDRESSES

STAY
Hotel Residence Villa Giulia – Loc. Lido di Capoliveri, 57036 Porto Azzurro. 7.5km/4.7mi NW of Capoliveri, heading towards Portoferraio. ℘0565 94 01 67. www.villagiuliahotel.it. Closed mid-Oct–Easter. 35 rooms. The hotel rooms are comfortable and well appointed, with rattan furniture, all with a balcony or a small terrace, garden. During the summer months meals (only for guests) are served on the terrace which has lovely views out to sea.

Da Giacomino – 57030 Capo Sant'Andrea. 6km/3.7mi NW of Marciana. ℘0565 90 80 10. www.hoteldagiacomino.it. Closed mid-Oct–Mar. 33 rooms. ⅍. The hotel rises up behind the cliffs; a wonderful garden runs to the edge of the sheer cliff-face with stunning views down to the sea, with a sea water pool and tennis court. Rooms are light and airy.

EAT
Da Pilade – Loc. Marina di Mola, 57031 Capoliveri. On the road to Capoliveri. ℘0565 96 86 35. www.hoteldapilade.it. Closed mid-Oct–Easter. This restaurant is not too far from the coast. Specialities include mouth watering Aberdeen Angus steak *alla griglia* (grilled) and a wide range of unusual antipasti. Also has rooms and self-catering apartments, with a little garden or a terrace.

Affrichella – Via Santa Chiara 10, 57033 Marciana Marina. ℘0565 99 68 44. Closed Wed. This little restaurant, which is renowned for its seafood dishes, is situated just behind the Duomo. Boasts a variety of both hot and cold *antipasti*, and an interesting wine list. In summer meals are served at candlelit tables on the adjacent *piazzetta*.

⊖❷ **La Lanterna Magica** – Via Vitaliani 5, 57036 Porto Azzurro. ℘0565 95 83 94. Closed Oct–May Mon and Dec–Jan. With its huge windows looking out over the sea in the direction of Porto Azzurro, this restaurant juts over the water. The menu has a regional flavour and features some local specialities. The wine and oil are produced on the family farm.

GOING OUT
Calata Mazzini – Calata Mazzini, 57037 Portoferraio. There are various caffès and tea rooms along this (somewhat noisy) street. A good place to watch the boats coming and going in the busy little harbour.

SPORT AND LEISURE
Centro Velico Naregno – Spiaggia di Naregno, NW of Capoliveri, 57031 Capoliveri. ℘338 92 40 201 (mobile). www.centroveliconaregno.it. This sailing club runs various courses and hires out equipment including sailboards, catamarans and dinghies.

Aquavision – ℘0565 97 60 22. www.aquavision.it. Panoramic tours along the coast and underwater sightseeing. Departures from Portoferraio or Marciana.

Volterra★★

A commanding **position★★** overlooking beautiful countryside makes a harmonious setting for the Etruscan and medieval town of Volterra with its well-preserved walls. Balzea, to the northwest, has impressive precipices, which are part of a landscape furrowed by gully erosion. Large salt pans to the west are used in the manufacture of fine salt and soda.

SIGHTS
Piazza dei Priori★★
In the piazza, the 13C Palazzo Pretorio has paired windows and is linked with the Torre del Podestà, also known as Torre del Porcellino because of the wild boar sculpted high up on a bracket. The early-13C Palazzo dei Priori, opposite, is decorated with terra-cotta, marble and stone shields pertaining to the Florentine governors.

Duomo and Battistero★
The Pisan-Romanesque cathedral stands in the picturesque Piazza San Giovanni. Inside is a lovely late-15C *Annunciation* and a 13C painted wooden sculpture, **Descent from the Cross**. The nave has a superb 17C pulpit with 12C bas-reliefs. The octagonal baptistery dates from 1283.

▸ **Population:** 11 136
♿ **Michelin Map:** 563 L 14.
🛈 **Info:** Piazza dei Priori 12, 56048 Volterra (PI). ℘0588 86050 03 53. www.comune.volterra. pi.it. Proloco: Piazza dei Priori 10, ℘0588 86150.
◖ **Location:** Volterra rises on a hill that separates the Cecina and Era valleys. The SS/SR 68 links Poggibonsi with Cecina.
⊛ **Don't Miss:** The Duomo, Battistero and the Etruscan displays at the Museo Etrusco Guarnacci.
◷ **Timing:** Allow half a day.

Via dei Sarti
At no. 1, Palazzo Minucci-Solaini, attributed to Antonio da Sangallo, houses the art gallery (◖*see Pinacoteca*), and no. 37, the **Palazzo Viti**'s superb Renaissance façade designed by Ammanati. In 1964 Luchino Visconti shot some scenes from his film *Vaghe Stelle dall'Orsa* here. Some beautiful Indian robes that belonged to Giuseppe Viti, a trader in alabaster who was also the Emir of Nepal, are conserved here. For opening time call: ℘0588 84 047. www.palazzoviti.it.

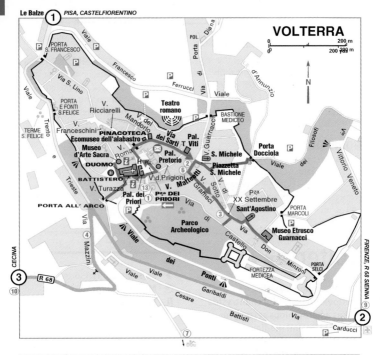

Pinacoteca

Via dei Sarti 1. Open daily mid-Mar–Oct 9am–7pm; rest of the year 10am–4.30pm. Closed 1 Jan, 25 Dec. 14€. ✆0588 87 580. www.comune.volterra.pi.it. The Art Gallery displays 14C to 17C Tuscan artists, notably Luca Signorelli and Rosso Fiorentino.

Museo Etrusco Guarnacci★

♿ Open daily mid-Mar–Oct 9am–7pm; rest of the year 9am–4.30pm. Closed 1 Jan, 25 Dec. 14€. ✆0588 86 347. www.comune.volterra.pi.it. More than 600 Etruscan funerary urns, made of tufa, alabaster and terra-cotta. ⊛Additional sights: **Porta all'Arco★** (Etruscan gateway); Teatro Romano; Porta Docciola; Viale dei Ponti.

EXCURSION
Larderello

▶ 33km/20.5mi S.

In the heart of the **Colline Metalliferi★**, the "metal-bearing hills", Larderello was mined for iron ore, copper and pyrites. An unusual Tuscan place; desolate landscapes, hissing volcanic steam and belching smoke from the blast furnaces.

ADDRESSES

🛏STAY

⊖⊕ **Albergo Nazionale** – Via dei Marchesi 11. ✆0588 86 284. Fax 0588 84 097. www.hotelnazionale-volterra.it. 🅿 50m/55yds (10€/24hrs). 40 rooms. - rest. Next to Piazza dei Priori, a hotel since 1890 near the major sights offers tranquil, comfortable rooms.

⊖⊜ **Hotel Porta all'Arco** –
Via Mazzini 2. ☏0588 81 487. www.
villaportallarco.it. 🅿 10 rooms. A few
steps from Porta all'Arco and near
the historic centre. Pretty garden and
rooms in this charming villa in antique
style. A panoramic view of the hills.

⊖⊜ **Villa Rioddi** – Loc. Rioddi.
2km/1.2mi W of Volterra on the SS 68 -
☏0588 88 053. Fax 0588 88 074. www.
hotelvillarioddi.it. Closed Nov–Feb. 🅿 ♨
♿ 13 rooms. This 15C relais decorated
in sober and functional style. A large
garden affords a lovely view of the
Cecina Valley.

♀/EAT

⊖ **Il Poggio** – Via Porta all'Arco 7.
☏Fax 0588 85 257. Closed Tue, Mar and
Nov–Jan. In an ancient tower, at the
town gate, this family-run trattoria
offers a summer terrace. Choose
medieval or Tuscan menus, and à
la carte.

⊖ **Ristorante Pizzeria Don Beta** –
Via Matteotti 39. ☏0588 86 730. Fax 0588
90 491. www.donbeta.it. Four fixed-price
menus and à la carte.

⊖ **Trattoria Albana** – Mazzolla,
2km/1.2mi S of Volterra. ☏0588 39 001.
www.trattoriaalbanamazzolla.com.
Reservation recommended. Majestic
cypress trees line the road to this
tiny village, where the friendly young
couple specialises in game.

⊖⊜ **Il Sacco Fiorentino** – Piazza XX
Settembre 13. ☏0588 88 537. Closed Tue.
A simple, unpretentious restaurant with
culinary specialities of Tuscany.

⊖⊜ **Vecchia Osteria dei Poeti** –
Via Matteotti 55. ☏0588 85 100. www.
osteriadeipoetivolterra.wordpress.com.
Closed Thu. In the historic centre, this
gourmet restaurant has a beautiful
room with stone walls.

Maremma★

There are two Maremmas: one with
its rich historic Etruscan and Roman
past and of medieval *borgos* built of
tufa; and the other of vast tranquil
virgin spaces, to discover on foot or
horseback. Combined, they are sure
to delight young or old.

A BIT OF HISTORY

Etruscans, Romans and reclaimed land
could summarise the history of the
Maremma. Etruscans founded *Populonia*, *Roselle* and *Vetulonia*, which began
to improve the area, greatly augmented
by the Romans' hydraulic expertise.
After the fall of the Roman Empire,
nature once again took over, and the
area became malaria ridden. Pirate
attacks along the coast and barbarian
invasions were especially dramatic in the
early Middle Ages. From the 10C under
Lombard and Aldobrandeschi rule, the
region enjoyed relative calm, although
Dante referred to the area as an earthly

▸ **Population:** 81 928
  (Grosseto)
⚭ **Michelin Map:** 563 O15.
🛈 **Info:** Viale Monterosa 206.
  Grosseto. ☏0564 48 48 48
  www.turismoinmaremma.it.
◐ **Location:** Parco regionale
  della Maremma. Via del
  Bersagliere 7/9. 58100
  Alberese. ☏0564 39 32 11.
🕐 **Timing:** Half a day for
  Grosseto and countryside.
👥 **Kids:** A bike or horseback
  ride in the park; Giardino
  dei Taraocchi (Tarot
  Garden) in Garavicchio by
  Niki de Saint-Phalle.

model of eternal misery. Reclamation
resumed in the 19C under Grand Duke
Leopold II, which continued with the
Unification of Italy through the Fascist regime, transforming the swamps
into an important agricultural area.

VISIT
Grosseto

Grosseto is the capital of the Maremma and is only 13km/8mi from the sea on the fertile Ombrone Plain. The town dates to the Middle Ages, although inhabitants claim their descendance from Etruscans. The province of Grosseto is known for its red wine, Morellino di Scansano, which pairs wonderfully with Tuscan dishes. Somewhat overlooked by tourists, its charming ancient centre, inside the hexagonal ramparts, is home to a superb archaeological museum, which alone merits a visit.

Duomo

The 12C cathedral dedicated to St Lawrence, inside has an Annunciation influenced by Andrea della Robbia. Strada Ricasoli leads to Piazza del Sale and the 14C Cassero del Sale, where salt was brought and distributed after being gathered along the coast, a commodity so valuable that the Sienese began to tax it in the early-14C.

Museo Archeologico e d'Arte della Maremma★

&. For opening time visit the website. Closed Mon, 1 Jan, 1 May, 25 Dec. 5€. ☏0564 48 87 50. www.museidimaremma.it.

The archaeological museum traces the history of Roselle, the Maremma and Grosseto. Museo d'Arte Sacra has works from the Sienese school. The small rooms give great attention to detail. The first room shows a lion devouring a man, and a 6C *bucchero* (black-glazed pottery) bowl with the Etruscan alphabet.

Chiesa San Francesco

This 13C church has frescoes (14C–15C) from the Sienese school and a beautiful 13C crucifix attributed to Duccio di Buoninsegna. The attached cloister has a well where buffalo, one of the Maremma animals, were depicted as coming here to drink.

Massa Marittima★★

Massa Marittima is an old medieval town that stands in rolling countryside and harmoniously blends mining, farming and crafts, all traditional sources of prosperity.

VISIT
Piazza Garibaldi★★

This square is lined by fine medieval buildings, three of which are of Romanesque origin – Palazzo del Podestà with its many double-windowed bays, the crenellated Palazzo Comunale and the cathedral.

Duomo★★

The cathedral built around the early-11C had Gothic-style features added in 1287 by **Giovanni Pisano**, its exterior adorned with a fine campanile.

▶ **Population:** 8 825
◔ **Michelin Map:** 563 M 14.
🛈 **Info:** Via Todini 3/5. ☏0566 90 27 56. www.altamaremmaturismo.it.
◖ **Location:** Massa Marittima is on the road that links Follonica with Siena.
☺ **Don't Miss:** The Duomo and the Abbazia and Eremo di San Galgano.
◷ **Timing:** Allow half a day.

The inside wall of the façade has striking pre-Romanesque bas-reliefs with Byzantine influence (10C). Note the unusual baptismal font (1267). The *Virgin of the Graces* is attributed to **Duccio di Buoninsegna** and the remains of the *Presentation of Christ at the Temple* is by Sano di Pietro (1406–81).

Palazzo del Podestà

The 13C palace residence of the town's most eminent magistrate *(podestà)* now houses the **Museo Archeologico**, with an interesting stela by Vado dell'Arancio, and splendid *Virgin in Majesty* by Ambrogio Lorenzetti (1285–c.1348). Open Tue–Sun 10am–12.30pm, 3.30-7pm (Nov–Mar 3–5pm). Closed Mon. 3€. ℘0566 90 22 89. www.coopcollinemetallifere.it.

Museo della Miniera

Guided tours only, open Tue–Sun Apr–Oct 10am–1pm and 3–6pm, Nov–Mar 10am–noon and 3–4.30pm. 5€. ℘0566 90 22 89. www.coopcollinemetallifere.it. The museum, which is situated near Piazza Garibaldi, evokes the mining activities in 700m/770yds of tunnels in the surrounding area; note the timberwork and extraction techniques.

EXCURSIONS
Abbazia and Eremo di San Galgano★★

▶ 32km/19.9mi NE. www.sangalgano.info. This Gothic Cistercian Abbey, the first Gothic church in Tuscany, 1224–88, is dedicated to **St Galgan** (1148–81), famous for plunging his sword into a stone in Montesiepi. This has cloisters, chapter house and scriptorium.

⌘/EAT

⊜⊜ **Osteria da Tronca** – Vicolo Porte 5. ℘0566 90 19 91. Closed Wed and 29 Dec–Feb. Regional cooking and rustic interior.

Promontorio dell'
Argentario★

This ancient promontory is now linked to the mainland by three ancient causeways formed by a build-up of sand *(tomboli)*.

🚗DRIVING TOUR

43km/26.7mi. Leave from Orbetello.

Orbetello

Train: Orbetello-Monte Argentario (Roma Ostiense 2hr 5mins).
Originally called Urbis Tellus, territory of the city (Rome), in AD 805 Charlemagne gave it to the Abbazia delle Tre Fontane in Rome. The **fortifications** are a reminder of the Sienese and, later, the Spaniards (16C–17C). The **cathedral** occupies the site of an ancient Etruscan-Roman temple.

Porto Santo Stefano★

The peninsula's main town is the embarkation point for the island of Giglio. Hillside houses are beside a 17C Aragonstyle fort with a superb **view★** over the **Talamone Gulf★**. Take the scenic

- ⌖ **Michelin Map:** 563 O 15.
- ⓘ **Info:** Piazza della Repubblica 1, Orbetello. ℘0564 86 04 47.
- ▶ **Location:** 150km/93.2mi south of Florence.

route north out of Porto Santo Stefano, with ascending fine **views★★** along the southwest coast, over the island of Rossa and the Argentario Promontory.

Porto Ercole★

This seaside resort has a tiny old urban district with machicolations linked to the fortress by crenellated walls. Caravaggio died here in 1610.

EXCURSION
Rovine di Cosa★

▶ 11km/6.8mi S of Orbetello, (opposite the bridge road to the Duna Feniglia reserve) take Via delle Ginestre. Open daily Nov–Feb 8am–5pm, rest of the year 10m–7pm. Museum 2€. ℘0564 88 14 21.
The ruins of Cosa, a 3C–4C AD Roman colony, have been found near the Via Aurelia, including an acropolis.

Pitigliano★

Situated between the sea and Lago di Bolsena, Pitigliano is perched on an outcrop of tufa. The view from Madonna delle Grazie is magnificent. Caves carved into the tufa were ancient Etruscan tombs, later used as stables.

▸ **Population:** 3 971 (Pitigliano)
🖈 **Michelin Map:** 563 O 16/17.
🚹 **Info:** www.comune.
pitigliano.gr.it.
◖ **Location:** From the Via Aurelia (SS1) the take SS 74 east.
🕑 **Timing:** Half a day.
👪 **Kids:** Explore Pitigliano and Le Vie Cave to see a city carved out of tufa.

🐾 WALKING TOUR

Arriving on the SS 74 to Pitigliano is especially striking. Remains of an Etruscan base and **aqueduct** south of town capture your attention. Piazza della Repubblica is a good vantage point to view the valley below, and makes for a pleasant walk.

The Medieval Borgo

The cobbled streets have retained their ancient lanterns, which linked walkways and stairs. The small 12C church of **San Rocco**, by the door, has an 11C bas-relief (a man with his hands in the mouths of two dragons).

Palazzo Orsini

The large square palace has kept its 14C appearance, crenelated with a loggia placed between two arches of different size. The courtyard inside has a Renaissance well, a ramp that leads to the Museo Diocesano, while the stairs lead to the Museo Archeologico.

Duomo

The 18C Baroque façade contrasts with the imposing campanile. Nearby a travertine column (1490) is sculpted with a coat of arms surmounted by a bear (symbol of the Orsini family).

ADDRESSES

🏠 STAY

⊜⊜ **Azienda Agraria Grazia** – Loc. Provincaccia 110, 58016 Orbetello Scalo. 7km/4.3mi E of Orbetello. 📞Fax 0564 88 11 82. www.agriturismograzia.com. 5 studios.

Light, airy studios; well equipped and comfortable, in modern-rustic style. An oasis of flora and fauna where deer, moufflon (wild sheep) and wild boar roam free.

⊜⊜⊜ **Antica Fattoria La Parrina** – Loc. Parrina, 58010 Albinia. 5km/3mi N of Orbetello Scalo. 📞0564 86 26 26. www. parrina.it. Closed Thu (winter). 12 rooms. A 19C villa, part of a working farm, is set in parkland. Elegantly decorated with antique furniture. Breakfast and dinner served on the terrace in summer. A stylish, rural retreat.

⊜⊜⊜ **Il Pellicano Località Sbarcatello** – Porto Ercole. 📞0564 85 81 11. www.ilpellicanohotel.com. 50 rooms. Exquisite cuisine in the terraced restaurant, a swimming pool carved out of rock, and rooms and cottages in an atmosphere private enough for guests like Charlie Chaplin and Jackie Onassis make for a memorable splurge.

🍽/EAT

⊜⊜ **Il Cavaliere** – Via Giancario Pantini 3, 58010 Orbetello Scalo (at the exit from the station underpass). 📞0564 86 21 87. Closed Wed and 10–25 Nov. Situated off the beaten track, away from the hordes of tourists, this restaurant is popular with the locals for its *antipasti*, as well as its fish-based starters and main courses. A simple, family-run restaurant (albeit a little noisy when the trains pass by).

Siena★★★

More than anywhere else Siena embodies the aspect of a medieval city. With its yellowish-brown buildings (after which the colour "sienna" is named) the city, encircled by ramparts, extends over three converging clay hills. As a centre for the arts, Siena is an enticing maze of narrow streets, lined with tall palaces and patrician mansions, that come together on the famous Piazza del Campo.

▶ **Population:** 54 526
Michelin Map: 563 M 15/16.
Info: Piazza Duomo 1.
☏ 0577 28 05 51.
www.terresiena.it.
▶ **Location:** Siena is 68km/ 42.3mi from Florence. Raccordo Autostrada Siena-Firenze links Siena with Florence.
▶ **Train:** Siena (Firenze SMN 1hr 23mins).
☺ **Don't Miss:** Piazza del Campo, the Palazzo Publico and Signorelli frescoes in the Abbazia di Monte Oliveto Maggiore.
🕐 **Timing:** Allow a day.
👫 **Kids:** Climb the duomo, explore Piazza del Campo.

A BIT OF HISTORY

Siena's greatest period of prosperity was the 13C–14C, when it was an independent republic with a well-organised administration of its own. During the Guelphs versus **Ghibellines** conflict, Siena was opposed to its powerful neighbour Florence. One of the most memorable episodes of this long struggle was the Battle of Montaperti (1260), when the Sienese Ghibellines defeated the Florentine Guelphs.

During this time Siena acquired her most prestigious buildings, and a local school of painting evolved that played a notable part in the development of Italian art.

In 1348 the plague decimated Siena's population and the city began to decline as dissension continued to reign among the rival factions. By the early 15C Siena's golden era was over.

The mystical city of Siena was the birthplace in 1347 of **St Catherine**. By the age of seven, it seems, she had decided on her spiritual marriage with Christ. She entered the Dominican Order aged 16 and had many visions and trances throughout her life. She is said to have received the Stigmata at Siena.

Piazza del Campo and Palazzo del Comune

©Aleksander Mirski/iStockphoto.com

Piazza del Campo hosts the popular festival Palio delle Contrade

G. Cianci/Fototeca ENIT

In 1377 she helped to bring the popes back from Avignon to Rome, which they had left in 1309. **St Bernardine** (1380–1444) is also greatly venerated in Siena. He gave up his studies to help the victims of the plague in the city.

At the age of 22, he entered the Franciscan Order and was a leader of the Observants, who favoured a stricter observance of the rule of St Francis. A great preacher, he spent much of his time travelling throughout Italy.

SIENESE ART

It was not only in political matters that Siena opposed Florence. In Dante's city, Cimabue and Giotto were innovators, but were greatly influenced by the Roman traditions of balance and realism, which led to the development of Renaissance art in all its glory. Siena, on the other hand, remained attached to the Greek or Byzantine traditions, in which the graceful line and the refinement of colour gave a certain dazzling elegance to the composition. **Duccio di Buoninsegna** (c.1255–1318/19) was the first to experiment with this new combination of inner spirituality and increased attention to space and composition.

Simone Martini (c.1284–d.1344 in Avignon) followed in Duccio's footsteps and had a considerable reputation in Europe, working at the Papal Court in Avignon.

His contemporaries **Pietro** and **Ambrogio Lorenzetti** introduced an even greater realism with minute delicate details. A favourite theme of the Sienese school was the Virgin and Child.

The Sienese artists of the Quattrocento (15C) continued in the spirit of the Gothic masters. While Florence concentrated on rediscovering Antiquity's myths, minor masters such as **Lorenzo Monaco**, **Giovanni di Paolo** and **Sassetta** continued to emphasise precision, flexibility and subtlety of colour.

In secular architecture, the Gothic style gave Siena its own special character. Windows became numerous, especially in the Sienese style with a depressed triple arch supporting a pointed one. Building activity was concentrated on the cathedral, over two centuries.

Sculpture, also influenced by the building of the cathedral, was enriched by the output of two Pisan artists, Nicola and Giovanni Pisano. The most important figure in Sienese sculpture is **Jacopo della Quercia** (1371–1438), who combined Gothic traditions with the Florentine-Renaissance style.

PIAZZA DEL CAMPO★★★

Visit: 1hr 15min.

This piazza forms a monumental ensemble. It is shaped like a scallop and slopes down to the façade of the Palazzo Pubblico. Eight white lines radiate outwards dividing the area into nine segments, each symbolising one of the forms of government that ruled Siena from the late-13C to the mid-14C.

At the upper end is the **Fonte Gaia** (Fountain of Joy), so called because of the festivities which followed its inauguration in 1348. Fountains were at that time a symbol of the city's power.

Twice annually the Piazza del Campo hosts the popular festival **Palio delle Contrade**, which recalls the medieval administrative organisation of Siena with its three main quarters, subdivided into parishes (contrade). The festivities begin with a procession of the costumed contrade, who then compete in a dangerous horse race around the square. The palio, a standard bearing the effigy of the Virgin, the city's protectress, is awarded to the winner.

Palazzo del Comune (Pubblico)★★★

Venue of the Museo Civico (open daily mid-Mar–Oct 10am–7pm; Nov–mid-Mar 10–6pm. 9€. ℰ0577 29 22 26. www.comune.siena.it).

The town hall, built between the late-13C and mid-14C in the Gothic style, has numerous triple bays under supporting arches. The **Torre del Mangia**, a tower (88m/289ft high) designed by Lippo Memmi, rises near **Cappella di Piazza**, a chapel in the form of a 14C loggia, built to mark the end of the plague. Tower: Open daily 10am–4pm (Mar–mid-Oct 10am–7pm). 10€. ℰ0577 29 22 26. www.comune.siena.it.

This palace was the seat of Siena's governments, and most great Siennese artists contributed to its decoration.

Sala dei Priori – Frescoes (1407) by Spinello Aretino recount the struggles between Pope Alexander III and the Emperor Frederick Barbarossa.

Cappella★ – Frescoes by di Bartolo, a **railing★** and early-15C **stalls★★**.

Sala del Mappamondo★★

In the Globe Room the **Maestà★★** (1315) is Simone Martini's earliest known work, and opposite is the famous **equestrian portrait★★** of the Sienese general, Guidoriccio da Fogliano, by the same artist.

Sala della Pace★★

In the Peace Room are the famous frescoes, although badly damaged (1335–40), of Ambrogio Lorenzetti, entitled **Effects of Good and Bad Government★★**, where the artist has combined a scholarly allegorical approach with meticulous narrative detail.

Torre★★

From the top there is a superb **panorama★★** of Siena's chaotic rooftops and the gently rolling countryside beyond.

SIGHTS

Duomo★★★

Open Mar–Oct 10.30am–7pm; Nov–Feb 10.30am–5.30pm. Closed Sun morning, 25 Dec. 4€ (includes Libreria Piccolomini; when pavement uncovered 7€); The OpaSi pass costs 12€ (Nov–Feb 8€, except Christmas hols, 10€) and includes all the below sights except the Gates of Heaven tour. ℰ0577 28 63 00. www.operaduomo.siena.it.

The façade of the cathedral was begun in the 13C by Giovanni Pisano.

The walls of the **interior** are faced with black-and-white marble. The 15C–16C **paving★★★** is unique. About 40 artists including **Beccafumi** worked on the 56 marble panels portraying mythological figures such as Sibyls and Virtues.

In the chancel is a 15C bronze tabernacle by Vecchietta and ornate 14C–16C **stalls★★**. At the entrance to the north transept stands the **pulpit★★★** carved from 1266 to 1268 by **Nicola Pisano**.

From the north aisle a doorway leads to the **Libreria Piccolomini**, built in 1495 by Cardinal Francesco Piccolomini, the future Pope Pius III, to house his uncle's books. The Umbrian painter **Pinturicchio** adorned it with **frescoes★★** (1502–9) depicting episodes in the life of Aeneas Silvius Piccolomini (Pius II). In 2013, for the first time the upper reaches of the Duomo were opened to visitors in the Gate of Heaven tour (mid-Mar–Oct, 15€, includes Cathedral and Libreria Piccolomini). The remarkable floor pavement panels were uncovered for a period in 2012 and 2013 for about two months beginning late Aug. The event will likely be repeated.

Museo dell'Opera Metropolitana★★

Opening time: same of Duomo. Closed 25 Dec. 7€ (includes Panorama del Facciatone). ☏0577 28 63 00.

The museum is in the extant part of the vast building started in 1339. The present cathedral was to have been its transept. The *Maestà (Virgin in Majesty)* by Duccio is in this collection.

Battistero di San Giovanni★

Opening time: same of Duomo. 4€. ☏0577 28 63 00.

The 14C baptistery is decorated with 15C frescoes. The **font★★** is adorned with panels by Jacopo della Quercia. The bronze panels are by Lorenzo Ghiberti and Donatello.

Pinacoteca Nazionale★★

♿ Open Tue–Sat 8.15am–7.15pm, Sun–Mon and public hols 9am–1pm. Closed 1 Jan, 1 May, 25 Dec. 4€. ☏0577 28 61 43.

The extensive collection of 13C–16C Sienese paintings is displayed in the 15C **Palazzo Buonsignori★**. On the second floor is the rich section of the **Primitives.** Beyond the late-12C to early-13C painted crucifixes are masterpieces of the Sienese school such as Duccio, with the **Madonna of the Franciscans.** The **Virgin and Child** is by Simone Martini. Works by the Lorenzetti brothers include the **Pala del Carmine.**

Via di Città★, Via Banchi di Sopra

These flagstoned streets are bordered by remarkable **palaces★**. In the Via di Città is the 15C **Palazzo Piccolomini**, its lower façade rusticated in the Florentine manner. Opposite stands the **Palazzo Chigi-Saracini**, now the Academy of Music. The **Loggia dei Mercanti** is the Commercial Courts.

The **Piazza Salimbeni** is enclosed by the 14C Gothic **Palazzo Salimbeni**, 15C Renaissance **Palazzo Spannocchi** and 16C Baroque **Palazzo Tantucci.**

Basilica di San Domenico★

St Catherine experienced her trances in this 13C–15C Gothic conventual church. Inside, there is an authentic portrait by her contemporary, Andrea Vanni.

In the Cappella di Santa Caterina *(halfway down the south aisle)* is a Renaissance **tabernacle★** containing the head of the saint. The wall **frescoes★** depict scenes from the life of the saint.

Casa di Santa Caterina

In the basement of St Catherine's house is the cell where she lived. Above is the 13C crucifix in front of which the saint is said to have received the Stigmata.

Chiesa di Sant'Agostino

This 13C church has a remarkable **Adoration of the Crucifix★** by Perugino, and **works★** by Ambrogio Lorenzetti, Matteo di Giovanni and Sodoma.

EXCURSIONS

Abbazia di Monte Oliveto Maggiore★★

▶ 36km/22.4mi SE of Siena.
Open daily 9.15am–noon and 3.15–6pm (winter 5pm). ☏0577 70 76 52.
www.abbazie.com/mom.

Cypresses hide this rose-coloured **abbey**, the Mother House of the Olivetans, part of the Benedictine Order. ⊘ Don't miss the **Signorelli** frescoes.

Chiostro Grande

The cloisters are decorated with a cycle of 36 **frescoes★★** depicting the life of St Benedict by **Luca Signorelli** from 1498 and by **Il Sodoma** from 1505 to 1508. The majority are by Il Sodoma, who was influenced by Leonardo da Vinci and Perugino.

The cloisters lead to the refectory (15C), library and pharmacy.

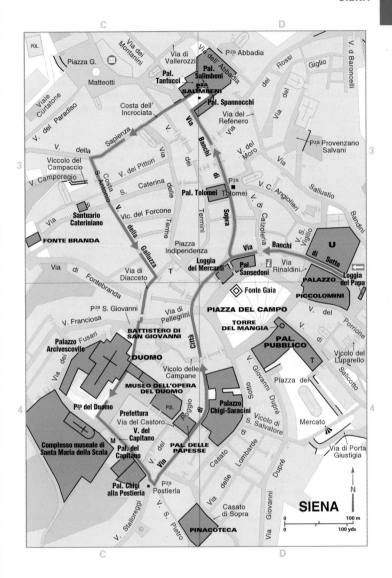

SIENA

0   100 m
0   100 yds

Chiesa abbaziale
This abbey church has inlaid **stalls★★**
(1505) by Fra Giovanni da Verona.

ADDRESSES

🏠 STAY

◻ Bed & Breakfast San Francesco –
Vicolo degli Orbachi 2. ☎0577 46 533. Fax
0577 23 63 46. www.bb-sanfrancesco.com.
6 rooms. ▭. Located near the basilica
complex, this welcoming establishment
have modern, functional rooms.

◻ Santuario Casa di Santa Caterina
Alma Domus – Via Camporegio 37.
☎0577 44 177. www.hotelalmadomus.it.
28 rooms. ▭. If luck is on your side,
you may get one of the rooms with a
balcony overlooking the Duomo. You
can always retire to the lovely reading
room or the little chapel (access on
the second floor). Ask for a "room with
a view"!

⊜⊜ **Albergo Cannon d'Oro** – Via Montanini 28. ℘0577 44 321. www. cannondoro.com. 30 rooms. ⊞. This was once the home of Sapia, who appears in Dante's *Divine Comedy* (Purgatory, Canto XIII). Guests must still negotiate the three flights of old stairs, although rooms are available on the ground floor.

℘ EAT

⊜ **Hosteria Il Carroccio** – Via Casato di Sotto 32. ℘0577 41 165. Closed Tue lunch and Wed dinner, Feb and 3 weeks Jan. Authentic Sienese cooking and delicious salads. Small and rustic but welcoming, popular with the locals. Minutes from Piazza del Campo.

⊜ **Osteria del Gatto** – Via di San Marco 8. ℘0577 28 71 33. Closed Sat lunch and Sun. Friendly, small, and casual trattoria attracts locals for lively banter and authentic Sienese cooking plus ethnic dinners twice a month.

⊜ **Osteria la Chiacchera** – Costa di Sant'Antonio 4. ℘0577 28 06 31. www. osterialachiacchera.it. You may have to wait a long time for a table, but it's worth it. In summer tables are out in the little street. Traditional Tuscan cooking.

⊜⊜ **Osteria Boccon del Prete** – Via San Pietro 17. ℘0577 28 03 88. www. osteriabocconedelprete.it. Closed Sun. Stylish in both atmosphere and food presentation at trattoria prices, with professional service. Try the homemade pici 'cord' pasta with black cabbage, toasted bread crumbs, and Pecorino cheese, or the creamy *crespelle di baccalà* (cod crepes), or braised beef. Even the house wine is good here. Plan on a full meal or reception may be cool, but excellent value for money.

⊜⊜ **Trattoria Papei** – Piazza del Mercato 6. ℘0577 28 08 94. Closed 10 days Jul. Classic, lively, friendly and unpretentious Sienese trattoria. Outside tables in the busy Piazza del Mercato. Torre del Mangia in the background. Good value for money.

⊜⊜⊜ **Antica Trattoria Botteganova** – Strada statale 408, 29 per Montevarchi. ℘0577 28 42 30. www.anticatrattoria botteganova.it. Closed Mon and Sun ev. Reservation recommended. Outside of town, but worth the detour. Vaulted ceiling, rustic atmosphere and Tuscan fare.

TAKING A BREAK

Nannini – Via Banchi di Sopra 22/24. ℘0577 23 60 09. Open daily. Sienese sweets are the specialities like *panforte* and *panpepato* in this caffè.

Pasticceria Bini – Via Stalloreggi 91/93. ℘0577 28 02 07. Open Tue–Sun 7am–1.30pm and 3.30–8pm. Siena sweets include *panforte margherita* (cake with honey, almonds and candied citrus fruit).

Bar Il Palio – Piazza del Campo 46-49. Tables facing the square and a good house Chianti Rietine and other wines.

WINE BAR

Enoteca Italiana – Fortezza Medicea, Piazza Libertà 1. ℘0577 22 88 11. www. enoteca-italiana.it. Open Mon–Sat. Closed 10 days Jan. In the castle ramparts, this wine cellar/bar promotes Italian and especially Tuscan wines.

EVENTS AND FESTIVALS

On 2 July and 16 August, Siena hosts the famous bareback horse race, the **Palio delle Contrade**; www.ilpalio.org.

Chianti ★★

A tour on roads that criss-cross the Chianti wine region leads not only to vineyards, but also to a landscape interspersed with olive groves set against dark forests rich with chestnut, oak, pine and fir. Spring splashes colour with red poppies and blue-violet irises. An abbey or castle crowns a hill. Arrival at a village heralds the moment to find a lovely square, seek a table, then sit and enjoy a glass of "Chianti Classico", perhaps accompanied by simple *bruschetta*, or better yet, a grand meal of Chianina steak or wild game. About 90 Chianti Classico wineries also bottle their own olive oil.

- ⚅ **Michelin Map:** 563 L15/16.
- ▯ **Info:** www.terresiena.it. www.provincia.firenze.it.
- ▶ **Location:** The Via Chiantigiana (SS 222) leads to most areas.
- ▸ **Don't Miss:** Wine tours.
- ⏱ **Timing:** Allow one and a half to two days.
- ♟ **Kids:** Castle of Meleto.

VISIT

The Chianti Classico area is bordered to the north by the suburbs of Florence, to the east by the Chianti Mountains, to the south by the city of Siena and to the west by the valleys of the Pesa and Elsa rivers. Siena and Florence are the capitals of Chianti, which includes the entire territories of the communities of Castellina in Chianti, Gaiole in Chianti, Greve in Chianti and Radda in Chianti, and parts of those of Barberino Val d'Elsa, Castelnuovo Berardenga, Poggibonsi, San Casciano Val di Pesa and Tavarnelle Val di Pesa. About 350 wineries bottle their own Vino Chianti Classico DOC and DOCG with the famous black rooster. When you do a driving tour, plan to stop in at least one of the nine Chianti Classico communities. Most driving tours branch off the Chiantigiana (SS 222), a 59km/36.7mi road that connects Siena to Florence.

A winery tour with tasting often takes an hour or two. You can also plan a wine tasting at a good *enoteca*. Order by the glass to sample. A good sommelier will suggest wines from small producers, as well as from the big names. Enjoy the wine with delicious Tuscan food. You can plan your own meanderings from the SS 222 Chiantigiana, the wine road that connects Florence to Siena, that goes through the heart of Chianti Classico territory. An ideal way to travel is to choose an *agriturismo* (farmstay) as a base, where your hosts may be winemakers too, and can share their experience of the land, wine, and cuisine.

Greve

As an agricultural and trade centre since medieval times, Greve, accustomed to travellers, still has a bustling atmosphere. There is a Chianti Classico wine festival every September. A town monument is dedicated to **Giovanni da Verrazzano**, who may have been born here, while another explorer, **Amerigo Vespucci**, hails from a nearby hamlet.

Castellina and Gaiole

Castellina has Via delle Volte, an underground arched walkway, and a 14C Rocca (castle) that houses an archaeological museum. The lovely Piazza Matteotti has a Saturday market. Montecalvario 7C BC Etruscan tombs and the Poggino Necropolis are just outside Castellina.

Gaiole in Chianti, in population in between that of Castellina and Radda, is home to the 11C **Castello di Brolio**, an important wine estate in the Ricasoli family. Baron Bettino Ricasoli is famous for his Chianti research and experiments, for which he wrote the formula in an 1872 letter.

The 11C *Pieve* dedicated to St Bartholomew once had a Simone Martini painting, which now hangs in Siena's Pinacoteca. In spring Gaiole also hosts a bicycle race on the local gravel roads.

Castellina in Chianti

© sumos/iStockphoto.com

Tavarnelle Val di Pesa

The main attraction here is the Medieval **Passignano Abbey**, with numerous other churches that merit a trip including Poggio's Pieve di San Donato that has a baptism shell by della Robbia and a stunning triptych. The town bridge crosses the Pesa River into **Sambuca**. **San Casciano** in Val di Pesa has a rich Etruscan heritage, as well as Medieval and Renaissance. Henry VII made this his base in 1312–13 and Machiavelli, exiled here in 1513, wrote *The Prince* and *The Mandrake*. Castles of Bibbione, Gabbiano, Pergolato and Montefiridolfi are all in the area.

Antinori is the big winemaker here, and there are many others to explore including **Poggio Torselli**. Still surrounded by its fortifications, **Barberino Val d'Elsa** has several interesting churches to explore including the 11C Sant'Appiano that now houses an Antiquarium, and Capella di San Michele Arcangelo, which has a dome said to be one-eighth the scale of the Duomo's in Florence. The Barberini family dynasty (see ROME) began here in the 11C.

Poggibonsi

A settlement since the Neolithic Age and one of the most beautiful of Medieval cities, Frederick II declared Poggibonsi an Imperial City, and in the 15C Lorenzo de' Medici began a plan to modify it as an "Ideal City". Palazzo Comunale has a palaeontological museum. The neighbourhood is rich with churches and castles, including one that belonged to the Knights Templar. **Le Fonti** and **Rignana** wineries produce excellent Chianti.

Castelnuovo Berardenga

This was the site of the bloody 1260 Battle of Montaperti, celebrated by the locals as one of the few major battles the Sienese won against the Florentines. The town has a nice laid-back atmosphere, with some thermal mudbaths. Castelnuovo Berardenga also hosts excellent Sunday bus tours from late spring to early autumn, where for 8€ historic sights and a winery visit are included. Or book a tasting at the **Fèlsina** or **MIscianello** wineries.

🚗 DRIVING TOUR

100km/62mi round tour. Allow a full day to a day and a half. This route passes through several Chianti Classico wine communities. Be sure to pause along the way for a lovely meal and a wine tour.

From Florence, begin the route south by **Certosa di Galluzzo★★** (charter house and distillery), then proceed south on Via Senese *(SR 2)* towards Sant'Andrea in Percussina, where you can see **Machiavelli's house** (now a restaurant). Continue south, passing Spedaletto, which has a lovely little castle *agriturismo*, to San Casciano in Val di Pesa.

Following along the Pesa River towards Sambuca, turn left *(east)* towards Passignano and **Badia di Passignano** (abbey). Return towards Sambuca and continue towards **San Donato** in Poggio, then to **Castellina** in Chianti, then turn north (SR 222) to Panzano. Stop along the way for a view★ of **Val d'Elsa**, then reach **Greve**. Turn west towards **Montefioralle** to see the town's circular medieval layout.

Return to Greve to continue north *(SR 222)* to **Impruneta**, a town with 15C kilns that made red tiles for roofs of local towns, including Florence's Duomo. Stop to shop for functional ceramics and to see **Basilica di Santa Maria dell'Impruneta★**.

San Gimignano★★★

Rising up from the Val d'Elsa like a city of skyscrapers, San Gimignano is surrounded by rolling countryside dotted with vines and olive trees. Its 14 grey-stone towers set on a hilltop are enclosed within an outer wall. This small medieval town has been amazingly well preserved.

▶ **Population:** 7 770
Ⓖ **Michelin Map:** 563 L 15.
🛈 **Info:** Piazza del Duomo 1, 53037 San Gimignano (SI). ☎0577 94 00 08. www.comune.sangimignano.si.it. www.sangimignano.com.
◗ **Location:** From Florence or Siena take the Raccordo Autostrada Siena-Firenze to Poggibonsi; follow the signs *(13km/8mi from Poggibonsi)*.
◎ **Don't Miss:** Collegiata frescoes and the view from the Palazzo del Popolo tower.

Piazza della Cisterna★★

The square is paved with bricks laid in a herringbone pattern and derives its name from a 13C cistern or well *(cisterna)*. One of the most evocative squares in Italy with its tall towers and 13C–14C mansions, an ideal pause for *gelato* or the local white wine, Vernaccia.

Piazza del Duomo★★

The collegiate church, palaces and seven towers line this majestic square.

Collegiata★
(Santa Maria Assunta)

Open Apr–Oct 10am–7pm (Sat 5pm); Nov–Mar 10am–4.40pm. Closed Sun morning, mid-end Jan, mid-end Nov, 25 Dec, 1 Jan, 12 Mar, 1st Sun of Aug. 4€. ☎0577 28 63 00. www.sangimignano.com. This 12C Romanesque church was extended in the 15C by Giuliano da Maiano. Inside are a *Martyrdom of St Sebastian* (1465) by Benozzo Gozzoli and an *Annunciation* by Jacopo della Quercia. **Frescoes★** by Bartolo di Fredi (14C) evoke **scenes from the Old Testament★★** (c.1350); others by Barna da Siena depict scenes from the Life of Christ. In the **Cappella di Santa Fina** designed by Giuliano da Maiano, the harmonious **altar★** is by his nephew Benedetto da Maiano and the **frescoes★** (1475) by Domenico Ghirlandaio.

Palazzo del Popolo★

The 13C–14C town hall has a tall **tower** with a **view★★** over roofs and towers. The Council Chamber has a remarkable **Maestà★** (Madonna and Child Enthroned in Majesty, 1317) by Lippo Memmi, restored c.1467 by

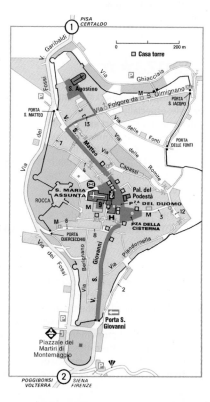

Benozzo Gozzoli. **The Museo Civico**★ is on the second floor.

EXCURSIONS
San Vivaldo★
▶ 17km/10.6mi NW.

In 1500 Franciscan monks built a monastery to honour St Vivaldo (d.1320). Its series of chapels, **Sacro Monte**, re-create Jerusalem in miniature. Open daily Apr–Oct 3–7pm, Sun and holidays opens 10am; Nov–Mar 2–5pm. 5€ ℘0571 699267 or 0571 699252. www.sanvivaldointoscana.com.

Certaldo
▶ 13km/8mi N.

In this hilltop village, above the wooded Elsa Valley, the great Italian writer **Giovanni Boccaccio** (1312–75), who wrote *The Decameron*, spent the last years of his life. In the upper town, **Casa del Boccaccio** is now a museum. The writer is buried in the church of San Jacopo. **Palazzo Pretorio** was rebuilt in the 16C. The town also has nice ceramic and print shops. **House-museum:** ℘0571 66 12 65. www.casaboccaccioit.

ADDRESSES

🛏 STAY

⊖ **A La Casa de' Potenti** – Piazza delle Erbe 10. ℘327 18 33950. www.casadei potenti.com. 11 rooms. ⊐5€. Central 14C palazzo; some rooms overlook the piazza and the Duomo.

⊖⊜ **Agriturismo Cesani** – Loc Pancole 82/A, San Gimignano. ℘0577 95 50 84. www.agriturismocesani.it. 10 rooms. ⊐. Vernaccia winemakers offer comfortable rooms. Lovely winetasting room.

⊖⊜ **Agriturismo Il Casale del Cotone** – Via Cellone 59. 2.5km/1.6mi N towards Certaldo. ℘0577 94 32 36. www.casale delcotone.it. Closed mid-Nov–Mar. 17 rooms. ⊐. An elegant 18C farmhouse with tasteful antiques and furnishings.

🍴 EAT

⊖ **Osteria del Carcere** – Via del Castello 13. ℘0577 94 19 05. Closed Thu lunch and Wed. Simple, rustic-style eatery near Piazza della Cisterna.

Pienza★★

Pienza displays a remarkable unity of style, especially in its main square, and is a perfect example of Renaissance town planning. It was commissioned by Pope Pius II, the diplomat and humanist poet, who wanted to build the ideal town. The architectural unity was intended to reflect the Utopian concepts of the "Ideal City", as conceived by the 15C humanist movement.

▶ **Population:** 2 190
⚲ **Michelin Map:** 563 M 1.
🚩 **Info:** Ufficio Turistico, Corso Rossellino 30, Pienza. ℘0578 74 99 05. www.comunedipienza.it.
▶ **Location:** Pienza lies off the SS 146, between San Quirico d'Orcia and Montepulciano.
🦋 **Don't Miss:** Abbazia di Sant'Antimo.
🕓 **Timing:** A day for the towns and Montepulciano wineries.

VISIT

The centre of Pienza is the work of the Florentine architect **Bernardo Rossellino** (1409–82), a pupil of Alberti, whose design centred on lining the town's main axis with principal monuments. The town hall is opposite the cathedral. The other sides of the square are framed by the Bishop's Palace and the Palazzo Piccolomini. There is a fine **view**★ over the Orcia Valley from behind the cathedral

Cattedrale★
The cathedral, which was completed in 1462, has a Renaissance façade. The interior (restored) contains paintings

by the Sienese school, including an **Assumption★★** by Vecchietta.

Museo Diocesano

Corso il Rosselino 30. ♿ Open Mar–Oct Wed–Mon 10am–1pm and 3–7pm, Nov–Mar Sat–Sun 10am–1pm and 3–6pm. For details, call ☏0578 74 99 05. 4.50€. www.museisenesi.org.
The cathedral museum contains pictures of the 14C and 15C Sienese school and a 14C English historiated cope.

Palazzo Piccolomini★

Piazza Pio II. ♿ Open Tue–Sun mid-Oct–mid-Mar 10am–4.30pm, mid-Mar–mid Oct 10am–6.30pm. Closed 2 weeks Feb and 2 weeks Nov. 7€. ☏0577 28 63 00. www.palazzopiccolominipienza.it.
Rossellino's masterpiece was greatly influenced by the Palazzo Rucellai in Florence (⚭see FLORENCE). The three sides facing the town are similar; the fourth, overlooking the Orcia Valley, looks onto hanging gardens, among the earliest to have been created. The palace still has its armoury, the incunabula and a Baroque bed from the Papal bedchamber.

EXCURSIONS
Montalcino★

◐ 24km/14.9mi W.
www.prolocomontalcino.com.
13C walls, and a magnificent 1361 **fortress★★★** shaped like a pentagon, where the Sienese government took refuge when the town was captured by Charles V in 1555.
Montalcino, famous for its **Brunello**, one of Italy's most prestigious red wines, makes a lovely stop to sample Brunello and Rosso di Montalcino (less expensive, but still delicious) wines.
The town's labyrinth of medieval streets leads to a Romanesque and Gothic church, the 13C town hall, the **Palazzo Comunale★**, or the small **Museo Civico e Diocesano**. ♿Open Tue–Sun 10am–1pm and 2–5.40pm. Closed 1 Jan, 25 Dec. 4.50€. ☏0577 84 60 14. www.prolocomontalcino.com.

Abbazia di Sant'Antimo★★

◐ 35km/21.8mi SW. Open Mon–Sat 10.15am–12.30pm and 3–6.30pm, Sun and public hols 9.15–10.45am and 3–6pm. Masses in Gregorian chant. Donations welcome. www.antimo.it.
The 9C abbey stands in an isolated hill **site★** amid cypress and olive groves. Its prosperity was at its peak in the 12C when the **church** was built. It is a fine example of Cistercian-Romanesque architecture with Burgundian (ambulatory and apsidal chapels) and Lombard (porch, bell tower with Lombard bands and façades) influences. The interior is spacious and austere. Columns topped by fine alabaster capitals divide the nave from the aisles.

Abbazia di Sant'Antimo

©Juergen Schonnop/Dreamstime.com

Montepulciano★★

Montepulciano is a lovely Renaissance town, a remarkably picturesque **setting★★** on the top of a tufa hill that separates two valleys. The town was founded in the 6C by people from Chiusi fleeing the barbarian invasions. The town rests on top of tufa wine cellars, full of the ruby-red Vino Nobile di Montepulciano, of which poets and travellers have sung its praises for centuries. Several wineries are right in town, while others dot the countryside. Some excellent winemakers are Sanguineto, Godiolo, Boscarelli, Bindella, Avignonesi, La Ciarlana, Le Berne, Tenuta Valdipiatta and Il Macchione. Crociani, Gattavecchi, Contucci and Redi have wineries to visit right in the centre,while Poggio alla Sala has accommodation.

- ▶ **Population:** 14 107
- **Michelin Map:** 563 M 17.
- **Info:** Piazza Don Minzoni 1, 53045 Montepulciano (SI). ℘0578 75 73 41. www.montepulciano.com.
- **Location:** Montepulciano lies off the SS 146, which goes from San Quirico d'Orcia to Chiusi.
- **Don't Miss:** The old town.
- **Timing:** Allow half a day.

●●WALKING TOUR

Città Antica (Old Town)★

Beyond the gateway, Porta al Prato, the high street, the first part of which bears the name Via Roma, loops through the monumental area in the old town.

At no. 91 Via Roma stands the 16C **Palazzo Avignonesi** attributed to Vignola; no. 73, the palace of the antiquarian Bucelli, is decorated with stone from Etruscan and Roman buildings; further along, the **Renaissance façade★** of the church of **Sant'Agostino** was designed by Michelozzo (15C); a tower opposite has a Pulcinello as Jack o'the clock. At the Logge del Mercato (Grain Exchange) bear left into Via di Voltaia nel Corso: Palazzo Cervini (no. 21) is a fine example of Florentine-Renaissance architecture with its rusticated stonework and curvilinear and triangular pediments designed by Antonio da Sangallo, a member of an illustrious family of architect-sculptors, who designed some of the most famous buildings in Montepulciano. Continue along Via dell'Opio nel Corso and Via Poliziano (no. 1 is the poet's birthplace).

Piazza Grande★★

At the centre of the city this square with its irregular plan is lined by the **Palazzo Comunale★** (town hall), which doubled as Volterra in the film *The Twilight Saga: New Moon* (2009). From the top of the square torre (tower) there is an immense **panorama★★★** of the town and its environs that includes Lake Trasimeno. **Tower:** Open Apr–Oct 10am–1pm, 2–6pm. 5€. ℘0578 75 73 41. The majestic Renaissance **Palazzo Nobili-Tarugia** facing the cathedral is attributed to Antonio da Sangallo the Elder. Palazzo del Capitano now hosts a wine-tasting area downstairs. Inside the 16C–17C **Duomo**, to the left, lies the recumbent figure of Bartolomeo Aragazzi, secretary to Pope Martin V; the statue was part of a monument by Michelozzo (15C). The monumental **altarpiece★** (1401) is by the Sienese artist Taddeo di Bartolo.

▷ Piazza San Francesco has a fine view of the countryside and of the church of San Biagio.

▷ Via del Poggiolo and Via dell'Erbe return to the Logge del Mercato.

Make a visit to the **Museo Civico Pinacoteca Crociani** for glazed terra-cotta by Andrea della Robbia, as well as 13C–18C Etruscan remains and paintings).

EXCURSIONS

Chiesa della Madonna di San Biagio★★

⯈ 1km/0.6mi.

This pale-stone 16C church at the base of town is an architectural masterpiece by **Antonio da Sangallo** and greatly influenced by Bramante's design for St Peter's in Rome. San Biagio's majestic design is a Greek cross crowned by a silver-coloured dome.

Chianciano Terme♯♯

⯈ 10km/6mi SE.

☎0578 67 11 22 (Info Point).

www.chiancianoterme.com.

The healing properties (kidney and liver disorders) of the waters were known to the Etruscans, Romans and Fellini, who put it in *8 1/2*. A new thermal pool, Theia, openend in 2013.

Chiusi

⯈ 27km/16.8mi SW.

www.comune.chiusi-della-verna.ar.it.

The little town of Chiusi was once one of the 12 sovereign cities of Etruria.

Museo Archeologico★ – Via Porsenna. &Open daily 9am–8pm. Closed 1 Jan, 1 May, 25 Dec. 6€. ☎0578 20 177. www. archeotoscana.beniculturali.it. Local Etruscan burial treasures, from sarcophagi to ex-votos and jewellery.

ADDRESSES

🛏 STAY

⯈ **Agriturismo San Gallo** – Via delle Colombelle 7. ☎0578 75 83 30. www. agriturismosangallo.com. 6 apts. Set near the vineyards, spacious and beautifully furnished rooms. Pool.

⯈⯈ **Albergo Meublé Il Riccio** – Via Talosa 21. ☎0578 75 77 13. www.ilriccio. net. 6 rooms. ⊂. 8€. Simple rooms in a medieval palazzo, terrace views.

❙/EAT

⯈⯈ **Hotel Tiziana** – SS 326 No. 154 Loc. Tre Berte. ☎0578 76 77 60. www.hotel-tiziana.com. This humble dining room lures local winemakers who want great *pici* and local fare, at economical prices.

Chiesa della Madonna di San Biagio

Agenzia turismo Chianciano Terme - Valdichiana/Fototeca/ENIT

Famous Inhabitants

Montepulciano was the birthplace of **Angelo Poliziano** (1454–94), one of the most exquisite Renaissance poets and a great friend of Lorenzo de' Medici, whom he called Lauro (Laurel) and whom he saved from assassination during the Pazzi Conspiracy (⯈*see FLORENCE: Duomo*). *The Stanzas*, Poliziano's masterpiece, describe a sort of Garden of Delight haunted by attractive women. Parallels can be drawn between Poliziano's verse and the paintings of his friend Botticelli. **Antonio da Sangallo il Vecchio**, of the famous family of Renaissance sculptors and architects, bequeathed some well-known works to Montepulciano.

⯈⯈ **La Grotta** – Loc. San Biagio. 1km/0.6mi lower Montepulciano near San Biagio. ☎0578 75 74 79. www. lagrottamontepulciano.it. Closed Wed. This fine 16C palazzo is Montepulciano's most elegant restaurant. Creative and traditional Tuscan fare. Al fresco dining.

TAKING A BREAK

Caffè Poliziano – Via Voltaia del Corso 27/29. ☎0578 75 86 15. www. caffepoliziano.it. Open 7am–midnight. First opened in 1868, this lovely caffè has long been popular with artists and writers, including Luigi Pirandello and film-maker Federico Fellini!

Arezzo★★

Arezzo is surrounded by a fertile basin planted with cereal crops, fruit trees and vines – and hidden from view, Arezzo is one of Italy's largest centres for trading gold. It is the birthplace of many an artistic genius including Guido d'Arezzo (997–c.1050) the Benedictine monk and inventor of the musical scale, Petrarch the poet (1304–74), Pietro Aretino the author (1492–1556) and Giorgio Vasari the painter and art historian (1511–74). But Arezzo owes its greatest artistic heritage to Piero della Francesca, although the artist was born in Sansepolcro, 40km/24.8mi down the road.

▶ **Population:** 94 675
🎢 **Michelin Map:** 563 L 17.
🚻 **Info:** Piazza della Libertà 1. ℘0575 40 19 45.
◖ **Location:** Arezzo is 11km/ 6.8mi from the Florence– Rome motorway, 81km/ 50.3mi from Florence.
◖ **Train:** Arezzo (Firenze Campo di Marte 51mins).
🐵 **Don't Miss:** The master- piece of the Affreschi di Piero della Francesca.
🕐 **Timing:** Allow a day to explore Arezzo fully.
👪 **Kids:** Picnics in the park around the Duomo.

SIGHTS

Chiesa di San Francesco

Reservation required. Mon–Fri 9am–7pm (winter 6pm), Sat to 6pm (winter 5.30pm), Sun 1–6pm (winter 5.30pm). Closed 1 Jan, 25 Dec. 8€, four sights 12€. ℘0575 35 27 27. www.pierodellafrancesca.it.
San Francesco was built in the 14C Gothic style for the Franciscan Order, who com- missioned Piero della Francesca to dec- orate the chancel with **Affreschi di Piero della Francesca★★★**. This fresco cycle (1452–66) is a Renaissance masterpiece, which depicts the **Legend of the True Cross**, revered by the Franciscans in the Middle Ages. The cycle is based on Jacopo da Varagine's *Legenda Aurea* (13C). 🐵*Binoculars recommended.*

👣WALKING TOUR

Piazza Grande★

The **main square** is surrounded by medieval houses, the Romanesque gal- leried apse of Santa Maria della Pieve (parish church), the late -8C law courts, the part-Gothic part-Renaissance Palazzo della Fraternità and the 16C galleries *(loggie)*, designed by Vasari. 🐵 *Fans of Oscar-winning film "Life is Beautiful" should recognise the square.*

Santa Maria della Pieve★

This superb 12C Romanesque parish **church** is crowned by a haughty cam- panile with 40 double bays, called the "One Hundred Holes". Giorgio Vasari made 16C alterations to the church. The **façade★★**, inspired by the Pisan- Romanesque style, has witty represen- tations of the 12 symbols of the zodiac. Some interior pillars are decorated with capitals carved with large human heads. Note two marble bas-reliefs – *Epiphany (rear of the façade)* and *Nativity*, dating from the 13C *(wall in the north aisle)*.

San Domenico

© ROMAOSLO/iStockphoto.com

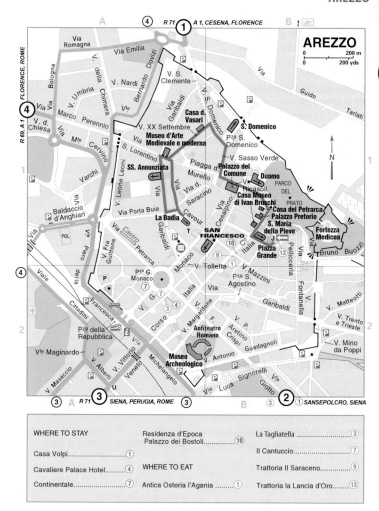

AREZZO

0   200 m
0   200 yds

The High Altar includes a superb **polyptych** (1320–24) by Pietro Lorenzetti.

Via dei Pileati

This **street** has palaces, Gothic towers, old houses and Palazzo Pretorio.

Duomo

Built from 1278 to 1511, inside the cathedral Gothic Revival façade are fine **works of art★** including stained-glass windows by Marcillat (*Moneylenders Being Chased from the Temple*) and a fresco of *Mary Magdalene* by Piero della Francesca.

▶ Take Via Ricasoli and turn into Via Sasso Verde.

San Domenico

This 13C Gothic **church** with asymmetrical façade inside has frescoes by the workshops of Duccio and Spinello Aretino. Cimabue's admirable **crucifix★★** is on the High Altar.

Casa del Vasari
(Vasari's House)

Open 8.30am–7.30pm (Sun to 1.30pm). Closed Tue. 4€. ℘0575 29 90 71.

Luxuriously decorated in 1540 by **Giorgio Vasari** – painter, sculptor, architect and writer – the artist's house also has works by Tuscan-Mannerist painters and a terra-cotta by Andrea Sansovino.

Museo Statale d'Arte Medievale e Moderna★

Open Tue–Sun 8.30am–7.30pm. Free.
℘0575 40 90 50.

The **Museum of Medieval and Modern Art** displays sculptures, gold and silverware and numerous paintings dating from the Middle Ages to the 19C, including works by Luca Signorelli, Andrea della Robbia and Vasari. Outstanding Renaissance **majolica ware★★** from Umbria is on display, as are 17C and 18C ceramics, glassware, weaponry, ivories and coins.

Museo Archeologico

♿ Open daily 8.30am–7.30pm (Sun and hol to 1.30pm). 6€. ℘0575 20 90 71.

Adjacent to the oval **Roman amphitheatre** (1C–2C), artefacts range from Etruscan and Roman bronze statuettes (6C BC–3C AD), Greek vases (Euphronios' *krater*) and Aretine vases to Hellenistic and Roman ceramics.

Santa Maria delle Grazie

1km/0.6mi S by Viale Mecenate.

An ethereal **portico★** designed by Benedetto da Maiano (15C) from Florence graces the exterior, while a **work★** by Andrea della Robbia frames a painting by Parri di Spinello (*Virgin Mary of Pity*).

ADDRESSES

🛏 STAY

♿♿ **Casa Volpi** – Via Simone Martini 29. 2km/1.2mi SW of Arezzo towards Sansepolcro. ℘0575 35 43 64. Fax 0575 35 59 71. www.casavolpi.it. Closed 10 days Aug. **P** 15 rooms. Panoramic terrace restaurant (20/40€). At the city gates in a large park, 19C rustic style with some frescoes. Warm hospitality.

♿♿ **Residenza d'Epoca Palazzo dei Bostoli** – B&B, entrance Via Mazzini 1, 2nd floor. ℘334 14 90 558 (mobile). www.palazzobostoli.it. 5 rooms. Flirty rooms in a 13C palazzo. Have breakfast at the caffè next door.

♿♿♿ **Continentale** – Piazza Guido Monaco 7. ℘0575 20 251. Fax 0575 35 04 85. www.hotelcontinentale.com. **P** car park (15€/24hrs). 73 rooms. Excellent value and spacious modern rooms in the centre.

🍴 EAT

♿ **Trattoria Il Saraceno** – Via Mazzini 6. ℘0575 27 644. www.ilsaraceno.com. Closed 6–30 Jan. A delightfully old-fashioned family place offers authentic regional specialities. Also pizzas cooked in a traditional wood-burning oven.

♿/♿♿ **Antica Osteria l'Agania** – Via Mazzini 10. ℘0575 29 53 81. www. agania.it. Open noon–3pm and 7–11pm. Closed Oct–May Mon. A simple family place to sample local fare and Tuscan wines.

♿♿ **Il Cantuccio** – Via Madonna del Prato 76, Piazza Guido. ℘0575 26 830. www.il-cantuccio.it. Closed Wed. Nice trattoria with traditional fare served under a vaulted ceiling.

♿♿♿ **Le Chiave d'Oro** – Piazza San Francesco 7. ℘0575 40 33 13. www. ristorantelechiavidoro.it. Closed Mon. Creative cuisine and modern decor. Well chosen Italian and French wines including Champagne, plus some Riesling from Germany.

♿♿♿ **Trattoria la Lancia d'Oro** – Piazza Grande 18/19. ℘0575 21 033. www. loggevasari.it. Closed Sun–Mon. Refined Tuscan cuisine in a historic setting.

♿♿♿ **La Tagliatella** – Viale Giotto 45/47. ℘0575 21 931. www. ristorantelatagliatella.it. Situated slightly away from the centre, this restaurant is decorated with motifs from the world of wine, as well as light colours, which give it a bright, airy feel. The menu features regional cuisine such as Chianina beef specialities. A particularly interesting wine list.

EVENTS AND FESTIVALS

In summer, the Piazza Grande hosts the **Giostra del Saracino** (Saracen's Tournament), when costumed horsemen lance an armoured dummy, the Saracen (Mediterranean pirate).

Sansepolcro★

This small industrial town (famous for its pasta) retains its old town walls and numerous old houses★ dating from the Middle Ages to the 18C. The finest streets are the Via XX Settembre and the Via Matteotti. Sansepolcro's main claim to fame is as the birthplace of one of the most important artists of the Italian Quattrocento (15C), Piero della Francesca.

▶ **Population:** 16 365
⚙ **Michelin Map:** 563 L 18.
🛈 **Info:** Via Matteotti 8, 52037 Sansepolcro (AR). ℘0575 74 05 36. http://turismo. provincia.arezzo.it.
◐ **Location:** Sansepolcro is off the E 45, near the borders with Umbria and Le Marche.
🐵 **Don't Miss:** Piero della Francesca paintings in the Museo Civico.
🕓 **Timing:** Allow two hours.

SIGHTS
Museo Civico★★
Via Aggiunti 65. ♿ Open daily 10am–1.30pm and 2.30–6pm (summer 7pm). 8€. ℘0575 40 33 19. museocivicosansepolcro.it.
See exquisite **paintings★★★** by **Piero della Francesca**: his *Resurrection*, rhaposodised by Aldous Huxley *as "the best picture in the world"*, the beautiful polyptych of the *Virgin of Mercy* and two fragments of frescoes, *St Julian* and *St Ludovic*. Other works are by Bassano, Signorelli and the della Robbia school. Upstairs is a beautiful view of Via Matteotti and 14C *sinopies* (red-chalk drawings).
🐵 Another sight you shouldn't miss is the **Chiesa San Lorenzo** for its *Descent from the Cross* by Rosso Fiorentino.

EXCURSIONS
Camaldoli★★
◐ 76km/47.2mi NW. www.camaldoli.it.
Camaldoli, situated in a great forest in the heart of the mountains, was the cradle of the Camaldulian Order, founded in the 11C by St Romuald. The monastery, rebuilt in the 13C, is now occupied by Benedictines.
Higher up in a grim, isolated site is the **Hermitage★** *(eremo)*, a cluster of buildings encircled by ramparts. These include St Romuald's cell and a fine 18C church.

Convento della Verna★
◐ 36km/22.4mi NW.
The monastery, pleasantly situated in the woods, was founded in 1213. Here St Francis of Assisi received the Stigmata. The basilica and the small church of Santa Maria degli Angeli are adorned with terra-cottas by Andrea della Robbia.

Poppi★
◐ 61km/38mi NW.
This town overlooks the Arno Valley. It's crowned by its 13C *castello★*, former seat of the Counts of Guidi, with a **courtyard★**. Open daily mid-Mar–Oct 10am–6pm (Jul–Aug to 7pm); rest of the year Thu–Sun 10am–5pm (Christmas hols daily). 5€. ℘0575 52 05 16. www.castel-lodipoppi.it.

Monterchi
◐ 17km/10.6mi S.
The enigmatic and compelling **Madonna del Parto** by Piero della Francesca, a rare depiction of the pregnant Virgin in Italian art, is set in the sterile room of a former school.

Cortona★★

Cortona occupies a remarkable spot on the steep slope overlooking the Chiana Valley, close to Lake Trasimeno. This medieval town, with walls commanded by a huge citadel *(fortezza)*, was annexed to Florence in 1411, and has barely changed since the Renaissance. It is the birthplace of artists Luca Signorelli (c.1450–1523) and Pietro da Cortona (1596–1669).

▶ **Population:** 22 008
⛭ **Michelin Map:** 563 M 17.
🛈 **Info:** Via Nazionale 42, 52044. ℘0575 63 03 52. www.cortonaweb.net.
◗ **Location:** Cortona lies off the S 71, linking Arezzo with Lake Trasimeno.
◗ **Train:** Cortona (Firenze Campo di Marte 1hr 15mins).
🕾 **Don't Miss:** The museum.
🕐 **Timing:** Allow half a day.

SIGHTS

Piazza del Duomo, against the ramparts, affords a lovely valley view.

Museo Diocesano★★

♿ Open Apr–Oct 10am–7pm; Nov–Mar 10am–5pm (closed Mon). 5€. www.cortonaweb.net.
This former church houses a beautiful *Annunciation* and *Madonna and Saints* by Fra Angelico and a remarkable *Ecstasy of St Margaret* by Crespi (1665–1747).

Palazzo Pretorio★

Open Apr–oct 10am–7pm; Nov–Mar 10am–5pm. Closed Mon (winter), 1 Jan, 25 Dec. 10€. ℘0575 63 72 35. www.cortonamaec.org.
Inside **Museo dell'Accademia Etrusca★** displays Etruscan exhibits including a 5C BC bronze **oil lamp★★** with 16 burners shaped like human figures.

Santuario di Santa Margherita

This enshrines the Gothic **tomb★** (1362) of St Margaret. Chiesa di San Domenico has a fine *Madonna* by Luca Signorelli and a fresco by Fra Angelico.

Chiesa di Santa Maria del Calcinaio★

3km/1.8mi W.
Built in 1485–1513, note the façade's stained-glass window designed by Guillaume de Marcillat (1467–1529).

ADDRESSES

Il Falconiere Relais – Loc. San Martino 370. ℘0575 61 26 79, www.ilfalconiere.it. 22 rooms. This 17C villa has beautiful rooms and a spa. Elegant, cheerful and airy. Tuscan cuisine with a creative twist. Wines include their own label.

Monte San Savino★

Monte San Savino, a medieval town, which dates back to the Etruscans, has a historic centre that has both a castle and a homey feel, especially lively on Wednesday when the market moves in. Famous sculptor Andrea Contucci del Monte San Savino, known as Sansovino (c.1467–1529), was born here.

▶ **Population:** 8 717
⛭ **Michelin Map:** 563 M17.
🛈 **Info:** www.arezzoturismo.it. www.monteturismo.it.
◗ **Location:** Monte San Savino is 21km/13mi southwest of Arezzo, on the SS 73, about 2km/1.2mi from the A 1 Florence–Rome.
🕐 **Timing:** Half a day.
👥 **Kids:** Climb Palazzo Pretorio tower.

WALKING TOUR

Porta Fiorentina leads to Corso Antonio da Sangallo. On Via Solomon Fiorentino is the **synagogue**, which served what once was a large Jewish community, massacred in 1799. **Piazza Gamurrini** has an obelisk erected in 1644, a 1385 Sienese tower, and the church of **Santa Chiara** with Sansovino terra-cotta sculptures of St Sebastian, St Roch and St Lawrence. The *Virgin and Child with Four Saints* is probably the workshop of Giovanni della Robbia.

Loggia dei Mercantia, attributed to Sansovino (1518–20), faces **Palazzo Comunale** (1515–17) by Sangallo the Elder. The Romanesque exterior of **Chiesa della Misericordia** leads to a 17–18C Baroque interior, where left of the entrance a tomb is the early work of Sansovino (1498).

San Giovanni Valdarno

An important Val d'Arno industrial centre known for its steel plants and lignite (coal) gave birth to **Masaccio (1401–28), born Tommaso di Ser Giovanni di Simone, whose nickname means "clumsy" or "messy". Visionary and precursor of the Renaissance, the artist introduced volume to paint.**

VISIT

The **Palazzo Pretorio★**, also called Palazzo Arnolfo, built in the 13C by Arnolfo di Cambio, is studded with coats of arms of podestas. San Giovanni Battista *(Piazza Cavour)*, an early-14C church, has elegant portico tondi glazed in the style of della Robbia.

Basilica Santa Maria delle Grazie (Piazza Masaccio; open Wed–Sun 10am–1pm, 2.30 (3.30 winter)–6.30pm, closed Mon– Tue; 3.50€. ✆055 91 22 445. www.basilicadel-legrazie.it), a 15C church, has a beautiful glazed ceramic *Assumption of the Virgin*

The 14C **Palazzo Pretorio** displays coats of arms of Florentines who lived there as podestas.

Note the beautiful Gothic portal on the 14C **Chiesa di Sant'Agostino**, and above it the rose window with stained glass by Guillaume de Marcillat (c.1470–1529). The cloister entrance to the arcades was designed by Sansovino, as was the baptistery door to San Giovanni.

A 14C **fortress** houses the **Museum of Ceramics** (phone, hours vary; ✆0575 84 30 98), medieval to contemporary.

ADDRESSES

⑂ EAT

Ristorante Belvedere – Loc. Bano. ✆0575 84 42 62, www. ristorante-belvedere.net. Tuscan cuisine. View.

▶ **Population:** 17 141
⚅ **Michelin Map:** 563 L16.
🛈 **Info:** www.arezzoturismo.it.
▶ **Location:** San Giovanni Valdarno is 40km/24.8mi from Florence on the A 1 towards Rome, and 37km/23mi northwest of Arezzo.
▶ **Train:** San Giovanni Valdarno (Firenze Campo di Marte 24mins).
◔ **Timing:** Half a day.

by **Giovanni della Robbia**. Inside, the high altar has a 14C fresco of Our Lady of Grace, which gives its name to the basilica; the right nave has a 15C *Virgin and Child with Four Saints* with two angels on a gold background.

Behind the choir, a small museum houses 15C–16C works of the Florentine school, including a beautiful *Annunciation★★* by **Fra Angelico**.

The 14C Oratorio di San Lorenzo, with modest brick-and-stone façade, has 14C–15C wall frescoes and an altarpiece by the Giotto school.

Umbria and Le Marche

Major Cities: Assisi, Orvieto, Perugia, Spoleto
Official Website: www.english.regioneumbria.eu

The Marches. Major Cities: Ancona, Ascoli Piceno, Fano, Macerata, Pesaro, Urbino
Official Website: www.turismo.marche.it

Highlights

1. Learn about winemaking at the **Museo del Vino** (p607)
2. Hear modern music at the **Umbria Jazz Festival** (p608)
3. Explore Giotto's frescoes in the **Basilica di San Francesco** (p609)
4. See the massive waterfalls at **Cascata delle Marmore** (p615)
5. Go spelunking in the **Grotte di Frasassi** (p632)

Separate Identities

Umbria and Le Marche, two central regions of Italy, have distinct personalities. Despite Umbria being the Italian peninsula's only landlocked region, of the two Le Marche has been more insular and less discovered by tourists, both Italian and foreign. Umbria has Assisi, attracting pilgrims there for centuries. Visitors that are nostalgic for the old Italy – where the dominant language is local, where there still is time for a languid lunch with wines made nowhere else, where artisans still are masters of trades long abandoned elsewhere – might just find that here is the Italy of their dreams, in both regions.

Local Industries

Industry ranges from textiles and furniture, to yacht-making in Fano, to metals in Terni. Artisans are a great treasure, and a major part of the economy, from potters, to carters (papermakers), to blacksmiths. In Le Marche look especially for shoemakers. Agriculture is a major economic force, which makes for excellent local meals and wines, as well as beautiful landscapes of vineyards, olive groves and fields of grain, tobacco, fruit trees and vegetables.

Le Marche's coast, once a seafaring power, still counts on its fishing trade, where trucks rumble into the hills travelling house to house. Some unspoiled beaches are near the Conero Promontory and Pesaro. The pretty hill towns offer delightful accommodation from castles, and historic palazzos, to monasteries, some still a spiritual base, others converted for modern sybarites. Or consider a stay on a working farm, an economical choice where they often serve delicious meals. The curvy hill roads are scenic and very historic, and Roman consular roads do indeed lead to Rome. From Rome the Via Flaminia winds through Lazio, Umbria and finishes on the coast in Fano, while Via Salaria concludes on the sea below Ascoli Piceno. Ancona offers ferries to Greece and Croatia.

Steeped in Historic Culture

Culture is no stranger to these parts. The ancient Etruscans, Umbri and Picenes had their own civilisations before Roman domination. Greeks founded Ancona, a reminder that for centuries the seafaring coast traded briskly with the Orient. Frederick II was born in Jesi, but it was in medieval Umbria where the Lombards ruled for centuries in the Duchy of Spoleto. Renaissance aristocratic Montefeltro and Malatesta families formed their grand courts in Urbino, Pesaro and Fano. Today small hill towns are a rich source of cultural life, from artistic treasures by Giotto, Cimabue, Lorenzetti, Simone Martini, Perugino, Crivelli, Raphael and Pinturicchio, to dazzling theatres. These historic 18C and 19C gems reach their highest concentration in Le Marche. There are atmospheric outdoor arenas too, from ancient Roman amphitheatres to Macerata's Sferisterio. Rather than ticking off long lists, mingle with locals and enjoy each discovery along the way.

Umbria

Umbria, at the heart of the Italian peninsula, is landlocked between elegant Tuscany, the hilly Le Marche and Imperial Lazio. Etruscans built – and later civilisations enhanced – commanding cities atop promontories of volcanic tuff, of which Orvieto and Perugia, the regional capital, were most prominent. St Francis took an oath of poverty and chastity and wrote his Canticle of the Creatures in the environs of Assisi, where upon his death, the magnificent Basilica di San Francesco, one of Italy's major places of pilgrimage, was built. Giotto, a forefather of Renaissance artists, decorated the Upper Basilica with frescoes from the life of St Francis. Artists who were born in Umbria include Perugino and Luca Signorelli, whose work is on display in Orvieto's Duomo.

Ancient Natural Landscapes

This region of evocative Perugino and Raphael landscapes still intact has dense mountain forests, slopes of vineyards and olive groves, valleys and river basins. The Clitumnus Valley (**Valle del Clitunno**), famous in ancient times for its oracles and pastures, today is fertile with crops of beet, wheat, saffron, onion, celery and tobacco. Black truffles, one of the region's precious products, are found mostly around Norcia, which is renowned for its butchery skills. Umbria has two lakes, **Trasimeno** and Piediluco, and many rivers, including the Tiber, which flows south to Rome. Medieval cities which succeeded Etruscan and Roman settlements overlook ravines and valleys.

They include haughty **Perugia** (the capital and university centre), Assisi, sophisticated Spoleto (site of a major arts festival), Spello, Montefalco, Todi and Gubbio. Others stand in the centre of a plain, such as lovely Bevagna, Foligno, a railway hub, and Terni, the metallurgical centre.

Highlights

1 Visit a Renaissance street in **Perugia, Via dei Priori** (p606)
2 Visit the medeival *gaite* of **Bevagna** (p611)
3 Taste **Sagrantino** wine in Montefalco, Bevagna, and Gualdo Cattaneo (p612)
4 Enjoy performing arts in sophisticated **Spoleto** (p614)
5 Hike across the **Castelluccio Plain** (p615)

Cascata delle Marmore

© silvano.audisio/Fotolia.com

Perugia★★

Perugia was one of the twelve Etruscan city-states known as *lucumonies* that composed the federation of Etruria in the 7C and 6C BC. After defeating the free city of Perugia in the 1540 Salt War, Pope Paul III erected a massive citadel (**Rocca Paolina**) over the city's original Etruscan bastions with the inscription "Ad repellandam Perusinorum audaciam" ("To curb the audacity of the Perugians").
The town has retained many lovely buildings from the Middle Ages. The Renaissance-era Collegio del Cambio houses frescoes by artist and master Pietro Vannucci, called Perugino, whose works are also in the Galleria Nazionale dell'Umbria and on the walls of Rome's Sistine Chapel. Umbria's capital and largest city today is an industrial and commercial centre and a vibrant university town. Also famous for its Perugina chocolates, it hosts a chocolate festival (**Eurochocolate**) each October.

▶ **Population:** 168 187
   Michelin Map: 563
   M 19 – Umbria.
   Info: Piazza Matteotti 18.
     ℘075 57 36 458.
     www.provincia.perugia.it.
     www.comune.perugia.it.
▶ **Location:** Perugia is perched atop a hill, in the heart of Umbria. The main access road is the E 45, which links the town with Emilia Romagna.
▶ **Train:** Perugia (Firenze SMN 2hr 7mins).
   Don't Miss: The National Gallery of Umbria, Chiesa di San Pietro and the Oratorio di San Bernardino.
   Timing: Allow a day.

SIGHTS

Piazza IV Novembre★★

Allow 2hrs.
This square in the heart of Perugia is one of the grandest in Umbria. The chief buildings of the city's glorious period as an independent commune are grouped here: the Priors' Palace, which houses the Collegio del Cambio, Collegio della Mercanzia and the Galleria Nazionale dell'Umbria, the Great Fountain and the cathedral. Leading off the square is **Via Maestà delle Volte★** with its medieval houses and passages.

Galleria Nazionale dell'Umbria★★

  Open Tue–Sun 8.30am–7.30pm. 6.50€ or Perugia Città Museo card for combined sights. ℘075 58 66 84 15. www.gallerianazionaleumbria.it.
The National Gallery of Umbria, housed on the top floors of the Priors' Palace, displays Umbrian art from the 13C to the late-18C. Among the highlights are a *Madonna* by Duccio, a **polyptych of St Anthony** by Piero della Francesca and works by Fra Angelico, Boccati and Fiorenzo di Lorenzo. Masterpieces by Pinturicchio and Perugino include a *Dead Christ* with its black background and an admirable *Madonna of Consolation*. Note also the marble statuettes by Nicola and Giovanni Pisano from the Great Fountain, and works by Arnolfo di Cambio. The 17C is represented by Federico Barocci, Pietro da Cortona and Orazio Gentileschi.
The 15C Priors' Chapel is dedicated to one of the city's patron saints, Herculanus and to St Louis of Toulouse, with a remarkable cycle of **frescoes** by Benedetto Bonfigli (d.1496). See also lovely 13C and 14C French enamels and ivories.

Fontana Maggiore★★

The Great Fountain (1278) has 25 side panels sculpted by Nicola Pisano (lower basin) and his son Giovanni (upper basin). Some of the replaced originals are on display in the National Gallery of Umbria.

Palazzo dei Priori★★

The grand impressive 13C Priors' Palace has a façade overlooking the square with

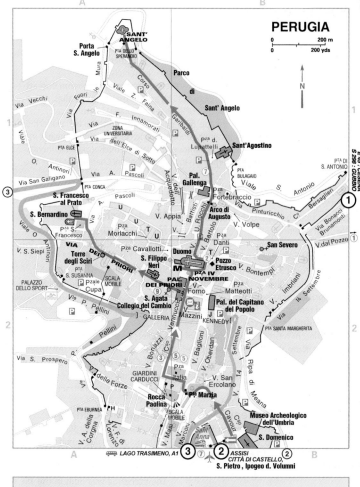

PERUGIA

0 _____ 200 m
0 _____ 200 yds

N

a majestic outside staircase leading up to a marble pulpit from which the priors harangued the people. The Corso Vannucci façade boasts a fine 14C doorway. Inside, the palace rooms are decorated with 14C frescoes or carved 15C panelling in the Notaries' Chamber and College of the Mercanzia.

Cattedrale★

The cathedral, dedicated to another patron, St Lawrence, is Gothic, but the Piazza Dante façade was completed with a Baroque doorway.

The south chapel contains an interesting *Descent from the Cross* by Barocci, which inspired Rubens in his *Antwerp Descent*. In the north chapel is a ring said to be the Virgin's wedding ring. In both these

Artistic Heritage

In harmony with their peaceful countryside, the Umbrian painters had gentle, mystic souls. Their atmospheric landscapes are punctuated with treesWomen are depicted with a tender gracefulness. Their extremely delicate draughtsmanship and soft colours characterise masters like **Giovanni Boccati** (1410–c.1485), **Fiorenzo di Lorenzo** (d.1520) and **Pietro Vannucci, alias Perugino** (1445–1523), the teacher of Raphael, celebrated for his sense of space, atmosphere and landscape. Bernardino di Betto Betti, alias Pinturicchio (1454–1513), employs Renaissance geometry, vivid colour, Flemish touches in detail and innovative landscape. Although he painted the Borgia Apartments in the Vatican, his real masterpiece is in Spello's Baglioni Chapel, where he also inserted his self-portrait.

chapels, note the superb **choir stalls** with 15C intarsia work.

Chiesa di San Pietro★★

Through **Porta San Pietro★**, a majestic but unfinished church is by the Florentine Agostino di Duccio, built at the end of the 10C and remodelled during the Renaissance. Inside are 11 excellent canvases by Vassilacchi, a Greek contemporary of El Greco. Note the **carved tabernacle** by Mino da Fiesole and the marvellous 16C **intarsia choir★★**, a masterpiece of inlaid wood.

Chiesa di San Domenico★

The interior of this imposing Gothic church, dedicated to St Dominic, altered in the 17C, has the 14C **funerary monument** of Pope Benedict XI.

Oratorio di San Bernardino

© O. Forir/MICHELIN

Museo Archeologico Nazionale dell'Umbria★★

& Open Mon 10am–7.30pm, Tue–Sun 8.30am–7.30pm. 4€. ℘075 57 27 141. www.archeopg.arti.beniculturali.it.
The National Archaeological Museum's prehistoric, Etruscan and Umbrian collections include funerary urns, sarcophagi, Etruscan bronzes and a vast display of amulets once used in southern Italy for religious or protective purposes. The 3C BC **Cippo Perugino** (Perugia Stone), a travertine slab, is believed to be an Etruscan property contract.

Collegio del Cambio★

Open Tue–Sat 9am–12.30pm and 2.30–5.30pm, Sun and public hols 9am–1pm; closed pm Nov–Mar. 4.50€. ℘075 57 28 599. www.collegiodecambio.it.
The Exchange was built in the 15C for the money-changers guild. In the Audience Room are the famous **frescoes★★** of Perugino and his pupils, which display the humanist spirit of the age that sought to combine Classical civilisation and Christian doctrine. The Justice statue is by Benedetto da Maiano (15C).

Oratorio di San Bernardino★★

To reach the Oratory of St Bernardino, walk along the picturesque **Via dei Priori★**. This Renaissance jewel (1461) by Agostino di Duccio is exquisite in its harmonious lines, the delicacy of its multicoloured marbles and its sculptures. The bas-reliefs on the façade depict St Bernardino in glory on the tympanum, the

Torgiano

© G. Cianci/fototeca ENIT

life of the saint on the lintel and delightful angel musicians on the shafts. Inside the church, the altar consists of a 4C early Christian sarcophagus.

Via delle Volte della Pace★

The picturesque medieval street is formed by a long 14C Gothic portico as it follows the Etruscan town wall.

Sant'Angelo★

The interior of this small 5C–6C circular church includes 16 ancient columns.

Rocca Paolina★

Access via Porta Marzia.

These are the remains of a fortress built in 1540 on the orders of Pope Paul III – hence the name "Pauline". The impressive interior still has huge walls, streets and wells dating from the 11C to the 16C. Escalators facilitate access within the fortress.

Arco di Augusto (Etrusco)★

This imposing Etruscan Arch is built of huge blocks of stone. A 16C loggia surmounts the tower on the left. Alongside, the majestic 18C **Palazzo Gallenga** serves as a summer school for foreign students.

Giardini Carducci

The superb **view★★** from the Carducci Gardens, which dominate the San Pietro quarter, looks over the Tiber Valley.

EXCURSIONS

Ipogeo dei Volumni★

▶ 6km/3.7mi SE. Open Jul–Aug daily 9am–7pm; Sept–Jun 9am–6.30pm. Closed 1 Jan, 1 May, 25 Dec. 3€. ℘075 39 33 29. www.archeopg.arti.beniculturali.it. This vast Etruscan *hypogeum* hewn out of the rock comprises an *atrium* and nine burial chambers.

The Volumnian tomb is the largest; it contains six rounded tombstones *(cippi)*, the biggest being that of the head of the family (2C BC).

Torgiano

▶ 16km/10mi SE.

This village above the Tiber Valley has the interesting **Museo del Vino★** (Lungarotti Foundation) showing wine-growing traditions in Umbria and Italy since the days of the Etruscans. &Open daily Tue–Sun 10am–1pm and 3–6pm (winter 5pm); Jul–Sept daily 10am–6pm. Closed 25 Dec. 7€ inc Olive Oil Museum. www.lungarotti.it/fondazione/muvit/.

Panicale

▶ 32km/19.9mi SW. Take the S 220, turn right after Tavernelle and follow directions. www.benvenutiapanicale.it. Panicale is a medieval town perched on a hillside overlooking Lake Trasimeno. The church of San Sebastiano houses a *Martyrdom of St Sebastian* by Perugino.

Città della Pieve

▶ 42km/26.1mi SW on the S 220.

This warm ochre-coloured town, founded in about AD 7–8 and originally called *Castrum Plebis*, was the birthplace of Pietro Vannucci, better known as **Perugino**. Some of his works are housed in the cathedral *(Baptism of Christ; Virgin with St Peter, St Paul, St Gervase and St Protasius)*, in the oratory of Santa Maria dei Bianchi *(Adoration of the Magi*, an elegant composition balanced by the portrayal of the gentle Umbrian countryside) and in Santa Maria dei Servi *(Descent from the Cross)*. In the oratory of San Bartolomeo there are mid-14C frescoes by the Sienese artist Jacopo di Mino del Pellicciaio *(Weeping of the Angels)*. City monuments date from the Middle Ages to the 18C. Palazzo della Corgna was built in the mid-16C by the Perugian architect Galeazzo Alessi and frescoed by Niccolò Pomarancio and Salvio Savini. Today, the city is also noted for its saffron production for which it hosts a lively autumn festival.

ADDRESSES

🏠 STAY

🛏🛏 **Hotel Priori** – Via dei Priori. ☎075 57 23 378. www.hotelpriori.it. A pleasant, no-frills hotel with splendid terrace over the little old alleyways and the roofs of the historic centre. Simple rooms, some with a view, have dark wooden furniture.

🛏🛏🛏 **Fortuna** – Via Bonazzi 19. ☎075 57 22 845. www.hotelfortunaperugia.com. 52 rooms. Ivy-covered hotel in quiet alley near Piazza IV Novembre. Charming old-fashioned rooms, frescoes in reading room, nice roof terrace.

🛏🛏🛏 **Castello di Monterone** – Strada Montevile 3. ☎075 57 24 214. www.castellomonterone.it. 18 rooms. This atmospheric 13C castle has lovely rooms with handsome wrought-iron furnishings locally crafted in Spello. In Superb chef Marco Bistarelli transferred his Il Postale restaurant here and also runs Il Gradale. Wellness centre, pool.

🛏🛏🛏 **Hotel La Rosetta** – Piazza Italia 19. ☎/Fax 075 57 20 841. www.perugiaonline.com/larosetta. 90 rooms. Some rooms have frescoed ceilings and gorgeous antique furnishings; others, although pleasant and spacious, feel cluttered and less elegant. Located in the vibrant heart of the city.

🛏🛏🛏 **Le Tre Vaselle** – Via Garibaldi 48, Torgiano. ☎075 98 80 447. www.3vaselle.it. 60 rooms. The Lungarotti winery runs this lovely hotel and restaurant in Torgiano. Cosy fireplace in winter. All modern conveniences.

🍴 EAT

🍽 **Dal Mi'Cocco** – Corso Garibaldi 12. ☎075 57 32 511. Closed Mon. Reservation recommended. An alternative establishment housed in former stables. Diners are welcomed with a glass of red wine. A 13€ fixed-price menu features Umbrian specialities. Bread and pasta are made on the premises.

🍽🍽🍽 **Antica trattoria San Lorenzo** – Piazza Danti 19a. ☎075 57 21 956. www.anticatrattoriasanlorenzo.com. Closed Sun. Reservation recommended. By the Duomo, in an intimate vaulted room, enjoy ultra-fresh Umbrian cuisine, refined, with bold touches.

🍽🍽🍽 **Collins** – Piazza Italia 12. ☎075 57 32 541. This elegant restaurant stands in the heart of the old town. It has a summer terrace overlooking the valley and a delightful fireplace for cold winter days. A good selection of regional specialities are served. Excellent standard.

EVENTS AND FESTIVALS

Perugia has been the backdrop for summer's **Umbria Jazz Festival** since 1973, then added Orvieto for a late December festival. www.umbriajazz.com.

Assisi★★★

The walled city of Assisi, birthplace of St Francis, transmits an aura of tranquillity, and figures in the numerous accounts of his life and work. Under the influence of the Franciscan Order of Minors founded by St Francis (c.1181–1226), a new, religious, artistic movement developed which marked a turning point in Italian art. The son of a rich Assisi draper, Francis preached poverty, humility, respect for nature and mysticism. His teachings gave rise to a new artistic vision expressed in the purity of Gothic art.

During the 13C the stark, austere churches were embellished with a new splendour to reflect the tender love of St Francis for nature and its creatures, as described in his canticles and the tales of St Bonaventure. From the end of the 14C famous masters came from Rome and Venice to Assisi to work on the Basilica of St Francis. These artists abandoned the rigid traditions of Byzantine art in favour of a more dramatic art imbued with a spiritual atmosphere. Cimabue and later Giotto were its most powerful exponents.

BASILICA DI SAN FRANCESCO★★★

Piazza San Francesco. Basilica Inferiore (Lower Basilica): Open 6am–6.45pm (winter to 5.45pm). Basilica Superiore (Upper Basilica): Open 8.30am–6.45pm (winter to 5.45pm). ℘075 81 90 01. www.sanfrancescoassisi.org.

From the valley, the road that winds up to town, or from the green esplanade, the basilica is an imposing and striking vision at all hours. The simple façade has a Cosmati rose window.

The complex consists of two churches, resting on a series of immense arches. The whole building, erected after the death of St Francis to the plans of Brother Elias, was consecrated in 1253. This monk influenced the Franciscans to use more splendour and decoration.

▶ **Population:** 28 147
⚫ **Michelin Map:**
563 M 19 – Umbria.
🔲 **Info:** ℘075 81 38 680. www.comune.assisi.pg.it.
◗ **Location:** Assisi spreads prettily across the slope of Monte Subasio and lies between Perugia and Foligno, on the SS 75.
◗ **Train:** Assisi train station.
◉ **Don't Miss:** Frescoes in the Basilica di San Francesco; enchanting Spello and Bevagna, Sagrantino wine in Montefalco.
◔ **Timing:** A day to explore Assisi and half a day for the excursions.

Basilica Inferiore – Beyond the long narthex, the walls of the dark, sombre four-bay nave of the lower church are covered with 13C and 14C **frescoes★★★**. From the nave, enter the first chapel on the left with **frescoes★★** by Simone Martini (c.1284–1344) illustrating the life of St Martin. These are remarkable for their delicate drawing, graceful composition and bright colours.

Above the pulpit is a fresco of the *Coronation of the Virgin* attributed to Maso, a pupil of Giotto (14C). The **choir vaulting★★**, painted by one of Giotto's pupils, has scenes symbolising the Triumph of St Francis and the virtues practised by him. The north transept is decorated with **frescoes★★** of the Passion. Those on the ceiling, attributed to pupils of Pietro Lorenzetti, are valued for their narrative design and charm of detail; those on the walls, probably by Lorenzetti himself, are striking for their dramatic expression (*Descent from the Cross*). In the south transept is the majestic work by Cimabue, a *Madonna with Four Angels and St Francis*. From the Sixtus IV cloisters make for the **treasury★★** with its many valuable items and the **Perkins collection** of 14C to 16C paintings. At the bottom of the steps, beneath the centre of the transept crossing, is **St Francis' Tomb**, which is both spare and evocative.

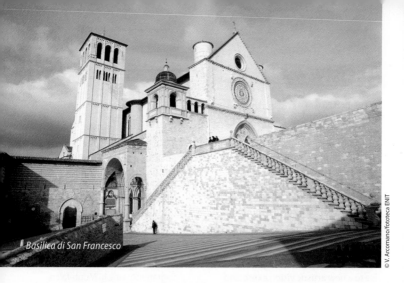

Basilica di San Francesco

© V. Arcomano/fototeca ENIT

Basilica Superiore – This accomplished Gothic work, with its tall and graceful nave bathed in light, contrasts with the lower church. The apse and transept were decorated with frescoes (many have since been damaged) by Cimabue and his school. In the north transept Cimabue painted an intensely dramatic **Crucifixion★★★**.

Between 1296 and 1304 **Giotto** and his assistants depicted the life of St Francis in a famous cycle of **frescoes★★★**. There are 28 clearly defined scenes, each showing a greater search for realism. They mark a new dawning in the figurative traditions of Italian art, which was to reach its apogee during the Renaissance.

Rocca Maggiore★★

The walls of this 12C fortress surround Assisi and they provide a spectacular **view★★★** of the Spoleto Valley below.

WALKING TOUR

This walk goes through the heart of Assisi. Begin in front of the Basilica Superiore of St Francis on Via San Francesco.

Via San Francesco★

This picturesque street is lined by medieval and Renaissance houses. At no. 13a the Pilgrims' Chapel (Oratorio dei Pellegrini) is decorated inside with 15C frescoes, notably by **Matteo da Gualdo** (open Mon–Sat, 10am–noon and 2–6pm (4.30 winter); ℘075 81 22 67).

▶ Via San Francesco turns into Via Seminario. Turn left at Via Fortini, then left again at Via Portica, where you can glimpse the Foro Romano ruins, then to Piazza del Comune.

Piazza del Comune★

Once the forum, on the square note the **Tempio di Minerva★** (1C BC), a temple converted into a church, and the People's Captains' Palace (13C).

▶ Walk E on Via di San Rufino to Piazza San Rufino.

Duomo di San Rufino★

The 12C cathedral has a Romanesque **façade★★** with a harmonious arrangement of its openings and ornamentation. Inside is the baptismal font used for the baptism of St Francis, St Clare and Frederick II.

▶ Return to Piazza del Comune. Take Corso Mazzini to Piazza Santa Chiara.

Chiesa di Santa Chiara★★

From the terrace in front of the church of St Clare there is a pretty view of the Umbrian countryside. The church was built from 1257 to 1265.

The Byzantine Crucifix brought here from St Damian's Monastery, which is said to have spoken to St Francis and called him to the Christian faith, can be seen in the small church of St George, which adjoins the south aisle. The crypt enshrines the remains of St Clare.

EXCURSIONS
Eremo delle Carceri★★
❯ 4km/2.5mi E.
The hermitage *(eremo)* stands in a beautiful site in the forest Monte Subasio. The hermitage was founded here by St Bernardino of Siena (1380–1444).

Convento di San Damiano★
❯ 2km/1.2mi S of the gateway Porta Nuova. Open daily summer 10am–noon and 2–6pm; winter 10am–noon and 2–4.30pm. ℘075 81 22 73.
St Damian's Monastery stands alone amid olive and cypress trees. Here St Francis received his calling and composed his *Canticle of the Creatures*, and here St Clare died in 1253.

Basilica di Santa Maria degli Angeli★
❯ 5km/3mi SW.
The huge 16C Basilica of St Mary of the Angels was built in the valley to house the **Porziuncola**, a small chapel named after the small plot *(piccola porzione* in Italian) of land on which it was built before the year AD 1000, later decorated with a **fresco★** (1393).
In Cappella del Transito Francis died on 3 October 1226. The St Mary Major Crypt has a **polyptych★** by Andrea della Robbia (c.1490).

Spello★
❯ 12km/7.4mi SW. www.prospello.it.
A picturesque hill town with bastions and gateways that bear witness to its past as a Roman settlement. The **Church of Santa Maria Maggiore** has the Baglioni Chapel with stunning **frescoes★★** by **Pinturicchio**. By the high altar are frescoes by Perugino. Nearby, in the **Church of Sant'Andrea**, built in 1025, is a painting by Pinturicchio and a crucifix attributed to Giotto. At the base of town Roman mosaics were discovered in 2005. In spring for Le Infiorate del Corpus Domini, inhabitants paint images on the streets with flower petals.

Foligno
❯ 18km/11.2mi to the SE. Train: Foligno Roma Termini 1hr 45 min. www.comune.foligno.pg.it.
Piazza della Repubblica is framed by the 14C Palazzo Trinci, built by the local overlords, and the cathedral *(duomo)* with its fine doorway decorated with Lombard-style geometric decoration.

Palazzo Trinci
⮾ Open Tue–Sun, 10am–1pm and 3–7pm. 6€. ℘06 399 67 444. www.coopculture.it.
This palazzo has fine **frescoes★**, executed with a firm grasp of perspective.

Bevagna★
❯ 24km/14.9mi S of Assisi. www.comune.bevagna.pg.it.
Bevagna, built in the valley, is a flat medieval town, divided up into four *gaite*, or quarters. Remains of various buildings bear witness to its Roman past, particularly from the 2C AD: ambulatory of the Roman theatre, temple and the **Terme di Mevania** (thermal baths) with enchanting marine mosaics. This town makes an ideal base for those who find the hill towns too daunting.

Piazza Silvestri
This beautiful square is captivating in its medieval asymmetry, overlooked by two churches – the late-11C church of San Michele and the late-12C church of San Silvestro (note the epigraph on the façade) – as well as the 13C **Palazzo dei Consoli**, which houses the charming **Teatro Francesco Torti**.

Montefalco★
℘0742 35 44 59. www.montefalcodoc.it. (Pop. 5 686). Ramparts from the 14C still girdle this charming little town, which sits above vineyards and olive groves, perched like a falcon on its nest, the Balcony of Umbria. **Sagrantino di Montefalco**, one of Italy's great red wines, is produced here from the Sagrantino grape, as well as in Bevagna, Gualdo Cattaneo and other designated communities. Also try Montefalco Rosso and the Sagrantino *passito*.

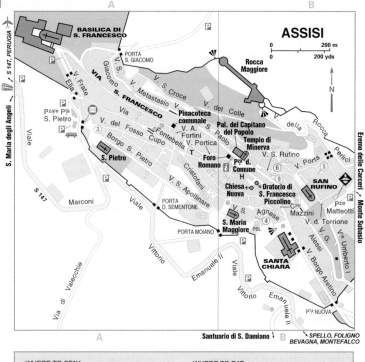

WHERE TO STAY		WHERE TO EAT	
Casa di Santa Brigida	④	Da Cecco	③
Pallotta	⑥	Da Erminio	⑤
		Piazzetta dell'Erba	⑨

Torre Comunale

The tower atop the city hall occasionally opens; enquire at tourist information on the piazza. It has a beautiful panorama★★★.

Museo Civico di San Francesco

Open 10.30am–6pm (Nov–Mar 2.30–5pm, closed Mon and Tue). ✆0742 37 95 98.

This Franciscan church converted to a **museum** has mid-15C **frescoes★★** of the life of St Francis and St Jerome by Benozzo Gozzoli, a *Nativity* by Perugino and an awe-inspiring crucifix by the Expressionist Master of Santa Chiara (active in Umbria late-13C–14C).

Chiesa di Sant'Illuminata

The Renaissance-style church has a doorway tympanum and several niches in the nave that were painted by Francesco Melanzio. Its most unusual display is a mummified pilgrim, who was preserved by micro-organisms similar to the Ferentillo mummies.

☙ An additional sight in Assisi is the Gothic Sant'Agostino, with frescoes by Umbrian painters of the 14C, 15C and 16C. Take an excursion to San Fortunato (1km/0.6mi S) for a superb **fresco★** by Benozzo Gozzoli.

ADDRESSES

🏠 STAY

ASSISI

🛏 **Casa di Santa Brigida** – Via Moiano 1. ✆075 81 26 93. www.brigidine.org. 18 rooms. ⌨. Tranquil spot run by nuns, with small garden. Light meals served, traditional cooking.

⊜ **Pallotta** – Via San Rufino 6. ℘075 81 23 07. www.pallottaassisi.it. 7 rooms. Centrally located medieval building with comfortable rooms, very busy.

NEARBY

⊜⊜ **Hotel Degli Affreschi** – Corso Mameli 45, Montefalco. ℘0742 37 81 50. www.hoteldegliaffreschi.it. An economical hotel right near the main piazza.

⊜⊜⊜ **Castello di Barattano** – Loc. Barattano, Gualdo Cattaneo. ℘0742 98 250. www.ilcastellodibarattano.it. ⅀. 6 apts. This medieval *borgo*, situated on a hill in Sagrantino wine country, has stone rooms with kitchenette and rustic furnishings.

⊜⊜⊜ **Hotel Palazzo Brunamonti** – Corso Giacomo Matteotti 79, Bevagna. ℘0742 36 19 32. www.brunamonti.com. 16 rooms. Lovely frescoes in the breakfast area, friendly staff, and bicycles to ride.

⊜⊜⊜ **Residenza del Marchese** – Via Villa del Marchese 15, Gualdo Cattaneo. ℘0742 91 340. www.residenzadel marchese.it. ⅀ 7 apartments. Each room or apartment has a kitchenette, the garden has a grill and swimming pool, and the owners make their own olive oil and wine. Dinner sometimes served.

⊜⊜⊜ **Tenuta di Saragano La Ghirlanda** – Loc. Saragano, Gualdo Cattaneo. ℘0742 98 731. www.laghirlanda.it. ⅀. 13 rooms. Classy country estate that has even hosted a Thai princess. Restaurant, bikes, horses.

⊜⊜⊜⊜ **Hotel Palazzo Bocci** – Via Cavour 17, Spello. ℘0742 30 10 21. www. palazzobocci.com. 23 rooms. Elegantly furnished rooms and frescoes in the reading room. On Spello's main street.

⊜⊜⊜⊜ **Hotel Villa Pambuffetti** – Viale della Vittoria 20. ℘0742 37 94 17. www.villapambuffetti.it. 15 rooms. Genteel villa at the edge of town. Pool.

⊜⊜⊜⊜ **L'Orto degli Angeli** – Via Dante Alighieri 1, Bevagna. ℘0742 36 01 30. www.ortoangeli.it. 14 rooms. Tasteful, comfortable rooms in medieval structure. Lovely sitting areas, and fireplaces in some rooms. An enchanting spot.

⊜⊜⊜⊜ **Villa Zuccari** – Loc. San Luca Montefalco. ℘0742 39 94 02. www.villa zuccari.com. ⅀. Lovely pink villa in the valley below town, with details from rose arbour to rooms.

ⵙ/EAT

ASSISI

⊜ **Da Cecco** – Piazza San Pietro 8, Assisi. ℘075 81 24 37. Closed Wed and 18 Dec–Feb. Rustic decor with Umbrian specialities in Hotel Berti.

⊜ **Da Erminio** – Via Montecavallo 19, Assisi. ℘075 81 25 06. www.trattoria daerminio.it. Closed Thu. Uphill near La Rocca, an open fire grills Umbrian dishes.

⊜⊜ **Piazzetta dell'Erba** – Via San Gabriele dell'Addolorata 15, Assisi. ℘075 81 53 52. www.osterialapiazzetta.it. Innovative cuisine, nice wines, good service, four outdoor tables.

NEARBY

⊜⊜ **L'Alchimista** – Piazza del Comune 14, Montefalco. ℘0742 378558. www. ristorantealchimista.it. Patrizia makes delicious pastas and local fare. Good Sagrantino wine selection. Tables outdoors in piazza or downstairs.

⊜⊜⊜ **La Vecchia Cucina** – Via delle Scuole 2, Marcellano. ℘0742 97237. Closed Mon. Simple decor but delicious bruschetta and grilled Chianina steaks.

⊜⊜⊜ **Villa Roncalli** – Via Roma 25, Loc. Sant'Eraclio, Foligno. ℘0742 39 10 91. www. villaroncalli.com. Closed Mon and Tue–Sat lunch. Sophisticated Umbrian cooking attracts diners to this lovely villa hidden off a commercial area. Food is prepared with great care and attention, with homemade bread.

⊜⊜⊜⊜ **La Bastiglia** – Piazza Vallegloria 7, Spello. ℘0742 65 12 77. www.labastiglia.com. Closed lunch and Wed. Creative cuisine, often variations on Umbrian classic fare. Good service, wines and food.

⊜⊜⊜⊜ **Redibis Ristorante** – Via dell'Anfiteatro, Bevagna. ℘0742 36 01 30. www.redibis.it. Closed Tue. Contemporary creative cuisine set in an ancient Roman amphitheatre foundation. Periodic themed dinners.

Spoleto★

Sophisticated, artsy Spoleto occupies the hill of this former Roman *municipium*, which was later capital of an important Lombard duchy from the 6C to the 8C. Crowned dramatically by the Rocca Albornoziana, it has graceful narrow streets, palaces, medieval buildings and a lively performing arts scene.

SIGHTS

Duomo★★

The street slopes dramatically down to **Piazza del Duomo★**, dominated by the cathedral façade with a fine Renaissance portico, a rose window and a 13C mosaic that gleams gold in the afternoon sun. Inside note frescoes by Pinturicchio, Fra Filippo Lippi's burial monument and **frescoes** depicting the Life of the Virgin by Fra Filippo Lippi and his assistants. *The Dormition of the Virgin* has a self-portrait of Lippi dressed in Dominican vestments.

Ponte delle Torri★★

A pleasant walk leads to the 13C Bridge of Towers (80m/262ft high, 230m/755ft long), with 10 Gothic arches built over a tall Roman aqueduct, which connects to dense forest on the mountain slope

Arco di Druso

This arch was built in AD 23 in honour of Tiberius' son, Drusus.

Chiesa di San Domenico

This lovely 13C church, dedicated to St Dominic, is decorated with 14C and 15C

▶ **Population:** 39 339
♿ **Michelin Map:** 563 N 20 – Umbria.
ℹ **Info:** Piazza Libertà 7. ☎0743 21 86 20. www.comunespoleto.gov.it. Parco dei Monti Sibillini: Casa del Parco, Via Solferino 22, 06046 Norcia. ☎0743 81 70 90. www.comune.norcia.pg.it.
◗ **Location:** Spoleto lies off the SS 3, Via Flaminia.
◗ **Train:** Spoleto (Roma Termini 1hr 27 min).
☺ **Don't Miss:** The Duomo's Fra Filippo Lippi frescoes and Cascata delle Marmore.
🕐 **Timing:** Allow three hours.

frescoes and the south transept contains a canvas by Lanfranco.

EXCURSIONS

Fonti del Clitunno★

◗ 13km/8mi N. For information on opening times, call ☎0743 52 11 41 or visit www.fontidelclitunno.com. 3€. Tempietto: Open Nov-Mar 12.15–5.45pm, closed Mon and Sun (the 2nd and 4th weeks of the mounth), Apr-Oct 2-8pm. ☎0743 27 50 85.

These crystal-clear waters in a pretty park were sacred to the Romans, who plunged animals into the water for purification prior to sacrifice. About 1km/0.6mi below stands the **tempietto★** of Clitumnus, originally a Roman shrine to the river god, where Romans, among whom Caligula, came

Ponte delle Torri

©Deniskelly/Dreamstime.com

to consult the oracle. An early Christian 5C structure was built over it.

Monteluco Road★

◔ 8km/5mi E.

A winding road leads up to **Monteluco**. Near the bottom, the church of **San Pietro** has a 13C Romanesque **façade★** with dramatic bas-reliefs. On the summit is Monteluco, once the seat of an ancient cult, later a resort. The monastery founded by St Francis still exists.

⊂ DRIVING TOUR

SOUTHERN UMBRIA

This long (155km/96.3mi) scenic route begins in Spoleto and leads to the Monti Sibillini.

◔ 16km/10mi. From Spoleto head SW for Carsulae along the SS 418 to SS 3bis S towards San Gemini and San Gemini Fonte (mineral water).

Roman Ruins: Carsulae

www.carsulae.it.

These are the remains of a Roman town destroyed in the 9C.

◔ Head S towards Terni along the SS 3bis. Follow the SS 79 S as far as Cascate delle Marmore.

Cascata delle Marmore★★

From the car park, 30min on foot there and back. For admission times and charges, contact Infopoint ℘0744 62 982. www.cascatamarmore.it.

This artificial waterfall created by the Romans falls in three successive drops down sheer walls of marble (*marmore*).

◔ Take the SR 209 to Ferentillo, approx. 10km/6.2mi NE of the fall.

Ferentillo

Two ruined castles dominate this village. *From here (5km/3mi N, then 2km/1.2mi further by a poor road) you can reach the solitary 7C abbey of* **San Pietro in Valle★**. The cloisters are decorated with fragments of 12C frescoes

and Roman sarcophagi. Open daily summer 10am–1pm 3–6pm; rest of the year by reservation only. Donation recommended. Across the road, the church of Santo Stefano has an odd collection of mummified corpses.

◔ Proceed along the SR 209 to the SR 320. Head in the direction of Norcia.

Norcia★

www.norcia.net.

Norcia, within the **Parco dei Monti Sibillini★★**, is birthplace of St Benedict, in 480. The town is known for its pork butchers, especially for salamis. Overlooking Piazza San Benedetto is the 16C **Castellina** fortress, which now houses the **Museo Civico-Diocesano**, and the 13C church of **San Benedetto**, with its Gothic façade. The frescoes inside date back to the 14C.

The High Plains of Castelluccio

Around 20km/12.4mi from Norcia, in the direction of Ascoli Piceno, the ramshackle hilltop village of **Castelluccio** is perched against a stunning backdrop of tundra-like scenery, an immense upland plain of the **Piano Grande★★**, which is carpeted with flowers in spring.

ADDRESSES

⌂ STAY

Prices increase during special events.

⊖⊜ **Hotel Aurora** – Via Apollinare 3. ℘0743 22 03 15. www.hotelauroraspoleto.it. 23 rooms. ⊑. Modern rooms near the Museo Archeologico.

⊖⊜ **Palazzo Dragoni** – Via Duomo 13. ℘0743 22 22 20. www.palazzodragoni.it. 14 rooms. ⊑. 14C palazzo beautifully furnished with antiques; some rooms have stunning valley views.

⊖⊜ **San Luca** – Via Interna delle Mura 21. ℘0743 22 33 99. www.hotelsanluca.com. 35 rooms. ⊑. At the base of town, many lovely details here like Deruta ceramics at breakfast, afternoon tea, fireplace in winter. Spacious rooms.

♀/EAT

🍽🍽 **Apollinare** – Via Sant'Agata 14. ☏0743 22 32 56. www.ristoranteapollinare.it. Elegant romantic atmosphere with cuisine that offers both tradition and innovation.

🍽🍽 **Pentagramma** – Via Tommaso Martani 4. ☏0743 22 31 41. www.ristorante pentagramma.it. Rustic stone walls. Wood-burning oven turns out excellent roast game. Pasta with fresh vegetables and saffron.

🍽🍽 **Tric Trac** – Via del Arringo/Piazza Duomo. ☏0743 44 592. www.ristorante trictrac.com. Outside seats have stunning view of the Duomo. Nice wine selection, and good specialities like game birds cooked in clay pots.

EVENTS AND FESTIVALS

Each summer the Spoleto Festival dei Due Mondi brings lively arts programmes. www.festivaldispoleto.com.

Todi★★

Perched on its own hill, Todi has retained walls from the Etruscan (Marzia Gateway), Roman and medieval periods. Side streets open to a lovely valley view★★.

SIGHTS
Piazza del Popolo★★

Todi's flourishing medieval commercial life is evidenced in the 13C palaces: **Palazzo dei Priori★**, **Palazzo del Capitano★** and **Palazzo del Popolo★**, one of the oldest communal palaces in Italy (1213), which houses art and antiquities. ♿Open Tue–Sun Apr–Oct 10am–1.30pm and 3–6pm, Nov–Mar 10.30am–1pm and 2.30–5pm. Closed 25 Dec, 1 Jan. 5€. ☏075 89 44 148. www.sistemamuseo.it.

Chiesa di San Fortunato★★

Piazza della Repubblica.
Gothic and Renaissance meet. Men and animals pop out of leaves carved around the **portal★★**. The lofty interior has **frescoes** (1432) by Masolino and the tomb of **Jacopone da Todi** (1230–1307), poet and Franciscan friar.

Duomo★

This early-12C Romanesque cathedral has a great and unusual rose window adorned with 36 *putti* faces.
Inside columns have medieval faces peeping out. Don't miss the beautiful **choir stalls**, its masterful intarsio panels depicting Renaissance street scenes.

▸ **Population:** 17 282
◉ **Michelin Map:** 563 N 19 – Umbria.
🛈 **Info:** Piazza del popolo 38, 06059 Todi (PG). ☏075 89 56 227. www.visitodi.it.
◗ **Location:** Roughly the same distance from Perugia, Terni, Orvieto and Spoleto.
◗ **Train:** Todi Ponte Rio (Terni 28mins).

ADDRESSES

🛏 STAY

🍽🍽 **Bed & Breakfast San Lorenzo Tre** – Via San Lorenzo 3 (2nd floor). ☏075 89 44 555. www.sanlorenzo3.it. Closed end Dec–15 Mar. 6 rooms. ⊂. A quiet, elegant establishment, with historic overtones but a homely feel. The rooms are individual in style and tastefully furnished with period pieces. Ask for a room with a view.

♀/EAT

🍽 **Antica Osteria De La Valle** – Via Ciuffelli 19. ☏340 818 47 75 (mobile). Closed Wed. A one-room rustic-style establishment complete with bar and bottles on display. The owner, who is also in charge of the cooking, offers a variety of dishes drawing on seasonal produce.

🍽 **Pane e Vino** – Via Ciuffelli 33. ☏075 89 45 448. www.panevinotodi.com. Closed Wed. Try chickpea soup with porcini mushrooms, roast fowl and other Umbrian specialities.

Orvieto★★

Orvieto rises dramatically from vertical cliffs of tuff, a remarkable site★★★. Once a major Etruscan centre, later Papal stronghold, here Clement VII took refuge in 1527 when Rome was sacked by French King Charles Via Vineyards below produce a pleasant white wine, Orvieto Classico.

VISIT
Duomo★★★

Cappella di San Brizio: Open daily. Closed Sun morning and during religious services. 3€ (ticket office in Piazza del Duomo 26). ℘0763 34 35 92. www.opsm.it/duomo/021.html.

The cathedral, in the transitional Romanesque-Gothic style, was begun in 1290 to enshrine the relics of the Miracle of Bolsena. Over 100 architects, sculptors, painters and mosaicists took part in the building, completed in 1600. The **Palazzo dei Papi★** now houses the **Museo dell'Opera** (open Nov–Feb 10am–1pm and 2–5pm, closed Tue; Apr–Sept 9.30am–7pm; Oct–Mar 10am–5pm, closed Tue; 4€: combined ticket with Palazzi Papali, Chiesa di Sant'Agostino, Palazzo Soliano, Libreria Albèri; ℘0763 34 24 77, www.museomodo.it).

Façade★★★

Boldest in structure and richest in colour among Italian-Gothic buildings, the original design was elaborated (c.1310–30) by the Sienese Lorenzo Maitani, and developed by Andrea Pisano, Andrea Orcagna and Sanmicheli. Maitani was also responsible for the **bas-reliefs★★** adorning the pillars which, reading from left to right, portray *Genesis*, *Jesse's Tree*, *Scenes from the New Testament* and the *Last Judgement*.

Interior

The nave and aisles are roofed with timber. Gothic vaulting covers the transepts and the chancel. Under the 16C organ is the entrance to **Cappella del Corporale**, the chapel which enshrines

the linen cloth *(corporal)* in which the bleeding Host was wrapped. A tabernacle encloses the **Reliquary★★** of the *corporal*, a masterpiece of medieval goldsmiths' work (1338).
A fine Gothic stained-glass **window★** in the chancel illustrates the Gospel.
The south transept gives access, beyond a wrought-iron grille (1516), to the famous **Cappella della Madonna di San Brizio**, painted with admirable **frescoes★★** (☉*see box, p618*). These were begun in 1447 by Fra Angelico, and then completed in 1490 by **Luca Signorelli** (c. 1445–1523).

▶ **Population:** 21 053
⚲ **Michelin Map:** 563 N 18 – Umbria.
🛈 **Info:** Piazza del Duomo 24, 05018 Orvieto (TR). ℘0763 34 17 72. www.inorvieto.it.
▶ **Location:** Orvieto is situated in southern Umbria, northwest of Lake Bolsena. The main access road is the A 1.
▶ **Train:** Orvieto (Roma Termini 1hr 11min).
🚏 **Don't Miss:** Underground Orvieto and Signorelli's frescoes in **Cappella della Madonna di San Brizio**.
🕑 **Timing:** Allow half a day.

In Step with Local Farmers

Umbria farmers aren't much for cinema or theatre, but love to dance. Look for postings of summer town festivals, sometimes called a *sagra*, sure to have food, an outdoor dance floor and music. Easter was the traditional time to open a bottle of Sagrantino *passito* wine, eaten with local cheese, bread, salami and boiled egg, all of which can make a lovely picnic.

A Few Minutes in Front of Luca Signorelli's Frescoes

The atmosphere that permeates the Chapel of San Brizio is even more disturbing if one considers the images as the anticipation of an apocalyptic day which could strike at any time. Monsters, the torture of the damned and the corpse-like colour of the demons all contribute to a sense of anguish. Every detail is imbued with a monstrous quality, even the grotesques. The frescoes should be read starting from the north wall. The first is a portrayal of the Preaching of the Antichrist; the Antichrist, who has the devil as his adviser, has taken on the appearance of Christ. Signorelli has portrayed himself in the noble dark figure on the extreme left. This image is followed by the Calling of the Elect to Heaven.

On the wall of the altar, on the left: the Angels leading the Elect to Paradise; on the right: Angels chasing out the Reprobates, with scenes of hell.

On the right wall: the Damned in Hell and the Resurrection of the Dead.

On the west wall, in the End of the World, the Sun and Moon have lost all traces of familiarity; the Earth is in the throes of an earthquake. A sibyl, a prophet and demons are all represented in this scene.

ADDITIONAL SIGHTS
Underground Orvieto

&. Guided tours only. 6€. 11am, 12.15, 4pm, 5.15pm. ℘0763 34 48 91. www.orvietounderground.it.

Orvieto lies on a bed of volcanic earth, with underground chambers (already present in Etruscan times) dug out of the hill, now cellars. These caves (more than 1 000 are officially listed) hold medieval niches for funerary urns, the foundations of a 14C oil mill and a 6C BC well.

Pozzo di San Patrizio★★

Open daily Mar–Apr and Sept–Oct 9am–6.45pm; May–Aug 9am–7.45pm; Nov–Feb 10am–4.45pm. 5€. ℘0763 34 37 68.

St Patrick's Well was dug by order of Pope Clement VII de' Medici to supply the town with water in case of siege. The well is over 62m/203ft deep.

Palazzo del Popolo★

The Romanesque-Gothic town hall has a majestic balcony, elegant windows and curious fluted merlons.

Quartiere Vecchio★

This quiet quarter has retained its old houses, medieval towers and churches, including **San Giovenale**, decorated by 13C–15C frescoes.

Museo Archeologico and Museo Faina

&.Open daily 8.30am–7.30pm. 3€. ℘0763 34 10 39.
Museo Faina: Open Apr–Sept 9.30am–6pm; Oct–Mar 10am–5pm. Closed Mon (winter), 1 Jan, 25–26 Dec. 4.50€. ℘0763

Marble, mosaics and intricate stone patterns enliven the façade of the Duomo

© Iteximage/iStockphoto.com

AREZZO A 1, FLORENCE, ROME

ORVIETO

WHERE TO STAY		WHERE TO EAT	
Albergo Filippeschi	①	I Sette Consoli	①
Corso	②	Palomba (La)	②
Palazzone	③		

34 15 11. www.museofaina.it. Two archaeological museums; the latter, a particularly rich private **Etruscan Collection★**, includes carved terra-cotta funerary urns and a rare 4C BC sarcophagus.

Piazza della Repubblica
Once the ancient forum, now dominated by the church of Sant'Andrea.
Etruscan Necropolis of Crocifisso.

ADDRESSES

STAY
Corso – Corso Cavour 343. 0763 34 20 20. www.hotelcorso.net. 16 rooms. This stone palazzo is a family-run comfortable hotel with pretty terrace.

Albergo Filippeschi – Via Filippeschi 19. 0763 34 32 75. www. albergofilippeschi.it. 15 rooms. A simple, family establishment housed in an old palazzo. Excellent location – ideal for those exploring the town on foot.

Palazzone – Rocca Ripesena 67. 0763 39 36 14. www.locandapalazzone. com. 5 rooms. Beautifully restored medieval cardinal's country house, set amid the vineyards of one of Orvieto's best wineries. An idyllic stay. Swimming pool. Restaurant open to outside guests.

EAT
La Palomba – Via Cipriano Manente 16. 0763 34 33 95. Closed Wed. Good traditional Umbrian food at reasonable prices.

I Sette Consoli – Piazza Sant'Angelo 1a. 0763 34 39 11. Reservation recommended. Imaginative cooking. Nice rustic-style interior, but garden with its wonderful view of the Duomo is stunning.

EVENTS AND FESTIVALS
Late December, Orvieto hosts the winter session of the **Umbria Jazz Festival** (*see PERUGIA*), with five days of music, culture and events culminating in a special New Year's Eve programme.

Lake Trasimeno★

Lago Trasimeno

Trasimeno, south-central Italy's largest lake, is fed by no springs or rivers. Its only water source is rain or snow, and its level fluctuates accordingly. You can swim in it, but the bottom is very muddy, making it better suited to boating, walks, bicycling or a ferry ride.

▶ **Population:** 15 618 (Castiglione del Lago)
⚅ **Michelin Map:** 563 M19.
🗎 **Info:** www.lagotrasimeno.net.
▷ **Location:** The lake is west of Perugia and east of Montepulciano.
🕒 **Timing:** Sunset is lovely.
🧍 **Kids:** Boat, fish, take the ferry, ride horses, picnic.

SIGHTS

The Islands

Isola Polvese, largest of the three islands, belongs to the province of Perugia, which has a research centre dedicated to biodiversity. An experimental olive grove occupies almost half of the surface, which tests ancient species that require less fertiliser that pollutes the waters. A road circles the island *(about 50min to walk it)* and offers pretty views of Castiglione del Lago.

Isola Maggiore★ counts some thirty residents. St Francis observed Lent on the island in 1211, which has the church of San Giuliano and the 14C Castello Guglielmi. The Marquise Guglielmi created a lace workshop there in 1904. Two other churches are Gothic-style Sant'Archangelo, and San Salvatore, in Romanesque style.

Castiglione del Lago

Train: Castiglione del Lago (Firenze Campo di Marte 1hr 27mins).
Castiglione del Lago is perched on a promontory. The tiny medieval town has Palazzo della Corgna, and the 16C Ascagnio delle Corgna, the palace with rooms decorated with frescoes by Niccolò Circignani, a Mannerist. Hannibal's

GETTING AROUND

Three islands float on the lake: **Isola Polvese, southeast, Isola Maggiore, north and Island Minore** (not served by the ferry).
Access by ferries *(traghetti)*: each line makes a dozen crossings a day, about 10 minutes from the pier. To **Isola Polvese from San Feliciano** (4.20€). To **Maggiore from Castiglione del Lago** (4.80€), **Passignano** (4.80€) and **Tuoro** (4.20€). The two islands are connected (6.60€). Direct links between **Castiglione del Lago and Passignano** for the day rate (14.30€). Times are displayed on the landing or from **Umbria Mobilità**, 📞075 9 637 637 or www.umbriamobilita.it.

route is illustrated including the Battle of Lake Trasimeno (⚅*see box*).
The 13C pentagonal Castello del Leone (Lion's Castle) was built by Frederick II.

Naturalistica Oasi La Valle

At Passignano, Magione fork *(oasilav-alle.provincia.perugia.it)* is a protected

The Battle of Lake Trasimeno

On 23 June 217 BC Hannibal destroyed the army of the Consul Flaminius near today's town of Tuoro sul Trasimeno. The legions formed a column along the lake when they fell into the Carthaginian general's ambush. Hannibal's attack, sudden and decisive, froze the Romans, unable to deploy. After several hours of fighting, 15 000 legionaries died, including their leader – the lake was red with blood, and 10 000 were taken prisoner.

wetland, with a bird and animal refuge. Bring binoculars, where along a jetty there may be herons, egrets, kingfishers and even raccoons.

Panicale

◗ 15km/9.3mi S of Castiglione del Lago.
This medieval village curls up a hill that overlooks Lake Trasimeno. The church of San Sebastiano (one of two churches and theatre offered in a tour, 5€) features the Martyrdom of St Sebastian by Perugino.

Città della Pieve

◗ 23km/14.3mi S of Castiglione del Lago.
Founded in the 7C–8C, here Pietro Vannucci, known as Perugino, was born. The cathedral has his *Baptism of Jesus* and the *Virgin between Saints Peter and Paul, Gervais and Protais*. The Oratorio di Santa Maria dei Bianchi has the elegant *Adoration of the Magi*, in harmony with the gentle Umbrian countryside, while the church of Santa Maria dei Servi has a *Descent from the Cross*.

Città di Castello

In northern Umbria, surrounded by an imposing wall, Città di Castello has a Renaissance historic centre. Contemporary artist Alberto Burri was born there and has two museums devoted to his work. The city has ancient Umbrian and Roman roots, with much of its plan revised by a Florentine architect in the 15C–16C.

▶ **Population:** 40 567
👟 **Michelin Map:** 563 M19.
🛈 **Info:** www.comune.citta-di-castello.perugia.it.
◗ **Location:** 53km/32.9mi north of Perugia, Città di Castello is served by the E45.
👁 **Don't Miss:** Alberto Burri contemporary art collection.
🕐 **Timing:** Allow half a day.

VISIT

🕙 Ask about a combined ticket valid for various museums.

Collezioni Burri★★

Palazzo Albizzini, Via Albizzini 1.
Open Tue–Sat 9am–12.30pm and 2.30–6pm, Sun and public hols 10.30am–12.30pm and 3–6pm. 6€.
📞 075 85 54 649.
www.fondazioneburri.org.
Alberto Burri (1915–1995) was an early proponent of Arte Povera, using humble, found materials with his 1950s focus on bags *(sacchi)*, later on flame-retardant plastic *(combustione)*, wood *(legno)* and iron *(ferro)*, then to sawdust and glue (Celotex) and resins.
Some 257 Burri works are spread over two buildings, the larger in the **old tobacco barns**, near the station (Ex Seccatoi del Tobacco, Via Pierucci; open Tue–Sat 9.30am–12.30pm and 2.30–6pm, Sun and hols 10.30am–12.30pm and 3–6pm (7

Jan–8 Mar only Sat pm); 6€, 10€ for both buildings; 📞 075 85 59 848).

🐾 WALKING TOUR

Begin in Piazza Garibaldi with its Renaissance palaces. Near Palazzo Albizzini is **San Francesco Vitelli**, a church with a chapel which was designed by Giorgio Vasari. In Piazza Matteotti, **Palazzo del Podestà** has a Baroque façade. Along Corso Cavour, a Gothic-style palace has bifurcated windows.

Museo del Duomo

Piazza Gabriotti 3a. Open Tue–Sun Apr–Sept 10am–1pm and 3.30–6pm, Oct–Mar 10am–12.30pm and 3–5pm. 6€. 📞 075 85 54 705.
www.museoduomocdc.it.
Religious art is on display here from the early Christian era to the 19C, notably the *Virgin, Child and St John* painted by Pintu-

ricchio. In Piazza Gabriotti, the Medieval **Palazzo Comunale (Municipal Palace)** faces the Torre Civica, the 14C civic tower.

Pinacoteca Comunale
Via della Cannoniera. Open Apr–Oct Tue–Sun 10am–1pm and 2.30–6.30pm, Nov–Mar 10am–1pm and 3–6pm. 6€.

✆075 85 20 656. www.cittadicastelloturismo.it. Among the artists displayed in the art museum are Maestro di Città di Castello *(Virgin and Child Enthroned)*, Raphael *(Holy Trinity)* and Luca Signorelli *(Martyrdom of St Sebastian)*.

Gubbio★★

The small town of Gubbio, spread out over the slopes of Monte Ingino, has preserved its rich cultural and artistic heritage almost intact. Encircling ramparts, buildings of warm yellow stone roofed with Roman tiles, and towers and palaces outlined against a grim landscape make it easy to imagine the harsh atmosphere of the Middle Ages.

▸ **Population:** 32 563
⏱ **Michelin Map:** 563 L 19 – Umbria.
🛈 **Info:** Via della Repubblica 15. ✆075 92 20 693. www.comune.gubbio.pg.it.
▶ **Location:** Gubbio lies off the S 298, 40km/24.8mi from Perugia.
👁 **Don't Miss:** The Old Town and pretty Fabriano.
🕐 **Timing:** Allow half a day.

OLD TOWN★★
Piazza Grande stands at the heart the charming but austere Old Town with its steep, narrow streets, spanned by arches. The houses, flanked by palaces and towers, often double as ceramic artist's workshops.

The façades sometimes have two doors; the narrower Door of Death was through which coffins were brought out. The most picturesque streets are Via Piccardi, Baldassini, dei Consoli, XX Settembre, Galeotti and those along the river, leading to Piazza 40 Martiri.

Palazzo dei Consoli★★
Open daily Apr–Oct 10am–1pm and 3–6pm; Nov–Mar 10am–1pm and 2.30–5.30pm. Closed 1 Jan, 13–15 May, 25 Dec. 5€. ✆075 92 74 298. www.comune.gubbio.pg.it.
Overlooking Piazza Grande, this imposing Gothic building, supported by great arches rising above Via Baldassini, has a majestic façade which reflects the palace's internal plan. The stairway leads up to the vast hall *(salone)* where

Palazzo dei Consoli

© vision images/Fotolia.com

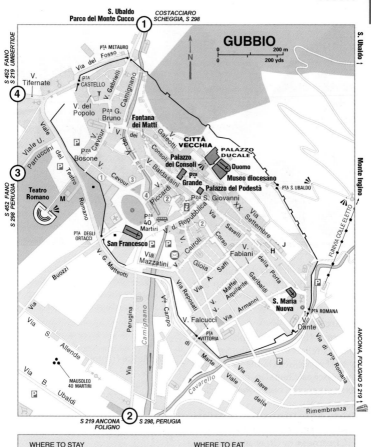

GUBBIO

WHERE TO STAY	
Gattapone	(2)
Le Logge	(4)

WHERE TO EAT	
All'Antico Frantoio	(1)
Fabiani	(3)

assemblies were held and which contains statues and stonework.

Its Museo Civico feataures the **Tavole Eugubine**, bronze tablets (2C–1C BC) which are inscribed in Umbria's ancient language. Unique in linguistic and epigraphic terms, the tablets record the region's ancient political organisation and religious practices.

Palazzo Ducale★

&Open Tue–Sun 8.30am–7.30pm. Closed 1 Jan, 25 Dec. 5€ (includes the Museo d'Arte). ℘075 92 75 872.

The Ducal Palace, which dominates the town, was built from 1470 onwards for Federico de Montefeltro. The design is attributed to Laurana, although it

Umbria Festivals

Annual festivals to enjoy: Medieval Gaite in Bevagna (May/June), Onion in Cannara (Sept), Infiorata in Spello (Corpus Christi), Sagrantino Wine in Montefalco (Sept), Jazz in Orvieto (Dec) and Perugia (summer), Due Mondi summer performances in Spoleto, Eurochocolate in Perugia.

was probably finished by Francesco di Giorgio Martini, who was inspired by the Ducal Palace at Urbino. The elegant

View of the old town on via Gattapone

© O. Fortr/MICHELIN

courtyard is delicately decorated. The rooms are adorned with frescoes and lovely chimneypieces.

Churches

Duomo – The cathedral's plain façade has bas-reliefs showing the Symbols of the Evangelists. Off the single nave, the **Episcopal Chapel** to the right is the room where the bishop would follow the services.

Chiesa di San Francesco – The walls of the north apse are covered with early-15C **frescoes★** by Ottaviano Nelli.

Chiesa di Santa Maria Nuova – Houses a fine **fresco★** by Ottaviano Nelli.

Basilica di Sant'Ubaldo – This church, on the top of Monte Ingino with a fine **view★** of the valley, is dedicated to Gubbio's patron saint. It is accessible via cablecar near Porta Romana. Inside the church are kept the remains of St Ubald.

Teatro Romano

This Roman theatre dates from the reign of Augustus.

ADDRESSES

🛏 STAY

😊😊 **Gattapone** – Via Beni 11. ☎075 92 72 489. www.hotelgattapone.net. 18 rooms. Charming small hotel near San Giovanni, below the Old Town.

😊😊😊 **Le Logge** – Via Piccardi 7/9. ☎075 92 77 574. 6 rooms. In a historic residence, spacious rooms are smartly furnished. Breakfast is in the garden, a bit dark.

🍴 EAT

😊 **All'Antico Frantoio** – Via Cavour 18. ☎075 92 21 780. www.allanticofrantoio.it. Closed Mon. The grand vaulted room with ancient press serves good *risotto con funghi* and pizza with white truffles.

😊😊 **Fabiani** – Piazza 40 Martiri 26. ☎075 92 74 639. www.ristorantefabiani.it. Closed Tue and Jan. Elegant ambience in this 15C palazzo which features Umbrian specialities. Meals served outside in the courtyard in the summer. Car park nearby.

EVENTS AND FESTIVALS

Most spectacular of Gubbio's traditional festivals is the Candle Race, Corsa dei Ceri, on May 15. Three "candles", or *ceri,* high wooden poles 4m/13ft tall, each carved with a saint (including St Ubald, patron of Gubbio), are carried through steep crowded streets in a frenzied 5km/3mi race to the Basilica of Sant'Ubaldo. "Candle" carriers, dressed in medieval costumes, must not drop their very heavy "candles", and must carry them into the church, before the doors are slammed shut. These three strange *ceri,* whose origins date back to the pre-Christian era, grace Umbria's coat of arms.

Le Marche

The Marches

A popular saying in Italy, "Better to have a corpse in the house than a Marchigiano at the door", refers to when men from Le Marche (Marchigiani) were tax collectors for the Papal States. Today, Le Marche is known for its hilly landscapes, the Sibillini Mountains, family-friendly seaside resorts, for shoemaking in Fermo and Macerata, and for the Renaissance city of Urbino, where painter Raphael was born and a lively university town. Ascoli Piceno with its medieval towers is lighter and more luminous than San Gimignano, its piazzas like grand salons. Fabriano, famous for papermaking, is lovely. The capital and port Ancona enjoys proximity to the rugged Conero. Tolentino's Cappelone has beautiful frescoes.

Suspended Towns

Apart from flat shoreline cities like busy Pesaro (a good base to explore San Marino) and Fano, an airy yacht-making town, most are picturesque hilltop towns, many graced with historic 18C and 19C theatres. Mac-

Highlights

1   Rent a boat and explore the coves of the **Conero** (p626)
2   Revel in the Renaissance court of **Palazzo Ducale** in Urbino (p628)
3   Walk, bike, picnic or ride horses at the medieval **Abbadia di Fiastra** (p631)
4   Go **spelunking** in the **Grotte di Frasassi** (p632)
5   Wander among the Medieval towers of **Ascoli Piceno** (p633)

erata has an outdoor arena, Sferisterio, Roman amphitheatre in Urbisaglia, and the medieval Abbadia di Fiastra, a lovely base for families. Hill towns are an economical refuge from the summer crowds.

Local cuisine can be simple, or delicate and complex. Look for *galatina*, local salamis like *ciauscolo*, grilled meats, white truffles, fish dishes, fried delicacies including olives, and *vincisgrassi*, a rich lasagna with chicken livers and béchamel. Local red wines like Rosso Conero, Lacrima di Moro d'Alba and Rosso Piceno, and whites like Passerina, Verdicchio and Pecorino are worth seeking out.

Riviera del Conero

©fotelo/Fotolia.com

Ancona★

Ancona, the capital, is a busy port that serves Italy, Croatia and Greece. The town's name derives from Greek *ankon*, elbow, the shape of its promontory. The historic centre has first-rate theatre, Trajan's Port and Arch, Vanvitelli's pentagonal building, churches, museums, and in summer hosts a jazz festival.

SIGHTS

Duomo★

Open daily 8am–noon and 3–7pm (winter to 6pm).
Dedicated to Ancona's patron, St Cyriacus, 4C martyr, this Romanesque cathedral combines Byzantine and Lombard architectural features.

Museo Archeologico Nazionale delle Marche

Via Ferretti 6, at the southern end of Piazza del Senato. Open Tue–Sun 8.30am–7.30pm. Closed 1 Jan, 1 May, 25 Dec. 4€. ☎071 20 26 02. ww.archeomarche.beniculturali.it.
Interesting prehistoric and ancient works, especially Roman bronzes.

Pinacoteca Comunale Podesti

Via Pizzecolli 17. Temporarily closed for restoration. ☎071 22 25 041.
www.anconacultura.it.
Works by Crivelli, Titian, Lorenzo Lotto, Carlo Maratta and Guercino. There is also a modern art gallery.

Chiesa di Santa Maria della Piazza★

This 10C Romanesque church façade (1210) is adorned with amusing knights, archers, animals and other figures. Built over two 5C and 6C churches, it retains some early mosaic fragments.

Loggia dei Mercanti★

This 15C hall for merchants' meetings has a Venetian-Gothic façade.

▶ **Population:** 102 997
⚙ **Michelin Map:** 563 L 22. Town plan in the Michelin Atlas Italy – Marches.
🅹 **Info:** Via della Loggia 50, 60121 Ancona. ☎071 35 89 91.
◖ **Location:** Ancona is accessible via the A 14.
◖ **Train:** Castelferretti (airport station) (Ancona Centrale 14 min).
◉ **Don't Miss:** The Riviera del Conero, the monuments in the city.
👥 **Kids:** Boat trips along the Riviera from Sirolo and Numana.

Arco di Traiano

The arch was erected in honour of Trajan, who built the port in AD 115. The fort nearby, designed by Vanvitelli, hosts occasional exhibitions.

EXCURSIONS

Jesi★

◐ 30km/18.6mi SW of Ancona.
Jesi's medieval and Renaissance nucleus is surrounded by fine **city walls★★** (13C–16C), gates and towers. Try to see a performance in Teatro Pergolesi, an 18C gem. Verdicchio di Jesi is the area's white wine.

Pinacoteca Comunale★

♿ Open Tue–Sat 10am–1pm and 4–7pm (summer 10am–7pm). 6€. ☎0731 53 83 42.
The municipal picture gallery, in Palazzo Pianetti, has a Rococo **gallery★**. The collection includes stunning paintings by the Venetian artist **Lorenzo Lotto** (ⓒ*see p112*).

🚗 DRIVING TOUR

LA RIVIERA DEL CONERO★

45km/28mi.

Portonovo★

12km/7.4mi SE.

The rugged Conero with its dense forests, cliffs and pristine waters is a welcome break from some of the modern coastal architecture.

Portonovo lies in a picturesque setting formed by the coastline of the **Conero Massif**. **Il Fortino**, the Napoleonic fort, now the lovely Hotel Fortino with good restaurant ($\mathcal{C}$071 80 150; www.hotelfortino.it). Private pebble beach area, but Portonovo also has a free beach nearby and camping (limited parking).

The panoramic road south for 20km/12.4mi winds through Rosso Conero (local red wine) vineyards, pretty villages including **Sirolo** (with a lovely small 1875 theatre) and **Numana**, from where there are boat trips to nearby coves.

▶ Porto Recanati has a lovely small beach area, nice for a swim.

Loreto★

Loreto is a pilgrimage site for its "House of Mary" in **Piazza della Madonna★**. Next to the **basilica★**, Palazzo Apostolico houses the **Pinacoteca★**, with **paintings★** by Lorenzo Lotto that include St Christopher. &Open Tue–Sun mid-Jun–mid-Sept 10am–1pm and 4–7pm (Sat–Sun to 8pm); rest of the year 10am–1pm and 3–6pm (Sat–Sun to 7pm). Closed 1 Jan, Easter, 1 May, 15 Aug, 25 Dec. 4€.

Il Santuario della Santa Casa★★

Open daily 6.15am–7.30pm (Oct–Mar 7pm). $\mathcal{C}$071 97 47 155. www.santuarioloreto.it.

Giuliano da Sangallo, Bramante and Vanvitelli contributed to the decoration of this church. Admire the triple **apse★** and Sangallo's dome from the outside. The **three bronze doors★★** are adorned with fine late-16C and early-17C statues. The **Sacristy of St John★** (San Giovanni) has a vault painted with frescoes by Luca Signorelli. The 16C **Santa Casa★★** was sculpted by Antonio Sansovino and others.

▶ Continue along the SS 77 for a further 7km/4.3mi.

Recanati

This little town, birthplace of the Italian poet **Giacomo Leopardi** (1798–1837), has his mementoes in **Palazzo Leopardi** (Tue–Sun 9am–6pm, fall–winter 9.30–1pm, 2–5.30pm, $\mathcal{C}$071 75 73 380; 7€ library, 10€ for exhibit and library combined ticket; www.giacomoleopardi.it). **Museo Villa Colleredo Pinacoteca Comunale** (Via Gregorio XII; Tue–Sun 10am–1pm, 4–7pm, Aug open daily; 4€; $\mathcal{C}$071 757 0410; www.villacolloredomels.it) has an astonishing *Annunciation* (1532) by Lorenzo Lotto. **Teatro Persiani** is a gem of a theatre.

ADDRESSES

🛏 STAY

🍽 **Hotel City** – Via Matteotti 112/114. $\mathcal{C}$071 20 70 949. www.hotelcityancona.it. 39 rooms. ➽. A good solution for those travelling by car and wanting to stay in the centre of town. Rooms are on the small side. Furnishings are modern and functional. In summer breakfast is served on the terrace.

🍽 **Rocco Locanda & Ristorante** – Via Torrione 1, Sirolo. $\mathcal{C}$071 93 30 558. Lovely modern restaurant with creative cuisine and good wines. Also pleasant rooms to rent.

🍽 **Hotel Fortino Napoleonico** – Portonovo. $\mathcal{C}$071 80 14 50. www.hotelfortino.it. Historic circular Napoleonic fort converted to charming hotel. Good restaurant set in cosy stone room or on the terrace, stunning at sunset.

🍴 EAT

🍽 **La Moretta** – Piazza Plebiscito 52, Ancona. $\mathcal{C}$071 20 23 17. www.trattoriamoretta.com. Closed Sun and 1–7 Jan. Run by the same family since 1897. Serves traditional, local cooking. Pleasant rustic-style interior, but for atmosphere try to get a table outside – the terrace looks out onto the square and the church of San Domenico.

Urbino★★

The walled town of Urbino, with its rose-coloured brick houses, is built on two hills overlooking the undulating countryside bathed in a glorious golden light. Urbino was ruled by the Montefeltro family from the 12C onwards and reached its peak in the reign (1444–82) of Duke Federico da Montefeltro, a wise leader, who created a court that attracted top talent in letters, the arts, philosophy, science and mathematics. Urbino was the birthplace of Raphael (Raffaello Sanzio) (1483–1520).

▶ **Population:** 15 627
🕑 **Michelin Map:** 562–563 K 19 – Marches.
Info: Piazza Rinascimento 1, 61029 Urbino (PU). ✆0722 26 13. www.turismo. pesarourbino.it.
▶ **Location:** Urbino is 36km/ 22.4mi from Pesaro, to which it is linked by the SP 423.
Don't Miss: Palazzo Ducale and Galleria Nazionale delle Marche.
🕐 **Timing:** Allow two days.
🕑 **Also See:** *SAN MARINO*.

SIGHTS
Palazzo Ducale★★★
Visit: 1hr 30min.
Begun for Duke Federico by Dalmatian architect **Luciano Laurana** and completed by the Sienese **Francesco di Giorgio Martini**, the palace (1444–72) is a masterpiece of harmony and elegance. The design hinges on the old town's west panorama, and the original façade overlooking the valley is pierced by superimposed loggias and flanked by two tall round towers. The inner courtyard, inspired by earlier Florentine models, is a classic example of Renaissance harmony with its pure, delicate lines, serene architectural rhythm and subtle combination of rose-coloured brick and white marble.

The ground floor has **Museo Archeologico** (lapidary fragments: inscriptions, stelae, architectural remains, etc.), a library, the **Biblioteca del Duca**, and cellars or **cantine**.

Galleria Nazionale delle Marche★★
🕭 Open Tue–Sun 8.30am–7.15pm, Mon 8.30am–2pm. Ticket office closes 1 hour, 15 min before closing time. Closed 1 Jan, 25 Dec. 5€. ✆199 151 123. www.palazzoducaleurbino.it

Duomo and Palazzo Ducale
© S.Bedessi / Fototeca ENIT

The palace's first-floor rooms with original decoration host the National Gallery of Le Marche with great **masterpieces★★★**: a predella of the *Profanation of the Host* (1465–9) by Paolo Uccello, *Madonna di Senigallia* and a curious *Flagellation of Christ* by Piero della Francesca (🕮 *see p109*), the *Ideal City* (🕮 *see PIENZA, p592*) by Laurana and the portrait of a woman, known as **The Mute**, by Raphael. Duke Federico's **studiolo★★★** is decorated with magnificent intarsia panelling.

A collection of 16C–17C Italian paintings and 17C–18C majolica is on the second floor. North of the palace is Valadier's early-19C cathedral.

Casa di Raffaello★

57 Via Raffaello. Open Mar–Oct Mon–Sat 9am–1pm and 3–7pm, Sun and public hols 10am–1pm; Nov–Feb Mon–Sat 9am–2pm, Sun and public hols 10am–1pm. Closed 1 Jan, 25 Dec. 3.50€. 🖉0722 32 01 05. www.accademiaraffaello.it.

Property of his painter father, Giovanni Sanzio or Santi, Raphael lived in this 15C house until the age of 14. The house contains mementoes and period furniture.

Oratori di San Giovanni Battista e San Giuseppe

Via Barocci. Open Mar–Oct Mon–Sat 10am–12.30pm and 3–5.30pm, Sun and public hols 10am–12.30pm; Nov–Feb 10am–1pm. 2.50€ (San Giovanni), 2€ (San Giuseppe). 🖉199 151 123.

Two adjacent churches, the first is 14C with curious **frescoes★★** of St John the Baptist's life, by the Saimbeni brothers. The second, dated from the 16C, has a colossal statue of St Joseph (18C) painted in grisaille, and a life-size stucco **crib★** by Federico Brandani (1522–75)

Strada Panoramica★★

Starting from Piazza Roma, this scenic road skirts a hillside and affords admirable **views★★** of the lower town.

🚗 DRIVING TOUR

IN THE FOOTSTEPS OF THE MALATESTA

60km/37.3mi. Allow at least one day.

▷ Follow the SS 423 to Montecchio, then turn left to Gradara.

Gradara

15km/9.3mi NW.

Gradara is a medieval town, almost intact. **The Rocca★** is a well-preserved example of 13C and 14C military architecture. Here Gianni Malatesta is said to have come upon and then murdered his wife, Francesca da Rimini, and her lover, his brother Paolo Malatesta, who as Dante recounts in *Inferno* "read no more that day", their fate, inseparable cranes perpetually batted by the wind. Open Mon 8.30am–1pm, Tue–Sun 8.30am–6.30pm. Closed 1 Jan, 25 Dec. 4€. 🖉0541 96 41 15. www.gradara.org.

An attractive stretch of **coastline★** extends between Gabrice and Pesaro *(15km/9.3mi S)*.

▷ Take the SS 16 S to Pesaro.

Pesaro★

Train: Pesaro (Ancona 30 mins).

A busy Adriatic port, Pesaro was the birthplace of the composer **Gioacchino Rossini** and every summer hosts a world-class opera festival. Rossini's house (no. 34 Via Rossini) is now a museum (same admission times and charges as the Musei Civici, below).

Palazzo Ducale – The 15C Ducal Palace, built for the Sforza, overlooks busy Piazza del Popolo with its fountain adorned with tritons and sea horses. The crenellated façade has an arcaded portico, with windows adorned with festoons and cherubs.

Museums★ – The Musei Civici has key paintings by the Venetian Giovanni Bellini, including the famous *Pala di Pesaro* (1475), an immense altarpiece with the Virgin. Note the fine Renaissance majolica in the **ceramics section★★**, along with Pesaro Rose china that became the fashion for the flourishing locals.

Gioacchino Rossini Tour (Pesaro 1792– Passy 1868)

Rossini's career was characterised by a "crescendo" which catapulted him from Pesaro into a realm of principal European courts. His work has an aloof sense of irony about the worries of the world, in the context of a typically theatrical humour, and ultimately attains a pessimistic view similar to that of Leopardi, who was also from Le Marche. Aged 37, Rossini stopped composing and retired from public life. Rossini Opera Festival in the summer is considered one of Europe's most prestigious opera festivals. Among his most celebrated works are *The Italian Girl in Algiers*, *The Barber of Seville*, *Cinderella* and *William Tell*.

Take a break next door at the historic *enoteca.* Open Jun–Sept Tue–Sun 10am–1pm and 4.30–7.30, Oct–May Fri–Sun also 3.30–6.30pm. Closed 1 Jan, 25 Dec. 10€ including Casa Rossini. ☎0721 38 75 41. www.pesaromusei.it.

Museo della Marineria (free; www.pesarocultura.it) has an archival display of maritime life, with a guided tour to explain it.

◉ Continue S on the SS 16. 11km/6.9mi SE.

Fano ⚓

This major yacht-building centre and seaside resort has new yachts that roll through town at night, a Guercino painting Robert Browning rhapsodised in a poem, the lovely Fortuna theatre, delicious *brodetto* (fish stew; try **Ristorante Casa Nolfi**, *Via Gasparoli 59*) and a church with paintings by young Raphael, his father Giovanni, and his maestro, Perugino.

Corte Malatestiana★ – Malatesta rulers between 13C–15C brought their Renaissance courtyard-garden and palace. This ideal theatrical set houses **Museo Civico.** Open Tue–Sat 9am–1pm, afternoon hours vary, Sun also. 4€. ☎0721 82 83 62. www.cultura.pesarourbino.it.

The **Chiesa di Santa Maria Nuova**, dating from 16C–18C has a **painting★** on the left side by Perugino, and across the nave, one by Giovanni Santi, father of young Raphael, who is said to have painted scenes on the predella.

Fontana della Fortuna – *Piazza XX Settembre*. This is a 16C fountain of Fano's protector, the goddess Fortune, near the lovely theatre named for her.

Arco d'Augusto – This 1C arch has a main opening and two side ones for pedestrians. Nearby a bas-relief on San Michele church's façade portrays the arch in its original forooms. To the left of the arch are the remains of the Roman wall.

ADDRESSES

🏠 STAY

😐😐/😐😐😐😐 **San Domenico** – Piazza Rinascimento 3. ☎0722 26 26. www.viphotels.it. In a former monastery that faces the Ducal Palace, this luxury hotel has all modern comforts. The family also runs economical hotels in the centre.

😐😐😐😐 **Excelsior** – Lungomare Nazario Sauro 30–34, Pesaro. ☎0721 63 00 11. www.excelsiorpesaro.it. This luxurious Pesaro beach hotel, with 1950s-inspired decor and whimsical touches, is tops in comfort, all run flawlessly by Antonella. Excellent spa, restaurant and lovely beach facilities.

🍴 EAT

😐 **Casetta Vaccai** – Via Mazzolari 22, Pesaro. ☎0721 69 201. Lively wine and coffee bar next to the Pinacoteca.

😐😐 **Il Cortegiano** – Via Puccinotti 13, Urbino. ☎0722 32 03 07. www.ilcortegiano.it. Have a snack at the bar or outside facing the Ducal Palace; even better in the back is the formal dining room with gourmet lunch or dinner, good wines.

Fermo★

Fermo, a lovely town, is the capital of Le Marche's newest province, Fermo, enriched by artisans in the shoe and hat industries. Enhanced by its hillside setting★, which overlooks the countryside and sea, the heart of its historic centre is the elegant Piazza del Popolo.

SIGHTS
Piazza del Popolo★
The piazza is surrounded by arcades, 16C porticoes and bordered by palaces, including the stunning 15C–16C Palazzo dei Priori (Priors' Palace), the Palazzo degli Studi, now the municipal library, and opposite, the Palazzo Apostolico.

Pinacoteca Civica
♿ Open Tue–Fri 10.30am–1pm and 3.30–6pm (Sat–Sun to 7pm); summer Mon–Thu 10.30am–1pm and 4–8pm, Fri–Sun 10.30am–7.30pm. 3€. ℘0734 21 71 40. www.comune.fermo.it.
The art museum boasts a fine collection, which includes elegant late -Gothic Scenes from the Life of St Lucy by Jacobello del Fiore (1394–1439) and the Adoration of the Shepherds by Rubens (1577–1640), one of the finest works produced by the artist during his sojourn in Italy. In the Map Room there is an 18C terraqueous globe.
Near the Piazza, in Via degli Aceti, are the Roman cisterns (same admission times and charges as the Pinacoteca) dating from the 1C AD; the 30 interconnecting chambers that are Italy's largest.

Piazza del Duomo
From this esplanade in front of the cathedral there are splendid views★★ of the Ascoli area, the Apennines, the Adriatic and Conero Peninsula.

Duomo★
Open daily Jul–Aug 10am–12.30pm and 4–8pm; mid-Sept 10am–1pm and 3.30–6pm (Sat 9.30am–12.30pm). Call for opening times rest of the year. Guided tour 2€. ℘0734 22 90 05.

▶ **Population:** 37 915
🚗 **Michelin Map:** 563 M 23 – Marches.
🛈 **Info:** Piazza del Popolo 6. ℘0734 22 79 40. www.comune.fermo.it.
▶ **Location:** Fermo is close to the Adriatic Coast.
👁 **Don't Miss:** Piazza del Popolo and local shoemakers.
🕐 **Timing:** Allow a day for the town and excursions.
👪 **Kids:** Papermaking at the Museo della Carta e della Filigrana and stalactites and stalagmites at Grotte di Frasassi.

www.fermodiocesi.it.
The Romanesque-Gothic cathedral (1227), built by the Maestri Comacini, has a majestic façade★ in white Istrian stone. Once the site of a temple, there are Roman ruins on the lower level.

EXCURSIONS
Porto San Giorgio
▶6.5km/4mi E. Train: PSG (Ancona 40 mins). A popular seaside resort with 3km/1.8mi of sandy beach and a modern marina.

Sant'Elpidio a Mare and Casette d'Ete
From Fermo head northwest towards Sant'Elpidio a Mare, which has a small shoe museum, Museo della Calzatura (www.sistemamuseo.it). Then head north to Cassette d'Ete. Castagno Village shopping centre (Via Brancadoro, Cassete d'Ete) sells shoes, including a Prada outlet.

Abbadia di Fiastra
▶ The SS 77 N.
The 12C abbey sits on a large nature reserve, perfect for walks, cycling and horseback riding.
Down the road, see a shoemaker at work at Lucina Calzature (Loc. Montedoro 25a, Urbisaglia, ℘0733 50 69 31; www.lucinacalzature.it), which now specialises in historic as well as contemporary styles.

Tolentino

◯ 50km/31mi NW.

The quirky **Museo dell'Umorismo nell'Arte** (&open May-Sept Tue–Sun 10.30am–6.30pm. Oct-Apr Wed–Thu and 2–6pm and Fri-Sun 10am–6pm; 3€; ℘0733 96 97 97; www.tolentino musei.it), in Palazzo Comune, has a collection of humour in art.

Basilica di San Nicola★★

Open 7am–noon and 3–7.30pm. ℘0733 97 63 11. www.sannicoladatolentino.it. The basilica interior is striking for its opulent marble, gold and stucco decoration, but its real gem is **Cappellone di San Nicola**, a chapel with beautiful 14C **frescoes★★** by an unknown master of the Rimini school, with period dress and scenes in the cycle.

Museums

The Castello Rancia below Tolentino lets visitors wander through the castle and up on the ramparts.

San Severino Marche★

◯ 65km/40.4mi NE of Fermo and 11km/6.8mi NW of Tolentino.
Piazza del Popolo is the main square.

Pinacoteca Civica

Palazzo Tacchi-Venturi, Via Salimbeni 39. Open Tue–Sun. 3€. ℘0733 63 80 95. www.comune.sanseverinomarche.mc.it. Of note are **Lorenzo Salimbeni** and his brother **Jacopo**, who revolutionised 15C painting, adding vivid realism to Gothic style. The 11C church of San Lorenzo in Doliolo's beautiful **crypt★** has frescoes attributed to the Salimbeni brothers and school.

Fabriano

◯ 38km/23.6mi E.
Famous since the 13C for paper manufacture, Fabriano's present speciality is printing money (euros and other).

Museo della Carta e della Filigrana★★

Largo Fratelli Spacca. &See website for hours. 6.50€. ℘0732 22 334. www.museodellacarta.com.

This lively museum illustrates the manufacture of paper through the reconstruction of an operative medieval workshop. The museum also has displays of antique Fabriano paper. Enquire about workshops.

▲▲ Grotte di Frasassi★★

◯ 55km/34.2mi NE. & Reservation required. ℘800 166 250. 15.50€. www.frasassi.com. ⊗Wrap up warm. Guides take visitors through this vast network of caves (grotte). Grotta del Vento is full of stalagmites and stalactites.

ADDRESSES

🛏 STAY

⊜ **Gusto Dop&Doc**– Abbadia di Fiastra. 0733 43 17 22. 3 rooms.

⊜⊜ **Il Gelso Agriturismo** – Frazione Melano, 102 Loc. Chigne Basse, Fabriano. ℘0732 73 60 99. www.ilgelsoagriturismo. com 10 rooms. This friendly farm has comfortable modern rooms. Its good restaurant features farm bounty, and is packed with locals.

⊜⊜⊜ **Hotel La Forestina** – Abbadia di Fiastra. ℘0733 20 11 25. www.laforesteria tolentino.it. 24 rooms. Ex-monastery, a great base for families.

⊜⊜⊜⊜ **Hotel Palazzo Romani Adami** – Corso Cavour 94, Fermo. ℘0734 22 66 79. www.palazzoromaniadami.it. 7 rooms and 2 apts. A lovely base in Fermo's centre, with apartments managed by the noble family that lives there, decorated in beautiful colours. Lovely furnishings and thoughtful conveniences.

🍴 EAT

⊜ **Da Rosa Ristorante** – Abbadia di Fiastra. ℘0733 20 16 61. Closed Tue–Wed lunch and Thu. The rustic restaurant here is delightful for lunch, dinner or a snack. Outdoor seating too.

⊜⊜/⊜⊜⊜ **Cobà Beach Restaurant** – Via Lungomare Gramsci, Bagni 13, Porto San Giorgio. ℘0734 677 569. www.cobabeach.it. This all-white restaurant overlooking the beach near Fermo is a great spot for a fish lunch or dinner, good Le Marche wine selection as well as Champagnes.

Ascoli Piceno★★

A luminous city of travertine and medieval towers, harmonious and elegant, Ascoli lies in a valley where the Tronto and Castellano rivers meet.

A BIT OF HISTORY

Some traces remain of the Roman town of *Asculum*. The Middle Ages and Renaissance brought bitter conflicts, although the town flourished. Its economic and artistic vigour attracted important figures like the Venetian painter **Carlo Crivelli** (1430–94), who settled in Ascoli permanently. Initially influenced by Mantegna and Bellini, Crivelli developed a highly original style and influenced painters throughout the region.

✦✦WALKING TOUR

Piazza del Popolo★★

The city's public drawing room is paved with large flagstones and framed by Gothic and Renaissance buildings and elegant arcades.

The 13C **Palazzo dei Capitani del Popolo★** (People's Captains' Palace) has an attractive courtyard (16C).

The 13C–16C **Church of San Francesco★** has several Lombard features. On the south side there is a fine 16C portal above which stands a monument to Julius II and the **Loggia dei Mercanti★** (Merchants' Loggia), a graceful early-16C building showing Tuscan influence. **Chiostro Maggiore**, 16C–17C, shelters a colourful fruit and vegetable market..

▶ Cross the square away from San Francesco and turn left into Via XX Settembre.

Duomo

Open 8am–12pm and 4–8pm. Donations welcome. ℘0736 25 99 01.

The grandiose Renaissance façade of this 12C cathedral was the work of

▶ **Population:** 51 081
🚗 **Michelin Map:** 563 N 22 – Marches.
ℹ **Info:** Piazza Arringo 7. ℘0736 25 30 45.
▶ **Location:** Via Salaria, 30km/18.6mi from Adriatic.
▶ **Train:** S. Filippo (San Benedetto del Tronto 40 mins).
👁 **Don't Miss:** Piazza del Popolo, medieval towers, and a drink at Caffè Meletti.
🕐 **Timing:** Allow a day.

Cola dell'Amatrice. **Porta della Musa**, on the north side, is a fine late Renaissance construction. Inside, the Cappella del Sacramento (Eucharist Chapel) has a superb **polyptych★** by **Carlo Crivelli**; the late Gothic grace of the Madonna and Child contrasts with the dramatic Pietà. To the left of the Duomo stands the 11C **baptistery★**, crowned by an octagonal lantern with graceful trefoil openings. Draining channels carved into the stonework above the portal are typical of local architecture.

Corso Mazzinia

This is the grand street of the city and is lined with old palaces of varying epochs, embellished with Latin and Italian inscriptions. At no. 224 the 16C Malaspina Palace has an original loggia with columns shaped like tree trunks. Sant'Agostino has a fresco of Christ by Colla dell'Amatrice.

Via delle Torri

Named for the many towers that once stood here, of these two 12C towers remain. At the end of the street is the 14C Church of San Pietro Martire.

Santi Vincenzo e Anastasio★

The fine Romanesque church with a 14C **façade★** is divided into 64 sections which were originally covered in frescoes. The simple interior has a 6C crypt with remains of 14C frescoes.

Ponte Romano di Solestà★

This Augustan Age bridge, with a 14C gateway, is supported by only one arch.

Via dei Soderini

Once the main medieval artery as evidenced by its numerous mansions, feudal towers and picturesque side streets, this street has **Palazzetto Longobardo** (11C–12C), a Lombard mansion which is flanked by the elegant Ercolani Tower (Torre Ercolani), more than 40m/130ft high.

ADDITIONAL SIGHTS
Pinacoteca★

Open Tue–Fri 10am–7pm Apr–Sep, to 5pm rest of year; Sat-Sun 10am–7pm. Closed 1 Jan am, 24 Dec pm, 25 Dec, 31 Dec pm. 8€. 0736 29 82 13.

The picture gallery in the town hall has a fine collection of art of the 16C–19C (Guido Reni, Titian, Luca Giordano, Carlo Maratta). Noteworthy from Le Marche region are the Carlo Crivelli, Cola dell'Amatrice and, of Crivelli's circle, Pietro Alamanno. Note the precious, delicately worked 13C English relic (**piviale★**), the cope. Opposite the town hall, in Palazzo Panichi, the **Museo Archeologico** displays relics of the Picene Age (9C–6C BC) and 1C AD Roman mosaics. Open Tue–Sun 8.30am–7.30pm. 4€. 0736 25 35 62.

EXCURSION
Civitella del Tronto★

24km/14.9mi SE.

This charming Abruzzo village perched on a travertine mountain enjoys a splendid **setting★★**. Its 16C **fortress★** (For opening times visit the website; 6€; 320 842 45 40 (mobile); www.fortezzadicivitella.it) is imposing, the last Bourbon stronghold to surrender to the Sardinian-Piemontese armies in 1861.

ADDRESSES

STAY

Az Ag Fiore Gioie di Fattoria – Contrada San Biagio 12, Controguerra. 0861 89 606. www.gioiedifattoria.it.

7 rooms. In the town of "Antiwar" south of Ascoli Piceno, this farm grinds its own organic wheat for bread and pasta, so be sure to book meals with Maria Antonietta. Pietro makes good organic wines including Passerina among other whites and reds. Rooms are simple, but comfortable. Swimming pool, ping-pong, weaving loom.

Casa Pazzi – Via Sotto Le Mura, Vie delle Loggie 8, Grottammare. 0735 73 66 17. www.casapazzi.com. 5 rooms. An 18C noble residence northeast of Ascoli overlooks the coast, with terraced gardens and stylish interiors.

Cento Torri – Via Costanzo Mazzoni 4. 0736 25 51 23. www.centotorri.com. 8 rooms. Lovely noble residence, with spa and gracious sitting areas, right in Ascoli's centre.

EAT

La Locandiera – Corso Trento e Trieste 33, Ascoli Piceno. 0736 26 25 09. A simple, informal restaurant, with tasty antipasti, pasta and lamb. Fried dishes are especially good.

Oasi degli Angeli – Contrada Sant'Egidio 50, Cupra Marittima. 0735 77 85 69. www.kurni.it. Winemakers of legendary red Kurni have a restaurant and rooms.

Osteria dell'Arancio – Piazza Peretti Grottamare. 0735 22 14. www.osteriadellarancio.net. Excellent creative and traditional cuisine, wines and service to match.

Zunica – Piazza Filippi Pepe 14, Civitella del Tronto. 0861 91 319. www.hotelzunica.it. On the village square, with views over the valley, this simple restaurant serves cuisine typical of Teramo (Abruzzo). Rooms are basic; some have views.

TAKING A BREAK

Caffè Meletti – Piazza del Popolo 2. 0736 25 55 59. Outside tables on grand Piazza del Popolo, inside a 1904 Art Nouveau jewel. It distills its own sweet *anisetta* liqueur.

EVENTS AND FESTIVALS

Summer brings **Torneo Cavalleresco della Quintana**, a pageant that was officially established in the Ascoli Statutes of 1377, with a jousting tournament and large procession.

INDEX

INDEX

D

INDEX

INDEX

INDEX

INDEX

🏨 STAY

♀/EAT

Thematic Maps

Maps and Plans

	Sight	Seaside resort	Winter sports resort	Spa
Highly recommended	★★★	⚐⚐⚐	❋❋❋	‡‡‡
Recommended	★★	⚐⚐	❋❋	‡‡
Interesting	★	⚐	❋	‡

Selected monuments and sights

	Tour - Departure point
	Catholic church
	Protestant church, other temple
	Synagogue - Mosque
	Building
■	Statue, small building
	Calvary, wayside cross
◎	Fountain
	Rampart - Tower - Gate
	Château, castle, historic house
	Ruins
	Dam
☼	Factory, power plant
☆	Fort
⌒	Cave
	Troglodyte dwelling
	Prehistoric site
▼	Viewing table
⋀	Viewpoint
▲	Other place of interest

Special symbols

◇	Police station (Carabinieri)
	Nuraghe
	Palace, villa
	Temple, Greek and Roman ruins

Additional symbols

		Tourist information
		Motorway or other primary route
❶	❶	Junction: complete, limited
		Pedestrian street
		Unsuitable for traffic, street subject to restrictions
		Steps – Footpath
		Train station – Auto-train station
	SNCF	Coach (bus) station
		Tram
		Metro, underground
		Park-and-Ride
♿		Access for the disabled

Sports and recreation

	Racecourse
	Skating rink
	Outdoor, indoor swimming pool
	Multiplex Cinema
	Marina, sailing centre
	Trail refuge hut
	Cable cars, gondolas
	Funicular, rack railway
	Tourist train
◆	Recreation area, park
	Theme, amusement park
	Wildlife park, zoo
	Gardens, park, arboretum
	Bird sanctuary, aviary
	Walking tour, footpath
	Of special interest to children

Abbreviations

H	Town hall (Municipio)
J	Law courts (Palazzo di Giustizia)
M	Museum (Museo)
P	Local authority offices (Prefettura)
POL.	Police station (Polizia) (in large towns: Questura)
T	Theatre (Teatro)
U	University (Università)

		Post office
		Telephone
		Covered market
		Barracks
		Drawbridge
ᴗ		Quarry
✗		Mine
B	**F**	Car ferry (river or lake)
		Ferry service: cars and passengers
		Foot passengers only
③		Access route number common to Michelin maps and town plans
Bert (R.)...		Main shopping street
AZ B		Map co-ordinates

Useful Words and Phrases

ON THE ROAD AND IN TOWN

	Translation
A destra	To the right
A sinistra	To the left
Aperto	Open
Autostrada	Motorway
Banchina	Pavement
Binario	(Railway) Platform
Corso	Boulevard
Discesa	Descent
Dogana	Customs
Fermata	(Bus) Stop
Fiume	River
Ingresso	Entrance
Lavori in corso	Men at work
Neve	Snow
Passaggio a livello	Level crossing
Passo	Pass
Pericolo	Danger
Piazza, Largo	Square, Place
Piazzale	Esplanade
Ponte	Bridge
Stazione	Station
Stretto	Narrow
Uscita	Exit, Way out
Viale	Avenue
Vietato	Prohibited

PLACES AND THINGS TO SEE

	Translation
Abbazia, Convento	Abbey, Monastery
Affreschi	Frescoes
Arazzi	Tapestries
Arca	Monumental tomb
Biblioteca	Library
Cappella	Chapel
Casa	House
Cascata	Waterfall
Castello	Castle
Cena	The last supper
Chiesa	Church
Chiostro	Cloisters
Chiuso	Closed
Città	Town
Cortile	Courtyard
Dintorni	Environs
Duomo	Cathedral
Edificio	Building
Facciata	Façade
Funivia	Cablecar
Giardini	Gardens
Gole	Gorges
Lagotto	Altar frontal
Passeggiata	Walk, Promenade
Piano	Floor, Storey
Pinacoteca	Picture gallery

Pulpito	Pulpit
Quadro	Picture
Rivolgersi a	To apply to
Rocca	Feudal castle
Rovine, Ruderi	Ruins
Sagrestia	Sacristy
Scala	Stairway
Scavi	Excavations
Seggiovia	Chairlift
Spiaggia	Beach
Tesoro	Treasure
Torre, Torazzo	Tower
Vista	View

Caro	Dear
La strada per .?	The road to .?
Si può visitare?	May one visit?
Che ora è?	What time is it?
Non capisco	I don't understand
Desidero	I would like

COMMON WORDS

	Translation
Si, No	Yes, No
Signore	Sir
Signora	Madam
Signorina	Miss
Oggi	Today
Ieri	Yesterday
Domani mattina	Tomorrow morning
Mattina	Morning
Sera	Evening
Pomeriggio	Afternoon
Per favore	Please
Grazie tante	Thank you very much
Mi scusi	Excuse me
Basta	Enough
Buon giorno	Good morning
Arrivederci	Goodbye
Quanto?	How much?
Dove? Quando?	Where? When?
Dov'è?	Where is?
Molto, Poco	Much, Little
Più, Meno	More, Less
Tutto, Tutti	All
Grande	Large
Piccolo	Small

NUMBERS

	Translation
Zero	0
Uno	1
Due	2
Tre	3
Quattro	4
Cinque	5
Sei	6
Sette	7
Otto	8
Nove	9
Dieci	10
Undici	11
Dodici	12
Tredici	13
Quattordici	14
Quindici	15
Sedici	16
Diciassette	17
Diciotto	18
Diciannove	19
Venti	20
Trenta	30
Quaranta	40
Cinquanta	50
Sessanta	60
Settanta	70
Ottanta	80
Novanta	90
Cento	100
Mille	1 000
Cinquemila	5 000
Diecimila	10 000

GASTRONOMIC TERMS

Brodetto:	a type of fish stew that has many regional variations; especially common in towns near the Adriatic Sea.
Caffè corretto:	*espresso* laced with brandy or *grappa*.
Caffè decaffeinato:	*(caffè "Hag")*: decaffeinated coffee.
Caffè latte:	mainly hot milk, with a splash of coffee.
Caffè lungo:	coffee which is not quite as strong as *espresso*.
Caffè macchiato:	*espresso* with a splash of milk.
Cannelloni:	large pasta tubes filled with a meat or other sauce.
Cappellini:	very thin spaghetti.
Cappuccino (or *cappuccio*):	coffee topped with frothy milk and a dusting of cocoa.
Cassata:	ice cream containing chopped nuts and mixed dried fruit (similar to tutti-frutti).
Crema:	cream.
Farfalle:	pasta bow-ties.
Fettuccine:	slightly narrower, Roman version of tagliatelle.
Fior di latte:	mozzarella cheese made from cow's milk (rather than buffalo milk); also a very creamy type of ice cream.
Fritto misto:	a mix of fried fish/seafood and vegetables.
Fusilli:	small pasta spirals.
Gelato:	Italian-style ice cream.
Gnocchi:	tiny potato dumplings.
Lasagne:	sheets of pasta arranged in layers with tomato and meat sauce (or other) and cheese sauce, topped with Parmesan and baked.
Maccheroni:	small pasta tubes.
Panino:	type of sandwich (bread roll).
Panna:	rich natural whipped cream.
Polpette:	meatballs.
Prosciutto:	cured ham.
Ravioli:	little pasta cushions, often enclosing meat.
Saltimbocca:	veal dish topped with prosciutto, so good it "jumps in the mouth".
Schiacciata:	type of sandwich (on a pizza-type base).
Spaghetti:	the great classic pasta.
Stracciatella:	chocolate-chip (ice cream).
Tagliatelle:	long narrow pasta ribbons.
Tiramisù:	coffee-flavoured gâteau *(semifreddo)*.
Tortellini:	small crescent-shaped pasta rolls filled with a meat or cheese stuffing, often served in a clear meat broth.
Tramezzino:	type of sandwich (on slices of bread).
Zabaglione:	dessert made from egg yolks and Marsala wine.
Zuppa inglese:	trifle.

YOU ALREADY KNOW THE GREEN GUIDE, NOW FIND OUT ABOUT THE MICHELIN GROUP